THE GLÉNANS

MANUAL OF
SAILING

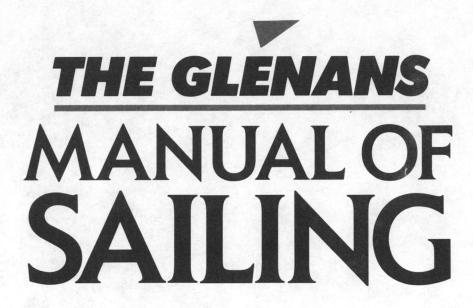

THE GLÉNANS
MANUAL OF
SAILING

Translated by Peter Davison
and Jim Simpson with
Ruth Bagnall and
Catherine du Peloux Menagé

David & Charles

A David & Charles Book

Translation copyright © Peter Davison
1992, 1993

First published in French as *Le Cours des Glénans*
Copyright © Éditions du Seuil 1990, 1992
ISBN 2 02 009963 2

English translation, *The Glénans Manual of
Sailing*, first published 1992, ISBN 0 7153 0016 4
Revised reprint, 1993

A catalogue record for this book is available from
the British Library.

ISBN 0 7153 0016 4

Typeset by XL Publishing Services, Nairn
and printed in Italy by OFSA SpA for
David & Charles
Brunel House Newton Abbot Devon

Contents

ditches, and the freedom of the waves

PREFACE

The Freedom of the Waves

The Glénans sailing school teaches people to sail; or rather, it is a place
where people learn to sail. In our experience, the act of taking responsibility,
the process of encountering an environment, is truly at the centre of learning.
For this reason, we do not feel we can prescribe any single theory of sailing.

Why, then, a sailing manual?

Because, over time, experience teaches you a way of doing things, and our
trainers and students have organised this experience in a form which can be
consulted before, during and after sailing, as a reference, to see what our
experience can tell you about the techniques used, rather than forcing you to
adopt them indiscriminately.

The manual brings together provisional conclusions, which continue to be
updated and renewed, mostly from our own experience, but many from other
sources. Thus the manual itself needs occasionally to be updated. This new
edition will be consulted by experts for the latest techniques and by pleasure-
boat sailors for everything they need to know in order to master wind and
sea.

The manual is an encyclopedia of the boat, with contents and index pages
and all the reference material you might need; it is also a fascinating story –
the sub-plots of a cruiser crew's movements while executing a tack, or a
funboarder 'helicopetering' are each small tales by themselves.

Above all, however, the manual is a book to be kept on board, to help the
potential purchaser, the anxious owner who wishes to help his guests avoid

spectacular mistakes, the adventurous or simply the prudent sailor who wants to sail for pleasure in safety.

So, we offer you the ocean not as an escape from real life, nor the ocean as consumerism, but the ocean experienced together, the sea as seen from les Glénans, and the freedom of the waves.

les **GLÉNANS**

PART I

The Practice of Sailing

Anyone who wants to sail should begin by avoiding theories and lessons: the best start is to get hold of a boat, rig it and head off out onto the water.

Sailing is not a sport which comes naturally: most of the actions it demands are new to the learner; many even run counter to one's natural instincts. This is one reason for not trying to learn how to sail from a book.

At the beginning, you will feel rather clumsy – not because you are stupid or inept, but because the daily routine of our lives suppresses those natural instincts of sense, smell, intuition and adaptation to the unknown. These will need to be re-learned.

The re-learning starts before you even venture onto the water, while you are discovering how to put this extraordinary combination of things together which go to make up a boat. And as for 'venturing onto the water' in a sailing boat for the first time: that's worth a chapter to itself.

Afterwards, we can supplement those re-awakened instincts by examining again our first experiences. This examination, again, deserves its own chapter, if not an entire book! We have mastered a few routines, found our balance (more or less), and begun to understand some of the behaviour of air and water. The learning process then enters another new phase as we encounter some of the surprising tricks our boat can perform if we learn to play the game according to the rules. Of course, our landlubbers' instincts will by then have been left miles behind us, as we start to become part of this new world we are exploring. Ultimately, even a measure of expertise may not be beyond our grasp ... but let's not get ahead of ourselves.

CHAPTER 1

Introduction

To paraphrase the title of a Woody Allen film, we might say that the purpose of this chapter is to sum up 'everything you ever wanted to know about boats but never dared ask'.

The chapter is a step-by-step guide through the phases of choosing a boat, getting the boat ready and making the first few forays onto the water. It contains all the actions and exercises the beginner must perform before setting out on that great adventure. Admittedly, all these explanations will fall into place only after the first sail ... but after that first sail, the novice re-reading the chapter will gain a better grasp of what happened on the water, and will understand the source of any mistakes. More experienced sailors may look up in this chapter any aspects of their initial training which were missed, and will find basic principles explained which are often overlooked or ignored.

In other words, in this part of the manual, which covers a wide range of learning situations, anyone can choose the sections they need, according to their own needs or experience.

We deal with three types of sailing vessel – sailing dinghies, catamarans and sailboards. Each has many similarities in terms of practice and technique with the other two; thus, just as the sailboarder will find questions answered in the section on dinghies, catamaran sailors will find the solutions to many of their problems in the pages dedicated to sailboards. Of course, each also has its specific peculiarities, which are dealt with fully.

Choosing a boat

This is a difficult decision, but an essential one. Many criteria besides technical ones must be considered: price, ease of

maintenance and transport, purpose for which the boat is to be used, etc.

Of course, one can start off right away with a large cruiser (a type of boat discussed at length later in this book). But for an introductory section, the catamaran, sailboard and single- or double-handed dinghy are perfect vehicles. They are affordable, manoeuvrable and require no special harbour facilities. They are also equipped with sails and not engines!

We consider the three types of vessel in two sections: the first dedicated to dinghies and catamarans, as two types of the same basic vehicle; and the second to sailboards, which require a section of their own due to the large number of specific techniques to be mastered.

Any details specific to monohull dinghies are marked

Any details specific to catamarans are marked

Dinghies and catamarans

Fitting out

Having chosen our boat, we now have to get it ready to sail. The following pages describe the fittings and equipment of a small two-handed racing dinghy (based around the 470 class) and a racing catamaran (based on the F-Cat). We take a fairly simple view; different classes will be arranged slightly differently.

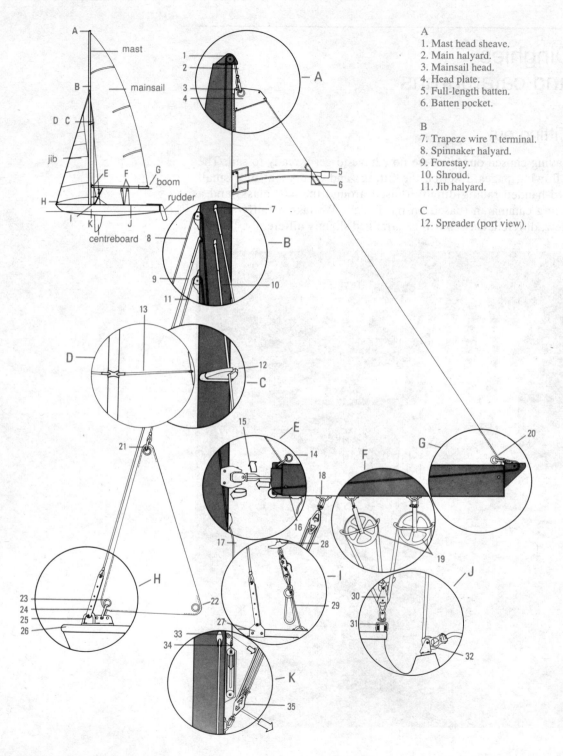

A
1. Mast head sheave.
2. Main halyard.
3. Mainsail head.
4. Head plate.
5. Full-length batten.
6. Batten pocket.

B
7. Trapeze wire T terminal.
8. Spinnaker halyard.
9. Forestay.
10. Shroud.
11. Jib halyard.

C
12. Spreader (port view).

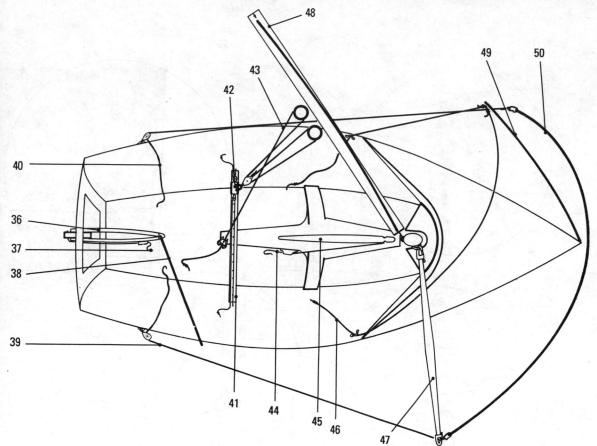

D
13. Starboard spreader (aft view).

E
14. Mainsail tack.
15. Gooseneck.
16. Clew outhaul jamming cleat.
17. Main halyard and cleat.
18. Kicking strap fixing point.

F
19. Mainsheet blocks.

G
20. Mainsail clew.

21. Jib head.
22. Jib clew.

H
23. Jib tack.
24. Chainplate.
25. Stem plate.
26. Bow.

I
27. Port shroud plate.
28. Trapeze handle.
29. Trapeze ring.

J
30. Mainsheet block with becket.
31. Mainsheet traveller.
32. Mainsheet jamming cleat.

K
33. Tube cleat for jib halyard.
34. Muscle box for main halyard.
35. Kicking strap tackle.

36. Tiller.
37. Rudder uphaul.
38. Tiller extension.
39. Spinnaker guy.
40. Spinnaker sheet.
41. Mainsheet traveller bar.
42. Mainsheet traveller.
43. Mainsheet.
44. Centreboard uphaul.
45. Centreboard.
46. Jib sheet.
47. Spinnaker pole.
48. Boom.
49. Jib.
50. Spinnaker.

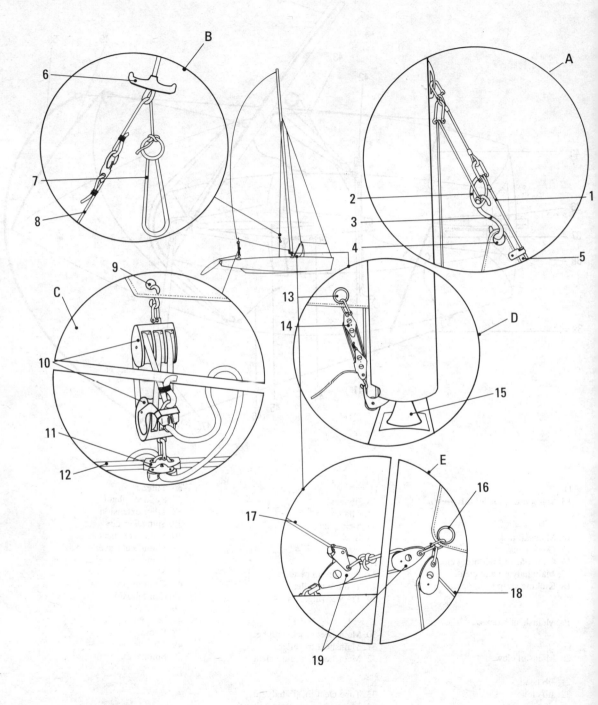

A
1. Forestay.
2. Halyard lock.
3. S-Hook.
4. Jib head.
5. Jib hank.

B
6. Trapeze handle.
7. Trapeze ring.
8. Shock cord.

C
9. Mainsail clew.
10. Mainsheet with jammer block.
11. Mainsheet traveller.
12. Mainsheet traveller bar.

D
13. Mainsail tack.
14. Mainsail downhaul tackle.
15. Rotating mast foot.

E
16. Jib clew.
17. Jibsheet.
18. Jibsheet.
19. Jibsheet blocks.

20. Rotating mast.
21. Mainsail.
22. Hounds.
23. Full-length batten.
24. Forestay.
25. Shroud.
26. Jib.
27. Crossbeams.
28. Forestay bridle.
29. Hulls.
30. Tiller extension.
31. Rudders.
32. Tiller.
33. Mainsheet.

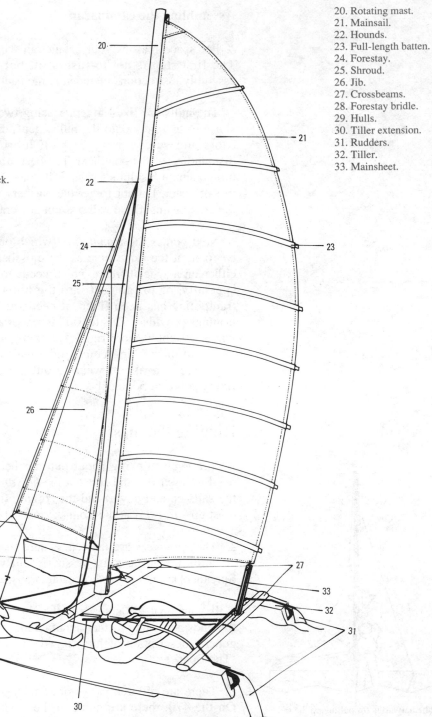

Assembling the catamaran

❱ For space reasons your catamaran will be delivered in pieces. The first step is not to rush at it, but to start by reading the assembly instructions included in the pack.

The hulls are fixed together using two crossbeams which will slot into or screw onto the hulls, depending on the class of boat. Slots and screws must be well lubricated to help the easy dismantling of the boat later. The best lubricant for this purpose is molybdenum bisulphide grease: it does stain, but will not dissolve in salt water. Do not forget the washers and spacers while fixing the crossbeams: these will prevent any cracking of the hulls.

Next comes the *trampoline* (which on some catamarans must be fixed at the same time as the crossbeams). This will be fitted either on a special frame which needs to be attached to the hulls specially, or to rails set into the hulls themselves. When the trampoline has been fitted, it needs to be tensioned, using the lashings provided. This tension is important, because it makes the whole assembly more rigid. The trampoline eyes must remain in line with their fixing points; otherwise the trampoline will tear, and there is a risk of wearing out the plastic grommets of the fixing points very quickly.

Rigging the mast

Before even thinking about putting the mast into position, you need to lay it flat and sort out the *halyards* (which are for pulling the sails up and down) and the *rigging* (the wires which hold the mast up – *forestay* at the front, *shrouds* at either side).

❱ The *spreaders* are there to ensure that the angle at which the shrouds meet the mast is sufficiently large to be efficient. Spreaders are not needed on catamarans.

If your boat has spreaders, the shrouds should be led through the ends according to the manufacturer's instructions. (There is a general description of jury-rigged spreader assembly in Part III, 'The Boat'.)

❱ There are different ways of attaching the rigging to the mast. On the 470, there are holes in the mast which the shrouds and

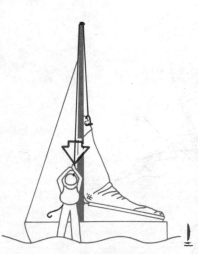

The halyard is for pulling up the sail.

forestay slot into. At the bottom, *chainplates* allow the tension of the rigging to be altered at deck level. The chainplates are attached to the *stay-plates* which are built into the hull.

The *halyards* must be fitted the right way round. Take care! There is usually a hard eye at one end which will be shackled to the sail head. Before you step the mast, tie the halyard ends together, and fit the trapeze wires. The final stage before stepping the mast is to lubricate the mainsail luff track, thus helping you to pull the sail up easily.

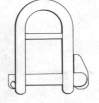

Quick-release shackle for fixing the main halyard to the head of the mainsail.

Stepping the mast

⚡ *Hull-stepped mast (as for most monohulls)*
When everything is ready, put the mast foot into the step and fix the shrouds into the topmost hole of the chainplates, which should be attached to the hull. These will be adjusted once the mast is upright. Do not step into the boat on dry land – you might damage the hull.

Two people can relatively easily step the mast: one holds the mast, while the other pulls gently on the forestay.

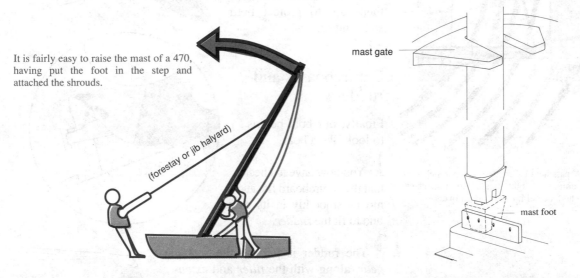

It is fairly easy to raise the mast of a 470, having put the foot in the step and attached the shrouds.

(forestay or jib halyard)

mast gate

mast foot

Detail of the mast step and gate of a 470.

When the mast is vertical, secure the forestay and adjust the length of the shrouds, with the two chainplates the same length, so

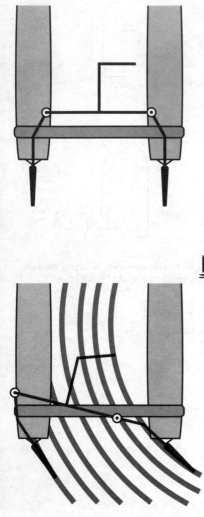

A catamaran's rudders are parallel when pointing straight, but at different angles when the helm is pushed far over.

that, with the forestay under tension, the mast stays upright without quite touching the end of the *mast gate*.

▶ *Deck-stepped mast (as in most catamarans)*
The mast foot is placed onto the universal joint and chocked so that it does not slip when the mast is brought upright. Most catamarans have a rotating mast, with a teflon-coated non-stick surface to help the rotation.

Having attached the shrouds as in the monohull, one person supports the mast head. The other, standing on the forward cross-beam, pulls the mast hard using the trapeze handles, while the first pushes the mast head up. Once the mast is upright, the forestay has simply to be fixed to the forestay bridle, and adjusted so that it is raked slightly aft (ie leaning towards the stern). Secure the shackle.

In all cases, secure the rigging by feeding stout twine through the shackle pin head, and whipping insulating tape round the split rings. Better still, replace the split rings with split pins, and tape them up, to protect both sails and sailors!

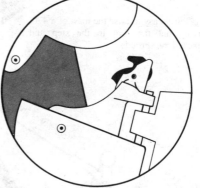

Centreboards and rudders

Finally, our boat begins to look like a boat.

You now have to check that the centreboard fits and moves smoothly in its case, and to fit the *rudder*.

The rudder is part of the *steering gear*, along with the *tiller* and *extension*, the *gudgeons* attached to the *transom* of the boat, and the *pintles* (part of the rudder stock) which fit into the gudgeons.

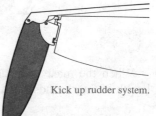

Kick up rudder system.

Although there is generally no centreboard on a small cata-maran, there are two connecting rudders. The bar between them is adjustable in length on some cats, so that your rudders are actually parallel. The tiller bars are slightly angled in toward the centreline of the boat. This way each rudder has the same angle of attack through the water, despite the different turning circles of the inside and outside hulls.

Most rudder blades can be raised or lowered: check that the system for locking the blade in place works properly and is kept regularly lubricated. The state of repair of the return shock-cord is particularly important.

The righting line

This is one thing that should on no account be forgotten. Tie it to the bottom of the mast, then stow the long end neatly on the trampoline where it cannot trail in the water. Without this you will have problems righting a cat after a capsize.

Rigging the sails

It is easy to ruin sails by:
– leaving them on sand, which gets into the seams and acts as an abrasive;

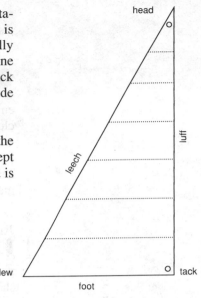

The edges and corners of a sail.

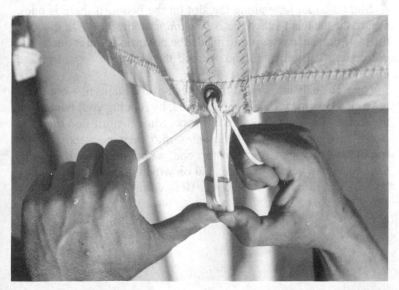

The right way to fit a full length batten.

– screwing them up into their bag (which cracks the sailcloth);
– smoking while handling them.

Begin by checking which edges and corners of the sails are which: the *luff*, *leech* and *foot*, and the *head*, *tack* and *clew*.

The mainsail is rightangled at the tack; it generally has a stiffening plate at the head, the sharpest angle; the *bolt rope* stops at the clew. There is no bolt rope along the leech. The luff is the long side with the bolt rope.

The jib has a wire along the luff, which is the longest edge. The sharpest angle is at the head; and the tack generally bears the sailmaker's mark.

Rigging the jib

Shackle the jib tack to the stem plate, just aft of the forestay itself (dinghy) or attach it to the bridle (catamaran). The head is shackled to the halyard, while the jibsheets are attached to the clew, either with a shackle or with a bowline. The sheets are then passed either side of the mast, outside the shrouds (most dinghies) or inside (catamarans), through the fairleads, and finished off with a figure-of-eight knot. Catamarans often have continuous jibsheets: this arrangement avoids the problem of ends trailing in the water. They usually have jib sheet tackles to provide the force needed to sheet the jib hard in.

Rigging the mainsail

Slide the *foot rope* along the slot on the boom (if there is one), secure the tack and attach the *clew outhaul* to the clew. On the 470, the clew outhaul passes along inside the boom and comes out by the *gooseneck*. It is adjusted and secured through a *tube cleat* on the underside of the boom.

Next, the halyard is fixed to the head of the mainsail – once you have checked that the sail is not twisted, by running your hand from the tack all the way along the luff rope. Slide the luff into the mast slot a few inches. Push the *battens* into their pockets, without forcing them – apart from the top one, which on many boats will have to be tied tightly in place, and on which the compression may be adjusted through the tie-cords (less compression is needed in stronger winds).

When threading a tackle, feed the standing part (the end which will be fixed) through the blocks, starting with the last one. This way you will not have to feed the whole rope through every block.

The mainsheet is fed through the blocks in the right order, without crossing. Tie a figure of eight at the end.

! Finally, the *kicking strap* is fixed between the boom and the mast. The main function of this piece of equipment is to keep the

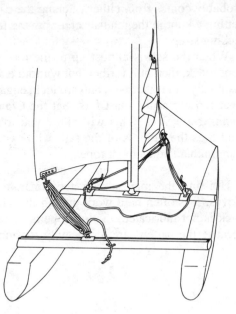

One way of feeding sheets in a continuous loop.

boom from flying up in the air. It also has further functions, which will be discussed later.

! On catamarans, the jib sheets pass through blocks and the mainsail is sheeted through a system of six blocks. This is because of the size of the sails: some mechanical advantage is needed to trim them. The end of the mainsheet is often used to position the mainsheet traveller: follow the manufacturer's instructions and check (while you are on land) that the system works in all positions.

Hoisting the sails

! First, place the boat head to wind (ie with the bow pointing towards the wind). Otherwise, when you raise the sails, they will fill, making the luff bind in the mast groove, possibly catching the ends of the battens in the shrouds, and maybe even tipping the boat over. Do not forget that when a sail is flapping it is wearing itself out, so do not leave the sails flapping for long before heading off. Raise the mainsail first; then the jib.

Raising the mainsail

Let the kicking strap and mainsheet well out. Then, with one hand, pull on the main halyard, while using the other to guide the luff into the throat of the mast groove. If there is any resistance, it probably comes from either catching the battens on the shrouds or getting a knot in the mainsheet, or having too much tension on the kicking strap.

When the sail is almost up to the top, put the boom onto the gooseneck, then pull further, but without excessive force. Cleat the main halyard. If there is a halyard lock, engage at the mast head and cleat loosely at the mast foot. Set the *Cunningham hook* into the *Cunningham hole*. This will allow you to adjust the luff tension (and thus the fullness of the sail) while you are sailing. Cleat the Cunningham adjustment rope.

Hoisting the mainsail on a catamaran involves a few tricky moves. It is often hard work pulling the sail up, because the mast track is not lubricated, the luff rope is in a poor state of repair, or because the battens are too heavily tensioned in light airs. Make

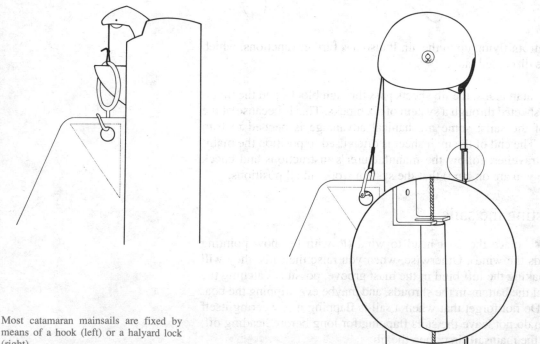

Most catamaran mainsails are fixed by means of a hook (left) or a halyard lock (right).

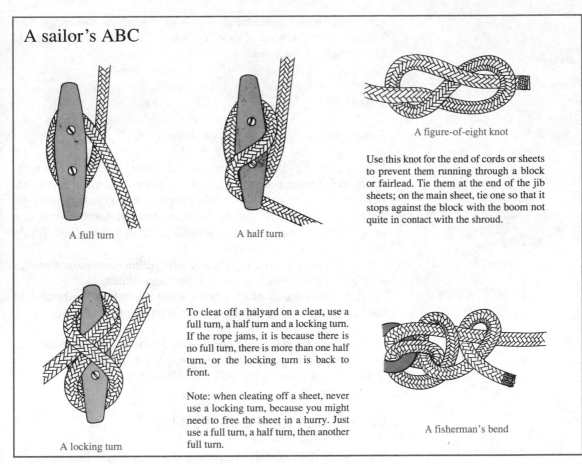

A sailor's ABC

A full turn

A half turn

A figure-of-eight knot

Use this knot for the end of cords or sheets to prevent them running through a block or fairlead. Tie them at the end of the jib sheets; on the main sheet, tie one so that it stops against the block with the boom not quite in contact with the shroud.

A locking turn

To cleat off a halyard on a cleat, use a full turn, a half turn and a locking turn. If the rope jams, it is because there is no full turn, there is more than one half turn, or the locking turn is back to front.

Note: when cleating off a sheet, never use a locking turn, because you might need to free the sheet in a hurry. Just use a full turn, a half turn, then another full turn.

A fisherman's bend

sure you are pulling the halyard in line with the pulley axis, and when the head of the sail reaches the top, fit it over the hook and cleat the halyard with only a little tension on it. To drop the sail, simply uncleat the halyard then disengage the halyard lock.

With a ring-type fixing, pull the sail up a little further, then rotate the mast fully to disengage the ring before dropping the sail. For a sleeve-type fixing, pull the halyard down and out from the mast to disengage the swage from the hook.

Raising the jib

There are two systems:
– either an S-hook at the head of the sail passed through a ring at the top of the forestay;
– or a halyard made of wire, with a rope tail. The jib luff generally includes a wire, so rig tension is achieved by tightening this so it

effectively replaces the halyard. A rope jib luff cannot replace the halyard, so rig tension is modified using the halyard, according to the strength of the wind.

Finally

To complete your equipment, you need:

– an anchor, 3–5kg, with an *anchor rope* of 30–60m length, attached to the anchor with a fisherman's bend. Do not forget to tie, or whip, the other end of the anchor rope either to the ring specially provided or to the bottom of the mast. Stow the anchor and line under the foredeck inside a small bag in a bucket and firmly attached;
– a scoop/bailer, if your boat is not self-bailing (catamarans are!);
– an oar, if you know how to scull, or two paddles;
– two buoyancy aids or lifejackets (not to be left in the bottom of the boat, but worn by the crew, and put on before leaving shore).

Now everything is ready, and you may set off, if the conditions are right. (Always drop the sails when transporting the boat to the water.) If the weather is not right, you can always practise your knots.

Conditions for the first sail ⚓ ⚓

The first sail absolutely must take place in a risk-free place, in docile weather conditions. You will have to start to think about the weather and your surroundings in a new way, and watch carefully and patiently. Your instincts, do not forget, were formed on land.

The place

You will not always be able to begin in an absolutely ideal spot, a small quiet lake or river, or enclosed bay on the sea. However, you should try to find a place as close to these ideals as possible, in order that you never get too far from land on your first excursion. Even such ideal waters as those described above may well have hidden currents or spots where the wind gusts.

Be sure not to venture onto waters too crowded with motorboats, fishing vessels or even other sailing boats. Your sailing dinghy has no provision for hoisting the two black balls up the mast which signify 'restricted in my ability to manoeuvre'! Equally, you should not choose an entirely deserted spot. However much seclusion you may desire, some supervision is necessary. Ideally, you should ask a friend in a motorboat to remain within sight. At the very least, leave a friend on shore who knows where help may be found if needed.

These precautions will not spoil your fun. Quite the reverse: they will leave you that much freer to discover and experiment for yourself without worries, and with room for mistakes. Nothing when you are afloat will be quite the way it looked from the shore. Distances, light, time, air, even the water will become a dynamic substance, full of life and movement.

The weather

In pleasant sunny weather one tends to underestimate the strength of the wind. We wouldn't go quite so far as to recommend a miserable overcast day for the first outing, but we should point out that a 'beautiful day' ashore can sometimes show its less attractive side once you are afloat.

It is particularly easy to be led astray by an offshore breeze. On the shore, maybe in the shelter of a sand dune or a hill, you might not notice it, but a few yards out an irresistible force could be lurking ready to push you off in the direction of the horizon. Unless the opposite shore is close and not too rocky, you should not set off for your first sail in an offshore wind.

If the wind is blowing towards the shore, you will at least be certain of getting back to where you left. In fact, it may be hard to leave! All in all, the best day to start is one where the wind is blowing parallel to the shore.

To begin with, you have to know how to check where the wind is coming from. The old moist finger held aloft is imprecise. Your ears are much better windvanes. They will hear the slightest wind noise; and that noise will be at its loudest (in both ears) when you are facing straight into the wind, or straight with the wind behind you.

You must train yourself to check the direction of the wind to the extent that it becomes automatic. *The wind is a sailor's most important point of reference.*

Beaufort scale of wind force

Beaufort number	Description	Windspeed (10m above sea level)		Sea conditions
		Knots	Km/h	
0	Calm	<1	<1	Mirror-like
1	Very light breeze	1–3	1–5	Small wavelets
2	Light breeze	4–6	6–11	Sharper wavelets, crests not breaking
3	Gentle breeze	7–10	12–19	Small waves, some breaking crests

Any more than this is much too much for a first sail.

When you get used to regarding the wind as a constant factor, and the shore as the part which keeps changing, you will begin to wonder how you once lived so many years in ignorance!

We specify the direction from which the wind is coming by using the points of the compass. It is of little use, navigationally, to say that the wind is coming from the direction of your sister's house, because a little further on the same wind will be coming from your aunt's house instead! It is a great deal more useful to say that the wind is coming from the west. That statement will remain true no matter which way the boat is facing.

Having worked out the direction of the wind, you then have to estimate its strength. You cannot go out if there is too much wind, and if there is none at all you are better off learning to row. The ideal beginner's wind is force 1–2. In a force 2, or light breeze, the sails will flap gently but noticeably. The jib clew moves to and fro but would not hurt you if it hit you in the face. The tell-tales lift, but do not reach the horizontal; smoke no longer goes straight up; kites fly, if lifelessly; you can feel the wind on your face, but it is not uncomfortable. The surface of the water is rippled, with perhaps some little waves if it is a large body of water. (Incidentally, if there is a swell, with breaking waves, even if there is no wind, it is best to stay ashore.)

The wind should be constant, not gusty. You should beware of stormy skies, or that clear light which comes just after showers. Showers are often accompanied by brief but strong gusts, known as squalls.

The wind can also change direction. This is one more reason to stay close to shore, even in ideal conditions. Sometimes, for instance in the summer, in the middle of a series of sunny days, the wind direction follows the sun round, so that by the end of each day it is coming from the west. Sailing off a south-facing shore will then give you a good day's conditions quite reliably. Come early evening, though, a land breeze from the north can set in quite suddenly, so you should ensure you are back on land in plenty of time.

There is much to be said on the subject of wind, and we shall return to the topic.

Dress

The pessimist, or optimist (!), who sets sail in a swimming costume is severely mistaken. It is never very hot in a boat (except on the sort of baking hot day when you should be in the shade anyway). It is cooler still after a quick dunking. Even wet clothes offer better protection than no clothes.

Wellington boots are not recommended. They inhibit your movement in the boat or in the water. Light shoes should be worn, as a stubbed toe is painful, and toestraps can also begin to rub after a while.

Sailing clothes have made great advances over the years: thermals, wetsuits, dry suits ... It is entirely possible to sail throughout most of the year, as long as you take care of your specialist clothing.

Wearing a wetsuit, which might cover the whole body or only a part, is often absolutely necessary and always reasonable. It might be 3mm thick or more, and you might want to wear an extra waterproof top. (A wetsuit is obligatory at the Glénans sailing school.) This is for two reasons:

– it gives you longer in the water without serious risks (an hour, rather than ten minutes);

– it gives beginners the sense of security necessary when they are experimenting with new moves which might capsize the boat, so that they can carry on and continue once the boat is righted, without being in any difficulties.

Buoyancy aids

Whatever the weather, a sailing dinghy must always be considered capable of capsizing. *Wearing a buoyancy aid is common sense.* It is hard, without a buoyancy aid, to swim around in the water, derigging the boat and waiting for rescue. The water is always colder than you think. You will tire faster than you think. You need a proper buoyancy aid. Does it impede your movement? Well, then, you'd better get used to it from the word go. Do you look inelegant? Well, floating inelegantly beats sinking in style.

The first sail

Preparation

Weather fine. Boat by the water's edge, with sails in place as practised earlier. Everything on board: rudder, tiller, centreboard, anchor, paddle, bailer. Now is the time to put on the lifejackets and to share out the jobs. One of you will be the 'helmsman' and look after the tiller and the mainsheet; the other is the 'crew', and will handle the jib and centreboard.

The hooks and rings involved in raising the sails of a catamaran make it sensible to put the sails up on dry land. The main is left uncleated, but the jib sheet should be cleated with the jib backed (that is, the windward sheet should be pulled tight). The boat is then taken all the way into the water.

In our ideal first-outing weather conditions, the crew then pushes the bows out to sea and jumps aboard. Next, the crew pulls in the mainsheet. The helmsman lowers the rudders and secures them fully down, as soon as the depth of water allows. This procedure requires the boat to be moving only slowly, so the sails must not be filling. If the rudders are not properly cleated down, the boat's speed will soon lift them up, at which point the boat becomes hard to steer and the pintles are put under a great deal of strain.

With dinghies, and on calm water, the boat can be put into the water before the sails are hoisted. If there are waves, follow the procedure given above for catamarans (not easy, since you must not get into the boat on land).

Carry the boat, don't drag it. A scratched hull is a sorry sight, and the centreboard casing can easily be jammed with sand, grass or gravel. Do not leave the boat half in and half out of the water, as this puts it under considerable strain.

If the boat floats completely straight away, the helmsman holds it by the forestay, which will naturally cause it to float head to wind while you are raising the sails. Holding it by the stern would allow the sails to fill, and the boat to become unmanageable. When the boat is held at the bow, it floats placidly, allowing the sails to be hoisted without trouble.

The crew gets in and starts to raise the mainsail, checking that the battens are not catching on anything. The main halyard is cleated on the starboard side of the mast. The main sheet should be running freely in its blocks. The kicking strap is then attached and put under moderate tension. Next the jib is raised, with the halyard cleated hard up on the port side. (The forestay might lose tension at this stage. This is not a cause for concern.) All control lines, sheets and halyards should now be stowed separately, clearly and accessibly.

Finally, the crew puts on the rudder and tiller. Ready for the off!

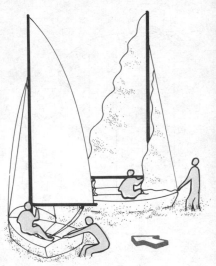

The boat will try to float off if you hold it by the stern. It floats gently head to wind if you hold it by the forestay, allowing you to climb aboard.

The helmsman climbs aboard, pushing the boat out to sea. If the first excursion is on a small inland water, one can choose a place where the wind is blowing off-shore (lightly, don't forget), so the boat will head off naturally. Otherwise, it is probably easiest to paddle out a short distance, so as to allow some sailing without the boat being blown back onto the land.

Starting out

Now one thing happens after another at such a rate that you are in danger of forgetting them all when you are back on dry land. The problem is one of organising and memorising appropriate responses and reflexes in a systematic manner for the situations which arise. For the situation itself is your teacher.

Since your aim is to get quickly to a level where you can take your boat out on any stretch of water, the best learning procedure is to put yourself deliberately in a range of situations which will equip you to overcome the challenges each of them throws up.

Our demonstration takes place on a stretch of water liberally strewn with landmarks: buoys, a chimney, a water-tower. The wind, illustrated by parallel lines, is coming from the top of the picture. It

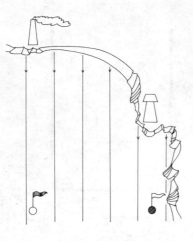

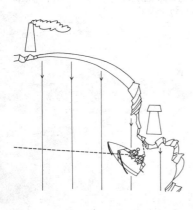

should be easy to transpose this picture to your own situation if you remember to take the wind as your reference point.

Let us suppose that the wind remains at force 2 for your first lessons. In practice, you will have to combine all your skills and knowledge from the beginning, maybe even consulting a map to get a really good picture of your water and its inlets, landmarks, sheltered spots, etc. It is hard to judge distances over water.

As the boat moves along, the coastline passes swiftly and the wind can shift. Nevertheless, since it is the wind by which you are sailing, it has to be regarded as the sole constant. It is also fair to point out that we are looking from above, and the system is simple from this angle. Down on the surface things are not so straightforward: you can see only a part of the picture, and your hands are full with the boat.

Finally, these exercises we suggest are only pointers. It is quite unlikely that your weather conditions and stretch of water will allow you to carry them out in precisely this order, though you will need to learn them at some stage, and the sooner the better.

Basic observations

You are in the boat, with rudder and centreboard both down. The first thing you both notice is that the boat is unstable. It's best not to sit on the same side, but to crouch in the centre of the boat, and to use gentle movements.

Before you can even start looking after the sails, the problem is to get used to this shifting, cramped cockpit space. All the rules you normally follow to keep your balance are suspended here. The only way you can control this moving world is by moving with it – your balance will constantly change, and the boat will begin to move once you find your balance. The boat itself will be somewhat hesitant until that point is reached.

There is nothing to be afraid of, even if you are now crouching in the bottom of the boat with the sails flapping around you. This, incidentally, is the first rule of survival: *whenever you find yourself*

The coastline as seen from above,
and as seen from the helm.

in difficulty, whatever the reason, it is better to abandon the usual survival instinct of grabbing hold of whatever is closest to hand; instead, *let go of everything and get down into the centre of the boat*. The boat will stop, become level and wait, sails flapping, for you to start anew.

Balance

The boat is at the mercy of the wind. It drifts downwind, but quickly finds a natural position in which it is side on, or beam on, to the wind. Every time you release the sails, the boat will find this position of its own accord. This is a basic point to remember.

The sails flap in the wind, more or less at right angles to the centreline of the boat.

Everything on the side of the boat from which the wind is coming is to windward. Leeward is the downwind side. The centreline of the boat divides the world very simply into two hemispheres: the windward and the leeward. The boat itself steers the line between these two.

The boat continues to float with the wind: we say it is making leeway. You can spot the drift by seeing how objects on land which were in line (transits) slowly move apart.

However, just as you are drifting to leeward, your landmarks ashore will start to show you that you are also sailing slowly forward. This is because the mainsail is not quite at right angles to the centreline; the boom is held slightly back from the mast, by the knot in the mainsheet. The mainsail is picking up just a small amount of wind, a few breaths, and it is this energy which is pushing you forward.

First lesson

Time to get on with it now. The helmsman takes hold of the tiller and the mainsheet; the crew holds the jibsheet, then they pull, to fill the sails with wind, and see what happens.

If there is an instructor on shore, at this point that person should look

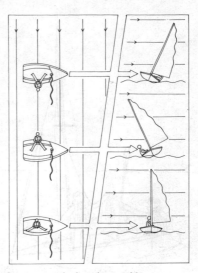

Lesson one: the boat is unstable.

When you let go the sheets, the boat heels less, settles down beam on to the wind and drifts gently downwind.

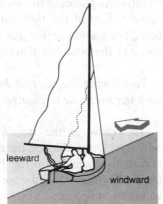

leeward

windward

Beginners must be left to make their own mistakes.

elsewhere. Above all, the instructor should not yell advice, which may be misunderstood or cause pointless panic, or just disturb the wildlife. In any artistic endeavour you learn by your own mistakes.

As you sheet in both sails, the boat comes to life. As each of you eases the sheets, the boat returns to its original semi-rest.

With the rudders down you already begin to move forward. In comparison with the dinghy, a catamaran can carry much more sail area due to the greater stability of the two hulls. The major part of the increase is accounted for by the mainsail, and this large power source is simple to operate. It does not even need to be perfectly adjusted in order to push you forward fairly swiftly.

In fact, the first problem you face once you have settled into position on the trampoline or one of the hulls is: how to stop! To stop, you ease both sails; if you are still travelling ahead, let go of the tiller extension and both move forward. The boat will now drift, sails flapping. Effectively you are in the same position as in a dinghy.

To progress beyond this point, you need to observe what happens with the tiller, the sheets and the weight distribution in the boat, still on calm water in a light breeze.

The sheets and weight distribution

Back to our boat, which is level, with the sails flapping. We now pick a course from one point, for instance a buoy, to any other point such that the line between the points is at right angles to the wind.

Sheet in; the sails fill; the boat speeds up and begins to heel slightly. As you ease the sheets, the sails flap and the boat becomes upright. Repeat the manoeuvre, sitting in different places in the boat. You should notice that adjusting the sheets alters not only the speed of the boat, but also its balance and that of the crew.

To balance the boat, ie keep it upright, you will need either to ease the sheets or to change your position in the boat.

The crew is the boat's ballast. Fortunately, the ballast is movable! Depending on the conditions, you will have to be moving constantly to maintain the balance of the boat, both side-to-side (obviously) and lengthwise (less obviously). Once the boat is balanced, it becomes a problem of sail trim.

Sheeting in/easing
To sheet a sail in, one pulls on the sheet to fill the sail: it then stops flapping (or lifting) and pushes the boat ahead. To ease the sheet, let it go until the sail is almost lifting. In other words, a sail which is flapping is definitely not sheeted in sufficiently; and just because it is not flapping does not mean it is correctly sheeted – it will benefit from being eased just to the point where it does not flap.

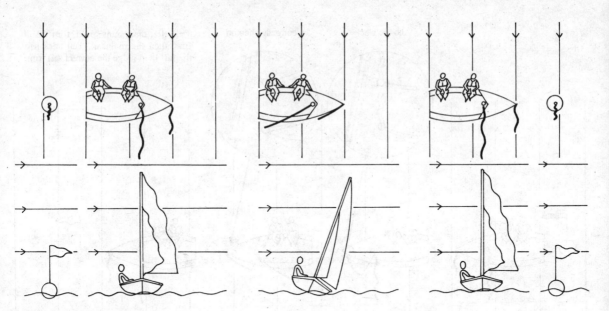

Trimming the sails

As you sheet in and the sails fill, the boat picks up speed. The fully battened mainsail is sufficiently large that it will pull you along without even needing to be sheeted in much; and the wide beam of the catamaran means that it hardly heels until on the point of capsizing.

If we return to our earlier situation, between the two buoys, the new objective will be to sail between them at top speed. You sheet the jib in until it is filling (and no further), then sheet in the mainsail.

Bearing away and luffing: using the tiller

Until this point, you have had your hands full with getting the boat to move, maintaining your balance, and all the other things going on. You reach the stage where heading for the buoy, and getting there, becomes repetitive. In order to expand your horizons, you need to use the tiller.

Begin by heading for the buoy. You have the sails correctly trimmed. You decide to change direction and head for the tower. Push the tiller away from you. The sails will begin to flap, the boat loses speed and comes more upright (noticeably in a dinghy, less so in a catamaran).

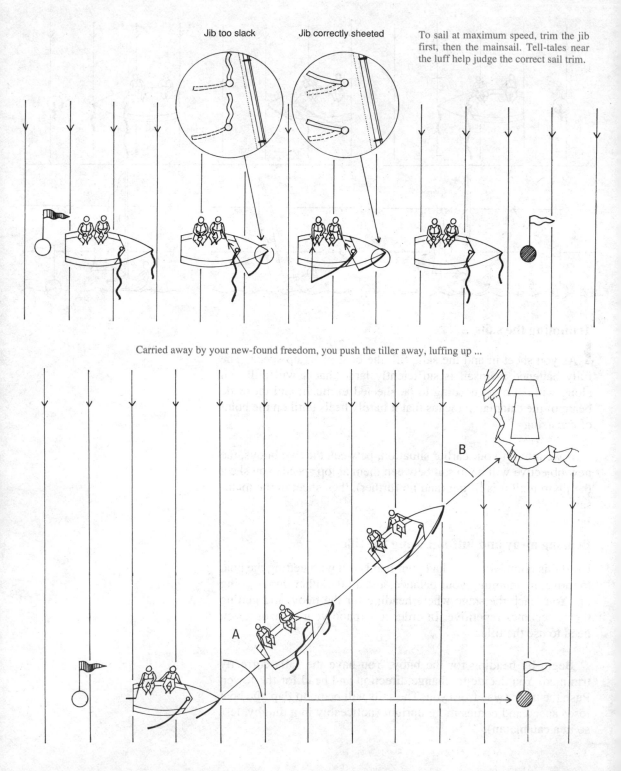

Jib too slack

Jib correctly sheeted

To sail at maximum speed, trim the jib first, then the mainsail. Tell-tales near the luff help judge the correct sail trim.

Carried away by your new-found freedom, you push the tiller away, luffing up ...

B

A

The sails are sheeted in – first the jib, then the main – just far enough to eliminate flapping. This was a luff, ie you were sailing closer to the wind. (In the diagram, angle A is greater than angle B.)

As you change your heading, you also change the point of sailing and you need to change the sail trim.

When you luff, or sail closer to the wind, you trim the sails by sheeting slightly tighter; instead of heading for the tower, though, you could have aimed back towards the buoy: in this case, bearing away, by pulling the tiller towards you. Trimming the sails when you bear away is done by easing them until they flap, then pulling back in just a little so they fill.

... then bearing away by pulling the tiller towards you, to head for the buoy.

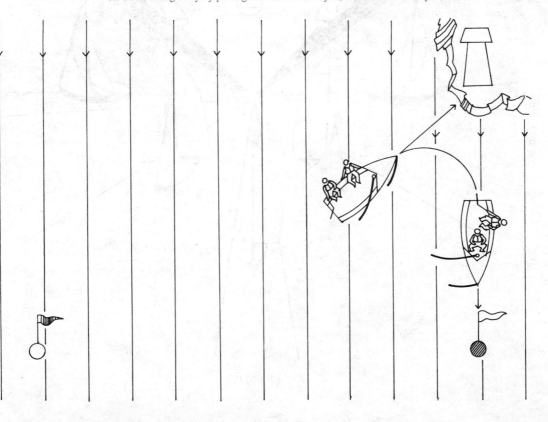

Points of sailing

Close-hauled, you sheet the sails in tight. They are still tight in when *close fetching*, though less flat; you head off onto a *reach* with progressive easing of the sheets through a *close*, *beam* and *broad reach*, until you are on a *run*, before the wind.

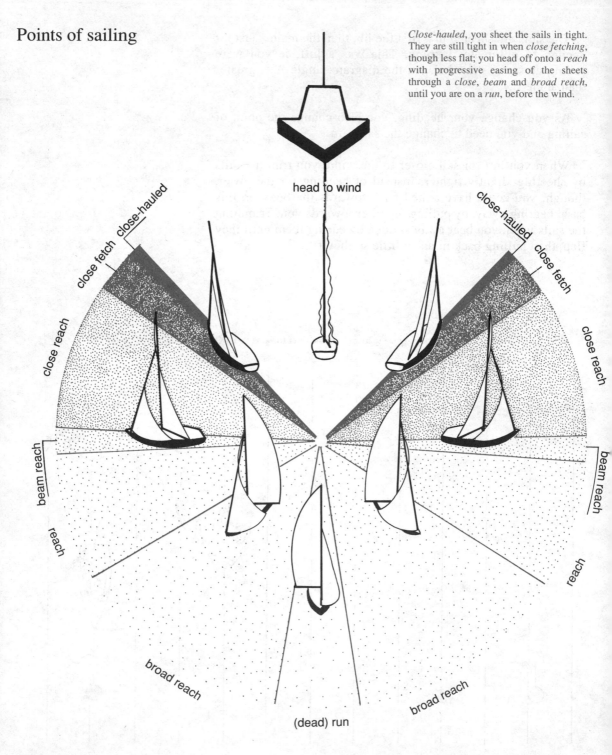

head to wind

close-hauled

close fetch

close reach

beam reach

reach

broad reach

(dead) run

Points of sailing

Definition 1:
By *point* of sailing we mean the angle between the boat's centre-line and the real wind. Once you know the wind direction, then this angle precisely describes your heading. Using the terms close reach, beam reach, running, etc means that both crew members understand what they are doing and can work together. For instance both know that luffing up means tightening their sails, all the way to close-hauled ...

Definition 2:
The above is useful to establish shared understanding on board. However, it is occasionally insufficient as a description of what is happening on a dinghy, and usually inadequate for a catamaran or a sailboard.

The boat's tell-tales or burgee do not indicate the true wind, but the apparent wind. It is the apparent wind which fills the sails and determines their correct trim. And *the apparent wind varies with the speed of the boat*: it is a combination of the true wind and the headwind caused by your motion. Effectively, the headwind component becomes relatively stronger the faster you sail, so the combined (or apparent) wind gets closer to the axis of the boat, and the sails have to be sheeted ever tighter. Catamarans and sailboards often reach the point where the sails are close-hauled, even though the course sailed is that of a broad reach.

Sailing to windward

You have decided to head closer to the wind. You centre the tiller and the boat luffs up. As you pass through a close reach, the sails flap, so you sheet in a little, just enough to stop them flapping.

From this point on, you are making ground against the wind, sailing upwind or to windward. The wind seems stronger and more lively than when it was coming side on, on the beam. The boat's tendency to heel increases; it feels firmer in the water; it is very responsive to the tiller. The hull vibrates slightly as it cuts through the water. The sails are still full, and you are close fetching, or driving to windward, sailing fast, comfortably and making very little leeway. Try not to wreck it by sheeting the sails in too tight: keep easing the sheets slightly and then pulling them back in, just enough to keep them filling and not flapping, with perhaps a hint of a flutter in the front edge.

You can get a touch closer to the wind; then you need to sheet the sails in tight, to flatten them. You are now sailing as much into the wind as possible, that is, close-hauled. This is a racing position, in which the boat-beast grows sensitive and tense. You have left the good-natured close fetch behind you. The wind hardens and stiffens in the sail, the boat heels more and the crew needs to move more energetically to keep it flat, especially if there is more than a little wind. You may need to pull the tiller towards you just to keep the boat moving on course; the hull gurgles and slaps a little on the wavelets, and the crew starts thinking about plans for the weekend off.

Close-hauled is an exciting point of sailing, which allows the boat to show its true spirit. Sailing close-hauled demands constant attention and sensitivity. The wind is never quite regular in either direction or strength; it can back you (come more from ahead) or free you (move round to the side), freshen or drop; the helmsman must constantly change course to keep close-hauled, and the crew must move around the boat constantly to maintain balance. It takes a long time to become an expert close-hauled sailor. The beginner tends to set course for a landmark on the shore, which is precisely the wrong way of doing it: one makes considerable leeway close-hauled, and to keep the landmark in sight you would pinch closer and closer to the wind, travelling ever more slowly forwards and making ever more leeway. Sailed this way, a beat (stretch of close-hauled sailing) can become a torture. If you put your trust in the wind as your guide and keep the sails filling, you will not point so high, but you will keep your speed up and make less leeway. Which of the two approaches is better? It depends whether you want fun and relaxation from your sailing or not!

Sailing downwind

Back to the beam reach. This time we shall explore the leeward side of the boat. You bear away, that is, pull the tiller towards you.

To begin with you are on a beam reach; you ease the sails out more, and everything begins to change. The wind feels less strong on your cheeks; you seem to lose some speed (which may be correct); and the water appears smoother as the hull glides through it. The boat stops slipping to leeward, and you may raise the centreboard; you do not need to lean out. The crew sits comfortably, the wind and the boat are travelling together, and you are on a broad reach.

You may indeed already be running, with the wind behind you. Off the wind, it is more difficult to be precisely sure where the wind is coming from: the burgee is less constant, and the tell-tales barely lift. You can try to fill the jib on the other side from the mainsail (goosewing). If it will not cross over easily, you are not yet running. If it does cross over, you are certainly running, but you may even – without realising it – be too far round and running by the lee.

Goosewinged, running before the wind.

At this stage the helmsman must be very delicate in using the tiller. Sailing downwind initially seems much more passive and easier than those hard upwind stretches, but the downwind leg has its tricky points:

– push the tiller too far down and the boat will luff quickly onto a reach, possibly encountering a stronger breeze than you expected;
– pull the tiller too far towards you and you can be sailing by the lee without realising it. The wind comes round behind the mainsail, picks the sail up and knocks it briskly across to the other side as easily as you would flick the page of a book. The sail, though, unlike this page, is equipped with a hard metal bar at the bottom known as the boom, which has a habit of clouting heads on its way across the boat. At this stage you also hope that figure-of-eight knot you tied in the mainsheet was far enough up to stop the boom short of the shroud. This is known as a gybe. In light winds, no problem. The wind, however, can push an unplanned gybe just that touch too far into a luff on the new tack, and that sudden change can lead to a capsize.

Anyway, whether you intended it or not, you have now changed tacks. For the first time, the wind is now coming from the other side of the boat: what was the leeward side is now the windward side, and vice versa.

With the help of a reasonably strong wind, a gybe can easily end in a capsize.

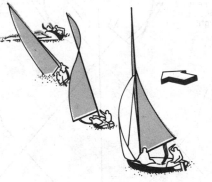

Changing tacks

Now that you have some basic survival skills afloat, you can start to try out some basic manoeuvres. To begin with, a few definitions:

Starboard: the right side of the boat as you look forward.
Port: the left side of the boat as you look forward.

On starboard tack: the wind is coming from the starboard side
 of the boat.
On port tack: the wind is coming from the port side of the boat.

To move from starboard to port tack, or from port to starboard
tack, you tack or gybe.

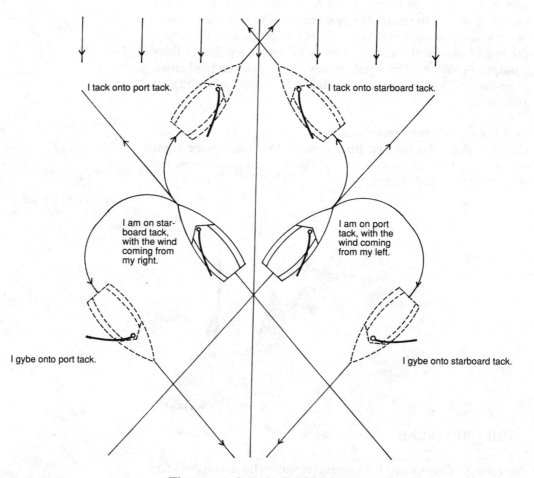

I tack onto port tack.

I tack onto starboard tack.

I am on star-
board tack,
with the wind
coming from
my right.

I am on port
tack, with the
wind coming
from my left.

I gybe onto port tack.

I gybe onto starboard tack.

The expression 'ready about' can mean either 'prepare to tack'
or 'prepare to gybe', depending on the situation.

Tacking

You have already seen that as the boat gets more and more close-hauled it actually stops in its tracks; it enters a sort of forbidden zone. Tacking means pushing the bows of the boat from a close-hauled course through this forbidden zone, the eye of the wind, onto a close-hauled course on the opposite tack.

As the bow passes through the wind, the sails are not full and pulling, so you rely on the boat's momentum, or way, to push you through. It is therefore most important that you should have some way on before attempting to tack.

Start by looking over your shoulder in the direction in which you will be travelling after the tack, ie at about 90° to your present course. Line up a landmark of some sort on a line perpendicular to the boat and to windward.

We start by assuming that you are close-hauled and travelling at a fair speed. The objective is to come out of the tack travelling at the same speed on the opposite tack, while keeping the boat upright …

Catamaran special

A catamaran tacks differently from a monohull, because the outer hull has a greater distance to travel than the inner hull during a turn.

The trick is to keep one's weight on the windward hull for as

---

The effect of the rudder
Weather helm and lee helm

We have already seen how if you push the tiller left, the boat turns right; push it right and the boat goes left. It is easy to come to terms with this if you think of the force the water exerts on the rudder blade.

In order to bear away, the helmsman sitting to windward has to pull the tiller towards him. To luff up, however, it is usually enough simply to leave the tiller centred. Why this apparent imbalance? Because most boats have a natural tendency to luff, known as weather helm. The opposite, which is rare, is known as lee helm and it tends to make the boat react less cleanly and quickly to the tiller.

To the beginner, the rudder seems so effective that it is easy to over-use it. *But once the rudder is at an angle to the centreline it acts as a brake.* It is not necessary, in a well-set-up boat, to make much use of the rudder to stay on course.

Tiller right, boat turns left.
Tiller left, boat turns right.

1. Close-hauled, ⚊ : port tack; ◖ : starboard tack;
Boat level, sails trimmed correctly. The helmsman looks for a
landmark, eg the chimney, to windward.
2. Having memorised this page, the helmsman luffs, sheeting in
and moving the tiller away gently.
3. As the boat turns, the tiller is moved further over. The jib
begins to flap, but the crew keeps it tightly sheeted.

⚊ The boat heels to windward and both crew members move
inboard.
4. Once the mainsail is in the middle of the boat:

⚊ The crew releases the now flapping jib. The helmsman
swaps hands for the sheet and tiller.

◖ The crew keeps the jib sheeted, until it fills slightly from the

other side (backs).
The mainsail might need to be freed slightly then re-sheeted to
help the battens re-shape themselves.

⚊ **5.** The helmsman sits down on the new windward side; the
crew pulls the jib in on the new tack and balances the boat.

◖ The helmsman changes sheet and tiller hands; the crew
releases the jib and pulls it in on the new tack.

⚊ **6.** Off on starboard tack.

◖ The helmsman trims the mainsail and the crew balances the
boat.

◖ **7.** Off on port tack.

long as possible, to lighten the outside hull and enable it to get round with little drag, at a fair speed.

Anyone accustomed to sailing old-fashioned boats will recognise these tips on tacking a cat, as boats of old also required the crew to pay a great deal of attention to the sails and tiller while going through the typical slow tack of these boats, correcting constantly as the boat turned.

If you went into the tack without sufficient way on, let go the jib too soon or pulled it in too quickly, or failed to follow the tack through with the correct movement of the tiller, you will fail to get through the tack. The boat will stop, then start to move backwards. Back to square one and try it again.

Gybing

First, free off until you are running downwind. The crew progressively eases the jib and ensures the boat remains in correct lateral trim (even in a catamaran) throughout the manoeuvre.

When the mainsail gets close to the shroud and as soon as the jib is ready to fill on the other side, you are running dead downwind. Do make sure you bring the jib over before you gybe, otherwise it can wrap itself round the forestay and make you go through the whole thing again. It's quite a good idea to centre the mainsheet traveller.

The burgee points straight back and you can hardly feel the wind any longer; in fact, you can hardly even feel the boat beneath your feet. Now you can start the gybe.

The helmsman changes sides and swaps sheet and tiller hands. He pulls the sail in to the middle of the boat; the crew changes sides; the mainsheet is released. You've gybed!

This is a simple manoeuvre in a catamaran because the boat remains so stable. It is all the simpler as most racing catamarans have no boom.

It feels worrying to begin with because the boat accelerates as you bear away. However, once you are actually running it soon slows down. It is most important that both crew members make sure they are free in their movements, to stop the boat luffing up on the new tack. And do make sure the battens don't hit the shroud!

Tacking and gybing are both ways of going about, or changing tack; however, tacking makes you gain distance to windward, whereas gybing means you drop off to leeward.

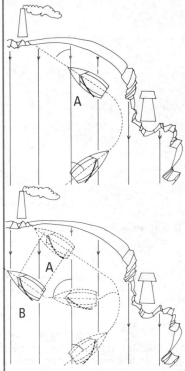

A good tack
You will know you have made a good tack if you go smoothly from one tack close-hauled and moving at a decent speed and come out of it on the other tack also close-hauled and travelling at a decent speed.

B bore off too far after the tack. They must now luff up excessively (pinch) and will never get on course for the chimney, whereas A, after a good tack, should get there with no trouble.

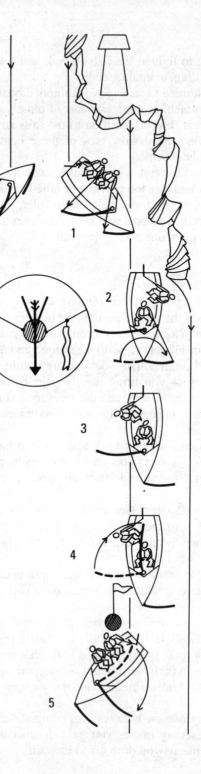

1. Bearing away:

The helmsman frees the mainsheet.

The helmsman frees the mainsheet traveller (and the sheet if necessary). The crew gradually frees the jib.

2. Downwind:

The jib is filled on the new side. The burgee is pointing straight back. The crew balances the boat.

The helmsman passes the tiller extension over to the new side, backwards.

3. The helmsman changes sides and swaps tiller and sheet hands, preparing to pull the mainsail across.

4. The helmsman pulls the mainsail over. In light winds, it is best to pull the mainsheet with your hand above the blocks, so the extra friction of the sheet running through the blocks does not stop the sail crossing over. In general, though, your aim is to soften the passage of the mainsail from one side to the other.

5. The crew changes sides. You may now start to luff up.

To windward/downwind

We have followed this basic introductory course with fixed reference points such as buoys, chimneys, etc. However, we all know really that the only proper point of reference for the sailor is the wind. For this reason, you will hear courses and headings described most often as being either 'to windward' or 'downwind'. This must become a natural reflex for you, because a clear understanding and correct use of these terms is essential for your safety afloat.

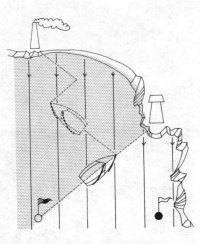

To windward
'I'm sailing to windward' is simpler to say than it is to do. In order to head towards the wind (in the diagram, towards the chimney) you will have to beat, that is, to tack repeatedly. In the olden days of sailing ships, a beat to windward was often said to take 'twice the distance, three times the time and four times the sweat'. Except for the sweat (let's not forget, we're still only sailing on flat water, in a force 2) this dictum is as true today as it was then.

Going upwind, ie towards the chimney, means that one has to tack – this is called beating.

Downwind
'I'm sailing downwind', in the diagram, means 'I'm sailing for the buoy'. This, to your relief and surprise, you find you can do in one. You could also say 'I'm on a run' or 'with the wind behind me'.

Capsizes

The main cause of capsizes is the wind; or, to be more precise, the wind in gusts or squalls. You reacted a moment too late and suddenly the boat is on its side with the rig in the sea, downwind of the hull. The first thing to avoid is walking on the mast. The mast looks like a convenient walkway, but this is the surest way known of 'turning turtle', ie going upside down, with the mast in the mud. Quite apart from the risk of breaking the mast, this is an extremely tricky situation to get out of …

When the boat is on its side, you make sure the sheets are uncleated. One crew member holds the bottom of the forestay to keep the boat head to wind, and the other clambers onto the centre-

Sailing downwind means heading straight for the buoy, carried along by the wind.

You have to hang on it with all your weight …

board. (You can generally stand on the centreboard, but not at the tip, because you might break it.)

In order to right a catamaran, you have to enlist the help of the wind. You need to get the masthead upwind. The best way to do this is to hold onto the submerged hull at one end so that you are a sort of pivot in the water and the hull can naturally drift downwind of you.

When you have got the boat into position, pass the righting rope over the upper hull and then hang on it with all your weight, to unstick the masthead from the water. Once the boat begins to come upright, duck down immediately to the submerged hull, because the top hull can come crashing down with quite a lot of force. (It sometimes has so much momentum that the boat capsizes the other way.) Flying hulls can give you a nasty headache if you get in the way!

Basic rule:
NEVER LEAVE THE BOAT.

For a practised team, re-righting a boat is a matter of a few seconds. Beginners tend to have a few more problems. You might even consider throwing out the anchor if the alternative is to drift onto a rocky coast or out to sea.

Avoiding collisions

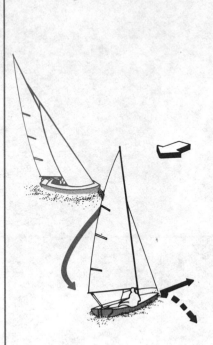

As you are seldom alone on the water, it is important to know what to do when you are close to other boats. There are precise rules for avoiding collisions; these state that of two boats on opposite tacks, it is the one on port tack which must take evasive action. Of boats on the same tack, it is the windward one which must take action to avoid the other. In both cases, when taking evasive action, it is better to aim to pass behind the other boat rather than in front of it. The manoeuvre must be clear, and begun in plenty of time, before the boats are too close together.

One thing must be clearly understood: this is not a question of right of way. It is not a matter of one boat being 'in the right' and the other 'in the wrong'. The boat which should not need, theoretically, to take evasive action is actually in the wrong if it does not do so when necessary.

The blue boat must take action to avoid the black boat. If it does not do so, black must tack (not bear away!).

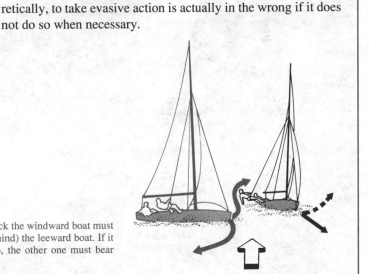

On the same tack the windward boat must avoid (pass behind) the leeward boat. If it does not do so, the other one must bear away.

Round-up

We have now undertaken a first trip through the wonders of steering a small sailing boat. Of course you will have to practise, look a few things up again, even train a little before these moves become a natural part of yourself. Re-reading this chapter might be a good start!

You will need to have assimilated these last few pages thoroughly before setting out in stronger winds. Your aim should be to tame the beast in peace and quiet before venturing forth in search of thrills and excitement in full safety.

Sailboards

Rigging a sailboard

You dream about it for ages before one day that dream comes true: you have your sailboard. But that's not even the beginning. First you have to learn to use it!

In the beginning was the board

The longer the board, basically, the easier it is to learn to sail on.

A beginner's board will generally be between 3.40m (if you are lighter than, say, 60kg) and 3.70m. The board will have a centre-board and will be relatively flat. Such boards are probably best termed multipurpose, or long funboards, because they can be used for lots of things besides learning! In fact, you can improve your boardsailing on these boards for a long time; and some of the high-performance boards are used in competitions.

Length and volume of sailboards

Length (metres)	Buoyancy volume (litres)	
3.89	340	Division II
3.70	230	Beginner/improver, raceboard
3.60	220	
3.50	210	
3.40	195	Funboards with centreboard,
3.30	180	improvers aiming for funboarding
3.20	165	
3.10	150	
3.00	135	First funboards
2.90	120	
2.80	105	
2.70	90	
2.60	75	Funboards
2.50	60	

The only boards which do not fit into our schema of length equalling ease of mastery are the long regatta boards, which are semi-circular in section and extremely unstable.

Do not be put off by the presence of *footstraps*. In anything over a force 3, you will soon come to appreciate them, but it is probably as well to unscrew them temporarily while you are in the early learning phases.

Board accessories

A board will come equipped with a fin, a centreboard, footstraps, a mast foot and a mast foot track.

The *centreboard* will have some mechanism for controlling how easily it moves up and down: either plastic chocks, or some sort of compression joint. If the centreboard moves stiffly in its casing, lubricate the sliding parts with paraffin wax.

The *mast foot* should be checked to see that it does not slip out of its housing too easily.

The *mast foot track* can also be problematic from the point of view of deciding how far forward to situate the mast foot. To begin with, keep the mast at the forward end of the track; we shall look later at occasions in which it might be moved.

Sail, boom and mast

There is no such thing as a beginner's sail. So long as you start off with a boom longer than 2m and a sail which is not too narrow, you will have a relatively sensitive yet forgiving rig.

The second criterion for choosing your first sail is weight, or rather the lack of it: you want as few battens as possible, and as simple a cut as possible consistent with durability. Do not succumb to the temptation of using a small sail (under 5sq m) for light winds: it is misleading to think that small sails are easier to handle, and this will slow your progress.

We use the conventional terminology taken from boat sails to refer to the eye at the bottom front of the sail as the tack eye, and the

A sailboard and accessories.

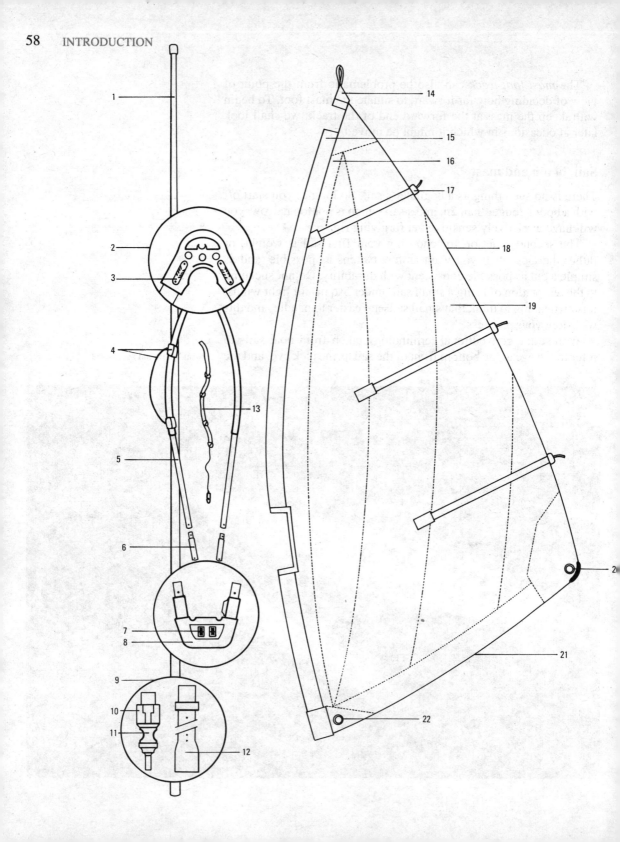

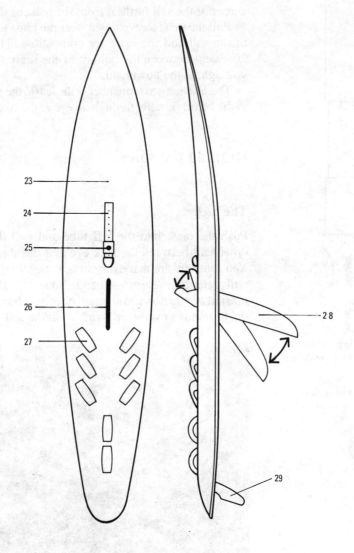

1. Mast.	11. Universal joint.	21. Foot.
2. Boom end.	12. Mast extension.	22. Tack.
3. Cleat.	13. Rig uphaul.	23. Board.
4. Harness line.	14. Sail head.	24. Mast foot track.
5. Boom.	15. Luff tube.	25. Mast plate.
6. Boom extension.	16. Luff.	26. Centreboard slot.
7. Clew outhaul sheaves.	17. Top batten (tied in place).	27. Foot straps.
8. Joint at the aft end of the boom.	18. Leech.	28. Pivoting centreboard.
9. Mast foot (complete).	19. Sail.	29. Skeg.
10. Mast base.	20. Clew.	

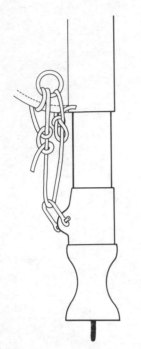

One simple method for tying the tack: use a bowline to attach the rope to the sail.

Tying the sail onto the mast, here with the help of a pulley and tube cleat.

corner of the sail furthest from the mast as the clew.

Pull the mast sleeve down over the mast to check that the lengths of the sail and the mast are compatible. There should usually be 20–30cm between the bottom of the mast and the sail tack before you tighten the downhaul.

The last thing to remember is the leash, the rope which ties the mast to the board (usually through an eye at the front of the board).

Rigging the sail

The tack

Push the mast into the luff tube and pull the luff tight using the downhaul between the tack eye and the sheaves on the mast foot. You must ensure that everything is tightly tied, as the tension here will determine the mast bend. You may also need to adjust the tension on the downhaul again once you have tied the clew outhaul up, to remove excessive wrinkles in the sail.

The boom

Now you need to fix the boom firmly to the mast. The illustrations show some ways of doing this.

In all the illustrations, you tie the boom on while it is placed parallel to the mast, and pull the boom down perpendicular to the

The boom is parallel to the mast while you tie it up. Bringing it down at right angles tensions the cords.

Two different ways of attaching the boom to the mast.

mast to tension the inhaul. The inhaul should therefore not be too tight to begin with: you are aiming to achieve a happy medium between over-tight (which can damage glass-fibre masts) and over-loose (which will mean that the boom slides up and down the mast). The boom should be tied onto the mast at about shoulder height.

The clew outhaul

Now you can tie the clew of the sail to the back end of the boom using the same principles as you did for the tack. There will be an eye in the clew and a couple of sheaves in the boom to give you

A comfortable position for pulling the clew outhaul tight on the boom.   The battens put a curve into the sail.

more power as you pull. Tie a bowline onto the sail, then pass the outhaul through one pulley, through the sail eye and back through the other pulley before cleating the outhaul on the boom. Tie up the loose end with a couple of half hitches. You are aiming to flatten the sail sufficiently to free it of vertical wrinkles. If instead you end up

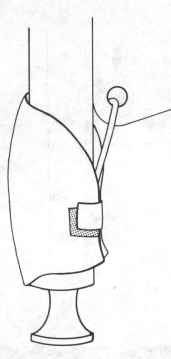

The mast foot protection sock.

with horizontal wrinkles, you need more tension at the tack. There will always be a few wrinkles at the corners, particularly at the mast head, which will only disappear once you have the battens tensioned.

The battens

The battens have the job of keeping a good shape to the leech of the sail. Full-length battens are there to control the curve of the sail, and only work when they are tied in with a certain amount of compression.

The final check

A sail's power derives from its curvature. This is to a large extent built in at the time of the sail being cut, but can be controlled somewhat by the tension you put on the downhaul and outhaul and the compression you give to the battens.

At the moment all you need to remember is that you need the sail flatter in stronger breezes: this is achieved by greater tension on the outhaul and downhaul, and relaxing the pressure on the battens.

The final attachments needed are the rig *uphaul* and the mast foot sock. The rig is now fully ready.

The first sail

Where do I start?

The usual advice to beginners is to start off in an onshore wind, so you are not blown out to sea. This good advice has a downside, however: with an onshore wind you are more likely to have a swell and waves to contend with, so it is a good idea also to look for some fairly sheltered water, say behind a sea wall or sand bar. In many ways the ideal wind to start out in is a wind parallel to the beach; and the ideal place is enclosed, with calm shallow water. At the beginning, it does wonders for your confidence if you know you can reach the bottom and stand up.

Wherever you start, there are some basic rules to observe:
– do not get more than a mile away from dry land;
– avoid harbour entrances, regattas and other crowded spots;
– ask the local authorities for guidance on areas where you may not boardsail (such as bathing beaches or shipping lanes);
– if there is an offshore wind above force 3, stay at home;
– wear your wetsuit, and don't worry about maybe getting too hot;
– do not boardsail on your own: whatever you might think, boardsailing is not a solo sport.

Taking responsibility for your own safety

If you feel you are getting a touch too far from home and you cannot make it back under sail power, don't wait to get any further away!

In *light* winds, place the boom flat across the back of the board, lie down along the front of the board and paddle with your hands. The sail has very little wind resistance when it is flat down in this way and you can quite easily move forward against the wind.

In *freshening* winds, use one of two solutions:
– de-rig the sail, lay all the parts of the rig along the board, lie down and paddle;
– call for assistance using the conventional signal illustrated.

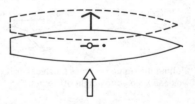

'I am unable to get back; come and give me a tow.'

First steps

Your first contact with the board

The classic boardsailing teaching technique would have you get to know the board on its own before introducing you to the rig and letting you start to pull the sail out of the water. Many of the exercises you would do on an unrigged board might appear absurd and repetitive, but the various games one can play with a board have a serious learning point as well as a value on their own: turning the board round, turning it over, pushing it sideways, falling off and climbing back on, paddling it and using it as a tame surfboard. The most important lesson to learn, though, is that falling off is an educational experience, and not a catastrophe.

Two crucial experiments

The board is in 50cm of water with the centreboard down. Push one end horizontally with your hand. You will notice that the board pivots on an axis more or less where the centreboard is. If, on the other hand, you push at the midpoint of the board, it will not turn: it will move sideways. The point at which your pressure achieves a sideways movement is known as the 'centre of lateral resistance' of the hull (ie of the board + centreboard + skeg). Any force applied at a point forward or aft of this point will result in the board turning. The point is movable: if you raise the centreboard you will notice

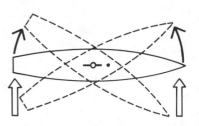

If you push the board horizontally at one end or the other with your hand, it turns. If you push at the midpoint of the board, it does not turn, but shifts sideways.

To windward/leeward

A straight line passing underneath the sailor's feet and perpendicular to the direction of the wind is the line dividing the world into *windward* (everything between the sailor and the wind) and *leeward*.

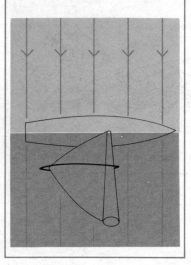

that the point moves aft. By the same token, if one end of the board is carrying more weight than the other, the centre of lateral resistance will move towards the submerged end; it will also move further forward as the board gathers speed.

The board is now in the water, beam on to the wind, with the centreboard down and the rig attached but downwind of the board. You climb onto the board, one foot either side of the mast. Try to move the sunken sail first towards the front of the board, then towards the back. You will notice that the board pivots beneath your feet, pointing either more into the wind or further away from the wind.

Pulling the sail up

Posture

The board and the rig are in the water. You are standing on the lake or sea bed, and can use this to position the board nicely across the wind. (This will not always be so easy in future.)

The board is beam on to the wind, centreboard down, sail to leeward, mast at the front edge of the sail.

Your doctor will no doubt have lectured you about the evil side-effects of pulling or lifting with your back bent. The doctor will have told you to use instead your leg muscles, just like a weight-lifter. This advice is equally applicable to a boardsailor trying to pull the rig out of the water. It is difficult to keep your back straight throughout the lifting process, but you must at least try not to bend your back too much. A long rig-uphaul rope is particularly helpful in encouraging good posture: with a rope of a decent length you can start with a good pull, leaning backwards while the sail is at its least willing, stuck to the water. You then use your weight, rather than your strength, to pull the rig up.

Technique

Your feet are still either side of the mast, and you are in the correct position to begin pulling the sail up. But the board starts to swivel the moment the sail starts to come out of the water, if you do not control its rotation.

You can control the rotation of the board by pushing and pulling with your feet: to turn the board away from the wind, you push with the front foot and pull with the rear foot, and vice versa. In this way you can counter the way the board tries to rotate as you are pulling the sail up. In fact, there is no harm in the bow coming up slightly into the wind as you are pulling the rig up, because the wind gets behind the sail and helps it up.

Pulling the rig up becomes much easier if you can keep your weight off centre.

Pulling the sail up.

The transmission of force through your feet

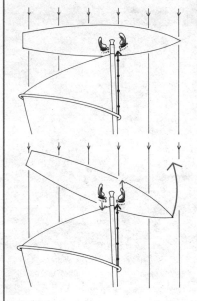

Have you ever taken part in a tug of war on slippery grass? The chances are, if you have, you ended up on your bottom at some stage or other.

Why did this happen? Instinctively, you leaned further and further back to pull more efficiently, but the ability of your feet to support this pull is limited by the slipperiness of the ground.

The board works the same way. All the force of your arms, either pulling the rig out of the water or actually sailing, is transmitted via your feet to the board, so long as the anti-slip surface permits.

The board, in turn, slips quite easily over or through the water, and so rotates either around the mast foot, which functions as a virtually fixed point while the sail is in the water, or around the centreboard, which is the pivotal fixed point once the rig is out of the water.

Your body is transmitting the force exerted by your arms, through your feet, to the board.

To visualise the process in operation, you can imagine the forces coming from the boom or the uphaul as a sort of current which you are channelling through one or other of your feet.

The wind operates on the uphaul creating a force which you channel back down through your feet.

Picking the sail up from the windward side

All too often the beginner will end up having to raise the rig from the 'wrong', ie windward, side, particularly if the wind drops suddenly and the rig falls into windward.

Solution No 1
Pull the sail partially out of the water and wait for the wind to turn you round so that the rig is on the leeward side. You are then back to your ideal starting position.

Solution No 2
Faster, but riskier. Pull the sail out of the water. The wind will get under it and flip it over suddenly to the leeward side. The process is a little sudden, but you can keep your balance if you anticipate it.

Balance

As the sail comes out of the water, it offers less and less resistance to your pull, so you have to decrease your effort gradually by leaning back less. Feed the uphaul through your hands so that you end up holding the uphaul next to the mast.

Once the sail is out of the water, it is in equilibrium only when perpendicular to the board.

You are still holding the uphaul, with the rig upright. Check that you can steer the board by altering the pressure of your feet and moving the rig forward and aft. It is rather difficult to balance in this position. You need a few more tips before you can balance with confidence.

Where do you want the board to head?

Hold on to the mast now, as the uphaul is too imprecise an instrument for you to use when steering. *As you lean the rig to the left, the board will begin to rotate clockwise. Incline the rig to the right, and it rotates anticlockwise.* You can hold the mast in one hand, and use the pressure of your feet and the rake of the rig to turn the board through 360°, first in one direction, then in the other.

The neutral position

This is the ideal position for the start. The sail flaps, the board is beam on to the wind and immobile, the body is relaxed. Your aim is to find a position where the rig does not weigh on your arms at all. The mast will have to be beyond the vertical, slightly to windward of the board, and you will need to position both feet aft of the mast.

When you are out on the water, with the sail at right angles to the board, you have to remember not to move your feet to the side in search of a better stance: that way you will fall into windward.

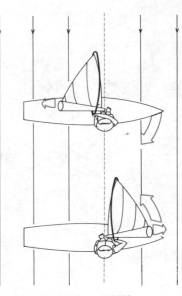

Turning the board through 360°.

The neutral position: side, rear and front view.

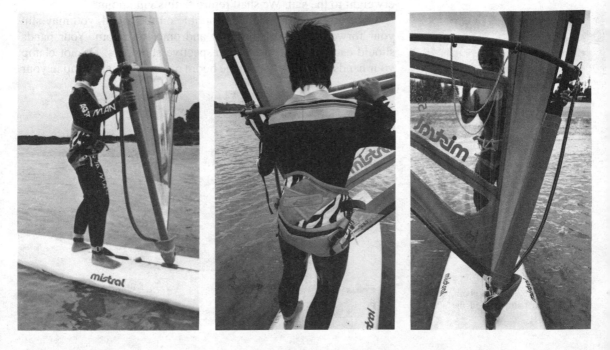

The neutral position.

Once you have found a neutral position, you have to maintain it, one hand on the mast, the other holding the boom opposite your shoulder, and the sail flapping.

The start

To get moving, leave your forward arm where it is and pull the boom with your aft hand. After a few yards, let the aft hand go completely, so that the sail flaps again. The board will slow and then come to a standstill; the flapping sail will be streaming out to leeward like a flag, telling you where the wind is coming from.

Use the flapping sail to check that you are still at right angles to the wind. If you are not, it is because you pulled the sail in too far forward or aft. The most common failing at this point is for the board to head up into the wind (luff). What has generally happened is that the sailor has pulled with the front hand as well as with the other, a perfectly natural reaction to feeling the force of the wind. The rig has then sagged off to leeward and the board has luffed up. Anyway, position the board back across the wind. To get used to the feeling of the wind in the sail, it is much better to keep going like this – start, release the aft hand, reposition the board, start again – than to press on heroically trying to keep the board moving.

You must be careful to use the strength of your arms, not your back, to counter the force of the wind, using your body as a counterweight to the sail. We shall return to this vital point.

Once you begin to feel comfortable on the board, you may slip your forward hand off the mast and onto the boom. Your hands should each be opposite their respective shoulders. Do not clamp your hands desperately onto the boom or you will get cramp in your

One way of holding the boom, with the forward hand palm up and the aft hand palm down.

forearms very quickly. For the hand which is palm down, try the 'hook' grip, with the thumb on the same side as the fingers; for the hand which is palm up, you should let your thumb round to the opposite side from your fingers.

Changing direction while moving

You can now balance and accelerate with the sail full. The things you needed to learn before you got this far were: to steer the board with your feet while the sail was in the water, and then with the sail flapping in the air. Changing direction while moving requires you to use the same basic tools: foot pressure on the board, and leaning the rig forward or backward. You do not need to make a great effort of strength to change direction, however, as the wind and water will help you.

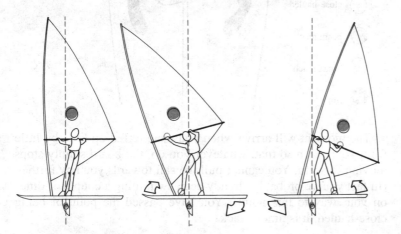

The tools of steering the board: pushing and pulling with hands and feet, rotating the board, leaning the rig forward and back.

Sail trim

The board is moving forward with the sail full. If you are still doing as we suggested above, you are beam reaching, with the sail about at right angles to the board and the board at right angles to the wind. If you let the sail out from this position, the luff (the part closest to the mast) will flap before the rest of the sail does. You pull the sail back in and it stops flapping.

Close-hauled

There is only so much one can theorise about sail trim on a sailboard. A great deal more is a matter of feeling. In order to balance yourself with the sail, your feet should be facing the sail.

Luffing up and bearing away

If you incline the mast
AFT   FORWARD

and push harder with your
AFT foot   FORWARD foot

the board will move
CLOSER to   AWAY from

the wind.
This is known as
LUFFING.   BEARING AWAY.

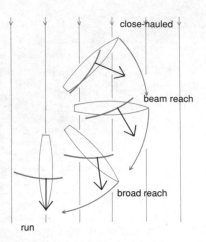

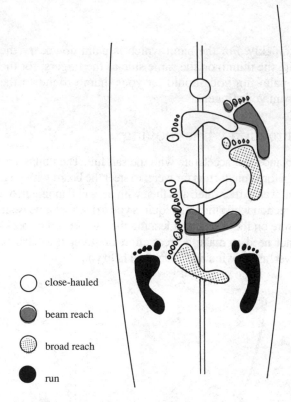

The further you bear away, the further you have to open the sail ...

close-hauled
beam reach
broad reach
run

... and you have to move your feet continually to keep them facing the sail. This diagram shows the positions as the board bears away on starboard tack from close-hauled to a run.

Walking round in front of the mast

The moment will arrive when you have luffed up little by little from your reach so that, whatever you do, the board simply stops moving forward. You cannot pull the sail towards you any further. (In fact you've probably already been swimming a couple of times on your way to this point.) You have passed the point of being close-hauled. It is time to tack.

Tacking

Tacking involves pushing the nose of the board through the wind. One needs to use the board's momentum to pass through the dead angle between the two close-hauled courses.

The steps to be followed are:
– incline the rig aft;
– put most of your weight on the aft foot;
– gradually pull the sail in;
– when the nose has passed through the eye of the wind, turn the rig round and pass in front of it to move off on the new tack.

So much for the theory. Some of these steps will need slightly closer examination.

Balancing as you luff up

As the board luffs up with the sail still filling, it is easy to keep your balance: your body weight balances out the force of the wind. As you get closer to the dead area beyond close-hauled, however, the wind loses its strength in the sail and then disappears altogether. Your balance is disturbed and the rig becomes a dead weight. You need to find a new equilibrium, which consists of you balancing the weight of the rig.

A beginner, the moment the rig becomes heavy, will be tempted to think that the board has already passed through the wind and it is time to nip quickly round to the other side. *But you must wait for the sail to be ready for the move, and change sides only when the board is pointing in the new direction.* This means:

– pushing the rig further aft still; and

– pulling on the boom to get the board to turn further.

In order to do this you need to bring your hand forward to grab the mast just underneath the handle, and pull the sail in hard with the other hand, until the clew of the sail has actually crossed the board. You can then stand up straight; the board will have passed through the eye of the wind. Keep holding the mast while you pass round in front of it, and then off you go ...

After you have been standing in front of the mast for a while, you have to lean the mast a little in the direction you want to go.

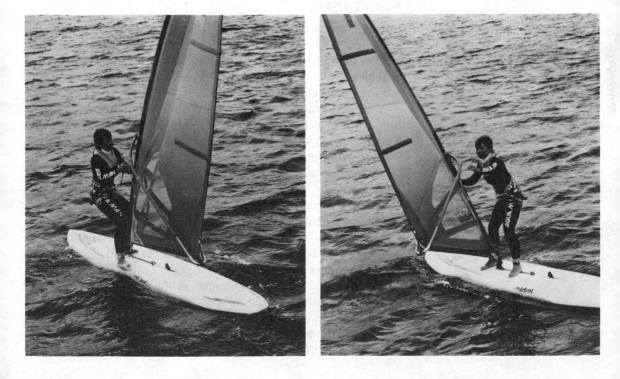

Balance while head to wind

The tack has gone correctly, the sailor has edged round in front of the mast and the board has passed through the wind. It is the easiest thing in the world at this point for the sailor, absorbed in staying upright, to let the clew of the sail drop into the water and stop the board.

In order to avoid this problem, it is best to stop for a moment while you are in front of the mast, with your feet both sides of the mast foot and your knees bent, and just concentrate on keeping the sail out of the water. To get moving again, you just have to lean the mast in the direction in which you want to go.

It should be emphasised that this technique is aimed at getting the beginner through the tack in simple steps.

Harmonising your movements

The successful tack is smooth all the way from the luff to bearing away on the new tack. The board quite often loses speed during the luff if the sail is not brought in far or firmly enough. If you find yourself in this position (and you have not fallen in!) you have to bear away with a big movement, pushing with your front foot, bringing the rig well forward and then starting the tack all over again.

Bearing away

Bearing away is easy in theory. You just push the rig forward and press hard with your front foot. In practice, however, it is bearing away which causes some of the most spectacular falls for the beginner, the so-called catapults. Let us take a look at the process, starting from a close-hauled course.

Your sail is pulled in close to the centreline of the board. As you bear away (ie as the board's centreline goes further away from the wind) you need to 'open' the sail; otherwise the sail will stall, as it is at the wrong angle of incidence to the wind.

As you bear away you need:
– to control the angle at which the rig is leaning, or you will be pulled off the board. The less wind there is, the greater the chance of losing your balance;
– to keep the sail correctly angled to the wind, and avoid it stalling;
– to bring your body weight gradually over the board and your feet gradually further aft;
– to come gradually more upright as the pressure on the sail reduces. You will also need to bring the mast head slightly further to windward as you stop bearing away, and to slide your hands slightly nearer the clew end of the boom.

As far as the centreboard is concerned, the best solution is to pull it up fairly promptly. It is best to pull it half way up before you even start the manoeuvre so you do not have to worry about it 'tripping the board up' as you bear away.

Running before the wind

'Before the wind' is not an expression limited to a precise angle of attack of the wind. It is more a 30–40° zone in which your position and the sail trim will be more or less similar. But some new problems of balance will crop up, as this point of sailing is one long battle for balance. At least it stops the run getting boring! Even the slightest imbalance on the sailor's part is transmitted through the sail straight down the mast to the board. This is the time for improvised swimming lessons.

First observations
– The board wobbles beneath your feet and tends to have little directional stability.
– If you have the centreboard down, the board wobbles less but is more difficult to steer.
– In light winds, the sail does not help you balance at all; in fact it is often an effort even to hold it up.

Basic position
The board is more or less in line with the wind and the sail is more

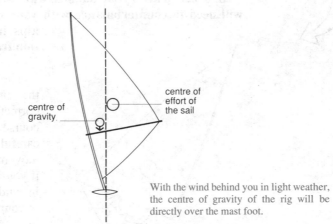

centre of effort of the sail

centre of gravity

With the wind behind you in light weather, the centre of gravity of the rig will be directly over the mast foot.

or less perpendicular to this line. The mast head is held to windward and the mast foot bisects the angle between the luff and the foot of the sail. Your feet are maybe 50cm back from the mast foot, placed symmetrically each side of the centreline, about as far in

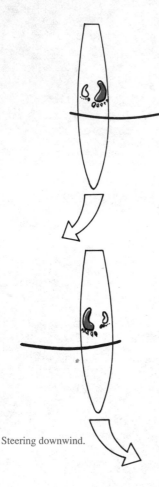

Steering downwind.

Steering downwind: the weight is on the left leg, with the hips out to the right. The board will therefore turn right.

from the rails (edges) of the board as they are from the middle. Your elbows are bent and your hands are a shoulder's width apart.

You will instinctively find the point at which the sail balances, and you need to position your arms so that they transmit equal force to each of your feet.

Balance

It may be relatively easy to keep the sail up, but it is less easy to keep your balance on the board, because of the waves and the swell. Your ankles and your hips will be working overtime. You do need to be quite supple, and you need also to avoid watching your own feet. In fact it is quite possible to sit down on the board while running. Try it: you'll find it surprisingly stable.

Steering

The slightest shift in your balance means you will also change course. You therefore need to keep an eye on where you are heading all the time, whether to change direction or simply to control the wandering tendencies of the rig. The theory is simple:

If you want to turn right:
– put your weight gently and progressively on your left foot;
– lean the rig to the left.
If you want to turn left:
– put your weight gently and progressively on your right foot;
– lean the rig to the right.

In order to keep your balance while steering in this way, you will need to counterbalance with your hips, by pushing your hips in the opposite direction from the sail.

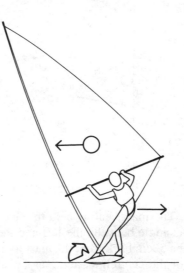

The firmer the movement, the more substantial the correction or change of course. You must therefore be careful only to apply these movements in measured doses if you are not to zig-zag along in wilder and wilder changes of course before finally falling in.

On the other hand, when there is little wind, you will need to make your movements exaggerated in order for them

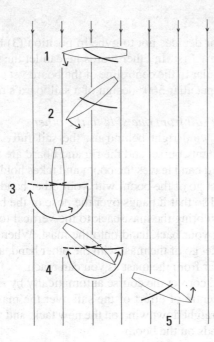

1. Beam reach.
2. Bearing away.
3. First chance to gybe, wind from directly behind.
4. Second chance to gybe, sailing clew first.
5. After the gybe, luffing up on the new tack.

to have any effect at all.

In general, you should aim to keep your knees flexed and to make your movements smooth but positive.

A good exercise for downwind boardsailing is to do a slalom. In order to make the board steer more quickly you will need to go further back along the board to take the front out of the water; and you will need to exaggerate your side-to-side movements in the opposite direction from the turn.

Gybing

Even if the peculiarities of the sailboard's rig allow one to sail a lot of different downwind courses, up to and including sailing clew first, the moment will come where you have to gybe.

Let us observe the progress of a sailor who decides to bear away from his beam reach (1) onto a broad reach (2). He continues to bear away until he is running dead downwind (3). He could gybe the sail now, quite easily. This would be the time for a gybe in a moderate wind and with flat water. You should note that we talk of gybing the sail: one does not necessarily have to change the course of the board at all. For this reason, gybing at this stage is a good way to learn how to change the sail over, because one can concentrate on that, and on the movement of one's hands on the boom, and repeat the move again in both directions.

If our sailor decides not to gybe in position (3) he can continue on, sailing clew first. In other words he can let the sail out beyond the perpendicular to the centreline of the board yet continue sailing, thanks to the peculiar 360° design of a sailboard's rig.

Handling the sail from one side to the other
We have the wind right behind us, the sail fully let out; we are sailing a constant course, and the rig and board are well balanced.

The forward hand leaves the boom and takes hold of the mast. As soon as you let go of the boom with your other hand, the sail begins to blow round so that it hangs over the nose of the board. You must make sure you bring the mast back to the vertical to avoid overbalancing. Bring your back hand onto the mast. When you have done that, you can let go of the mast with the other hand, and grab hold of the boom as far from the mast as you can reach.

You should correct the course automatically by sloping the mast to bring the centre of effort of the sail over the mast foot. You are still sailing straight downwind on the new tack, and you should now have both hands on the boom.

Summary

We have now gone through all the basic moves you need to learn for handling a sailboard in moderate winds and calm water. Now you must take some time for practice.

Just as with the dinghies and catamarans, anyone who wishes to build on the foundations acquired over the last few pages can do so, and proceed to more advanced practice.

CHAPTER 2

More advanced practice

In order to understand better how a boat uses the wind and to learn how the boat itself can be used better, we need to examine some parts of the theory of sail power. The theory applies to all types of boat and, properly used, can elevate sailing almost to the status of art. To reach this level, of course, requires not just knowledge, but thought, practice and a long period of maturation. It requires real love for the sport, and a certain deftness in applying the things one has learnt.

In this chapter we shall limit ourselves to the vital elements: trim, boat speed, and the finer points of some of the manoeuvres covered earlier. This chapter also contains the introduction to funboarding, for those so inclined.

One point before we start this section on techniques: the reason dinghies, catamarans and sailboards these days are capable of such high performance is that yacht designers and sailors have established with considerable precision and learnt to exploit all the different forces which act on a sailing vessel. These forces will be explored in the second part of this book, 'The Mechanics of Sailing'.

Dinghies and catamarans
Leaving and coming back to land

The beach from which you launch your dinghy is strewn with natural obstacles. It is worth spending some time thinking about and choosing the point on the beach from which to launch or at which to return to land. You will have to take account of the slope of the beach, the wind direction, the state of the sea and numerous other factors.

You should generally try to avoid launching or coming back too close to any obstacle, whether a rocky outcrop or simply a moored boat; you should certainly not launch just upwind of an obstacle and try not to launch just downwind of one. It is quite easy to lose control of the boat momentarily as you launch or land, and a bump in the breaking surf can do you or your boat a lot of damage.

What is true one day may not be true the next. The state of the sea and the wind direction are important variables. Waves break close to the beach if the sea bed is steeply shelving, so you are quickly past them on your way out; but where the bottom shelves more gently, the breakers stretch a long way out, and you will have to pull the boat all the way out through them to have enough depth of water to put the centreboard down. As you come back to land any breakers present problems, whether close to the beach or not. In fact, you should always launch and land at the place on the beach where the waves are least fierce. This is generally the most windward end (and a moment's thought will tell you why that is the case). In any case the direction of the wind is the determining factor.

Leaving

The boat is prepared on land, with all the equipment put on board and the sails in position.

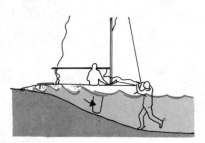

Too steep.

↳ Assuming the water is calm, it is always best to pull the sails up when the boat is afloat and you can get into the cockpit without the risk of damaging the hull. This is the job of the crew, who should also clear the sheets, put the rudder on if possible, and ensure the paddle is accessible.

↳ Pulling the sails up on a catamaran is sufficiently complicated that it is a job always best carried out on land. So long as you back the jib, and do not tension the mainsail luff, the sails will not flap them-

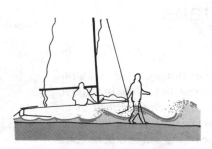

Too flat.

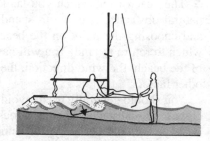

Just right.

selves (or you) to death, and they should not develop enough power to capsize the boat ingloriously on dry land.

⚓ ⚓ The boat is carried into the water. Carrying boats is a wearisome pastime, so you should generally head straight for the nearest water and then pull the boat round by the forestay to your preferred launching spot once it is floating clear of the sand.

Once you have reached your launch site, the helmsman continues to hold the boat by the forestay, head to wind. The crew jumps aboard, pulls the sails up and checks that the sheets are free. If the water is deep enough the crew also puts the rudder(s) on and lowers the centreboard a little. Now you are ready to launch, and the way you do this depends on the wind direction.

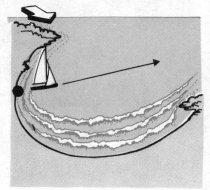

The rollers are usually weaker at one spot on the beach.

Offshore wind

⚓ ⚓ When the wind is blowing from the land, it is fairly easy to launch. The sea is usually well behaved and the breeze light (at least it is light next to the beach), and the boat is just waiting for you to say the word to be off. Nevertheless, there are some points you should watch: the boat really will sail off on its own if you are not careful, and that well-behaved sea and pleasant light wind flatter to deceive. Particularly if your beach is a little sheltered, it is often advisable to take a stroll to the top of the shelter (cliffs, dunes, sea wall) just to get an idea of how strong the wind really is.

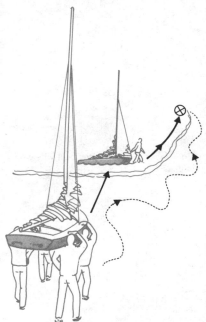

Boats are easier to move on water than they are on land.

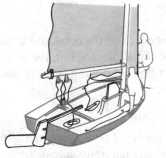

While the helmsman holds the forestay, the crew finishes getting the boat ready, pulls the sails up, disentangles the sheets, puts the rudder on and lets the centreboard down.

! The helmsman holds the boat head to wind, ie with the bow pointing towards the land. In order to leave, the boat will have to turn through 180° and the helmsman will clamber in over the transom. If there is not enough depth of water to lower the rudder, use the paddle to steer (as no boat will sail happily downwind without a rudder except in a very light breeze). The mainsail will make the boat luff up quickly until you are beam on to the wind. On the other hand, you will at least be drifting slowly in the right direction, that is downwind, so there is no urgent hurry and no real need to follow a very strict procedure. Some helmsmen prefer to get aboard before the crew does, so that they can take precautions against any tendency to luff up.

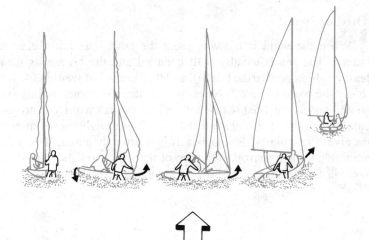

Do not wait too long or the boat will leave without you.

! Both crew members sit on the bows and let the wind push the boat out. When you are some distance out, the helm goes aft and lowers the rudders. Only when everything is ready does the crew move aft, and you bear away.

Onshore or side wind

Those days when the wind is blowing along the beach are rare but welcome. The boat sits naturally across the wind, finds its balance quickly and heads out making little leeway. For this reason a beam reach launch is highly recommended. You need very little centre-board; the sail trim does not have to be perfect; and any slight mistake with your steering is unlikely to cause a great mishap. If you have the chance of launching on a reach, take it! Do not go looking for difficulties by setting off on a beat.

Sometimes there is an onshore wind and a straight stretch of coastline. There is nothing for it but to set off close-hauled. If you can get the rudder and the centreboard down fairly soon after leaving the shore, and the sea is calm, there should not be any great difficulty. But if there are waves breaking and the bottom shelves slowly, you have to sail rudderless and with little centreboard. For that reason, we shall go through the procedure in some detail.

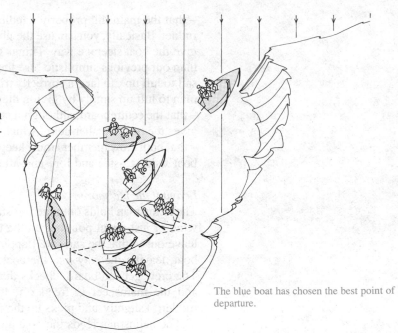

The blue boat has chosen the best point of departure.

Balancing the boat

Think back to what you know of the factors influencing the boat's stability.

A boat luffs:

– when it heels to leeward
– when the centreboard is fully down
– when the mainsail is sheeted in
– when the weight is kept forward.

A boat bears away:

– when it heels to windward
– when the centreboard is pulled up, even only partially
– when the mainsail is freed
– when the weight goes aft.

Boat speed is vital in getting off a lee shore: a boat is not even steerable unless it is moving! *The faster a boat travels, the more manoeuvrable it is.*

Catamarans have hulls which resist sideways forces in much the same way as the centreboard of a dinghy. However, these hulls are hydrodynamically efficient only above a certain speed. *Slowing down has the same effect as raising the centreboard!*

If you read the above list, you will see:

– that the mainsail, properly handled, can work more or less like a rudder. Basically, you can use the jib to give you forward motion and give the boat steerage way. Things then become a little more subtle than our previous simplistic 'use the jib to bear away, and the mainsail to luff up'. In fact, a correctly trimmed jib will permit the helmsman to luff up simply by giving the boat enough speed to steer by;
– that the centreboard, although it stops you drifting to leeward, also gives the boat weather helm, which is not our current aim;
– that both crew members must keep moving constantly to adjust the boat's side-to-side and fore-and-aft trim.

Leaving the lee shore
The helmsman holds onto the forestay as usual with the boat head to wind or just about pointing on the tack which you have decided to leave on, so that the sails are flapping just over the other side of the boat, leaving the way into the cockpit or onto the trampoline free. The crew gets on board, checks that none of the sheets are tangled and the mainsheet is freed off, lowers the centreboard and the rudder(s) slightly, and picks up the jib sheet.

The helmsman feeds the boat along past him, jumps aboard and takes hold of the mainsheet and the tiller. The crew then sheets in the jib just as much as is necessary to help pick up speed quickly. The centreboard should be lowered further whenever possible, but this is not so urgent that you need to get obsessed by it. For the moment, you are quite happy for your boat to have a little lee helm.

The most important thing at this stage is to get up some speed. On no account should you try to sail too close to the wind, because the moment you start to pinch, the boat will slow down and you've had it! As the boat picks up speed it will in any case try to luff up, so the helmsman should sit a long way aft, try to heel the boat to windward and steer very gently with the semilowered rudder (so as not to put

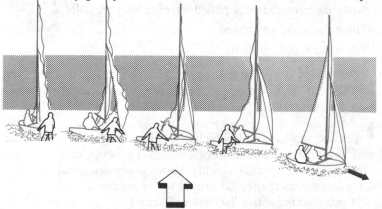

Giving the boat a good push to start off helps you get away.

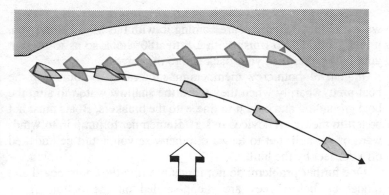

Pinching to windward will land you back on the beach.

too much strain on the pintles). If the boat still luffs up too much, free off the mainsheet and lean further back. All this time the crew is intent on keeping the jib correctly (not excessively) trimmed.

As soon as you can get the rudder down, you are in the clear and you can luff to your heart's content.

Launching without the help of your rudder is easiest when the wind is on the beam. When one launches into the wind, one is over-come by this terrible fear of not being able to get off the beach, and the temptation to pinch is strong. But the penalty for giving in to temptation is severe: as soon as the boat loses speed, it starts to make leeway and there is nothing one can do about it. *This is usually a result of having sheeted the mainsail too tight and the jib too slack.*

Without the use of your rudder (and maybe your centreboard) you cannot sail at closer than 70° to the wind. It is far better not to try, but to build up some speed sailing along the shore line with your sails nice and full. *The only way you will get away from a lee shore is by pretending that getting away was the last thing on your mind.*

Coming back to land

Some of the problems of leaving the beach crop up again when you come back to the beach, particularly the matter of choosing a point at which to make your landfall. If you are close-hauled, choose a spot where the beach is fairly steeply shelving. That way you can keep your centreboard and rudder down almost until the final moment. If there are breaking waves, come in at the spot most to windward, where the rollers are smallest.

In some ways, breakers are more of a problem when you come back to land than they were when you left. The boat is travelling with the waves and there is a chance that it will accelerate at just the wrong moment. The boat is also more open at the transom than at the bow, and can be picked up and swung round side on to the waves. In fact, when you are coming in with the wind behind you, it is a good idea to finish with a little 180° hook so as to present your bow rather than your back end to the waves.

In general, both crew members must be ready to hop out of the boat pretty sharply when they reach the shallow water, to stop the boat grounding and hold it in line with the breakers. Boats must not be left to their own devices in surf. Remember to jump in to windward of the hull, not to leeward; otherwise you could be knocked off your feet by the hull.

One further problem: do not forget to bring the centreboard and rudder up before they are rough-sanded on the bottom. It is commonplace, but regrettably true, that the most careful crews when getting their boat ready tend to leave all their care behind them when they are surfing back into the beach.

The essential point is to arrive back at the beach as slowly as possible, or better still, to stop before you arrive.

Downwind

When there is not much wind you can sail straight back to the beach with both sails filling, then luff up in a hook at the last moment, with your centreboard and rudder raised, and drift in the last few yards.

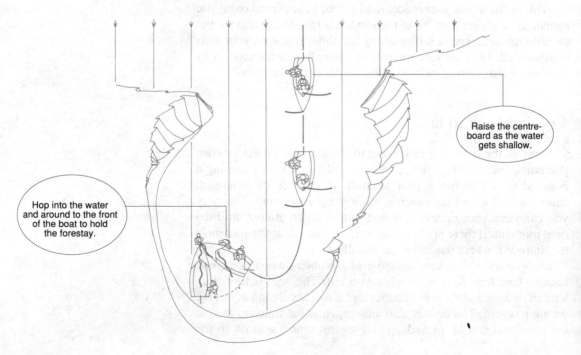

Raise the centre-board as the water gets shallow.

Hop into the water and around to the front of the boat to hold the forestay.

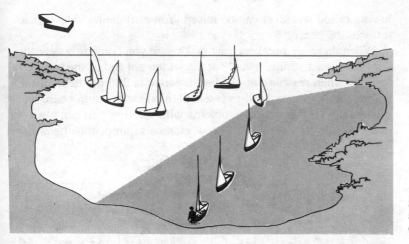

Sailing under jib alone, one can go anywhere in the blue area, not only dead downwind.

It gets a bit trickier when there are breaking waves. The safest technique is to position the boat directly upwind of the planned landfall, drop the mainsail and come in under jib alone, making sure you keep the boat at precisely 90° to the line of the breakers. *To drop the mainsail, you need to be almost close-hauled,* not dead head to wind, because the boat will not stay head to wind long enough.

It is not possible to drop the fully battened mainsail of catamarans and some dinghies while on the water. If there really is an enormous amount of surf, the real sea dog's solution would be to anchor outside the surf, gradually let the anchor line out until the boat reaches the beach, back end first, de-rig on land, pull the hull back out to lift the anchor then paddle back ashore.

Catamaran sailors can exploit one of the twin-hulled boat's party tricks, which is using the lateral stability of the twin hulls to sail backwards in a straight line with the sails freed:
– about twenty metres out from the beach, put the catamaran head to wind;
– raise the rudders and free the sheets;
– both go and sit on the bows;
– the catamaran will back slowly onto the beach.

Reaching

Coming into the beach on a beam reach is ideal, just like setting off in the same conditions. In fair weather, you just head straight for your preferred spot, then hook towards the wind at the last moment, having raised whatever can be raised. You drift gently sideways in towards the beach.

When there are breakers, just make sure you come in where the waves are least strong, usually at the windward end of the beach.

Even when reaching in, the best solution is to drop the mainsail before coming in, and sail in under jib alone with centreboard and rudders up. (If this causes problems with steering you can always use a paddle to steer.) Both crew members jump into the water

Reaching in with fair weather. The boat drifts sideways for the last few yards.

It is safest to come in under jib alone in a fresh breeze. You can even drop the jib just before you reach land.

If you cannot drop the main, you must make sure you meet the breakers head on. The 180° turn is a tricky manoeuvre.

when it is shallow enough, hold on to the boat to make sure it does not get across the waves, and pull it out of the water immediately.

If you cannot drop the mainsail you will have to sail in with the waves behind you. You head straight for the beach with board and rudder up. You luff hard at the last minute, preferably just after a wave has passed. The boat goes head to wind, with the sails freed, and stops. The crew jumps into the water and holds the forestay so that the boat is head on to the next big wave. Be sure always to jump in on the windward side of the boat, or you might end up underneath the hull.

Coming in on a beat

There are generally no breakers when the wind is blowing off the land, but there is another problem. You would like to come in to land close-hauled but you have to pull the centreboard and rudder(s) up as the water gets shallower.

You have to see if there is a bias to be found in the approach. By this we mean that the wind might not be quite at right angles to the beach, or there might be a little indentation where you could get in on a close reach. You approach the beach with the sails hard in, from the more windward side. Keep checking the depth of water with an occasional glance over the side.

The crew brings the centreboard up as slowly as the depth of water allows, and keeps checking the depth by looking over the side. The helmsman bears away a touch and frees the sheet just slightly, to keep the speed up and leeway to a minimum. A good luff at the end should allow you to reach the beach with the boat's own momentum, so long as you have remembered to pull the board all the way up by now.

The manoeuvre is simplified by the fact that you have not got a centreboard to worry about. Do watch the rudders though!

Summary

All that sounds difficult. And it can be. But the moment when you have to start raising the centreboard or the rudders is probably also the moment when you could reasonably hope to stand on the bottom without too much trouble. There is no harm in pulling the boat a little way, particularly when that is going to conserve your mirror-finished centreboard.

A pivoting centreboard which hits an underwater obstacle can be damaged; a dagger board is more likely to get stuck in its case.

A rudder can break, stick, or be torn off the transom. Two rudders can do it together.

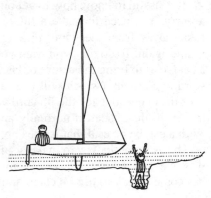

In almost every case, if you need to raise the centreboard, the water is shallow enough for you to stand up.

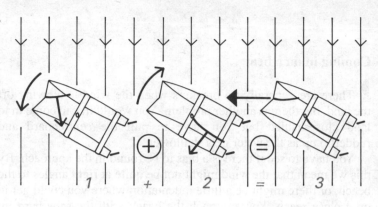

The equation of heaving to: 1 + 2 = 3. With the sails trimmed as above, the boat will move forward, facing as if close-hauled but making a course perpendicular to the wind.

If any of these problems happen, do not try to fix things from inside the boat. It is much easier to jump out and try to put things right from the outside. This also lightens the boat and lessens the chances of further damage.

Heaving to

Boats do not stop themselves. You stall them.

A boat hove to will drift gently downwind. With the aid of the tiller, you can make it drift facing more or less wherever you like. What you need to keep in mind is that:
– a backed jib will tend to drive you backwards and make you bear away (1);
– a mainsail sheeted in hard will drive you forwards and make you luff (2).

You can exploit the particular characteristics of the two sails to bring the boat to face more or less into the wind at will (3).

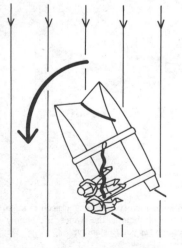

You can create a pivotal point for the catamaran to rotate around by sitting aft on the leeward hull with the mainsail freed.

Bearing away quickly

It is useful to know how to get out of a head-to-wind position in a hurry. You need to make a fulcrum around which the boat can rotate away from the wind, pick up speed and become manoeuvrable again. To do this, you want your weight aft and to leeward in a cat (so as to bring the centre of lateral resistance aft) and to windward in a dinghy (which will bear away as it heels to windward). Free the mainsail, back the jib until you are almost at right angles to the wind, then sheet in normally and the boat will sail off again. With a cat, be careful that it does not 'submarine' backwards.

This is a classic way to make a sailing boat bear away quickly. It was widely used in the days of long, shallow-draught vessels, and has come back into use on catamarans with no centreboard.

Controlling a dinghy
or catamaran to windward

For our first few lessons we were careful to venture out only in moderate wind, not too strong and not too weak. Sooner or later, though, you will want to go out in a stiffer breeze.

When that day comes, you can definitely feel the wind on your face. Your hair blows about and the flapping of the sails has a harsher quality to it. As we have already seen, for an experimental day it is best to choose a day with an onshore breeze, so we shall have to start off by looking at the close-hauled point of sailing.

Into the boat, along with your crew: this is going to be one of those days when you appreciate each other's company. You sheet the mainsail in, from your position on the catamaran or on the dinghy's side deck, the boat heels or flies a hull, and it luffs up. You pull the tiller towards you, but the boat continues to luff.

Why? Because the stronger wind produces a stronger heeling force. Any attempt to bear away is in vain; rudders lose their effectiveness under these conditions, partly because they are mostly out of the water anyway. (In fact, for the rudder to operate at full efficiency, the boat needs to be flat.) Anyway, the boat keeps heeling, and you are going to have to do something else to bring it back to an even keel.

Thus far, we have covered only sail trim, basically as a function of the point of sailing. Now we move to consider the boat's stability. To remind ourselves: both dinghies and multihulls need to be sailed as flat as possible. To keep them flat the crew need to lean out, and to control the power in the sails by changing their shape.

The Righting Moment

When the wind freshens, the increased force on the sails needs to be balanced out by the righting moment of the crew: either through putting their feet under the toestraps and leaning back on the windward side, or (if that is not enough) through using the trapeze.

Sitting out

Depending on the type of boat, you will slip your feet under the toestraps and lean your body horizontally out with either your bottom, your thighs or even the backs of your knees on the windward rail. The hands are used only for holding the sheet or the tiller.

The righting couple.

Trapezing involves hanging from a wire, suspended at the same height as the shroud fixings. This allows you to take your whole body outside the boat.

Sitting out is the solution adopted in dinghies. Their side deck is designed to make it comfortable to lean out; you can go so far as to fit the hollow of your knees over the rubbing strake.

Leaning out on a catamaran is usually uncomfortable and inadequate. The trapeze is generally preferred.

The trapeze

If you are going to trapeze you need a trapeze harness, with a hook on the front to fit through the ring on the end of the trapeze wire.

To get out on the trapeze, you fit the harness hook through the trapeze ring, then slide out until you can prop your front foot against the shroud plate. Take the handle in your front hand and swing out gently, putting most of your weight on the front foot. The positioning of the foot is important, since your foot stops you from swinging round the front of the shroud if you slip or the boat thumps into a large wave.

To avoid swinging forward, the aft leg is kept gently flexed, and the body slightly behind a right angle with the boat's centreline.

You must ensure the boat remains in longitudinal as well as lateral trim. On many catamarans, both crew and helmsman can trapeze.

Lateral trim is controlled as soon as the strength of the wind demands it by leaning out or hooking onto the trapeze, keeping the windward hull in contact with the water. When the wind really picks up, you can try to sail with one hull out of the water. Since the two bows are effectively hitting different waves at different times, having both in the water actually disturbs the move-

Getting out onto the trapeze. The forward leg is carrying most of your weight, but it is the aft leg which needs to be flexed to control your own and the boat's balance.

ment of the boat; and some cats even have asymmetric hulls, so that the shape of the hull is more efficient at stopping you slipping down to leeward when it is at an angle. But you do have to be careful. It is a thin line between flying a hull and capsizing.

Longitudinal trim is important for ensuring that the boat responds to the tiller, and sails a straight course. The stronger the wind, the further aft both crew must go, to stop the bow from burying and the whole boat from 'submarining'.

Sail shape and sail tune

Either the righting moment of the crew is sufficient at this stage or it is not sufficient. If not, you have to alter something else. Now is the time to learn about all the strings which lie in the bottom of the boat, and to start really using the rigging.

If the boat's fuel is the wind, the sails are the engine. You need to adapt the shape of the sails to the demands which the wind makes on them, so that they propel you as fast as circumstances allow. Ideally, you should observe the effect of the changes you make so that you know how your sails should be trimmed for the best results in a given wind.

The main variables which make up the shape of a sail are its camber and its twist.

The camber

A sail is not a flat cloth triangle stretched between the mast and the boom: it has had camber, or fullness, built into it with varying panel shapes. It is this fullness which determines the strength of the forward thrust the sail generates. You can change the degree or even the position of this fullness according to the effect desired. In light airs, you want a full, round sail, whereas in stronger winds you will tend to want it flatter. The more camber, the more power the sail has, but the more heeling force it also exerts. You will have to find the best compromise. The point of maximum fullness tends to move aft in stronger winds, and you can alter the sail shape to keep it in the right place.

The twist

A sail full of wind naturally tends to twist slightly, so that it is, in effect, sheeted harder at the bottom than at the top. In light winds, this phenomenon can be useful, as the apparent wind higher up is freer than that near the water; in moderately fresh winds, however, one needs to limit the twist, as the wind direction is comparatively uniform over the whole sail.

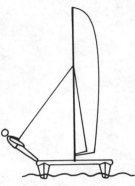

Insufficient heel.

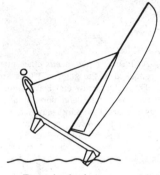

Excessive heel.

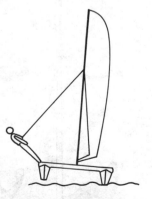

Just right.

Tuning

Even when one simplifies the principles of sail trim and cut to the extent we did above, the difficulties in quantifying and measuring the concepts involved become apparent. It is an over-simplification to say 'For wind X you need your sail adjusted like Y'. Getting the trim right comes only after long experience and detailed observation. You also need to be aware of the means at your disposal for adjusting the sail trim. We are now going to look at each aspect of each sail, while not losing sight of the fact that the two sails actually form an indivisible whole. Of course all the adjustments interact with all the others; and some things need to be adjusted on land, while there are others you can carry out afloat.

Tuning on land
Basically we are talking about adjustments to the mast.

On the 470, you can adjust the mast chocking at the mast gate. Depending on whether you chock the mast more forward or more aft, the degree of bend in the mast can be increased or decreased, and you can control the height at which it bends.

As the width of the mast gate is not variable on the 470, the only

A heavy crew needs the mast fully chocked at the gate, and long spreaders. The lighter crew can leave some play in the mast gate, and should take shorter spreaders. Chocking leaves the sail with camber low down; removing the chocks de-powers the sail from head to foot.

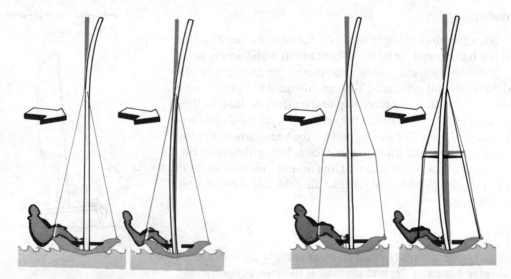

way of controlling sideways bend is at the spreaders: the longer the spreaders, the greater the tension on the shrouds, and the less the mast will bend. Equally, the shorter the spreaders, the less the shroud tension and the greater the mast bend.

The top batten is tied in. If the ties are tight, the sail becomes fuller, which is useful in light airs. The sail can be flattened for strong winds by decreasing the tie tension.

The jib draws best with its luff straight, so the halyard is always kept tight, except in the very lightest breeze, when it may be slackened a touch.

Catamarans generally have stiff masts, so the shape of the mast remains constant; only the rake can be adjusted. You need generally to rake the mast further aft on catamarans in strong winds, to help reduce the tendency to bury the bows.

All the mainsail battens are full length. The stronger the wind, the flatter the sail should be, so the less tension is needed on the ties. In lighter wind, the battens need to force shape into the sail. Whatever the weather, all the battens should be under the same compression.

On a fully battened sail, you cannot tell by looking whether the sail is correctly trimmed, so it is easy to oversheet. To avoid this, you need to prepare before setting sail.

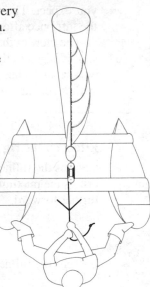

The initial tuning of the mainsail.

The preparation is done on land, in light weather. The boat is set up close-hauled, with the mainsheet traveller centred. You walk back several metres, sighting along the boom, and pull the sheet in until the mast begins to disappear behind the leech. This gives you the maximum mainsheet tension for light winds. Mark the spot on the sheet with a marker pen or gaffer tape.

The jib luff needs to be tight, so cleat the halyard hard down. (The only exception is in very light winds.)

Many jibs have a plate at the clew, so the sheets may be attached at varying heights. You need the sheets fixed higher up in stronger winds, to reduce jib twist.

Tuning afloat (dinghies)

On the 470, you can adjust the mainsail using the following means: the traveller, the sheet, the halyard, the Cunningham, the kicking strap and the clew outhaul. The jib can be tuned using the halyard and the fairlead slide.

The main halyard tensions the luff. The tighter the

On this cat, the mast has been raked so far aft that one can sheet the main in block to block. This is a way of ensuring that one does not oversheet

halyard, the flatter the sail and the further forward the draught. Thus, in strong winds, you need more halyard tension. As the luff tension can also be changed once you are afloat, using the Cunningham, the luff tension should be set up for the lightest wind you expect. The Cunningham may be used for further tensioning the luff once afloat.

The clew outhaul may be used to tension the foot and flatten the sail; it is generally adjusted at the same time as the Cunningham.

The mainsheet traveller permits you to trim the sail in or out without changing the sheet tension. In strong winds, therefore, one

Tuning afloat

Tuning action	Effect on the rig	Visible consequences
Tightening the luff with the halyard or Cunningham hole.	Lessens the fullness and brings the maximum belly further forward.	The mainsail has a crease down the mast. This should disappear when the sail is full; otherwise the halyard is too tight.
Tightening the outhaul.	Lessens the fullness.	The mainsail has a crease along the boom. This should disappear when the sail is full; otherwise the outhaul is too tight.
Tightening the kicking strap.	Keeps the boom down; puts a bend in the mast low down; absorbs the fullness of the sail.	The main becomes flatter.
Letting off the traveller and tightening the sheet.	Stiffens the mainsail leech; flattens the sail by bending the mast at the top; reduces sail twist; tensions the jib luff.	The main is very flat at the back and has no twist in it.
Centring the traveller and freeing the mainsheet.	Keeps the fullness in the sail and increases twist.	The mainsail acquires a pronounced twist.
Moving the jib fairlead aft.	Increases twist in the jib; opens the jib leech.	Opens the slot between the sails high up.
Moving the jib fairlead forward.	Flattens the jib; closes the leech and reduces twist.	Narrows the slot between the sails high up.

can pull the mainsheet in hard to flatten the sail and limit its twist, to bend the mast and keep the jib luff taut; and play the traveller instead of the sheet itself.

The traveller can be played in light winds, either centred or brought slightly to windward, so that the sail is pulled inboard but not down, and thus remains full and with some twist.

The kicking strap prevents the boom from flying upward when you are sailing downwind. In strong winds, it can be used to bend the mast low down and thus flatten the mainsail. The jib fairlead can be brought forward on its slide to tension the jib leech and cut the twist, or aft in lighter weather to allow more twist.

Tuning afloat (catamarans)

Most of the the tuning apart from sail trim is carried out ashore. Only the mainsheet traveller and jib fairlead track can be adjusted while sailing.

The traveller allows you to change the set of the sail without tightening or slackening the sheet. This allows you to keep the forestay taut and prevent excessive twist in either sail. This technique reaches its limit in very strong winds, when you have also to ease the sheet, or else a hull will be buried. The fully battened mainsail can cope with this handling quite well; and the loss in power from the (relatively small) jib is unimportant.

In light winds, the sail can be kept twisted by leaving the sheet slightly eased and bringing the traveller into the centre, or even slightly to windward.

The jib fairlead is usually mounted on a transverse track. Moving the fairlead outboard allows you to open the 'slot' without altering the sheet trim in strong wind; you can bring the sheeting point further inboard as the wind eases.

Checking sail trim

Flattening, twisting, easing and sheeting in the sails is certainly entertaining, but you need some means of checking how much benefit all this action is bringing you. Racing, especially against more experienced sailors, is an excellent and important means of measuring one's performance. Among the other checks, however, we must also mention tell-tales.

Tell-tales are thin pieces of wool or strips of cloth fed through the sail about thirty centimetres aft of the luff. They are particularly helpful on fully battened sails, which do not flap even when they are poorly trimmed.

In theory, your sail is correctly trimmed on the beat when these tell-tales are both streaming out horizontally. In practice, the mast tends to cause so much turbulence that only the higher tell-tales are actually giving useful information. Anyway, if the lower leeward tell-tales are also horizontal, the sail is correctly trimmed; if the windward ones are horizontal, the sail is too tight.

When you are a touch tighter than close-hauled, correct trim is indicated by a slight lifting of the windward tell-tales.

Some helmsmen prefer streamers fitted to the leech of the sail. These stream out horizontally when the sail is correctly trimmed and drop to leeward when the sail is too tight.

The jib and the slot
The slot between the jib and the leeward side of the mainsail needs to be 'trimmed' just as carefully as the two individual sails. The main tool for controlling the slot is the jib fairlead track: the further forward the fairlead, the more constricted the slot.

Sailing the waves

There is one further important external influence on the boat's behaviour: the state of the sea. When the water is flat, the boat goes in a straight line and the angle of attack of sails and hull remains the same. In rough water, on the other hand, the boat slows down up each wave. You then have to power up the waves by freeing off slightly to get over the crest. Pinching will slow you down so much that the waves virtually stop you in these circumstances.

Light winds

You've dealt now with moderate winds and tried your luck in a heavy blow; but the lesson is not over yet. You have still to confront those special days where searching for the slightest breeze becomes as obsessive as searching for the suntan lotion.

Catching the breeze is a game of waiting and watching, cunning and sometimes sheer desperation. The first thing to do is to reduce your air resistance by both getting down into the boat; you should also aim to eliminate any sudden movements which might shake the air out of the sails. And whereas until now you have been trying hard to keep the boat flat, in light winds your aim is to reduce the wetted area of the hull.

The sails need to be specially adjusted for light winds: nice and full, and with a good twist in them to make the most of the difference between real and apparent wind at surface level and higher up.

Heel the boat over to leeward to help the sails fill and to reduce the wetted area of the hull. Keep your weight far enough forward to lift the transom out of the water, thus reducing the drag still further.

You need your weight so far forward – probably forward of the shrouds – that the tiller pulls quite hard, and the boat even becomes a little unmanageable in the small gusts.

Controlling a dinghy or catamaran downwind

The moment you bear away from the beat, the atmosphere on board changes almost tangibly: finally a bit of space to breathe in! All those worries about staying precisely on course disappear, and you can get down to the business of boat speed. From a close fetch all the way round to a broad reach, you will be surprised by the speeds of which your boat is capable. In the right conditions, you can plane, virtually take off ... However, before we leave planet earth altogether, a few observations about the boat on a reach.

The apparent wind

So far we have written of the wind as though there was only one. However, you need to consider several different winds: the true wind, the headwind due to your speed, and the combination of these two, the 'apparent wind'. Despite its name, this apparent wind is actually the one by which you sail. You trim the sails to the apparent wind, and it is that wind you can feel on your face.

The true wind is that which is blowing over the water, and which you would feel when standing on the beach.

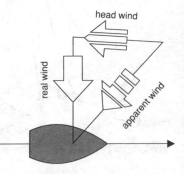

The real wind combines with the headwind caused by your speed to give the apparent wind. It is this apparent wind which powers the boat.

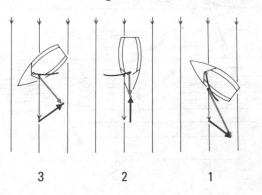

3   2   1

The apparent wind is stronger when you are close-hauled (1) than on the run (2) or the reach (3).

The headwind, or relative wind, is the one which is always blowing in your face once you start moving forward.

The apparent wind is the one which actually propels the boat, and the only wind you can actually perceive on board.

The apparent wind is always further ahead than the true wind; the difference between the two is frequently as much as 20° and can even go above 60° on a reach. The apparent wind is up to 80% stronger than the true wind when you are sailing to windward, and as much as 50% weaker when you are sailing downwind. The difference is most noticeable as you pass from one point of sailing to another.

The difference in strength and direction is greater on catamarans than on dinghies. The faster you go, and the more wind there is, the closer you are to making your own wind!

The dinghy off the wind

In strong winds

As you bear away off the beat, gradually freeing the sails, the boat will tend to bury its bow; at the same time it picks up speed rapidly, the mainsail develops a large crease along the luff and the jib leech twists excessively.

You will already have concluded that you are going to have to re-tune the rig for the reach.

You can remove the crease from the main luff by freeing off the kicker and maybe the Cunningham a touch. Bring the jib fairlead forward to reduce twist. Most importantly, move your weight aft to

In order to get the boat to plane, you have to play the waves.

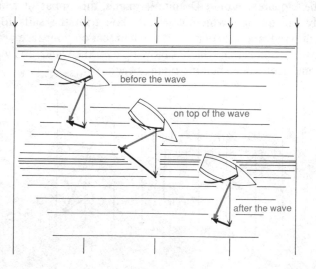

before the wave

on top of the wave

after the wave

bring the bow up. Now raise the centreboard a little and concentrate on keeping the boat flat. While you were close-hauled you were having to push your way through the waves; now you can use the force of the waves to push you forward even faster. As you do so, the apparent wind increases; you can use the stronger wind to go faster still, and so on. This seems unending, but in fact there is a maximum possible speed.

You are now perfectly set up for planing.

Planing a dinghy

Quite by chance, a wave catches you and you accelerate down it at a fearsome rate, sails flapping, until you hurtle into the back of the next wave and judder to a halt like a watch spring breaking.

You need to get to know how waves affect the boat downwind. We can divide their action into 'before the wave' and 'after the wave' phases.

Before the wave

You are travelling along at a given speed, with a given real and apparent wind, and the appropriate sail trim. As you get ready to go down a wave coming over your quarter, you bear away slightly. The boat takes off down the wave and the apparent wind heads you. You must sheet both sails in to take account of this new apparent wind.

After the wave

Either you bash straight into the back of the next wave, in which case you stop in your tracks, or you can luff up slightly along the slope of the wave. If everything comes together at the right time – sail trim, rudder angle and wave phase – you can stay on the plane almost permanently.

The catamaran off the wind

As you bear away onto the reach, the boat accelerates rapidly. A catamaran is sailing at its fastest somewhere between 105° and 110° to the real wind. The apparent wind actually becomes stronger than the real wind and you can sheet the sails in as if for a beat. To keep the boat correctly balanced the crew has to go quite far aft and keep an eye on the leeward bow so as to react immediately if it looks like submarining.

As you bear away on to a broad reach you need to ease the sails; however, you also need to keep the air flow over the sails regular.

This is possible a long way off the wind, so long as you keep your speed up! The flow can be checked by looking at the tell-tales and making sure they stay horizontal. You will also need to fight against the boat's natural tendency to bury the bow. Both crew move as far aft as possible, and keep the mainsail twist at a minimum, by letting the traveller out as far as it will go before freeing the mainsheet.

Depending on the type of cat you are sailing, there are two ways of coping with this tendency to bury the bow. In a cat like a Dart, for instance, which has a lot of buoyancy in the bow and a high aspect ratio sail, you bear away and free the main, which relieves some of the pressure on the leeward hull. The boat regains its balance and quickly picks up speed again.

A catamaran with sharper bows and a lot of roach on the sail, such as a Hobie Cat 16, demands a quick luff and no freeing of the sail. Any other way, and the boat will be tripped up long before the force in the sails diminishes. In light airs, loosen the jib halyard to help the mast to pivot.

'Tacking downwind'

This slightly misleading term is applied to sailing a downwind leg not as a straight run but as a succession of very broad reaches (and gybing between them), thus exploiting the boat's very fast reaching speed. This is particularly important on a catamaran. There are two questions to keep in mind while sailing this course:
– are we sailing the fastest course? (Or, more precisely, are we getting downwind at the greatest possible rate?)
– are we on the best tack?

When the windward tell-tale on the bridle is pointing forward of the bow, you are sailing too far off the wind, and when the tell-tale is flying back, you are heading too close to the wind. Although this general rule of thumb applies for most boats in most conditions, you will soon tell if you have got it right, as the boat will sail fastest when the apparent wind is approximately beam on.

You cannot tell whether you are on the best tack unless you use a compass or have some landmark to head for.

The one time when there is nothing to be gained by 'tacking downwind' or luffing in the gusts is when the wind is light. In light weather you are better off sailing straight for your target.

1. Tell-tales flying back: you are too close to the wind.
2. Windward tell-tale touching the bridle: just right.
3. Tell-tales flying forward: you are sailing too far off the wind.

Sail trim under acceleration

The apparent wind comes ahead, or heads you, as the boat picks up speed. You need to change your sail trim immediately to avoid the boat slowing down. It is almost always better to bear away than to pull the sails in. The converse is also true: when the boat is slowed and the apparent wind frees you, it is better to luff up than to ease the sheets.

Thus, even when the wind is relatively constant, sailing a catamaran is quite similar to sailing a dinghy in gusty weather.

Gusts and squalls

We shall refer to a temporary sudden increase in otherwise light wind as a gust; a sudden increase in already strong wind is a squall. The two require different treatment on the part of the sailor.

Before the gust or squall strikes, the boat is heading in a certain direction, with its sails trimmed for the course being sailed. As it hits you, the real wind component increases in strength. The apparent wind increases and frees, so you luff a little or ease sheets a little; then the boat starts to accelerate, the apparent wind becomes stronger still, but heads you. You then have to bear away or sheet in harder until the wind strength drops again. As it drops you bear away or sheet in a touch more, before luffing or freeing the sheets at the end.

Which is better? Changing course, or changing the sail trim? The answer depends on the point of sailing, the wind strength and the boat.

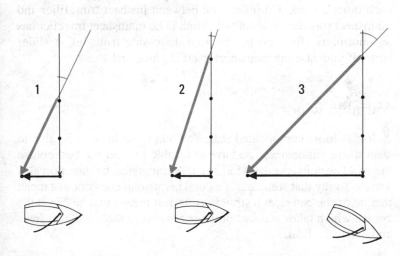

Using gusts on a reach

1. The normal course.
2. As the gust arrives, the apparent wind frees you briefly, because your headwind has not yet increased.
3. The apparent wind heads you and increases in strength during the gust, due to your increased headwind: you have to bear away.

In strong winds, you bear away during the gust, then harden up after it.
In light winds, you luff during the gust then bear away afterwards.

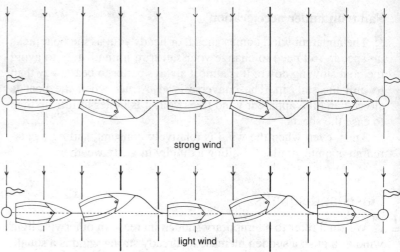

strong wind

light wind

The closer you are to the wind, the more likely you are to change the boat's heading. In light winds, you should change the heading, but in strong winds change the sail trim. In a dinghy, you can use the sheets, but catamarans seldom give you time for this option, so using the tiller may be preferable!

There is a risk of capsizing when a really severe squall hits you. At such times it is vital to keep both crew members working together to maintain the boat's side-to-side and front-to-back trim. You might consider it worthwhile to swop jobs between helm and crew for a few gentler days just to heighten your appreciation of each other's work. Co-ordination between jibsheet trim, tiller and mainsheet traveller is absolutely vital. (The mainsheet traveller has an enormous effect on the boat's side-to-side trim, but it slides better if you ease the mainsheet itself slightly first.)

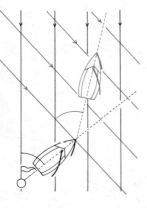

Luffing up
As the wind frees you, or lifts, the boat can luff up to take advantage.

Variable winds

It gets more complicated still. You don't just have to be able to steer a straight course; you have to be able to steer the best course the wind permits. As the wind strength fluctuates, its direction also varies. To say that someone is a good helmsman does not just mean that he or she can steer a straight course: it means that he can sail a course which takes account of the variations in the wind as it frees and heads the boat.

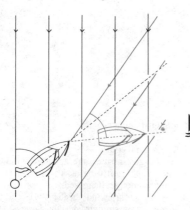

Bearing away
As you are headed, you must bear away.

Playing the shifts

Imagine two buoys positioned one directly downwind of the other. There are two possible courses to sail from the downwind buoy to the windward buoy if you want to get there with only one tack. We shall call the more-or-less square shape formed by these two courses the 'frame'. Within this frame there is a wide range of possible courses one can sail.

Sailing outside the frame is an unnecessarily long route, since it is unlikely that any gains in speed would be sufficient to offset the increase in distance. The edges of the frame are lines drawn at the optimal angle for a close-hauled course for a particular boat. All the boats on the same heading and within the frame are equidistant from the buoy.

The frame shifts if the direction of the wind changes, even though the buoys stay in the same place. In the diagram below, boat A set off on starboard tack, staying within the frame. When the wind shifts (shown by the blue lines), boat B, which set off on port tack, loses out, and is left outside the frame. The lines drawn at right angles to the new wind show A to be clearly ahead of B.

The rule is quite simple: *if the wind shifts, sail into the shifts.*

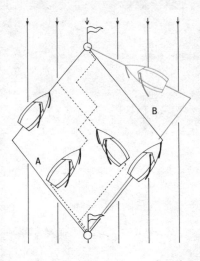

The blue boat will take longer than the others to reach the windward mark, as it is sailing outside the frame.

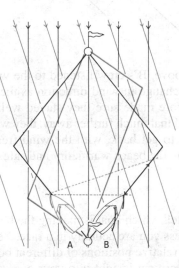

A wind-shift.

Learning to play the shifts is not only important for winning races; it is also a vital part of your safety afloat.

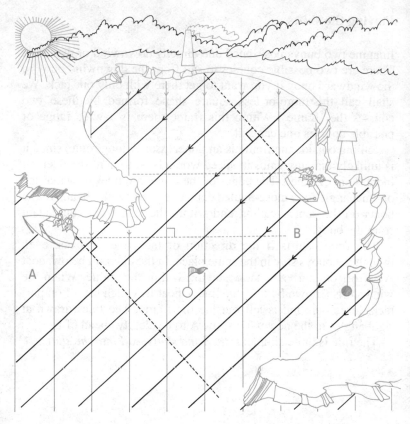

In the diagram above, B's crew listened to the weather forecast and anticipated the change in wind direction as the stronger wind arrived. They therefore made sure they stayed well to windward. Although A is not all that much further away, they will now need to put in several tacks to get back, with the wind freshening all the time, and B sitting on the beach warm, dry and safe.

Who is leading?

You cannot always tell which boat is making the best use of available conditions, unless you are actually in a race. Yet some idea of how to compare the relative positions of different boats is essential if you are to gain a critical insight into your own sailing. We can talk of making ground on the other boat, either to windward or to leeward. You simply have to imagine lines drawn from the bows of the boats perpendicular to the wind. The ground made is the distance between the lines, nothing more, nothing less.

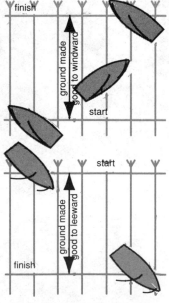

Making ground to windward/to leeward.

Spinnaker work with a dinghy

We picked up a lot of speed in the last section, surfing down the waves on a reach, powered by main and jib alone. We can get more power still, all the way from a close reach to a dead run, by using the spinnaker.

The spinnaker is a rather strange-shaped sail with a strange name, but it is best considered just like any other sail. Except for the fact that it is rigged differently from the others, and has rather more fullness cut into it, it shares with the other sails the same three corners – head, tack and clew – and the same three sides – luff, foot and leech. Unlike other sails, these corners and sides change names as you change tacks: the luff and tack are the side and bottom corner to windward; and the leech and clew are always the leeward side and corner.

In the same way, the ropes which you use to trim the sail also change names: the guy is the rope to windward, and the sheet is the one to leeward.

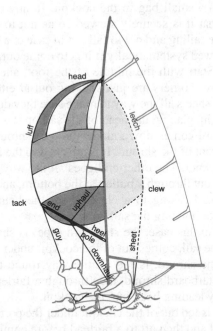

A dinghy with the spinnaker rigged.

The spar on which you push the tack up to windward is known as the spinnaker pole or boom. It has a clip on each end, through which the sheet will run. In almost all dinghies the two clips are identical, so either can be used at the tack or in the mast fitting.

The remaining two spinnaker fittings are the uphaul, which prevents the pole dropping onto the foredeck, and the downhaul, which stops it from flying up the mast.

Rigging the spinnaker

A spinnaker is rigged outside everything else: outside the forestay and outside the shrouds. You have therefore to think quite hard about where exactly the sail will end up once it is pulled out of its bag, and how it is going to get there.

You will have to get the spinnaker ready before you leave the beach, and this will generally involve deciding which side of the boat you want to raise it on. For the purposes of this explanation, let us assume we shall raise it on starboard tack. As a spinnaker is flown to leeward, this means we shall need to prepare it to come up on the port side.

The sail is stored in a chute under the foredeck, or more frequently in a small bag in the cockpit. In any case, you should make sure that it is securely stowed so as not to get in your way when you are sailing and not to fall out in case of a capsize. The sail has to be stowed systematically if it is to come out of the bag in the right order. Start with the middle of the foot, and feed the sail in until the lower corners are just sticking out at either side (having followed the sheets all the way to make sure they do not cross); then feed the rest in, placing the head of the sail on top.

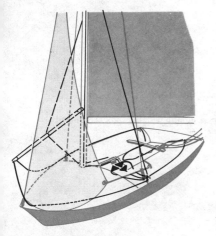

Ready to fly the kite: halyard, guy and sheet all come out of the cockpit forward of the shroud and under the leeward jibsheet.

The halyard comes down along the port shroud and under the jibsheet in front of the shroud. It is attached to the head of the spinnaker with a knot. The other end goes all the way down inside the mast, comes out through a pulley at the bottom, and is fed aft along the centreboard casing to a cleat where the helmsman has easy access to it for hoisting the sail.

The *guy* (in this case, the starboard rope) is shackled or tied to the tack of the sail, comes out of the cockpit under the port jibsheet in front of the shroud, is fed all the way round the forestay and outside the starboard shroud, then through a fairlead quite well aft before finally leading back into the cockpit.

The *sheet* is fed out of the cockpit under the port jibsheet in front of the shroud and then aft to a fairlead before coming back into the cockpit.

Many boats are set up so that the sheet and guy are one continuous rope with one end attached to the spinnaker clew and the other attached to the tack. The rope has to have some length to spare: it does not just go all round the cockpit, but it should be loose enough for the guy and sheet to be played independently, and if necessary to be freed in an emergency.

All three ropes – halyard, sheet and guy – can be clipped under the leeward reaching hook, by the shroud, while the sail is being stored. We shall talk more of the reaching hook in a few minutes.

The uphaul and downhaul are usually permanently fixed in place on the mast. The uphaul may be a simple length of shock-cord; the downhaul will be a rope which leads back through a pulley to where the helmsman can adjust it.

The spinnaker pole has a cleat or some other fixture half way along, to put the uphaul–downhaul system in. The uphaul and downhaul are positioned and the pole put in place, with the guy running through the windward boom-end clip, before you start to raise the sail. The height of the pole can then be adjusted from the cockpit with the downhaul.

Raising the spinnaker

If you are sailing a triangular, Olympic-style course, you can put the pole in place on the last close-hauled tack before you round the windward mark and bear away. That way you can begin to fly the spinnaker from the moment you round the mark.

When you are just starting to practise your spinnaker drill, you should make sure you are sailing a reach somewhat freer than on the beam. Of course the spinnaker is a large and powerful area of sail, and you can anticipate that flying it will have a significant impact on the boat's balance! If there is much wind and you are on a beam reach, the crew will have to hang out hard to ensure that the boat is not blown over on its side as the spinnaker fills for the first time. On a broader reach, the effect is not quite so dramatic, as the wind is blowing more nearly in the same direction as the boat is sailing, and the force of the wind is slightly lessened by the turbulent eddies from the rest of the rig. However, you should be very cautious indeed when hoisting the spinnaker on a run, as the boat is less stable anyway on this point of sailing.

The helm pulls the spinnaker up fast. You need to get this bit over fast, because the spinnaker will not wait. It will begin to draw (and acquire the potential to get tangled) the moment it leaves the bag or chute. As the sail is being hoisted, the crew pulls hard on the guy to bring the pole and tack round to windward. You want the pole at right angles to the wind. If you are on a reach, the crew clips the guy under the reaching hook, thus adding to the force of the downhaul and also freeing up some space for leaning out.

It is worth making sure that the centreboard is fairly well raised when you fly the spinnaker on a reach, because the moment the sail fills you will find that the boat wants to slide off to leeward. The centreboard would 'trip it up'.

Trimming the spinnaker

The spinnaker works the same way as the other sails, effectively by deflecting the wind. Due to its fullness, the spinnaker can deflect the wind through a considerable angle, and thus develop a great deal of force. In fact, in any decent wind, the boat will change character completely once you raise the spinnaker, and its power will surprise you. You will quickly appreciate that mastery of the spinnaker is not a matter of brute strength on the part of the crew, but that you will have to make full use of your agility and cunning too!

There are three basic rules for trimming the spinnaker:
– open the sail to the wind as much as possible, by keeping the pole at right angles to the wind;
– balance the spinnaker, allowing it to keep its symmetry, *with tack and clew at the same height*;
– keep the spinnaker sheeted as little as possible: just enough to stop it collapsing, but letting the air escape easily at the leech.

These rules apply to all points of sailing with the spinnaker, though the precise shape of the sail will vary from close reach to dead run.

Close and beam reach

The spinnaker has to be kept fairly flat on a close or beam reach, since the apparent wind is coming in on the boat from a quite acute angle; especially as you sail faster, the difference between real and apparent wind can become considerable. You might even have to let the spinnaker pole come round until it is pointing straight ahead, next to the forestay. When you reach this point, the clew will be pulled down a long way by the sheet, so you will need to tighten the downhaul to keep the tack at the same height.

It is vital that the boat be kept balanced, because otherwise, in any decent wind, it will career off, and you will not be able to keep control by using the rudder. The most serious loss of control occurs when the boat luffs up suddenly, so you must keep the boat flat or even heeled slightly to windward (as we already recommended for when you are close-hauled). This will allow you time to react when

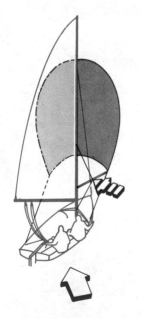

The pole needs to be kept perpendicular to the apparent wind. The more the sheet pulls the clew downward, the more tension you will need on the downhaul to keep the sail corners balanced.

a gust does come. You should also make sure the centreboard is raised well over half way, and both crew are sat well back to keep the bow lifted (within reason). And do remember to keep the tack and clew at the same height: *any imbalance in the spinnaker will inevitably imbalance the boat.*

Broad reach and run

As soon as you bear off for a broad reach, you can allow more fullness into the sail to deflect the wind by rather more. You can allow both the clew and the tack of the sail to rise. Unhook the guy from the reaching hook, and try to fill the spinnaker as far forward as possible, so that its wind is not disturbed by the main. Do not over-sheet the spinnaker: let the air circulate and escape easily.

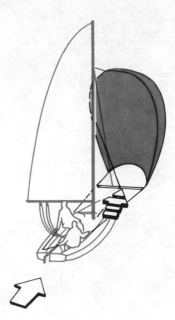

Keep the pole perpendicular to the apparent wind. You will find that the spinnaker clew tends to rise up, so you should ensure the tack is free to do so to the same height.

There are different problems of balance on the broad reach and run from those we encountered earlier. The boat will not be heeling so much; and the simple fact of having the mainsail out to one side and spinnaker off to the other should in theory help keep the boat balanced. However, the boat does need a little sideways force to help keep it stable. If you are running dead downwind, the slightest unexpected wave or ill-timed movement can set an unfortunate 'death roll' off which it is difficult to stop.

To prevent the onset of the dreaded roll, you should keep the main sheeted a touch in from the shroud, the centreboard down just a little, and even slightly over-sheet the spinnaker (thus flattening it and lessening its tendency to swing from side to side).

The crew members should sit sufficiently far aft that the flattest part of the hull is in contact with the water. Both will need to be able to foresee the boat's reactions to its surroundings, and to move quickly but smoothly to keep the boat in constant balance.

In waves, you will need to learn surfing skills: you move forward as the wave hits, to unstick the transom and get carried forward on the flat part of the hull, and then aft before you shoot down the wave into the back of the previous one. Then you start all over again ... forward, then aft ...

While it is true that the crew members' movements around the boat are of central importance in sailing, it is virtually impossible to be prescriptive about the exact timing or manner of the movements. The real truth is that it is largely a matter of feeling. If there were real rules, we would all be champions. The real experts are those who become part of the boat as they move around.

Gybing

Just as you've worked out how to keep the boat level downwind, it's time to disturb that delicate balance, and gybe. You will have worked out from our remarks above that the gybe is best done quickly and in one go. In fact, each crew do things in their own order – some move the main across before the spinnaker, others the other way around – but in reality everything happens more or less simultaneously anyway!

The first thing to get out of the way is the centreboard. Keep it raised, especially in fresh winds. It might make the boat steer more sluggishly, but at least you won't trip over yourselves in an uncontrollable luff after the gybe.

You should not even think about gradually sheeting in the main before pushing it over to the other side of the boat. The boat is not stable enough under spinnaker for you to start worrying about balancing it all the way through an extended manoeuvre. Basically, you leave the main to its own devices and let it come across when it is ready. You will have your hands full gybing the spinnaker. You will need to bear away until you are definitely sailing by the lee, so that the wind will push the sail across without you touching it. When the sail does fill on the new tack, you will find that you are virtually on a reach, and you might need to lean out immediately if there is a reasonable wind ...

We have covered all the warnings and caveats. Now let's get on with the gybe. The crew sits down to leeward, in front of the main, ready to lean out when the main crosses the boat. The helmsman moves aft and keeps his wits about him: he has the jobs of

1. Having already gybed the main and jib, the helmsman takes hold of the spinnaker sheet and guy, and balances the boat, standing up.
2. The crew detaches the pole from the mast ...
3. ... and clips the free end onto the new tack of the spinnaker.
4. The crew detaches the other end of the pole from the old tack, and clips that end onto the mast.

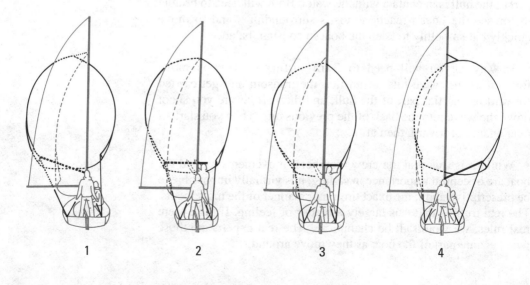

1   2   3   4

balancing and steering the boat through the gybe as well as trimming the spinnaker. The helmsman holds the spinnaker sheets, ready to ease or pull them as necessary to help the crew.

At the agreed moment, the crew unclips the pole from the mast and clips that end onto the sheet by the old clew of the spinnaker (which is now becoming the tack). Then, the other end is unclipped from the guy and fitted onto the mast eye. All this should take a few seconds. If you have not already gybed the main, now is the time. The crew leans out, and takes the guy and sheet back from the helmsman, who has already adjusted them for the new tack. Once the boat is level and correctly balanced, you can bear away back onto the run. It's over.

Dropping the spinnaker

Dropping the spinnaker (ie letting it down) is largely a matter of bringing it into the boat to leeward, back along the path it followed on the way up. You release the guy and the halyard. The crew pulls the sail back into its bag, taking hold of it by the clew. Tuck the sheet, guy and halyard under the reaching hook ready for the next spinnaker leg. Finally, unclip the pole.

It can be advisable to drop the spinnaker on the windward side if you expect to have to raise it next time on the other tack. In that case, you release the sheet and the halyard and the crew takes hold of the tack to pull the sail back into its bag. The only thing to watch out for is the jibsheet on the other side. You should pass the slack jibsheet over your head while you are stuffing the spinnaker into its bag, so as to ensure that the spinnaker comes out neatly from under the jib.

On paper, this may all sound rather idealised and academic. In practice you will discover hundreds of little details to make the procedure easier for yourselves. You should certainly aim to develop techniques which 'feel right' for your boat as well as you. The day will come when you suddenly notice that the boat which you are steering so skilfully and carefully actually seems to know what to do all of its own accord (for instance as it comes up onto the plane). At that moment, you will begin to see that part of the art of sailing is simply letting the boat express itself.

Of course this does not mean that you can survive without exercising firm control over things; but your control should be able to become strategic. Rather than dealing with individual events, you should aim to create conditions which help you and your boat overcome obstacles without needing to analyse each action.

The conclusion of all this should be that a boat needs to be treated with the same firm kindness as a horse. You should not attempt to master it with strength or to drive it faster and further than its nature allows. A whipped horse grows stubborn; and many a sailor has deserved that clout on the head from the boom.

More advanced sailboarding

Or, saving energy and using energy efficiently

So, you want to stay out for a long time, sail in strong winds, sail fast, sail stylishly ...

There's only one way to achieve all this: practise what you know already and add a few new advanced techniques.

Stance and harness

The theory of sailing suspended from the rig

The joint at the bottom of a sailboard mast allows you to adopt positions which would be impossible in a boat, and which use the wind more efficiently, by exploiting its ability to drive things not just sideways, but upward. This ability of the rig to give lift is effectively the aspect we use when getting a dinghy or catamaran to plane.

You can use the wind on a sailboard to suspend yourself from the rig. The weight of your body and the weight of the rigging will be cancelled out by the upward force of the wind; all available energy is then directed to steering the board and trimming the rig.

The board only becomes a displacement vessel when there is little wind or at certain stages of certain manoeuvres, when you slow down.

In order for you to hang from the rig as comfortably as possible, you need to find the ideal position for your hands on the boom and for your feet on the board.

Your hands should be the same distance apart on the boom as the width of your shoulders. Any further apart, and you will get tired quickly. Where exactly you place your hands is a function of the angle of incidence and strength of the wind on the sail. You will need constantly to keep seeking the best place for your hands, so that you feel comfortable and you are sailing the board efficiently. You can use lighter winds to move your hands along the boom and back as you look for the ideal place, and you can even hang there on one arm alone!

Just like the hands, *the feet should not be placed too far apart* in

Keep changing the degree of force you exert on the boom, to balance the changing strength and direction of the pull from the sail. This in turn varies with the angle at which the sail is held to the wind.

order to balance and transmit the various forces involved. The forward foot will take most of the strain, so you will need to lean slightly aft so as not to overstress it.

If you can position your feet and hands correctly, you only need to lower your centre of gravity and keep your body well out from the sail to balance out all the other forces.

Hanging from the rig: practice on land

It is a good idea to experiment on land with suspending all your weight from the rig. It will be harder to hold onto the sail than it is when you are afloat, because the force of the wind which is usually transferred into forward motion will all have to be contained by the strength of your arms!

Put the board on the sand, beam on to the wind, or just draw for yourself the shape of a board on the sand, just so you know where you may and may not put your feet. Starting from standing upright, you lean far enough back so that your weight is countered by the full sail. Now you are using your arms and legs to keep yourself away from the sail, and balancing your own weight against the force of the wind. Above all, keep your back straight. Now we're going to play 'lifts'. You tighten the sail in to go up, then free it off to go down. It is not easy to keep your balance playing this game: you have to use your arms as shock absorbers, while your feet are stemmed against the sand which is slipping away between your toes.

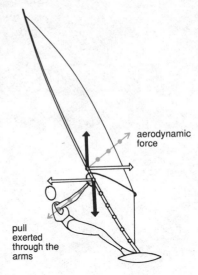

aerodynamic force

pull exerted through the arms

Suspended in balance: with your body weight correctly positioned, you can balance out the force of the wind with a varying pull through your arms.

Playing 'lifts' on the sand:
1 and 2. Instead of pushing the 'up' button, you just tighten the sail in.
3 and 4. To go back down, you free the sail off.

If the sail overpowers you, you must get your body further away from it by pushing with your legs.

If you feel yourself falling backward, you must bend your knees and lift yourself up by pulling on the boom with the sail held hard in. As you are pulled higher, you will feel the pressure on the sail growing less. Then you have reached a point of equilibrium again, so you can take your finger off the 'up' button.

Thus, it is your arms which tell you how much to lean back. You flex and extend your legs so as to balance the wind by bringing your body further away or closer to the sail. You do need to separate the movements required of your arms from those performed by your legs. Some of the freestyle exercises from page 121 will help you practise.

Harnesses

To extend your range, you will need to pass over the lion's share of the pulling at some stage from your arms to the harness. You have relieved your backache by learning to hang from the rig; now give your forearms a rest. We shall stick with our aim of saving energy, and use the weight of the body as efficiently as possible.

You can see harnesses which fit over your back and shoulders, round your waist like a belt, or ones which you sit in like a pair of shorts. All will have a hook on the front which clips over a rope hanging off the boom. Thus your arms are freed for adjusting the angle of the boom, and the sailor is still free to move relative to the rig, as the hook will slide along the rope.

Of the three types of harness, it is the seat harness which is most comfortable. The force of the sail is transmitted to your pelvis, and the upper body is left free. If you prefer the harness which fits over your shoulders and down your back, make sure you keep the hook as low as possible, or you will end up with a nasty backache. Ultimately, the choice is a matter of taste.

NB The base plate of the hook should be low and wide enough so that the load is carried by the back without constricting the chest. Foam padding also increases comfort.

Just as you would position your hands on the boom either side of the centre of effort of the sail to even out the force on both arms, the harness rope is attached similarly.

Use a robust rope, as the hook will rub through it rapidly otherwise. It should be 8–10mm in diameter. The rope is attached to the boom either with velcro cuff fasteners or with a slip knot (see diagram). The ends should be no further apart than the width of your shoulders, or they will be too far away from the centre of the sail; and the rope should not be too short, as it is important for you

Seat harness.

to be able to move your body independently of the sail. Ideally, you should have your arms slightly flexed when you are hooked on and holding the boom.

You should certainly experiment on land before using the harness on water. Hang backwards, then simply bend your elbows to hook on. If you can stay hanging without using the pull of your arms when the sail is filling, you have found a point of balance. If you are still having to pull with your front arm, the rope is too far aft; and if you are having to pull with your aft arm, it is too far forward.

The harness rope should be tied to the boom with a slip knot finished off with a figure of eight.

The ends of the harness rope should be shoulders' width apart, and long enough for your arms to be just slightly flexed when you hold the boom.

The long board

Setting off and coming back to land
You must get used to putting the rig and the board in the water in one, because it is much easier to put the mast on while you are still on dry land.

Carrying the board
Carry the board and rig as close as possible to the water's edge.

First, the board (it is best to leave the rig out of the wind, or it might fly off in a gust!):
– in light winds, the board is best carried on your head;
– in strong winds, carry the board by your hip and to windward of you. One hand should be in the mast step, and the other about level

Using the mast foot track

The board has a foot button which you can depress in order to be able to move the mast foot forward and aft. Here are some simple rules for you to start using the track:
– you want the mast forward for beating or tacking;
– you need the mast foot aft for reaching, running and gybing;
– between the two ends, you will find your own ideal positioning. For instance, you are less likely to bury the bow if you keep the mast foot back; but when there is a light wind, keeping the foot forward stops you dragging the rear end of the board.

with the centreboard. You can lean into the wind against the force provided by the board.

Next, the rig. Hold the mast in one hand, the boom in the other, the sail above your head and the mast to windward.

Keep the sail downwind of the board and put the mast foot in place. Tie the mast on using the leash so that you do not lose the rig if it detaches itself for some reason. This is an important safety precaution.

Now all you have to do is carry the whole lot to the water:
1. The least tiring option (albeit hard to balance) is to stand between board and rig, holding the back of the board in one hand and the boom in the other. You then simply push it into the water.
2. From the same stance you can grab the centreboard or fit your hand inside the centreboard case. Then you can carry everything.
3. It is possible to carry the sail on your head and the board on your hip. The mast needs first to be upwind of the board. You then flip the board on to its side, take the mast between the tack and the boom, and put the sail on your head. In your other hand, you grab the centreboard or centreboard casing. Then you can pick it all up, with the board on your hip.

Beach starts

The board is on the water. It is far less tiring and much quicker to use a beach start than to haul the rig out of the water.

Preparation
Stand upwind of the board, with the sail out of the water, one hand holding the mast and the other on the boom. You aim to steer the board *without filling the sail*; you will simply press down or pull up on the mast to make the board bear away or luff.

Carrying the sail: one hand on the mast, the other on the boom. Do not forget to keep the mast to windward.

Carrying the board

1. Pushing, standing between rig and board.
2. Carrying rig and board from the same position.
3. Mast to windward, rig over your head and board carried against your hip.

Beach start

A. Preparation:
1. Push the mast away and the board bears away.
2. Pull the mast towards you and the board luffs up.

B. Starting off:
First, you put your rear foot on the board, pointing at the sail so as to provide a good foothold against the force of the sail. Your pelvis should be swung towards the sail. Your front foot pushes you off.

If you pull the sail in and push on the mast, the wind will pull you over on top of the board. If you pull the sail in and also pull on the mast, the rig will simply fall on top of you.

If the sail falls on top of you and pins you down in the water, you have to get out to the mast and unstick the rig from the water, taking great care not to leave the end of the boom trailing in the water – otherwise the wind will flip the sail over pivoting about the clew, and your sail will be back to front. If you do find the sail back to front, pick it up at the clew and let the wind flip it over with the mast as a pivot.

If the sail is blown over to leeward because you tried to pull the sail in as you pushed on the mast, you will almost certainly have had to let go. To bring the sail back to windward, you pick the sail up, lifting the clew slightly, and bring it back to where you were standing. The wind will get underneath the sail and flip it over. You then just have to take hold of the mast and bring it back to windward of the board. *You should exert pressure on the rig through pushing and pulling on the mast: that will provide all the force needed to pull you onto the board at the right time.*

Starting off

You begin by putting your back foot (ie the foot which will be further aft once you are up and sailing) onto the board, facing towards the sail to give you a better push against it. Swing your hips towards the sail as well, to help resist the force. You then push off with your front foot.

It is very important to be in the right position relative to the board at the moment when you want to step on. If you are too far aft, the rig will give an immediate luff and you will be swimming. *You need to be level with the centreboard casing.*

Once your front foot leaves the ground, you are going to need to control the sail. If it is pulling too strongly, you need to let some of the pressure off by relaxing your rear arm.

If the wind is strong enough to pull you onto the board before you have completely filled the sail, you can start to lean back immediately, then pull the sail in to start using all the available wind power.

Coming back to land

Wherever possible, you should aim to come in on a reach. That way, you will not have to change course when the centreboard is pushed up. Depending on how you like to carry the board, you can step off either between the board and the rig (which is the fastest and easiest) or to windward, keeping hold of the boom. That way you will not drag the sail in the sand or water, and should avoid annoying other beach users.

Dealing with waves

The moment you leave the beach on a day when there is a lively wind, you will encounter waves. You need to know how to cope with them.

If the wind is ahead, the waves will be almost like fences to jump. You will have to ride the front of the board up the wave, or you will crash straight into it, stop and fall in.

To succeed in riding up the waves, you need to have a fair amount of way on, and you need to be able to tell how serious an obstacle the wave represents, so as not to bury your bow in it. *You use your legs as shock absorbers, but there is one golden rule to follow: do not move your upper body.*

With an onshore wind, there will be turbulent, frothy water between the rollers coming in and the retreating waves or undertow. As the board travels over the froth, it loses its 'grip' on the water as though you were sailing sideways on ball bearings. You need to try to sail straight at the waves over the froth, to get through the obstacle as quickly as possible. As the board slows, going through the breakers, the pressure in the sail from the wind will increase. *You must completely dissociate the actions of the upper body from those of your pelvis and legs.* The upper body is controlling the rig, while you steer and balance the board with your lower body.

If you fall off in the surf, it is best to come back to the beach in order to get through the surf with your speed up.

With an offshore wind, you can surf out with your centreboard retracted, taking the waves diagonally, as the force of the water will be pushing the board along. As you sail down the wave and pick up speed, the apparent wind will come ahead, so you must pull the sail in.

If the wave is travelling faster than the board and you want to catch it to surf with it, you can temporarily accelerate by 'pumping'. Taking care not to overbalance, the sailor gives the rig a hefty pull from front to back and from the leeward side to windward, meanwhile counterbalancing with movements of the hips.

With the wind on the beam, you can use the waves by surfing the down-slopes and then heading up quickly through the front of each successive new wave. You should not be worried if this means your course is rather zig-zag: you will more than make up for the extra distance sailed with the speed you gain.

Pumping: for a momentary burst of acceleration, you can pump the sail by swinging the rig and moving your hips to balance: 1, 2, 3 and then 1 again.

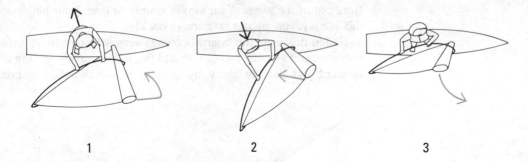

1   2   3

Improving your technique with some freestyle figures

Freestyle practice is essential, whether you are a beginner or a national champion. It is the only way to explore comprehensively the board's (and your own personal) limits.

You will develop essential boardsailing skills, speed, agility and suppleness through these exercises.

Turning the board through 360°

This manoeuvre will take you back to your first days on a sailboard. Let the sail hang loose, hold the mast in one hand and use the other to balance. Use your feet to push the board round. Then try the same with the sail filled, and using your arms to resist the force of the wind.

Sailing back to front.

Sailing back to front

Instead of pulling the boom against the force of the wind, you push. In other words, you will be standing on the convex side of the sail. When you sail like this, you will quickly realise just how far towards the wind you need to push the mast, even to get started; and in stronger winds, you will have to push it further still. If you can imagine yourself back on the usual side of the sail, you will see how necessary it is to lean back as you sail, to balance the force of the wind.

Sinking the tail

When you are on a run, you walk back along the board until the water reaches at least your ankles. The board will rear up, with its front out of the water. Your aim is simply to keep your balance. If this is easy, you are not far enough back!

Sailed this way, the board becomes very sensitive to your foot pressure, and you can swing it to and fro, luffing up by heeling it to leeward and bearing away by heeling to windward. The board

reacts less quickly if the stern is only just under the surface, but you only need to press hard with one foot and it will turn on the spot. This is the quickest way of changing direction when going down-wind. You can even gybe in this position. But for the moment, our objective is merely to hold the position. You should still be able to feel the sail pulling on your arms. If it is only pulling weakly and all your weight is on your legs, you need to trim the sail more.

Flare tack

You can also use the technique of sinking the stern to luff up quickly. If you try this manoeuvre, you will have to be nimble on your feet.

You move back along the board, luffing as you do so. The bow rears up out of the water, and the sail comes in towards the board as you harden up into the wind. The moment will come when you run out of space on the board. At that moment, you drop the bow back down and hop neatly round to the other side to finish the tack.

This is a particularly interesting demonstration of the effect of the sailor's position on the board's behaviour: you get to the limits of your balance to turn the board quickly in a very restricted space.

Sailing inside the boom

Instead of using your arms to pull on the rig, you can use the strength of your back by sailing inside the boom. You then need to use the pressure you can feel on your back to determine the amount you lean back and the way you trim the sail.

This technique means you have to judge the degree of lean quite precisely. As all your upper body is trapped in the narrow cage of boom and sail, any excess of lean will make you fall over.

Sailing clew first

Both these boards are sailing at the same angle to the wind. The one above is sailing normally, broad reaching on port tack.

The board below has its sail clew first, or forward of the mast.

Sailing this way, the belly of the sail, which is normally a third of the way back from the mast and the front of the sail, is now two thirds of the way back from the front edge of the sail, which was the leech! It is thus hard work for the front arm to keep the leading edge correctly positioned. One false move and you're swimming. If the wind pressure is too great, the front hand lets go and the sail flips round in line with the wind.

In order to keep some control over the sail as it flips round, the aft hand holds the mast as the leading hand lets go of the boom. That then leaves you free to gybe ... but that is another tale.

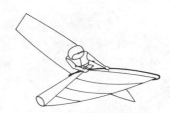

Both these boards are broad reaching, but the lower one has its sail clew first.

Head dips

From a starting position hanging on to the boom, this move involves leaning your head back until you can dip it in the water.

You lose sight of where you are going (or indeed of any of the normal reference points which tell you how you are sailing). You have to rely purely on the pull through your arms to let you know what is happening.

If you go so far back as to dip your whole head in, you might find yourself back to where we started this section: leaning so far back that you overbalance, and with your bottom almost touching the water. You need to flex your knees to bring your centre of gravity quickly much closer to the board. This is why the head dip is worth practising. In gusty conditions, you will need constantly to use your knees this way to stay on the board.

Going about quickly

You are already practised in tacking and gybing your sailboard, but still every time you go about the board slows down or even stops. Now we shall look at quick tacks and quick gybes, to avoid these dead patches.

Quick tacks

You can break a tack down into three phases:
– the initial phase, in which the board luffs up;
– the moment of actual change from one tack to the other;
– the final bearing away onto the new tack.

Although the phases are in practice one continuous movement, they are broken down here into their constituent parts for analysis.

The luff

We have already looked at quick luffs by sinking the stern. Your sudden move to the back of the board makes it luff hard, and as you pull the sail in you have to spring round to the other side fairly swiftly, because the sail would otherwise push you off your perch. A quick tack begins in much the same way, except that here you try to keep your movements rather smoother so as not to lose speed; when you first experimented with sinking the stern it was precisely in order to stop, so you could turn on a sixpence.

1. As you start the luff, the rig is inclined aft and your weight is on the rear foot.

2. The forward hand holds the mast to guide it aft.

3. The leading foot comes round in front of the mast, but the sail is still kept drawing, even though it is now over the rear quarter of the board. The weight is maintained on the back foot for as long as possible.

The dead phase of the tack is kept as short as possible using this technique by making sure that the sail is drawing throughout.

The luff phase is rather long, and can be considered the most important phase. You actually continue the luff even after passing through the eye of the wind, so as to make the board pick up more easily on the new tack.

The luff begins by bringing the rig as far aft as possible, and putting almost all your weight on the back foot. The sail must be kept drawing throughout the manoeuvre, so you will have to keep pulling it further and further across, controlling the change of direction. Do not forget that you can speed the luff up still further by heeling the board. While you are preparing to pass round the front of the mast, you can keep pulling the sail in most effectively if you put your front hand on the mast.

It is hard to stay on the same spot on the board after you have brought the sail across the back of the board. You should put your front foot forward of the mast, but keep the weight on the back foot for as long as you can.

Through the eye of the wind

The front hand is holding the mast and the front foot is forward of the mast. Your body should be away from the sail, but still using the drawing sail as a stabiliser. You should now be ready to spring round the front of the mast quickly.

Move forward just for the length of time it takes to change your hand grip. The longer you stay at the front of the board the more you will slow down, and the likelier you are to lose your balance.

4. You are through the eye of the wind. You are using the mast as a support.

The new tack 1
The front hand is still holding the mast; the mast is raked forward; the forward foot is still next to the mast, but the sail is already pulled in and drawing.

The new tack 2
Back in normal position, both hands on the boom and both feet aft of the mast.

During this phase you should be using the mast as a rest, and also as a help for the turn. When you had the mast raked to the rear, you were luffing up. Now you want to start bearing away, so you should lean the mast forward.

The new tack

You had enough momentum to come out of the turn already on the new tack. You should now be facing the sail, with your front arm extended. The mast is raked forward, helping you bear away and accelerate again.

You should aim to get the sail filling again as soon as you possibly can, even while you still have one foot in front of the mast. You finally take up the customary position again and lean back, with both your hands on the boom and both your feet aft of the mast.

Extreme conditions: light and heavy

In light winds, you will need to exaggerate all your movements in order for them to have the necessary effect. Your start on the new tack will certainly be helped by a hefty pump.

When the wind is livelier, any small motion on your part will translate into a fast reaction from the board. Do not let things go too fast for you! You should still be hanging from the boom as you start the luff. You really need to get round in front of the mast fast, to balance yourself again on the other side by leaning back against the force of the full sail. Every movement will need to be planned ... and before you fill the sail completely on the new tack you must

Sailing with the sail clew first. To counter the force of the wind in the sail, you need to hang on the boom, with your body leant forward.

have both feet aft of the mast, or you will be catapulted forward.

Quick gybes

A quick gybe is part of a smooth continuous movement from one broad reach to a broad reach on the new tack.

Coming out of a gybe is easier than coming out of a tack, because the board loses much less speed. You are therefore also less likely to lose your balance. But in order to carry out the gybe successfully, you will need to sail through a broad reach, a run and another broad reach in quick succession, and stay in control throughout. You really need to be able to sail a slalom downwind on either tack using the sail clew first.

The gybe is easier with the centreboard retracted. Again, to help our analysis of the manoeuvre, we shall break it down into bearing away, luffing and coming out of the gybe.

Bearing away

You are sailing on a broad reach, both hands in front of you on the boom and transmitting the wind to the board through your legs. Most of your weight is on the front foot. When you decide to start bearing away, you must plan for more pressure on your front foot, heeling the board to windward, with the rig over to windward and forward of the centre of rotation of the board.

The boardsailor will be aiming to lean into the curve, balancing by keeping board and rig inclined towards the outside of the curve.

To increase the turning moment, you have to be prepared to bring your hands further back along the boom, to lean the rig further into the wind and keep your balance by keeping your body weight on the opposite side.

As the board turns, your feet need to follow the sail round, always facing the sail to keep your balance correct and transmitting the force of the wind squarely into the board. As the board is sailing dead downwind you will have both feet close together facing straight forward. In order to get more purchase in this position for stemming yourself against the force of the wind, you will need to move back along the board. You only need the mast raked forward to turn at the very beginning of the manoeuvre, as you start to bear away. After that, all the turning will be done by your feet on the back of the board.

The moment where your feet come together facing forward marks the beginning of the luff with the sail clew first.

Luffing up

Once the board has started luffing up, you can bring the mast in towards the centre of the board, and you can also bring the mast more upright, as your hands move along the boom closer to the mast.

As you keep your feet following the direction of the sail, your windward foot, which was the rear foot, will find itself at the front. For the moment, though, you should keep your weight on the rear foot. Now you have passed through the wind, the board will tend to heel to leeward and will want to luff up on the new tack.

Remember that when we were doing our introductory freestyle exercises, the sail being held with the leech forward was trying to swing quickly back round to its natural position.

We have now luffed up to the position where the sailor and board are stable and are ready to finish the manoeuvre off by gybing the sail.

Quick gybe

1. You start to bear away: the front arm straightens and pulls the sail forward and to windward; the front leg straightens and heels the board to windward.

2 and 3. You move back to assist the turn and keep your balance ... the stern crosses through the wind as your feet are together, pointing straight ahead; and you begin the luff.

4 and 5. You then bring the mast into the centreline of the board and lessen the aft rake. Your weight shifts onto the front foot; the front hand lets go of the boom and the mast rotates, held by the rear hand.

6, 7 and 8. You push the mast aft, allowing the sail to catch the wind and keep propelling you forward. As the sail catches the wind, your mast hand pulls the rig forward and to windward.

Coming out of the gybe

Now you have to shift your balance. For a brief instant, as in the tack, your only support will be the mast itself. So you will need to lower your centre of gravity by bending your knees.

You simply let go of the boom with your front hand and take hold of the mast so that your rear hand can grab the boom on the other side. The sail, suddenly free to pivot, will move on its own all the way round onto the new gybe, while your front hand supports the mast through the rotation.

As the mast rotates, you must keep the mast pushed towards the stern of the board so that the sail catches the wind and keeps propelling the board forward. The hand which is holding the mast meanwhile pulls the rig forward and to windward.

You know the rest. You start off again, picking up speed, facing the sail and leaning back as necessary.

Extreme conditions: light and heavy

Just as with the quick tack, you need to exaggerate your movements in light airs and to moderate them in heavy winds.

Exaggerated movements in a light wind can easily cause you to lose your balance. To prevent this, it is best to bring your hands really far back along the boom, even as far as taking hold of the leech with one hand.

Since you have exaggerated the movements of the sail, it does not matter if you minimise the heel to windward (particularly as you have so little wind in the sail to balance yourself against). You do have to move back along the board, but not too far: if your feet are getting wet in light airs, you are slowing the board and decreasing the board's fragile stability.

One final point: in light airs you must allow the board time to turn round. If you try to move the rig too much too soon, you will fail to catch any wind in it on the new gybe, and you will end up in the water.

In a strong wind, you absolutely must pull the centreboard up, or the hydrofoil effect of the board will trip it up and flip the board over upside down.

Since you will already be hanging backwards on the rig you will not need to bring it any further to windward. You do not need to move your hands on the boom either; it is sufficient to lean the rig slightly forward.

As the turn begins, you will need to come aft and bend your knees to lower your centre of gravity and make it easier to lean back. You can happily heel the board quite hard to windward, as the sail will have plenty of power to support you.

The spell with the sail clew first will be necessarily brief, because it makes great demands on your strength. It is therefore best to cut it short and gybe the sail early, bringing the mast aft. It will be easier to start off again this way, and the sail will keep drawing throughout. You need to be leaning back as soon as possible on the new tack to prevent the sail from flapping and the board from slowing down.

Funboards for beginners
Choosing your equipment

The board

The characteristics of the board will be determined largely by who is going to sail it. It must have a volume sufficient to support the sailor and rig. It will be in the region of 2.80 to 3m long. (Any longer than 3.20m and the board does not require special instructions, as it will have a centreboard ... which is not to say it will be any less fun!)

There is a wide variety of underwater shapes available, and all differ slightly in the way they handle. One thing the funboard must have is a good clean edge, to 'grip' on the water when turning. At the very least, you should ensure that the aft third of the board has underwater edges.

On a funboard, you can make (and learn from) all the classic mistakes of the beginner without paying for them too dearly, because the board will have enough volume for you to use the uphaul, and you can tack it and sail it to windward (even without a centreboard), carry out freestyle tricks, jump and surf.

If you weigh, say, 70–80kg, you need a board with 110–120 litres of volume, 2.80–3m long and 56–60cm wide.

Fittings

Foot straps

These must be easy to get your foot into (ie they have to spring back into shape after they have been stepped on). They must not move even slightly on their fixing plates. Nylon foot straps rub on bare feet and should be avoided. The front foot straps will be diagonal, pointing across the board in to face the sail as you use them; the rear ones will be straight along the centreline of the board.

Skeg (or skegs)
There is an infinite variety of skegs, differing in shape, cross-section and rigidity. They should all have a wing cross-section, but as far as shape is concerned, there is an enormous choice. The only sort you should avoid are the weed-catcher type (!) which slope forward. Some clever shapes have been invented to reduce the development of air bubble streams down the skeg of the board, which would make steering difficult; the most common of these is a slot high up towards the back of the skeg. Rigidity is of course a factor of the material used. Carbon fibre is stiffer than polyethylene.

Mast foot
It is most important that this link between board and rig should be utterly reliable. It should be up to you to decide when you want to detach the mast, and not up to the whim of the elements. Do not forget the safety leash.

Mast foot track
Most modern funboards have a mast track, so that the foot of the mast can be slid fore and aft. It is adjusted when you are afloat using a foot-pedal. Some old-fashioned models need to be adjusted using a screwdriver (ashore, of course). The panel entitled 'Setting the position of the mast foot on a funboard' gives you some points to look out for when deciding how far forward or back you want the mast foot to be. You must in any case experiment to find what suits you best.

Setting the position of the mast foot on a funboard

With the mast foot forward	**With the mast foot aft**
The board feels quiet.	The board feels lively.
You might bury the bow.	You might luff up too much.
You increase the length of the board in the water.	You have less of the board in the water.
You maintain directional stability. You move in wide curves.	You can carry out extreme moves.

Rig

There are several different types of rig. The chief variable is the sail. The choice of the sail determines your choice of mast and boom.

Camber induced sail.

Sail

There are two major types of sail: camber-induced and rotational.

Camber-induced sails produce a great deal of power, which derives from the camber. They have a very full entry, ie a lot of fullness in the front third of the sail. These powerful sails are designed for experienced funboard practitioners.

Most readers will use lighter, rotational sails, which are easier to manage and altogether better for one's initial funboarding experiences. They are easy to pull up owing to the fact that they have a short boom. They can have either full-length battens or leech battens only. In a fully-battened sail the belly cannot move forward and back so much, giving a feeling of stability. Leech battens allow the luff to flutter, so the sail is rather easier to control.

Sail with rotational mast sleeve.

Mast

The mast is generally made of glass fibre for rotational sails, and of aluminium alloy for camber-induced sails. Glass fibre masts can break, but they can also be repaired. Alloy masts can get permanently bent, and have to be thrown away if they break. Glass fibre masts, being flexible, actually break less easily, and they are certainly more forgiving for beginners.

A flexible mast cushions you from gusts, whereas an alloy mast will transmit to the board every shock it receives. The choice is yours. The mast must be plugged to ensure that it is watertight. It is often a good idea to put a protective sleeve or some tape on your mast at the point where you fix the boom, to avoid excessive wear.

Boom

The boom has to be rigid to ensure the sail is held in a constant shape. Above all, the boom must be curved to accommodate the curvature of the sail. Some booms can be lengthened to suit the sail being used.

The boom has to be watertight: make sure any holes or fittings are properly plugged.

Leaving the beach

Carrying the board

It is easy to carry your equipment down to the water's edge, as it does not weigh much. You should learn to save yourself the effort of the extra journey and carry both rig and board down to the water's edge in one go. The following techniques use the force of

1. Board on the hip and sail above the head.
2. Board and sail above the head.
3. Between board and rig.
4. Board and rig against the waist.

the wind to help you lift the rig and board together. Do not try to fight the wind: use it on your side.

Board on the hip and sail above the head

You stand to windward of both parts, with your front hand on the mast and your rear hand holding a foot strap. Then lift it up in one go and put the sail over your head, shifting your grip as necessary. You can balance when you have the board resting against your hip and the whole lot somewhere between beam on and in line with the wind. You have to hold it more in line with the wind the stronger the wind is. Leave the rig and board in the same alignment with the wind irrespective of the direction you are going. Holding the equipment in this way you can carry it a long way, and walk relatively fast, as you will be leaving your legs unencumbered. When you do reach the water, you will find the rig is already in the right position for the beach start.

Board and sail above the head

Pull the rear of the board, skeg up, through inside the boom. You can then carry the sail on your head, with the mast held to windward. Your hands are needed to balance everything, but they do not bear the weight. This technique also leaves you very mobile, but you will need to stop before you reach the water to put the board down in a position which permits a quick getaway.

Between board and rig

Stand between the board and the rig, board to windward and rig to leeward, with the mast to the rear of the sail. Hold a foot strap in one hand and the boom in the other. When you lift, your boom hand will force the mast in to rest against your waist, stabilising the sail. The board is held up by the cantilever effect, through the mast foot as well as by the foot strap. You can either carry the equipment, using one of the forward foot straps, or push the nose of the board along the ground, holding one of the rear straps.

Just as with the other methods, the direction in which you hold the board is determined by the wind direction rather than by where you are going. In this case, you are using the strength of your arms, which makes this technique heavy going over anything other than short distances.

Board and rig against the waist

You stand to windward, with the mast facing aft. Prop the sail and board against your waist by carrying the boom in one hand and a forward foot strap in the other. This position is uncomfortable, but it does allow you to put the board into the water and sail off immediately from a beach start.

Uphauling

Before you get carried away with speed, you must master the art of uphauling. It is one way to avoid long inadvertent swims.

The board is in the water.

The rig and board are in the basic starting position, with the board to windward, the rig downwind and the mast forward of the sail.

You need to find out where on the board you can balance. There is not a great deal of space between the front foot straps and the mast foot. You have no room for moving side to side while the board is not moving forwards, so you do need to have considerable control of the trim and reactions of the board.

The best position for rotating the board is with your feet either side of the mast foot. As the sail comes out of the water, the bow of the board will begin to sink – since the mast is only a third of the way along the board. In order to correct this tendency, which might be quite pronounced on some boards, you need to slide your rear foot further aft, and place more weight on that foot. As when starting on the long board, remember to keep your back straight.

It becomes more and more difficult to keep your balance as the sail comes out of the water, so you need something stable to hold onto. Your first concern should therefore be to fill the sail with wind, no matter where the board and rig are facing. You can always steer once you have found your balance.

Beach starts

In theory, a beach start on a funboard is no different from a beach start on a long board, but the practice is slightly changed, due to the small size of the board.

As the board is light, it is easily pushed or pulled into position by pressure on the mast; but the fact that it has less buoyancy means it is also less stable when stopped or moving slowly.

For this reason you need to place your rear foot on the board with some precision. If it is too far forward, the board will nosedive and you will be pulled off. Too far back and the board will luff immediately. You should not start by putting your foot into a foot strap, since the straps are not necessarily in the spot where you need them for balance at this stage. The foot is better placed forward of the foot straps as you set off. Once the board picks up speed you can of course slip your feet into the straps.

Water starts

A water start requires the same sort of preparation as a beach start.

You will soon discover that the water offers a base to push against in the same way as the beach did: you have to paddle with your feet, or tread water. With a water start, however, your body will be much lower relative to the board than it was for the beach start, so it is worth practising beach starts in deeper water to get a feel for it.

Preparation

You have only to swim, and let the wind do the rest. There are four possible starting positions:
– sail to windward, clew forward;
– sail to leeward, clew forward;
– sail to leeward, mast forward;
– sail straight down in the water.

Preparation for a water start (1)

Sail to windward, clew forward:
1. Hold on to the clew to pull the board head to wind.
2. Lift the sail for the wind to flip it over.
3. Ready to go.

Sail to leeward, clew forward:
1. Swim round to windward and pull the stern of the board round to the mast.
2. Grab the mast by the boom ...
3. ... and prop the rig up on the board.

Preparation for a water start (2)

Sail to leeward, mast forward:
1. Swim round to windward and lift the clew.
2. The wind will flip the sail over ...
3. ... so that the clew is facing forward and you can prop the rig on the back of the board.

Sail straight down in the water:
1. Swim to windward with the mast in your hands.
2. The sail will come to rest lying flat in the water.

Sail to windward, clew forward
You swim round to the end of the boom and hold onto it. Your body will work as a floating anchor, and the board will drift downwind of you. If you have not the patience to wait for this to happen, you can swim and tow the clew upwind.

All you then have to do to reach the right position is lift the boom. The wind will catch under the sail and flip it over, leaving the mast where it is.

Sail to leeward, clew forward
Swim to windward and bring the rear of the board in towards the mast. Hold the mast about at the boom, and prop the boom up on the stern of the board. This will hold the sail clear of the water and you can pull it round to windward of the board.

Sail to leeward, mast forward
Combine the two techniques above, first moving the sail round then across to windward.

Sail straight down in the water
Take hold of the mast and swim to windward. The sail will then come to rest lying flat in the water. If it is not already in the right position for the start, follow one of the previous recipes in order to set it up.

The water start

The first job, having got the board and rig into the starting position (sail to windward, mast forward), is to unstick the sail from the water. If you can keep the mast between 45° and 90° from the wind, you will find the wind helps you. (The bigger the angle, the more difficult it gets.)

You should be treading water level with the boom; then you can unstick the sail, lifting and pulling the mast towards you. (If you lift but forget to pull, you will sink the clew, and the wind will flip the sail over.)

The moment the sail comes out of the water, you need to grab the boom in both hands. You can then ease and pull the sail in to keep it balanced, and keep the heading of the board correct, while you tread water.

Just as for the beach start, you should aim to achieve a strong pull from the sail, without it becoming overpowered. If you bear away too much the sail will pull too hard, and if you luff up too much the sail will crash down on top of you.

Water start

1. Swimming, pulling the rig towards you, you unstick the sail.

2. You push down on the mast to make the board bear away and keep the sail out of the water.

3. Bending your rear leg accentuates the bearing away.

4. Bend your foot, knee and hip forward to keep the pull under control.

5 and 6. As you come up out of the water, you ease the sail.

When you have got everything pointing in the right direction, you can put your back foot onto the board without pushing it off course.

You put your foot diagonally across the board, at 45° to the centreline, with the inner side downmost. Keep treading water with your front foot.

Now you have to imagine you are climbing a wall. Both hands have got a grip above your head; you have one toe- and knee-hold at hip height, with your other knee dangling. In order to get your front foot up next to its partner, you need simultaneously to pull with your arms and to push with your bent leg on its grippy surface. You swing your hanging leg to help yourself up.

The water start involves the same movements.

Your hands are holding onto the boom. You need to ensure that the handhold is secure enough to take your weight, but you do not make the climber's typical 'chin-up' move – this would probably not work and would certainly tire you out. Your aim should be to let the sail offer as much surface to the wind as soon as possible, so as to provide as much power as possible. Your arms should be fairly straight, and you should aim to make up for the lack of pull in your arms by pushing with your legs. With the back foot resting on the board and the front one pushing against the water, both will help you on to terra firma.

You need to get close to the board before trying to climb onto it, so you must bend the rear leg. If your foot has the inside resting on the board, then your knee will automatically be pointing forward. This way your leg will supply the most force for getting your weight above the board; your other leg will be helping as you paddle with it, and your arms should be devoted to keeping the sail correctly trimmed.

As soon as your body weight is over the board, your success is virtually guaranteed, so long as you then retain control over your ascent. If you do not, the sail will carry your weight over to leeward and you will have to start again from square one. Do not forget that your weight is much easier for the sail to lift once you come out of the water.

Going about

Tacking

Your board has sufficient buoyancy to keep you and the rig afloat when stopped, so it is possible to tack.

Tacking

1 and 2. As you luff and lean the rig aft, your weight is on the back foot.

3. Moving round the front of the mast. Your weight comes briefly onto the front foot.

4. Moving round the front of the mast (continued). As you bury the bow, you change hand and foot positions.

5. Your front arm pulls the rig forward, and your front foot prepares to move aft of the mast.

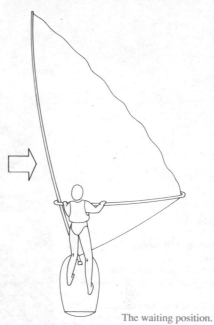

The waiting position.

Tacking is often useful, since you do not lose ground to windward by going about this way. You can sail to windward and tack even without a centreboard.

You start the manoeuvre with the sail, but as you proceed with the tack, it is your feet which do the work by controlling the board.

You must ensure that your feet spend as little time as possible outside the stable central zone of the board, between the front foot strap and the mast. You therefore stay close to the mast and move round quickly as you go, in order to stop the bow sinking.

Unlike quick-tacking a long board, you must pass round the front of the mast and move the mast forward to bear away in two entirely separate movements:
– first you move round the front of the mast, holding the mast vertical, right next to your body;
– then you continue the movement, pushing the mast forward once you have actually reached the new side.

Once you have got hold of the boom on the new tack, you can either shoot off immediately or take your time about it. You can actually remain stopped in this position, balancing by pulling the sail in and easing it. We call this the waiting position, and it is similar to the starting position we used in the first sailboard lesson.

Short boards are hypersensitive to any movement. Remember to move your upper body and your lower body separately. Any sudden or heavy movement will destroy your balance. Do not try to be super-fast at the beginning, as this is bound to send you for a swim.

1. Sailing at full speed, harness still hooked up.
2. Harness unhooked, accelerating as you bear away. The back foot comes out of its strap.
3 and 4. From bent knees, push forward inside the curve, depressing the lee rail.
5. You push the board round further with your feet, while the rear hand pushes the boom round and you change hands.
6 and 7. You wait until the sail is filling on the new gybe before changing feet.

Carve gybes

Gybing this way keeps your speed up throughout, and the board never comes off the plane.

Both feet are in the straps and you are sailing at full speed. Pull the aft foot out of its strap and put it down in front of the strap.

Unhook your harness and lean the board in towards the centre of the turn. The board will accelerate and bear away.

Your body weight should be over the board; the sail is pulled in more than usual and your knees are pointing forward and into the turn.

When the sail stops pulling, you are through the wind, and you push the boom round with your back hand before letting go, so as to make the rig rotate faster.

With this free hand, catch hold of the mast. The board will lose some speed, but should still be moving quite fast and should still be heeled towards the centre of the turn. If you leave the gybe too late, the sail will back and you will be in the water.

You start to bring the sail in with one hand still on the mast and the other on the boom, taking care not to luff up too far. As you pick up speed, you can change your foot positions and put your feet back in the straps, hook the harness on and finally bring both hands back on the boom.

The difficult part of this manoeuvre is keeping your speed up. You need a good burst of acceleration to begin with and then you need to find the right angle of heel through the turn: too much or too little and you lose your speed completely.

With a bit of practice, you should be able to gain a further couple of seconds by making the gybe without touching the mast and just taking your hands from one side of the boom to the other.

Clew first

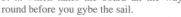

1. The board is travelling relatively slowly
2. ... so you sail clew first ...
3. ... which takes the board all the way round before you gybe the sail.

Clew first gybe

When the wind is too light for a carve gybe, or when your balance is too precarious for some reason, you will need to sail clew first. Since this manoeuvre is carried out at lower speeds, the board will be less stable, so your movements will have to be more cautious.

Unlike the carve gybe, where you can use the rails to do your steering since you are travelling at a considerable speed, you need to use the sail as a rudder to get you through this manoeuvre. The upper body controls the rig as it is tipped forward and to windward. You need to incline the rig further the less wind there is.

The lower part of the body controls the side-to-side trim of the board and starts the turn by heeling the board. At the same time you must also keep an eye on your fore-and-aft trim to conserve your balance.

You begin the turn with your feet, then as the board slows down you bring the rig into action, leaning it forward and to windward.

You change foot positions as the board turns through the wind, and luff up clew first onto a beam reach.

The board accelerates and gains stability as it does so. When you feel the board is stable enough, you gybe the sail.

Some freestyle manoeuvres

Practising freestyle manoeuvres is an excellent way of getting to know your board and how it will react to the demands you make on it.

When the wind is light, don't turn your nose up and go for a bike ride: use the opportunity to practise your balance afloat (not forgetting to fix your uphaul). Try the following light-weather exercise programme: uphauling, 360° turns, tacks and gybes, helicopter tacks and water starts.

Just because you can carry out these manoeuvres in light winds does not necessarily mean you can do them in a gale. It does make sense to keep trying them again and again, perhaps adding a back-to-front water start and a clew first gybe for variety.

All these freestyle manoeuvres will help you one day in an unexpected situation: when you need to stop suddenly, for instance, or turn in a tight spot. Here are some to be getting on with.

Helicopter tack

This is an easy tack for light winds, which avoids the need to walk

Helicopter tack
1. Luff up with the leading hand on the mast.
2 and 3. Once you have passed through the eye of the wind, you push the rig away, making the board bear away as it goes into reverse. You let go with your front hand and put all your weight on the back foot.
4. When the board has turned far enough, you shove the boom away ...
5. ... sending the sail through 360°.

round the front of the mast. It is often used to tack boards without much buoyancy, which do not tack easily using conventional techniques.

What you are aiming for is to luff beyond head-to-wind, putting one hand on the mast and standing with your feet either side of the mast. Then, with a single sweeping movement, you push sail and mast forward and deliberately back the sail.

When this happens, the board starts to travel backwards, turning as it goes. The pressure on the sail builds up as you turn away from

Water start in light weather

1. Take the rig with one hand low down on the mast and the other on the boom ...

2. ... as you try to get the rig as close to upright as possible, to make the most of what wind there is.

3 and 4. Off we go. Note that the rig is eased out as you come out of the water.

the wind, and you will have to push very hard against the boom. With one large shove of the back hand, and while you hold the mast in your front hand, the sail will rotate through 360° about the mast, and you change over your hands and feet to start off on the new tack.

Water start in light weather

This move uses what wind there is to get started. It takes more physical strength than a normal water start, and uses both arms and legs.

You pump the sail to create a temporary handhold strong enough to lift yourself out, and you also need to push harder with your legs.

In order to get the sail further out of the water and closer to the

Two types of quick water start.

vertical you might need to put your hands on the mast and the foot
of the sail rather than the boom. The role of the legs is to position
your pelvis above the board: the front leg will be paddling hard, and
you might end up kneeling on the back leg.

Quick water start

The thing which takes most time in a water start is getting the sail
in position. In fact you can cut this phase out: so long as you can
hold the sail up and reach the board with your feet, you can get
going, whether the sail is facing the right way or not.

Once you are up, you can start putting the sail the right way
round.

Slam gybe
1. Shift your weight aft.
2. The board pivots about the submerged end.
3. Find your balance with the sail clew first.
4. Gybe the sail.
5. And off!

Slam gybe

Rather like tacking, this is one way of going about which is often used in order not to lose too much ground to windward when changing tacks.

Since what you are aiming for is a fast turn, you start the manoeuvre not by moving the sail but by transferring your weight aft and sinking the stern. As the board rears its front up out of the water, it will pivot around the submerged end. You can keep relying on the full sail as a source of stability throughout ... so long as you do keep it full. As soon as you have the board travelling fast enough on the new gybe with the sail clew first, you can gybe the sail.

Safety afloat

All the remarks made in Chapter 1, 'Introduction', about safety for the beginner apply just as much to the more experienced practitioner. Although some of the precautions might seem less important for better sailors, it is just as necessary for experienced sailors to keep their boat in good condition, unsinkable, equipped with anchor and anchor rope, bow fairlead, bailer and paddle as it ever was for beginners. Equally, there is no level of experience at which the buoyancy aid becomes an optional extra.

Having said that, there are some further comments to be made regarding safety. Beginners tend to stay within earshot and sight of land. As one develops one's skills further, learns how to handle equipment and how to right a capsize, one tends to sail further afield to use one's new-found independence ...

In fact, you are never truly independent in a boat of the type we have examined so far. Even championship-level sailors cannot always guarantee to get back to shore under their own power. When you find yourself in difficulties, you will need outside assistance ... and that is precisely the problem.

Weather and place

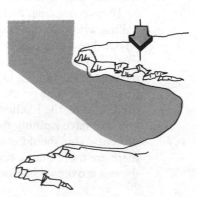

The safe area to sail a dinghy in varies with the wind direction. In all these cases, one can reach the shore by sailing downwind from the shaded area.

French law requires that light dinghies and racing keelboats must stay within two miles of a point on the coast where they can take refuge, unless they are sailing with 'appropriate accompaniment'. This common-sense rule should be observed even where it is not law.

Two miles is a long way. This minimal precaution is just that: all it means is that potential rescuers can reach you in a certain time. And it becomes quite meaningless as a safety measure unless the area in which you are sailing is actually being watched by someone, and the weather is genuinely suitable for setting out to sea.

It cannot be considered prudent to sail on your own, on a deserted stretch of sea, in any weather. Even a stretch with lots of traffic is less dangerous: you might capsize there, but at least you have a chance of someone in a passing boat noticing you – even if there is not much they can do to help you.

If you are sailing without 'appropriate accompaniment', the only solution you can adopt is to have someone on the beach who knows what they are looking for and where, and who knows where help can be found if it becomes necessary. In order for this arrangement to have any sense at all, the boat must clearly stay where it can be seen.

Those sailing the boat must have a certain amount of knowledge of the water on which they are sailing. It is a good idea to look at a map before setting off (and a nautical chart, rather than a tourist map) and to check for local hazards: unmarked wrecks, currents, tidal rips which can cause problems on the nicest of days.

As far as the weather is concerned, we may as well keep it simple. A gusty force 4–5 or a steady force 6 is too much for most crews on the sea. You are practically certain of capsizing and you will probably have difficulty righting the boat. Equipment failure is likely. It is much harder for would-be rescuers, and you can endanger the lives of others as well as yourselves.

It is necessary, but still not quite sufficient, to have someone watching you, and to check the weather.

There is one final factor to think about: how long you will be out. Sailing a boat takes a certain amount of physical exertion, and your physical resources are not immediately renewable, at least not on a small sailing boat, which remains upright only so long as you are paying close attention to it, to say nothing of the actual effort itself. So plan your time on the water to suit your own strength. The more tired you are, the likelier you are to capsize and the more difficulty you will have righting the boat. If you are out in charge of a group of boats, you should ensure the group heads for home as soon as there are more than a few capsizes. In any case you should ensure the sail is over well before sunset: the chances of finding people lost in a capsize after dark are minimal.

The main difference between beginners and advanced sailors from the point of view of safety is this: advanced sailors will travel further from land and will not be watched so closely. They will therefore inevitably have to wait longer for help to come should it be necessary. As the wait lengthens, the real dangers are those of cold and tiredness. You should learn to recognise the symptoms and effects of these.

Cold and tiredness

In general, there is no problem with staying for several hours in water which is above 20°C. But the temperature of the Channel and the Atlantic is well below this: about 17°C in summer and 10°C in winter. Especially in winter and in inland waters, the temperature can drop well below these average figures.

Any prolonged exposure to cold water causes the body to become exhausted quickly due to heat loss. Scientific test results show the average period before losing consciousness to be 20–60 minutes at 10°C, and 2–3 hours at 17°C. (Losing consciousness in such circumstances of course usually means death.) These average figures are for normally clothed individuals in good health, in calm water, not making any particular physical effort.

There are further points to be made to gloss these bare statistics:
– there are two separate phases to the period before loss of consciousness: at the beginning the person can still move and is capable of participating in the rescue. Although still conscious in the second phase, that person will no longer be capable of helping the rescuers. The first period becomes shorter in relation to the second as the water temperature becomes lower;
– any physical effort, and particularly any protracted physical effort, although it initially keeps the body warm, will exhaust one's energy and contribute to a faster rate of heat loss than otherwise, thus reducing the chances of survival.

There are four conclusions to be drawn from the above:
– you must dress properly. Any clothing, but especially woollen clothing, slows heat loss. (One point, though not strictly related to this, is that you should usually make sure you are carrying a knife when sailing in case you need to cut yourself free from tangled sheets);
– in cold-water areas, the best solution is to be wearing a wetsuit.

This will keep you conscious three to four times longer;
– a lot of heat is lost through the head. Your lifejacket should be of a type which keeps your head clear of the waves;
– if you find that you cannot right the boat, avoid physical effort. Preferably, pull yourself onto the hull; if you cannot manage this, stay next to the hull, tying yourself on if possible, and keep still.

Decision-making

When you cannot right the boat and help seems a long way off, you face two decisions: whether to anchor the boat, and whether to leave the boat.

If you are being taken out to sea by wind and/or tide, you should certainly drop the anchor. Obviously, if you are drifting towards the shore, it is better to wait until you are close in. The right answer depends on the circumstances: just make sure you take your time before you decide what to do, and check which way the boat is drifting.

You absolutely must not leave the boat. If you can stay with the upturned hull, you will stand an infinitely better chance of being spotted and rescued quickly. Your chances of reaching the beach by swimming are slim. The average swimmer cannot manage 300 metres in waves, fully clothed, despite the aid of a lifejacket. We usually underestimate the distance to the shore; and even if the shore is close by, you still have to bear the current in mind. You will not make any progress against the tide. Staying with the boat will help to conserve your energy and can provide shelter against the waves and wind. Thus you will survive for longer than if you swim out into the open sea. The longer you survive the more time you give to be spotted and rescued.

We are aware of only one case when the above advice would have been wrong. On 6 July 1969, in a fearsome storm, the crew of a capsized boat was found exhausted but alive, having swum to and held onto a nearby rock. The helmsman stayed with the boat and was drowned. The sea that day was so rough that holding onto the hull was too difficult, and there was no hope of rescue.

These were exceptional circumstances. We mention them because this episode does constitute an exception to our absolute rule; but you should not seek to generalise from this one case.

Conclusion

In conclusion: the essential safety precautions are:
– to make sure that you are fit
– your boat correctly prepared
– the weather is fine
– someone is on the beach watching.
If you consider a dinghy, a catamaran or a sailboard to be a boat, then their sailors should conduct themselves in a seamanlike fashion. This means deciding not to go out if the wind is too strong or if you are feeling off-colour. It means coming back to land before you are tired out and night falls. These are what is really meant by safety precautions. Following them shows that you have come to

An upturned hull is easy to spot. A lone swimmer is not.

know your own limits, those imposed by the sea and those of your craft. Your greatest enemy is your own vanity. Do not let it lead you astray.

PART II

The Mechanics of Sailing

However you learnt to sail, whether through studying the first part of this book or elsewhere, you are now a capable sailor. In other words, you can set off confidently from a beach and head in the direction of your choice, quickly or slowly, in heavy or light winds.

Still, there will be a number of aspects of sailing which escaped your notice and that of your crew. It all seems to work, but why? Now is the time to look a little deeper.

In this part of the manual, you will learn more of the subtle craft of sailors, marine architects and boatbuilders who have been harnessing the forces of nature; we shall examine those forces and their effect on the balance of your boat and its hull.

CHAPTER 1
Origin of forces

Air or water flowing over a solid surface creates force: aerodynamic or hydrodynamic force. We shall attempt to provide here some intellectual tools for the understanding of key situations, but we shall not proceed to a general discussion of fluid mechanics. The theory might appear dry and abstract, but it is worth spending some time on it in order to understand what is going on and how your actions can influence it.

A sailing boat is knocked and battered by opposing forces, which are all subject to the laws of fluid mechanics. These forces are just like the Greek gods of Mount Olympus: they can work in harmony, or individually. And each has potentially terrifying power in its own sphere of influence.

Definitions

Air and water are *fluids*. A physicist would say that they are continuous isotropic homogeneous media which behave as if noncompressible in equilibrium. When static, at any one point, they *exert the same pressure in all directions*.

We should distinguish between gases, which will take up all the space available to them and are therefore said to be compressible, and liquids, which are practically incompressible. However, in the case of a body floating on water, both *water and air act as incompressible media*.

The essential difference between air and water derives from their specific density. Water is very gravity-sensitive and has a free horizontal surface when static. The weight of air is practically insignificant as the air flows round or acts on a sail or aerofoil.

Fluid mechanics

To explain the movement of a fluid round an obstacle, one can either follow the fluid's action as it moves (such as you would see from inside a moving boat) or observe it from a fixed point or obstacle (such as a boat anchored in a current).

When a fluid is in motion, the *speed* of the 'particles' or individual little pockets of air or water varies across time and space.

Each small part of a fluid can move (translation), pivot (rotation), or be deformed, just like a tennis ball.

This variation causes both rotation (turbulence) and deformation.

Since both air and water are continuous media, any local change transfers itself and changes the surrounding areas.

As the water flows, an image (here, a series of squares) is deformed as it moves.

Turbulence

Any phenomenon occurring within a relatively stable fluid environment can be considered as turbulence. It is vital to look at the phenomenon, however, from the point of view of scale.

The atmospheric disturbances which the human eye perceives represent a turbulent air flow on a planetary scale, such that an eye out in space could also see them. On a rather more localised scale, we are daily confronted with turbulence in fluids: columns of smoke, water jets from a hosepipe or a basin as it drains ... these turbulences are small and localised in time and space, yet they impose themselves on and over whatever general movement or

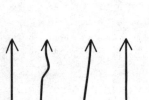

Quite apart from any atmospheric disturbances, your sails are subject to any turbulence created by sails or other obstacles situated upwind or earlier in the flow.

Even when sailing close-hauled, with the wind slipping apparently smoothly over the sails, the air flow over a sail is turbulent. There is intense turbulence on a very small scale, mixing up all the individual air streams.

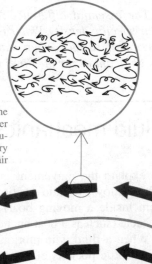

flow is taking place. We can observe some pattern, however, to their action.

A scientist would talk of fluctuations in velocity, turbulence chains and disaggregations ... all phenomena which occur within a single water flow or which are produced by the action of wind on an obstacle.

We can distinguish between the fine structure of air flowing over sails on the one hand, and the sort of turbulence in the air which leaves a boat as nothing more than a straw in the wind on the other.

Beneficial turbulence

As a boat passes through water, the water acts on it as a brake, and turbulence can be seen in the wake. The water is turning in opposite directions, and the whole effect of the phenomenon is to waste energy and slow the boat down.

On the other hand, when some action of the crew produces rotation of the wind or water all in the same direction (such as when you turn the rudder to tack, trim the sails or the boat), this need not slow you down. If you can produce a clockwise rotation in the water while you are on port tack, this will actually propel you and the boat along. This is one of the forces at work when, in a flat calm, you waggle the tiller from side to side and begin to move forward.

The same phenomenon arises with a sail. It is accompanied by eddies at the trailing edge. The intensity of these eddies varies

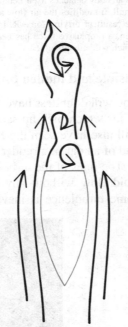

Energy is being wasted by confused turbulence.

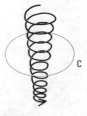

As water drains from a sink, with all the turbulent rotation in the same direction, it exerts a force proportional to $2\pi r v$. In general, whatever the size of the enclosed circle C, we can define the force arising from the turbulence, which is called circulation of a vortex.

with the trim of the sails or other rig changes; it is a necessary component of the aerodynamic force which pushes you forward on a close-hauled leg.

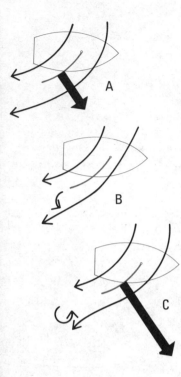

As an eddy detaches itself behind a sail or a hull, it modifies the air flow and affects the resultant driving force R. In figure C then, a propulsive force has been created which will strengthen $\vec{R}$.

Air eddies are invisible. In the water, however, you can spot them when you change tack, trailing out behind you. In fact, although the eddies you see at the surface are well aft of the boat, the stream of turbulence they show originates at, and is still attached to, the trailing edge of the rudder, rather like a ball of string unravelling.

Visible and hidden turbulence

You will doubtless have seen little 'sand devils', turbulent columns of air which pick up sand off a beach or a stretch of tarmac. You will also have seen the eddies behind a buoy in a tidal way, at the end of an oar or a rudder as you change direction.

The lines of the turbulence can run continuously throughout the fluid flow without any particularly well-defined outward signs: some turbulence is inevitably present when there is flow over a

Visible turbulence about an axis rotating with speed r.

A physicist would call one of our individual eddies, which go to make up the phenomenon known as turbulence, a vortex. They may be characterised by their intensity and by their circulation. The local speed of rotation of a vortex is the speed at which a theoretical tiny floating body would rotate when caught by the vortex. Seen or unseen, vortices play a determining role in certain points of sailing. They give aerodynamic or hydrodynamic lift which helps propel the boat forward.

Inside the vortex

surface, and it results from the rotation of individual particles trapped, as it were, between the fast-flowing liquid and those particles which have been slowed by friction with the surface. This hidden but regular turbulence plays an important part in the distribution of effort over any of the boat's surfaces: hull, rudder, rigging or sails.

In any real flow system, turbulence will develop and be distributed in the immediate vicinity of the obstacle. The effect of this turbulence has actually been harnessed and used for propulsion in several inventive schemes, such as Fletner's 'rotor' system and Father Malavard's 'windmill'. As a classical sailing boat travels to windward, turbulence effects are closely linked to the motive force of the wind on the sails and the water on the hull.

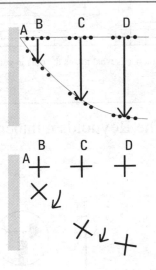

Flow

Mixing of fluids

Air flow over a sail is always turbulent, due to effects of diffusion (interpenetration of fluids at the molecular level), friction and mixing. Within a scale of a millimetre or so, there is a constantly changing disorder of molecules mixing with and flowing over each other in minute eddies. This sort of turbulence is quite unrelated to the sort of atmospheric disturbances which the eye can see and which operate at the level of hundreds of metres.

Flow is said to be laminar when the currents run parallel to each other, not mixing. With a very smooth hull on very calm inland water, there will occasionally

As a fluid travels along a surface with friction, eg as water flowing along a hull, the fluid is forced to rotate over itself, thus causing small amounts of hidden turbulence distributed throughout the fluid.

If, for instance, we consider point A as a flat surface along which a fluid is travelling, we can see that the speed of the flow past that surface at points B, C and D (represented by the length of the arrows) is greater as the distance from the surface increases. The molecules of water which are moving past the hull will be distributed along the curve described by the ends of the arrows; and the rotation of those molecules can be represented by imagining them as frozen in the form of a cross, which is turned further the closer that cross is to the hull.

Cigarette smoke rises in a brief laminar flow before beginning to diffuse and become turbulent.

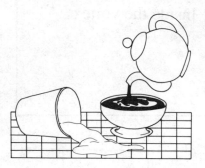

Turbulence is what mixes the milk in your coffee.

be laminar flow. In general, though, there will be so much mixing that any theory which uses laminar flow or 'the ideal fluid' as its basis has to be considered oversimplified.

When flows differ in *speed* or in *direction*, this causes *variation in pressure*. The resultant motive or resistant forces are studied under the name of fluid dynamics.

Laminar and turbulent flows

If you pierce a few small holes in a sachet of bubble bath and let the contents flow slowly out into the bath water you will see that the lines of liquid stay separate, not mixing with each other, for quite a

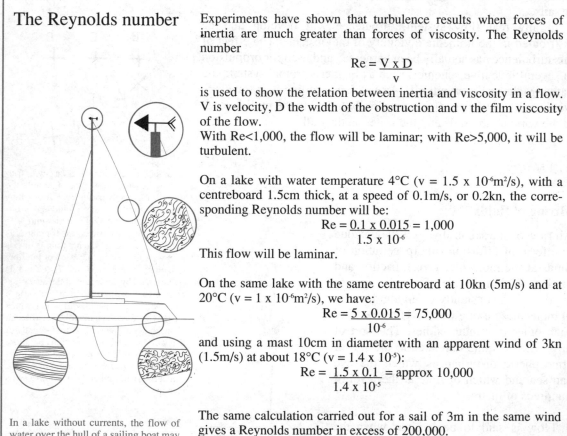

The Reynolds number

Experiments have shown that turbulence results when forces of inertia are much greater than forces of viscosity. The Reynolds number

$$Re = \frac{V \times D}{v}$$

is used to show the relation between inertia and viscosity in a flow. V is velocity, D the width of the obstruction and v the film viscosity of the flow.

With Re<1,000, the flow will be laminar; with Re>5,000, it will be turbulent.

On a lake with water temperature 4°C ($v = 1.5 \times 10^{-6} m^2/s$), with a centreboard 1.5cm thick, at a speed of 0.1m/s, or 0.2kn, the corresponding Reynolds number will be:

$$Re = \frac{0.1 \times 0.015}{1.5 \times 10^{-6}} = 1,000$$

This flow will be laminar.

On the same lake with the same centreboard at 10kn (5m/s) and at 20°C ($v = 1 \times 10^{-6} m^2/s$), we have:

$$Re = \frac{5 \times 0.015}{10^{-6}} = 75,000$$

and using a mast 10cm in diameter with an apparent wind of 3kn (1.5m/s) at about 18°C ($v = 1.4 \times 10^{-5}$):

$$Re = \frac{1.5 \times 0.1}{1.4 \times 10^{-5}} = \text{approx } 10,000$$

The same calculation carried out for a sail of 3m in the same wind gives a Reynolds number in excess of 200,000.

These last three flows will all be turbulent.

In a lake without currents, the flow of water over the hull of a sailing boat may be laminar; but the air flow is turbulent, however regular it may appear.

distance, with their 'strands' parallel even when the flow line itself curves. This is laminar flow, even when there is a certain amount of molecular diffusion on the edges (the speed of which increases with the temperature). If, on the other hand, you carry out the same experiment near where the tap is running into the tub, the liquid will mix in so quickly that you will no longer be able to trace where an individual trace of colour has gone. In this instance, the flow is turbulent. No liquid can stay separate from its neighbour for long in conditions of such chaos.

Differences between fluids and solids

A picture drawn in air with coloured smoke or in water with coloured liquid will quickly lose its shape and become unrecognisable. Fluids such as water and air do not possess a shape of their own. They cannot, therefore, cause friction unless there is movement in the system. For instance, air pressure bears straight in on our eardrums and remains constant whichever way we turn our head.

Once there is movement, however, one surface rubs against the other and the pressure is no longer quite perpendicular to the surface of the obstacle. So the water 'rubs' against the hull of the boat and slows it down. Water and air both behave in this way and are therefore said to be viscous fluids. We can simplify greatly by pretending that these are 'ideal fluids' and that the effects of this friction are negligible compared with the much stronger force exerted by normal pressure. This simplification does actually permit us to explain almost all aerodynamic phenomena.

'Almost all' phenomena will not quite be good enough for us in seeking to explore the real flows which occur, since it does leave out some essentials. The theoreticians prefer to be able to explain things and quantify results in a more comprehensive way which takes account of localised forces known as drag. This comprehensive approach is known as the dynamics of incompressible fluids, and it comes closer to explaining the real behaviour of the viscosity of air and water.

This advertising logo on the (solid) sail remains legible even when the sail bulges and moves. A similar logo traced in the sky by a plane would not last long before becoming illegible.

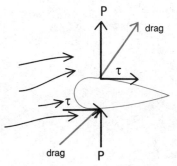

When water flows over a surface, it 'rubs' or causes friction, just as oil and air do. The drag which this causes is related to the surface area and is composed of the normal surface pressure (p) and a tangential force τ. In the case of 'ideal fluids' the tangential τ may be omitted as it equals zero.

The 'ideal' and Newtonian 'viscous' models do not successfully represent all the real behaviour of air and water, as they cannot deal either with mixtures or with the more general case of turbulence.

The simplified 'ideal fluid' model and its applications

The vast majority of observed phenomena on a sailing vessel when close-hauled can be explained by demonstrations and the use of a few appropriate mathematical tools. In fact, so long as there is no separation of flow (ie so long as the air or water stream remains in contact with the sail or hull) and little wake created, the entire geometry and speed of flow, and therefore the pressure of the fluid, remain very close to those predicted by our ideal model. Under these conditions we can explain the direction and strength of the lift provided by an immersed foil, using the idea of the circulation of vortices.

In general, when close-hauled, an effort should be made to avoid or limit separation as far as possible. The effects of separation are

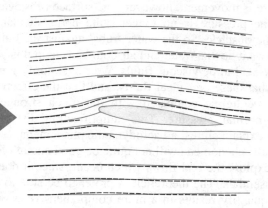

We can compare the flow around a foil as it actually is (black lines) in an air stream which strikes it at a small angle of incidence, and as it is predicted by the theory of the ideal fluid (blue lines).

unpredictable when the interactions of water on hull and air on sails are combined. Because of this unpredictability we adopt special measures to avoid separation on the upper or outer surface. These measures can include a foil on the leading edge, or a sail fulfilling the same function; alternative methods can include inducing a rotating air stream, or various designs of slot to induce limited and controllable turbulence in the boundary layer of air over the top surface and thus prevent separation. C class catamarans, for instance, use slotted flaps in a series to produce a wing effect.

The woollen tell-tales which indicate the air flow are important indicators of separation taking place, and can thus indicate correct trim.

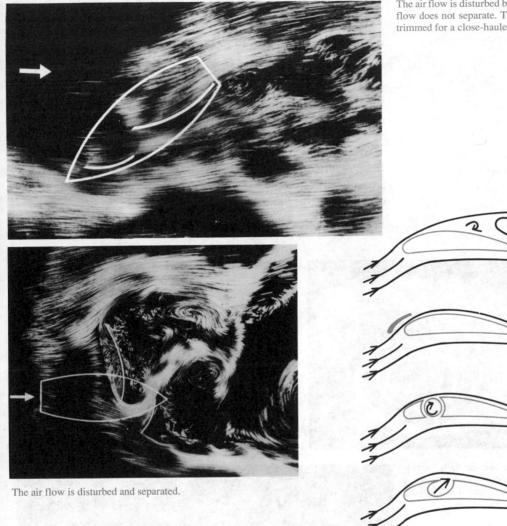

The air flow is disturbed by the sail, but the flow does not separate. The boat is nicely trimmed for a close-hauled course.

The air flow is disturbed and separated.

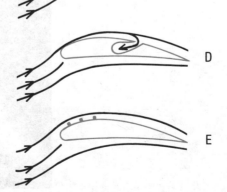

A. A leading-edge foil.
B. A mechanically induced vortex.
C. Blowing the boundary layer out from the surface.
D. Sucking the separated boundary layer back in towards the surface.
E. Generating a turbulent boundary layer.

There are several ways to produce a real effect which simulates the flow of an ideal fluid:

Air and water viscosity

Turbulence arises and is distributed throughout the flow of both air and water as a result of the viscosity of the fluids, on the relatively small scale of a sailing boat. On a much larger scale, that of the planet, turbulence such as a cyclone arises also due to the rotation of the earth.

We can show that zones of turbulence arise in real fluids in the wake of any obstacle and beside an obstacle, beginning as soon as any movement enters the system. Once the motion is established consistently, this has several further consequences:

Turbulence arising and setting in permanently as movement is introduced into a system by an obstacle placed in a flowing viscous fluid.

– a vortex arises on the surface of the foil as a result of the combination of the starting vortex linking with the tip vortices. Some part of this action can be observed in the laboratory or outside, as dust or bubbles follow the route of the circulation. You can also arrange woollen tufts to trace the flow;

– the air flow over (or outside) the foil is faster than that inside or under it, and the pressure is thus less. This 'speeded-up' air flow has added induced speed which can then modify the shape of the flow round a further obstacle, such as when a jib deflects the flow round a mainsail;

– resistance is built up to both forward motion and drag.

The starting vortex does not separate from the foil surface; it is held there by the self-cancelling action of the tip vortices.

How a vortex arises

Let us return to our flow around a foil. There is generally a vortex which corresponds to the lift created. We can see how this vortex is created by observing the flow over time around the foil in figures 1–6.

• In figure 1, there is no motion.

• In figure 2, the foil is set in motion at a uniform velocity through the fluid; any fluid particle meeting the obstacle can travel either over (outside) the foil or under (inside) it.

• In figure 3, the system moves from rest to continued action. Because the particles travelling along the underside have a shorter path to follow than those on the topside, they emerge at the trailing edge with different velocities.

• This in turn causes a deflection or curvature of the flow at the trailing edge (figure 4).

• The curvature continues (figure 5), setting up a real circulation of the flow.

• Finally, in figure 6, the circle is closed and a starting vortex is formed. As this vortex separates from the surface, it equalises the speed of flow of the fluid particles arriving from the underside and those from the topside. As this happens, there is a lengthening of the trailing tip vortices.

The diagrams show the formation of a starting vortex from rest (figure 1) to separation and continued action (figures 6–8).

We can demonstrate using Kelvin's law that the circulation will be equal and opposite to the circulation of the vortex round the foil.

This description applies to the period when the system is entering motion, ie when it is gaining speed from a start or changing speed. Each time the velocity of the system changes, a vortex will form, giving lift *p*. Whenever you set off from the beach or from a mooring, you will set up several starting vortices, both from the sails in the air, and in the water, from the hull.

Perhaps surprisingly, given the importance of the fluid's viscosity in this initial phase, viscosity may safely be ignored once the system is in continuing motion. We can then use the theory of ideal fluids, with vortices. The correspondence between theory and reality only breaks down in the region very close to the obstacle around which the flow is taking place, known as the *boundary layer*. Outside the boundary layer, the theory is an excellent representation of what actually happens.

The boundary layer and separation

Let us consider water flowing around a hull.

The pressure and speed of flow of the water are constant at a given distance from the hull. As we get close to the bow, the pressure increases as curvature is forced into the flow. Then, alongside the hull, a slight depression in the water may be observed as the curvature of the flow is inverted. The particles closest to the surface of the hull are simultaneously slowed by the friction with the surface, and sucked back against the current by the differences in pressure in the water. If this combined braking effect is sufficiently strong, the particles will stop flowing along the surface altogether and break away, rotating, creating turbulence and a wake.

At some point downstream, the wake will actually 'follow' (that is, flow upstream in the direction of) the moving body.

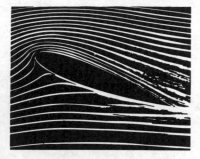

This permanent air flow is the same as one would expect to see in an ideal fluid with vortices, except at the very thin boundary layer which can be seen next to the surface of the foil.

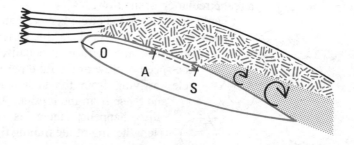

When a foil meets a flow of viscous liquid at a small angle of incidence, the current is initially accelerated in the boundary layer (between O and A) then slowed (from A to S), remaining laminar. After point S, the boundary layer can separate from the surface and create a wake.

All the above phenomena can be observed with the eye in the case of water, but the effects are there also in the case of air; with a light apparent wind, the flow can be curved very significantly. The angle through which the wind can be bent without separation grows smaller as the wind increases in strength. When particles are slowed down by too great an angle of curvature they are no longer capable of laminar flow alongside the surface; separation can be avoided then only by various techniques aimed at making the real flow as like the flow of an ideal fluid as possible.

Important note: the pressure and other phenomena observed in the separation zone are quite separate from those to be found in the rest of the fluid flow outside this zone. The rest of the fluid flow continues to behave very similarly to our theoretical ideal fluid.

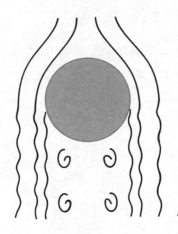

Separation and the wake

Separation and the wake are both consequences of the fact that the fluids with which we are dealing are viscous. The wake can actually be thought of as a sort of dead zone. The wake is visible on the surface of the water as the wash created by the boat. The behaviour of this flow is quite different from that around the sides of the hull: the eddies are much larger and they mix in with each other, dissipating energy as they do so. This energy is taken from the hull of the boat, and thus lost to you.

In the air, you cannot see this turbulence and eddying which you leave in your wake. It is nevertheless there, in the area downwind of you. Any racing sailor will be all too aware of the influence which this dead zone can have on one's competitors!

Friction

Every fluid particle is subject to a number of forces:

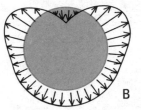

Due to the effects of separation and the wake, the pressure and speed of flow are different from those in an ideal fluid. If we look at a cylinder, as shown above, there is no symmetry along the axis of the stream, and a drag effect is created.

Figure A shows lines of flow; figure B shows the distribution of pressure.

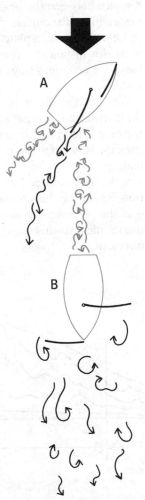

In theory, the wash from boat B's hull should give a push to boat A; and the strong laminar flow from A's sails should give more power to B. In practice, this situation is so transient that it is seldom of use.

– gravity;
– forces arising from pressure;
– forces arising from viscosity;
– forces of inertia arising from the acceleration caused by changes in the direction of flow.

In the case of the *ideal fluid*, the forces of viscosity are negligible compared to those of inertia. The opposite case is an extremely viscous fluid in which the *forces of inertia are negligible compared to those of viscosity*.

In order to move a hull through water, or any solid through a real fluid, there will be a certain resistance to be overcome. This resistance is due in part to the viscosity of the fluid, but also in part to the roughness of the surface of the object. We call the average distance between the peaks and troughs on this surface, divided by the length of the surface, 'relative roughness'.

Let us consider a plate in a flow at a zero angle of incidence over it (as, for instance, a centreboard). The coefficient of friction will vary, in a turbulent flow, according to the relative roughness of the surface.

The smaller the irregularities on the surface, the lower will be the friction coefficient and the less will be the friction. For this reason it is tempting to sand centreboards and rudder blades mirror-smooth. However, the problem is slightly more complicated than that:

– at the upstream end of the plate there will be a zone of laminar flow where the fluid remains parallel and does not mix;
– as the particles are slowed, there will be local disturbances and instabilities. At this stage the boundary layer thickens and becomes turbulent;

Over a thin plate in a fluid at zero angle of incidence, flowing at velocity Vo, the fluid will be slowed after a certain distance and will become turbulent.

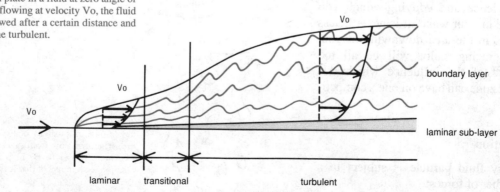

Vo

boundary layer

laminar sub-layer

laminar   transitional   turbulent

– once the turbulent boundary layer has formed, it tends to separate. (This often happens where the surface is curved, as in the case of sails, centreboards and hulls.) A certain amount of turbulence within the layer generated (primarily) by surface roughness can delay the separation or even avoid it altogether. There are therefore instances in which a rough surface, despite the greater friction it creates, has better characteristics than a smooth surface. The grooved underwater surface of *Stars and Stripes*, which was used in the 1987 America's Cup in Australia, was based on this principle.

Cavitation

Cavitation is a phenomenon similar to boiling, but without the heat. The bubbles and cavities created in the process are not stable or predictable, however. The bubbles can implode, causing fine but powerful water jets. This implosion can be harnessed, as in industrial cleaning equipment, but can also work destructively, actually wearing away the surface of a hull quite quickly. For this reason, hydrofoils and propeller blades are actually designed so that the implosion takes place away from their surface. This is called supercavitation.

The speeds reached particularly by sailboards and catamarans can be such that cavitation occurs on the centreboard or the end and downwind side of the fin (within the tip vortices).

Cavitation can cause not only wear but also vibration and resonance, and a loss of hydrodynamic power. The vacuum reduces the lift of the foil; this loss of lift is in turn accompanied by increased drag.

The answer is either to avoid cavitation altogether or to convert it into supercavitation.

Cavitation arises in the low-pressure zones which form downstream of any bump, or in the turbulence which streams off the tip of any foil or blade-like surface. We therefore try to keep the tips of any foils to a shape which will maintain horizontal flow across any underwater foil such as a rudder, limiting the circulation of vortices. Let us not forget that if we are suppressing vortices at the tip of the centreboard, the vortices will arise elsewhere instead, with an intensity proportional to the rate of circulation; their intensity will also increase as the centreboard supplies more lift.

The best course of action is to ensure that you keep as few underwater surfaces as possible which might cause cavitation. A more acute leading edge to your underwater surfaces will encourage supercavitation instead, which is far less harmful.

For the same speed, a boat will create cavitation more readily in warm and rough waters than in colder and calmer waters.

Curvature and pressure

Curvature and pressure gradients

As soon as any surface deflects flow, that flow will tend to exert pressure towards the outside of the curve. The pressure is thus less on the inside of the curve than on the outside; we say that the pressure gradient is towards the outside of the flow curve.

The curvature of the flow causes acceleration and thus a pressure gradient.

In the case of a sail, neither weight nor atmospheric pressure enters into the equation: there is a high-pressure area on the inside of the sail belly and a low-pressure area on the outside of the sail.

In the case of a hull on the surface of the water:
– there is high pressure by the bow;
– there is low pressure aft of the shrouds;
– there is high pressure by the stern.

This can be seen in the form of variations in the height of the water flowing along the hull, the bow and quarter waves.

The region of lowest pressure is where the curvature of the (well-trimmed) sail is greatest. A sail with a lot of belly (or camber) built in creates more effort than a flat sail ... at least up to a certain wind speed. Once the flow 'overshoots the bend' the air stops behaving like an ideal fluid. You need to flatten the sail to counter this effect.

In a constant flow, the pressure varies inversely with the speed along a given trajectory.

This law is a result of Bernoulli's theorem, which is widely known and almost as widely misapplied. It is valid only for stable flow along a given trajectory.

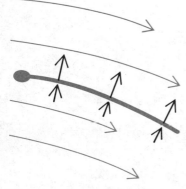

The pressure gradient in a curved flow goes from the outside of the curve to the inside. The curvature of the sail causes the sail to be 'sucked' to the outside and accelerates the flow on the outside (convex) face of the sail; the flow on the inside, or windward, face of the sail is slowed down and made denser.

Pressure and speed

In a horizontal air flow, the speed increases as the pressure decreases, and vice versa. The air flows fastest where the pressure is lowest, ie at the point of maximum curvature on the outside face of the sail. At this point, any small obstacle to the flow can create a pressure build-up which will destroy the speed of the flow.

In the water, you will notice that the self-bailer in the bottom of a dinghy is placed at the low-pressure point (ie the point of maximum curvature of the hull) to accelerate the emptying of the water out of the boat.

The relationship between effort and flow deflection

To create the maximum effort, a sail has to deflect the air flow on both its concave and its convex faces. In order to maximise the deflection, the sail must be trimmed so as not to allow flow separation, since the effect of the separation would be to reduce the effective deflection.

Euler's theorem

From Euler's model of steady ideal fluid flow, we can relate the entry velocity $\vec{V1}$ (that is speed in a given direction) of the fluid to its exit velocity $\vec{V2}$. For a flow Q of density P, the sum of external forces $\Sigma\vec{F}$ ext. acting on the flow boundary is given by:

$$\Sigma\vec{F}\text{ ext.} = PQ\,(\vec{V2} - \vec{V1})$$

The greater the difference in direction (ie the curvature of the flow) between $\vec{V2}$ and $\vec{V1}$, the greater will be the force exerted.

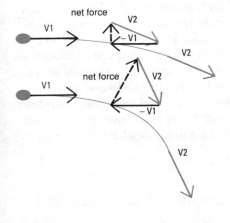

If the flow is only slightly deflected, the net force resultant is low. The greater the deflection, the greater the force resultant.

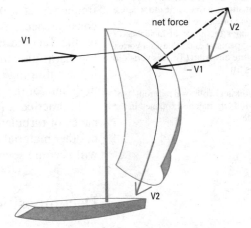

Regular users of a spinnaker will have discovered one application of these laws already: a spinnaker has to be flown high in order to lift. In effect, what this means is that air has to be allowed to escape towards the bottom, thus creating a net outward force which also points upward. If the only net outward force was dead ahead, the spinnaker would end up collapsing.

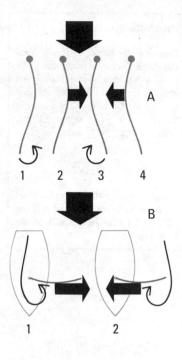

A. The thin turbulent boundary layer on the pennant allows a free vortex to separate off (1). This vortex creates lift (2), which in turn changes the angle of incidence of the flapping pennant and releases a vortex in the opposite direction (3). This vortex in turn creates lift.

B. The rhythmical roll, or death roll(!), of the downwind leg may be explained in the same manner.

Vortices and resultant forces

There will always be a thin turbulent boundary layer around any sail or foil, with a corresponding vortex which gives a greater lift component as the vortex flow is faster.

Any change in the shape (curvature or camber) of the foil or in its orientation to the flow will also change the vortex and the resultant force. Each time a change is introduced a starting vortex is released equal and opposite to the change on the foil surface. Unfortunately, these starting vortices cannot be seen in air, or we should be able to tell immediately the direction of any change we have caused or undergone.

When the boat rolls or pitches the angle of incidence inevitably changes; from this change arises a variation in the circulation. This leads to the phenomenon known as the rhythmical roll:

– as a vortex becomes free it causes a lateral force P which rocks the boat; the rocking creates a further vortex in the other direction, which, when it in turn detaches itself, will create a lateral force of –P, etc.

This is the same effect which makes a pennant flutter or your rudder blade vibrate on certain points of sailing. If the changing emission of vortices happens to coincide with the resonant frequency of a mast or cable, this can actually have disastrous consequences, as happened most famously in a storm force wind on the Tacoma Bridge in the USA in 1940. More common and less harmful manifestations of this can be observed all around us, in the galloping motion of electrical power cables overhead or the high hum of the rigging and mooring cables down at the harbour.

In practice it is not possible to predict the effects of this resonance of turbulent flows, as we do not know enough about metal or other material fatigue to be able to say at what point the effects will become severe.

Decomposition of forces of resistance in a hull

It is well known that a so-called aerodynamic shape creates less resistance to forward motion than a circular or square shape. The resistance comes from two sources:

– friction on the hull arising from the viscosity of the water, which is not an ideal fluid. The result of this friction is known as *frictional drag*;

– pressure arising from the shape of the hull and the water flow around it. This causes *pressure drag*. Since one of the boundaries between substances, that between the air and the water, is free, increased pressure results in a rise in the surface level of the water; in other words, the boat causes waves as it moves forwards. Those surfaces of the boat which are always entirely under water, such as the centreboard, create negligible pressure drag; however, the windward force, which the centreboard creates to stop downwind drift, does cause considerable drag. In fact, that drag is a necessary result of the lift created, and it is therefore called 'induced drag'.

It is customary to draw a distinction between the resistance arising from waves made by the boat's motion and that arising from the boat's underwater shape and any induced drag.

The total resistance to motion of the hull is the sum of all these forces, and their relative contribution varies according to the speed of the boat through the water:

– the wave resistance is small at low speeds, but can increase to 60% of the total as the boat nears the *hull's maximum displacement speed*;
– the induced drag can account for 10% of the total, when it is present;
– the friction drag increases as the boat travels faster, but its relative share of the total resistance actually decreases, declining to minimal importance at high speeds.

The total resistance to forward motion can reach 15–20% of the boat's weight at top speed, and drop as low as 1% in the lightest breeze.

Wave resistance

The 'flow' of still water around a moving hull is identical to the flow of moving water around a static hull. The flow is deflected such that there are variations in pressure. This can be observed in the variations in the water height, or waves: the water is highest at the bow and at the stern, and lowest about half way along. These variations in height are greater as the speed increases and the relative deflections of the flow are less.

When you throw a stone into a pond, concentric circular waves are formed on the water's surface.

In the case of a moving hull, this wave formation occurs in two systems:

– the 'divergent' system, which has little effect on the resistance of the boat to forward movement;
– the 'transverse' system, which determines the shape taken by the free surface of the water in the immediate vicinity of the hull.

What actually happens is that the bow wave combines with the waves created amidships and at the rear of the boat. Depending on

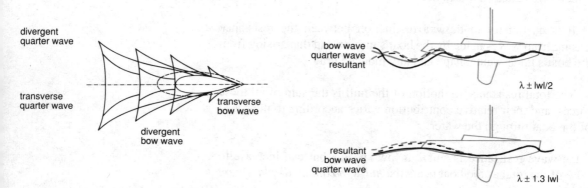

As the hull is in motion, the visible wave system created by the hull is much more complex than the circular ripples from a stone thrown in a pond.

As the boat travels faster, the length of the wave (viewed from the boat) increases to more than the length of the waterline (lwl).

the speed of the boat, these will then give a varying wave on the surface of the water, as shown in the diagram.

As the speed increases, so does the resistance. This is partly because the boat is creating bigger waves and partly because the waves combine less and less favourably. Once the length between the tops reaches the same value as the length of the waterline, we can talk of 'sailing on the bow wave'.

At this stage the wave resistance becomes very high, and a great deal more propulsive force becomes necessary for even the slightest increase in boat speed. At this stage the displacement hull is reaching its top speed.

Depending on the shape of the hull and the displacement weight, one can still overcome this theoretical top speed by further increasing the propulsive force. The approximate top speed is given by $V_e = 0.4 \times g \times lwl$. We shall return to this point.

When the boat starts to travel faster than the hull's maximum displacement speed, it begins to plane. The phenomenon of planing is analysed in the next chapter.

Induced resistance

Induced resistance depends above all:

– on the cross-section of the foil (eg the centreboard);
– on the angle of incidence of the flow. In practice, with any angle of incidence over 8°, drag is dramatically increased with no corresponding increase in the lift provided. There may under certain conditions even be a reduction in lift. The underwater shape may be deformed by the forces acting on it, particularly if these forces lead to some twist so that the angle of incidence itself changes along the foil surface. Because the angle of incidence is so critical, it

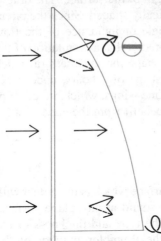

becomes vital that the foils are constructed of material which resists twist or torsion (quite separate from resistance to flexing).

Inevitably, we are dealing here with three-dimensional flow and not two-dimensional or planar flow. The tip vortices play a vital role in this.

In the diagram, you will see that these vortices arise on a limited

sail cut

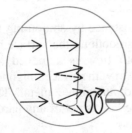

centreboard section

Tip vortices exist both in air and in water. These vortices explain the fluttering upwards or downwards of your woollen tell-tales. In the figure, the boat is close-hauled on port tack.

surface in any fluid flow. In positive (water or air) flow, there is a low-pressure area on the upper or outside surface which pulls the flow back in towards the surface; overpressure on the underside pushes the flow out.

The tip vortices take on a cone shape. They are due entirely to the fact that the surface is not limitless.

The tip vortices are linked to the starting vortices. As they are left behind in the flow, the circulation of the vortex on the surface is distorted.

The shape of the tip vortices at the bottom of a keel can be altered by building in a bullet-shaped bulb. This changes the circulation over the whole foil surface, but the vortices cannot be suppressed altogether except by stopping the circulation entirely, which would in turn destroy the lift created by the foil.

The induced resistance is also dependent on the aspect ratio of the surface. For a given value, the induced drag depends on how the circulation is distributed over the length of the surface. The drag is minimised if the distribution is elliptically shaped. Since the circulation depends so heavily on the angle of incidence of the flow against the surface, we can actually predict that a circulation of the desired shape will be obtained on a shape the thickness of which itself varies elliptically. In this, the shape of a boat's underwater foils is similar to that of many aeroplane wings, which are of elliptically varying thickness in order to benefit from the enhanced lift this gives.

Friction resistance

Some friction will be caused at any surface which is in contact with the water. A boundary layer will be found at any plane surface, whether of the hull or of the foils. The type and thickness of the boundary layer are determined by the Reynolds number of the surface.

The value of the friction resistance is proportional to the area of the surface in contact with the water. For a given area, the friction is proportional to the square of the speed of flow and to the drag coefficient (Cd).

We aim to reduce the Cd value, for instance by smoothing the surface (though beyond a certain point, smoothing the surface has no further effect). Hydraulically smooth flow is achieved, for instance, over the hull of a 10m boat at 10kn with surface roughness of 0.3mm, which is the same as that of unpainted metal. This example shows that a mirror finish on the hull is not of any particular use.

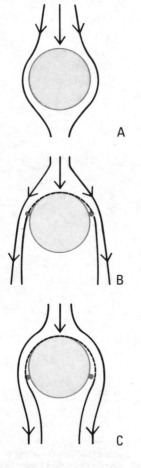

Techniques of drag reduction can avoid the separation of flow which occurs here in figure B.

In order to reduce the drag due to friction, we must reduce the surface roughness. However, it is often useful to have a certain amount of turbulence over the surface, since this can encourage the boundary layer to 'stick' better.

Impregnating the surface of the hull with special liquids which modify the behaviour of the boundary layer is neither legal in races nor particularly economical (though it has been shown to have spectacular results under laboratory conditions). This technique has been used on the walls of Paris's drainage system to improve flow rates under storm flood conditions. The search for that magical coating or for a perfectly adapted 'living' surface like that of a dolphin's skin has not yet borne fruit …

At very low speeds more efficient flow could be achieved by the use of capillary (surface tension) phenomena, but for the moment this too would require the use of impregnation with chemicals.

In theory, the most efficient sailing vessel would be one the hull of which was entirely beneath the surface, at a sufficient distance as to be unaffected by the waves, joined to its sails by a slender, rigid and aerodynamically shaped rig. In practice, the best we can do is to overcome the waves' resistance by escaping upwards and out of them, by getting the boat to plane.

CHAPTER 2

Interaction of forces

The interaction of air and water flows creates new forces of its own; the interplay between these two elements must be understood by the sailor if the boat is not to become a plaything! Since the playing field is three-dimensional, it is sometimes hard to grasp the laws of the game. For this reason, we begin this chapter with a simple description aimed at helping you to understand what is actually happening on a moving sailing boat, a sort of gazetteer of all the forces which play on a boat and their names.

We shall then look at where and how these forces are generated, both in the air and in the water.

There follows a set of practical applications concerning boat trim in general and sail trim in particular.

Summary of forces and their component parts

Wind and sails

When the wind encounters an obstacle, for instance a sail, it is deflected from its original course. Just as every action has an equal and opposite reaction, the sail is operating on the wind to deflect it, and the wind is exercising an equal and opposite force on the sail. We are most interested in this last force – the propulsive force of the wind – and we shall start by seeing how it is created.

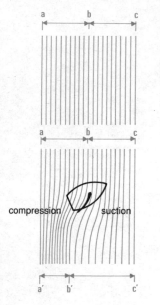

Compression + suction
= aerodynamic force.

Creation of force

Let us take a totally empty stretch of sea with a constant and regular wind. The air flow can be represented by straight parallel lines. If the scene is then divided down the middle, it is clear that there is the same amount of air flowing between points a and b as there is between b and c.

Enter a boat. The sail causes a deviation in the flow of air, and we can make the following observations:
– the air flow is deflected only in the immediate vicinity of the sail. Any air stream a certain distance away remains straight, as c->c', or regains its original course quickly, as a->a';
– the air which hits the sail on its windward side is forced to change direction. The air flow between a and b is compressed against the sail. *The air on the windward side of the sail is compressed as it is deflected;*
– if the air downwind of the sail continued to flow straight, there would be a vacuum behind the sail. In order to fill the vacuum the air flows along following the vacuum: it is thus being pulled in by the vacuum and pulled out by centrifugal force. The air flow itself is pulling the sail outwards. There is a low-pressure region behind the sail because of the bend which has been forced into the flow. *The downwind side of the sail is thus subject to suction.* There is pressure acting to windward, and suction to leeward of the sail. The combination of these two forces constitutes the total *aerodynamic force on the sail.*

Direction of force

The force exercised by fluid flow on a plane surface is perpendicular to the plane, whatever the angle of incidence. We can go further and state that the force applied at any point is perpendicular to the surface at that point. In practice, this means that the resultant total force created by the forces of compression and suction on a sail is perpendicular to the chord of the sail.

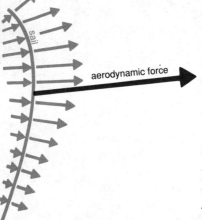

The distribution of pressure over the surface of a sail remains the same through all points of sailing.

Strength of force

If we remain for the moment in the area of general physical laws, we can say that the aerodynamic force is more or less:
– proportional to the area of the sail: if you halve the size of the sail, you will halve the force created;
– proportional to the square of the wind speed: if the wind speed doubles, the force quadruples.

Returning to our earlier principle of action and reaction, one might think that the force also becomes greater the more the wind is deflected. In fact you will quickly have noticed that this is not the case.

As you trim a sail gradually to catch the wind, the force created increases very noticeably to begin with, but then decreases rapidly past a given angle and then remains at a constant low level for any further increases in the angle of incidence.

Water and keel

A keelboat's keel and the centreboard of a dinghy both have the same function: that of stopping the boat drifting to leeward. In this section we shall use the word keel to refer to any fin under a sailing vessel which has this function.

In effect a keel functions in water just as a wing does in air. The interaction between surface and flow is the same whether we are dealing with a surface moving through a fluid or a fluid passing over a surface.

As a boat moves forward, its keel cuts through the water at an angle, which we can call the 'angle of attack'. A force is created almost perpendicular to this angle, known as *hydrodynamic force*. It is a sort of partner to the aerodynamic force we encountered above.

Just as the shape of the air stream over the sails was related to the angle of incidence between wind and sail, the flow of water over the keel is influenced by the angle of attack, which is the difference between the direction in which the boat is heading and the course it is actually making good through the water. When this angle is small, the flow is regular and smooth. There is, however, a critical angle above which flow separation takes place. The keel causes large amounts of turbulence and the boat starts suddenly to sideslip, as the flow becomes irregular.

Hydrodynamic force is produced in different ways depending on whether the flow is smooth or turbulent. In smooth-flow conditions, force is produced by the action of the stream flowing along the keel surface. Once that flow becomes turbulent and eddying, the lift can be produced only as a reaction to the force caused by the boat's downwind drift.

The strength of the hydrodynamic force is more or less:
– proportional to the surface area of the keel;
– proportional to the square of the speed of the boat (in smooth flow);
– proportional to the speed of drift (in turbulent flow).

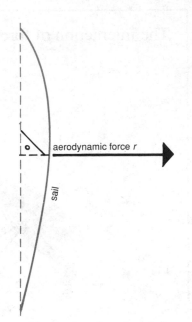

The direction of aerodynamic force.

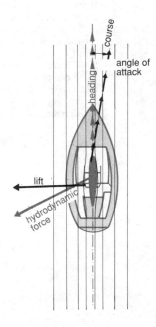

The interaction of forces as the boat gets under way

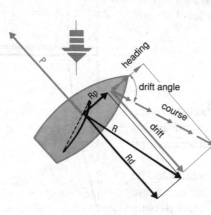

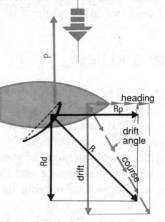

1. *Flow separation over the keel.*
If the sails are sheeted in too tight while the boat is on a close-hauled heading, the drift component becomes very large and causes an equally large lift component P. This lift component is obtained only by a considerable speed of drift. The forward thrust component Rp is small so the boat picks up little forward speed; as a result, the drift angle is large and has no prospect of being reduced.

2. *Flow separation over the keel.*
As you start off, you pull the sails in only once the boat is heading some way off the wind; this way the aerodynamic force is directed well ahead and the drift component is kept as low as possible. Little lift is required, but for the moment even this lift will come from a fairly noticeable sideways drift, since the flow over the keel is still turbulent.

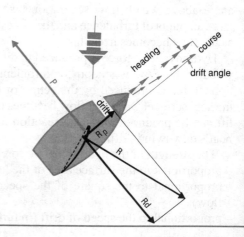

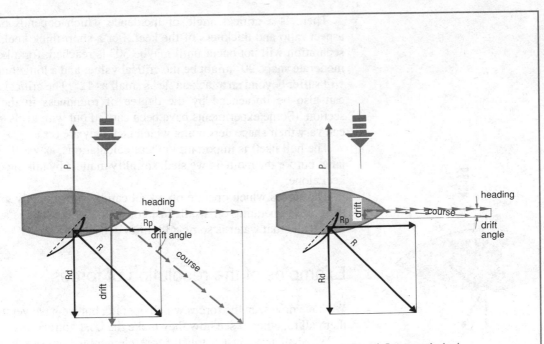

3. Flow separation over the keel.
The boat is now picking up speed. The drift component and the lift are still as they were; the boat is still moving sideways at the same speed, but since it is now also moving forward with increasing speed, the drift angle begins to reduce.

4. Smooth flow over the keel.
As the speed increases still further, the drift angle becomes smaller still and the keel suddenly 'bites' as the flow becomes smooth. From this moment, there is considerable lift generated but with a negligible drift angle.

5. Smooth flow over the keel.
You may now luff up. With smooth flow, the lift P can balance out even a very strong drift component Rd, still giving a small drift angle. You will notice that the force vectors appear the same as in figure 1, yet the result is entirely different, due exclusively to the fact that you now have smooth flow over the keel.

There is a critical angle of incidence which depends on the aspect ratio and thickness of the keel. For a short thick keel, flow separation will not occur until maybe 30° is reached; for a keel of moderate shape 20° might be the critical value; and a long thin keel will suffer beyond an attack angle as small as 12°. The critical angle can also be influenced by the degree of roundness in the keel section. (Some experiments have been carried out with keels which can vary their shape depending which tack they are on.)

The hull itself is important in these calculations, as we shall see later, but for the moment we shall simplify matters by talking of the keel alone.

The forces which operate on a keel can be considerably greater than those operating on a sail. Just consider that the keel is a rigid shape, and that water is some 838 times denser than air!

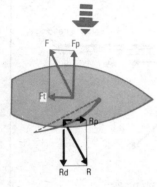

R : aerodynamic force.
Rp : forward component.
Rd : drift component.
F : hydrodynamic force.
Fp : lift.
Ft : drag.

See illustrations on two previous pages.

Examples of the resolution of forces

We have now seen the forces which operate, but we have yet to join them all together to see how they make the boat go forward.

We shall need just a touch more elementary physics here. In order to work out how best to use the forces our boat is generating, we need to resolve them into a parallelogram showing those forces which operate fore-and-aft, and those which operate sideways. Thus we can break down the aerodynamic force into a *forward component* and a *drift component*; and the hydrodynamic force into *lift* and *drag*.

It is sufficient initially to know that *the lift is always equal and opposite to the drift and the forward component equal and opposite to the drag*.

The interaction of forces as the boat gets under way

Let us take the example of a moored boat. As it slips its mooring, it begins by drifting slowly backwards, then bears away, still drifting downwind. The angle of attack of the keel on the water is about 90°, and the flow is so turbulent you can see the eddies to windward of you in the water.

If the sails were sheeted in as soon as the boat reached close-hauled, the aerodynamic force would be mostly in a straight down-wind direction, with a considerable drift component and very little forward thrust. The only way the lift component of the keel can be equal to the drift is by the boat sideslipping fast. The boat would end up back at the jetty or aground.

But if the crew sheets in only once the boat has come onto a beam reach course, the aerodynamic force which the sails create will be pointed much more ahead, with a strong forward component and relatively little drift component. There is more force in general, because the sails can be perfectly sheeted to the angle of the wind.

The boat, while still drifting downwind, gets on some forward way. This lessens the angle of attack, until the angle actually goes below the critical angle for the keel, and the flow becomes suddenly smooth. From this moment on, the lift is provided by the fluid stream over the foil surface; the boat will heel a little and leap forwards. It becomes easy to steer and stops drifting. At this stage you can begin to luff up quite happily.

Generation of forces

The complexity of real flows

Even the simplest swell will cause some circular flows.

It is comparatively easy to grasp the idea of two-dimensional flow. In reality, however, afloat, even without breaking waves, there is a swell to complicate the speed and direction of both horizontal and vertical flows over all the boat's underwater surfaces.

Air flows next to the boat's superstructure, behind the mast or the boom or next to any one of the sail's corners, will never be horizontal nor even straight.

The three-dimensional nature of the real flows has an effect on the upward component of any forces created, and complicates any numerical or theoretical model we might make. In any case it renders our understanding of phenomena less immediate.

Before the invention of the sailboard, vertical aerodynamic forces (Z) used to be largely ignored, and the assumption was of a

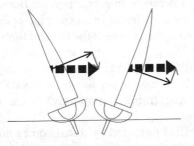

When the boat rolls, the relative wind exercises a fluctuating 'vertical' force component parallel to the mast.

Air turbulence can occur also on a horizontal axis.

Migratory birds flying in a V-formation are using the upward air flows generated by the bird ahead.

well-trimmed sail somewhere close to vertical, with an air flow more or less horizontal over the water. In fact, vertical air flows close to a cliff, for instance, or thermal currents, can be strong enough to knock an airliner out of the sky.

The vertical air flows are associated with air turbulence about a horizontal axis. The air eddies can be tens of metres across, or even a few hundred metres across. They are invisible, unless one uses tracer smoke. They occur more frequently close to the fronts you see on a weather chart, and they can be just as large and powerful as any vertical-axis turbulence.

Partly because it is less familiar, and partly because it is often a temporary phenomenon due to the boat's rolling or pitching, or due to tip vortices, the vertical component of the force on the sails is often ignored. For the most part, we can do the same.

There are, however, some areas in which these effects are important for the sailor. In particular, we are interested in the way in which the air flow off a head sail can alter the flow onto a following sail. This is the phenomenon used by wild geese when they fly in the lift generated by the lead goose's wing tips.

The compressibility of air and the generation of aerodynamic force

You have all seen that air can be compressed ...

Everyone knows that air can be compressed, unlike water. However, even in a storm force wind, this fact is of *virtually no importance* in driving a sailing vessel forward.

The fact that the air is not subject to compression does not mean that there is no variation in pressure in a constant air flow. In the same way, the water pressure is different in a hose pipe at different points, as it flows uphill and down, through the tap and through the nozzle.

The pressure alters at different points over a sail or any other obstacle in an air flow. It is higher on the (windward) inside, concave part of the sail and (more importantly) lower on the outside.

... but this phenomenon is of little practical relevance for the sails of your vessels. When Paul Maka set a former world sailing speed record of 38.86kn in 1986, at no point over the rig did the pressure build-up exceed the ambient atmospheric pressure by more than 0.7%.

The major part of the effort provided by a sail comes not from the pressure build-up on the inside of the curve, but from the depression on the back of the sail ... just as an aeroplane does not rest on a cushion of air but derives its lift from creating an air stream which sucks it upward.

Since the force is created by the low-pressure zone, we are most interested in the area of lowest pressure. An important role is played by the sail's curvature, the fore-and-aft position of the 'belly', or any obstacles to smooth flow. The variation in pressure is not great in air. In a 20kn wind it amounts only to a few hundred grammes per square metre. Spread over a few dozen square metres, however, this can amount to the equivalent of several men's weight.

The tent and the roof of the 2CV are sucked out by the low-pressure zone created by the curvature in the air flow.

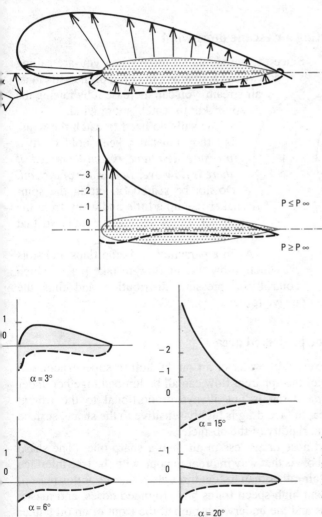

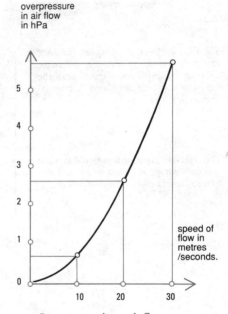

overpressure in air flow in hPa

speed of flow in metres /seconds.

Overpressure in an air flow
The maximum over-/underpressure in an air flow is weak compared to an average atmospheric pressure of 1,000 hectopascals (hPa).

The underpressure on the outside (pressure P lower than ambient pressure P∞) creates more force than the overpressure on the inside (P greater than ambient pressure P∞) for any angle of attack less than 15°. The shaded area corresponds to the total effort produced.

Compare this with the effects of pressure variation in water flow, which are altogether more dramatic, as water is so much denser than air. Areas exist under the hull of the boat where the pressure is only half the ambient pressure. This creates a force on the hull equivalent to 5 tonnes per square metre.

Increasing the propulsive forces

Increasing the propulsive forces operating on the sails is not only achieved by changing the size of the sail area or the speed of the air flow.

Letting air escape downwind

The air needs to escape from the spinnaker so as to create a pressure difference between the inside and the outside of the sail. Unfortunately, this flow cannot be seen as one is sailing.

The sails should not be kept reined in when you are sailing downwind; you should aim to free them of each other's influence.

Since the aerodynamic force when you are sailing downwind is in effect the drag of the sails in an air stream, you can increase it by raising the spinnaker to 'catch' more wind.

The sails do need to catch the wind, but they must not keep hold of it: *a pressure gradient is only created if there is flow over both sides of the sail.* Do not be scared of letting the spinnaker rise up a little and away from the mainsail, or of setting the sails so that some air can 'escape'.

As in a parachute, it is the flaps and slots which allow the air flow to take place, which control the pressure distribution and thus the propulsive force.

Drag and the projected area

The forces exerted by water or air on the hull or superstructure in the direction of the apparent flow can all be lumped together under the term *drag*. Drag is not always proportional to the frontal projected area; in fact, drag is highly sensitive to the shape, surface roughness and rigidity of the obstacle.

A rounded nose drags less in air than a sharp one. (The sharp shape of the bow is that way in order to cope with the free interface of water and air rather than to 'cut through' either.) For this reason, submarines and high-speed trains have rounded noses, and masts, cycle helmets and the underwater bulb at the front of an oil tanker are all designed with this principle in mind.

The geometry of flow is dictated by local phenomena, such that maximum drag is not always caused by the biggest projected area. It is for this reason that three small sails are preferable to one large one on downwind legs, since they allow for controlled interaction between the flows.

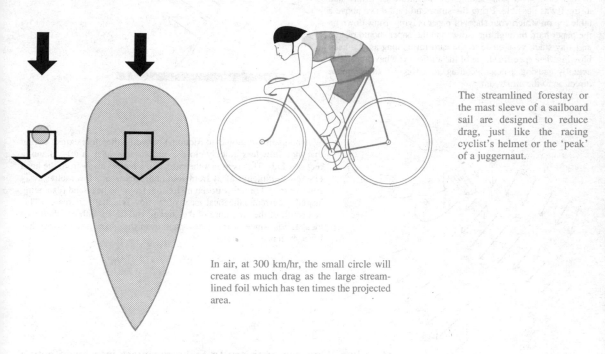

The streamlined forestay or the mast sleeve of a sailboard sail are designed to reduce drag, just like the racing cyclist's helmet or the 'peak' of a juggernaut.

In air, at 300 km/hr, the small circle will create as much drag as the large streamlined foil which has ten times the projected area.

The influence of the standing rigging

Sails are held upright by a set of equipment which contributes nothing to the forward effort and just adds drag: mast, halyards and stays. Whereas the shrouds are at some distance from the 'business area' of the sails and only ever contribute drag, the forestay and mast are positioned much more critically, at the leading edge of their respective foils.

Wind-tunnel experiments have shown that a circular-section mast has a slowing effect on the performance of a mainsail. It should be clear that we aim to find the most slender mast possible, consistent with the stiffness and other attributes required. A shaped mast goes some way to improving the situation, so long as that shape can then be swivelled to present its most favourable aspect as part of the overall foil it makes with the sail on all points

A simple experiment to show that it is possible to pick up a piece of paper by blowing down on it!

Unexpected things can happen when fluid flows across an obstacle ...

Cut out a circular piece of card about thirteen centimetres across and push a drinking straw though a hole in the middle of the card. The hole should fit the straw as firmly and airtightly as possible. Bring the straw and card down above a table top on which your sheet of paper is lying. Blow down on the paper hard through the straw, and the paper should rise up and stay stuck very close to the card for as long as you keep blowing. The specific shape of the air flow you have created is actually causing a negative drag, ie a force in the opposite direction to the air stream.

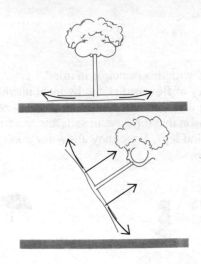

Water and air are subject to friction. You would therefore expect to find that they flow less quickly close to an obstacle such as a headland, a reef or a hull. This is in fact the case, a few metres away from the head or a few centimetres away from your hull. However, a few metres away from your hull or a few dozen metres out from the headland (excepting any eddy currents) the local speed of the flow is actually increased. This is a result of the curvature of the stream, and fits in with our theory of ideal fluids, since at these distances from the obstacles viscosity has little influence.

of sailing. One can even try to make the mast into an effective contributor to the forward propulsive force, eg with a wing mast, which is the current state of the art for very high performance boats.

Increasing the surface area in a flow is less important than achieving an efficient shape for that surface.

Optimal direction of aerodynamic force

When the wind gets stronger on a beam reach, your boat heels. You will have been told that a boat sails fastest when it is kept upright. This is true, though you have to go one step further if you want to plane the boat. You actually need to heel the boat to windward a little to step up onto the plane. By doing this, you will have created

a vertical component which lifts the boat up and reduces the hydro-dynamic drag. Under these conditions, the speed of the vessel which maintains equilibrium among the various forces acting on it is much higher.

This is one of the reasons that sailboarders will often start off in a high wind by lying back in the water and letting the sail pull them up. This water start technique is the only one possible for very short boards, known as sinkers.

Trimming the sails

Polar diagrams for sails

Pressure differences arise from the changing speed or direction of the wind and the boat. The forces arising from these differences can be broken down into vectors of forward thrust and drag.

When a sail is hanging free, it flaps, in line with the wind, producing an alternating and regular stream of starting vortices. There is no sum lift, and the only resultant force is drag. If, on the other hand, the sail is trimmed, it fills and the *aerodynamic force* can then be resolved into *drag* (T) and *lift* (P), or a drift component Rd and a propulsive component Rp, if you prefer.

We can look at the polar diagram of a sail in a constant wind.

Values are given below for the results obtained in a wind tunnel using models giving lift P and drag T at different angles of inci-dence to the wind.

In practice, one further value must be added to these. That is the vertical force Z, which operates upwards.

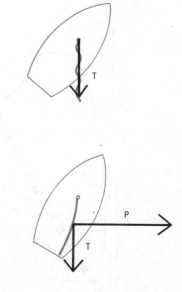

A flapping sail creates only drag; a trimmed sail generates drag T and lift P.

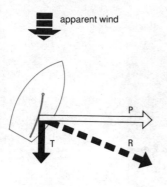

The lift P and drag T are the aerodynamic components from the apparent wind, resolved into a force in the direction of the wind, and a perpendicular force to that.

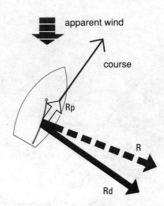

The components can equally well be resolved into one propulsive force Rp in the direction of the boat's travel, and one drift component at right angles to that, Rd.

In order to obtain the propulsive force Rp, you need to plot on the diagram the angle between the course made good and the apparent wind.

You will note that the resultant force R is more or less at right angles to the average chord of the sail, or to the boom, just as our ideal fluid theory predicts. Depending on the position of the maximum fullness in the sail and the consequent low-pressure area, it might move slightly forward or aft and deviate slightly from the perpendicular.

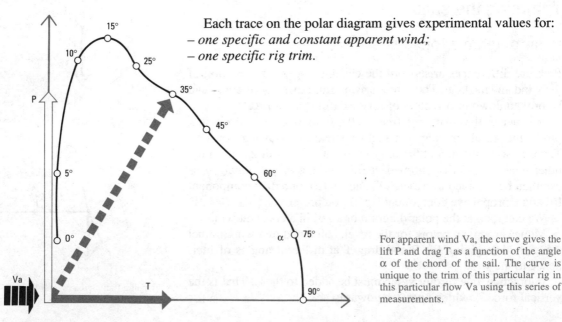

Each trace on the polar diagram gives experimental values for:
– *one specific and constant apparent wind;*
– *one specific rig trim.*

For apparent wind Va, the curve gives the lift P and drag T as a function of the angle α of the chord of the sail. The curve is unique to the trim of this particular rig in this particular flow Va using this series of measurements.

The polar diagram does not remain the same relative shape for different wind strengths; in other words, when the wind doubles in strength, the drag and lift for a given trim are not exactly quadrupled.

The main factor which changes the shape of the polar diagram is the shape of the sail, and notably the shape and position of the maximum draft of the sail, as well as the aspect ratio:
– a 14% fullness in the sail will produce more power than 5% fullness. However, in stronger winds, the fuller sail will suffer more from flow separation;
– a high aspect-ratio sail will give its best power at around 15° to the apparent wind, whereas our gaff-rig sail with a ratio of only 1.5 is most powerful at around 40°.

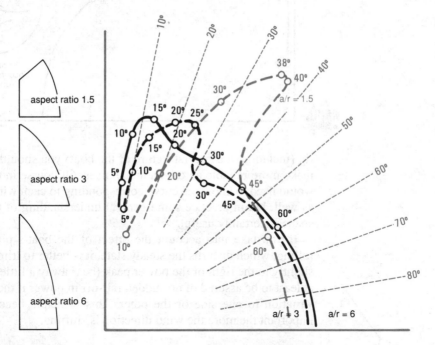

These curves, worked out in laboratory conditions, can help us to understand what is going on, but they are of little immediate practical use, when the boat is subject to *varying winds*, sailed at *varying angles* of heel and with *different parts of the hull* in the water.

The force components which can be read off on the polar diagram are correct for *steady state*. They assume no change over a period of several seconds. Knowing the shape of this graph for your

Examples of polar diagrams for different sail shapes.

The sail is trimmed for the wind between points a and b. At this stage, assuming no pitching or rolling, the ratio of lift to drag is at its highest; from point b onwards, some separation of flow occurs; there is turbulent flow downwind of the sail from point c on.

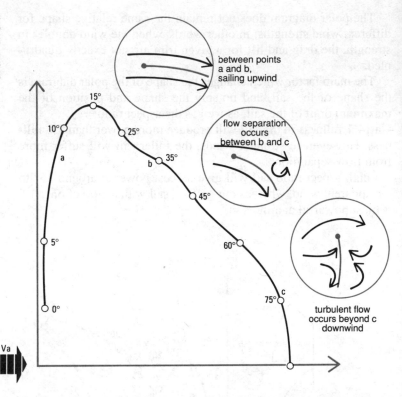

rig (including the superstructure of the boat) you should be able to make more reliable aerodynamic choices. Of course in theory you would need to know the curve corresponding to each wind strength as well, but in practice some general understanding of the overall shape is certainly useful.

If you take into account the effect of the boat's pitching and rolling, which disturbs the steady state, it is better to trim for a spot slightly to the right of the power peak (bear away a little), and thus at least to be assured of no sudden fall-off in power if there is some variation to one side or the other. This principle becomes more important the more the wind direction is shifting.

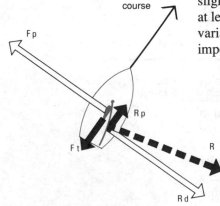

We can break the *aerodynamic* force down into propulsive force Rp and drift Rd; the boat's *hydrodynamic* system must then create the lift Fp and drag Ft.

The most effective strategy is not always that of maximising Rp. Close to the wind, the drift component Rd is so high that it may be better to seek to reduce that instead.

Sail adjustment

The sails are the propellant of your boat. Their shape influences the strength and the direction of the propulsive force produced.

We can adjust:
– the camber of the sail at different heights, ie the length of the chord and the position and depth of maximum fullness;
– the angle of incidence between the sail and the apparent wind at different heights.

It is extremely difficult to adjust only one of these variables at any given time. We shall look later at some techniques for achieving this, but for the moment it is enough to note that the cut and material of some sails gives us more room for manoeuvre than others.

Adjusting the fullness

Our polar diagrams show that a fuller sail is a more powerful sail. This is true so long as there is no separation. On the outside of the sail, there is a boundary layer of slowed-down air, due both to friction with the cloth and to the pressure difference along the curve. This slowing becomes relatively more exaggerated the higher the apparent wind speed and the fuller the sail. Once the wind goes above a certain critical speed for its angle of incidence and the fullness of the sail, the air particles are slowed so much that separation takes place and some of them actually start to move against the direction of flow. Correctly placed woollen tell-tales can alert the sailor when this is happening.

The sail adjustment for a close-hauled leg must be such as to avoid separation. One way of doing this is to flatten the sail. There is thus less pressure gradient and the particles along the outside of the sail are slowed less; the flow thus remains laminar. Another solution is to reduce the angle between sail and wind, but this will also have the effect of changing the direction of the forward force.

Downwind, the propulsive force of the rig is actually due to drag. You therefore need to keep this as high as possible. You should encourage turbulence on the back of the sail, and a very full sail is an effective aid in this.

Adjusting the angle of incidence

As the air flows over the surface of the sea or the land it creates a boundary layer, just as it does when flowing over any obstacle. This boundary layer can be of any thickness from a few metres to tens of metres. The true wind is therefore seldom the same at the bottom of the mast as it is higher up, and the apparent wind therefore varies vertically in strength and direction.

If your aim is to achieve the same angle of incidence all the way up the sail, you need to introduce twist into the sail, so that the chord of the sail at different heights is at different angles to the centreline of the boat. As the apparent wind is slightly freer higher up the mast, you need the angle to be greater higher up the sail.

Theoretically, even if the apparent wind was the same all the way up the sail, it would still be in your interest to allow twist, to vary the angle of incidence as a function of height and the shape of the sail: to minimise drag, you will recall, the ideal is to have an elliptically circulating vortex on the upper or outside foil surface, and this is assisted by the twist. In practice, it is difficult to work out what the optimum degree of twist should be, so you have to proceed to some extent by trial and error.

Bear in mind that twist is not an absolute necessity forced on us by the variation in speed of the wind at different heights; and that what is right for one sail in one set of conditions is not necessarily applicable to all sails or all conditions.

The position of the sum resultant of all the local pressure areas on the sail depends on how the pressure is distributed over the sail. The optimal sail adjustment does not always mean maximising the value of the resultant force. In particular, you might actually choose to take some of the power out of the sails by increasing further the angle of incidence at the top of the sail to the wind. This has the dual benefit of bringing the centre of effort of the rig lower down and thus reducing the heeling moment, and angling the effort slightly more forward. This is called opening the sail or opening the leech.

The interaction of the sails

Many boats have a total rig consisting of more than one sail. We therefore have to think of the effect on the other sails when we adjust each individual sail.

Let us take the simple case of a jib and mainsail:
– the jib blows wind into the back of the mainsail through the slot, thus ensuring that any separation happens later or not at all. This

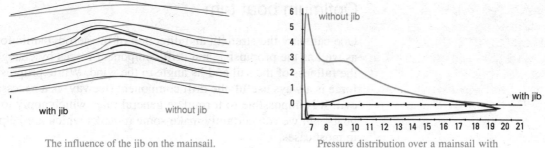

The influence of the jib on the mainsail.

Pressure distribution over a mainsail with and without a jib. The presence of the jib considerably weakens the underpressure on the back of the mainsail.

allows higher angles of incidence than for a single sail, and is an *advantage of having a jib*.
– the jib disturbs the air flow and deflects the stream, thus pushing the forward component of the mainsail's effort aft. This, therefore, is a *disadvantage of having a jib*.
– the presence of the mainsail aft of the jib accelerates further the flow of the air stream over the back of the jib, thus reducing the likelihood of flow separation. This is an *advantage of having a mainsail behind the jib*.

There is no universally correct optimum solution to these problems, which are a matter for boat designers.

In classical sailing-boat design, the division into jib and mainsail was primarily for reasons of manoeuvrability. There are two major options:
– one can treat the mainsail as the priority, with the jib being used much as one would use an engine cowl or leading-edge slot on an aeroplane, to accelerate the flow over the outside edge. The jib's own power is then less important. This is generally the case in multihulls and fractional-rig monohulls with a smaller jib;
– one can prioritise the jib. The function of the mainsail then becomes one of improving the flow over the outside of the jib, much as a trailing-edge flap is used on an aeroplane wing. The mainsail itself loses power in this model due to the deflection of the air stream, and the increased size and efficiency of the jib has to compensate for this. This is the way masthead rigs are designed.

For a given surface area of sail, the single-sail rig (for instance of a C-class catamaran) is actually more powerful. With this type of rig, attention is usually paid to alternative methods of ventilating the outside sail surface, such as slotted or foil-shaped standing rigging.

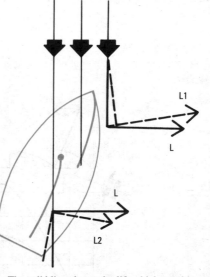

The solid line shows the lift which would be generated by each sail if it were separate. The dotted line shows the lift of the two sails combined. Putting the two sails together in this way backs the jib and frees the mainsail. This is why the jib luffs and flaps earlier than the mainsail does.

Optimum boat trim

One can vary the strength and direction of the aerodynamic force as well as the propulsive and drift component forces by changing the fullness of the sail and its angle to the wind. While propulsive force is always useful, the drift component (leeway) is a necessary evil. It is impossible to formulate general rules which apply to all boats, but we can certainly make some remarks which are helpful in most cases.

Maximum speed and direction of force

The drift component is never entirely absent on the reach, but its influence is negligible until one reaches a close-hauled course. If we superimpose different polar diagrams on a graph we can see that the power generated varies only slightly with different angles of the sail to the wind, whereas the amount of drift generated increases dramatically as the angle increases. As this generally also means that the boat heels over at the same time and presents a less efficient underwater shape, thus causing increased drag, it is best not to trim the sails exclusively for maximum power.

Off the wind, any attempt to limit the propulsive force will end in problems of stability, both directional stability and side-to-side stability.

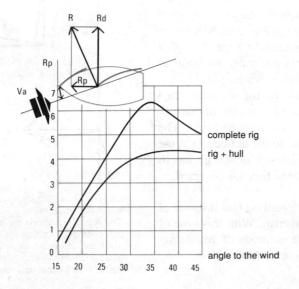

The polar diagrams shown were derived in a laboratory with constant wind and constant sail trim.

As the angle between the sail and the apparent wind increases, the propulsive force Rp increases quickly to its peak.

As the power declines from its peak, the drift component continues to rise. The lower curve in the figure, showing the rig with the hull, is flatter, showing that after a certain point increasing the angle between the sail and the wind becomes less efficient. It is far better to seek to reduce the angle of attack through the water by cutting the drift.

In extreme conditions, the limiting factor to the power developed by the boat and its rig can be the point of mechanical failure of the components.

Polar diagrams

These few remarks on optimising the boat trim will have given some idea of the complex interactions between the variables involved; this shows how impossible it is to make choices between trim settings automatic, and shows how vital the crew's role is in making these choices.

In order to make the right choice, you need to know how fast your boat is on different points of sailing in different conditions. The variables are, in decreasing order of importance:
1. The true wind speed and your course relative to the true wind.
2. Boat and sail trim (including sail choice).
3. The state of the sea.

The first set of variables can be adequately defined and quantified, so long as there are no complications of current. The second set of variables is less easy to deal with, since the shape and trim of the sails is constantly changing. The third set can only be dealt with very approximately, as there is an infinite number of combinations of wave height, direction and length.

It is possible to plot graphically the most important variables, ignoring current and waves. For a true wind of a given strength and direction, you can read off the speed of the boat sailing at a given angle to the true wind; you can then plot the optimum sail trim such that this approaches the theoretical boat speed at all given angles.

It is important to note that the angle to the true wind does not correspond to the course actually made good, since it does not allow for any drift. By plotting the speed through 360°, we can obtain a *speed curve* or *polar diagram* which shows what a boat is capable of under ideal conditions.

This curve is of course symmetrical about the axis of the real wind. Needless to say, there are as many curves to be drawn as there are wind strengths, but it is customary to draw them at 5kn intervals.

It is theoretically possible to derive these values by calculation if you know all the wind speed and direction values. In practice, however, one will never know exactly all the values of the forces

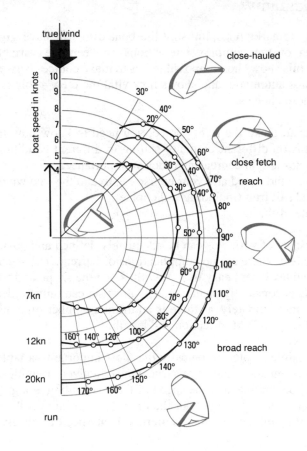

Performance curve of a 12 m JI. The three speed curves correspond to real wind strengths of 7, 12 and 20kn. For any angle to the real wind, one can read off the angle to the apparent wind and the boat speed in knots.

applied; after numerous wind-tunnel experiments, empirical observation has given us the ability to plot 'theoretical' polars. These will never be anything more than an approximation, but they do allow us to make meaningful comparisons between different course decisions and different types of boats.

We shall next move on to look at the practical uses of these speed curves, and at polar diagrams for fin sections.

Practical uses of polar diagrams

Let us now suppose that we have a polar diagram for all values of
the true wind.

On board, we can measure:
– the strength and direction of the apparent wind;
– the speed of the boat through the water and the heading measured
against the land.

From these known values, we can only work out the strength of
the true wind and the boat speed over the ground if we know the
speed of the current and our angle of drift. We should theoretically
be able to work these out by using earth-related navigational
systems (taking land fixes, Loran or satellite systems).

Assuming you have got access to this information, the polar
diagram to use is that which gives you the apparent wind related to
the current.

You can then check your measured values against your theoretical position on the curve: you will generally find that your
measurements are very close to those predicted by the curve, but
you should not draw over-quick conclusions from this. In practice,
the state of the sea also plays an important role, and a sail or boat
trim which is fine in one set of conditions may be suboptimal in
others. This is particularly the case in multihulls, which are very
sensitive to the direction of the swell.

It is interesting to collect data of this kind on your own boat, but
to exploit it practically, you need to process the data quickly. Some
racing yachts are now experimenting with the technology necessary
to do this.

*The general shape of the speed curve should, in most circum-
stances, be sufficient to inform your choice of the optimum course
and trim.*

If we take the example of a course from A to B with a constant
wind blowing from B to A, we need to beat into the wind to see
which tack is the optimum closehauled angle. Our speed curve
shows us that the most effective angle to the real wind is about 45°;
this angle gives us the highest VMG (velocity made good). You can
quickly work out a similar result for the downwind leg.

This elementary example shows the potential of the speed curve
as a tool, even if you do not know the precise values for your own
craft. Whatever else you do when deciding your optimal course,
keep the polar diagram in the back of your head.

Polar diagrams and fin sections

Unlike the rigging, which is always the same shape in the air, the underwater shape of the boat is constantly changing. The problem is thus rather more complex. The proximity of the surface of the water adds a series of further complications, such as wave formation and air bubbles. For this reason it is not generally productive to try and draw a polar for the whole hull.

It is, however, possible to draw a polar diagram for the side-on underwater shape and for the section of the underwater fins.

The simplest keel one might make would be a thin sheet. These, however, have a very poor hydrodynamic performance. The National

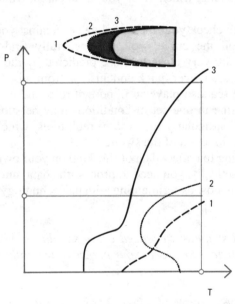

For these three fin sections, the relationship between lift P and drag T varies noticeably as a function of their shape, with constant angle of incidence and speed. It is particularly noticeable that the rounded nose creates much more lift than the other two.

Advisory Committee for Aeronautics (NACA) has carried out a series of tests which aim to establish the most lift-producing shapes. For a fin which has to work equally well on both tacks, the ideal section is symmetrical, and can be defined by the relationship betwen thickness and length and the position of the maximum thickness.

Comparing the polars of a flat sheet and a shaped foil demonstrates the superiority of the foil: for the same angles of incidence, the fin produces more lift, and the lift is directed further forward. These fin shapes, known as NACA sections, are important, though they are not the only solution to the lift-versus-drag problem. For reasons of ease of manufacture, one has generally to be content with a flat sheet with a rounded leading edge. Experiments show that the polar is very sensitive to the shape of the foil: *you should not use a tapered edge fin*.

The sudden drop in lift at angles of incidence above approximately 8–10° is due to separation of the fluid streams (stalling). Separation is a function of the angle of incidence, but also of the speed of flow, surface roughness and any vibration. There is thus a critical separation speed.

If we look at the lift curve plotted against the angle of incidence of the flow, we can see severe separation above a certain angle. Section A stalls at 12°; section B above 8°.

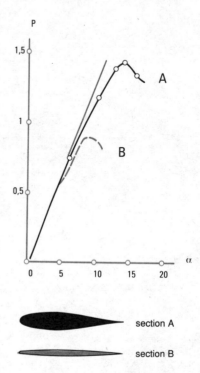

CHAPTER 3

Equilibrium of a sailing vessel

A boat has to deal with constantly changing speeds. It is at the mercy of wind and tides. To begin with, we shall define some terms and look at some surprising phenomena. Only after this shall we look at what forces actually get the boat moving.

Definition of velocity

Movement can be defined only in relation to a reference point. The velocity of a boat relative to the earth can be shown by a trace on a chart. Velocity is speed in a given direction, and can be defined as the relationship between time taken (t) to cover a given distance (l). Velocity can be represented mathematically by a vector, an arrow showing both direction and (by its length) speed of movement.

This can be the average velocity over the distance during time t; when time t is very short we can talk of *momentary velocity*. More often than not, we are interested in the boat's *speed over the ground* rather than through the water, so we shall continue to use this measure, abbreviated Vf.

Force and speed

The concept of forces operating on an object is fairly widespread; it can be a pull on a boat's painter, or on any other sort of object. At the moment you exercise this force, it is static, ie there is force with no movement and no speed. It is more difficult to imagine there ever being speed with no force. Nevertheless, for constant speed, no force is required, contrary to what the ancient Greeks believed at the time of Aristotle. They knew nothing of friction or of the fundamental law $F = m\gamma$.

Once a satellite has been put in orbit it continues to move without consuming energy: the net resultant force operating on it is zero, yet it maintains a speed of 28,000 km/h.

An aeroplane or a sailing vessel also has a net resultant zero force at constant speed (zero acceleration, $\gamma = 0$). In the case of an

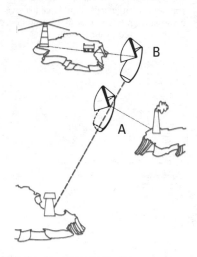

Velocity is represented by a vector showing speed and direction. The average speed over the ground (Vf) can be shown on a chart.

A satellite with no engine orbits at considerable speed (once round the earth every few hours). Its weight and momentum cancel each other out.

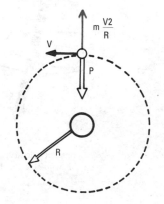

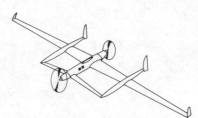

An aeroplane or a car at constant horizonatal velocity needs some force to move it forward: in effect, a push, to cancel out the drag caused by air friction.

aeroplane its weight is balanced out by the low pressure above the wings (lift) and the air resistance or drag is cancelled out by the engines, whether jet or propeller.

In the case of a sailing craft, Archimedes' principle stops it sinking, and the hydrodynamic resistance on the hull is balanced out by the motive force of the aerodynamic thrust caused by the wind in the sails. If this thrust is changed, the velocity will also change so that a new equilibrium is established, with the hydrodynamic force again balancing the aerodynamic force.

When there is a swell running, the result is a permanent disequilibrium between the forces in operation and the zero-sum equation ... a waste of energy, in other words.

True and apparent wind

Over a stretch of water, the *true wind* has velocity Vr in relation to the ground. This is the wind which you feel while your boat is anchored.

If your boat is moving at Vf (velocity over the ground) the wind which you will feel is the apparent wind, travelling at velocity Va.

These three vectors are related as follows: Vr = Va + Vf.

This equation can be drawn by measuring Va and knowing Vr and Vf. They form a triangle, as shown.

When sailing to windward, the apparent wind is stronger than the true wind and it meets the boat at a more acute angle. This becomes more noticeable the greater the value of Vf. In this way, a fast boat such as a catamaran can sail a beam reach with its sails close-hauled.

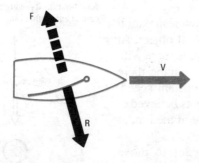

At constant velocity, the forces operating on the *whole* of the boat are in equilibrium.

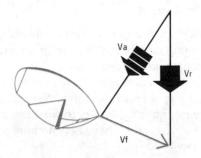

The apparent wind has strength and direction Va. This vector, added to the velocity of the boat over the ground Vf, gives us the value of the true wind, Vr.

Off the wind, on the other hand, the apparent wind becomes less strong. This is more and more noticeable as the boat travels closer to the axis of the true wind.

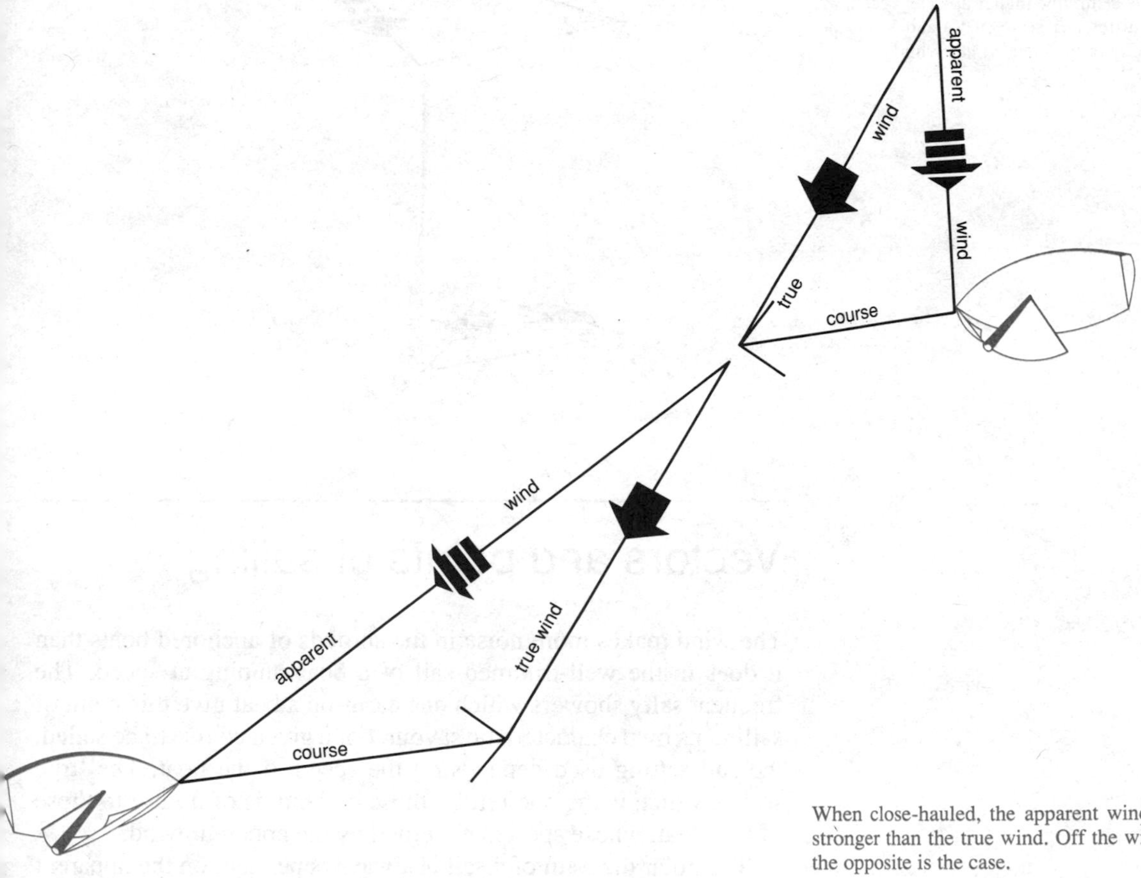

apparent wind

true wind

course

wind

wind

apparent

true wind

course

When close-hauled, the apparent wind is stronger than the true wind. Off the wind, the opposite is the case.

This is why you can be sailing close-hauled in a strong breeze and pass a boat sailing off the wind whose occupants' hair is unruffled.

The burgee at the mast top indicates the direction of the apparent wind; on a beat, the apparent wind is also a tangent to the luff of your sail all the way up if the sail is correctly trimmed.

It is worth changing the angle of attack by allowing the sail to twist, partly because the true wind is not the same at the top of the mast as it is at the gooseneck, and partly because the wind is deflected in any case by the jib. For this reason, the apparent wind is slightly further ahead on the jib than on the mainsail.

Since the real wind is stronger at the mast head than at deck level, the luff of the sail can also be at more of an angle to the boat's centreline higher up. The vector Vv (the difference between Va and Vr) is the velocity of the induced headwind.

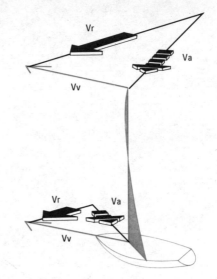

Vectors and points of sailing

The wind makes more noise in the shrouds of anchored boats than it does in the well-trimmed sail of a boat running at speed. The frequent salty showers which one earns on a beat give this point of sailing its own characteristic savour. For a given course to be sailed, the sail setting used depends on the speed of the boat. The 'true wind', which is the one felt by those on land, is of no use to those of us afloat, whose sport is governed by the apparent wind.

The polar diagram of a sail is always dependent on the apparent wind; this in turn is dependent on the performance of each boat in a given true wind. Thus, sailing the same north–south course in the same force 4 north-westerly, a heavy cruising yacht will be broad reaching at 3kn while a sailboard might be close-hauled at 12kn: *your point of sailing depends on the speed of your craft.*

It is therefore unproductive to talk of points of sailing by reference to the true wind: the terms beat, broad reach, etc are imprecise and unrealistic in terms of modern sailing craft.

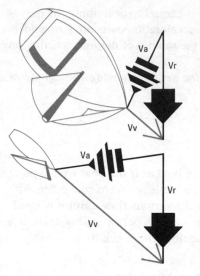

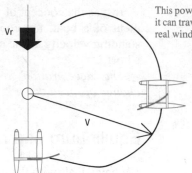

This power curve for a Tornado shows that it can travel three times as fast at 90° to the real wind as it can straight downwind.

Although they are travelling on the same course and with the same true wind, this boat has its sails trimmed out, while the sailboard has its sail close-hauled. This is a result of their different values of Vv: a very fast craft will have its sail in tight on any point of sailing other than a dead run.

From a theoretical point of view, there are two points of sailing only, characterised by the different air flows around the sails:
– laminar flow;
– turbulent, or separated, flow.

In general, a boat will be sailing with laminar flow when it is travelling to windward, and with separated flow when it is travelling downwind. In laminar flow, one's aim is to minimise drag, whereas downwind, drag is the very thing pushing you forward.

These definitions apply to the flow of air round the sails. As far as the flow of water under the hull is concerned, this should always be laminar. In any case, it is hard to sail for long in separated water flow: this is a transitory phase while getting started and bearing away, or a tactic such as a deliberate sideslip in strong weather to reduce the heeling moment of the wind.

Varying velocity and acceleration

If the boat is travelling in a constant direction at a constant speed, it is said to be in steady flow. If, on the other hand, its velocity changes, either because the direction or the speed has changed, then the boat is subject to an acceleration.

The state is said to be steady when the velocity is the same at one moment as at another moment. If the velocity has changed, it is not steady.

Acceleration does not necessarily mean a change in speed: it can also mean a change in direction.

Just as the concept of velocity is central to describing the movement of a boat, the concept of acceleration is central to understanding velocity as the effect of the totality of the forces acting on a boat.

The 'acceleration' vector is the vector showing the 'speed of change of speed'.

Equilibrium of a boat

We have dealt with the motion of a boat as if the boat were a point on a chart table. This was adequate while we were concerned with analysing the forces arising from the various flows. But it is insufficient once one starts to look a little deeper: a sailing craft is a collection of equipment joined together either solidly or flexibly.

The boat or board as a collection of solids

A solid is a substance within which the distance between two points does not vary. In very many cases, the behaviour of a boat can be analysed by considering it as a collection of three basic solids:
– solid S1 covers all the parts of the boat which are normally in the air. It is this part on which the wind acts, meaning primarily the sails, but every other exposed surface as well. *The speed of the apparent wind determines the strength of the force on these solids, Av;*
– solid S2 is the underwater part of the boat, which is subject to the forces created by the water. *The speed through the water determines the force Ae;*
– solid S3 is made up of the crew, which has a changing mechanical function depending on the type of boat: movable ballast in a dinghy, and the link betwen S1 and S2 on a sailboard.

These three solids are said to be in relative equilibrium if their spatial relationship to each other remains constant over time, and all three are moving with the same velocity over the ground, or Vf.

The forces Av (operating on all the above-water parts of the boat) and Ae (operating on the wetted surfaces) determine the velocity Vf. Since these forces are equal respectively to Va and Ve, you cannot change one variable without changing the other, even if the true wind vector Vr and water vector Ve remain constant. There is an infinite number of possible combinations, and the skill of the crew consists in finding the solution which will result in the highest velocity made good over the ground.

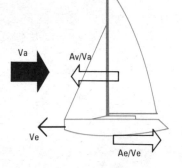

The action of the wind Av is dependent on the vector of the apparent wind Va. The action of the water Ae is dependent on the speed vector of the hull through the water Ve.

Definition of the equilibrium of a sailing boat

Let us assume our boat to be a collection of solids in relative equilibrium. If the wind is dead astern, the action of the wind Av is reduced to the aerodynamic thrust Rp in the direction of travel of the boat. If the boat is travelling at a constant velocity Vf, the action of the water Ae can be reduced to a force Ft equal and opposite to Rp. There is zero acceleration and the system is stable. The essential point in this is that *the sum of the actions of wind and water is zero*.

In fact a boat's motion is a succession of temporary states. The speed of the hull relative to the water (with all associated forces) varies simply as a result of the swell. We therefore simplify by regarding the motion as a steady state with small variations; and we know that on average the forces of the wind R will balance out those of the water F.

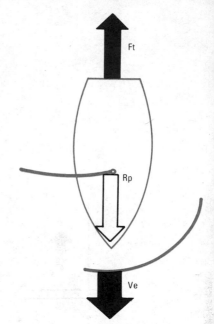

If we plot on the same graph the variation in force exercised on the rig (Rp) against the forces on the hull (Ft) as a function of velocity (Vf) – which is itself a function of the velocity of the true and apparent wind – at the point where the two graphs cross there is a velocity over the ground Vfo for which the propulsive force Rp equals the resistance Ft.

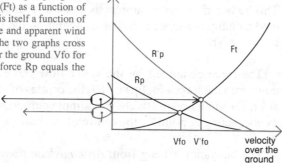

Velocity through the water Ve is constant when the aerodynamic force Rp is equal and opposite to the hydrodynamic resistance Ft. In this case, with the wind dead astern, Ve (velocity through the water) is in the same direction as Vf (velocity over the ground).

Representation of forces on a run

When the boat is running, the apparent wind drops as the velocity of the boat over the ground increases. The sum of the boat's velocity and the velocity of the apparent wind equals the velocity of the true wind: Vf+Va=Vr.

The force exerted by the wind on the sails reduces as Vf increases, thus Rp reduces with increased velocity Vf. The resistance from the water (Ft), on the other hand, increases with increased speed. Thus, at a certain velocity (here called Vfo) Rpo and Fto will be equal.

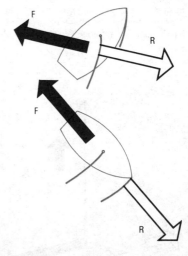

At a constant velocity, a boat is always in equilibrium between the forces F and R, even if not sailing dead downwind.

Having made this generalisation, we can continue on to study many situations; the validity of the statement is limited, however. For instance, as you are reaching harbour, you will have noticed that the boat does not stop as soon as you take away the power. *The transitory phase is therefore vitally important.*

By definition, a sailing boat is in mechanical equilibrium if its parts are undergoing uniform translation, ie the boat is sailing a constant course at a constant speed, neither rolling nor pitching.

The forces acting on a sailing boat in equilibrium

The forces acting on a boat arise from:
– the wind;
– the water flow under the hull;
– friction from the water;
– the weight of the boat.

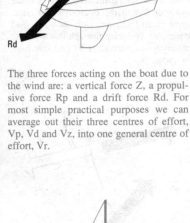

The three forces acting on the boat due to the wind are: a vertical force Z, a propulsive force Rp and a drift force Rd. For most simple practical purposes we can average out their three centres of effort, Vp, Vd and Vz, into one general centre of effort, Vr.

The force of the wind can be further broken down into the three forces, Rp, Rd and Z, which act on the three points Vp, Vd and Vz. This rather rigorous treatment is generally unnecessary, and we tend to lump the three together as acting on the overall 'centre of effort' or Vr.

The force generated by the water flow can equally be broken down into the forces Ft, Fp and Fz, the centres of effort of which are at Et, Ep and Ez respectively. For simple purposes these are treated as one, acting at point C, the centre of the hull.

The buoyancy arising from *Archimedean flotation* acts at point C. This is a vertical force which balances the weight of the volume of water displaced by the vessel. P, the weight of the boat, acts at the centre of gravity of the hull plus rig plus crew. This may be assumed for practical purposes to act downwards at the same point as the upward force of flotation.

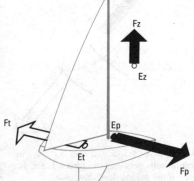

The forces acting on the hull due to the water flow are due to drag (Ft), lift (Fp) and an upward force (Fz). These three act at points Et, Ep and Ez respectively, but can be dealt with more simply by placing the centre of effort and resistance at C, the centre of the hull.

The laws of equilibrium

Since Newton, we know that a solid or group of solids is in mechanical equilibrium if and only if the sum of the forces acting on it is zero.

When a solid or group of solids is in equilibrium there is no acceleration: speed and direction are constant. *Mechanical equilibrium does not mean zero velocity.*

It should be pointed out that interactions between the solids within the group (the internal strains) are irrelevant, so long as these remain in relative equilibrium.

When a crew member falls overboard and is attached to a harness and cable, the force on the cable will be the same whether the cable is fixed to the rail or handheld by another crew member; the internal strains between the elements of the human body, by contrast, are greatly different, depending on where and how the force is applied.

We can use the word action to designate the effect of the wind or the water on the sailing boat. A mechanical action has both force and moment. For instance, if you exert a force F down on the lever of a door handle, this becomes an action bearing on the axis with both the force component F and a turning moment. In the same way, pulling a boat's tiller towards you will apply a turning moment to the rudder as well as a linear force which must be compensated by sideways pressure on the pintles.

As a general rule the moment M caused about point P by force F is proportional to the strength of F and the distance from P at which F is applied.

Mathematically, it is the same whether we say a group of solids is in equilibrium or:
– the sum of exterior forces is zero;
– the sum of the moments of exterior forces about one point is zero.

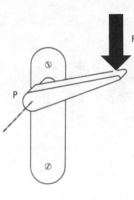

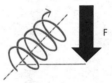

The moment M at point P due to force F is here shown by a right-hand screw thread.

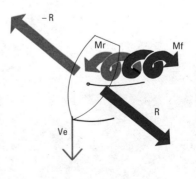

If the opposing forces of air and water are equal (R = –F) and the moments also cancel each other out (Mr = –Mf), the boat will move at a constant velocity Ve.

Translational equilibrium

When the boat is travelling without heeling, as is the case with multihulls, sailboards, and monohulls sailing downwind, the resultant of the forces which cause translational equilibrium is as follows:
– the aerodynamic propulsive component, Rp is equal and opposite to the hydrodynamic drag component Ft, ie Rp = –Ft;
– the aerodynamic lift component Rd is equal and opposite to the hydrodynamic drift component Fp, ie Rd = –Fp;
– the Archimedean thrust A cancels out the weight of the boat P, less the hydrodynamic and aerodynamic vertical components Fz and Z, ie A = P – (Z + Fz).

Everything is much simpler when the boat is not heeled over.

Translational equilibrium is characterised by the zero sum of all forces.

P and A are parallel and vertical; Z and Fz are parallel to each other and to the keel. A balances out P, plus Z less Fz. Z and Fz are small.

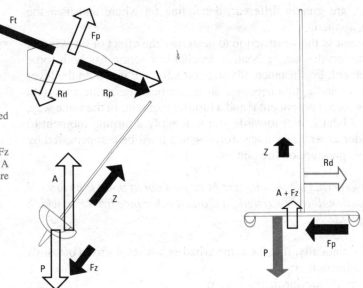

Longitudinal equilibrium

The boat's longitudinal equilibrium is governed by the relationship between the aero- and hydrodynamic thrusts (Rp = –Fp), for a given value of the thrust produced by the rig Rp.

The expression 'to reduce drag' means that you are changing the point at which equilibrium is established between drag and thrust. Thus, *with the same value of Rp, you obtain a higher value for Ve.* It is not actually true that the drag is reduced, but that the same drag is achieved at a higher speed.

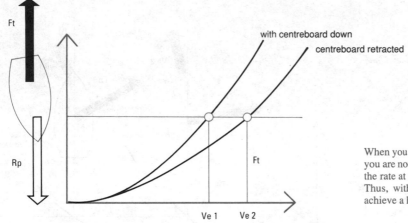

with centreboard down

centreboard retracted

Ft

Rp

Ft

Ve 1   Ve 2

When you retract the centreboard on a run, you are not reducing the drag, but reducing the rate at which drag is induced by speed. Thus, with the same sail thrust Rp, you achieve a higher speed Ve 2.

Lateral equilibrium

The aerodynamic drift component Rd and the hydrodynamic lift component Fp determine the lateral equilibrium of the boat. A drift component Rd is unavoidable on any laminar point of sailing; on the wind, there is no way of creating a propulsive force (Rp) without also creating a drift component.

The hydrodynamic lift component Fp varies with the velocity through the water Ve and the angle of drift (or angle of attack) β. For a given value of Fp, the higher the speed Ve, the smaller will be the angle of attack β. If we plot a graph of velocity against angle of drift for a given value of Fp, we can see that there is a sudden increase in drift below velocity Vec, because it is at this point that the centreboard 'stalls', ie the flow separates. Since it is in your interest to avoid high values of β, you should aim to avoid travelling slower than Vec at any price.

If this does happen, you should bear in mind that the lift component Fp is imposed by the drift component Rd of the sail thrust, and that the value of Ve is determined by the longitudinal equilibrium. Under these conditions, the only way out is to find a new equilibrium position in which Rd is weaker, with a weaker value of Ve. This is part of any compromise between speed and the course made good.

The flow separates suddenly at attack angle c, which corresponds to velocity Vec. Boat A, travelling more slowly than Vec, and therefore with a high β, is losing a lot of ground to windward, whereas boat B is sailing normally.

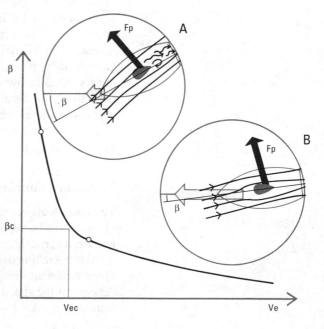

β

Fp   A

β

Fp   B

β

βc

Vec

Ve

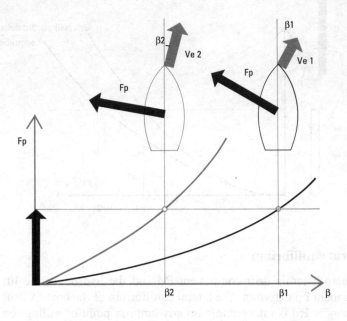

For the same propulsive thrust, the angle of drift increases as the speed through the water decreases.

Without wanting to insist that you carry equations round in your head, we would suggest that this is a lesson worth learning. If, from a standing start, you create a propulsive force R which has any component Rd other than zero, the value of β resulting will be not far from 90°, ie the boat will move sideways. This is the case with any start to windward. Usually, the boat picks up some speed, so Ve increases, so β is reduced to a reasonable value in the region 5–7°. Occasionally, though, Ve does not increase sufficiently, and you cannot get β below about 60°. You will notice this quite quickly, particularly on a sailboard, and then you need to reduce Rd to an equilibrium level where β is reduced to an acceptable level. You can then proceed to try to increase your speed from this course and build up Rd again.

Vertical equilibrium

The boat floats because $A = P - (Z + Fz)$. Its vertical equilibrium, in other words, depends on Z, a vertical force due to the air flow, and Fz, a vertical force due to the water flow.

A, the Archimedean thrust, is a static force which is equal to the volume of water displaced. P is the weight of the boat. Z and Fz depend on the speed of the boat and are dynamic. Before the boat started, then, $A = P$ was enough for the boat to float!

The moment one reduces the volume of the boat in the water, A is reduced, as is Ft, the hydrodynamic drag component. Reducing A

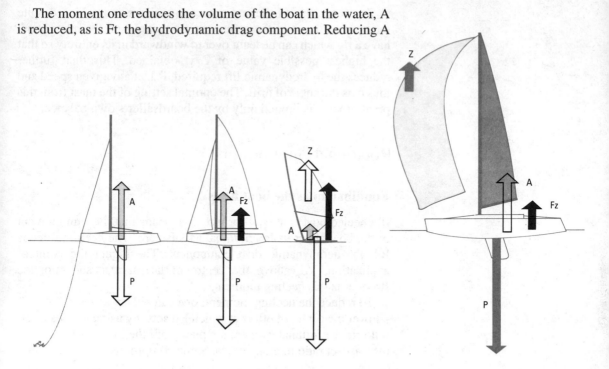

The first boat is moored. Z and Fz are both zero since the boat is not moving.
The second boat is a classical keelboat. It does not create a force Z when close-hauled.
For the funboard (right), the forces Z and Fz are the main things stopping the board from sinking!

With negligible heel, the Archimedean thrust A is occasionally added to by a Z force arising from the air flow and an Fz force from the water flow.

thus 'cuts drag', or, more precisely, increases the equilibrium speed (where $Ft + Rp = 0$). For a given weight, A is smaller where Z and Fz (the aerodynamic and hydrodynamic upward thrust) are both large and positive.

Fz can be either positive or negative depending on the curvature of the water flow over the hull. The curvature needs to be downwards to provide hydrodynamic lift, which can be achieved in some boats by modifying the fore-and-aft trim; and the swell can achieve the same effect and play an important role in changing the value of Fz. Some fairly flat-sectioned hulls are particularly effective in generating positive values of Fz, and many sailboards have an undersurface designed specifically to encourage this effect even at relatively low speeds.

Once Fz becomes fairly large, the boat is said to have started *semi-planing* or *surfing*. When Fz approaches the value of P, one starts to *plane*.

Z is generally of little importance to cruisers or dinghies, despite the upward thrust of the spinnaker. Sailboards, on the other hand, have a rig which can be leant over to windward in its entirety so that the highest possible value of Z is obtained. This then further reduces the hydrodynamic lift required, Rd, at any given speed and thus cuts the angle of drift. The optimal setting of the mast from this point of view is limited only by the boardsailer's own balance.

Rotational equilibrium

Equilibrium as the boat heels

If a heeled boat is at equilibrium, this means that the sum moment of the boat about its longitudinal axis is zero. The heeling force is Rd, the aerodynamic drift component. The higher the point of application, Vd, above the centre of lateral resistance Fp, the stronger is this heeling moment.

To reduce the heeling moment, one can either:
– lower the centre of effort at which Rd acts, by using a low aspect-ratio rig. Unfortunately there are plenty of other reasons for using a high aspect ratio in many cases. Some compromise must be found; or
– raise the centre of lateral resistance of the hull, Fp. This may be achieved in a dinghy by raising the centreboard, but raising the centreboard will also tend to reduce the boat's resistance to drift, and thus increase angle β.

The force which tends to right the boat is the Archimedean thrust A, which acts at point C, the centre of gravity of the volume of water displaced by the boat. When the boat heels, this changes the point at which A acts, and C moves away from the centre of the boat.

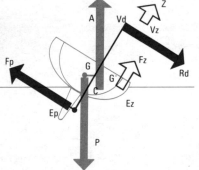

Forces acting as a boat is in equilibrium at a heel are: Rd, the aerodynamic drift; Fp, the hydrodynamic lift; P, the weight applied at G, the centre of gravity; and A, the Archimedean thrust applied at C, the centre of displacement. G' is vertically above C.

The moment acting on a heeling boat may be written:
$$A \times (GG')$$

ie the Archimedean thrust times the distance between the centre of gravity of the boat and the point on the boat's centreline which is level with the centre of gravity. In the diagram, C has moved to the right as the heel has increased. The value of (GG') increases. For a given strength of the heeling couple, one of two outcomes may be expected:
– either equilibrium is reached and the boat keeps on a given angle of heel;

– or GG' is not sufficiently large and the boat capsizes.

Depending on the shape of the hull, the centre of displacement moves out from the centreline more or less quickly as the boat heels:

– for a monohull or a sailboard, C moves out further the flatter the hull;

– for a multihull, as soon as any heel is achieved, there is a substantial change in the share of the flotation provided by each hull, so that even at small angles of heel, the centre of displacement moves quite suddenly. This is why multihulls are so stable.

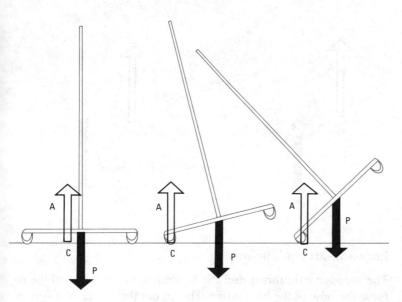

So long as the windward hull is fairly close to the water, the boat remains very stable. Once it starts to heel a long way, the righting couple reduces.

Cruising yachts are generally designed so that equilibrium is possible at any angle of heel, even under extreme conditions. Generally this is helped by the fact that as the rig becomes less effective when heavily heeled, Rd is generally reduced.

With a multihull, the value of GG' does not increase at all after the initial 'unsticking' of one hull. That is why multihulls can capsize!

One further way of increasing the distance GG' is to move the centre of gravity of the boat:

– in a light dinghy or a sailboard, you can move G by moving the crew, whose body weight makes up a significant proportion of the whole. This movement is most effective when simply side-to-side;

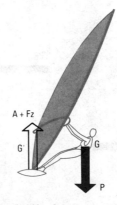

A lateral shift of the centre of gravity G increases the distance GG' and thus the strength of the righting couple.

Heavy ballast, or ballast placed low down, gives an increased righting couple as heel increases.

– in a cruiser, the crew weight is not the determining factor, even though it should not be completely ignored. G can be moved by weighting the bottom of the boat; this is what is achieved by the heavy bottom of the keel. It has to be said that this passive ballast is less efficient in creating a righting moment than lateral movement of G.

In planing conditions, the vertical hydrodynamic thrust Fz can reach strengths comparable to A, and it then acts similarly. For even small angles of heel, the centre of effort of Fz can move considerably. For this reason, a planing hull is very stable.

Fore-and-aft equilibrium

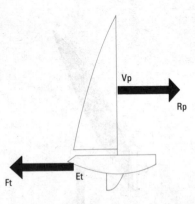

A boat pitches fore and aft as a result of the couple Rp/Ft (aerodynamic thrust/hydrodynamic drag).

The aerodynamic thrust and the hydrodynamic drag combine to force the bow of the boat down. The higher the centre of effort of the rig, the more noticeable this tendency.

If the centre of displacement of the hull is forward of the centre of gravity, the water will tend to push the bow back up.

When the boat is static, ie subject only to the action of its own weight, G and C are in the same line. Once the boat starts to move, the waterline shifts. The boat's longitudinal stability is greater if C moves a long way for only a small degree of pitch.

If the hull shape is such that the bow encloses considerable volume, there will be great longitudinal stability. If one examines the volume distribution along the hull, one can learn a great deal about this problem, particularly noticeable in multihulls. One does not generally imagine having problems in achieving longitudinal stability; nevertheless, in some conditions, the bow can be buried so deep that there is a sudden shift downwards in the point at which drag Ft is applied. The forward rotating couple is thus increased and the boat can capsize over its own bow.

In light dinghies, the position of the crew can markedly alter the position of the centre of gravity, so the longitudinal trim may be maintained by moving aft. *A small change in the longitudinal trim can enormously change the hydrodynamic forces Ft and Fz, so balancing the two can be very difficult.*

When a boat is planing, Fz plays the role normally occupied by A. The point at which Fz acts is determined by the water flow under the hull. When Z acts upward, the tendency is for this to lift the bows; this is the case with a well-trimmed spinnaker.

Directional equilibrium

When a boat moves forward, the forces acting on it are never all in one line. There is therefore a turning moment, represented in the diagram by the couple Fp and Rd, which tends to make the boat bear away, and the couple Rp and Ft, which makes it tend to luff up. Depending on circumstances, the direction in which these couples act and the points at which they act may be reversed.

For a given force on the sails, Fp is fixed by the translational equilibrium, and the only thing which you can change is the point, Ep, at which it is applied:

1. You can move the tiller, thus changing the underwater shape and shifting Ep (though not changing the force Fp, which is determined by the action of the wind on the sails). For the same value of Fp, it can be shown that the angle of drift decreases if the underwater shape is changed by the tiller being pulled to windward. *This is why it is in your interest to tune the boat to have weather helm.*

However, by moving the tiller you also 'increase the drag', thus slowing the boat down and increasing the angle of drift again. This increased drift is generally negligible until the tiller angle goes past about 7 or 8°. For this reason you should aim never to move the tiller by more than this amount. (Applying fluid flow theory will lead to the same result.)

2. You can also move the point Vd at which the

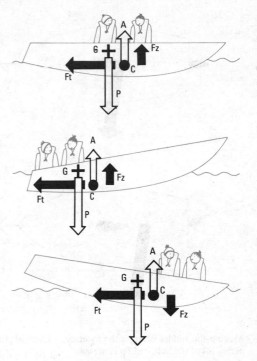

The position of the crew can change the centre of gravity G at which the weight P acts; it also changes the centre of displacement C at which the Archimedean thrust A acts.

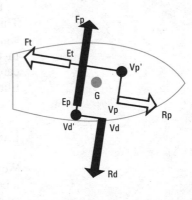

Directional equilibrium
The couples Rp/Ft (aerodynamic thrust component and hydrodynamic drag) and Fp/Rd (hydrodynamic lift and aerodynamic drift component) interact to steer the boat. Archimedean thrust is irrelevant if the boat is not heeling.

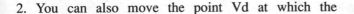

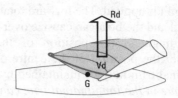

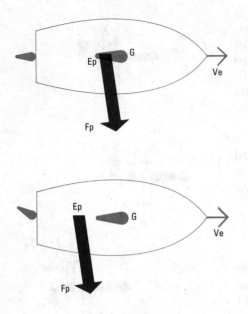

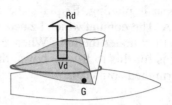

On a sailboard, moving the rig aft also moves the point Vd aft at which the drift component Rd acts: the board then luffs up to find its new equilibrium.

Moving the rudder changes the hydrodynamic lift of the hull, and Fp is moved.

aerodynamic drift component Rd acts, as is done by moving the rig of a sailboard fore and aft. If Vd is moved forward, the board will bear away; moved aft, the board luffs up. Although it feels to the boardsailor as though the feet are directing the board, in fact the board's 'steering' is the result of these external forces on the sail.

In some conditions, it is impossible to achieve an equilibrium. This is the case when you are sailing under spinnaker, which has a significant value of Rp: under these circumstances, a small increase in the angle of heel greatly increases the couple Rp/Ft. If you cannot increase the couple Fp/Rd correspondingly by pulling the tiller up, the boat will luff up uncontrollably.

Elements of the theory of boat control

We have looked at the mechanical equilibrium of the boat. In fact, a boat is never strictly in equilibrium, but varies between successive equilibrium states, rather like a baby, tottering but never quite falling over.

It is practically impossible to quantify and study all the forces which are actually involved in sailing in a swell with a constantly varying wind.

Instead, we simplify matters by assuming the boat to be in constant steady-state motion with small variations superimposed on this.

For most cases, this hypothesis holds up. What distinguishes the talented sailor is an ability to spot these small variations and respond accordingly.

The steady-state hypothesis is clearly flawed when certain manoeuvres are being carried out, such as tacking. Let us now study some of these transitional states.

Trimming a boat consists in finding an equilibrium which corresponds to the directional objectives you have imposed on the boat. This might include getting there at high speed or in relative comfort; but you have a choice in deciding how to go about it. You can either find out for yourself through trial and error, or start by testing some of the principles outlined above.

The tack

Tacking is the most frequent manoeuvre you will have to make. The equations we developed for looking at mechanical equilibrium states are of no use here, because there is no directional momentum to fall back on. We can simplify the problem by taking a single point of effort for the aerodynamic forces Vr, and assuming all the hydrodynamic forces to be acting at C.

In our starting position (A), the aerodynamic force R and the hydrodynamic force F are in balance: the boat is travelling at constant velocity. To change direction or go about, if you are on port tack, you need to create a turning couple to the right to bear away, or to the left to harden up. You can choose between two methods:
– moving the point of application of the hydrodynamic force F, as in a boat with a rudder (B);
– moving the point of application of the aerodynamic force R, as on a vessel without a rudder, such as a sailboard (C).

Combining the two methods increases their effectiveness.

With the tiller

Let us assume your intention is to turn to the left, in the diagram. You need to bring point C forward, which involves reducing the anti-drift component of the rudder. To do this, you need to reduce or

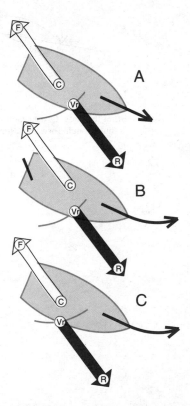

In A, the boat is in equilibrium. The two forces R (aerodynamic) and F (hydrodynamic) are in line.

In B, moving the rudder changes the point of application of the hydrodynamic force: the resultant couple turns the boat.

In C, the rig is moved, thus changing the point at which the aerodynamic force acts: a couple is created.

reverse the angle of incidence, s, of the water flow over the rudder blade. This creates a turning moment to the left which is then super-imposed on the translational movement of the boat.

Just as the true wind combines with the speed of the boat to give an apparent wind, the boat's translational speed is combined with the speed of rotation, and each part of the hull is moving through the water at a different velocity. Thus, point E at the bow is moving

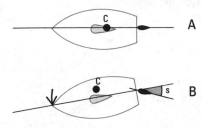

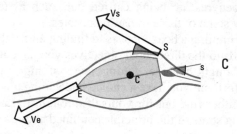

In A, the boat is in equilibrium.
In B, the rudder has been turned, thus producing less lift at the back. C, the centre of the underwater shape, is thus brought forward. A turning couple is created.

In C, the translation and rotation are combined. Point E at the bow has speed directed more to the left than point S, at the transom. The water flow around the rudder is reorientated and angle s is reduced. There is hydrodynamic resistance to the rotation, and point C moves aft. To bring C further forward, the tiller has to be pushed further over.

at speed Ve which is directed further left than Vs, the speed of point S at the stern. The angle of incidence of the water flow over the hull thus varies, increasing from front to back.

At this stage, the hydrodynamic force moves aft, operating against the change of direction. The angle of incidence s of the water flow onto the rudder is reduced, so the rudder has to be moved further over if the turn is to continue: thus, during a tack, the increased angle of the rudder has to be synchronised with the turn. This is particularly important because s should remain relatively small throughout the manoeuvre for efficient flow to be achieved.

The polar diagram for an underwater foil shows flow separation at an angle of 10° or more. In order not to create unnecessary drag and lose the lift which provides your steering ability, s should remain below 10°.

The sudden loss of lift above this angle means that the turn is less efficient if the rudder is turned so far and so suddenly that separation takes place.

The angle of the rudder should increase as the change in direction of the boat through the water becomes greater; your aim is to maintain a constant angle of incidence of the water flow over the blade.

What is happening to the aerodynamic force as all this is going on? If you are tacking, the apparent wind will change direction and strength, just as the aerodynamic force will. For a short part of the manoeuvre, there will be no propulsive force; and as the speed of the boat drops, so will the hydrodynamic force and the efficiency of the rudder. Occasionally, the boat will lose its way before the manoeuvre is completed: at this point you will lose your ability to steer, as it is impossible to steer using non-existent forces.

With no tiller

Generally, if you have no tiller with which to shift point C forward, you need to bring Vr aft. In a dinghy minus its rudder, you do this by sheeting in the mainsail. In some craft, the rig will not allow you to steer this way; on a surfing catamaran, you have to shift C forward or aft by changing the longitudinal trim (ie burying the bow or the stern).

On a sailboard, the desired effect may be obtained by leaning the rig aft. As soon as you start to turn, the speed of the water flow under the board changes, and the wind speed changes due to the speed of turn of the board. The centre of effort of the sail moves back and to the side, and the apparent wind heads you. You need to pull the rig towards you to maintain an efficient angle of incidence to the wind for completing the manoeuvre.

Just as with a boat with a rudder, the shift in position of the rig relative to the board should be synchronised with the speed of rotation of the board: if you harden in too soon, the aerodynamic force will be so directed that it actually slows you down, and if you leave it too late the sail will not be pulling fully and the board will stop dead before you have pushed the nose through the wind.

We have looked only at the visible mechanics of these manoeuvres so far, and related them all to relative speeds:
– while a boat is travelling at constant velocity, it is in equilibrium, and each part of the boat is travelling at the same speed relative to the ground;
– when a boat tacks, the speeds over the ground of the different parts of the boat are different, which in turn means that their speed relative to the apparent wind and to the water changes.

During this transitional phase, momentum plays a vital role, but one which is difficult to model mathematically. For that reason, we

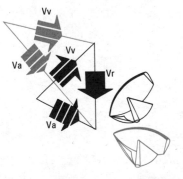

When the black boat starts to turn, the direction of the apparent wind changes; it freshens and comes more from the right as you turn to the right. When the boat reaches the position shown in blue, the apparent wind has freed, so you can continue to keep the jib sheeted in. It will continue to fill until almost head to wind.

have to take a pragmatic approach, and deal with the 'special cases' as they come up.

Planing

The coefficient of maximum hull speed of 0.4 which we derived earlier gives us a value of about 5kn as the maximum displacement speed for a sailboard and about 8kn for a 10m keelboat. These speeds can be considerably exceeded when planing, and indeed there are some sailboards (known as sinkers) which can only be sailed on the plane.

Getting up onto the plane

Our equilibrium equations show that the immersed volume A can be radically reduced when the hydrodynamic force Fz and the aerodynamic upward force Z are both positive and substantial in relation to the weight of the boat P. In practice, this only happens with an angle of heel close to 0. In the case of monohulls, Z is small in relation to the other forces.

When a boat is moving at a moderate speed, Fz is generally negative, since the overall underwater shape of the boat produces concave flow. This means that the boat floats slightly more bow-down than when it is static.

Once the speed begins to increase, the nose lightens. If the hull is suitably shaped, a shift of weight towards the transom can cause the concavity of the water flow under the hull to invert. The lift then becomes upward, and Fz is positive. The centre of effort of hydrodynamic action moves forward and the boat leans back a little.

The boat's displacement volume (A) decreases, since A is equal to the weight of the boat less the lift, and the water drag decreases correspondingly. In order for planing to start, the fore-and-aft trim needs to change sufficiently far for the curvature of the water flow under the hull to invert, but not so far that you bury the transom and create extra drag that way.

Planing only starts when the boat trim and underwater shape are precisely right. The crew of a dinghy plays an important role in achieving this condition.

In the case of sailboards, one can of course change the direction of the aerodynamic force to produce upward thrust Z from the rig.

This encourages planing, but the underwater shape must be correct also for a sailboard to get up onto the plane.

Summary

More than any other vessel, a sailing boat is subject to changes in its motive power, whether from the waves or the wind. In practice, few air or water flows are constant and correspond neatly to the theoretical cases we have examined.

Even if the external forces are steady, with a very constant wind, no swell and with constant course and sail trim, the flow of the air and water can still produce irregularities, because of simple mechanical instability, rather like trying to stand still on a bicycle.

Instability has advantages and disadvantages. On one hand, it means that irrotational field flows cannot become set up when you are running downwind, for instance; however, if you deliberately induce instability in your sail when on the reach, you might find that this enables you to set up a laminar flow and a stable boundary layer when before the flow was separated.

You cannot see what is happening under the hull, and in any case the angles of incidence in the water are generally smaller. This makes it more difficult to influence the hydrodynamic forces, but you should at least make sure your boat and rudder are free of vibration.

Our theories and models remain insufficient confronted with the instability of real flows; for this reason, you should digest our advice and diagrams, but not let them blind you to the need to develop your own feeling for what is going on. Even with the help of all this science, sailing a boat well remains an art.

To trim a boat, you need to choose among variables which are mutually dependent. Passing from one stable state to another means that you need to co-ordinate a number of actions over time. Your reflexes will improve if you understand the physics of the processes involved, but understanding alone is not enough. The processes are so complex that they can never be described exhaustively: the art of a good sailor is to learn practical lessons from one's own experience just as much as to learn the theory.

Equilibrium and points of sailing

A. The boat is close-hauled, in equilibrium. The aerodynamic force R and the hydrodynamic force F are aligned.

B. The same boat heels. The centre of effort of the sail drops off to leeward and the centre of lateral resistance of the hull moves to windward. The resulting couple causes the boat to turn. This boat has weather helm and luffs up.

C. The boat heels to windward, reversing the couple. It bears away.

D. The jib is freed in the hope of bringing the centre of effort of the sail aft and luffing up. The centre of effort does actually move aft, but the jib is freed a touch too far, and R becomes weaker, even though pointing more forward. The boat slows and the centre of lateral resistance moves aft. The luff is only temporary.

E. The jib is lowered. The centre of effort moves aft. The flow over the mainsail is disturbed, so R is weak and more side-on. The boat slows and the centre of lateral resistance moves aft. The boat bears away.

F. The wind freshens. The fullness of the sails moves aft, as does the centre of effort. R is mainly directed sideways and the boat slows. The centre of lateral resistance moves aft, but not far enough to prevent the boat developing extreme weather helm.

G. The boat is beam reaching, and has light weather helm.

H. By pulling the centreboard up, one is bringing the centre of lateral resistance aft and so balancing the boat. If the boat heels, it will develop weather helm again.

I. Spinnaker reaching. R increases, the centre of effort of the sails is brought noticeably forward and to leeward. You are travelling fast and the centre of lateral resistance is well forward. Even with the centreboard retracted, you will find that the boat still has weather helm.

J. Broad reaching under spinnaker, in a swell, with the boat rolling side to side. The mainsail begins to lose power as the flow separates, so the centre of effort is well forward. As the boat rolls, R moves alternately to windward and to leeward of F, with the boat trying alternately to luff then bear away. Hard work for the helm ...

K. Running, with the spinnaker out to windward. The boat has lee helm, exaggerated by the slight tendency to heel to windward.

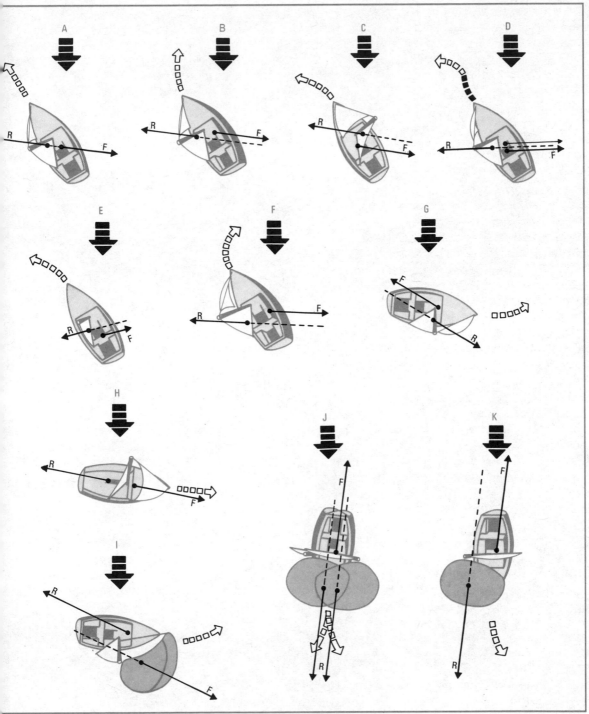

PART III

The Boat

So now we know a boat does not sail all by itself. It's hard enough work trying to sail it in a straight line; before the boat starts to give up its secrets, you have to get really deeply involved with it, to try and understand the forces which drive it and the subtleties of sail and boat trim.

This is not all. We would maintain that you need to get to know the inner workings of the boat itself. You cannot just pick up a boat, use it and put it down like you might some other objects; if you try to treat a boat that way, you will never be admitted to the inner sanctum. To get to know the sea you must first understand your boat, and build up a relationship with it which should end up as a partnership.

In the second part of this book, we looked at what makes a boat move (or stop!). In this part, we are going on a tour of the machine itself. This will not amount to a series of lecture notes on marine architecture, nor an analysis of building materials; it will be much more utilitarian. Since we are about to use the boat, we might as well get to know its weaknesses, how and where it ages fastest, and how to maintain it. Our aim will be to supply the tools for looking at boats with a critical eye, whether you are choosing one, preparing, using, maintaining or repairing one.

A critical eye is a considerable advantage. It makes you self-sufficient, which is a comforting thought, when you are afloat miles from the nearest port. You will be forced, not to take your problems to the nearest 'expert', but to solve them yourself. It is a question of attitude. That same critical eye will stop you from regarding your boat as some sort of luxury toy requiring expensive and frequent servicing. At the same time, it will make dealing with professionals, on those occasions when this becomes necessary, a pleasure rather than a strain, and it will enable you to instruct them and inspect their work that much more precisely.

The questions raised in this part are quite varied and some are dealt with in greater detail than others. You should certainly not attempt to read straight through. It is intended more for a reference, for you to dip into with the help of the index. It is not exhaustive, and in any case equipment develops and is invented at such a speed as to make exhaustiveness a fruitless quest. If we can guide you through some occasionally murky waters, assist you at the places where you need to stop, and speed you through the more straightforward passages, we shall be happy and you will be developing the necessary eye as you go.

CHAPTER 1

The rigging

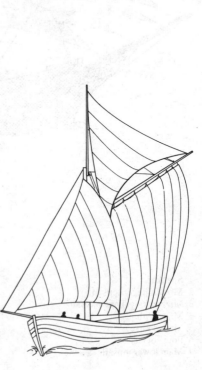

The term rigging, used in its collective sense, means all those elements of the boat aimed at propelling it forward: spars, ropes and sails.

Standing rigging and running rigging

The spars and standing rigging are the framework on which the sails are hoisted. By spars we group together masts and spreaders, booms, spinnaker poles and even yardarms. The standing rigging is the collection of wires which hold the mast up: the forestay and shrouds, their fixings and adjustment fittings, as well as the gooseneck and the spreader anchorages.

The running rigging covers all the necessary equipment for handling the sails, whether hoisting them, trimming them or changing their shape. Halyards, sheets and guys, the kicking strap, are all part of the running rigging.

Designing the rigging

There are three requirements that this construction in the air must fulfil:
— it must be thin, to offer as little wind resistance as possible. Extra windage would slow the boat down and disrupt the air flow onto the sails;
— it must be light, as any weight high up destabilises the boat;
— it must be strong, and to some extent stiff. This last requirement of course determines how far we can go in satisfying the others.

There will inevitably be compromises necessary in designing spars and rigging. Depending on the boat, each of these requirements will be weighted differently. Dinghy rigs are designed with light weight and low windage uppermost in mind. This occasionally means they lack strength, though it is rare indeed for equipment failure to endanger the crew. On a cruising yacht, on the other hand, one cannot run any chance of breakages.

1. Spanker.
2. Mizzen jigger topsail.
3. Mizzen topgallant staysail.
4. Mizzen jib.
5. Main course.
6. Fore course.
7. Main lower topsail.

8. Fore lower topsail.
9. Main upper topsail.
10. Fore upper topsail.
11. Main topgallant.
12. Fore topgallant.
13. Main royal.
14. Fore royal.

15. Main topmast staysail.
16. Main topgallant staysail.
17. Main royal staysail.
18. Fore topmast staysail.
19. Inner jib.
20. Outer jib.
21. Flying jib.

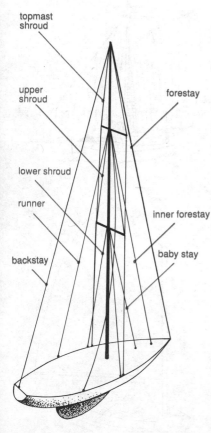

topmast
shroud

upper
shroud

forestay

lower shroud

runner

inner forestay

backstay

baby stay

As materials and designs progress, rigging and spars have become much lighter over the years without compromising their strength. This in itself must contribute to active security, as it makes today's boats more stable.

The distinction we have made between standing and running rigging is convenient, but should not deceive you.

For the rigging to function properly, neither its fixed nor its movable elements should be adjusted in isolation. It is all part of a single system, and should be treated accordingly. The mast and boom are not just a fixed frame on which to drape a mainsail. The frame they provide can change shape in a number of ways, some desirable and others imposed by the elements, which the crew must try to limit.

The problem is to suit spars and sails to each other so as to achieve a harmonious and efficient whole, which works in a wide range of winds and conditions on all points of sailing.

Before we start to study the different parts of the rigging, then, we need to know how the rigging as a unit functions, and to look at some of the ways in which it can be adjusted.

Different rigs

The aim of the rig designer is to allow the most efficient sail setting for the boat, its crew and its purpose, whether cruising or racing.

The preliminary questions one faces are:
— is the boat a monohull, a catamaran or a trimaran?
— is it made of flexible (eg plastic) material or very rigid material (eg moulded wood)?

– is the boat going to race at sea or inshore? Is it going to cruise in coastal waters or on the ocean?
– will it be sailed only in fair weather or does the crew like a bit of a blow?
– is it to be sailed single handed or by a pair of gorillas... ?

Technological progress, economic constraints and our increasing understanding of aerodynamics have all tended to push rig design in one direction over the last years: the sloop rig. There are variations within this basic plan:

– *masthead rigs,* so called because their jib is run up to the masthead. The mast is held rigid, and the sails have to adapt to this shape. This rig is appropriate for cruisers in which mast tuning is not an issue for the crew;
– *fractional rigs,* so called because the jib goes only five sixths or seven eighths of the way up the mast. The mast is flexible, and can be bent into the most useful shape for the sails and weather conditions on the day. This rig is most often used on small cruisers and dinghies. It is gradually finding favour with those sailing larger craft, particularly those who want high performance;

The *Glénan,* a masthead-rigged cutter.

A Coco-class fractional-rigged sloop.

Royale, a sloop with wing mast.

Côte d'Or, a sloop with four sets of spreaders.

Sinagot-class cruiser, unstayed mast.

Objectif 100, experimental rig.

– *self-supporting rigs* are rather complex. They can work with either rigid or flexible masts. They can be rotating, with bracing or stiffening supplied by spreadered stays fixed high up and low down on the mast. *Wing masts*, where the foil shape becomes part of the sail design, are self-supported, as they must also be able to rotate. This technique is also used with very tall, slender masts, such as that on a 12-metre yacht;

– finally, you will come across *unstayed* rigs. The mast is simply placed in a hole in the deck and held there. The Finn class or the OK are examples of this type. It has recently been extended to cruisers, such as the Freedom class, and, last of all, to the Sinagot, where even the jib is rigged on its own free-standing mast. Sailboards also come into this category.

There are various intermediate types of rig and some further subtle differences, but the above are the major distinctions necessary. The way in which the mast is held up determines its behaviour and most of the adjustments you can make to your boat's trim.

The first thing to make sure of is that the mast *is* held up.

Staying the mast

Principles

Imagine a radio mast held up by four stays. The mast is tall, but you can anchor the stays as far away from it as you want. The forces acting on the stays are of two types: the useful type is the horizontal component, which actually keeps the mast in place; the vertical

At rest, the mast is held up by all the stays together. When the wind blows, only the windward stays are under load. Vector a represents the horizontal vector necessary for holding the mast up. As the angle between mast and shrouds diminishes, so the compression loading on the mast (C1, C2, C3) increases, as does the tension needed on the shrouds, T1, T2, T3.

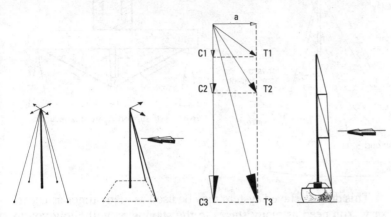

component is wasted and absorbed by the mast itself as a compression strain. When there is no wind, the four stays each bear the same horizontal force and the system is in equilibrium. When the wind does blow, a greater horizontal component will be exerted through the windward stay. This increased strain also increases the vertical component. The leeward stays, on the other hand, hang loose, doing no work.

Let us bring the anchorage of the windward stay closer in to the foot of the mast. As the angle between mast and stay reduces, the parallelogram of forces changes shape. In order to reach the same horizontal component, the tension on the windward stay and the compression on the mast both have to increase substantially. When the angle gets too small, these forces become excessive and either the stay snaps or the mast buckles.

A boat mast faces the same problem, except that you cannot put your stays anywhere you like on a boat, since the fixed platform is limited in size and you need some space for trimming the sails, etc.

Let us now look at what we need to do to hold a boat's mast upright.

Sideways support

A shroud at 10 or 13° to the mast would need to be fixed outside the boat, if we did not use spreaders to angle the shroud back in. The shroud does then exercise a compression force on the spreader itself, squeezing the mast inward at spreader height. For this reason, then, on many boats, an additional stay is placed with its anchorage on the mast at spreader height.

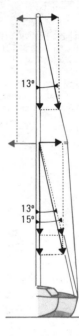

Do not be misled by the tall elegance of racing rigs: a cruising boat should have a fairly large angle (around 13°) between the mast and the shrouds. A lower shroud should come in at an even larger angle, and/or have a thicker wire section, since the lower shroud has to take up the added pressure from the spreader, as well as being only half way up the mast; there are significant sudden stresses at this height on the mast. You should be sure to check the rigging design when buying a cruiser.

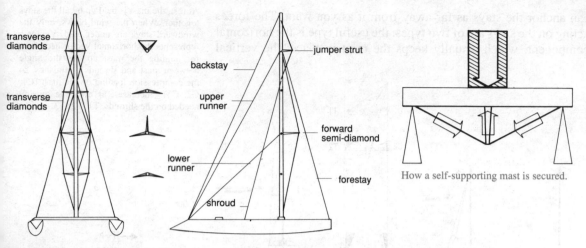

transverse diamonds

transverse diamonds

jumper strut

backstay

upper runner

forward semi-diamond

lower runner

forestay

shroud

How a self-supporting mast is secured.

This catamaran has a particularly thin mast supported by two shrouds swept well back and far apart, and a forestay. There are two sets of transverse diamonds, a semi-diamond forward and a jumper strut to keep the top of the mast steady. There is also a backstay and two running stays aft.

This double-stayed system may be used as many times as necessary. You need as many stages to the staying as will allow you to reach deck level with each stay held at an efficient angle to the mast. The final stays should be particularly strong, as they are subject to the greatest stresses. It is quite frequent for the lateral standing rigging to be designed narrower than the boat itself, to permit closer sheeting of the jib. The chain plates are then in the middle of the side deck rather than at the rail.

Self-supporting masts have made a reappearance recently. Instead of supporting the mast in a number of places, one needs only to support it with one set of stays swept wide apart. The mast needs to be very strong in order not to flex between the shroud fixings and the deck, or above the shroud fixings, so it is reinforced with diamond stays. In this system, the downwind stay holds the mast stiff through the spreaders pressing in on the mast.

Fore-and-aft support

It is more difficult to support a mast longitudinally than laterally, because one cannot add stays at will fore and aft. The most one can usually do is to set up a forestay to stop the mast falling back and a backstay which stops it falling forward. The mast is under a great deal of compression; the forestay needs to be kept in line, so the whole system of triangulation has to be rigid. For this reason, most masts are oval in section, so that the mast itself plays a part in resisting longitudinal bend.

Under some circumstances, lower-mast staying can be incorporated, with an extra inner forestay and aft runners (movable stays). One can also use a fore-and-aft self-supporting system with spreaders pointing in line with the centre of the boat – known as jumpers.

Rigid and bendy masts

These general principles of mast support are subject to variation, depending on how rigid or flexible you want your rig to be.

On many masthead-rigged boats, one's aim is to achieve a rigid mast which does not change shape whatever the point of sailing. In this case, you tune your rigging once and for all.

On other boats, particularly those with fractional rigs, one's aim is to let the mast bend, so that one can change its shape depending on the wind strength and the point of sailing. Under these circumstances, you need to be able to adjust the rig, though all parts of the rig – standing and running rigging as well as sails – play their part in the rig tune.

Again, we are talking in general principles here. One mast might be more or less rigid, another more or less flexible, or any point in between.

In any case, the problems of rig tune are most clearly dealt with when the boat is sailing to windward. We shall therefore examine windward rig tune in most detail, starting with the relatively simple case of the rigid rig.

Rig tune

Masthead rig

On boats with a masthead rig, the genoa is often very large indeed, and this automatically means you need a large-sectioned mast. The mainsail is in any case smaller, and slightly in the wind shadow of this large mast, so its efficiency is reduced. With this type of rig, one sets the mainsail up for the average course and then devotes one's attention to tuning the jib.

Tuning the mast

When we talk of mast tune, the first thing people think of is the mast *rake* (ie the degree to which it leans aft). This is in fact the second thing to worry about. First of all you should check that the mast is upright side-to-side, and straight.

For the jib to work effectively to windward, the forestay needs to be as tight as possible. The forestay will sag if the mast is allowed to bend. *The mast should be tuned afloat, when you are close-hauled*: this is the most demanding point of sailing for the rig.

Masthead sag

With a masthead rig, the forestay will remain taut so long as the mast is straight. If the mast is bent to begin with, it will bend more when it is under more compression. As the masthead sags, the forestay becomes slack; in turn, the jib fullness moves aft and you can no longer sail a good close-hauled course.

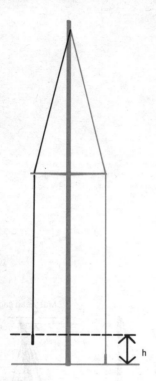

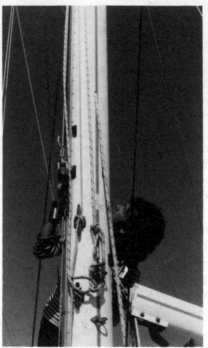

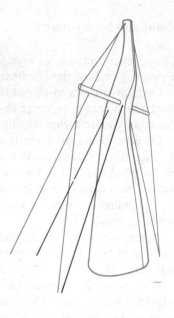

The only way you can spot small bends or distortions in the mast is by looking along the sail track.

The two shrouds should be the same length. If they are not, you should note the difference and compensate for that when tightening the bottlescrews.

Tightening the masthead rig in harbour

Adjust the mast rake approximately (or exactly if you have a way of measuring it). Tension the forestay to its maximum, using the backstay(s), even if you have a running tension-adjustment wheel. This is vital for the jib's close-hauled performance. Be careful, though, not to distort the hull, which is often less stiff than you might imagine.

Tension the bottlescrews, making sure the mast is not leaning to either side. This should be the case when the bottlescrews are turned equally far, so long as the two shrouds themselves are the same length. Check that the masthead stay fittings are in order. Adjust the lower shrouds so that the mast is more or less straight.

Adjusting the mast afloat

In order to get the tune right, you should be sailing quite hard, in a decent wind but without too much of a sea running. Ideally, this should be done in a force 3 or 4 wind, with no waves.

The tuning operation consists of adjusting the lower shrouds on the windward side to straighten the mast.

You are sailing close-hauled. One crew member stands at the foot of the mast, looking up the mast track and shouts out which shrouds need to be tightened or loosened. You should be adjusting only the fore-and-aft stays and the shrouds on the windward side.

The leeward stays should be slack.

Let us take as an example a rig with one set of spreaders and an inner forestay. The first thing to do is to check the overall rig tension. This is done by seeing that the lee shroud is slack without being positively loose. If you need to make any adjustments at this stage, adjust both sides together, and check that no irregularities are introduced in the process.

Next, you turn your attention to the lower shrouds. If the boat is on port tack and the mast is bent out forward and to starboard, you need to slacken off the inner forestay and tighten the port lower shroud to straighten it. Be sure not to tighten the windward shroud so much that the lee shroud also becomes tight.

When you have finished this phase, you tack and then do the same thing on starboard. If all you need to do to get the mast straight this time is to tighten the lower shroud, then you have finished. If, however, you needed to readjust the inner forestay, you will need a further tack onto port to check that the process is finished ... and so on until you are satisfied.

It may appear unnecessary to mention that no crew member should be hanging on to any part of the rigging while this procedure is going on ... otherwise you will have to start all over again.

The same process is required with two sets of spreaders. It takes a little longer, but it need be no more difficult.

In theory, your boat should sail well after just the above operation. If the mast is wrongly raked, however, it is only now that you will start to notice. If that is the case, start again.

Mast tune will always take at least an hour, and often four or five, particularly with a brand-new boat which is still stretching and adjusting itself to the pressures of life afloat.

There are several simple rules which should be borne in mind while you are carrying out these operations:
– do not touch the masthead rigging except to change the overall tension;
– aim to slacken off rather than tighten;
– ensure that the lee shrouds remain slack;
– keep your patience!

If the mast is well set up for the beat but not quite straight when you are running or at rest in harbour, don't worry.

It would be wrong to think that you have now tuned the rig for ever. Every time the mast is unstepped the rigging will have to find its position again. This takes more than just one day afloat. The hull changes shape slightly over time as well. It is well worth looking up the mast track regularly, just to make sure nothing has stretched or distorted over time.

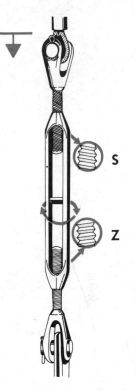

It is infuriating to try to adjust rigging if your bottlescrews are the wrong way up. It is the right way up when the bottom screw has a right-hand thread. You should be able to tighten the screw by turning the centre section clockwise.

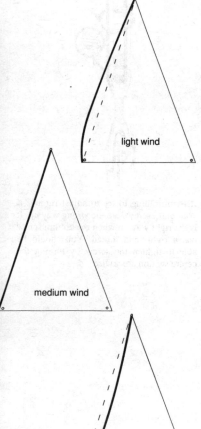

Three genoa jibs, cut for different wind strengths.

light wind

medium wind

heavy wind

Slackening the rig for downwind work
Some boats have a facility for slackening the forestay while sailing. This is usually accomplished by letting off the backstay using a control in the cockpit. You set up the initial mast tune as before, with the forestay taut, then you reduce the tension progressively as the course sailed goes further off the wind or as the wind speed drops.

Whenever you change your point of sailing or the wind strength changes, you need to check that the mast is still straight. So that the mast does not bend excessively off the wind, you might need to set up control lines to tighten the inner forestay or the lower shrouds.

When you come back onto a beat, the rig should return to its initial setting – but not further.

Adjusting the jib

The point of maximum fullness in a jib moves aft when the wind freshens: the cloth stretches a little, and the forestay becomes not quite straight. It is difficult to adjust the jib much, so the best solution is to change it for a jib with a different cut depending on the wind strength.

Choices
The three genoas in the diagram are all the same size and for the same boat:
– the light-wind genoa has a rounded luff, giving a very full sail when the forestay is straight;
– the medium-wind genoa has a straight luff; when the forestay sags slightly to leeward, the belly of the sail will remain in the right place;
– the genoa for heavy winds has a cutaway luff so that it will remain reasonably flat even when the forestay has a heavy sag.

Adjustments
Some jib luffs stretch more than others. If your luff wire does not stretch, you will need to change jib as the wind drops or increases. Some luffs can stretch by as much as 20cm, and the belly can be held forward in increasing wind to a certain point by increasing the luff tension.

Once the luff is tensioned to the last notch and the jib is still flogging, you do need to change it.

To reduce the strain temporarily without changing the jib, you can bring the jib sheet fairlead aft or upwards. This has the effect of freeing the jib leech, thus reducing the heeling moment while still keeping your speed up.

Adjusting the mainsail

When the wind freshens, you can flatten the mainsail by increasing the foot tension, and if necessary bending the boom with the kicking strap. Tightening the luff rope keeps the belly forward.

With a rigid mast, the only further way of flattening the sail is by taking in a reef. The reef not only reduces the area of the sail, but also reduces the belly.

Second and third reefs are intended primarily for reducing the area of the sail.

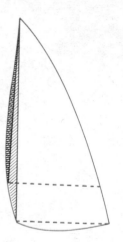

Fractional rig

With a fractionally rigged boat, the mainsail will be the more important, and the mast will bend more than in a masthead-rigged boat. A thin, bendy mast can ensure excellent windward performance, by reducing the air disturbance over the sail and bending to suit your sail shape needs, so that the boat has as much power as it can handle at any time.

The tuning of a fractional rig is the same for keelboats as for dinghies. As the wind freshens, you need to flatten the main by bending the mast; as it freshens further, you need to open the leech at the top, to keep the boat moving without too much heel. At the same time, you need to reduce forestay sag as much as possible to keep the jib pulling.

Just as in dinghies, the aim is to have a rig which will bend automatically into the best shape for the wind. On cruisers, one cannot take too many risks with materials, so that the active intervention of the crew is often preferable. A poorly adjusted bendy mast can have disastrous consequences: it breaks. Before you buy such a mast, it is important to know exactly what you are doing with it!

Adjusting the mast

Static tuning

With a very bendy mast, the lateral support usually comes from two or three sets of spreaders; the fore-and-aft support comes from a forestay and a backstay, with an inner forestay and two pairs of runners. All this fore-and-aft rigging can be adjusted.

Flexible rig with two sets of spreaders, twin backstays and an inner forestay.

When the boat is not being sailed, the mast is straight. It is generally raked fairly well aft, with the lower shrouds quite heavily tensioned, the intermediate shrouds moderately tensioned, and the upper shrouds fairly slack. The mast should be central in the axis of the boat, with each pair of shrouds adjusted to the same length (see the masthead rig for this adjustment).

Tuning afloat

We are tuning, as already noted, primarily for windward performance, and particularly for the beat.

The first adjustment to make is an approximate lateral trim. If there is not too much wind, the mast should be straight. In a fresh breeze, the top of the mast should fall away to windward slightly. If you need to adjust any of the shrouds at any height, be sure to adjust both to the same length.

Once lateral control of the mast has been established, we can turn our attention to longitudinal control. Except for the odd tweak, the side-to-side rig tune can be left alone from now on. The fore-and-aft tune, on the other hand, will be constantly adjusted.

Tuning the mainsail

As the wind freshens, the mainsail needs to be flattened. Initially, this is done by tensioning the foot and the luff. The next step is to introduce mast bend using the kicking strap and the mainsheet. However, as the mast bends, forestay tension is lost, so you need also to tension the upper runner to straighten the forestay. The upper runner meets the mast just above the forestay, so the mast bends more, and the mast bend is then kept modest lower down by the inner forestay and lower runner. The bend should be regular from top to bottom, or the mast can buckle.

As the breeze gets stronger, you can let the mast bend still more by tightening the kicking strap and the upper runner, and if

Given the importance of mast bend control, you might find it useful, to begin with, to take a thin fishing line attached to the top of the mast and led down to the mast foot. The line should be very tight. You can then read off the degree of bend against markings on the sail.

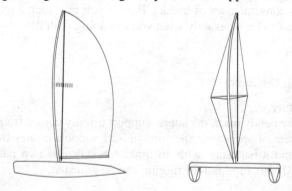

necessary slackening off the lower runner. This will flatten the main sufficiently for any wind until your third change of jib.

In a gust, the mast head will 'fall off' of its own accord, since the upper shrouds are fairly slack. This opens the leech at the top of the sail. You can open it still further by 'playing' the backstay. You tension the backstay in the gusts, pulling the mast head further back still, then let it off in the calm patches, to allow the sail to develop its full power. This keeps optimum power on at all times.

Once we stop sailing to windward, there is no further purpose served by having a flexible rig. You need to bring the mast back upright, with the forestay slacker, to ensure that the sails are nice and full.

Other rigs

Self-supporting rig

With this type of rig you can step a rotating mast or a very thin mast, whether rigid or bendy.

Before stepping the mast
The diamonds need to be adjusted before you step the mast. This is a question of strengthening the mast, which on its own would be insufficiently strong to keep its shape. The diamonds should be tight, but not like piano wire! Each pair should be matched for tension, so that the mast is straight. The longitudinal diamonds should be as tight as possible, without bending the mast. You can check the mast for lateral straightness by looking along the track.

In harbour
Check the rake and tension the forestay.

Under way
The final tuning is done at sea, close-hauled. If you have a bendy mast, follow the instructions for a fractional rig; for a rigid mast, tune as for a masthead rig. The only difference is that if you need to change the tune of the self-supporting part of the rig, you have to adjust the leeward shrouds. A curve to windward is corrected by slackening the leeward diamond.

Unstayed rigs

If there are no shrouds, everything depends on the quality and

Checking the standing rigging

It may be standing rigging at the moment, but can you be sure that it will still be standing at the end of the day?

Of course the best insurance policy is well-maintained rigging ... but regular checks should be made even so. On a cruising yacht, you should be checking the rigging every week or every fortnight, climbing up the mast some way and checking shrouds, pulleys and blocks, the state of the halyards and shackles, for any wear and tear. As an extra precaution, five minutes spent on your back each day with a pair of binoculars are an excellent investment. You should get into the habit of it, so that anything out of the ordinary is immediately apparent. If you make this inspection first thing in the morning, you can combine it with checking whether the night's manoeuvres have led to any tangled halyards aloft!

design of the mast. The only thing you can adjust is the sail shape, which has to be suited to the spars. These rigs behave similarly to fractional rigs.

Summary

The main difference between a rigid rig and a flexible rig is one of feel.

You can leave a rigid rig to look after itself for long periods. This is the rig for long calm passages, where your principal interest may be in admiring the scenery rather than demonstrating your stamina.

A flexible rig demands almost constant attention. This is the racer's solution, which gives you an optimum setting for any course and any conditions, so you can squeeze that last fiftieth of a knot out of your boat and crew. It will test the most obedient and enthusiastic crew's good humour.

It's a matter of taste; and you can find a middle way with either sort of rig, slackening off a backstay downwind or leaving the rig tight for a while as the lunch is prepared ...

The elements of a rig

Ropes and cables

Ropes and cables of some sort are involved with just about any activity on board a sailing boat, whether we are dealing with a shroud with a breaking strain of a couple of tonnes (sorry, a couple of thousand kilo-Newtons), or a reefing point made out of a shoelace.

The subject is worth spending some time on, and we shall look at all these cords, their uses and functions.

Cables

There are five basic types of commercially available metal cable designed for use on a boat. They are made up of varying numbers of strands: 1, 19, 49, 133 and 259.

Each type of cable has its uses and its disadvantages.

To take a slightly theoretical example, each of the following cables has the same amount of metal per metre, and thus the same strength:

– 8mm rod, 1 strand;
– 9.17mm wire, 19 x 1.84mm strands;
– 10.29mm shroud wire, 49 x 1.14mm strands;
– 10.41mm flexible wire, 133 x 0.69mm strands;
– 10.44mm superflexible wire, 259 x 0.5mm strands.

Each cable, though, is differently made up, of different thickness and with widely different uses. The finer the strands, the more flexible is the wire, the easier it frays and the more it stretches under load. The more strands there are in the wire, the fatter it is, so the more windage it causes. If, on the other hand, there are lots of strands, it's no great problem when one breaks.

Each cable thus has its own precise area of use.

As far as rigging is concerned, the five sorts of cable used are these:

• *Rod*, the simplest, which, as its name implies, is a single strand threaded at each end.

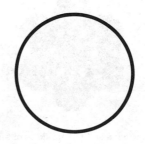

Rod

Use: Permanently fixed shrouds, such as diamonds, or side shrouds where the lee shroud remains taut. Usually racing use only.
Advantages: Smooth surface, small diameter, maximum aerodynamic efficiency for minimum sail wear.
Disadvantages: expensive and brittle, susceptible to vibration, bending and shock. If one strand goes, the race is over. It has to be stored straight or coiled in very wide coils (2m for 6mm cable). Difficult to check for fatigue.

• *Single-twist wire* is made up of 19 strands, twisted as follows: a single central core, with 6 strands twisted around the core and a further 12 twisted around them, either in the same direction or in the opposite direction: 1 + 6 + 12 = 19.

Single-twist wire with 1 + 6 + 12 = 19 strands, for straight applications only.

Use: Virtually any shroud on any type of boat.
Advantages: Best strength/price ratio. Fairly attractive appearance. Smooth, so little wear on sails; and relatively thin, thus low windage. Minimal stretch. If a strand breaks, you will be able to sail home under reduced sail.
Disadvantages: Weak point where it emerges from eyes/terminals. So long as you use this wire straight, it has no other disadvantages.

• *7 × 7 shroud wire* has 6 + 1 twists of 6 + 1 strands. Each twist is made up of a core strand plus six outside; one of the twists then serves as a core for the others.

7 x 7 shroud wire, made up of 6 + 1 twists of 6 + 1 strands.

Use: Traditional for shrouds, but single-twist wire is now more popular, except where the rigging needs frequent adjustment, as is the case with runners.
Advantages: Rather more flexible than single-strand, and thus less weak at the terminals. Stretches more under load.
Disadvantages: Rough surface, rather large diameter and comparatively expensive, as it is becoming less widespread.

• *Flexible wire* is made up of 6 plus 1 twists of 1 + 6 + 12 strands. Also known as 7 x 19.

Flexible wire, or 7 x 19, made up of 6 + 1 twists of 1 + 6 + 12 strands.

Use: Running rigging, especially used for halyards and other purposes where it must run over pulleys.
Advantages: Little stretch compared with rope; moderate price.
Disadvantages: Minimum radius of curvature quite large, c12. This means that the cable cannot run smoothly over blocks the radius of which is less than twelve times the diameter of the cable. An 8mm cable thus needs a sheave 192mm across. In practice, one can use

blocks only 60% of this size, but one loses so much strength this way (about 30%) that it is better simply to use smaller-diameter cable.

• *Super-flexible wire* consists of 6 + 1 twists of 1 + 6 + 12 + 18 strands. 8mm is the maximum diameter for this wire.

Use: For running rigging, where one cannot fit sufficiently large blocks for other wires; generally only used on very large yachts.
Advantages: This cable is so flexible that it can be used with a radius of curvature of 8, ie for 8mm cable, 64mm-radius blocks may be used. You can even use blocks only 60% of this size so long as the strength loss is not unacceptable.
Disadvantages: The strands are so thin that the wire frays extremely easily.

Super-flexible wire: 6 + 1 twists of 1 + 6 + 12 + 18 strands.

Wire breaking strains table

	Breaking strains of steel rigging wire (kilo-Newtons)								Elasticity	Curvature
Diameter (mm)	3	4	5	6	7	8	9	10		
Single-twist	8	14	22	30	41	53	-	83	127/147	-
7 x 7 shroud	5	9	14	22	-	35	-	61	88/110	-
Flexible	6	10	14	22	-	36	-	56	88/110	12

NB These figures are approximate. Refer to manufacturer for precise information.

– In order to choose the right wire for your rig, you need to know the elasticity, E. You can then tell by how much a wire will stretch (the stretch coefficient, A) under a given load, C. The formula is: A = C / E. Thus, a wire with elasticity 100 would stretch by 5% under a load of 50 kilo-Newtons.
– The curvature is the minimum figure by which you need to multiply the diameter of the wire to find the radius of a curve around which the wire is to bend, eg over a pulley sheave.

Types of metal

Galvanised steel has practically disappeared, due to its unattractive appearance and difficulty of upkeep. It is worth using galvanised steel for wires which run on winches, or wires which end in a fixed shackle, since it does resist rust better than stainless steel.

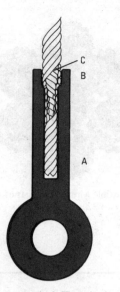

Clamp-on terminal. The wire is squeezed and held tight at A; at point B, the wire is fed through to prevent bending at the neck; and the neck, C, is rounded to prevent damage to the wire.

Stainless steel has conquered the world, it seems, despite its weakness when led round corners or scratched. Although it always looks good, it can hide defects as it ages.

Terminals and eyes

Before you can use a wire, you need some means of fixing it to the spars, hull, or other cords. There are different ways of doing this.

All terminals are expensive; however, saving money in this area is as shortsighted as trying to scrimp on the wire itself. In the end, it might cost you much much more ...

Threading
This is the solution for rod cables. You can screw whatever you like straight onto the rod, then fix it there permanently with a suitable cement glue.

Clamp-on terminal
This is a long stainless steel sleeve fitted over the end of a stainless wire. The wire is not bent, so this terminal may be used with single-twist wire. This is one of the best fixing methods for the ends of the standing rigging.

It has two shortcomings, both arising from the neck of the sleeve. The wire is so much more flexible than the sleeve that it can easily become permanently bent at this point. The wire can also be damaged as the sleeve is put on.

Screw-on terminals
This terminal is easy to put on using the tools you have on board, such as an adjustable wrench. For this reason you should carry a couple on board as spares. It is particularly suited for use on running rigging, and if you put the terminal on well, it will be just as reliable as any other.

Thimbles and ferrules
The wire is passed through a Talurit ferrule, or sleeve, and around a thimble. It is then led back into the ferrule, which is crimped in place. The technique produces a good strong fixing. In order to avoid corrosion, copper ferrules are used with stainless wire, and alloy ferrules with galvanised wire. This is the standard wire terminal for the running rigging.

Screw-on terminal.   Thimble.

Eyesplicing wire

A. Preparation: Bind the wire at the point where it must stop unravelling. Unravel it and cut out the central strand next to the binding. Form your eye and bring the unravelled end back down, two ends either side of the wire and two ends along it.

B. The far left end (1) passes under two twists of the wire, and the next left (2) under one twist, against the twist, ie right to left.

C. In the same way on the other side, the far right end (6) is passed under two twists and the next right (5) under one, with the twist.

D. Check: The ends should each poke out separately, one twist apart.

E. Pass ends 3 and 4 under their nearest twists, each in a different direction.

F. Now there should be an end sticking out of each slot, and the first wrap is complete.

G. Make two further full wraps, passing each end over the twist to its left and under the next twist. Keep the splice long by pulling the ends along the wire, not down. When you have finished each wrap, use a hammer to flatten the splice.

H. Three wraps are complete. A further two are done with the even-numbered ends only, passing under two twists at a time. The ends are then cut off flush with the wire and the splice is whipped.

NB The easiest material for binding is adhesive tape, such as insulating tape.

Wire-clamp.

Splicing

Splicing is an ancient craft, but one which is almost forgotten today, as it is costly in terms of time and care, needing to be finished off with whipping and protected against corrosion. It is only possible with 7 x 7 or more flexible wires.

It is not terribly difficult to eyesplice flexible wire if you keep referring to the pictures (or better still, to the photographs entitled 'Eyesplicing wire').

You will not always have time to splice wires. It is therefore useful to keep a few wire-clamps aboard, well greased and packed. U-clamps are the simplest to put on, though you do need two to be certain the wire will not slip. They cannot be put on without a ring spanner. (Open-ended spanners will not work.)

Stowing wire

You roll wire just as you would a garden hose or an electrical cable. If you have not got the space to roll the wire, you coil it, which means turning it as you form the loops (as you should with the garden hose, incidentally): a loop then a half-hitch, a loop then a half-hitch, and so on. The difference is that you absolutely cannot coil wire any other way.

When you need to use the wire, you unwind it (if you rolled it in in the first place) or uncoil it. If you make a wrong move, the wire will end up kinked, and should be thrown away.

Do be careful not to coil the wire too tightly: if you coil it too hard close to the terminal, the wire will not recover. And if you try to bend it back straight again it will break quite easily.

A wire is coiled by making first a loop then a half-hitch. The loop is just like coiling a rope, but is followed by a half-hitch, for which you need to turn your hand over.

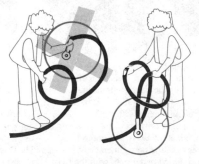

How to do it and how not to do it.

Cutting wire

As an elementary precaution, before you cut any wire, whip both parts either side of the cut with adhesive tape, or the wire will unravel in both directions.

You can cut wire:
– with a chisel, using the anchor as an anvil or chopping block. Cutting this way is easier if you heat the wire up to red hot 1cm either side of the cut;
– or with wire cutters, which you should be carrying on board anyway.

Ropes and sheets

Synthetic materials have now completely replaced natural fibres for marine ropes. Their major advantage is that they will not rot, though they are damaged by the ultraviolet rays of the sun.

It is quite possible to make good rope and bad rope out of the same material. Almost any rope will shrink by 5% or so of its length in the first year, while one made with inadequately stabilised fibres might lose as much as 15% of its length. This is 1.5m over a 10m rope, which is substantial! In general, the materials are seldom to blame: it is the manufacturing process which makes the difference, so it is as well to get to know which are the reputable makes. Price is not always a guarantee of quality.

Materials

The most frequently used materials are:
– polyamide (nylon): this barely stretches at all until it reaches 25% of its breaking strain, at which point it stretches a lot. Nylon is very susceptible to ultraviolet light;
– polyester (Terylene, Dacron): fairly high elasticity up to 25% of breaking strain, virtually nil thereafter. Not very susceptible to ultraviolet light; expensive; less strong than polyamide;
– polypropylene: low elasticity; very susceptible to ultraviolet light; cheap; much less strong than polyester;
– Kevlar deserves special attention, since it is currently very popular. Kevlar actually has a higher elastic limit than steel weight for weight. As its breaking point is very close to its elastic limit, it is recommended to buy Kevlar rope with a breaking strain 5 times the expected maximum load, as against 3 or 4 for steel. Despite this, in every respect except windage, Kevlar has to be seen as the best solution.

Twisted rope and plaited rope

Rope is made in any number of ways for different specific uses. The same material can produce ropes which differ widely in their strength, elasticity, chafe-resistance and resistance to UV light, depending on how it is used. For a long time twisted rope was the most widespread for most purposes, but it is now on the retreat, and plaited rope is being ever more widely used.

Twisted ropes are susceptible to chafe. Once the strands start to break, the rope begins to unravel and loses part of its strength all the way along its length. The rope is then useless very soon. If you do not whip, or bind, the end of the rope the same thing will start to happen. Even if you melt the twist ends together, you will find the same thing happens quite quickly. Twisted ropes do have two points in their favour, however: they are easy to splice; and they are stronger than plaited ropes.

Plaited or braided ropes come in all shapes and sizes. They tend these days to be of composite manufacture, with a central core (which may itself be plaited, twisted or bunched) of strong fibres, and a covering sheath layer. The outside layer is often made of different fibre, but its prime purposes are protection against chafing and ultraviolet light. There are also plaited hollow ropes with no core, which are very elastic; and plaited flat straps.

Plaiting has one major advantage, which is its resistance to chafing. A single broken strand does not ruin the whole rope. Admittedly you cannot splice a plaited rope, but you can sew it if needed. Talurit eyes and ferrules are becoming more widespread. Plaited straps can be sewn either by hand or with a sewing machine.

It is difficult to knot many synthetic ropes, especially if they are stiff and smooth. Many knots simply will not hold on such slippery material. However, matt-finish synthetic ropes are also available, which make for easier knotting and lighter work on the hands.

Radii of curvature

The minimum radius of curvature for a nylon or polyester rope is four times its diameter (thus, 12mm rope will run over a block with radius 48mm, say a diameter of 100mm). It can run through a tighter curve but it will be weakened and wear out more quickly. Rope does not suffer from over-bending so much as wire.

Kevlar is more vulnerable to over-bending than steel. It has to have a block with a radius at least six times the diameter of the rope (thus, a 72mm radius for 12mm rope). The same is true when choosing winch sizes, and you should aim for these values in your

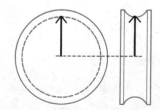

How to calculate the radius of curvature of a block or pulley.

mast sheaves, too. With Kevlar ropes, one should avoid the use of tubecleats or clamcleats. Any knots are to be avoided. If you are using Kevlar stays, get a specialist to fix the terminals.

Knots and ropecraft

In order for a rope to be useful on a boat, you need to be able to work on its ends to ensure that they link up solidly with other elements of the rigging. This section is to show a variety of ways of working ropes and cords.

Knots

There are so many knots, but it is sufficient to know a few of them and where and when they are to be used. Some can be tied and untied when the rope is under tension, others cannot. Some knots tighten over time and others are easy to undo at any time.

It is not enough to know your knots and how to use them. You have got to be quick at tying them. We must begin by tying them correctly.

We have chosen to illustrate only the most widely used knots. If you know them so well you can do them without thinking, these are all the knots you need for your voyage round the world.

Slip reef knot
Easy to undo in a hurry, but quite easily comes undone of its own accord. Useful only for reefing points and tying your shoes.

Reef knot
The only reason for illustrating this famous knot is to show how little use it is to the sailor. It either jams or comes undone.

Double sheet bend
For joining a thin rope and a thick rope. Make sure the double turn is made with the thinner rope.

Sheet bend
Use this in place of a reef knot. The sheet bend is to be used in joining two ropes. It does not jam and does not slip. It cannot be tied or untied when the ropes are under tension.

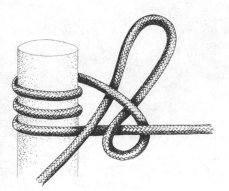

Round turn and two half-hitches
Very quick and easy to make. Used for tying up, eg to a jetty.

Slip half-hitch
Very useful. A few turns round a post allow you to stop a line escaping when the pull is too strong. The slip half-hitch can be tied and quickly slipped even when the rope is under tension. Used for towing and reefing.

Ring hitch
Simple and useful. This knot may be used for fixing a sheet to the bottom of a reefed sail, or to attach an anchor rope to the boss of the anchor. It is equally useful in the cabin for tying things temporarily to a handrail.

Double thumb knot
So difficult to untie that it has to be regarded as permanent, this is used for tying jib sheets to each other at the clew of a dinghy jib, or for tying fishing line back together again when you have had to cut it out of some entanglement.

Sewn eye
For a sewn eye, use thick double nylon thread and a size 15 needle or larger. It is practically impossible to sew through the whole rope, so you should aim to pass through a quarter of the rope with your stitches.

For a very neat finish, you can whip the sewn ends and seize them, as follows. Take a thick thread, and whip it round the joined pieces of rope, having jammed the free end under your first few turns. When you are two thirds of the way along, put a thin pencil or other obstacle in the way and continue whipping, but pulling less hard. Finish the whipping, then pull the pencil out and push your thread through the space. Finish by pulling these turns tight one by one and cutting the end off flush.

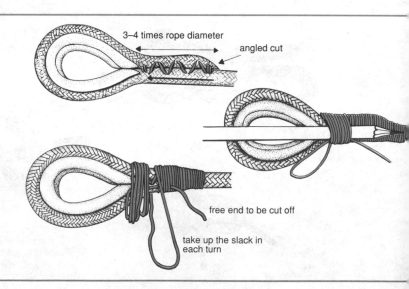

3–4 times rope diameter

angled cut

free end to be cut off

take up the slack in each turn

Eyes

You should always make an eye if you are going to need a permanent loop at the end of a cord, whether you splice it, sew it or clamp it.

Eye splice (twisted rope)

Hold the eye as in the picture. You need the black, left-hand end on top, and the blue, right-hand end underneath. Start by making an eye of the desired size, if necessary using a centre thimble.

A. First push the middle end through (pale blue).

B. Then the left-hand end (black).

C. Turn the eye round, so as to see the back. Now pass the blue end from right to left under the free twist. (This may appear to be going in the other direction from the first two.)

D. At this point, check the splice, pulling it tight. The blue end should be parallel to the twist to its right.

E. The three ends should be coming out of the rope at the same height, and at an angle of 120° to each other.

F. Continue the splice, passing each end from right to left over the first twist, then under the following one. To avoid making mistakes, work round the rope systematically to the left. Pull the splice tight after each tuck. Four tucks should hold well enough, but a really beautiful result can be obtained by making six tucks, with a few threads being taken out of each end to thin it down after the third tuck.

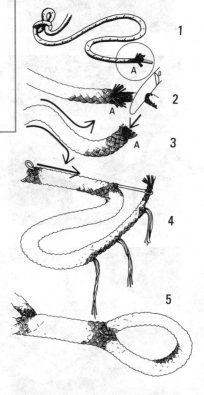

Simplified eye splice for plaited ropes over 9mm diameter, such as dinghy sheets

1. Knot the rope about 1.80m from the end. Slide the sheath back to reveal the central core.

2. Cut off 67cm of the core.

3. Put the sheath back *completely* in place, leaving 67cm of hollow sheath.

4. Push the needle into the rope about 68cm from the end, and push it back out again from the hollow sheath about 28cm up. Thin the sheath out so it will pass back inside, by cutting off 1 strand about 7cm from the end, 1 at 5cm and 1 at 2.5cm. Feed the sheath into the needle eye.

5. Pull the sheath back along inside rope. It will then fill the hollow sheath and finish the splice. Roll the rope between your hands to make sure all the fibres are in place.

Bear in mind that this splice weakens the rope substantially. It should only be used on dinghies.

Bowline

The bowline does not slip or jam and can be used with any rope. It can be used for mooring, tying on a ladder or fixing a rope to a ring. You should learn to do a bowline quickly in the dark. It is tied differently depending on whether the loop (the bight) is towards you or away from you.

Bight away from you.
1. Make a turn round the ring to stop it chafing, then an overhand knot.
2. Pull the free end towards you in your right hand, while releasing some tension from the fixed end with your left hand.
3. Pass the free end under the fixed rope ...
4. ... and back through the hole.

Bight towards you.
1. Take the free end in your right hand and cross it over the fixed end. Roll your hand over, to turn the cross upside down ...
2. You're most of the way there.
3. Pass the free end underneath the fixed part ...
4. ... and back through the hole.

1

1

1

2

3

1

2

3

2

3

4

2

3

4

4

4

Clove hitch

The clove hitch was never intended to be used on a post, but it is very quick, holds well if kept under tension and does not slip sideways. It enables a running line to be stopped extremely quickly. It should be used on posts where a bowline, for instance, might jump off. You can move the knot along the rope without untying it, but it does jam.

Tugman's hitch

This knot is ideal for towropes. It can be tied as the line is running out, and tied and undone under tension. It does not jam. The free end has to be at least 1m long, and wrapped round a cleat to be sure the rope does not run out.

1. The first half-hitch is made by making a loop over the free end.
2. From now on, you should already be able to stop a line running out.
3. A second half-hitch is made, the same as the first ...
4. ... and the knot is done! Be sure not to make a round turn before your first half-hitch, or the rope will jam very quickly.

1. A half-hitch stops the rope running out. Note: this should be a half-hitch and not a round turn, so that if the rope does start to run out at this point it will drop down the post and not flip up over the top.
2. Five or six more turns ensure that the rope will not slip.
3 and 4. Make the knot secure by slipping a loop over the post.

Cutting a cord with a hot knife.

Cutting and whipping ends

Ropes made with synthetic fibres should preferably be cut with a hot blade. You heat up a penknife blade then cut the rope with the back of the blade. This gives the strands time to melt and reseal themselves either side of the cut as you pass through the rope. Only the sheath of a Kevlar rope may be cut in this way as the Kevlar itself does not melt. Care should be taken not to heat the rope up as the knife is being heated.

Heat-sealed ends do not last long. It is best to finish the end with a whipping. In the case of composite ropes, whipping is absolutely necessary to hold the sheath and the core together.

When you cannot cut a rope with a hot blade for some reason, it is best to whip both sides of the proposed cut before making it.

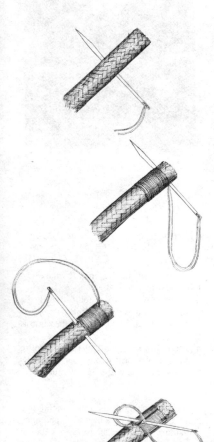

Whipping

Use a double-threaded nylon thread through a size 15 needle , or larger (say 14 or 14.5). Bring the thread through the rope, then wind it tightly round the rope for a length about equal to the thickness of the rope. Pull it through the rope again. Then seize the thread with three tight loops which pass over the whole whipping and about a third of the way through the rope. The seizing should be straight down a plaited rope, but slanted following the twist of a twisted rope.

To finish, make a half-hitch on the last seizing and bring the thread back through the rope at an angle before cutting it off flush.

An essential tool:
the hacksaw blade

Rather than ruining your knife, use a hacksaw blade for your hot cuts. There should always be a blade or two in your tool box. In fact, a hacksaw blade is such a useful item that you should have one always hanging up in easy reach. (One wonders whether that is actually what the hole is there for.)

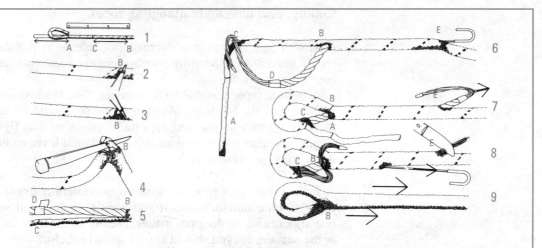

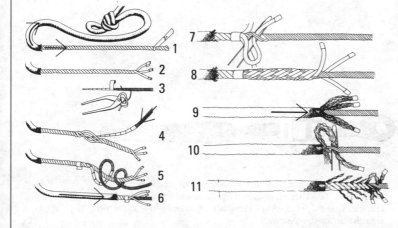

Spliced eye in plaited rope

1. Form the eye, mark point A. Measure 30cm, mark point B. Mark point C the same distance from B as point A is from the end of the rope.

2 and 3. Using a marlin spike, pull free four strands of rope at point B.

4. ... so that you can see the core of the rope through the hole.

5. Pull the core out completely and mark point D on the core with sticky tape, level with point C on the sheath.

6. Push the special needle, eye first, into the rope at point E, 28cm from B. Push it all the way to C between core and sheath. Having cut off half the core strands from D onwards, you can thread the core through the eye.

7. Pull the core back along the rope until there are only 2cm of core showing.

8. The final part of the operation is to bring the sheath back inside in the same way. Unravel the final 5cm of the sheath, cut off half the strands, then tape the tip. Insert your needle, eye first, about 13cm from the centre of the eye, on the opposite side of the rope from point E; slide the needle along between core and sheath. Thread the taped sheath strands through the needle, then pull the sheath back inside the rope. When the end shows, pull the sheath and the core separately through, keeping the eye in shape. Cut the ends.

9. Roll the rope in your hands, starting at the eye end, to smooth bumps and take the cut ends past the holes in the sheath.

Splicing plaited rope to wire

1 and 2. Tie a knot 1.80m along the rope to stop the sheath slipping back down the rope. Push the sheath back to expose 1.20m of the core. Cut off 15cm of the core. Tape the three ends of the core strands.

3. Cut strands off the wire progressively further back from the tip, about 22cm, to taper the wire. Tape the end.

4. 75cm from the end of the rope, twist the core twists apart and insert the wire end.

5. Tape the wire and the rope core together and manoeuvre the wire inside the core working back until you reach 20cm from the end of the rope.

6. Slide the sheath back over the core and the tape.

You now splice the three twists of the rope core into the wire (7), taking two wire twists per tuck. Make three complete tucks (8). For the fourth and fifth tucks, thin the core twists by cutting off a few strands (9).

Next, you whip the sheath at the point where your core splice stops. Then you unravel the sheath strands from each other, divide them into three equal bunches and tape these. These new twists then need to be spliced into the wire (10) *in the same direction*, so as to cover the wire up for a length.

In each of the final three tucks, separate out a few of the strands from each bunch, to taper the splice. Cut off the loose ends and your splice is complete.

Coiling, uncoiling and untangling ropes

A tangled rope does as much damage to the rope as it does to the crew's nerves. It is therefore worth spending some time learning how to coil correctly.

A twisted rope should always be coiled clockwise, since this is also the way the twists go. At each turn, you should let the rope twist over gently so you end up with loops rather than figures of eight. Even after you have done this, you should leave an end free so the rope can untwist itself.

In the same way, a rope should be uncoiled starting from its fixed end, this time anticlockwise. If you want to undo a coil which is free at both ends, it does not matter whether you start at the inside or the outside, but you should always uncoil anticlockwise.

If a rope is still kinked despite your care, you should be sure to straighten the whole rope out before you try using it.

Plaited ropes may be coiled in either direction. However, they should always be uncoiled in the opposite direction to the way they were coiled. It is convention that they are coiled the same way as twisted ropes. Start at the fixed end, as before, so that the free end can unwind itself.

As soon as any rope gets tangled, knots seem to start to multiply mysteriously. In fact, these are not knots at all, just kinks and twists. You just have to pull them apart without touching the ends, otherwise you will start making them into real tangles.

Kevlar standing rigging has screw-on terminals like those used for steel wires. These terminals should be attached by a professional. One can find the same sort of terminals for running rigging, which are suitable for self-assembly.

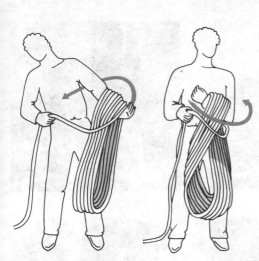

If you have a large coil and short arms ... turn the coil round.

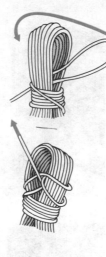

Finish it off with a few turns as above to keep it from getting tangled up.

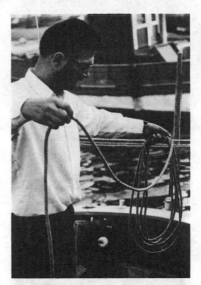

Coil rope clockwise. With each loop, turn the rope over a half turn, holding it between thumb and forefinger. This should prevent it forming figures of eight. When you need to stow a coil, make a few turns around it with the free end, then pass the end back through the coil.

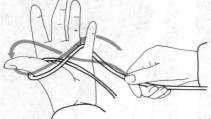

Coiling string. Make figures of eight around your thumb and little finger. Finish off with a few turns around the hank.

When you are untangling a rope, pass it doubled through the 'knots'. This will ensure that you do not make new knots.

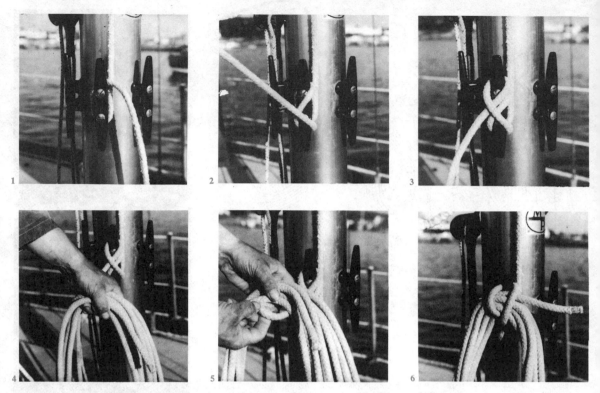

Cleating a halyard and stowing the free end: Turn the halyard round the cleat in the usual way: 1. a round turn; 2. a half figure of eight; 3. a half-hitch. Do not let the free end obstruct the working area: 4. coil it; 5. put your hand through the coil and pull a small loop of the halyard which is close to the cleat back towards you; 6. fit the loop over the top of the cleat and pull it firm.

Cleating a sheet: One round turn, a figure of eight and another round turn. Occasionally, one more figure of eight and another round turn. Never use a half-hitch to cleat a sheet.

Bits of string

It would be unfair to conclude a section on ropes and cables without an honourable mention for the seafarer's trusty friend, the spare bit of string. How many times has it saved your glasses, your dinner, your reefs and even the sails themselves? The hemp and cotton strings of yesteryear have been chased from their place by the products of international chemical research; yet it is still true that the more bits of string you have, and the greater variety, the more unexpected occasions you will be able to deal with calmly and capably.

Fittings

There is an infinite variety of gadgets under the general term 'fittings'. We could spend pages describing these gadgets, and be out of date by the time we finished, because new ones are appearing daily. One can spend a lot of money on some of these goodies, and just as much on a lot of the less good ones.

For this reason we are going to limit ourselves deliberately to a short list of the principal types of fittings; their use will be described as they are brought into play. The fittings will be grouped by purpose. The purposes, of course, existed long before the items themselves.

Shroud tangs and chainplates

Tang fittings
This is the commonest form of fixing. The bolts need to be washered or even cemented in place with Loctite or a similar product, and nuts or clevis pins need to be moused to be really safe.

To prevent your halyards becoming slack when the sail is not in use, you can rig up an arrangement as shown. Place the sail-head snap-shackle about 1m above the cleat, then take a round turn around the cleat and feed the free end through the shackle before making it fast finally round the cleat.

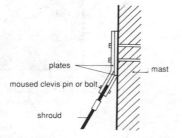

plates

mast

moused clevis pin or bolt

shroud

Tang fittings.

40°

screw-in eye

Avoid subjecting screw-in eyes and U-
clamps to any prolonged tension at a
greater angle than that shown by the
cone.

Chainplates
The traditional chainplate needs the shroud to be secured by a
moused pin.

U-clamps
Very convenient, but to be avoided for shrouds, since it is not very
strong if subjected to shear force at more than 20° to the axis of the
screws.

Screw-in eyes
Again, convenient, but not very strong. Avoid shear forces at more
than 20°.

Hook-in fittings
Very reliable, except that the connection between the mounting and
the mast needs to be inspected closely. (See section on spars.)

Chainplates do wear out, and it is difficult to spot wear. Just occasionally, measure the thickness of the load-bearing metal to check
that it is at least as strong as the wire.

In order to join permanently wires to plates, or wires to wires, use
fixings which cannot be knocked out of place, or moused pins. Do
not use split rings to mouse your clevis pins, as these bend and catch
any moving ropes and wires. Use only split pins.

You should not put your trust in fittings which have been screwed
into place, unless there is a nut on the end or a mouse through the
thread. Do not use shackles for standing rigging. They are not strong
enough.

U-clamp

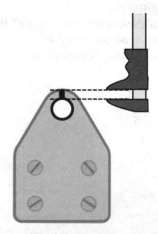

Calculating the strength of a chainplate:
Section = height × width
Strength = section × breaking strain
(Stainless steel has a breaking strain of
40–60kg/mm²)

Shroud adjustments

Closed bottlescrew
The most attractive device, but difficult to secure in place unless the throat is slotted or there is a hole in the centre for passing wire through.

Open bottlescrew
Less attractive, but easier to secure and easier to check the screw threading.

Adjusters with handles
One can find screws with an external handle, which are particularly useful for stays which need frequent adjustment, such as the backstay. One can even find tensioners which operate on hydraulic pressure, rather like a pump-up car jack.

Locking the screws
Your bottlescrews need to be locked to stop them coming undone as you are sailing. *Do not use locknuts for this purpose, as they do not work.*

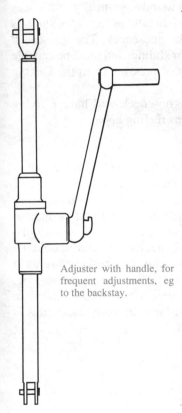

Adjuster with handle, for frequent adjustments, eg to the backstay.

> **Calculating the breaking strain of a bottlescrew**
> The breaking strain equals: The breaking strain of the metal (60–80kg/mm² for steel) x π x $(d - 1.3t)^2$, where d = the nominal diameter of the screw, and t = the thread thickness.

Note: a stainless steel screw can easily stick if you attempt to adjust it while it is under tension. Use graphite or molybdenum bisulphide grease.

Plates with holes in
This venerable method is certainly the simplest available, and it will not let you down. It is very hard to adjust, however, and its use is not recommended if an alternative is available.

Threaded cord
An extremely simple solution is to make a quadruple-purchase

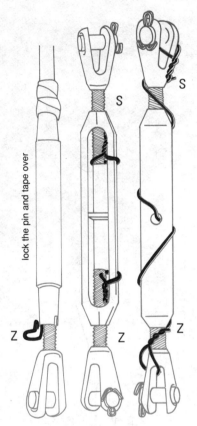

lock the pin and tape over

The bottlescrews need to be locked so they do not come loose when you are sailing. Locknuts are widely used, but they are not secure, and there are better ways of locking the screws:
– pins which sit in a slot on the bottle throat and lock into the screw thread;
– a mouse which is bent round with pliers, for open bottlescrews;
– a simple brass/copper/steel/nylon wire wrapped round and led through the hole in the middle.
A bottlescrew needs to be secured by one of these means as well as using locknuts.

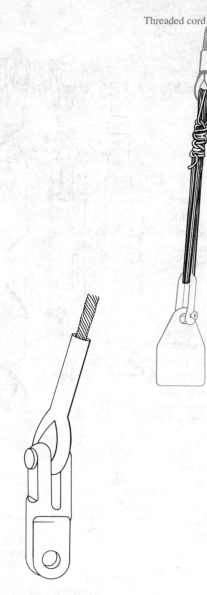

Threaded cord.

Toggle.

attachment by threading nylon cord four times up and down through the eye and the chainplate. Four thicknesses of 4mm nylon are as strong as 3mm steel wire. This arrangement is recommended if you are aiming for some stretch in the system.

Universal joints and goosenecks

The gooseneck is a universal joint allowing the boom to move both horizontally and vertically. The boom should be able to move vertically through as much as 50°, and horizontally as far as the shrouds without damaging the gooseneck. The gooseneck may be either fixed or sliding, and must be capable of withstanding a lot of pressure from the kicking strap.

A good cruising gooseneck will have a fixing point for the tack, plus reefing hooks.

Toggles

A toggle is a necessary fitting between the bottle-screw and the chainplate, to allow some articulation. Otherwise, damage would be caused every time someone held onto the shroud a bit too hard or if you hit the jetty or another boat a bit awkwardly. A bent toggle has done its job and should be thrown away. Toggles can also be very useful at each end of the forestay, if you have a flexible rig, to take some of the strain which would otherwise be borne by the mast tang. In many cases, this is

If the boom can pivot in all directions, it is subject to much lesser forces and can therefore be made of lighter material.

where the forestay will end up breaking.

Tiller extension
This is virtually a necessity to be able to steer correctly and comfortably.

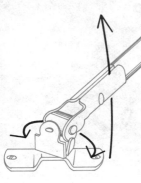

Tiller extension joint.

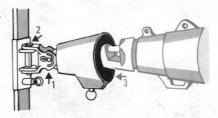

Spinnaker boom cup fitting.
1. Vertical articulation.
2. Horizontal articulation.
3. Fixing clip.
Three quite separate functions.

Spinnaker boom ends
With a symmetrical, or double-ended pole, both ends are the same. If the pole is asymmetrical, one end is designed to fit on the mast, and the other to catch the spinnaker guy.

In either case, the mast attachment fitting must be sufficient to allow 180° of horizontal movement and at least 90° of vertical movement. On smaller boats, up to 5m length, the fitting will usually consist of an eye on the mast and a clip on the boom.

On larger boats, such an arrangement is insufficient. The functions of fixing the boom and allowing it to rotate have to be separated. You will then find a real gooseneck fitting on the mast rather than a simple eye. The cup system works well for securing the boom end, particularly as it reduces the chances of the boom twisting.

The other end of the pole has a clip or a snap-fastening which can be opened at a distance, for the spinnaker guy to run through. It will also have an uphaul and downhaul fitting. Some older designs have a hook for fitting through the spinnaker tack eye. This is an unsafe arrangement, as it can make it very difficult to detach the pole from the sail.

Swivels
Swivels eliminate torsion and are therefore vital in all sorts of places. You will find them incorporated in shackles, pulleys, etc.

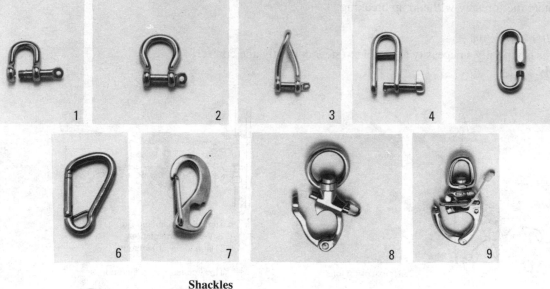

Shackles

1. D shackle.
2. Harp shackle.
3. Half-turn shackle.
4. Long safety shackle with key closure.
5. Screw shackle/karabiner.
6. Sprung safety snapshackle. Useless if the spring breaks. Oil weekly.
7. Jib snap-shackle.
8. Swivel snap-shackle for halyards.
9. Swivel remote-release snap-shackle. Good with the string, better without: then it can only be opened with a splicing knife, levered under the crossbar.
10. S-ring. Cheap, simple, and particularly useful for discouraging petty thieves if you squeeze the ends together in a vice.

If the bar of your shackle bends, you need a stronger shackle. A bent snap-shackle can be straightened, however, and will work better with a drop of oil.

Pulleys

Nylon and similar plastic sheaves change shape slightly if subjected to constant pressure in the same direction. After a while they will not rotate ...

Steel wires can melt Tufnol sheaves if they are pulled through very fast or under heavy loading.

Steel sheaves will survive everything, but they are often too heavy to be used with sheets.

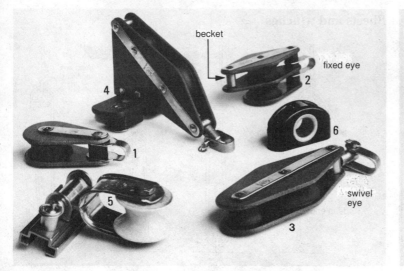

Better still, but dearer too: an openable block with a swivel snap-shackle.

1. Single block (with fixed eye).

2. Double block with becket and fixed eye. The fixed end of the mainsheet is attached to the becket. For this block to work properly, the sheaves need to be turning together, but since they are often bearing different loads, the block tends to skew.

3. Swivel block. The swivel eye allows the block to align itself with the rope. With the rope pulling only in one direction, the block does not skew. If there are two sheaves, they must turn in the same direction.

4. Swivel block with built-in jamming cleat.

5. Roller fairlead. This thumps the deck less than normal blocks, and brings the sheet down to deck level. When it is put on its track, care should be taken that the stopper is forward of the block, so that the sheet does not chafe on it and you can move the fairlead when the sheet is under tension. If you use a split ring, rather than a pin, to secure the stopper, the ring will get lost. You should be able to fit two sheets through your roller fairleads simultaneously.

6. Fairlead. Does not bash the deck like a block, but does cause significant friction.

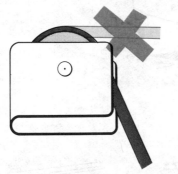

The rope must meet the pulley at a point where the pulley is enclosed, or it will jump off. There should be no more play between the sheave and its housing than a third of the width of the rope. If the sheave is distorted, it will not rotate, however much you lubricate it.

If a sheave squeaks, oil it.

A B C

A. A rope wears less if it fits the sheave correctly.

B. This sheave has too small a diameter for wires and it will ruin your ropes.

C. The ideal sheave for Kevlar ropes is one which allows the rope to flatten as it runs through.

A: *Double-purchase sheet*. Excluding friction, this arrangement uses half the effort of a simple downward pull. It requires 1m of rope to be pulled in to bring the boom down by 50cm.

B: *Triple-purchase sheet*. One third of the effort. Pulling 1m of rope brings the boom in by 33cm.

C: *Combination sheet*. The middle block is mounted on a block leading to a dead end. This gives a six-times mechanical advantage (3 x 2), but you have to pull in a lot of sheet.

D: A mainsheet cannot be rigged up just any way. In order to gain maximum efficiency, you need to be pulling in the desired direction of travel of the boom. If, as here, you pull upward to bring the boom down, you lose one part of your mechanical advanage. This is a two-part purchase system, although it looks more.

When threading a mainsheet, you always start by threading the dead end (the one which will be tied) through the blocks, so as not to have to pull the whole length of rope through each block. In the case illustrated, then, it goes forward from the cockpit, back over the forward boom pulley, back again through the traveller block, forward over the aft boom pulley and is then made fast on the traveller block becket.

Winch. This piece of equipment performs many of the functions of a block-and-tackle. It gives a mechanical advantage which is the length of the handle over the radius of the winch drum. One can buy variable-speed winches where a switch or internal gearing allows one to choose levels of purchase. Most winches revolve clockwise.

A self-tailing winch cleats the sheet progressively as it is wound in. This frees both hands for use on the handle.

Sheets and winches

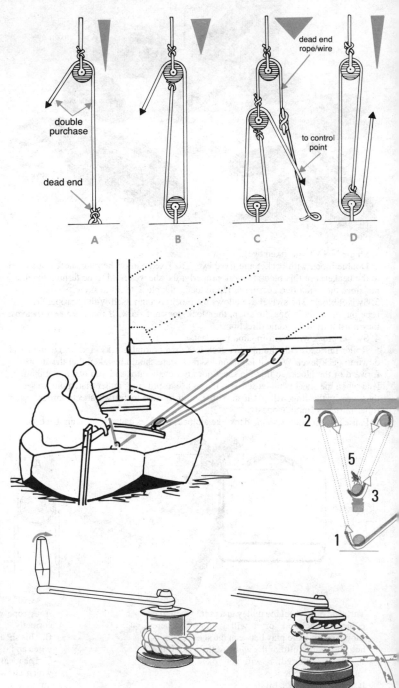

Cleats

6. Quick-release clamcleat. Can be released while under tension. Compulsory for multi-hull sheets.

6

1. The classic cleat, suitable for virtually any use.

2 and 3. Cleats which hold the rope firm after the first turn. No 2 is for halyards and No 3 for sheets.

4. Jamming cleat. The most widely used sort of cleat for sheets. If in doubt, buy a large size, because this design does not stand up to very large strains. It can jam if sand gets into the mechanism. Do not use grease, as it retains the sand. Use oil.

5. Clamcleat. This was invented by a genius. No moving parts to go wrong, cleats beautifully and does not cost much. Minus points: It allows some slack back into the rope after cleating (about 5mm) so is not suitable for halyards. It will catch any rope of the right diameter, including the ones you did not want cleated. It wears out fairly quickly, particularly if made of plastic.

All cleats should be glued in place as well as screwed or bolted.

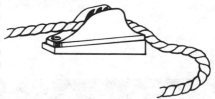

A clamcleat correctly mounted, so that the rope can drop down on the after side.

Clutch stopper (spinlock jammer). Some of these can be released while the rope they are holding is under tension. Others cannot. Check before you buy.

Tracks

Three sorts of track are used, depending on the conditions under which you need to slide equipment along the track:
– metal-on-metal, for occasional adjustments under zero load;
– metal-on-plastic, especially Teflon, for frequent sliding under small loads;
– runners and bearings, where the slide will bear major loads.

Mainsheet traveller

This track is known as a traveller, although it is actually the track along which the travelling is done. The mainsheet block slides along the track, and can be stopped at any point.

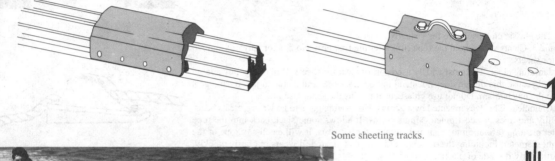

Some sheeting tracks.

Mainsheet traveller track.

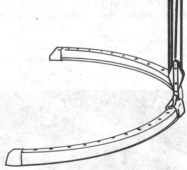

Multihull kicking-strap or mainsheet traveller.

Depending on the type of truck used on the tracking, it will have different sections. So long as the traveller track is not subject to enormous loads, a simple slide is quite adequate, perhaps with Teflon inserts.

If the traveller is going to come under considerable load, one will need a truck equipped with multiple roller bearings.

Jibsheet fairlead tracks
The jib fairlead block will generally be a roller type, which can be moved to a limited extent along a track screwed onto the side decking. The screws should be strong, close together, and the deck reinforced, since there will be considerable vertical forces acting on the track. Metal-on-metal runners are adequate, since you will not usually need to move the fairlead under load.

Roller-reefing

With a roller, one can reef the sails extremely precisely, even reducing the effective sail area to zero, without leaving the cockpit.

There are three roller types:

– the jib roller, which has been around longest and is now fairly well perfected. The roller is rigged on the forestay;
– the mast roller, for rolling up the mainsail around the luff, either inside the mast or outside;
– the boom roller, for rolling the mainsail around the foot, generally inside the boom itself.

A roller-reefing system needs to have some sort of mechanism also for taking some of the bag out of the sail, and needs to be adjusted for the sail you are using; otherwise, the results can be disappointing. Although rollers are very convenient, they cannot satisfactorily be used with very full sails. At the current stage of development mainsail roller reefing systems tend to be heavy, bulky and unreliable, but development is fast ...

The genoa jib roller is already pretty fully developed, and we should look at it in some detail.

The only major problem is that if the roller does get damaged, it could be difficult to roll the genoa up or pull it down. For this reason you should pay particular attention to the following rules of use:

– keep the forestay well tensioned, so as to be sure the roller tube does not swing from side to side and knock one or other part out of alignment. If this happens, you will not be able to roll the sail any further or pull it down, as the sail track will not be straight;

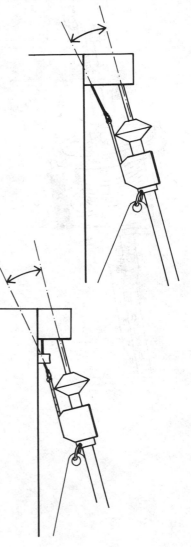

Make sure that the halyard and the roller are not in contact: keep the forestay and the halyard at a slight angle.

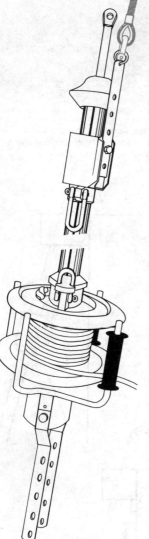

Jib roller mechanism.

– keep the halyard and the roller mechanism well apart so that the halyard does not get rolled round the forestay. If this happens, the sail is stuck;

– ensure the control line leading to the roller drum has a clear route from the cockpit, otherwise the friction in the system is too great. You will almost certainly need a winch anyway;

– buy a roller with stainless-steel ball bearings;

– protect the furled sail against ultraviolet rays by adding a protective or sacrificial strip on the leech (see p325);

– make sure the spinnaker pole does not bash against the forestay on any occasion, or the roller will get damaged;

– make sure you have the manual and correct tools with you at all times, so that you can fix the roller or at the very least take the sail down in an emergency;

– ensure that you are equipped at least to hoist a storm jib in case of breakage.

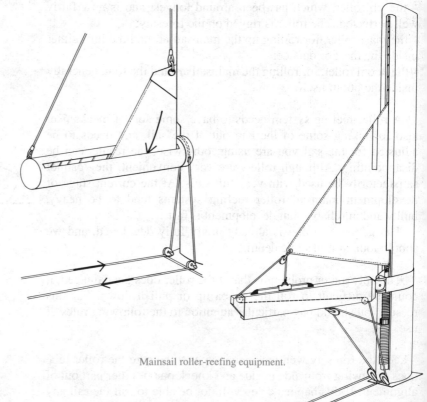

Mainsail roller-reefing equipment.

Gear: selection and maintenance

There is an infinite variety of types of gear, and new models and designs appear weekly for most of the jobs which need to be done.

Bear at least the following criteria in mind when choosing:
– is it strong?
– is it reliable?
– is it light?
– is it inexpensive?
– is it designed for the job you have in mind?
– is it easy to maintain?
– does it work with the rest of your equipment?
– can it cope with the likely conditions of use?
– is the supplier well known and well distributed, nationally and internationally?

It might be made of stainless steel, aluminium alloy, bronze, or plastic (Tufnol, Delrin or Duratron).

Do not forget the likelihood of electrolytic action and corrosion, especially if you have copper items touching aluminium. It is always prudent to put a thin plastic film between any two metal surfaces. Also be careful with carbon-fibre hulls. Plastics can be used next to virtually any other material.

If it is to work well, gear must be put to the use for which it was designed. If you use a ring or a screw for a purpose which it was not intended to fulfil, it does not matter how heavy or large it is, you are increasing the likelihood of some gear failure. Size in itself is no sort of guarantee of safety: a super-heavy block attached to your boom will smash itself and the boom to pieces gradually, every time you go about. If something has been built light, it is often because the materials are very strong.

The simpler your equipment, the more reliable it will be, and the easier to fix if it goes wrong. If you use fancy gear, you will need appropriate tools, spare parts and diagrams of the insides. And you will still need a potential jury-rigged solution: just because you are mending the halyard winch does not mean you can survive without the mainsail for long …

Lubrication

Take a pinch of sand, mix with plenty of salt water and a fingerful of axle grease … and you've made a lethal cocktail for any marine equipment.

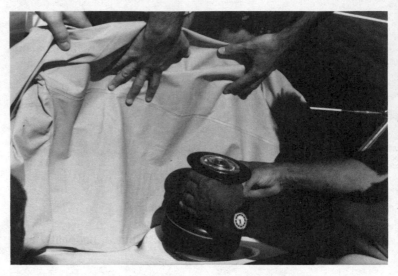

When you take a winch apart, you should have a cloth over the top (not shown) and one underneath, to catch the springs, etc, which will fly out in all directions!

Forget about tallow, axle grease and other 'traditional' products. They will pick up sand and grit, and almost certainly emulsify in salt water.

The accepted solution these days is to use light lubricating oil. Since this does not last long, you need to oil fairly frequently, say, once a fortnight, in small quantities.

Greases used on gear which is not in the open air (such as the inside of winches, or shroud toggles), should be those with solid lubricant bases, such as molybdenum sulphide. Grease lightly, once a year, having cleaned off the old grease first.

Slide runners should be lubricated with silicon grease, unless the sliding surface is plastic, in which case cleaning with paraffin is more effective.

De-ruster is an extremely useful item to have on board, just in case you are a bit late getting to any item with your oil can. Careful, though: even though the de-ruster might be called oil, it is not a good lubricant and should not be used as such.

Repairs

There is not much you can do afloat unless you have the spare parts and diagrams of how the broken equipment works. One absolute rule: you should never carry out repair work except inside the cabin. If you must work in the cockpit, bung up all the drain holes and spread a net or cloth underneath any part which might fall, spring off or otherwise escape, such as the ratchet mechanism of a winch. This precaution should even be taken when the boat is in port.

Spars

Metal spars

These days almost all spars are made of metal. Most are in some sort of aluminium/magnesium alloy (for instance, AG4 is aluminium with 4% of magnesium), with the addition of a little manganese and chromium.

Masts are also made in titanium, but so far only experimentally.

Most AG spars are extruded, ie they are produced as constant-thickness tubes. They are then tapered to produce different bend characteristics, reduce weight and improve the aerodynamic shape high up.

Masts are also manufactured from specially cut panels, which are welded together. This technique is used only for very big masts or highly specialised racing yacht masts.

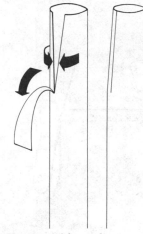

How a mast is tapered.

Construction

The maximum length of one section is generally 15m or less, for reasons of price and transport. Longer masts are generally made in two sections which are either welded together or sleeved.

Sleeving is done by joining the two sections together and attaching both to an inside sleeve of slightly smaller section. This sleeve is riveted or bolted to the two outside pieces, as well as being stuck with epoxy glue such as Araldite, to ensure there is absolutely no movement to hinder the smooth sliding of the main luff in the track.

Welding as a means of fixing mast sections together is becoming more widespread, but only specialists can carry out this type of welding. It is widely used in mast repairs.

Maintenance

Light alloy masts need little upkeep, especially if they are anodised, which is usually the case. Anodising is a surface treatment carried out in the factory which more or

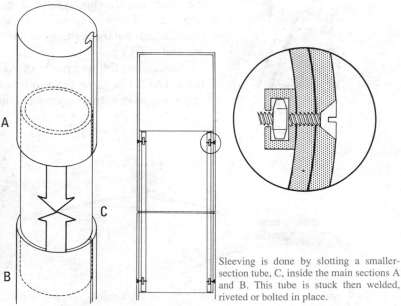

Sleeving is done by slotting a smaller-section tube, C, inside the main sections A and B. This tube is stuck then welded, riveted or bolted in place.

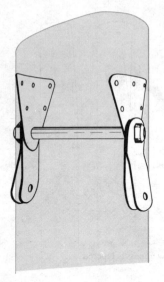

less prevents surface oxidation taking place. The anodisation is broken at those points where the mast has been worked, welded or just scratched. It is also broken by electrolytic action. For that reason, the less work you do on your spars, the better. Try to protect them from unnecessary wear and electrolysis. Non-anodised spars need to be painted, as do aluminium hulls.

Wherever possible, one aims to leave the mast in place even when the boat is laid up over the winter. The running rigging should then be removed so it does not cause surface wear by banging against the mast.

If you do need to take the mast down, the main precaution you can take is to ensure that it is not in contact with copper, brass or bronze during storage.

Mast fixtures
You do need to watch out for electrolytic effects with alloy masts. We shall spend more time on this topic with metal hulls. The main point to make at this stage is that one needs to choose fixtures carefully for AG masts. Copper compounds are not usable. Steel can be used, but one should aim to insulate the two metals by the insertion of a plastic sheet.

It is easier to mount fixtures on a metal mast than on a wooden mast. You can use bolts, pop-rivets or tapped screws.

Some boatyards use self-tapping screws. These look like wood-screws, and one is supposed to be able to screw them straight into the sheet metal. This system is extremely cheap and extremely unreliable. There is usually galvanic action between screw and mast, which enlarges the hole. Get rid of them and use a proper method of fixing.

Sometimes, fixtures made of AG are welded straight onto the mast. Welds like these need to be carried out by specialists, in the same way as structural mast-welding does. Since masts are hollow,

Ways of attaching mast fittings.

No entry: the self-tapping screw.

halyards can be run down inside the mast and shrouds anchored inside the mast, thus reducing windage.

Composite spars

Only competitive racing yachts and sailboards have composite or glass-fibre masts. The wing masts of some multihulls are of composite construction.

Wooden spars

Wood is the traditional material for spars, but it is hardly used at all these days. Still, for the traditionalists among us – who seem to be growing in number – we should spend some time looking at the maintenance and repair of wooden spars.

Maintenance

Wooden masts are usually varnished rather than painted, for aesthetic reasons. You will need to put five to seven coats of varnish on each winter to ensure the mast makes it through the rest of the year without the water penetrating. Make sure the head and foot of the mast are well impregnated with varnish, or the water will creep along the grain, leading to rotten wood and loss of adhesion.

You can recondition an old mast with a light touch of the plane, though this of course will only work two or three times. If you need to lay a wooden mast or boom down flat for an extended period, make sure it is laid very flat, in a dry place where the air can circulate. It should be placed on the sail track, which is the only flat face.

Fittings

Fittings should be attached to the spars with a great deal of care, as wood is quite delicate material. There are two ways of attaching fittings:
– woodscrews, which hold the wood well if they are sufficiently long and thick; they grip well against sideways pull, but less well if pulled straight;
– bolts, which hold well in all directions.

You should only attach fittings to the mast where the mast has been reinforced, and ensure that screws are subject to sideways force only.

Wherever possible, bolts should be used to ensure that screwed fittings cannot be pulled out; this is especially important when the fittings will be subject to sudden pulls.

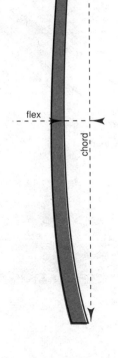

Masts can be made in quite radical shapes. The wing mast of *Royale* flexed by more than 2m.

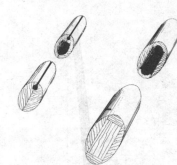

Spars are hollow, and fittings should only be attached where the spar has been reinforced.

Holes in masts weaken them. Even if you fill the hole, you have still cut the wood fibres. Before you get out your drill, think where you need to make the hole, then check twice, then think again!

Any hole in a mast is a potential entry point for water. You should therefore dribble some varnish down the hole and grease the screw before putting it in.

If you do have any holes which are no longer in use, do not force in a dowel which is too wide. This will lead to cracking as the wood expands and contracts.

Repairs

Any repairs to wooden spars should be made with spruce. Screws or tacks should not be used to join pieces of wood: they should be glued. In order to join two pieces of wood end to end, you need to cut half-wedges at a slope of about 10%.

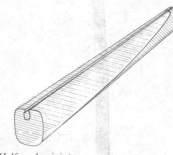

Half-wedge joint.

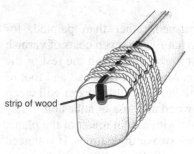

strip of wood

In order to repair a broken or damaged track in a mast or boom:
– push a strip of wood into the track to support the piece which is being replaced;
– glue the pieces together;
– bind the join tightly with 1 or 2mm nylon twine, wound at least every 1cm.

The mast

Choosing masts is a specialist skill. Buying a mast which is too strong is almost as bad as buying one which is too weak. It is worth acquiring a few bits of general knowledge on the subject, but you should not be carrying out much work on the mast or tinkering about yourself.

Mast fittings should generally have zero play. They should have absolutely no play between mast and mast foot, or one day you will find yourself watching the mast keel over like so much overcooked asparagus. If the mast does fall down in this way, the bent section has to be cut away and a new piece Aralditd in place, with plenty of bolts or pop-rivets as insurance. Any further accidents and the mast will need to be welded back together.

Get to know your masts

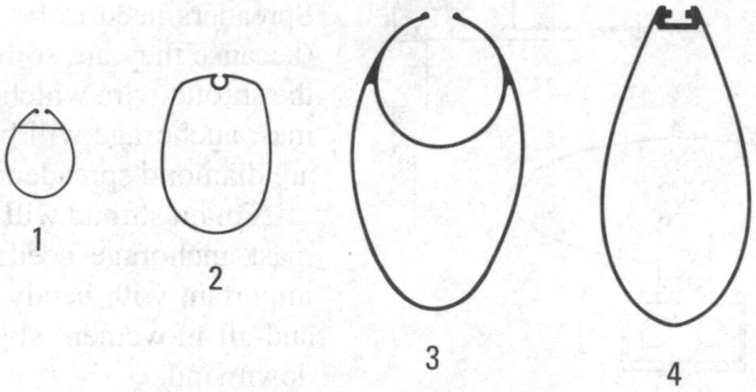

Masts are a highly specialised subject, but you should at least know your own mast. You should know:
– what alloy it is made of;
– how thick the walls are;
– its sideways inertia (xx') in cm^4;
– its longitudinal inertia (yy') in cm^4;
– its weight per metre.

1
2
3
4

If you know these details and do lose your mast, for instance while you are abroad, you should be able to acquire a replacement with little risk of error. You will also have an idea of what you need in a stiffer or bendier mast: for instance you might specify more sideways inertia, while keeping the same weight per metre.

The above mast sections show some of the possible variety: the first is a dinghy mast; the second might be for a 7 or 8m boat, with a tack rope of the right shape for the mast track; the third is for a ten-tonner with a mast-track roller-reefing system; and the fourth is a wing-section catamaran mast.

Pop-rivets

Pop rivets will be either 4 or 5mm in diameter, made of aluminium alloy (respective shear resistance 190kg/310kg). The length of the pop-rivet depends on the thickness of the mast wall. Use this table as a reference.

Aluminium alloy pop-rivets

Length of rivet (mm)	Wall thickness (mm)	Length of rivet (mm)	Wall thickness (mm)
6	2.5–3.5	6	2.5–3.5
7	3.5–4.5	–	–
8	4.5–6	8	3.5–5
10	6–7.5	10	5–7
12	7.5–10	12	7–9.5
–	–	14	9.5–11.5
15	10–12.5	–	–
4mm diameter		**5mm diameter**	

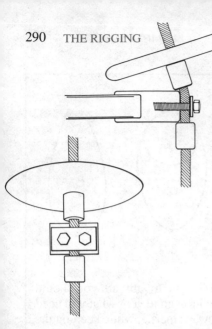

Spreaders

Spreaders need to be strong but slim (for less windage) and light (because they are so high up). They need to be attached solidly to the shroud wire which they are holding out from the mast, but their mast anchorage will be quite different depending on whether they are diamond spreaders or actually attached to the main shrouds.

A main shroud will hold the spreader in the right position, so the mast anchorage needs to be hinged. This hinging is particularly important with bendy masts, but the spreaders need to resist fore-and-aft movement slightly, so that the mast does not flop around downwind.

Diamond spreaders have to be fixed in their anchorages with no play, even if the mast is flexible. The anchorages need to be well attached to the mast.

The spreader is held in place on the shroud by the screws, which press in on the wire, and the sleeves, which stop the arm sliding up or down. (One of these methods alone is sufficient.) The disc is there to stop the sail brushing against any sharp edges.

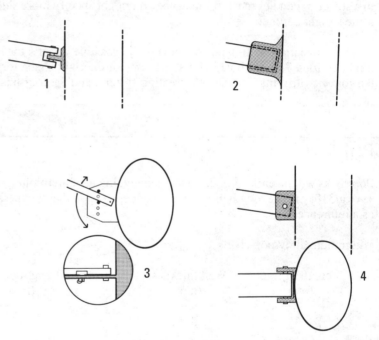

1. Vertically hinged spreader. Ideal for main shrouds.
2. Fixed spreader for diamonds and other supporting stays. This is the commonest design.
3. Dinghy spreader with adjustable fore-and-aft movement.
4. Horizontally hinged spreader. Useful only for saving space when storing the mast over the winter.

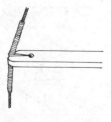

This jury-rig arrangement can be used on all spreaders. It is fastened the same way as you finish off a sewn eye in a plaited rope.

The boom

The boom needs to be light for two reasons: it is fairly high up; and when it moves across the boat, especially as you gybe, it can exert considerable strain on the rigging (as well as on the back of unwary heads). Nevertheless, you should not go too far in seeking light-ness: the boom is subject to considerable vertical and compression stresses when your sheet is in tight on the beat and when you take in a reef or two; and to flex stresses when you gybe or tighten the kicker.

Some boats made in the 1970s have bendy booms for taking the belly out of the sail. This solution has been largely abandoned these days, as the same result can be achieved more simply through other means.

The spinnaker pole

The spinnaker pole keeps the tack of the spinnaker out to windward; similarly, some boats will use a jib pole or whisker pole for holding the jib clew out on a dead run.

These poles can be subject to considerable compression stresses, but they do also need to be very light, for reasons of manoeuvrability and personal safety (since the pole is at crew head level!). It is easy to lose a spinnaker pole, so it must be attached at all times when it is used, by the uphaul/downhaul. Whatever it is made of, whether wood, metal or plastic, the pole should ideally be tapered at the ends. It is easier – and cheaper – to make them as a simple tube, but this is a less efficient shape.

The spinnaker pole is normally the same length as the foredeck, whether for racing or cruising.

The jockey pole

This short pole can be used for holding the spinnaker guy away from the windward shroud when close-reaching. The effect of this is to reduce the strains and friction on the guy. It is extraordinarily easy to lose, so make sure your pole is tied on to the foot of the mast with a thin safety cord.

1. Spinnaker sheet.
2. Spinnaker pole.
3. Jockey pole.

Standing rigging

The standing rigging is what holds the mast up, so it is worth spending time and attention on choosing and maintaining it. It will usually be made of Kevlar or steel wire. In matters of standing rigging, you should never be saying to yourself: 'I guess that'll hold.' You should be absolutely certain. Although testing your rigging might be a job for the specialist, it is up to you to ensure it is correctly put together and maintained.

Shrouds and stays

The shrouds will generally be made of single-twist wire. They should have a toggle to allow twist at the bottom fixing, particularly if the rigging is to be slack on any point of sailing. Straps and cords, for instance at the bottom of a fractional-rig forestay, are simply not up to the job: they do not allow enough twist, so the wire stay itself will end up breaking at the swage.

The twist problem is not so severe with Kevlar stays.

You have a variety of mechanisms for adjusting the standing rigging, from bottlescrews and chainplates to levers and cords. Whenever you can, use the chainplates for setting up the stays which will remain fixed: that is, if you have an adjustable backstay for your mast rake, use a plate on the forestay; if the mast rake is effectively controlled by the jib luff wire, as on a small racing cat or a dinghy, use plates for the shrouds.

You may use threaded cord where you need the rig to be slightly elastic, as on many flexibly rigged small boats.

Bottlescrews are the best answer for most standing rigging. If you have the choice, it is best to have the bottlescrew attached to the cable via an eye rather than directly onto the wire. They are easier to maintain and less likely to twist the stays this way, since there is an extra link. The main disadvantage of bottlescrews is that they occasionally catch on the sheets.

Runners and other movable stays

These should be made of shroud wire (7 × 7) or of flexible wire (7 × 19). Single-twist wire or Kevlar is liable to break at the sleeve.

Adjusting these stays takes a lot of force, with not much available length for the required mechanical advantage. If your boat has a rigid (masthead) rig, the runners should be adjustable by levers, which are very powerful and allow you to achieve a consistent tension. With a flexible rig, the best solution is a Terylene line wrapped over a winch. There is some 'give' in this arrangement, due to the considerable length of line involved, although the line itself is not really elastic.

Wear

It is rare for rigging to show obvious wear before it breaks; and of course the break never occurs when you are safely in harbour. You have to inspect the rigging to spot any impending problems.

Stretch in a shroud rod.

If a strand breaks in a shroud, no problem: change the shroud. Generally, though, the only visible sign that a shroud has suffered excess strain is that it stretches slightly: some strands will have been stretched beyond their elastic limit and permanently deformed. These signs of stretch usually appear at the point where the wire comes out of the eye-sleeve, where it is no longer clamped in place. The metal will be extra shiny where it has been pulled. Only a practised eye will spot the tell-tale signs, and then only if they are not hidden by a plastic sleeve!

The other method for telling if a wire is still in order is to subject it to its maximum admissible load (just less than the elastic limit of the wire), and see whether it returns to its original length. If not, there are broken strands inside, even though you might not be able to see them. Then the only thing you can do with the wire is throw it away.

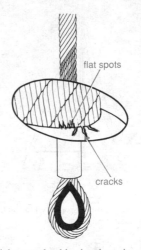

Stainless steel cables break at the sleeve. When there are shiny flat spots by the top of the sleeve, it is time to change the shroud, since it is already partly broken. In this case, the cracks in the sleeve show that the sleeve is just ready to give way.

Running rigging

Halyards

A halyard needs to be:
– light, so as not to weigh down the top of the mast;
– thin, so as not to cause unnecessary windage, especially if it is not run straight down or inside the mast (a halyard 5mm out from the mast causes the same extra windage as a mast 5mm wider);
– as inelastic as possible, so that you are able to stretch the sails exactly.

There is only one fabric which is practically non-stretch: Kevlar. Its combination of strength and light weight make it ideal for halyards. The same simple halyard arrangement is as appropriate for a dinghy as for a 50ft yacht.

Steel wire should be used on larger yachts, and Terylene on small boats.

All-fabric and all-steel halyards

The simplest and usually cheapest solution is to have the entire halyard made of one material. The masthead sheave will have to be of a suitable size, and there will need to be appropriate cleating arrangements for whatever material is used. *Sheaves need to have a diameter at least 8 times that of the halyard for Terylene, 12 times for Kevlar and 22 times for steel.*

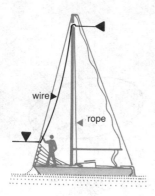

When the the jib is lowered, you should be able to catch hold of the wire.

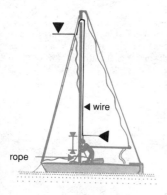

When the jib is up, the wire should stop short of the cleat.

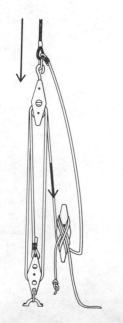

Mixed steel-fabric halyards

The steel wire and the fabric rope can be joined in a number of different ways:
– a tail splice is the neatest, but not the simplest or cheapest method. The splice will pass through all your sheaves;
– an eye on the end of each part can be joined by a shackle;
– the eyes can be spliced through each other (and the join thus made permanent).
    These last two are only possible if the halyard is made off at the mast foot.

The rope part needs to be long enough for you to turn it onto the cleat once the sail is lowered (not forgetting that a rope will shorten by about 10% in its first year of use).

The wire part should be as long as possible so that there is relatively little elasticity in the assembly once the sail is up – an obvious plus point. If the wire is joined to the rope by a tail splice and you have a winch at the mast foot, you can even winch directly onto the wire. (Two turns on the drum are enough.) You should cleat the rope part, though: never the wire.

Tightening mechanisms

There are numerous mechanisms in use. These are the most widespread:

Winches are the simplest and commonest equipment for this purpose, and they can be used with any size of boat, any halyard system and any type of sail. The winch can have a cleat attached, but you should be very careful when using the winch, because it is an extremely powerful tool and you can easily end up damaging the sail if, for example, a hank gets caught somewhere.

Block and tackle can be installed at the bottom of the mast for any foresail. The sail is pulled up using the tackle and the rope end wound onto the cleat. The upper block is hooked into the wire eye, and the tackle rope is cleated onto the same cleat used for making off the halyard tail. Using only one cleat in this way ensures that no mistakes can be made when you let the sail off. The upper block can be lost unless there is a figure-of-eight knot in the end of the tackle rope.

The block-and-tackle system is less common nowadays for tightening halyards.

You can use a block at deck level to lead the halyard to a winch at the mast foot; this allows the halyard to be cleated inside the cockpit.

The most widely used system for tightening a halyard.

If the winch breaks down ... you can rig up a tackle as illustrated, complete with stopper knot, to last until you have time to make a tail splice.

This system is becoming less common, but is certainly useful if your winch breaks down. The hook is replaced by a short (1.5–2m) rope fastened onto the halyard, whatever it is made of, with a whipping knot.

Simple tackle is a system using no blocks, in which a loop of the tail rope is used to give a purchase once the sail has been pulled up. The rope is caught at point P, a loop is made, the tail is then fed under the cleat and back through the loop. To let the sail down, you allow a little slack, then unhook the long loop from the cleat before letting all the rope out. This system may be used for jibs of up to about 10sq m.

Reel winches may be used for all-steel halyards on boats of 12m or over. If the mechanism is well lined up, the wire will coil on neatly and the system will work beautifully. This is rare, however: usually one coil will slip between two others and will need to be carefully unjammed when the sail is pulled down. In any case the wire must not be pre-bent; if your wire bends and is then difficult to straighten, you need a less thick wire, which will make the whole system work better.

P

Simple tackle: the 'splice' is a simple sewn eye, with the three ropes sewn together in a triangular shape (see cut-out).

Tack-tightening arrangements are common on mainsails. The sail is fully pulled up, the halyard cleated and the sail hooked on at the mast head (where applicable). There are then three options for tightening the sail:
– pulling the boom down by hand and fastening the gooseneck on its slide (small boats);
– pulling the boom down with block and tackle or winch;
– tightening the Cunningham eye. (This is an eye above the tack which shortens 'over-length' luff ropes, on mainsails or on jibs, particularly for racing use where sails are often generously cut.)

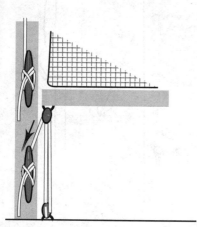

If the jib is not fixed on its luff wire, the luff tension can be controlled by a block at the tack, through which a rope is run from the tack eye back to a winch or tackle in the cockpit.

Wire-rope combination halyards. So that the bottom end of the wire part of the halyard is kept at the same height no matter which jib you are using, it is common to add a length of wire at the head and even occasionally at the tack of the smaller jibs.

Luff-tightening devices:
1. using your hand;
2. using a block and tackle;
3. using a Cunningham eye led back to the cockpit.

Simple purchases are rather out of date now, but some large boats still use them. There is a two-part purchase on the bottom of the halyard which is itself attached to a block on another two-part purchase used to tighten the halyard once it is cleated. This gives a total four-part purchase.

Joining the halyard to the sail

You need a quick joint which will not get lost. The simplest joint is a snapshackle, which is permanently fixed to the halyard eye. It is tempting to attach a pull-cord to the plunger, but this is generally unwise, as the cord can get caught and open the shackle when it is least wanted.

If the head eye is too small for a snapshackle, then use a shackle with a crimped pin, so that you do not lose the pin. A hook is adequate for dinghies, and much less attractive to petty thieves than the alternatives.

Where to run the halyard

You should aim to run your halyards through swivelling pulleys rather than boxed sheaves. The reason for this is that the halyards are occasionally used for other purposes than pulling up sails, such as attaching a boat to a jetty from which it was drifting away, or throwing to a crew member who falls overboard.

If your halyards are led outside the mast, they should go forward of the spreaders, so that they are not jammed in place by the mainsail when you are sailing downwind.

Many modern boats have the halyards led inside the mast, which reduces windage and simplifies the rigging. The halyards *must* go inside the mast if it is a flexible one; otherwise the sails will sag as soon as the mast bends. Leading the halyard inside the mast means that the halyard must be either entirely of wire or entirely of rope; if it is a combination, the only possible join is a tail splice; and the halyard needs to be replaced before it breaks, or life gets very complicated!

Changing the halyard inside the mast is accomplished by using a fishing line which is pulled all the way down the mast bringing the new halyard on its end.

If an inside halyard does break, replacing it is theoretically simple. You climb up the mast and drop your line down the mast, hooking it out at the bottom sheave (when it reaches there) with a bent wire. The new halyard is then pulled through on the end of the string.

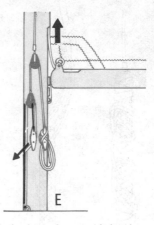

A simple purchase on a halyard.

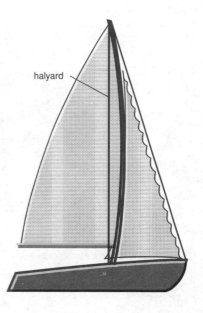

halyard

The sails sag as soon as the mast bends, unless the halyards are led inside the mast.

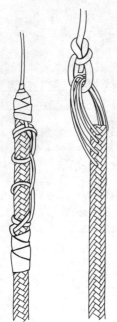

Two ways of attaching fishing line to a halyard end.

The main difficulty is dangling the line down inside the mast without it snagging something on the way. You can take precautions by ensuring any other halyards are kept tight, and weighting the bottom of your fishing line. Your aim should be to let the weight down as quickly as possible so it does not catch. This does not always work straight away; and if the halyard does end up wound round one of the others, they will both wear out quickly due to the friction. When the season is over, it is worth taking the top and bottom off the mast and checking that nothing inside is tangled.

Where should I cleat the halyards?

The traditional place for halyard cleats and winches is at the mast foot. This spot is now unfashionable, but by far the best. There is less friction, so the sails go up more easily, and the halyards do not join the tangle of ropes in the cockpit. If you are using a deck- or roof-mounted winch, it may take two of you to pull the sails up, one in the cockpit, the other standing at the bottom of the mast. The halyards should be stowed in the cabin so as to be out of the way: either free, or hung up in a little bag (which the boatbuilder will almost certainly not have supplied).

How many halyards should I take?

Halyards occasionally break. More often they are dropped overboard. You should carry a spare with you. Alternatively, the topping lift could act as a stand-in for the main halyard, the spinnaker halyard could be used for the jib, and the spinnaker pole uphaul for any inner jib (though this might have to be tied with some imagination). A spare jib halyard is certainly worth taking along on long voyages.

Halyard wear

The halyard does not wear out at the same speed over all its length. It wears out fastest at the places where it is attached once the sail is up: the masthead and foot sheaves, and the cleat; any fittings it bangs against when the sails are up or down also cause points of wear, inside and outside the mast. You should be merciless in rooting out sources of such problems, and it is worth padding the inside of the mast, against the wear you cannot see.

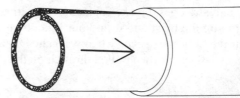

Slide a rolled polystyrene sheet inside the mast as padding.

There are worthwhile savings to be made by buying a halyard which is a bit too long initially. You can then shorten it, since it will almost always wear fastest at the ends. It can also be turned end to end so as to change the places where it is wearing. You should turn or shorten the halyard well before it breaks, of course ...

The wire part of the halyard is of course more robust than the rope part, though it will wear out very fast if, for instance, it is wrapped round the forestay.

Typical wear to look out for:
– If the wire is wearing out next to a sheave, you probably need a stronger wire.

– If the wire is wearing out at one spot half way along, or over a fair length, it is probably rubbing against some other part of the rigging or mast.

– If a jib halyard is going about 20–30cm above the head of the jib, maybe it is wrapped around the forestay.

– If the wire is permanently bent, you need to change the way you wind it onto the winch or capstan drum. The bend will end up as a break.

If the masthead sheave is too small, deformed or not straight in its box, points of wear will appear all along the wire, and it will form itself into corkscrew shapes. You need either more flexible or thinner wire; or you need to change the sheave; or you need to switch to Kevlar halyards with appropriate sheaves.

Your halyard will wear out fast if you let it wrap around the forestay.

The wise sailor keeps an eye out for signs of wear.

Spare halyards

Since wear is inevitable, you should ensure that you have some material on board with which to replace halyards if this becomes necessary, particularly when cruising:
– a length of wire a little longer than your longest wire halyard, with an eye bent into one end. Cut it to length when you need it. The second eye can be put on with a couple of clamps or a Talurit swage. Alternatively, you can make a splice;

– if you know the sheaves are big enough, you can have a rope
halyard for temporary use (preferably one made of pre-stretched
Terylene);
– finally, you might choose to have a complete spare halyard for
each sail.

Any wires you keep aboard as spares should be well greased and
wrapped in an oily rag.

The sheets

The sheets should be:
– made entirely of rope: they should ideally not stretch, but the
important thing is that they should be easy and safe to handle;
– preferably plaited and sheathed. The sheets will be pulled to and
fro constantly, and are subject to wear all along their length, as they
rub over your anti-slip deck, against the shrouds and bottlescrews,
on the winches and through the fairleads. Twisted rope wears out
quickly and then starts to unravel. Plaited sheathed rope is much
more wear-resistant;
– sufficiently fat, since they are often subject to considerable pull,
and they need to be kind to your hands. Thin sheets would be strong
enough on a small boat, but would tear your hands to shreds. The
sheets should be at least 8mm in diameter.

Jibsheets

Length

A jibsheet should be the length of the jib foot, plus the length from
the forestay to the fairlead, plus whatever you need for holding. The
optimum length is best worked out on the spot: tie a bowline
through the jib clew eye, then take it all the way round, to the
forestay plate, through the fairlead, winch and cleat, plus a metre to
grab onto, plus another 10% for shrinkage. Any more than this will
simply add to the serpent's nest of ropes in the bottom of the
cockpit. If you are going to use the same sheet for several jibs,
measure it for the jib with the longest foot.

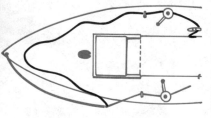

How to measure the length of the jibsheets. Check that the sheets will reach if
you use a whisker pole with the genoa.

Design

It is usual to have two separate sheets; however some smaller boats
use a continuous sheeting system, which runs all the way across the
cockpit, with the two ends tied to the jib clew with bowlines. This
type of sheeting arrangement needs to be measured for length with

the jib poled out, with half a metre of slack added, plus the 10% for shrinkage.

Joining the sheets to the jib

The join between sheets and jib needs to be light but strong. It is simplest to splice or knot the sheets through the clew eye of the jib. This is probably the best method for boats with only one or two jibs, such as dinghies.

If you will be using the same sheets for several jibs, you need to be able to change over easily. Shackles are rather heavy, which can be dangerous in a strong wind and annoying in a light wind. It is probably better to tie each sheet onto the clew with a short bowline, making sure that the knot does not butt up against the fairlead or any intermediate block.

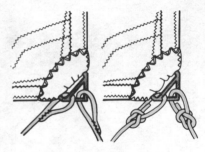

You can join the sheets to the jib either by making sewn eyes, or by tying small bowlines.

Precautions against wear

You need to ensure that the sheets are not regularly snagging on anything, or they will wear out very quickly. Check the lower shrouds and stays, bottlescrews, lifelines and pulpit, and the fairleads themselves. When the source of friction cannot be removed, you just have to reduce it, for instance by fitting a length of plastic tube around the shroud fixtures, or sheathing the lifelines.

Some wear is inevitable where the sheets run through blocks or fairleads. You can limit wear by using blocks which turn easily and swivel: oil the blocks when necessary, and ensure they are fitted in the most logical place.

Some anti-slip deck treatments really give sheets a hard time. You might consider removing the heavy-duty anti-slip on the deck area over which the sheet usually runs.

Sheets will wear out at different speeds at different points on their length. You can get the most mileage out of your sheets by reversing them before they are thoroughly shot.

Sheet ends

It is not adequate to cut the sheets with a hot knife and trust this will stop them fraying. It won't. They should be whipped at the ends, especially if they are made of plaited rope with a sheath (since the rope slips through the sheath quite easily). A figure-of-eight knot at the end also helps keep the core and the sheath together.

Main and mizzen sheets

The mainsheet should be a powerful purchase. The sheet not only controls the angle of the sail, but (in boats with a flexible rig) often the mast bend and jib luff tension too. It is fairly simple to set up a system where the sheet gives sufficient mechanical advantage that it actually becomes easier to pull in than the jib.

Length
The simplest method, as for the jibsheets, is to measure the length with everything in place. You should have sufficient length to hold when the traveller is centred and the boom is out against the shrouds. Don't forget to add 10% for shrinkage.

Design
The blocks need to be large, and well apart, to ensure that the sheet feeds through them easily. If you need a double block, it is better to use one where the pulleys are placed one above the other than one in which they are side by side. The pulleys should be turning both in the same direction, and they should be able to swivel to give the sheet a clear run whatever the position of the boom. The block should generally run straight along the boat's axis.

The mainsail on some boats is so big that you will need lots of purchase. Consequently you have yards of sheet in the boat when

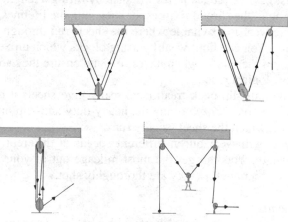

Four ways to rig up a mainsheet.

close-hauled. Placing a wire strop between the boom and the top block helps overcome this problem, but this may mean that the top block is then cunningly positioned at head height. Look out for it!

Wear
A mainsheet wears fastest when you are close-hauled, at the end next to the boom. You can treble its life expectancy by reversing it once, then cutting off both ends.

Mainsheet mounted with wire strop.

Ends

You need to whip both ends of the mainsheet. There is no point in splicing the boom end: just tie a bowline, which will enable you to untie it when you need to reverse the direction of the sheet.

Quick-release clamcleat.

Quick release

On a multihull you will occasionally need to let go of the sheet very quickly indeed. It is best to have a quick-release clamcleat which the helm can get at from anywhere in the boat.

Control lines for the mainsail

Traveller

Depending on the size of the boat, the traveller will be controlled by either a single cord run through a clamcleat (B) or a small pulley arrangement on either side (A). It might even be led to a winch.

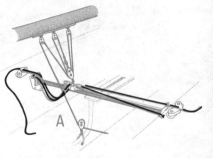

Kicking strap

The kicker needs to be powerful and non-stretch. There is a wide variety, from the ingenious 'three hole' set-up to a hydraulic bar which also serves as a topping lift.

Roller-bearing traveller. The block can slide even while the sheet is under tension. The control lines can be adjusted while the boat is sailing.

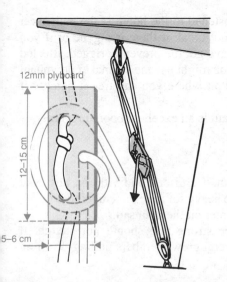

12mm plyboard

12–15 cm

5–6 cm

Take a piece of 12mm ply, about 15cm long, with three holes through which your kicker rope will run. The plate is fixed half way up the first purchase of the strap. Pass the cord through the bottom hole, tie a knot, run it through the top hole then fix it to the boom pulley becket. The free end of the strap comes up from the bottom pulley and is led through the centre hole. The strap is tightened by pulling down; it is fastened by a simple turn round the back of the plate. When you let off the main halyard, the turn will unwind and the kicker will ease automatically.

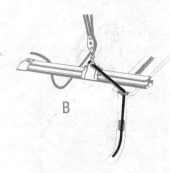

Sliding traveller. The control line is fixed very firmly. The traveller can be released under tension, but not tightened.

Generally the kicking strap will be a three- or four-part purchase between the boom and the mast foot. One can make sure it does not stretch too much by using Kevlar rope or by using only a short purchase with a wire strop. The kicking strap often needs a lot of power on it, and one can lead it round a winch, but winches are so powerful one can end up breaking something.

Hydraulic kicking strap which also serves as a topping lift.

On older boats, the kicking strap is sometimes a movable tackle which can be fixed to various points on the deck. In such cases, it is used only for keeping the boom down when off the wind, and has no mast-bending function.

Such a kicking strap also functions as a boom preventer, but if you are dead running it can be a little risky to rely solely on this, as an inadvertent gybe could break the boom. It is better to rig a real boom preventer so as not to run this risk.

Boom preventer

A boom preventer is a rope tied between the end of the boom and the front of the boat when you are running in heavy seas, to prevent accidental gybes.

It must be rigged so you can release it from the cockpit, because if the gybe does happen despite your precautions, you will need to let the preventer off quickly, rather than performing acrobatics at the bow.

The preventer should be fastened to the boom at the mainsheet block, so that the boom will not break if there is a gybe or if you sheet in, forgetting that you have got the preventer rigged. It is led through a block at the front (you might use the spinnaker downhaul block) and back into the cockpit where you can free it quickly if necessary.

The spinnaker pole downhaul is an excellent boom preventer.

Topping lift

A topping lift is useful on small cruisers, and vital on any boat which has a boom which is too heavy for a crew member to hold up, for instance while taking in a reef on the mainsail.

The topping lift should be strong and should not stretch. It should bear the weight of several crew members pulling down on the boom.

The topping lift (here in blue) will rub against the mainsail head plate. A larger block should be used.

The topping lift is normally made of rope. If you do use wire, make sure the wire is not chafing on the mainsail head plate; one can use a combination, with a tail splice so that there is no wire in contact with the sail.

There are good reasons to use a strong topping lift: you might need to convert it into a substitute main halyard, or even to pull a member of the crew up the mast for repairs.

Clew outhaul

The clew outhaul is for holding the clew of the mainsail at the end of the boom.

A simple cord is adequate for small cruisers and dinghies, but on some larger boats one wants to be able to adjust the tension on the clew outhaul while sailing. The clew is then run on a boom slide, and is adjusted with the outhaul rigged like an internal reefing pennant.

Reefing pendants

Reefing pendants are the clew outhaul for each stage of reefing.

They should be flexible enough to be knotted, but as non-stretch as possible. The best material to use is pre-stretched Terylene. Kevlar is to be avoided, unless you are certain it will not be bent over an excessively small radius. Modern cruisers tend to have a

reefing pennant led back inside the boom and adjusted at the mast or on the deck with the aid of a winch. It is not always possible to use this set-up with older boats. The diagram above shows one system which can be used with almost any metal boom.

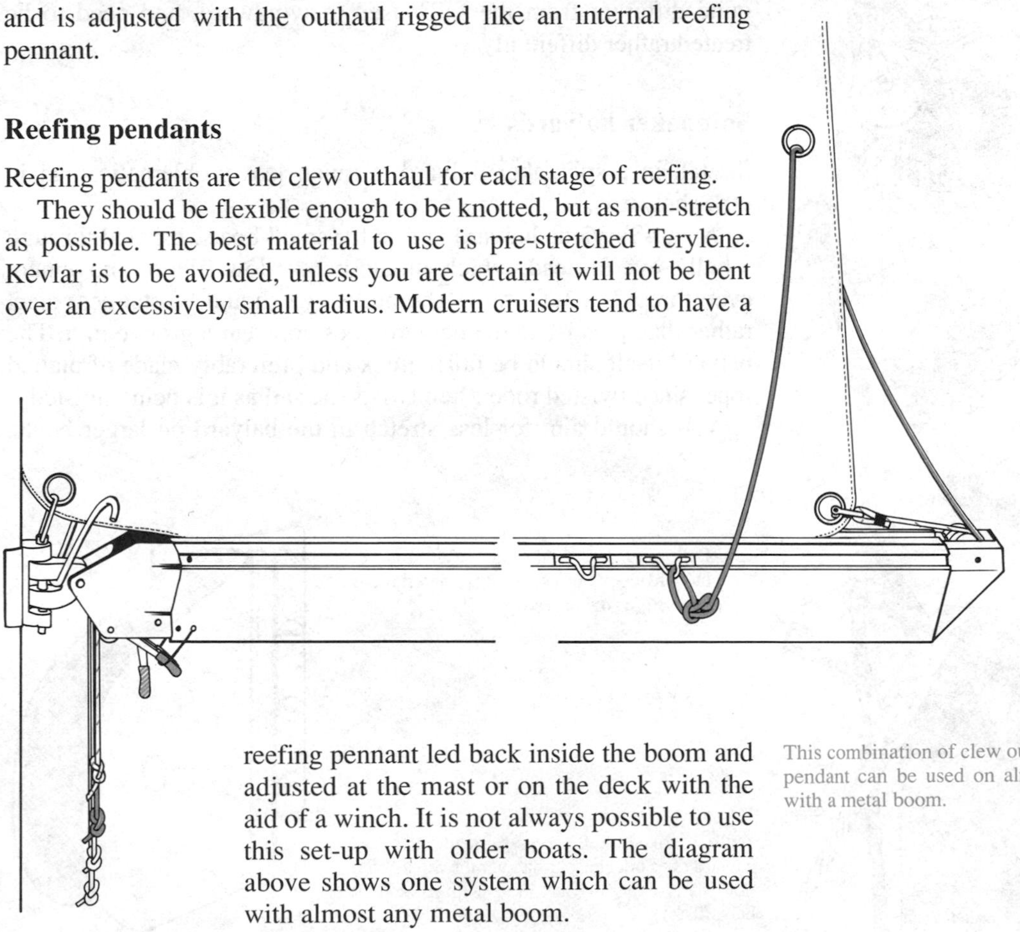

This combination of clew outhaul and reef pendant can be used on almost any boat with a metal boom.

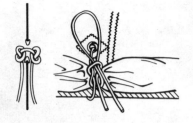

Reefing points, as they are tied through the sail and under the boom.

Reef points

These are small strings led through the sail to enable you to gather up excess cloth when reefing. They should be easy to tie. Plaited polypropylene cord is ideal for the purpose.

The reef points should be sufficiently long (ideally about a metre) to allow you to make a slip-reef knot. If possible, they should be tied between sail and boom; otherwise tie them underneath the boom.

Rigging the spinnaker

Spinnakers and other specialist downwind sails (big boys, etc) are quite different from the sails used to windward, and need to be treated rather differently.

Spinnaker halyards

Stretch in a spinnaker halyard is much less problematic than in other halyards.

An all-Terylene halyard is fine for small boats. It is led through a bull's-eye fairlead, which should permit low-friction movement even through a 180° turn. The bull's-eye should be stainless steel rather than plastic, so the halyard does not wear a groove in it. The halyard itself should be fairly thick and preferably made of plaited rope, since twisted rope often twists the sail as it is being hoisted.

You should aim for less stretch in the halyard on larger boats.

If the block can swing too far, the spinnaker halyard could end up chafing on the forestay.

Pulleys on a vertical hinge ensure that the halyard does not chafe. Any material can be used for the halyard.

With a fixed bull's-eye fairlead, the halyard does not chafe, whatever the direction. This can only be used with rope halyards.

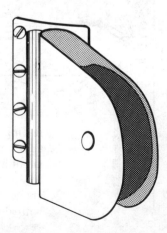

The halyard runs over the pulleys every time it stretches and will wear out very quickly if it is too elastic; it also lets the spinnaker seesaw up and down. It is better to use pre-stretched Terylene or Kevlar than steel wire. The forces involved are too great for a bull's-eye and you will need a swivelling block – which must not be able to move so far that the halyard snags on the forestay. It is worth setting it slightly out from the mast on a crane.

Big boats will often have a swivel at the end of the spinnaker halyard so that the spinnaker can untwist itself, compensating for any twist in the halyard. On smaller boats, the sail can be tied on with a bowline if the halyard is made of Terylene, or snapshackled on if the halyard is of Kevlar.

You will need a winch for pulling up the spinnaker if it is bigger than 40sq m, in case the spinnaker fills before it is all the way up.

Do not economise on spinnaker halyard length: you should be able to catch the snapshackle at the stern of the boat while your crew is holding onto the other end at the mast foot. Do not forget the 10% for shrinkage!

Spinnaker sheets

The spinnaker has two sheets, which are known as the *guy* (to windward) and the *sheet* (to leeward) to differentiate them when you are sailing.

The sheets must be able to run very freely, and they should not stretch. Use plaited rope.

The sheets can be tied onto the spinnaker with bowlines on smaller boats (up to 8m). Bigger boats should have a snapshackle which can be opened under tension. The snapshackles should be the sort which can be opened only with a marlin spike, rather than needing a pull-cord which will catch on something sooner or later and unexpectedly free your spinnaker.

The sheets will usually be led through blocks at the transom, from where they come into the cockpit. These transom blocks take quite a lot of strain, so they should be large and securely fixed. The sheets should be very long, so as to allow the spinnaker tack to come very far aft if necessary on the run: at least twice the length of the boat. You should also have a spare length of cord for use as a light-weather sheet.

With a spinnaker of over 150sq m it is best to have two independent sheets on either side, which can be used as either sheets or guys; these are led through different fairleads, one set aft and one set further forward, so you can choose which sheeting point is best suited to circumstances.

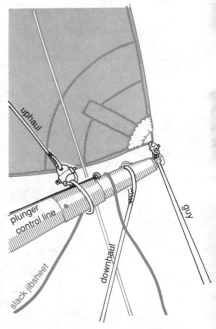

Spinnaker tack arrangement on a large boat. The guy runs through the pole-end fitting. The downhaul is sewn on and fixed. The uphaul is attached some way along the pole rather than at the end, thus leaving some space for the slack jibsheet.

This is an adequate set-up for spinnakers of less than 20sq m.

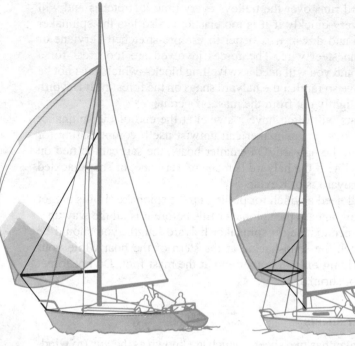

The uphaul and downhaul need to be attached to the end of the pole for larger spinnakers.

An arrangement with rope spans will serve for spinnakers between 20 and 50sq m.

Pole downhaul

The downhaul prevents the spinnaker pole from skying.

There are three methods for rigging the downhaul, depending on the size of the spinnaker. For small spinnakers of under 20sq m, the downhaul is attached to the middle of the pole and led into the cockpit via the mast foot. The pole is subject to greater forces as the spinnaker becomes larger, and these can be offset for spinnakers of 20–50sq m by rigging a wire span; this relieves the pole of any forces other than compression. With either of these systems, the pole can swing around the mast without you having to adjust the downhaul.

For really large spinnakers, the downhaul will be attached to the end of the pole, and led back to the cockpit via the bow. With this system, you have to trim the downhaul at the same time as you trim the spinnaker itself. The downhaul needs to be nearly as long as the sheets, even if it is not quite so thick. In practice, one can use a slightly worn sheet for the downhaul in this set-up.

It is worth pointing out one final purpose of the downhaul: as a security rope for the pole! So long as the downhaul is permanently fixed, you need not worry about dropping the pole overboard. (Of course, if it is fixed to the pole but you have forgotten the figure-of-eight knot at the inboard end, you will just lose both in one go!)

Pole uphaul

The main purpose of the spinnaker pole uphaul is to keep the pole up while the sail is being hoisted or dropped; once the sail is actually filling, the pole needs to be kept down rather than up.

A shock cord will usually do the job with small spinnakers (up to 15sq m). If it is thick enough, a shock cord will even hold up the pole for a 30sq m spinnaker.

For larger spinnakers, you need an uphaul made of sufficiently thick rope that you can handle it without wrecking your hands.

There are three options for rigging the uphaul, which correspond to the downhaul systems above: centred or on a span for smaller sails; at the pole end for larger ones. As the diagrams show, the mast fitting for the uphaul is lower than the inner forestay in both the first two cases, whereas in the third the sheave has to be above the forestays. This ensures that the pole can be passed from one side of the boat to the other without undoing either the uphaul or the downhaul.

If you are using a twin-pole system, then you will clearly need a pole uphaul either side.

Spinnaker pole mast fitting

On dinghies and small cruisers, the pole clips onto a mast fitting which is immovable. Medium-sized cruisers may have a track on which one can move the pole up and down by hand, and then lock the heel in place. For larger boats, the pole heel cannot easily be moved by hand, so an adjustment mechanism is needed.

You fix an endless line to the car, lead it up to a block at the top of the rail and back down again, through two cleats. Thus, one line can let the pole up and down. If there is a lot of wind, you do need to be careful using this sort of set-up: the pole can easily slip right up or right down the track, as it is subject to considerable compression force. It is vital to ensure that the pole remains at right angles to the mast as it is moved up and down.

Sails

Sail technology has moved forward considerably over the years. Not all that long ago, sails were made of cotton canvas, which was an excellent material despite certain drawbacks which made life complicated for captain and crew. Cotton sails tended to change shape depending on whether they were wet or dry, new or old; and they began to rot if ever they were put away damp. The sailmaker's art began to change very quickly in the 1950s, with the invention of new synthetic materials which were much stronger and more controllable, and rot-resistant. From the fifties onwards, advances have been made in every area – surface finish, materials, weave – so that a sail is today almost as controllable as the equivalent rigid shape.

Progress continues to be made through experiments in wind tunnels and by attaching measuring devices to sails in use. The computer age allows much more complex calculations, paid for in part by the enormous budgets generated for events such as the America's Cup and multihull offshore races.

In order to gain some sort of perspective on all this development, it is best to start out from the users and their actual needs. Many areas of current development are really pure research, and the avenues being pursued could easily turn out to lead nowhere. At the very least, there are commercial interests mixed in with those of 'pure' science, with all the attention to fad and fashion that implies.

Materials

The main fibres used for making sailcloths are:

Polyester, turned into cloth which weighs from 80 to 450gsm. The trade names vary from country to country: Dacron, Terylene, Tergal, etc. Polyester stretches only very slightly and is used for any sort of conventional sail apart from spinnakers and the like. It is the standard sailcloth.

Polyamide stretches rather more and is used for light downwind sails, such as spinnakers and big boys. It is known commonly as nylon, and used for cloths from 16 to 120gsm.

Kevlar is a very strong amide fibre, very light and with minimal stretch. It would be the ideal sailcloth material if it did not suffer in the sun's UV light. At the moment, it lasts no longer than one season, and it is very expensive; it is thus the exclusive reserve of top-class racers and the moneyed cruising set. Available in 110–350gsm.

Realistically, the average pleasure sailor will use polyester or nylon sails with conventional finishes.

Cloths

Cloth is made from crossing two sets of fibres. The up-and-down fibres are known as the *warp*, and the cross fibres are the *weft*. Cloth behaves differently depending on the direction in which it is pulled, in other words it is non-isotropic. If it is pulled straight along the line of the fibre weave, it does not lose shape much at all, and it has about the same elastic properties as the fibres themselves. (It is slightly more elastic along the warp than along the weft.) If it is subject to a diagonal effort, ie on a bias, it is less strong, and loses its shape more easily. Various techniques are used, separately or together, to combat this.

• A close weave cuts down the play between the fibres by locking them into place. The weft becomes slightly more elastic. One can stabilise the fibres after weaving, which pulls them closer together, and slightly shrinks the fabric.

• Cloth can be treated by 'ironing' it at high pressure to partly melt the fibres into each other.

• The cloth can be 'finished', or treated by impregnating it with a resin which sticks the fibres together, such as Mylar.

The sail loft does not limit itself to using these classic materials and treatments, however: they will use one-directional weaves, which have Kevlar or polyester fibres that stretch in one direction only, or they might use 'scrim', a transparent film with a net of carbon or nylon fibres actually in the film. The more elaborately treated or finished sails are often also the most fragile. It is as well to bear this in mind when handling them. Some cloths should only be rolled, rather than folded: you can usually tell these because they have a stiff, board-like feel to them. If you let these sails flog at all they will be shot within a very short time.

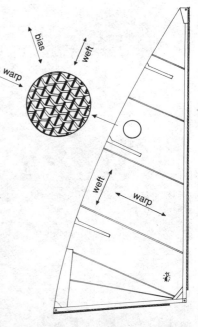

Cloth retains its shape well when pulled along the fibre weave (warp or weft), but can be deformed easily at a bias. The panels of the sail are therefore cut so that the main stresses operate along the weave.

Cut

A sail is a complex shape of which you need to control the surface. You might want the shape to remain constant all the time, you might want a shape which you can change, or a shape which changes of its own accord to suit the conditions. The ideal shape will never be achieved of course, but improvements are being made all the time, which goes some way to explaining why boats are constantly getting faster.

The ideal shape of a sail is dictated by the laws of aerodynamics, and its construction by the forces to which it will be subjected. Let us now look at how a sail is made up.

Panels

The panels of a sail are the strips of material which are put together so as to ensure that the maximum stresses are along the weave of the fabric, so giving the minimum deformation. If one took this to its logical conclusion, the seams would follow the stress lines and one would have a geodesic sail. This would look magnificent and perform superbly. Unfortunately, it would be extremely difficult and expensive to manufacture: even a simple version, the tri-radial mainsail, would be out of the reach of most of our pockets.

The ordinary sailor does have a satisfactory solution to hand. So long as the weave is aligned with the main forces acting on the foot and the leech of the sail, you should be content. The weft is less elastic than the warp, so the panels are laid at about right angles to the leech and foot.

Above and opposite:
Examples of complex sails in which an effort has been made to align the panels with the main forces acting on the cloth.

Camber

The panels of a sail are cut to shape to give the sail its fullness, and darts are put into the ends of the panels.

Since the sail will be hoisted on spars which might be stiff or flexible, the degree of fullness built in by the darts will have to vary to allow for different amounts of bend.

Mainsails

For reasons of tradition and also because of the racing rules, only

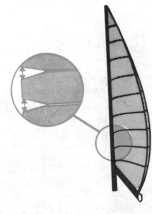

Darted sail panels.

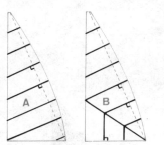

The two most common panelling arangements.

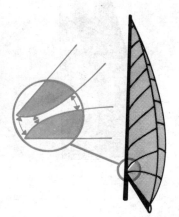

A dart cut on the twist at the foot of the sail.

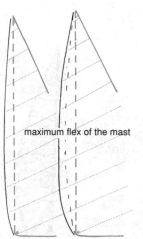

maximum flex of the mast

The luff on the mainsail cut for a rigid mast (left) and a flexible mast (right).

one mainsail is used. This mainsail has to function in all winds and on all points of sailing, so it is a very complex item.

Panelling

Sail A is panelled in the classic manner. The panels are at right angles to the leech (with no allowance made for the sail's camber). The weft carries the major force. This is the cheapest and most widespread design.

Darts are put in the panels to take the sail closer to a right angle with the boom, but the darts can never be quite big enough to achieve all the roundness needed. It is more effective in fact to fan the bottom panels by cutting them on the curve. The two panels are then sewn together along the rounded seams to give the required draught.

Sail B has the weave at right angles not only to the leech but also to the foot. These sails are attached to the boom only at the tack and clew, thus giving the sailor more control over the sail draught. There is a skirt of light cloth loosely stitched at the foot to prevent air escaping between sail and boom.

The luff

It is not sufficient just to put tucks in between the panels: to get a decent fullness in the sail you also have to build fullness in at the luff.

If the sail is designed for a stiff mast, the camber is built in all the way up the sail. It is most noticeable at the bottom of the sail, where there is most cloth. The maximum luff fullness occurs a fifth of the way up. It is minimally full at the top, just enough to ensure the sail does not lose all its shape if reefed.

If you are aiming to rig the sail on a bendy mast you have to build in fullness to take up the maximum curvature of the mast. Since the mast does not bend uniformly along its entire length, cutting the luff curve is something of an art:

– the mast bends uniformly up to the forestay, and the luff is curved largely as a function of the sail width, so it is cut widest at the bottom, and it reduces regularly as it goes up;

– where the shrouds are attached, the mast begins to bend more markedly, so more fullness needs to be cut into the luff;

– the very top of the mast bends little, so little roundness is required. The top of the sail should in any case be quite flat in fresher winds.

As the luff is cut on the cloth's bias, you can take out some of the sail's fullness by stretching the luff rope. If the luff is too long to be stretched by the halyard alone between the gooseneck and the mast head, one uses the Cunningham eye, which is a supplementary eye just above the tack. This method is widely used in racing, where it is important to have as large a sail as allowed. In cruising boats, it is a good inexpensive way of making a sail usable which was a touch too big.

The leech

The leech should not curl over or close, so it is generally left with little reinforcement, apart from a single thickness of cloth, which must not be stretched too tight.

Battens are used to hold the roach of the sail up (ie all that part which would fall outside a straight line drawn from the clew to the head). The battens need to be thin at the end closer to the mast, so as to fit in with the curvature of the sail, but progressively stiffer towards the leech.

The topmost batten is often full length, and rests up against the mast. It stretches the cloth so that the roach, and thus the overall sail area, can be greater. The top batten has to be very bendy, so as not to force the sail into an unnatural curve, and its pocket will need to be reinforced. The lighter the wind, the more compression there should be at the top batten, so as to give the sail the curvature which the wind is too weak to provide.

There is an increasing tendency to use full-length battens further down the sail, which allows greater control over the shape; it also prevents flogging, which is deadly for modern sails. You do of course need good, appropriate battens which are properly fixed.

The foot and the reefing points

The cut of the foot is less crucial than that of the luff. It may be given a regular curvature, which is between 1.5 and 10% of the length at its maximum. This curvature in part determines the fullness of the sail.

If you reduce the sail area, one of the lines of reefing points becomes the sail foot. The reefing points are placed so as to maintain some belly in the sail, but relatively little, since you do actually want a flatter sail in high winds. The cringles at the ends of each reefing line are reinforced like the tack and clew of the sail.

The three corners

• *The tack* is subject to very little effort and is therefore minimally

The slide is attached to the halyard eye, thus relieving the horizontal effort on the sail.

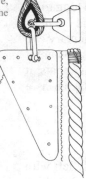

reinforced.

• *The clew* takes a lot of strain parallel to the leech, so the eye has to be sewn into several layers of cloth. The foot rope sliding along the boom tends to rub a lot and sails have a tendency to wear between the eye and the foot rope. *The eye must be attached to the boom properly.*

• *The head* of the sail suffers from wear between the head plate and the luff rope. Keep an eye on this spot and make sure any signs of wear are dealt with before the sail rips. There is a considerable vertical force acting on the sail at this point, which is taken up by the plate. There is relatively little horizontal force. If the sail is pulled up on slides, you should ensure that the top slide is particularly well sewn in place (and preferably shackled separately to the halyard eye). One can even attach a slide to the halyard itself in the mast track.

Genoas, jibs and staysails

Traditionally, and thanks to racing regulations, one brings as many jibs on board as one is likely to need. Some people take different jibs for each point of sailing and each wind strength. Every jib, certainly, is cut for a precise purpose, even if the genoa (plus roller gear) is now becoming something of an all-rounder. All-purpose genoas are not particularly excellent sails yet, but the search is on ...

Panels

Sail A has a good panel arrangement for smaller jibs, so long as the clew makes a 90° angle and the panels are straight across the leech. This arrangement produces moderately good jibs.

Sail B has panels perpendicular to the leech over most of the sail and parallel to the foot at the bottom. It is thus more resistant to deformation.

Sails C and D are cut with no bias on the foot, which is a necessary precaution against excessive stretch in big jibs. The panels are

Jibs have different names depending on their shape and function:
B, C and E are *genoas*, because their foot sweeps the deck;
A is a *jib*;
D is a *yankee*.

joined at an angle which bisects the clew. Yankees (sail D) and most genoas are cut this way.

The luff

The luff needs to be cut differently to its forestay for light and heavy weather, and differently for bendy rigs and stiff rigs.

So long as the forestay is straight (ie in light weather) one aims for a rounded luff to the jib. This way the jib retains its draft despite the straight stay. When the forestay sags, however, as the wind gets up, this is doubly bad news, because the sag causes more draft still, just as you need a flatter sail. You then need a straight luff to the jib. If the wind freshens more, the forestay will sag more, and you actually need a concave luff on the jib.

Jibs for stiff rigs do not need so much cut away on the luff as jibs for bendy rigs.

Some people use an S-shaped luff to their genoas, so as to keep the maximum draft in the right place. This ensures that the genoa keeps its draft lower down, while it flattens out towards the head as it becomes narrower. One can achieve the same result by making larger darts in the bottom part of the sail than those higher up.

Darts are vital in concave-luff heavy-wind jibs. If it were not for the darts, in fact, these sails would be completely flat and would therefore produce very little power.

You adjust the jib according not only to the shape of the luff but also depending to a certain extent on how the luff is made.

There are three sorts of luff:
A: those in which the fabric sleeve is sewn onto a steel luff wire. These cannot be stretched by halyard tension.

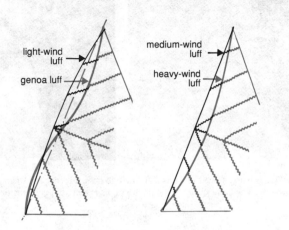

Jibs have different luff shapes depending on the weather for which they are designed.

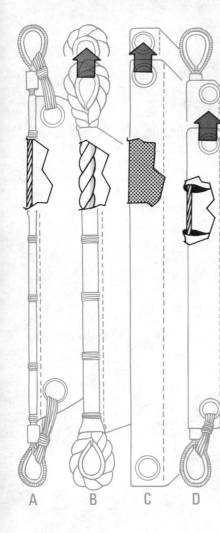

A   B   C   D

B and C: those in which the sleeve is attached to a fabric or rope core. These can be adjusted by halyard tension.

D: those with a steel luff wire on which the sail sleeve is free to move. The jib can be adjusted independently of the halyard tension.

If your jib is of type A, the jib is set up on the luff wire to cope with a particular wind strength. If the wind changes, you have to change jibs.

Types B, C and D allow you to adjust the luff tension. It is possible to stop the belly moving aft, up to a point. Each jib is therefore capable of dealing with a range of wind strengths. Some boats take the logic of this knowledge to its conclusion on the beat, by cleating the sheet hard in, then adjusting the luff tension (by as much as 10–20cm, depending on the size of the jib).

If the luff rope is so long that you have no freedom to tighten it (whether this came about deliberately or not), you can have a Cunningham eye on the jib just like that on the mainsail.

We should conclude by pointing out that there are alternatives to the usual hanks for attaching the jib halyard to the forestay. Some modern boats have a headfoil with a groove along which the jib luff rope is pulled; and there are roller-reefed jibs which can be rolled round the forestay depending on the wind strength, and can be made to roll up entirely when you are in harbour.

The leech

A light strip of fabric will be sewn on the leech, rather than any real

When one is using a headfoil, it is usual also to have a feeder for keeping the luff lined up correctly. The large spring in the photographs is there to keep tension in the system.

reinforcement. The leech will generally be concave for heavy weather and straight for light weather. (One cannot build much roach into a jib, as it is difficult to support it with battens.)

The foot

Jibs normally have a straight or concave foot. For light winds, some genoas have a full foot, so that the 'skirt' of the deck-sweeping jib prevents any wind escaping between the sail and the deck.

The three corners

• The jib luff should always be pulled tight, so the fittings at top and bottom of the luff need to be good and solid.
• There is also tension at the jib clew, between there and the luff. The clew is constantly being dragged across the decking, rubbing against the rigging and flapping to and fro. The clew must be particularly well constructed.
• The tack and head of the sail are subject to lesser strains, but they do need some reinforcement, particularly if the luff runs in a roller reefer or hollow forestay. If the jib is attached to the forestay with hanks, there must be hanks at or close to the two ends.

Cunningham eye system on a jib.

Spinnakers

Spinnakers are all made of nylon, which may be light or heavy depending on the size of sail and the sort of winds it is designed for. Reaching spinnakers are made of slightly heavier material than running spinnakers, so that they keep their shape better.

Panels

Spinnaker panels can be arranged in a huge variety of ways: you can get some idea of the potential diversity if you just watch a downwind start to a race. In general, one is aiming for a configuration which will allow the spinnaker to take on and maintain a reasonable shape, particularly on the leeches. Most people like to have the edges aligned with the weave, but some prefer the leeches to be on a bias, for reasons to do with cut and manufacture.

The commonest arrangements are the following:
Sail A Panels leading from all three corners: *star cut*. Holds its shape extremely well.

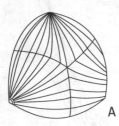

The dedicated follower of fashion ...

Sail B Panels at right angles to the leeches, made in two parts: the upper panels are joined in the middle and perpendicular to the leeches, while the lower panels are horizontal.

Sail C is a mixed design, with a star cut at the top and horizontal panels lower down.

Sail D is another mixed design, with stars cut for all three corners, and horizontal panels in the centre, known as a triradial design.

All these designs have their advantages and their disadvantages. The general tendency is to ensure that the leeches are aligned with the weave, just because any loss of shape at the leech means that the spinnaker does not empty correctly.

Spinnaker shape

A spinnaker should be cut in the shape of half a cylinder, topped off with a quarter sphere. The peak of the sail should be almost horizontal. The fuller the sail is higher up, the more upward lift it will generate. The shape of the top part of the spinnaker has an inordinate influence on the way the whole sail behaves: quite often you will find that a poorly shaped central section is actually due to a bad cut at the top of the sail.

Spinnakers are just like any other sail in that you need them to be flatter the stronger the wind is and the closer to the wind you are trying to sail. Some people are now using asymmetric spinnakers which are cut quite similarly to full genoas. One noticeable advantage of the flatter spinnakers is that they let the air out more easily if you are caught by a broach and luff uncontrollably.

Some spinnakers are specially designed for particular wind strengths and precise points of sailing, but a cruiser should have a general-purpose spinnaker which gives reasonable performance on all points of sailing.

Asymmetrically cut spinnaker

The edges of a spinnaker

The three corners of a spinnaker are heavily reinforced, because they take all the force which the sail generates.

• The leeches are simply edged with a moderately light binding. The binding should be of the same elasticity as the sail cloth, or the leeches will curl.

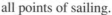

• The foot drags over the pulpit and forestay. However, if you reinforce it, it will stiffen what is supposed to be a stretchy sail. For this reason, you will see that many spinnakers get their first repairs and patches along the foot.

Manufacture

Seams

Originally, sails used to be hand-sewn, but these days all sails are sewn by machine in either a zigzag stitch or a running zigzag. The size of the stitching is determined by the need to make a profit: the larger the stitch, the quicker (and weaker) the seam. The thread used in machine stitching is rarely pulled hard enough for the purposes of sailmaking, so the stitches are subject to wear when they rub on anything. You should always keep an eye on the seams of your sails and have them restitched before they split.

Any thread used for machine sewing should be continuous, and treated against UV light. For stitching panels together, two seams are the minimum, and you should have three or four in the more heavily

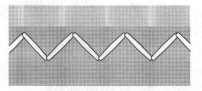

These large stitches are keeping the panels together. The edges of the panels could fray unless the cloth was hot-knived.

Half of these small stitches are keeping the panels together; half keep the edge down. This otherwise excellent stitch has the disadvantage that it can damage the edge of any cloth which is not reinforced.

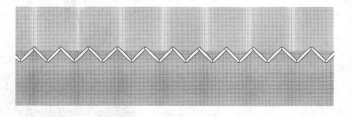

stressed areas.

Glues are often used before sewing to make the assembly easier. It would probably be possible to make sails simply with glued panels, but no one has yet dared try this with mass-produced sails.

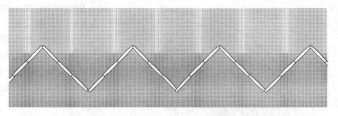

This running zigzag stitch is the best solution: the seam is held down by small stitches, but the panels are held together by well spaced zigzags.

Punched eye.

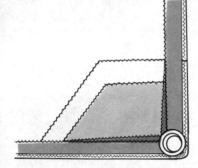

Mainsail tack with cringle.

Triangle held by reinforcing strips on a mainsail.

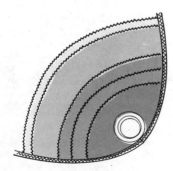

Spinnaker clew.

Eyelets

There are three sorts of eyelet:

• *Punched eyes* are simple rings with teeth punched into each other through the sail. They cannot be used where there is a lot of force, as they will tear the cloth. They are best kept for use on your sailbag only.

• *Press rings* are eyes put in with a very large machine. They are fairly strong. Of course, the eyes need to be of a suitable size for your boat.

• *Rings or triangles* are often sewn onto the edge of the sail and held in place by reinforcing strips. They are still stronger than press rings. Any cringle at the jib clew must be large enough for two sheets to fit through. On mainsails, the tack and clew cringles can often give trouble, so should be regularly checked.

Reinforcing

The sail needs to be reinforced where it will be subject to the most force. A look at the clew of a spinnaker will provide a good example.

If we assume that there will be a 600kg force on the cringle, which has a half-circumference of 6cm, and the sailcloth can withstand 10kg/1cm, then we shall need ten thicknesses of cloth to prevent the cringle being torn out.

Going further away from the cringle, the same force will be spread over, say, 10cm, so we shall only need six thicknesses to support it. Where we have 12cm of cloth, only five layers will be needed, until we reach an arc at 60cm, where our final double thickness can stop.

Reinforcing layers are not an insurance policy in case one layer tears: they are an integral part of the sail's strength. Any seam in a reinforcing patch which starts to come undone must be re-sewn immediately.

Edging

There will be reinforcing patches sewn along each of the sail's edges, to stop the edges losing their shape. The edge strips can also be controlled to move the position of maximum fullness in the sail. In the past there were ropes sewn along the edges, whereas nowadays there are simple cloth strips with the weave at 90° to the edge.

The means of attaching the sail to the rigging are fixed in these edge strips: clips and/or a luff wire/rope in the jib; slides and/or a rope in the mainsail.

Patching

Patches which protect the sail against wear are important, though they are not strictly speaking part of the structure of the sail. They should be added after the sail has had a few outings, so you can tell exactly where they are needed. Their main job is to protect the seams; they should not influence the shape of the sail, so they should be of lighter cloth than the rest, and sewn on with some slack left in the thread.

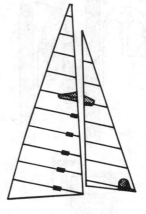

Batten pockets

The first place to need a patch is always the end of a batten pocket. The pictures show the reinforcement necessary. So that battens which are not tied in do not slip out and get lost, you should pay particular attention to the end of the pocket next to the leech. This should be at least 2cm in from the leech, and the batten itself should in turn be 2cm shorter than the pocket. Some sails have an elastic strip in the mast end of the pocket, to force the batten against the pocket top. This strip is of dubious usefulness. It does mean you get an extra layer of reinforcement.

Batten pocket.

Tied batten pocket.

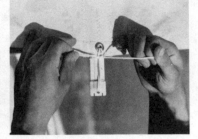

Knotting a full-length batten in place.

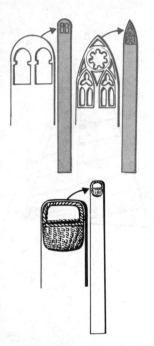

The tip of the batten should be the shape of an old basket handle, not a romanesque or gothic arch!

We cannot overstress the importance of tying in any full-length battens with a sensible knot.

Battens

Although the battens might appear to be an optional extra, the wrong ones can cause considerable loss of power in your mainsail.

Battens come in wood, plastic-coated wood and reinforced plastic. Wooden battens are gradually dying out, as it becomes harder to find the right wood: ash, acacia, spruce, red cedar, etc. Wooden battens are limited in their maximum useful length, and it is difficult to achieve a good combination of strength and flexibility. Decent wood reinforced with plastic or glass fibre, on the other hand, can make highly sophisticated battens. They are not commercially available: you have to make them yourself, tailored to the size and weight of your sail.

The best solution for the average cruising sailor will be a simple plastic batten the same width all along. It can be cut to the desired length and then fitted with end-pieces so it does not ruin the pocket.

The boat's sail-wardrobe

The number of sails you take on board depends less on the size of your boat than on the type of sailing you plan to do. The more ambitious you are, the more sails you need.

• *Dinghy racing*. A mainsail, a jib and usually a spinnaker. Rich sailors might have several sets of sails, but only one will actually be with the boat once you are afloat.

• *Day-sailing and fishing trips*. A mainsail, a jib and a storm jib.

• *Coastal sailing*. A mainsail, a number one jib, a storm jib and (on cutters) a staysail. Genoa and spinnaker are recommended but not essential.

• *Coastal cruising*. A mainsail, a genoa, a number one jib, a storm jib; if possible a number two jib, a spinnaker and a storm mainsail. Cutters should also have one or two staysails.

• *Ocean cruising*. A main, a storm main, a spinnaker, a genoa, a number one and number two jib, a storm jib, and for cutters, two staysails.

• *Cruiser racing*. A main, a trysail and all the jibs and spinnakers necessary to ensure you are carrying as much sail as the weather will allow.

A genoa rigged on a roller can replace all the jibs except the storm jib. With the roller, you can theoretically reduce the genoa's surface area to that of a storm jib, but you should take some precaution against the roller packing up.

Along with the storm jib, then, you should also pack a spare luff wire, and ensure that there is one halyard rigged separately from the roller gear; as well as a spare. These need not be specialist items: by all means use the spinnaker pole uphaul as a luff rope and a topping lift as the halyard. So long as you've thought about it in advance, and practised, a problem will not throw you off balance.

Maintenance and repairs

Wear

Wear is the greatest enemy of long life in sails.

One barely thinks about it, but the sail itself is the prime source of its wear, as it flaps to and fro. You should not allow the sail to flap excessively, and you should not hoist it up half an hour before rigging the other sails, or leave it up long after mooring.

Wear on the areas of the sail which naturally touch other parts of the boat is inevitable. The other parts should be kept as smooth and free of sharp points as possible. The shrouds should be cased in plastic, split pins taped up, spreaders wrapped or provided with a ping-pong ball over their ends and plastic discs rigged at the spreaders.

Attention paid to this preventive medicine will save wear on the edges of the jib, the mainsail from the boom all the way up the lower shrouds, and the spinnaker clew.

You should not forget, either, that the boat is constantly in motion, even when it is moored. If you leave the luff rope in the jib, or do not roll the main onto the boom properly, the sails will slowly deteriorate even in harbour. It is always preferable to take the sails off the boat completely, particularly as this will also save them from the effects of UV rays as well. Jibs rigged on roller gear should have a strip of coloured cloth round the leech and foot so as to protect these exposed parts from the effects of UV radiation when the jib is furled.

Be particularly careful not to let heavily treated or complex sail-cloths flog: they are easily destroyed.

Drying and storage

Rot-resistant though they may be, synthetic sails still need to be put away and stored with care.

For a day or two, it does not really matter if you put a sail away in its bag while it is still wet with sea water; but you still need to dry it out when you can, or it will end up covered in unsightly, if not actually damaging, little black spots.

If you make the sail bags different colours for the different sails, it will aid fast retrieval. If the bags are all the same colour, they should have the name of the sail written on them in a dozen places, in large letters. Banana bags are expensive (unless home-made), but very convenient, as they can be fed through hatches so easily. For very stiff or heavily treated sails, they are the only sort of bag you can use. You can also tie the furled sail into a sausage, with knots every two feet, like on the old three-masters. This is particularly useful with larger sails – so long as you are good at making the knots!

To tie a furled sail correctly, make a loop in a ribbon using a bowline, feed the other end through the loop and tie with a slip-half hitch.

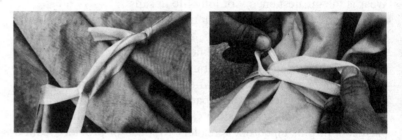

You can protect a mainsail furled on the boom with a cover. If the cover bears the boat's name, your friends will be able to spot you more easily in the harbour.

It is worth rinsing the sails from time to time in fresh water. The salt crystals formed by drying sea-water make a good abrasive, as does sand.

How should you rinse the sails? They should be soaked and stirred around in a tub for five to ten minutes. In fact, you can even rinse them in sea water, which might sound stupid, but in fact there is so much salt deposited on sails after a longish trip with water repeatedly drying on the sail, that a good rinse with sea water will actually clean off most of it.

How should you dry the sails? Depending on whether you need to dry the sails on land, at sea, or at a mooring, there are different answers.

On land, you can hang them up, or lay them on grass to dry. (Do not put them on sand, concrete or gravel, where they will pick up the grit in all the seams.) Do not leave them in the sun longer than necessary.

If you are moored, you can hoist the sails up the mast with the tack uppermost, but this can only be done on calm days: it is ten times worse for a sail to flog than to stay damp in its bag.

When you are at sea and you have wet sails to dry out (generally the smaller, storm sails) you just have to wait for better weather when you can hoist them, either on their own or alongside the usual sails, downwind. If nothing else, they make good decoration!

How should you store the sails? If sails are to be stored for any length of time, they should be put in a safe dry place, away from light and rats. Whatever you do, make sure everyone who might find them knows that they do not need to be folded or ironed into good sharp creases ...

Repairs to stitching

A little practice can make an expert sail-stitcher of any of us. A 1m seam should take you no more than ten minutes – though ideally you should have grabbed your needle and thread before repairs over this length became necessary. As soon as a seam begins to show signs of loosening, you should attend to it.

If the sailcloth is no heavier than 300gsm, you can use an ordinary domestic sewing machine on it. Any more than that, and you will need to sew it up by hand. You do not need much in the way of equipment: needles and thread, beeswax, a sailmaker's or cobbler's palm and a hook.

The needles to use are: No 17 for cloth over 300gsm; No 18 for cloth of 200–300gsm; and for lighter cloth you can use a No 19 or a domestic needle.

Cotton thread is easier to use than Terylene, and just as strong. The beeswax is used not so much to protect the thread as to ensure it does not get tangled while you are sewing. *The thread should always be used double, so as to fill the hole left by the needle.*

Sticking a patch

Amateurs will have problems sewing a patch as well as a professional would do. On the other hand, sticking a patch in place and then reinforcing it with some stitching is within the abilities of most of us.

Surgical plasters or self-sticking material make good patches. You can of course use ordinary sailcloth, with a sufficiently strong adhesive.

Your patch will not stick unless all the surfaces are clean and completely dry. You can dry a piece of sailcloth in next to no time by filling a normal bottle with boiling water and laying the cloth over the top of that.

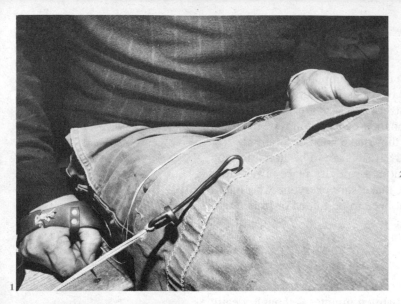

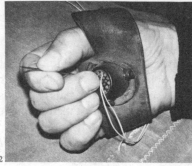

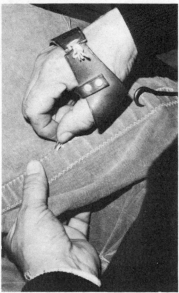

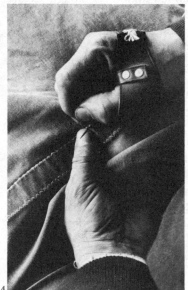

When handsewing a seam, always use a simple sailmaker's stitch rather than a zigzag stitch.

1. To remake a seam, sit down with the sail folded double on your knees. The hook keeps tension on the sail, so the cloth stays straight. The seam is made from right to left, with a slanting oversewn stitch at about 30° to the weave of the sail. Do not try to make a zigzag stitch like a sewing machine: the sailor's stitch you are using is better than any machine can do!

2. The palm enables you to push the needle through the cloth without hurting your hand. Hold the needle as shown in the photograph, between thumb and index finger; use your middle and ring fingers to keep the end in place on the palm heel.

3. Begin to sew just above the loose seam. Push the needle through until it hits the second thickness, then pull it back a touch so as to unstick it. (You should hear it come away from the second layer.)

4. Push the needle so that it comes out again below the seam. Your left hand is simply keeping the cloth flat, while it is being held still by the hook.

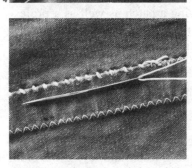

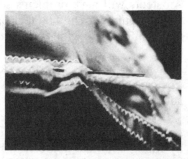

5. Once you have the needle out, pull the thread fairly hard with your left hand, then start the next stitch.

6. Aim to make twelve stitches within one needle length.

7. If you do not have a hook available, you can use a string pinned in place.

The sail should then be laid flat with the torn edges drawn together into the right shape. Make sure the weave of the patch is aligned with that of the sail.

The same hot-water bottle can be used to heat the whole area, so the glue will stick better.

Such a repair is temporary unless, of course, you sew it as well as glueing it.

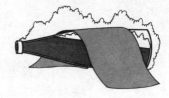

The cloth will dry in three minutes.

Sewing on a slide

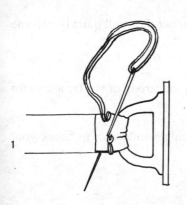

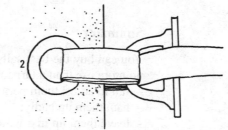

To fix a slide to a sail using webbing:
1. Attach the webbing to the slide using a running stitch.
2. Give the webbing three or four turns through the sail eye.
3. Finish off with another running stitch on the webbing between the slide and the luff rope.

Running stitch.

Darning

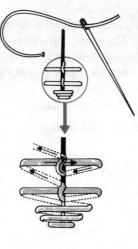

Darning is useful for repairing small tears of up to 3 or 4cm. (Anyone who darns a tear of 20cm is being optimistic.) Sew from right to left and away from yourself. Follow the diagrams exactly, with two or three stitches to the centimetre. The stitches should be 1–1.5cm long.

Summary

You can buy the best sails available, but they will quickly become no more use than a tarpaulin if you:
- fail to adjust them periodically to the rig;
- haul them up badly;
- leave them up in a wind which is too strong or too far ahead for them;
- let them chafe;
- repair them yourself without getting a sailmaker to check your work;
- store them badly.

CHAPTER 2

Motors and electricity

More and more, the motor has become essential in cruising yachts. Access to marinas is often difficult, and regulations tend to forbid the use of sail within their precincts. Moreover, it is not easy to find the power for navigation lights, electronic equipment and lighting on board without a motor. Finally, the knowledge that in a tricky situation it is possible, with a motor, to get out of a strong current, or compensate for lack of wind, makes for peace of mind on board.

The famous 'Perkins breeze' (or the Volvo, or Couach) well conveys the newly found esteem in which amateur sailors hold their motors, where formerly they were thought unacceptable to the purists. Nonetheless, *the motor is there for convenience only, and should not be regarded as a guarantee of safety.*

The only useful motor is a reliable one. And a motor is only reliable if its owner knows it well, services it regularly and uses it often. This is only achievable if the necessary time and money are available. It is not like an automobile engine; its environment is cramped, humid and salty, factors which affect its performance if proper attention is not paid to them.

The many stories one hears of motors which refuse to start just when they are needed are obviously not all fictional, but it is always partly the owner's fault if the motor won't start – it may be down to incompetence or neglect. A motor should be looked after with the same care as the sails. A daily half hour run for man and motor – that's how to keep fit.

This book does not claim to be exhaustive on the subject of motors but rather to set out the basic information.

How to choose your motor

Only two kinds of motor are suitable for a cruising yacht: either a fixed diesel or an outboard petrol motor. You should not even consider a fixed petrol motor because it is a fire hazard and there is the risk of explosion from petrol stored on board. Whether you choose an outboard or diesel motor depends on the type of boat and how powerful you want the motor to be.

Outboard motors are always cheaper than diesels. But if the motor is a powerful one – above 20hp – then petrol consumption is very high. Bear in mind, however, that four-stroke motors are more fuel-efficient than two-stroke ones. Above 25hp, outboard motors are very heavy and are not practical on yachts.

A diesel motor is better if you want to be able to run the motor for a long time at moderate speeds – while fishing or to recharge the batteries for example. This obviously means that there must be enough space on board and that the boat can bear the relatively heavy weight involved.

When you have decided on the type of motor you want, you then have to decide how much power you need. The salesman will of course know the maximum possible power, but this will not give you any idea of the practically usable power. In short, you must know first of all what you want. If you want to be able to get back on time when there is no wind, to manoeuvre in a port and to recharge the batteries, even the smallest motor will have sufficient power. For example, a motor of 15kW on an 8 tonne boat will provide enough power to do 5 or 6 knots when there is no wind/in a flat calm. This provides enough speed for manoeuvring. To charge up batteries, 150–200W are quite enough. A bigger motor can only be justified if you want to be able to move quite fast at all times, but in that case perhaps you should buy a motor boat or a real speedboat. Small motors are slightly cheaper to buy, a good deal cheaper to fit and very much cheaper to maintain than large motors.

Outboard motors

An outboard motor for your boat is always second best choice, but justifiable on grounds of purchase cost, ease of maintenance and storage in winter. The greatest problem with this sort of motor is the fuel, which can be very dangerous unless proper care is taken.

Safety

An outboard motor with an internal petrol tank is dangerous, for two reasons. When you lay the motor down on its side petrol can leak through the air intake valve of the tank. More serious still is the risk that eventually you will give in to the temptation to fill it when it is running and start a fire. On the other hand if the motor and the tank are separate, it is much safer. When you lower the motor, it cannot leak; the tank is not near the motor and sparks. Furthermore, since the tank has a larger capacity, there is less temptation to fill the tank while the motor is running. Since petrol is sucked up by the motor, there is almost no danger of leaks along the pipes.

Finally, one must not forget the dangers of using a motor which is not enclosed; it is easy to burn yourself on it and particularly to hurt yourself on the flywheel.

Never bring the motor and the petrol tank into the boat, even into the cockpit lockers. If for any reason you have to do so, they should be put into a cockpit locker which is completely watertight, both at the bottom for the fuel and at the top for fumes. If the cockpit is drained while afloat, remember that any petrol which may have been spilt is lighter than water and that it will stay in the draining pipes and could well catch fire.

Installing the motor

One of the advantages of outboard motors is that they are very easy to install; it takes only minutes to set them up on the boat or take them ashore. When they need to be repaired or laid up for winter they are very easy to carry to the dealer; it is easier and cheaper than having to call in a specialist to look at the motor *in situ.*

When installing an outboard motor, there is one major point to be taken into account; when the motor is running, the propeller and the cooling water intake must both be completely submerged. Since this cannot be guaranteed at all times, *you should never use the motor in a rough sea or if the boat is rolling.* When the motor is not in use, it is best that the propeller be completely out of the water. Ideally, it should be possible to lower and raise the motor without having to take it off its mountings. The best solution is to have a well, preferably one which can be blocked off when the motor is removed. If this is not possible, the motor should be mounted on the transom of the boat, or on a movable mounting. Unfortunately, this means that the motor is vulnerable to shocks if a false movement is made, and if it is particularly heavy it can encourage the boat to pitch.

When under sail, if the motor can't be removed altogether, it should be lifted off its mountings and laid on the deck, either hanging upright on the back rail, or lying on the deck. Wherever it is stored, you should put a cloth cover over it, but keep the side which faces down uncovered to allow water and air to pass through. If the motor is put in the cabin, it will make anyone prone to seasickness very unhappy, and means a very high risk of fire.

The sea water intake must be completely submerged, even when the boat rolls.

Things are rarely as easy as they look here. The mounting must be able to move up and down on the transom.

While you are handling the motor, it is wise to keep it tied to the boat with a safety chain.

Using the motor

Most modern outboard motors work reliably as long as they are properly used. Problems tend to be the result of incorrect use rather than of mechanical defects.

The petrol supply

If the motor stops, it is very often because there is a problem with the petrol supply. If the feeder pipe is wrongly connected the motor won't work; this may seem obvious, but it is the most common reason for motor failure. You should also remember to check that the motor is not starved because the screw which allows air in has not been adjusted (not all tanks have a screw).

There may also of course be some water in the fuel. In this case, you should:
– empty the carburettor; you must know how to do this and make sure that the tools you need are on board;
– clean out the fuel tank itself, either by emptying it, or preferably by siphoning out all the fuel;
– clean out the fuel feeder pipe or you will immediately break down again.

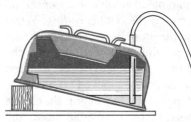

To stop an outboard motor you can simply disconnect the feeder pipe. This empties the carburettor and when the motor is laid down, there is no longer any risk of it leaking.

To clean out the reservoir, use a rubber pipe with a rigid intake.

Ignition

Over a period of time, the sparkplugs will become clogged and show signs of wear. They should be cleaned occasionally and the electrodes should be tightened (they should be 0.6mm apart; that is about three times the thickness of a marine chart.) Since sparkplugs do not last for ever, it is better to change them after they have been in use for one hundred hours. For other problems with the ignition, you will need to go to a good mechanic. Remember to get him to waterproof the whole circuit each time.

Cooling the motor

It is very dangerous for the cooling system to break down; if the motor is not being properly cooled it can burn out in less than a minute. There is a very small amount of water in the water cooling circuit, so it is crucial that there should be a constant, rapid flow of water to keep the temperature low.

Firstly, remember that the water inlet should always be below water level. This may not be the case, say, when one or more of the crew goes to the front to moor the boat.

You must also be careful to make sure that water inlets do not get clogged up with the marine rubbish which is common in ports – algae or pieces of plastic, etc. On most motors there is a warning light connected to the cooling system. Remember to keep an eye on this all the time. If the pump develops a fault, you will have to call in a mechanic.

Lubrication

A two-stroke motor is lubricated by oil mixed with the fuel. It is important to follow the manufacturer's recommended percentage for the mixture; this usually varies from 1 to 4% depending on the make of the motor. It is important to mix the fuel and oil properly, either by mixing it vigorously yourself, or by getting your supply from a pump which will mix the two for you.

Four-stroke motors have a sump which contains the oil. Check the oil level regularly and clean out the sump completely every fifty to one hundred hours.

It is easy to forget to lubricate the subsidiary parts of the motor like the throttle, the clutch cable, the steering pin, the screw clamps, etc.

Running speed

Two-stroke outboard motors are built to run at high revs; they can quite happily run for several hours at 90% of their maximum speed. When they run slowly for a long period of time, they become clogged up and are then difficult to start. To make it easier to start up the motor next time, you should run the motor for a few seconds at very high speed before shutting it off.

Four-stroke outboard motors are much more flexible to use and can run for extended periods at low speed; in this case, it is best to run the motor for four minutes at low speed before shutting it off.

Fuel consumption

Above 80% power, the fuel consumption doubles, but the speed of the boat only increases by 5%. You can draw your own conclusions.

The propeller

The propeller often contains a shear pin which will break if the propeller is jammed (by a piece of rope, for example). It is therefore useful to have spare shear pins on board.

Broken starter

Even if the starter is broken, it is always possible to start up a motor; just wrap a length of cord around the flywheel. You will have to take the broken starter off some motors, which will involve using a screwdriver. (Don't forget to take the screwdriver with you when you set up the motor on the tender.)

Motor overboard

If the motor falls into seawater, it must be looked at by a mechanic as soon as possible and cleaned out. Until the mechanic arrives, keep the motor submerged in water – but preferably in fresh water. If the motor falls into fresh water it can simply be dried off, and it should then start up again.

Essential spares

- An electrical insulating spray.
- At least two sparkplugs and a good sparkplug spanner.
- One or two shear pins for the propeller.

Diesel motors

These are bigger and more complicated than outboard motors. To use them most effectively, you need to have a basic understanding of mechanics; you need to know how to prime the fuel system, change a rubber hose, tension the alternator drivebelt, drain the motor and do a grease and oil change.

Installing the motor

Diesel motors must be installed according to certain fixed guide-lines, and there are very strict regulations about this. Despite this, the errors listed below can occur quite frequently.
• The fuel tank's valve is not accessible in case of fire; to avoid this you should make sure that you can close the valve from the deck at a distance.
• Very often, to save money, the flexible piping linking the fuel tank to the filler cap is cut from a longer piece of piping; this means that only one of the ends is smooth and the fuel inlet is not watertight. Consequently, when the tank is filled, diesel fuel leaks into the bottom of the boat.
• It is also very often impossible to empty the drip tray, the waterproof container which has to be placed underneath the motor to catch any fuel overflow. The container ought to have a clear mark, low down its side, at which it is possible to introduce a syringe to siphon out the fuel. You should check that the leak tray is of the right shape and that the siphoning point mentioned above is accessible.

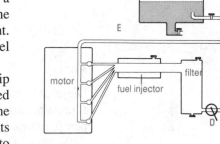

Diagram showing how a diesel motor should be installed on board.

A. Deck plate, which can be tightened with a winch crank.
B. Rubber seal, which is totally water-proof.
C. Jubilee hose clip.
D. Feed pump, which is necessary if the tank is lower than the motor.
E. Fuel return from injectors.

You should also remember that the flexible hoses used in motors do not last for ever. The rubber shock absorbers and hoses will eventually perish through continued contact with diesel fuel. They should be changed frequently, at least every year or every two years.

The fuel tank needs a special note. Ideally, the tank should be below the motor and the fuel should be pumped up to the motor . In this way, if there were a leak in the piping, the pump would take in air and the motor would stop, but no diesel would be spilt in the boat.

When the motor is running there can be problems; the most serious ones will be problems with the oil and the cooling system. In a car, any lack of oil or water is shown up by the oil and water lights on the dashboard, which the driver can see at all times, but in a boat you will not be constantly looking at the instrument panel. For this reason it is a good idea to back up the instrument panel with an alarm which will go off if there are problems with the level of oil in the motor or problems in the cooling system. As soon as you hear the alarm, check the instrument panel to find out what the problem is, then turn off the motor. If the system has been properly fitted, the alarm will go off at the same time as the motor starts up and stops, just as the oil light comes on in a car.

The sea water inlet should be easily accessible and everyone on board should know where it is. It should have a fixed handle so that it can be closed immediately in case of any leaks.

Finally, you should remember to take on board all the tools and equipment that you will need for basic repairs and ongoing maintenance. Obviously, you will only bring with you the tools for the jobs you know how to do. If you can't carry out even the most simple repair jobs, the first problem will leave you just as if you had no motor, so it is worth learning the basics.

Operation

Fuel

Diesel motors only use ordinary diesel fuel as used in cars and lorries. It must be absolutely free from any impurities because the injection pump cannot tolerate water or impurities over 4 microns in size (0.004mm). The motor therefore has two filters: first of all a pre-filter with a transparent reservoir where water collects, then a filter with a filter cartridge, generally made of blotting paper, which holds all the solid impurities; this filter should be replaced at each grease and oil change. If you can see water in the first filter reservoir, the reservoir must be emptied and cleaned out, either by draining it if that is possible, or if not, by pumping out the bottom of the reservoir with whatever you have available – either a hand pump, or a syringe fitted with a pipe which can be put at the bottom of the reservoir.

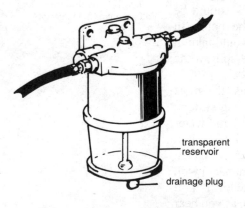

transparent reservoir

drainage plug

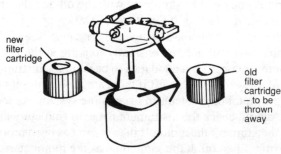

new filter cartridge

old filter cartridge – to be thrown away

A diesel filter showing both a water filter and a filter for solid impurities.

If there is any air in the fuel system (which can happen particularly if you have run out of fuel), the motor will not work. It will stop or fail to accelerate as soon as any air reaches the injector pump, and the air will not 'go through'.

Cleaning out the system should be done in two stages:

1. Loosen the fuel filter pipe at the point where it goes in to the injector pump (assuming there is no tap to empty out the system); allow the fuel to run through or pump it through by hand until there are no bubbles left; tighten up the pipe again.

2. Loosen the nuts which hold the pipes onto the injectors; make the motor turn over if possible by cranking it until all the air has been expelled from this part of the system too; then tighten up the nuts again.

The cooling system

Most diesel motors are cooled by fresh water which in turn is cooled by sea water. This means that there are two water cooling circuits.

The fresh water circuit is closed, just as in a car. It should be kept full, and you should have a supply of fresh water on board to top it up if necessary. It is dangerous to introduce any sea water into this circuit, even for a short time, because it will corrode the steel engine lining.

The sea water circuit is an open one: water is sucked in by a pump through a strainer located below the waterline; it goes through a heat exchanger where it cools down the fresh water then it is ejected from the boat, usually through the exhaust.

If the alarm signal goes off because the motor is overheating, stop the motor immediately and first of all check the level of water in the fresh water circuit. If there is not enough water, you should top it up when the motor has cooled and you have checked for leaks.

If the water level is satisfactory, you should still let the motor cool down, then start it up again and check that the sea water circuit is working as it should. If this is also working normally, the water pump has probably broken down, and you won't be able to repair this yourself.

If the sea water is not circulating, there are several possibilities:
– the seacock may be closed;
– the strainer may be blocked; to find out, close the cock, remove the pipe, open up the cock again and see if the water is flowing;
– if both the cock and the strainer are letting water through, you've got a bigger problem on your hands; the entire circuit may be blocked or the pump may be malfunctioning, and you will need to call in a mechanic.

The sea water inlet valve is usually kept open as long as you are living on board; it should simply be tested once a week. If the boat is not being used, the valve should be closed, and you should find a way of reminding yourself to open it before starting up the motor next time, because it's easy to forget. For example, you could hook the key over the valve.

Lubrication

A pressurised oil circuit keeps the engine lubricated. The pressure must not fall below a certain level and the level can be checked on a pressure gauge. An oil filter with a cartridge which is changed when the oil change is done keeps the system clean. You should use the make of oil recommended by the manufacturer; always using the same oil and the recommended quantity. It is just as bad to use too much as too little. It is better to change the oil more often than strictly necessary (every 100–200 hours) than to do it less often. Even if the engine has not been used much, you should not run it on oil which is more than three months old.

If the alarm system goes off because of a problem with lubrication, you should stop the engine and check the level of oil. If it is low, just top it up. Otherwise, there is likely to be a serious problem which you cannot fix yourself, so get ready to sail back.

If the gearbox has a sump which is separate from the engine sump, you should check the level at least every two weeks and clean it out at least once a year. Don't forget the subsidiary parts either: the fresh water and sea water pumps, the coupling, the clutch and throttle cables. These should be oiled at each oil change but more frequently if the engine is used a lot.

Electricity

As soon as the engine runs, the alternator should recharge the battery. You can check this on an ammeter. After the engine has been running for a period of time (anything between five minutes and several hours), the rate of charge will decrease but it should never stop completely. If the alternator is not charging the battery, it is often because the drive belt is loose and this can easily be repaired.

Starting the engine manually

It is very useful to be able to start the engine manually if the battery is flat or waterlogged. This is only possible if you have a small engine equipped with a fly wheel and if you are reasonably strong.

It's important to try to start the engine before buying it. Don't be convinced just by the salesman's patter and the fact that the engine has a cranking handle.

Maintenance

The reliability of the engine depends to a large extent on good maintenance. The owner needs to pay careful attention to maintenance, even if this means in practice entrusting the engine to a competent mechanic. Only the person who actually uses an engine knows its foibles, and it is important therefore that the owner is the one to arrange for work to be done on the engine when necessary. Keep a note in your logbook of maintenance activities and any malfunctions. The manufacturer's servicing recommendations should be closely followed. Associated components also need maintenance. Here is a practical list of what should be done and when.

At the annual fitting out
– clean out the diesel tank completely;
– empty the pre-filter reservoir/bowl;
– change the fuel filter cartridge;
– drain all the fuel from the engine;
– check that the fuel cap is waterproof;
– calibrate and check the injectors;
– refit the starter, alternator and batteries if they have been taken out; if they haven't been taken out, tension the fanbelt, top up the level of electrolyte and clean the battery terminals;
– drain the oil from the engine and the gears; lubricate all the moving parts as well as the gear and throttle;
– clean the strainer, including the inside: it may have become blocked with barnacles or other animal or vegetable matter;
– grease the seacock;
– check the condition of the rubber hoses. If you can see cracks when you squeeze them, they must be changed. Top up the level of fresh water;
– if there is one, loosen the stern gland and add more packing.

At laying-up
– close the fuel cock;
– it is best to remove the alternator, starter and battery. They can also be left on board, but if so it will be necessary to run the engine for at least an hour every two weeks or preferably an hour a week;
– put a little oil into each cylinder and turn the engine round twice

to make sure that the oil is evenly distributed on the sides of the cylinder;
– close the seacock;
– put some antifreeze into the fresh water;
– check that the stern gland is waterproof; if you need to, tighten it further;
– clean and lubricate all electrical connections with a silicon based lubricant.

Operation

The reliability of the engine also depends to a large extent on how it is used. Users should therefore follow the manufacturer's instructions to the letter. But, as for maintenance, use involves more than running the engine itself, and another practical list of things to do is given below.

When you go on board
– open the seacocks;
– check the fuel level;
– check that there is no water in the pre-filter reservoir;
– check the level of oil in the engine;
– check the level of the fresh water;
– switch on the electricity.

Ignition/starting the engine
– with the motor in neutral, open the throttle a bit;
– preheat if necessary;
– start the engine without draining the battery for more than five seconds at a time;
– let the engine run at one-third power for at least three minutes to warm it up; in the meantime check the battery is charging, the sea water cooling system is working, and the oil pressure is normal.

   If the engine fails to start, in 90% of cases it is because of a problem with the diesel supply, and in 10% of cases because the temperature is too low.

Under way
– give the engine time to warm up by running it at half power only for the first five minutes you are moving;
– go into gear properly; never slip the clutch;
– remember to go into neutral for a moment when changing direction;

– avoid accelerating suddenly;
– don't run the engine at over four-fifths power, particularly on long journeys;
– if you want to run the engine at slow speed for fishing, it may be worth having it retuned.

Stopping
– run the engine for at least five minutes at reduced speed to cool it down;
– turn off the fuel;
– check the fuel level;
– switch off the engine after it has stopped turning;
– check that there is no water in the pre-filter reservoir;
– check the level of the engine oil after you have been stationary for five minutes;
– when you're stopping for the day, check the fresh water level.
By doing all of these, you ensure a quick start in any situation.

On leaving the boat
– close the seacock;
– make sure that the stern gland is not leaking;
– disconnect the battery.

Engine safety

If your boat is equipped with an inboard diesel, you should carry:
– a set of tools;
– a spare injector;
– fuel/lubrication oil filter elements;
– spare hoses, fuses and gaskets;
– spare drive belts.

Electricity

It is now almost essential to have an electricity supply on a cruising yacht. But since the boat can't be plugged into the mains, there is always a limited amount of electricity available. You therefore need to learn how to manage intelligently the production, storage and consumption of electricity so that what should be a blessing doesn't turn out to be a nightmare.

How much electricity do you need?

To find out how much electricity you need, you have to assess your needs in relation to two factors – the time you are prepared to spend on charging up the battery, and the facilities you would like to have available on board. Obviously, the money you have available will affect your decisions. Before beginning to make the assessment, you will need some background information.
• An incandescent lamp will provide the same intensity of lighting but not the same mood as a neon lamp. It uses twice as much

---

How to check an electrical circuit

- With an ohm meter measure the resistance of the circuit from the switch or the fuse.
- Then measure the resistance of the individual piece of equipment (bulb, Satnav, etc).
- The difference between the two readings will give you the resistance of the circuit. It should be very low. If not the circuit needs to be checked.

---

electricity, although it is cheaper to buy.
• Even if you are very careful, the more lamps you have on board, the more electricity you use.
• A navigation aid consumes very little electricity, provided you can cut down on the lighting.
• Mooring lights consume a lot of electricity, because they are never turned off at daybreak.
• Three navigation lights consume three times as much as a tricolour masthead light; and the masthead light is much more visible.
• A radio receiver and transmitter consume a lot of electricity and you are tempted to use them often.
• A pressurised water supply system uses much more than a foot pump and also increases water consumption enormously.

What kind of electricity?

Most boats use 12V direct current. This is the voltage on which the explanations given in this book are based. People who use a lot of electricity may prefer a 24V supply on larger boats, but that will cost more simply because the appliances themselves are more expensive. Some boats also have a 240V alternating current supply, but this lies beyond the scope of this book. One thing is clear – you should only have one type of voltage on board; either 12 or 24V, otherwise chaos ensues.

Storing electricity

The heart of the electrical system is the battery which stores the current generated by the engine and supplies electricity when needed for the various appliances on board. Batteries should be chosen, installed and maintained with care.

Batteries consist of separate cells, each of which can supply 2V; 6 cells make up a 12V battery; 12 cells make up a 24V battery.

Choosing a battery

The four main types of batteries are given below. You must choose the most suitable one for your needs and your means.

1. The standard lead acid accumulator batteries, which contain a liquid electrolyte of sulphuric acid. If they are knocked over, the electrolyte will leak since it is not sealed. Some electrolyte is always lost when the batteries are charging and you can compen-

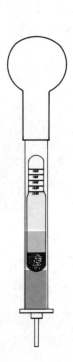

A hygrometer.

sate for this by adding distilled water to keep the correct level, at 1cm above the plates. Never top up the batteries with acid. You can easily measure the charge of the batteries by using a hygrometer.

2. Sealed batteries. These are very similar to lead acid accumulators, but they contain a sufficient supply of electrolyte to last for the life of the battery. This means that they can be sealed and they don't need to be put in a waterproof container. The level of charge must be measured with a voltmeter. These batteries have a limited life, particularly if they are not treated carefully.

3. 'Solid electrolyte' batteries. These have the same characteristics as the previous batteries and can have a very high capacity. They give off no hydrogen.

4. Alkaline batteries (nickel-cadmium), with a potassium-based electrolyte. These are very expensive but are not damaged by being allowed to run down completely. They are not widely used.

Choosing the number of batteries on board

For small systems, and on boats where the engine can be easily started by hand, one battery is enough. But if it is not usually possible to start the engine in this way, it would be wise to have two different batteries. One will be needed for starting up the engine and should only be used for that purpose. The other (or eventually others) should be suitable for supplying low current over a long period of time.

The first battery must be completely insulated from the rest of the electrical system and should always be kept at least 75% charged, which is the minimum level necessary to start up a cold diesel engine. If you have several batteries, you will need an electronic current distributor which will automatically direct the appropriate amount of current to each of the batteries.

Installation

Given their weight, it is tempting to put batteries as low as possible; this helps when moving under sail, but the first big wave might soak them and make them ineffective. Once again you need to find a compromise. They should be covered with an insulated cover, so that no accidental contact can run between the two terminals.

Finally, they should be strapped down securely with nylon or Terylene rope to prevent them from shifting position even if the boat rolls more than 90°. Liquid electrolyte batteries should be kept in an acid-resistant container (made of polyester for example), so that if they overturn accidentally acid should not be spilt in the boat.

When the batteries are charging, both hydrogen and oxygen are released creating a highly inflammable and explosive mixture. The battery compartment should therefore be ventilated from above and you should not go near it with a naked light.

Charging batteries

The main features of batteries are as follows:
– their voltage (12 or 24V);
– their maximum output current (150, 200, 300A);
– their capacity (55 or 95A hours).

A 12/325/95 battery then, is a 12V battery which can supply 325A for short periods to start up the engine, and which has a capacity of 95A hours.

If a battery is less than 75% charged, it will not in theory be capable of starting up a diesel engine, particularly if the engine is hard to start.

In theory, batteries should never be allowed to run down more than 80%. If this does occur, it is likely that one time out of two there will be no lasting damage, but batteries age a lot if they remain flat for more than a few hours.

Batteries run down on their own. If they are new, they will last for three months without being re-charged, but if they are more than a year old, they should be re-charged on average at least every other week.

The regulator will monitor the charging process. At first batteries charge very fast, then the rate decreases progressively until the end of the process. (This can be measured on the ammeter.) On average, the charge is equal to 15% of the capacity of the battery and it is limited by the power of the alternator. So, to re-charge a battery of 55A hours which is 80% flat, you will need 80% of 55A hours worth of power, or 44A hours.

The average output of a typical 40A alternator here would be 15% of 55A hours, which makes 8.25A hours. It will therefore take 44/8.25A hours or 5.33A hours (or about 5 hours 20 minutes) to re-charge the battery. But in theory, it should only take 2 hours 40 minutes to charge up 44A hours in a battery of 110A hours with the same alternator, in perfect condition.

After this time, the battery will be adequately but not totally charged, if, as is likely to happen, the voltage and the density of the electrolyte have not remained constant over three hours.

To know how charged or flat a battery is, you will need an electronic voltmeter, which can always be left on. The reading it gives is only valid when the battery is being used, not when it is being charged. For example:
– the needle is in the yellow part of the dial when everything is off.

It is still there when everything is switched on. This means the charge is satisfactory;
– the needle is in the yellow part of the dial when everything is off, but moves into the red part when everything is switched on. This means that you need to charge up the battery;
– if, when the engine is off and the lights are on, the needle stays in the green part of the dial, the battery is fully charged.

Maintenance

1. Keep the battery as fully charged as possible.
2. Keep the level of electrolyte at least 1cm above the plates; top up with distilled water when necessary, never with acid.
3. At least once a year, unplug the leads, and clean and lubricate the terminals.
4. Keep the battery as clean as possible to avoid the risk of salt-laden dirt which can collect on it, running it flat.

Producing electricity

Electricity is nearly always produced with an alternator, driven by the engine. It should not be forgotten that some boats use other means, often auxiliary alternators.

The alternator

In everyday language, we say that the power you need in an alternator is around a quarter or a third of the power of the batteries. If you fit a high-powered machine, you will only use its extra capacity very rarely; if it is too low-powered, it will take longer to charge the battery.

Alternators should be fitted with a suppressor (to eliminate the possibility of interference) if you want to be able to use the radio equipment (communication and navigation equipment) while the engine is running.

If its output is disconnected whilst it is running, the alternator will immediately burn out. To make sure this doesn't happen, you must make sure that the circuit breaker is fitted with a surge protector. They do exist and you simply need to insist that you want one fitted. Some fitters don't know about them, so get a different fitter if necessary.

If the alternator isn't running, that means it isn't charging up the battery. This happens more often than you might think and it is usually because the drivebelt is loose. If, when you push down firmly on the belt, you can depress it by more than 1cm, it needs re-tensioning. The maintenance of an alternator is straightforward. It should simply be kept clean and overhauled every 500 hours to check the condition of the brushes, and to lubricate the bearings.

Other methods of producing electricity

The quayside supply in the UK is 240V supply of alternating current from the mains. Obviously, it is possible to use this current at 240V on board, but we don't advise you to do so because it would involve an expensive installation and two sets of equipment. However, it is well worthwhile supplying 240V current to a charger which can then charge up the batteries and keep them fully charged. But you must remember that if corners are cut when doing the installation, it can be very dangerous. Sea water, which gets everywhere on a boat, is almost as good an electrical conductor as copper.

Here is a list of some precautions you should take:
– you should always leave the mains supply plugged into the battery charger and make sure it is properly earthed;
– the supply should be made of heavy duty three wire cable (2.5 mm^2);
– the supply should be fitted with a socket which is (a) impossible to unscrew; (b) filled with elastomeric sealant; and (c) click-water-tight. If you use different ports which require different plugs, you should build up a stock of ad hoc adaptors along the same lines.

The battery charger includes a regulator which will adapt the charge to the level required by the battery. It should always be switched on and may need to be fitted with a diode to prevent battery discharge.

Wind generators and solar panels are other possible power sources. They are not usually able to maintain an adequate supply of electricity, but they can keep the batteries in reasonable condition when the owner is away for long periods of time.

Alternators run by the propeller shaft (or by an underwater propeller) can produce a significant amount of power, assuming you will be travelling a good distance.

Installation

It is essential that the wiring be well thought out; unfortunately, it is often done badly in modern boats. Here is a list of the main points to look out for:

Main circuit breaker

The wiring must be completely insulated from the batteries by a circuit breaker. In line with regulations it should be a double pole breaker, but this is not always the case. This is only a problem on boats made of light alloy.

It is a good idea to have two circuits, one for navigation, and one for creature comforts. When the battery is low, one can then cut the second one and keep the main one in working condition. It is also possible to buy automatic discharge limiters.

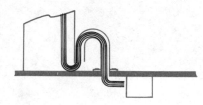

Swan neck to protect wiring from moisture as it passes through the deck.

Wiring

The wiring must be twin core, except for the engine. This very important point is nearly always observed. One should add that on a metal boat, especially one made of light alloy, it is not a luxury to use twin core cable throughout – even on the engine – because this is the way to avoid those little electrical surprises.

Since we are dealing with direct current, the cables should be colour-coded throughout the system, because many electrical items (navigation aids, neon tubes, etc) are dependent on the correct polarity being observed, and they will not withstand being connected the wrong way around. Most builders do not worry about this as much as they should, and even if the cables come in several colours, it is best to check the system.

A good durable and reliable electrical system is made either of flexible plated cable or of a single conductor per cable – better still one with its ends soldered. This type of set-up will last twenty years and more. Always make sure that the cable near the motor is flexible, because of vibration there.

Using slightly thicker wire means you will use less current. We recommend $2.5mm^2$ wire for boats up to 12m length.

Some production boats, even those from major builders, are fitted with ordinary flexible cable which is really pretty useless. The wires quickly oxidise and blacken. Every connection becomes resistive after a year or two so that between 10 and 30%, even as much as 50% of the power is being used up in the wires themselves. And by this time it is impossible to do anything about it.

One can choose to put the wiring in conduits, thus making replacement easy. Or to make it visible, as in cellars.

Builders prefer to conceal wiring behind the lining, without any concern for the need for future repair work. It is quite common to find vulnerable spots behind the lining with no protection.

In the mast, electrical cables, like the antenna cables, must be in a conduit. If not, they will quickly be damaged by bolts, screws or pop-rivets, and short circuits will occur.

Connections

It is best to solder connections when the installation is new, before there is dirt or corrosion to cause resistance. One might also tin the ends of the wires, or solder the flat crimped connectors and grease all connections to reduce oxidation. This operation is not feasible after one winter's oxidation of the wires.

The control panel

The modern practice is to put the control panel in a visible position near the chart table. This is not necessarily the best position; experience has shown this to be too damp because the back of the panel then rests against the hull. By far the best solution is to fit the panel on the ceiling, or against the engine box which is generally warm and therefore drier. The somewhat oily atmosphere contributes in no small measure to maintaining the equipment in good order. The front must, of course, be completely protected from water.

Ancillary equipment

Fuses

Every system needs to be protected against fire. Today it is the fashion to use circuit breakers which double up as switches. This is nice and practical, and sensible, but it is much too complicated and delicate to be used in a marine environment. A good old-fashioned cartridge fuse is much more reliable and easier to repair.

Main switches

Rocker switches are best – and the simplest. They do not even have to be waterproofed if they are mounted on the ceiling.

Ceiling lamps

Ceiling lamps with bayonet fittings are better than hanging lamps which are rarely well enough fixed. Neons are best, anyway.

Navigation lights

The further they are from the water the better. For a boat under 20m in length, use a single tricolour light at the top of the mast. When running under engine power, display three lights (red, green and white) as high as possible on the mast. A stern light must also be fitted.

Total electrical usage

Every skipper needs to work this out if he is to realise what kind of risk he runs every time he adds what seems like an improvement. The three following examples apply to three boats of around 10m involved in similar activities – twelve hours sailing (four of them at night) and the rest of the night at anchor. The battery is an 80A hour one, and the alternator a 20A model. There is only one difference – the idea one has of cruising.

First example

The skipper is economical. He uses paraffin lamps in the cabin and when he is at anchor. He starts the motor by hand.

	Power (in watts)	Time (in hours)	Consumption (in watt-hours)
1 3-colour lamp at masthead	10	4	40
1 small 3W neon in galley	3	2	6
1 small 3W neon (chart table)	3	4	12
1 compass light	3	4	12
1 navigation aid	1.5	12	18
Lighting for above	3	4	12
Various lights	5	.5	2.5
Total			102.5

With a 12V system, this makes 102.5W hours which equals 8.54A hours. The system has been checked over, and all connections are tinned; losses are negligible. If the battery is charged at a steady 15A, that makes 8.54 divided by15 which makes .57 hours, or 34 minutes of motor running in order to recharge.

Second example

A good recreational sailor, who has rented a basic boat which has been on the water about a year.

	Power (in watts)	Time (in hours)	Consumption (in watt-hours)
3 navigation lights	30	4	120
1 neon in galley	8	2	16
1 neon in cabin	8	2	16
1 chart table lamp	5	4	20
Navigation aids	2	12	24
Lighting for above	3	4	12
Various lights	5	1	5
Total			213

This is a standard one-year-old set-up; one must add 15% for losses. At 12V, the total is 245W hours which makes 20.4A hours, to which we must add 1.5A hours for starting the motor (400 A for 15 seconds). To charge 21.9A hours at 15A and thus replace the electricity consumed will take 1 hour 46 minutes, nearly three times as long as in the previous example. If the gear is two years old, 30–50% will be lost, increasing the charging time needed still further.

Third example

The kind of person who doesn't keep a tally.

	Power *(in watts)*	Time *(in hours)*	Consumption *(in watt-hours)*
3 navigation lights	30	4	120
1 anchor light	10	7	70
1 neon in galley	8	2	16
2 neons in cabin	16	2	32
1 chart table lamp	5	4	20
4 navigation aids	4	12	48
Lighting for above	5	4	20
1 bridge spotlight	40	.25	10
Various lamps	5	2	10
1 fresh water pump	40	.5	20
1 bilge pump	40	.25	10
One VHF set	7	18	126
Receiving	18	1.25	22.5
Transmitting	60	.5	30
Refrigerator	60	4	240
Total			794.5

Assuming it is a standard set-up about a year old, add 15% for losses, making 914W hours which at 12V makes 76A hours. Add 1.5A hours for starting the motor. Charging at 15A, 5 hours 6 minutes will be needed to replace the electricity used – and this is hard to justify. By doubling the capacity of the battery and the power of the alternator one could reduce the charging time to 2 hours 53 minutes. With a two- or three-year-old boat the calculation becomes horrifying.

CHAPTER 3

Hull and accommodation

We have devoted a lot of time to the boat's rig, since that is one area in which you, as a pleasure-boat sailor, are constantly confronted with choices about the materials or designs suitable for your particular boat, where and how to arrange things and how to look after them. When you buy a hull, of course, you are rather more limited in your scope for changing things, but there are nevertheless major areas where your influence can be crucial. You do not need to know how to build a hull, but it is important to know where a hull's weak spots are likely to be, both for when you buy a boat and for when you have to maintain one; you should try to learn enough to carry out some tasks yourself, whether you set your own limit at screwing fittings onto the deck, or rendering the boat unsinkable; and you should certainly know where to start looking if your boat starts taking on water. This chapter contains advice on all these things, and our only starting assumption is that you can hammer a nail straight and use a screwdriver.

The weak spots of a hull

The points to watch, no matter what the hull is made of, are joins and seams, strengthening points and the superstructure. It is worth keeping an eye out also for the effects of galvanic action in the hull itself and on the fittings.

Seams
The parts of a hull are joined in a variety of ways: nailed, glued, bolted, welded ... any of these can turn out to be the chink in your boat's armour, and one chink is all it takes.

Strengthenings
There are strengthened panels wherever the hull takes particular strain: the mast foot, the anchor housing, etc. Such strains should be spread out over a large area, and the strengthenings themselves should be kept in good condition. If you are planning to fit an item which will take any real strain, you should make sure it is anchored to a sufficiently strong strengthening plate.

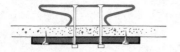

Any fitting should be mounted with sufficient strengthening.

When a bolt is put through a conductive deck, it needs to be insulated all the way through, not just at the surface of the deck.

If you are fitting a cleat to the deck, for instance, it should have a backing plate underneath.

The superstructure

Some of the strongest hulls come with alarmingly delicate superstructures. The cabin roof is often designed more with sunbathing in mind than resisting the onslaught of a fierce wave. In other cases, strength has been sacrificed to the demands of headroom or economy. We cannot emphasise the point enough: the roof and hatch-covers should be robust beyond reproach. The same goes for any closing or locking mechanisms: the sea can cause you more problems than any thief!

Galvanic action

The presence of an electrically conductive medium such as salt water, or the salt layer itself which forms over much of the boat, can allow electrolysis whenever two different metals are together. The less electropositive metal begins to corrode as it gives out a positive current.

There are certain pairs of metals which should not be allowed to come into contact on a boat: aluminium or galvanised steel in contact with cuprous metals (such as a galvanised steel chainplate with a bronze bottlescrew) will not last long at all. Some will survive if you can fit an insulating layer of plastic, such as stainless steel and aluminium; and others are entirely unproblematic, such as aluminium with galvanised steel (though the zinc coating will not last for ever).

Carbon fibre is an excellent conductor, so it has to count as an 'anti-insulator'. With carbon in the deck or spar between them, two pieces of metal several metres apart can set up an electrolytic current.

The aim should be to use alloy fittings wherever possible on alloy spars; if this is not suitable, one should use stainless steel (appropriately insulated) or any non-conductive material such as nylon or other plastics.

Beware of galvanic action when you are carrying out repairs or improvements: if your battery or electrics are poorly insulated, most pieces of metal can become anodes, and corrode quite rapidly. One more example of this would be an uninsulated stainless steel chainplate on a hull with galvanised rivets: the rivets would corrode away rapidly in the area around the chainplate.

1. Deck beam.
2. Scuppers.
3. Quarter rail (above bulwark).
4. Coaming.
5. Engine bed (or engine bearers).
6. Handrail (or grab rail).
7. Cabin trim.
8. Frame.
9. Shelf.
10. Mast step.
11. Half beam.
12. Deck joint.
13. Bulwark.

14. Bow.
15. Stem.
16. Floor.
17. Garboard strake (the first plank, rabetted into the keel).
18. Limber holes.
19. Garboard seam.
20. Garboard return (zone of inverse curve of the hull).
21. Rib.
22. Carvel planking.
23. Mast pillar.
24. Bilge stringer.
25. Ballast keel.

26. Wood keel.
27. False keel.
28. Sternpost.
29. Rudder.
30. Sterntube.
31. Propeller shaft.
32. Rudder shaft (or stock).
33. Rudder shaft tube (or trunk).
34. Counter extension.
35. Heel.
36. Transom.
37. Taffrail.

It is not always practical to use insulation in this way on the outer surface of the hull. A simple and effective alternative is to use consumable anodes. These are zinc plates attached to the hull; the galvanic action is attracted to the plates and put almost entirely out of operation elsewhere. This method is used when the propeller is made of bronze and the hull rivets are galvanised steel. The anodes must of course be replaced before they are completely corroded.

Types of construction

A variety of materials are used in the construction of yacht hulls: the classic all-wood construction, plywood, glass-reinforced plastic (GRP), steel, aluminium, carbon, titanium, Kevlar, even concrete.

We shall look briefly at the advantages and disadvantages of each of these materials, but it should be made clear that our main aim is to look at the type of care and maintenance which each demands if it is to serve you well in a particular type of hull. The materials themselves are not bad, but it is quite possible to choose them badly or to use them badly.

You should be sceptical of those yards who like to do everything in 'their' material, whether all-wood or all-alloy. It is often far more sensible to use a combination of materials, such as an aluminium hull with a plywood deck and a laminated roof.

All-wooden hulls

Until 1950, almost all hulls were made of wood. Many of these beautiful vessels are still sailing today, though few are being built these days.

A wooden hull: lots of bits, with lots of joins and lots of things to worry about.

All-wooden hulls are usually built with a round bilge. They are hard to sink, at least for smaller boats, but they are relatively heavy and not particularly stiff. The techniques used in making solid wooden boats do not lend themselves to mass production; or at least mass production does not enable significant savings to be made in the manufacture. Moreover, they require a lot of upkeep. For these reasons, this type of construction is being replaced by newer materials and methods.

The owner of a traditionally built boat has plenty to worry about. Almost all the sources of worry can be traced back to the fact that the boat is made of so many separate pieces.

Strength. There are so many joints, and they are so difficult to keep an eye on, that they inevitably lose some of their strength over the years as the boat flexes.

Leaks. It is hard to achieve a totally watertight finish, due to the large number of joins and the fact that they are mostly reliant upon narrow connecting surfaces.

The caulking material is least reliable in the seams at the join between hull and keel. If the boat needs re-caulking, you should use the services of a professional, and not try to do the job yourself. You will do more harm than good.

With a wooden board deck, which is alternately dry and wet, it is also difficult to achieve a leak-free finish. One can use elastomers – a sort of rubbery compound which stretches a long way but which sticks well to planking. The same materials should be used for the joints between the deck and the cabin, and the deck and the hull. These are the traditional points to ship water!

Durability. Wood rots. And many of the wooden surfaces, notably the surfaces inside a joint, cannot be reached with a paint brush.

A sworn enemy of wooden boats is the gribble or shipworm. The gribble is a tiny mollusc which is found in temperate seas and which sticks to underwater surfaces. It cannot be seen or heard. The boat needs either three months in fresh water or one month drying out to kill the worm. However, one should not allow wooden boats to dry out too much, or the wood starts to shrink. This is particularly true during the summer months.

There are two tests which you can carry out to see how leaky a traditionally built hull is: try to stick a knife into the wood around the keel-hull join, both inside the boat and outside (the knife should not go in more than 2mm); and then sail the boat hard in windy weather to see whether she takes in any water. (You should be careful with this second test, since an otherwise tight boat can take a little water if the deck has been allowed to dry out too much.) A leak below the waterline is usually due to an untight seam.

Maintenance. The maintenance of a wooden boat is a real labour of love: it must be taken out of the water and repainted yearly; the caulking will need to be replaced every five to ten years; and when the boat is afloat it will probably need regular draining or pumping out.

Repairs. Repairing a solid wood hull yourself is a chancy business. Even small repairs should be entrusted to a professional. If the boat takes a really hard knock (so hard that it has a hole knocked in it) it will almost certainly have had a large number of joints distorted and may well be irreparable.

Glued wooden hulls

Solid wood is less strong across the grain than along it. By using glued construction, one can achieve a shape which is strong and of consistent thickness in all directions. The hull is made out of thin layers of planking laid crosswise over each other – between three and nine layers, usually.

Cold moulded hull.

Frame of a plywood hard-chine hull.

A plywood hull will be made up from panels of ply pre-cut in a factory; moulded hulls require the pieces to be cut in position after they have been stuck together. The outside skin of the hull will in both cases be stuck in place over the structure of keel and ribs, and the combination of skin, glue and structure gives the hull its stiffness.

Glued wood construction is excellent for one-off boats and can even be used successfully by amateur boat-builders, but as wood has become more expensive, it is no longer used in the series manufacturing of boats. Glued construction makes boats with a first-class combination of lightness and stiffness, which are easy to render unsinkable.

A modern variant on the glued construction theme is the West System, which uses wood soaked in epoxy resin as well as glued. The resultant material is so strong it is used for aeroplane propellers, windmill blades and multihull wing masts.

Strength and watertightness. The glue provides both the hull's strength and its watertight finish. If the boat does start to leak, you have a problem, because it means there is a poor join somewhere, so the hull is also less strong than it should be.

The seams of a glued wooden hull have to be inspected closely to tell what sort of state the hull is in. If the joints are visible, either as cracks in the finish or as lumps, there is clearly poor adhesion, even if the boat has not yet started to leak.

Durability. Plywood is fairly rot-resistant, so long as water is prevented from entering through the grain end. If the protecting strakes covering the edges are not watertight, however, the boat can age rapidly. Shipworm does not damage glued hulls badly, because the first layer of glue stops it.

Maintenance. Although maintaining a glued wooden hull is less demanding than looking after a traditionally built one, you do occasionally have to dry it out and repaint it.

Repairs. The average sailor can carry out certain minor repairs, as we shall see at the end of this chapter. For general upkeep and important hull repairs, you should use a properly equipped workshop, which can dry the boat out and do any gluing necessary with heated equipment, so that the adhesives are at the peak of their efficiency.

A well-glued hull can sustain considerable damage without being made irreparable.

Making a GRP hull.

Fibreglass hulls

Most mass-produced boats are made of plastic. This generic term covers a variety of composite materials, even reinforced concrete (a composite of sand, iron and cement, see page 363).

A composite material will have some of the properties of its main constituent parts: reinforced concrete has the compression resistance of sand and the traction resistance of steel, while the cement holds it together.

A composite boat is usually made of two types of material: for traction resistance, there will be fibres of glass, carbon or Kevlar; and epoxy or polyester resin to resist compression and hold the structure together.

The boat's structure is determined by the correct arrangement of the resin and fibres. The hull and decking will each be made of a single piece. The point where these two pieces join can be a weak spot.

Composites are particularly well suited to mass production, as they can be spread or poured inside a single female mould.

For one-off manufacture, it is more usual to build the boat as a sandwich of two layers of composite plastic separated by a foam core. An inexpensive male mould is used.

Plastic has one major disadvantage: it burns very easily, much more readily than wood, and gives off toxic gases as it does so. Even a small flame can cause a major problem.

Strength and watertightness. A plastic hull is usually stronger than a wooden one, in large part because it is more flexible and cracks less easily. Angles and corners can be weak points, particularly on the deck; and you should watch the chainplate and rudder mountings. The hull is watertight so long as the outer gel coat remains intact: if this is damaged, water can seep in.

Maintenance. Plastic hulls have a major point in their favour: ease of maintenance. They can be left in the water for a couple of years: they will still look smart and will suffer no damage.

If you want to keep a good finish on your hull, it does need to be polished occasionally; and when it grows too old for polishing to work, it needs a coat of paint once in a while. The gel coat will be worn out after several years. The boat then needs to be repainted with polyurethane paint, which takes very well, or paraffin-based gel coat (if it is not paraffin-based, it takes for ever to dry out).

Repairs. Small repairs are not beyond the ability of the average sailor, but any structural damage needs to be taken to a professional.

Our vote would go to sandwich construction, which has the enormous advantage of making boats inherently unsinkable.

Steel hulls

Steel is of no interest as a construction material for boats of less than 12m in length. Hulls any shorter than that would need to be made too heavy. For boats of 18m or more, on the other hand, steel can be one of the least expensive materials to use, and it is quite suitable for amateurs to work on.

Steel can be used for round or hard chine hulls. The latter are better value. They are almost impossible to make unsinkable, however, given their size, and the density of steel.

Steel creates a set of new problems for the boat owner. The on-board compass needs to be checked and realigned regularly; a hand-held bearing compass is simply unusable. The steel hull also becomes a Faraday cage, making radio bearings from inside the boat an impossibility.

Strength and watertightness. A steel hull is quite uniform in construction, with the steel plates welded to each other. It is very resistant to collisions, as the steel will bend or dent, but it will not crack. It is perfectly watertight.

Durability and maintenance. The most feared enemy of the steel hull is rust ... and of course rust flourishes in the least accessible recesses of the hull. A continual battle has to be fought against rust: the slightest speck needs to be knocked out with a pointed hammer and then painted over. As soon as you've done one spot, there will be another to knock out and repaint. As the years go by, a steel hull can become dangerously thin.

The rust problem can be almost completely overcome with an expensive cold galvanisation of the entire hull.

A relatively recent step forward has been Corten steel, which creates its own protective layer as it oxidises, in the same way that aluminium or copper does.

Repairs. Both large and small repairs need to be carried out by the boatyard.

Aluminium alloy hulls

There are a huge number of aluminium alloys available, but the alloy best suited to boat construction is AG4MC. One cannot recommend other alloys, and we have to positively advise against any alloy containing copper. (These will have the code letter U, such as AZ5GU.)

Aluminium was first used for making boats in the sixties, and it has proved its worth since then, for limited mass production as well as for one-offs; from the 2.3m Optimist to the 23m-long JI 12 m yacht and big racing multihulls.

There are two ways of using aluminium in building boats:
1. Chine construction involves joining together panels with a hard angle between them. This process is relatively inexpensive.
2. Round-bilge boats need to have beaten panels, which can be considerably more expensive. The structural supports, such as ribs and floor, are pre-cut in standard shapes.

Aluminium does not disturb the compass, though it does make an effective barrier to radio navigation from inside the cabin.

An aluminium hull. Note that the deck is put in place before the topsides.

The wire mesh for a concrete hull.

Like steel hulls, aluminium hulls are very strong and watertight. They dent rather than crack when there is a collision.

Durability and maintenance. Oxidation is virtually non-existent. Galvanic action, on the other hand, is a constant worry. The hull can be corroded fast by a paint with copper in it; or a bronze coin dropped and left in contact with the hull will eat into it over a period. These problems can be quite unexpected. You should even be careful not to moor for an extended period alongside a boat which has a bronze or copper treatment on its hull.

The great advantage of aluminium is that it is virtually maintenance-free. Its surface oxidation protects the metal, and you can even leave it unpainted.

If you do wish to paint the hull for aesthetic reasons, you should follow the paint manufacturer's instructions to the letter, particularly in the way you prepare the surface.

Concrete hulls

Concrete hulls were much in vogue in the seventies. They are made by constructing a metal frame which is then covered with a watertight concrete coat.

Very large yachts can be made in this way, even by amateur builders if the material is handled correctly. Concrete is losing favour nowadays, because the results are almost invariably too heavy for any boat under 25m long.

Maintenance

Painting

Painting can protect the hull as well as improve its appearance.

It takes several coats of paint to protect a hull; each coat has a separate and precise function, and one generally uses different paint for each coat.

• A primer has two functions: protecting the base material and sticking fast to it. The manufacturer will give indications of which paint is appropriate for which base.
• A topcoat or finishing coat is primarily to protect the boat from the effects of knocks and scratches, sun, sea and air.
• There will usually be at least one undercoat between these two. The purpose of this is to even out any irregularities in the primer. Undercoat does not hold particularly well, and its main function is to allow a perfect finish to the topcoat.

Repainting a hull

The secret lies in the preparation of the surface. Preparing the surface takes three-quarters of the total time for the job: you need care and infinite patience.

In order for the paint to hold, it needs to be applied on a clean, rough surface. The surface should be cleaned of grease and dirt by a good wash, if necessary with detergent, then sanded to even the surface out and roughen it. The aim of this is to get rid of the top surface of damaged paint, and to reveal the sound layer beneath. If the sanding is done well, drops of water will no longer stay on the surface: they will spread over it and wet it.

Fold the glasspaper in three to get a good hold when rubbing down. If you fold in two, the smooth faces will slip over each other; and if you do not fold at all, your hand will not get a good grip.

The join between the first and second coats is clearly visible, showing that the second is not adhering well to the first.

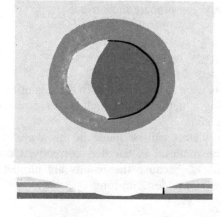

The cleaning and rubbing down can be done at the same time. Use wet-and-dry paper, soaked in water with detergent in it. For inaccessible places or very rough surfaces, use scouring powder and a stiff brush.

Throughout the rubbing-down process, you will have time to check the state of the underlying paint. If it is still holding well, it will make the best foundation coat you can get. Unfortunately, this is not always the case. You can tell when one layer is not holding well, because its edge is clearly defined when you rub down a rough spot. Any imperfect paint must be removed.

If the existing layers are too thick (any more than 2mm) you might have to strip them down to the bare surface with a blowtorch or chemical stripper. If you do this, you must take particular care to clean the surface before painting. Chemical strippers can also attack certain metals (such as zinc galvanising).

After the hull has been cleaned and rubbed down, it should be washed with clean water. It needs a good hard rub with a sponge, not just a gentle rinse. When the surface dries, you should be able to run your finger over it without picking up any dust.

At this stage, you're over the hard bit: now you can start with the paint.

If you have rubbed the hull down to the bare material, the protective layer has to be put back on coat after coat. One coat must be allowed to dry completely before another is applied. If you apply more than one coat of topcoat, each must be lightly rubbed down before the next is put on, to provide light scratches for the next coat to 'key' into. (Undercoat layers should also be rubbed down, to get a more regular, even surface.)

If the paint has not been taken all the way down to the hull, you start off by touching up any bare patches, applying one or more new coats as necessary. After every coat (apart from the primer coat) you should rub the paint down slightly to give the next coat a key. The coats should be thin and evenly applied, and the same colour as the rest of the hull. The final coat should cover the whole surface.

What paints to use

Paints can be classified into families. You should always use the same type of paint on any hull; and if possible you should use the same brand. The commonest sorts of paint used by small-boat sailors are:

How to paint:
1. Apply paint in the middle of the surface to be covered.
2. Spread it in one direction ...
3. ... then in the other.
4. The final strokes should all go in the same direction, towards the part which has already been painted.

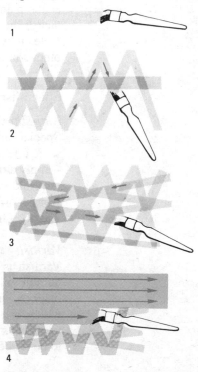

• Enamel paints. These are easy to put on but not very durable. Enamel can be applied in temperatures from 5 to 25°C, and even in conditions of high relative humidity (up to 90%). The foundation coat should be well dried and you should avoid putting the paint on in direct sunlight. Some enamels can even be painted on while it is raining.

• Alkidurethanes. These are moderately durable paints which should not be applied when it is too cold or too humid (no less than 10°C, no more than 70% relative humidity). The foundation coat should be dry.

• Polyurethanes. These are exceptionally hard paints, made of two ingredients mixed immediately before use. They are difficult to apply, and need a high temperature (18–25°C) and low relative humidity (under 60%). The foundation coat needs to be absolutely dry and completely free of grease.

Polyurethane paints have a few special characteristics. On a wooden hull, you can use the same paint for the primer coat (diluted) as for the undercoat and topcoat. You can also start to apply one coat when the previous one is not yet quite dry. As soon as the paint no longer sticks to your finger (though while it is still tacky) the next coat can go on, with no need for rubbing down. Note, however, that polyurethane paints will not stick on top of other sorts of paint.

Specialist finishes

Anti-slip paint
Special anti-slip paint is commercially available, but exactly the same effect may be achieved by doing what we do at les Glénans:
– apply a thick coat of polyurethane;
– sprinkle immediately with clean, fairly fine sand;
– brush off the excess lightly, once the paint is dry;
– apply a further one or two coats of polyurethane.

Varnish
Varnish is a beautiful finish but unfortunately not a particularly durable one. If varnish cracks, the wood underneath will start to blacken, and later re-varnishing is of no use. Unlike old paint, which can be rubbed down, old varnish needs to be completely taken back to the base surface. Varnish in good condition still needs to be rubbed most of the way down to the wood.

Wood needs five to seven coats of varnish each year for adequate protection, which is a lot of work. There are boat owners who are never without their glasspaper and pot of varnish: they seem to be at it all year round. As soon as a spot of dry weather comes along, they sand and revarnish a rubbing strake here, a tiller there ... these are the ones whose boats have that perfect, glossy look.

Underwater paints

Bronze bottom
A range of bottom treatments consisting of copper powder in suspension are known by this term. Most bronze finishes are applied in the same way as enamel, as they are chemically similar to it.

Bronze-bottoming works quite simply: the outer surface oxidises, and since copper oxide is poisonous, for a while no animal or vegetable life attaches itself to the boat's undersides. A good rub down with fine (400 – 600 grade) glasspaper will restore the properties of the finish. Ten to fifteen coats create a finish so thick that the boat's bottom is virtually copper-sheathed.

Antifouling
Antifouling is more toxic than bronze bottom but less durable. Many antifouling paints break down in air, so they have to be applied at the last moment before the boat is put in the water in the spring.

At les Glénans we treat hulls with ten coats of bronze, then one of antifouling, so the toxic properties do not need such frequent renewal.

Special precautions
If you are going to use a copper-based treatment on any hull with galvanised rivets, make sure you apply marine stopper to any sharp irregularities, or the resulting galvanic action will corrode your hull.

It is worth a reminder that aluminium hulls should be painted either with special paint designed for aluminium or (preferably) not be painted at all.

Paints using tin compounds and most lead-based paints are no longer permitted for use on boats in Europe because they are harsh on the environment.

Galvanising

Steel needs re-galvanising once a fleck of rust appears. There are three ways of doing this, which are not all as good as each other:

1. *Hot galvanising*. The piece of steel is left in a bath of molten zinc. This method is very effective.

2. *Cold galvanising*. The zinc is sprayed onto the metal. This is the only possible method for large areas of metal, such as hulls. It is often used for smaller pieces as well, which is a pity, as it is not so effective as hot galvanising.

3. *Electrolytic galvanising* is quite inadequate. It should not be used except on screws, which cannot be galvanised any other way.

Running repairs

Making sure the boat is watertight

You will need to spend a lot of energy to ensure your boat is made watertight and remains so. This should be one of your main concerns as captain.

The task of preventing leaks is different depending on whether you are dealing with the deck or the hull, covers or hatches.

Fixed joints

Elastic sealants are particularly effective at closing off fixed joints such as those between deck and hull, deck and cabin, and some portholes, because they hold even when there is play between the pieces. The elastomer is applied directly at the joint, and it becomes rubbery either through simple contact with the air or when you add a catalyst.

The elastomer should not be stretched to more than twice its normal thickness, so it is best applied thickly, and the joint left fairly wide. If the elastomer is applied very close to a join between two surfaces and the surfaces move apart, it will be enormously stretched and will tear. You can avoid the sealant sticking at the joint by inserting a piece of paper or thin cotton as you apply it.

Some sealants are also powerful adhesives which will hold two surfaces together made of different materials; others are purely designed to seal a static join. Check you have the sealant for the job.

Elastic sealant usually needs to be applied onto a prepared surface. It is often a good idea to put a thin primer film of sealant onto the surface, before you apply the thick second layer. The film

aids adhesion. Whatever you do, make sure you follow the manufacturer's instructions.

Movable joints

Making hinged hatches watertight is an entirely different problem.
The join has to be made watertight using a compressible rubber
insert. For large openings like hatches, the only solution is to set up
a system of obstacles to the flow of water. The first obstacle slows
the water down (particularly water running over the deck); the
second limits the quantity able to get in; the third is an expansion
chamber where the water loses its remaining energy before it is
drained off; and the fourth is the rubber joint to catch any drops.

You can even buy products which re-establish a seal around, for
instance, an opening porthole. A putty-like substance is applied to
one of the surfaces; the cover is closed so that the putty moulds to
the necessary shape. After a while, you can open and close again,
with a perfectly watertight join.

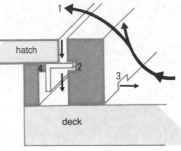

The fast-flowing water passes over the top
of the hatch cover (1). The water which
drains down is slowed by the barrier (2)
before flowing back out onto the deck (3).
The foam rubber insert (4) prevents drips.

Large openings

Water can easily get into the cabin through the main hatch, for
example, when it is left open. You do not want the water to drain
into someone's bunk, though, or onto the chart table, so you should
set up a system of barriers and gutters to channel any water which
does get into the cabin straight down to the bilges.

1. Flat-headed nail for solid wood.
2. Countersunk nail for plywood.
3. Panel pin.

Attaching accessories

Methods of fixing

Nails

Nails can be made of stainless or galvanised steel or of copper.
They are designed only for fixing pieces of wood together.

If the nail is to go in straight, the hammer must be clean. The
hammer they hand you at the fair, offering prizes to anyone who
can drive the nail in with three hits, has got grease on the striking
surface, so the nail bends, you go home empty-handed and the stall-
holder hangs onto the fluffy animal!

We start, therefore, by cleaning the hammer. The second step is
to pick a nail of the right size: too big, and you will split the wood;
too small, and the nail will not hold.

You do need to take certain precautions in order to avoid

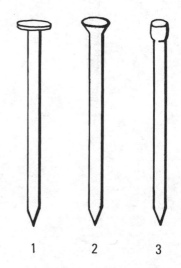

1   2   3

splitting the wood:
– use a nail which is about four times as long as the wood to be fixed is thick;
– take care not to nail too close to the edge or the end of a piece of wood;
– always nail the thin piece to the thick piece rather than vice versa;
– slightly blunt the tip of the nail if necessary.

Nailing becomes more problematic when the nail to be used is a big one. You might well find that the hammer you usually use on board is too light for the job. It is best in such cases to make a small hole in advance to hold the nail straight and lessen the chances of splitting the wood. This is done by taking a smaller nail, maybe three-quarters the size of the large one, cutting off the head and using it as a drill bit. This will produce an excellent result, even if the hole is rather short. If the two pieces of wood are stuck together as well as nailed, better still.

There are two good ways of ensuring you do not hammer your own finger:
– hold the hammer in both hands;
– get someone else to hold the nail!

Woodscrews
Screws are used for joining two pieces which might have to be taken apart again; they can be used for fixing plastic or metal to wood.

Screws can be made of stainless, galvanised or cadmium steel, or brass (though brass is not recommended for outside use, as it does gradually deteriorate). When choosing screws, beware of potential galvanic action.

It is best to use screws which are threaded all the way up. The traditional woodscrew has no particular advantages over this type, and has several disadvantages.

When screwing a fitting on:
– put it in the desired position;
– mark and start the hole by pushing a drill bit of the appropriate size through one of the holes in the fitting;
– using a drill bit the same size as the screw shank (ie, the width of the screw minus the depth of the threads), bore a hole to the same length as the screw;
– screw the fitting in place; mark the remaining holes in the same manner and repeat the procedure.

In soft wood, you can make the starter hole with a simple gimlet.

You should not attempt to put screws into soft wood without a pre-drilled hole, as any hard grains in the wood will knock the screw off course.

Do not forget to grease screws before putting them in. (If you have not got any grease to hand, cooking margarine will do.)

Rawl nuts/neoprene dowels

These are a type of bolt which holds well in any material. The nut is threaded along its bottom end, and when a bolt is screwed into it, the nut rides along the bolt, squeezing the neoprene washer. If the piece being attached is thin, the neoprene flattens against the back surface; if it is thick, the neoprene will actually be drawn into the hole. This holds as well as a conventional nut and bolt, but also helps waterproof and shockproof the attachment.

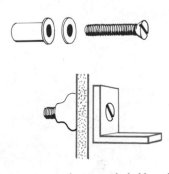

A neoprene rawplug not only holds well, but it also forms a watertight seal.

This is the cheapest and safest method of attaching fittings to plastic, when a backing piece cannot be used. Since it means you have to bore a fairly large hole, the force is spread out over a wide area.

If you use this method on a metal surface, be sure to remove any burrs, or they will cut the neoprene.

Neoprene dowels are very useful in wood as well, since they permit you to use old holes which might have been slightly spoilt, when woodscrews are no longer an option. They can also be used for mounting things on plywood without a reinforcing panel.

The main disadvantage is that items attached using neoprene dowels can move around slightly.

Glue

Adhesives are an excellent means of attaching things. They are often stronger than the material being stuck. (This is especially true of wood.) If you attempt to pull a well-glued joint apart, the wood will usually break before the glue does.

If you use glue, remember that only the surfaces of the items to be joined are actually attached to each other. With weak materials (such as plywood, which has little strength through its thickness) you should reinforce the join with nails, rivets or some other positive means.

There is a staggering variety of glues available, for just about every imaginable material. Apart from polyethylene, virtually any material may be glued.

Every glue needs to be applied in a particular way. Make sure you follow instructions. In general:

– glues are less effective in damp surroundings (whether the material itself or the atmosphere is damp);
– they stick less well or not at all when it is cold: most are intended for use between 18 and 25°C;
– the pieces to be glued should be kept absolutely static while the drying process is going on, which might be anything from ten seconds to twenty-four hours.

Adhesive mastic is worth a separate mention. It is virtually the only way to stick things onto a plastic hull, especially for finishing off the internal fittings. Before applying it, you should get rid of any trace of grease, preferably through rubbing hard with glasspaper. This elastomer glue is moderately strong, giving 20–40N/sq cm. It is thus best used to stick in place fairly large thick sheets of ply, to which you can then screw anything you like. The ply should be held in place for twenty-four hours by adhesive tape while the mastic is hardening, before anything is attached to it.

Cleats

On board a boat, there are generally too few cleats, often in the wrong place, and sometimes even badly fixed. You need to know how to add, move and unscrew them.

Cleats need to be attached to a strong point, and they also need to be strong in themselves. Ideally, you should be able to fix them absolutely fast by using adhesive as well as bolting them in place. Screws may be used in place of bolts, but then you really do need the adhesive; otherwise the screws will work themselves loose and the cleat will tear off.

If the cleat is poorly positioned, the best fixing in the world will not help. The cleat should always be placed along the line of pull. It will be easier to take turns on the cleat if it is up to 10° out of line, but you should not twist it by any more than that.

Cleats should have perfectly smooth surfaces so that the ropes do not wear out. A quick rub with a file or with sandpaper can save you a lot on ropes!
Jamming cleats and clamcleats are easy to fix in place without gluing, since they have fairly wide base-plates. The critical question with clamcleats is *where* they are fixed. A clamcleat will not hold a rope properly unless the rope can drop down after the cleat. Depending on where you put it, the cleat might have to be mounted

on a slight slope or wedge. It is also important to ensure the rope will not catch again in the cleat once it has been released.

Winches

Winches need to be solidly bolted on a good strong base. Again, the important question is one of position. The rope should meet the winch at 90° or preferably slightly more. If this angle is not big enough, the rope will ride up on the previous turns and jam so that it is difficult to free off.

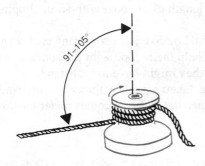

So that the turns do not ride up, the angle between the drum axis and the rope should be slightly over 90°.

If the winch is to be used for several diferent ropes, each of them should meet the drum at the correct angle. If necessary, you should set up a movable block for all the ropes to pass through.

Stanchions and guard rails

Stanchions bend easily, but this does not matter. The stanchion itself is not the safety component; it is the wires or rails between them which do the job. In fact, reinforcing a stanchion so it does not bend is not necessarily a good idea, because there is then a danger that the foot will be torn out of the deck in the event of a collision. The best solution is to have stanchions which are easily removed and easily put back up.

The guard wires are actually stronger if they are left with a certain amount of slack in them. The fore-and-aft pulpit fixings should of course be very strong.

The four feet of the pulpit together support the weight of any crew member on a guard wire.

The pulpits themselves should be securely fixed at all four feet. They should be capable of bending without breaking. They are therefore better made of galvanised steel rather than stainless, because stainless steel does not bend much and breaks more easily at weld points.

Jackstays

The jackstays should be made of flexible steel wire, Terylene plait or preferably nylon webbing (coloured so as to offer protection against UV radiation). There should be one stretched down each side of the boat from bow to stern. This way a crew member should be able to move the length of the boat without unclipping from the jackstays.

The jackstays should be fixed to very strong anchorages, but left quite slack, so as to help them cope with the sudden large pulls of up to a tonne which they might have to withstand.

The slack can be taken up by a thin cord or band which is designed to break when the jackstay comes under tension.

This jackstay is kept under a certain amount of tension by stitching it half way. The stitching pulls out when the line is subjected to sudden tension.

A

Centreboard and rudder

The weak spots to keep an eye on are not only those above the waterline. The centreboard casing and the rudder fixings need particularly frequent attention.

If your boat's ballasted centreboard develops any play in its slot, this can cause serious problems. At least once a year you should arrange to operate the board from underneath so you can check for excessive play. This can be done while the boat is in its cradle or by careening the boat over onto its side. The boat can be put on its side in the water by pulling on the rigging, or on land by resting it on some tyres. (You should not pull on the rigging when the boat is on land, or you might break something.)

Losing a rudder can be infuriating, and it does happen. The screws and bolts on the rudder can develop play, come undone and wear out quite easily, since the rudder is constantly being moved. The fixings should therefore be checked frequently. It is worth trying to cut down the chances of bolts working loose by using Loctite or some other adhesive on the thread.

Built-in buoyancy

If your boat has built-in buoyancy, leaks and capsizes lose their fear for you. A cruiser with adequate built-in buoyancy can be full of water and nevertheless capable of sailing back to harbour (at reduced speed).

Buoyancy can be provided by the use of expanded polystyrene or inflatable bags.

Polystyrene has the advantage that it never needs to be maintained and will always be reliable; it has the disadvantage that it can get in the way (unless it is sandwich-built into the hull skins).

Inflatable bags have the advantage of leaving plenty of free space in the boat and providing almost limitless buoyancy. On the other hand, they do need frequent checking, and they have to be used correctly.

One can render one's own boat unsinkable using inflatable bags, using the following method:

You calculate the buoyancy required:

– add the weight of everything which you need to remain above the waterline: the crew, half the hull, spars and rigging; plus the underwater weight of the ballast, the anchor, etc, and the other half of the hull weight;

– bear in mind that a quarter at least of the boat's volume must be left above the water, if the boat is not to lose its stability.

As a general rule of thumb, if you divide the weight in kilos by three, then multiply by four, this should give you the volume required.

The buoyancy should be well distributed along the length and over the whole depth of the boat. At least a quarter of the buoyancy should be immediately below the deck, about half way along the boat; at least half the buoyancy should be below the average waterline level.

The buoyancy needs to be fixed in place securely. Do not forget that the bags will be thrusting upward when the boat is upright, and towards the centre of the boat when it is heeling. If you put a bag under a bunk, for instance, the bag must not be able to escape as soon as the boat starts to heel. A bag under the deck needs to be securely fixed in place, not free to move if the boat heels.

If you are using air bags, you need to follow a few rules:

– the air bottles must be well maintained;

– you should calculate for medium pressure only (8 bar);

– the bags should be only 80% inflated;

– the bottles should contain the exact amount of air necessary;

– one bottle may be used to blow up either one bag or two of equal volume;

How to calculate the buoyancy required for a plywood boat 8.5m long

Hull	800kg
Rig	100kg
Ballast	900kg
Anchor plus chain	150kg
Crew	600kg
Equipment/luggage/food	300kg
	———
Total weight	2,850kg

Rig is entirely out of the water	100kg
Crew is entirely out of the water	600kg
Hull is half out of the water	400kg
Half under water 400kg – 620kg	–220kg
Equipment is a quarter out of the water	75kg
Three-quarters under water, effective weight	0
Anchor plus chain entirely under water 150kg –20kg	130kg
Ballast entirely under water 900kg –125kg	775kg
	———
Weight to be buoyed up:	1,860kg

or approximately 1,860 litres.

Add a third for safety and stability: total buoyancy required *2,480 litres*

How to calculate the buoyancy required for the same boat with an aluminium hull

The half under water has an apparent weight of

400kg –145kg thrust	255kg
The hull does not float, so an extra	220kg
is needed to compensate.	

Total extra buoyancy needed: 475kg

plus the one-third safety/stability margin, giving an extra *633 litres* of buoyancy needed.

– if two, the feed tubes should be the same length;
– the bags should be held in place by solidly fixed webbing straps and loops;
– the bags should be protected from damage while they are folded up.

The only way you can be quite sure you have made your boat unsinkable is to try it out. It is suggested that you do this before the boat is completely fitted out. If in doubt, overdo the buoyancy.

You may decide that the buoyancy you have given the boat is sufficient even though you have not rendered it completely unsinkable. The primary role of the buoyancy is to give you time: time either to stop the leak, to get back to land or to abandon the boat without panic.

Repairs

Cutting off a leak

We are not talking here about caulking leaky boats which have been inadequately maintained. You should not be sailing one of these at sea anyway. The problem we are addressing is that caused by an accident at sea: hitting a rock or a wreck, or damaging the decking due to a broken spar or a capsize. A cruiser captain should have considered these possible incidents and worked out how to deal with them.

The fastest and simplest response to a holed boat is to wrap a sail around the hull on the outside. Ideally, you should use one of the large jibs, the luff wire of which will reach all along the boat. If we assume the hole is on the starboard side, you should drop the head and tack of the sail over the starboard rail, having weighted them and attached cords, and pass them under the boat forward and aft of the keel respectively. (Thus, the luff is up against the starboard side of the keel.) The head and tack are then fastened on the port side of the boat, fore and aft (see diagram) and the clew is pulled up tight to starboard so that the sail is flat over the hole. Half of the hull will be wrapped in the sail, and although the leak will not be completely stopped, the flow of water should be very substantially stemmed while you work out a more substantial repair.

The next stage of repairs depends on what the hull is made of. On a wooden hull, you can nail a panel of plywood. A plastic, metal or concrete boat can be patched from the inside with ready-mixed cement which you have stored aboard in plastic bags. A few rags mixed in with the cement can help it stick together.

Of course you have to use common sense when this sort of thing happens, and the best solution will depend on where the hole is as well as how big. If you are short of repair material, you can even stuff clothes or a corner of a mattress into a hole, but it is worth carrying a few bits of plyboard with you aboard, even if your boat is made of plastic or some other material. Plyboard is always handy for repairs to the superstructure, and it can delay the moment when you have to chop up the chart table ...

Whenever possible, try to plug a hole from the outside.

Repairing a plywood hull

In most cases, anyone who is reasonably good with their hands can fix a hole in a plywood hull. Plastic fillers are a tempting solution, but not recommended. Polyester does not bond permanently to wood. Epoxy resin will do, if you must.

The only tools you need are those for cutting: chisel, plane and saw. Do not use glasspaper or a file, as these are not up to the job. The method described below is recommended for small holes. Bigger holes can be dealt with in the same way, but the wood will need to be glued as well.

Cutting out the hole

1. Trace a trapezium around all the damaged area.
2. Drill through diagonally opposite corners. Using a keyhole saw, cut out a shape 2 or 3mm inside the shape.
3. Attach a batten very precisely to one of the lines of the trapezium, using thin nails. Do not hammer the nails all the way in.
4. Cut off the wood which is proud above the batten, using a sharp chisel, held as in the photograph. You should make a straight cut, at 90° to the surface of the wood. Be careful not to cut the batten.
5. Cut the other three sides in the same manner.

The chisel should be used like a knife, pulled towards you, down to the left. Do not try to push it.

Keep the plane flat with the thumb and index finger of your left hand. Use the middle and ring fingers to guide the plane, pressing against the surface of the wood. The right hand keeps the plane level and pushes it.

Making the patch

1. Using plywood of the same thickness as the hull, cut out a piece roughly the same shape as the hole, but a few centimetres bigger in all directions.

2. Plane the longest side flat and straight. Hold the plane as shown in the photograph, pressing down on the front of the plane at the start of the stroke, and on the back as the stroke ends.

3. Hold the patch against the hole and trace side B. Cut and plane side B. Offer the piece up to the hole and check that both sides fit straight. Make corrections if necessary.

4. Cut side C in the same way. If you plane a little too much off, you can still use the patch by trimming side B a little more. This is the advantage of a trapezium over a rectangle.

5. Cut the final side. Be very careful with this one. If you make a mistake, you will have to start again.

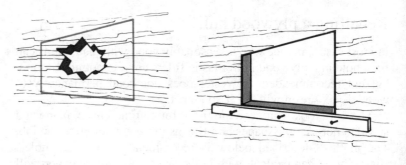

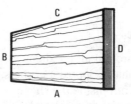

Making the backing piece

Make a backing piece out of plywood of the same thickness or slightly less. It should be 3cm bigger than the patch all around, so the sides will be 6cm longer. Chamfer the edges.

Fixing the backing piece

1. Apply a thick coat of paint to the side which will press against the hull. This should ensure it is watertight and does not rot.
2. Nail the backing piece to the inside, one nail every 3–4cm, in a zig-zag shape around the hole.
3. Clench the nails.

Fixing the patch

1. Paint the inside face and the edges. Do not apply too much paint, because the patch should be exactly the right size, and there will be no room to squeeze the paint out!
2. Nail in place. Put a few nails in the middle, then in a zig-zag row around the outside.
3. Clench the nails in the same order.

How to nail

1. Use thin galvanised nails.
2. Nail from the outside, with an assistant holding a dolly (a heavy object) firmly against the inside. The dolly should be held still, avoiding the nail.

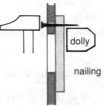

How to clench

1. Cut the nails on the inside to a length of 3mm maximum, and bend them over.
2. Finish by tapping the nail while the dolly is held over the bent end.

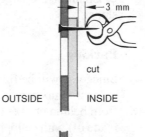

Special cases

If the hole is next to a rib or frame piece, cut the shape to half way across the rib, but do not cut the rib itself. The difficult part of the exercise is removing the ply without damaging the solid wood. It is a good idea to use an old chisel for the first part of this job, to make sure you do not ruin your good chisel on the original nails.

   If the ply is only slightly caved in,

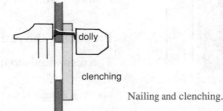

Nailing and clenching.

you might be able to survive without removing the damaged part: just put a backing plate in place.

Repairing a plastic hull

Repairing a plastic hull might appear difficult, but it is generally quite simple, certainly easier than fixing plywood. You need only a file, saw, brush and scissors.

You should take account of the weather conditions, temperature and humidity before starting the repair work. You should also bear in mind that your repairs will be less strong than the rest of the hull, however well you carry out the work. Basically, the glass shell has been holed, and there will never be a perfect bond between your new resin and the old resin of the hull.

Minor damage can be 'plastered over' quite satisfactorily.

Conditions

1. Minimum temperature: 18°C.
2. Maximum relative humidity: 60%.
3. The glass matting needs to be very dry, which is not easy, as it is hygroscopic.
4. The edges of the hole need to be very dry.
5. The resin needs to be fresh (under four months old).

Cutting the hole

1. Cut out all the damaged part of the hull. The hole can be any shape.
2. Chamfer the edges of the hole quite roughly, to about a 10% slope.

Backing

Since you will be filling the hole with a liquid, you need to provide at least temporary support by putting a plate over the hole either from behind or over the top. Cover the backing plate (whatever it is made of) with cellophane so it can be removed once the resin is dry.

Preparing the resin

The resin needs to have about 1% hardener mixed in with it before

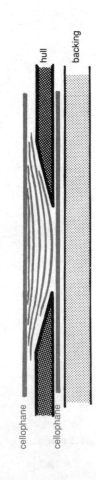

Repairing a plastic hull.

it will polymerise, or dry hard. In order to speed up the process of polymerisation, an accelerating compound is used, usually cobalt acetate, in a proportion of about 1 to 3%. One uses less the higher the temperature.

Take care when mixing the ingredients, as the hardener and the accelerator should not come into direct contact: they give off a lot of heat when they react together, and can even explode. One can buy resin mixes with the accelerator already in them.

Impregnating the fibre mat

A glass fibre mat is used and cut to shape to match the hole. The mat is impregnated with resin, either before you put it in place or afterwards. The important thing is that it should be thoroughly impregnated but with as little resin as possible, and with no air bubbles left in. The brush should be used vigorously to get rid of any bubbles.

Stopping the hole

1. Soak the edges of the hole in resin.
2. Build up layer after layer of glass matting to the thickness of the hull.
3. Cover the area with cellophane to stop drips and also so you can flatten or otherwise shape the surface with a roller or with your fingers.

Finish

1. Wait for the resin to set, but not until it is very hard.
2. Pull off the cellophane and rub the surface down with a file or abrasive paper.
3. Take off the backing if it is still accessible.
4. Smooth down with 600-grade wet-and-dry.
5. Paint over with paraffin-based gel coat or epoxy or polyurethane paint.

Looking after your tools

You do not need many tools to carry out the repairs described. However, the tools you use absolutely must be properly looked after and used correctly. Some advice on this topic will not go amiss.

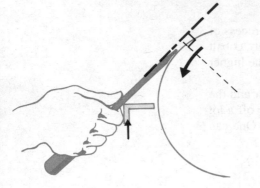

Find a comfortable position at which to hold the screwdriver. Rest your index finger against the bracket so as to be sure to find the same angle again when you bring the blade back after cooling it in the water. Note the wheel is rotating towards you.

Screwdrivers

A screwdriver must fit the head of the screw as perfectly as possible, so the faces need to be parallel, as wide as the screw head and as far apart as the slot is wide.

A screwdriver can be filed to the right shape on a grinding wheel. The faces should be ground on the curve of the wheel so that they are parallel at the point where they are in contact with the screw. Be careful not to press too hard. The steel loses its tempering if it gets too hot. At 200°C it will turn pale yellow; but if it reaches 600°C and turns blue, it is useless. You should aim not to let the metal get above 200°C, which is easily done especially on a thin blade. If the blade is thin, keep a pot of water nearby to cool the metal every five seconds or less.

You should hold the blade at a constant angle to the wheel and keep hold of it in the same place until the operation is finished. Use the rest on the wheel for this purpose.

Wood chisels and planes

In order for a chisel or a plane blade to cut properly, the back of the blade needs to be flat all the way to the cutting edge. The grinding should be done on one side only, at a cutting angle of between 20 and 30°.

The grinding is done in the same way as for a screwdriver, leaving a slightly concave face. The cutting edge will have a thin wire of scrap on it.

The face is then polished by rubbing the chisel at the correct angle along a flat oilstone, until the whole cutting edge of the bevelled surface shines consistently.

The wire on the edge is removed by rubbing the face and the back of the chisel alternately on the oilstone. Make sure you are not lifting the chisel handle as you rub down the back: if you start a bevel on the back of the chisel, the tool becomes useless. Check the edge by shaving the hairs on the back of your hand.

The cutting edge of a wood chisel is quite delicate, and there are some precautions to take so as not to lose the edge too quickly. Make sure you leave the chisel lying on a wooden surface, with the cutting edge uppermost; planes should be left lying on their side. When the tools are put away in their box, wrap the chisel blade in an oily rag and retract the plane blade completely.

Penknives

No sailor is complete without an adequate sailor's knife. The knife does not have to have hundreds of accessories. A really good blade will stand up to most of the tasks you might demand of it: marlin spike, corkscrew, tin-opener, bottle-opener, nail clipper and toothpick!

Ordinary steel keeps a better edge than stainless steel, though you should ensure that stainless steel is used for the rivets.

Knives should not be sharpened on a grinding wheel. You might use a lubricated wheel for thinning a new blade, but the blade should only be honed on an oilstone. Push the blade on the stone with the cutting edge forward, otherwise you will make an edge wire and your knife will have a problem cutting through warm butter ...

The knife should be equipped with a hole in the handle and a lanyard threaded through the hole. That way it need never become separated from its master.

Taking off the wire edge
Position the bevel flat
on the oilstone.

Position the back of the blade
flat on the oilstone.

The bevelled edge after removal of the wire. A sharp chisel should be able to cut the hairs on the back of your hand.

Accommodation

A hull is not a simple shell which floats and moves over water. It is a place in which members of the crew will expect to be able to satisfy many of their physical needs, such as the need for warmth.

Some boats have cabin accommodation which would not disgrace a palace – or so we are told – with soft music and even softer furnishings. Those are not the sort of boats we shall be discussing. Quite apart from the fact that such furnishing is more useful in harbour than out (which may account for the inordinate length of time some sailors spend in harbour) we are ill qualified to pronounce on such luxury. We would firmly maintain that perfect comfort may be achieved in a boat at sea so long as the following conditions are met: a cosy bunk, adequate sources of heat, light and air, a functioning lavatory and well-thought-out storage room. And a good atmosphere – which cannot be bought from a chandler.

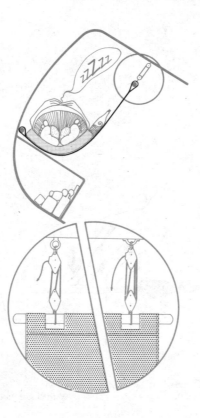

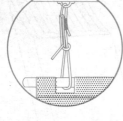

Simple tackle for lee cloth.

Bunks

In harbour, a 60cm-wide bunk allows you to sleep like a log. Out at sea, such a bunk is too wide: you will spend the night hanging onto the mattress, wide awake and remembering that night you once spent in a tent on the north face of an alp ...

To sleep at sea, you need to be snug, and the old hand who turns up with a long sausage-shaped cushion to wedge himself in at night is not so stupid as he looks. Ideally, we would all like adjustable bunks. Some approximation to this luxury may be achieved by rigging up a lee cloth. This rectangular cloth is wrapped round a mounting at one side of the mattress and passed under the mattress to a fixing on the roof. A strong batten passed through a sleeve at the top of the cloth keeps it in shape and acts as a mounting point for the drawstrings which hold the cloth to the roof hooks. The cloth needs at least 50cm in height above the mattress, or the batten will get in the sleeper's way. If the cloth goes most of the way to the ceiling, better still, as it will give a little privacy and darkness to sleep in.

The drawstrings and hooks should be very strong, since they will often be called on to support the sleeper's weight.

Ideally, one should have ropes the length of which can be adjusted to suit the sea conditions and the boat's course to the wind.

• The cloth should be wrapped round the mounting with no creases, or it will be uncomfortable.

• Each hook should be able to bear a weight of 80kg.

• A fixed supporting rope should at least have two lengths: light and heavy wind.

• The best solution is a three- or four-part purchase. If you can attach a clamcleat as well, you have achieved heaven.

All you need to do to make the bunk narrower is to tighten the drawstrings. This will be necessary when the boat is off the wind, and may be rolling. The mattress will then be half hanging and half lying, and curved, with you well tucked inside. When the boat's angle of heel is relatively constant, as on a beat, the strings can be loosened and the occupant then rests either against the hull or against the cloth.

On board the *Iroise*.

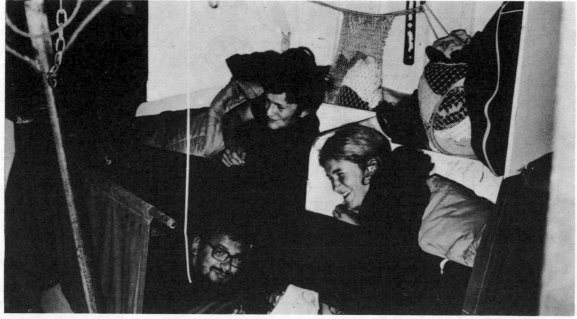

If the mattress is too thick, it will amplify the boat's movements. Ideally the mattress should have a removable plastic cover, with a synthetic foam stuffing. This should be comfortable and quick-drying.

Your sleeping bag should also be of synthetic material for the same reasons. Forget the down bag you bought for going to the Himalayas. It is wetness rather than cold which is your enemy on board boat: so long as you stay dry, you should not get cold.

The chart table

The boat's chart table is usually placed just opposite the galley, or kitchen, so long as one can find space for it there. You have to plan the area devoted to navigation in great detail. Every item the navigator will need must have its own place allocated, where it can be put or retrieved quickly and with one hand. Be careful of the likely effect the different compasses, echo sounders and radios might have on each other. (Do not forget there is a magnet in the radio speaker!)

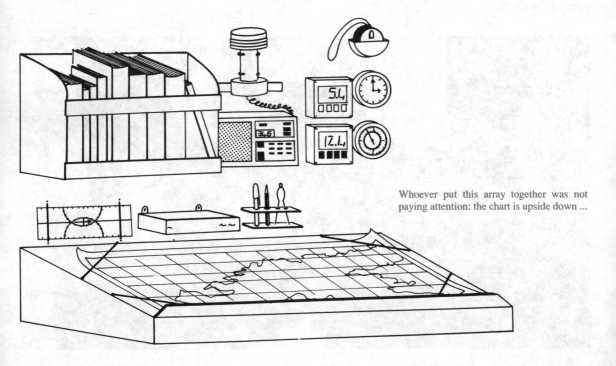

Whoever put this array together was not paying attention: the chart is upside down ...

The chart table needs to be the right size to cope with your charts. You might not have enough space to lay an entire chart out flat, but you should at least ensure it is as wide as your biggest chart and at least two-thirds as long. (Half as long is not good enough, because then you have no choice where you fold the chart.)

The shelves should be mounted at a slope so that documents cannot fall off them. It is worth also spending some time on little tricks to make your life easier. It is useful, for instance, to stick coloured tabs in your tide tables so you find the right place quickly; you should store your drawing implements in a perspex case so you know what is in there before the case is open …

Lighting the chart table is always problematic. It is important that the lighting should not be capable of blinding the helmsman. Ideally, a red light should be used, though you should make sure you know where any red-coloured symbols are on the chart and mark them. You should also have a reading glass with built-in light such as the one illustrated, for examining parts of the chart in detail. If you do decide to use white light, at least set it up so that the person steering cannot see either the light source or the chart (which will be very bright).

With a glass such as this one you can magnify and light the chart up.

On a small boat, with little space for a chart table, the navigator still needs a place to store all the necessary paraphernalia in an orderly fashion. A large box with a flat lid held down at all corners by elastic bands can be used as a table and storage box in one.

On large boats with electronic navigation, and on those boats whose designers did not expect them ever to leave harbour, the chart table tends to be rather skimpy or even not to be there at all. Do not be misled by this triumph of modern design over common sense: *chart tables are not optional extras.* You may be able to find out where you are by electronic means, but you still need to be able to plot on a chart where you have been and where you are going.

Galley

The galley has a reasonable claim competing against the chart table for the most stable and best ventilated spot on the boat. It is generally right next to the companionway, either to port or to starboard, right by the step down into the cabin.

Some boats have galleys which are extremely luxurious – or so we are told. On our boats, the kitchen or galley is the place where the stove is situated, so we shall concentrate on that.

A good stove is one which heats things quickly, is easy to light and uses non-dangerous fuel.

It is not uncommon to find a stove which serves both as cooking spot and as source of cabin warmth. Such stoves may be fuelled by coal. A coal stove, however, needs a fairly large boat to be built around it, and demands a fair amount of attention once it is lit.

Petrol cookers should not be allowed on board, for the same reason as inboard petrol engines: the fuel is dangerous to store and dangerous to handle.

Primus stoves work well, even though they are occasionally difficult to run. You need a little patience (not to say obstinacy!) to light them and clean them, but they do give out a great deal of heat. The main danger they present is that they can cause the methylated spirit primer to catch light easily. This is mainly dangerous if the meths is not being correctly handled or if it is stored in a plastic bottle. For this reason, we now tend to use solid meths (Meta) tablets.

Alcohol-fuelled stoves are similar, though they are easier to light than Primus stoves. They give out rather less heat, however, and they can be rather smelly. The fuel is also expensive.

The cleanest stoves and easiest to maintain are butane gas stoves. However, they give out noticeably less heat than Primus stoves, and they are less safe in use. If you have one of these on board, you should consider it a constant risk: all it needs is an untight seal or a badly closed valve, and gas will leak out gently into the bilges, waiting for someone to cause a spark.

If you are going to use a butane gas stove, you should take the following precautions:
• Ensure the screw threads on the regulator and burner are not damaged, and any flexible tubing is well away from the flame, including when the boat heels. For these reasons, camping stoves should under no circumstances be used.
• If possible, use burners with a safety switch which is tripped by heat.
• It is better to have two stoves with one burner each than one stove

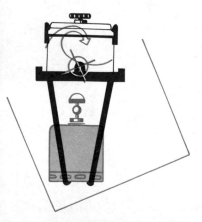

The cooker and canister are mounted so that the join between them comes under no pressure. When the wind gets up beyond a certain point, the only pot you can use is a pressure cooker.

with a double burner. If one stops working, the other will still be usable.

• When you change the gas canister, check all the seals are tight by wiping over them with a sponge soaked in soapy water.

• Make sure you always put the stopper back in empty canisters. There is always a little gas left inside, and some start to leak if the stopper or the burner valve is not on.

• If you are not certain the stove is in perfect order, throw it away without mercy.

For long voyages or boats with a large crew, we recommend a butane gas stove for warming up small snacks, and a Primus stove for cooking major meals.

If you are planning to sail outside Europe, you might not be able to get hold of the gas you prefer, so plan to adapt.

Some boats have built-in gas appliances which run a water heater and a fridge. These appliances are not free of risk any more than cookers are; our own preference is to do without. (Small gas-powered refrigerators, on the other hand, are completely acceptable so long as they are kept in a well-ventilated spot.)

As a general principle, once you are bringing gas on board, you should install a *gas detector*. These are now available at affordable prices. You should make a quick daily check that the detector is working by opening the valve of a gas cigarette lighter next to the filament. If there is no reaction, change the filament. The filament should be positioned low down in the boat, but in a dry place, since it will not work when it is wet.

Back to the galley. Whatever sort of cooker you choose, you need it to provide a stable base for your pots. It should therefore be mounted on gimbals, or at least hinged and able to swing on fixing points placed lengthways in the boat. So that the cooker remains horizontal rather than actually swinging to and fro, the fixing points should be a little higher than the centre of gravity of the pot.

The contents of the cooking pot have to be considered a potential hazard in themselves, as they can slop around easily. You should therefore use only pots with a large base (which incidentally helps the heat distribution) and high walls, and you should not over-fill the pots. In bad weather, you should limit your use of cooking pots to pressure cookers and others with a fixed lid.

The cook needs space to stand in front of the stove and use both hands. Ideally, the cook should be able to sit; but if the only space available is standing space, the person cooking should at least be able to wedge their feet or elbows firmly against some support, or even use a webbing strap as a fixed belt. The cooking utensils and ingredients should be within reach. You should ensure that there are plenty of conveniently placed sloping shelves, cupboards, drawers and secure hooks arranged so things cannot fall out accidentally. These should contain ingredients for one to two days' worth of cooking in case replenishment is difficult in lively sea conditions. The replenishment stock can be around the boat in less convenient locations.

The galley will often be equipped with a sink, which is useful only if it is deep and narrow enough to function at something of a slant.

You should check that the sink does not let water in with the drain open and the boat heeled to its maximum. If it does let water in, keep the seacock immediately to hand. The water supply to the sink can come straight through a tap from the fresh water tank, if the tank is a reasonable size and a certain amount of waste is acceptable. You should also have a reserve pump which brings in sea water in case it is needed.

Interior lighting

You can use electric or oil lighting on board a boat.

Electricity
Fluorescent lights consume much less power than incandescent lights, and are therefore preferable. Fluorescent lighting is also less warm, so you might want to supplement it with some oil light.

Paraffin
Huddled away in the shelter of their cabin, with wind and water safely outside, many sailors have discovered the joys of oil lamps. Oil can give a warm, soft light and an atmosphere of days gone by. It need not smell bad unless the wick has been wrongly trimmed.

One can get beautiful oil lamps in gimbals, but hurricane lamps are quite acceptable to most of us. They should be in secure mountings, and at appropriate places around the cabin walls. Plastic boats need to have the ceiling protected from the heat which the lamp gives off. Marine ply is a good protector: not only is it difficult to burn, but it also has excellent thermal insulation properties.

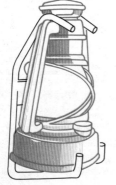

This lamp is ideally fitted in a bracket with clamp-on arms.

Oil lamps can be extinguished by blowing. If you wind the wick too far down, it will fall into the reservoir ... which is as good a place as any for storing your spare wicks.

Even if your boat is electrically lit, you should have one hurricane lamp aboard in case of a breakdown in the electric system, and also to use as an anchorage light.

Emergency lighting
If you have no electricity supply, you should nevertheless be able to switch on one electric light which is powered by normal batteries (like the ones used in caravans, which are even available as fluorescent tubes). This is vital when you need instant illumination – for instance when you are looking for your matches.

It is worth bringing some Cyalume lights aboard with you which will produce a fluorescent light for an hour or more by chemical reaction.

Toilets

The most widespread toilet is the marine head, effectively a sort of pump which allows you to flush straight into the sea. In theory, this sort of installation should be just as reliable and easy to use as a domestic WC, but in practice the pumps tend to break down. The pump handle needs gentle but firm treatment. The pump seldom works twice in succession after it has been used with a closed valve. The head is easily blocked and any but the lightest paper will clog it; in fact, many cannot deal with any paper at all.

The heads can be a source of·leaks, and you must remember to close the seacock after every use. It needs a certain amount of maintenance: the seacock and the plunger need greasing at least once a year. Of course it should not be used in port – especially in a port where there is little tidal action, which would rapidly get turned into a sewer.

Chemical toilets have a number of advantages. Apart from the top-of-the-range models, they are generally inexpensive,

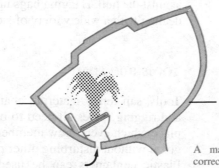

A marine head which has not been correctly installed can change from a convenience into an inconvenience all too easily.

and they save you any mechanical worries. They are clean and do not pollute the harbour. There are of course some associated chores, such as emptying the container and re-filling it with chemical fluid. Make sure you do not spill the fluid, as it can corrode metal and glass fibre.

Storage space

Space aboard a boat is at a premium, so everything you are not using needs to be neatly stowed. Every object should have its own spot, come out to be used and be put back immediately afterwards. This applies just as much to the bearing compass as to your spare pullover and the vinegar bottle. Your storage space should be planned with this in mind. On modern boats, this aspect is frequently ignored. The lucky owner gets the job of interior designer ...

Sails

Sails are traditionally stowed under the foredeck, and are put below through a large hatch without the need to pass through the cabin. The hatch needs to be particularly large if you use cylindrical sail-bags.

If the space under the foredeck is sleeping space, opening the hatch in heavy weather is not an option. And if you are concerned to lighten the bows, you should perhaps use the cockpit locker instead. One good solution is to use the forward berth for light-weather sails and the cockpit lockers for heavy-weather sails.

The sailbags should be hung up on hooks, with shock-cord holding the bottom of the bag firm, so the bag does not chafe against the hull. Hanging bags up on hooks is in fact a good way of dealing with a wide variety of stowage problems.

Tools and spares

Tools, sail-repair material, chandlery such as shackles and pins, and rigging spares all need to be stored together in an accessible place which every crew member is familiar with, so that it can be got at without disturbing other people at any time of day or night. Plastic containers can be used, so long as they close tightly. Anyone who is good with their hands might try rigging up a series

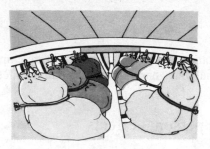

Every bag neatly hooked in place and all held down with shock-cord: too good to be true!

of plastic drawers. (Whether you decorate them is up to you.) Drawers are always more convenient than boxes, so long as there is some sort of system to prevent the drawer and its contents landing on the floor. There should be an automatic stopper for when the drawer is closed.

This is a simple stopper system. The drawer is locked in place when it is closed. It is opened by lifting and pulling, but will not come out of its own accord.

Food

You need to be able to store food not only in the space immediately around the stove, but also in bulk under the bunks and in the bilges. This way you can distribute the weight in the most sensible way, with the heavier items in the centre of the boat and low down.

You should not forget that on a modern boat (and particularly on multihulls) the crew and their food and gear are a high proportion of the weight of the craft. Eight people plus gear weigh a tonne.

Fresh water is very important when you are at sea. It is usually kept down in the bottom of the boat, in either rigid or flexible containers, and pumped up through a system of pipes and tubes to where it is needed. The more complicated the system is, the more immediately available the water will be, and the greater is the chance of things going wrong. And of course if the container itself is damaged, you lose all your water. If you are planning to go a long way it is probably safer to have a series of small containers into which you insert the feed pipe as each is sucked dry. Small containers have other uses as well, when they are empty: have you ever been in a small busy harbour with no public toilet?

Clothing and personal effects

Once you have organised the spares and so on which are necessary for keeping the boat running, the remaining space is for your own effects. The room for storage is a function of the waterline length of the boat and the size of the crew.

On a small boat, personal storage is often no more than a personal kit bag each. You can put up nets in the angle between deck and hull for storing items in, which is convenient and dry if not particularly attractive.

On boats with a little more space, each crew member can have their own locker.

Whether you use bags, netting or lockers, we recommend that you put each item of clothing in its own plastic bag (use the bags which come on a roll). This is the only way you can be certain of always having something dry to put on.

Up to four people can easily store their boots and shoes in the same place. If there are more of you, everyone should have their own shoe space, to avoid unnecessary mess and confusion. (Rolled up boots plus a pair of shoes take up about 13 litres.) Nothing will dry in the boot and shoe cupboard, but then it would not dry in a hanging cupboard either. It is reasonable to store the lifejackets in the same place all together, particularly if they are all of similar size.

Smart clothes for shore use can be hung up in a hanging cupboard, which need be no wider than a clothes hanger and no longer than a dress, say, 0.5m x 1m. The bigger the hanging cupboard, the more the clothes move to and fro, which is not desirable.

Finally, you have to find a spot for those little personal items: lighter, tobacco, glasses, camera ... these are best stowed in a hanging strip of pockets by your own bunk. A similar device should be hung up by the entry to the cabin, containing pocket torches.

Gear

Under the general term 'gear', we shall cover all those items which are not actually part of the boat but which are directly necessary nevertheless. The first major group of such items are those which contribute to the safety of boat and crew; then there are navigation aids, without which real cruising would be impossible; and finally the odds and ends, by which we certainly do not mean useless clutter, but rather those uncategorisable objects without which you would never dream of venturing to sea: paddles, fenders, mooring ropes and legs for when the boat needs to be propped up on the ground.

The chapter is not encyclopedic, but it does aim to give you a view of the methods and materials we have found the most useful and safest. One of the items we omitted under the list of odds and ends is the boathook, the long pole with a metal (or more likely plastic, these days) rounded hook for pulling and a rounded point for pushing on the end. The French word for a boathook is 'gaffe', and this is emblematic for the whole chapter. What follows is the collected wisdom of all our gaffes and mistakes down the years, put together in the earnest hope that you will avoid some of them!

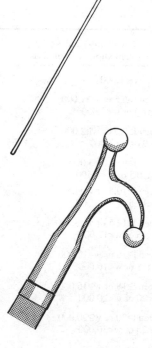

Safety equipment

There are people who start from the view that since humans were not designed to live on water, anything which allows them to do so must by definition be safety equipment, starting with the boat itself. This view has its merits, and we are happy to agree that the first line of safety defences is a perfectly maintained boat, from stem to stern.

Whether you belong to that school of thought or to the opposing school (those who maintain that the sea is a darn-sight safer than the average road), there is an entire range of equipment designed to ensure you and your property make it home in one piece. We shall

A plastic-headed boathook.

look at the range starting with those items aimed to ensure the boat is safe (anchors, signalling aids, fire extinguishers and water pumps, as well as the tools for looking after this lot); then on to those items designed for crew safety: lifejackets, harnesses and safety lines. The final section is devoted to those circumstances in which the crew's interests and those of the boat diverge: namely, when you need to use the life raft.

Anchors

You may be surprised to find anchors at the head of a list of safety equipment, but you should not be. Boats are not like cars: they have no brakes, and the anchor is the only means you have of stopping and staying stopped. The anchor can keep you out of dangerous situations in the first place, and it is worth expending time, effort and money on getting it right.

Experience is the best guide in such matters, and what follows is a condensation of our experience at les Glénans.

As a general point, you should not be tempted to choose the lightest and cheapest anchor and rope from the following table. That would be a false economy.

Length (l, in metres) and weight (w, in kilograms) of boat	anchor weight (in kilograms)	chain Ø (in millimetres)	rope Ø (in millimetres)
l<6.5 or w<1,000	8	6	10
between l>6.5 or w≥1,000 and l<7.5 or w<2,000	10	8	14
between l≥7.5 or w≥2,000 and l<9 or w<3,000	12	8	14
between l≥9 or w≥3,000 and l<10.5 or w<4,500	14	8	14
between l≥10.5 or w≥4,500 and l<12.5 or w<8,000	16	10	18
between l≥12.5 or w≥8,000 and l<16 or w<12,000	20	10	18
between l≥16 or w≥12,000 and l<18 or w<16,000	24	12	22
between l≥18 or w≥16,000 and l<20 or w<20,000	34	12	22
between l≥20 or w≥20,000 and l<25 or w<30,000	40	14	24
l>25 or w≥30,000	60	16	28

If the anchor gear is too heavy for the crew ... really, the crew is too light for the boat.

The anchor weights in our table must be considered a minimum. The length of chain and rope attached are also important for the anchor to hold well.

We never go on a cruise with less than 40m of chain and 100m of warp.

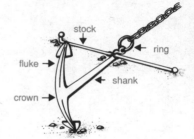

Anchors

An anchor is described by its shape and its weight, thus you might use a 15kg fisherman anchor. Some shapes are defined by the name of the manufacturer, so that you could talk of a 10kg Danforth or a 10kg FOB, although both are the same basic shape.

Let us look at some of the pluses and minuses of different anchor designs.

The fisherman

This is the oldest and one of the safest types of anchor. It will hold any bottom which an anchor can hold: sand, mud, gravel, weed and even rock (though it is sometimes hard to extract from a rock crevice). It holds predictably, if not brilliantly. Even if the anchor is dragging, it will slow you down at a constant rate.

Fisherman anchor:
1. Holding.
2. Fouled on the stock.
3. Fouled on the fluke.

A fisherman anchor can be one of a variety of shapes. Some are fat, with wide flukes which hold mud very well but can sometimes fail to reach the bottom if there is a lot of weed around. Others are longer and thinner, and they are less strong, but they do find the bottom more easily and grip deeply.

The very qualities which make the fisherman anchor effective on the sea bed make it a nuisance on board. It is hard to store and handle on a small boat. It needs a pin to be inserted and tied in place before you drop it. (Use rope for the tie, rather than a metal clip, which will not hold.)

If the anchor is not dropped correctly, it can foul quite easily at either end, then drag.

The grapnel

This is also a traditional anchor design. It has four or five flukes. It does not hold quite so well as the fisherman, except in weeds, where it performs at its best. It is rather clumsy to use and handle, like the fisherman.

The grapnel is widely used on cruisers but does not hold particularly well and is really suitable only for light strains. The flukes are held out by a metal ring, but you should secure this with a string as well, as the ring can slip and the flukes close.

The stockless anchor

This is a more recent invention which does not have the disadvantages of the fisherman. It has no stock to foul, and seldom fouls a fluke. It is easy to stow and handle.

It holds sand and mud very well, and gravel reasonably well. It performs poorly in weed. Its hinge can be jammed by pebbles or shells, or clogged by weed.

If this type of anchor starts to drag, it seldom catches again of its own accord, and it will not slow you down at all.

Stockless anchor.

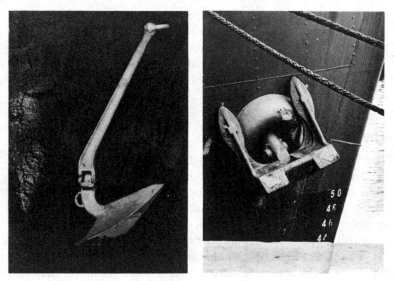

CQR/plough anchor.   Very handy for this sort of yacht.

There is a wide variety of models available. Some are good, others are very poor.

There are some stockless anchors which only hold under ideal circumstances. The best models currently available are the Danforth, the FOB H. P. and the Brittany.

The CQR, or plough anchor

The plough anchor is one of the best types available. It holds at least twice as well as a fisherman, though it is less good than flat anchors on mud bottoms. Except in weed, it will hold on any sort of bottom. It rarely fouls.

The plough still offers some resistance as it is dragging. It is easy to handle and takes up little space on board.

Which anchor?

When you are choosing anchors, you need to have some idea of the weight range within which any type of anchor is most efficient. A 2.5kg FOB H. P. is very reliable for its weight, while a 2.4kg CQR is not. (CQR anchors are not effective below 7kg.) If any further example were required, a Marel anchor weighing half a tonne will hold a cargo ship, whereas a 20kg Marel will not hold a one-tonner. The one-tonner will be safe with a 9kg CQR, on the other hand ...

How many anchors?

Dinghies need to carry one anchor. Other boats should have at least two. That way you can use one as a kedge or you can moor fore and aft. One can be used as a depth gauge, or in case the other is lost.

For serious cruising, you should have three anchors, one heavy anchor, a medium anchor and a light one. We shall go into the use of these in Part IV.

Anchor chains

The primary attribute of a chain is its weight, which makes it sink to the bottom so that the force exerted on the anchor itself is horizontal. The sag caused by the weight of the chain also acts as a shock absorber for the irregular tension of the boat on the rope.

A secondary attribute is that chains are very resistant to chafing. Chains will not wear out on the bottom or on the fairleads and rollers on the foredeck.

The weight of the chain is not an unalloyed advantage: it makes it hard to handle aboard, and it weighs the boat down. Since the weight is at the bow, it increases the boat's pitching.

At les Glénans, we use standard chain, which has a breaking strain of 15kg/sq mm. You might prefer proofed chain, at 25kg/sq mm. A standard chain with diameter 10mm (1,180kg breaking strain) could be replaced by a proofed one of 8mm (1,250kg breaking strain). Whether there is much to be gained from this is debatable: a lighter chain is a less efficient shock absorber for sudden pulls, so one needs a longer length which, in turn, gives you more to haul back in when you leave the mooring.

In practical terms, one should not put too much trust in thin chains, and our advice would be not to use any chain of less than 7mm diameter.

Chain weights per metre	
ø6	0.75kg
ø7	1.05kg
ø8	1.35kg
ø10	2.10kg
ø12	3.00kg
ø14	4.10kg
ø16	5.60kg

The length of the mooring chain should theoretically be three times the depth of the water. Depending on the area in which you sail, you might need to moor in considerable depths of water. In practice, this is what will determine the length of chain you use. The minimum length of chain you need is 30m.

It is just as much a false economy to provide your boat with an insufficiently strong or insufficiently long chain as it would be to buy too small an anchor. When your boat is bumping up against the rocks is not the time to start thinking about those extra 5m of chain you might have bought at the chandler's.

A simple and effective method of fixing the anchor chain to the boat.

The rope tail to the chain must be long enough so that the end of the chain can be put on deck. The tail is fastened to the chain with a sewn eye, with the other end either fed through a panel and blocked with a figure-of-eight knot behind a strong panel (A), or tied to an eyebolt (B).

Making the chain fast

The chain is shackled to the anchor. The shackles used should be at least as strong as the chain. Since shackles are less strong than chain of the same diameter, you should use, for instance, a 12mm shackle with a 10mm chain. The shackles should be moused so as not to lose the pin, even if you are at anchor only for ten minutes.

The boat end of the anchor chain should be tied with strong rope, not with a shackle or wire, because these are difficult to release in a hurry if necessary. The rope should be made fast to the chain with a sewn eye, and blocked off behind a strong panel with a figure of eight or attached with a bowline to a bracket or strong hook in the chain locker. The rope should be sufficiently long that the whole chain can be piled on deck if necessary, with none in the locker.

Maintenance

The thin layer of zinc covering a galvanised chain

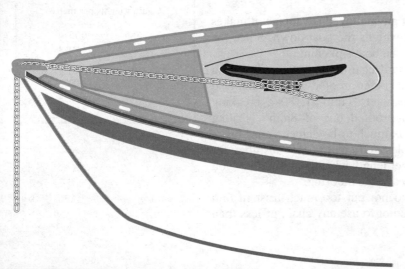

deteriorates slowly, and rust begins to appear. As soon as rust appears, the chain begins to wear out, as the rust operates as an abrasive. To delay the onset of rust, you can spray the chain with motor oil yearly when the boat is laid up for the winter. By the spring, the oil will have dried off so should not soil your boat.

Once the chain begins to rust, it needs to be regalvanised. A chain which receives no maintenance would last on average five years: it can be re-galvanised a couple of times and its life extended to fifteen. The two galvanisations between them would amount to the same cost as one new chain.

However much care one takes of a chain, it does wear out slowly. The most wear is caused at the water's surface, so it is worth reversing the chain annually to spread this.

The chain needs replacing in the end when its weakest link is reduced to 75% of its original thickness.

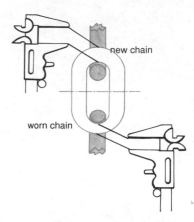

Measure the wear on a chain at the point of contact between links to check how much load it will bear.

Warps

Every boat needs at least one long warp, for use in mooring and towing. The warp should be bought at twice or three times the strength of the chain, as ropes age and wear more quickly than chains, and you do want it to last a while. The warp should be at least 60m long.

It is extremely useful to have at least two warps when you are on a long cruise:
– one thick one with a breaking strain equal to the weight of the boat (up to three tonnes). This thick warp can be used for towing, tying up, anchoring or trailing. It can be made of polypropylene, which is light and bulky and therefore particularly useful for streaming;
– one that is two or three times as strong as the chain, which will frequently be used for anchoring. This rope should be of nylon, which stretches slightly, unlike Terylene, and sinks, unlike polypropylene (so running less risk of damage from, or damaging, propellers). Plaited nylon is more chafe-resistant than laid nylon.

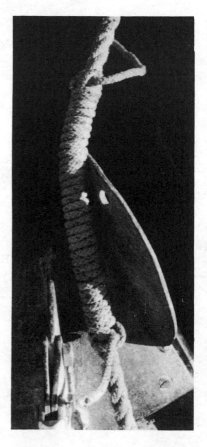

Warps are expensive and wear quickly. Where you expect a lot of wear, the warp can be protected by whipping with thinner line: simply a clove hitch, turns, then another clove hitch. This is a more elegant and more seamanlike solution than the lengths of plastic tubing you will see hung over the bows of many boats. (The tubing quite often has a rather unfriendly sharp edge, too, which makes rubber a better bet.)

Anchoring the tender

We use a thin 150m rope and a 3kg anchor. As well as being used to anchor the tender, it can actually be used in a flat calm for anchoring the yacht itself against a contrary current. (If you use it for this purpose, it is as well to have a top-action handled winch mounted on the mast to help pull it back in.) The line can also be used for taking depth soundings, so long as you have not tied knots in it.

Moorings

If you are going to moor the boat regularly in the same place, whether a favourite picnic or fishing spot, or an overnight haven, it is worth putting down a fixed mooring so as not to have to worry about how well your anchor will hold. The base of a fixed mooring is usually a concrete block. In most cases you will need permission from the port authorities/harbour master before dropping such a mooring.

The block

The block needs to be square, or it will roll. A slightly concave lower surface will help it stick. It should be as thin as possible: a 500kg block should be 10cm thick, and a 2.5 tonne block 20cm thick. The weight should equal the breaking strain of the anchor chain; thus, we use a 600kg block for our Mousquetaire, which has a 7mm chain with a breaking strain of 580kg.

The line

To reduce the radius of swing, the line should be shorter than the boat's line, at about one and a half times the maximum depth of water. The line should also be stronger than the boat's line, so that it does not break when you lower or raise the block. If you use chain, choose a heavy one: it will double as a shock-absorber. If you use rope, make sure you use nylon for its elasticity. The rope should be sheathed with plastic tubing over most of its length, to reduce wear on the bottom, and there should be chain for the last 1 or 2m before the block. Each part of the line needs to be joined to its neighbour by a very

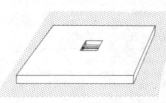

A mooring block should be in cast concrete, with a hole in the middle made by leaving a large piece of polystyrene there as the block is cast. The bar for fixing the chain should be as big and strong as possible for the eye on the end of the line. The block in the diagram can be left on the bottom either way up.

large, adequately moused shackle. Finally, to ensure the rope is not cut by propellers, it should be weighted 2 or 3m below the surface. Rope is less heavy and deteriorates less quickly than chain. The chain should be shackled to the block with the strongest available shackle: for a 10mm chain, use a 12 or even 14mm shackle if it will fit. The shackle should be moused with wire or nylon cord of at least 3mm diameter.

Fixed mooring chains do not need to be galvanised because they have no contact with the air so they will not rust. They wear out most quickly at the end nearest the bottom, and the only way to check the condition of the chain is by sending your crew down as a diver.

At some moorings, the boat swings round in the same direction all the time, so the anchor line gets twisted. One way of dealing with this problem is to mount a large swivel or bearing between the block and the line. Unfortunately, even this solution is imperfect: the swivel seldom turns freely and the line will need a manual untwisting every three months. Without a swivel, the line will need to be untwisted every month.

Mooring buoys and pick-up buoys

There are alternative ways of joining the line to the buoy. We shall call those arrangements in which the chain is fixed directly to the buoy *mooring buoys*. Those where there is a top line will be called *pick-up buoys*.

The only reliable way to rig a mooring buoy is with the chain running right through it. That way there is no weak spot at the fixing point, and one can pick up the ring on top of the chain directly.

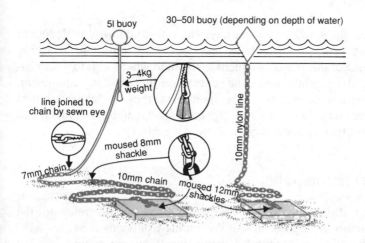

600kg concrete blocks, maximum thickness 10cm

Fixed moorings for a 1.2 tonne boat. Pick-up buoy on the left, mooring buoy on the right.

Mooring buoys
The buoy must be made of cellular material so that it is unsinkable. It needs a buoyancy of twice the weight of the line at spring high tide.

There is a disadvantage to this type of buoy. Since the chain passes straight through it, there is constant friction between the chain links due to the motion of the water, even when there is no boat attached.

Pick-up buoys
When there is no boat attached to a pick-up buoy, the line rests on the bottom. The nylon line should be one and a half times as long as the water is deep. There needs to be a small length of chain attached to the line near the buoy end for cleating on board. The chain needs to be thin enough for you to handle on board and pass through the anchor chain fairlead, and long enough to reach from the cleat to below the surface of the water.

The major disadvantage of pick-up buoys is that the line can be cut by propellers. For that reason, it is as well to weight it 2 or 3m below the surface with a weight of 500g, or with lead weights plaited into the rope. The ideal is rope which has been weighted by the manufacturer.

Pick-up buoys are usually white, as required by French regulations. However, white is a poor choice of colour for buoys, as they are hard to pick out in a rough sea.

Signals

At sea, the smaller you are, the more effort you need to devote to getting yourself seen. Being seen is just as important as seeing others. For this reason we include any item which adds to your visibility, day or night, under the general heading of safety equipment. The signals themselves can be divided into those which warn others to stay away, like radar reflectors and lights; and those which call others urgently towards you: distress signals.

Navigation lights

Before fitting lights to your boat, you should refer to the International Regulations for Preventing Collisions at Sea.

The rules on positioning navigation lights are precise, and we shall enumerate the basics here:

• boats of more than 20m overall underway must show two side-lights, a red light to port and a green one to starboard, and a white sternlight (three separate lights);
• boats of less than 20m need the same lights, but they may be shown as one combined centreline lantern at or near the masthead;
• boats of less than 7m are not obliged to show these lights, but they must carry a white masthead light or be able to signal their position at any time;
• sailing boats under power must show an additional white mast-head light (or, by day, a black cone, hoisted point downwards, forward of the mast). A combined masthead lantern may not be used;
• a moored boat over 7m must show a white all-round light (or, by day, a black ball hoisted forward);
• sidelights show for 112.5° from ahead to abaft the beam. They must be visible from 1 mile away in conditions of 10 mile visibility;
• the sternlight shows for 135°, ie 67.5° either side of dead astern, and must be visible for 2 miles;
• a masthead light (obligatory when under power) shows for 225°, ie 112.5° either side of dead ahead and must be visible for 2 miles.

Black balls and cones
Any shapes hoisted aloft will be blown around by the wind. Reduce their wind resistance by making the shapes out of fine wire mesh.

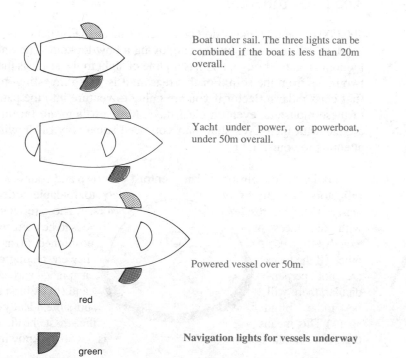

Boat under sail. The three lights can be combined if the boat is less than 20m overall.

Yacht under power, or powerboat, under 50m overall.

Powered vessel over 50m.

red

green

Navigation lights for vessels underway

The nautical almanac will give you the heights at which these lights are to be displayed. In practice, there are only two points on a sailing boat where they can be displayed without interfering with the sails on one tack or other:
– the bow pulpit for the sidelights, where the lights will certainly not get in the way, though this spot does have the disadvantage that the lights are not highly visible;
- the mast head, which has the disadvantage that it is difficult to change a bulb if one blows.

The lights should be perfectly watertight, and powerful enough for the job (which is not easy given the limited power sources on board, unless you use high-output bulbs). A storm lantern is perfect for use as an anchor light.

It is also useful to have a very strong battery-powered torch on board. This is especially handy for drawing attention to yourself when the other boat appears not to have noticed your ordinary lights, but it has other uses too: picking out marker buoys in a channel (especially if the buoys have reflective paint on them), or picking out a crew member who has fallen overboard (again, it helps if their lifejacket has reflective strips on it).

The radar reflector

500,000 tonne oil tankers do not come cheap, so the owners have a habit of saving money by not employing a bow lookout. The only lookout is on the bridge, and has no line of sight to the sea less than two miles from the ship. For this reason, it is worth investing in a first-class radar reflector if you are going to venture into the paths of these monsters, even on clear days. Most of them are hurtling around with their eyes shut, and you need some way of drawing attention to yourself.

In order to do their job, radar reflectors need to be at least 45cm across, with flat faces at exactly 90° to each other. (If the faces are not perpendicular, there will be radar blind spots.) This means that you should not entrust your own and your boat's safety to foldable reflectors. The reflector needs to be correctly positioned: (a) as if it were resting on a plane surface; and (b) as high as possible, ideally at the mast head. It is worth knowing

Radar reflector correctly positioned. Note that it is face-upward, not point-upward.

Spherical radar reflector

something about the way a ship's radar operator actually works: when the sea is rough, the waves actually give a radar echo which the operator has to over-ride in order to see other objects. In effect this means that only objects above a certain height are radar-visible.

Distress signals

You must have distress flares and rockets aboard. The number depends on the type of sailing you do. Every crew member should know where they are kept and exactly how to use them: if anyone has never taken part in a practice drill (which should not be the case!), make sure they read the instructions on all the flares and rockets on board … and do not listen to their protestations that all flares work the same way. They don't! And at night it can be hard to decipher that small writing.

Of flares, rockets and regulations

Flares and rockets can only be used once, and their light does not last long. They should be used advisedly, ie when you think there is a chance of their being noticed. There is no point setting off a smoke flare in anything over a force 3; nor in sending up a rocket when it is foggy or there are no other boats in sight; nor even when there is a boat in sight but it is sailing away from you, or you are between it and the sun. On the other hand, it is certainly worth trying a rocket at 4 o'clock in the morning off most areas of the coast, as that is when the fishing fleets will be setting out.

You will have noticed also that rockets and flares have a date stamped on them after which they are not to be used. Your boat's regulation flares must be within the date.

There is no regulation, though, prohibiting you from keeping your old flares as well. We have tested a lot of old flares at les Glénans, and found that the vast majority which appear on a visual inspection to be dry and in good condition are perfectly usable for several years after the date stamped on them.

Within a few years, you can build up quite a stock of old but quite usable flares, which mean that you can continue your fire-work display long after you have used up all the regulation flares. There is no shame in owing your life to a non-regulation flare.

The prudent multihull sailor bears in mind the possibility of a capsize, and stores the flares so they can be got at even if the hull is upturned, or even when one hull is under water.

Parachute flares

These are big flares which can be shot high up and should theoretically be visible for at least thirty-five seconds as they come down. In fact they are rather hard to see in daylight.

They are easy to use, but it is easy to make mistakes with them at night if you have never used one before and cannot read the instructions. It is best to hold them out over the water when letting them off, because they occasionally fail to launch properly. If a parachute flare malfunctions, you should not keep it in your hand

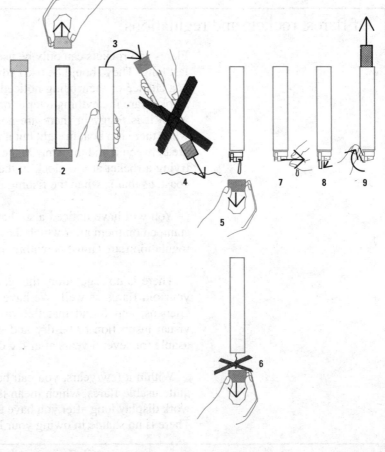

When you buy flares, make sure you know which is the top and which is the bottom. You should be able to tell the difference by sight and touch (1).

Once you have taken off the top (2), do not turn the flare upside down (3), or it will fall into the water (4).

If, when you take off the bottom stopper (5), you see a pull-string, buy a different sort of flare next time, because this sort of flare takes a terribly long time to go off.

A safety flare with a firing pin needs you to take off the catch (7), releasing a lever (8) which is then pulled (9) to set the flare off.

any longer than fifteen seconds and it is even worse to try to look down the hole! Drop the failed flare into the water.

Automatic handheld red flares

These flares have to be held at arm's length. They are simple and safe to handle, and they last about as long as a parachute flare. They are perhaps better than parachute flares in daylight, as they burn at a more visible height. In theory, they should last for over forty-five seconds.

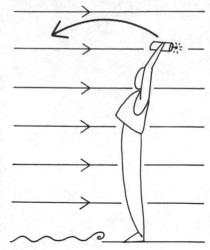

Automatic handheld flare.
Do not panic: you will not burn your hand if you make confident gestures. The flare should be held downwind and over water so that you can drop it once it goes out.

Floating smoke flares

These flares let off orange smoke for a period of at least three minutes. The smoke is visible five miles away in daylight, but this sort of signal is little use when there is anything over a force 2 wind, as the smoke is blown along the surface of the sea.

Signaling with a mirror

Mirrors have one major advantage over rockets and flares: they do not go out. Assuming of course that the sun is shining, a mirror can be extremely handy for drawing attention to yourself.

A signalling mirror will have a hole in the centre which allows you to direct the beam as much as 80° away from the sun. You will need to shine the beam right in the passing sailor's eyes for long enough to get them really annoyed before they will notice you.

SARSAT/COSPAS radio beacons

This system has been in development for a number of years. It now

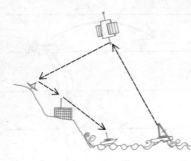

covers the entire surface of the globe, and gives virtually immediate response times in the northern hemisphere. (In the southern hemisphere response times are under three hours.)

The beacon sends a coded signal to a satellite which in turn transmits the signal to a shore base where it is decoded. The shore base then tells the coastguard where you are.

Multi-frequency radio beacons

These send a distress signal on two or three frequencies, usually the VHF band 16 and the marine call band 218kHz. They cost only £300–600, so should be considered a good investment. These beacons are personal equipment, and need to be handled with care and checked regularly.

Firefighting equipment and waterpumps

Fire

There is a fire risk on board in the form of the various flammable items you take aboard, particularly fuel. The ideal is to avoid taking flammables on board, but if they are used, *they must be stored in their own compartment away from the cabin.*

We have already made our opinion of petrol engines known. At les Glénans, we have got rid of any petrol engines on decked craft; and we use outboard motors only on open boats.

If you are using a motor which takes petrol, you must avoid handling fuel while the engine is running. Equally, there should be no cooking or smoking near the engine.

Methylated spirit also burns readily. It should not be poured into a lamp or a heater unless the flame is thoroughly extinguished first.

Fire spreads very fast on a fibreglass boat, though noticeably less fast on a wooden boat. Metal or concrete boats will not burn ... though the furnishings will.

The regulation requirements as far as fire extinguishers are concerned are not excessive: they relate to the potential dangers afloat. Do check and follow the regulations for your type of boat. Fire extinguishers need to be placed with care, so that they are accessible wherever the fire has broken out. (The best place for a fire extinguisher is usually right next to the cabin entrance, on the side opposite the galley.) Every crew member needs to know exactly how to operate the fire extinguisher, and the skipper should

---

Recommended (and French regulation) number of fire extinguishers for cabin sailing boats of various lengths with a single engine of under 150bhp:

• under 10m	1 extinguisher
• 10–15m	2 extinguishers
• 15–20m	3 extinguishers
• 20–25m	4 extinguishers

take time to explain it to any new arrival on board – even if they are only a passenger.

Lightning

Lightning can cause a disaster on board a boat. It can literally blow the boat up, or at least set fire to it. There is no sense in bringing a lightning conductor on board; the mast and shrouds are perfectly adequate conductors so long as they are earthed (that is, connected to the sea) either by very long chain plates, or by making sure the anchor chain is wound round and making contact with each stay as well as with the water.

The mast and rigging make a good lightning conductor so long as they are properly earthed.

Water

Any cruising boat needs at least one pump, and at least two if it is over 15m long. It also needs two buckets with cords tied to the handles.

The pump needs to be solidly fixed and housed, in a spot which is easy to get at, in case you have to sit there pumping for a couple of hours with a big leak. The pump handle should also be fixed, or

the handle is accessible when not in use

This pump is well housed and fixed, so that a long session on the pump will not cause you permanent damage. The handle is also nicely accessible ...

... and secured with a string so it will not get lost.

Strong bucket.

at least very close to hand; if you stow it somewhere else you can guarantee it'll get lost just when you need it.

Single-action diaphragm pumps are the best type. Choose one which is easy to take apart and clean. The suction pipe should be either rigid or properly reinforced so it does not distort under decompression; and it should be fitted with a removable strainer. The strainer should itself be equipped with holes big enough to fit, say, a match through (but not big enough for a match box).

The outlet pipe should also be permanently fixed and lead to the outside of the hull – though it can lead to the cockpit if the cockpit is self-draining.

When there is only a little water in the bottom, a pump or a bailer is a perfectly adequate means of emptying the boat. When the boat is swimming, however, there is nothing to beat the good old-fashioned bucket, preferably the thick black plastic sort used for cement, containing 7–10 litres and equipped with a sturdy handle and a strong rope. Using the bucket will wear you out but it will also empty the boat far quicker than any other method, down to the last few centimetres. From then on, the pump and the bailer take over.

Tools and spare parts

Just as we included the anchor and chain among the boat's safety equipment, this is also the category for tools and spare parts. You are your own guarantee of safety when cruising, and there would be no sense at all in all these other elaborate precautions if you were not also to bring along some spares and materials to replace things that break or wear out. This precaution is also (some might say, especially!) necessary on brand-new boats.

Tools you absolutely must have on board include:
– an adjustable wrench which can fit the biggest bolt on the boat;
– a medium-sized screwdriver with a square-section blade (so that you can use a wrench on it);
– a crosshead screwdriver;
– a small electrical screwdriver;
– pliers with variable-set jaws;
– two centre punches;
– a carpenter's hammer;
– a marlin spike;
– wire cutters, for cutting shrouds in emergencies;
– a sailmaker's palm, a set of needles (Nos14–18) and a sailmaker's hook;
– and all the tools necessary for maintenance and simple repairs to the auxiliary engine.

You need special wire cutters for shrouds. A bolt-cutter will not do.

This list is a minimum, and you would do well to supplement it with those objects you think you will not need, but which could help out immensely one day:
– a corkscrew;
– a hand saw, with a sharp blade, not rusty;
– a hacksaw and several blades;
– a cold chisel (use the anchor as your anvil or base);
– a drill and a set of bits;
– a wood chisel (with the blade protected);
– an oilstone;
– two vice-clamps;
– sundry spanners, pliers and screwdrivers in different sizes.

No precaution is stupid. The *Sereine* could easily have been lost when she developed a leak off the coast of Scotland, if the chartering skipper had not chanced to discover in a locker an enormous bit and brace bought for some extraordinary reason by a previous hirer.

It is hard to produce an exhaustive list of spares, as this all depends on the type of boat you are sailing and where. Making up the list of spares is one more job for the skipper and the skipper's powers of imagination.

We have pointed out as we have gone along those items on the hull, the rigging and the sail wardrobe which need spare parts to be stocked. We should add to that list:
– a spare for every thickness of rope used aboard, as long as the longest piece used. If, for instance, the boat only has one thickness of plaited rope (all the same diameter and the same material), the only spare you need carry would be one of the same length as

the mainsheet, along with spare reefing ropes, which are probably thinner anyway;
– some sailcloth of the same weight as the chief sails used: self-adhesive Dacron or Terylene is now available in various weights, and is very easy to use; adhesive spinnaker cloth; sail thread and thread for whipping the ends of ropes; wax;
– one or two battens, as long as the longest used;
– one or two blocks;
– shackles, universal joints and bearings for the rigging;
– brass wire and iron (or better, steel) wire;
– stainless steel bolts in all sizes used on board (stuck together between two lengths of adhesive tape, so that none are lost);
– galvanised nails in various sizes (about 300g for a Mousquetaire);
– stainless steel woodscrews in various sizes (from 4×25 to 5×50). It is preferable to use special screws designed for composite panels, as these are easier to use and hold better than conventional woodscrews;
– a few pieces of plywood, for blocking off broken windows, leaks or more mundane repairs; a tube of mastic; and for concrete or metal boats, 4 or 5kg of ready-mixed cement in plastic bags which should be replaced annually;
– bulbs, batteries and fuses;
– tallow for screws and shackles; oil for blocks and sheaves; grease for winches and other items; and a couple of bottles hidden behind the bulkheads ...

Personal safety equipment

Every crew member on board should have their own personal safety equipment, tested and approved by the regulatory authority. An approved safety harness, buoyancy aid or lifejacket will bear the authority's mark (in the UK the British Standards kitemark).

Harnesses and lifejackets

The harness and lifejacket need to be dealt with together since we believe they are, or should be, inseparable. This belief arises from experience: there is always some reason why you need to unclip your harness from the safety line for a moment; and that is the precise moment at which you are likeliest to be washed or knocked overboard. For that reason you should never be without supplementary buoyancy. Equally, if you are wearing buoyancy, that will be because there is some risk of falling in the water: for that reason you should always be clipped onto the safety line. The logical solution is to wear an efficient combination life-jacket/harness, made of material which is comfortable and strong enough to withstand the pressures to which both uses will subject it.

Comfort

Gear should be easy to put on and wear. Considering the number of amateur sailors who do fall in the water wearing no harness or lifejacket, comfort should perhaps be your over-riding criterion.

Using a combination lifejacket simplifies the problem of what else to wear. We suggest that all the jackets on board should be the same size, and should adjust to fit any adult on board, from a sylph in a bathing costume to a gorilla in three sweaters. This way, no one will pick the wrong jacket in the dark when they are in a hurry. Any decent chandlers will have a wide selection of lifejackets from which to choose. Take along possible members of your crew, or as wide a range of physical sizes as possible, when you go shopping for your jackets.

The gear should also be easy to move around in, on deck and at the chart table. Your lifejacket should be normal on-board wear, just like your waterproofs. Just getting into the habit of wearing it is half the battle.

Strength

The harness part needs to be particularly strong – though the jacket must also stand up to prolonged use without wearing out.

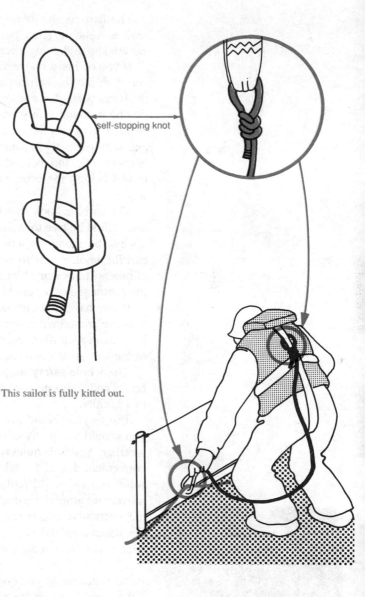

self-stopping knot

This sailor is fully kitted out.

The harness should be of the same type as a parachute harness, with a webbing strap passing between the legs to ensure that it cannot slip under any circumstances.

If you do insist on wearing separate harness and lifejacket, make sure you put the harness on first: otherwise you will probably get the harness tangled and certainly fail to tighten it correctly.

The personal safety line which joins you to the jackstay should be between 1 and 2m long, made of nylon rope, preferably plaited, and with perfectly sewn eyes. The line should be attached to your harness at the top, behind your head, so that if you do end up being towed behind the boat, your head will be held safely out of the water.

The carbine hook should be of the correct shape for its purpose and should be free to swivel. This way the pull exerted on it should always be along its axis of maximum strength. Of course, the carbine hook needs to be kept perfectly maintained. Do not use climbers' hooks or aluminium karabiners, as these will not stand the prolonged exposure to salt water: use stainless steel.

If you have two carbine hooks, you should theoretically be able to move around without ever unhooking. In practice, a second hook is often an encumbrance, and a lot of people prefer to hook it up out of the way so as not to be constantly tripping over it.

The whole safety assembly – from the lines themselves to the hooks and fixing points – should be capable of withstanding a strain of 15,000N.

Just as you should get into the habit of wearing your lifejacket, you should habitually clip yourself onto the jackstay, even in good weather. You will quickly notice that the harness is an extremely convenient device for taking the strain when you need to get into some otherwise difficult positions: paradoxically, it frees your movement around the deck considerably. You will also get to know the alternative points for clipping onto: not only the jackstay, but the stanchions and rails (so long as they are firmly anchored) and even some parts of the running rigging when properly secured.

At no time should you clip yourself onto:
– the shrouds, as, in the event of you falling overboard, the top end of the chainplate would be subjected to a great sideways strain which it is not designed to take;
– any eyebolt, as experience has shown that these can actually open the carbine hook from a given angle.

Do not clip onto eyebolts.

Efficiency

A jacket made of strong, comfortable material is already most of the way to being an efficient lifesaving device. But we should also look at the requirements on a lifejacket once the wearer is in the water and not clipped onto the boat. This event can take several courses:

• Crew member overboard in rough sea, not attached to the boat. The lifejacket needs to keep your head sufficiently high above water that you do not swallow a mouthful of every wave which comes along. For this requirement to be fulfilled, the lifejacket needs to be very large (and thus clumsy) or to cover only the upper part of the body and be fixed with a firmly fastened strap between the legs.
• Crew member overboard while the boat is sailing downwind under spinnaker. Rescue could take some time. The jacket should therefore be designed so that the wearer reclines slightly backward, face up in the air, with the back of the head protected.
• The final course is hypothetical, but we are required to mention it, as it is a specific design requirement on lifejackets. The crew member is knocked overboard and unconscious by a blow to the head from the boom. The lifejacket should hold the unconscious wearer's head above the waves, which is only possible if the jacket is allowed to ride up the body, ie has no strap between the legs ...

The choice you need to make is quite clear. Our preference is for the type of jacket *with* straps between the legs, easy to wear, which saves lives every day and works in the great majority of cases. We are happier using this type than the sort which conforms to the regulations on unconscious wearers but is so uncomfortable that by the time you are knocked overboard you have probably taken it off ...

Clothes with built-in buoyancy

The problem is a complex one. You must have the regulation lifesaving material on board, but it is not forbidden to save lives using non-regulation gear! For this reason, we advise regular cruising sailors to buy clothes with built-in buoyancy which will be worn regularly and happily and which will save lives.

We have actually invented our own *Glénans multipurpose jacket*. This is a garment which arises from all our worries about personal safety expressed above, and comes close to solving them.

It has six separate functions:
– it is waterproof;
– it has two layers, so keeps the wearer warm;
– it has a built-in harness, so you can clip on;
– it has built-in permanent buoyancy sufficient for you to stay afloat while you come to, but does not encumber your swimming;
– it has an inflatable chamber, which can keep your head further out of the water during a long wait, and a dayglo hood;
– it has pockets for your flashlamp, whistle, inflatable marker buoy, and even a piece of chocolate.

Flashlamps, whistles and inflatable buoys

It is not sufficient for the person overboard to float high and comfortably; it must also be possible to fish them out! In the slightest swell, even in daylight, you can sail back and forth very close to a crew member who has fallen overboard, and fail to spot them. Any lifejacket should have compartments for a lamp, a whistle and a marker buoy, and these accessories should be of the right sort.

The flashlamp can be:
– either a good quality waterproof torch;
– or a small flat torch wrapped and sealed into a plastic bag.

An affordable waterproof flashlamp.

This torch should on no account be used on deck at night, as there is a risk of blinding the helm (and if it is in a plastic bag it has a good chance of blinding its user, too). The most you should do is check from time to time that the torch works, by turning it on inside the cabin; its purpose, however, is exclusively to draw attention to yourself if you fall in the water.

It is certainly worth sewing reflective strips onto your jacket. These shine out in the beam of a searchlight. A number of people like to sew these strips onto their hat, and this is also a wise precaution.

The whistle is particularly useful for drawing attention to yourself in conditions of poor visibility, and will not run out. Do ensure that the whistle you buy is one which will not rust or bend and in which the pea does not jam. It is worth spending serious time trying whistles out. The whistle needs its own special pocket, and should not be left dangling at the end of a string where it can too easily become detached.

The inflatable buoy can be blown up by mouth and held by hand at the end of a string. It is much easier to see in daylight than any crew member's head. It is worth keeping a couple in your pocket, considering how much extra visibility a few more pounds can buy you.

Lifebuoys, lifelines and lifebuoy lights

The lifebuoy and light are only useful if they can be thrown immediately to any crew member who falls overboard. It is vital to choose the right equipment and maintain it properly. Failure to do so could lose a crew member's life.

The lifebuoy

A traditional lifebuoy is perfect if the hole is big enough for anyone to fit through without difficulty; however, these lifebuoys take up a lot of space and are difficult to stow on board. Rather than buying a circular lifebuoy which is too small, you would be well advised to take a horseshoe-shaped belt, held in place close to the helm either by a shock-cord or in a suitable frame holder. It needs to be firmly fixed so as not to be taken off by a stray wave, but easy for the helm to pull out and throw in one movement.

The lifebuoy needs a floating sea anchor so that the belt is not driven downwind away from the unfortunate crew member. A small (0.8sq m) weighted skirt will do the job.

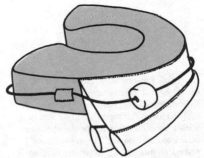

The skirt attached to this horseshoe lifebuoy works as a sea anchor, or drogue.

The lifebuoy light

Lifebuoy lights these days are all electrical, and light up automatically when turned the right way up.

There are three sorts:
– fixed lamps, giving off a continuous light;
– flashing lights of various speeds;
– flash flares, which give off a momentary very bright light like a camera flash, at longish intervals.

We recommend only the fixed lamps, because it is virtually impossible to steer around a flash flare at night, and very difficult to manoeuvre around a flashing light. Quite apart from this, the flashes can easily coincide with a high wave between the swimmer and the would-be rescuer, leaving very long periods in which nothing can be seen.

Lifebuoy lights can be held at a considerable distance above the waves by a sufficiently large float. The larger the float, though, the less easy it is to handle. There is no rule that says you cannot have two: a large and a small one.

Unfortunately, these lights are generally not very reliable. The floats often leak and the bulbs tend to come unscrewed.

We suggest two simple operations to increase the reliability of your lights:
1. A drop of domestic glue will hold the bulb in place.
2. The float can be waterproofed by swathing it in electrical 'gaffer' tape.

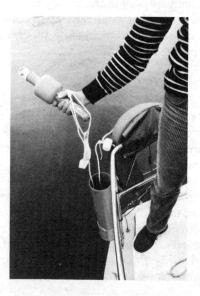

Essential for rescuing anyone who falls overboard: a combination lifebuoy light /lifebelt/rope. The flare has to be immediately to hand; the rope should be 50m long with a loop on the end for the man overboard to hold on to. The rope should be flaked at the bottom of its housing so it runs out smoothly, and tied to the lifebuoy. It must be possible to pick the lifebuoy out of its fixing with a single move.

The IOR pole/dan buoy

This is a floating pole about 2m long, weighted at one end and with a flag and a light at the other, visible from a mile away. (It is named after the International Offshore Rule, which requires offshore racing yachts to be equipped with such an item.)

This is particularly useful in larger boats which take a while to turn round and can sail a long way from the person overboard before reaching them again. It is stowed in a horizontal tube, or upside down along the backstay. It must be stowed so you can grab it in one movement, but where a wave will not rip it away.

Some big catamarans have a sort of gun for their IOR pole, so it is ejected from its tube when a lever is pulled.

The pole should only be attached to a lifebelt if you are completely sure this will not delay getting either of them into the sea. In any case, since the pole is fairly heavy and deep, it does not drift much, despite the lack of any sea anchor.

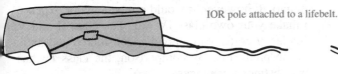

IOR pole attached to a lifebelt.

The heaving line

The line used for pulling anyone to the boat should be 50–100m long and 5mm in diameter, with a loop at the end which can be fitted over a wrist like the loop of a ski stick. In order to help you throw the line anything over 10m, you need a weight on the end. The lifebuoy light is perfect for this purpose, and we assume that you use one of these in the instructions that follow.

Assembly

– tie the lifebuoy to one end of the line and the lifebuoy light to the other;
– put the lifebuoy in position;
– flake the line in its housing, starting with the end nearest the lifebuoy;
– stow the light upside down on top of the line.

You must make absolutely certain that the line is not tangled or tied onto any part of the boat. Check this before you set off on your sail, pulling the line all the way out of its housing.

Liferafts

There are currently three types of liferaft on the market:
– the class V raft for category 4 yachts (cruising limit 20 miles to the nearest safe haven),

–   the class IV raft for category 3 yachts (60 miles to nearest haven),

–   the class II raft for categories 1 or 2 yachts (200 miles or unlimited range) dependent upon inventory.

The class IV liferaft specification is undoubtedly the best for yachts. Unfortunately it is not currently available on the market; however, it would not be a major expense to make your own class IV raft. The class II and V circular liferafts can only be considered as static rescue platforms. By comparison, the class IV has two distinct advantages:

1. It is the yacht's tender, all the crew use it frequently and are familiar with the launching procedure in case of emergency.

2. This type of dynamic liferaft can be sailed out of trouble. Tests have shown that this type of semi-automatic liferaft can sail at 80° to the wind, at a speed of 2 knots in a force 3–6 wind, thus enabling the crew to reach

The following French regulations are recommended by Glénans to sailors in all waters.
–   Over 60 miles from a safe haven a class II liferaft is required.
–   Less than 60 miles, class II or class IV liferaft required unless the yacht is unsinkable (under 8 metres overall length, class V raft accepted).
–   Less than 20 miles, class V liferaft required, unless the yacht is unsinkable.
–   Less than 5 miles, crew floatation equipment required, unless the yacht is unsinkable.
–   Dinghies and racing keelboats must be unsinkable, and may sail up to 2 miles from a safe haven.

Equipping your tender with an air cylinder

Materials

– a transomed tender with interconnecting compartments (if the tender has two separate inflation compartments, you need two identical tubes on the gas bottle);
– a 10–12l compressed air cylinder;
– two bent fixing rods (see diagram);
– a regulator valve;
– a piece to braze onto the valve stopper (see diagram);
– a brass Zodiac valve with base and stopper;
– a 120mm (30mm centre) diameter neoprene washer to reinforce the dinghy at the point where the valve is positioned.
Major inflatable dinghy manufacturers, such as Avon, provide the necessary equipment packaged together as a CO_2 inflation pack.

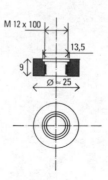

M 12 x 100
13,5
9
Ø ≈ 25

Piece to braze onto the valve stopper (to scale).

Assembly

Fix the cylinder horizontally on the transom, either inside or outside the dinghy. The cylinder must not get in the way of the sculling notch, nor must it obstruct any drainage bungs.

The valve should be at the bottom end of the cylinder so that the pipe reaches the valve without stretching. The pipe should be led through the fixing rods for protection.

r = 78

Drawn stainless steel rod 6mmØ, length straightened 460mm.

To find out how much air you need in the cylinder:
– weigh the cylinder empty (tare weight);
– weigh the cylinder filled to 200 bar (Filled Weight, or FW);
– inflate the dinghy to the desired pressure, from the cylinder;
– weigh the cylinder again (New Weight, or NW);
– the amount of air needed (AN) equals FW minus NW;
– thus, the weight of the cylinder ready to use is tare plus AN.

Placed here, the cylinder is easily fitted and will not get in the way even when you are sculling.

land unaided or at least to get into a frequently used shipping lane. This capability to move under the liferaft's own power is extremely important, not least from a psychological point of view: a crew actually involved in doing something, in contributing to their own rescue, loses heart far less easily than a group of people huddled together just waiting to be picked up.

For years, the prevailing view of liferafts was that they should ideally stay as close as possible to the spot, to aid the search. We can concede that this view has merits for large ships, which can (assuming the crew has time) signal their position by radio to the shore before the ship sinks. If the coastguard is able to send out rescue forces immediately, then it is indeed best to stay in one place.

But when was there last a shipwreck which was foreseen and followed such a textbook course?

One competitor in the *Figaro* offshore race of 1984 was only picked up five days after his boat was lost, despite the boat having VHF equipment, the fact that the race organisers knew his course and had requested all other competitors to keep a look out, and that he was in the middle of a shipping lane where it crossed a fishing ground. Basically, you need to be able to fend for yourself.

We actually carried out an experiment, with two semi-automatic liferafts released into the sea forty miles south-west of Concarneau. They made it back to land at Port-Manech within twenty-six hours. If they had really been shipwrecked, they would have been back on dry land before anyone missed them.

We are so convinced of the advantages of this type of liferaft that we would advise all cruising sailors to carry one, whatever their boat and wherever they plan to sail. A class V liferaft is basically a large inflatable lifebelt which is little use to anyone except a bureaucrat. And if you are sailing further out to sea, then take the tender with you as well as the legally required liferaft.

Protecting the liferaft

You can use either a bag or a rigid polyester box. Bags are only really suitable for protecting class V liferafts from water and knocks. A box offers better protection against both, so long as you do not walk or sit on it. If you do that, any box will quickly lose its watertightness. The best protection of all is a vacuum-sealed bag *and* a box outside.

Remember though, whilst it is important to protect the liferaft to keep it in good, functional condition, it will be of no use at all if this protection makes it difficult to open in an emergency. In an emergency the boat may be upright, on its side or upside down, and the

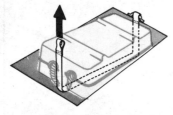

Most boats built since 1980 have had a specially designed housing for the inflatable liferaft. The housing has to be easy to open from above, and the liferaft must come out easily. A webbing strap laid under the folded liferaft saves time and effort. Test your design a couple of times to be sure it does allow quick and easy access to the dinghy.

liferaft must be obtainable in all these situations. You need to strike a balance between protection and accessibility.

Stowing the liferaft

Since about 1980 most boats have had a compartment housing the liferaft. It has to be easy to open from above, and the liferaft has to be easy to pull out. Unfortunately, most of these compartments are poorly designed, such that the liferaft cannot be pulled out in the event of an accident.

If your liferaft is out in the open, exposed to the elements and knocks from the crew, at least cover it up with a plywood sheet and tie it down with a slipknot. If the liferaft is stowed in the cockpit and gets a regular soaking, it will deteriorate very quickly unless it is vacuum-sealed.

On a multihull, the liferaft must remain accessible if the boat is upturned, so you need a flap which can be undone from below to gain access to the liferaft. Do not forget that a multihull will be unsinkable, and that the upturned hulls make a safe and stable platform for the shipwrecked sailor. Make sure there is some means of fixing yourself and your gear to this platform from underneath.

Dinghy tied down with a slipknot.

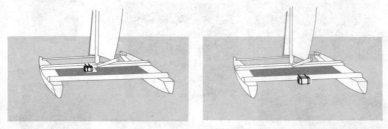

Two ways of fixing the dinghy on a catamaran.

Releasing the liferaft

The release mechanism must be instant and must not need any tools. A simple slip half-hitch is your best friend, though a knife will do if there is always one to hand.

However the liferaft is released, you must make sure that the drawstring which triggers the air cylinder valve is made fast at the other end to a strong part of the boat ... otherwise the liferaft will leave of its own accord.

Equipping the liferaft

Liferaft equipment should be kept to a minimum. This means that you must think long and hard about the items you decide to take. It is actually worth reading the true-life story of life adrift in a liferaft, told best by Dr Bernard Robin in his *Survivre à la dérive,* a good read partly because it is difficult to imagine life in a liferaft for days on end, and partly because we all know these things only happen to other people.

1. Floating rope.
2. Floating knife.
3. Bailer.
4. Sea anchor.
5. Paddles.
6. Sponges.
7. Repair kit.
8. Pump.
9. Survival manual.
10. Instructions for the dinghy.

11. Fishing equipment.
12. Empty bags.
13. Lengths of cord.
14. Signalling mirror.
15. Whistle.
16. Watertight flashlamps.
17. Parachute flares.
18. Hand-held flares.
19. Light and signal tables.
20. Medical kit.

The official inventory for a class II liferaft (up to 60 miles out).

From experience, we suggest including the following supplementary items:
– firstly and most importantly, some means of propulsion (sail and paddles);
– secondly, and vitally, some means of protection from cold. Shipwrecked sailors report that hunger becomes a problem only after about a week, and thirst after a couple of days, whereas one can start suffering very severely from cold within a few hours of a shipwreck, even in summer. You need to take proper precautions against this: aluminium overblankets are cheap, light and effective (and make superb radar reflectors);
– a sizeable water supply. We suggest a 20 litre canister, four-fifths filled, so that it floats;
– extra ropes;
– a proper knife (whereas the regulation kit prescribes one with a round end);
– serious fishing gear. Most people who have been in this situation claim they were constantly surounded by fish and birds, often quite close. It would even be worth taking along a sort of makeshift harpoon. Plankton can be caught in a stocking (and twice as much can be caught in a pair of tights!);
– plastic bags which can be easily sealed to keep food fresh, and clothes dry;
– and finally, several small flashlights. The single torch you take with you will always be full of water, and there can be few things more depressing than a totally dark night in a dinghy at sea.

Navigation aids

Navigation aids are all instruments for measuring something, and they are generally fragile and expensive. You should spend time working out where to put them.

Instruments which are handheld need a storage place which is well shielded from knocks but at the same time handy, so you will always remember to stow them in the correct spot after use. Fixed instruments need to be positioned well away from the main passages, and some need to be kept in a dry place.

As the chart table is invaded over time by ever more sophisticated instruments, each one a better and more powerful electronic equivalent of some traditional tool of the sailor's trade, it becomes ever more necessary to protect them from the elements.

One of these electronic crew members is the navigator. The electronic navigator can work out everything for you, from where you are to when you will arrive. Wonderful though this facility can be, it needs to be treated with caution and realism.

On-board electronics

You need to have the manual equivalent on board of every electronic instrument: a plumb line for instance, and not just the depth sounder.

The instruments themselves do no more than give precise measurements of their dedicated parameter: boat speed for the log, wind speed for the anemometer. The measurements cannot replace the knowledge of what these measurements mean, and you should not put your faith in them to the extent that you lose the ability to judge for yourself.

All electronic instruments use power, some more than others. A boat which is well equipped with electronic wizardry needs a reliable source of power.

It is always possible that some accident might deprive you of all your electricity, and you must ensure that such an accident does not cripple the boat.

Wiring electronic instruments needs to be carried out with considerable care, using plated copper wire to attach the instruments to the power source. The instruments need to be protected from knocks and from salt water – whether the water comes from contact with wet fingers or some other source. They are best installed, therefore, at ceiling level, with their buttons and keys protected by transparent plastic sheeting.

Any wires running between the instruments themselves and their displays need to be all in one piece, with no junctions, and protected from wear. The best way of protecting them is to pass them along conduits, for instance down the inside of the mast, and to make sure they do not run through the bilges.

Compass

A compass gives direction relative to magnetic north.

It is made of one or more fixed magnets on a circular plate marked from 0 to 360°, pivoted at the centre and floating in a liquid in a closed bowl. Depending on the type of compass, this liquid can be oil, white spirit, glycerine or a water/alcohol mix.

The magnets follow the direction of the earth's magnetic field (or, to be precise, they follow its horizontal component!) and the disc markings are arranged such that 0° points to magnetic north.

Steering compass

The steering compass is aligned with the axis of the boat, shown as a line drawn on the compass bowl. This allows the helm to read off the boat's course directly from the intersection of this line with the disc markings. The compass is hung in gimbals so that the disc stays horizontal.

There are several types of steering compass:

The traditional compass is very simple and therefore cheap. One can read off one's course at any time, but you need to keep the really rather faint degree markings in line with the lubber line, which can be inconvenient. This type of compass is really only usable if it is divided into the thirty-two points of the compass card as well as having the degree markings. This way, the markings will be rather clearer.

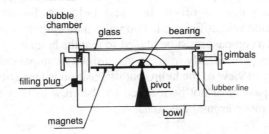

The domed compass works on the same principles as the traditional compass but has several centrelines marked and a domed top glass which magnifies the markings for the helm who is sitting in line with the centrelines. This type of compass is particularly useful on large yachts, but of little interest for small-boat sailors, as it can be fragile and one does need to move around to get the best effect from the magnifying lens.

The bulkhead compass is widespread and extremely convenient. There are generally two, sited one on each side of the aft bulkhead of the cabin.

The lubber line is marked at the back of the bowl, so the helm needs to read off the markings the other way round from normal

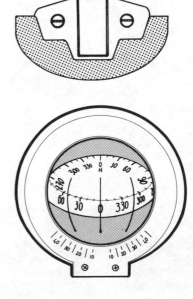

Bulkhead compass.

compasses.

The electrical compass is found on steel and reinforced concrete boats. The compass can be insulated from the magnetic properties of the hull by siting the instrument itself up the mast, with a display by the helm. These compasses are expensive.

The simple compass is one which is not mounted on gimbals, probably fairly small: it is perfectly adequate (and actually very useful) for small boats.

Installation

A compass should be installed as far away as possible from any metal on board, and in particular away from any variable magnetic fields such as those created by the radio, any loudspeakers, radio direction-finding devices, other compasses and any switch gear. It should of course be in a place where it will not be clouted regularly by winch handles, and it deserves its own cover for when it is not in use.

If the compass is not away from the influence of other magnetic fields, it will *deviate* from magnetic north. However, this can be *compensated* by a specialist who will place further magnets around the compass disc to offset the local fields. A further step, if compensation is insufficient, is known as adjusting the compass.

A domed compass must be placed so that the helm has one of the lubber lines permanently in sight. An ordinary compass also needs to be easily in view of the helm, but its position is less critical. Any fixed compass must not be masked by the crew as they sit in the cockpit or move around the boat.

Lighting

The compass should be lit moderately: if the light is too strong it will blind the helm. It is therefore best to use a low-wattage light bulb, preferably red.

Some compasses have the correct built-in lighting, but these tend to be rather expensive. For most of us, do-it-youself lighting is the order of the day. It is fairly simple and effective simply to solder a wire directly onto the bottom of a bulb, with the end leading to batteries or some other power source; the bulb can then be stuck onto the compass glass with plasticine, which also has the effect of shading the helm's eyes from the glare.

We advise strongly against using a pocket torch to light the compass: the batteries will not necessarily be antimagnetic, even if they look like plastic. You will most likely have a false reading while you hold the torch close to the compass, then the compass will return to its true reading when it is back in darkness ...

Maintenance

A compass does not need much maintenance, but you do need to remember to keep the gimbals lubricated.

If a bubble appears in the liquid, turn the compass upside down for a moment then bring it slowly back upright. If this does not get rid of the bubble, you will need to get extra liquid added by an expert or the manufacturer (or add it yourself if you are certain what sort of liquid it is).

Hand-bearing compass

This is an ordinary compass which is held in the hand and which has a built-in prism which allows you to see the bearing displayed as you look along the centreline.

This hand-bearing compass is easy to use as the bearing is read off from a focal point at infinity, allowing you to focus on the mark at the same time as reading the bearing, if you keep both eyes open.

Although this is a handheld compass, it is not designed to withstand knocks: *it must be kept in a pocket or in its own compartment, not left in a corner somewhere 'temporarily' or worn around your neck like a pendant.*

If the hand-bearing compass is battery-lit, make sure you use antimagnetic batteries. Check that they are antimagnetic by running them around the edge of the compass and watching the reactions of the rose. Check each battery, as even two batteries of the same type might well have different characteristics.

Since a hand-bearing compass is mobile, it cannot be compensated in the way that a fixed compass can be. Compensation only works for a specific, precise position. If your boat is made of steel or concrete, you will need a fixed bearing compass. The alternative is to use an azimuth bearing ring, which will not measure the bearing of the landmark, but will give you the angle between the boat's centre axis and the direction of the mark.

Log

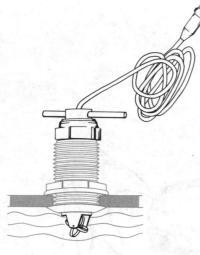

The boat's speed and thus the distance covered can be measured by using an item called a log. The log is generally an electronic instrument, but it is also easy to make your own simple mechanical log, which works in just the same way as an old-fashioned ship's log.

Electronic logs

This is a sort of distance counter operated by a slotted rotating drum or paddle wheel underneath the hull. The turns are counted electronically and the speed and distance covered are displayed on a screen by the chart table and/or by the helm. The readings given are usually accurate to within .5–1kn.

Electronic log sensor with paddle wheel.

The sensor needs to be situated forward of the keel, close to the centreline of the boat, with the rotor blades or paddles some 2–4cm out from the hull so that they are not affected by the boundary layer.

The blades must be retractable so that they can be cleaned of any flotsam that might upset their functioning. Keep your foot over the hole while you are cleaning them! It is crucial to get the wheel pointing in the right direction, so that the correct speed is registered.

The log can be wired straight into the electronic navigator, so that the navigator does not miss out on any information.

Dutchman's log

This is a flat piece of wood, ballasted so that it floats vertically, and attached to a line by a span. Knots are tied in the line at intervals of 7.71m (ie 1/240 of a nautical mile).

The log is dropped in the water and the line let out. The knots are then counted as they slip through your hands.

Making a Dutchman's log

The float. Take a piece of ply 8–10mm thick, a small wedge-shaped sliver of wood, a piece of lead sheet and join them together as in the diagram. The lead should weight the wood so the tip sticks just out of the water with the float upright.

The span. Take two lengths of 3–4mm line about 80cm long, and a clothes peg. Tie a small loop in one end of one of the pieces of line, put an overhand knot in the middle of the line and fix the other end through the hole in the wedge at the top corner of the float. The other length of line should be fed through the spring of the clothes peg and fixed there with a figure-of-eight knot either side of the spring. Both free ends should be fed through the bottom holes of the float and tied.

Now feed the top line through the gap in the clothes peg so it is above the overhand stop knot. This should then give a collapsible log (useful when you want to pull it in, since a single sharp upward tug on the line will snap the cord through the peg and collapse the span).

The line. Use a 2–3mm line at least 70m long (or longer if you plan on sailing that fast ...). A loop on the end, big enough to fit the float through, will allow you to fix the line easily to the span.

The first knot in the line should be about 10m above the float, and subsequent knots should theoretically be 7.71m apart. In practice, 7.5m is about right, as there is always a certain amount of drag as the line is let out. If you tie a tuft of wool in each knot, with a different colour for each, you should be able to read off your speed that much more quickly. As the log is pulled back in, drop the line into a bucket fixed to the aft pulpit.

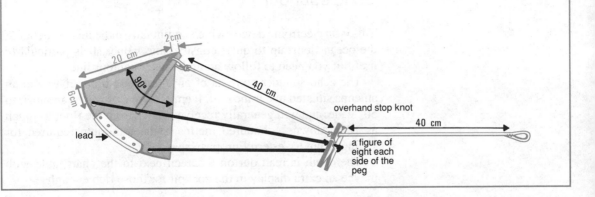

2 cm

20 cm

6 cm

90°

lead →

40 cm

overhand stop knot

a figure of eight each side of the peg

40 cm

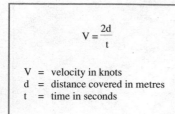

$$V = \frac{2d}{t}$$

V = velocity in knots
d = distance covered in metres
t   = time in seconds

Your speed in knots is the number of knots that go out in 15 seconds (ie 1/240 of an hour).

An alternative way of measuring the speed is to measure the amount of time taken to travel a known distance. Simply make two knots in the line, say 25 or 40m apart. You then measure the time taken for the second knot to slip through your hand. Since we know that 1kn equals almost exactly 0.5m per second, the sum is simple …

The ship's log is not only simple to make, it actually gives reliable results. Use yours to check the accuracy of your electronic log.

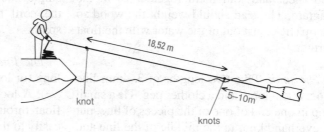

Better still, and cheaper.

Emergency log

When in need, you can make a replacement log using the plumb line and a bottle nearly full of water (so that it just about floats). Let out the first few metres of line so that it is free of any turbulence created by the boat and check the time the boat takes to cover 18.52m (1/100 of a nautical mile).

The approximate speed can then be found by dividing 36 (about twice the distance) by the time taken. Thus, if you take 18 seconds, your speed is 2kn; 9 seconds means you are travelling at 4kn; 4 seconds means 9kn.

This method is not exactly precise, but it's quick, simple and cheap. If you have no bottle to hand, then you really are in desperate straits, and worrying about your boat speed probably is not your prime concern!

Echo sounder

This is an electronic device which continually indicates the depth of the ocean floor, up to quite considerable values. It is particularly useful if you need to follow an underwater contour line.

The echo sounder consists of an ultrasound transceiver and an antenna situated under the hull. It emits a cone of waves about 20 to 50° wide, and will generally receive echoes from the floor as much as 100m down. A hundred metres is the minimum required for sailing around Western European seas.

The depth is read out on a screen next to the chart table with maybe an extra display in the cockpit for those rich enough.

The transceiver head needs to be placed forward of the keel so as not to pick up false echoes. The angle of heel of the boat must be less than the angle of transmission of the sounder. Otherwise, you need two transceivers, one either side of the centreline, and an automatic switch which activates the one lower down. The head needs to be kept free of weed and paint.

The echo sounder should tell you the distance between the sea bed and the sounder head, but this point is worth checking.

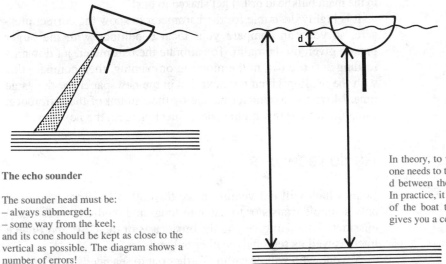

The echo sounder

The sounder head must be:
– always submerged;
– some way from the keel;
and its cone should be kept as close to the vertical as possible. The diagram shows a number of errors!

In theory, to work out the depth of water, one needs to take into account the distance d between the sounder and the waterline. In practice, it is better to add the total draft of the boat to the sounder readout: this gives you a certain margin of error.

Manual soundings

Manual soundings are carried out with a weight of 0.5–1kg and a line about 50m long, with depth markings. Ideally the weight should have a slightly concave bottom; you can then put some grease in it and take a sample from the bottom, or at least check that it did reach bottom.

Mark the line with indelible marker ink, with one colour for every 10m (1 stroke for 10m, 2 for 20, etc) and another for the 5m intervals (1 at 15m, 2 at 25, etc). Only the first 10m need to be marked with individual metres. Do not forget that the line will stretch as you are sounding the depth, so be sure to do your marking with the line taut.

The leadline can be kept in a bucket, a bag or a basket. It must be tied to the bottom of its container and flaked in carefully between your hands. (If you throw it in a heap or try to coil it, it is bound to tie itself in knots.)

Most boats need only a leadline. All boats should have one, since the electronic echo sounder (a) can break down, and (b) cannot tell you about the nature of the sea floor.

Barometer

'Stop tapping my face, I'm doing my best. And please don't attach me to the main bulkhead or I'll get shaken to bits!'

It is highly desirable for the barometer to show the correct pressure, so you can compare your local conditions with the larger picture given on the radio. To calibrate the barometer, jot down its reading at 6 o'clock in the morning or evening, then compare this with the reading given the next day in the newspaper for the same time. Move the barometer needle by the amount of the difference, using the little screw on the back. Check it again the next day.

Radio receivers

Boats which will not venture more than 60 miles from land need only a simple transistor to listen to long- and medium-wave transmissions. This will give you the broadcasts of the BBC and France Inter, as well as regional weather bulletins.

Anyone who will be sailing further out to sea needs to be able to listen in by radio telephone to the maritime stations of Boulogne, Le Conquet, Grasse and so on which transmit on the Single Side Band (SSB) between 1.6 and 4MHz. Any receiver which bears the letters A3J or J3E can pick out these stations.

Your radio reception will be much improved by the addition of a good aerial. This will stop you needing to turn the transistor round for long wave stations, and will drastically improve your SSB reception. A backstay (suitably insulated at the top and bottom) makes an excellent aerial. On metal boats, you will need an extra earth.

For radio direction finding, you need to be able to receive radio beacons which transmit on around 300kHz, and you need a directable aerial which has a compass attached so that you can take a bearing on the transmitter. The directable aerial can be linked into your main radio system, but it is better rigged separately.

Any radio equipment needs its own place on board, preferably out of the way of water and knocks. The radio should be some distance from the compass, because the loudspeakers have a large magnet inside them. The radio direction finder needs to be stored somewhere safe but quickly accessible: it is even more fragile than your hand-bearing compass and should be put back in place the moment it is no longer in use.

Radio transmitters

Many pleasure-boat sailors have a transmitter on board so that they can make contact with the land and with other boats.

Short distance VHF communication systems are improving as their price is coming down. A portable system may be had for less than £400, and will allow you to transmit over a radius of several miles or several tens of miles depending on the height of your antenna. Theoretically, two portable sets 2m above sea level can communicate over a distance of 6.5 miles; or each can communicate with a coastal station 100m above sea level from 25 miles away. With a powerful transmitter, a fixed masthead antenna and an appropriate budget, you can use the system like you would your own phone.

VHF radio is not exactly a safety device, but it can fulfil some safety-related functions which contribute considerably to your comfort:
– distress signals can be sent out on channel 16;
– other boats can be asked for assistance;
– medical advice, weather forecasts and port information may be obtained;
– radio telephone contact can be maintained with home base;
– in certain cases, one can obtain information on one's own position.

A simple 4- or 5-channel handset, protected by a watertight pouch, is adequate for asking passers-by for a tow, drawing attention to oneself and communicating with other boats in your flotilla. The handset can also be taken with you in the liferaft should you need to abandon the boat. You should have a re-chargeable battery, but you need a couple of spare batteries as well. You need a charge-testing device to tell whether your set is capable of transmitting or not. If you are going a long way and you absolutely must stay in touch with land, you need an SSB transceiver. This sort of equipment is expensive and quite demanding to operate, and lies outside the scope of this book.

You may only use a transmitter if you have passed a simple test administered by the RYA (see their booklet G26). The set needs to be checked by an inspector and you have to pay an annual licence fee. *Important:* Make sure you have an adequate source of power for all the electronic items you plan to run on board. They are quite draining on a battery, and you should ensure that the VHF is not used excessively, both for your own good and for the good of others who need to use the frequency you are transmitting on.

Windvane and anemometer

These two pieces of equipment are generally combined in one assembly at the mast head. They are expensive, and usually found only on the best-equipped boats. Buying them is really only justified if you plan to race a lot.

They give an exact reading, undisturbed by the effect of the rig, so long as the sea is relatively calm and the wind relatively constant. When the boat is rolling in a heavy sea with light winds, there are too many variables for the equipment to give a reliable reading.

As an alternative, an effective windsock can be constructed for next to nothing out of 1.5m of steel wire and a length of spinnaker fabric!

Sextant

The sextant is an optical instrument for measuring angles very precisely. It is used particularly for measuring the angle above the horizon of a heavenly body.

Theory

A lens and a small mirror are fixed on a frame which is shaped like an arc of a circle. The arc is marked from 0 to 120° and toothed. A large movable mirror, the index mirror, travels along the arc. The index mirror is moved by a lever called the index and adjusted by a micrometer screw which is marked in minutes and tenths of minutes. The smaller mirror is most often a piece of highly reflective transparent glass.

As you look through the lens, you see the horizon through the small mirror, and the image of the star is superimposed, reflected by the index mirror and the small mirror. As you move the index

Micrometer sextant.

mirror, you can bring into alignment the two points between which you wish to measure the angle: the lower edge of the sun, for instance, and the horizon. You can then read off the angle: the degrees are shown on the index and the minutes on the micrometer screw.

Older sextants will have the small mirror silvered only on the right-hand side. The border of the silvering is in the sight line. There will be no micrometer screw, so the degrees and minutes are marked on the arc and read off on the vernier on the index.

Adjustment

The sextant is a very precise instrument but can easily be knocked out of adjustment. It needs checking periodically:
– before each season, check the alignment of the mirrors;
– before each observation, check the index error.
The index mirror must be at right angles to the arc. Two stops are supplied with the sextant for checking this. The sextant is placed flat on its side, with the stops at each end of the arc. You need to sight as shown in the diagram A. The index mirror is perpendicular when the directly visible left-hand stop appears to form a continuation of the reflected image of the right-hand stop in the mirror (which is adjusted by a screw on its back). This is the case in the photograph B.

The small mirror must be at right angles to the arc. Hold the sextant flat, with the index mirror at zero. Look through the lens at a distant horizontal line, for instance a roof of a house, or the horizon itself on a calm day. Turn the adjusting screw until the direct and reflected images align (diagram C).

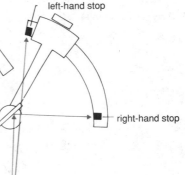

A. The mirrors are adjusted by sighting as shown.

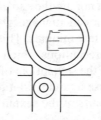

B. The index mirror is perpendicular to the arc. 1. The right-hand clip is seen in the index mirror. 2. The left-hand clip is seen directly. 3. Their edges are aligned.

C. The mirror is not quite perpendicular to the arc.

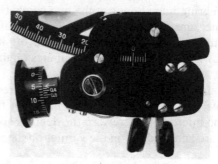

D. There is index error of –5′.

Index error can be measured by holding the sextant vertical and aligning the direct and reflected images of the horizon. The angle on the arc should be 0°; if it is not, the value shown is referred to as index error (see photograph D). The error needs to be known so you can subtract or add it to observed values (subtract if the error was read to the right of zero, add if it was to the left).

Maintenance

Sextants are fragile and must not be shaken even slightly. The sextant should be regularly lubricated by wiping it with cotton wool with a small amount of Vaseline. It must be kept in its box, away from water. Older models of sextant have such fine teeth on the arc that it is best not even to touch the arc.

Plastic sextants

Plastic sextant.

Plastic sextants have been on the market for a number of years. They are nowhere near so precise as metal sextants, as they bend a little, but nor are they so expensive. If you take a few precautions in use, they can manage good measurements which are correct to within a few minutes. This is generally as accurate as one needs.

The precautions which should be borne in mind are:
– to take the sextant out of the cabin at least ten minutes before you plan to use it, and hold it by its handle throughout. This will ensure that all parts of the sextant are at the same temperature by the time it is used;
– to hold the handle as lightly and with as constant pressure as possible, so as to minimise any distortion;
– to check the index error before every observation;
– to use it just as you would a metal sextant;

– to check the index error again after the observation, if desired. If the error found is approximately the same as that found earlier, use the average of the two values as the correction factor in your calculation. If it is a long way from the previous reading, start the whole procedure again.

Electronic navigation

Satellite navigation

The receiver picks up information from the five satellites of the TRANSIT system which are in polar orbit round the earth, and take 105 minutes on each orbit. On average, you will pick up one satellite every four or five hours, and the electronic navigator uses the sighting to plot your longitude and latitude. If you then feed in your speed and heading, either by hand or by plugging it into the log and compass, it will calculate your position constantly. It can also calculate the course required to a given point, estimate the time required to get there, and perform many other useful functions.

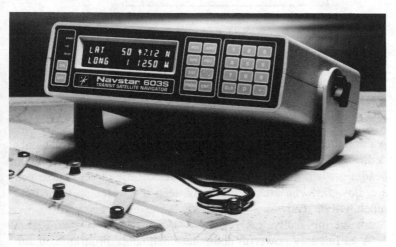

Your on-board box of tricks.

Hyperbolic navigation systems

These systems cover a given limited area of sea, outside which your machine cannot be used. They pick up a signal every 10–30 seconds and constantly update your position; they then use the stored information to calculate your average heading and course made good over a given period: 3, 5 or 10 minutes depending on what you need. A hyperbolic navigation system can also estimate an arrival time, calculate the best moment to tack, etc, so long as the operator spends a little time exploring all its facilities and learning to use them. Incidentally, a seasick operator is the source of most navigation mistakes ...

All this wizardry is wonderful, but one must also know how to navigate manually.

Area covered by Decca in Europe.

Area covered by Loran in Europe.

Navigation by computer

A computer on board is like an extra crew member permanently dedicated to letting you know where the boat is, where it should be heading, when it is best to tack, how far off the direct course you are, how fast you are sailing, how deep the water is, what time lunch will be ready ...

Staggering, really.

A sufficiently powerful computer adequately programmed can perform all these functions if it is hooked up to the necessary sensors (log, anemometer, windvane, navigator, electric compass, radar – if you have one – and electronic weather-map decoder). This can save the captain an awful lot of headaches. There are specialised programmes (such as Mac Sea on the Apple Macintosh) to do all this. One can even feed in electronic maps of the sea area you are covering and the computer then takes on the job of pilot as well!

Charts and documents

The member of your crew who is responsible for navigation will be recording all the information gathered on a nautical chart (as opposed to a land map, which many people use but which really cannot be recommended).

The best charts are Admiralty charts or their French equivalent, SHOM (Service Hydrographique et Océanique de la Marine). There are commercially published alternatives such as the charts of Stanford or Imray, which have different graphical symbols. Paper charts such as these are vulnerable to water, and need an HB or B pencil for drawing on them.

The charts of the areas most widely used by pleasure-boat sailors are available plastic-laminated, which is greatly preferable to paper if they can be found for the area you are interested in. To draw on plastic-covered charts you need a soft pencil, 2B or 3B, or a dry laboratory pencil.

Caring for your charts

Charts are fragile and expensive. They need to be looked after if they are to remain legible.

If you do not have space to store the charts flat, they are best rolled. Unrolling them can involve some acrobatics, but it is better than folding, as they quickly become illegible and tear at the folds. If you must fold a chart, fold it where the folds will matter least. Do not just fold it down the middle.

Tears in charts can be repaired by gluing a sheet of old chart paper onto the back, using ordinary office glue. Sticky tape is not recommended, as it tends to shrink slightly after it has been stretched onto the paper, and makes the chart wrinkle.

If there is one area in which you cruise regularly, it is worth sticking the chart onto a sheet of plywood. The chart can then be plastic-coated with transparent film or even varnished (though check before you proceed with the varnish, as some varnishes can erase the print on the map ...).

Storing paper charts

On a long cruise, it is worth storing several charts together by area, so that you group them, for example, as 'Western Channel, West of Cherbourg', or 'Northern Spain, St-Jean-de-Luz to La Coruña'. All you actually keep on the table is a list of which charts you have in store; or better still, the general map of the region divided up and numbered into the individual charts and the areas they cover.

If you roll your charts, make sure you do so with the printed face outside; otherwise it is impossible to stop them curling up on the table. Any charts you are not using can be stored in a 120cm plastic tube with one stopper glued in place and the other a watertight screw fit. The tube can then be stowed virtually anywhere (above the bunks, in the forecastle or sail locker).

Admiralty chart formats

Chart Format	Paper Size
Half DE (unfolded chart)	711×521mm
DE (single-folded chart)	$1,041 \times 711$mm
Long DE (double-folded chart)	$1,270 \times 711$mm
A0	$1,189 \times 841$mm

There is always too much to carry. Better use a semi-automatic liferaft, not a beach toy.

Odds and ends

The phrase 'odds and ends' covers a multitude of different items, but you must not infer that any disorder is intended. We shall be systematic and selective in our coverage of boat bric-à-brac.

The tender

The tender is the largest loose object on board and also the most abused. The average amateur sailor has conflicting demands on their tender: it must be cheap, since it is not a 'real' boat; it must be light, since one often has to carry it; and it should not get in the way on board. However, given that we are sailors and not rowers, it should also be large enough to carry all the crew, gear and food in one go: thus it has to be roomy, strong and stable, just like a real boat. Oh, and it must be unsinkable. And you should be able to use it to pick up a mooring in a stiff breeze, or a crew member who has fallen overboard while you are anchored in a tidal rip …

Any vessel which is capable of satisfying most of the above conditions must be extremely adaptable. The only material which comes into consideration is rubber (or, more precisely, neoprene or PVC).

The tender needs to be a fair size: at least 3.10m long for four people, and 3.60m for six people. It needs to have the fattest tubes practical, a rope which goes all way round and good built-in oar notches. It need not have a stiff floor, even if you will be using an outboard motor, so long as the tender is blown up hard. And it can be fitted with an air inflation cylinder (see the section above on inflatable dinghies) and stored in a container made the same way as that of the rescue dinghy.

We strongly recommend that the tender should be made of hypalon neoprene: it costs 20% more than PVC, but will last fifteen seasons instead of three, and is easy to repair.

Precautions

A good quality inflatable tender does not lose air or spring a leak unless it is really badly treated. A few elementary precautions are all that is needed to keep it in good condition:
– do not walk on it when it is folded or deflated;
– jump out before it touches the bottom or the bank;
– do not leave it in the surf at the water's edge: the dinghy should either be floating or on dry land, not in between;
– do not leave it fully inflated for a long time in strong sunlight, or it might burst;
– do not tie it up by a stone quay, which is too rough (though tying the tender alongside the boat will not damage either boat or tender);
– do not tow it at sea, as there is a risk of it flipping over, which could damage the nose ring or fender.

Problems with the airtightness of the tender arise most frequently at the valves. It is worth lubricating the valves every fortnight or so with mineral oil.

Propulsion

As it has considerable windage, the tender needs an efficient means of propulsion to push it forward against wind and waves. Sculling is insufficient, even if there is a reasonable notch built into the tender transom. You will need to row the tender, with proper oars (which disqualifies most collapsible oars) and decent rowlocks. You need to be seated at the right height, for instance on an upturned bucket. There is no harm in having a couple of paddles as well as the oars. If you plan to use an outboard, check that the transom can take the weight and the power.

Laying up

Before you put the inflatable away for the winter, it should have a good rinsing in fresh water. It should be stored semi-inflated, away from heat and light if possible. If you absolutely have to fold it, at least make sure it is completely dry and dust it down with French chalk to make sure it does not stick to itself.

Repairs

Do not wait until your inflatable has a puncture before starting to fix it. If you can patch places which show bad scuff marks, you will save yourself a lot of troubles. You can also find anti-scuff adhesive tape to put on the spots which receive the most wear. There are certain places which are weak, such as the join between the transom and the sidewalls, and these should be reinforced before they tear or unstick.

With a punctured tender:
– find out where the air is escaping, by pumping it up then wiping it all over with a sponge full of soapy water. You should see bubbles at the puncture;
– carefully roughen the area around the hole with a file or glass paper. You need to remove the film coating of the neoprene which prevents adhesion. Roughen the patch similarly;
– apply a first layer of adhesive to both faces to be joined, and wait a quarter of an hour for it to dry thoroughly;
– apply a second coat and wait for that to dry so that it is tacky but does not come off onto your finger. Then press the patch into place.

There is one essential requirement for this procedure to work successfully: the temperature of the air and of both pieces to be joined must be at least 20°C.

The sculling oar and rowlock

Modern boats have a lot of freeboard, so the sculling oar needs to be quite long: the blade must be entirely submerged, and the sculler

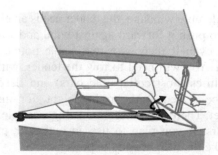

The sculling oar has a high-priority position on board.

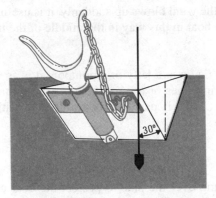

The sculling oar will only work properly with a well-fixed rowlock which cannot fall out.

must be able to stand comfortably. It is unusual for the boat cabin to have space for an oar this long, so it is stowed on deck. It needs to be readily accessible, yet firmly held in place, and not held bent. It makes sense to stow it on the same side as its rowlock.

For a right-handed sculler, the rowlock needs to be to port. It should be angled 30° aft so as to give a good push. On most cruisers, this rowlock will have to be permanently fixed, but on some it is important to have a removable rowlock so as not to get in the way of sheets and the crew when sailing. Removable rowlocks should be equipped with a safety chain.

If the transom is higher than the deck it is best to cut a sculling notch in it, rather than attaching a rowlock. This rounded notch should be lined with brass.

Rowlocks and sculling notches need to have smooth inside surfaces if the oar is not to be worn away very quickly.

Mooring warps

Two lines 20–30m long are absolutely necessary, and three or four are better.

One is quite likely to find oneself in a situation where one needs to cut a mooring warp, and the warp will wear out fairly fast anyway, so you should choose a cheap but strong rope. At les Glénans, we use thick-section polypropylene rope (12mm for a Mousquetaire, 16mm for a Galiote and 18mm for the *Sereine*).

In the Mediterranean, it is worth taking along some lengths of steel cable, maybe 4–5m, with an eye on each end, so you can tie straight onto the rocks in a bay or inlet where the bottom will not hold an anchor. The steel cable is passed around a rock at either side of the inlet, and the boat then tied to the cable with nylon rope (which can be quite light, say, 5mm for a Mousquetaire).

A mooring-line spring.

Particularly if the wind blows up suddenly, it is useful to be able to immobilise the boat in this way in the middle of the inlet.

The spring

Whenever you tie up at a jetty or a pontoon, it is as well to spring the main mooring lines or to cross them over so that they have a springing effect. This is particularly worthwhile with lines which are slightly too short.

Fenders

Fenders are hung over the side to protect the boat against bumps with other boats or jetties. They can be made of almost anything and in almost any shape. The one criterion all must fulfil is that they stay in place once positioned. For this, they should be flat, which very few are. It is worth noting that bow fenders are very effective as side fenders when hung over at the beams. But the best fender is a car tyre (or even better, a scooter tyre). The only shortcomings of a tyre are that it can get in the way when not in use, and that it makes everything dirty if it is not kept in a casing. (The casing should be made of oilcloth or similar, as any other cloth will pick up all the filth from a dirty harbour.)

As well as the normal fenders, it is worth keeping a few blow-up buoys on board for those few times where you are really hemmed in, with a lot of sea running.

The fenders need to hang vertically, or they will ride up. They will work best if you hang three or four on each side, with the biggest front and aft and the smallest amidships.

Legs

Legs are metal or wooden stilts which hold the boat upright when it is beached.

They need to be 8–10cm shorter than the keel so that they are not carrying the whole weight of the boat if the keel sinks into the ground a little.

The legs need a base plate which should be bigger for heavier boats and smaller for lighter boats. If the plate is too small for the weight of the boat, it will dig in at the wrong angle and can break; if it is too big, it will not dig in at all and can be knocked. We use the following guidelines: 500sq cm for a Corsaire, 800sq cm for a Galiote and 1,000sq cm for an Arpège. 1,000sq cm for a Corsaire would be too much.

The legs are generally bolted in place either to the hull directly or onto specially made plates. Either way, the fixing points need to be reinforced, of course … and you must not forget to plug the holes when you unbolt the legs!

Even on a small boat, the leg bolts have to be strong, or they will bend. To give some idea, we recommend 14mm bolts for a Corsaire, 20mm bolts for a two-tonner and 25mm bolts for a ten-tonner.

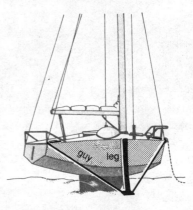

The legs are held in place by guys made off at the bow and transom. The feet are splayed slightly out from the boat to aid stability. The beach is sloping at a rate appropriate for the slope of the bottom of the keel.

The legs are kept at the correct angle by guys leading from the foot of the leg to cleats (not the pulpits) each end of the deck. Polypropylene ropes are good for this purpose as they barely stretch.

CHAPTER 5

Laying up and fitting out

When a boat is sailing, it knows no rest. Sea and wind put it under considerable strains and the salt water and sea air corrode every part of it. Your maintenance, repairs and watchful eye are weapons in a ceaseless battle against those enemies of the boat: wear and corrosion. Running maintenance of the sort covered in the chapters to date will not hold out for ever against these powerful foes, and one day the boat and its crew will have to withdraw, regroup and prepare properly to face the challenges to come.

This regrouping is done at the end of every season when the boat is laid up for the winter ... at least for those of us who live in climates where year-round pleasure sailing does not deserve the name. At the time of laying up, you can go into details and check for signs of fatigue in the hull, rigging and any other material. This is the time to look to the future: if you get the laying-up right, fitting out the next spring will be that much easier and faster.

Since any time spent on laying up or fitting out is time lost to sailing, it is worth planning and organising yourself to keep that time to a minimum. Actually, you should be preparing for laying up throughout the season; then there should be a few days of intensive preparation right towards the end of the season. This can be done most effectively by keeping a notebook on board and just jotting down daily all the things which annoy you on the boat or don't work. The things that can be done at a short stop in port can be ticked off then; but the ones remaining at the end of the season are the ones you need to sort out when laying up. Write down any possible improvements which occur to you, or any items which need replacing. If you use a good thick notebook, it will last several years and end up as a valuable addition to the logbook, a sort of maintenance manual. The book can give you the detailed picture as well as an overall perspective, and it will also save you forgetting anything in the long winter nights between laying up and getting ready for the next spring.

Laying up

Enjoying leisure is an essential qualification for being a pleasure-boat sailor. We can take this further and say that a good sailor is one who plans their activity so as to avoid wasting energy.

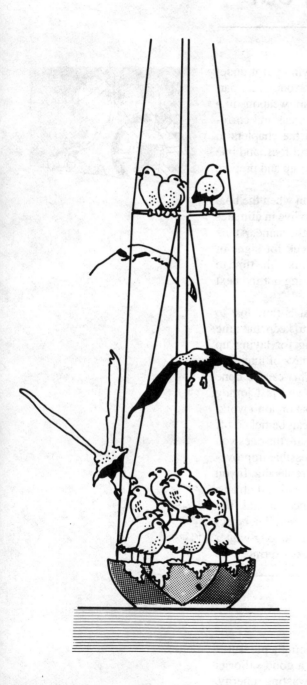

Applying this dictum to the activity of laying up a modern cruising boat, we find that the materials are generally on our side: they are mostly hard-wearing and easily maintained, quite apart from the fact that the boat has not been sailed full-time over the season. The main principles of laying up, then, are:
– repair immediately anything that needs it;
– leave everything in place that can be left in place;
– protect as much as you can from the ravages of the weather.

We are not absolutely forbidding you from de-rigging the boat entirely, so you can while away the long winter evenings picking over the shrouds … but if that is your plan, you need to have the boat kept close to home, which is impossible for most of us. Basically, the type of processes involved in laying up are determined by the site you have chosen for the boat to spend the winter.

Wintering

A sailboard is easily stored over the winter: you rinse it in fresh water, sling the mast, boom and board from the garage ceiling and spread the sail on top.

A dinghy is little more trouble: it can be kept anywhere, with the hull turned over, the mast stored somewhere under shelter if possible, and all the gear taken away in a box or two in the car boot. But a larger boat is more problematic and more complicated. If your boat can be trailed and stored near your home over the winter, fine; but if not, that is where your worries begin. Depending on what the boat is made of, where you live and how much you can afford to spend, you will need to look at different solutions.

Wintering afloat

This is the simplest answer: very little de-rigging

to do, and the boat is practically ready to go whenever you are. But wintering afloat can only be recommended if you have a very shel-

Dinghies can overwinter outside perfectly well. They need to be turned over, held above the ground so that air can circulate underneath, and firmly lashed down so they are not blown away in a gale.

tered berth in a well-equipped harbour with twenty-four-hour surveillance and someone who will pop over to the boat regularly to air it, check and replace as necessary any mooring parts, fenders or other items before they break, and dissuade any would-be squatters.

The mooring itself will be the least expensive part of this solution: the 'babysitting' service is likely to cost a fair amount if it is reliable; and your paint will be exposed to the weather at an inhospitable time of year, while various forms of marine wildlife make their homes in your hull.

Depending on what they are made of, some boats will withstand wintering afloat better than others. A classically built wooden boat will be prevented from drying out, though it will still need a month in the dry at some stage to get rid of any shipworm. Any glued wooden boats will become a little heavier, and less well-built ones will age rather faster if kept in the water. Glassfibre boats will cope perfectly well, however, so long as you are prepared to expend a bit of elbow grease on polishing the hull the next spring. Steel and aluminium boats do not suffer from spending the winter in the water, unless they are tied up close together, or a nearby hull has copper paint on.

This particular problem can be avoided if you fit your hull (correctly!) with sacrificial anodes.

Wintering on the beach or in a mud berth

The boat can be left on a beach if it is adequately supported, and sufficiently far up that it will only be reached by the high spring tides. (It is worth checking that the March springs will reach as high as the September ones, or you will have problems floating it off again!)

This is the traditional mode of wintering in areas with a long tidal range; it is particularly suited for traditional wood hulls, which dry out enough to kill off the shipworm and lose some of their moisture. It is also cheap (since the spot on the beach is usually free), at least if you can float it on and off the beach yourself. You need to catch the autumn and spring equinoctial tides, and the boat will need checking occasionally in between at the time of particularly high tides. No valuables should be left on board, since you cannot keep a constant watch on the boat.

Wintering on the mud without legs is also a good way to lay up a traditional wooden boat, which is thus prevented from drying out completely and is not subject to any great stress. The boat and its moorings need to be checked regularly, and it will need pumping out occasionally.

These two solutions can only be recommended for owners who live relatively close to their boats.

Wintering outside on dry land

The ideal and the cheapest solution for those whose garden can take it is to lay the boat up there.

Any boat too big to be towed can be left on legs in a chandler's

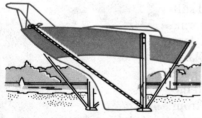

Quite safe until the next high spring tide.

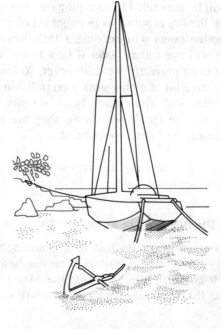

yard or the sailing club car park. This is a moderately costly solution. If the boat is sufficiently far from vandals, you can leave most of the gear on board and just take the radio and other expensive items with you. The paint will survive fairly well.

A classically built boat which is left out in the dry in this way needs to be put back in the water early in the spring; others can wait until midsummer if you want.

Wintering under cover

This is the most expensive solution but also the least problematic. It should be considered if there are significant repairs to the hull proposed. It is also recommended for wooden racing yachts which need to dry out to keep down to their design weight. (They should be sufficiently soundly made that the hull is not stressed.) It is especially good for those yachties who like to have a gleaming finish on their hull. There are no problems with moisture, and you can leave all your gear on board.

Take it home with you if you want to work on it over the winter.

Laying up, in detail

Let us now look at the individual operations involved in laying up, according to the method of storage chosen for the boat.

The boat should be laid up as soon as possible after the last cruise of the year, while all the boat's weaknesses are still fresh in your mind, and you are still firmly intending to sort them out. Later on, you forget and your interest turns to other things.

We shall look at each part of the boat in order.

Hull

The inside of the boat must be cleaned thoroughly and systematically; your brush should reach every corner and every cranny, dry out the bilges completely so there is no chance of any moisture remaining in the boat to rot the upholstery and greet you with an awful stale smell six months later. As far as possible, the inside should be washed out with fresh water, which will reduce the humidity further. A high-pressure (30–40 bar) water pump with a fine nozzle is good for getting into awkward corners, and a little detergent may also be used, so long as you rinse afterwards.

While you are cleaning the boat is also the best time to check for cracks and weak spots. Look in all the places you might expect to weaken first: the join of hull to deck, rudder pintles, keel bolts, and

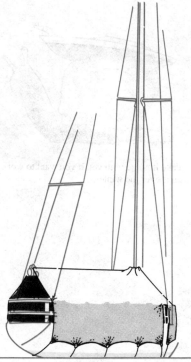

any bulkheads or angles.

Next, lubricate any moving parts: winches, rails, blocks, windlasses. Lightly grease aluminium and chromed surfaces.

Finally, do not forget that it is absolutely vital to ventilate the cabin adequately. Make sure you have any equipment necessary to get air to circulate: hatch cover props so that the hatches can be locked ajar;

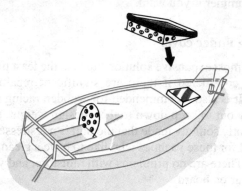

However you lay the boat up,
make sure the cabin is well aired.

perforated covers for the companionway. Inside the boat, leave the cupboards open and the floors up: everything to get the air circulating.

Depending on the style of laying up you choose, it may be worth covering the boat with a tarpaulin (though with the air still allowed to circulate). This is only crucial for traditionally built boats with a planked deck. You need to be very careful fixing the tarpaulin if it is to do its job properly without forming little pockets for rainwater to collect in and without being blown off by the winter gales ... There is only one effective means of tying a tarpaulin on: shock-cord.

Painting the hull is becoming less of an issue as fewer boats are made of wood. A boat which sails all year needs to be repainted every two years; one which is sailed only in summer needs it three- or four-yearly.

Do not forget that the painting needs to be completed a good week before the boat is fitted out again, so the paint is fully hardened.

Rigging

Leaving the mast up

If the boat is wintering afloat, in a mud berth or by the jetty, the mast and rigging can usually be left in place, so long as you know what condition the rigging is in (ie you have been checking it regularly and thoroughly). Only strike the mast if there is some major repair work needed or if you cannot climb up it.

If the mast is staying stepped, you need to give it the once-over with a long-nozzled oilcan and a greasy cloth, to lubricate blocks, sheaves, halyards and other moving parts. You should be particularly careful to immobilise the running rigging so that it cannot beat against the mast; or better still, temporarily replace the halyards with light cords which will allow you to store the halyards themselves away from the UV light. In general, you should not rig any new gear at the time of laying up: this gives it six extra months to wear out. Do, however, make a careful note of anything which will need changing in the spring.

Mast unstepped but fully rigged
There is one important precaution to take when unstepping the mast: *let the bottlescrews out from the top – the shroud end – rather than from the chainplates*. Otherwise there is a good chance of losing a part of the screw, and chandlers no more stock bits of bottlescrews than they do shackle-pins! Similarly, when the mast is being stepped again, *the bottlescrews should be fastened first to the chainplates*, and not to the shrouds.

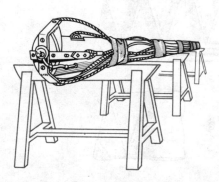

Always lay the mast with the track down.

The mast should be stored horizontal, fully rigged, and preferably indoors, as water does not run off a mast easily if it is horizontal. A wooden mast only has one flat face to be laid on: that is the side with the track. A metal mast needs to be kept away from any cuprous metals to avoid possible galvanic action. If the mast is not stored indoors, you should take off any parts of the rigging made of stainless steel.

Mast unrigged
Completely de-rigging a mast is a considerable job, and offers lots
of chances to lose things. Resort to this (reluctantly) only if the
mast needs to be repaired or revarnished.

Sails

All sails should be carefully rinsed in fresh water, dried out and
painstakingly inspected before they are put away for the winter.
Small repairs should be carried out immediately (or at least noted).
Any which need more complicated attention should be sent off to
the sail loft now.

Terylene sails can stay on board if you are leaving the boat afloat
and planning to use it over the winter, so long as it is dry inside. Do
not leave them in their bags: drape them over the bunks to give
them something of an airing.

Otherwise, your sails should be stored in a dry place. You can
fold them in a zig-zag shape along the foot, then roll them round the
luff rope so they do not take up too much room; heavily finished
sails or those which are partly of Mylar should be rolled into a
sausage around the luff.

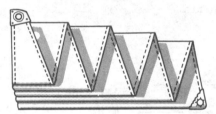

Sails should be folded in a zigzag along the
foot, then rolled from the luff.

Other gear

While you are cleaning the boat out, cast a pitiless eye over the gear
and contents: throw out the ever-so-slightly rusty cheese grater,
those little bits of string that were bound to come in useful some
time, the improvised ashtray made of a corned-beef tin, the ball-

point pen that works when you jam a matchstick in the top and the pretty flowers you picked up in the Scilly Isles but which are now wilting in their jam-pot. It is better to throw out now all those items you will not be able to face in six months' time.

As for the rest of the contents of the cabin: as far as possible, leave everything where it is. That way, you won't lose it.

Everything you do take off the boat in the autumn should be noted down in your exercise book. You might even think it worth sticking a little label on the spot from which you have removed an item, with a note on the label of where you have put the item at home. This is a particularly worthwhile precaution if you will not personally be refitting the boat in the spring.

There are some groups of items which nearly always need to be taken off the boat; others which can be left on board in almost all cases.

Electronic equipment
All the electronic gadgets should be removed even if the boat will be stored in a hangar. They should be put in a warm dry place, such as the mantelpiece in the living room. This will give you fond memories of your time afloat every time you look at them. Before you unplug everything, mark the wires. (An electrical store will sell you stick-on numbers which serve this function well.)

Take the batteries out. Do not forget to clean out and rinse any sensors or other underwater parts. Anything you are unsure of, take to the specialist.

Electricity
If the boat is to sit idle for a number of months, the batteries are best taken out and handed to someone who can maintain them and keep them charged. All contacts should be carefully cleaned: switches, light sockets and control consoles, before sprinkling with a water-repellent spray.

Inboard diesel engine
If the engine is still to be in good condition when you come back to it in the spring, you must take the following precautions:
– trickle a little oil into each cylinder;
– clean out and empty the cooling water, to avoid any risk of freezing;
– take off the dynamo and starter motor and give them to a local garage to look after (you have already done the same with the battery);
– clean and lightly oil the outer surface of the engine;

– turn the engine over by hand a few times, once or twice a month, to prevent the pistons sticking and ruining the sleeves and rings;
– tighten the stern gland a little more than usual and grease it generously;
– shut the seacocks (and if possible, grease the underwater surface of any metal flaps);
– stick a big sign by the ignition switch, saying: 'Have you remembered to open the seacocks and loosen the stern gland?'.

Outboard motor

This has to be taken off the boat in any case. First, get rid of the salt from the system by running it in fresh water for at least twenty minutes, then clean it off on the outside with a brush and fresh water with a little detergent, again, to get rid of the salt. (Do clean under the cover, but do not get the electrics wet.) Put a few thimblefuls of oil into each cylinder then turn the motor gently to spread the oil. Finally, silicone-grease the whole thing.

You can give the outboard to a mechanic for all the above jobs, but you need to be certain the work will be finished by Easter ...

Navigation material

The compass, sextant and binoculars should be taken ashore, and any moving parts Vaselined. You will also need the charts and tide tables at home for updating, planning future cruises and repairing any tears.

Safety equipment

If your dinghy is one of those which needs an annual check, leave it with the stockist. Rinse in fresh water and carefully dry any life-jackets, harnesses and lifebelts; then leave them hanging up inside the boat. Grease any snapshackles. Take your waterproofed torch to pieces, throw away the batteries and smear Vaseline on the contacts.

Flares should be kept carefully in a dry place. As we noted earlier, most of them will still be serviceable a couple of years after their expiry date. It would be a shame to throw them away when they could be such a useful backup to the new ones you will buy in the spring.

Take the fire extinguisher to the stockist for its annual check and maintenance. Make sure you do not pay for a check and maintenance on a fire extinguisher which would be cheaper to buy new!

Medical kit

Take it back home, use any items that you can and throw away any which are out of date.

> Your dinghy needs an annual check-up. If you can, you should try to watch the checker at work, as this will give you a good idea of what points need looking at, and what sort of condition they should be in.

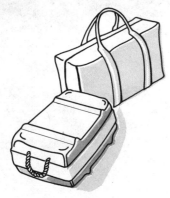

Textile material

Rinse in fresh water and dry out; hang any lee cloths open inside the boat; and put the mattresses on their side if there is no one who can pop in to turn them periodically.

Household items

Clean all the galley with care (as you normally would); lightly grease any aluminium utensils. Beware of any galvanic effects and do not leave a stainless steel ladle, for instance, in an aluminium box. Clean the cooker thoroughly (as usual) and grease it. Any slightly dubious-looking gas burners should be thrown out rather than left to leak. Pumps and taps need to be greased, the water tank emptied and any containers thoroughly cleaned out with bleach solution. Finish any last-minute washing-up.

Any part-used gas bottles should be taken from under their burner valves and re-stopped with their original stoppers. Swill the water tanks with water plus a little bleach for an hour, then empty and rinse. Dry out any tanks, pipes and pumps.

Give any containers the same treatment.

Grease under any seacocks, including the toilet valve, and close them. We recommend emptying the toilet of water and sluicing it through with cooking oil if you have the boat out of the water. The water inlet needs to be disconnected from its seacock.

Finally, take all the food out, including spices, condiments and preserves.

The dinghy

Wash the dinghy with soapy water and check it thoroughly, including the pump. If repairs are needed, use a specialist. Otherwise, dust with French chalk and store semi-inflated if you can.

Odds and ends

Make sure the anchor and chain are stowed somewhere other than in the bilges, as water will always collect down there over the winter. Tools should be left under oil, for instance in a bucket. The paddle can be hung from the cabin roof, by at least three points, so it does not warp.

When you have gone through all the above procedures, look back over your notebook for items you have not yet ticked off: make a detailed and coherent list of the repairs to be covered and contact all the people to whom you plan to give the work. You need to be able to give precise indications of the work to be done; especially if there is a leak somewhere, you need to have found out exactly where it is before the boat is laid up, because it is not always easy to locate leaks while the boat is at rest.

Any new material you will need to order should be listed, and ordered immediately, so long as the high autumn springs have not coincided with a low ebb of your finances. Even if you do have a temporary cashflow problem, it is best to have a word with the stockists, get the gear ordered now and offer to pay and collect at whatever date you think reasonable.

Fitting out

If the laying-up was done well, fitting out the next spring is child's play, or should be. You just have to put things back where you took them from, install any new equipment and check that it all works. Simple ... except that it is seldom so simple. You will always forget something, and the effect of forgetting will be to waste some time in the spring. Just as the first beautiful sailing weather of the spring comes along, you leaf through your notebook to check those last details ... but you forgot to write them down in September. If this happens to you, make a note to make a better job of it next time. Otherwise, even the best of resolutions can be forgotten.

When you have tracked down that missing batten, changed the sheave which was jamming, bribed the local welder to fix your pintle at five minutes' notice, sent your spouse to the garage ten times to check how the battery charging is getting on; when you have ticked off every item on your exhaustive list of the boat's equipment, then you might be justified in thinking you are almost ready.

You are not almost ready. The boat looks prepared and the crew is raring to go, but you have no grounds for believing it will all work. Rather than heading off immediately on a nice long cruise, you should spend just one night on board and make a quick trial outing.

The first outing

Before even going on board, check from the jetty that the boat's trim is correct. Then sort out the sails and gear, and check the running rigging is all straight, pulling the sails up and letting them down, pulling on the sheets and trying out the winches. Start the engine. Have a trial scull with the oar to check nothing breaks. Spend a few minutes reading our chapter on safety.

Every crew member should try on their own personal safety gear: lifejacket, harness, lifeline clip, watertight flashlamp. This process should allow you to check not only that the gear itself is in good order but also that the crew knows how to use it. They must also be reminded of how to use the lifebelt and its light, as well as where the rocket flares and smoke flares are kept and how they are used. Check the liferaft is properly attached and drill the crew in launching it.

Setting everything up can be laborious. But the moment you leave port, the boat and crew will all wake up. The first job to be done at sea is to adjust the standing rigging. Then you check the rest of the boat, systematically; go through every normal basic manoeuvre, try out all the sails and take in and shake out a reef. Only this way can you be sure that the sheets have not shrunk, all jib shackles are properly attached and the reefing points still there.

When you have checked the boat over once and got your eye in, practise the 'man overboard' drill until you have got it right. Make sure that if you are the one who falls in, your crew knows how to fish you out! When that point has been reached you can return home with a light heart.

It would be surprising if the first outing were entirely problem-free. Note the niggles as they crop up and then, once you are back in harbour, set to work on your new list of items to be sorted out.

The first night

Your aim should be to duplicate the conditions of a night aboard on a cruise, so you should eat at least one meal and sleep one night before you go setting off on this year's adventures. The meal should be a feast to celebrate the start of the season, as well as allowing you to check that the galley really is fully equipped with food and crockery, the stove works, there is salt and pepper, the lights are all in order and the radio picks up all the frequencies you need. After

the feast, everyone retires to their bunk and finds out whether there is anything wrong with it.

You will not be able to set off at dawn the next day, because there will be a substantial shopping list generated by the evening's activity. Do not forget your waterproofs, your pen, the tender ... then up anchors and away ...

One last check that the boat is sitting in the water correctly trimmed.

PART IV

Boat handling

While you were learning to sail, we followed a sort of syllabus. This becomes difficult after you have mastered the basics, such as how to point the boat in the right direction and how many hulls to have in the water: then a whole range of new experiences opens up in front of you, and route planning among all these new areas becomes more difficult. Circumstances will help you fill in the gaps in your knowledge, teach you more about old topics, and throw new difficulties in your path. Some manoeuvres you will master immediately; others will take an age. Gross mistakes, though, are still perfectly possible at this stage of expertise; and there is no substitute for trial and error in learning.

There will therefore be no attempt in this detailed look at boat handling to treat topics in any artificially imposed chronological order. First we shall study the behaviour of the boat on different points of sailing. The accompanying tasks of changing sails, mooring, manoeuvring in harbour will be learnt as we go along, and as you acquire greater familiarity with the boat and its reactions.

The basics of these manoeuvres will be the same for all types of boat. Most of them have already been touched on earlier in this book, while we were talking about dinghies and racing catamarans. This by no means implies that all boats need to be handled the same way. The differences are largely a question of style. Small boats are like acrobatic apparatus, over-canvassed and flighty; for the few hours you are sailing, your main interest is speed and you can take all the risks you like while pushing the boat to its limits, since there will always be someone watching the area in which you are sailing. A cruising boat is designed for different requirements, whether it has one, two or three hulls. You have to be able to live aboard, including eating and sleeping; you have to be able to survive the widest range of weathers without any help, so the boat will inevitably be less extreme in its design criteria.

When we get down to questions of specific manoeuvres, we shall have to distinguish between light and heavy boats, monohulls and multihulls. A lighter boat stops and starts easily; a heavier boat carries much more momentum, but reacts more slowly to the influences of wind, water and helm. The crew represents a high proportion of the total weight of a dinghy and the positioning of their weight has a vital influence on the way the boat sails. This is a far less important factor on a one-and-a-half tonner, and becomes a minor point only on a large cruising yacht (though even then it is never quite irrelevant). On a light catamaran, the very idea of the 'real' wind becomes relative in strength and direction; and quite fundamental fixed points of orientation are called into question.

Precise rules and categories are hard to lay down: a fairly large but light boat can respond to the tiller like a dinghy, while a small and relatively heavy boat often handles like a large cruiser. Every boat has its own personality, which you will discover as you live with it. There are no absolute truths, nor should there be.

CHAPTER 1

Control

Boat control depends vitally on how much attention you pay to the wind. This basic truth should be tattooed on the forehead of every sailor: *the wind is your only valid reference point, and you will achieve nothing in a sailing boat until your sails are in harmony with the wind.*

This reference point, of course, changes constantly. If you try to extract maximum performance from your boat, you must face up to needing to readjust your perfect trim of a moment ago, and you must live with constantly changing reality. The best sailor is the one who first notices and adapts to a change in the wind strength or direction. There is no other secret to it (as far as we know), and such skills only develop with practice.

Adapting to circumstances means, in essence, changing the sail trim, the boat balance and the way you steer.

Throughout this chapter we shall return to these three points as they relate to each point of sailing and every wind strength. In reality, of course, there is more to sailing well than the combining of these elements; but the relationship between them will be shown to be fundamental. *Changing one aspect of a boat's trim alters all the others, and boat speed depends on the balance between the forces at work.*

Analysing the various situations helps us not to produce ready-made answers, but to indicate the directions in which you should search. There is no precise standard by which you can say, at such and such a time that boat is perfectly trimmed. For that reason, though you might come to know your boat intimately, the only real yardstick you have is that of the boat next to you; by comparing, you can make progress, and this is no less true for those who have no desire to enter into competition afloat. (The proximity of other boats does impose certain restrictions on the way one handles a boat, and we shall cover the 'rules of the road' in this section. See pages 515–21.)

We shall start by looking at sailing to windward. The boat is set up and tuned to windward, and it is also when sailing to windward that you will gain or lose the most by the degree of attention you pay to the wind. We shall examine the windward leg in some detail.

Which wind?

1. *True wind*. This is the wind which is blowing over a given stretch of water, and which you can feel on your face when the boat is moored.

2. *Headwind*. This is the wind created by the speed of the boat itself, also known as the relative wind.

3. *Apparent wind*. This is the only wind you can actually feel (or use) while the boat is moving.

The apparent wind is always further ahead than the true wind; the difference between their angles of incidence is often as high as 20°, and can reach 60° on a reach.

The apparent wind is stronger than the true wind when the boat is close-hauled, and weaker when the boat is running. It can be as much as 80% stronger or 50% weaker. The difference can be noticed most strongly when you change course.

These differences in direction and strength are very marked on multi-hulls. These can be said to make their own wind, as they go faster and faster.

The masthead wind vane is a superb tool for checking the apparent wind. It is precise, reliable and cheap, and you should consult it constantly. It gives a more reliable reading than streamers lower down in the rigging, where the air is bent by the sails.

headwind

true wind

apparent wind

The apparent wind is a combination of the true wind and the headwind.

headwind

true wind

apparent wind

Catamarans have a higher headwind because of their greater speed. The apparent wind therefore comes from further ahead, and the sails have to be sheeted more tightly.

Windex wind vane with close-hauled indicator blades.

To windward

Finding the best course

The ideal close-hauled course

Sailing to windward, one has to trim the sails to close-hauled. There are degrees of closeness, however! As we saw in the first chapter of Part I, a boat which luffs up from a beam reach finds itself first on a close reach, then on a close fetch, then close-hauled, then pinching. If you pinch any further, you find yourself unable to make headway without tacking, and you are said to be head to wind.

Your best windward course is that which the boat should take ideally when it needs to make ground to windward by tacking. We should at this point make the distinction between this and the simple fact of heading for a given point which happens to require a close-hauled course to reach it in one tack. The case we are concerned with involves tacking, and choosing a course not by reference to any specific fixed point, but by reference to the wind (which is of course constantly changing). One is therefore interested in taking advantage of the variation in the wind to gain ground to windward while keeping speed up, and effectively reducing the angle which constitutes the head-to-wind zone. This zone varies in size depending on the wind and the state of the sea, the number of hulls and the way you sail the boat. In general, a boat making an angle of 50° or so either side of the wind can be said to be making a good windward course. Some narrower-hulled boats can manage as little as 85° between tacks; but in a very strong or very light wind this can become 120–140° in the same boat. (The best windward course can be made in moderate weather.)

Your ability to make a good course is limited by the need to keep your speed up. When you are close-hauled, the force of the wind on the sails has a strong sideways component and heeling couple and a relatively weak forward component. The boat's leeway is only limited by its speed, which provides lift over the keel. To keep your speed up, you cannot afford to sail too close to the wind. *The optimum windward course is a compromise between heading and boat speed, and a battle against leeway.*

Depending on the strength of the wind, the state of the sea and the tactical demands of the race, one of the requirements may have higher priority than the others: *you might pinch to reduce the*

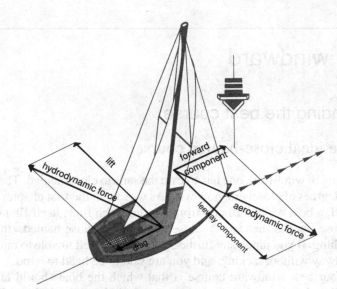

The force exerted on the sails by the wind (aerodynamic force) is at right angles to the sails, and is applied (simplifying slightly) at the centre of effort of the sail area. It can be broken down into a forward component parallel to the boat's axis, and a leeway component at right angles to the boat's axis. When the boat is close-hauled, the leeway component is always much stronger than the forward component.

Hydrodynamic force (that of the water on the underwater surfaces) is applied more or less at the centre of lateral resistance of the hull; it will be equal and opposite to the aerodynamic force. It can be broken down into drag, parallel to the boat's axis, and lift, at right angles to it. The lift is equal and opposite to the drift component.

overall distance sailed, at the risk of slowing down and increasing leeway; or you might sail slightly faster, further and freer, making less leeway.

For example, you might head at 45° to the wind, making 5kn, with 5° of leeway; if you were to head at 49° to the wind, making 5.25kn and only 3° leeway, you would only lose a total of 2°. Would this be offset by the extra speed? The problem is to know at what point the extra speed gained by sailing slightly freer is cancelled out by the extra distance to be covered. You can make a good comparison with other boats sailing the same course to experiment on this point; or you can even carry out the calculations if you have the necessary instruments on board. But you usually find out the answer in a race only at the windward mark.

There is unfortunately no general rule we can cite: any results will be valid only for the precise situation in which they were derived. The compromise between heading and speed is a

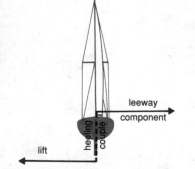

The leeway component and the lift determine the heeling couple: the bigger they are, the greater the heeling couple.

You have to make the hard choice: do I pinch and reduce the distance to be covered, or do I sail further and faster?

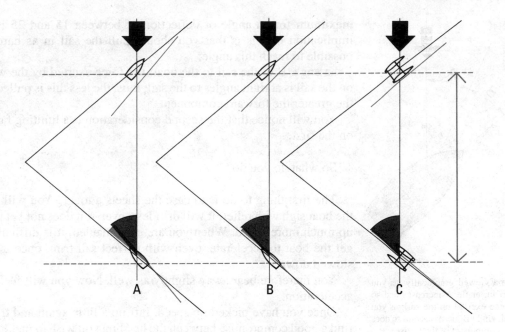

constantly shifting one. Since conditions will always be changing, the search for your ideal is never-ending.

These three boats have taken three different routes but arrive together. Boat A has sailed the least distance.

Almost close-hauled

Let us leave the lofty heights of theory and look at what happens on the water to a beginner trying to make the best course possible to windward.

Our novice crew in the first chapter of Part I set off from a reaching course, trimming the sails and gradually luffing up. We defined close-hauled as that point of sailing reached when the sails were completely pulled tight and to luff any further would cause them to flap.

The result of looking at it this way is often dreadful. The boat thuds into the waves, pinching hard, with its air flow restricted, making massive leeway. The beginner often sails in light to moderate winds with the sails in too tight and the boat pointed too high.

To get out of this position, work out:
– the angle A of the sail to the wind: we know that the force exerted on the sail by the wind is due to the air being deflected, and is at a

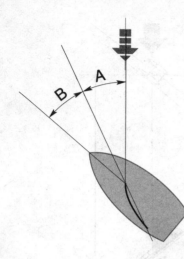

The dilemma viewed graphically: as you pull the sail in, angle A increases and so does the force exerted on the sail; as you ease the sail, angle B increases and so does the forward component of the thrust.

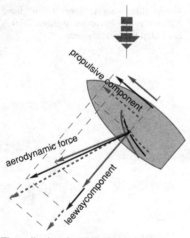

The sail trim shown in black is the best compromise: the aerodynamic force (Fa) is large and pointed fairly forward, the propulsive component (Cp) respectable and the leeway component (Cd) modest.
The dotted sail is too hard in: Fa has been increased, but so too has Cd.
The blue sail has been freed too far: both Fa and Cp are smaller. This trim is recommended only in strong winds, when the boat would otherwise heel excessively.

maximum for an angle of deflection of between 15 and 25°; the implication of this is that you should pull the sail in as hard as possible to reach this angle;
– the angle B of the sail to the boat: the force exerted by the wind on the sail is at right angles to the sail; thus, the less this is pulled in, the greater the forward component.

You will notice that the second consideration is a limiting factor on the first.

So what do you do?

The first thing to do is to ease the sheets a touch. You will feel the boat sigh with relief; it will drift less, even if it does not yet pick up much more speed. When you are close-hauled, it is difficult to get the boat to accelerate, even with perfect sail trim, once it has slowed down.

You therefore bear away slightly as well. Now you will feel the acceleration.

Once you have picked up speed, luff up a little again and try to find a good compromise between the heading you wish to make and boat speed.

The correct compromise is a series of approximations, as you adjust the sails to your course, and the course to the set of the sails … the lighter and faster the boat, the more difficult it is to achieve this compromise.

Achieving optimum sail trim

Let us consider the effect of three different trims for a sail:
• The dotted sail is very hard in, drawing all the way to the luff, exerting considerable force directed mostly sideways: the boat heels and makes leeway. This sail trim has no virtues to recommend it.
• The coloured sail is very free, such that the luff is flapping. It exerts less force (the propulsive component is weaker), but the force is at least directed mostly forwards. This is not ideal, but we shall see that it has some advantages in a strong breeze when the heeling couple would otherwise be too strong for the boat and crew.
• The best trim is clearly the middle one, in black. The force is almost as great as in the first instance, but there is noticeably less leeway. The sail luff quivers slightly, as it is trimmed until the sail 'lifts'.

Sailing the optimum course

The sail trims we were just considering related all to a single course; we also need to see whether the course itself can be improved.

When we look at the speed curve of a sailing dinghy on different headings, we notice immediately that we have a certain amount of choice: OA might be our ideal course, but OB and OC are not vastly different in terms of the progress to windward they permit. (OY is very little smaller than OX.) Thus one can vary the heading to suit the sea conditions and any tactical considerations. This freedom, however, only extends a few degrees either side of the ideal, and is reduced in strong winds or with a poorly trimmed boat.

Although you have now achieved a compromise between course and sail trim, you cannot relax. Even in a constant wind, your ideal compromise will be undermined by a number of factors.

Particularly at the beginning, you only need one mistake with the tiller to destroy the whole balance:
– *bearing away* will cause the boat to speed up but will take you further from your destination;
– *luffing up* will bring you back to the first mistake we looked at: this mistake will be swiftly punished by your making less speed and more leeway. We make no apologies for repeating this point: there is a chain reaction here which destroys the boat's momentum and can even leave it dangerously hard to control, if you are just to windward of the shore, for instance. The boat stops and drifts round as the flow of wind over the sails and the flow of water over the underwater surfaces become turbulent. There is only one way out of this situation: admitting it has happened, freeing the sails to re-establish a smooth flow and bearing away to induce laminar flow over the centreboard. Only then, when you have regained sufficient way to steer, can you think about hardening back onto a close-hauled course, slowly, so as to pick up speed on the way.

At this stage we shall venture a general recommendation: particularly in the early days, you should sail to windward in a series of gentle, short luffs. This is known as feathering; on the one hand, it ensures that you are not gradually bearing away without realising it, and on the other, it ensures that you do not miss any chances if the wind frees you to make a better course.

Multihulls cannot be feathered to windward, as the apparent wind is so dependent on the boat's own speed. All this is approximate. Sailing really well to windward is a skill which takes a long time to acquire. Sailing downwind, the consequences of a mistake

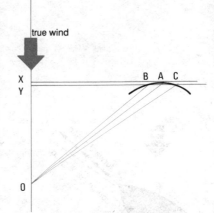

This graph shows a sector of a normal boat's speed curve, obtained by applying a vector representing the boat's speed for each course sailed in a given wind, from point O. The curve is always seen as one approaches the close-hauled area. In theory, point A, at which the tangent of the curve is perpendicular to the true wind, is the ideal point to aim at for making ground to windward. In practice, there is a certain latitude around this point; although OA is the ideal close-hauled course, the ground made to windward varies little for courses a few degrees either side.

are less severe, and differences between boats tend to be less marked; to windward, even boats of the same class will make noticeably different progress without any obvious reason. This shows that there is a certain skill involved in trimming the sails, steering and balancing the boat. It is time to go into detail on these topics.

This is a good compromise. Despite a considerable drift component, the boat is not making excessive leeway.

If you luff excessively, for instance to avoid an obstacle, the flow over the keel separates and the boat drifts sideways. If you then find you need to tack, you could find this is impossible because you have not got enough speed for the rudder to work. The only way out is to bear away drastically.

After bearing away drastically, the boat has picked up enough speed and the drift has reduced sufficiently for the flow over the keel to become laminar again. Now you can luff up again.

Direct and indirect courses: making ground to windward

• If you can reach your goal in a single tack, you should head straight there trying to maximise boat speed for that course.
• If your goal lies in the 'dead angle' to windward, you will have to head for it indirectly, by tacking. At this point, you are seeking not to maximise boat speed, but to maximise the ground made good to windward. This involves optimising the projection of your speed vector against the wind axis.

Better than almost close-hauled

You need to draw a speed curve for different wind, sea and sail conditions, which will permit serious study of your close-hauled course.

We have combined diagrams below for a catamaran and a monohull. The shaded sectors show the acceptable courses, with OA as the ideal course. The catamaran has a wider range of acceptable courses than the monohull.

Its speed continues to pick up considerably further off the wind than OC.

How can you weigh the potential 10% gain to windward of sailing OA against the extra 2kn achieved by sailing OD? Monohulls are simpler, but studying the diagram is useful nevertheless.

Best of all, but most expensive is the on-board computer which can store all the data necessary to work out boat speed against angle to the wind. It can then suggest what it believes (on the basis of the information you have given it) to be the optimum course to sail in the conditions.

This expensive gadget is most worthwhile for a racing catamaran, where you are always travelling very fast, so that it is easy to forget that it might be possible to add another 10% or so to your speed.

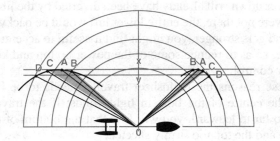

On these combined speed curves for a catamaran and a monohull, one can see how difficult it is to pick the best close-hauled course, particularly for a catamaran. If the catamaran chooses option OD, it will lose considerable ground to windward, despite sailing 2kn faster.

Trim to windward

Sail shape

When you are sailing close-hauled, as we have seen, the sails need to be trimmed to the point where they lift. We can state this more precisely: *the sails are correctly trimmed when the luff lifts slightly, simultaneously over its full length.* Achieving this ideal state means looking not only at the angle of the sails to the wind, but also at their shape. Shape and angle are closely related.

Camber

Controlling the curve of the sail is essential for windward sailing. Two properties of the curve need to be adjusted according to the strength of the wind:
– its position. The maximum camber of the sail should always be about at the centre of the sail. When the wind freshens, the draft tends to move aft. It can be pulled forward (on the mainsail) by tightening the luff or (on the jib) by using the backstays to tighten the luff;
– its depth. The stronger the wind, the flatter the sails need to be to reduce the deflection caused. You should bear in mind that *the reason for flattening the sails in strong winds is not so they can be sheeted tighter, but so they can be freed further before they start to flap.*

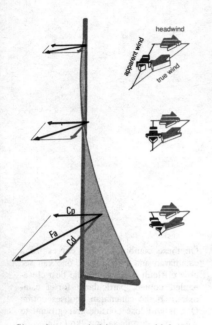

Since the true wind is stronger higher up the sail, the apparent wind is freer. A certain amount of twist in the sail gives you an aerodynamic force which is directed further forward, and a smaller heeling couple.

Twist

Sails have a greater or lesser tendency to twist, with the higher part of the sail (which is less controlled than the bottom) falling away under the wind. Although this tendency has to be controlled, it is not in itself a problem: the wind is stronger higher above the water (about 10% stronger 10m up), so the apparent wind comes freer the higher up the sail you go. For this reason the sail can be sheeted in less tight at the top than lower down. As the aerodynamic force has a stronger forward component higher up, it creates less of a heeling couple.

The twist should be stronger still for a mainsail set aft of a jib, as the air lower down will already have been diverted by the jib, and if the twist were not there, the entire lower luff would be backwinded. As the wind gets stronger, you might find it useful to accentuate the twist more, so as to reduce some of the power up top and keep the heel under control.

For these reasons the mainsheet traveller needs to be brought towards the centre of the boat in light winds; if the traveller is cleated too far to leeward, you will find that the bottom of the sail is too free and the top too firmly sheeted.

We studied the reasons for needing to control sail shape in Part II; here we shall just quickly revise the means at your disposal.

Means of controlling the jib

The degree of camber in a jib is generally invariable. When the wind changes in strength, you need to change jibs. In a few cases, you can control the camber by tightening the luff.

The twist can be controlled by moving the fairlead fore and aft, or by changing the height of the tack.

Means of controlling mainsail shape

The position of the camber can be altered by luff tension; the degree of camber is determined by the foot tension and by the degree of bend you put in the mast by using the kicker, the mainsheet traveller and the backstays. Twist can also be controlled using the kicker and traveller.

Trimming the sails

Armed with these new techniques, we are getting closer to a definition of close-hauled sail trim.

The jib is trimmed almost as far as it will go. The boat's course

Using the mainsheet traveller

The mainsheet traveller is used basically when sailing close-hauled; if it is very long it can also be very useful on other points of sailing. It allows you to control the twist in the sail as you change the sail angle. Playing the traveller either close to the centreline or down to leeward, you can ease or trim the sail without changing the tension on the sheet. You are opening or closing the slot by doing this. You can use the traveller to increase the twist in the sail, bringing it slightly up to windward and letting the sheet out.

If you have a bendy rig, you can use the traveller to flatten the sail by bending the mast, without necessarily sheeting the sail in.

When you gybe, the traveller can slam from one end of its bar to the other and cause itself a fair amount of damage. It is a worthwhile precaution to centre the traveller when you are running, to avoid this problem.

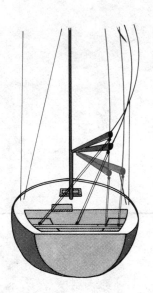

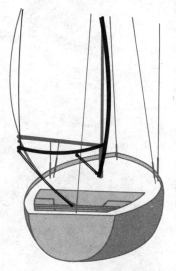

Using the kicking strap

The kicking strap can be used when you are close-hauled, to control the twist in the sail if you have no traveller. It is used for this purpose on all boats when sailing off the wind, when the sail is too far out for the traveller to be of use. It also partly takes up the belly in the sail by helping to bend the mast.

is then dependent on the jib: you head up until the luff lifts all the way up, then bear away by 2 or 3°.

The mainsail is sheeted in as little as possible, just enough for it not to be backwinded by the jib. The slot between the sails is then being made to work to its best effect.

The best sail trim is one in which both sails lift at the same time, from top to bottom of the luffs.

This is a question of cunning and subtlety, since the boat, to a large degree, makes its own wind. Particularly on a fast, light multi-hull, if you decide to feather into the wind just to check that you really are sailing as close to the wind as possible, you will just lose all that extra apparent wind and bring the whole painstakingly achieved trim to nought. When this happens, there is nothing for it but to ease the sails and bear away, trimming them back in as the speed gets up, and so on ...

Aids to correct sail trim

When there is a bit of a chop, you can check quite easily whether the sails are correctly trimmed or not: well-trimmed sails will lift slightly at the top when you are on the crest of a wave. This is

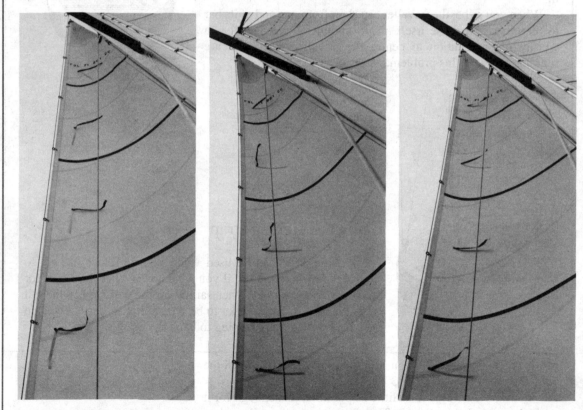

Jib sheeted much too tight, with the lee-ward tell-tales hanging down.

Jib eased too far, with windward tell-tales lifting.

Jib correctly trimmed, with both sets of tell-tales flying horizontal.

caused by the top of the mast rocking forward and causing a temporary increase in the headwind, thus bringing the apparent wind further ahead. You know that you are too close to the wind if the sail is lifting constantly, and if it does not lift at all, you are sailing too free.

Tell-tales sewn on the sails can also be used. The ones on the jib should be kept horizontal. If the jib is too tight, the leeward tell-tales will flap; and if it is much too tight they just hang limp. If the jib is excessively eased, the windward tell-tales are the ones which start to dance.

Tell-tales on the mainsail should stream out in the same direction as the sail; if it is sheeted too hard, they will fall off to leeward.

If not all the tell-tales react in the same way, you can tell that you have too much or too little twist in the sail.

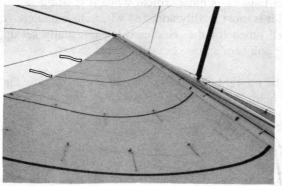

This mainsail is well set up, with the camber nicely situated and the tell-tales flying out straight.

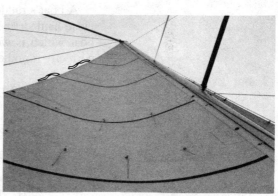

This mainsail has the luff too slack, with the result that the camber has come aft and the sail has lost drive. The tell-tales fluttering to leeward indicate that the sail is trimmed too tight.

Tell-tales and streamers
Coloured cloth strips may be stuck or sewn onto the sail horizontally, a third of the way back and two-thirds of the way back. These can help you to see where on the sail the belly is and how big it is. Tell-tales can also be attached to the leech of the mainsail to assist correct trim.

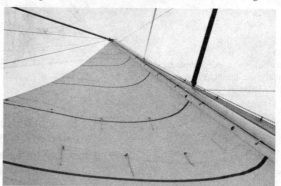

The luff rope on this sail is too tight: the curvature has been brought unnecessarily far forward.

Boat trim

Sailing against the wind is almost unnatural, and the boat needs a lot of help to drive itself against the combined might of wind and waves. Balance and trim, both lateral and longitudinal, are especially important in this.

Rudder balance

When a boat's sails are correctly trimmed and the tiller centred, yet the boat tends to luff up, it is said to have weather helm. Lee helm is the opposite of this. In either case, simply keeping the same course necessitates the use of the tiller, which is obviously damaging to boat speed, since the rudder acts as a brake when it is not straight.

A boat's rudder balance is most critical when it is being sailed close-hauled; and it is most readily adjusted when close-hauled. A boat which is well tuned for the windward leg is usually set up correctly for other points of sailing as well.

The mast can be brought forward or raked forward to give the boat less weather helm; it will have more weather helm if the mast

Watching a good boardsailor, you can quickly see the effect of mast rake on the craft's balance.

is brought aft or raked aft. It has to be said that moving the mast usually affects the boat's tune in other ways, and can produce the opposite to the effect you are seeking. The experimental approach is the only one which works.

The centreboard should theoretically be pushed completely down for the windward leg to offset the drift component which is strongest on this point of sailing. Nevertheless, if the board pivots, you might find it useful to lift it just a touch, which will not reduce the surface but will bring the centre of lateral resistance aft and slightly change the balance of the boat. If you have two centreboards, only the leeward one needs to be used.

▶ There are cases in which these theories must be treated with caution. The faster you travel, the more lift the centreboard creates, so you need less of the board in the water. Catamarans above a certain speed can quite confidently raise one centreboard when travelling above a certain speed.

You can choose which centreboard to raise depending on your objectives: if your main concern is safety, raise the leeward centreboard, so that the boat will sideslip rather than heeling; and if your aim is to sail fast, you can raise the windward plate, thus encouraging the early flying of the windward hull.

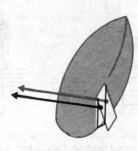

If you pivot the centreboard aft, the point at which the hydrodynamic force operates also comes aft, thus changing the balance of the boat.

Should a boat be perfectly balanced to the helm, or should it have a little weather helm? There are a few who like lee helm, but these are rare birds.

Certainly excessive helm pull in either direction is damaging. For beginners, we reckon that a little weather helm is useful, as it keeps the boat feeling lively and reactive to the helm. A boat which is perfectly neutral to the helm requires a great deal of skill and concentration to sail well. In the end though, a dinghy sailor can tune the boat to their own taste; a cruiser which will be helmed quite possibly by a number of people over the day should definitely be set up with weather helm, since this gives a 'feel' which most people become accustomed to more quickly.

Longitudinal trim

A boat will only sail well if it is floating on its designed waterline, thus neither too light nor too heavy, and with neither the bow nor the transom excessively weighted down.

In general, weight should be kept to the centre of the boat. It will pitch excessively in choppy water if there is too much weight toward the ends, and become quite uncomfortable – for instance, when a member of the crew goes forward to the bow to change a sail, or someone is fishing from the aft pulpit.

These principles hold for all boats, large and small, heavy and light, but they are particularly important when the weight of the crew and material represent a large proportion of the total weight at that point.

The reason this boat is pitching so much and burying its bows, strangely, is that there is so much weight concentrated aft.

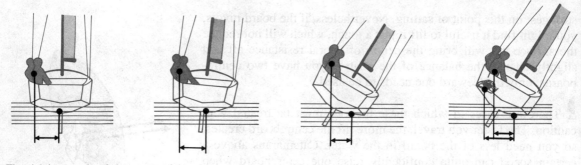

The righting couple of the crew weight increases when the boat starts to heel, but reduces as soon as the angle of heel increases further. Sleeping crew members below decks can make a significant difference.

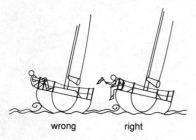

wrong   right

These two figures are helping to keep their respective boats flat. The person on the right is reminding the one on the left that it is forbidden to race with one's body outside the safety lines.

The optimum angle of heel of a catamaran is when one hull is just skimming the surface of the water.

Lateral trim

A boat should be sailed as flat as possible. Once it starts to heel, the hull loses its designed underwater shape, and the boat is slowed. Heel also causes excessive weather helm in almost all boats.

Heel can be controlled by a combination of correct sail trim and the correct disposition of crew weight, usually by leaning out. There are two essential rules which apply:

Leaning out is very efficient when the boat is still almost flat, but its efficiency reduces considerably once the boat moves beyond a minimal angle of heel. A small amount of heel may occasionally be desirable, particularly in light winds, to keep the sails filled and reduce the wetted area.

Some narrow yachts are designed to be sailed heeled over, since this lengthens their waterline. These include the Dragon and International 5.5m class.

Leaning out is more efficient the closer you are to the water. This is particularly true if boats are wide at the waterline, such as those with a hard chine: you can exert more righting moment by lying down quietly in your bunk than by clinging on grimly to the top edge of the deck.

▶ *Multihulls* are so wide that any lateral crew movement has a considerable effect. You can exploit this fact in a catamaran to reduce the wetted area, by raising one hull just above the water. A few degrees of heel will give optimum power without destroying the efficiency of the underwater shape for the windward course. But be careful: you are then literally sailing 'on the edge'. This is not advisable when you are miles offshore.

How to steer

The basic principle to be followed is that the helm should not be used excessively or too suddenly. Speed is your vital weapon, so it should not be thrown away thoughtlessly; every twitch of the rudder reduces your speed slightly.

Beyond this fundamental rule, good steering is largely an intuitive matter which depends on your paying attention to everything which is going on. The experienced helmsman will feel the whole life of the boat through the tiller, especially if there is a touch of weather helm. When you are sailing close-hauled at a reasonable speed, you should find that the tiller becomes quite hard to move; and as you gain in experience, the sensation in the tiller can be used to give you all sorts of information about how the boat is sailing. The tiller moves more easily and has less 'feel' as the boat slows, and you know something is amiss.

The function of the tiller in a boat is similar to that of the reins for a horse: it must not be used to slow you down with excessive control, but to guide your steed to give its maximum performance in the desired direction. A well-tuned boat knows what it has to do. You need, in turn, to learn what the boat will do of its own accord and what you need to make it do. As you learn its habits and its limits, you will use the tiller less as a way out of trouble than as a way to avoid it in the first place.

Everyone has their own style and their own philosophy of steering. One of the chief variables, we suspect, is the captain's age.

The boat cannot be tuned in a day. You need practice together over a period of medium-strength winds (which is a rather vague expression, meaning something different for every boat and every crew, but which in effect implies that you do not need to go looking for the wind, but you are not suffering severe problems with excess power either).

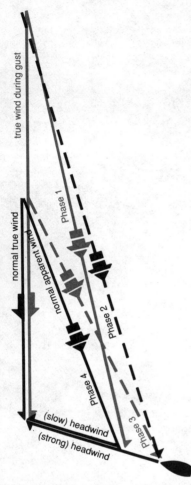

true wind during gust

normal true wind

normal apparent wind

Phase 1

Phase 2

Phase 4

Phase 3

(slow) headwind

(strong) headwind

Changes in the apparent wind during a gust

Phase 1: freshening, freeing.
Phase 2: freshening further, heading.
Phase 3: heading further, lightening.
Phase 4: back to original values.

You also need the practice wind to be constant, a still more questionable concept when applied to wind. We have maintained throughout this book that there is seldom such a thing as a wind which is constant in direction. To approach a feeling of what relative constancy might mean, we have to look more closely at its (very common) opposite: variability. We shall follow this up with a look at fresh and light winds.

Gusts

A temporary increase in wind speed is a gust, when the wind is otherwise light to medium in strength. An increase in an already strong wind we shall refer to as a squall. There is no clear boundary between the two: it depends on the size of the boat and the state of mind of the crew.

What happens in a gust?

The apparent wind, which is the one which fills your sails, is a combination of the true wind and the headwind created by the speed of the boat. It comes from a direction between the two, which is therefore always further ahead than the true wind. The point to be noted here is that *any change in strength of either of its component parts changes both the strength and the direction of the apparent wind.*

The gust hits you.

Phase 1. The true wind increases in strength. The boat does not react immediately, so the headwind remains the same. The direction of the apparent wind comes closer to that of the true wind, and you are freed.

Phase 2. The boat, sails correctly trimmed, accelerates. The headwind increases in strength. The apparent wind heads you.

The gust passes.

Phase 3. The true wind subsides. The boat has momentum and does not slow down immediately, so the direction of the apparent wind moves even further ahead and you are headed still more.

Phase 4. The boat slows and the apparent wind returns to its original direction.

How does one react?

Particularly when you are close-hauled, a gust is an opportunity to make more ground to windward than the true wind would normally permit. In order to take advantage of the opportunity, you have to see it coming and immediately trim the boat correctly for the new wind.

On a small boat with quick reactions, you can luff and trim the sails in; for the mainsail, this usually means pulling the traveller in.

On a larger boat, with the sheets made off round winches, you will not have time to re-trim the sails, so you simply change your heading, by luffing up when the gust arrives, thus keeping the sails at the correct angle to the wind.

As soon as the headwind component increases, you need to bear away so as not to let the sails flap and to maintain the extra momentum you have been given by the gust.

Of course, wind variations are not always this predictable, but the principle remains the same: keep an eye out to weather.

Strong winds

Strong winds usually make sailing less comfortable. In heavy weather the boat begins to heel excessively and becomes difficult to handle, you are unsure how to go about launching the boat and landlubbers' faces turn green at the sight of the waves.

There is no way of making an ideal course to windward in heavy weather: with reduced lift from the sails, heavy wave motion and increased windage on the hull, it is more a question of limiting your boat's heel and finding ways of conserving its momentum.

Reducing the lift of the sails

As the wind freshens to a point where the weight of the crew and the natural tendency of the boat to sit flat in the water are not sufficient to keep it correctly trimmed, the sails need to be flattened and eased.

As the wind freshens, you need to reduce the angle through which it is deflected by the sails. (Initially, this measure is sufficient on its own.) *This ensures that the aerodynamic force does not increase in the same proportion as the wind strength. The angle of deflection is reduced by flattening the sail and easing it out.* The diagram shows that by easing the sail (in black), you can increase the propulsive component Cp without an increase in Fa, the aerodynamic force.

Trimming the mainsail

The curvature of the mainsail is reduced and kept in

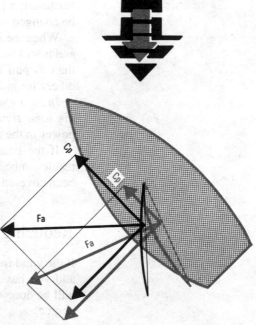

When the wind freshens, the sails need to be freed. The total aerodynamic force may not increase, but the forward (propulsive) component does, and reduces the leeway.

the same place. The sail is then trimmed until it lifts, with the traveller fully to leeward. If you need to, you can increase the amount of twist in the sail until the head is not pulling at all. This will have the effect of reducing the heeling moment.

Trimming the jib

Before you trim the jib, you have to decide which one to rig for the wind. One can adjust certain jibs by stretching the luff, which flattens the jib somewhat and prevents the camber from moving aft. Other jibs can be rolled around the forestay, bringing the camber forward. Often you will use a flatter jib with the same area.

So as to stop the jib losing its shape, you need the forestay to be as tight as possible. A slack forestay sags to leeward, causing the sail to belly out and the camber to move aft, while the leech tightens and closes the slot. At this stage the jib is not pulling the boat forward properly: it is just heeling the boat.

It is possible also to let the head of the jib twist: if you bring the sheet fairlead aft and up, this will tension the foot and slacken the leech.

The interaction of the sails: the 'slot'

The jib can tend to backwind the main. If this happens, it is usually because the jib is too full. It then needs either to be flattened or to be changed.

When the jib has been flattened and trimmed as much as possible and is still backwinding the main, it is better to let the main luff flap than to pull it in any further and kill any boat speed you might otherwise pick up.

In strong winds, the boat is correctly tuned when both sails lift at the same time, on the top half only. This way you can reduce the power in the sails by a small luff.

If the boat has a flexible mast, like many dinghies, the same result can be achieved using mast bend. This technique has already been covered in an earlier section.

Reducing sail

If the wind freshens still more, these techniques will be insufficient, and you have to think about actually reducing the sail area. This will be done earlier on some boats than on others, and to a varying degree.

First reef

The main function of the first reef is to flatten the sail. For this reason the first reef is usually smaller than the others and is sometimes called a flattening reef.

The first reef will certainly reduce the area of the mainsail, but above all it will cut the curvature of the luff of the sail, taking up most of the fullness.

The first change of jib (or No 1 jib) is often no smaller than the light-wind genoa, but is considerably flatter.

Second reef

When cutting the power by flattening the sail is no longer enough, you have to start cutting the surface area. Two or three reefs can be taken in a mainsail, and the jib can be made successively smaller, allowing you to take some power from the jib despite the inevitable sag in the forestay. If you have a roller jib, start rolling!

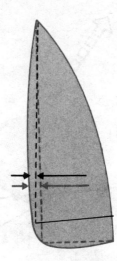

The first reef is intended primarily to take up most of the luff curvature.

Balancing the sails

As you reduce the sail area fore and aft, your main aim is not to unbalance the boat. Do not be misled by the fact that a boat develops weather helm when it heels, into the mistake of leaving too much sail up forward.

Let us look at a typical example: two Frégates (five tonners which have weather helm when they heel) are sailing together in the Western Channel in a wind freshening to force 8.

One of them reduces its sail area regularly as the wind increases, fore and aft, so that it soon has only a storm jib and the mainsail down to the last reef. With both sails sheeted tight but the mainsheet traveller fully eased, this boat will be sailing well on a close fetch.

The captain of the other is concerned to ensure that the boat does not develop weather helm, so keeps a fair-sized jib up as long as possible. As the wind freshens, this boat makes each change a little later than the other: thus, the No 1 jib is hoisted when the other has its No 2 up, and the No 2 is only hoisted when the other has already resorted to the storm jib. On the other hand, this boat does treat the mainsail with caution and takes in a reef one stage earlier. Finally, as the boat continues to heel alarmingly, they are left with the No 2 jib, and no mainsail. The boat is still heeling badly and still has weather helm; the jib is too full for the weather conditions and the forestay sags slightly: this boat is going nowhere fast.

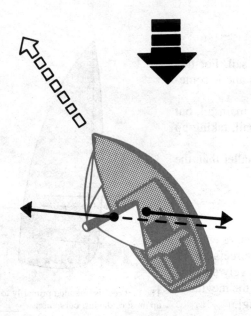

The reef is in place with the main flattened and a suitably sized jib hoisted: the boat is nicely balanced.

With the jib too large and too full, the boat will heel excessively and develop a lot of weather helm, despite the fact that the mainsail area has been cut.

This instance gives us a further principle to follow when choosing sails in fresh weather: *to keep the boat balanced, you need to pay as much attention to the shape of the sails as to their surface area.*

Balancing the boat

A boat can still heel considerably under reduced sail: your aim should still be to sail it as flat as possible. A small cruiser such as a Corsaire or Mousquetaire, with a moderate hull shape, can be kept driving in winds up to force 7 or 8, as long as it is sailed as flat as possible, with flattened sails, eased as the occasion demands.

Working the waves

Even if the boat is sailed with a good fore-and-aft trim, you will find that the waves begin to cause problems as the wind gets up. This is especially the case with light boats and multihulls.

Heavy cruisers

The heavier the boat, the more momentum it has, and consequently the less it is affected by this problem.

There are two ways of dealing with the waves to windward:

1. Sailing up the side of the wave at a slight slant, then luffing as soon as the crest of the wave passes; if the waves are coming from the same direction as the wind, you will probably find that the boat does this of its own accord.

2. Luffing and sailing straight up the slope of the wave, then bearing away down the back of the wave to regain speed; this is usually the only way to cope with waves which are coming straight at you, from further ahead than the wind.

When the waves are breaking, you have no choice: you must take them bow on, even if this slows the boat considerably. (This recommendation is slightly optimistic, as a wind strong enough to cause breakers out at sea is likely to be too strong for you to luff up under perfect control at will.)

Even with a heavy boat, your prime aim must be to keep the boat's momentum up, simply as a safety precaution. If you feel the boat slowing too much, bear away and keep your speed up rather than sticking to your heading and letting the boat lose way.

Light cruisers

A light cruiser has much more difficulty in waves: the dilemma is that the boat will be severely slowed if it crashes into the waves, and it will also be severely slowed if its sails stop drawing. The aim, then, must be to steer up the side of the waves without losing the wind from the sails.

The procedure should be as follows:
– at the top of a wave, the relative wind is noticeably stronger, so the apparent wind shifts further ahead; you need to bear away to keep the sails drawing;
– at the bottom of the wave, with less relative wind, you are freed by the apparent wind and can afford to luff up.

In fact this only works in a sea which is moderately rough and in a wind which is moderately strong. As the waves and wind build up more, things change; between waves, you might not even have any wind in the bottom half of your sails, and you need to respond as follows:
– bear away in the hollows, so as to keep the tops of your sails (which are the only parts with wind) drawing;
– luff hard at the crests so the boat does not heel too badly.

You will see that the two techniques are exactly opposite, and you will quickly notice which is the appropriate method for the wind and sea conditions you are in. The principle of both is that you keep the sails drawing, to gather as much forward force as possible and prevent the boat being stopped in its tracks by the waves.

Catamarans

If you are flying a hull (which you will not be doing often on a cruise!) or if both hulls meet the wave together (probably equally rare), the techniques to use are the same as for the light cruiser. The reality is much more likely to be that the windward hull hits the wave before the leeward one does. The windward hull is then lifted up by the wave, and the crew begins to think that the boat is heeling and flying a hull, though it is in fact still sitting on the water. At this point, you need to luff in anticipation of the second hull hitting the wave and the boat being brought back level. The technique is thus very similar to what you would do if you were working the wave with only the leeward hull to think about – it just feels rather different.

This situation, in which you are forced to luff, should not be confused with the situation which arises when one hull leaves the water because the boat is overpowered. If that happens, you should not luff at all, as that could well lead to a capsize.

In practice, one only has to work the waves in a catamaran if they are very steep. In any other case you just let the bows cut through them as you fly on!

Squalls

On a heavy cruiser it is best to use medium-weather sails, so that you can survive the squalls without being flattened, but still make progress in the calm patches. A reasonable compromise is to have a fairly flat jib which works well in the heavy gusts, and a rather fuller main which is of little use in the squalls but gives you a fair amount of power in the calms. The jib is left sheeted in during the squall, and the boat luffs, with the main freed off if necessary to stop the boat heeling further. When the wind drops, the main is sheeted back in and you bear away. With a flexible rig, you may not need to change course: the backstay runners are tensioned in the squall to open the top of the sail, and they are let off again when the wind drops.

On a light cruiser sailing in squalls can be rather demanding: you need to be on your toes constantly to keep the boat moving.

Some people reckon that you should keep the jib sheeted in through the squall to maintain power, with the mainsheet eased as necessary to keep the boat flat, while the crew sits as hard out to windward as possible.

This can have undesirable effects, however: the mainsail can become fuller when the sheet is eased; so too can the jib, if you have a fractional rig without backstays. In the end you can make the boat harder to control rather than easier.

There are two ways of avoiding this problem:
1. Luffing, rather than easing the mainsheet, so that the sails almost completely stop drawing. You need to carry out this manoeuvre with a great deal of skill and precision if you are going to do it: you should aim to respond to the strength of the squall as it passes, keeping the boat flat but moving.
2. Easing the traveller rather than the sheet, so that the sail keeps the boat moving forward without excessive heel, and remains flat.

You are likely to need to apply both these solutions in practice.

On a catamaran the second of the above solutions is almost certainly going to be the most effective measure you can adopt: the mainsheet traveller is long enough and the mainsail sufficiently big for it to become a much more effective weapon than it ever can be on a monohull. The procedure, then, in the following order, is:
– mainsheet traveller down to leeward;
– mainsheet eased;
– jibsheet eased.

This only works if you react quickly to the squall.

Your reactions will be speeded up if you are holding the mainsheet throughout. If this is too demanding, you should have the quick-release mechanism in your hand instead.

Light weather

We pass now to the gentle breeze that you can barely feel on your cheek. The first problem is telling exactly where the wind is coming from. Cigarette smoke is most effective. An alternative is to take your shirt off and see where the first goose pimples appear ... Quite frequently, in fact, there may be no wind down where you are sitting, but a little way up there will be enough breeze to stir the telltales or the burgee.

A real close-hauled course is impossible in these conditions, as the resistance of the water on the hull is greater than the forward component of the thrust on the sails. You need to bear away if you are to gain any speed.

Everything in place. The sails are full, with both luff and foot slackened off, the traveller in the middle of the boat and little kicker tension. The sails are also well eased, the boat slightly heeled and the transom out of the water; the crew is still ... and you have the suspicion of a wake.

Sail trim

Since there is so little wind, it needs the greatest possible deflection, so you need the sails to be very full, and eased as far out as possible to bring their force well forward.

The sea will generally be calm in light airs, though there can be a swell; the regular flapping of the sails caused by the rolling motion of the waves can be harnessed and used to your adavantage.

Boat trim

The crew sits well inside the boat to reduce windage. If you sit rather further forward than usual, this will pick the transom out of the water and also give a touch of weather helm. The boat should be slightly heeled to reduce the wetted area and keep the sails filling on the right side. Any abrupt movement should be avoided. You have at all costs to maintain your momentum.

Steering

The tiller needs to be handled with extreme care. More than ever, sudden changes in direction must be avoided.

If you pinch into the wind, you will feel the boat slow down immediately. Since your own headwind was contributing a significant part of the total apparent wind, this is serious. You need to bear away and ease the sails considerably to pick up speed again.

If you bear away too far, you will 'stall' the sails. At this point the boat will slow and the wind will seem to have left you forever. Ease the sails out, then luff back up again on to your course gently, bringing the sails in tighter as you go.

In this wind, every manoeuvre takes time, and mistakes take a very long time to put right.

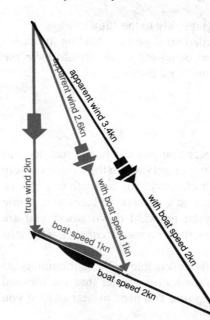

In light airs, boat speed has a considerable influence on the direction and strength of the apparent wind.

Variable light airs

The slightest puff of wind is a treasure. You need to take from it everything you can get, without being hasty. When a puff hits you, since your sails are very full, you can sheet in and luff at the same time, thus gaining speed as well as ground to windward. But you must not try to stick to this new course: you should bear away as soon as the wind drops again, to keep whatever speed you have. Paradoxically, the boat's own headwind is playing a major role in propelling it forward.

To make decent progress to windward in a light breeze is largely a matter of feel. It is a question of finding a point of sailing at which the wind feels strongest. When you achieve that, you know you are making the best windward progress you can.

Close fetching

The close fetch is that comfortable point just off the wind from close-hauled, at which the sails are full and drawing hard.

Trimming the boat for a close fetch is not all that different from trimming it for the close-hauled leg, but it will feel quite different. You no longer need to worry about playing games with the fickle wind to get to some point in the dead zone to windward of you: from now on you have a fixed point to sail at and you can head directly for that point without difficulty.

Sail trim

The sails will be fuller and sheeted less tight than on the beat. Your aim on a close fetch should be to deflect the wind through as large an angle as possible while minimising the sideways component of the force generated. For this reason you should not ease the sheets as much as you might suppose from the change of heading.

When the wind freshens, you will not always need to flatten the sails. This depends to some extent on the sort of boat you are sailing: while some small boats cannot carry very full sails on a close fetch, this is less of a problem on heavy or large boats.

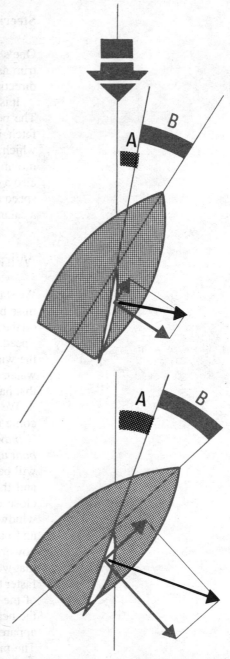

When you bear away from a beat onto a close fetch, the angle of deflection A increases to reach its optimum, of about 20–25°. Rather than easing the sheets you should aim to increase the fullness in the sails.

Steering

One's aim should be to stick to the desired course, changing the sail trim as necessary according to the variations in wind strength and direction.

It is usually easy to maintain a steady course when close fetching. The boat is stable and easily controlled; for this reason the close fetch is the recommended point of approach to any manoeuvre which requires great precision, such as coming into a channel, moving around a crowded harbour or coming up to the jetty. It is also a catamaran's best point of sailing: if you analyse and compare speed curves, you will always find that the ideal windward course of a catamaran is less close to the wind than that of a monohull.

Windward sailing summed up

We started out by defining the ideal course to windward as a compromise between speed and heading; ever since, we have been insisting on the need to maintain boat speed. Without speed there is no course. Speed, in the final analysis, has to be considered the prime concern of the windward leg. The boat needs to remain easy and strong in the water, and consequently needs to be left a certain margin as it steers that narrow fringe along the side of the 'dead zone'.

We should just explain one piece of terminology which will come up again and over which there should be no confusion: *by 'windward sailing' we mean sailing on any course which takes the boat upwind of where it started*. It follows that this point of sailing will be characterised by a certain set of the rig relative to the mast and the hull. For most monohulls, the act of hauling the sails in close can therefore easily be confused with the close-hauled, or windward course, which is sailed in this way. However, light boats and particularly multihulls derive such a high proportion of their power from headwind, which they effectively generate themselves, that we need to distinguish the sail trim from the course sailed. The faster the boat, the more significant this headwind is as a proportion of the apparent wind which powers the sails. Since, by definition, the headwind always comes straight at the boat from the front, the apparent wind always comes from further ahead than the true wind. The practical consequence of this is that the sails of a cat may be trimmed as if close-hauled, all the way through to a beam or even a broad reach. *Throughout this book, we reserve the terms 'to windward' and 'close-hauled' for a point of sailing which takes the boat upwind.*

Downwind

In theory, sailing downwind is sailing with the wind directly behind the boat at 180°. In reality, this would be an extremely difficult course to sail for any length of time. We therefore define 'downwind' sailing as being in that sector which is 30° either side of dead downwind, and we therefore include a broad reach in this section.

In a moderate wind, running and broad reaching are extremely comfortable points of sailing. There are no complicated sums to work out and no particularly difficult strategic considerations: the wind pushes, the boat moves whether the sails are trimmed or not (in fact, whether the sails are hoisted or not!). You do not need any great speed to maintain your course, as there is no sideways drift. There are no problems with heeling. You can design magnificent spinnakers in your mind, as you sit there pleasantly at your ease. The boat runs with the waves rather than bashing into them. There is little apparent wind and the world is in harmony.

There is treachery afoot: the wind flatters to deceive. As soon as the wind freshens, all those charms seem a little less certain. The boat is still not slowed at all by the waves, and its carefree progress becomes a headlong rush, requiring every ounce of your concentration to keep it on course. Dangers beckon either side of the thin line you are sailing: one side of the road is marked 'gybe' and the other, 'broach'.

Sail trim

Downwind, you will be showing off the full contents of your sail locker: mainsail, spinnaker, possibly a big boy and a few further exotica … if you are confident that you can use all these without getting into a muddle.

Mainsail

Off the wind, the air flow over the sails is non-laminar: it swirls around, and so the mainsail lacks power. To maximise its potential, you need to put shape into the mainsail, limit its twist and offer the maximum possible surface to the wind.

The mainsail works downwind through drag rather than lift. For the first time, your aim will be to maximise drag!

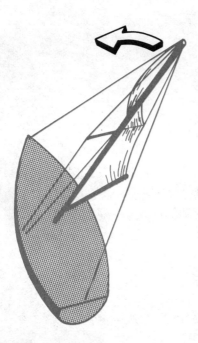

Twist in the sail is harmful downwind: the aerodynamic force on the top part of the sail acts in the wrong direction and heels the boat to windward. Here, the kicking strap needs tensioning.

If you sheet the mainsail in slightly, air flows into and around the spinnaker better; since the forces acting on the two sails are in slightly different directions, the combination gives the boat some sideways 'grip' and prevents it rolling.

Fullness and twist

You can slacken the luff and the foot of the main, and even bring the mast more upright to accentuate the fullness.

Use the kicking strap to reduce the amount of twist in the sail. Off the wind, there is no particular reason to have the head of the sail fall away to leeward; in fact, quite the contrary, since twist in the sail will encourage luffing and heeling towards you at the same time. This in turn can set up a rolling motion which makes it difficult to keep to your course.

Trim

Ideally, the mainsail should be at right angles to the wind, ie let out as far as it will go. There are a number of reasons not to go quite that far, however. For a start, the less sideways force there is on the sail from the wind, the more easily the boat will roll. Secondly, a fully eased main has the effect of disturbing the air flow around the spinnaker. And the final consideration has to be that if you let the main out all the way, it has a good chance of ruining itself by rubbing constantly against the shrouds.

Beware of the accidental gybe: make sure there is a figure-of-eight knot in the sheet to stop the boom hitting a shroud if it is whipped across; cleat the mainsheet traveller in the middle; and ease the runners if you have them (since there is no reason to tension the forestay when you are on a run).

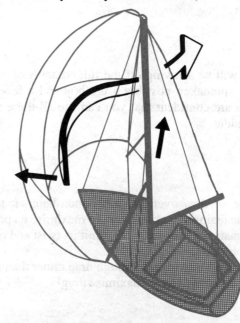

Spinnaker

Downwind, the spinnaker is usually raised. Just like other sails, the spinnaker is there to deflect the wind; because of its round shape it can deflect the wind through a very acute angle. The spinnaker is trimmed so as to get the air circulating as much as possible, which means that it needs to be set well forward and to windward so as to keep it away from the other sails. For this reason, you need to:

• *Open the spinnaker up to windward* by poling it out such that the spinnaker pole is at right angles to the apparent wind. If the pole also travels round so it is at right angles to the boat's centreline, you know that you are sailing dead downwind. This is harder to achieve than it sounds, and you have to keep a certain scepticism about the wind you can actually feel down at deck level; it is better to put your faith in what the burgee is telling you, or (in light winds) to have a little tell-tale fixed to the middle of the spinnaker pole. It is fairly rare to manage to get the spinnaker pole exactly at right angles to the wind: in general, sea and wind conditions plus the predispositions of the boat and crew combine to move the pole as much as 10 or 15° from this 'ideal'. If you pull the pole round further, you increase the lee helm, and if you let it drop to leeward, you increase the weather helm.

• *Make the spinnaker fuller* by letting the foot rise up as high as possible, especially in light winds; this in turn may mean rigging it with very light sheets, or the clew will not rise enough.

The spinnaker should be *symmetrical around a vertical axis* (note, this really means plumb vertical, as opposed to the line of the mast). The foot should therefore be *horizontal*. The foot can only rise up if the tack goes first: it cannot be pulled up from the clew. Thus, the pole has to be raised, and the clew kept level with it; if you raise the pole too far, the clew will flop back down and will have to be fished back up again by dropping the tack and starting anew.

On monohulls, the pole also needs to be kept at right angles to the mast by means of the uphaul–downhaul assembly; otherwise there is a chance it will wear the sheets or slide up the mast. It is not always possible to trim the pole this way on small cruisers, and the pole has to be allowed to rise slightly.

• *Ease the sheet as much as possible.* Of course, this is how all the sails should be trimmed, but it is particularly important with the spinnaker, which *loses power unless it can empty itself of the air it has deflected.* A spinnaker which is sheeted in too hard traps the air and will collapse from the middle, wrapping itself firmly and affectionately round the forestay. Whatever else you do, you should not sheet the spinnaker so tight that the foot touches the forestay.

Like other sails, spinnakers should be eased until they just lift. When a spinnaker is well trimmed, you will see a faint crease along the luff. This crease is not problematic in itself, but it tells you the spinnaker has been eased to its optimum point and will collapse if it goes out any further (not from the middle, in this case, but starting at the luff). A collapse can be quite sudden and upset the trim of the whole rig. For this reason it is best to sail with the merest flutter in the luff rather than a noticeable crease.

Trimming the spinnaker

You cannot trim the spinnaker and then leave it there. It can be knocked off balance by the boat rolling or any slight 'hole' in the wind. While the spinnaker is up, therefore, one crew member will be exclusively dedicated to its care and trim, playing it constantly.

Adjusting the uphaul
Logically, you would expect to have to trim the sheet every time the spinnaker loses power, like any other sail. However, the spinnaker, as we saw above, needs to be kept symmetrical about a vertical axis: it will collapse primarily if this condition is not fulfilled, and only much later as a result of being incorrectly trimmed at the sheet. Thus the uphaul is critical in balancing the sail consistently; once you have achieved a balance, the pole can then be held in place by also tightening the downhaul. Do not forget that the clew will flop down just as readily if the tack is too high as if it is too low.

Just as you need to keep a constant eye on the uphaul, you need to watch out that your angle to the wind has not changed; the tell-tale on the spinnaker pole will usually be the first indicator of a change in wind direction (or of the helm not paying attention). If you stray seriously from your course, the spinnaker itself will alert you to the fact, by flapping if you have luffed up or by collapsing if you have borne away too far.

Trimming the sheet
Some people prefer to use the sheet to trim the spinnaker. This is a more laborious way of doing things, particularly in light airs; if the luff starts to fold, you need to grab an armful of sheet then let it go again once the sail fills; and if it starts to collapse from the centre, you have to ease the sheet rapidly. The tack height is adjusted afterwards: upwards if the luff folds high up, and downwards if the fold is close to the foot.

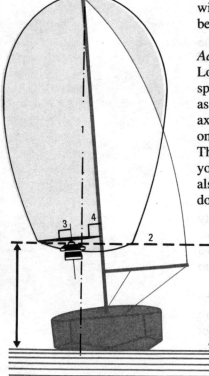

The spinnaker is perfectly trimmed when
1. it is vertically symmetrical;
2. the foot is horizontal;
3. the pole is perpendicular to the apparent wind ...
4. ... and perpendicular to the mast as well.

! Off the wind, one can generally do without a spinnaker pole, which is a relief. So long as the sheet and guy are trimmed symmetrically, the spinnaker should take shape naturally.

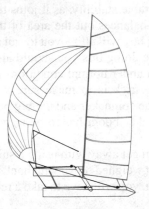

The spinnaker on a multihull
Catamarans are usually wide enough to allow a spinnaker to be used without a pole, which simplifies life, especially when gybing! With the sheet, guy and downhaul set, the sail can then be trimmed as on a monohull, except that you will not have to contend with the boat rolling or suddenly broaching. Yet another good reason to swop your monohull for a cat! Some boats have a sort of spinnaker pole used with flat reaching spinnakers, more like an adjustable bowsprit, to allow them to be used to windward.

Racing catamarans sometimes have a fixed spinnaker pole rather like an adjustable bowsprit, but this is for reaching, not running.

Other sails

Once you have trimmed the spinnaker successfully, why take the chance of wrecking that fragile balance by adding yet another sail? Why not? Logically, it must be possible to find more power somewhere ... If you take a good look, there are still gaps in your rigging, where the air is slipping through without being put to work. Are you going to let this continue? There are at least two obvious places to catch more of the available air: one is underneath the spinnaker, where a spinnaker staysail can be set; the other, more important gap, is opposite the spinnaker, to leeward but away from the mainsail, where a big boy sail can be set in any wind of over 10kn.

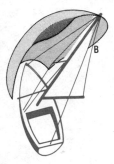

The big boy is a sort of loose genoa, made of spinnaker cloth, with the clew high up, the foot longer than the leech and a heavily cut-away luff so that the sail sags well downwind of the spinnaker.

The sail is set flying. It is shackled onto the stem and hoisted downwind of the spinnaker sheet, with a fairly slack halyard so that the head is maybe 30% of the mast height down. The foot should be set down by the surface of the water and the sheet fairlead should be as far aft as possible.

The big boy fills in the opposite direction from a genoa: the air enters at the leech and leaves via the luff. It follows that when the

Spinnakers without tears, part 1
A. Spinnaker sheeted too hard, collapsing from the middle, just about to wrap itself round the forestay.
B. Spinnaker trimmed correctly, with a faint curl appearing at the top of the luff.
C. Spinnaker insufficiently sheeted, on the verge of a major collapse starting from the luff.

sail flaps it needs to be eased; at the same time the halyard needs to be tightened or the sail will droop in the water. When it stops flapping, you can sheet in a little again and let off the halyard. As you will appreciate, one member of the crew needs to be assigned permanently to the halyard.

The big boy gives the boat considerable stability, as it joins the area of the mainsail and more or less balances out the area of the spinnaker on the opposite side. The big boy will allow you to sail as far as 15° by the lee (though if you are doing this you should also rig a boom preventer). It will function under normal conditions as far as 40° from dead downwind. The trick is to make sure you always leave a sizeable slot between the spinnaker and the big boy to let the air escape freely. The spinnaker boom has to be rigged very square to allow this.

If you do not have a big boy, you can get away with using a suitably cut genoa (so long as the luff is not weighed down with hanks). In order to let enough air into the genoa, you will have to take a reef or two in the main.

Jib

Occasionally there will be too much wind for you to hoist the spinnaker. At this point you will have to make do with the jib.

You can pole a reasonably large genoa out to windward on the run, with the main reefed to the same size as it would be on a beat in the same wind (or perhaps a little larger). If there is a heavy swell, you must bear in mind the possibility of the pole catching a wave; to avoid this, use a smaller genoa or at least one with the clew cut higher. On the run, you can complete the picture with a big boy ... but then again the boat is probably already virtually flat out, so the big boy might not help much.

If you are sailing too close for the genoa to pull when it is goosewinged, you can choose either to bear away a little to help it draw properly, or to harden up and set it in its usual position, to leeward. You have to decide how much of a hurry you are in.

We are not trying to push you into hurtling around at breakneck speeds, far from it! If you are at all nervous of the ideas presented, it is perfectly acceptable, and very safe, to sail downwind under jib alone, or with two jibs of which one or both are loose-luffed. If you do use two jibs, make sure there is a good gap left between them so the air can flow through.

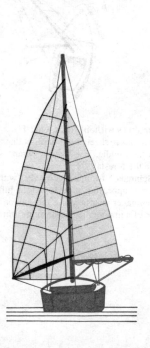

If you have no spinnaker ...

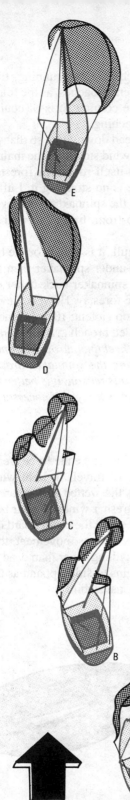

Twin staysails

There is good reading matter to be found in sailors' tales featuring long days spent with a favourable trade wind across the Atlantic. If you are not obsessed by speed, twin jibs or twin staysails are a wonderful way of profiting from a constant wind from behind.

You need to use two whisker poles, preferably the telescopic sort. You will not need the mainsail: since the centre of effort is well forward, the boat has immense directional stability, and the autopilot (or just the piece of shock-cord attached to the helm) works at its best.

There is a more modern version of the twin-staysail arrangement, known as the booster. This is a double jib rigged on a single, central luff rope; it does have an alternative use, as a very full jib, doubled over. It has to be said that this sail is designed for peace of mind and tranquillity, rather than high performance.

One note of caution on these long downwind stretches: if you have no mainsail up, it can take ages to get back to any crew member who falls overboard. Clunk click on the safety harness is greatly preferable to the sickening splash of the first mate's belly-flop.

Boat trim

Downwind, the boat's balance to the helm is dependent on the asymmetry of the sails as they are set:
– with the mainsail well eased, and no other sail up, the boat tends naturally to luff up;
– with a jib drawing to windward (ie the boat goosewinged), you can balance the helm by heeling the boat slightly to windward;
– the spinnaker offsets the imbalance from the main more or less completely, but it can make monohulls heel to windward, giving an uncomfortable degree of lee helm.

Spinnakers without tears, part 2
A. Either the spinnaker was sheeted in too tight or the helm has borne away too far and the boat is sailing by the lee ...
B. ... leading to this.
C. You therefore gybe the mainsail and rig a boom preventer.
D. The next step is to bear away again so as to be sailing by the lee on the new tack, and the spinnaker unfurls of its own accord.
E. You can now gybe back onto the original tack and sail as you were before, trimming the guy and (most importantly) easing the sheet. No problem!

In pleasant weather, without much of a sea running, the boat holds its heading easily. You can prevent broaches, as the fold in the spinnaker luff will warn you they are coming. It is of course less easy to spot a lurch to leeward approaching.

If you bear away a touch beyond dead downwind, so that you are by the lee, the spinnaker can have its wind stolen by the mainsail; it will then instantly collapse and wrap itself round the forestay in a wineglass shape. Once it starts, there is no stopping it. Luffing up just makes matters worse. To unwrap the spinnaker, you have to go through the whole procedure back-to-front, by gybing and sailing by the lee on the opposite tack.

As a general principle, in a monohull, it is better for the helm to luff up when something goes wrong under spinnaker than to bear away; it is easier to bring a flapping spinnaker back under control than one which is wrapped around the forestay. However, even this reflex needs to be controlled, and not too violent: 10 or 15°, no more, or your luff can turn into an uncontrolled broach ... *A multihull must under no circumstances be allowed to heel uncontrollably, and there is in any case less chance of wrapping the spinnaker around the forestay, since the boat rolls less. For this reason, it is better to keep the wind behind you, even going so far as to gybe if necessary.*

The centreboard

The centreboard is of little use downwind, since the force created by the sails is in line with the direction of travel. In light wind, the centreboard is harmful, as it increases the wetted surface area. It is thus better to retract it completely. In fresher winds, if your boat has no fixed underwater foil, it is worth keeping the centreboard down a little way. If there is no resistance to sideways movement, the boat becomes less controllable once it is anything other than dead downwind; the moment you head up, it begins to sideslip, and as there is no resistance to rolling, it loses directional stability.

With no underwater foil, the boat sideslips, and the heading bears no relation to the course actually made good. With a touch of centreboard, the boat is much more obedient to the helm.

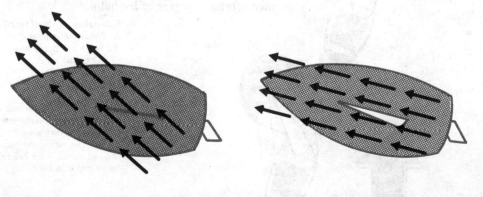

The efficiency of the centreboard increases with the square of the speed through the water. If you are sailing fast, with little sideways pressure on the board, you do not need it very far down.

Strong winds

Downwind, things begin to liven up as the wind freshens. The waves begin to take on more definite shape just as you become aware of the amount of sail you are carrying and the speed at which you are travelling. You suddenly find the tiller demands much more attention ...

At this stage, your first thought should be for the safety of boat and crew. It is hard to stop when you are sailing downwind, and if the spinnaker is up, every manoeuvre will take twice the time: retrieving a member of the crew lost overboard can take a while.

The first rule, which is valid for all points of sailing but especially vital downwind, is to clip yourself onto the safety line in plenty of time, ie in anything but the lightest wind. The next rule is to know how long to keep the spinnaker hoisted. Different boats behave differently when the crew makes a mistake: a light dinghy will capsize without any breakage, though it might tip the crew in; a heavy cruiser will resist the capsize so hard that something might well break; and even a stable multihull can be flipped over *in extremis*.

The spinnaker can be kept up for a long while, so long as you have things under control. How long you leave it up depends largely on the skill and experience of the crew. You will only improve your spinnaker handling if you try it out in progressively stronger winds (making sure that any mishap will not have grave consequences, by sailing in suitably safe waters). We shall look shortly at the factors to take into account when deciding whether or not to carry the spinnaker.

The main problem when you are sailing downwind in heavy weather is staying on course. It is much easier to be slewed round by the sea or the wind than on any other point of sailing, and causes far more problems when it happens. It is seldom advisable to sail dead downwind: 10–15° off will give you much improved stability.

Clunk click ...

rather than splash!

Helm balance

Instability caused by the sails

In a strong wind, the spinnaker can seriously upset the boat's directional stability. It becomes more difficult to keep the boat upright, and the spinnaker tends to heel the boat to windward, giving it lee helm. Before you know it, the boat can start to roll, the tiller pulls in an alternate direction and the helm starts to sweat ...

It can also become more difficult to keep correct fore-and-aft trim, as the spinnaker can easily pull the top of the mast forward and lift the transom. The braking action of the water causes the hull to bury its bows. You can move aft to bring the bows up, but the best way to stabilise the boat is to flatten and steady the spinnaker by using a barber hauler or hook to bring the clew tension down and forward, then keeping the foot horizontal by doing the same for the tack.

If you will be subjecting the spinnaker to a long period of sustained tension, it is best to let the halyard up or down a few centimetres every couple of hours, just to prevent excessive wear at any one point. Mainsail twist should be minimised by using kicking-strap tension; and the main should be trimmed so as to counteract any rolling motion.

Instability caused by waves

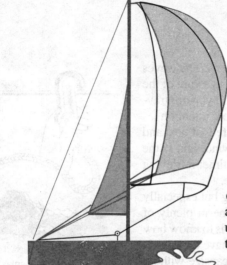

In a strong wind, the boat tends to dig its bow in, so the spinnaker needs to be flattened by bringing the sheeting point forward. This reduces the thrust from the sail and points it more directly forward.

The combination of waves and rolling sends a monohull off course. When a wave catches the boat on the windward quarter, it tends to make it luff up; and the boat will bear away when caught by a wave on the leeward quarter. This pivoting effect can be added to by the action of the wave in heeling the boat, which increases the tendency to go off course.

It is crucial to have a sensitive hand on the tiller in waves. Once the wave has caught the boat, the rudder has no effect, so you actually need to anticipate its action. If the swell is coming at your windward quarter, you need to bear away before the wave, so that it puts you back on course; if it is coming from the leeward quarter, you will need to luff before the wave and then let it push you back down to leeward with no fear of an accidental gybe.

All this requires firmness and skill on the tiller. In stormy seas, you maintain the harmony of boat and sea by adopting your best Wagnerian style, and you can conduct the pizzicato of the wavelets with suitably delicate strokes of the stick. In effect this means pushing or pulling the tiller only when there is most force from the wave trying to send it the other way: your aim is actually to keep the rudder as steady as possible – which can be exhausting.

One added complication: you need to learn different reflexes depending on the number of hulls your boat has!

Spinnakers without tears, part 3.
The end of a broach: the boat has stopped on its ear, and has no particular reason to pick itself up until you help it! Just letting go of the sheet will probably be inadequate. You need to let the guy off as well, and then probably drop the spinnaker. This will achieve the desired long-term effect.

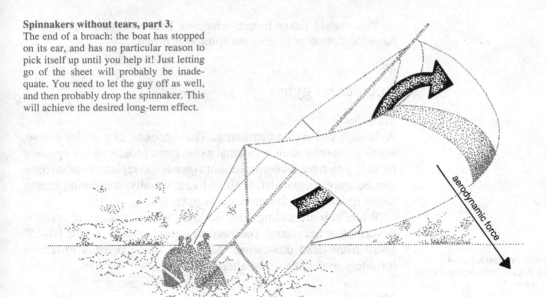

aerodynamic force

Broaching

The boat can escape from the grasp of even the most attentive helm at times and luff up uncontrollably. Adding a spinnaker makes this situation even more delicate. Once the boat heels over on its ear and slows down with the wind on the beam, it has a nasty habit of staying that way, because the air flow over the spinnaker becomes reversed: it flows up from the foot and escapes around the sides.

If you react to the luff sufficiently quickly while your boat still has enough way on, by pulling the tiller up to windward and letting go the spinnaker sheet, you can sometimes save the situation. If the boat has slowed down so much that it barely responds to the helm, it will simply stay there, with the spinnaker flogging. You need to get out of this position, and quick. There is one simple and fast way out. Let off the guy. The boat will come upright, the spinnaker will deflate and you can then pull it down without difficulty.

If broaching is a worry for a monohull, it is fatal for a multihull. There can be no question of happily recovering from the broach, whichever way round it happens: it is always preferable to get the spinnaker tangled or gybe. Since you can never be entirely sure that the wind will not cause a sudden broach, the spinnaker guy *should not be cleated, but should be held in the hand with two or three turns on a winch, ready for instant release if the situation demands.*

At the top of a wave, the surface water moves in such a way as to turn the boat round and make the helm ineffective. At the bottom of a wave, the rudder works well and the boat is not turned in either direction. You should therefore use the hollow between waves to make the adjustments to the boat's heading which you know the next wave will require.

You should never forget, whatever boat you sail, that you do have the option of pulling the spinnaker down.

Accidental gybes

Monohulls

A broach can be embarrassing. The opposite can be far worse, leading not only to an accidental gybe, but a broach on the opposite tack. If you have a boom restraint rigged, the resultant catastrophe can be truly spectacular, if short-lived: usually, something breaks rather quickly, and the spectacle is over.

When you are sailing downwind in waves, a boom restraint is nevertheless necessary. You need to ensure you are a safe 10–15° away from dead downwind. All in all, the risk of a broach is infinitely preferable to the alternative.

Spinnakers without tears, part 4
This situation did not last long enough for the artist to capture it.

Multihulls

An accidental gybe following an uncontrolled bearing away is considerably less fearsome, and the chances of it happening are lower, since the boat rolls less. Since a broach can have horrible consequences, your reflex response to a problem should be to bear away, taking the chance of an accidental gybe. You should therefore be prepared for this eventuality. You can prepare by:
– eliminating mainsail twist;
– cleating the mainsheet traveller in the middle of the boat or even to windward, so that the boom gybes automatically a long way over toward the shrouds without you needing to ease the mainsheet;
– ensuring the mainsheet is always free to run out;
– keeping your head (and everyone else's) well below boom height;
– not using a boom restraint, unless it is one which can free itself automatically.

The general principle is: a multihull's safety depends on speed. You should do everything possible to prevent it slowing down, because once the rig is travelling faster than the hull ...

Reducing sail

Sailing under spinnaker in a fresh breeze is not always easy. You have to know when enough is enough, and cut your cloth, as it were, according to your means.

Above a certain wind strength, in fact, the problems caused by carrying the spinnaker start to outweigh the potential benefits.

The spinnaker starts to cause an almost permanent roll which in turn makes the boat difficult to steer. The risk of burying the bows increases drastically, even for a blunt-nosed boat; and if you do not break the mast, you might send the whole boat down.

Crew tiredness is a perfectly valid reason for taking the spinnaker down. You need to be alert and fit to tend a spinnaker in strong winds. It is also difficult to change places at the helm, because whoever has been steering while the wind was freshening will have been getting slowly used to the conditions, learning to react appropriately; any replacement, coming fresh to the job, is thrown in at the deep end, with no time to adjust to the situation before that wave or gust comes along which might cost you your spinnaker or your mast if incorrectly handled.

Running downwind under spinnaker in a big sea causes nervous exhaustion. Nobody on board can relax properly. Tiredness in turn can cause rash decisions to be taken. Then there is the possibility of losing someone overboard …

Knowing when you should not be carrying the spinnaker is thus essential for anyone thinking of using one in strong winds. It is seldom an improvement to use a smaller spinnaker, as the problem is less one of area than of balance: since the spinnaker is only held fixed at two points, it can subject the rigging to considerable strain. It is often much better to pole out the genoa or another jib, or to use an asymmetric spinnaker (which is by definition rigged without a pole). You may lose some speed, but you will make up for this by being able to hold your heading.

Taking in a reef on the mainsail has little effect on boat speed downwind. *If the main is reefed, it gets in the way of the spinnaker far less. This is particularly true when the boat needs to be turned around quickly. The boat is easier and safer to handle under the same sail area as it would carry on a beat.*

One more good reason for reducing sail in a strong wind. With a reef in the main, the air empties better from the spinnaker.

Light weather

In very light winds, it is just as exhausting running before the wind as in a strong breeze. In fact you can even find yourself longing for a few more of the problems which the excess of wind was giving you earlier. In light winds you can play with the spinnaker, which is not helping you along much, or you can amuse yourself by inventing go-faster tricks. The boat's rolling motion becomes your greatest enemy; and on a heavy boat (so long as you are not racing) you might just decide to drop all the sails for a while to give boat and crew a rest while you drift along.

It is worth knowing how to get your boat to move in the lightest of airs: this skill can be vital in a tricky passage as you need to make a few extra miles to avoid a foul tide, or to get back home on time.

Is it worth mentioning sail trim?

When you are running, the apparent wind is less strong than the true wind. As soon as the boat starts to move forward you cannot feel any wind at all.

A light spinnaker (26gsm) with light sheets (4mm diameter for a 100sq m sail, for instance) might just about be persuaded to fill … but once you have got it filling, you have to keep it that way. You will almost certainly need to make constant adjustments to the tack height to keep it level with wherever the clew happens to be floating.

You might need to ease the halyard out slightly to keep the spinnaker well clear of the mainsail. This in turn has the disadvantage of decreasing the stability of the tack.

You can try to play the sails by letting them fill while gently easing the sheets, then holding them once they reach the correct trim. You might even have to hold them in place by hand when there is virtually no wind.

The sails need to be as full as possible, of course, and if they flap a little as the boat rolls, all the better: the flapping can be used to propel the boat forward.

The boat needs to be heeled slightly in order to get the sails filling in the right position. The crew should remain as still as possible. There is no point crouching down in the boat: you actually want all the windage you can get. If your boat has a centreboard, pull it up.

Whistling is said to encourage the wind to come …

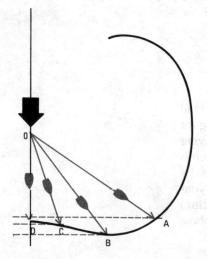

The boat which sails the course OB makes the most ground to leeward.

To run or to reach?

Making ground to leeward

Modern boats, particularly multihulls, tend to be slow and uncomfortable on a run, so it is usual to avoid the run. Just as we were interested, when beating, to find the course which offered the most ground made good to windward, we seek the downwind course which makes most ground to leeward by exploiting the superior performance of our boat on a broad reach.

The diagram on this page shows that route B allows the most ground to be made good to leeward. The best downwind course is thus one which involves regular gybes from one broad reach to the other.

Reaching

The reach is that wide area between beating and running, which brings freedom and ease to the boat and its hard-pressed crew.

Reaching is the boat's natural and favoured condition. It travels fast and uses the wind efficiently. When the wind freshens on a beat, one's correct response is to ease the sheets; on the reach, you simply sheet in a bit more and travel all the faster. It is less a question of trimming them until the luff lifts than of working out the optimum angle through which they should deflect the air flow to give maximum power.

There is nevertheless one trap in store for the unwary. The boat can stall, slowing down suddenly and with no apparent reason. When this happens the wind seems to have disappeared completely and nothing you do has any effect.

Multihulls set one further trap for their crews: there is a risk of capsizing on the reach.

Points of reaching

There is a considerable difference in feel between sailing a boat with regular, laminar air flow over the sails, and the moment where the flow becomes turbulent. In the first case, we can speak of close or beam reaching, while the moment at which the flow becomes turbulent indicates that we are almost on a run: this is the area of the broad reach.

It is conventional, in fact, to divide the reach into close reaching and the rest. We shall begin by looking at the points of similarity between these two points of sailing, and then look at those areas which are unique to each. The differences in how you sail the boat on each point of sailing are as much a matter of personal preference and mood as of technical constraints. A reach can give you one of the most carefree rides in a boat or one of the most uncomfortable. It is perfectly possible to sail a reach without stalling, and even if you do stall, the effects need not be catastrophic; so long as you do not over-sheet the sails, the boat will continue along quickly in any case. Nevertheless, there is always a risk with catamarans (especially the lighter types), that a mistake on the tiller will lead to a capsize, no matter how correctly you trim the sails.

If your aim is to extract maximum performance from your boat, you have to take the issue of stalling rather further. The greatest power is obtained from the sails when they are eased to the point of lifting (ie just when flow separation is about to take place). At this point you need to stay on your guard.

Flow separation

This is a matter we have dealt with several times. For the moment, we need to bear in mind simply that the sail creates gradually more power the closer it is sheeted, until it reaches a critical angle, at which it is said to stall, and the power falls away suddenly. This critical angle is that at which the sail becomes an obstacle to the air flow rather than a deflector. The flow ceases to be regular and becomes turbulent, and the pressure of the wind on the sail suddenly drops.

When you have just stalled the sails, your first reaction is one of surprise. Nothing you noticed had prepared you for the stall, and you will take a moment or two to get over it. You need to free the sheets considerably or luff up a fair way to drive the turbulence off the sails before you can get back on course. If your boat is heavy, and the wind light, it can take a very long time to build your speed back up.

The apparent wind and its whims

One further important point to bear in mind is that the difference between the apparent wind and the true wind is greater on a reach than on any other point of sailing. The apparent wind comes from much further ahead than the true wind, and the difference increases the faster you go. (It can easily reach 30° on a dinghy and as much as 60–80° on a multihull.) The smallest acceleration or deceleration can therefore mean a radical change in wind direction.

Whenever the boat slows for any reason, the wind frees to such an extent that the sails are suddenly over-sheeted; the air flow, which had been laminar, separates and becomes turbulent; the sails stall, and the initial slight deceleration can become a sudden stop if you maintain both sail trim and helm heading as they were initially.

When you are bearing away from a close fetch, you can begin by increasing the fullness in the sails and thus the angle through which they deflect the wind. This gives maximum power as quickly as possible.

The further you bear away, the greater the difference in angle and strength becomes between true and apparent wind; this limits your ability to respond by easing the sheets, but it does mean that the boat accelerates to its critical speed more readily, as the increasing boat speed increases the headwind, which in turn strengthens the apparent wind, giving yet more speed ... So long as the boat does not go beyond its critical speed, any further bearing away will decrease the headwind component of the apparent wind in proportion to the change in angle between the boat and the apparent wind. These two changes cancel each other out, so the boat can keep its speed, with the air flow over the sails remaining laminar, all the way round to about 140° from the true wind, so long as you do not stall the sails.

If the boat starts to plane, it will continue to accelerate as the angle between the boat and the apparent wind increases (even if the wind strength begins to drop). The most noticeable phenomenon in this case is that the apparent wind moves ahead only very slowly, and can stay below 50° even when the boat is sailing at 140° to the true wind (always assuming you have succeeded in keeping it on the plane). Once the boat's own speed becomes an important element in keeping it balanced, you can imagine the concentration required on the part of the helm!

On a reach there can be considerable variation in the apparent wind.

Boat speed

On a multihull the effect of slowing down is well known, and any crew will be wary of it. Basically, even a large boat can capsize simply as a result of slowing down suddenly. Let us spend some time looking at how this happens.

If we take the example of a catamaran which buries the leeward bow in a wave, the boat is suddenly slowed, the wind swings round to the side and the aerodynamic force on the sail suddenly increases and changes direction before the flow separates. The boat develops weather helm and luffs, unless the helm has previously borne away in anticipation of the problem. If it is allowed to luff, the bow will be buried deeper, slowing the boat still more. Meanwhile the mast head continues forward at its usual merry pace and pow! the boat somersaults, throwing both of you into the water.

This chain of events explains our earlier comment that the speed of a multihull is what ensures its safety. You must never allow a multihull to be slowed suddenly, especially on a reach.

The crew's instinct should be to maintain boat speed at all costs, even if this means losing ground to windward. If you do need to slow the boat down, by all means luff up, but do so gradually and sparingly.

On a monohull you will in any case be travelling less fast. The boat can heel without any great danger, so feels quite different. Slowing down suddenly does have the same aerodynamic effects, but the boat can respond by heeling and losing power, so there are generally far fewer problems caused.

Sail trim

You should constantly be changing the angle at which you trim the sails, to correspond with the speed of the boat. The faster you travel, the further ahead the apparent wind comes, and the further in you need to sheet the sails to keep them at the optimum angle to the wind.

When the wind freshens, you do not need to flatten or twist the sails: it is enough simply to ease the sheets. This means that they deflect the wind less, but the force exerted on them by the wind will stay the same and will be pointed further forward, thus increasing the usable power at your disposal.

As always, the sails should be sheeted in until they just about stop lifting at the luff; they should not be over-sheeted, which runs the risk of stalling them. You can spot a stall coming if you have tell-tales sewn into the sails; keeping a close eye on the tell-tales allows you to trim the sails perfectly, just to the limit of flow separation.

Spinnaker trim

The same principles apply as to spinnaker trim downwind. To recap:
– the pole should be at right angles to the apparent wind;
– the spinnaker should be vertically symmetrical;
– the pole should be at right angles to the mast;
– the spinnaker needs to be flattened in strong winds.

These principles are subordinate only to the need to balance the boat, which might mean that you have to change the angle of the pole to the apparent wind; occasionally the pole will also have to be at a different angle to the mast, in order to keep the foot horizontal.

On a reach, the spinnaker generally flattens itself naturally, since you are pulling the clew further down the closer to the wind you go and the further inboard you sheet the sail. In light winds, the sheet should be led further back and higher (up to the level of the rails, or even the boom) to keep the sail full; as the wind freshens, the sheet fairlead should go forward and down to flatten the sail.

The spinnaker foot needs to be kept horizontal on the reach, despite the angle at which the boat is heeling. The clew can be raised by bringing the sheet up over the boom and round the reefing hook. A jockey pole set forward of the shroud to windward is useful for spreading the strain on the guy.

You can also buy reaching spinnakers which are cut less full than running spinnakers and are designed to allow you to carry them closer to the wind. The tack of these spinnakers needs to be set fairly low: you can tell the correct height by checking the position of the fold on the luff of the spinnaker when you ease the sheet. Most spinnakers curl first at the shoulder, ie about two-thirds of the way up. If the fold appears higher up, you have the tack too low; if the fold is lower, the pole is set too high.

Some reaching spinnakers are trimmed the opposite way round from downwind spinnakers. The tack height is adjusted first, using the luff fold to find the correct height; the clew is then trimmed to make the foot horizontal. Starcut spinnakers need the luff rather tighter than others, as they are used more like a genoa, and on these the fold should appear half-way up. Asymmetric spinnakers are intermediate sails between spinnakers and genoas, and these too should set with the foot horizontal.

> **A point to remember**
> If the fold is too high, raise the pole.
> If the fold is too low, lower the pole.

Boat trim

Many monohulls tend to develop strong weather helm on a reach, since the centre of effort of the sails is so far down to leeward.

It is very difficult to counter this tendency. If you have a pivoting centreboard, you can raise it most of the way and offset most of the weather helm. The important thing is to ensure that the boat stays flat, since the slightest heel increases the weather helm further.

Close to beam reaching

In non-planing conditions, a boat sails fastest on a close or beam reach. The air flow over the sails is regular, with the aerodynamic force strong and pointed well forward. In a fresh breeze, however, the boat can develop a considerable heeling couple, and you will need to lean well out to keep the sails trimmed at their optimum angle to the wind. It is hard work, but worth it!

The reach is a sort of half-way house between a run and a beat. It gives you the greatest freedom of choice in how you trim the boat and sails. The sails can be sheeted anywhere between their stalling point and flapping. Even if they do stall, the recovery is quicker on a reach than otherwise: you simply let them go to get rid of the turbulence, then sheet back in gradually, picking up power and speed as you re-establish laminar flow.

In the gusts, you can choose whether to luff, as if you were on a beat, or to bear away and ease the sheets, depending on the conditions and where you are headed.

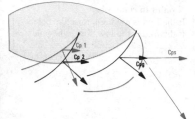

Cp1 + Cps = Cp2 + Cpg.
Or in other words, the spinnaker and
genoa are equally efficient.

Spinnaker or genoa?
Deciding which foresail to use can be a tough problem. You cannot
always tell in advance which will be more efficient. In the diagram,
we show the borderline case where either one, along with appropriate mainsail trim, will give the same result. In order to keep the
spinnaker drawing, you have to sheet it in fairly hard, with the result
that its power is not directed so far forward as you would like. The
genoa gives less power, but it is directed further forward. Even so,
the spinnaker has the advantage at this point. Under genoa, however,
you can afford to ease the mainsail further, giving much better-
directed power than under spinnaker. The greater power of the
combined spinnaker and mainsail has to be weighed against the
better direction of the force provided by genoa and main together.

When you do decide to raise the spinnaker, you can get a very
approximate idea of the direction in which it is pulling by looking at
the halyard. The only time a spinnaker is really useful on a close
reach is in light airs. When there is more wind, any speed gained has
to be offset against the extra distance you will need to sail due to the
inevitable luffs, plus the time needed for pulling the sail up and down.

Multihulls
Some multihulls start to plane even on a close reach. Since the
apparent wind is then well ahead, the sails will be sheeted almost as
tight as for a beat. The only difference should be that you increase
the angle of deflection by allowing more fullness in the sails.

The boat needs to be sailed differently on a close reach, because
of the risk of a capsize. You must not allow the boat to broach or to
stop suddenly, and you must be very careful not to allow it to bury a
bow. At the slightest hint of a problem, you should react by bearing
away. This is a difficult habit to pick up if you have spent years in a
monohull before changing over to a multihull, but it must be
acquired if you want to hang on to your new boat!

Beam to broad reaching

Beyond the beam reach, there should be no question about it: up
with the spinnaker!

It has to be said that the boat is in the greatest danger of stalling
on this point of sailing. As you bear away from a close reach, you
ease the sails gradually to keep them correctly trimmed to the wind,
until the moment comes where the main is against the shroud. At
that stage, bearing away any further will result in flow separation.
Even if you keep rigidly to that course, there is still a good chance of
losing laminar flow at some stage, simply if a little wave slows you

a touch. When this does happen, you cannot recover by easing the sails any further, so you need a good strong luff, almost such that the sails flap. Then you can start to bear away carefully back onto your course.

There is an enormous difference between sailing the reach with laminar air flow and sailing it with turbulent flow. It is quite possible to see two boats sailing the same broad reach, with the same sail trim, at markedly different speeds: one of them has borne away onto the reach, maintaining laminar flow, and is still sailing fast; the other has just luffed up from a run and is still dawdling along with turbulence on the downwind side of its sails. It can pick up speed by a short, hefty luff, but until it does, it might as well be in a different world from its faster neighbour.

There can be no question about the correct way to sail a broadish reach in a more-or-less constant wind. When a gust hits, you have nothing to gain by luffing up: that will simply overpower the boat. You should always bear away and ease the sheets, in monohulls or in multihulls. If the gust is really strong, bearing away sharply can take the sting out of it by stalling the sails. As the flow becomes turbulent, it exerts less force on the sails. You can use the stall as an important safety valve on multihulls when absolutely necessary.

The cargo vessel is still in alignment with the corner of the cabin roof and the boom end on the third sighting. This signals danger.

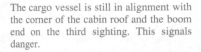

The 'highway code'

Rules of the road

Sailing a boat well, alas, is not simply a question of correct sail trim and choice of heading. The best technique in the world for dealing with variations in the wind is no use if there is an obstacle such as a boat in the way of where you want to go. This is a frequent problem, and all boats should aim to avoid getting in each other's way. At this point, we need to refer to the rules for avoiding collisions when boats are sailing in company with other vessels. The first principle is to keep a good lookout. The second, to assess the chances of a collision occurring; and the third is to know what to do to avoid these chances from turning into unpleasant reality.

The basis of our 'highway code' is vigilance. This vigilance must not be allowed to be compromised by tiredness or by seasickness. You should be aware that there are large sectors of the horizon permanently obscured from the helm's eyes by the sails and parts of the boat's superstructure.

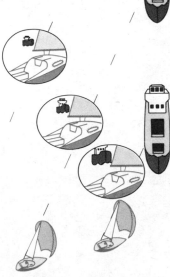

Risk of collision

When is there a risk of collision? We begin by quoting from the admirable Rule 7 of the *International Regulations for Preventing Collisions at Sea*:

'Every vessel shall use all available means appropriate to the prevailing circumstances and conditions to determine if risk of collision exists. *If there is any doubt such risk shall be deemed to exist.*'

The prime consequence of this rule is that you must not allow all eyes on board to be fixed on the spinnaker luff. Someone should be keeping a constant lookout, especially ahead and to leeward of you. As soon as another boat is sighted, you should work out whether you are on a potential collision course.

Two boats are on a collision course if the bearing from one to the other does not vary, or varies only slightly. The first thing to do when you spot another boat, then, is to take a bearing on it, ie read off on your compass the angle between it and your own heading. You can avoid the need for calculations by using a sight line, for instance, looking at it along a certain rail on the deck. If the boat can still be sighted along the same rail later, the bearing between you has not changed and you are on a collision course. You need to take avoiding action.

At night, you can tell the approximate heading of a boat from its lights. All boats carry a green light to starboard and a red light to port, with a lit sector of 112.5°. They must also carry a certain number of white lights. (You can check the precise list in your nautical almanac.)

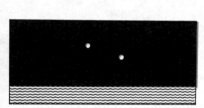

If all you can see are these two masthead lights, you can tell that the boat is travelling from left to right.

White lights are visible at a much greater distance than coloured lights (10, as opposed to 2 miles). The masthead lights are the first ones you will see which can give you an idea of where the boat is headed. On a big ship, the aft masthead light is higher than the forward one, and they are both raised above the ship's superstructure. If you see one light directly above the other, you know the ship is coming straight at you.

Coloured lights can be seen as the boat comes closer. (7 x 50 binoculars are useful for picking them out.) There is no risk of collision if you can see the other boat's red light in the sector covered by your own red light, or the other boat's green light in your green sector.

When you are catching up with a big ship (it can happen!) you will see its stern light only.

Right-of-way rules

Collisions at sea can only be avoided if we are all following the same set of rules. The rules are both strict and flexible, as they are based not on a boat's rights, but on its duties. The expression 'right of way' implies some priority; it would actually be more correct and more subtle to speak of a duty of care. The situation is: this boat has to keep clear of that boat; that boat, in turn, has to maintain its current course unless the first has clearly not seen it. You need to learn not just a set of rules, but also a new mentality.

This mentality is clearly shown in the official text of Rule 14, which stipulates that if you are in any doubt, you should consider your boat to be subject to a duty of avoidance: 'When a vessel is in any doubt as to whether such a situation [a likely collision] exists she shall assume it does exist and act accordingly.'

The rules may be learnt by heart if you want (and this is actually very useful if you plan to take a powerboat licence), but everyone should ensure they grasp at least the basics, and know enough of the rest of the text to look in the right place when in doubt. We shall limit ourselves here to the basics.

Under sail

You must avoid:
– any vessel which you are overtaking;
– when you are on starboard tack, any sailing vessel also on starboard tack and to leeward of you;
– when you are on port tack, any sailing vessel on starboard tack as well as any sailing vessel on port tack and to leeward of you.

This generally means that if you are close-hauled on starboard

The windward boat must keep clear.

The port-tack boat must keep clear.

The boat on the right is under engine power (as can be seen from the inverted cone) and must keep clear of the left-hand boat, which is exclusively under sail power.

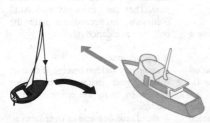

When both boats are under motor power, the one which has the other on her starboard side must keep clear of the other. (This generally means crossing behind it.)

Two boats under motor power heading on reciprocal courses must pass each other to the right.

tack, others will need to avoid you. However, you will quickly find that this does not mean that you rule the waves, Britannia-like, as you steer your 24-footer through a busy shipping lane! Even when you are close-hauled on starboard, you still need to avoid any other boat which has failed to spot you or which cannot change course for any reason.

As a general principle, any boat showing cones, balls or other shapes during daytime, or lights one above the other during the night should be avoided. Once you have taken avoiding action, you can check your nautical almanac to see precisely why that vessel had priority over yours!

Under power

You must keep clear of:
- any boat which you are overtaking;
- any powered vessel forward of you and to starboard (to be precise, any vessel in the 112.5° sector of your starboard light);
- any sail vessel and any vessel showing cones, balls or other shapes, or lights one above the other;
- if two boats are travelling directly towards each other, they pass on the right.

Traffic separation lanes

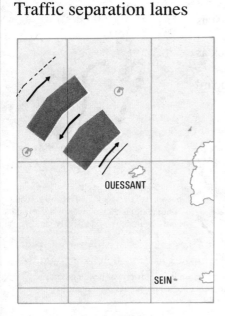

OUESSANT

SEIN

1. The use of lanes is optional

A boat need not use the traffic separation lanes in all cases.

It may choose either:
- to pass outside the lanes, leaving a good distance between itself and the lane;
- or to use the inshore navigation zone (between the lane and the land).

The captain of the vessel has the responsibility for making the choice on the basis of the relative safety offered by each course.

2. Within a lane

All vessels must follow the general direction of traffic flow within their lane. They may manoeuvre to avoid collisions, in accordance with the collision avoidance rules.

It is prudent to:
- avoid any sudden change of course;
- keep your distance from other vessels by using the entire width of the lane;
- avoid crossing into or over lanes or separation zones (the central reservation between lanes).

Whether you are steering under sail or under power, it is as well to keep two basic principles in mind:
• When you are taking avoiding action to keep clear of another boat, this action is always preferable if it leads your course *behind* the other boat rather than in front.
• Avoiding action should be taken clearly and early, so as to leave the skipper of the other vessel in no doubt as to your intentions.

Traffic separation lanes

Shipping lanes have been established in certain very busy sea areas to give large ships an exactly defined corridor which they must use. We should not need to say that pleasure-boat sailors are not supposed to sail around in these corridors. In fact, you should avoid shipping lanes like the plague; and if you do have to travel across one, do so without delay, and at right angles to the traffic.

In a channel

The rules which apply to boats at sea are effectively in abeyance once you enter a channel. Within the channel there is one essential rule, which is to keep to the right.

3. Entering and leaving a lane

Vessels are normally expected to enter and leave shipping lanes at the lane ends.

They may, if necessary:
– enter from the side of a lane if they are travelling in the same direction as traffic in that lane;
– leave by the side of a lane, but at the smallest angle practicable.

4. Crossing a lane

A vessel may cross a lane or both lanes, but must do so at right angles to the general direction of the traffic in the lane or lanes.

The following rules apply:
– *in a shipping lane, fishing vessels, vessels of less than 20m in length and sailing vessels* must not obstruct the passage of shipping;
– *in the separation zone:*
• fishing is permitted;
• traffic is prohibited except in case of emergency or cutting directly across lanes at right angles.

Radar reflectors
Boats that do not have a metal hull must be *fitted* with a radar reflector, and not just have one on board. The octohedral reflectors should be installed correctly, and must not point upwards.

Sound signals
In theory, a sailing ship under way in fog should sound three blasts, one long and two short, at intervals of not more than two minutes.

Even this simple rule needs some explanation. For very large ships, steering in a channel is an extremely delicate operation: there is generally insufficient room to manoeuvre, and if the ship slows down it can end up without sufficient way to steer by. In a channel, a sailing cruiser should not only keep right, but should ensure it does nothing which might obstruct a large ship, even slightly. In many cases, it is perfectly possible for a small pleasure sailing boat to move along just outside the limits of the channel, thus leaving the really deep water to those who need it.

Fog

The rules governing right of way do not change, but it becomes difficult or even impossible in fog to tell if you are on a collision course with another vessel. Sailors have two systems to help them avoid each other in fog: radar and sound signals.

Big fishing boats, cargo ships and warships have radar equipment. To be picked up by their radar a pleasure boat must have a radar reflector, preferably at the mast head. The reflector needs to conform to very precise design requirements, but if it is correctly positioned, and large enough, it can be seen on a radar screen as well as a 10m metal hull can.

Sound signals cannot be relied upon. If you sound a foghorn, the only people who will hear it are other sailors: smaller motor boats will drown it out with the noise of their engine, and larger boats will have the door to the bridge closed anyway.

If you hear another boat sounding a foghorn, you know it is somewhere near, though you cannot tell precisely how near, nor where it is headed. The propeller noise of a large ship can be heard from inside your own cabin at quite a distance, through the water, but again the knowledge that a boat is somewhere near does not help much.

In fog, it is sensible to avoid lanes in which you know there to be heavy traffic, particularly freighter traffic. If you cannot avoid them entirely, at least make sure you cross the lanes at a right angle, to keep the risk of a collision to a minimum.

Let us not forget the gravestone inscription: 'Here lies the body of Johnny Gray, who died defending his right of way'. Small sailing boats are the pedestrians of the sea: it does not matter how right you are when you are in collision with a steel monster twenty times your size. Bear this in mind when you are on collision course with a large freighter who might not have seen you. If you are not sure, then change course yourself, early and noticeably. Remember:
– large ships cannot always change direction quickly, as they are

travelling fast and respond slowly to the helm;
– out at sea, it is quite common for freighters to be sailing on autopilot, with no one on the bridge (particularly at supper time);
– at night, the lights of a small sailing boat are virtually impossible to spot from the bridge of a cargo ship.

It is not always sufficient to change direction in order to be sure of avoiding a collision. Use all the means at your disposal if necessary: shine a powerful spotlight at the bridge of the ship, if you have one; if the boat seems in imminent danger of being hit, even fire off a flare or two in the direction of the bridge (preferably using green or white flares).

Let us not forget that fast multihulls pose problems all of their own for ships' captains. If you are travelling at the sort of speeds of which these boats are capable, well in excess of 15kn, the person looking at that weak radar reflection shooting across their screen is quite likely to disbelieve the evidence of their own eyes, especially if they are used to the more sedate pace of traditional cruisers. You do need to be extremely vigilant if you are travelling this fast, and you should always be ready to take avoiding action yourself.

Once the metal monster has passed safely by, you can drink to the captain's health using all the rude words you wish, before returning to the important business of preparing your own supper, or re-trimming that spinnaker you have just spent a quarter of an hour getting right …

CHAPTER 2
Going about

Going about is a peculiar moment on board a boat, and an activity unlike any other: very briefly, the boat actually pushes either its bow or its stern through the eye of the wind. The sails, which are normally trimmed in or out fairly gradually, are subjected to sudden movements from one side of the boat to the other. In all this motion, there is a momentary hiatus, an instant of uncertainty, which you must learn to control.

The eye of the wind is like a wall: you can luff up close to it, travelling forward as you do so, but to get over the wall, you need to use all the momentum you have been able to build up. Just as when you are beating, keeping way on is of paramount importance when you tack.

Gybing can be done without much concern for boat speed. It is more important when you gybe to ensure that you have your course under control, as any deviation from the plan can foul everything up. When you are running before the wind, it is a little like balancing as you walk along the top of the wall, and the gybe must not be allowed to knock you off!

There is thus a world of difference between the two ways of going about.

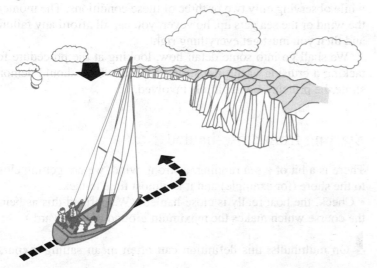

Tacking

Tacking is a decisive sort of manoeuvre. The boat heads up into the wind beyond its close-hauled course, continues luffing right through the eye of the wind, and you end up close-hauled on the opposite tack. Nothing simpler!

However, as this manoeuvre is taking place, the sails flap, and the boat is supposed to travel through an angle of 90° powered by nothing more than its own momentum; if there is insufficient momentum or it is used incorrectly, the boat might fail to make it all the way through the eye of the wind, and you can be caught *in irons*, that is, stuck temporarily head to wind. This is usually no more than embarrassing, though it can on occasions be dangerous.

We do not want to exaggerate the chances of a tack turning dangerous, but *a tack should not be allowed to fail*. A failed tack in a fresh breeze, just off a lee shore, has to be one of the most common causes of serious yachting accidents. And failing to tack means that you have failed to come to terms with the way the boat interacts with the sea and wind around it.

For a tack to succeed:
– *the boat must be balanced, and neither under- nor over-canvassed;*
– *take account of the waves, and choose the right moment;*
– *start from a close-hauled course, with way on;*
– *both tiller and sheets must be correctly handled throughout, and the boat's trim needs appropriate adjustment.*

When the weather is kind, it is possible to tack successfully while observing only two or three of these conditions. The moment the wind or the sea gets up, however, you can ill afford any failure, and then you must get everything right.

We shall go into some detail now, looking at the procedure for tacking a cruising yacht in a strong breeze, which should demonstrate the principles and pitfalls involved.

Starting from close-hauled

There is a bit of a sea running, a strong wind, we are getting close to the shore (for example) and it is almost time to tack.
• Check: the boat really is close-hauled. (We defined this as being the course which makes the maximum ground to windward.)

▶ On multihulls, this definition can often mean sailing a course which is some way freer than desirable for the tack, as it still leaves a considerable dead angle. It may then be worthwhile adopting a rather closer course than that you would normally expect to sail.

• Check: the boat is 'well set up'. We take this as meaning that the sails are correctly trimmed, just short of lifting; the windward runner (if you have one) is tight and so is the forestay; all crew members are well back from the bow so they do not slow its turn through the wind and waves, and nor do they get in the way of the air flow in the slot between jib and main; the boat is correctly canvassed, so it has enough power but not so much that it is hard to control. Basically, the helm should feel confidence in the boat.

You can tell that a monohull is correctly set for the tack by checking that it is not heeling excessively. This check is meaningless on a multihull, so you need to spend a little more time feeling your way into the boat's movements to gauge whether it is ready.

• Check: the boat is travelling fast enough: the lighter the boat and the less momentum it has, the more important speed becomes as you go into the tack. This is true with most catamarans.

Make sure all the conditions for a successful tack have been fulfilled, ie that when you choose to tack, you will be able to do so.

All the above conditions, in reality, are nothing more than you

The left-hand boat is ready to go about:
– it is close-hauled;
– the sails are well trimmed;
– the forestay is tight;
– it is correctly canvassed for the wind;
– it is heeling only slightly;
– the crew members are in position;
– the sheets are free.
If only we could say the same for the right-hand boat!

would expect of a boat sailing a good close-hauled course.

All the same, you should try to choose your moment to tack, so that there is no chance of the sea itself destroying your carefully acquired momentum or turning you off course. This means avoiding any waves which are particularly large or powerful-looking. (This is particularly important on a multihull, which will end up going through the same wave two or even three times as it tacks.) You need to be able to delay the tack if the boat is suddenly slowed for any reason, since speed is the most important basic condition for getting started.

Successful tacking is also the result of perfect co-ordination between crew members: everyone has their own precise job to perform at a precise moment. In order to co-ordinate all the separate activities, there is no harm in the captain giving direct orders loudly as the tack takes place. Some picturesque cries from the age of the square-rigger have been lost as tacking becomes less dramatic with ever more modern materials, but there is still a fairly well-established sequence of orders: 'Ready about!' is the first, followed by the confirmation from the crew that they are indeed ready, then the order to put the helm down, 'Lee-oh!', and soon after, the order to let the sheets fly. We shall use this sequence of orders to go through the whole procedure for tacking in some details, as each of them corresponds to a precise set of actions. Of course, you are welcome to try your own variations on this procedure and these orders. There are certain captains we know who prefer four-letter words to these more traditional phrases, and who feel the need to whip obedience into their reluctant crew. Others prefer to do the whole thing themselves, performing all the actions in sequence.

'Ready about!'

This serves as a general alert to all those on board. Everyone drops their nonchalant pose and heads for a predetermined position. You check that all the sheets are free to run.
• The windward jib sheet should have some slack in it, and be lying free on the foredeck, so that the jib pulls it across the deck, clear of the numerous obstacles in its way. It is pointless, and can be positively harmful, to take a pre-emptive turn on the winch before tacking, because all this will mean is extra work for whoever is looking after the winch handle.
• Check the winch handle is where it should be, in easy reach.
• The leeward sheets should be ready to be released, and free to run easily. If there are a number of turns on the winch barrel, you might think it worthwhile to let off one or two turns so as to let the jib out more quickly when the time comes; but *do not lose hold of the jib*.

The only way to ensure the sheet is free is to leave it flaked on the cockpit floor, but not to coil it.
• If the leeward runner can be tightened before tacking without

ruining the shape of the mainsail, now is the time to do so. Otherwise, this needs to be done as you begin the tack, just when the mainsail starts to flap. The other runner is eased only after the tack.
• When the crew is ready, they confirm 'jib ready' or 'staysail ready'. The helm also should confirm their readiness for the manoeuvre, if it is actually being directed by someone else. If a mealtime is coming up, check in the galley to see that there will be no massive upset in there as a result of the change in angle of heel.

You still need to choose exactly the right moment, with the boat in tune with the rhythm of the swell rather than just at the beginning of a series of huge waves: there is nothing so destructive to a boat's momentum as a massive wave pushing it back onto the original tack a third of the way through. (This is particularly true in multi-hulls.) If the waves are really steep, the turn should be begun high on the back of a wave, just after the crest has passed, so that you are

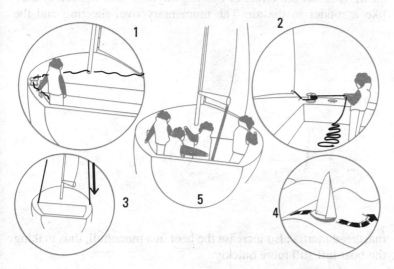

1. There is slack in the windward jibsheet.
2. The leeward sheet is flaked on the cockpit floor.
3. The leeward runner is tightened.
4. The big wave is safely out of the way.
5. Time to go about.

in the trough between waves as the nose of the boat passes through the wind, and the following wave then gives its impetus to the move off on the new tack.

'Lee-oh!'

This is the point of no return, the order to charge. It commits you, your boat, your crew, even the sea itself, to a course of action. When you say 'Lee-oh!', the boat has to make its turn, and every available means has to be used to this end. Let us look at who does what.

What does the helm do?

Any sudden tiller movement can stop the boat in its tracks: the rudder acts as a brake, and the boat is halted by the attempt to turn too tight a curve.

On the other hand, handling the tiller too timidly means that the boat luffs up too slowly, losing momentum all the way.

Theoretically, then, what the helm needs to do is to push the tiller gently at first, then increase the angle as the boat turns, accompanying the tack with the tiller movements. Often, however, the boat can tack just as well or even better if left to its own devices. The helm can actually push the tiller away, then leave it and turn to looking after the mainsheet. Whether or not you need to keep hold of the tiller, you can help the tack by pulling down on the mainsheet above the bottom block without letting it out of the cleat. This has the effect of making the boat luff: the sail is used like a rudder in the air. The momentary over-sheeting and the

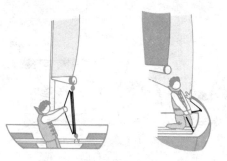

'Strength means knowing the right way to tackle the job.' – Turkish proverb.

masthead inertia also increase the heel in a monohull, thus making the boat luff still more quickly.

What does the crew do?

If necessary, one crew member can help trim the mainsail, or take this task over entirely. One tightens the jib, by pulling sideways on the sheet between winch and fairlead (with the sheet still cleated, of course).

As you luff up, the other crew members should move forward and to leeward, to accentuate the heel and make the boat luff faster. If the boat still will not tack after you have gone through all this, there is only one thing for it: get a new boat.

apparent wind over the jib

apparent wind over the mainsail

As the boat rotates, the apparent wind frees the jib and backs the main.

'Let go the sheets!'

This order is directed at the foredeck, or jib hand only. For the first time, the jibsheet is brought into play properly.

Do not release the jib too quickly

It is important to have the jib as tight as possible as the tack begins, since it should be drawing as long as possible as you luff up; and it will keep drawing for longer than you think. The rotation of the boat causes a particular effect, so that the jib is actually freed by the apparent wind as the boat turns, and the mainsail is backed. The main starts to flap early on (at which stage the mainsheet can be eased), but the jib will continue to fill until you are almost head to (true) wind, using the apparent wind caused by the turn. This extra

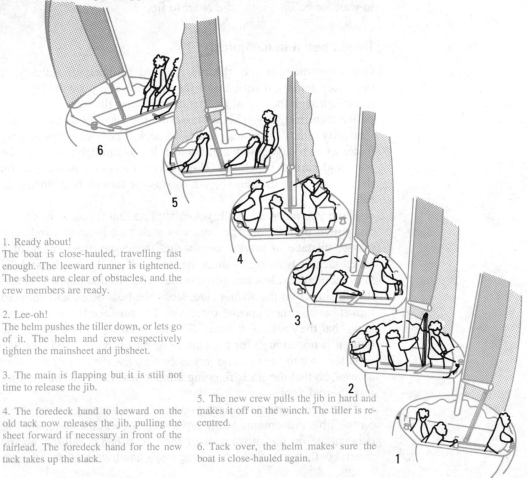

1. Ready about!
The boat is close-hauled, travelling fast enough. The leeward runner is tightened. The sheets are clear of obstacles, and the crew members are ready.

2. Lee-oh!
The helm pushes the tiller down, or lets go of it. The helm and crew respectively tighten the mainsheet and jibsheet.

3. The main is flapping but it is still not time to release the jib.

4. The foredeck hand to leeward on the old tack now releases the jib, pulling the sheet forward if necessary in front of the fairlead. The foredeck hand for the new tack takes up the slack.

5. The new crew pulls the jib in hard and makes it off on the winch. The tiller is re-centred.

6. Tack over, the helm makes sure the boat is close-hauled again.

Ready about: this jibsheet is turned once only around the winch, no more.

little bit of thrust can be precious indeed, quite apart from stopping the jib flapping, which would in itself slow you down severely. The jib should be released only once it has backed. This is the moment to wait for before giving the order to free it.

Do not pull it in too quickly

One crew member lets the old leeward jibsheet off quickly, if necessary pulling it forward of the fairlead. The jib will flap as it passes through the eye of the wind, so long as the new sheet is not pulled tight instantly. This ensures that the sheet pulls clear automatically of any obstacles on the foredeck. The boat keeps turning under its own momentum at this stage. It gets through the eye of the wind and starts to bear away. The mainsail fills of its own accord on the new tack and the helm begins to stop the turn by re-centring the tiller.

Have you made it? Well, yes, assuming that the new sheet was not pulled tight before the boat was well past head to wind. The classic mistake of novice crews, and the commonest cause of a failed tack, is wanting to sheet the jib in before it is ready, and the very moment its clew has got past the mast. All that happens is that the jib fills from the wrong side, stops the boat dead, and starts to turn it back in the opposite direction. The mistake lies in not realising that the fairlead is some distance from the centreline of the boat. It is not enough for the boat to be past head to wind: *the line from the tack to the fairlead has to be through the axis of the wind as well*, so that the jib is flapping almost next to the shroud before it is sheeted tight.

To spot the correct moment, you have to be keeping a careful eye on the jib's movement. Many novice crews, at this stage, start to concentrate on the movement of their own hands pulling on the sheet; but the time to start admiring one's handiwork is after the job is done, not during the manoeuvre. It is generally the case that one should be carrying out common manoeuvres without looking at one's own hands, but in the case of tacking this general rule becomes the first condition of success.

Do not pull it in too slowly

Once the jib has made it all the way across the boat, and it is time to sheet it in, do not waste any time about it! Once the jib fills with wind, it can become very difficult to control: ideally, you want to sheet it tight just at the instant where it cannot quite fill. After only a little practice, it becomes quite easy to spot this precise instant. If you miss it, and have to pull the jib in while it is already filling, you will need strong arms and a good winch! If you have no winch, you might even find it necessary to bear away so that the air flow becomes turbulent and there is less power in the jib. This might be a fairly crude solution to the problem, but it is certainly better than luffing up and slowing the boat down entirely.

Very large jibs

There are special difficulties associated with tacking with a large jib (and some boats can sail with their biggest jib up even in quite fresh weather). As the jib foot extends back well aft of the mast, it is sometimes hard for the clew to make it round the front of the mast as you carry out the tack. If the clew does not get caught on a shroud, it catches on a halyard or some eye on the front of the mast. You will find that you quite often need someone to give it an extra hand round.

Heavyweight crew member after going one round with the genoa clew.

The most efficient procedure is for the person who releases the old sheet to hold onto the clew and walk it all the way to the mast, keeping hold throughout. On a fresh day, this job should be entrusted to your best heavyweight crew member. Even so, a moment's inattention can leave the heavyweight looking like an amateur boxer after going ten rounds with a professional.

On a large yacht, having a crew member perched in the bow will make little difference to the boat's fore-and-aft trim. This allows you to rig a so-called tacking-line, which is strapped onto the jib at the centre of the foot, with a small sheet either side running forward to the tack. The foot is then pulled forward sufficiently far for the clew to make it round the mast. This frees up the jib hand in the cockpit to help get the jib sheeted in on the new tack: firstly, by helping pull the old jib sheet forward, then by pulling down on the clew until the jib is properly sheeted in and cleated.

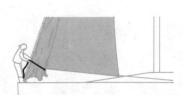

Correct use of the tacking-line.

Twin jibs

If your boat has twin jibs, you need to sheet in the jib first, then the staysail. One crew member can handle the pair of them in succession. If you do it the other way round, the jib clew flaps furiously against the back of the tight staysail, and both sails can wear out very quickly. What is more, sheeting the jib in actually makes it easier to sheet the staysail. The opposite does not work.

To conclude:

Whatever else happens, one thing should now be clear: that no crew member should be sitting idle while the boat tacks. The success of the whole manoeuvre depends largely on the co-ordinated activity of all on board: the tack can be ruined by an attack of excess zeal; or it can be just as seriously hindered by a laid-back attitude along the lines of 'What's the point in pulling the sheet in when we're just about to let it off again?'.

The stronger the wind, the more important it becomes to prepare for the tack calmly and spend time getting every condition right for success. It is far better to take your time and be certain you will make it (even if that means you sail very close to some obstacle while making sure you have enough boat speed), than to throw your boat around in a series of hasty and ill-executed attempts at a tack.

Making sure of the tack

There is one technique you can use to ensure a successful tack.

You can actually tack without touching the jib. Once you have made it through the eye of the wind, the jib fills from the other side and pushes the boat round. It is then released and sheeted in only after the tack is complete. Doing it this way, you will certainly not come out of the tack with much speed on, and you will have to bear away considerably to pick up speed again.

If you find yourself head to wind with the sails flapping, either because of a wrong move, or because you had insufficient way on to make the tack, you can still get round if you react swiftly.

If, for example, you are caught head to wind while you are trying to tack onto starboard:
– hold the jibsheet out against the wind, with the sail backed, on the starboard side of the boat;
– push the boom out to port, leaning down on it to limit the twist;
– reverse the tiller (ie push it over to port), as the water will flow over the back face of the rudder as the boat sails backwards.

The combined effect of the two sails and the rudder will push the boat round so it comes out on starboard tack.

Once the boat is well on its way on starboard tack, you can let go the boom, release the jib, pick up some speed on a beam reach and then come back onto a close-hauled course, sheeting the sails in progressively as you go.

On a catamaran, you need to release the sails the moment the boat starts to move backwards; otherwise the boat picks up too much speed as it travels backwards, and puts excessive strain on the rudders and fittings.

If you do not respond sufficiently quickly with this backward tack, the boat will fall back onto the original tack and you have no choice but to start again from the beginning. This means picking up some speed on a reach before doing anything, so you can ease the sheets and wait for the boat to come round onto the reach of its own accord. Alternatively, you can speed the manoeuvre up by going through the same

1. The boat runs out of steam, head to wind.
2. Jib and mainsail are held out deliberately backed, with the tiller reversed.
3. Jib and tiller are still reversed.
4. The boat bears away hard onto the new tack, and the jib is then released. The tiller returns to its usual position.
5. You pick up speed on the reach before beginning to luff back up onto the close-hauled course.

routine as above, but in the opposite direction: the jib then needs to be backed to port with the boom pushed out to starboard, and the tiller down to starboard. This will give you a quicker re-start.

If you absolutely cannot afford for the tack to fail, you can always give a push round with the paddle: this can give you just that little bit of extra force which makes all the difference and saves the tack. It might even save the boat ...

If things are really that difficult, it is tempting to use the motor to ensure that the tack succeeds. If you do take this step, remember that there *must not* be any sheets trailing in the water, and that the motor should not be run for extended periods while the boat is heeling. In other words, the motor should be on only briefly, and this might have the effect of running down the battery, since you cannot run it for long enough to re-charge after using the current for the starter.

Using the motor should therefore be an exception.

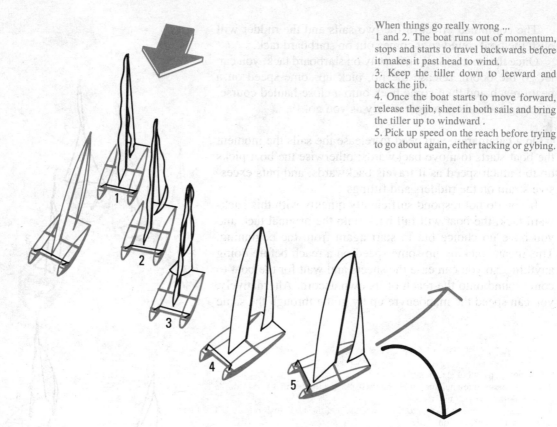

1 and 2. The boat runs out of momentum, stops and starts to travel backwards before it makes it past head to wind.
3. Keep the tiller down to leeward and back the jib.
4. Once the boat starts to move forward, release the jib, sheet in both sails and bring the tiller up to windward .
5. Pick up speed on the reach before trying to go about again, either tacking or gybing.

Handling characteristics

Not all boats handle similarly when they tack. The weight of the boat is more important than its size in this respect, as in many others. A light boat lacks momentum but can turn quickly; a heavier boat will keep its way on but turn slowly, no matter how small it is; and a multihull is light but turns slowly.

Some boats will tack more easily than others of the same weight, since factors such as hull shape and tuning also have an effect. In general, it is true to say that multihulls and boats of older designs are less willing to tack, whereas modern monohulls are much more obedient. Either way, you must get to know the reactions of your boat and not try to impose any unnatural rhythm onto your tacks.

As we conclude this section, what exceptions have we discovered to the rules covered at the beginning? We have spent this section describing techniques appropriate for relatively inexperienced crews and difficult weather conditions. In good weather, with a slick crew, a tack can be carried out flawlessly in less time than it takes to describe it. For instance, it is perfectly possible to tack from a point of sailing other than close-hauled if you can accompany the tiller movement with progressive changes to the sail trim. Just because your jib is allowed to flap too early does not necessarily mean your tack will fail, so long as the boat is travelling fast enough; and you can even carry the tack off with very little boat speed so long as you co-ordinate the tiller and sail movements perfectly.

This is no reason to get casual about it. One of the main perils with a monohull is that precisely because the boat does so much of the work itself, you tend to let the tack happen without paying much attention. *After a while, you actually forget how the tack works and you fail at precisely the point when you can least well afford to: in bad weather, when you have not left yourself enough of a safety margin to recover in case of failure.*

If this does happen to you, do not lose hope. You might not be able to tack round, but you may well be able to gybe.

Gybing

Gybing involves changing tacks with the wind behind you, but it does not necessarily mean changing direction. The mainsail will be completely eased for the run, and it rotates through almost 180° as it crosses the boat; the spinnaker also needs to change over to the new windward side, and the spinnaker pole needs to be moved on a monohull.

Gybing is probably the most delicate operation in all sailing as soon as there is more than a little wind. This is due in the first instance to the impossibility of 'turning the sails off'. When you tack, the mainsail flaps and loses all its power as you go through the manoeuvre; when you gybe, the mainsail is always drawing, even if you sheet it all the way in. (In fact, when that happens, the leech becomes the leading edge. Since it is not rigid, the leech flops from one side to the other, but the sail stays full either way.) The spinnaker never stops pulling; and in fact it goes through a phase in the gybe where it is pulling but not stabilised by the pole, so it really can develop a mind of its own!

The main problem in gybing is the risk of broaching. Although any downwind sailing carries this risk, the change in the boat's balance which occurs as the sails change sides aggravates it. Downwind, as we noted earlier, the boat is balancing along the top of a wall, and the available space between falling off either side is not great.

Unfortunately, the boat devotes most of its time to trying to fall off! The helm needs to remain highly vigilant: otherwise the boat heads off on a wild broach to windward, or it ends up sailing by the lee and you find yourself gybing accidentally, the boom sweeping across the deck, destroying everything in its path, knocking the boat into a broach on the new tack and tying the spinnaker (sensitive soul that it is) in knots around itself. This sort of gybe usually ends up breaking something.

There are certain precise conditions under which you can be sure a gybe will not end in this sort of disaster:
• *The boat should be sailing dead downwind*, and retain exactly the same heading throughout the manoeuvre.
• *Monohulls should be kept dead flat* throughout. The worst enemy is the rhythmical downwind roll known as the 'death roll'. This leaves you one-legged on top of your wall!
• Even more than usual, *sheets and controls must be kept clear*. In particular, the mainsheet, which might need to run free at any time, must be ready for an immediate release.
• Last but not least, *do not hurry*! Unlike a tack, the gybe does not suffer from being done at a snail's pace, and boat speed is unimportant. The manoeuvre itself does not necessarily mean that the boat is actually changing course, and you have some flexibility over the time you elect to take over it. All the same, whether you work out your gybe routine in minute detail or not, there should be one person on board co-ordinating the work, as the individual crew members are working fairly spread out, and someone is needed to retain an overall view of what is going on at any one time.

Just as for the tack, we shall now go through the essentials of gybing a one-, two- or three-hulled vessel in a fresh wind and moderately rough sea, since only in this case will really interesting problems crop up.

Bearing away to a dead run

Steering on a run is never easy: it is difficult to feel where the wind is; your tell-tales do not give a clear picture; and the boat barely changes its angle of heel as you alter course. Nevertheless, before gybing, you need to be sailing dead downwind. How can you go about achieving this?

The spinnaker can give you the best rough guide. Assuming it is correctly trimmed, it will have the pole guyed right out across the line of the boat and the clew not far from the forestay. If there is a

Down with tangled sheets!

fold to be seen on the luff, this shows that you are a good 15° above the dead run. If, instead, the spinnaker is a little floppy and seems to be in danger of collapsing, you are already sailing by the lee. In fact, this guide is at best rough: a real dead run is much more precise than this, and spotting it is largely a matter of practice: the helm's ears can sense the wind, just as the burgee can; and the direction of the waves and behaviour of the boat can give a good idea too.

You decide to gybe. Your mental check-list should ensure you do not forget any of those little things which cause great upsets:
– *have you eased both runners?* This should have been done as soon as you bore away below a beam reach;
– *is the kicking strap tight?* Doing this limits mainsail twist, thus also limits the boat's tendency to roll; it also ensures you do not make the famous boom-in-the-air 'Chinese gybe';
– *is the mainsheet traveller cleated centrally?* This should be done in case you need to be able to sheet the main in centrally as you gybe; and in any case, it is a simple matter of looking after your equipment to ensure that the traveller cannot shoot all the way across the boat at top speed following the sail;
– *have you let off the boom preventer?* Forgetting to do this is a more frequent cause of upsets than you would believe …

As all this checking is going on, the helm must also keep an eye on the boat's course to ensure that it stays on the dead run. Nothing must be allowed to obstruct your view of what is going on (including affectionate spouses, children or others sitting on your knee). Many people prefer to helm through the gybe while standing – though making allowance for the boom coming across – as this gives a good feel for the balance of the boat and can help you respond more quickly to the movements of the mainsail and the spinnaker.

At the same time, in a monohull, in waves, you have to be careful not to allow the 'death roll' to get started. A good way of stopping a death roll is to give the tiller a good hard shake to left and right. (Trying to steer against the roll directly seldom works, and often makes it worse.) We do not know exactly why this works, but it does seem to.

Now you can carry out your gybe. Every crew member should have a clearly defined job, and there are plenty of jobs to be done: both spinnaker sheets need to be handled, as does the mainsheet; and you probably want someone on the foredeck to look after the spinnaker pole if there is one rigged.

There are three phases to the operation:
– moving the pole from one side to the other;
– passing the mainsail across;

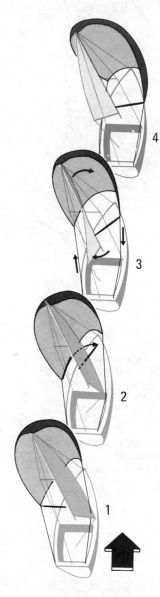

1. Position the boat on a dead run.
2. Pass the pole across.
3. Change sides for both sails.
4. Trim the sails.

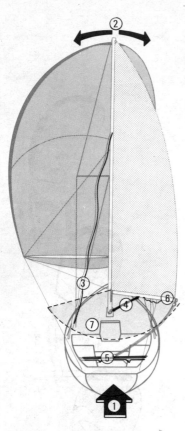

The helm's mental check-list:
1. Are we really on a dead run?
2. Has the boat stopped rolling?
3. Are the runners eased?
4. Is the kicking strap tight?
5. Is the traveller at the middle of the horse?
6. Did we remember to take the boom preventer off?
7. Is anyone standing in the way of the boom?

– passing the spinnaker across.

The final two phases have to occur at about the same time and they effectively constitute the gybe itself.

Moving the pole

The first thing to do is to make some space on the foredeck, so take down any big boy, reacher or spinnaker staysail you might have rigged; you also ease off the pole downhaul.

There are a number of different techniques for transferring the spinnaker pole over from one side to the other. Whichever method you use, it will work only if *the spinnaker will hold itself up and full without the pole, so long as the boat is held on its course dead downwind* throughout the manoeuvre. In fact, when you are on a dead run, the spinnaker pole's function is less to hold the tack out from the mast than to keep the sail in. (This is because the sail has a natural tendency, on a run, to come round to windward.) This should mean that you can completely unrig the pole if you want, without needing to hurry to rig it back up.

How you move the pole across depends primarily on the rig of the boat.

If there is no inner forestay, or the inner forestay is movable, the pole can be swivelled round on its mast fitting in a circle, passing between the forestay and the mast. This is a simple procedure: you unclip the guy from the outer end of the pole, turn the pole round and clip it onto the sheet. (Occasionally, you will have to ease the sheet a little in order to be able to catch it; if your boat is rigged with double sheets, you need to catch the slack one.)

If the inner forestay is fixed, the job becomes a little more complex. The pole is unclipped from the mast, pushed forward so that its inner end passes in front of the inner forestay, then brought back on the new side to bring the outer end past the forestay.

A twin-pole system can simplify matters considerably. As you start the gybe, the second pole is clipped to the leeward side of the mast and also to the sheet. (If you have double sheets, the pole can be rigged well in advance and attached to the slack sheet.) After the mainsail has been gybed, the new spinnaker guy is trimmed for the new tack and the first pole, which is now no longer in use, is removed.

One important detail should not be missed: *the moment a spinnaker pole is unclipped from the guy, the uphaul must also be eased. If this is not done, the pole will stick up in the air by the spinnaker, with a chance of making a hole in the sail.*

Whichever method you use, moving the spinnaker pole can become a tricky and often acrobatic job in a fresh wind and a swell. In these conditions you can see how huge are the forces acting on the spinnaker; trying to work against these forces is fruitless and exhausting. It is far better to use some cunning and ensure the forces are working with you, by watching the spinnaker's movements, waiting and then making your move at the instant when the force is pushing the sail where you want it to go. Once the sail is detached from the pole, it is free to move (and does, in the most disconcerting way). There can be no hard and fast rules about how to deal with this: the helm holds the key to the problem, by controlling the boat's course, so it is up to the helm to control the spinnaker for this difficult period.

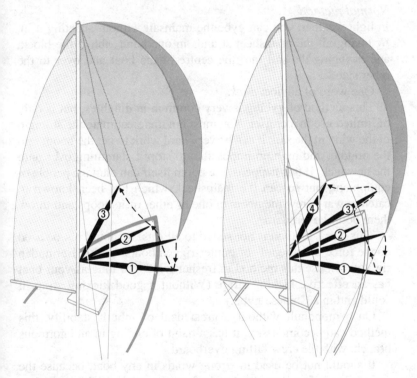

1. The uphaul is eased, then the pole unclipped.
2. The pole is passed under the forestay.
3. The pole is clipped back onto the sheet.

1. The uphaul is eased, then the pole unclipped.
2. The outer pole end is rested at the bottom of the forestay.
3. The pole is unclipped from the mast and the outer end passed over to the other side. The inner end is passed in front of the inner forestay.
4. The inner end is clipped to the mast and the outer end finally clipped onto the sheet.

If you cannot manage the situation perfectly, you should not feel obliged to gybe the spinnaker by putting the pole up with the sail still flying. It is perfectly possible to drop the spinnaker, gybe the main, put the pole up on the new tack and then hoist the spinnaker once more ...

Gybing the sails

Once the spinnaker pole is in place, to leeward, you can begin the gybe proper, which consists in passing both sails, the spinnaker and the mainsail, to the other side of the boat, ideally at the same time.

Gybing the mainsail

Normal method

In light weather, you can gybe the mainsail without sheeting it in, by taking all the mainsheet strands in one hand, above the block, and swinging the sail into the centre of the boat and over to the other side.

One word of advice: *duck!*

This method of gybing is very common in dinghies, but is only of limited use in a cruiser. You must not underestimate the strength of the wind in the sail: it can be very hard work to get the boom into the middle, and nigh on impossible to stop it slamming over onto the new tack. If this happens, the boom itself can damage people or equipment, but so can the mainsheet, which has been known to catch unwary crew members in one or other of its loops and throw them bodily overboard.

This quick method is not suited to all rigs. It should not be used above force 2 with gaff- or gunter-rigged boats. With a Bermudan rig you can use this method in fresher winds, so long as your boat has an effective kicking strap. (Without a good kicking strap, it could end in a Chinese gybe.)

On a monohull without a great deal of inbuilt stability, this method can become risky: it has a habit of ending in an enormous broach, with the crew falling overboard.

It should not be used in strong winds in any boat, because the mainsail transfers stress too suddenly to the rigging, with a substantial risk of breakage.

Traditional method

The traditional method of gybing is a better bet in fresh winds. Keeping the boat sailing straight downwind and well balanced, you begin to sheet in the mainsail. This gives the boat a tendency to luff

It is also possible to gybe the mainsail by pulling the kicking strap across – more easily done under spinnaker than jib.

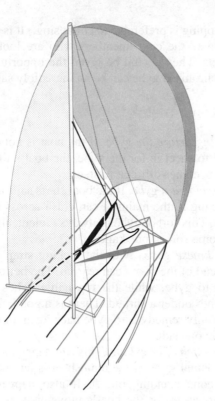

This boat has a complete set of sheets and poles for both tacks.

The guy for the next tack can be put in place well before the gybe. It is attached to the clew, run through its own pole end and back down to the block on the deck. When you gybe, you simply need to tighten the guy and adjust the pole height.

The sheet which is currently not in use stays in position and will only come under tension when the guy is eased, before the pole is lowered down to have its outer end placed on the deck.

In the diagram, the boat has just gybed, and the only job remaining is to lower the outer end of the port pole to deck level.

up, and you will need to offset this by pulling the tiller. Once the sail is entirely sheeted in, you need only a slight change in direction, and the mainsail will fill from the new side; you can then free the mainsheet very quickly, and again compensate for the boat's tendency to luff up on the new tack. To avoid the possibility of a broach, the sheet has to run all the way out to the figure-of-eight knot (which stops it in the bottom block before the boom hits the shroud).

... and gybing the spinnaker

Ideally, the spinnaker is gybed across at the same time as the mainsail, so that the two sails swop sides. This is the most sensitive moment in the manoeuvre. The mainsail must not be allowed to blanket the spinnaker at any stage, or the spinnaker will simply collapse around the forestay as it is starved of air. Similarly, the spinnaker needs to be transferred from one side of the boat to the other in a smooth movement: if you sheet in the new guy without letting off the sheet, the sail will stall and collapse; and if you let the sheet off without pulling the guy in sufficiently quickly, it will flap.

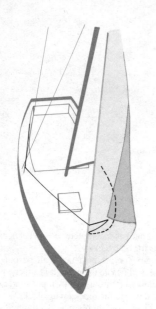

If you let the starboard sheet out completely without taking up the slack with the port sheet, there is a good chance that the jib will blow in front of the forestay and catch so that it is impossible to pull in.

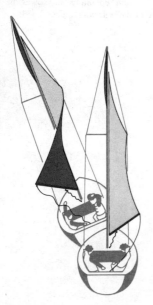

Chinese gybe.

(Flapping is preferable to collapsing.) It is therefore essential to co-ordinate the crew members who are looking after the spinnaker sheets. They should be given the opportunity to practise. A well-synchronised gybe can be an incredibly satisfying achievement.

Classic mistakes

Luffing before the gybe. If the boat is not on a dead run when you start to sheet in for the gybe, the boat will tend to luff up strongly and becomes difficult to steer.

Accidental gybe. If the boat starts sailing by the lee without your noticing it, the mainsail can crash across the boat quite unexpectedly. This sort of gybe is always violent, and often ends in a capsize or some sort of breakage.

Chinese gybe. With the kicking strap insufficiently tensioned, the end of the boom can rear up. The bottom half of the sail is then free to gybe, while the top half catches a spreader, or a batten catches under a shroud. There is a good chance of tearing the sail. The only remedy is to gybe back again quickly so as to get the sail all on one side.

Broach after gybing. This can happen after a planned gybe or an accidental gybe, if the mainsheet is jammed at all (for instance by someone standing on it). It also happens if the helm fails to compensate for the boat's movement, or simply if a large wave catches you unawares.

Gybing an asymmetric spinnaker

An asymmetric spinnaker is rigged like a genoa, in theory, with sheets to both sides from the single clew, and is carried on the reach. However, in racing fast boats, it can be necessary to gybe the asymmetric spinnaker as you round a mark, since the apparent wind can move round from 90° on one tack to 90° on the other. The only difficulty in gybing can arise if there is too narrow a gap between the forestay and the luff of the sail: the tack should be allowed to blow some way out as the sail is gybed, to allow all the cloth to pass through the gap.

Gybing after failing to tack

There are two circumstances in which you might decide to gybe when a tack would be the normal method of going about: either you have just failed to tack and you have not got enough space to leeward of your normal close-hauled course to try again; or you are certain that if you tried again you would fail anyway. The gybe is a sort of last resort on these cases, but it is better to use a last resort quickly than none at all …

If your boat has just failed to tack it will be stopped, facing across the wind, with the sails flogging. Even if you bore away

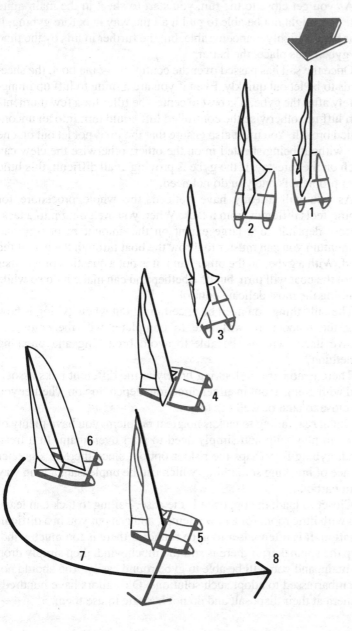

1. The boat runs out of momentum and stops.

2 and 3. You need to bear away as quickly as possible, so you back both jib and main, and the boat bears away and moves backwards.

4. At this point the jib is freed and the tiller reversed.

5. If the jib is left backed, at this stage the boat stops bearing away and the boat goes nowhere.

6. The boat picks up speed more quickly if you play the sheets to suit your direction.

7. You gybe quickly but not hastily.

8. Finally you are in a position to luff up on the new tack.

quickly from this position, say, by backing the jib, you can go no further without building up some speed first. The sails are therefore pulled in for the beam reach (the jib can happily be a little over-sheeted and the main still a little slack). As you bear away, you can let the sails out slowly in order to keep accelerating.

As you get close to the run, you start to sheet in the main quite fast. You might not be able to pull it all the way in before gybing, if your boat is highly manoeuvrable, but the further in it is by the time the gybe takes place, the better.

Once the sail has passed over the centreline of the boat, the sheet needs to be let out quickly. Even if you are aiming to luff up immediately after the gybe, it is best to centre the tiller for a few moments then luff up; otherwise the controlled luff could turn into an uncontrolled broach. You must also ensure that the jib is not let out on one side without being sheeted in on the other; otherwise the clew can catch on the forestay. If the gybe is proving at all difficult, this little extra problem is one you do not need.

As you will already have noticed, the whole procedure for gybing feels different from a tack. When you are going into a tack, success depends to a large extent on the amount of energy and momentum you can muster to throw the boat through the eye of the wind. With a gybe, on the other hand, it is not a question of whether or not the boat will turn, but of whether you can make it do so while retaining the most delicate control.

The only thing you need be uncertain about when gybing is how long the manoeuvre will take to complete: will the spinnaker behave itself; will we be able to avoid broaching and breaking something?

There is no harm in looking briefly at the different risks associated with going about in either direction, depending on whether you are close to land or well out to sea.

Out at sea, failing to tack is no great problem: you have plenty of space to play with and simply need to start over again. In a fresh wind, gybing is perhaps the riskier option, since there is a greater chance of breaking something, which can be unpleasant a long way from harbour.

Closer to land, the opposite is the case. Failing to tack can leave you with little room for a new attempt, and can put you in a difficult situation. It is often wiser to gybe round: if there is too much wind, drop the spinnaker; if there is still too much wind, then simply drop the main, and you will be able to gybe round easily. You should not be embarrassed to adopt such solutions. Old sailors have hundreds of them at their disposal, and do not hesitate to use them.

CHAPTER 3
Changing sail

We have already looked at some of the alterations to sail trim and shape which are necessary as a result of changes in the weather or the course to be sailed.

Altering the sails in the ways covered so far is an aspect of boat handling. You need to be able to carry out the various routines involved just as smoothly as any change of course. Some of the alterations mean you have to slow the boat down momentarily, such as when you change sails or take in a reef; others, such as hoisting the spinnaker, roller-reefing or unreefing the jib, should not slow you down at all. However, any of them can cause chaos aboard the boat if you fail to carry them out precisely and correctly.

In matters of changing sail, everything depends crucially on details. It is extraordinary how the smallest detail can cause the greatest bother if not attended to properly.

Changing sail usually involves handling cloth in conditions which can be fairly difficult. The fate of the sails hangs literally by a thread: you can lose a jib simply because you omitted to attach one of the hanks to the forestay; or you can tear the mainsail if you forget to attach a single reefing point.

Changing sail includes dropping and raising the sails, tightening them, sheeting and freeing them. Although every one of these operations is basically simple, they can all cause major problems if certain rules are not adhered to. Ignoring the rules leads to jammed pulleys, blocked cleats, and ultimately it can incapacitate the entire boat.

Most of this chapter is devoted to describing the operations involved with changing sails, but you should also read it as a sort of manual of sail care and sail use. We analyse in detail not only what you need to do to carry out a given operation, but also how to look after your sail wardrobe.

Whatever operation you are engaged in, there are a few principles which should be borne in mind:

1. You should aim to leave the boat minus its sail for the shortest time possible. Some crews, after a lot of practice, can change a jib

or take in a reef in under a minute, or break out the spinnaker in 10 seconds. One should not be over-hasty and run the risk of hoisting the jib upside down, turning the spinnaker into a fishing-net or tying a reefing point around a control line, but one should be brisk about the operation.

2. Whenever the sea is at all rough, every crew member should be clipped on with a safety harness. This is the only legitimate circumstance under which you can ignore the old dictum of 'one hand for you, one for the boat'. With the harness on, you can use both hands without fear of falling in.

3. The time and place for the operation should be consciously chosen, wherever possible. The boat loses power when it has less sail up than usual, particularly on the beat, and it slows down and starts to drift sideways. You should therefore ensure there is free water to leeward.

4. The operation should always be carried out in the same order, and every crew member must know the routine. The operation should be begun only when everyone is ready.

5. Remember that even simple operations become more difficult and more delicate, the stronger the wind is.

We shall now look in detail at some of the more widely used systems for changing sail. There is not space to look at the most up-to-date designs, which will in any case change annually and are often specific to one design of boat. We shall also limit ourselves to operations which can be carried out without specific tools and which can be used in emergency on any boat.

Clunk click ...

rather than splash!

The jib

As far as foresails are concerned, modern-day boats can be divided into two types:
– those which have several jibs, each of which serves a specific purpose: when you need to change the way the sail at the front of the boat works, you simply swop jibs;
– those which only have one, all-purpose foresail, which is roller-reefed to a greater or lesser extent to reduce the surface area.

Rigging of jibs

Jibs can be dropped or hoisted on any point of sailing, but it is easier off the wind for various reasons: the foredeck is then less cluttered with flapping sails and clews with murderous intent; there is no risk of the halyard catching in the spreaders; and it is less hard work pulling the jib up tight and sheeting it in. Finally, if there is a bit of a swell, the foredeck hand is less likely to get soaked than on a beat ...

For all these reasons, if you face a long downwind leg with a jib which you know is too large for the beat which follows, you are well advised to swop jibs before luffing up onto the beat. This advice is given as part of our energy-conservation campaign.

How you change jibs depends on how the boat is equipped.

Some cruisers are equipped with two of everything: forestay, halyard and sheets. This is excessive. If we are being selective:
– a double forestay is utterly indefensible: it is impractical, since the jib hanks always get caught between the stays; and it is even theoretically problematic, since the two forestays can never be maintained at the same tension;
– two tack attachments are worth having, since they can be arranged simply, cheaply and they ease the changeover noticeably. It would be silly not to use this device;
– using two halyards is acceptable, though there can be a risk of confusion;
– two pairs of sheets can be useful.

In reality, the more equipment you have, the less quickly you can sort things out. A tidy foredeck is the best guarantee you can have that any operation will be carried out quickly and efficiently.

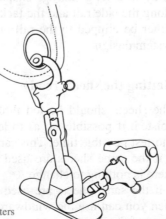

Having two tack attachments simplifies matters considerably.

Changing jibs

Getting the new jib ready

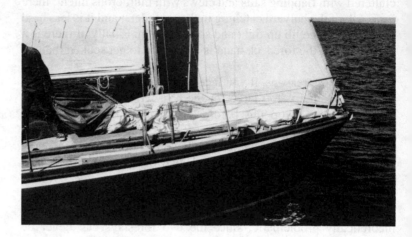

Know how to take the jib out of its bag.

Small jibs, up to 20 or 30sq m are normally stowed in a bag, with the tack at the top. The bag is taken onto the deck and the tack attached to the stem fitting. (If you have only a single fixing point for the jib tack, then you clip the bottom hank to the forestay.) The bag is then brought back into the cockpit, so that the jib is fed out along the foredeck, saving time and energy.

The next step is to clip all the hanks onto the forestay at the bottom, and unclip any you can reach of the current jib hanks.

If the jib is larger than this, it will in any case have been rolled away in a long sausage-shaped 'banana bag'. The bag is placed along the side rail and the tack of the sail is attached. The bag can either be clipped to the rail or removed below, depending on the system design.

Getting the sheets ready

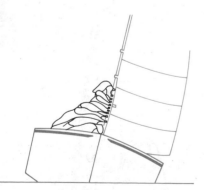

Unclip any hanks you can reach of the jib in place. This gives you more space for arranging the new jib.

The sheets should be led through the fairleads before the jib is hoisted, if possible, so as to leave the boat underpowered for the shortest possible time. This can be done in a number of ways:
– if the same sheets are used for each jib, in the same fairleads, there is nothing to change;
– if the same sheets are used but led through different fairleads, then you can use the windward sheet of the old jib as the leeward sheet of the new one;

– if the new jib has its own sheets attached, then they can be put in place immediately.

If the fairleads have no room for two sheets at the same time, you simply have to wait and put the sheets in position all at the same time.

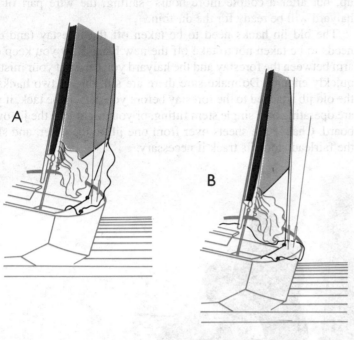

A   B

A. The windward sheet is taken from the old jib to be used as the leeward sheet on the new one.
B. The new jibsheets are put in place before the old jib is lowered.

Lowering the jib

One crew member lets the jib down, using the halyard which is normally made off to port. If you are sailing downwind, it is best to cleat the sheet in, to prevent the jib falling in the water. If you are on a beat, you might have to ease the sheet a little so that the hanks slide down the forestay more easily.

The foredeck hand should try to pull the jib down as quickly as possible to limit the amount of time it spends flogging. Stopping it from falling in the water is useful but of secondary importance: the sail will not dissolve in salt water.

Changing the three corners

As soon as the jib is down, the halyard end must be cleated. The heads of the two sails should then be brought together and the halyard shackle transferred from one to the other.

You need to pay attention at this stage. If it takes any time at all to transfer the halyard from one jib head to the other, the boat's natural movement will be enough to wrap the halyard round the forestay. You will not always notice this happening, especially at night. The infuriating thing is that you can usually still pull the jib up, but after a couple more hours' sailing, the wire part of the halyard will be ready for the dustbin.

The old jib hanks need to be taken off the forestay (and care needs to be taken not to take off the new hanks!). If you keep one arm between the forestay and the halyard you can spot your mistake quickly enough. Do make sure there are still one or two hanks of the old jib attached to the forestay before you detach the tack, if you are operating on a single stem fitting, or you might lose the jib overboard. Change the sheets over from one jib to the other, and slide the fairlead along its track if necessary.

With one jib lowered on top of the other, there will be a succession of hanks to unclip, which all look the same. If you pass one arm through between the forestay and the halyard, you will notice as soon as all the old hanks are undone.

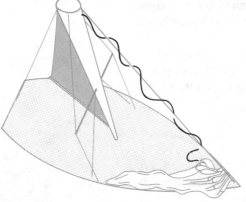

If you transferred the halyard from one jib to the other correctly, any apparent tangles between halyard and forestay are unimportant, as they will unwrap themselves automatically as the jib is hoisted.

Old sailors' tricks

Changing jibs is a wet, tiring and occasionally dangerous job. You can make your life simpler as follows:

On the beat
Lower the jib just as the tack commences (or just as soon as you are sure the boat has passed head to wind, if there is a fresh breeze, to avoid any risk of failing the tack), and hoist the new jib after the tack.

An alternative method is to sit with the wind on the beam and the mainsail just tight enough to avoid flogging. This makes the foredeck rather drier and safer, at the expense of losing some ground to windward.

Downwind
The new jib can be positioned on the windward side, the old one lowered and then the boat gybed. The new jib is hoisted after the gybe.

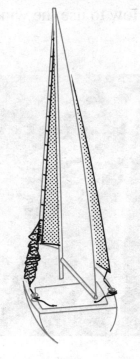

The new jib is set up to windward. The old jib is lowered as you tack, and the new one hoisted once you are on the new tack.

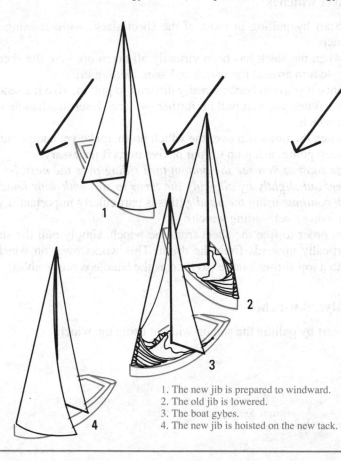

1. The new jib is prepared to windward.
2. The old jib is lowered.
3. The boat gybes.
4. The new jib is hoisted on the new tack.

How to use the winch correctly

Fouling a sheet on the winch. This is a so-called riding turn, with the bottom turn riding up over the next, so that the sheet is jammed and cannot be eased.

Freeing a riding turn. The only problem is to ensure the free end of the sheet does not catch in the winch drum. Hold the sheet out with your left hand then pull straight upwards with your right, with no attempt at any rotational movement.

Almost all winches turn clockwise. (If your winch turns anticlockwise, the ratchet has been set up wrongly.) The sheet which needs to be winched in is therefore fed onto the winch in the same direction.

Theoretically, the more turns you make on the winch, the less effort is needed on the rope end in your hand. It makes no difference to the winch handle, however. If there are too many turns, they can jam, with the bottom turn riding up on the others such that you cannot free off the top turn.

If this happens, it can cause serious accidents, so you should approach the use of any winch with this in mind. Do not use more turns than you need.

Sheet winches

– Start by pulling in most of the sheet slack, without using the winch;
– when the slack has been virtually all taken up, give the sheet a single turn around the winch and keep hauling in;
– once it starts to become really difficult to pull in, give it a second turn. When you can pull no further by hand, insert the handle into the winch;
– when the turns slip over the winch drum, make yet another turn;
– keep going, using up to four or five turns if necessary;
– *as soon as you see the bottom turn riding over the next, let the sheet out slightly by allowing the turns to slip with your hand as you continue using the handle* (this is particularly important if you are using a self-tailing winch);
– in order to free the sheet from the winch, simply pull the sheet vertically upwards from the drum. This works even on winches with a top-fitting handle (so long as the handle is removable).

Halyard winches

– Start by pulling the sail up without using the winch;

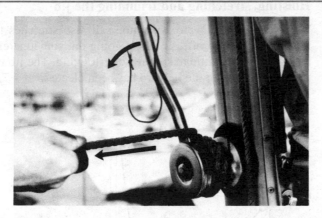

Freeing a halyard winch. This winch needs to be freed with a horizontal tug. The fixed winch handle does not get in the way, as it can turn.

– as the sail reaches the top, put a few turns on the winch, then continue adding turns (as for the sheet winch) as the resistance increases;
– the sail can be at the top between ratchet clicks: you therefore continue turning the handle without pulling on the halyard tail, thus allowing the next ratchet tooth to engage;
– a halyard winch is freed the same way as a sheet winch.

Important precaution

Do not touch a sheet which is running directly between the winch and the sail. Any slight slackening of the sheet as it comes onto the winch drum encourages riding turns. You might not even notice this happen (especially at night), and you can then find yourself suddenly unable to free the sheet off when you need to tack or make some other sudden change of course.

Bringing the halyard into the cockpit

These days, most halyards are led back into the cockpit. Pulling the sail up from inside the cockpit demands a lot of strength, and the problem is generally dealt with by using two people. One hoists the sail, standing at the bottom of the mast, while the other takes up the slack and then winches from inside the cockpit.

    You can end up with a real bird's nest of halyards in the cockpit. To avoid this, the halyard should be stowed neatly in a small bag which is hung up by the companionway or put in a safe place on the floor.

This is the only way of getting a really good purchase on the jib. Do not worry about standing close to the edge while you help pull the jib in: so long as you are pulling on the sheet, you are holding onto the boat!

Hoisting, stretching and trimming the jib

The crew member who hoists the sail also stretches the luff and makes the halyard off. As this is going on, someone else needs to sheet the jib in a little to stop it from flogging. The jib is sheeted in properly only after the halyard has been cleated.

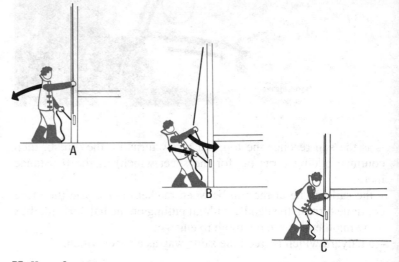

Sweating the jib up

Anyone can get the halyard as tight as a harp string, but not everyone succeeds in stretching the luff correctly. Once the sail is up to the top, the halyard should be led under the cleat and held steady in your left hand. You can then steady yourself against the mast foot and take hold of the halyard at shoulder height with your right hand, leaning back to tension it. The halyard can then be pulled down the mast with a strong downward tug, while you take up the slack with your left hand.

Hollow forestays

The same procedure is used when the jib luff runs inside a headfoil forestay, except that there are no hanks. The jib is slightly harder to drop and hoist because there is greater friction, and it is not always easy to guide the luff rope into the headfoil. The only real problem is the halyard: if you wrap the halyard around the forestay at any stage, the track can become bent. If this happens, either it becomes impossible to pull the jib up any further, or – which is worse – the jib goes up easily enough but will not come down.

If you have a headfoil with twin grooves, you can hoist one jib before dropping the other. This operation can be difficult, because the two sails rub against each other as well as in the track. It is really only possible in light winds.

Rolling the jib

This operation is as simple as it sounds. The jib should already be flat, as you tightened the luff when the wind freshened, so you simply need to pull in the roller drum, letting the sheet out as necessary while you are reefing (not too fast, or the sail will flap), then sheeting in again once you have reduced the sail area to the desired extent.

Even with a jib which is rigged on a roller-reefing attachment, the all-purpose jib is never quite that. Even the most carefully made all-purpose jib will be either a little too flat for light airs or too full for heavy winds. As a compromise, too flat is preferable to too full.

Raising the storm jib

The storm jib is an absolute must on board. You need to give particular attention to arrangements for its use.

A storm jib designed to be used with a headfoil is pointless. The purpose of having such a sail on board is for when your normal system is broken or unusable, in an emergency.

The storm jib should not be hoisted using only its own luff wire. You should therefore have a wire halyard, preferably one which is always in place and shackled down the front of the mast for when it is needed. If you have not got such a wire, then a normal halyard can be used, but the storm jib must have a steel or Kevlar wire down the luff sleeve if it is to be hoisted independently of the forestay.

It is worth having a second jib halyard, especially if the main jib uses roller gear: if something goes wrong with roller gear, it can be very difficult to recover the halyard out at sea.

Tidying up

Lead the windward sheet through its fairlead if you have space.

Stow the jib away.

Small jibs are stowed in a bag, according to a precise routine:

Sails should be furled using a loop with a bowline on one end, which is then tightened and made fast with a half-hitch.

When you have lowered a large jib, it is best furled in a sausage before you take it off the forestay.

first the head is put away, then the sail is fed into the bag so that the tack is uppermost, this being the part to which you will need most immediate access next time you use the sail.

Large jibs are furled in a sausage shape along the side deck then put away (either in their banana bag or straight down the fore hatch) clew first, so that you have immediate access to the tack next time you want to use the sail.

The mainsail

Mainsails are generally less easy to handle than jibs. You cannot lower the sail or hoist it on every point of sailing; keeping the boat on course with no mainsail is a tricky business; and as the weather deteriorates and you need to reduce the amount of sail area up, you are more likely to roll the sail or reef it than to swop it over. (Generally, you will only have two mainsails anyway.)

Although changing or reducing the mainsail is not complicated, there is a right way to do it, and we shall study that in detail once we have dealt with some general principles.

Hoisting and lowering the mainsail

The wind must be forward of the beam. In order for the sail to slide along the mast track, it needs to be more or less along the centreline of the boat, not resting on the rigging. This is generally possible only somewhere between a close reach and head to wind. Even with the wind on the beam the slides are under too much sideways pressure and will jam in the mast track.

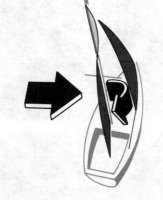

If necessary, the main can be dropped with the wind on the beam. You need to over-sheet the jib so it backwinds the main, taking it inboard of the rigging and making it easier to pull down. The mainsail can be hoisted using the same technique.

The jib can be very handy as the mainsail is being raised or lowered: if it is slightly over-sheeted, it can backwind the main, thus allowing you to keep working even with the wind on the beam, even if the topmast shrouds are fixed to the deck aft of the mast.

The boom must be supported, at least during two stages of the operation: when you are finishing hoisting the sail or beginning to let it down. If you do not support the boom, the sail stretches the luff rope at an angle and pulls it out either at the track throat or at the last slide. This is a good way of stretching your sail permanently out of shape, tearing it, losing a slide or bending the track.

The usual way of supporting the boom is to let the kicking strap off and use the topping lift. Smaller boats will not have a topping lift, so a member of the crew supports the boom by hand. In order for that person to reach the boom, it needs to be central, so the boat

A mainsail ages quickly with this sort of treatment.

has to be close-hauled. *The person supporting the boom needs to be to leeward and fairly well forward*: if they stay too far aft or in the middle of the boat, they will not have a good angle of purchase on the boom.

Ways of reducing sail

There are two alternative systems for reducing the mainsail area: reefs and rollers.

• Reefing is the traditional way of reducing the area of the mainsail. The reefing points run in lines along the sail, with bands hanging down either side from reinforcing patches. When you need to reduce the sail area, you fold that part of the sail between the boom and the reefing points over on itself, tying the reefing bands around and under the boom.

The boom can never be supported too much! This is the best method to make sure that the luff rope slides properly up or down the mast track. In order to be able to get a good grip on the boom without risking falling in the water, you need to stand well forward and to leeward.

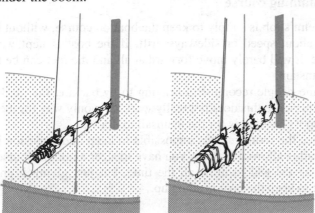

When you need to tie part of the sail along the side of the boom because it will not all fit on top, you must be careful not to wear the sail out against the shrouds on a run.

Reefing has one major shortcoming: since there are only a few rows of reefing points, you always have to take away a large and invariable part of the sail area. On occasions, this will be more than you want to reduce. It is easy, however, to keep the sail a good shape so that it continues to set properly. The operation is simple and involves no machinery, so it cannot break down.

• Roller reefing involves rolling the sail inside the mast or boom in much the same way as a jib roller works.

Roller reefing appears quick and easy, and it is fair to say that it does have certain advantages over traditional slab reefing: you can reduce sail by exactly the desired amount, and you do not have to be close-hauled to carry the operation out. However, mainsail rollers are a relatively recent invention, and it is early yet to judge the complete balance of their advantages and disadvantages. Certainly, if you are equipped with roller gear, there is no harm in having reefing points as well, as a second line of defence!

The oldest method of reducing sail was to roll it around the boom. This method has died out these days because it makes it difficult to keep the sail in shape, and involves expensive items of extra gear.

Reefing

You need to arrange your working conditions so as to ensure a quick and efficient reefing procedure.

The boom needs to be well supported and the sail must not be drawing. The best course to sail is therefore a close reach or close fetch.

Maintaining course

The helm's job is simply to keep the boat on course, without bothering about speed or sideways drift. If the boat is kept well on course, it will barely move forward at all and the reef can be taken in an instant.

Some people recommend heaving to by backing the jib, but in our experience this does not really work. The only way for the boat to keep its heading is for the mainsail to draw …

Since the foot becomes impossible to keep under tension if the mainsail is allowed to draw, you have to steer a middle course, not allowing the sail to draw all the time, but just giving it enough power to keep the boat heading up.

Necessary precautions

The sail must not be allowed to flap hard or for long. Flapping makes it lose its leech tension, and can even cause the battens to break and tear the cloth. This is one reason to get the reef over with quickly. (The sail will flap harder as you are carrying out the reef if it is under too much tension, so you should ensure you support it using the topping lift.)

It is not usually necessary to take the bottom batten out, unless through some design fault its pocket is at the same height as the reefing points.

Keeping the sail shape

A sail which sets well despite the reduction in area is a major advantage to anyone trying to sail in heavy winds. As we noted above, keeping a good shape to the sail is one of the major advantages of reefing; and it is possible to get a perfectly shaped sail if you adjust the tack, clew and reefing bands properly.

The tack should be as close as possible to the gooseneck. This is usually accomplished by a simple hook.

The clew should be held down on the boom if possible. It should not be pulled too far aft, however. The important issue is to control the foot tension: if there is too much, the sail creases along the foot at the reefing points; and if there is too little, the reefing points themselves carry too much of the load and might tear. The foot tension is what controls the shape of the sail, so you need to find a good medium setting.

The clew is usually held on a pendant, which will be designed so that the reefing operation works quickly and easily, and also so that you can control the foot tension precisely.

The reefing points hold down the folded part of the sail. Ideally, they should pass between the foot rope and the boom, if the foot is on a slide track, as this gives a better 'grip' on the sail. If the foot is fed along an internal groove, they will have to be knotted around under the boom. This allows the sailcloth to slip around, and can easily rub against the shroud when you are on a run. (This is another good reason for tying that figure-of-eight knot in the mainsheet just below the bottom block, so that the sail and boom do not come into contact with the shrouds.)

Most modern sails have a high aspect ratio, and a relatively short boom. The function of the reefing points is thus largely one of keeping the sail tidy. It is possible to sail without knotting the points, even if the aesthetic and aerodynamic effect is unfortunate.

With a relatively long boom, the reefing points help to keep the sail flat (though they should not be used on their own to flatten a sail with a slack foot).

Taking in a reef

There are many reefing systems. Most of them work very well. The method we shall describe here uses the most widespread system, with hooks at the tack and reefing pendants at the clew.

The tack hook

The hook is very simple to use: it might need to be put in place, but the only real mistake one can make would be to fit the sail cringle over it the wrong way round.

The clew pendants

The reefing pendant is run along inside the boom, with a figure-of-eight knot at the end. The aft end of the pendant is fed through the clew reefing cringle and fastened to an eye on a track at the end of the boom. (If there is no eye, the pendant is led under the boom and tied to itself with a bowline between the cringle and the end of the boom.) This operation should be completed before you let the sail down, so that you do not have to go to the end of the boom again. If you feed the pendant through later, the reef will take longer and be more difficult.

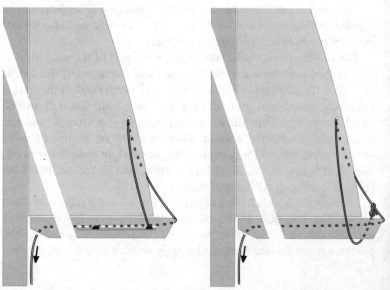

Two systems for the clew reefing point.

Letting the sail down

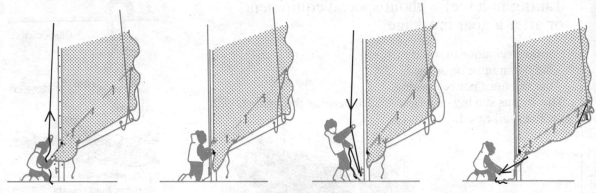

Come onto a close reach or close fetch. Let out the mainsail and the kicking strap and support the boom at about 30° above the horizontal. Let the halyard down just enough to be able to fit the tack cringle over the hook.

> *If the clew pendant is not put in place before you let the sail down,* the procedure takes longer, and observes the following order:
> – ease the mainsheet and kicking strap;
> – support the boom slightly;
> – drop the sail by two reefs;
> – sheet in and cleat the mainsheet;
> – feed the pendant through;
> – ease the sheet;
> – support the boom at 30°;
> – fit the tack cringle over the hook.

Taking in the reef

– Hook the tack cringle on at the gooseneck, ensuring that the sail is not twisted;
– pull the sail back up and cleat the halyard;
– pull the clew pendant tight and adjust the foot tension. This can only be done if the boom is thoroughly supported. You have to choose your moment for tightening the pendant, and maybe help the pendant into place at the boom end as you are tightening it.

Starting off again

Ease the topping lift, pull the sail in, tighten the kicking strap and start back on your course.

Ready to take in the reef …
1. Take the strain on the topping lift. Let down as much mainsail as needed, taking out any slides from the mast track if necessary.
2. Fit the tack cringle over the hook the right way round.
3. Sweat the mainsail back up.
4. Tighten the clew reef pendant, then wait for the right moment to finish off with the reefing points.
Once this is over, you just let off the topping lift, sheet in, tighten the kicker and set off again.

> If a luff slide is very close to the tack reef cringle, it should be taken out of the track. It is no problem if that one slide remains outside the track when you hoist the sail back up again fully.

Taking in a reef without special equipment, or after a gear breakage

For this technique to work:
– the boom must be inboard;
– the sail must not be drawing.
This means staying on a close-hauled heading throughout, with the mainsail eased.

Clunk click …

rather than splash!

If the boom is properly supported, you can lean on it while working.

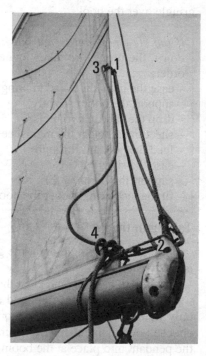

• The jib is sheeted tight and cleated.
• The helm keeps the boat on a close-hauled heading.
• The mainsail has been lowered a long way.
• The tack is tied down.
• The foot is tensioned.
• The mainsail is hoisted again.

Jury-rigged clew reefing pendant ready for use.
1. Attached to the reefing cringle.
2. Passing through the boom end.
3. Back through the reefing cringle.
4. Made off at the clew.

The procedure is:
– to come up to close-hauled;
– to lower the main a long way, as if for two reefs;
– to cleat the mainsheet or tighten the topping lift so as to immobilise the boom (to make sure it does not knock anyone overboard);
– to fasten the tack down;
– to tension the foot;
– to tighten the topping lift and pull the sail back up.
The boat is then ready to sail. You just need to sheet in and take up your original course again.

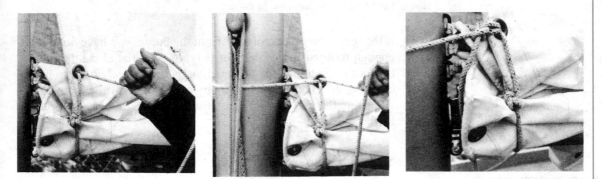

Jury-rigged tack arrangement.
A. Tie the pendant onto the tack reef cringle with a bowline, pass it under the boom then back through the cringle to bring the tack tightly down ...
B. ... then around the mast to bring the tack well forward, then back through the cringle again ...
C. ... and finish off with two half-hitches tied on the rope which goes around the mast.
You need to ensure that the rope does not drop down between the boom and the mast. If it jams in the gooseneck it will wear through very quickly.

Jury-rigged clew arrangement.
A. Tighten the foot.
B. Make a turn around the boom and pass the cord back through the cringle without losing the foot tension.
C. Finish with a single slip half-hitch around the rope, aft of the turn under the boom. Tighten the half-hitch by the cringle.

Checking the sail

Foot too tight: you are ruining the sail cloth.

Foot not tight enough, reefing points too tight: there is a chance of tearing the sail.

Just right.

If the reef curves markedly out from the boom, you have not put on enough foot tension. If the reef is lying dead flat along the boom, the foot is too tight. A happy medium is for the reefed sail to bulge out from the boom at the middle by about 3–5% of the foot length. Adjusting the foot tension is relatively simple, though you need to let the sheet off while you do so.

Stretching the sail

Bring the boat onto a close-hauled course so that all the foot of the sail is within reach. All the bottom part of the sail which will not be used should be pulled down from the windward side and rolled into itself tightly. Tie the reefing points in a bow.

If you need to sail a course other than a beat, the reefing points should be left untied for the time being. This is not too inconvenient.

The only thing left to do is to tighten the kicking strap.

Although the operation may appear long, as described above, it can be carried out with a practised crew so as to leave you without the mainsail for little more than half a minute, during which time the boat will not have moved far at all.

If you need to take your time about taking in the reef (for instance when the crew is tired) then you can simply drop the whole sail while doing it. It has to be said that there are few advantages to doing this unless the boat is sailing a course very far off the wind and there is little chance of the boat rolling dangerously in the swell. If you do drop the main, you should take particular care to ensure all the reefing points used are in the same row; it is also very easy to tie the mainsheet, the guard rails, the lifebelt and any other nearby pieces of rope in with the reefing bands.

One quick tug and the reef is shaken out.

One final detail: if the breeze has really freshened very suddenly, you may need to take in a double reef in one go. If you have sufficient time (and sufficient water to leeward), it is actually better to take in the first reef and then the second, rather than going straight for the second. Otherwise, when the wind moderates again, you will have to let go of everything in order to take in the first reef then.

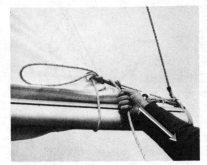

Shaking out a reef

This is a simple and quick operation. There are a few necessary precautions, the most important of which is making sure that you have first untied all the reefing points. One crew member carries the job out, and another must follow, checking everything is free. No one should resent having their work checked in this manner: it is so easy and so disastrous to miss one, that the whole boat and crew might suffer to save the pride of one person.

The reef is shaken out on a beat. The rest of the operation consists of:
– letting off the kicking strap;
– supporting the boom;
– letting off the clew pendant; unhooking the tack cringle;
– feeding the luff rope or slides into the mast track;
– hauling the sail up and cleating the halyard, tightening the kicking strap and setting off again;
– stowing any loose reefing gear.

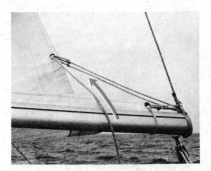

Unlucky! This can easily happen.

If you have no topping lift, you must remember to support the boom at the moment you release the clew pendant; otherwise the boom will crash onto the deck.

Changing mainsails

At sea

This is a long operation which can take 10–20 minutes in fresh winds, even with a modest-sized sail.

The boat needs to be close-hauled for dropping and hauling the sail up; but once the main is lying on the deck, there is no need to prevent the boat bearing away naturally.

The main problem in this operation is to get a clear view of what is going on. You should only have one sail on the deck at a time, and the change sail should be correctly furled so that it is easily slipped onto the boom without needing to be unfolded.

A mainsail really needs to be flaked on top of the boom with the foot straight and the luff rope folded in concertina fashion down to it. It is not possible to make a good job of this afloat: it needs to be done on land, where you can prevent the wind blowing the sail about.

Afloat, then, you need a simple short-cut. You fold the foot up to about half the height of the first reef to make it into a pocket, then drop the rest of the sail into the pocket in as regular a manner as you can manage, taking the battens out as you flake the sail. Close the pocket around the sail and tie it together.

In port

In port, when you want to leave the sail along the boom, you can make it into a pocket in the same manner and flake the top of the sail in, leaving the battens in place and any slides still in the mast

Furling the mainsail:
– make a pocket;
– flake the sail;
– roll the sail into itself;
– pack and tie tightly.

track. It is vital that the sail is packed tightly so it does not rub and wear itself out. The halyard should also be tight (though not pulling the sail up), so it needs to be made off onto an appropriate fitting on the mast or elsewhere, or at least hooked on somewhere if you do leave it shackled to the sail head.

The furled sail can be tied up either with a series of independent sail ties, with shock-cords or in a chain knot using a few of the reefing pendants. There are two methods which cannot be recommended: using the mainsheet means that you cannot change the position of the boom without undoing the whole lot; and using a double chain knot means that the ties will become slack as time goes on.

The spinnaker

The spinnaker (or 'kite', to the initiated), started life as a racing sail, and this racing pedigree is apparent in the way it is used even in cruising yachts. It is a minor aristocrat among sails, and needs to be pampered and attended to by its own accessories; nor can it stand waiting around at anything less than full power once it is up. Sailors of little faith speak of their spinnakers as being contrary, whereas in reality they are just spirited, like highly strung racehorses. Certainly their retainers can get a nasty shock at the ease with which the aristocratic sail turns ill-tempered.

We have already studied the handling of the spinnaker once it is up, and looked at how to gybe it. However, hoisting and lowering the spinnaker are subjects worthy of study in their own right, as these stages (at least initially) are among the most problematic aspects of spinnaker handling.

The sail

Early racing spinnakers looked rather like two staysails sewn together at the luff. Over the years, the sail has become fuller and the edges more rounded, so that what we have nowadays is like a rather bulbous isosceles triangle which is vertically symmetrical.

The top corner of the sail (which can make any angle up to 180°) is the head. The two bottom corners are known alternately as the tack and clew, depending on whether they are to windward or to leeward. They make an angle of around 135°. The windward edge of the sail is the luff and the leeward edge the leech; the bottom edge is known as the foot.

Spinnakers come in all shapes and sizes. They are made of more or less light cloths, depending on the wind strength for which they are designed. A reaching spinnaker can be carried even on quite a close reach, and has to be flatter than a running spinnaker. In the same way, cruising spinnakers tend to be flatter and heavier than racing spinnakers.

The equipment

Spinnaker equipment consists essentially of:
• the halyard, led through a block or pulley above the forestay. The bottom end of the halyard is usually made off in the cockpit or at the port side of the mast foot, like the jib halyard, though aft of this to avoid mix-ups;

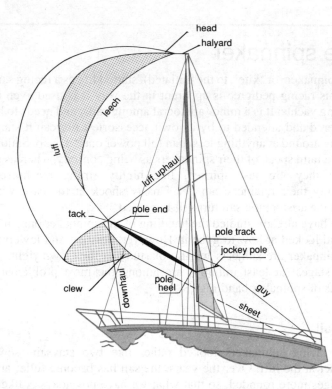

head
halyard
leech
luff
luff uphaul
tack
pole end
pole track
jockey pole
clew
downhaul
pole heel
guy
sheet

Spinnaker equipment.

• two ropes (called collectively sheets), one on either of the bottom corners, for trimming and directing the spinnaker; like the corners themselves, the ropes change name depending on whether they are to windward (the guy) or to leeward (the sheet). Both are led aft to fairleads well back along the boat and close to the outside. They need winches for controlling them, and should be at least twice as long as the boat itself.

Some boats use double sheets on both sides;
• a pole, which holds the tack out from the mast; the tip of the pole which is next to the mast may be called the heel, while the other is just known as the end. Multihulls are wide enough not to need a pole. On small boats, the ends of the pole are usually identical, so either end can be used as the heel; on larger boats the ends tend to be different, and there will usually be a track on the front of the mast so that the inboard end can be set at different heights;
• an uphaul, which supports the pole and allows you to raise the outer end. This will be fixed either in the middle of the pole (on small boats) or at the outer end (on larger boats);
• a downhaul, which prevents the outboard end lifting. On small boats, the downhaul goes from the middle of the pole to the mast foot, so the pole can be directed without changing

the downhaul setting. On larger boats, the downhaul goes from the end of the pole to the bow; any change in the direction of the pole thus means that you have also to alter the downhaul setting.

On many boats, all the controls for the spinnaker are led back to the cockpit, so that it is possible to trim it entirely without sending anyone up onto the foredeck.

Rigging the spinnaker

All the control lines for the spinnaker (guy and sheet, uphaul and downhaul, etc) are kept in place whether the sail is up or not. The sail is brought onto the deck only when you are just about to set it.

Preparing the sail

As a rule, the spinnaker is made ready down in the calm of the cabin. (No smoking or cooking is allowed while this is going on.)

The first question is whether you are going to furl it or not. This is seldom absolutely necessary, though it is sensible in certain circumstances, such as when you are dropping the jib, or if you plan to hoist the sail up while you are setting the pole at the same time. (We shall return to this 'quick' method later on.) It is usually worth keeping the jib up, even if that means some of the operations become more complicated: the jib prevents the spinnaker filling before you have got it fully hoisted, and, most crucially, stops the spinnaker from wrapping itself round the forestay.

Whether you elect to furl the spinnaker or not, one of the most practical ways of getting the spinnaker ready is to use a bucket with the bottom cut out of it. (Any other rigid ring of about the same diameter will work just as well.) You pull the sail through the hole, head first, guiding the edges of the sail in and making sure they do not twist over each other, all the way down to the bottom corners. You then take a bag and pack the sail into it, starting with the cloth which has not been through the bucket, keeping the bottom corners out of the bag and well apart; this process is continued until you

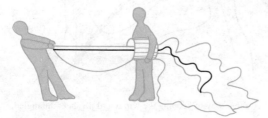

Sorting the spinnaker out with the bucket.

have pulled all the sail back through the bucket and into the bag, keeping an eye on the edges of the sail as you go. The head of the sail is kept out of the bag and between the two bottom corners.

If you intend to furl the spinnaker, then the preparations have to be made as the spinnaker comes through the bucket the first time. You tie thin strands of cotton or wool around the sail, which are designed to break as soon as you tighten the guy and sheet. The top tie must be 2m or so beneath the head, as it will not break if it is higher up. The lower ties should be made tighter as they get closer to the foot.

Novice crews or those who have few spare hands are recommended to use a spinnaker squeezer. This is a long thin bag, the length of the spinnaker sides. The bottom end has a rigid ring built in it; the top end has a snapshackle on the inside which can be attached to the head of the sail, and a ring on the outside which the halyard is passed through. There is an uphaul–downhaul system for raising the bag up above the sail once it has been hoisted, by pulling the ring up, and dropping it down over the sail to re-furl it before you strike it.

The bag is placed and *tied at the aft end of the foredeck*, ideally just in front of a shroud. This is an important detail, as it ensures the spinnaker is hoisted in the wind shadow of the jib and will not fill until you guy the pole into place.

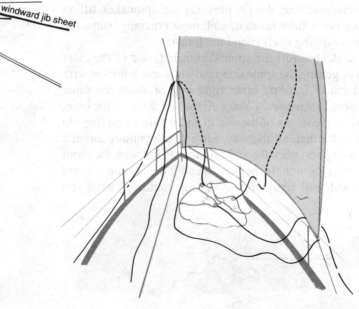

Another way of keeping the windward jib sheet untangled.

Preparing the sheets

You must keep a keen eye on every rope and the course you are asking it to take. The whole stage must be perfectly set before you dare raise the curtain. The skipper must take time to examine everyone's work and check that the diagrams below have been followed in the minutest detail.

The skipper's checklist

Windward side:
– the guy should come from the stern of the boat outside everything, through the end of the pole, in front of the forestay and into the spinnaker tack, passing over the guard rail, under the jib and under the windward jibsheet;
– the downhaul comes from the end of the pole, over the guard rail, then through its pulley into the cockpit, underneath all the other control lines and sheets.

Leeward side:
– the sheet should come from the stern of the boat outside everything and be attached to the clew, passing over the guard rail, under the jib and the windward sheet;
– the halyard is normally made off on the port side, but here it has needed to be moved round since the boat is on port tack, and it would have been on the wrong side of the forestay. It is led around the front of the jib and onto the spinnaker head over the guard rail, under the jib and under the windward sheet.

The three main ropes attached to the sail are thus fed through the same 'gap' in the boat's rigging to reach the sail.

With the boat set up this way, you are still free to tack if needs be, because you made sure that the windward jibsheet was led over the spinnaker pole.

Final preparations

1. Come onto the correct course, ie a beam reach. You should aim not to have to raise the spinnaker on a broad reach or run because then the mainsail and jib make an effective screen which stops the wind filling the spinnaker.

2. Let the mainsail fully out, to prevent the spinnaker coming between the spreaders and the mainsail.

3. Trim and cleat the jib, so it does not get in the way.

4. Let off the pole downhaul.

5. Raise the pole so it is horizontal and pointing straight forward, against the forestay.

6. Do not tighten the sheet! It should be released as the spinnaker is hoisted, so that there is no danger of the spinnaker filling prematurely.

7. Remember the essential rule: from the moment you start to hoist the spinnaker, *everyone on board must be clipped on.* As soon as you are sailing under spinnaker, it takes at least twice as long to turn the boat round and fish any crew member out of the sea if they fall overboard.

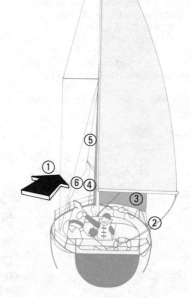

Hoisting the spinnaker

The sail must be raised quickly. If there is a strongish wind, you should take a turn round a winch, so that the crew member who is hoisting the sail does not have their arms pulled out of their sockets if it fills too early. It is helpful for one member of the crew to stand by the bag and help the sail out of it.

Adjusting the guy

When the halyard has been cleated, pull the guy round so as to position the pole at right angles to the apparent wind.

If the spinnaker will not unfurl, it is probably twisted on itself. This can happen when you put the sail in the bag, if you hoist it when too far off the wind, if you are slow bringing the tack round to the pole end or if you pull the sail up too slowly. It can often be untwisted before it fills with wind, by a short tug on one edge. If this does not work it is better to drop the spinnaker by pulling on the luff, sort it out on the foredeck, then hoist it again.

The spinnaker has come out of its bag nicely in the wind shadow of the other sails. The main is well eased so the spinnaker cannot catch on a spreader, and the presence of the jib prevents it from getting wrapped round the forestay. Both the guy and the sheet are slack, so the sail will not fill. What else is there to do but wait?

You now need to adjust the guy and pole, and sheet in.

So long as the sheet is not pulled, the spinnaker will not fill. To stop the spinnaker twisting, the guy is pulled first, so that the tack reaches the end of the pole. The halyard is cleated as soon as the sail is fully raised.

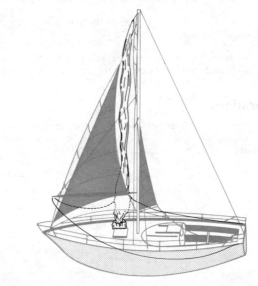

Sheeting in

When the pole is in position you can begin to sheet in. There is no great urgency to this: so long as the sheet is not pulled, the spinnaker will not fill. If you are using a squeezer, this is the moment at which you slip it up to the top and sheet the spinnaker in.

Trimming the sail

After a while, you are back on course, so you can begin to adjust the sail to the precise wind and to the course you are sailing.

On a beam reach, you can keep the jib up, which might give a little extra power. An alternative is to use a specialist sail which might be more appropriate, such as a spinnaker staysail.

On a broad reach or a run, the jib gets in the way, so it is better to drop it and hoist the big boy.

Important rule: the jib halyard must not be left along the length of the forestay, because if the spinnaker does collapse and wrap itself around the pair of them, it will be virtually impossible to undo.

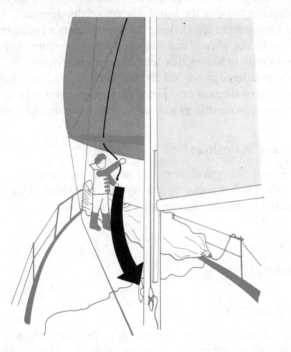

When you have dropped the jib, the first job is to make the jib halyard fast at the mast.

The quick method

With a little practice, you can pull the spinnaker up and fill it more quickly; if necessary, you can do this on a pretty close reach.

The spinnaker turtle bag is tied by the forestay. The tack is pulled up to the pole end just before you start to pull on the halyard, and the pole is guyed round to the correct position. The sail is then pulled up very fast, not forgetting to take a turn on the winch: you need to get the sail up before the wind manages to fill it.

If the sheet is properly eased, this should work smoothly.

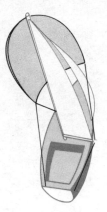

Raise the jib and ease the mainsail a long way out.

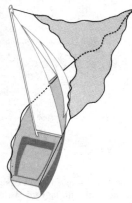

Let off the guy, unclip the snapshackle, and watch the spinnaker fly out ...

... before it subsides gently in the lee of the mainsail, allowing you to bundle it inboard and drop it very easily.

Lowering the spinnaker

Pulling the jib up

The jib should be hoisted immediately before you drop the spinnaker, so as to take some of the wind out of it and prevent it wrapping round the forestay.

You need to ensure before hoisting the jib that the sheets are well clear of the spinnaker gear, so that the foredeck remains in order.

Coming onto the right course

Just as when you were pulling the spinnaker up, you should aim for the spinnaker to be in the wind shadow of the mainsail.

The ideal course for striking the spinnaker is a broad or maybe a beam reach. You should not attempt to drop the spinnaker on a dead run, especially in waves, for fear of accidental gybes.

Once you have mastered the technique, you will find you can drop the spinnaker on any point of sailing, even a beat. You will need to learn to do this as part of the 'man overboard' drill.

Easing the mainsheet

As you drop the spinnaker, you need to increase the size of the mainsail's wind shadow by easing the mainsheet. This also helps prevent the spinnaker catching on the spreaders.

Danger

No smoking!

Freeing the tack

The guy should be freed a long way so that the pole is against the forestay with the spinnaker flapping in the lee of the mainsail. The guy needs to be let off fairly quickly, especially in a fresh breeze, if you are not to broach. Once the pole is against the forestay, the tack plunger can be released and the sail is free to come down.

Dropping the sail

Before you drop the sail, you need to be sure it is no longer filling, and is resting behind the mainsail. If you have a squeezer, you can let it down at this point, and the operation is complete.

If you have no squeezer, the delicate part of the procedure is letting the halyard off in time with the crew bundling the sail inboard. The halyard needs to be let down quite slowly. One or more crew members pull first on the sheet, then on the sail itself, holding either the cloth or one of the edges (though not both, or it will fill again).

The spinnaker can subside happily on the deck, though it is often not keen to lie down, and it is easy for the crew to slip on. The best thing is to pull it inboard under the boom and take it straight below deck: there it can be packed away in its bag with the three corners poking out of the top, and the neck of the bag tied tightly.

Making off the halyard

Once the head has been detached from the halyard, the halyard can be clipped onto its usual bracket at the port side of the foot of the mast. Careful, though, if you pulled it down while on port tack: it will have to be led back round the forestay before being made fast.

If your halyard is made of rope, it can be clipped onto the bow pulpit, though it will cause windage. Wire halyards must under no circumstances be left at the pulpit, as they catch in the jib hanks.

Tidying up

The pole is put back in its place and the downhaul tightened. The sheets are clipped onto the pulpit, tightened aft and held along the outside of the boat. If you were not prepared to hoist the jib at the beginning of the operation, you can do it now, with everything tidy.

Careful where you lead the halyard.

The quick method

The decision to drop the spinnaker is often made when the wind backs you on a reach and you can no longer sail as high as you would like. Sometimes you even need to drop the spinnaker as you are luffing up, either because the wind has changed, or because you are entering a channel or rounding a mark in a race. You certainly need to drop the spinnaker in a hurry if someone falls overboard. In such cases, you bring the sail down using a short cut: the guy is completely released, the spinnaker flies out behind the main and you then bundle it inboard hand over hand at the back of the boat and to leeward. The halyard is let down as the sail comes into the boat, and you might find it worthwhile to take a turn round the winch to stop it coming down too quickly.

This emergency method only works if the spinnaker sheets have no figure-of-eight knot in the end, so do not tie one.

How much sail can we carry?

A little practice goes a long way to help you change sails efficiently; but you need a lot of experience to decide when and by how much you need to reduce or increase the boat's sail area. You cannot always solve the problem with a rule of thumb along the lines of 'take in the first reef at force 4'. There is an infinite variety of solutions, according to your boat and the conditions prevailing. We can only give a few general hints, returning to points made in earlier chapters.

A boat's performance is partly predetermined by its shape, weight, size and sail design. It can be either 'stiff' or 'tender', ie capable of carrying a lot of sail as the wind increases, or needing to reduce sail fairly early. As the wind increases, the boat might develop more or less weather helm on the beat, and roll either more or less on the run. You can get an idea of when to change the sail area from the angle of heel or the degree by which it becomes hard to steer.

To get the right sails for the condition, you must pay as much attention to the shape of the sails as to their surface area. They should be full in light winds, then progressively flattened as the wind freshens. If the wind is really gusty, you are often best advised to flatten the jib so that it continues to be usable in the gusts, with a fairly full mainsail so that you have some power in the calm patches.

The state of the sea is also an important variable: on a sheltered stretch of sea you might be able to keep all sail on in a given wind, while the same wind on a rough sea would force a reduction on you.

There are also subjective factors to consider: how experienced your crew is, what sort of sailing you are doing. If you are racing, or your crew is keen and eager, your primary concern might well be speed, and any changes you do make to the boat's sails will be carried out swiftly and efficiently. You can also look at the problem from the other end: a novice crew should be encouraged to make as many changes as you think prudent, so as to gain confidence and skill. However, if you are cruising, and the crew is inexperienced, of course you will leave a greater margin of security, reducing the sail area earlier, knowing that any operation becomes more difficult when the wind is stronger; in the same way, you will probably think twice before shaking out a reef or hoisting the spinnaker.

There is no hard and fast rule. At best, there is a basic principle: you need your boat to be manoeuvrable at all times. This means it should have enough power to steer by, but not so much that it is out of balance. Speed is also an element which contributes to your safety and comfort, even if you are not competing with anyone. Under-canvassed is no better than over-canvassed: one boat floats but does not move, and the other lies on its ear. Neither is a pretty sight.

Manoeuvres in the harbour

Entering and leaving port, whether a giant marina or a tiny sheltered cove, can be among the most difficult, the most spectacular and the most public operations you perform in a boat. They test your skill, sense of humour and your crew's cohesiveness. There will almost always be someone watching and enjoying every minute as you miss the mooring buoy the second time round, or tangle spars, sails and sheets as you rig in a hurry to catch the tide. If the only thing you damage is your pride, you can consider yourself well off.

Almost all cruising boats these days are equipped with an engine, which helps enormously; you should not, however, be misled into thinking you will always be able to manoeuvre around the harbour under engine power ...

You must never forget that a sailing vessel under engine power is still a sailing vessel: it is always subject to the effects of the wind, and any successful operation carried out using the engine must take account of the wind as well.

It is also enormously satisfying to carry out a manoeuvre in port under sail and in such complete silence that the would-be spectators do not even notice.

There is one final reason for concentrating in this chapter on sail power: engines just occasionally break down. Any peculiarities of using the engine instead will be mentioned as we go along.

Theory

Speed

In all manoeuvres in a harbour, you must bear in mind that a boat cannot steer unless it has a certain amount of way on. You thus need to pick up some speed as soon as possible after starting, and keep speed on until the very last moment, at which stage you need to slow down quickly. In either case, the general principle is to reduce to a minimum that embarrassing interlude when the boat is floating, but with insufficient way to steer by.

Setting off and arriving

Under sail, as you set off, you need to get the boat onto a downwind heading (or at least a beam reach). As you arrive, you should aim to finish up on a course which slows the boat as much as possible: head to wind, or at least pinching close-hauled. If you are on a broad reach or further off the wind, the boat will not stop of its own accord.

Under engine, starting off is easiest with the wind dead ahead (though no direction is difficult). Arriving is best done with the wind either dead ahead or dead astern, since you need to make more delicate adjustments in all other cases.

This simple advice needs to be considered in the context of the specific harbour, wind and sea conditions you are dealing with: perfection will not always be possible.

Practising

Before you start to practise your manoeuvres in a real harbour, you should get to know the boat's handling characteristics in a less busy spot, in a variety of wind conditions from, say, force 2 to force 6.

You should aim to find out:
– your stopping distances;
– your minimum steering speed;
– the turning circle under different conditions;
– any points at which the boat is in stable equilibrium.

You should experiment with different amounts of sail up, including using the engine. There is no need to practise with sails you would never dream of using in harbour, such as a spinnaker or genoa.

You start by putting out a few marks fairly close together (fenders or the boat's dinghy will do), mooring them separately and weighting the mooring line about 2m down so as not to catch your rudder or propeller.

The marks are fixed at known intervals, about 10m apart, in a line from windward to leeward. You should aim to stay within 10–20m of the buoys for the practice session.

Here are a few of the areas you might like to check:
– stopping distance under full sail;
– stopping distance under no sail;
– effectiveness of various methods of braking:

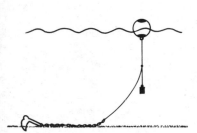
An improvised practice buoy.

backing the sails;
dragging a bucket as sea anchor;
paddling backwards;
– speed of drift under full eased sail;
– speed of drift under no sail;
– speed ahead with sails flapping or backed;
– speed ahead with all crew paddling in a wind.

A few boat positions to be checked:

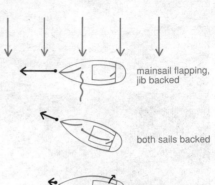

mainsail flapping,
jib backed

both sails backed

both sails flapping

mainsail only

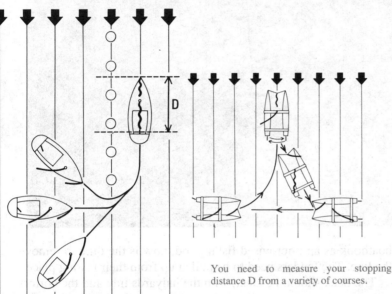

You need to measure your stopping distance D from a variety of courses.

Emergency stop and reversing round corners.

Approaches

Preparing the boat

As you near harbour, particularly after a few days out at sea, the skipper should cast a careful eye over the boat. You have been used to long gentle tacks made with nothing around you; over the last few days, all the equipment you need in harbour has been relegated further down in the cockpit locker, under a pile of other gear which was all more immediately useful at the time.

Now it all needs to be brought up from its hiding place and put in position. You need to check that any fixing lines are untangled (and present!) and that the anchor chain is not jammed in under a pile of sail bags and other jumble. If you have been using the

A natural harbour: the inlet at Fazzio, near Bonifacio, Corsica.

boathook as an improvised fishing rod, now is the time to remove the line. The fenders need to be pulled up from their resting place.

The deck should be clear, with the halyards tidy and the correct sails up. (You may well need to change sails for coming into harbour.) You need enough sail to keep the boat steerable on all points of sailing, in a wind which will almost certainly be less regular and less strong than that out to sea. You should not have too much sail up, however. It is often dangerous to sail around in harbour with the genoa up: it takes a long time to tack, obscures your view and is easily backed. An everyday jib is preferable. Check that the engine is ready in case you need to use it. You should enter harbour with the boat tidy and everything in place.

Preparations for entering harbour should be made some way in advance. Inevitably, the crew begins to take interest in the land once it is in sight, particularly if the coast you are approaching is unknown to them. It would be a shame to spoil the final phase of the voyage with mundane housekeeping.

If the boat is not quite ready for entering port, it is better to heave to for a few moments and go through the order of service, so that

All peacefully
tied up.

Entering harbour: order of service, part 1

The first part of the order of service begins an hour or two before you reach the harbour entrance channel.

A pious crew preparing to enter harbour

1. Take the chart out and study it.
2. Read carefully your nautical almanac and any guide you may have.
3. Analyse the chart of the harbour and draw the wind direction on it in pencil. (Beware, though: the wind in the harbour may be swirling or behaving in unexpected ways.)
4. Check the currents in the harbour for the estimated time of arrival, using the arrows on the harbour chart.
5. Check the scale of the harbour plan and work out how much space you will have to manoeuvre.
6. Calculate the time of high tide.
7. Check that the depth-sounder is switched on and working correctly. If necessary, recalibrate the alarm.
8. Identify the main landmarks (or the main light characteristics) and the bearing to them from the harbour mouth on the map; tell the rest of the crew about them.
9. Tune the radio direction finder to the frequency of the landfall transmitter.
10. Tune the VHF radio to the harbour frequency.
11. For the traditionalists among us, pull the log back in when you enter the harbour channel, and reel in any fishing lines.

Order of service, part 2

1. Hang three fenders on either side.
2. Keep one large fender in the cockpit in case of emergency.
3. Tie on one rope at the bow as a bow warp, and one aft as a stern warp. Keep a rope in the cockpit for use as a breast rope.
4. Slot the sculling oar in place.
5. Keep the boathook ready at the bow.
6. If the hedge anchor is accessible in an aft locker, make it ready. Otherwise, ensure the main anchor is ready at the bow with about 10m of chain ready to be let out.
7. Turn off the autopilot if it is on.
8. Start the engine and disengage the clutch, so it is ready for use.
9. Put the sails in order for the harbour:
– the spinnaker and all its gear should be stowed away;
– the boom restraint and barber haulers should be slackened;
– the genoa should be dropped and stowed, and replaced by a No 1 jib, so as to keep the foredeck clear, to improve visibility forward and keep the boat manoeuvrable. If your boat is easily steered under main-sail alone, then you only need a small jib; with roller gear, no problem;
–   reef the main or shake out any reefs so that the power in the main corresponds to the size of the jib.
10. Ensure all halyards for any sails in use are clear and can be released quickly.
11. Tension the topping lift so that dropping the mainsail does not cause any head injuries.

    All this routine should be gone through before you get into the harbour entry or channel.

you enter in a state of something approaching grace.

Entering any harbour, even a familiar one, can bring surprises, and you can easily find your usual route (or the one you have just worked out on the map) blocked for some reason. Good sailors always have an alternative up their sleeves. If the engine conks out, you hoist the sails which you had ready in place; then you round the corner and find a dredger blocking your usual channel, so you luff up and out (since of course you were using appropriate sails) …

Choosing your spot

As you get into harbour, the landmarks fall into place and you recognise the points on the chart. The plain permanent description given by the almanac comes alive with the fleeting impressions of that day, that weather, tide, currents, the light and the other boats around. In fact, any other boats can provide valuable clues for your sailing, whether they are themselves sailing or moored. Particularly if you are thinking of anchoring in a natural harbour such as a little inlet or creek, you can guess how deep the water might be from the size of any boats already there, and you can tell a lot about the current and wind from watching them swing at anchor. Before you get inside a harbour, you can tell by watching the forest of masts how much activity there is, and how full the jetties are. Smoke from a boat tells you it is inhabited but also gives valuable wind information. The size of moored boats or those tied up by a jetty can give you an idea of where you should look for a suitable spot.

As you get closer into the harbour, you must keep a perfectly clear view of the situation at all times. This means handing the tiller over to someone else, so you can lend a hand wherever it is needed: helping the navigator with a bearing, getting the main halyard or the anchor chain unjammed, etc. You must also make sure that everyone on board knows the procedure and their role within it. Nevertheless, if you need to change plan en route, they will have to put up with that too: if you decide it is better to pick up a mooring (or even to go back out to sea) rather than head for the jetty, that is their hard luck.

Ideally you should sail once round the harbour to look for likely spots to moor. However, if there appears to be a prime spot free in an otherwise busy harbour, there is probably a good reason. The best spots are usually reserved for fishing vessels or the harbourmaster's craft anyway. You must be sure that you can get out of the hole you steer the boat into. The wisest course in a strange harbour is therefore often to tie up temporarily on a pontoon, a mooring buoy or even next to another boat while you take a proper close

Look out for the entry and exit signs at the harbour mouth.

look. Any well-organised pleasure-boat harbour will have an information office which you can sail up to, rather like the reception desk in a hotel: you go there in effect to be given your room number and your map of the premises.

Once you are in a channel, do not forget that the rules for avoiding collisions change: all boats, large and small, sail or power, keep to the right, and small boats should not get in the way of large ones.

In high season, moorings are not cheap. You might choose instead a natural harbour, which you must then check with great care: how the coastline runs, what the currents, tides and state of the sea bed are like there. Further aspects to consider are the length of stay you envisage and the weather (current and expected). If there is already a boat there, it is probably in the best place for mooring, and it may well be possible to tie up alongside, leaving something of a gap, of course. You should also bear in mind that two boats tied together behave differently from one on its own, and it is seldom pleasant to be in the lee of a large boat in a storm when it starts to drag its anchor …

Anchoring

Mooring at one's own anchor these days is only generally done in a natural harbour. Since even the most sheltered cove seldom offers the same sort of protection as a real port, you need really robust anchor gear. We have said it already, but twice is better than once: your anchor belongs in the category of safety equipment, since it is the closest thing the boat has to a brake. It can stop you almost anywhere in a time of need. You should take care over choosing and using an anchor for various weathers and locations.

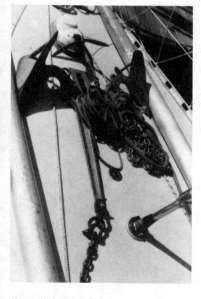

Katsou's three anchors:
– one everyday, medium anchor;
– one light anchor (grapnel type);
– one heavy anchor.

Anchors

You need at least two anchors. Three are preferable on large boats, or on small boats which sail in tricky waters such as the Channel. You will need:
– a light anchor, for use as a temporary mooring or at a short stopover when you will be keeping watch and staying on board throughout;
– a medium anchor, which is for the average mooring in a safe place, whether for a few hours or a few days, when the crew need not be staying on board;
– a heavy anchor which is generally used for long-stay mooring or in a rather unsafe spot; this is also the anchor of last resort when all

else fails to stop you.

Although these terms may sound general, they will be widely understood in the specific sense in which they are used here.

Mooring cables

You need three cables for mooring: a warp, a chain and a light line.

A warp has the advantage that it is light and easily handled, though it is not very wear-resistant. You need a length of chain between the warp and the anchor, to prevent the warp chafing on the bottom; and you also need to wrap extra cord around the warp where it passes through the fairlead. You need to let out a length of warp around three or four times the depth of the water at high tide in average to good weather, and around five to seven times the depth if the weather is rough.

Chain has two advantages: it is heavy so it rests on the bottom and presents the anchor to the sea bed at the correct angle; and it is strong and does not wear out when it rubs the bottom. The chain needs to be three times the high-tide depth of the water to give a good grip and a limited circle of swing. This figure of three repre-sents a minimum, and you will need more if the boat is particularly large or the water particularly shallow: 45m of chain is fine in 15m of water, but you should use at least 10m in 2m of water. The weight of the chain is not always a positive factor: if you anchor in more than 15m of water the chain becomes difficult to handle and almost impossibly heavy to pull up.

A long light line is useful in a wide variety of circumstances, and particularly for a temporary mooring. If, for instance, you need to anchor in a flat calm, with deep water, a long line is the only answer.

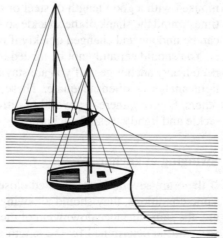

A light line is not much subject to the current, whereas a heavy line can be very seriously affected. It can become impos-sible to raise the anchor until the tidal flow slackens.

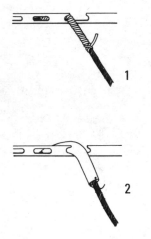

1. The simplest, fastest and most efficient wrapping for the warp where it crosses the rail is a length of 25mm webbing (or alternatively 4 or 6mm twine) wrapped diagonally down the rope and finished at both ends with a clove hitch.

2. If you really hate even the simplest of knots, a length of fairly wide rubber tubing is just about an acceptable substitute for real wrapping. Even this needs to be secured with a little knot, however.

Permanent mooring ropes should be equipped with a vinyl tube through which the warp does not slip. This is the ideal solution.

Which to choose?

Almost all combinations of anchor and line are possible. As the final choice depends on specific circumstances, we shall not run through them all here. As a general rule:

– the heavy anchor should be used with a warp in emergencies, bad weather and deep water; and used with chain in shallow water, for long spells and when it is important to limit the circle of swing;

– the everyday medium anchor is usually used with the warp, though it can be used either with chain (to reduce the swing) or with a light line (in a tide);

– the light anchor may be used with a warp, for instance if you are moored in a safe place in fair weather but with a very rocky bottom (such as is found in some Mediterranean inlets): if you are going to lose an anchor, make sure it is the light one;

– the light anchor is used with a light line out at sea, in a flat calm, while you are waiting for the tide to turn in your favour. (Our boat the *Glénans*, which is a ten-tonner, uses 6mm rope and a 7kg anchor for this purpose.) Assuming you are really out at sea rather than close to a rocky coast, the anchor does not even need to 'bite' particularly well, just so long as it prevents the boat from being driven by the tide at full speed.

In practice, you will generally leave two combinations permanently in place:

– *the light tackle*, which consists of the heavy anchor with a length of chain and the rope readily to hand;

– *the heavy tackle*, which consists of the medium anchor, attached to chain, and which should be almost as readily accessible as the first.

Anchors need to be shackled onto their line and the shackles moused with a good length of steel or brass wire twisted just a few times round the shank of the shackle so the anchor–line combination can be undone and changed quickly if necessary.

You should certainly not be misled into thinking that you always need heavy anchor gear. If you are staying aboard, in fine weather, a light anchor is often adequate. These are much less trouble than others. Even so, there is a world of difference between light anchor tackle and lightly tackled anchoring!

Swinging at anchor

If there are several boats moored close together, all subject to the same conditions, they should all swing together, ie all in the same arc, the same distance downwind of their anchors. Whether they do so or not is determined by the length of the lines: if these are the

The right way to mouse an anchor–line shackle.

same length, the boats will not come into contact with each other.

This ideal situation is very rare (if indeed it exists). All the lines would need to be the same length and all the boats of similar design, say, all modern keel boats between 8 and 10m in length. But as soon as everyone uses their own mooring, and a few multihulls and old wooden coastal cruisers are mixed in with the fleet, any semblance of order disappears. If there is a current as well, the likelihood of the boats behaving similarly vanishes virtually to zero. The only solutions, except at properly designed moorings, are either to make sure the boats are anchored a good distance apart or to leave someone on board to handle the inevitable bumps and move the fenders around at need.

Since the last boat to arrive has to fit in with the others which are already there, it is as well to have some sort of idea of how these might swing at anchor.

The first thing to look out for is what sort of mooring the other boats are using: they might have a fixed mooring (in which case the small buoy will be hitched up on the foredeck or the can buoy visible in the water), a chain or a warp. In the case of a fixed mooring, the boats will swing very little, as the line is short. With a warp you can be fairly sure they will swing in a wide arc, especially if the warp is a long one. There is no telling with a chain, as the chain limits the swing in light airs, but allows the boat much more freedom as the wind increases or as the tide goes out.

The next thing to consider is the type of boats you can see. They will swing more, the lighter they are, the more windage they present or the less lateral resistance their hull has. Fast catamarans and monohull centreboarders are thus likely to swing the furthest in the wind, whereas old, heavy boats with considerable lateral resistance stay put. In a current, however, the lighter boats are relatively immune, whereas the deeper hull sections mean that heavy boats can drift and swing considerably. You can attempt to fit your boat in with the estimated swing of its neighbours by raising or dropping the lift keel, if you have one.

Preparing the mooring

Light tackle

Some of the roughest-looking crews can occasionally be seen picking carefully coiled anchor warp out of the foredeck locker with touching maternal care. Such care is wasted on a coiled warp. *A coiled warp must not be touched.* The moment it is moved it will

A warp needs to be pulled straight up if it is to be uncoiled without tangling. A simple but effective trick is to rig a pole horizontally and pull it out over that pole.

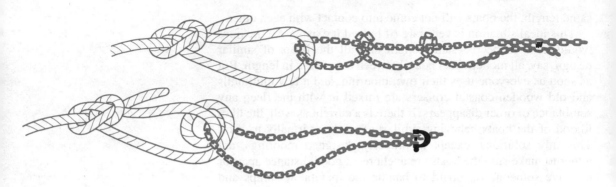

Two methods of attaching a warp to a chain. The round turn is optional in both cases.

tie itself into knots. If it must be moved, you have to uncoil it, transport it, then re-coil it. All this work takes time, care and patience. Coiling has to be done clockwise, in an oval shape and flat onto the deck; it also has to be done in layers. Each layer is started from the outside and finished in the middle; otherwise the whole warp is pulled into the water as soon as the first loops start to move.

In fact, expending all this effort on coiling is pointless. The best way to stow a warp is in a well-ordered pile at the bottom of a locker. By well-ordered, we mean that it should in fact be flaked in a zig-zag or concertina fashion, snaking to and fro but not looping or crossing over itself. The end of the warp is attached to the chain which is then shackled to the anchor, and the shackle moused. All you should then need to do is fish the anchor out of the locker and take it (under all sheets and control lines) to the roller. The anchor is then ready to be dropped.

If the chain is allowed to run out of the locker and over the deck once the anchor is dropped, it will scuff the deck and the edge of the locker very badly. It is actually better for a crew member to feed the chain over by hand, then to let the rope warp down on the roller. The warp can run out unattended all the way to the end if necessary.

Only when the warp is over the roller are you actually really ready to anchor: when the chain is still on deck, there is still a chance that the knot joining it to the warp can jam on the roller. The chain and knot should follow the anchor overboard rather than being allowed to run across the roller.

It is perfectly possible to stow the anchor line right at the bottom of the foredeck locker (for instance) even if it is then covered up with sails and other items. The only points which do need to be observed in this case are: that the anchor itself should always be accessible to your hand; and that anything stowed on top of the line should be large, with no hooks, eyes or other attachments which will catch in the warp as it runs out.

Heavy tackle

The chain is normally stowed in its locker, with the inner end made fast to a sturdy ring; the outer end is shackled to the anchor (and the shackle moused) and the anchor is accessible from the deck.

The first step to take is to pull a length of chain out onto the deck which is at least three times the depth of water you expect. This length of chain is known as the *bitts*. The end is wrapped with three turns on the anchor post, or samson post, such that the top turn is the one nearest the inboard end of the chain. This way, it is always possible to slacken the chain off in a controlled fashion (not the case if the top turn is closest to the outboard end). Never tie a half-hitch in a chain. It will jam and you will need a hammer and cold chisel to undo it.

Chain stored on deck gets in the way and is always likely to slide overboard if the boat heels. It should therefore be left in its locker until the last moment. When it is on deck, it must be kept clear to run out smoothly: the best method of doing this is the well-ordered snaked pile.

You begin by piling the desired length of chain on the deck, as it comes out of the locker. Ideally you will have marked the chain in

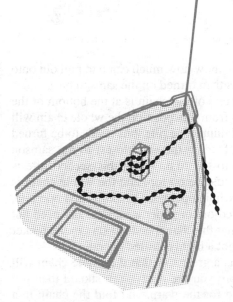

Correct. This way you can slacken the chain as necessary.

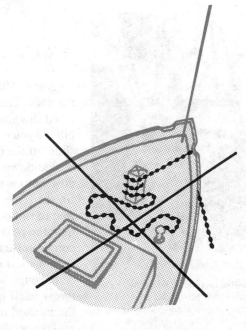

Incorrect. It is impossible to slacken the chain without removing the top turns from the post.

A well-ordered pile of chain.

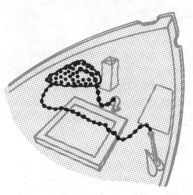

A. Pull the chain out and pile it up.

B. Take three turns on the samson post.

C. Make another pile, the other way up
from the first.

D. Ready to drop.

Alternative method: flaking the chain
The chain is fed through the roller, and you
can reduce the danger of it coming out by
placing a (suitably shod) foot on it as it
runs out. The chain is neatly and correctly
flaked, and the anchor can be dropped.

lengths of 50cm, so that you know how much chain to pull out onto
the deck. The inboard end is then turned on the samson post.

At this stage, the anchor end of the chain is at the bottom of the
pile. If you drop the anchor from this position the whole chain will
slide off the deck in a solid lump. The pile thus needs to be turned
upside-down. You start by feeding the end closest to the samson
post onto a new pile next to the first. When this second pile is
finished, the anchor end should be on top, and the whole chain is
free to run out easily. The whole operation (making first one pile,
then the next) may be carried out in under a minute, and need not
compromise the principle that the chain needs to stay in the locker
until the last moment. It is not a highly skilled operation.

In rough weather, there is a great risk that the whole chain will
throw itself overboard before you are ready. You should then use
the method described above for the warp, and fold the chain in a
zig-zag on the deck, a little more in advance of needing it. This is
known as flaking the chain. It can then be lashed down if need be.

The final step before you are ready to drop anchor is to place the anchor itself outboard, out of its support, and the chain over the roller.

If you leave a little slack chain between the roller and the anchor, it will hang down neatly at the bow and make sure that the chain does not jump the roller when it is released.

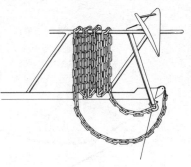

Ready to drop anchor:
– the chain is hung on the pulpit;
– the knot joining the warp to the chain is past the roller;
– the anchor is hanging ready.

Light tackle

A well-ordered pile is the best way of stowing a light line. The light line may be stowed in a bucket so as to be permanently ready. About 1m from the inboard end, the line should be tied to the bucket handle, with the remaining metre being used to attach the line to the boat itself. The line is arranged in the bucket in the same way as a chain in a locker. A bag is also usable, so long as it is not too long.

Tripping line

Anchors can get caught in almost anything on the sea bed. You should bear this in mind before you drop the anchor: a moment later is too late. It is worth attaching a tripping line to the anchor (at the blade, not the stock), so that you can pull the anchor from the bottom rather than the top if it does get stuck. The tripping line leads from the anchor either to the boat itself or to a separate buoy. It can be useful, but is also beset with problems.

The first problem is choosing what diameter line you want. It needs to be strong enough to lift the anchor once it has come unstuck; but it should not be so fat that the current takes it with it and drags the anchor. (We have seen some boats dragged for several miles because of an over-diameter tripping line.) Nor should it be too thin: the light anchor line and the lead line are usually too thin and generally not strong enough for use as a tripping line. You should use 8mm rope as a minimum.

Length is also an issue: if the rope is not too fat, neither should it be too long, because this will also give more frontal area for the current to work on.

The tripping line must not float, or it will catch in propellers: it should therefore be made of nylon or polyester.

The final tricky question is what to do with the top end of the rope. There are three possibilities:

1. Tie the top to a buoy. Get everything ready on deck before letting the anchor over the side: the tripping line should be carefully stowed, with one end tied to the anchor and the other to a buoy. As one crew member lets the anchor down, another should feed the

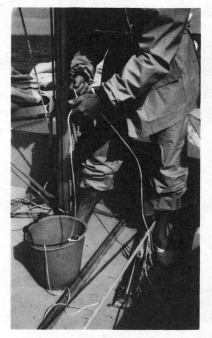

Light line has two bad habits:
1. tying itself into knots;
2. jumping overboard in its entirety if the inboard end is not made fast.

To rid it of these habits, you must:
1. stow it in a pile rather than looping it, inside a bucket or bag;
2. tie the line to the bucket handle a metre or so from the inboard end;
3. fasten the inboard end to the boat.

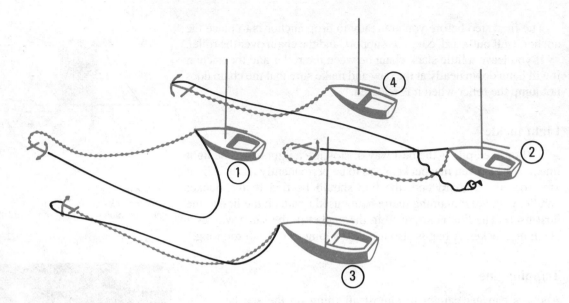

1. *Tripping line too long.* The current can take the line and drag the anchor.
2. *Tripping line too short.* This will pull the anchor upside down.
3. *Tripping line the right length.*
4. *Tripping line too long with buoy.* This will get caught in someone's propeller, a different boat's mooring, the rocks ... you are unlikely to be able to find it!

tripping line out before finally letting the buoy into the water. The line should be only slightly longer than the depth of high water, because it can wrap around the chain if it is any longer. What is more, the longer it is, the more grip the current can take on it. This solution has a few shortcomings: when you are getting ready to leave, the tender will be needed to fetch the tripping line, unless the wind and current happen to be in the same direction; and the line is always at the mercy of a passing propeller (of which there can be a good number in a busy harbour).

2. Keep the top end of the tripping line on board. This requires the line to be about 3m longer than the length of warp you are using, so that it does not drag the anchor. Measure the three metres before dropping the anchor and mark the tripping line at the point where it should cross the roller. The operation is handled as above.

3. Fix the tripping line to the warp itself. Again, the tripping line needs to have about 3m of slack. Even though there is a chance of the tripping line and the anchor line getting twisted round each other, this is definitely the best solution.

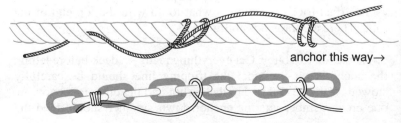

anchor this way→

Two ways of attaching a tripping line to the anchor line.

In common with most safety devices, the tripping line appears to be in the way when it is not in use. Nevertheless, when you are anchoring over a tricky patch of sea bed, you cannot afford to be without it. When in doubt …

Anchoring head to wind

This is the traditional position. You approach your anchorage from the leeward side, ensuring that the boat is on a course which leaves it freedom to be steered and slowed: a beam reach is ideal. The jib should be dropped as early as is practicable, to clear the foredeck, though you should not pack it away in case you miss the mooring and need it again. If your boat is very clumsy under main alone, keep the jib up a little longer, but not too long: whoever has the job of picking up the mooring or dropping the anchor will quickly find the foredeck too small for the pair of them; what is more, the jib can easily back at an awkward moment and make the boat bear away just when you are luffing head to wind.

It does not matter which direction you approach from if you are using the engine, but you must keep the sails ready for re-hoisting.

Just downwind of your chosen spot, you luff suddenly and sheet in the mainsail if needed. The boat should have enough way on to keep going for about twice its own length: if it is moving at the right speed, you may now drop the mainsail; if it is moving too fast, you keep the main up, because its flapping will slow you down.

Under engine power, you put the boat head to wind, then just switch off at the chosen moment, or even go into reverse for a moment to stop the boat and start it moving backwards. The skipper should be checking for the moment the boat stops, by looking at a few transits and aligning them. The order to drop anchor should be given at the precise instant when the boat stops. If the boat is still moving, the anchor rope will 'overtake' it and make the anchor come down flat, so that it will not grip.

Aligning transits. The boat is only stopped when near objects are no longer moving relative to distant objects as you look abeam of the boat.

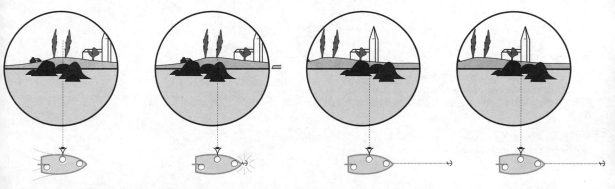

The foredeck hand lets the anchor down quickly, but just until it hits bottom and no further: if too much chain is let out and falls on the stock, the anchor can foul.

At the same time, the mainsail should be dropped, but held ready to be re-hoisted in case the anchor does not bite. As the boat starts to drift backwards, the foredeck hand lets the chain out, braking slightly, so that the boat stays head to wind as it gathers way backward. The anchor line can be braked with a well-shod foot.

When the line has gone out to its full length, the skipper checks the alignment of the transits again to be sure the boat has stopped and the anchor is gripping. Occasionally, if the line has been let out badly, the anchor grips but the boat continues to go backward for a little while. You will soon learn to recognise the difference between this and real drift: don't panic!

Even if the anchor really is *dragging*, there is still no real cause for alarm, because the boat will be pulled back to windward in any case once you start pulling the anchor line in.

The ten commandments of anchoring head to wind

1. Thou shalt approach on a broad reach at a fair speed.
2. Drop the jib just before luffing up (or earlier if the boat sails well under main alone).
3. Luff quite sharply, though not sufficiently to stop the boat, as you sheet the mainsail in.
4. Drop the mainsail.
5. Find the precise head-to-wind course. This can take at least two boat lengths, during which the boat is sailing on momentum alone.
6. Check the transits align and stop, so you know exactly when the boat is no longer moving.
7. Anchor away!
8. Let the anchor line out gradually, braking a little.
9. When you have reached the correct length of anchor line, check the alignment of the transits again.
10. Check the transits are still aligned 10 minutes later. If so, you have stopped!

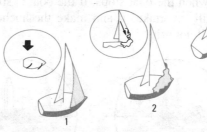

If you find that the boat is still travelling too fast when you reach the fourth commandment, you may put it off for a moment, but no later than No 7!

When anchoring under engine power, there are only five commandments, Nos 6–10. The engine is turned off before No 7.

Anchoring with the wind astern

There are a number of reasons you might choose to anchor with the wind astern:

– in very light weather, the boat does not drift backwards in the head-to-wind position to stretch the anchor line properly, whereas if the anchor is dropped over the stern while you continue on your course, it will drop to the sea bed at the correct angle;

– *in any weather, this method ensures a better grip in a grass- or weed-covered bottom, especially for a plough or pivoting-fluke anchor, which needs the extra momentum to penetrate the bottom covering*;

– assuming you let the anchor out at a sufficient speed (say, 2kn), you will be able to tell instantly whether the anchor has bitten, as it should make the boat stop on its nose as soon as the chain is stretched. If it slows you down, rather than stopping you, you know that it is not holding properly and it is time to move on.

You need to prepare particularly well for anchoring downwind. The line must be perfectly free and ready-tied to the right length. If the anchor bites, it should pull the boat up with something of a jolt. Chains are preferable to rope warps, for this reason.

You need to close fetch up to windward of the desired anchorage, dropping the mainsail as you do so. You then bear away under jib alone, and sail at a reduced speed towards the spot. Above the point you are aiming for, the boat should be on a dead run if it was not already; then the anchor is dropped and you continue straight ahead until the anchor pulls you up. Ideally, you should be doing about 1kn at this point.

To regulate your speed, you might need to drop the jib earlier; in very light airs, though, it should be kept pulling even until the boat is stopped.

Under engine power, the procedure is the same, though you need to switch off at the latest when you drop the anchor overboard, to avoid any chance of catching the line in the propeller.

Anchor in the desired location by letting the chain out rather fast over the front of the boat. Do take care of the paint finish on the hull!

When the chain has all run out, the boat will need to be turned head to wind. The helm helps the process by luffing in the direction of the chain. If you have two anchor line rollers, you can choose which side you are going to turn to in advance. If you only have one, the foredeck hand must signal to the helm just before the chain goes tight, which side to turn. A moment or two after the sound of the chain running out over the deck stops, the helm pushes the tiller down.

Anchoring with the wind astern
1. Close fetch to windward of the chosen location and drop the mainsail.
2. Position yourself directly to windward of the spot.
3. You should now have about four boat lengths to position the boat on a dead run, and adjust the speed, if necessary easing the jib if the wind is strong.
4. Drop the anchor fairly briskly.
5. When the line has run out, put the tiller down to help the boat come round head to wind.
6. Take a transit alignment.
7. Ten minutes later, check the transit again: if it is the same, the anchor has held.

Under engine power, start at 2 and turn off at 4.

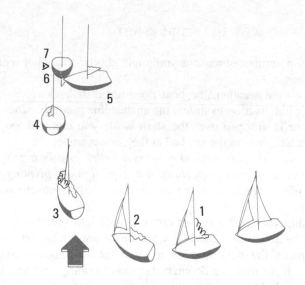

Anchoring with the wind astern in this manner can be very convenient, and yet many sailors are reluctant to use it, fearing that they will drag the anchor. In fact, though, if the anchor does not grip, you always have time to hoist the mainsail again and start afresh. (In fact, you have time however you try to anchor: no boat sails fast trailing its anchor and chain over the bottom.)

Anchoring in a current

The operation can get noticeably more complex if there is a tide or other current when you are trying to drop anchor.
    You should start with a tour of the anchorage:
– initially, to enable you to estimate the strength and direction of the current;
– subsequently, so you can get an idea of how much the boat will swing at anchor (more precisely, how the line will swing and how far the boat will follow). If there are other boats around, they can give you an indication, but your own experience is also a good guide.

    The wind and current can interact in a variety of ways:
• *Both in the same direction*. This does not present any particular difficulties, even if they are only within 20–30° of each other.
• *Wind perpendicular to the current*. You should approach the mooring sailing upstream on a beam reach, with both sails up if needed, and taking account of any drift to leeward. To stop, you just

let the sheets out, and then drop the anchor and the sails as soon as the boat starts to drift backward.

• *Wind and current in opposite directions* (and up to 80° different). This situation can cause real difficulties, and the way round them depends on the shape of the anchorage as well as the relative strengths of wind and current.

As a general rule, you need to drop the anchor with the wind astern, under jib alone, but behaving as if you were anchoring head to wind. (Do not leave the mainsail up, as it will be flat against the rigging, very difficult to pull down and causing all sorts of other problems.)

You might find yourself having to anchor head to wind, with some forward momentum. In this case, the main problem is pulling the mainsail down completely before the current turns you round. After that, it is like anchoring with the wind astern.

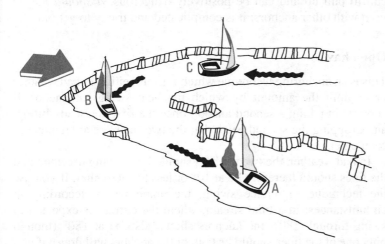

Anchoring in a current
A. Anchor in the normal manner.
B. Anchor facing upstream, both sails up.
C. Anchor facing upstream under jib alone.

Two boats anchored in the same current will not necessarily swing at anchor in the same manner, even if they present the same windage. The underwater shape makes the biggest difference, so it is as well to give other boats a wide berth.

When you anchor in a current, the tiller must be tied in the middle of the boat. If you are staying on board, you may move the tiller a little in either direction to remain clear of other boats.

You must also remember that conditions can change completely the moment the tide turns. If several boats are tied up close to each other, it is worth making sure you are aboard at slack water just to keep an eye on things.

If you are at anchor out at sea in a current, say, because there is no wind, you will need to pull the anchor up and then drop it again every time the tide changes, so as to avoid the line catching in any rocks on the bottom as it goes round. This is less likely to happen with a light line than with a medium-weight warp, which is one good reason for using a light line for this job.

Anchoring with more than one anchor

Backed anchors

Backed anchors are anchors rigged one above the other. The technique involves attaching an extra anchor below the main anchor by fixing a length of chain to the anchor crown. This works well with fisherman anchors, but used with other types, it makes them difficult to pull up and can be positively dangerous. *It should not be used* with other anchors: it is complicated and tricky to get out of.

Open hawse

This is an anchoring technique which is useful either in bad weather or to limit the amount by which the boat swings at anchor. It consists in taking a second anchor, once the first is already biting, and dropping the second, such that the two lines are at an angle to each other.

In bad weather, the two anchors should be working together, and the lines should therefore be at 10° or less to each other. If you use the technique to reduce swing, the angle varies according to circumstances: in a tidal stream, where the current is expected to swing through 180°, the anchors should also be at 180° (though only one of the lines should be taut, or the anchors will drag); if you are anticipating a change in wind direction or strength, the second anchor should be placed in the direction of the expected wind.

If the angle between the anchors is acute, the two lines should be different lengths, so as not to get mixed up in each other.

Dropping the second anchor

In this case, a well-ordered pile will have the anchor at the bottom. The two people paddling simply concentrate on that: the helm's job is steering the tender and letting out the line.

It is worth looking at the technique for carrying an anchor in the tender, either for an open hawse mooring or because you have gone aground. If there is any serious wind, the operation can be quite delicate, and can easily fail if any part of it is carried out half-heartedly or less than perfectly.

You start the operation by *loading the whole anchor assembly into the tender* in a well-ordered pile: anchor first, then the warp or chain. If you are using a warp, leave the inboard end tied to the boat. If you are using chain, it should be loaded entirely aboard the tender, with the inboard end attached to a 20m rope which is then tied to the boat. The tender is really too light to be used for feeding out a heavy chain, so the rope is used for bringing the chain back to the boat once you have thrown it overboard.

It is worth having three people in the tender for this job. Two should be at the bow, each with a paddle and a single idea in mind: to paddle, without bothering about where they are heading or how the anchor line is fed out. The third member of the crew looks after the direction, using a sculling oar, and feeds out the line. The major part of the job is getting far enough to windward of the boat: this is best done in a short spurt of intense energy, rather than a sustained gentle paddling session. You can get your breath back once the anchor is safely unloaded and the line nicely taut.

Emergency second anchor

When the weather turns nasty and it would be risky or impossible to paddle out with a second anchor in the tender, you can use the second best method of dropping your support anchor as a weight.

The operation is carried out as follows:
– in a calm patch, pull in 3–5m of the line which is already out;
– drop the second anchor straight down (or better still, 1–2m away from the boat, off to the side from which you think the wind might strengthen);
– let go the main anchor line, letting out the secondary line as you go;
– if the secondary line is a chain, either you can bundle it all overboard in a pile, since there is no risk of it fouling the anchor; or you can leave it tied with sailmaker's thread in a zig-zag pile on deck – if the boat starts to drag its anchor or the wind veers, the thread will break, the chain will drop, slithering over the deck as it does and alerting the slumbering crew to the fact that there is something amiss. This technique is actually useful at night if you just want to know when the wind changes direction;
– if the secondary line is a rope warp, it should be neatly stowed on deck so that it can be pulled out when necessary: if it was allowed to go overboard all at once, it would wrap round the rudder or the other anchor line for sure!

This style of secondary anchoring is not a real solution: it is more a precaution so that you are warned and ready if your main anchor starts to drag.

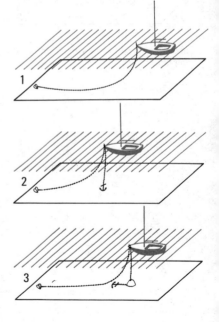

1. At anchor normally.
2. Take in 3m of line and drop the secondary anchor.
3. Drop back to your normal position and let all the chain out in a pile into the sea floor ... or set it up as an alarm system on deck.

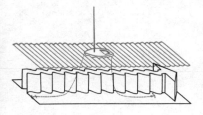

Mooring fore and aft.

Mooring fore and aft

One anchor out the front, one at the back. This is a method used occasionally in rivers to reduce swing, but it does not work well. The boat is for ever ending up beam on to the wind and the current, pulling both anchors sideways at once. This can be uncomfortable, and difficult to get out of without undoing one of the anchor lines and letting it go (buoyed up, of course, so you can fetch it back).

There is a similar technique which works better. Both anchors are dropped from the bow, but one is also attached to the stern on its way down, in a manner which allows it to be released quickly if the boat does go side on, and you will be moored in a 180° open hawse.

Anchoring a catamaran

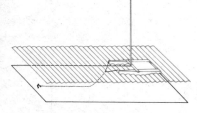

Catamarans need to be anchored from the centre line.

Catamarans need to be anchored from the front of one hull, making sure the line is kept well clear of the craft so that it does not catch a rudder or centreboard if the boat turns round.

So that the boat does not swing badly once the anchor line is taut, make a span of rope across the front by tying another line to the anchor line from the front of the other bow. You can use the roller mounted on the front crossbeam, if there is one, but the span arrangement is better if the crossbeam is set too far back from the bows.

Weighing anchor

Preparation

For a boat to weigh anchor is effectively the same as transforming it into a sailing boat from a simple floating object in a matter of seconds, once the anchor starts to slide. This transformation demands considerable subtlety on the part of the crew.

Everything should be ready before you touch the anchor line: the jib should be hanked on, the mainsail run along the boom and ready to go up the mast, the deck clear and the sheets in place. The procedure is just the same if you are leaving the mooring under engine power, but take care of those ropes hanging near the propeller.

When this is done, you can begin on the anchor gear. If you have used two anchors, you can start by pulling one of them up, preferably the heavier one. It is easier to get under way from a light anchor. You can try to bring the first anchor back on board from the boat, but this will only work if the second line can be lengthened sufficiently.

You will frequently find that the only thing for it is to fetch the anchor using the tender, though this is a good deal less tiring than carrying it out. You simply haul yourself out along the anchor line until you are directly above the anchor itself, then you start to pull it in. The anchor line is pulled in from the boat, which has the effect of dragging the tender back to the boat at the same time. The chain or the warp are then piled neatly into their lockers as they come aboard, and the whole procedure has been accomplished without touching a paddle. The first anchor line should be thoroughly stowed away before you start work on the second.

When getting under way using sail power, the tripping line is nothing to worry about, but with a start under engine power, be sure to have the tripping line inboard before the clutch is let out.

Bringing the anchor gear back on board

Everyone on board needs to know the stages to this operation.
• A boat is said to be *anchored* so long as it is held firm by a rope or chain which is of sufficient length for the anchor not to drag.
• A boat is *hove short* when the anchor gear is partly hauled in, but there is still enough line out for the anchor to hold (at least for a while). One's safety margin has been reduced to nothing, but the initial position is recoverable simply by letting out some chain.
• A boat is *up and down* when the bow is almost directly over the anchor, and the anchor, while still gripping, is about to drag. This moment is hard to spot, but if the anchor was holding well, you may feel its resistance to your pull suddenly increase. This position is over in an instant, and you might be able to re-anchor, but only if you are very quick … otherwise the anchor will drag or foul on something. As soon as the crew member who is pulling the anchor in announces 'up and down', the boat must be readied for the off.

The difference between hove short and up and down is actually a matter of judgement, and you need some practice. 'You have to

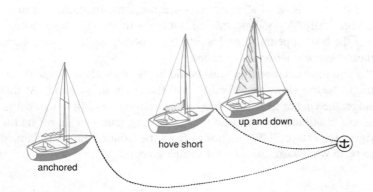

up and down

hove short

anchored

You can be technically up and down in a strong breeze, with the anchor ready to drag, long before the bow is over the anchor.

guess when you're hove short, but you can smell when you're up and down.' (Cyrano de Bergerac.)

Getting under way

The boat is shipshape, with the sails ready for hoisting and everyone in position. You have decided which tack you are going to leave on (or decided that it does not matter), and everyone knows what they're doing.

As you reach the hove short position (and only then) the mainsail can be hoisted. There is no point doing it earlier: it will flog unnecessarily and wear itself out, quite apart from the extra windage it causes, so that you have to pull all the harder on the anchor warp.

As you are hoisting the mainsail, the skipper (who should be managing by walking around, rather than tied to a specific task for this period, encouraging and showing as necessary) checks a few transit alignments, just to be sure you are not already drifting.

The mainsail flaps happily, and the tiller is centred.

The foredeck hand keeps pulling the anchor in slowly.

When the foredeck hand announces 'up and down', the skipper has a few seconds to decide whether to go or not, depending on whether the chosen course appears possible. (If the boat really is up and down, you have about 5 seconds; if it is already past that stage, you have correspondingly less time to decide!)

There are several scenarios for which you must be prepared:
– if it does not really matter which way you break out, by the time you have the jib up and the anchor on board, the boat will have swung one way or the other;
– if the boat is already heading the right way, you can break out, helping it to bear away if necessary, as follows (assuming you have chosen to leave on starboard tack): the jib is hoisted and backed by being sheeted to starboard; the boom is pushed out to port so that the main backs; the tiller is right down to port. You sail backwards and bear away onto starboard under the influence of sails and rudder;
– if the boat is head to wind, you use the same method, just more energetically! A good alternative is a few strokes with the paddle!
– if the boat appears to be leaving the mooring on the wrong tack, then *re-anchor without hesitation;*
– if you have decided that you should break out and mechanical aids might be too slow, you need to pull the chain in by hand. At this stage, the anchor gear is no heavier in a strong wind than in a calm;
– on a multihull, the simplest way of making sure you set off on the right tack is to pull the anchor in from the front of the hull planned to be to windward: this should assure success.

You can bear away onto the correct tack by backing the jib, the main and the tiller.

If you are getting under way using engine power, you can use the engine to move the boat slowly forward as the anchor warp comes up. There are two important rules to keep in mind while doing this:
1. The helm must know and follow precisely the direction of the anchor, and supply only 95% of the necessary power from the engine. The foredeck hand who is pulling the line in is thus spared unnecessary effort, but is still keeping the boat on course, and the boat will not run over the anchor.
2. The sails may be hoisted before, during or after the raising of the anchor, but you must make sure of your tack before cutting the engine, by using the rudder.

The 'flying start'

If there is little wind, light cruisers can attempt to get under way on the chosen tack simply by using the momentum acquired by the boat as it is pulled upwind by the raising of the anchor. As the boat is moving forward, it will respond to the rudder. If you want to head off on starboard, you put the helm down to port, the boat veers right, but then is pulled back by the anchor and turns onto starboard at the up-and-down position. This trick can be used up to a force 2.

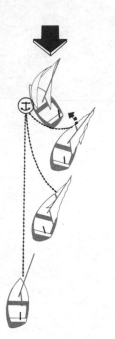

One way of making sure you set off on the correct tack is to pick up some momentum on the opposite tack, then get the anchor to swing you round.

If the wind or the boat is very light indeed, you can make a real flying start, pulling the anchor up in one go and letting the boat be pulled forward without bothering about the tack. There is no in-between position: the boat is suddenly moving, the anchor broken out, and you can bear off onto your chosen tack. You should only be careful of the boat's own acceleration as the warp is pulled in: ideally you should pull fairly slowly to start with, or else the boat will pick up too much speed by the end and will move forward faster than you can pull the line in. You then overtake the anchor before it is torn out of the mud, it brings you to a juddering halt and you have to start again.

Drifting under way

This has to be the most economical and the most stylish method of getting under way, particularly for those without strong arms when they have to start off in a strong wind.

It is economical, because:
– it looks after your sails, rather than wearing them out by letting them flog for ages;
– it looks after the crew: the boat is easier to pull along without flapping sails, and the whole crew is available for pulling the chain in.

It is stylish because it shows that you have your boat well under control. You do need the sails in position for hoisting, of course. The technique should only be used if you are not worried which tack you will leave on, if you can guarantee your preferred tack (either because of the wind direction or because you are using a sculling oar), or if you have some spare water to leeward.

Drifting under way
Even if you take your time you will not drop below the dotted line.
The boat stays to windward of its initial resting place, even if the operation is handled in a leisurely fashion.

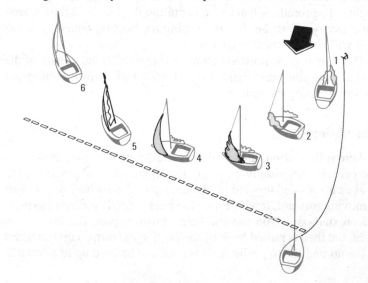

Whipping a rope on

You can find yourself unable to pull the anchor line in at all, for instance in a strong wind or tide, despite everyone on board lending a hand. If the warp is very taut, there is no room for extra helpers between the roller and the samson post, so what do you do? If you were to untie the warp, you would risk losing the whole lot overboard. You therefore *whip* a rope onto the top end of the anchor warp, just aft of the roller, and attach that rope to a strong point. At that point, the warp can be untied from its ring and led back over a block or two to the jibsheet winch. You can then winch it in. If you have a chain on the anchor, you need to use two whipped ropes alternately, each one being winched in turn.

Whipping is a useful skill …

Whipping can come in handy in a variety of situations. If you notice, for instance, that a rope halyard is coming detached from its wire part, and you do not want to take the sail down for running repairs, you can hitch an extra rope tail onto the wire and make it fast at the mast foot. The sail remains solidly up, and you can repair the halyard at your leisure.

Chains can of course also be whipped in the same way.

Cow hitch.
1. Two or three turns under the end which will be pulled.
2. Four to six turns in the opposite direction, well spaced out.
3. Finish with a clove hitch.

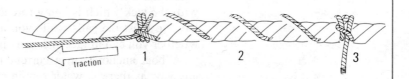

traction   1   2   3

It is carried out as follows:
• Pull up and stow the anchor.
• Let the boat bear away backward, keeping the tiller down to leeward, and hoist the jib (though not the mainsail, which will stick in the mast throat or catch on a shroud if you pull it up off the wind).
• Trim the jib as necessary, then come onto a close fetch when you have picked up enough speed, and hoist the mainsail.

You might feel uneasy at allowing the boat to drift downwind with no means of power. There is no need to worry: a boat without the sails up, and with the tiller hard to leeward, makes slow leeway. On most occasions, you will have the boat moving and under way well before it drifts as far back as its starting position.

Dragging the anchor

If you are hemmed in on both sides by other boats, and any wrong move would mean leaving the mooring on the wrong tack, you can decide to use the spare space to leeward by deliberately dragging the anchor. You bring the boat to the up-and-down position, then, when the anchor starts to drag, the boat starts to move gently backward. We cannot recommend this method for use in a built-up harbour, because the anchor is bound to catch on an underwater cable, or worse. If you are going to try this technique, make sure there is a tripping line on the anchor.

It is certainly preferable to use the sculling oar, though this is heavy work! There are few people who can scull to windward in anything over force 2.

You can always use the engine instead of the oar.

Weighing anchor in a current

If you need to weigh anchor in a strong current or tidal flow, spend a moment first working out what is likely to happen. To start with, you will probably not be able to choose your tack, unless you are lucky enough to have wind and current in exactly the same direction. The next problem is that if the wind is light and the current strong, the boat will not handle in any case.

On the one hand, then, you have to work out what you can do with the tack which is being forced on you; and on the other, you have to hoist the sails while you are still firmly at anchor, to see whether you can in fact make any headway against the current.

A boat anchored in a current is steerable to a certain extent anyway, as there is water running over the rudder. It is therefore usually possible at least to get the boat pointed in a direction which

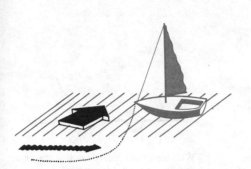

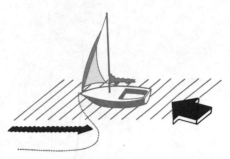

The mainsail can be raised, as there is no danger of it catching in the rigging.

It is impossible to hoist the mainsail. You have to start out under jib alone.

will fill the sails. It is usually also possible to keep the boat headed in such a way as to help the foredeck hands bring the anchor up. This should also mean that the boat is fully steerable as soon as the anchor does start to slip.

There is one further peculiarity of this situation: as soon as the anchor breaks out, the apparent wind is different from the one you had at anchor. In the worst case, the wind and current arc in the same direction and have the same strength ... and the wind disappears completely.

There are two main scenarios:

1. *Wind and current in the same direction*, or at least no more than at right angles to each other. The wind is thus ahead, and you can raise both sails. You can often even get them filling before you start pulling up the anchor, which saves some effort for the foredeck hands.

2. *Wind and current in opposite directions*. If you cannot make the boat move far enough downwind at its anchorage to be beam on, you cannot hoist the mainsail. You therefore need to start out under jib alone. Before you leave the anchorage, it is worth checking that the jib gives you enough power to breast the current, or that you at least have enough space to hoist the mainsail.

If the conditions are sufficiently favourable, and you have some space downstream, you can even let the boat drift as you raise the sails. First you hoist the jib, then use the jib to bring you close-hauled before hoisting the main.

The anchor is stuck!

Finally, the tripping line comes into its own. Usually, a simple tug sideways on the anchor by the tripping line will be enough to break out the anchor. There are two situations in which even the tripping line will not help, however: if it is wound round your anchor line; or if another anchor line has been allowed to pass above it.

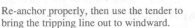

With the anchor already out of the mud, drop the ring over the stock.

Re-anchor properly, then use the tender to bring the tripping line out to windward.

Now use the tripping line to raise the anchor.

If you have not used a tripping line, you can try to free the fouled anchor by turning it with sudden tugs at 45°, then at 90° to the initial mooring angle. A final try at 120°, then if that has not worked on one tack, try on the other. In such situations, you might be glad you have the engine!

One further option is to rig a sort of ring around the anchor line, for example with a length of chain tied into a tight noose with a shackle, and use this to trip the anchor line. You bring the boat right up and down to slide the ring down over the anchor stock. You then return the boat to its original anchored position, then head off to windward of the anchor in the tender, taking the tripping line with you, and pull the anchor upwind. The crew member who succeeds in this operation is awarded a Mars bar.

There is one solution we have left until last: the heroic one. You take a large rock under your arm (so as to sink quicker), and let yourself down the anchor line, which should be straight up and down. As soon as you reach the bottom, those left on the boat should free the anchor line a little, to give you some working slack. Before you start this operation, it is wise to have set out a further reserve anchor (complete with tripping line).

If you are setting off under engine power, pay particular attention to the tripping line: propellers eat them for breakfast!

At the mooring

We shall make the distinction in this section between pick-up buoys and mooring buoys. A pick-up buoy is tied by a light line to the mooring chain, which lies on the sea bed; in the case of a mooring buoy, the chain is led right through the buoy itself. Since a mooring buoy has to hold the weight of the chain, it is generally larger and heavier than a pick-up buoy: it also stands up for itself when it comes into contact with a passing hull …

Picking up the mooring

Almost by definition, moorings are picked up in a limited and crowded space. Failing the pick-up can be a real problem, as you might have difficulties coming back for a second try, especially if your boat is difficult to steer at low speeds, like a multihull. Whatever sort of boat you have, you should make sure you have the anchor gear ready in case you miss the mooring.

Whether you are picking up a mooring buoy or a pick-up buoy, the operation must be carried out with precision. The boat's momentum has to be judged so that it slows down not too early and not too late. Too early, and you will witness the contortionist act of the foredeck hand with the boathook, vainly trying to catch a buoy just a foot or two out of reach; too late, and assuming you have got hold of the mooring, the boat will whirl round on the spot, tacking as it goes, spreading confusion among your crew and delight among the observers who are hurriedly putting fenders in place. Gone is the peace of the harbour at dusk.

Nevertheless, a little too much speed is preferable to not quite enough. There is no harm in keeping going for another couple of metres when you pick up a mooring buoy; and any extra momentum picking up a pick-up buoy can be used to bring some extra of the light line aboard.

This operation is simplest to do under engine power, since then the boat can be made to stop dead head to wind.

The approach

You approach the mooring on a close fetch, preferably with the jib already dropped, so as to leave the foredeck clear. Most boats are still perfectly steerable without their jibs on a close fetch; they can be made to speed up or slow at will and make only a little leeway. If your boat is not one of these, just keep the jib up until the last

Choose your tack to approach the buoy: the right tack is the one which leaves you room to leeward in case you miss the buoy.

moment. If you aim straight for the buoy, the leeway will bring you just to leeward of it.

It is vital to choose the correct tack for the approach, so that you have some space to leeward if by chance you miss the buoy first time.

Luff up to the buoy when you are a boat's length or less away. You need enough speed on for the boat to respond to the tiller, but not enough for the boat to plough on for more than a boat's length. The sheets should be thoroughly freed so that there is no chance of the sails filling even if the boat drifts round to beam on.

If there is a current, of course this makes the operation more tricky. You need to take into account all the factors which operate when you are anchoring in a current, plus the extra precision required for picking up a mooring. Once again, the most complex problems arise when the current and the wind are in opposite directions, and there is also your leeway to take into account. But this is enough preaching from us: you need to try it out for yourself a few times. (And let him who has never missed a mooring cast the first stone!)

As soon as you have hold of the mooring buoy or the pick-up buoy, you tie up temporarily while the sails are dropped: first the jib, if you have not been able to drop it earlier, then the mainsail. Only when the sails are down do you tie up properly.

If you are using engine power, approach the buoy head to wind, slowing down gradually until the boat stops with the bow nudging the buoy. You should not switch the engine into reverse except in a flat calm: using reverse almost guarantees failure.

Tying up to a mooring buoy

You cannot pick up a mooring buoy from the trampo-line of a catamaran using a boathook: the buoy will disappear under the boat, taking the hook and half of your arm with it.

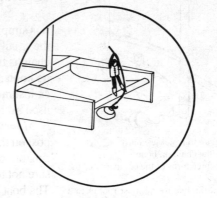

Emergency stops with a catamaran

On a catamaran, one can sweep up the pick-up buoy with a length of rope hung between the hulls. This slows the boat if you are travelling too fast, which is not possible with a boathook speared through the top ring of a mooring buoy as you sail over it!

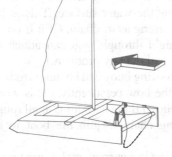

The cowboy approach

A few metres of rope weighted with fishing weights make a very good lasso for catching a buoy which is just out of reach.

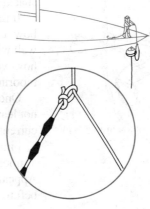

You can now buy well-designed boathooks specifically for picking up moorings.

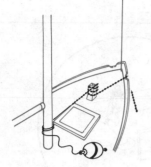

Mooring up to a pick-up buoy:
1. Bring the chain on board.
2. Make three turns of the chain around the post.
3. Fasten the line to the mast foot or to a cleat.

Loop a rope through the top ring before shackling a chain on.

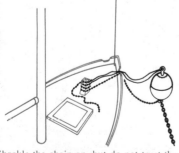

Shackle the chain on, but do not trust the buoy for too long.

Mooring up

It is simple to catch a *pick-up buoy* with the boathook. You then bring the small buoy on board and pull the line until the chain appears. The chain is then fastened to the anchor post with at least three turns (and no knots, please!); the top rope can be tied to the mast or onto a cleat as insurance in case the chain slips. The rope is not designed to be used as the main mooring line, however.

Mooring buoys can be picked up with a slip of rope tied onto a post on the boat, and about 4–5m free. The free end is fed through the ring on top of the buoy and then back up to the boat to be tied on. Be sure not to use rope which is too thick to pass freely through the ring! The boat is then temporarily tied up, for a very short stay at most.

If you plan to stay longer, you can still leave the rope in place, as it will be useful for when you decide to leave, but you need to find some way of fastening the boat more securely. In pleasant weather, for a limited-length stay, you can shackle a chain to the buoy ring (rather than passing the chain through the ring, as doubling back on itself is not good for chain). In more difficult weather or for a longer stay, the boat should be attached to the mooring chain by a strong, moused shackle on the chain *below* the water surface. This is just because the buoy itself is never so strong as its chain. (If it is one of those which the chain passes straight through, you can attach the shackle to the top ring of the chain without any problem.)

If the harbour is sheltered, the mooring buoy can be hung from the bow, to avoid it bumping against the bow persistently. (This works well with a large boat and a small buoy.) If the harbour is at all rough, however, it is better to use a long chain to join the boat to the mooring.

Once you have tied up to a mooring in a current, make sure you do not leave the boat without tying the tiller amidships: the action of the current on the rudder could swing the boat around wildly.

Finally, whether there is a current or not, do not attach your boat to a mooring unless you know what is on the other end of the chain! Appearances can deceive, and you should ask the harbourmaster before abandoning the boat on an unfamiliar mooring.

Leaving a mooring

This operation poses similar problems to leaving an anchorage: the boat needs to head off on the correct tack. From a fixed mooring, however, it is easier, since you do not have to bring the mooring on board at the end!

Leaving a mooring buoy

Start by unshackling the chain. The boat is still tied onto the ring on the top of the buoy by the length of rope. You then pass another length of line through the ring and tie the inboard ends to the boat at the spot which will swing the boat round at the desired angle. Thus, if you wish to leave on port, on a close fetch, the line is attached on the port side just forward of the shroud; and if you want to leave on a reach, you just tie it a little further aft.

When you have pulled the sails up and everything is ready, you release the mooring rope and the boat will swing round on the slip rope. You can release this line just before the boat comes to rest on the new course, because it will continue to bear away naturally until it starts moving forward.

This slip rope is not necessary if the boat and wind are light: you can make the boat bear away by pulling the mooring rope round to the desired spot.

If you are using the engine, you drop the buoy, let the boat drift back 2 or 3m and you're off!

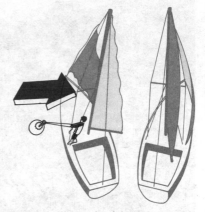

Attach the line to the right spot to ensure the boat sets off on the correct tack.

Leaving a pick-up buoy

This operation is slightly less simple. In light winds, you can carry the mooring chain round to the side of the boat so that the boat bears away from that point. You can even use the top rope for this part of the job (if it is fairly strong), by bringing it round to the side before you let off the chain. The top rope is seldom designed to withstand this sort of tension, however, and if there is much wind you should set the initial tack by using an extra line led through one of the chain links, then proceeding as above.

When you let go of the top rope, make sure you feed it out and do not drop it all into the water in one go. If the rope does not disentangle itself, the weight of the chain will sink the buoy. This advice is especially important if you are using the engine to get under way.

In a tide or current, setting off from either sort of mooring is easier than setting off from your own anchor. You can set off on the correct tack quite easily by using the top rope on a pick-up buoy or pulling the extra line round to the side with a mooring buoy. This means that you will often have a choice about which tack you set off on.

If the wind and the current are in opposite directions, you may well find that it is impossible to turn the boat round into the wind sufficiently to hoist the main. You are then forced to set off under jib alone.

Saint-Malo harbour after the Cowes –Dinard race.

The quayside

In a busy port, the wisest course is often to use the engine or the sculling oar to manoeuvre, but you should use sails where possible. On one hand, sails are a perfectly good means of power; and on the other, only by using them in a tight corner will you find out what you and your boat are really capable of: how the boat deals with shifts in the wind, what is its lowest steerable speed, how it holds its way … a successfully completed manoeuvre in the harbour shows a considerable degree of harmony between boat and crew.

Manoeuvring in port and up to a jetty are to be carried out with caution. As you arrive, reduce your speed, and keep a lookout for fixed and moving obstacles, especially to leeward. You need to be able to change course or even stop at a moment's notice; and you should be holding a light anchor line ready for use in emergency.

How you manoeuvre your way into position depends on the position of the wind relative to the obstacles, the current, and your own boat's abilities. Any description of what goes on will appear a little abstract, because it cannot possibly account for every eventuality; the description will be limited to the fundamental principles, but you will have to invent a new solution to the problem each time.

There are many different ways of tying up, and you will choose whichever is most appropriate in the circumstances.

Tying up parallel to the quay is convenient, as it allows you to move people and gear ashore and back again easily and swiftly (at least at high tide). But you need to keep adjusting the warps, and there must be a lot of room along the quay to permit such luxury. These days, it is most uncommon to find a length of jetty to yourself: it is more likely that you will have to tie up alongside a boat which is itself alongside another … and so on, up to the jetty.

Tying up to another boat or to a pontoon is a very comfortable solution, as you are not left constantly worrying about the warps. (You do need to show consideration for your neighbours, though.)

The most widespread position for tying up in modern harbours is perpendicular to the quay, jetty or pontoon.

Tying up parallel to the quay

With the quay to windward. The first thing to do is to ensure you come up to the quay with the wind from forward of the beam, otherwise you will not be able to stop the boat when you want to.

Ideally, approach on a close fetch, jib down (if the boat can be steered under main alone) and the main just sheeted in enough to keep you moving; alternatively, come in under very low engine revs, with the main down but ready to be re-hoisted as necessary. Either way, do not head in at right angles to the quay: approaching at an angle gives you more freedom to veer away if you need to.

If there is plenty of room, no problem: you end up next to the quay, having slowed to zero, with the sail out or the motor idling. If you are coming in too fast and the boat can still be steered, head off for another approach at a more appropriate speed; and if you come in too slowly, then simply let the boat drift sideways and start again, or give a little help with the sculling oar or a burst from the engine.

With a little practice, you can even time it so you arrive with both sails already dropped. (You let the mainsail down just in time, so the boat comes up to the quay on its own momentum, or with a few last-minute paddle-strokes.) One crew member hops out onto the quayside as you arrive and ties the boat up immediately, starting with the bow warp. If you start with the stern warp, there is always a chance that the boat will swing round and the mainsail will fill again if it is still up. If you are coming up to the quay too quickly and the approach is at enough of an angle, the bow warp can even

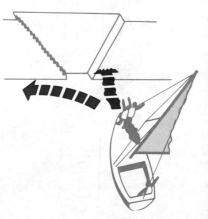

It is better to come in at an angle, since boats veer off more easily than they stop!

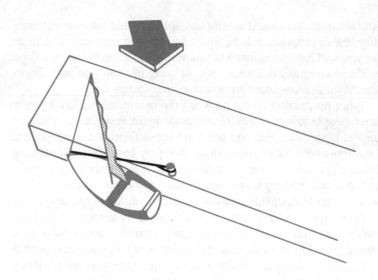

A boat should normally be tied up at the quayside using the bow warp first. If the quay is to windward of the boat, this is absolutely vital, in order to avoid the wind catching the mainsail.

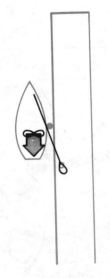

Under engine power, just let in the clutch, and the boat will stop.

be used as a brake: the crew fends off the quay, to stop the boat actually making contact. The mainsail needs to be dropped as quickly as possible.

There is frequently so little room beside the quay that you are forced to approach beam on, or even to tie up temporarily to another boat if it is a question of fitting in between two of them. You can then tie onto the quayside at your leisure. It is simpler to make the approach in one go if using the engine, even against the wind.

With the wind parallel to the quay. Adopt the same procedure as for a mooring buoy or a pick-up buoy, head to wind, whether under sail or engine power.

With the wind onto the quay. This is a delicate operation, and you should look for other ways of approaching if possible.

If you have no choice, then sail to windward of the quayside and drop the mainsail. You then sail to the quayside under jib alone or using the engine (or even drop both sails and just drift gently in).

If you do tie up to windward of the quay, there is no room for mistakes, and nor will you be able to leave the quay under sail. It is therefore worth dropping an anchor (using rope warp rather than chain) on the way in. Once you have dropped the anchor, you continue to sail in toward the quay, letting the anchor warp out over the bow. An alternative if you have anchored directly to windward is to turn the boat round and let the warp out slowly, so the boat reverses in toward the quay. If you do this, look out for all those parts of the boat which project aft of the stern: rudder, boom, etc.

Dropping an anchor as you come up to the quay is also worth doing when the wind is not blowing onto the quay at the moment, but you suspect it might be when you want to leave!

In a current. Any current must be parallel to the quayside. If the current and the wind are in the same direction, you need to come up to the quay head to wind. If they are not, you make a choice.

• In general, tie up head to current, with the wind behind, under engine or jib alone. You might need to use a genoa to give the boat enough power. Even if the genoa is not powerful enough to pull you forward, at least it will stem the current enough for you to drift toward the quay with a few strokes of the sculling oar.

• The wind might be strong enough to offset the effect of the current. In this case you can tie up head to wind, but do not forget that the current will play with the rudder once you have stopped, as though the boat was travelling backward, and this can have quite uncomfortable effects. It is often preferable, even in quite strong winds, to moor bow to current.

Tying up windward of a jetty is not recommended. Fortunately, you will seldom be in a position to do this even if you want to; but if you must, make sure you do it using an engine with a strong reverse.

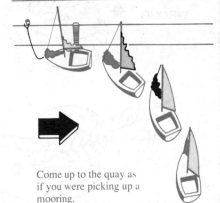

Coming into a jetty under engine.
You can exploit the fact that the boat continues turning even after you have applied reverse thrust.
At point 2, push the tiller down hard, just before applying reverse thrust. The boat will stop parallel to the quay without you needing to pull the tiller back up.

Come up to the quay as if you were picking up a mooring.

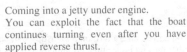

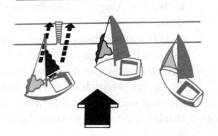

The stylist's trick: drop the jib on the reach; drop the main when close-hauled, then drift gently to the quayside.

Braking with a warp

You can use a warp to brake the boat, by letting it out slowly, so the boat is not brought to a juddering halt. The anchor warp is used in this way when you anchor in a strong current or strong wind, so that the boat is not stopped too suddenly; equally, excessive speed as you come up alongside the quay can be reduced by braking with the mooring warp.

The same technique can be used to avoid a jolt when the boat is about to be speeded up suddenly, as, for example, when you are being towed.

As the general aim of the technique is to act against over-powerful forces, you always need to start by taking a turn round a fixed object, generally a Samson-post. You can use a winch if there is nothing else to hand, but never a cleat, as the rope can catch too easily; on land, you can use a bollard or an iron ring.

WRONG

RIGHT

When you take a turn on a Samson-post, be sure to loop the free end under the part which is attached to the boat. The pull will thus be down rather than up on the loop, and there is less chance of it riding up over the top.

Tying up

Alongside a quay where there is no tide, tying up presents few problems. The warps should be good and tight, so there is no play in them.

It is usual to use *bow and stern warps*, led as far forward and aft as possible on the quay from their respective ends of the boat. If you have no room for these, you can tie up using *springs* instead. These are warps led forward from the stern and aft from the bow, thus crossing over each other. They need to be supplemented by small *breast ropes* to keep the boat parallel to the quayside.

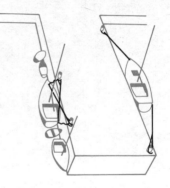

If there is any play in warps or springs, you should use the winches to tension them. The breast ropes should be tight as well, but not as taut as the other lines.

Alongside a quay where there is a tide, it is impossible to keep the boat immobile, but you can at least restrict its sideways movement. This is accomplished by tying the warps as far forward and aft as possible, and not at the height of the quay top, but to the rungs of the ladder which you will always find nearby, at the half-tide height. If you tied the boat up at the top, you would need to leave enough slack for when the boat drops at low tide: this would then leave too much slack at high tide. If you tie at the half-way mark, there will be no play at high and low tide, and a limited amount at half-tide.

With nicely taut springs or bow and stern warps, the boat can never pick up speed forward or aft. This in turn means that the warps never have to stop the boat and come under excessive strain.

With the warps fastened half-way up the quay wall, there is no play in them at high tide or low tide. If you will be leaving harbour at high tide, you must remember to tie bowlines with a long loop!

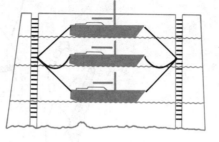

Tying up alongside another boat

Tying up alongside another boat is just like tying up alongside the quay, except that the boat is shorter, private property, and rather fragile. The operation therefore demands a fine touch.

Tying up alongside a moored or anchored boat

There are a variety of reasons why you might want to tie up alongside another boat. Let us suppose that you are out cruising with your friends, and you want to tie up alongside them in a little bay far off the beaten track for supper.

We have actually already studied a similar case to this one. In effect, their boat may be regarded as a quayside, with the wind blowing parallel to it. The quay in this instance is not solid, however, and you do not want to come up against it at an angle. Ideally, you will not come up against it at all!

The approach is made on a close fetch, with the jib dropped, passing behind your friends' boat on whichever tack leaves most safe water to leeward in case you miss them first time round. When you are just to leeward of their boat, you luff up head to wind and drift up to them using your boat's momentum. The vital point is of course to guess how much momentum you need. It is better to have too little than too much, since you can always throw them a line to pull, or scull a few strokes with the oar. If you discover you are moving too fast, there is only one responsible course to take: head off, bear away and come round again, more slowly.

Under engine power, you plan the manoeuvre as if you were picking up a mooring buoy placed a metre or two behind the stern of your friends' boat.

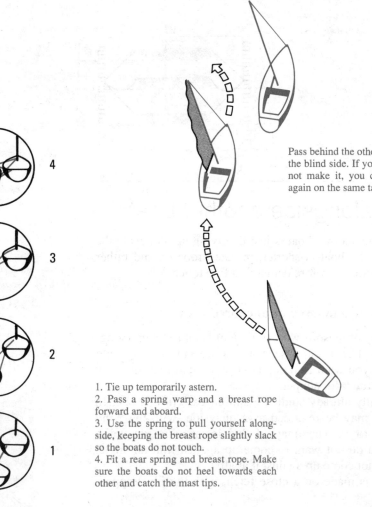

Pass behind the other boat and come up on the blind side. If you can tell that you will not make it, you can simply bear away again on the same tack.

1. Tie up temporarily astern.
2. Pass a spring warp and a breast rope forward and aboard.
3. Use the spring to pull yourself alongside, keeping the breast rope slightly slack so the boats do not touch.
4. Fit a rear spring and breast rope. Make sure the boats do not heel towards each other and catch the mast tips.

Once you have a line attached to the stern of the other boat you can drop your sails, tidy everything away and put your fenders over the sides.

Lying alongside another boat then involves:
– passing a spring from the stern of your boat to the bow of the moored boat;
– passing a breast rope from the front of your boat to the front of theirs;
– pulling on the spring to bring your boat forward, while leaving a little slack on the breast rope so the boats do not bump together as you come up parallel (or, better still, pointing slightly apart);
– passing over another spring from your bow to their stern, and a rear breast rope; the springs are then tensioned.

The picnic can be ruined if you do not observe two crucial rules: as the operation progresses, do not allow your crews all to get onto the same side of their respective boats, or the masts and safety rails will lock in an inextricable embrace; nor should the warps be tied so that the two boats are exactly level, or the masts will clash every time someone moves from one boat to the other.

Lying alongside a boat which is at the quayside

A summit meeting …

This works similarly to tying up parallel to the quay itself, and the same set of scenarios applies. If the wind is parallel to the quay, you should sail up behind the boat; again, the most sensible course of action is to tie temporarily to their stern, drop the sails and tidy your decks before pulling up alongside them.

The actual tying up process is identical: use two well-tensioned springs and slightly slack breast ropes. Again, beware the summit meeting of the two masts …

Approaching at right angles to the quay

In any harbour with strong undertow, or in modern marinas where mooring space is at a premium, the boat is tied up with one end at the quay and the other end anchored or moored.

In the case of marinas, it is seldom possible to sail right up to the quayside except in very light winds or with a highly practised crew. It is more advisable to use the sculling oar or the engine to bring you in.

Whatever the wind direction, the approach will finish with the boat travelling in at right angles to the quay for two or three boat-lengths.

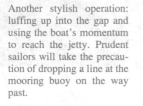

Another stylish operation: luffing up into the gap and using the boat's momentum to reach the jetty. Prudent sailors will take the precaution of dropping a line at the mooring buoy on the way past.

The operation demands the exact co-ordination of three actions:
1. Anchoring, using a chain (for fear of passing propellers) or catching the mooring buoy with a line.
2. Letting out the anchor chain or mooring line.
3. Attaching a line to the jetty or quay.

The difficulty in all this is that the boat becomes more difficult to steer as it is slowed. If the mooring line is not let out fast enough, if the knot onto the buoy takes too long to tie, or if the boat drifts with the wind (unless you are on a dead run), you will miss the gap and fail to tie up. And what is more, you cannot sail straight up to the quay: you want to sail just close enough for a crew member to hop out and tie you up, not a step further.

If you can put a line onto the quay, it is perfectly possible to let the line out gradually so that the boat leaves the gap slowly, turns round and is then brought back in stern first.

Tying up

The boat needs to be tied very firmly, so as not to bump against the next boat, and most importantly, so as not to move fore and aft. This is particularly important in a port with any amount of undertow or swell, since the continuous movement between a mooring (which stretches) and a line to the quay (which does not) makes for considerable wear and tear on the boat: as it gets closer to the quay, the mooring line pulls it back, then it is brought up with a jolt by the quay ropes. If this motion is other than minimal, it will build up a rhythm and never stop until something snaps.

The boat can be tied up with the ropes taut, even in a tidal port, so long as the boat is sufficiently far out from the quay wall, because the distance between the quay and the anchor does not change, however high the water is.

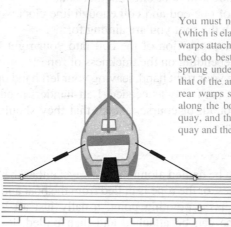

You must not allow the boat to start swinging between its anchor rope (which is elastic) and the warp which ties it to the quay (which is not). The warps attached to the quay have the function of taking up any slack, which they do best if they are tied in a V-shape, spread fairly well apart and sprung under tension. This should then give them an equal elasticity to that of the anchor rope, and the whole system remains under tension. The rear warps should not be too short: it is best to tie them about half way along the boat. The boat should be a reasonable distance out from the quay, and the crew can use a short (2–3m) gangplank to get between the quay and the boat.

A long anchor line will remain tight whatever the state of the tide. If the system is sufficiently long, with the boat somewhere in the middle, the line to the quay will also remain tight throughout.

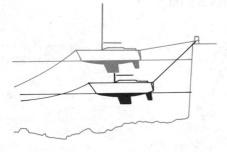

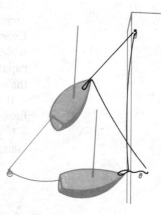

If you have enough space, you can tie up at an angle. The mooring as a whole can thus be longer, and this will make it hold better. It also means you can pass between boat and shore without touching the anchor rope. This is also the best way to moor a tender.

There is one final precaution you must take when tying up to a quay, whether parallel to it or perpendicular, and that is to check the depth of water at low tide, so that if the boat is going to ground, you have plenty of time to prepare.

The correct use of heaving lines and warps

Throwing a line

To throw a line ashore or onto another boat:
– take hold of one end and coil enough line clockwise in your left hand to reach the spot you are aiming for;
– then take a proportion of the coil into your right hand (three to five turns, depending on the thickness of rope);
– throw with your right hand, leaving your left hand open so that the rope can run out freely as needed. Left-handers need to do this the other way round, of course, except that they should also coil the rope clockwise!

Warping

The boat can be hauled along in two ways: either the point which is on land moves, or the rope is pulled from the boat and fixed on land. Every boat has a pivoting point, usually just aft of the mast, at which a rope can be attached and then pulled, leaving the boat capable of maximum manoeuvrability even at low speeds. Often the mast itself is an adequate approximation.
– If the boat is being hauled from on land, the warp should be fastened to the boat at this pivoting point.
– If you are hauling the boat forward on a warp which is fixed on land, you should stand at this central point.

1. The hauling warp should be fastened at or around the centre of the boat.
2. If you are hauling on a fixed warp, stand at or around the centre of the boat.
3. Someone was not paying attention to the lesson!

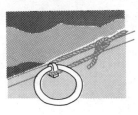

Tying up

A warp is not to be used as a leash, for pulling the boat along by. If you need to carry a warp on land, it is best to have plenty of slack in it, so you can make it fast as quickly as possible on a fixed point. The slack can then be taken up by those on board.

You should only bring as much of the warp on land as you need for the purpose of tying the boat up. If you bring the whole coil onto the quayside, you will get in everyone's way ... quite apart from the possibility of someone passing by and thinking you have so much spare warp that you couldn't possibly miss just a few metres.

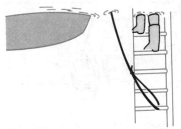

It is worth preparing in advance a warp with a very large looped bowline (maybe 1.5m in circumference) at the outer end: once you are on land, this can then be hitched over a bollard in a single move.

If you are tying the warp onto a quayside ring or a ladder which is submerged at high tide, do not forget to make the loop long enough for you to undo it at all times ...

If you have looped a warp round something on the quay, make sure you undo the correct end of the loop. This is:
– the windward end if the warp is round a post;
– the lower end if it is passed around the rung of a ladder.
    This should ensure the rope does not jam.

Wear

Warps chafe on everything, and wear out correspondingly quickly unless you take a few precautions. The first of these is to make sure the rope is not actually moving over any part where it is also taking strain: always make a round turn on any ladder rung or quayside ring; also try to make the warp fast on the boat as close as possible to the point at which it is being pulled. You can occasionally choose the spot where the warp takes the strain so as to minimise wear, eg by leading the stern warp through the spinnaker block before tying it onto the cleat.

Keep the warps good and tight: as far as possible, use warps which do not stretch, such as polypropylene.

If you know you will not be able to immobilise a warp, serve it (ie wrap it with thinner rope) at any strain point.

Tying up at a cat-way

This is a fairly common arrangement in marinas: it consists of a long pontoon with smaller pontoons about 5–7m long leading off it at right angles.

You approach this sort of pontoon in much the same way as you would a mooring spot at right angles to a quay, with the difference that you should not drop a stern anchor. You almost always, therefore, have to put the boat's engine into reverse to pull up. This in turn means that you have to work out what will happen to the boat's course once the propeller starts turning the other way, and, if the wind is fresh, how much leeway the boat will make once it stops.

You tie up between a pair of these mini-pontoons, and the boat is thus prevented from swinging back and forth between an anchor line and a warp. A note of caution: the boat is much more buoyant than the small pontoon, so the fenders can easily be knocked out of place every time someone leaves the boat or boards it.

The boat should really be tied up very tight indeed, with the warps winched in. You should use:
– a spring from the bow of the boat to the outer end of the cat-way;
– a stern warp from the stern of the boat to the outer end of the cat-way;
– and two lines in a V at the bow, spread as wide apart as possible, to prevent the boat twisting in its berth.

The best way of protecting the boat is to use fairly long cylindrical fenders, tied top and bottom (ie underneath the boat). You should also tie a vertical line from the side of the boat to the outer end of the cat-way to prevent it sinking when someone stands on it. No method of tying up is perfect, however, and if the water is at all disturbed, boats can take quite a beating from this pontoon arrangement.

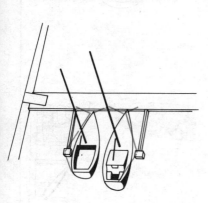

Variations on a familiar theme: the springs are winched tight.

Leaving the quay

Under sail

Leaving a quay is simple when the wind is blowing you away from it, though you need the wind ahead to be able to hoist the mainsail. If the wind is coming from abaft the beam, you can sometimes head off under jib alone; but if you are going to need the mainsail as well, you will have to take the boat round through 180° to get into one of the more-or-less head-to-wind positions shown in the diagram.

In the pale blue sector the wind is blowing from the quay, so you are lucky: you can hoist both jib and main. The boat is held to the

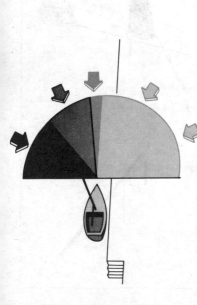

quay by the bow warp which is looped back to the deck. You now proceed as for leaving a mooring. If you want, you can use an aft spring to make sure the boat bears away.

In the dark blue sector the wind is blowing just about onto the quay, but you have still got room to hoist the mainsail without it blowing into the wall.

The boat is held by the bow warp and the aft spring which is looped back. You should ensure the area at deck level around the rear pulpit has plenty of fenders hung over it, because it will knock against the quay wall as you bear away.

The bow warp is untied and you push the front of the boat through the wind with the boathook. The boat will bear away, still tied by the rear spring, and you can release the spring and trim the sails once the boat reaches a close fetch.

In the grey sector the wind is blowing onto the quay and you dare not hoist the mainsail; it is still possible to get under way under jib alone, however.

First the bow warp is untied, then the bow is pushed round using the boathook until it is through the eye of the wind. Only then do you hoist the jib and back it to bring you round. The boat will bear away, pushing backward against the quay wall with its stern. Once you are round so that the wind is on the beam, you can pull the jib in normally and undo the spring. The boat will move off rather sideways, so you need some room to leeward.

In the black sector the wind is pinning the boat to the quay, and you cannot move off under sail.

If you took the precaution of dropping an anchor as you came into the quay, you can always pull the boat round on the anchor so

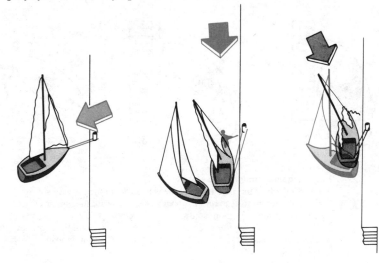

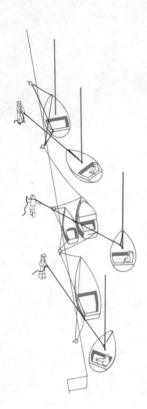

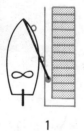

it is head to wind and the sails can be hoisted. If you did not drop an anchor, it is not too late: you can send the tender off to put one out. And of course you still have the possibility of using the sculling oar, pulling a warp round, or even (gasp!) starting the engine, to bring you to a spot where you can anchor or drift and pull the sails up at your leisure.

Under engine power

Getting under way using the engine is much simpler than using the sails: there are only two scenarios to work through, and you do not need the wind to be forward of the beam.

In the grey and black sectors you start off with the engine in reverse. The operation relies on the fact that (whether you are using the engine or not), the front of the boat does not lead the turn: the stern slides out round any corner. As the boat turns, it is as though it was pivoting about a point situated just aft of the mast.

If you are tied up alongside a quay and you try to leave in forward gear, the rear quarter of the boat will press against the wall and scrape along as you turn.

For this reason, you need to take the stern of the boat out from the wall, using a spring tied between the bow and a point on the quay as far back as, and at about the same height as, the boat's widest point. You can move gently forward until the spring goes tight, then put the boat into gear, pulling the tiller so as to turn the bow in toward the quay. The stern then drifts out until the boat reaches a sufficient angle for you to reverse out of the gap.

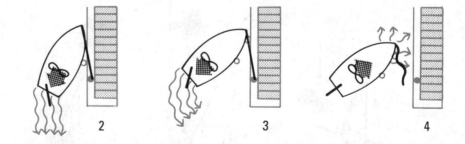

1   2   3   4

Leaving a quay under engine power
1. Put out the fenders and take in all the warps except the forward spring.
2. Pull the tiller up so as to turn the boat's bow in toward the quay wall, gently at first to tighten the spring, then more confidently, so the boat pivots.
3. The longer you keep this operation going, the easier it will be to get out.
4. Engage reverse gear, centre the tiller and bring the spring inboard.
This procedure works for all wind directions.

In the blue sectors you start out as though you were using the sails, but using the tiller only when the boat is sufficiently far out from the wall not to scratch the rear quarter. If there is too great a risk of scraping along the wall, you can set out in reverse gear.

Going aground

It is better to go aground in harbour than out at sea or by accident. To landlubbers, going aground sounds shameful however it is done, but we should distinguish firmly between the two ways it can be done:
1. Deliberately and after careful planning: the boat can *take the ground* if you decide to ground her in a harbour which dries out at low tide, or to carry out any work on the underwater hull surfaces.
2. Accidentally, as a result of some navigational mistake: this is known as *running aground*, and tends to happen on a shoal or sandbank.

Taking the ground

Not all boats are equally well equipped for taking the ground. We can distinguish between three main types:

1. Those which were designed without considering the possibility of taking the ground: these generally have a deep draft and a narrow underwater shape.
2. Those which were designed to take the ground simply and frequently, such as twin-keeled boats and most boats with a retractable keel or centreboard.
3. Those which were designed with the possibility in mind that they might take the ground occasionally: this accounts for most modern single-keeled yachts.
   There is little point spending time on the first sort of boat.
   Twin-keeled boats, in the second category, are masters of taking the ground. So long as there is no serious chop or undertow, they will cope with any reasonable bottom surface. Drop-keel or centreboard boats, *however many hulls they have*, can cope only with even, homogeneous surfaces which have no sharp objects (rocks, old anchors, etc) sticking up. They still have a rudder to worry about, and you should not allow this to take any weight. If these conditions are fulfilled, there will be no stability problems.
   It is the third category which we need to spend some time looking at.

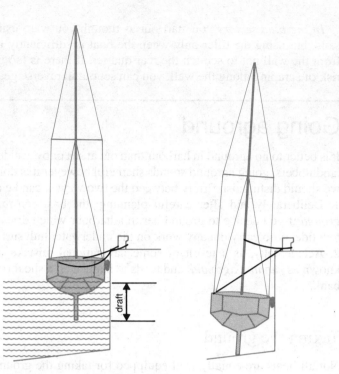

Do not forget that the fenders will be compressed, and the shrouds must not be allowed to bear on the quay.

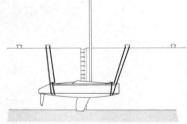

Taking the ground by the quay
Boats with a deep narrow keel can easily tip forward or aft, so they should be equipped with a vertical rope at the stem and stern which passes underneath the hull. (If the rope is attached to the deck, it will rip something out.)

Taking the ground alongside

When you are tied up alongside the quay wall, you can take the ground, so long as the boat is leant slightly in toward the wall.

The first thing to check is that the keel will have a decent spot to rest on; then you need to heel the boat to the wall by 2 or 3°, no more. Once the boat grounds, the fenders will be compressed against the wall and the boat will naturally heel further over; it should not be allowed to heel so far that the shrouds begin to bear on the wall. (If this does start to happen, slacken the shrouds immediately.)

The boat can be tied against the quay using a warp fastened on the outside rail, so it presses more firmly inwards. Use warps and breast ropes for this. A warp wrapped around the mast is not up to the job.

The warp network needs to be tightened just before the keel touches bottom: as you touch, the boat needs to be firmly pressed to the wall by the warps. If this is not achieved, it will heel excessively.

If the keel is narrow, you might find it necessary to attach extra lines to the bow and stern to make sure the boat does not tip forward or aft.

This is a very agreeable way to take the ground: you will not need your waders or the 'legs' to support the boat.

If you take the ground anywhere other than by the quay, you will need to use legs or accept that the boat will lie over on its side.

Taking the ground on legs

Legs are put in place to make sure the boat balances on its keel. They are not designed to take significant strains themselves, and nor are their mounting points. This means that a boat can only take the ground on legs if the ground is flat and all the same degree of hardness or softness. It must not be allowed to lean.

Before you fit the legs, you need to check the ground, prodding all around the boat with a boathook. It is rare for a rocky bottom to be flat. Muddy bottoms are rarely even-textured: they almost always have a rock or old paving stone hidden in them which means that one leg or one part of the keel is better supported than the rest. You should really only ground using legs on sand or shingle bottoms.

If the ground is on a slope, such as on a beach, you need to ground the boat facing up the slope. If it is across the slope it will lean, and if it is facing down the slope, it might fall on its nose.

Laying the boat on its side

If the boat is dried out on its side, the chances are that everything on board will fall out of its rightful place and there will be chaos in the cabin. However, *the boat is safer and in a more natural position when it is lying on its side than it is when taking the ground in any other way.* This technique can only be used on a soft mud bottom; and remember that the mast needs a lot of space off to the side.

Drying out for scrubbing

On legs

A low tide in harbour can be used to best advantage if you want to scrub the bottom of the boat, but beaches are generally cleaner, and since they are sloping, you can calculate very precisely where you need to beach the boat for the minimum length of stay. (You simply take the ground when there is still a depth of water approximately one-and-a-half times your draft to drop until low tide. You can beach earlier if you want to take your time.)

Before you take the ground on a beach, you need to check that it has a regular texture to it, with no hard and soft patches, rocks, etc. (To be certain, check at the previous low tide, prodding with the boathook or a paddle.) You also need to check the weather forecast and that there is no surf on that part of the beach just before low tide.

How to take the ground. Before you reach the beach, anchor over the stern as far as possible out from the water's edge. This should allow you later to pull yourself out to sea without the anchor dragging. Use a warp as the anchor line rather than a chain: it is lighter, longer and runs out more easily.

Take the ground at a fair speed, say, 2kn, and with the boat slightly heeled, so that it is properly immobilised straight away. If you cannot take the ground fast enough (or dare not), take an anchor ashore to hold the bow fast that way.

Once the boat is stopped, and only then, put the legs out. If you try to do this while the boat is still floating and mobile, the legs become dangerous weapons. *A boat which is allowed to move with its legs in place ages 10 years in as many minutes.*

If you beach at a reasonable speed, and with the boat heeling, the operation will run more smoothly and the boat will suffer less.

In practice, you can even wait for the sea to go down another 20cm before putting the legs in place (which might take only a few minutes on some western Channel beaches at spring tides, or as much as half an hour in the Glénans islands at neap tides).

How to move off. The legs must be removed as early as possible when the sea comes in again, without waiting for the boat to start moving! Particularly if there is any surf or undertow, the legs should be removed as soon as the whole keel is submerged.

Drying out by the quay or on your side

Both these methods have the same disadvantage: it is impossible to clean both sides of the hull in one tide. If you dry the boat out by the quayside, you can usually not reach the side near the wall, unless you have a very large incompressible fender or can manage to wedge some sort of prop in-between. To finish the job if you cannot do this means you have to heel the boat away from the wall once it will float, and complete the scrubbing from the tender, or just take the ground again on the other side at the next tide.

Drying the boat out on its side on the sand is the best way of dealing with wide or shallow-draft vessels: this makes scrubbing considerably easier than if the boat is left on legs. Unless your boat is small or you have a lot of helpers, you will need two tides to complete the scrubbing, though.

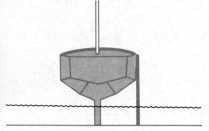

There is already enough water for you to take away one leg.

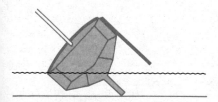

If the boat tips over, no harm is done.

Scrubbing afloat (careening)

The hull can be scrubbed without taking the ground (ie while the boat is still afloat). This is known as careening, and is a particularly useful technique in areas which are virtually tideless, as it is the only way of getting at the bottom of the boat without paying slipway fees. *The operation must be carried out with great precision, or it could cost you your mast, which is more than a year's slipway fees ...*

You need to heel the boat over until the keel is horizontal. This is done from the tender, using a rope which has been *attached to the mast at the hounds* (the shroud fixing points) and not elsewhere. If the jib halyard is led over a block, rather than through a sheave, and if there is a shroud fixed at the same height, you may use the halyard. The operation is easier if a member of the crew clambers up the mast to the same spot (not elsewhere). The point is worth repeating: *any force must bear at the hounds, and nowhere else, or there is a strong possibility of breaking the mast.*

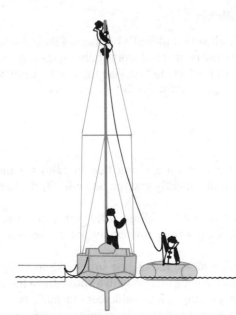

The nimblest member of the crew climbs up to the hounds and attaches a line.

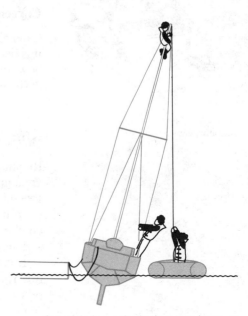

One of the less enthusiastic mountaineers on board heels the boat slightly, so that the boat can be pulled down by the sailor in the tender. Note: the boat is only loosely tied up; and our climbing expert has not moved from the hounds.

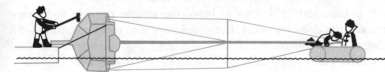

The boat remains held at the hounds.

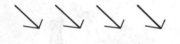

There is no shortage of helpers, but nor is there any guarantee of success.

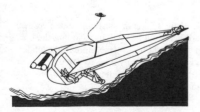

The most effective rescue operation is carrying the light anchor gear off, so you can haul the boat along on that.

Once the boat is horizontal, you might find you can rest the keel on a pontoon, which makes the hull easier to work on. Otherwise, you need to continue holding the boat flat for the whole duration: this means you need a second tender and at least one extra crew member to do the scrubbing. To bring a 6.5m boat over on its side takes three people. Once it is laid flat, two can hold it in place while the third scrubs it down.

You can also careen a boat next to the shore, *so long as the hull is not allowed to touch the bottom.*

Once one side is clean, the climber sits back at the hounds and the boat is allowed gently back upright. It can then be brought over to clean the other side. When you have finished the whole job, you can let the boat upright with no one on the mast, just by letting go of the line on the mast. Righting the boat is not very spectacular, though: it is actually a little disappointing!

Careening multihulls

Careening is difficult with multihulls because of their shallow draft. It is better to beach the boat at a steeply shelving spot, then prop the bows on old tyres or fenders, and support the rear by using specially designed cradles slung just forward of the rudders.

Running aground

Running aground gently, on a rising tide in calm weather, is no great matter. You wait patiently and the tide will lift the boat off the ground.

In bad weather, or with a falling tide, you need to react very quickly indeed if this simple mishap is not to become a more serious problem.

It is often enough to use the engine in reverse to push the boat off. You might need to back this up with a shove from the boathook or a paddle, or by picking a few volunteers to jump out and push (thus also relieving the boat of their weight). If these first efforts show no sign of bearing fruit, you need to put the light anchor gear in the tender immediately and send it off as far as possible, drop the anchor and then heave the boat along on that line. (Do not use chain for this task, as it is much too short and much too heavy.)

It is especially pointless to leave the engine running for long periods if it does not work fairly quickly: it is too weak to be of more than incidental use. When you are using the engine, make sure there are no rope ends floating about or hanging over the side.

Heeling the boat

Heeling the boat before you are ready to get the boat off the bottom using other means is likely to result in you grounding it higher up the sandbank! If you are ready with the anchor line, paddles and crew members pushing, on the other hand, then you should be prepared to heel the boat considerably (to at least 30–45°). There is only one way of achieving so much heel: sending your resident monkey up the mast. Using legs in this situation is the surest way of wrecking your boat, since the legs are designed for holding a boat upright, not heeling it over. You have no way of knowing whether the boat will remain vertical once the tide goes further out, and if it leans over to one side, a leg can slip or break, causing considerable damage. *In all cases, it is less dangerous to let the boat dry out on its side.*

If the bottom is muddy or sandy, there is no risk at all. If it is rocky, you need to provide the boat with a soft landing. You can protect the sides of the hull by putting down fenders, coils of rope or even mattresses.

Then you sit and wait. If you are in a hurry, just make sure you do not run aground at spring high tide ... or in the Mediterranean.

The tender

We cannot conclude this chapter without a few remarks on the subject of the boat's best friend, its tender. The tender is a faithful servant, though of occasionally uncertain temper: we ask it to perform remarkable feats, then to curl up in a corner, forgotten until it is next needed.

Whenever the tender was needed over the course of this chapter, it has been mentioned. It will turn up again regularly in the chapter on towing. We shall limit ourselves here to talking about the tender in those situations where you let it off the leash, and it becomes the boat's link between itself and the land.

Travelling in an inflatable dinghy is not entirely risk-free. On the one hand, the poor dinghy is generally overloaded with people and gear, in the forlorn and unreasonable hope of saving that one extra shuttle journey. On the other hand, it is difficult to steer, since the person paddling it will not always be in a position to use all their strength on such a light vessel, and has probably less elbow room than they would like. The most significant hazard for those using the tender, though, is the combined force of wind and current, which can easily sweep it off course.

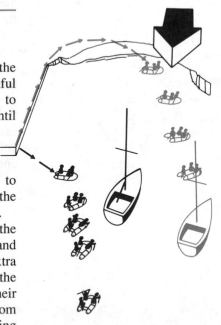

Carrying a boat round on land is almost as tiring as paddling against wind and current, but a whole lot safer.

Good sailors may be recognised by the way they use the tender. In strong wind and strong current, they will carry the tender round on land to the spot from which it can drift to its destination. If they need to make headway against a wind, they will sit on an upturned bucket and paddle with short fast strokes. When they come up to a boat, it will be alongside and head to wind. (If you need to, you can come alongside facing downwind, but you must never come crashing straight into the side of your boat.)

Within the limits of its size, a tender should be as safe and usable as a proper boat. It must be unsinkable and be permanently equipped with a suitable anchor (say, 3–4kg) and line (50m or so). If it is to be rowed, you need to have a spare oar. It is also worth keeping a couple of paddles on board. And you must all wear life-jackets on board. You can buy rigid tenders (usually made of glass fibre) or inflatables. We prefer the latter, which are very safe and take up little space on board.

When you are on land, make sure you tie up the tender so that it does not scrape against the quay wall or the beach. It should be moored diagonally to the jetty, or better still, pulled out of the water altogether.

Coming into land, you suddenly realise why you like being away: the wind is less regular than at sea, the currents more fickle, the water shallower and the mud stickier. What is more, there are boats everywhere! You need to take great care coming into the land. You might plan to approach the beach in one way, but your plan must always be flexible and capable of last-minute changes: you must keep your eyes and mind open and your vessel moving. Not all the land's tricks work against you: you can use the current and the wind eddies to your advantage. Even the presence of other boats can be very useful. But this list of factors which influence the way you handle your tender in a harbour would be incomplete without one further item …

That item is the welcome you get when you arrive. You should never rely on this to cover up for poor boat handling, but nor can you ignore it. There is always someone hanging about on the quay-side, only too happy to pick up the warp you throw, and tie it onto a ring. The general mood on the water in a harbour is a happy one. The harbour itself is protected not only from the open sea, but also from the rush of the big city: it has a more relaxed atmosphere, and ill-temper is even more out of place than petrol fumes. The people who inhabit the harbour share a secret, which begins when one hand throws a warp, and a different hand ties it onto a post to help out. That secret is the community of the sea.

CHAPTER 5
Man overboard

This is our final chapter on handling a boat under sail. It is rather different from the previous chapters. Manoeuvring the boat is only a small part of what needs to be done when a crew member falls overboard: we also have to cover prevention techniques, how to pick people out of the sea and any first aid that might be necessary. We have chosen to include all these topics here, although they are not all questions of boat handling, and in part because of the light they throw on the preceding chapters. This chapter shows the difficulty of combining good theory with good practice, and it should serve as a reminder of the need for rigour and crew training in the use of your boat. It is fine to be able to make a boat move, but complete mastery involves being able to stop the boat and hold it in one place under sail while the crew is occupied with other things. This is at least as important. Knowing that you can manage these things can give a whole new sense of relaxation to your everyday sailing … and it might one day help you to save a life.

The risk

Of all the risks we take at sea, the risk of falling in is the most frequent and the most serious. Jonah will never forget his experience of it, for he was one of the lucky ones who made it back to terra firma. Whales are dying out these days, so there are certain issues about which we need to be quite clear:

• There is a permanent likelihood of falling overboard. You are just as likely to fall overboard in nice weather as in a gale, but the risks associated with doing so are smaller.
• Picking up someone lost overboard in good weather is easy, given a certain minimum crew training.
• In very bad weather, the chances of picking anyone up are slim.
• At night, whatever the weather, anyone lost overboard cannot be found unless they are equipped with a light.
• Downwind, by day or night, such accidents are more serious than they are when the boat is close-hauled: you move on past the person

in the water very fast, and matters are not made any easier by the fact that you are using a spinnaker or a poled-out genoa.

• The victim is frequently the skipper, who tends to think that normal rules about clipping on apply only to other people. The crew is often less skilled at carrying out the recovery operation without the skipper's directions to help.

• This accident can happen to anyone on board, not only those on deck. On one of the Glénans boats, the *Arche*, one crew member was literally caught by a turn in the mainsheet as the boat was gybing, and thrown overboard. On another occasion, aboard the *Glénan*, someone stuck his head out of the cabin to take a bearing just as the boat was knocked flat by a squall: the next minute, he was picking himself out of the guard rail where the sudden knock-down had thrown him. And we all know someone who is so prone to seasickness that they have the habit of rushing out of the cabin on a rough day with neither safety line nor lifejacket on …

• Falling overboard is by definition unexpected, and often caused by the stupidest things. You can predict sudden broaches or the occasional big wave, but there are always unexpected variations in boat speed, false moves made with a paddle or a boathook, over-anxious grabs after a slippery fish, bailing buckets which pull you off balance, and so on.

• You can easily fall overboard while the boat is at anchor. This can become serious if you are anchored in a current, for instance.

Let's face it, having human beings sailing the seas always involves some risk, and you can never make an exhaustive list of the cases in which an accident might happen. For the same reason,

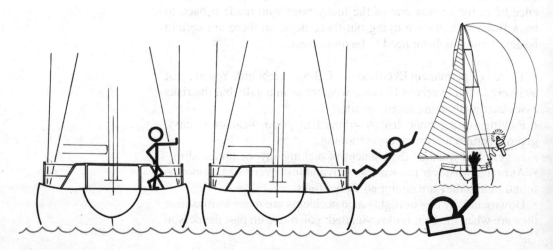

there is no known anti-accident panacea. There will always be some new situation which involves you taking a fast decision, on your own: you need to be ready and aware of this.

We should not overdramatise the need for quick decisions: you can avoid much of the risk and much of the need for decisions by taking a few simple precautions. We shall begin by looking at various sorts of precautions, then continue with a look at what to do if an accident happens despite your precautions.

Precautions

Since the beginning of seafaring, people have applied their industry and imagination to the dangers of the sea and invented means for avoiding or minimising the dangers one by one.

There is an enormous range of safety gear available today. Let us run through it quickly in a logical order:
– the boat's deck is covered in anti-slip material;
– if our would-be swimmer slips despite the anti-slip surface, there is a foot strap or handrail to grab onto;
– having missed the handrail, the swimmer next has to overcome the obstacle of the guard rail;
– once the swimmer has vaulted the gaurd rail, their own harness wire comes into play and holds them fast against the side of the boat;
– if the harness line breaks (or was not attached in the first place, more likely!), then the swimmer will thank their lucky stars for their lifejacket (if they are wearing one);

– the lifebuoy light is the next thing into the water, attached to a long line, the other end of which is the horseshoe lifebelt. The lifebelt will keep the swimmer afloat while the boat turns round and comes back;
– the spot at which the person was lost overboard is marked by an IOR pole buoy;
– the swimmer should be equipped with a watertight light, a life-jacket and a whistle; there should also be reflective strips stuck to everyone's waterproofs, lifejackets and hoods, so as to aid recognition in the water (this is one of those rare times in life when you might be thankful for a garish taste in clothes);
– once the swimmer has been spotted and has a firm grip on a rope or some part of the boat, you must use anything available to get them on board: ladders, ropes, the tender;
– anyone who has spent a while in the water can be in a sorry state by the time they are back on board: you then need to go through a routine of resuscitation and warming them up to get them back on their (hopefully non-slip) feet.

We have described the equipment for these procedures in the chapter entitled 'Gear' in Part III, but we need now to look in more detail at how it is used. In doing so, we make two logical assumptions which are actually the opposite of what we would like to believe, namely: that the person was perhaps not tied onto the boat, and was perhaps not wearing a lifejacket. These are the psychological links in what is otherwise a perfectly logical chain.

This is actually the heart of the problem: if you are tied on, you have little to worry about; if you are not tied on, you should be worrying; and if you are short of buoyancy, expect the worst ...

When should I clip on and put on my lifejacket?

At what stage does the precaution of clipping your safety harness on become worthwhile? We have gone through a number of situations above in which clipping on seems to us absolutely imperative. In general, though, this must be left above all to the captain's judgement. The question the captain should have constantly in mind is: 'If someone were to fall in the water now, could we rescue them easily?' If so, fine. If not, harnesses and lifejackets must be worn and used. If either the crew is inexperienced or the boat is unfamiliar to them, the skipper should have a further question in mind: 'If I fell in now, could this bunch rescue me?' If not, the skipper should be clipped on even in the most perfect conditions.

The moral is: *you need to take extra precautions not because the risk of falling in has increased, but because the chances of being rescued if you do fall in have decreased.*

Recovery manoeuvres

Let us now assume that our Jonah has fallen overboard; despite all our warnings above, he didn't clip on, and his life now depends upon our reactions and the crew's skill.

There are as many correct recovery manoeuvres as there are potential precautions. If the first option fails, the second should be there ready to take its place, and a third after that. If that fails, start again from the beginning. Nor is there a general rule of what you need to do: we shall propose a few courses of action which have been found effective, but our list is not exclusive. What you do depends on external circumstances, on your crew and your boat. However, there should at least be an agreed procedure for your boat, and everyone must know what it is, they must have practised it and they must know what to do in all foreseeable situations, including knowing who takes over if the skipper falls overboard.

The first moments

The first few seconds are vital. Immediately (and preferably simultaneously), the following things must happen:

1. Shout '*Man overboard!*' to alert the whole crew.
2. Try to *maintain contact* with Jonah by throwing him the lifebuoy and light, with the line running out behind it.
3. Drop the IOR pole dan buoy over to mark the spot.
4. *Stop the boat* as close as possible to Jonah.

The first three actions are easy, and should be automatic reflexes. Stopping the boat is not always that simple.

Let us look at a few scenarios:

• The boat is sailing along under plain sail. Whatever point of sailing you are on, the helm can stop the boat by throwing it past head to wind without touching the sheets. This gives you time to think.

• The boat is under sails which make steering difficult: a spinnaker or poled-out genoa. You still have to stop. The helm luffs up and lets off the spinnaker guy completely. (This shows the importance of not tying a figure-of-eight knot in the end of the spinnaker sheets: you might need to get rid of the spinnaker completely, letting go the guy, sheet and halyard.) If you are using a poled-out genoa, you luff until the genoa collapses under the main. Clearly, the crew will need to practise these manoeuvres to find out how the boat responds.

• The boat was in the middle of some manoeuvre. (This is a common time to lose someone overboard.) Everyone will be on deck anyway, so you can respond quickly, and you can decide which way to go depending on circumstances.

In gentle weather, even under spinnaker, Jonah will be able to catch the floating lifebuoy without you throwing all the line overboard. The only change you need to make to the sails is to let out the spinnaker guy.

If there are not enough of you to drop the spinnaker, you just need to let off the halyard and sheet to get rid of it. The spinnaker is comparatively worthless anyway.

It does not matter how much chaos there is on deck: if the boat is moving sufficiently slowly, you will be able to haul Jonah back on board even with a 5mm diameter rope. Note: *the tiller is hard to leeward and stays there.*

In many cases, Jonah will be able to grab the lifebuoy with a short swim of 10 or 20m. He then slips his hand through the loop in the line (or better still, clips his harness onto the loop). When he has done this, those on board make two round turns and two half-hitches with their end of the line around the stern pulpit. It does not matter how much of a mess the jib or spinnaker is in: you have a line to Jonah, and that is the important thing.

With a trained crew, you can get a solid line to the person in the water in the first few seconds in the majority of cases.

If not, you have a few decisions to take, depending on whether you were able to stop the boat or not.

If you can stop

If you were able to stop before all the line was fed out, but you threw the lifebuoy too late for Jonah to catch it, then the situation is by no means lost: you have time to get everyone on deck and prepare the boat for the return to the scene of the accident.

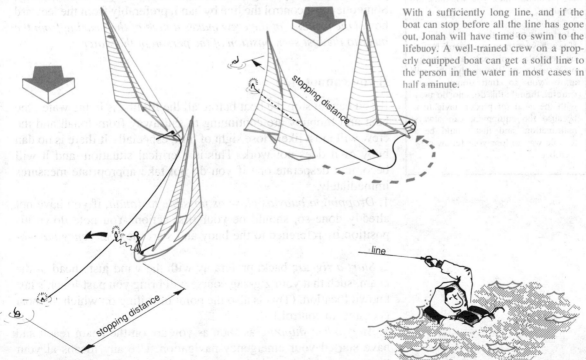

With a sufficiently long line, and if the boat can stop before all the line has gone out, Jonah will have time to swim to the lifebuoy. A well-trained crew on a properly equipped boat can get a solid line to the person in the water in most cases in half a minute.

With a lifebuoy which is properly installed and easy to throw, it is easy to make up for the stopping distance of the boat.

The line should be held above the head to avoid being towed under the water.

Emergency navigation

The log book
You need to keep a very precise log for a very short time. In one corner of the chart, you note down as you go along, as precisely as you can: the time of the accident, the precise time (to within 10 seconds) of any change of course, all compass headings and speeds. The emergency log is maintained until you have recovered the lost crew member.

Proper navigation
From a chosen point, ideally the middle of your chart, trace all the compass headings as though they were real courses sailed, and all the distances covered, according to a simple scale, say, 1cm per knot per minute. This should allow you to give the helm a precise bearing once the boat is ready, and to predict accurately the point at which you will pick up Jonah.

Electronic navigation
If you have a 'man overboard' button on your electronic navigation equipment (and press it promptly), this will allow you to find Jonah again. Careful, though: this does not do away with the need for proper navigation, because the equipment can always malfunction, and that would be a terrible way to lose your fellow crew member.

While you are waiting:
– the most important thing is to keep Jonah in sight. If you dropped the dan buoy, there is no immediate risk; otherwise, one person should take on exclusively the job of watcher, announcing what they are doing;
– and there is an urgent decision to be taken regarding the float line: whether to pull it in or leave it trailing?
• It should be pulled in if the weather is good and there is plenty of daylight, as the boat will be turning round quickly anyway. As you approach Jonah, you will need the line again to reach him.
• It should also be pulled in if the dan buoy is floating visibly and close to Jonah.
• It must be left trailing if you have a second line, if it is night, if the pole light is not working, in bad conditions or if it will take you a while to turn the boat round. Under these circumstances, the lifebuoy light is actually a useful marker for the place you lost touch, and can be a good place to meet up again. Be careful, though: it is hard to keep the flare in one place if you heave to and tack round, as you will inevitably drag the flare downwind as you make leeway. Someone must control the line by hand, preferably from the leeward bow. *One member of the crew makes a note of the bearing from the buoy to the last seen position of the person in the water.*

If you cannot stop

If you cannot stop the boat before all the lifeline is in the water, the boat and lifebuoy are continuing to sail away from Jonah and the crew will most likely lose sight of him, especially if there is no dan buoy or it does not work. This is a critical situation, and it will become a desperate one if you do not take appropriate measures immediately.

1. *Dropping a buoy as close as possible to Jonah*, if you have not already done so, should be your first action. You note down his position by reference to the buoy and start the *emergency navigation*.

2. *Start a zig-zag* back, preferably with the wind just ahead of the beam, such that your zig-zag course will bring you past Jonah's last known location. (This is also the point of sailing on which the boat is easiest to control.)

3. *Alert other shipping* as soon as you are on the beam reach and have started your emergency navigation. Use any means at your disposal: rocket flares if there are other boats in sight, VHF radio on band 16 or single side band at 2182kHz. This is entirely justified by the situation.

Spotting the man overboard

If Jonah or the pole are in view, sail back towards them; if not, follow the directions of the emergency navigator. Dropping a buoy is so important we cannot stress it sufficiently. The only way this emergency can become fatal is if you fail to find the person in the water. Doubtless some people have drowned fairly soon after falling overboard, but how many more must there be who have been perfectly conscious, watching their boat criss-crossing a route leading gradually further away? A person in the water with no life-jacket has a chance of being seen as much as 100m away, but you need to be less than 50m away to be sure of spotting them. This illustrates how precise your emergency navigation needs to be and how important it is to drop a marker right at the spot of the mishap: the marker is the *only* way you can be sure of finding Jonah again.

If Jonah is not found immediately, start combing the area.

It is possible to increase the distance at which a person in the sea is visible, especially if the person is wearing bright clothing or a reflective life-jacket. This is done by posting a lookout up the mast, at the hounds. Make sure the lookout is not easily seasick!

Combing the area

Combing an area means crossing it back and forth so that you go within a maximum of 50m of every point in the area at least twice. We recommend the following method: take two points about 200m to windward and to leeward of the estimated location of the fall, and tack from one to the other. Each tack should be 100m long, ie take about a minute in the average boat, including tacks. You then extend the area to be searched by another 200m to leeward and to windward, making your tacks 200–300m long, say, 2 minutes including the turn. The tacks should be less close to the wind than usual so your zig-zags do not take you more than 50m from any point in the area. You can mark the area to be searched with floating objects (such as fenders) equipped with sea anchors (buckets, coils of rope, lightly weighted clothes) so they do not drift too far.

But are you searching the right area? This is the question everyone asks themselves, especially if they failed to put out markers in time. While the boat is combing back and forth, one crew member should check the emergency navigator's calculations.

The search must continue while there is still a chance of finding Jonah alive. *In the Atlantic, in temperate latitudes, you should not give up searching for a person in a lifejacket for 8–10 hours.*

What if I am Jonah?

You do not just lie back waiting to be rescued. You can contribute to your own rescue.

HELP (Heat Escape Lessening Position), which gives the slowest possible rate of heat loss.

The first thing to do is to try and catch hold of the line if it is within reach. Do not attempt to swim long distances, because this could be exhausting, and you might be in the water for some time. Of course, if you are not wearing a lifejacket, it is worth trying a little harder to reach the line, because there is a lifebelt on the end.

As soon as you have hold of the line, or have worked out that you will not be able to get hold of it, you need to improve your flotation, if necessary by blowing up your lifejacket or climbing into the lifebelt. You also need to check and adjust your harness fitting.

Ensure that you lose heat at the slowest possible rate, by fastening your clothing and keeping your shoes on, reducing movement and taking up the HELP position if possible.

Establishing a line

Once Jonah has been found, he needs to be attached to the boat quickly, easily and precisely. While a boat is reaching it can sail quickly, and steering becomes more precise at speed. The boat should pass close to Jonah (3–5m away) and the lifebuoy light should be thrown 2–3m in front of him so as not to knock him out. The boat then continues onward for another two or three boat-lengths before heaving to and tacking without letting go the sheets.

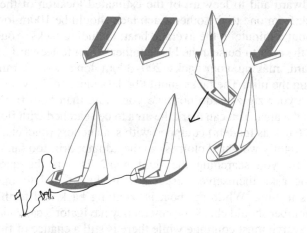

Is it better to pass to windward or to leeward? It does not matter much, so long as you pass close. Nevertheless, it is easier to throw downwind than upwind …

If you miss Jonah, start again in the same way, but leaving more space and time. You need to remain calm and overcome the anxiety which influences everyone's behaviour in this situation.

If you left the line floating and Jonah caught it, then pull the line along forward and 20cm below the surface using the boathook. The boat should be stopped as soon as there is a line established to Jonah.

If you have more than one line on board, you can attach a small float to a warp about 20 or 30m long, with a loop on the end.

If the search took a long time or Jonah appears exhausted, and especially if he is not wearing a lifejacket or harness, someone should go and fetch him. One crew member, warmly dressed, fully equipped and firmly attached to the boat, should jump in and take hold of Jonah around the middle to keep him buoyed up. As soon as possible, there should be another line made fast: you do not want to take the chance of losing the person you have just rescued. Any line used should be supple and with a little 'give' in it. To avoid jolts, the lines should be handheld on deck; and to avoid accidents, made fast around a cleat, leaving a little slack.

What about the engine?

We have so far limited our description of the search to using the sails. However, the engine can be of great assistance in this exercise. No one cares about style: it's results that count, and just as you need to be able to use the sails in case of engine failure, you need to be able to use the engine in case the sails will not work.

On a sailing vessel, you are probably under sail when Jonah falls overboard; for this reason, we have assumed at least that the recovery manoeuvres begin under sail. Once you have dropped a marker buoy or established his position, once you have got the boat and the emergency navigation sorted out, you can think about continuing the operation under engine power.

If the engine is to be used, it must be sufficiently powerful to allow you to manoeuvre exactly as you need in the prevailing conditions, the sails must be dropped and stowed; and all trailing ropes which might get in the way of the propeller must be brought inboard.

A mixture of sails and engine is not recommended, as there is too great a danger of catching a rope in the propeller.

If you manage to fulfil all these conditions, retrieving your lost crew member could be easier under engine power than with sails. There are still problems, though: the rescue line in particular, and Jonah, whom we do not wish to injure as we come to collect him!

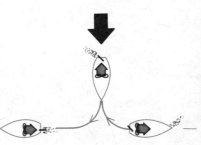

If the weather is really awful, some sailing boats will not be able to turn their bow through the wind, in which case they have to be turned stern to wind. This inevitably means losing ground to windward, so the engine should be used in reverse until you are facing dead downwind; you follow this by luffing up as fast as possible, engine full speed ahead and tiller right down to leeward.

Bringing Jonah aboard

Occasionally you will have a couple of gorillas on board who can pull their shipmate out of the drink straight away, and he'll be right as rain. This is the exception. Even in pleasant weather, the person who falls overboard falls into another world: paralysed by fear and stricken by a panic attack, even the soberest individual cannot be immune. No training can prepare you for the real thing: every instinct works against an efficient rescue, as you clamp your fingers white-knuckled to the nearest rail, and your rescuers may well have to unclamp them for you, forcibly. A moment later every ounce of strength ebbs away and you would fall back into the water unless firmly held. Add to that your weight: you may weigh only 75kg dry, but a suit full of water can make that up to 110–120kg, and any heeling of the boat can add enough momentum to make you seem 200kg. If you are not wearing a harness, it will be difficult to get hold of you, especially in rough weather. Your rescuers need to know what they are doing; they need the correct gear; and they need to have practised.

Bringing Jonah alongside

Once attached to a line, he needs to be brought round to a spot from which he can be hoisted aboard. On a monohull, this spot is slightly aft of the mast and to leeward, where the boat has least freeboard, and even that can be reduced by heeling the boat; you are also sheltered from the worst of the waves, and drifting slightly downwind, thus keeping Jonah firmly alongside. There are two problems with this: it is occasionally difficult to get Jonah in place; and once there, he may be so well pushed up against the hull that he can be washed under it. If the boat has a transom scoop, Jonah can be manoeuvred into that and hoisted up, though any pitching of the boat in the sea can render this operation dangerous. Multihulls have such narrow hulls that Jonah should be brought on board wherever there is room for the rescuers: in this case, freeboard is a secondary consideration.

Unfortunately, the likeliest place for Jonah to end up is behind the boat and to windward, and *it is to avoid this that we tack and heave to several boat-lengths after we have passed the line to him.* If you do this and then pull the line from the foredeck, Jonah will arrive naturally at the right spot. If he is behind the boat and to windward, you can pull him all the way round the stern, so long as there is someone in the water to help him fend the boat off, or he is capable of doing this himself; alternatively, you can tack round, giving slack but not letting go. This is rather easier under engine than under sail.

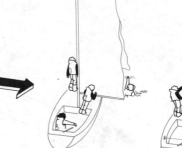

Hoisting Jonah aboard

You should now waste no time in pulling Jonah aboard, as experience shows that it is difficult to keep him in the right place for long.

On a small boat with little freeboard, the operation is fairly simple: the boat is hove to with the crew to leeward accentuating the heel. The rail is thus at about water level, and you only need to undo or cut the lower guard rail wire for Jonah to be rolled on board. There is no real hoisting involved. If there is a little too much freeboard for you to do this, you might be able to drag Jonah out of the water by seizing him under the armpits. If you do this, he should be facing away from the boat, or his knees will catch on the way up.

On a large boat with lots of freeboard or a multihull the operation is quite different. The first solution that comes to mind is the boarding ladder. If this is to be used it must be up to the job: rigid and solidly attached to the transom, with at least three rungs below the water surface. If Jonah has the strength to grab on and climb up, then the problem is solved; and this is the case sufficiently often to justify the presence of the ladder. If Jonah is too exhausted to climb the ladder, the situation is entirely different, depending on whether he is wearing a harness (with a crotch strap, of course) or not. Assuming Jonah is wearing a harness and has been able to hook onto a line, you are in no further danger of losing each other. So long as the hook holds, it is a question of strength, and a well-rigged block and tackle should hoist a giant aboard without much effort.

If Jonah has no harness on, you are still not on the home straight. There are instances of boats managing to bring a crew member alongside, only to find their efforts to hoist them aboard ending by pulling their clothing off piece by piece, while the person stays firmly in the water. It may be appropriate to send a harnessed crew member overboard to help, or to use the tender or the liferaft. If you use the liferaft, be very careful with its painter and fixing points, which were not designed for this sort of use.

Using a block and tackle

Often it is not possible to bring Jonah aboard without using a block and tackle. The rope should reach at least 2.5m at its full extent, plus the height of the boat's freeboard. It should be a four-part purchase, with a self-cleating block at the top and a figure-of-eight knot 2m in from the free end. The block and tackle may well be used for something else most of the time: it might even be the kicking strap.

The tackle is used only after attaching the top block to a halyard. The top block must be kept close to the mast to ensure the halyard does not jump off the sheave, and the free end must be pulled out of the cleat.

Once the tackle is in use, you should always be able to reach the free end, thanks to the figure-of-eight knot. When you pull, Jonah will be hoisted out of the water.

Never use a halyard on its own to hoist someone out of the water: this can easily cause the halyard to jump off the sheave.

A block and tackle can be put to use immediately only if it is:
– correctly rigged, with a well-tightened figure of eight one block's length from the free end;
– correctly stowed, either completely extended, with the strands held by cotton snap-bindings every 20cm, or pulled block-to-block with the rope coiled separately.

First aid

You have brought your shipmate back on board. If he is still in good shape, celebration all round. Occasionally, though, he will be less than fully fit. If he is just generally frozen, it is still relatively simple. It would be a terrible shame to have got this far and then to lose the battle … so on we go.

Warmth

If anyone has spent a considerable length of time in the water getting cold, even if they did not lose consciousness, they need to be warmed up. This must not happen just anyhow. The usual techniques one hears about – undressing the person, rubbing them or giving them a draught of Scotch – are not only useless, they can actually do harm.

When the body cools down, a number of reactions take place to restrict the blood flow. Firstly, the blood vessels around the outer parts (or peripheral zone) of the body constrict, then those a little closer in (the intermediate zone), leaving blood flowing properly only around the vital organs such as the heart and brain and keeping these warm. If the vital organs begin to cool down even by tenths of a degree, things can become serious.

When someone has been badly exposed to the cold, the first step to take is to avoid any further reduction in body temperature. They should not be undressed, but insulated from the outside air by being put in a big plastic sack and pressed close between two or three other people. (A sleeping bag will do if there is no survival bag on board.) The person should not be rubbed, nor given alcohol to drink. Both of these would dilate the blood vessels at the outer edges of the body, causing blood to rush to the outside while it is still relatively cold. This cooled blood can then return to the vital organs and damage them.

Giving hot drinks to anyone who has been pulled out of the sea is acceptable, as this warms them from the inside. If you cannot warm the person quickly, you should head for land and the nearest doctor as soon as possible.

Resuscitation

If Jonah is unconscious, there are two possible reasons:
– asphyxia due to swallowing too much water, which might leave

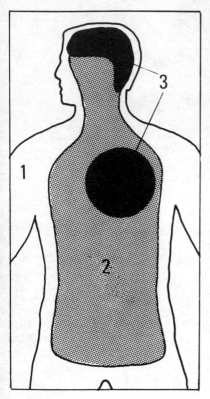

1. Peripheral zone.
2. Intermediate zone.
3. Vital organs.

him no longer breathing for the moment, but with his heart still beating;
– immersion syncope, which is a sudden loss of consciousness due to the difference in temperature between the body and the surrounding water, with loss of heartbeat, followed (if the body is still in the water) by asphyxia.

Once he is back on board, you need to check that his heart is still beating, and at the same time start artificial respiration. The best place to find a pulse is not on the wrist, but inside the groin, on the femoral artery. If there is no heartbeat, you need to carry out heart resuscitation at the same time as getting him breathing.

Mouth-to-mouth

Believe us, the slightest loss of time can mean disaster. Now is not the time to teach yourself mouth-to-mouth resuscitation. You need to have attended a course, learnt and practised it previously, and carried out exercises using a dummy. If any crew members have not been through such a course, it is by no means ridiculous for the skipper to carry out a training session before setting out from harbour on the first day.

Mouth-to-mouth resuscitation is carried out as follows:
– the patient is laid out flat on their back, with their head facing to one side; remove dentures, spittle or any foreign bodies. This must be done very quickly;
– the head is taken in both hands and stretched well back. This is essential: the patient's throat should be stretched so that the air can get into their lungs. (It is useful to pile clothes under their shoulders.);

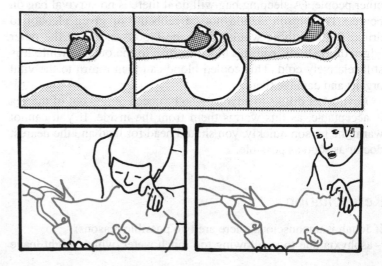

The patient's head needs to be put well back so as to open the top of the windpipe, or no air will be able to pass.

Pinch the patient's nose shut and press your mouth against the patient's. Let the air escape naturally, then start again, with about 12–15 breathing cycles per minute.

Man overboard

The purpose of drilling is so that the reflexes which could save your shipmate's life become second nature. You should drill as often as possible without letting the drill become monotonous.

There are three phases to the man overboard drill:
1. Throwing the line and the dan buoy pole over.
2. Getting into position for the pickup.
3. Bringing Jonah on board.

The exercises can be broken down further.

1. Throwing the line

The purpose of practising this is that the crew should learn the fastest way to the lifebuoy, light and heaving line, and learn about the surroundings, so they know which direction it is easiest to throw in and where one can throw the line so as not to tangle it in the rigging. You can practice this en route, throwing at no particular target to start with, then maybe aiming at a lobster pot buoy. It is preferable for the skipper to order: 'Jim, throw the light at the pot!' rather than 'Man overboard!' when practising this part of the drill. Once every member of the crew has practised throwing the line out three or four times it is worthwhile proceeding to a fuller drill.

2. Positioning yourself for the pickup

You need a dummy for this exercise: anything that floats, such as a lifejacket, weighted down with a sea anchor such as a bucket, and with a 4–5m line attached which has a lump of wood or cork on the end. The exercise consists of dropping the line less than 4 or 5m from the dummy, then stopping the boat before you reach the end of the line. Once the practice session is over, the dummy can be picked up by catching the boathook under the floating line.

3. Bringing Jonah on board

This is an important exercise. It does not matter how quickly you can find and get a line to a crew member in a force 10: if you cannot bring them on board, they will not survive.

The exercise really only has validity if you have a crew member to play dead, lying in the bottom of the tender. It should be carried out with and without harness.

You will quickly realise that a Jonah with no lifejacket needs a rope tied around his chest if he is not to be lost. You will also notice that it becomes very difficult to lift a limp body.

Note: it is considerably easier to hoist a dry and comfortable person feigning unconsciousness than it is to bring a wet and scared (or worse still, panic-stricken) Jonah on board.

Man overboard drill

– press with one hand on the patient's forehead. With one hooked finger of the other hand, pull their lower lip down so as to open their mouth wide;
– press your lips close around the patient's mouth, pressing your cheek against their nostrils to avoid air escaping that way;
– blow hard. You should see their chest rise. If it does not, this is probably because the head is not far enough back;
– draw back slightly to let them breathe out, then blow again according to whatever rhythm suits you (about 12–15 cycles per minute).

A few special cases:
– if the patient is rigid and you cannot open their mouth, you have to use mouth-to-nose. The head position is the same; use one hand to press their forehead back and down; use the thumb of the other to keep their lips closed. Blow, but be careful not to obstruct the nasal passages. Part the patient's lips to help them breathe out, then start the cycle again;
– if the patient is a child, put your lips over mouth and nose together. Stop blowing as soon as the chest inflates and blow in a faster rhythm than for adults (about 20 cycles per minute);
– there are special tubes available for artificial respiration, which are particularly useful for preventing the patient's tongue falling back.

Cardiac resuscitation

If the patient's heart has stopped, you need to re-start it at the same time as carrying out mouth-to-mouth resuscitation. If you are carrying out the operation alone, you carry out five cardiac massages between each breathing cycle, as follows:
– place the heel of your left hand on the lower third of the breast-bone, *in the middle* of the chest, and place your right hand on your left;
– with your arms straight, press down with all your weight on the breastbone. Make a series of short, sharp pushes in groups of two.

If the patient is old or a child, you should avoid massaging too hard or you might break one of their ribs. The massage is then better carried out one-handed; for very small children, use just two fingers.

Mouth-to-mouth resuscitation and cardiac massages need to be carried out with the same commitment and perseverance as any of the preceding operations. You must not give up hope: 'drowned men' have been known to open their eyes after 6 hours of no apparent success. If there are several of you, keep going in relays until you see some sign of life.

Afterwards, it is best to visit a doctor as soon as possible with the newly revived patient.

Summary

The only operations described in this chapter are standard ones, requiring standard, cheap, reliable and simple equipment: a floating line, an IOR pole dan buoy and a block and tackle. All three items have a right to be on board any boat, and you must practise their use. The drills we propose are easy to carry out and will not disturb your cruising even on the calmest of days.

Bringing a member of the crew back on board when they have fallen over the side in the daytime, in pleasant weather, is a simple operation for a trained crew. A trained crew also has a good chance of success in carrying out the same operation in bad weather.

But if a member of a poorly trained crew falls overboard with no lifejacket and no harness on, they do not stand a chance, whatever the weather.

There is no harm in admitting it: some of us are here to tell the tale today because we were fortunate enough to be fished out quickly after nasty accidents; some of us have helped others out of difficulty; and all of us are the heirs to a strong tradition of safe sailing in the Glénans school. Over the thousands of miles covered by members of our community, the number of accidents has been astonishingly small, and this testifies to the traditions of safety. Alas, even at les Glénans, the number is not zero, however.

In case we have not made ourselves clear enough already,
let us just repeat once more:

I PRACTISE
I ENCOURAGE OTHERS TO PRACTISE
WE PRACTISE TOGETHER.

CHAPTER 6

Manoeuvres under engine power

There is an artificial rivalry between sails and engines, with both sides fuelled by pseudo-philosophical arguments. The rivalry is absurd these days, as a well-maintained engine seldom refuses to work, and indeed is an almost indispensable supplement to the sails, even if it is only used for manoeuvring in over-full harbours where you cannot (or are not allowed to) use the sails.

Engines have other obvious advantages: they enable you to get home on time when the wind dies, they can get you out of tricky situations, rescue you when the rigging breaks, and speed up the process of fishing a man overboard out of the sea if they are strong enough to cope with the conditions (not forgetting the danger to the person in the water from the propeller).

Engines can also be extremely dangerous if they make sailors over-confident.

It is important to define the role of the engine without ambiguity. An auxiliary engine must not be considered part of a boat's safety equipment; or, to put it another way, you should take the same precautions whether you have an engine or not. If you rely on the engine, there is a great temptation to take short cuts, or to end up in tight spots where the boat can be in real trouble if the wind dies or gets up suddenly. You absolutely must not look at the engine this way. The engine *is an extra*. If it works, great. If it does not, you must not allow this to cause problems.

It should be clear that we are talking about auxiliary engines here, those which are not powerful enough to withstand absolutely every situation, especially heavy weather. Our attitude is that a 5 tonne boat, 10m long, can manoeuvre in harbour or pull itself through a flat calm perfectly adequately with a 9–14hp engine. Such an engine could also help you tack in a heavy breeze or reduce your leeway while you are taking in a reef, but it would not push you forward with a fresh headwind: that would take 40–55hp.

Quite apart from the fact that a large engine costs more than a small one one to buy, maintain and run, it is heavier and bulkier – indeed, it probably takes up so much space in a confined area that it is difficult to reach all the parts needed for routine maintenance. You should beware of anyone who tries to sell you an oversized engine: they probably don't sail.

What can the engine do?

The first property of an auxiliary engine should be to make the boat as manoeuvrable as possible. This in turn is dependent on whether or not you can direct the thrust of the propeller.

Propeller thrust

There are three alternatives:

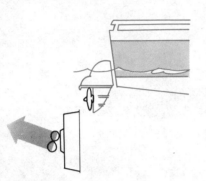

A. The propeller thrust itself can be directed.

1. The propeller itself can be directed. This is the case with an outboard engine which can pivot. This gives the boat a great deal of manoeuvrability, as the propeller gives full thrust, no matter which direction it is pointed in. Even when the boat is at rest next to a quay, the engine can be used to bring the stern to either side (diagram A).

B. The rudder steers the propeller thrust.

2. The propeller is fixed but its thrust is directed over the rudder. By turning the rudder, the thrust can be steered to a certain extent, and the boat is still quite manoeuvrable, even when stopped (diagram B).

3. The propeller is so situated that the rudder does not affect the direction of its thrust. This is unfortunately the case with many older sailing boats and on smaller modern boats with a fixed outboard. This arrangement does not give much manoeuvrability unless the boat is moving at speed, just as when it is under sail (diagram C).

On many boats, the propeller is not even in line with the keel.

You also need to take account of the paddle-wheel effect of the propeller: there is a difference in pressure between the water on the upper part of the propeller and that on the lower part, which can unbalance the boat's steering. This is occasionally noticeable when you start the engine, and particularly when you reverse thrust.

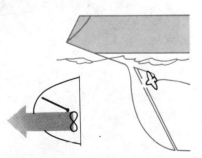

C. The rudder and propeller are offset, so on one side the rudder has no effect and on the other it directs the thrust only slightly.

Any boat should be tested individually at rest, when there is no wind, to check in which direction the screw tends to make it turn. The same experiment needs to be conducted in reverse gear.

Reverse gear

You cannot hope for delicate manoeuvres in reverse gear, as everything to do with the engine is designed for going forward:
– the propeller itself is less efficient when turning in the opposite direction; what is more, it is poorly positioned in relation to the hull;
– the thrust is not directed over the rudder and so cannot be steered;
– the rudder itself is poorly positioned for steering.

As soon as there is a decent wind, using the engine with reverse thrust will always make you bear away; and if you keep going in reverse, you will finish up with the bow facing dead downwind. This position can be regarded as reasonably stable.

The main function of reverse gear is as a brake. It can break the boat's momentum, which is a pretty useful function!

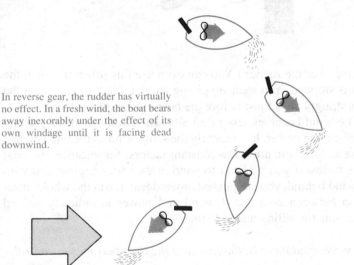

In reverse gear, the rudder has virtually no effect. In a fresh wind, the boat bears away inexorably under the effect of its own windage until it is facing dead downwind.

The effect of the wind

Even under engine power, you still have the wind to contend with. The boat's windage can have a considerable effect, especially with shallow-draft boats such as catamarans: the wind action on rigging and superstructure will always tend to bring the boat to its natural rest position of beam on to the wind. It is therefore always possible to get into the beam-on position, however you start out; on the other hand, in a lively breeze, it can become difficult to luff or bear away out of the beam-on position.

The stronger the wind, the more speed you need to be able to steer accurately. (To be precise, the more speed you need the water

---

The paddle-wheel effect
Memory aid
You can find out which direction the propeller is turning in by looking at the shaft. It is easy to work out which direction the screw effect will operate in, by imagining the propeller turning against the sea floor.

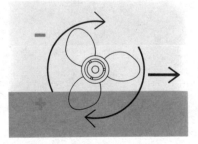

Propeller seen from the rear in forward gear, left-handed propeller.

Propeller seen from the rear in reverse gear, right-handed propeller.

The water pressure increases with depth.

A boat under engine power can easily reach the beam-on position, though it may have some difficulty getting out of it.

1. This boat is in its rest position, side on to the wind.
2. The boat luffs slowly.
3. If you want to luff further, you need more revs.
4. If you are heading for an obstacle in this position, do not slow down, as the boat will drift back to beam on. You need more speed, to luff up and 'shoot' the obstacle.
5. The boat has made it past head to wind, so you do not need to accelerate at all if you want to bear away.
6. You simply need to sit in neutral and wait. If you want a really tight turn, you can reverse the engine thrust.
7. Past beam on, it is easy to bear away, but since the wind is also pushing the boat forward, the turning circle becomes relatively large.
8. Again, if you want a tight turn, you can use reverse thrust.
9. Putting the engine in neutral will bring the boat back to beam on faster than using forward thrust.

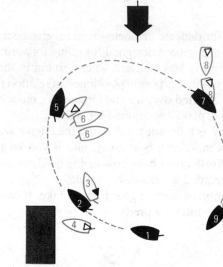

to have over the rudder.) You can even use this principle when the boat is stopped. You steer by giving a quick burst of revs with the tiller straight ahead just before the boat moves off.

The wind becomes less of an ally when you are moving along under engine power. It is scarcely the same wind as the one you had in the sails! There are some constant factors: for instance, the boat stops fastest if you go head to wind, even under engine; and with the wind behind, you are pushed onward faster. But the whole interaction between boat speed, wind and power is radically altered when you are sailing under engine.

The more wind there is, the less easy the boat becomes to control.

In lighter winds, on the other hand, you might find the boat overpowered.

As a general principle, when you start the engine of a sailing boat while sailing along, the boat seems subject to entirely new laws which can disturb its steering and actually give the helm a disagreeable surprise. *There is no room for improvisation in steering a boat under engine.* It is worth practising your engine manoeuvres at least once on a deserted stretch of water: practise tying up alongside, rigging the sails, and try to learn how the boat behaves and turns, and how you can best slow it down, so that when the time comes when you need a fast manoeuvre under engine power, you are ready and able to carry it out.

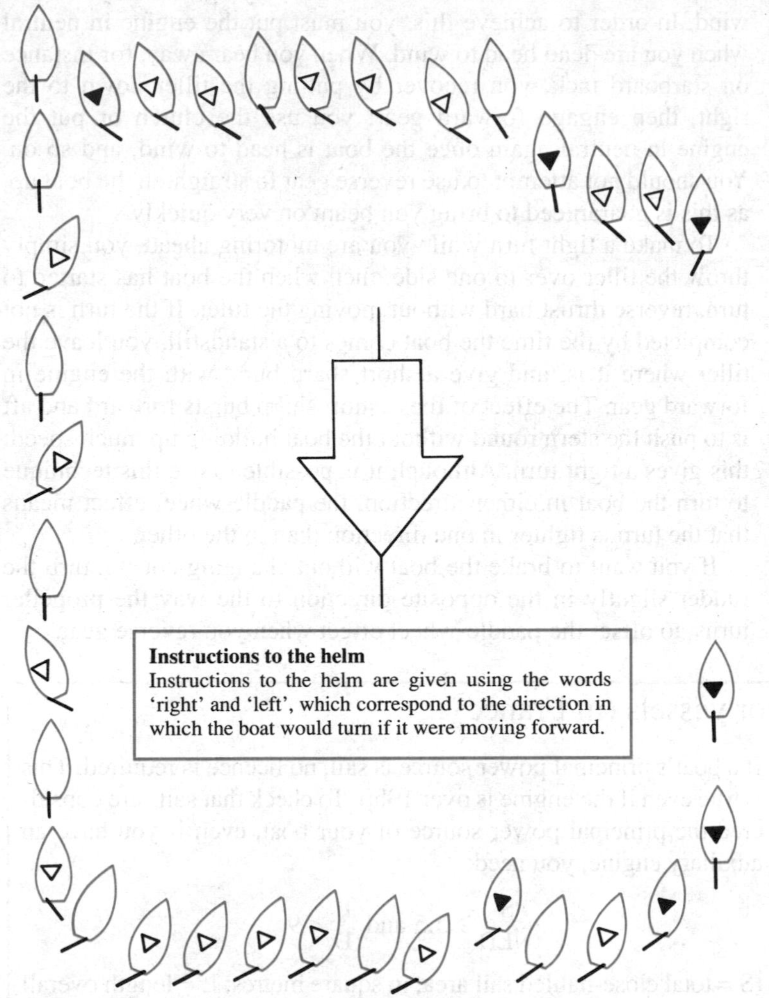

A short steering exercise under engine power (boat equipped with tiller).

The basic technique for steering a boat without moving forward is to push the tiller hard over before revving the engine.

The boat starts out from top right.

Phase 1. Try to move from right to left, across the wind, maintaining the boat's heading relative to the wind. Every time you bear away too much, the boat can be brought back into the wind by pushing the tiller hard to port and accelerating more or less.

Phase 2. Allow the boat to move downwind, keeping the bow into the wind. Every time you bear away, rev the engine and throw the tiller over to the side the boat is moving toward. Do not use reverse, as this will push you beam on. If the wind is strong enough to push you back with the engine in gear, you just have to stay head to wind at low revs.

Phase 3. Same as in phase 1, but from left to right.

Phase 4. Head back straight upwind and start again.

You may consider yourself a master when you can manage a perfect square.

Instructions to the helm
Instructions to the helm are given using the words 'right' and 'left', which correspond to the direction in which the boat would turn if it were moving forward.

Steering

Steering a boat under engine power is a good deal simpler than steering under sail, but nothing is quite so easy as it seems, and it is certainly harder than steering a car.

If you can manage the exercise illustrated above in a variety of wind conditions, you will have confronted most of the problems steering under engine power can throw up. Above all, though, you will have sharpened up your reflexes.

This exercise will only work if your boat is equipped with an 'active' rudder, ie one which can steer the propeller thrust, or where the propeller itself is steerable. The aim of the exercise is to stay in one place or even drift backward while staying virtually head to wind. In order to achieve this, you must put the engine in neutral when you are dead head to wind. When you bear away, for instance on starboard tack, you recover by putting the tiller down to the right, then engage forward gear; you use the clutch or put the engine in neutral again once the boat is head to wind, and so on. You should not attempt to use reverse gear to straighten the boat up, as this is guaranteed to bring you beam on very quickly.

To make a tight turn while you are motoring ahead, you simply throw the tiller over to one side, then when the boat has started to turn, reverse thrust hard without moving the tiller. If the turn is not completed by the time the boat comes to a standstill, you leave the tiller where it is, and give a short sharp burst with the engine in forward gear. The effect of these short sharp bursts forward and aft is to push the stern round without the boat building up much speed; this gives a tight turn. Although it is possible to use this technique to turn the boat in either direction, the paddle-wheel effect means that the turn is tighter in one direction than in the other.

If you want to brake the boat without changing course, turn the rudder slightly in the opposite direction to the way the propeller turns, to offset the paddle-wheel effect when you reverse gear.

Driving licences for motor vessels (in France)

If a boat's principal power source is sail, no licence is required. This is true even if the engine is over 10hp. To check that sails are considered the principal power source of your boat, even if you have an auxiliary engine, you need:

$$\frac{S}{\sqrt{LD}} \geq 5.5 \text{ and } \frac{P}{D} < 9$$

(S = total close-hauled sail area, in square metres; L = length overall in metres; D = displacement in tonnes; P = maximum engine power in HP DIN.)

Pleasure-boat skippers do not need a licence in UK-registered vessels.

For any other French vessel, a licence must be acquired.

• Licence A permits cruising up to 5 miles from the coast.

• Licence B permits unlimited cruising for boats of up to 25 tonnes displacement.

• Licence C permits unlimited cruising for pleasure boats of any size. More details are available in Yvonnick Guéret's book, *Permis de conduire en mer*.

One final reminder: a boat with a rudder which does not steer the propeller thrust is less manoeuvrable than a boat under sail, but the propeller thrust in reverse has a good braking effect.

> Beware: some engine lubrication systems do not function correctly when the boat is heeling.

Passage-making

There are limits to one's ability to make passage under engine power:
– wind strength;
– fuel consumption: one seldom carries enough fuel for a long journey, especially one against the sea and the wind.

In general, the engine is of most use in a flat calm, and you will drop the sails for motoring along unless there is a heavy swell, in which case the mainsail can be left up and sheeted in tight to reduce the rolling.

If you need to make ground to windward, it is generally more effective to sail close-hauled under mainsail and engine only (ie with the jib dropped) than to drop sail completely and motor straight upwind.

> The *Regulations for Preventing Collisions at Sea* require that a sailing vessel which is using sails and an auxiliary engine should exhibit an inverted cone forward, at the most visible point.
>
> On large boats, the cone must have a base diameter of at least 0.6m, and must be the same height as it is wide.
>
> The size of cone is not specified for boats of less than 20m. It must simply be in proportion to the size of boat.

Catamarans

Catamarans are light, with little 'grip' in the water and considerable windage: these characteristics give a catamaran a large turning circle and little momentum, quite apart from their occasionally awkward width. Any boat with these characteristics will have problems making headway into the wind at low speeds. On the other hand, it can fairly easily be held stern to wind with the engine in reverse.

On small catamarans, a small outboard engine attached in the centre of the boat will have little thrust effect on the rudders; the boat can be turned in a tight circle nevertheless, by shuttling the engine from one side, on reverse thrust, to the other, on forward thrust.

Any catamaran over 12m long should ideally be equipped with a small inboard engine in each hull.

Manoeuvring with twin engines

The first point is that if you have two engines, their controls should also be dual. The boat can be turned on the spot by reversing thrust on one engine at the same time as running the other forward. The rudder must also be used to increase the effect of the engine which is running forward. Elementary, my dear Watson ... if you create a couple, the result will be rotation!

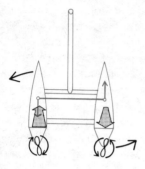

The boat can be turned on the spot by running one motor forward and the other in reverse.

CHAPTER 7

Oars, paddles and tow ropes

There is such a phenomenon as a flat calm, so let us speak about it. Strangely, in a sailing manual, the only context in which flat calms are mentioned is when the authors are telling you how to escape them! This manual will be no different, at least in this respect. (Anyone who has found a use for flat calms is probably best advised to keep the fact to themselves ...)

Let us then look at ways of moving the boat once the sails are of no further use. The techniques covered are useful for various situations as well as when there is no wind: for instance if you need to catch a rope which has been lost overboard, manoeuvre in a busy port or pull yourselves out of a sticky situation.

We have already dealt with the engine. The sculling oar is a logical extension of this, but if neither of these two solutions works, you can still be towed. Despite appearances, however, towing is not the most relaxing way out of trouble.

Sculling

Sculling is an art, and mastering it can be one of the would-be sailor's most useful accomplishments. It can be of extraordinary use in an enormous number of situations. There can be few tools so economical, effective and reliable as a correctly used sculling oar.

Theory

It is not easy to define exactly what sculling is, where it begins and ends: we could perhaps best describe the sculling oar as a sort of manual variable-pitch propeller. Even if we managed to describe the item and the action required, putting it into practice would still be another matter. Even the movement of the sculler does not carry immediate promise of advancement: it looks more as though it belongs as an illustration in a book on *The Psychoanalysis of Angles*. Still, its definition remains somehow elusive.

1, 2 and 3 and the job is done.

You can also reverse using the sculling oar.

Take up the same position as for sculling forward; place the oar blade in the water at an angle of around 45° and the handle on one shoulder; press on the oar with both hands and push it in figures of eight keeping it at the same angle throughout. Do not move your hips.

This is not such an easy movement as that needed to propel the boat forward, but it is useful if you want to reverse the boat a few metres in a straight line without getting involved in complex manoeuvres.

The best way to start learning is on a heavy open boat, with no wind and no waves. You might also prefer a spot where no one is watching. The sculler stands facing aft, legs apart and body erect. The oar handle is held in both hands, thumbs pointed downward, at shoulder height. The blade must be completely immersed, and as vertical as possible, and the oar should balance so that its weight is taken by the rowlock or the sculling notch in the transom.

If the blade is held flat in the water and moved from side to side, the sculler will feel no resistance, and will achieve nothing. If the blade is placed perpendicular to the surface of the water, on the other hand, there will be a great deal of resistance but still little appreciable result: if the boat moves forward slightly, it is probably because the movement has caused eddies which are streaming away from the boat.

The blade needs to be held at a certain slant, and angled slightly left as you pull the oar right, then slightly right as you pull the oar left. Simple! The upper face of the blade does not push the water back forcibly, it moves the water off to one side as it presses through. It must be possible to explain how it works more scientifically than this, but let's just leave it that sculling works best if the oar is angled in this way.

Not like this, or like this ...

... just act natural!

The real problem in practice is getting the correct movement at the end of the stroke. *Do not let your hands slip on the oar handle; you turn the blade by rolling your wrists.* At the same time, the upper face of the oar must not be allowed to stop pressing on the water, or the oar will no longer be held down in the notch and will slip out. Beginners always have this problem.

If you lose control of the oar, the only course is to start again. The average apprentice sculler takes about an hour to reach modest competence. Thereafter, it is more a question of perfecting your technique. If you need to turn the boat, just slant the oar slightly more in one direction than in the other. If you need to stop sculling but do not want the oar to jump out of the notch, just stick the oar in at right angles to the water surface like a rudder.

You will need a few further hours of advanced practice before you reach the stage of freestyle sculling: a really experienced practitioner can be seen sculling their boat one-handed (with the other hand in their pocket, of course) through a crowded harbour, facing forward, ostentatiously concentrating on something else.

The uses of a sculling oar

The main benefit of the sculling oar is that it can be readied for action in an instant to help you through a difficult manoeuvre in a critical moment, such as a tack in light winds. It can also be used for very precise operations in a confined space. It has clear advantages over engines. It does not annoy anyone, as it makes no noise; it keeps the environment clean and does not smell; and it gives you a sense of security as there are no mechanical parts to go wrong or catch on warps.

The sculling oar does have its limits: even the strongest sculler cannot work up much speed; it cannot make headway against any sort of current or any but the lightest breeze. However, if you have no engine, it is certainly much more effective than beating the water with a couple of oars in rowlocks, at least on a boat of any size.

As far as we are aware, no one has yet honoured the humble sculling oar by using it for an Atlantic crossing (preferably one-handed), but that day cannot be far off.

The sculler on the left has his woolly hat on and his oar dug deep in the water. He is moving slowly but powerfully. Minus the woolly hat and with the oar at more of an angle, the sculler on the right has less power, but is moving faster.

Keep your arms straight and let your chest do the work.

Paddling

We should mention in passing the even humbler paddle, which is usually used for sailing dinghies or inflatables. In a dinghy, paddles have the advantage that they take up little room and can be used without any special notch or rowlock. On an inflatable dinghy, even if you can scull, you need to paddle as soon as there are waves or if you have to make headway against a breeze.

There is no apprenticeship with a paddle as there is with a sculling oar, and no great initiation rite to pass through before you start to get anywhere. Even the worst paddler usually makes some progress, but this should not be a reason not to learn to paddle better (after all, we live in an energy-conscious age). Good paddling technique involves using your arms straight, putting the blade in the water well forward of your sitting position and using your chest to pull, without flexing your arms.

If you are the only paddler on board, you can use the paddle on one side of the boat only, rather than constantly changing sides. Sit well aft in the boat and to leeward (assuming there is any wind). If you are sitting to starboard, for instance, the boat will turn to port with the first paddle stroke, so you finish the stroke by using the paddle as a rudder to correct your direction. You can even overcorrect a little, so the boat moves less off course with the next stroke. On a centreboard dinghy, it is worth lowering the centreboard in order to maintain course better.

Towing

There are two very different but utterly complementary ways of looking at towing, depending on your perspective: whether you are the one doing the towing, or you are being towed.

As far as the boat doing the towing is concerned, we shall limit ourselves to those manoeuvres which can be carried out by a sailing boat under engine power. The question for the person being towed is: how much of this sort of kindness can I stand? You may find yourself putting up with an infinite variety of good intentions.

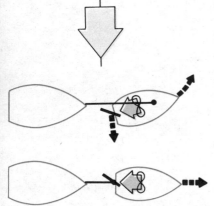

Towing a boat larger than oneself
The boat above can steer, because its stern is free to move round as the rudder is moved.
The lower boat cannot steer (or only just) because the towing warp is attached to its stern, preventing the stern from swinging round. It is particularly hard to luff up.

On board the towing vessel

Ideally, the towing vessel or tug should pass the warp across, and not the other way round: the operation is easier this way, and helps the boat being towed in a number of ways.

The tow rope is subject to violent jerks. It is therefore worth picking one of the best ropes you have (generally the mooring warp). The rope should always be too thick rather than too thin, and it should be as long as possible: the longer it is, the easier it will be to start the tow.

The tow rope should be made fast aboard the towing vessel at a solid point well forward of the propeller. If the tow rope is tied at the rear of the tug, it becomes virtually impossible to steer. The best place to tie the rope is at the point about which the boat rotates.

Also think about where the rope runs across the boat: unless you lead it to windward of the mainsheet and the backstay (or between the backstays if you have two), the tug will not be able to luff up.

If the tow rope has been properly stowed in a locker in an orderly pile, you should not need to take it all out in one go. You simply bring out one end and feed that aft along the chosen path, from the point at which you plan to fasten it, to windward of the mainsheet and the backstay. You then pull out a sufficient length to pass to the boat you are towing, then let the full length of the warp out only once the two boats are tied together. This should ensure that the rope does not tangle and catch everywhere just when it is least convenient …

Normally, this part of the operation is carried out under engine power. The tug can hoist sail again once both are back on their way.

Make sure you pass the rope to windward of the mainsheet and the backstay, or you will only be able to sail on a broad reach!

Passing over the tow rope

The towing vessel should position itself to windward of the boat to be towed (always assuming it is not drifting downwind even faster than the boat it is helping). The rope can be thrown downwind more easily. The easiest of all is to use a light *heaving line*, which is a light rope with a weighted knot at the end, allowing it to be thrown further and more exactly. The tow rope itself is then tied to the end of the heaving line and pulled across from one boat to the other.

There are several possible scenarios:
• *Taking a drifting boat in tow.* This is the easiest case. You come up to the boat as slowly and as close as possible to windward, throw the line across, then let the tug drift downwind in front of the boat needing the tow while the line is being made fast.
• *Taking a boat in tow as it is sailing.* This works similarly: catch the boat up and pass to windward to throw the line over. While the line is being tied on, both boats should be sailing at a similar speed.
• *Taking an anchored boat in tow.* This one is slightly more complex. The ideal solution is to let the anchor slip so that the boat starts to drift and you are back to the first scenario. This is not always possible, however, especially if there is no water to leeward.

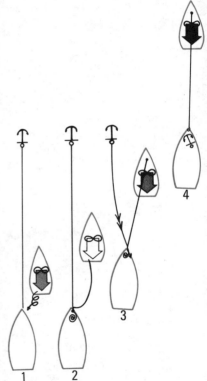

1. Throw the line over.
2. Stop the tug while the line is made fast.
3. Pull gently to help the anchor slip (though you must not let the boat move ahead of its anchor).
4. The anchor is up and clear, and you can be off.

If you can direct the thrust of your engine and have practised the moves on page 661, there is no problem: you simply stay in one place, head to wind, upwind of the boat you are about to tug while they fasten the tow rope and pull the anchor up.

If your engine thrust cannot be directed, you have a problem, because you cannot stop, and everything has to be done while the boat is in motion. The tug positions itself fairly far behind the other boat and then draws alongside slowly, so that everyone has time to get ready. When the tug is level with the boat in difficulty, the line is thrown across and the tug sails as slowly as possible into the wind, while making sure it has enough way to steer by. The tow rope needs to be fed out quickly. For this operation to run smoothly, you need a very long rope, and the boat in difficulty should pull up part of its anchor chain before the manoeuvre begins.

Throughout the operation, the tug must take great care that the

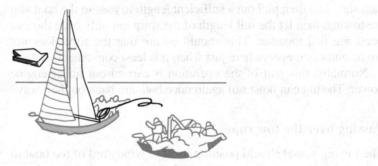

The tug passes to windward of the other boat and then heaves to in front of it while the crew makes the rope fast.

rope does not catch in the propeller. There is a particular chance of this if you make the mistake of reversing the engine at any stage.

Setting off

So that the start is not too bumpy, you should move forward gently until the tow rope is tight, and only then accelerate properly. If you time the acceleration well, both boats will speed up together and the rope will remain taut. As the rope tightens, there is a good chance it will make the tug bear away, so the helm should pre-empt this by luffing up higher than would normally be necessary.

Once you are under way, the tug can adjust the length of the rope. This should be sufficiently long that it sags slightly in the water, though even with a very long tow rope it is difficult to avoid the occasional jerk, especially if you are travelling downwind, as the two boats will rarely be travelling at the same speed together.

A tack while towing
1 and 2. The tow rope is shortened slowly so as not to lose momentum.
3 and 4. As you tack, the tow rope is let completely slack.
5. The tow rope is passed round to the other side.
6. Pick up speed as fast as possible.

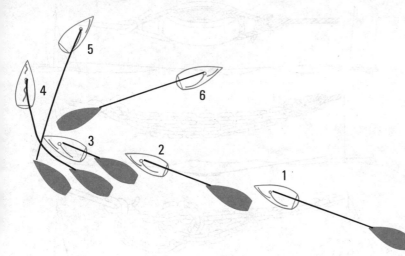

Towing under sail power

Towing another boat while sailing has to be the ultimate in skill! Well, at least it requires a certain minimum level of competence, and especially a good idea of one's own boat's power.

The preparation for the tow and passing the rope over are theoretically no different from the routines described above.

There is nevertheless one particularly difficult case. Again, it's the anchored boat. You need to be able to stop and wait while it makes fast the tow rope and pulls up the anchor. The best option may well be to anchor yourself, then to set off at the same time as the boat you are towing, or even slightly later, once the tow rope is in position. You also need to be able to set off with the wind a little behind the beam, so you can pick up speed before luffing up.

Sailing close-hauled while towing another boat is difficult whatever you do, since your own sails are not giving much forward thrust. Tacking is also a problem, because the tug will need to free itself of its burden for an instant during the turn. In order to manage this, a good length of the tow rope needs to be pulled back in, then let go just at the moment you go about. This should ensure it remains slack throughout the turn. Once you have completed the tack, the rope needs to be brought round to the new windward side.

If you cannot manage a tack, you can always gybe.

Watching the tow rope

The best way of ensuring the rope does not jerk too violently is good boat control. If the line goes slack:
– the tug must slow down, and not speed up again until the line is

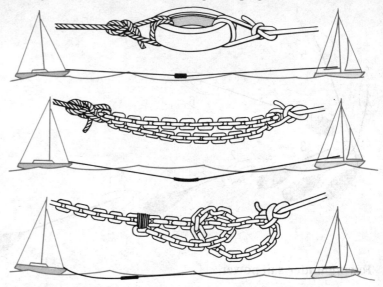

A car tyre makes a good shock-absorber; the tow rope can also be made more 'elastic' by weighting it.

taut once more;
– the following boat should change course, so that the first strong pull on the line simply pulls it back on course rather than dragging it suddenly forward.

You can also give the rope shock-absorbing properties by:
– tying a car tyre in the middle of it;
– weighting the middle;
– tying the anchor chain (or at least 20–30m of it, in bad weather) of the following boat onto the end of the tow rope.

The tow rope can be chafed and worn through by the anchor chain fairlead. If the tow is intended to last some time, the crews of both boats should check for any points at which the line might chafe, and parcel it at those points.

On board the boat being towed

Making fast the line

The crucial thing is for the boat to be tied on properly. This means making the tow rope fast to the strongest point on board. This should in theory be the samson post or the mast foot, but unfortunately even these points are not always as strong as they should be on modern-day boats. If there is a rough sea and the tug is fairly powerful, it might be sensible to run the rope all the way round your boat.

When you tie the tow rope, make sure you use knots which can be untied and which will not jam. In effect this means bowlines or tugman's hitches. It does not mean a clove hitch!

Problems

As soon as the tow rope is made fast, the trouble starts. In fact the trouble can usually be traced to a single source: the tug almost always goes too fast. The following boat suffers the consequences and can do nothing about it.

The captain now has plenty of leisure to think about what might be done better next time:
– you might choose a less powerful boat (assuming there is a choice, and you are not in immediate danger);
– you should use the tug's warp rather than your own, firstly because it is easier to take hold of, and secondly because if things get rough you will worry less about untying it;
– you might elect not to tie it fast immediately, but just to take a few turns around a post and hold the end in your hand while you wait and see what sort of treatment will be meted out.

To a certain extent, you can influence the tug, so long as it is not a huge boat (and particularly if you notice the rope has been tied aft rather than in the middle). If you want them to turn left, for instance, you only need to steer hard right and the tug will obey.

As you are being towed, it is best to stay slightly to windward of the tug's wake. This is especially important when travelling down-wind, so as to avoid any risk of being washed into the leading boat's transom by a big wave. This can happen quite easily, especially if the boat being towed is bigger than the one doing the towing.

You must also pray that when the tug reaches harbour, its captain remembers that you have no reverse gear, and stops head to wind.

There is one further potential worry: how much will the tow cost? Salvage fees are nothing to do with this chapter, theoretically, but we must mention that any wrong move when you are asking someone to tow you home can be very expensive. Any boat towing another home is entitled to a large sum of money if it wants, so you must make sure you agree terms before accepting help (unless you are in imminent danger, of course). Many would-be rescuers will be content to settle for a bottle of your best Scotch, but others might insist on their rights.

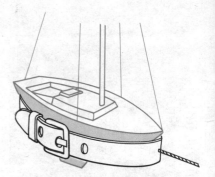

It may be wise to fasten the rope all the way round the boat: anything to avoid further damage to a battered craft.

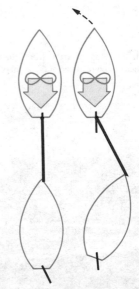

If the tug ties the warp aft, the following boat can 'steer' the tug.

Pushing the boat along with the tender may not be the solution which springs to mind, but it is certainly more effective than towing.

Using the tender

One simple and cheap solution to the problem of the auxiliary engine is to equip your tender with one instead of fitting one to the boat itself. This can be an outboard of anything from 1.5 to 10hp, and will certainly cost less than any engine you might buy for the boat. It can certainly not carry out the same range of activities, but it can help in a variety of cases. And an outboard on the tender certainly makes the multiple trips in harbour less tiring.

Pushing

You have the choice of pushing the boat or towing it. Pushing actually works better, though it can only be done in an inflatable.

You simply push the nose of the tender up against the transom of the boat (ideally in the middle, though off to one side will do if the rudder gets in the way). You should tie on with a very short warp to improve your ability to steer: if the tender steers hard right the boat will turn left fast, and vice versa.

An inflatable dinghy is very safe when used this way, even offshore in waves. It can be put over the stern some time before you enter harbour and tied there with one member of the crew inside. This ensures that the tender is ready for use as soon as it is needed.

Towing

It is also possible to tow the boat using the tender, whether the tender is rigid or inflatable.

The tow rope is fastened to the front of the tender (or if

To pull the boat from the front, the tow rope needs to be fastened at the front of the tender.

The tender can be used to pull from alongside. The spring rope (in white) should be under tension; the breast ropes just tight.

absolutely necessary, to the middle), even if this gets in the way of the person steering; if the rope is fastened to the stern, you cannot steer.

The person steering the tender has to pass the rope over either side of the engine when changing direction. Steering is actually quite easy, as the rope itself can be used: if you push it to the left, the dinghy veers left, and if you push it right, the dinghy goes right. This works because the boat is so much heavier than the tender.

The last and least satisfactory technique is to drive the boat from the tender placed alongside. This really only works in the flattest of calms or in very sheltered havens: any chop will soak the person in the tender and probably wreck the tender too, since there are no good spots to make the warps fast.

The obvious technique to use in a catamaran is pushing. Depending on how large the boat is, one or two dinghies fit in between the hulls at the rear of the boat. This also makes communication very easy! When you are manoeuvring in harbour, two dinghies nestling under the rear in this way can achieve spectacular results if one motors forward and the other uses reverse thrust.

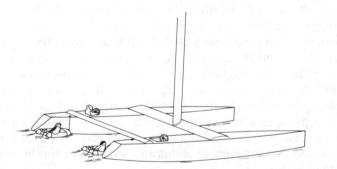

The obvious way to deal with a catamaran is to push it.

Special technique for large catamarans
If you have only one engine, you can rig a line between the two bows and attach a tow rope to the centre of that. If the tow rope is forward, as in the diagram, it can be difficult for the person steering the tender to communicate with the person helming the boat. The technique does allow one to push forward, backward or sideways (by pushing up against one of the hulls).

Engine or sail?

We conclude by making the point very firmly that half measures are not good enough for anyone travelling by sail: sailing is too demanding a discipline to excuse sloppiness. From the moment you first stepped onto a boat (probably someone else's) you will have noticed that a botched manoeuvre puts everyone in a generally bad mood: it can expose the boat and crew to the whim of the elements, such that any attempt to put things right instead makes them worse, and then circumstances combine to cause complete confusion. Every action and every part of the boat depends on every other action or part, and things can happen fast. On a badly sailed boat, you are never far from danger, whether it has an engine or not. If you are committed to carrying out your manoeuvres under sail, then common sense dictates that you ignore the fact that you have an engine, and you must concentrate on getting things perfect under sail power.

Unfortunately, we have noticed an attitude becoming ever more widespread which is the exact opposite of that outlined above, particularly in those cruising ports where manoeuvring under sail has actually been prohibited. This sort of prohibition seems to encourage mediocrity and negligence rather than precision and judgement. If someone cannot handle their boat in harbour, they are hardly likely to get far out at sea in a gale, or be up to facing unexpected situations with calm and expertise. If harbours need to become more regimented as the number of pleasure cruisers increases, surely it must still be possible to arrange them so that one can sail up to a mooring and then use the tender to land? We have no doubt that everyone would prefer to sail under these circumstances, and that the harbour authorities would also find it made their lives easier.

True safety afloat is not the result of simple solutions, however: it is actually part of one's aim throughout, and must not be regarded as separate and potentially contradictory. If you decide to go sailing, then you have accepted the sport as a universe in itself: you do not go looking for problems, but you do not shy away from them when they crop up. Safety is achieved by playing by the rules of the game … and rule number one is that you handle your boat with care and precision. So long as you keep to the rules, you will see the game through from start to finish, thereby ensuring your position in the sun … or wind … or rain … throughout.

PART V

Meteorology

Tomorrow's weather is an important question for all those at sea: unfortunately, it is difficult to arrive at a forecast without help. In days of yore, people looked to the colour of the sky, the way the ship's cat behaved and the captain's rheumatism; the predictions that were made on the basis of these were not always far wrong. We no longer have the knack for such insights. On the other hand, thanks to the various weather bureaus we now have access to information on the weather that nobody would even have imagined in days gone by. It is particularly with the help of this information that one can gauge what the weather is going to do.

Meteorology has traditionally been the object of scorn and scepticism – it still is from time to time. A meteorologist's life is not an easy one. Meteorologists work on a complex and shifting mass of information, which can be interpreted differently by any individual at any given point. Their frame of reference in dealing with these phenomena is not that of the man in the street, which leads to bitter disappointments for the latter, and can give the impression that forecasting is all guesswork. In fact, the people who make proper use of this information – sailors and pilots to take two notable examples – know full well that it is of a very precise nature. The use of satellites and radar to map out the sky, and of computers to process the information received, along with the less spectacular but no less astounding evolution of the methods of interpretation themselves means that the value of this information is constantly increasing.

If weather reports occasionally fall under suspicion, it is probably because one tends to consider them as products for the mass market, to be taken as you find them. Now, the first thing to remember is that the forecasts presuppose a modicum of knowledge on the part of the consumer, and secondly that the forecasts provided deal with vast areas and cannot take account of shifts and nuances in particular locations. We must do some of the work ourselves. For the amateur sailor, as for everyone else, accurate forecasting depends on two prior conditions: the correct interpretation of the forecasts, and the capacity to modify the general forecast to take account of our observation of local conditions, so as to see what the weather will do in the area in which we are sailing.

It's best to admit it straight away: we'll understand nothing from the weather forecasts until we actually get down to a little bookwork, in order to acquire some elementary knowledge of the more significant atmospheric phenomena, why they occur and what relation they bear to the whole. This is why we have taken the step of devoting an entire chapter to the earth's atmosphere and the air currents. Treating such a vast subject in a few pages was evidently a risky business: sometimes we had to tack rather carefully between not oversimplifying on the one hand and making things clear on the other, trying not to lose sight of either of these important marker buoys.

We wanted to provide information for the second part of the task: the observation of the weather at a local level. This observation is only useful if you know what the situation is when, from the deck of your boat, you see the clouds scudding past, and you are aware of the position of depressions and anticyclones. From that point of view there is not one weather for the ocean and another for the Mediterranean, but rather, one weather system for the whole of Europe.

The last chapter in this part is given over to weather reports and the sort of forecast you can make from them. If you are already aware of the basic principles, you can look back at these pages to find the necessary meteorological information.

As they stand, these chapters can only provide a simple introduction to a vast subject. It falls to you, the reader, to follow up on this, on the one hand by reading the works we have cited in the bibliography (and on which we have drawn extensively), and on the other by getting into the habit of looking at the sky, and acquiring a feel for this incredible world, whose power and splendour cannot be dulled by even the most dusty treatise.

CHAPTER 1

Air movements

Meteorology is an honourable science, first of all because it tries to answer honestly the questions that determined children put to it. The sun warms the earth, everyone knows that, but then why does it get colder when you go up in a plane, even though you are nearer the sun? Why is it cold at the poles and hot at the equator? Why is that cloud staying where it is over the top of the mountain when there's a wind blowing? Why are there clouds or winds? Where do they come from and where are they going?

Those of you who find this all a bit obvious will just have to bear with us for a while.

The sun radiates energy towards the earth, a ball surrounded by an atmosphere. A part of that energy is directly reflected back out into space when the sun's rays reach the planet, and has no influence on it. A small proportion is absorbed by the atmosphere itself, which is slightly warmed by this (a light ray absorbed by an object is transformed into heat). The greatest proportion is absorbed by the earth and heats it up considerably.

Let us note straightaway that if the transfer of energy was a one-way process, the earth's temperature would increase continuously, and we wouldn't be around to talk about it today. However, the earth, like any body that is heated up, radiates energy in its turn. On a global scale, it radiates as much energy as it absorbs – there is therefore an equilibrium.

The first important thing to observe is this: in the same period, the land absorbs three times as much energy as the air above it. The land is therefore warmer than the air, and warms it from the ground up. This warming continues up to an altitude of 12km or so. From the ground up until about 12km temperature therefore decreases with altitude. This is the principal characteristic of this lower stratum of the atmosphere, which is referred to as the *troposphere*. The thickness of this layer varies according to latitude (12km is an average: the layer is much thicker at the equator than it is at the poles); it also varies from one day to the next, according to what the weather is like. The upper limit of the troposphere is known as the *tropopause* . Beyond that, up to an altitude of about 50km, there is the *stratosphere*, a region where the temperature rises slightly and where the winds are variable and can be very violent. If you want to know what happens after that, talk to an astrophysicist – we don't need to worry about that here.

The troposphere, a mere 12km in depth, seems rather thin compared to the 6,400km radius of the globe itself: it's rather like a layer of tissue paper around an orange. Nevertheless, this thin film contains 80% of the total mass of air, as well as 90% of the water in the atmosphere; it is here that all the clouds are to be found, and where all the phenomena of interest to us occur.

Second question: *Why is it cold at the poles and hot at the equator?*

The sun's rays run parallel – or can be considered so to do for all practical purposes – but the earth is spherical. The polar regions are therefore at a disadvantage: they receive fewer of the sun's rays per square metre than is the case for the equatorial areas, which are well exposed.

This simple answer, although it appears satisfactory, is in fact a trap. It begs another question, and this will take us a long way. Calculating the amount of energy absorbed by the poles and the equator respectively reveals an immense imbalance between these two regions, an imbalance that ought to translate into a much greater temperature difference than is actually observed. Going by this simple calculation, the equatorial regions ought to be incredibly hot and the polar regions incredibly cold: the one place as inhospitable as the other. If things are not so, if the temperature is pretty much tolerable virtually everywhere (as long as you pack a few warm pullovers), then this is because there is an exchange

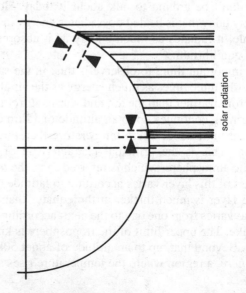

Solar radiation is uniform, but in the higher latitudes it spreads out over a greater surface area than at the equator.

between the equator and the poles. So, the question arises, how do these exchanges take place? The answer to this one takes up a bit more space, and is the object of the science of meteorology itself.

Physicists tell us that any body which is heated at a particular point tends to transfer that heat throughout the entirety of its mass. This spreading out can occur through *conduction*, that is to say by contact between molecules throughout the mass of the object. But this is not the case for the planet earth, because the ground is a bad conductor of heat. The transfer can also occur through *radiation*, except that the heat radiated by the earth goes almost entirely out into space and is lost. Only a small proportion is reflected back by the clouds (this is why it is often less cold on cloudy nights), and this is not enough to create an equilibrium between the equator and the poles, because the amount of heat that has to be transferred is considerable.

Conduction and radiation are the sole means of exchange on the moon for example. Temperatures of 200°C have been recorded in those regions exposed to the sun, compared with –100°C in those regions that are in darkness.

However, the earth has both an atmosphere and oceans. Air and water are in themselves bad conductors of heat, but they can move around. The air can also carry water, taken off by evaporation from the warmer, wetter areas of the planet. Could not these two elements, apparently subject to a constant churning, contribute to the equalisation of temperatures on the earth's surface? Furthermore, would this equalisation of temperatures not be the reason for this very movement?

This is precisely what the meteorologists have shown; on earth, thermic exchanges take place by means of the large fluid masses that move from the equator to the poles and from the poles to the equator. These exchanges take place by *convection*.

There are also warm ocean currents – such as the Gulf Stream – which transport heat from the tropical seas towards the north, along with cold currents – such as the Labrador Current – moving in the opposite direction. These currents are very slow, but nevertheless account for just as much of the heat exchange as does the movement through the atmosphere: the equatorial air masses (which are warm) tend to move towards the poles, while the polar air masses (cold) tend towards the equator.

Following this schema, it would appear that one could very easily arrive at an explanation to account for the winds. Now, it is tempting to conclude that the winds would blow mainly either from the north or from the south. However, if we consider general tendencies across the globe as a whole, drawing on observations made over many years, then we would have to admit that this was not the case.

The north and south components are of little significance (they cancel themselves out); instead, winds generally come from either the east or the west: east winds in the equatorial and polar regions, west winds in temperate areas. It also appears that these winds are, on average, very gentle: barely 2m/second. Of course, we all know that some are stronger.

As we can see, those childish questions are beginning to present a number of sticking points. We could come up with a rather peremptory and schematic answer to them, which might well run along the following lines: we know that the earth rotates on its axis. Given that it is covered with lumps and bumps and holes, this movement creates eddies in the air, some up and some down. At the same time, the oceans and the continents are warming and cooling at different rates: this imbalance creates other eddies which appear and disappear periodically. The hot and cold air masses, which are trying to keep the exchange of heat between the poles and the equator going, get drawn into all these movements, and from there on follow rather unexpected paths. What is more, when a cold air mass and a hot air mass meet, they refuse to mix, and so collide instead. This creates further eddies, in which you find strong winds, and which whizz around in between all the other eddies we've been talking about. It's all a question of cogs and wheels, or even just one big circle.

Now, nobody really needs to know any more than this. However, those who want to will have to roll their sleeves up. Time to leave such lofty speculations, to turn the telescope round, and start from the beginning. Let us look at what makes up the air that we breathe. Moreover, what is an 'air mass' anyway? How does it get around? What about clouds? If we have a look at some of the processes involved, we might see a bit more of what is going on.

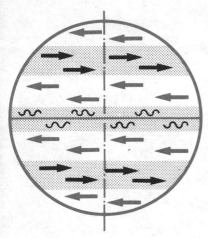

According to latitude, winds come from either the east or the west.

The atmosphere

The first astronauts called the earth the 'blue planet'. In fact, seen from space, it appeared blue to them, surrounded by a bluish ring created by dust in the atmosphere which breaks up and diffuses the sun's rays.

Even though it was pretty easy to see the atmosphere from up there, for us down here it is rather difficult to say how thick the thing actually is. What we do know is that this enveloping layer, compared to the size of the earth itself, is really rather thin: 90% of its mass (5,300 million megatonnes, give or take a gramme) is to be found in the 16km directly over our heads. What is more, thanks to the satellites, the first observations of this gaseous layer were made from about 130km up – which could be regarded as the top of the atmosphere.

This thin film of air in which we live (a bit like fish in water), which protects us from the sun and nourishes us, is basically made up of dry air and water vapour, as well as a large number of solid particles, impurities and debris, bacteria and so on. Of course, these are all microscopically small … even the ice crystals.

Water in the atmosphere

The composition of dry air, determined for the first time by Lavoisier, is practically invariable: 78% nitrogen, 21% oxygen, 0.9% argon – these acccount for 99.9% of the components. The other gases are only present in traces. But, in fact, meteorologists are not all that interested in dry air, which is almost never found in the lower layers of the atmosphere. They are mostly interested in the mixture of dry air and water vapour – this last gas, whose quantities can vary considerably, plays a key role.

In fact, water exists in the atmosphere in three physical states:
– *gaseous state*, water vapour;
– *liquid state*, water droplets in clouds, rain, dew;
– *solid state*, ice crystals in higher clouds, hail, snow, frost.
There is constant change from one state to another. These changes of state take up or release heat (latent heat). For example,

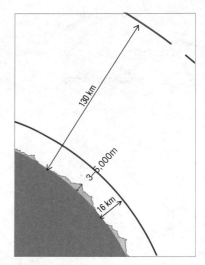

A fine film of air surrounds the earth. Mountain ranges have a by no means small influence on air movements.

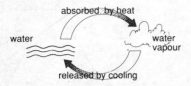

to transform water into vapour (evaporation of the oceans, transformation of a water droplet into water vapour) you need heat. On the other hand, condensation (the change from water vapour into water droplets) produces heat.

The story so far

Let us summarise what is happening in the atmosphere:

As the ocean surface is warmed, water evaporates.

The resulting water vapour mixes with the air, yet the quantity of water vapour the air can contain is limited. Once this limit is

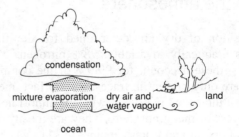

reached, we say that the air is saturated; if we go beyond that limit, the excess water vapour condenses out in the form of water droplets, forming clouds. The limit of saturation depends on the temperature of the air: warm air can contain more water vapour than cold air.

For example, in the lower layers (where the air pressure is 1,000 hectopascals [hPa]), at a temperature of 20°C the atmosphere can contain up to about 15g of water per kilogram of dry air, whereas at 0°C the atmosphere can only contain about 4g. Let us imagine a quantity of air at 1,000hPa at a temperature of 20°C, containing 14g of water vapour. It is not saturated, since air under these conditions can contain 15g of water vapour, but if it cools for whatever reason, then it will rapidly become saturated, and condensation will occur.

If the air in question cools to 0°C, the 10g of excess water vapour (14−4=10) will be transformed into water droplets.

Note that:
– the change from the state of water vapour to that of water releases heat, which slows cooling considerably;

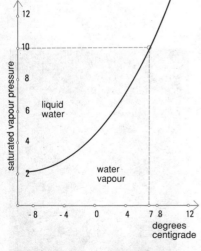

By experiment we can show that the saturation level of air rises in proportion to its temperature. 'Relative humidity' is the percentage of saturation level reached by a given air mass for a given temperature.

– condensation is helped by the presence in the air of miniscule hygroscopic (water-absorbing) particles, which are referred to as condensation nuclei: dust, salt crystals, etc;
– in the atmosphere, water vapour can condense out in the form of water droplets, even in sub-zero temperatures. There can therefore be water drops (and not ice crystals) down to temperatures of –15°C (supercooling).

It is therefore important for the meteorologist to know the amount of water contained in the air (humidity), but also the possible reasons for cooling of the air. The principal causes are radiation and fall in pressure. These will be discussed in detail below. (We should also note as less common causes the mixing of air and turbulence.)

Clouds cause precipitation. Water falls on the ground; a part of this evaporates; some waters vegetation, which returns it to the atmosphere in the form of vapour through *transpiration*; another part either collects in streams or soaks into the ground and returns to the ocean.

The cycle is complete. Water, in the course of its movements through the atmosphere, changes state and can also absorb and distribute significant quantities of heat.

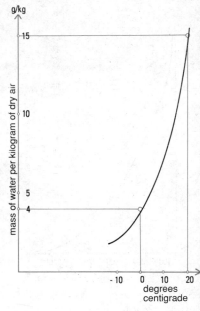

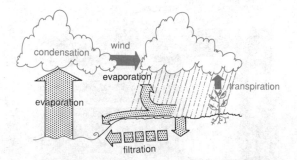

At a pressure of 1,000hPa:
– at 20°C, the atmosphere can contain approximately 15g of water vapour per kilogram of dry air;
– at 0°C, the atmosphere can only retain just over 4g of water per kilogram of dry air.

Defining a state

The state of a gas is defined by its pressure, its temperature and its volume. The volume of the atmosphere is virtually unknowable. The first two parameters that are used, because they are easily accessible, are pressure and temperature. To find out the composition of the mixture of dry air and water vapour, we define also a parameter 'humidity'. Since the atmosphere is also a fluid in perpetual motion, we must also allow for the parameter 'movement', ie the wind.

To study these parameters, the meteorologist, like the geographer about to make a map, must define a scale. The one most frequently used, because it is imposed by the distance between each measuring point (weather stations), is the synoptic scale. Synoptic areas within which the different parameters are considered to be uniform, have a horizontal dimension of several tens of kilometres, and a vertical dimension of 10m or so.

Atmospheric pressure

On 19 September 1648 at the Puy de Dôme, Pascal and his brother-in-law, Périer, showed that atmospheric pressure falls with altitude. This drop in pressure is easy to understand: it is obvious that if the vertical dimension of a column of air falls, then so does the pressure exerted. Things are a little more complicated, however, because we must also take into account the density of the air. On average, in the lower layers, the drop is 1hPa per 8m of elevation, but the drop is faster in cold air than it is in warm air, and the fall slows with altitude.

Atmospheric pressure is measured with compensated aneroid

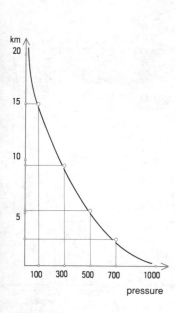

Average fall in pressure in relation to altitude
On average, an altitude of:
3km corresponds to a pressure of 700hPa;
5.5km corresponds to a pressure of 500hPa;
9.1km corresponds to a pressure of 300hPa;
16km corresponds to a pressure of 100hPa.

The barograph
The sensitive element is a partially evacuated capsule, whose contraction or expansion is amplified. The capsule is linked to a needle or to a pen, which then leaves a trace on graph paper.

barometers. These indicate pressure with reasonable accuracy, but they require frequent re-setting. Barographs allow changes in pressure to be observed. It is often very useful to know the rate of change. A sudden, and significant, drop or rise is a warning that should not be ignored. Without wishing to over-state the case, barometers also remain vital pieces of equipment for sea-going vessels.

Aneroid barometer compensated to allow for direct readings.

In moderate latitudes, such as Europe, atmospheric pressure varies between 950 and 1050hPa, the average pressure (often referred to as normal) being 1013.25hPa.

There is a daily rise and fall in air pressure which is known as the 'barometric tide'. The range of this rise and fall is limited (about 1hPa) and hard to detect in recordings. Suffice it to say that, through the day, the pressure rises between 0400 and 1000 and then again between 1600 and 2200, and that it falls between 1000 and 1600, and then again between 2200 and 0400.

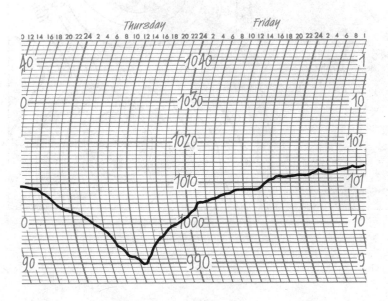

Diagram showing the rapid variation in air pressure recorded on a graph: fall between Wednesday and Thursday (1300), rise from 1300 Thursday on into Friday.

Variations in atmospheric pressure play a very important role in meteorology. At sea level, the air pressure is not the same at all points around the globe. There are regions where the air pressure is relatively low, which are known as *depressions*; and areas where the pressure is relatively high, which are referred to as *anticyclones*. It is important to know this horizontal distribution, because it has a direct influence on the wind direction.

We must therefore analyse the pressure areas. For practical reasons, this analysis, which is done by tracing on the isobars, can be done in one of two ways, depending on whether one is at sea level, or a higher altitude.

At sea level, by definition a constant altitude of 0m, we join up the points having the same air pressure. The isobars are marked at intervals of 5hPa.

Analysis of air pressure at sea level

The analysis on a pressure map brings out the high pressure zones or *anticyclones* (marked A), and the low pressure areas or *depressions* (marked D).

A trough extends from a depression, a ridge from an anticyclone.

A col lies between two low pressure zones, and two high pressure zones. The isobar marked 1015, showing the normal pressure (1013.25hPa), is often marked in bold.

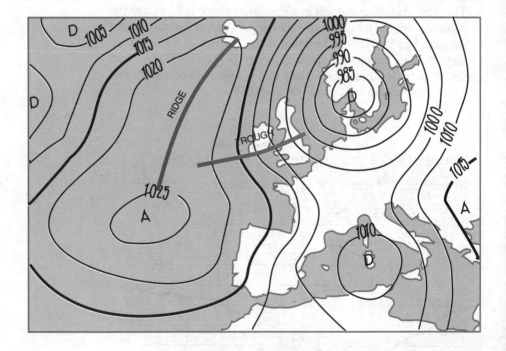

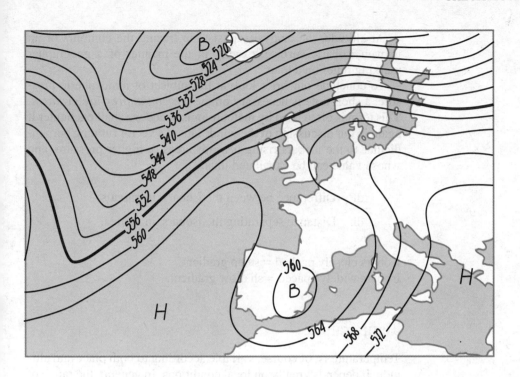

Analysis of a high air chart (here at 500hPa)

The contours of the surface at 500hPa are marked in geopotential decametres. The 'normal' contour at 556 decametres is marked in bold.

Example of a calculation of the horizontal pressure gradient

dP = 5hPa
dl = 500km

$$\frac{dP}{dl} = \frac{5hPa}{500km} = \frac{1hPa}{100km}$$

The pressure gradient is 1hPa per 100km.

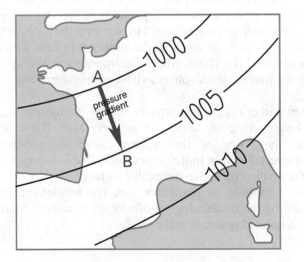

At altitude, the analysis consists in tracing the contours of an uneven isobaric surface, exactly in the manner of a geographer marking relief on a map.

To conclude our brief look at the subject of atmospheric pressure, a short note is necessary on the *horizontal pressure gradient*. This term is often used by meteorologists, and we shall encounter it again in our discussion of the wind. This is a vector running perpendicular to the isobars rising towards areas of higher pressure, and whose value can be calculated thus:

$$\frac{dP}{dl}$$

dP   Difference between the isobars, in pascals.

dl   Distance separating the isobars, in metres.

Isobars closely packed = steep gradient.
Isobars widely spaced = shallow gradient.

Temperature

Temperature is, of course, variable according to both place and altitude. It depends greatly on local conditions. In general, the range of temperature variation is greater in the interior of continents than by the sea, and also greater under clear skies than under cloud. The change in average temperature in the vertical plane allows us to see the different layers in the atmosphere more clearly: in the troposphere (whose depth varies from 4 to 8km over the poles to between 15 and 17km over the equator) the temperature falls with altitude by about 0.6°C per 100m. Above the troposphere and up to about 50km, we find the stratosphere, whose temperature rises with altitude.

Even further up, the mesosphere and the thermosphere are very high layers where air molecules are very rare. These layers lie outside the scope of this section, since all meteorological phenomena take place in the troposphere, that is to say, within the 12km or so directly above the earth's surface.

It is important to remember that the temperature readings provided by the meteorological offices are measured from a sheltered, ventilated space, ie in the shade.

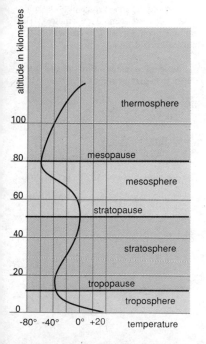

The variations in temperature with altitude help to establish the atmosphere's layers.

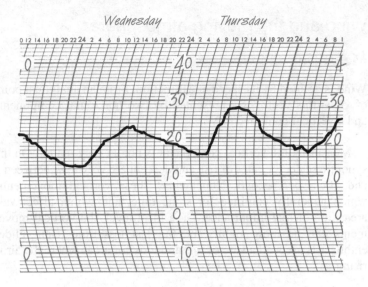

From a temperature recording taken in sheltered conditions, the times of the maximum and minimum temperatures can be determined, as well as for what length of time the temperature was higher or lower than a particular threshold. (Here, on Thursday 22nd, the temperature had been at 20°C and over for 7 hours.)

The diurnal amplitude is the difference between the maximum, which generally occurs in the early afternoon, and the minimum, which generally occurs just after dawn. On Thursday the 22nd, the amplitude was 12.5°C.

Humidity

The third parameter relating to the atmospheric conditions, and certainly one of the most important, is humidity. The water vapour in the air comes from the lakes, seas, rivers and other inland water courses. There is also vegetation, which takes up water from the ground through its roots and returns it to the atmosphere by transpiration. As a consequence, humidity, ie the amount of water vapour contained in the air, depends on the amount of water to be found in the area: it is greater at sea than on land (particularly over deserts). The further away from potential sources of water, the less water vapour there is: there is less at higher altitudes than in the lower layers of the atmosphere, for example.

Obtaining an absolute measurement of humidity is difficult, and relative measurements of humidity are not always precise.

Summary

Determining the three different parameters described here allows us to know the atmospheric conditions. Meteorological stations therefore measure these both at the surface and at altitude. However, as we have said, the atmosphere is also a gas in constant movement, both vertically and horizontally.

Wind and the moving atmosphere

Measuring the wind

Wind is defined by its speed and direction. From an analytical point of view, this vector is represented by two horizontal components and a vertical component, V.

Measuring the vertical component is not an easy matter. On the synoptic scale, the rates of rise and descent are very low: between 1 and 10cm per second. Nonetheless, these vertical movements, which generally continue for some time, and which affect vast areas, are of real importance. On a local level, the vertical movements can be more significant, but last less time. Hang-glider enthusiasts are well aware of this and look for areas where the air is rising.

While still looking at the synoptic scale, we note that the main movements in the atmosphere are essentially horizontal. It is this horizontal component, UV, that is measured by meteorological stations. It is important to note that the windspeed at ground level is always measured at a height of 10m. The measuring equipment is fixed to a pole that creates the least possible disturbance in the air flow.

To see the wind direction, we use a weather vane. The pointer is fixed at 360° (true north) and the other points of the compass are marked on the rose attached to it.

1. A turbulent wind.   2. Recording of average speed over 10 minutes.   3. A regular wind.

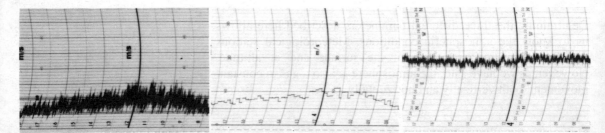

The Beaufort scale

Force	Description	Land specifications	Sea specifications	Equivalent speeds (at height of 10m over level ground)	
				Knots	Miles per hour
0	Calm	Smoke rises vertically.	Sea like a mirror.	-	-
1	Light air	Direction of wind shown by smoke drift but not by wind vanes.	Ripples like fish scales form.	1–3	1–3
2	Light breeze	Wind felt on face; leaves rustle; ordinary vane moved by wind.	Small wavelets, still short but more pronounced.	4–6	4–7
3	Gentle breeze	Leaves and small twigs in constant motion; wind extends light flag.	Large wavelets; crests beginning to break.	7–10	8–12
4	Moderate breeze	Raises dust and loose paper; small branches are moved.	Small waves becoming longer; fairly frequent white horses.	11–15	13–18
5	Fresh breeze	Small trees in leaf begin to sway; crest wavelets form on inland waters.	Moderate waves taking more pronounced long form; many white horses formed. Chance of spray.	16–21	19–24
6	Strong breeze	Large branches in motion; whistling heard in telegraph wires; umbrellas used with difficulty.	Large waves beginning to form; white foam crests are more extensive everywhere. Probably some spray.	22–27	25–31
7	Near gale	Whole trees in motion; inconvenience felt when walking against wind.	Sea heaps up and white foam from breaking waves begins to be blown in streaks along the direction of the wind.	28–33	32–8
8	Gale	Breaks branches off trees; generally impedes progress.	Moderately high waves of greater length; edges of crests beginning to break into the spindrift.	34–40	39–46
9	Strong gale	Slight structural damage occurs (chimney pots and slates are removed).	High waves. Dense streaks of foam along the direction of the wind. Crests of waves begin to topple, tumble and roll over. Spray may affect visibility.	41–7	47–54
10	Storm	Seldom experienced inland; trees uprooted; considerable structural damage occurs.	Very high waves with long overhanging crests. The resulting foam is blown in dense white streaks along the direction of the wind.	48–55	55–63
11	Violent storm	Widespread damage.	Exceptionally high waves sometimes concealing small and medium ships. Sea completely covered with long white patches of foam. Edges of wave crests blown into froth. Poor visibility.	56–63	64–73
12	Hurricane	Widespread damage.	Air filled with foam and spray, sea white with driving spray. Visibility bad.	>64	>74

The wind gauge is used to measure the speed (or force) of the wind. The units used are metres per second and the knot (1 kn = 0.51m per second). The average wind speed measured over 10 minutes is referred to as the *mean wind*. The gust speed is the maximum force of the wind at a given instant in time and is read from the recorder. The difference between the maximum and the synoptic wind speeds gives an indication of the turbulence.

The real wind

Wind is vital in navigation so we will devote a little more attention to it.

We have seen that the analysis of the pressure fields brings out the depressions and the anticyclones. One might think that the air would move quite naturally from the areas of high pressure to those of low pressure. This is almost what happens, although things are not quite that simple. In fact:
– the earth rotates on its axis;
– its surface is not regular;
– it is not a smooth ball.

The earth's variation creates a deviating force which acts perpendicularly to the direction of the air flow (to the right in the northern hemisphere, to the left in the southern hemisphere). This is known as the *Coriolis force* or the *geostrophic force*.

In the northern hemisphere, the air coming from the anti-cyclones, twisted to the right, goes clockwise. The air going towards the depressions, pushed to the left, goes anticlockwise.

Departing from this observation, the meteorologist Buys-Ballot, at the end of the last century, established a rule: an observer who stands facing into the wind always has low pressure to his right and high pressure to his left.

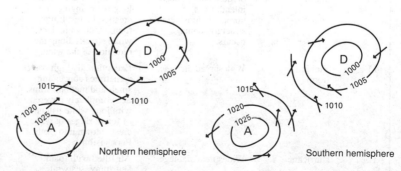

Buys-Ballot's law (here for surface winds). (A = anticyclone, or high-pressure area. D = depression, or low-pressure area.)

All atmospheric movements go in the opposite direction in the southern hemisphere, so the opposite rule applies in that hemisphere: low pressure on the left, high pressure on the right.

However, the earth is not flat in the lower layers at least, and the wind encounters friction that affects both its direction and its speed.

Buys-Ballot, demonstrating his famous law.

If, at high altitudes, it is shown that the wind runs parallel to the isobars this is not the case for the lower altitudes: it blows out of anticyclones and it blows into the depressions. Its angle in relation to the isobars is about 30° on land and 10° at sea. Its actual speed is therefore about half its theoretical speed on land, and two-thirds its theoretical speed at sea.

The wind speed can therefore be correctly estimated using a map of the pressure zones which has been analysed. Identifying the anticyclones and depressions, as well as the route of the isobars, allows us to mark the direction of the wind at any point. The distance between the isobars informs us of the wind speed.

Some small corrections must be added, however:

1. Where there is a *strong cyclonic curve,* or if the air is warmer than the water, then the speed calculated must be reduced by 1–2 Beaufort.
2. In case of an *anticyclonic curve,* or if the air is cooler than the water, the speed calculated must be raised by 1–2 Beaufort.
3. On a flat gradient, the lower the latitude, the higher the speed.

Horizontal convergence and divergence

Let us examine a few consequences:

Winds blowing in an anticlockwise direction are associated with a depression, and in the lower layers of the atmosphere, the wind spirals into the depression. There would therefore be an accumulation of air particles towards the centre of the depression. This accumulation can only be accommodated by a rising vertical movement over the depression. The vertical movement leads to a drop in pressure. Therefore the rising air mass grows *in volume*. This expansion naturally requires some exchange of energy. Given that air conducts heat badly, and can only take heat on from the surrounding environment (*adiabatic process*), it will therefore exhaust its own reserves, and its temperature will drop.

Lift, whether due to convergence or to another cause, is one of the principal causes of air cooling in the atmosphere.

We can summarise this phenomenon:
Depression → horizontal convergence → air rising → decrease in pressure → cooling.

Horizontal convergence: the air moves back into the centre of the depression, the accumulating air rises and cools.

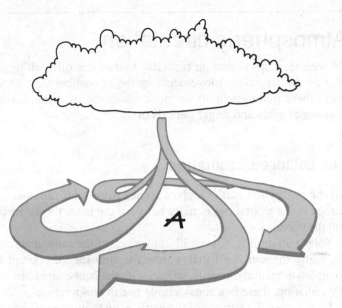

A

In the case of an anticyclone we observe the opposite effect. The wind leaving the anticyclone creates horizontal divergence. This leads to a dispersal of air particles towards the exterior. These are replaced by air sinking down from above. The sinking produces compression and warming.

Sinking is one of the principal causes of warming in the atmosphere.

Let us see what the consequences of this are:
• Lift causes cooling, and therefore condensation.
• On the other hand, sinking leads to evaporation: the water droplets in clouds are vaporised (and are therefore invisible).

We can summarise this:

Depression → horizontal convergence → lift → fall in pressure → cooling → condensation (clouds).

Anticyclone → horizontal divergence → sinking → compression → warming → evaporation (clearing skies).

Atmospheric circulation

On weather maps drawn up from day to day, it is difficult to get an idea of the larger air movements in the atmosphere. In order to make these more apparent we must make use of maps drawn up over wider areas and larger periods of time.

The balance of radiation

All the energy the earth receives comes from solar radiation. This energy is not shared out equally between the land, the atmosphere and the oceans.

Solar radiation is not readily absorbed in the atmosphere. It is not really the sun itself that warms the atmosphere (except from about 50km up and onwards, where, with the ozone layer absorbing UV radiation, there is a considerable rise in temperature).

By contrast, the surface of the earth, even though it reflects some of the sun's energy, also absorbs a good proportion of it. It is therefore much warmed by the sun. (Note that water absorbs more energy than the land, which is why the seas appear dark on satellite photographs.)

Once the earth is warmed, it radiates heat in its turn (infra-red radiation), and this radiation from the surface of the earth is almost entirely absorbed by the atmosphere. It is therefore principally the earth's surface that warms the atmosphere, which explains the drop in temperature experienced with altitude in the troposphere. The lower layers situated near the heat source, ie the earth, are warmer than the upper layers.

At night, the earth continues to radiate energy back into the atmosphere, but receives no further energy and therefore cools.

If we calculate the annual balance of radiation, we note that the earth's surface absorbs more than it radiates, whereas the atmosphere radiates back more than it absorbs. There is therefore an imbalance, but since the earth cannot go on warming indefinitely, its energy is transmitted to the atmosphere by other means.

Transfer of heat

The other means are:
• *Molecular conduction*, which is very limited since air is a bad conductor of heat. Exchange through conduction is only really

found in the lower layers of the atmosphere in contact with the surface of the earth. Cold air coming into contact with a warm surface will be slightly heated in the vicinity of the ground, and warm air cools on contact with cold ground. This is what happens at night for example: the ground cools by radiation, and transmits this cooling little by little to the lower layers of the atmosphere. As a result, there is a progressive drop in temperature, and, in certain conditions, the condensation of water vapour in the form of dew, fog or low clouds (stratus), and sometimes the appearance of frost.

• *Thermal convection* is considerably more efficient than conduction in exchanges of heat between the ground and the atmosphere. In all fluids warmed from the bottom up, thermoconvective columns appear, characterised by a rise in the centre, with fall off at the sides. The air warmed therefore rises and carries the heat into the higher reaches of the atmosphere.

• *Water changing state* is another important means of heat transfer. You will remember that in order to change from a liquid state to a gaseous state (vaporisation), energy is required and that the change from a gaseous state to a liquid state releases energy.

The water of the oceans evaporates into the atmosphere. The water vapour mixes with the air and, by rising (this being through a process either of horizontal convergence or of convection), it condenses to form clouds, thereby transferring to the atmosphere the energy taken from the oceans. The amounts of energy thus exchanged between the surface of the earth and the atmosphere are considerable.

It is estimated that 75% of the excess energy received by the land by radiation is released back into the atmosphere by means of water changing state.

A balance is therefore established between the earth and the surrounding atmosphere. However, the surface of the earth does not receive the same amount of energy from the sun at all points; nor can it transmit the same amount of energy to every corner of the globe. The polar regions, because of the shape of the earth, are less well off when compared with the equatorial regions. Further, in the general system of exchanges between the earth's surface and the atmosphere, there is an imbalance between the poles and the equator. Thermic exchanges take place between the two (otherwise both the polar and equatorial regions would rapidly become uninhabitable). These exchanges, which cannot take place via the ground, operate both by means of those ocean currents flowing along the meridian (north–south/south–north: eg the Gulf Stream and the Labrador Current) and by currents of warm air moving towards the poles and cold air moving towards the equator.

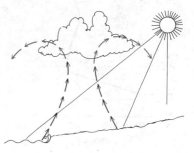

Thermal convection
Warm air rising leads to a drop in pressure, and therefore to condensation. Naturally, thermoconvective columns can be greatly distorted by the wind. Nonetheless, they continue to exist. The warm air of the lower strata rises in places, which leads to a drop in pressure, and therefore cooling and condensation.

General circulation

The movements of the air that we have so far described determine what is known as the general circulation. They become apparent when the general distribution of pressure zones is worked out, and if we know the temperature at the relevant points. As we have seen, if we know where the pressure zones are, then we can calculate the speed and the movement of the winds.

The meridian profile of the air pressure measured *at sea level* shows that on average there is a minimum in the region of the equator, a sub-tropical maximum, another minimum at a latitude of 60°N and S, and a polar maximum.

The minimum, or equatorial depression, is linked to thermal exchange (warming in the lower layers, whence convection, lift and convergence). The tropical anticyclone is essentially a dynamic anti-cyclone (as the vertical view on page 703 shows, these zones show sinking and divergence). The depressions around 60° latitude are also dynamic in origin (convergence in these zones, resulting in lift), while the polar surface anticyclone is the result of the high density of the cold air in the lower layers.

Of course, the average winds at the surface are subject to devia-tion due to the rotation of the earth.

The average meridian circulation viewed from above also reveals a certain number of columns, the most important of which are known as Hadley's cells, found on either side of the equatorial depression. These allow the excess energy from around the equato-rial region to be transported into the high troposphere as well as towards more northerly and southerly regions.

We can therefore note that:
• The equatorial depression, or Inter-Tropical Convergence Zone or meteorological equator, is not to be found at the geographical equator, but rather to the north (the uneven distribution of the conti-nents leads to the different energy balances in the two hemispheres).

• The distribution of pressure zones and their circulation vertically vary according to the season. We also note an oscillation along the meridian of the centres of activity, and the appearance of anticy-clones and thermal depressions on the continents (Siberian anticy-clone in winter, depression over the Sahara in summer).

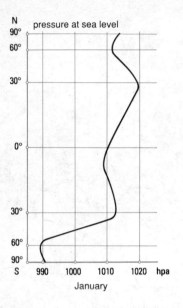

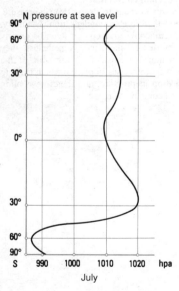

Meridian profile of pressure at sea level.

Average pressure at sea level (northern hemisphere).

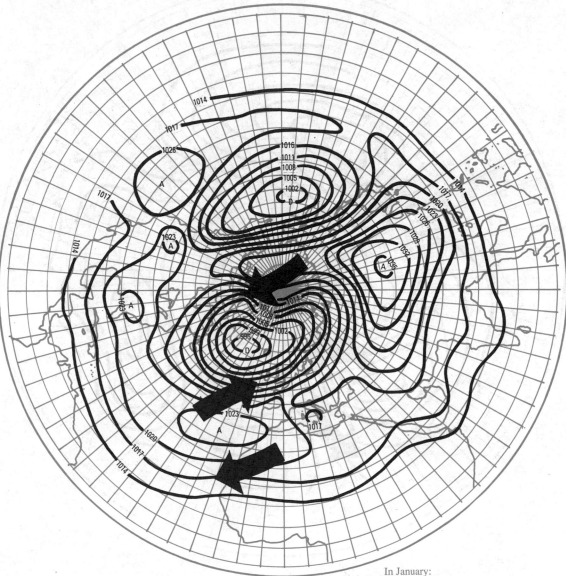

In January:
The high pressures on the American continent and over Siberia are thermal in origin (cold air).

The average winds blow from the SW or west on the Atlantic at temperate latitudes, and from the NE or east (trade winds) in tropical latitudes.

In July:
The low pressure area extending from the Sahara to China as well as the one covering California are due to the warming of the lower layers of the atmosphere over these regions.

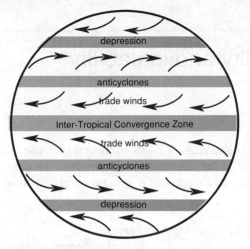

Average surface winds.

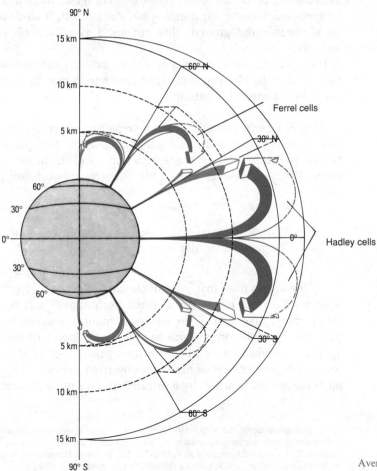

Average vertical meridian circulation.

Stability and instability

Theory

If an air particle rises, it cools by decompression. This cooling is independent of the surrounding air (adiabatic process). Let us take, for example, an air particle at ground level and raise it to a given altitude.

There are two possible scenarios:
1. If the particle is at a lower temperature than that of the surrounding air, then it forms a bubble, so to speak, of air at a lower temperature than the surrounding air. As a result, it tends to sink back towards the ground: this creates a condition of vertical stability.
2. If the particle enters a colder area, it is consequently warmer than the surrounding air, then it tends to continue to rise: this creates a condition of vertical instability.

This process is complicated to a greater or lesser degree by the amount of humidity (particularly if condensation takes place while the air is rising), and by the temperature gradient in the vertical plane. We can, however, reduce the question to two broad principles:

Cold air with warm air above it = stability
Warm air with cold air above it = instability[1]

Following on from that, we can conclude that:
– air cooled from below (or warmed from above) will be stable (temperature inversion). This occurs at night, for example, when heat loss from the ground reaches the lower layers of the atmosphere by conduction, or when warm air passes over a cold surface for a sufficient amount of time (cooling from below), or by warm air being pushed upwards by a disturbance (warming from above);

[1] In meterological terms, the notions of warm and cold refer to potential temperatures.
   In order to compare the temperatures of two air particles, those temperatures must be taken at the same level (generally at 1,000hPa). The potential temperature is therefore the temperature of the particle raised adiabatically to a level of 1,000hPa.

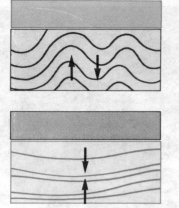

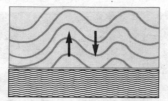

Whether cooled from above, or warmed from below, air becomes unstable.

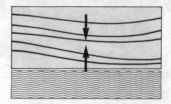

If warmed from above, or cooled from below, air becomes stable.

– air that is warmed from below (or cooled from above) is necessarily unstable. This occurs during the day, with the warming by convection of the lower layers of the atmosphere, or when cold air passes over a hot surface (warming from below), or, again, by cold advection to altitude (cooling from above).

Clouds: a manifestation of instability

The stability or instability of the different layers in the atmosphere can easily be determined by observing the clouds (assuming there are any, that is!).

Clouds indicating stability

High clouds: cirrus, cirrostratus.
Medium-level clouds: altostratus, nimbostratus.
Low clouds: stratus, stratocumulus.

Clouds indicating instability

High clouds: cirrocumulus.
Medium-level clouds: altocumulus.
Low clouds: cumulus, cumulonimbus.

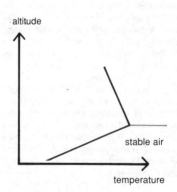

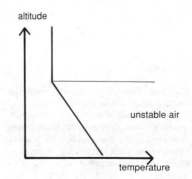

Clouds indicating stability

High clouds

Cirrocumulus. Granules and lines leaving no shadow associated with fibroid elements at the same level are characteristic of cirrocumulus.

You can also see here some cumulus *fractus* or *humilis*.

Medium-level clouds

Altocumulus. There are numerous varieties of this sort of cloud. The type illustrated is an altocumulus *translucidus*. The elements of this cloud-layer, all at the same level, present quite definite gaps between the 'balls' which form into parallel undulations (hence, altocumulus *undulatus*). These differ from cirrocumulus by their thickness.

There also exists the variety altocumulus *lenticularis*, which takes the general shape of lentils or almonds. These are generally found in mountainous areas. There are also the varieties altocumulus *floccus* (clouds broken up into small tufts) and *castellanus* (horizontal base topped with small crenellations or turrets).

Low clouds

Cumulus. This variety shows a moderate vertical development (cumulus *mediocris*). The summits show undeveloped protuberances. You can also see some small clouds that are of the variety cumulus *fractus*. When these show little vertical development, they are referred to as cumulus *humilis*.

Medium-level clouds

Nimbostratus. Grey cloud-layer, often dark, which is often indistinct in form due to almost constant precipitation.

Low clouds

Stratus. This cloud type appears very uniform, and has a low, rather misty, base only a few tens of metres above the ground. It is reminiscent of a fog that does not reach down to ground level. The change from stratus to fog, and vice versa, is common and can be very rapid.

Stratocumulus. The individual clouds appear like large grey shingle. A thin layer often has gaps showing blue sky between the clouds.

Clouds indicating instability

High clouds

Cirrocumulus. Granules and lines leaving no shadow associated with fibroid elements at the same level are characteristic of cirrocumulus.

You can also see here some cumulus *fractus* or *humilis*.

Medium-level clouds

Altocumulus. There are numerous varieties of this sort of cloud. The type illustrated is an altocumulus *translucidus*. The elements of this cloud-layer, all at the same level, present quite definite gaps between the 'balls' which form into parallel undulations (hence, altocumulus *undulatus*). These differ from cirrocumulus by their thickness.

There also exists the variety altocumulus *lenticularis*, which takes the general shape of lentils or almonds. These are generally found in mountainous areas. There are also the varieties altocumulus *floccus* (clouds broken up into small tufts) and *castellanus* (horizontal base topped with small crenellations or turrets).

Low clouds

Cumulus. This variety shows a moderate vertical development (cumulus *mediocris*). The summits show undeveloped protuberances. You can also see some small clouds that are of the variety cumulus *fractus*. When these show little vertical development, they are referred to as cumulus *humilis*.

Cumulonimbus. A powerful-looking cloud of considerable size, with a rather vague outline; when this variety of cloud is topped by an anvil, then it is referred to as cumulonimbus *capillatus*.

Underneath the clouds you can see a heavy shower falling.

Air masses

The different types of air mass

These large movements in the atmosphere set in motion enormous quantities of air. It is estimated that by means of the trade winds in the northern hemisphere more than 200 million tonnes of air a second move towards the equator.

In the course of these movements, air masses from different points of origin meet, but only mix with great difficulty – Siberian air, which is cold and dry, and air from the Azores, therefore warm and humid, are very different things. There is consequently a sort of partitioning of the atmosphere into great air masses separated from one another by narrow, turbulent boundary zones.

We can follow these air masses, recognise them as they move and study their evolution.

They can be classified into three broad types:

1. *Radiation mass* (cold continental anticyclones) characterised by a strong cooling from below, which tends to lead to stability.
2. *Convection mass* (cold invasions) characterised by warming from below, and therefore tending towards instability.
3. *Film mass* (warm advection) which groups together the changes undergone during the various movements.

European air masses

Europe comes under the influence of three air masses:

Arctic air
Cold, dry and initially radiative, it becomes progressively more humid and prone to convect in the course of its move southwards (warming from below and passing over the sea). Squally showers begin to appear.

Polar air
Less cold than the above, because it originates in more southerly climes, it also becomes humid and convective when it reaches Europe after passing over the sea (patchy with showers). On the other hand, if it comes in over the land – say, over Russia in winter – then it is very cold, relatively dry and radiative on arrival.

Tropical air
Warm, more or less prone to convect and very humid, this air is accompanied by many clouds after it passes over the sea. It gives good weather in summer when in anticyclonic conditions (hence divergence and sinking).

These movements of the air masses depend on the distribution of pressure centres and the position of centres of activity: anticyclones and depressions.

Fronts

The creation of fronts

If two air masses of different temperatures (polar air and tropical air, for example) meet and if the paths they follow keep them in close contact, then a *front* is created. This front is basically the boundary between two air masses, and it is a place of considerable activity. If either of the two conditions specified above ceases to apply, then the frontal activity tends to die down rapidly – this is known as frontal decay.

Certain regions of the earth provide ideal conditions for the creation of fronts. An example of this is the Inter-Tropical Convergence Zone, which is to be found near the equator; another is to be found in the more temperate latitudes of the Atlantic, where air coming from the poles and tropical air, driven by the anticyclone found over the Azores, come into contact.

This polar front will be distorted under the influence of two principal forces:

1. The warm air and cold air tend to follow opposite paths, cold air moving towards the equator, warm air towards the pole.
2. The warm air, being less dense, moves more quickly.

These two influences will create an eddy with a vertical axis turning in the direction of a cyclone. This produces a wave-type distortion in the front.

A depression is created at the top of the warm updraft, where the pressure drop at ground level is at its greatest as a result of the warm air rising as it meets the cold air (cyclogenesis).

Creation of a depression

After a few hours, the wave-type distortion deepens and develops. In the warm front, the cold air replaces the warm air at a gradient of between 1 in 200 and 1 in 1,000. In a cold front, the cold air replaces the warm air along a gradient of between 1 in 10 and 1 in 200.

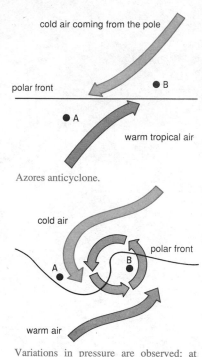

Azores anticyclone.

Variations in pressure are observed: at point B, where the warm air is replacing the cold air, the pressure falls. On the other hand, at A, where the heavier cold air is replacing the warm air, the air pressure rises.

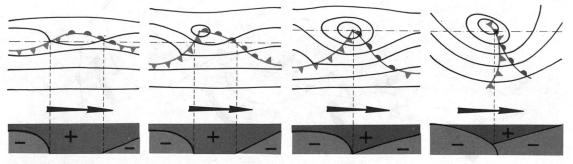

Birth of a depression
The warm air from the disturbance that is forming is 'captured' between the two areas of cold air. Since the warm air is lighter, it rises gradually along a shallow gradient, above the cold air in the rear, which is generally colder than the air that precedes it. The creation of fronts is an important source of lift.

The disturbance is being occluded. The cold air in the rear, which is 'active' and fast-moving, gradually joins up with the cold air ahead. Soon, all the warm air will have been pushed up to higher altitudes.

Occlusion

At this point, some new phenomena appear. The cold air ahead is different from the cold air in the rear. The latter, less well developed, is generally colder. It also moves faster. Consequently, the warm air between the two masses of cold air is gradually pushed upwards, forming a warm front that stretches from the summit of the warm sector to the depression: this is known as occlusion.

Trains

At any given moment, there is of course more than one wave distortion on the polar front. This series of depressions is referred to as a 'train', moving towards Europe from the west. The whole process takes about 48 hours in disturbed conditions in the west and between 24 and 36 hours in the NW.

A train of wave disturbances
The wave disturbances that are created turn into depressions which are gradually occluded as they move from west to east.

CHAPTER 2

Today's weather

Having discussed the principal atmospheric phenomena in the preceding chapter, we must now see how these affect sailors, and what the general weather conditions are in the areas that they will normally be travelling, ie the Northern Atlantic, the Channel and the Western Mediterranean.

It is more difficult to talk about the weather conditions in a given area than it is to describe the atmospheric conditions. One can outline the larger movements of the air masses without running into too many difficulties, but it is a rather more dangerous enterprise to try and work out the weather conditions on a day-to-day basis. So as not to get too enmeshed, we will start with what we can learn by using our eyes.

First of all, we will look at the clouds. There is an infinite variety of cloud types, but long observation has allowed meteorologists to arrive at a system of classification.

Since we can read the clouds, and the weather conditions that they imply, we must now learn to read the different types of weather that we might encounter. This will be done through case-studies.

Cloud systems

From a boat, we can observe the clouds, which are organised into systems and which behave regularly.

Air rising at the frontal boundary gives rise to large cloud masses, often accompanied by rain, snow and hail (all referred to as precipitation), over a distance of hundreds, if not thousands, of kilometres.

The movement of fronts, which are organised into atmospheric disturbances, will be marked by often extreme and violent variations in the various meteorological parameters, which would take too long to discuss in detail here, but which will be summarised in the panels giving the relationships between the disturbances and the different meteorological parameters.

By following the organisation of the cloud systems it is possible to know, from the ground, whether the approaching air is stable or

Warm, stable air

TEMPERATURE	Falling	Stationary		Rapid rise		Weak rise
PRESSURE	Rising	Falling	Stationary or falling slightly	Falling rapidly	Moderate fall	Weak fall
WIND	NW turbulent	Veer	SW to W	S to SE rising	SE to S	Weak
PRECIPITATION	Showers Rain Storms	Rain	Mist Fog	Rain Snow if below freezing		
VISIBILITY	Very good (reduced in storms)	Good	Mediocre to poor	Fair to mediocre		Good
CLOUD SECTORS	TRAIN	MAIN BODY	Warm sector	MAIN BODY		HEAD

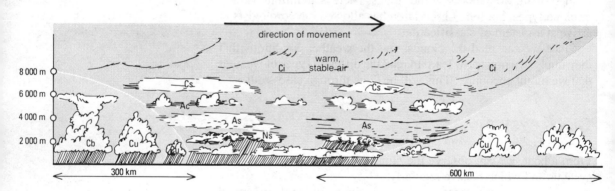

Ci: Cirrus
Cs Cirrostratus
Ac: Altocumulus
As: Altostratus
Ns: Nimbostratus
Cb: Cumulonimbus
CU: Cumulus

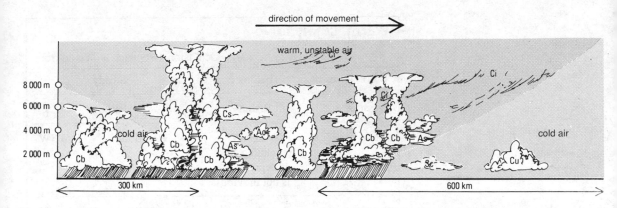

Warm, unstable air

TEMPERATURE	Falling	Slight fall	Rise with sudden falls in showery conditions	Sudden fall in showers		
PRESSURE	Rising	Uneven fall	Very slight fall	Falling, with sudden rises under cumulonimbus		
WIND	NW blustery	S to SW, blustery in storms		Weak S to SE with gusts		
PRECIPITATION	Rain showers, hail or snow Storms	Rain showers or hail Scattered showers		Rain	Showers	Storms
VISIBILITY	Good to very good (reduced in showers)	Mediocre to bad		Good, reduced under showers		Good
CLOUD SECTORS	TRAIN BODY	STORMY WITH HEAVY, SQUALLY SHOWERS		BODY STORMY		HEAD PRE-STORMY

unstable (or, better, if it is convectively stable or unstable). The cold air in either the rear or the van is generally unstable, except in the winter when you can encounter stable radiative air masses.

Warm, stable air			
			Occlusion associated with cold front
TEMPERATURE	Falling	Steady	
PRESSURE	Rising	Falling	
WIND	W to NW remaining SW if depression is not moving	Rotation	S to SW
PRECIPITATION	Rainshowers, snow or hail	Rain Snow if below freezing	Rain
VISIBILITY	Good or very good (reduced in showery conditions)	Mediocre	Good
CLOUD SECTORS	TRAIN	BODY	HEAD

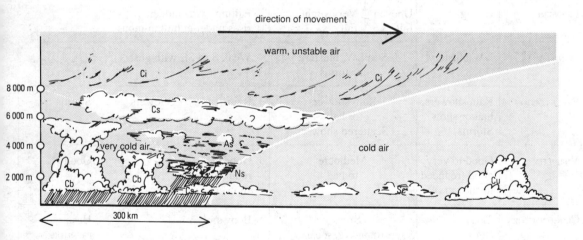

Ci: Cirrus
Cs: Cirrostratus
Ac: Altocumulus
As: Altostratus
Cb: Cumulonimbus
Cu: Cumulus

The cloud system

From the preceding vertical sections, or by observing the satellite photographs of several disturbances, one can see that the clouds occupy quite precise positions, as if they were organised into a system of several characteristic cloud sectors. It is useful to know the various names which recur frequently in the weather bulletins.

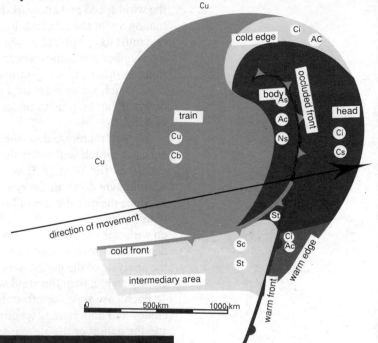

Cloud System
The clouds that make up the head and the body are unstable or stable according to the characteristics of the warm air. Around the edges, we find cirrus and altocumulus clouds; stratocumulus in the intermediary areas, and finally in the train, cumulus and cumulonimbus, with clear patches (changeable weather).

Case-studies

We have now discussed all the elements necessary for an under-standing of the weather. However, it is not enough to observe the cloud systems, read the barometer and the thermometer, measure the wind speed and know its direction, even along with all the infor-mation about the air conditions. In order to interpret them correctly, one must have to hand all the different parameters at once, because the weather conditions where we are depend on the weather condi-tions in other places. Fortunately, there are typical sorts of situa-tions which we can use as a guide, in the same way that a wiring diagram can help us to understand an otherwise confusing bundle of wires.

We will therefore describe five typical cases, with a few of their variants, which will cover the spread of the main possible weather situations for Western Europe, Ireland down to Spain, and from Scandinavia down to Greece.

Since the distribution of high and low pressure zones is bound up with the movement of the air, then the wind at all altitudes depends on variations in air pressure both at the surface and at altitude. If the depressions and anticyclones, whose positioning is determined by the analysis of the parameters we have already described, are suffi-ciently stable, then the wind will keep a fairly steady direction.

Each case type therefore depends on the position of the anticy-clones and depressions (centres of activity), from which the winds and the nature of the air masses can be deduced.

Case No 1: arctic air from the north

Centres of activity

We find the following:
• A ridge of high pressure over the Atlantic at about 20° W.
• A depression over Southern Scandinavia.

This configuration, which is often encountered in winter and spring, leads to a rapid flow from the north over Western Europe. The arctic air, which is cold and radiative initially, passes over the surface of the sea, which becomes warmer as one moves south. The air warms progressively from below and therefore becomes convective and humid. The clouds are therefore generally of the cumulus and cumulonimbus types, accompanied by showers of rain, snow/hail and squalls. The winds can be quite strong or very strong (according to gradient and pressure), with gusts blowing from the north to the NW.

It is important to remember that this type of advection of arctic air occurs frequently towards Labrador (giving an anticyclone over Canada). In the winter, arctic air can also pass over NE Europe.

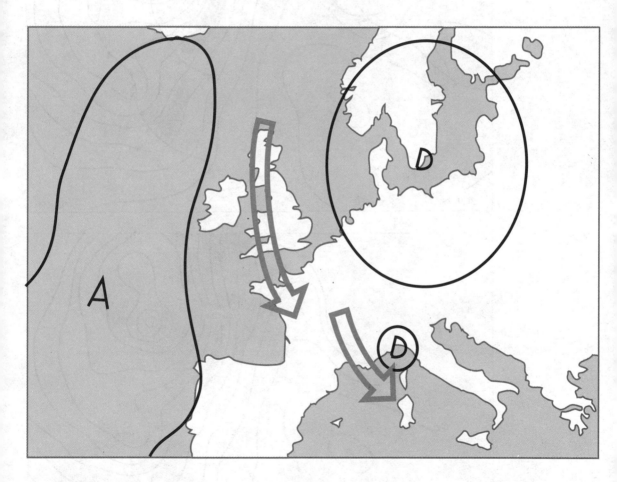

24 January 1986

24.1.86

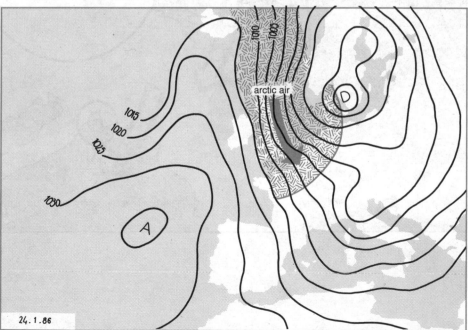

arctic air

24.1.86

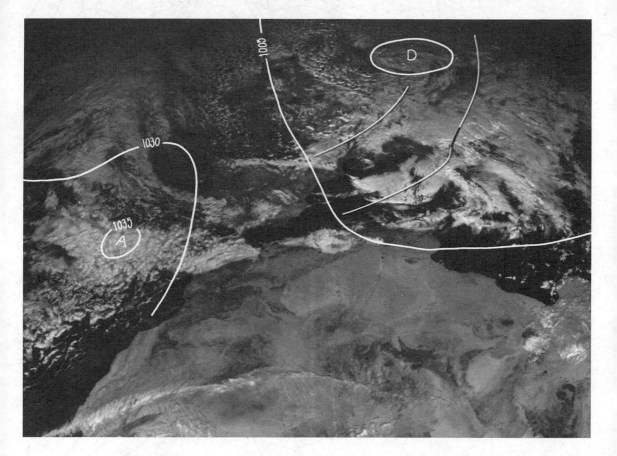

The anticyclone over the Azores stretches towards Iceland.

Between this anticyclone, and the depression over Scandinavia, the strong current from the north brings cold, unstable arctic air to France. This produces a good number of showers.

Note the heavy cloud build-up to windward of the Pyrenees and the Cantabrian mountains.

25 January 1986

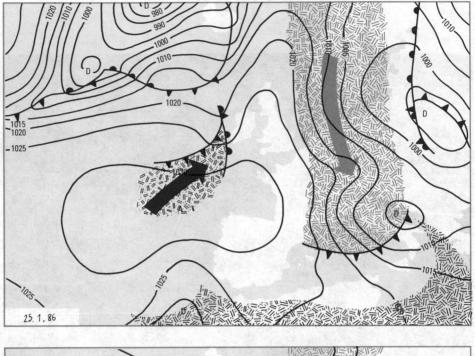

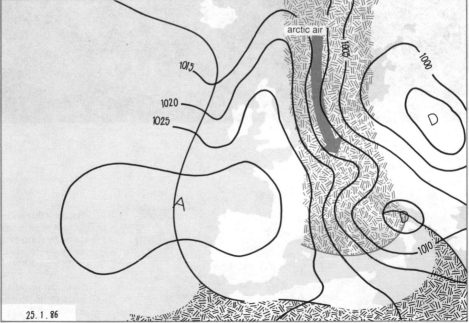

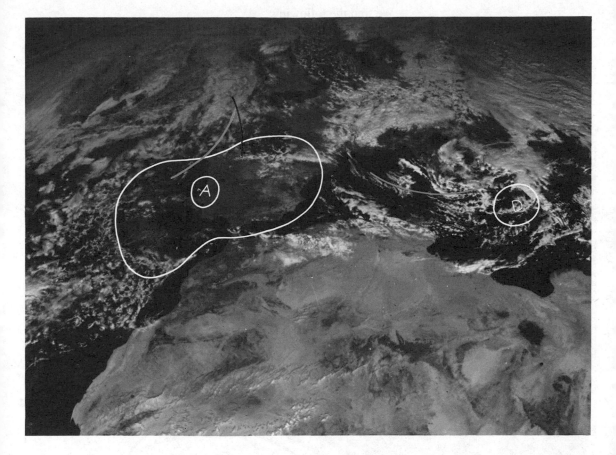

The combination of anticyclone and depression moves towards the east, the arctic current from the north affects Germany and Eastern Europe.

Looking to the west of the anticyclone, note the advection of tropical air, which circulates west to east and cuts the supply of arctic air to Europe.

Case No 2: arctic air from the east

Centres of activity

We find the following:
• An anticyclone over Scandinavia and the North Sea.
• A more or less clearly-defined depression over Southern Europe and the Mediterranean.

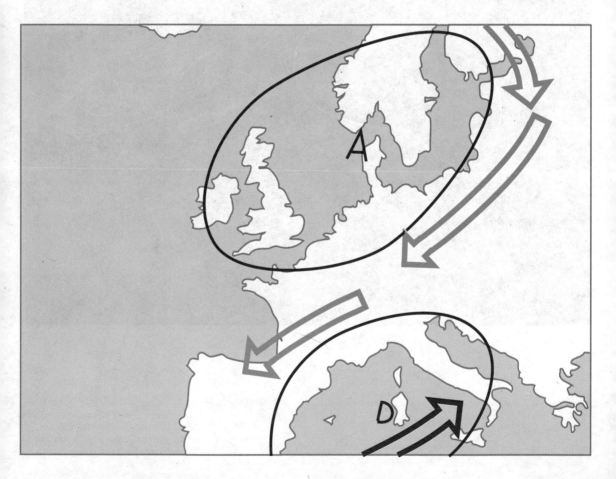

Case No 2: the depression is centred over the Eastern Mediterranean.

The arctic air coming into Russia is next pushed towards Western Europe in a flow from east to NE. Originally dry, cold and radiative, it keeps its properties, which may become even more strongly marked in its passage over snowy regions of the continent. When it reaches us, it is referred to as continental polar air: very cold, radiative and dry. It then causes waves of intensely cold weather which can last for a considerable time. The clouds found with it are of the stratus and stratocumulus varieties, with very little precipitation. The weak or moderate winds, which are fairly steady, blow mainly from the NE. They can be strong, north to NE around the Gulf of Lyons and in Provence (mistral, tramontana) if the depression is centred over the region of the Gulf of Genoa or over Italy (Case No 2.1).

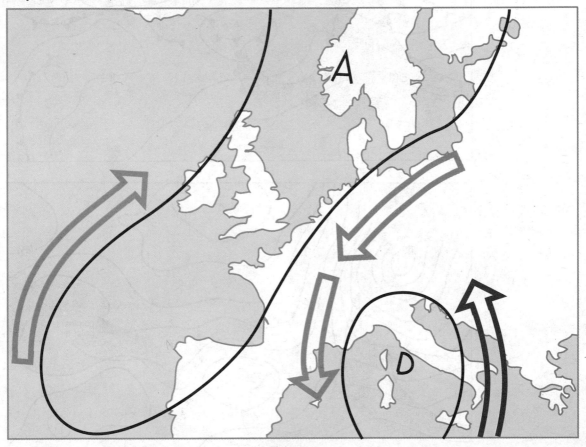

Case No 2.1: the depression is centred over Italy and the Gulf of Genoa.

7 February 1986

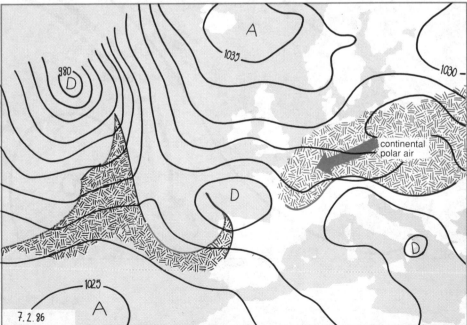

The continental anticyclone stretches towards Iceland. On its southern edge, the continental polar air circulates east to west, and passes into France. The depression over the Bay of Biscay is moving towards the Mediterranean.

8 February 1986

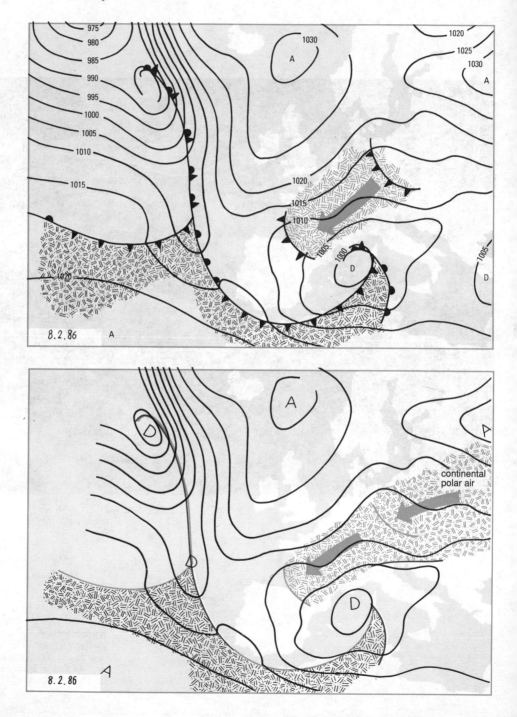

8.2.86   A

8.2.86   A

continental polar air

The next day, the depression is over the Mediterranean, the high pressure zones stretch more to the south, towards France. The advection of continental polar air becomes more widespread. The movement of the depression over the Mediterranean towards Italy is reminiscent of Case No 2.1, discussed on page 725.

Variations on case No 2: 9 February 1986

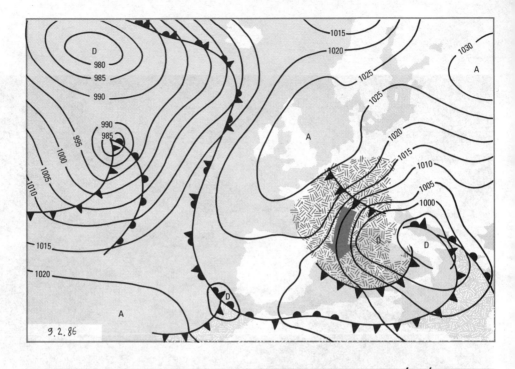

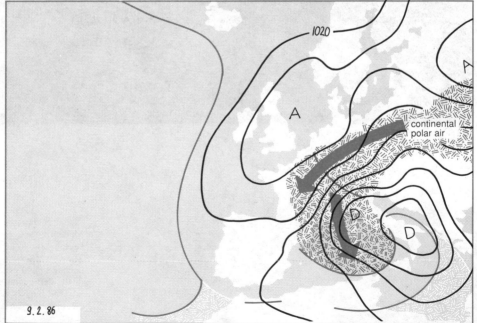

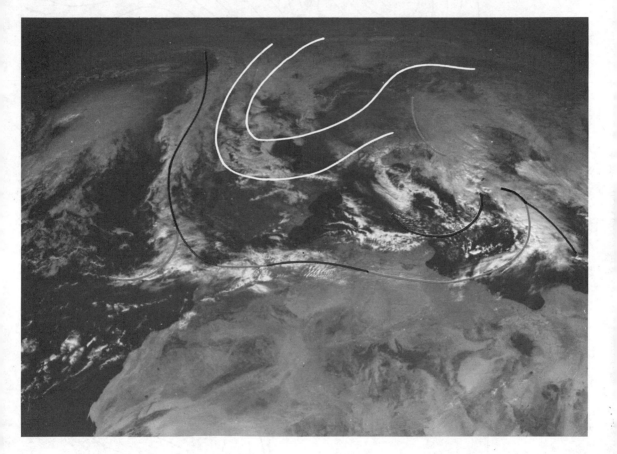

Centres of activity:

• Anticyclone over the North Sea, stretching towards the Bay of Biscay.
• Depression over Italy.

The very cold continental polar air (−2°C over Marseilles–Marignane) is being pushed north-south and channelled by the valley of the Rhône; it causes storms over the Mediterranean. The 'warm returns' from higher altitudes bring snowfalls over the Côte d'Azur.

11 February 1986

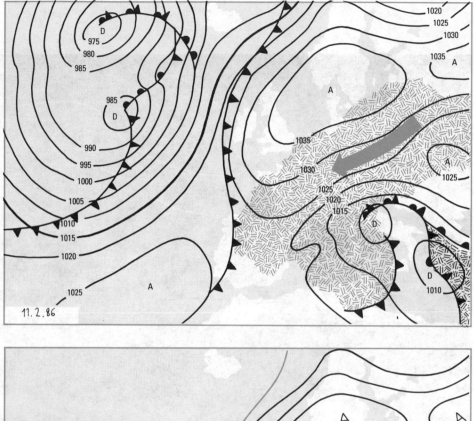

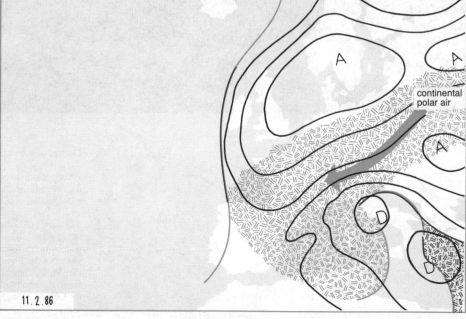

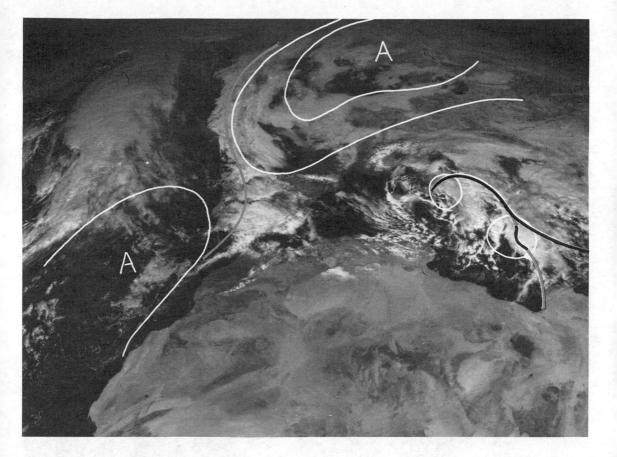

The anticyclone persists, still bringing very cold continental polar air to France, but the depression over Italy is filling in quite rapidly.

The mistral weakens. Note the 'warm returns' from higher altitudes, giving precipitation over the Adriatic.

Case No 3: maritime polar air over the British Isles, circulating west-east

Centres of activity

• The anticyclone over the Azores moves northwards.
• A depression persists near Iceland.

This sort of situation is often found in summer (see page 700). The maritime polar air circulates west to east around the level of the British Isles, the North Sea and Scandinavia. Because the air is unstable and humid, cumulus and even cumulonimbus clouds are found in places, as well as showers and strong west winds, gusting at times. Advections of maritime tropical air occur at the north edge of the anticyclone, leading to the creation of fronts between 50° and 60° N.

Over France, fine, warm weather without too much wind, except for some warm breezes.

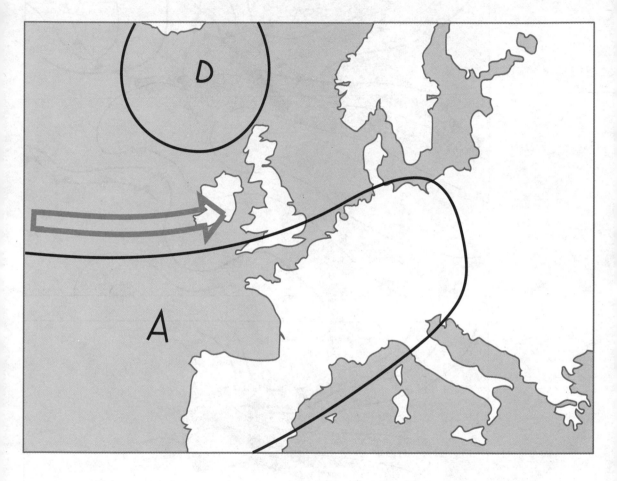

14 July 1986

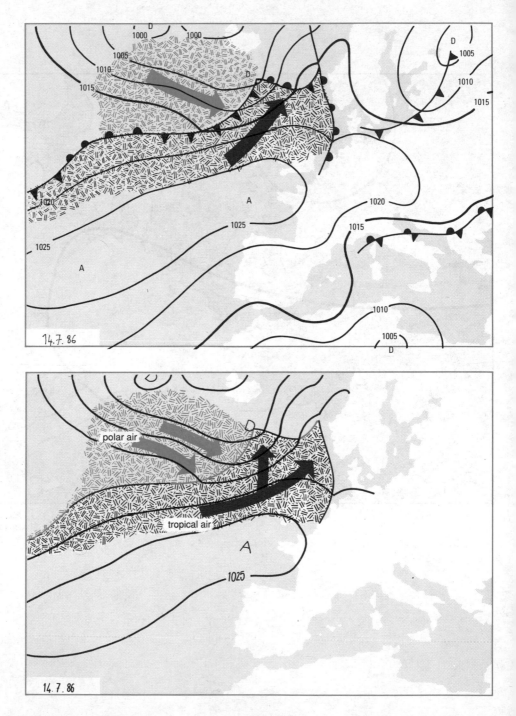

• The anticyclone stretches from the Azores to England and France.
• The depression is in the region of Iceland.

There are disturbances in the polar front in northerly latitudes. Over France, fine, warm weather with little wind.

16 July 1986

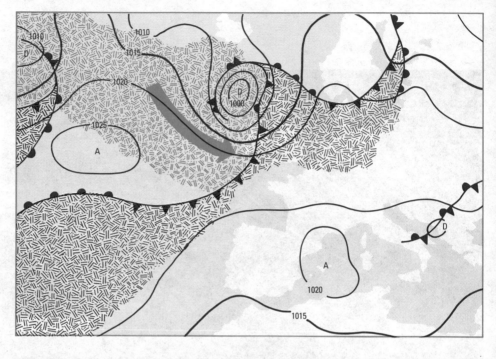

A depression is opening up off the Scottish coast.

Polar air is moving towards France with the arrival of the cold front at centre left showing very little activity in a field of relatively high pressure.

18 July 1986

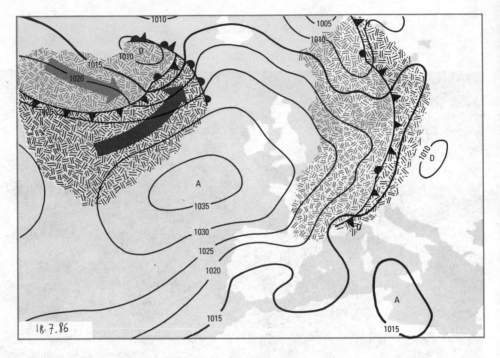

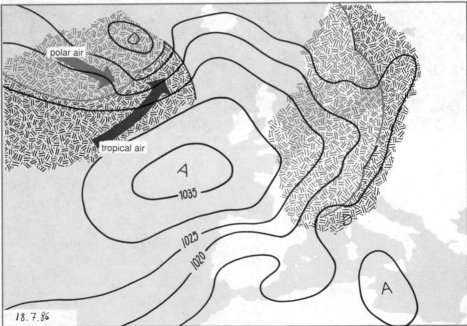

The anticyclone is re-forming behind the cold front. Some polar air is heading towards the Mediterranean, where there is a shallow depression over the Gulf of Genoa (reinforcing the north to NW winds from Provence to Corsica).

Case No 4:
the Azores anticyclone

Centres of activity

- The Azores anticyclone is … over the Azores.
- The Icelandic depression is … over Iceland.

This is the situation most commonly encountered: the centres of activity are where they should be, with the air flow from the west affecting most of Western Europe.

The convergence of the tropical and polar flows leads to the formation of disturbances circulating rapidly from west to east. The tropical air then forms the 'warm sectors' and the polar air the 'trains' of these disturbances.

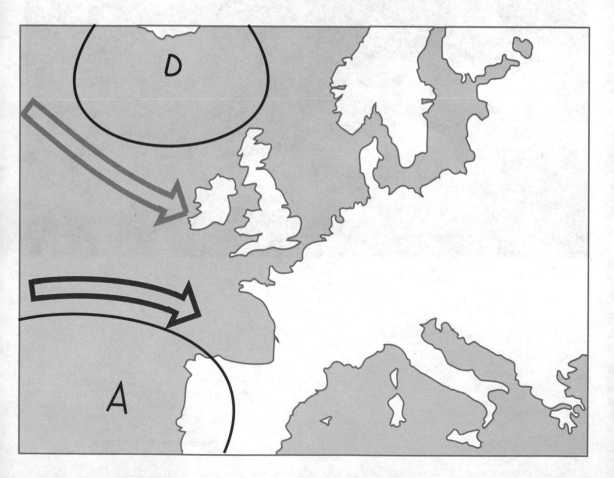

The clouds which develop in the warm air (stratus, altostratus, nimbostratus) are generally stable in winter, but often become unstable (altocumulus, cumulonimbus) in summer. In the cold air we see cloud types characteristic of the 'train': cumulus and cumulonimbus.

The wind varies as is usual in the regions of the disturbances. If the contrast in temperature between the two types of air masses is sufficiently large, then violent storms can result (so keep a weather eye on the barometer, which might well indicate the depression associated with the disturbance).

As the cold season approaches, because of the seasonal displacement of the centres of activity to the south, the Azores anticyclone can take up a more southerly position, and the depression around 60°N can spread towards the central Atlantic. The convergence of tropical and polar air then occurs in lower latitudes, and the disturbed air current from the west also affects Spain and the Mediterranean, giving rise to conditions rather like those we saw in case No 1.

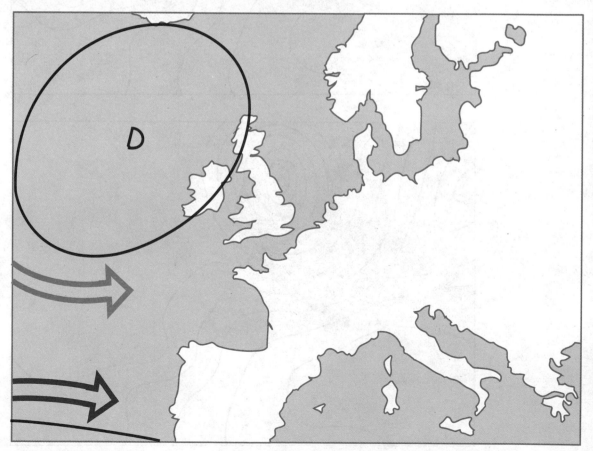

19 April 1986

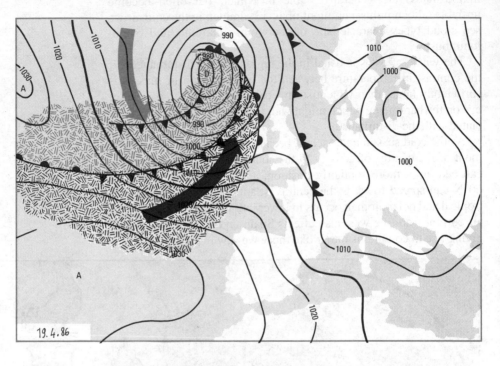

19.4.86

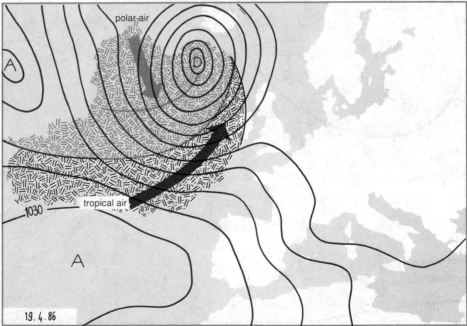

polar air

tropical air

19.4.86

• Depression immediately to the south of Iceland.
• Anticyclone over the Azores.

Between these two centres of activity, the WSW flow over the Atlantic veers to the NW over France (continental depression). There is a very active disturbance over the British Isles.

20 April 1986

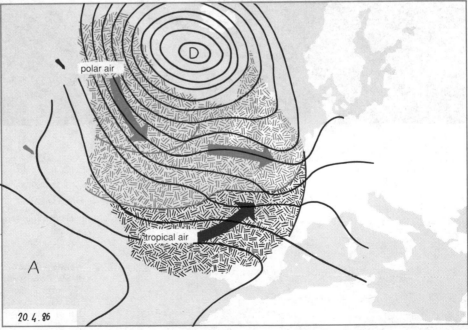

The next day, between the two centres of
activity, the disturbance circles from west
to east and moves across France. Polar air
moves rapidly in its wake.

Case No 5:
tropical air from the south

Two variants are characterised by slight differences in the position of the centres of activity.

Centres of activity

• Depression situated over the near Atlantic in the region of the Bay of Biscay.
• Anticyclone stretching towards Italy.

Tropical air originating in the arid regions of the Sahara (strongly warmed from below, and therefore hot and unstable) gradually becomes more humid in the course of crossing the Mediterranean (warm sea) and causes precipitation on arrival in Southern France. Conditions on land can be very stormy – a fact that is accentuated by the mountainous terrain in that area, which accelerates the rise of the incoming air. Cloud associated tends to be of the type cumulonimbus.

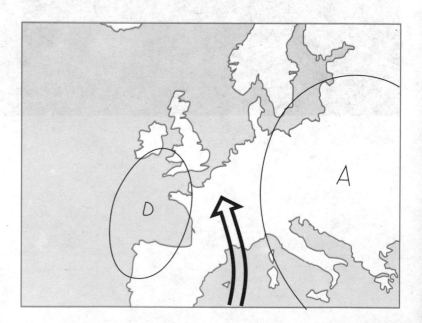

Strong sea winds blow from the SE. If the horizontal pressure gradient between the Atlantic depression and the continental anticyclone is significant, then violent storms can result.

Centres of activity: a variation on case No 5

In this variation on case No 5, the centres of activity are positioned as follows:
• Continental anticyclone stretching towards the British Isles and over half of France.
• Depression in the region of the Balearic Islands.

The tropical air from the Sahara circulates towards Italy, and then comes back towards the Gulf of Lyons and the Pyrenees (warm return). The heaviest unstable precipitation is to be found on mountain slopes facing into the wind, notably in the area of Roussillon and the Eastern Pyrenees. The strong wind (strength varying according to gradient) blows from the east to the NE in coastal regions. This is known locally as 'The Greek'.

In winter, these conditions give a situation rather like case No 2 discussed above.

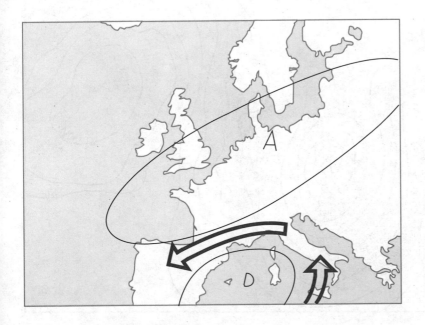

6 November 1982

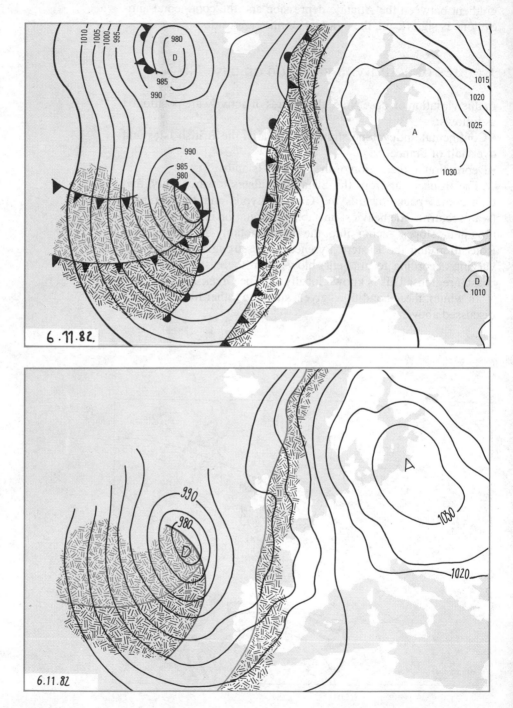

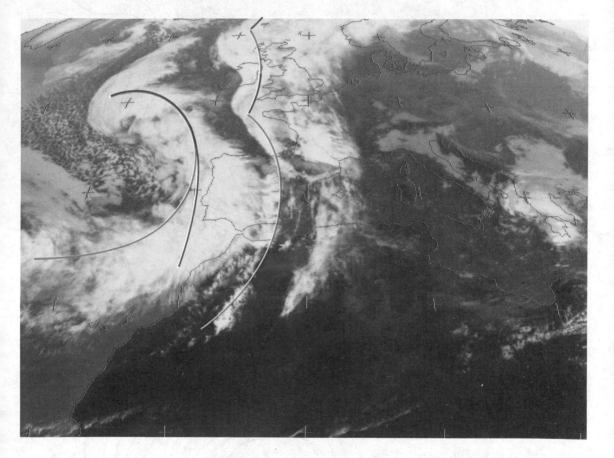

Note the positioning of the centres of activity:
• The continental anticyclone, static between the Balkans and Scandinavia, stretches out by means of a ridge towards the plain of the Po.
• The depression moves towards the Bay of Biscay, deepening.

The pressure gradient rises (between the anticyclone which is maintaining a steady high pressure and the depression that is deepening), particularly between Cape Finisterre and the plain of the Po. This gives rise to a violent wind from SE to east over the south of France and the Gulf of Lyons. The tropical air, which is warm, humid and unstable, pours into France.

7 November 1982

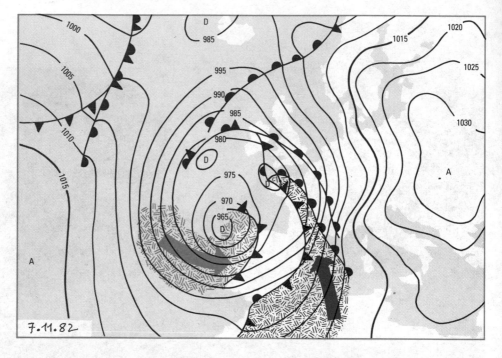

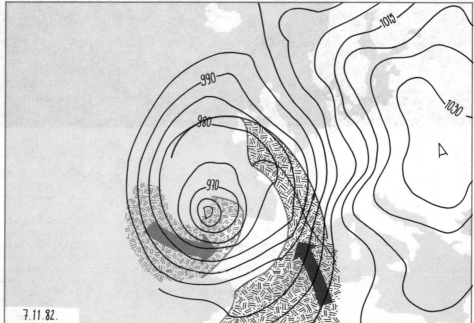

On 7 November 1982, a storm rages over the Gulf of Lyons (winds of 60kn observed by a ship). The pressure gradient reaches its maximum. There is considerable precipitation over the south-facing slopes of the mountain ranges.

8 November 1982

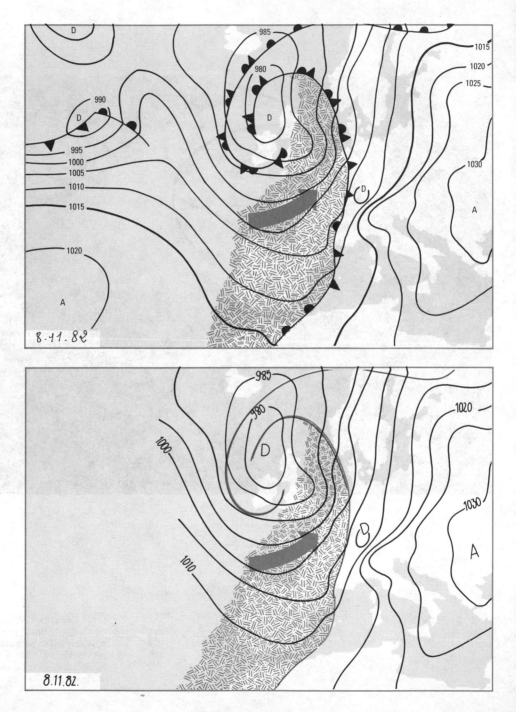

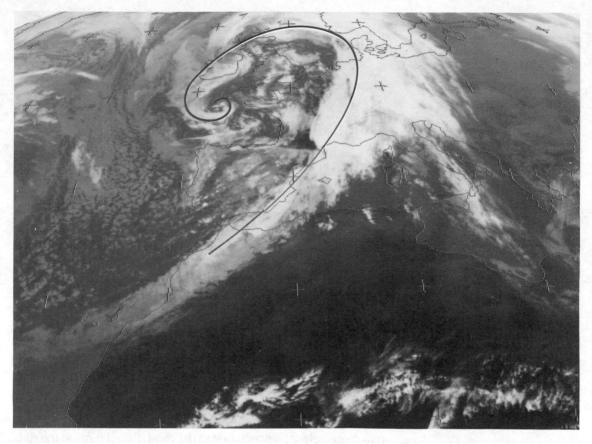

8 November 1982.

Over the day the depression moves to the NE, filling up as it goes; the pressure gradient decreases over France. Maritime polar air gradually replaces the tropical air over a large area of the country. The storm dies down.

Summary

With these five case-studies and their variations, we have covered the main scenarios to be found over Europe. However, in describing these phenomena, we have only spoken of the 'synoptic situation', ie what appears to be happening from an astronaut's point of view, and what determines the main movements in the atmosphere that are responsible for the wind that fills our sails in the here and now.

Yet this is precisely the point: the weather that we should have – if we follow the general synopsis – does not occur in the here and now. Local conditions can either cancel out or reinforce the general situation.

Local effects

There are two types of local effects: thermal and dynamic.

Thermal action: land and sea breezes

In good, calm summer weather, yachtsmen sailing in coastal areas will notice a light wind which varies in direction throughout the day: the sea breeze.

The breeze is thermal in origin and the mechanisms behind it are easy to explain.

Land and sea are warmed and cooled at different rates under the influence of solar radiation. During the day, the land becomes warmer than the sea, but it cools down faster at night. The lower layers of the atmosphere are subject to the same variations. As a consequence, at night, the cooler air over the land flows slowly towards the sea: this is the land breeze. During the day, the very warm air over land tends to rise by convection and is replaced by cooler air coming from the sea: this is the sea breeze.

If there is sufficient humidity, then the updraft, caused by convection over land, can be detected by the formation of cumulus clouds.

The sea breeze starts after sunrise in general (when the land has been warmed sufficiently). Initially, the breeze is quite weak and runs more or less perpendicular to the coast, then it turns to the right during the course of the day (if the observer is facing into the wind) and tends to run parallel to the coast. Its strength varies, generally between 1 and 4 Beaufort, although it can rise to 5 or 6 Beaufort.

Land breeze: during the night, the cool air from the lower layers over the land flows towards the sea.

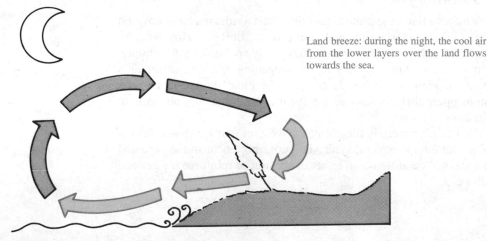

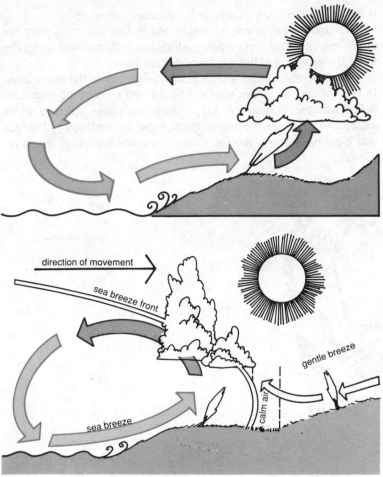

Sea breeze: during the day, the warm air over the land tends to rise and be replaced by cooler air coming in from the sea. Normally, the breeze begins to blow when the difference in temperature between the air over the land and the air over the sea reaches about 4–5°C.

The breeze front advances in an irregular manner over the land. It can become apparent by the formation of cumulus clouds. As the breeze front passes, there is a period of calm wind, which usually lasts for a short time.

The breeze appears as soon as conditions are favourable: different temperatures over land and sea, combined with a certain instability. The breeze can be obscured if there is a strong synoptic wind, linked to the wider pressure field. If the latter is moderate, then it influences the strength and direction of the breeze.

The arrival of the sea breeze is preceded by the passing of the sea-breeze front – a line of convergence which is created offshore and which moves inland in an irregular manner.

The shape of the coast, and its relief, play an important role in the evolution of the sea breeze in a given area.

Wind roses have been constructed statistically by means of wind measurements taken every three hours by the coastal weather stations over a number of years now. These can guide sailors on the probable evolution of the wind during the course of the day (if there is no other significant change in the weather situation).

The land breeze is much weaker and it does not carry very far out to sea, except in certain cases which can be accounted for by the lie of the coast (eg at the mouth of certain valleys).

These thermal effects are also experienced up in the mountains. In the valleys, on slopes exposed to the sun's rays (and therefore being warmed during the day), rising breezes – referred to as *anabatic winds* – are created; at night, these are replaced by breezes that blow back down into the valley (these are known as *katabatic winds*).

anabatic wind

katabatic wind

Dynamic action

Mountains, valleys and, in a general way, all natural obstacles cause local changes in the synoptic conditions.

Orographic lift

In general, mountains cause a rising movement of the air passing over the windward side and a falling movement over the lee side.

Cloud waves

At the summit of a mountain, or over the regions situated on the windward side of the mountain, and where there is stable, sufficiently humid, air, there occasionally form almond-shaped clouds, which are sometimes stacked, rather like plates. These are referred to as lenticular altocumulus clouds. They are virtually immobile, and indicate areas of rising air (therefore cooling), which lead to condensation in the air flow deformed by the mountain. Their presence gives a useful clue to the direction of the wind at medium altitudes.

Orographic lift
If the rising air is dry enough, then there is no condensation due to the fall in pressure, and, once over the mountain, it warms at the same rate that it cooled previously.

On the other hand, if the air is cool and humid initially, then there is condensation, causing cloud to appear which often gives precipitation.

In this case, in the lee of the mountain:
– the air is drier, because it has lost water with the rain, and the cloud disappears rapidly;
– the àdiabatic warming that the air undergoes through compression in the course of its descent does not evaporate the water droplets, but rather raises the temperature of the air instead. The air is therefore warmer and drier to lee than to windward.

This phenomenon, the foehn, occurs in the lee of mountains and mountain ranges.

Valleys

Valleys act rather like corridors channelling the wind. If the valley narrows, the wind speeds up.

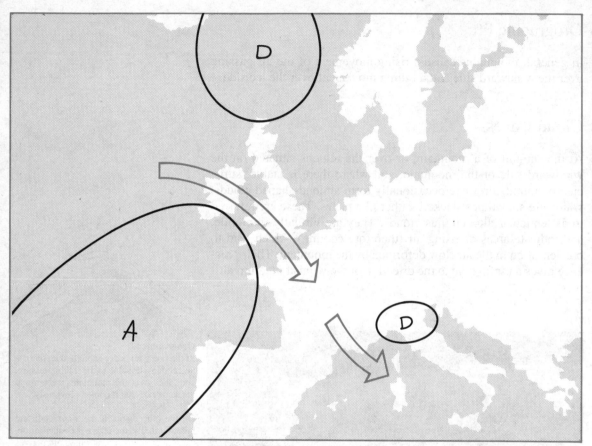

The mistral

This wind is linked to a depression over Northern Italy and the Gulf of Genoa, blocked by the curve of the Alps. Its northerly direction, its turbulent and often violent character that it takes on over land and maintains until far out over the Mediterranean, are all due to the unusual contours of the valley of the Rhône, a narrow corridor running along a north-south axis. It is thus a wind very much dependent on local conditions. Cold and dry, blowing from somewhere between north to NNW at the mouth of the Rhône, the wind stretches out into the Mediterranean, where it becomes more humid and more gentle, turning west as it gets down towards Corsica.

While it is a local phenomenon, the mistral is also a synoptic one, since it is created by a particular position of the centres of activity (notably the depression in the region of the Gulf of Genoa).

There are three typical isobaric situations connected with this, although many variations can and do exist:

1. The Azores anticyclone stretches towards the Bay of Biscay:

The general air flow moves along an axis running NW–SE from Iceland to Italy. Since this sort of situation can persist, the mistral can last for several days, rising and falling over the period. Statistics show that it is in April that the mistral usually lasts longest.

2. The anticyclone lies along a north-south axis over the Eastern Atlantic (case No 1):

There is a flow of air over the north of France, which suffers an invasion by arctic air. This generally lasts for a shorter time than the preceding one, but is accompanied by a very cold mistral.

3. The continental anticyclone stretches towards the British Isles (case No 2.1):

This situation, which generally only occurs in the winter (advection of very cold continental polar air), can sometimes last for several days. Warm returns at altitude around the depression over the Gulf of Genoa can cause snowfalls right up to the coast.

The strength of the wind can be estimated by means of the pressure gradient (between Perpignan and Nice, for example):

– 9hPa of difference in pressure between these two stations would correspond to a mistral of force 8 Beaufort in general;

– a 12hPa difference normally indicates a mistral of about force 10 Beaufort.

The tramontana

Of course, we cannot devote so much space to the mistral without mentioning the tramontana.

The tramontana is a wind from the NW, blowing into the southern areas of the Languedoc, as well as across Roussillon. Like the mistral, it is also generally associated with a depression over the Gulf of Genoa; in fact, it is often associated with the mistral.

The acceleration of the air flow is due to narrowing of the valleys between les Corbières and the Montagne Noire (of the Massif Centrale), or in the valleys of les Corbières.

In order to get some idea of the wind speed of the tramontana, use the difference in pressure between Toulouse and Perpignan as a guide, or that between Perpignan and Montpellier (a difference of 5hPa between Perpignan and Montpellier corresponds generally to a tramontana of force 10 Beaufort).

CHAPTER 3

Tomorrow's weather

So, now we know what the weather is like today, still, there is one tiny problem: now that we know what today's weather is, it isn't today's weather any more and you can't sail in it. While reminiscing nostalgically about the weather in days gone by is all very well, it is much more useful to know what the weather is going to be like tomorrow. This has a variety of uses, allowing the sailor to choose the best route, to be aware of the approach of bad weather, and to work out what tactics to use in a race.

Knowing about weather conditions in the past is obviously a great help when it comes to forecasting weather conditions in the future, since it allows us to make use of certain constant features, characteristic evolutions and the signs that tell us that these are going to occur. However, when it comes to finding out what the weather is going to be like for the next few days to come, it is certain that we cannot merely rely on our own observations, however good at gathering such information we may be. The analyses that we have discussed so far have shown that the weather conditions in any particular area are only one aspect of a situation that goes way beyond the horizons of the individual observer. Local conditions are often the product of what was happening yesterday, hundreds, or even thousands, of miles from where we are now; their evolution in the longer term depends above all on changes and tendencies in the general situation. These changes can only be mapped out by referring to information supplied by the meteorological services, whose stations cover the entire world.

Our own observations are a supplement to the information we gather from these other sources. We must compare the local weather conditions with the other facts at our disposal, in order to see from the barometer, from the appearance of the sea and the sky, whether the information we receive from the weather services corresponds with what we can observe, whether the local situation is evolving more quickly or more slowly than the synoptic situation, as well as what the changes will be along the route that we wish to take – will the weather be better or worse in the place to which we are going?

Defined thus, the role of observation seems rather limited. In reality, it takes years of practice to obtain such results. This is why

The National Meteorological Service of France publishes a leaflet in March every year, giving all the necessary information (frequencies, times, telephone numbers) pertaining to the PTT and France Inter transmitters, or to the answering services. This leaflet is available (or ought to be) from the various offices of the Affaires maritimes, as well as from harbour master's offices. It can also be ordered direct from the Météorologie nationale (National Weather Bureau), Service des relations extérièurs, 73, rue de Sèvres, 92100 Boulogne. Also consult the SHOM (vol 196) and *Reed's*.

there is so little advice to give when it comes to weather forecasting; as we said at the outset, the most important thing is to have a clear understanding of the weather bulletins, and to have devoted a considerable time to understanding the forces behind the prevailing weather conditions, both on the synoptic and the local levels. No amount of advice can replace the time and effort involved.

The best way to progress in meteorology is to study the forecasts systematically every day and to watch the sky and the barometer carefully.

The weather report

The BBC shipping forecast

The BBC shipping forecast can be heard on BBC Radio 4 on 198kHz (1515m) and local MW frequencies daily at 0033–0038 (including area Trafalgar), 0555–0600, 1355–1400 and 1750–1755. The bulletins include a summary of gale warnings, a general synopsis for the next 24 hours giving wind direction and speed, weather and visibility.

The 0033–0038 and 1355–1400 broadcasts for Monday to Friday include 24 hour forecast for the Minches (between Butt of Lewis and Cape Wrath in the north and between Banna Head and Ardnamurchan Point in the south), after area Hebrides. The 0033–0038 is further followed by a forecast for up to 1800, covering coastal waters to a distance of 12 miles offshore.

A detailed guide to the shipping forecast is given on pages 767–770.

Automatic telephone weather service – Marinecall

Meteorological Office weather forecasts covering an area up to 12 miles offshore are available by telephone, and are updated twice daily (three times daily in summer). The forecasts also give details for the Channel and Irish Sea crossings, Isles of Scilly, Channel Islands, Orkney and the Isle of Man. The area around Britain is divided into 15 sections, and the numbers are given below. The number in all cases consists of the 0898 code, followed by 500 and then the three figures for the area required. Calls are charged at 38p per minute for peak and standard rates, and 25p per minute for evenings and weekends (VAT included). Calls can also be made via British Telecom coastal stations when the VHF tariff is 95p per minute.

458   South West (Hartland Point to Lyme Regis)
457   Mid-Channel (Lyme Regis to Selsey Bill)
456   Channel East (Selsey Bill to North Foreland)
455   Anglia (North Foreland to the Wash)
454   East (The Wash to Whitby)
453   North East (Whitby to Berwick)
452   Scotland East (Berwick to Rattray Head)
451   Scotland North (Rattray Head to Cape Wrath)
464   Minch (Cape Wrath to Ardnamurchan Point)
463   Caledonia (Ardnamurchan Point to Mull of Kintyre)
462   Clyde (Mull of Kintyre to Mull of Galloway)
461   North West (Mull of Galloway to Colwyn Bay)
460   Wales (Colwyn Bay to St David's Head)
459   Bristol Channel (St David's Head to Hartland Point)
465   Ulster (Carlingford Lough to Lough Foyle)
992   English Channel
991   Southern North Sea

Facsimile broadcasts

Fax machines can be used to receive a variety of meteorological information, such as isobaric charts, sea and swell charts, cloud satellite images, sea temperature and wind field charts.

Radio telephone broadcasts

Meteorological Office forecasts are transmitted by the British Telecom coastal radio stations on both Medium frequency and VHF (where available) twice a day at either 0703 and 1903 GMT or 0733 and 1933 GMT according to area. For VHF broadcasts, an initial announcement is made on channel 16, and the broadcast proper on another channel. Details of channels and times can be found in the *Macmillan and Silk Cut Nautical Almanac*. The coastguard also broadcasts strong wind warnings for the local area on VHF channel 67 after an initial announcement on channel 16.

Gale warnings

British Telecom coastal radio stations transmit gale warnings on receipt. The radio-transmitter Medium frequency silences are from 00 to 03 and from 30 to 33 each hour. Gale warnings are repeated at the next of the following times: 0303, 0903, 1503, and 2103 GMT. The warnings are preceded by the radio-transmitter signal SÉCURITÉ (pronounced say-cur-e-tay).

Other sources

Scheduled broadcasts are available on NAVTEX. This is part of the IMO's (International Maritime Organisation) Global Maritime Distress and Safety System (GMDSS), operational as of August 1991. At present, broadcasts are made on 518kHz, information generally being provided through a dedicated receiver. In Britain, the warnings are broadcast from Portpatrick (for the west coast of Scotland and England), Cullercoats (east) and Niton (Channel and south coast). Further details can be found in the *Macmillan and Silk Cut Nautical Almanac*.

Reports in French

Telephone recorded message services

There are telephone recorded message services all along the French coast, on telephone number 36 65 08 08; if you know the number of the département, a more local forecast may be obtained on 36 65 08 + number of the département. They provide a brief summary of the broadcast given by the nearest PTT transmitter, edited for the coastal area in the immediate vicinity of the particular station. They are very useful on short outings.

PTT transmitters

These transmitters, situated at Boulogne, Le Conquet, Saint-Nazaire, Bordeaux, Marseilles and Grasse, broadcast a report twice a day for the sea and coastal areas in their region. In order to receive this, you will need a radio that can receive the shipping waveband (SSB). The report is dictated at a reasonable speed, and then re-read: it can be taken down virtually word for word. Its content is simple to understand, perhaps a little too simple though, since there is only really a cursory description of the general situation, which does not really allow one to understand what is actually happening.

Fax receivers

These machines allow weather maps to be received directly on board ship. Forecasts for 3, 6, 12, 24, 48 and 72 hours later are available, as well as maps of conditions at altitude, of temperature, and even satellite photographs. Although these are useful for ocean-crossings, they are rather expensive and bulky for coastal navigation.

VHF transmitters

In certain areas, the CROSS broadcast one or two bulletins a day on channels 9, 11 or 13, following a signal given on channel 16.

France Inter

France Inter generally broadcasts two bulletins a day, morning and evening. These are prepared by the Météorologie nationale (National Weather Bureau) and cover the Atlantic and Mediterranean. They give gale and storm warnings, and present a detailed and informative account of the general situation. The position of the centres of activity and the fronts with their direction and their speed of movement are clearly defined; the forecast by area is then given, but the summary of information from coastal stations is omitted.

Special weather reports and gale warnings

These bulletins are broadcast as soon as the information is collated, and are repeated regularly by the various transmitters for as long as the warning remains relevant:
– they are repeated on the hour and on the half hour by the PTT transmitters and the BBC;
– they are repeated continuously by the answering services;
– they are repeated every two hours on the VHF transmissions.

Bulletins in English

It is often said that the English are the worst nation in Europe when it comes to learning foreign languages. Fortunately for us, most European countries (and those in other regions, too) give their main weather reports in English.

However, even English listeners will find that the weather report has a language all of its own. Listening regularly to the BBC broadcasts is the best way to become familiar with the terminology that is used. These are, after all, probably some of the best weather forecasts available – the French version of this book recommending them unreservedly.

The reports are broadcast regularly at useful times. The report given at 0555 is especially useful: you can listen to it in bed. If the forecast is good, then it is the ideal time to make ready to get under way, and if it's bad, then you can treat yourself to a lie-in.

The forecasts are always given in the same order, one area after another, the forecast being for the centre of the area; they are given in a calm, confident voice, in the most impeccable BBC English, and the expressions used will rapidly become familiar. This is the order in which the different items usually appear.

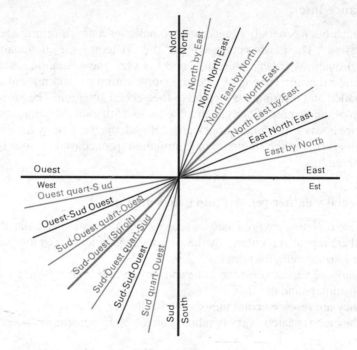

The BBC: a user-friendly guide

1. *Gale warnings are in operation for all sea areas* … This is the usual opening for a weather report when conditions are poor.
2. There then follows the *general synopsis*, with information on the distribution of depressions and anticyclones, along with their movements and the pressure reading for that particular area. For example: *High 1013 moving slowly east and weakening*, or *Low 985 centred over sea area Rockall, moving eastwards at 25 knots and deepening, is expected 956 in sea area Forties at 0700 tomorrow.*

   Remember: depressions can be *filling* or *deepening*; an anticyclone where the air pressure is falling is said to be *collapsing* .
3. *Area forecast*. The areas always occur in the same order as found on the preprinted weather charts on which you note down details of the weather conditions. They run clockwise from Viking to South-east Iceland.

Wind direction

Wind direction is given by means of the points of the compass. The divisions are quite fine, and so it is worth taking a little time to memorise them. A small chart with the directions marked might well come in handy if you're not sure about the finer gradations.

Winds from the south or north are *southerly* or *northerly*. When the wind is turning left, it is said to be *backing*; when it is turning right, then it is said to be *veering*. If it is tending to become a northerly wind, then it is *becoming northerly*. If it seems to have no definite direction, then the wind is said to be *variable*. In a depression, the wind is *cyclonic*.

Wind force

The force of the wind is given according to the Beaufort scale (see above). If there is no wind, then it is *calm*. If there is a strong wind, then the forecast is more specific, eg gale 8, severe gale 9, storm 10, severe storm 11, hurricane 12. The wind is either *increasing* or *decreasing*.

The sky

The sky is rarely described, but the various types of precipitation are: *rain*, *continuous heavy rain*, *drizzle*, *intermittent slight drizzle*. All these are pretty much self-explanatory.

Showers can be either *scattered* or *isolated*. There are also *squally showers* with sudden, unpredictable gusts of wind. For the area South-east Iceland, precipitation can show either *icing* or *no icing* (frost or no frost).

Rain can either be *spreading* or *clearing* , depending on whether it is, obviously, spreading or dying off. The direction of this movement is also given: *rain spreading from the west*, *rain clearing from the north-west*.

Of course, sometimes it isn't raining, and the weather is said to be *fair*. Not that you'll have to worry about that too much.

Visibility

Visibility can be either *good*, *moderate* or *poor*. In addition, there are some nuances: *mainly good*, *moderate to good*, *moderate or poor*. It can get worse (*good becoming poor*) or improve (*moderate improving good*).

If the visibility is poor, then the reason is usually given: *locally poor with fog patches*, or *with coastal fog*. Fog can vary in density from *thick fog* to *haze*.

Both wind direction and visibility can change over time. This change can take place more than 12 hours from now (*later*), between 6 and 12 hours from now (*soon*), or within the next 6 hours (*imminent*).

4. *Weather reports from coastal stations.* The coastal reports go in a fixed order clockwise from *Tiree* to *Malin Head*. They use many of the terms already encountered. They will say what the weather conditions have been like recently (eg *rain in past hour*), whether the barometer is *rising*, *falling* or *steady*, and how rapidly these changes are taking place (*slowly*, *quickly* or *very rapidly*).

How to take down a weather report

The BBC weather reports are read at a normal speed. However, since the items always occur in the same order, it is possible to be prepared in advance. There are a variety of ways to make the task more simple:

1. Use a pre-prepared map, marking the conditions (in abbreviated form) on the different areas. Wind directions are marked by arrows with force in degrees Beaufort given above. Precipitation can be marked in lower case characters (*r* = rain, *s* = showers, *ss* = squally showers). Visibility can be marked in capitals (*MG* = moderate to good, *MoP CF* = moderate or poor with coastal fog.

2. A grid could also be used, with conditions marked according to your own abbreviations.

3. Alternatively, you could take the entire broadcast down in shorthand or record it onto a cassette.

Once you have taken down the report, it is quite possible to build up a simple weather map. Once the isobars and fronts have been marked, there should be no more surprises.

Sample weather reports

Bulletins in English

Most European countries also broadcast a weather report in English. The Italian report for 7 February 1987 is given on page 778.

The BBC's own report is given in a highly structured predictable format, which makes life particularly easy!

And now the shipping forecast issued by the meteorological office at 0505 on Saturday 07 February 1987

There are warnings of gales in Viking, North Utsire, South Utsire, Forties, Fisher, German Bight, Sole, Shannon, Rockall,

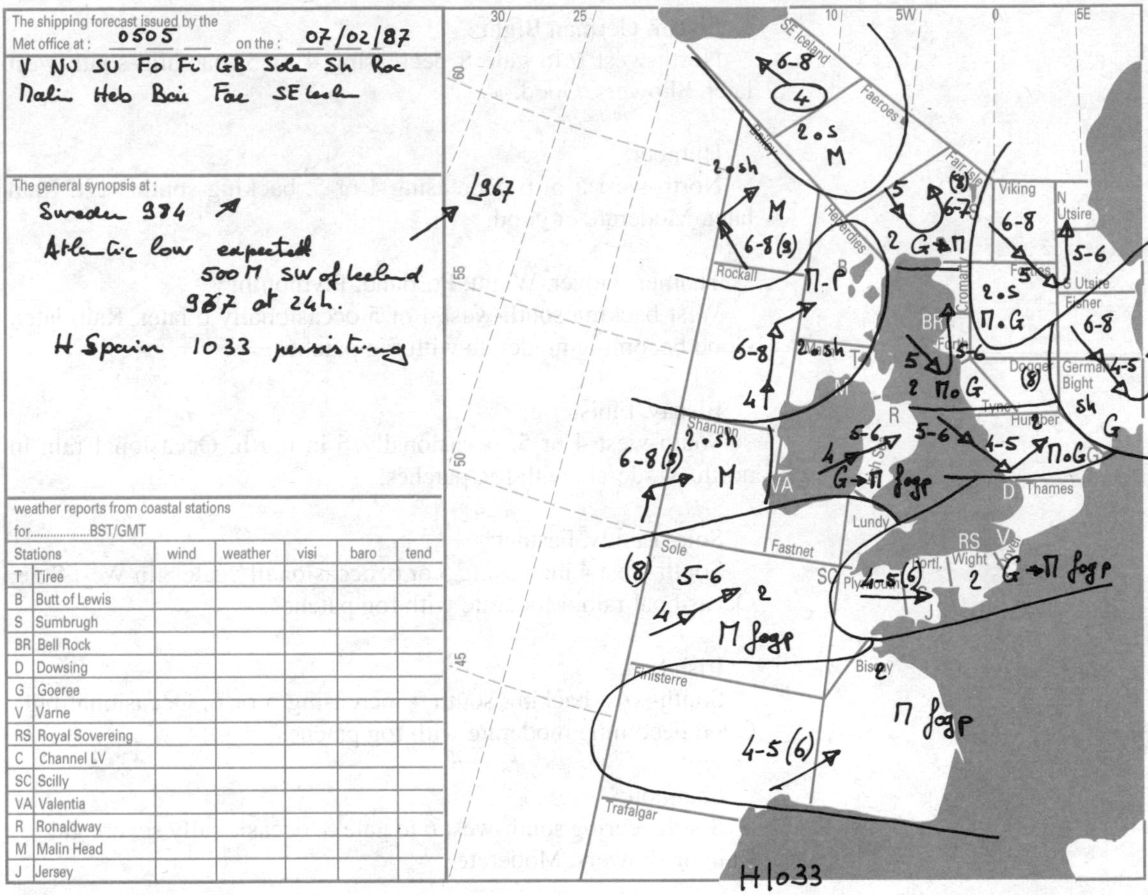
The shipping forecast issued by the Met office at : 0505 on the : 07/02/87
V NU SU Fo Fi GB Sole Sh Roc
Mali Heb Bai Fae SE Iceland
The general synopsis at :
Sweden 984
Atlantic low expected 500 M SW of Iceland 967 at 24h.
H Spain 1033 persisting
L967
weather reports from coastal stations
for................BST/GMT
Stations
wind
weather
visi
baro
tend
T Tiree
B Butt of Lewis
S Sumbrugh
BR Bell Rock
D Dowsing
G Goeree
V Varne
RS Royal Sovereing
C Channel LV
SC Scilly
VA Valentia
R Ronaldway
M Malin Head
J Jersey
SE Iceland
Faeroes
Bailey
Fair Isle
Viking
N Utsire
S Utsire
Forties
Fisher
Hebrides
Rockall
Cromarty
Forth
Dogger
German Bight
Tyne
Humber
Shannon
Thames
Lundy
Fastnet
Sole
Wight
Portl.
Plymouth
Dover
Biscay
Finisterre
Trafalgar
H1033

Sea areas and coastal stations for English reports as marked when carefully listening to a weather bulletin.

Malin, Hebrides, Bailey, Faeroes, South-east Iceland.

The general synopsis at midnight:

Low Sweden 984 moving steadily north-east. Atlantic low moving slowly north-east expected 500 miles south-west of Iceland 967 by midnight tonight. High Spain 1,033 persisting.

The area forecasts for the next 24 hours:

Viking, North Utsire, South Utsire, Forties:
North-west 6 to gale 8 decreasing 5, backing southerly 5 or 6 later. Rain or snow later. Good.

Cromarty, Forth, Tyne, Dogger:
North-west 5, occasionally 6 in Dogger, backing southerly 5 or 6 later. Rain later. Moderate or good.

Fisher, German Bight:
North-west 6 to gale 8 decreasing 4 or 5, backing south-west later. Showers. Good.

Humber:
North-west 5 or 6 decreasing 4 or 5, backing south-west. Rain later. Moderate or good.

Thames, Dover, Wight, Portland, Plymouth:
West backing south-west 4 or 5 occasionally 6 later. Rain later. Good becoming moderate with fog patches.

Biscay, Finisterre:
South-west 4 or 5, occasionally 6 in north. Occasional rain in north. Moderate with fog patches.

Sole, Lundy, Fastnet:
South-west 4 increasing 5 or 6, occasionally gale 8 in West Sole. Occasional rain. Moderate with fog patches.

Irish Sea:
South-west backing south 4 increasing 5 or 6. Occasional rain. Good becoming moderate with fog patches.

Shannon:
South veering south-west 6 to gale 8, occasionally severe gale 9. Rain or showers. Moderate.

Malin, Hebrides:
Southerly 4 increasing 6 to gale 8, veering south-west later. Rain or showers. Moderate occasionally poor.

Bailey:
South-east 6 to gale 8, occasionally severe gale 9, veering south-west later. Rain or showers. Moderate.

Fair Isle:
North-west 5 backing south-east 5 to 7, perhaps gale 8 later. Rain later. Good becoming moderate.

Faeroes, South-east Iceland:
Variable 4 becoming south-east and increasing 6 to gale 8. Rain or snow. Moderate.

The navigator's thoughts on Saturday evening 7 February 1987.

We have rented a boat for a week at Brest and we're toying with the idea of going up to the Scilly Isles if only for a day, where the daffodils are already in flower.

The navigator is at the chart table, the crew are preparing the dinner.

The boat is in good condition, and we have spent the day going through the inventory, and checking that we have all the necessary provisions for winter sailing. If you want to sail at this time of year, you have to be sure that you've not left anything vital out.

We've just spent a good hour or so circling around. All we have to do is to decide on a possible course, and it's the weather forecast that will tip the balance one way or the other.

For about the umpteenth time, the navigator looks at the depression that is on its way. He has no idea what to make of it, since the ridge of the anticyclone is protecting the area. However, the weather report says that this ridge is collapsing. Moreover, although the depression which has opened up is staying where it is for the time being, it is bound to start moving again and will complete its crossing of the Atlantic. According to the forecast, the disturbance associated with it will pass across Britain tonight.

So, the centre of the depression isn't moving that much, but, as is so common in this sort of situation, the isobars are bending with the movement of the front, and the ridge is not putting up much resistance. It's often like this in winter. The vast area of low pressure off the coast of Iceland is continually fed by the other Atlantic depressions; the situation is relatively stable, the isobars are bending a little as the disturbances pass, and the winds remain westerly.

In these conditions, we'll spend the night in port. Tomorrow, the weather report will tell us what has become of that depression and if there is another one on the way. If, as one might think, these are classic winter weather conditions, then the wind will not move up into the NW, and we'll continue to get a moderate west wind. In that case, we'll start as early as possible so as to get past the channel of the Four with the current, calculating our speed to the inch in order to arrive at the Scillies in daylight, because the area isn't very well lit and the nights are long at this time of year.

If, on the other hand, the ridge takes up its place behind the disturbance again, there will be very little wind tomorrow. In that case we'll have a look around the harbour …

Inter-Service mer du samedi 7 février 1987 au matin

1. Avis de vents forts:

Pour Ouest-Irlande: avis de grand frais force 7 de Sud à Sud-Ouest pour cet après-midi.

Pour Ouest-Écosse, Nord-Irlande: avis de grand frais force 7 de Sud à Sud-Ouest pour ce soir.

Pour Cromarty: avis de grand frais force 7 de Sud à Sud-Est prévu la nuit prochaine.

Pour les zones Lion et Ouest de Provence: avis de grand frais force 7 à coup de vent force 8 de secteur Nord prévu en fin de matinée.

2. Situation générale et évolution:

– Dépression 985hPa sur la Baltique se décale vers l'Est.

– Anticyclone 1, 030hPa des Açores au Nord-Ouest de l'Espagne se prolonge vers le Nord par une dorsale au niveau du 10e Ouest.

– Dépression 975hPa à 450 milles au Sud du Groenland se décale vers le Nord-Est. La perturbation associée abordera l'Irlande ce matin.

– En Méditerranée: flux de Nord-Ouest à Nord-Est modéré se renforçant ce matin.

3. Prévisions par zones:
Mer du Nord:
– Cromarty, Forth, Viking, Forties:
Pluie la nuit prochaine. Vent de Nord-Ouest force 3 à 5 virant Sud-Est à Sud cet après-midi et fraîchissant force 5 à 7 la nuit prochaine d'Est en Ouest. Mer peu agitée devenant agitée.
– Utsire, Fisher, German:
Vent de Nord-Ouest force 4 à 6 avec rafales à force 8 ce matin près de la côte norvégienne et virant Ouest force 3 à 4 puis Sud-Ouest force 4 à 6 demain. Mer peu agitée devenant agitée demain.
– Tyne, Dogger, Humber, Tamise:
Vent de Nord-Ouest force 3 à 5 virant Sud-Ouest cet après-midi et fraîchissant force 3 à 5 cette nuit du Sud au Nord. Mer peu agitée.

Chart of areas and coastal stations for weather bulletins (North Sea, the Channel, the Atlantic).

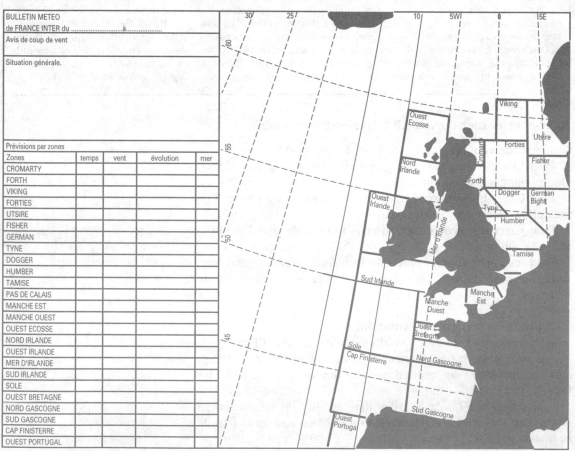

Manche:

– Pas de Calais, Manche-Est:

Vent de Nord-Ouest force 2 à 4 virant Sud-Ouest en soirée. Mer devenant peu agitée.

– Manche-Ouest:

Vent de Sud-Ouest force 2 à 4. Mer peu agitée et petite houle d'Ouest.

Atlantique:

– Ouest-Ecosse et Nord-Irlande:

Pluie ce soir. Vent virant Sud à Sud-Ouest force 4 à 5 puis fraîchissant la nuit prochaine force 6 à 7. Mer devenant agitée, voire temporairement forte la nuit prochaine. Houle modérée de Sud-Ouest.

– Ouest-Irlande:

Pluie. Vent de Sud force 4 à 5 fraîchissant force 5 à 7 cet après-midi puis mollissant à Sud-Ouest force 4 à 6 la nuit prochaine. Mer agitée à forte s'atténuant la nuit prochaine. Houle modérée de Sud-Ouest.

– Mer d'Irlande:

Quelques pluies. Vent de Sud-Ouest force 2 à 3 fraîchissant force 4 à 5 en soirée. Mer peu agitée.

– Sud-Irlande et Sole:

Pluies ou bruines. Vent de Sud-Ouest force 3 à 4 fraîchissant force 4 à 6 du Sud au Nord cette nuit. Mer peu agitée à agitée et houle modérée d'Ouest.

– Ouest-Bretagne et Nord-Gascogne:

Vent d'Ouest force 2 à 3 fraîchissant force 3 à 4. Mer belle à peu agitée et houle modérée d'Ouest.

– Sud Gascogne et cap Finisterre:

Vent d'Ouest force 3 à 4. Mer peu agitée et houle petite à modérée d'Ouest.

– Ouest-Portugal:

Vent variable faible sur le Nord et d'Est force 2 à 3 sur le Sud. Mer belle.

Méditerranée:

– Lion et Provence:

Vent de Nord-Ouest à Nord force 4 à 5 fraîchissant force 6 à 7 puis 7 à 8 en soirée. Mer devenant agitée à forte.

– Nord-Baléares:

Vent d'Ouest force 3 à 4. Mer belle.

– Ouest-Sardaigne:

Vent de Nord-Ouest à Ouest force 4 à 6 d'Est en Ouest. Mer

devenant peu agitée à agitée.
– Gênes, Ouest et Est-Corse:
Vent de Sud-Ouest à Ouest force 3 à 5. Mer agitée.

Terminé.

Since we are in the Mediterranean we should also listen to the Italian broadcast.

Bollettino del mare
dal Servizio Meteorologico dell'Aeronautica
alle ore 12 del 7.2.1987.

Nessun avviso da segnalare.

Sea areas and coastal stations for weather bulletins (Mediterranean).

Situazione: alta pressione su Mediterraneo Occidentale; moderato

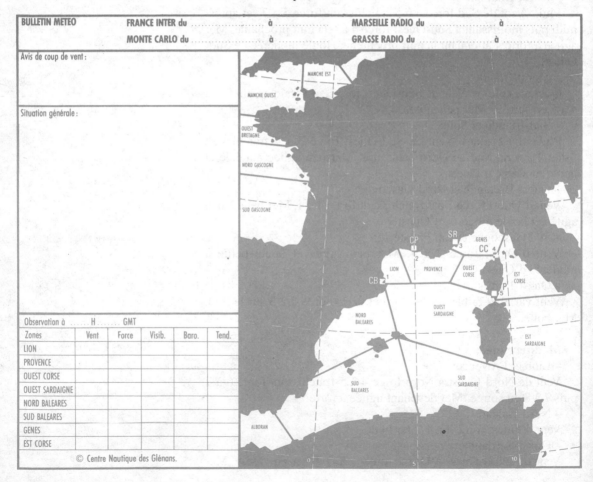

BULLETIN METEO	FRANCE INTER du .... à	MARSEILLE RADIO du .... à ....
	MONTE CARLO du .... à	GRASSE RADIO du .... à ....

Avis de coup de vent :

Situation générale :

Observation à ...... H ...... GMT

Zones	Vent	Force	Visib.	Baro.	Tend.
LION					
PROVENCE					
OUEST CORSE					
OUEST SARDAIGNE					
NORD BALEARES					
SUD BALEARES					
GENES					
EST CORSE					

© Centre Nautique des Glénans.

fronte freddo su Adriatico Settentrionale si muove velocemente verso Sud-Est; flusso di aria instabile su Mediterraneo Orientale è in attenuazione e si muove verso Est.

Tempo previsto fino alle 6 di domani e tendenza per le 12 ore successive:

Mare di Corsica, Mare di Sardegna: venti da Ovest forza 3 in intensificazione e rotazione a Nord, parzialmente nuvoloso, visibilità buona, mare mosso. Tendenza: attenuazione dei venti.

Canale di Sardegna: venti da Nord-Ovest forza 4 in intensificazione e rotazione a Ovest, parzialmente nuvoloso, visibilità discreta, mare mosso. Tendenza: attenuazione dei venti.

Mar Ligure, Tirreno Settentrionale: venti da Sud-Ovest forza 3 in intensificazione e rotazione a Nord-Est, parzialmente nuvoloso, visibilità discreta, mare mosso. Tendenza: Nord-Est 4.

Tirreno Centrale: venti da Ovest forza 3 in rotazione a Nord-Ovest, parzialmente nuvoloso, visibilità discreta, mare poco mosso. Tendenza: Nord 3.

Tirreno Meridionale: venti da Nord-Ovest forza 3, parzialmente nuvoloso, visibilità discreta, mare poco mosso. Tendenza: Nord 4.

Canale di Sicilia: venti da Nord-Ovest forza 4 in intensificazione, parzialmente nuvoloso, visibilità discreta, mare mosso. Tendenza: Nord 5.

Jonio Meridionale: venti da Nord-Est forza 4 in rotazione a Ovest, sereno o poco nuvoloso, visibilità discreta, mare mosso. Tendenza: possibilità di temporali.

Jonio Settentrionale, Adriatico Meridionale: venti da Nord forza 3 in intensificazione e rotazione a Nord-Ovest, locali pioggie, visibilità discreta, mare mosso. Tendenza: possibilità di temporali.

Adriatico Centrale: venti da Ovest deboli in intensificazione e rotazione a Nord, rovesci isolati, visibilità discreta, mare poco mosso. Tendenza: Nord-Est 5.

Adriatico Settentrionale: venti da Ovest deboli in intensificazione e rotazione a Nord-Est, rovesci isolati, visibilità discreta, mare poco mosso. Tendenza: Nord-Est 4.

Mediterraneo Occidentale: venti da Nord forza 3 in intensificazione, sereno o poco nuvoloso, visibilità buona, mare mosso. Tendenza: attenuazione dei venti.

Mar Libico: venti da Nord forza 3 in rotazione a Nord-Ovest, locali pioggie, visibilità buona, mare poco mosso. Tendenza: Nord-Ovest 4.

Mediterraneo Orientale: venti da Nord-Ovest forza 4 in attenuazione, rovesci isolati, visibilità buona, mare mosso. Tendenza: miglioramento.

Italian bulletin broadcast in English

FXIY71 — LIIP 070640
METEOMAR 07 FEB 87 06.00 GMT
METEOMAR — WEATHER FORECAST OVER MEDITERRANEAN OF 06 07 02 87
WINDS BEAUFORT FORCE

1/WARNINGS
GALES UNDER COURSE: NIL
THUNDERSTORM UNDER COURSE: NIL
GALE FORECAST: NIL
THUNDERSTORMS FORECAST: CHANNEL OF SICILY SOUTHERN IONIAN SEA NORTHERN IONIAN SEA

2/WEATHER SITUATION
HIGH OVER WESTERN AND CENTRAL MEDITERRANEAN
LOW OVER SOUTHERN ITALIAN SEAS MOVES TOWARD SOUTH-EAST
UNSTABLE AIR FLOW OVER EASTERN MEDITERRANEAN

3/FORECAST TO 18 GMT OF TODAY AND FURTHER 12 HOURS OUTLOOKS FOLLOW

SEA OF CORSICA SEA OF SARDINIA CHANNEL OF SARDINIA NORTH-WEST THREE — PARTLY CLOUDY — VISIBILITY GOOD — STATE OF SEA SMOOTH — OUTLOOK SIMILAR

LIGURIAN SEA NORTHERN TYRRHENIAN SEA CENTRAL TYRRHENIAN SEA NORTH-EAST THREE — CLEAR — VISIBILITY GOOD — STATE OF SEA SMOOTH — OUTLOOK SIMILAR

SOUTHERN TYRRHENIAN SEA NORTH-EAST FOUR — LOCAL RAINS — VISIBILITY MODERATE — STATE OF SEA SLIGHT — OUTLOOK IMPROVEMENT

CHANNEL OF SICILY EAST FIVE WEAKENING — OCCASIONAL THUNDERSTORMS — VISIBILITY MODERATE — STATE OF SEA SLIGHT — OUTLOOK IMPROVEMENT

SOUTHERN IONIAN SEA NORTHERN IONIAN SEA NORTH-EAST FIVE WEAKENING — OCCASIONAL THUNDERSTORMS — VISIBILITY MODERATE — STATE OF SEA MODERATE — OUTLOOK IMPROVEMENT

SOUTHERN ADRIATIC SEA CENTRAL ADRIATIC SEA VARIABLE CALM INCREASING AND BECOMING NORTH-WEST — PARTLY CLOUDY — VISIBILITY POOR — STATE OF SEA SMOOTH — OUTLOOK PHENOMENA ARE INTENSIFYING

NORTHERN ADRIATIC SEA NORTH-EAST THREE INCREASING — LOCAL RAINS — VISIBILITY POOR — STATE OF SEA SMOOTH — OUTLOOK PHENOMENA ARE INTENSIFYING

WESTERN MEDITERRANEAN NORTH FOUR — PARTLY CLOUDY — VISIBILITY MODERATE — STATE OF SEA SLIGHT — OUTLOOK SIMILAR

LIBYAN SEA VARIABLE THREE INCREASING AND BECOMING NORTH — ISOLATED SHOWERS — VISIBILITY MODERATE — STATE OF SEA SLIGHT — OUTLOOK SIMILAR

EASTERN MEDITERRANEAN VARIABLE THREE — LOCAL RAINS — VISIBILITY MODERATE — STATE OF SEA SMOOTH — OUTLOOK SIMILAR

PART VI

Seascapes

To sail is to journey across the seas; a journey which stories of the sea can evoke but never quite explain. At sea, the eye of the landlubber loses its familiar points of reference. One must learn to find one's bearings in a changing world which is constantly transformed by the winds, the waves and the currents. There are no signposts, no roads, no crossroads, no villages, no ordnance survey references. It is a world of moving contours, and one must learn to decipher its signs – to read the clouds, listen to the sounds of the sea, watch the rise and fall of the waves and feel the fog falling.

Charts offer no fixed routes. Only cargo ships have to follow predetermined ocean traffic lanes when near ports and in very busy seas like the Channel. One is therefore free to choose any route one wishes using marine charts which only show the coastline (with land shaded in grey), depth markings, a few reference points – lighthouses, buoys, deeps and wrecks … But what will the sea be like where the sea bed shelves or if you cross the tide in full flood? How will you learn to recognise the landmarks at the entrance to a port at twilight? A chart will not help a fisherman to find his lobster pots offshore in a labyrinth of islands and rocks. He finds his way by noting signs which would be invisible to the casual sailor.

How many tales would one tell before communicating that understanding of the sea which analysis alone cannot give? Instead, in these pages, we have sought to present some guidelines which may help you understand the clues offered by the sea and the coasts. To complement the serious study of navigation we offer a kind of user's manual to the sea, to help you open your eyes and ears, and learn to recognise the ways of the sea. This knowledge may help you see through certain traps and avoid those surprises that the charts do not show.

We will do this in a journey of three chapters. First of all we must describe and explain just what a seascape is from a yacht's eye view. The very notion of a seascape warrants an initial definition, as the term is a rather broad one. There are all sorts of seascapes and different ones are crossed in different ways. This examination of the idea of the seascape will give you a way into the subject, and basic method for exploring the sea in all its variety.

Then we will discuss the land as seen from the sea, an inverted view, full of surprises and so unfamiliar to the land-dweller. Ultimately we will speak of the sea itself with its extraordinarily complex and vibrant depths, its temperature, colours, currents and tides, its ceaseless movement fuelled by the wind and obstacles in its path. The world of the sea is a mysterious one which yields its secrets reluctantly. We will try therefore to be as practical as we can in our analysis of the variety and forms of the sea's movements, and how a sailor can be harmed or helped by them.

We can only offer a brief introduction. When you are sailing you will make your own discoveries which cannot be touched upon here. In fact, the more you get to know the world of the sea, the more you understand why it used to be seen as magical, and why the ancients projected onto it both good and evil powers. The sailor who is up against the sea will find it an unpredictable lover; the ocean can smile or rage, be generous or mean, wonderful and awful. As an old sailor from Saint-Malo used to say: 'There is nothing more beautiful or treacherous than the sea'.

CHAPTER 1

The concept of the seascape

Some things are not easy to capture in words. They are too rich, complex and can only be understood through analogy with other parts of our experience. They must be seen in relation to other things rather than on their own.

Landscapes

A landscape has a close affinity with ideas like country, situation, place and space. A landscape is what a specific place conveys; a space with its own atmosphere and its specific characteristics which serve to distinguish it, sometimes in very subtle ways, from other places even very close by. To know a particular landscape truly is to use all one's senses to be aware of its lines, volumes, lights, colours, sounds, smells, temperatures, winds, humidity and dryness, the nature of the soil, and animal and plant life. Landscapes also evoke the geological and human past, and the current ecological balance. The mineral composition of the landscape is the result of the ancient events recorded in the physical features of the place. The developments of the land, of the flora and the fauna, tell a story about the secular compromise between man and nature. Military, religious, urban, mineral and industrial activities mark off the passage of time.

A landscape, in sum then, is a picture. The adjectives we use to describe its character – tragic, soothing, harsh, wild, romantic – reflect the relationships between landscape and the human sensibility, those relationships which are expressed by painters and writers, and which vary in different eras. We need to look again and again at landscapes to understand them, to see what changes and what remains the same. They are like people; to understand them, one has to get to know them over a long period of time. The first impression is oversimplified and superficial; it must be expanded and enriched by further acquaintance. Some aspects will recur, but other, new nuances will appear and increase one's understanding. In fact, you learn to understand a landscape as you learn to read.

Venice.

Seascapes

The word landscape is not only used to refer to dry land. There are also marine landscapes or seascapes. Thirty years ago, this idea seemed strange to everyone except sailors. But like all new ideas which are disturbing at first, and then shed light on all others, this concept is beginning to be accepted. Nonetheless, for many land-lubbers, the sea and its domains are all the same. The sea is just the sea – a vast expanse of salt water which is more or less cold depending on whether it is in the north or the south, with waves if it is windy, with rocks, beaches, ports, fish, shells and birds. People go to the seaside.

Yet the sea and its seascapes show as much individual character and diversity as do landscapes. The sea is not the same everywhere. It might be surrounded by land, or totally open. It can be unsettled or calm depending on the region. Its depth varies greatly; it is fringed by a varying continental shelf; the temperature of its waters depends on the currents and on the movement of water from tropical or polar regions or on the circulation of water from the great deeps at the edge of the continental basins. Just as there are many continents, countries and provinces, there is not one sea, but many. All of them are different. This variety is not faceless or haphazard.

Tuna fishing boats at Concarneau.

There are frontiers and border areas, and each sea or part of a sea has its own characteristics. This makes different seas definable, understandable and recognisable.

We need to understand not only that the Channel and the Mediterranean are different, but also that within both of them there are very different areas, sometimes with their own names, such as the Tyrrhenian, Ionian or Aegean seas. There are also widely differing seascapes in the Channel and the Mediterranean where sailing will vary depending on the place and the season. It is easy to understand that coastal areas are different from each other, because they look different, but offshore areas are also different – the Sole Bank is not the same as the Adour or the sandbanks of Newfoundland.

Experiencing a landscape

Seafaring peoples have always understood the concept of the seascape. The ancients invented the Seven Seas. The nature of the Mediterranean and its different regions, at least in the Eastern Mediterranean, was described in the *Odyssey*. Norwegian sagas tell of the Baltic and North Atlantic which the Vikings had discovered. The long journeys made by the Phoenicians and the Carthaginians

Praos from Java.

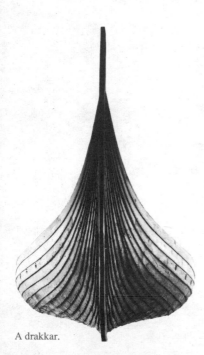

A drakkar.

mapped out several seas on either side of the Pillars of Hercules. The names given by history to oceans and seas, to gulfs and bays are part of an attempt to define them and classify them. If you know how to listen to sailors and in particular to fishermen, they will talk about certain areas of sea, be they large or small, just as farmers, shepherds or foresters talk about an area of land, be it a valley, a plateau, or a mountain, with its fields, its pastureland and its forest clearings.

To understand this, you must have had the experience of going out with a fisherman to lift his lobster pots, 10 miles offshore in the early morning, sailing without a compass. It is fascinating to see him

'This is how we used to go to Saint-Pierre: you sail towards the setting sun as long as a particular type of seaweed is floating on the water; then you sail so that the sun is to your left a little. When everything goes very blue (you can't miss it) you come to the places which the dolphins love, then those where the prevailing wind blows in small gusts. Then you come to the place where the waves are low, then there is the big grey square. After that, you cross the big breakers; when you have seen them, the first sandbanks are not far, to leeward.' The captain could speak forever about this and could have carried on all night. He had observed the things he was telling us since adolescence; he had seen the changes around him while he was sailing. Nobody had taught him any of this, because his two skippers had not uttered a word all day except that sometimes when the boat was going about or changing speed, they would wave their hands to point out the shimmering expanse of sea around them, this composite surface which was as full of variety as any old-inhabited countryside.

Michel Serres, *Le Monde* (The World)

Sinagots from the Morbihan region.

A Phoenician ship.

A fishing boat from Nazareth.

find his floating markers topped with a black pennant, often straight away. This makes you understand how two small areas of sea – which look identical to each other for the person who doesn't know them – are in fact entirely different, because of the colour of the water, the direction of the waves, the nature of the deeps, the aspects, or the style. This is not magic; it is knowledge, born of experience.

'I know the area from Penmarch to the Talut Point. In one place, the sea is always calm, whereas in another it is often rougher, and in this corner, the wind is always strong; you can anchor behind this rock but it is not really sheltered enough, and the swell comes round, particularly when the wind comes from the north-west. In this place here, you must beware of the south-easterly wind which raises the groundswell. This is as far as my knowledge extends.' Similarly, you can find sailors who have sailed around Cape Horn, or skippers of wind-powered tuna fishing boats, or sailors from boats which have fished off Newfoundland who can tell you about the high seas, where there are just as many strongly marked differences, although the setting is much more stark.

A landscape of shapes

A fascinating way to grasp the reality of marine landscapes is to look not only at the seascapes themselves but also at the shapes and the rigging of different types of boats created by different seagoing peoples. They vary from the pointed shapes of Mediterranean vessels, to the caiques of the Aegean, closed on top, flat-bottomed with long, straight prows; there are sardine and tuna fishing boats from Portugal, with their backs like upside-down crinolines, the heavy sinagots from the Morbihan region, the pinnac from Andernos and Arcachon, floating light on the water, inherited from the Greeks. There are the powerful pilot boats of the Channel, the large, heavy, flat Dutch barges, with their leeboards.

In one type of sea, you need to have a huge and very light sail to make the best of even the faintest breeze, but it must be a sail which can be taken down very quickly if the mistral suddenly begins to blow, and you also need to be able to pull your boat up onto the beach because few moorings are safe in all weathers. Elsewhere, you fish from the back of the boat and the waves are strong when you come back into the port. Some boats will need to be able to sail in shallow water. Where the current is strong, the boat will need to go deep into the water to hold its sail and counterbalance the strength of the current. In one situation, the boat will need to weather heavy seas with strong winds, whereas in another it will be necessary to ride over small waves and sail in shallow water. In some seas, it may not be possible to avoid running aground on sandbanks occasionally. These different situations will require different types of craft. Visiting small fishing ports on the Atlantic coast of France, on the Channel, in the North Sea or in the Mediterranean and talking to the fishermen has taught some of us from Glénans far more than any lectures. And we still know nothing about the reasons behind the shapes and structure of Chinese junks, Polynesian pirogues or North American schooners!

A Kuwaiti dhow.

Landscape and culture

Seeing and understanding a landscape gives more than aesthetic and intellectual pleasure. It also provides the basis for an approach to our environment which respects the inherent balance of nature and the order and harmony of the natural world. All those whose profession means that they will be involved in physically altering the landscape, be they agricultural or civil engineers, foresters, architects, town planners or administrators, should have a detailed understanding of the countryside. It would have been better to use the knowledge of the farmers of high alpine valleys, of the guides and shepherds, before putting up buildings which were subsequently destroyed in avalanches. Similarly, so as not to damage the coast and sometimes even cause catastrophes, to sail safely and make the most of one's time at sea, to understand local traditions which are often fascinating, the sailor needs to gain access to another culture, to learn to read seascapes.

How can we do this? Initially, it will be more difficult than learning to read landscapes, because we already have the basic alphabet for reading landscapes. There are geography books of varying quality, which we will have more or less read at school, we may have family in the country, we may have taken part in harvests, we have probably all been on walks to discover the countryside or the town. We may also have read articles about how to appreciate landscapes and finally we will have experience of tourism. We are educated to be land-dwellers. There is no doubt still much to be done to develop a really good and in-depth understanding of the environment, but there is already a basis on which to build. None of this applies to the sea, except for those who were born near it.

Sea-going kayak by the Raz Point.

We must therefore begin by educating our senses, by learning the marine alphabet, and getting used to a new way of seeing, of touching, of tasting, of smelling and of hearing before we can even begin to learn this new alphabet. Just as those of us who were not brought up with music, before learning to read or play music, need to learn to hear sounds, to become capable of recognising the quality of different sounds, their differing intensity, their pitch, their organisation, and their movement. Another analogy is with modern methods of learning languages, where we are taught first of all to hear sounds and words before learning the rules of writing or constructing a language.

Learning to read a seascape

The best way to go about this learning process is to choose a place which contains the greatest number of discrete components which can be separated out and recognised. Some bays in southern Brittany like the mouth of the Aven or the Bay of Odet can be an excellent base for this initial sensitisation to the sea, and for your first experience of undertow, swell, currents, shelter, rocks, breezes, and light. A small yacht or better still a kayak or best of all a set of goggles and flippers are the tools to have in this voyage of discovery. As Antonio, in Giono's *Le Chant du monde* (*The Song of the World*), becomes one with the river, you must become one with the sea.

Once this first stage is complete, rather than trying immediately to acquire encyclopedic knowledge by sailing in very different types of sea, it is better to aim to get to know one very rich and varied region, for example, the whole of southern Brittany. Very often, the same elements will recur in different forms everywhere. It is better therefore to acquire a solid foundation which will allow you subsequently to interpret correctly situations and places which you haven't yet physically experienced, but which you will find in books and papers. Like mountaineers, sailors, even when out of their own environment, are better off with in-depth knowledge of one specific region; when you know where you come from, you can belong anywhere.

It is obviously useful though not to restrict oneself to local knowledge, and to obtain more general information about the different aspects of seascapes, on a more scientific basis. The following chapters attempt to describe the deeps and the coasts, the sea and its movements and the traces left by human beings in terms which are accessible to all. Our descriptions are based on observation and they are the basis for our attempts to analyse and generalise. But it must always be clear that this factual information is only fully meaningful when it leads to true knowledge, that combination of facts, experience and sensitivity which a few sailors possess.

Cape Pertusato.

Summary

This is an outline of the approach we suggest, which in fact involves complementary approaches, constantly moving between theory and practice, between raw experience and an analysis of that experience. Nevertheless, there is no substitute for experience. It is crucial to live inside a seascape, to observe it again and again, to ask questions about it, to return to it to try to understand more, to find new answers to new questions. You need to learn to observe the sea. We are more used to seeing fields of wheat swaying in the wind than the living waters of currents whipped up by the wind. You must learn to notice what the surface of the water looks like above the deeps, where there is a break in the swell. You must learn to see the rivers in the sea, the swaying movement of seaweed and of lobster-pot markers, the green, black, or white of the ocean bed, the huge swell of the open sea beyond the protection afforded by islands. You must learn to recognise the full and overwhelming nature of the water at high tide and the respite of low tides.

You need to learn to look at the land from the sea. It can be a wonderful sight. If Corsicans and the administrators who are responsible for protecting areas of natural beauty were used to seeing Corsica from the open sea, they would immediately have declared the whole island an area of natural beauty, and part of the national and international heritage. From a boat, the sea becomes the foreground of a theatrical set, with mountains, greenery and villages in the background. From another angle, the view is horizontal, not vertical and has a different, more subtle beauty. From yet another angle, the coast is a menacing wall, in which you have to look hard for a welcoming inlet. And we should not forget how beautiful towns can look from the sea.

You must also learn to understand the pacts and alliances made between the land and the sea. This is clear when you are about to enter an unknown harbour and you are looking for the key of the sights you can see. 'How do this steeple, these cliffs, these quays, these buoys, all of which are difficult enough to find, relate to each other? And how can I find my way through?' Which sailor has not felt this anxiety, during the day more than at night, when the horizon offers only undecipherable clues and the boat seems to be moving at the speed of a torpedo?

You must also learn to read the sky; to learn to tell the difference between a storm cloud in the Western Mediterranean and a cloud which promises good weather. You must learn to distinguish between the different types of cirrus clouds, some of which can bode ill for the sailor, and you must be able to tell from looking at the horizon that a squall is on its way and how fast it is moving.

In the final analysis, to know a seascape properly, you must have felt really involved in it, threatened and reassured by it; you must have sweated with anguish in the fog when everything on the sea takes on terrifying proportions; you must have asked yourself what is hidden under those glaucous, calm surfaces of water which dolphins love; you must have listened out for the whistle of the wind in the sails and guessed that fine weather was on its way. Then and only then will you truly understand that a seascape is not a stable entity, with well-defined surfaces and planes like a landscape, but that it finds its coherence in perpetual change. It consists in fact of a number of factors whose rhythms change with time. Linked to this is one's own sense of time, the time spent at sea, time wasted or gained, the time it takes to sail off, to seek shelter, to run aground or struggle vainly against the current, or to escape to the open sea; your experience of a seascape can include near misses and successful manoeuvres.

CHAPTER 2

From the sea to the land

Navigation can be rigorous and based solely on geometric calculations on charts, but there is another way of navigating, based on
one's own perceptions and knowledge of a seascape. Part VII,
'Navigation', explains how to find your position on a chart, work out
exactly where you are, take your bearings, plot your route and use
astronomical data. On paper a boat is a point in space, in a world of
straight lines, right angles, and vectors. This is an abstract universe
and the sailor always needs to check the real world by leaving the
chart to look at the horizon. Who has never felt first of all apprehen-
sive, then delighted when actually succeeding in coming ashore in
poor visibility? You have a tangible proof that your calculations are
correct when you find a marker where you expected it to be.

But the navigator must move from the chart table and look for
reference points, thus learning to find directions and getting to know
the sea. This process of discovering the sea is one of the real plea-
sures of sailing. Referring constantly to the reality outside the charts
is also the only way to ensure that you are not sailing blind and it
confirms that your calculations are correct.

The open sea

The heart of the marine universe is the open sea, the high seas, the
vast oceans. To sail offshore, in the open sea, is to cross a space
which seems to have no boundaries, to push back the horizon one
wave at a time. This is the true sea voyage. When you are sailing like
this, charts can offer no concrete reference points. The boat's position
is the point where co-ordinates intersect. The world is made up of
lines, criss-crossing on the charts, and these are what you follow.
There are no physical markers to tell you where you are, although
you might happen to catch sight of a cargo boat or a whale.

In the open sea, the weather conditions, the light, the wind, the
swell are not mediated by the presence of land. The water is deep
blue in colour. These are the deeps (average depth 4,000m).

It has been discovered recently that this hidden face of the earth
consists of underwater plains and mountain ranges, of networks of

Some boats we have encountered: a light vessel near the Scilly Islands, the lifeboat of the island of Ushant, a trawler in the bay of Audierne, a malamok at the entrance to the port of Lesconil.

deep rifts which divide up the very crust of the earth. But the sailor in the open sea sees nothing of these hidden regions, since the geography of the depths has no effect on the surface of the water, except for the occasional sight of a few volcanic peaks, breaking the surface of the water in the shape of atolls.

The approaches to land

As you get closer to land, you are still in the open sea, still in the territory where you will sail for long stretches without seeing land, but the sea begins to fill with other ships and with signs which tell you that land is close. These are areas crossed by a constant procession of large vessels, converging on straits or big ports and they can be unaware of the presence of smaller boats. Crossing a cargo route helps you locate your position quite accurately, but you need to be careful to avoid a confrontation with these metal giants. These are areas fertile in fish, so, depending on the seasons, they are criss-crossed by trawlers, which can make unexpected changes in direction, trailing huge nets, drag lines and other cumbersome equipment.

You might also come across warships on exercise or on more or less covert reconnaissance missions, in waters which border more than one country. You will also come across the strange shapes of oil-drilling platforms, in the middle of the North Sea, in the Persian Gulf and on the coast of the Gulf of Guinea.

Near a continent, the colour of the water can vary and you become aware of the proximity of land under the water. This is the continental shelf, a shallow ledge (less than 200m deep) which slopes gently up to the coast. The edge of the shelf juts out suddenly from the deeps and is indented with great gashes which are underwater canyons. The extent of the continental shelf varies. It is particularly wide where it borders plains or hills (on the Atlantic coast of Europe for example or the western coast of the USA) and is practically non-existent near mountainous regions like the Western Mediterranean or the Bay of Biscay.

The relief and the depth of the water varies in these areas. There are ranges of shallows, banks, plateaux, and complex underwater networks of valleys and canals. The state of the sea is directly affected by the uneven relief; the sea is difficult around offshore banks such as the Sole and the Rockall plateau off Scotland. Areas of shallows can be dangerous, like the Dogger and Viking banks in the North Sea, the Rochebonne plateau in the Bay of Biscay or the Wild Bank to the south-west of Ireland; the deep clefts in the sea floor and in particular the sudden rises in terrain affect the swell

The continental shelf in Western Europe.

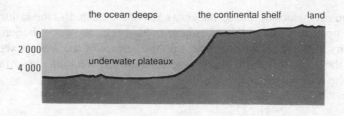

the ocean deeps   the continental shelf   land

0
2 000
4 000

underwater plateaux

From the continental shelf to the deeps.

(near Penmarch, on the Birvideaux plateau, and the Adour Deeps). The closer you get to the coast, the more effect the relief has and the more difficult the sea becomes.

Coastal areas

Coastal zones are areas bounded by the land on one side and the open sea on the other, and therefore have clear boundaries. Boats sailing here are in changeable and dynamic conditions, but within a framework as specific and clearly defined as contours on the charts. Land is usually clearly visible on the horizon and may even appear when you are further off shore in the shape of banks, outcrops of rocks and islands. The ocean no longer reigns supreme with its high waves crashing down on the shallows and the reefs; the movement of the water is contained and directed within specific compartments, be they channels or passages, which take their structure from the relief of the nearby land mass.

It is not enough for you to keep track of changes in the weather and the effects on the sea; you must also take bearings frequently and know the exact position of the boat within the seascape. You learn to look out for the most varied signs, ranging from a line of cumulus clouds above the land, to choppy water on the shallows. Sailors who are familiar with a particular coastline can find clues in anything from the colour of the water, the sound of waves breaking on the reefs, or a shoal of fish quivering near the surface of the water. They can navigate in a seascape which they know well by recognising where they are, but they are lost when out of these familiar haunts.

Markers

Sailors who do not know an area or those on a pleasure cruise cannot rely on vague impressions. They need to use specific markers which can be located on a chart; these may be landmarks, small islands and rocks with names which evoke their appearance such as Bull Rock, Needle Rock, Tête de Mort or Castle Point. They may also be whitened rocks or buildings on the coast, such as church steeples, watchtowers, factory chimneys, or tower blocks. There are also purpose-built aids to navigation such as landing markers, beacons, turrets built on reefs or on the mainland, marker buoys to indicate danger, or mark out a channel. Some buoys are mounted with lights and others with whistles or bells to make it easier to find them at night or when visibility is poor. These markers constitute a sort of network of reference points at sea. In foggy weather, the fact that it is possible to navigate from one buoy to the next makes it possible to keep track of one's position.

The Ferlas channel.
... you will need to change direction again when you see to port a house above a whitened stone.

There are also sound signals over moderate distances, such as fog horns, automatic gunshot sounds, and medium range direction-finding radio (VHF, consol or Decca) which help navigate near coastlines in all weathers. At night, lighthouses are the reference points for navigating; these are positioned in the front line, at the tip of a promontory, at the end of a rocky causeway or on a reef. A few lightships shaken by the waves also help the sailor. To tell the story of the construction of the big isolated lighthouses such as the Eddystone, Ar Men, Jument, or Fastnet would be to relive the relent-less determination of the men who built them, working in impos-sibly difficult conditions. The story of the keepers of these lighthouses is the story of the rhythm of the lights, of nights and days in rhythmic succession and ultimately of the rhythm of the sea itself.

Night-time navigation takes place within a world lit by powerful landing lights, lights at the entrance to a port, or smaller-scale lights marking out a channel. Sailing at night within coastal areas means living in a world defined by the beams of light from lighthouses. Areas which during the day were capes, channels, chains of shal-lows, rocky islets, are transformed at night into zones of darkness, white areas, red areas, or particular alignments of lights. When it is foggy and reference points fade into the mist, the sea becomes a mass of sounds – reassuring sounds like the bell on a buoy, or worrying ones like the sound of engines or the rumbling of water breaking on the reefs.

Passages

The extent of the coastal zone varies greatly on different coastlines. Sometimes, it can be represented by a mark on a chart, and consist of endless cliffs or beaches, but on more jagged coastlines, land and sea can be interwoven over distances of 10–30 miles. There are huge coastal basins, sheltered from heavy seas by a network of shallows and islands; examples include the great inlets of southern Brittany between Penmarch and Le Croisic, the channels of the Charente, the sea of the Hebrides, the bays of south-west Ireland, the bays of western Corsica and the Bay of Douarnenez. In other places, areas of calm water wait behind a promontory or a jutting out piece of land. Examples here include the Bay of Quiberon, the harbours of Chichester, Weymouth, Hyères and Villefranche.

There are natural harbours totally surrounded by land, like the harbours of Brest, Cork, Lisbon and even the Solent. There are inland basins with many inlets such as the ria of Arosa, in Galicia, or dotted with islands, like the Gulf of Morbihan or Clew Bay, or there are the intricate networks of the Norwegian fjords. Access to these inland areas of water is only gained through a bottleneck at the entrance, and this narrow pass may be swept by strong currents. There are also labyrinths of broken up rocks and small islands forming long barriers which hide the shore; in northern Brittany, there is a band 4–30 miles wide consisting of channels which are difficult to negotiate in order to reach the shelter of the coast; and part of the coastline of Scandinavian countries is a real minefield of reefs.

Sailing near the coast means learning to deal with changing conditions; the play of converging winds in a bay can leave the headland under complete calm; the play of strong currents in bottle-necks and near headlands can cause fierce undertows. Tides may cover then uncover a three-dimensional scene. You must keep your distance when sailing near a coastline open to the ocean and swept by strong winds, but you can come in close to a sheltered coast to recognise coves and moorings. You must also plan your route carefully to avoid areas where the sea breaks on the reefs.

Anchorages

It is also crucial to learn how to choose an anchorage, not only in relation to the shelter which the coastline and the wind direction afford you, but also in relation to the sea bed. In many cases the nature of the sea bed will tell you a lot about the quality of the anchorage and the shelter it will offer.

Generally speaking, if the sea bed consists of gravel and shingle, the sea will be rough and it will be difficult to get a good anchor hold. A sea bed covered with seaweed is no better because the anchor will slip and slide around on the blanket of weed and will not be able to get a proper grip. You should therefore beware of rocky floors covered with seaweed, and also of the grasses which cover the bottom of sandy coves. There are fields of grasswrack with flat leaves – this is known as varech in Brittany and was used in the past to stuff mattresses. In the Mediterranean, there are the mattes, which are fields of slender green strips undulating on the sea bed, some-

Will she drag?

times up to 1m in height. Charts often indicate these areas, but they may expand, and contract or shift. Have you ever noticed in our clear waters in the Glénans, that there are very fine and supple weeds (*Himanthalia elongata*) which are the only ones which can survive in areas where there is a strong current? In the Mediterranean, certain types of gelatinous weeds indicate water polluted by sewer outfalls. Simply look carefully at the sea bed or use a spot of tallow on the end of your lead line to make sure that you choose a good anchorage.

Sand usually provides enough purchase for an anchor, provided that it is deep enough. But that does not mean that it is possible to anchor anywhere sandy! For example, you could get some unpleasant surprises trying to moor on a sandbank or off a straight lee shore. Only mud usually provides a good place to moor even if there is a current.

The shore

The shore is both land and sea, in turn covered and uncovered by tides, high water and storms. The first part of the shoreline is the area which is covered by the sea at high tide; the low tide mark is the zero point at which chart depths begin, and the high tide mark is the beginning of terra firma.

The tidal zone

The width of the area of the shore affected by the difference in level of the sea at high and low tides varies, depending on the slope of the land. In some places there are sudden differences in level, forming cliffs, vertical drops beaten by the waves. In these cases the tidal zone is almost vertical and forms a natural quayside and it may even be possible to draw up alongside it. In other places, it slopes more or less gently and can be constituted differently in different parts.

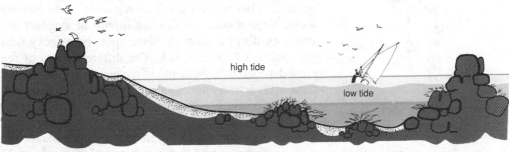

high tide

low tide

A granitic coastline.

Laminaria saccharina.

Laminaria digitata.

The extent of the tide also affects the extent of the tidal zone. In areas with a wide tidal range, like northern Brittany, the sea goes out several miles, uncovering damp beaches and rocky plains; on the contrary, in the Mediterranean, where there is almost no tide at all, the tidal zone is nothing more than a narrow border on beaches and rocks.

We should also point out that the high water mark is not always really the highest point which the sea reaches; it is impossible to imagine the wide beaches of Languedoc without remembering the waves which sweep over them in bad weather when the water goes far beyond the usual high tide mark; the same is true of the beaches of Penfret when they are washed over by waves in winter. Tidal zones must be seen as parts of the sea in their own right, with their own characteristics; their uneven topography, their channels, their holes full of water left by the full tide, their boulders, all make them a self-contained little world which can have a lot to say about the sea to the person who knows how to look.

Whatever the nature of the tidal zone, the sailor who wants to bring a boat in to the land will have to take it into account and bear in mind all the hazards described above. You will need not only to know how to assess the depth of the water in a particular spot, but also to decide whether the water is likely to be calm or rough. You will also need to be able to recognise the features of the sea bed which will become the ground when the tide is low; is the tidal zone rocky, spiky or slippery? Is the beach firm and sandy or soft and muddy?

Rocks, beaches and mud flats

Seaweed found around a rocky tidal zone can give precious clues about the nature of the area. Firstly, it may stand out by its absence. Completely bald rocks around a headland are a bad sign. It probably means that the waves are so strong that no vegetation can survive, except in nooks and crannies. Limpets and barnacles will probably survive because of their grip on the rock.

Seaweed develops in those parts of the sea which are least beaten by storms, but where there is nevertheless some movement of the water, since it does not flourish in still or stagnant water. It will attach itself to the most sheltered spots on a rocky tidal zone, the gaps and cracks in the rock. The different types of seaweed will grow depending on the depth of the water and the length of time the seaweed is actually underwater, and their distribution can be identified quite precisely on the basis of those two criteria. At the lowest level, below the zero contour on charts, you will find deep water wrack, which consists of big strips fixed onto the rocks by flexible stalks, sometimes branching, and several metres long. The longest,

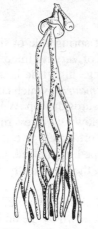

Himanthalia elongata.

Fucus serratus.

Fucus vesiculosus.

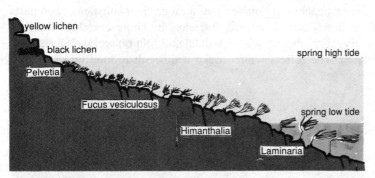

yellow lichen

black lichen

spring high tide

Pelvetia

Fucus vesiculosus

Himanthalia

spring low tide

Laminaria

The distribution of seaweed on a rocky tidal zone.

Pelvetia canaliculata.

the *Macrocystis*, can be up to 80m long and create serious problems for shipping. In our regions, we would only see the fronds of these at low tide, when the water is less than 1m deep. Wrack has the effect of slowing down waves, and cushioning their full impact. This means that at low tide, the sea often beats less strongly on the shore.

In the main areas affected by the tides, you will find a different type of seaweed, known commonly as 'shore wrack'. Continuing to go up towards the beachline, you will find the following types of seaweed. There is more seaweed with strands, dark in colour (*Himanthalia*), only visible at the spring low tide. This is followed by a slippery carpet of *Fucus*; either *Fucus serratus* whose edges are serrated, or *Fucus vesiculosus* which can be recognised as the name suggests by the small bladders which can be popped between the fingers and which act as floats for the plant. Further up, you will find the branching type (*Pelvetia caniculata*) and small green weed.

At the top of the shore, a fat necklace of 'wreck seaweed' torn

away by storms marks the level of the last spring tide or the last storm. Here you can find all sorts of things of varying interest. On the rocks themselves, the level of the average high tide is usually shown by a band of dark lichen (*Verrucaria maura*), which consists of a number of black patches, crumbling towards the top. When the top consists of a black band which spreads downwards evenly, you are not looking at lichen or seaweed but unfortunately at oil.

Tidal zones made up of soft soil are shaped by the sea, and the amount of sediment can give a good idea of the force of the waves which have been breaking on the shore.

Shingle – small more or less rounded pebbles – is washed up on the tidal zone by the rollers and washed back down by the undertow of the retreating waves. During storms, waves wash most of the shingle up above the high water mark. Shingle beaches not recommended for yachts: they usually slope steeply, and you can only land when the sea is calm. It is not sensible to stay long.

Sandy beaches are made up of a much finer substance, and parts of the beach can be moved sideways by shore currents. Beaches usually 'slim' during winter winds, and 'put on weight' during the summer. The rollers which make it difficult to load up or to land

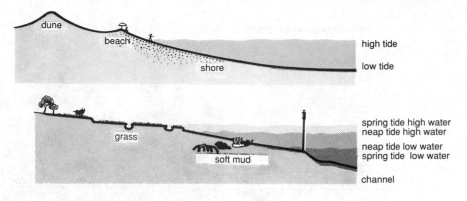

without running some risks, also dig a treacherous step at the edge of the tidal zone. These beaches are ideal for children and swimmers, and contain shells, clams, crabs and marine worms. Boats can sometimes lie up on them but you only need to look at a few grains of sand under a magnifying glass to understand the dangers.

The best place to clean or repair your hull is on a sheltered beach, with firm sand. Rough sand is usually too soft and loose to hold the weight of the legs and the sand is rapidly undermined by streams of water from the lower part of the beach. The ideal place

Asphodel (*Asphodelus albus*).

Oyat (*Ammophila arenaria*).

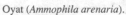

Sand convulvulus (*Calystegia soldanella*).

Hare's tail (*Lagurus ovatus*).

Thistle (*Carduus nutans*).

is a nice flat tidal zone of fine hard sand which remains damp for the entire period that the boat is out of the water.

The smooth surface of mudflats, criss-crossed with deep sinuous channels is revealed when the tide is low. The mud is made up of extremely fine particles which are brought in by the tide and stick to the ground during the slack of the high tide, in very calm areas such as the bottom of sheltered bays, estuaries, the back of ports. Their smell can be explained by the amount of decaying and fermenting organic debris. The mud may be hard, settled or mixed with sand or gravel. Most commonly it is a soft substance into which things sink easily. Mudflats are a perfect place for wintering, since the hull of a boat can settle comfortably into the mud provided that there are no foreign bodies underneath, such as rocks or sharp-edged wrecks.

Now, let us progress on to dry land. As we go back up to land, we should not overlook the marvellous orangey-red lichen (*Xanthoria parietina*) which cover the rocks (and also the old slate roofs of nearby houses). They are out of the reach of the sea, but not of the seaspray. Without them, the quality of the light of Breton beaches would not be the same. Further inland you can still sense the presence of the sea, up to a certain distance, particularly in the dunes, where you can find willowy plants, which may sometimes be spiky, with astonishing flowers, forming a precious and varied universe. This is also a fragile world and visitors are advised to watch where they walk and use paths if they exist.

Beyond this we will not venture, because we would be walking on private property. The fierceness of the dangerous dogs which lie in wait for us there can easily match that of the ocean.

Europoort, near Rotterdam.

Harbours

All sailors must eventually return to port. The port is the starting and end point of any journey; the port can be home base, port of call, or safe haven.

The definition of a port varies depending on the type of craft. A windsurfer and a dinghy only need a piece of land which slopes towards the sea, a dock or a beach sheltered from the water. A boat can stop for a few hours in the relatively exposed mooring which an inlet can offer, provided wind and weather are favourable, but on the whole boats will need to put in at a port.

The facilities offered by ports depend on the type of port and whether it is dedicated to one type of shipping. It is not advisable to slip into an oil terminal in a yacht and try to moor the boat using huge mooring rings intended for much bigger craft. Neither is it a good idea to stop amidst the clouds of dust of a port for ore tankers. Naval military bases do not extend a warm welcome to visitors who have strayed off course. You may prefer the facilities of a marina with landing stages in neat rows. They are really yacht parks, and although they do provide adequate shelter, they are also very crowded. You can also try small fishing ports which are less comfortable but much more personal and where you have to be discreet to appreciate the warmth of other sailors and their world. However, you must make sure that you know the timing of the movement of the fishing boats from the port to avoid crossing the path of trawlers as they leave in the early morning, or being caught up in their rush to get back to port for the evening fish auction. You will also be able to listen to the tales of sailors who have extensive experience of the sea.

The choice of a port does not only depend on the type of facilities and shelter that you need. The draught of some large yachts and the width of some multihulled boats may limit the number of possible

The port of Sète.

The port of Paimpol at low tide, showing the docks and the lock. The downstream gate of the lock is.open. The lock itself is empty. This is how the lock operates at the neap tides. At high tide, the downstream gate is closed behind the boats which are in the lock. Then the sluice gates let water into the lock from the dock until the levels are the same. The upstream gate is then opened. The process is reversed to let the boats out.

The procedure is easier during the spring tides. Both gates can remain open at high tide, during which time the water level in the lock and the dock even out. The dock is then simply tidal. The spillway to the right of the lock plays an important role here. Sea water can pass over the top, to avoid there being a strong current within the dock itself. The spillway has two other roles to play. It contains gates through which excess water can be expelled during sudden rises in water level; at the same time, the access channel is cleared of mud. Its second role is to lower the level of water in the dock when tides are low. At the ebb tide, it is crucial to close the gates before the spillway is uncovered, otherwise the current would rush into the lock and smash everything.

The port of la Rochelle.

The entrance to the port of Granville. Here is a gate at full tide. The entrance to the port looks vast and there is nothing visible to suggest any problems. In fact, you must go in between the two posts, above the gate (which is lowered), because on both sides there is a wall, just below the surface of the water.

ports of call to large, deep harbours. Obviously, if your boat suffers any damage, you will need to make your way to the nearest and most accessible port where the damage can be repaired.

Ports are basically sheltered areas fitted out for boats. Things are changing. The small creeks where small boats could be pulled up onto the sand, the sheltered inlets, the deep estuaries have all been gradually fitted out with quays to make boarding possible, with walls to act as breakwaters, with docks, with lights, and a harbour-master.

There are two sorts of ports. First of all, there are inland ports, built on estuaries within lagoons, or even dug out of coastal plains. These sites are usually very well sheltered, but they are also hidden from the sea; access to them is likely to be through a channel and the current may cause problems. Other ports are built on the sea, behind huge quays which act as breakwaters. Waves break on the harbour walls and there is a strong undertow in the channel. The water in the front part of these ports is rough, and the back part of the ports with its sheltered basins and docks offers really still waters. In areas with a wide tidal range, docks have been set up behind locks. This is one facility which makes it possible to avoid running aground, but it requires a precise knowledge of the timetable of the opening and closing of lock gates and difficult manoeuvres to avoid collisions between boats while going through the locks.

Sailing within a port is not without its dangers. If the water is still, the wind might be unpredictable and changeable. If the wind falls, one might easily be swept up by the current; a gust of wind may mean that one is suddenly heading towards the quayside or towards another boat. This is why moving under sail within a port demands good co-ordination between all crew members, great precision and the ability to anticipate. Holding the anchor gear at the ready, having the motor running and an oar in the right position can help avoid disasters.

Manoeuvring within a port involves being able to move without collisions within a confined space. You must be able to pick up your moorings, tie up alongside a large boat, board a landing stage. You also need to be able to know exactly where you are within a complex space divided up into docks, full of other boats and buildings. You must be careful to avoid colliding with other boats which are also manoeuvring near you. Finally you must know how to undertake complicated manoeuvres with the warp to make sure you are properly moored. The moorings must be adjusted in relation to the wind conditions and the tide; you must know how to choose your mooring ring, tie up with the right knot, which is both secure yet easy to cast off, and organise the deck appropriately.

In the final analysis, calling in to a port means confronting the dangers of land before being seized by the desire to be back on board and out at sea.

CHAPTER 3

The sea and its movements

The sea covers three-quarters of the earth's surface, and under the water there is still more water. Yes, there is water at the bottom of the ocean. The earth consists of lumps and bumps, with quite a few more deep ravines than high mountains. In fact, if the earth was levelled out then there would be nothing but ocean, 2,000m deep all the way round.

As things stand, the water is rather unevenly spread over the surface. There is a great deal of it in the southern hemisphere – rather more than in the northern, in fact, as the oceans take up almost all the room. In the north, there is more land, and enclosed bodies of water which are referred to as seas, when they fulfil certain characteristics. There is a whole field of terminology that distinguishes secondary seas, inland or Mediterranean seas and so on. The important thing for the navigator is the way in which these seas join up with the oceans, which then either favours or obstructs the swell, ocean currents and tidal streams, and which allows for exchanges of water.

One of the essential characteristics of the sea is that it is salty. In the Atlantic, it is very salty in regions like the tropics, where there is a great deal of evaporation and very little rain. It is also very salty in enclosed seas such as the Mediterranean and the Red Sea. It is rather less salty at the equator, where there is a good deal of rain and where the great rivers meet the sea. The cold seas are not very salty, because there is little evaporation and there is a good deal of fresh water flowing into them.

Just as the degree of salinity varies, so does the temperature. On average, the temperature of the surface waters diminishes as you move from the equator to the poles (the temperature can also vary according to latitude and seasonal changes, although these are rather less significant than those variations experienced on land: the sea has a high specific heat capacity, which explains some of the difference between the maritime and continental climates). Generally speaking, the water temperature also decreases with depth.

Temperature and salinity determine the density of the water. Cold water is denser than warm water (this is very easily observed in the bath, where, when you top up with warm water again, the latter remains on the surface). Very salty water is denser than less salty water. This means that the sea water is not the same density everywhere. As a result of the various influences – temperature difference at the equator and the poles, between the surface and the deeper regions, the formation and melting of ice, the shape and depth of the sea bed, rivers, evaporation and rain – it becomes apparent that there are masses of water which are very different from one another, and which do not like to mix.

The last characteristic of the sea, and not one of the least important is that it is in constant motion. Some of these movements are readily visible, such as the tides, waves and the swell. Others are rather less obvious, such as the many currents which run in all directions, and it is probably best to start with these.

Currents

Currents can be either massive or highly localised, regular, or just appear on the odd occasion. Even up until recently, the movements of the currents were little known. We are beginning to measure them with greater accuracy thanks to techniques used on board ship and also thanks to satellites which can detect minute differences in temperature and translate them into different colours on a photograph or a chart.

Establishing a classification is still rather a delicate matter, and whatever model is established will look a little mechanical compared to the real thing. Furthermore, every current has its counter-current. Specialists generally classify them in terms of their causes, which can be either internal or external. There are therefore *density currents*, which are caused by differences in temperature and salinity between different neighbouring masses of water. There are also *drift currents*, which are linked with the wind, and *slope currents*, which are a result of the latter. However, it must be remembered that a current is a combination of a variety of forces, that density and wind can work together and that a current is always connected with a gradient (the sea is far from flat, and the notion of sea level as a uniform plane is actually rather relative).

In order to give a slightly clearer picture, we will say that there are large general regular currents, and rather more local, occasional currents. Tidal streams are local regular currents, but they are of quite a different origin, and we will deal with them later.

General currents

The oceans are made up as we have said of large masses of water of varying density which do not want to mix. These water masses move along at greater and lesser speeds than each other, side by side, or one on top of the other, often covering thousands of miles while preserving perfectly their own characteristics, before they finally blend with the waters around them. These vast movements are the general currents. Since they frequently flow between one continent and another, they have helped the great migrations of people over the centuries and have influenced climates. If we never really think of them during our coastal navigation in Europe, then it can nonetheless happen that we are reminded of their existence by some bottle or other with a piece of paper and an address, thrown into the sea in a far-off country.

On a more practical level, why does all the water move around so much? The force behind these and other movements is, of course, the sun. Not all points on the globe are equally warmed, and the water masses attempt to equalise this imbalance by moving either towards the poles or from the poles towards the equator, according to the principle of convection. We have already dealt with this topic in some detail in the Part V, 'Meteorology', since the winds do the same job in a more spectacular fashion.

General circulation at surface level.

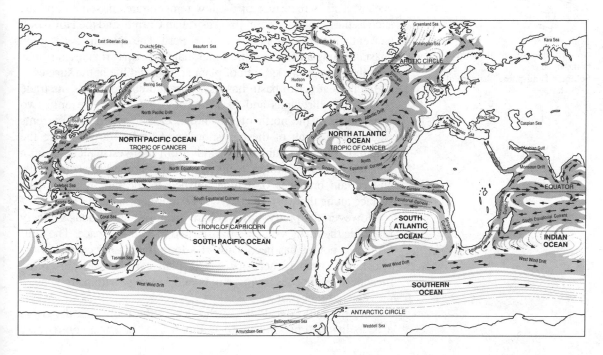

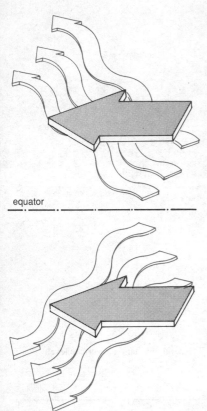

equator

Northern hemisphere: the current deviates to the right.
Southern hemisphere: the current deviates to the left.

Having said that, the rotation of the earth also causes the Coriolis effect, which deflects moving objects towards the right in the northern hemisphere and to the left in the southern hemisphere. If you examine a map of the general circulation of currents over the globe, then you will note that the main currents turn in a circle in each ocean with remarkable symmetry on either side of the equator. In the northern hemisphere, the currents turn towards the right, leaving the less dense water to the right, and the heavier water to the left. Look at the Gulf Stream, which is the current best known to schoolchildren, and which is warm: it moves up the American coast, curving in towards the NE (since the cold Labrador Current is to its right), and then is pushed across by the North Atlantic Drift, one of whose branches continues to turn right in order to come down the African coast. At this point the current is taken over by the trade winds, winds blowing regularly from east to west, and becomes the great North Equatorial, which closes the circle and carries a good number of round-the-world sailors towards America.

One of the characteristic features which is revealed by the charts is the existence of cold currents on the western edge of the continents. These currents are linked to the north-easterly trade winds in the northern hemisphere and to the south-easterly trade winds of the southern hemisphere between the 15th and 35th parallels, and which correspond to the *upwelling* of cold water from the deeper parts of the oceans. This is the cause of the low temperatures in some currents, such as the Canary Current, the Australian Current and the Humboldt Current which runs along the coast of Peru. The upwellings are good coastal fishing areas, since the water that flows up is rich in nutritious salts that support the growth of plant and animal life at the surface.

Each great ocean basin has its warm and cold currents, its trade winds, its whirlwinds and its areas of calm. There are only two exceptions: in the north of the Indian Ocean, where the currents change as a result of the monsoons, and further down where the Antarctic Ocean is subject to winds from the west which set up a general drift of the waters from west to east around the south pole, and certain branches of which, pushed to the left, return to the surface along the western coasts of various continents.

However, the pretty current charts from our childhoods scarcely resemble the images that are transmitted to us from space. The Gulf Stream is not, as has been said for a long time, a large river in the sea, but a complex network whose path can change, presenting meandering stretches, veins, knots and U-turns, within its general movement to the east.

And the more one looks at the ocean, the more one discovers aspects that had previously gone unnoticed. The latest controversy concerns the gigantic whirlpool which go back and forwards under the sea, which can be more or less stable and which can retain their basic identity for anything up to several months.

Heat is exchanged by contact between neighbouring masses of water, the process working in both directions. As they cross the globe, the currents have a considerable effect on the climates of the regions through which they pass. The warm current that forms the North Atlantic Drift takes the warmth of tropical regions to the north of Europe: life can be quite comfortable even in Spitzbergen. The cold Labrador Current that sticks to the North American coast like glue keeps the weather there appalling, while the other side of the continent, at the same latitude, the weather is much nicer. It is much warmer in the Channel than on the St Lawrence river, and much more

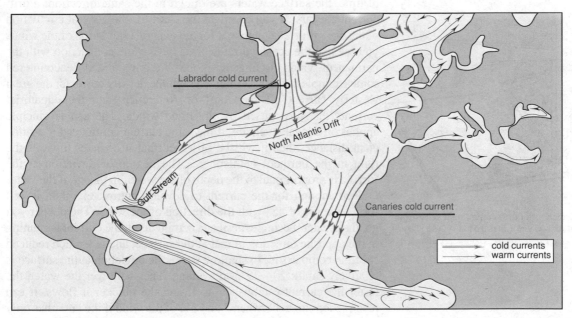

pleasant in Lisbon than in New York.

For transoceanic navigation, it is vital to know the currents. Even if this is not a problem in Europe, where we are on the receiving end of warm currents, the same is not true for Chile, where you have to cross the Humboldt Current to find good sailing conditions, and certainly not for the Florida coast, where the speed of the Gulf Stream can vary between 3 and 5kn, nor up on the NE coast of the USA where the Gulf Stream and the Labrador Current meet.

On boats entered in the round-Bermuda race, the thermometer is an essential piece of navigational equipment, which allows you to know exactly when you pass from one current to another.

Principal currents in the North Atlantic.

Local currents

We'd better define what we mean by local currents. The term can refer to currents that are a considerable distance across, and which can just as well be quite a way out to sea as near the coast. Nonetheless, it does cover currents that are a product of random factors, linked to drift, gradient and a variety of other circumstances. Offshore, it is hard to observe these currents, and we will deal with those that are to be found nearer the coast, and whose activity can cause considerable changes in the tidal stream.

Drift currents

When the wind blows in a certain direction for a considerable length of time, the surface waters are drawn in the same direction: a drift current appears. If you compare the chart for the general circulation of the ocean currents with that for the general circulation of the winds you see that the ocean currents often have some connection with the permanent winds circling the globe. We have already encountered some examples of this, connected with the density currents: the great westerly current off the coast of Antarctica, and the equatorial currents that are caused by the trade winds. The same principle applies on a local level, and if the same current continues for a sufficient distance, then it will be observed that it deviates towards the right in the northern hemisphere. The degree of deviation at the surface is proportional to the depth of the water. In theory, if the water is deep enough for the current to develop completely, then it will form an angle of 45° with the direction of the wind. The deeper you go, the greater the angle, until at a certain depth the current is running in the opposite direction to that at the surface, and at a much reduced speed in comparison. In shallow water, the deviation at the surface is relatively small: 20–25°, on average. The shallower the water, the faster the current establishes itself and the quicker it flows. It can reach speeds up to between 3 and 6% of the wind if the latter has only blown for a couple of days at force 4. From the point of view of coastal navigation, particularly in closed basins such as the Mediterranean, it is a good idea to bear in mind the weather conditions of the previous few days in order to be able to take account of currents that might persist a certain time after the wind has stopped.

Near the coast, a drift current can have quite particular effects. Depending on the direction of the wind that caused it, the current can cause an afflux or reflux of water towards the coast. This is why we talk about reflux and afflux winds, a notion that is intriguing from several points of view.

Winds from the shore are, naturally enough, reflux winds, since

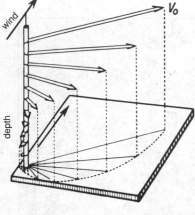

Directions of drift current relative to depth of the water (after Ekman). (*La Terre, l'eau, l'atmosphère*, Gauthier-Villars.)

they draw the water from the coast back out to sea. Thus, in the case of a reflux wind in front of a sheer cliff, the water level can drop in the region of the coast, and the surface waters that are thereby pulled back out to sea are then replaced by colder waters from the depths (upwelling). It is for this reason that along the Atlantic coast of Morocco which receives the trade winds from the NE in summer, for example, the waters are very cold. This is also the explanation behind the cold Canary Current, as well as the majority of the cold currents on the globe. Another more local example is when the mistral blows on the Côte d'Azur – bathers note that the water temperature drops rapidly; this is because it is no longer the same water.

Afflux winds cause the water to rise towards the coast. However, sea winds are not afflux winds because the currents that they create are then subject to the Coriolis force and deviate. Imagine that an observer in the northern hemisphere is out at sea facing towards the coast. The winds that come from his right are afflux winds, because the current that they create, which deviates to the right, heads for the coast. However, the winds that come from his left are reflux winds, because the current that was running along the coast, and which then deviates to the right, heads out to sea.

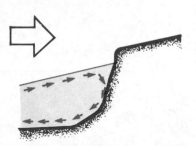

Afflux winds: the surface water is pushed towards the shore and the level rises.

Generally speaking, the rise in water level due to afflux winds is negligible, and simply translates itself into a tide that is either slightly higher when high (or slightly less low when low) than marked in the tide tables. However, the effects of afflux winds, when combined with shallow waters and a depression, can be violent and spectacular. The waves whipped up in these conditions are referred to as storm surges, or abnormal tides. This is often the case in the North Sea, where the sea is rarely deeper than 50m in the south, and is frequently disturbed. A zone of very low pressure can make the sea rise as it is pushed along, and the wave that is created can be maintained and accelerated by a violent wind, causing damage to both the coast and shipping. This is what happened in Holland in 1953, when a NE wind combined with a very deep depression at the time of the spring tides: for several tides in succession, the water remained well over its normal level, broke through the dikes and flooded large areas.

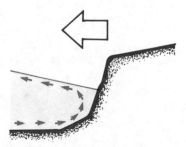

Reflux winds: the surface water is pushed away from the shore by the wind and then replaced by colder water rising from deeper down, leading to a drop in the level.

In order to protect against the risks of flooding, the Dutch have raised the dikes higher and barred the rivers in their deltas. In England, there is the Thames flood barrier, to protect London.

The water pushed up by an afflux wind cannot rise continuously. It must escape. When the water is sufficiently deep, the waters drop down in the reverse of the phenomenon we have just described. When the water is shallow, on the other hand, the water can only escape by the side: an example of what we refer to as a slope, or gradient, current.

Gradient currents

On the coast, as at sea, when there is a current, such as a drift current created by a wind that has been blowing for some time, then the sea ceases to be horizontal and a gradient forms that is linked with another current, which tends to restore equilibrium. This current naturally tends to follow the gradient, but like the others we have seen, it is also subject to the Coriolis force and deviates. Offshore, the current runs parallel to the contour lines, and therefore perpendicular to the gradient (in the same way that the wind at altitude is parallel to the isobars), whereas near the coast, friction against the ocean bed causes the current to turn in towards the land. A component running in the direction of the slope then appears, in the case of both afflux and reflux. In the case of an afflux to the coast, gradient currents more or less parallel to the shore can be observed. Such currents transport sand and sediment, and therefore have a considerable influence on the shape of the coastline.

Gradients created close to the shore are especially marked in seas where the flow of the tide is less large. In the Mediterranean, where the tide is so small as scarcely to be noticeable, the distortions in the water level can be as great as 2m. When the wind ceases to blow, then the current created by the gradient can remain very strong until the two levels even out.

Inequalities in atmospheric pressure can also create a gradient in the surface of the sea. In a depression (low atmospheric pressure), the level of the sea tends to rise, while it can tend to drop under an anticyclone (high pressure area). If these areas are next to one

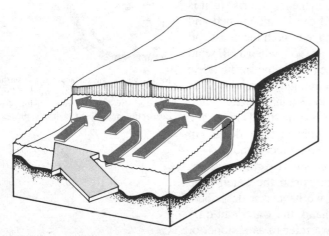

Currents created by an afflux wind.

depression

anticyclone

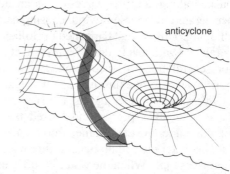

The surface of the sea hollows out under an anticyclone, and rises up under a depression; this then results in a gradient current.

another, then a gradient current is created running from the area under the depression towards the area under the anticyclone, with the current trying to restore equilibrium.

Another case is found in the Strait of Gibraltar. The level of the Atlantic is on average 30cm higher than the level of the Mediterranean (which receives very little fresh water and is subject to intense evaporation: the sun removes 150cm per year). A strong current forces the lighter waters of the Atlantic in between the Pillars of Hercules into the Mediterranean. There is also a deeper current that carries the heavier, saltier water of the Mediterranean out into the Atlantic. However, if we start talking about deep currents, we'll never stop, and we're not dealing with submarines, after all.

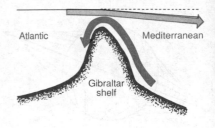

Tides and tidal currents

Animal respiration, fever, and the special intervention of Providence letting the boats get into le Havre are some of the many strange explanations that have been given for the tide over the centuries. For a long time, however, people have noted the connection between the tides and the phases of the moon. Pliny notes in his *Natural History* that the seas purge themselves at the full moon. However, we had to wait for Newton's theory of universal gravitation to begin to have some rather more precise ideas on the question.

The stars exert a gravitational attraction on one another and this influence depends on the mass of the star, and distance, which causes that influence to decrease. Although the stars have this influence, it scarcely affects us, because they are too far away. The sun, on the other hand, has a great influence, although it is the moon which has the most important influence on the tides (twice as great as that of the sun) because it is nearer. The effect of this attraction on the sea is spectacular, but the effect on the land is harder to see, although there is one, and these 'land tides' can be more than 20cm in amplitude (as is the case in Geneva, for example).

The tide and its rhythms

The moon exerts its greatest gravitational attraction when at its zenith over a given point; its influence is at its weakest when its orbit and the rotation of the earth place it on the other side of the world from that point. Curiously enough, the effect is the same: on the one side of the earth, the waters rise up because they are attracted by the moon, and on the other, they rise up because the moon is exerting less

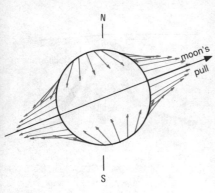

The force generating the tides (from *La Terre, l'eau, l'atmosphère*, Gauthier-Villars).

of an influence on them than on the rest of the earth's sphere. Thus, there is a high tide on opposite sides of the world at the same time, whereas there is a low tide for all the other places where the body can be seen on the horizon. This is the principle, at least, because the inertia of the water also has to be taken into account, and the sea is always late in comparison to what it is supposed to be doing at the time.

The action of the sun, although it is less strong, is nonetheless not to be discounted. It reinforces the action of the moon to a considerable degree. When the two bodies both fall on the same line and are in conjunction (both on the same side of the earth) or in opposition (on either side), then they are said to be in syzygy (from the Greek word, *suzugia*, meaning coming together or reunion), and their effects are combined. At this point, the attraction is at its greatest, and we are in the period of the great or spring tides. At the opposite extreme, when the sun and the moon are at right angles in relation to the earth (in quadrature), then their influences oppose each other and

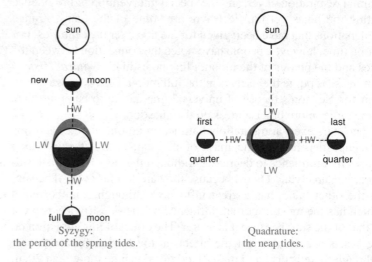

Syzygy:
the period of the spring tides.

Quadrature:
the neap tides.

it is the period of little tidal movement known as the neaps. At this point, the first or the last quarter of the moon can be seen in the sky.

Since the moon orbits the earth in about 29 days, there are two spring tides and two neap tides during the complete cycle. During the year, however, other factors complicate the question: the relative distances of the moon, the sun and the earth vary constantly, which explains why no two successive spring tides have the same heights. It will be easy enough to understand if you read our chapter on astronomical navigation in Part VII, 'Navigation' (and perhaps even if you don't read it), that the largest tides occur at the new moon and at the full moon, and that the even larger ones occur around the equinoxes, when sun and moon are over the equator. At the solstices, in June and December, on the contrary, the spring tides are at their lowest.

On the other hand, the lunar day lasts 24 hours and 50 minutes (we know that the moon gets later every day, which explains why the tides are later, too) and that during that period at any given point there should be two high tides and two low tides.

On our coasts, this is exactly what happens. The sea rises for 6 hours and 12 minutes during the flood or rising tide. At the end of the flood, the level remains about the same for a certain period of time – this is the high water slack (HW in the reference works). Then the sea goes down in level for about 6 hours and 12 minutes – this is the ebb tide, which continues until the low water slack (LW), and then the whole cycle starts again.

However, the same thing does not happen everywhere on the planet, and the observation of the tides in various places shows that there is quite an amazing diversity. Tides can be semi-diurnal (occurring twice a day) on our Atlantic coasts, with two high and two low tides per lunar day, but in the Gulf of Tonkin or the Gulf of Mexico, the tide is diurnal, with only one low and one high tide in a solar day. Some tides are mixed (sometimes diurnal, sometimes semi-diurnal),

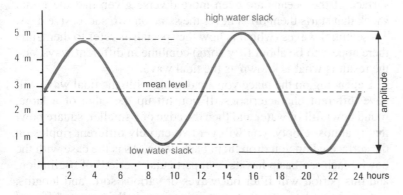

Semi-diurnal tides in the Atlantic.

or they have an uneven daily cycle, and then show inequalities of height between two low and two high tides. This type of tide pattern is to be found in Venice and on the Pacific coasts, for example. Finally, in certain places, the tidal range (the difference between the levels at high and low water) can vary considerably over comparatively short distances.

These particularities of the sea, local deformations of the initial tidal surge, are due to the shape of the coastline and the Coriolis effect (surprise surprise!).

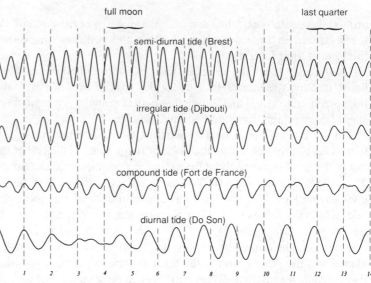

full moon   last quarter

semi-diurnal tide (Brest)

irregular tide (Djibouti)

compound tide (Fort de France)

diurnal tide (Do Son)

0   1   2   3   4   5   6   7   8   9   10   11   12   13   14

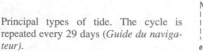

Principal types of tide. The cycle is repeated every 29 days (*Guide du navigateur*).

The tidal wave

If you raise the edge of a pan of water a bit and then let it drop back down again, this causes an oscillation and the creation of various sorts of wave. In the case of the tide, the waves that appear on the surface of the oceans are even more diverse given that the initial shock that starts them off is never the same on two successive days. These initial waves (which is how the specialists refer to them, and there appear to be about fifty sorts) combine in different ways, and the result is what is known as the tidal wave.

Depending on the place you are dealing with, the tidal wave will have different characteristics. If you lift up the edge of a large, round bowl full of water and then the edge of a smaller, square bowl that is almost empty, you will get two entirely different ripples on the surface when you drop them back down. As is the case with the bowls, each sea basin has its own particular 'period' of oscillation, and this period will filter out waves of various sorts and lengths, just in the same way that certain concert halls favour different frequencies, and therefore produce a different sound.

This is why there are tides that follow the rhythm of the moon, others that follow the rhythm imposed by the sun (in this case, the tides appear at the same time every day), and then a whole range of variants. There are also basins that have no particular rhythm, such as the Mediterranean, for example.

When the difference between the period of the oscillation peculiar to the basin and the period of the tidal wave is small, a phenomenon known as *resonance* is produced. When this happens, the wave has a tendency to take on the form of oscillation of the sea basin, and is considerably amplified as a result: this is the reason for the size of the tidal range in Mont-Saint-Michel bay, or in Fundy bay in Nova Scotia: 18.5m during the spring tides. The forms and dimensions of this bay mean that it has a natural period of oscillation that corresponds precisely to the semi-diurnal tidal wave.

In order to understand in what direction the tidal wave is propagated, account must be taken of the effect of the Coriolis force. As far as the tide is concerned, the force causes centres of immobility, of zero tidal range (where the level does not change throughout the tide), around which the tidal wave seems to be propagated by rotation. In some aspects, the surface of the sea takes on the appearance of an inclined plane pivoting around an axis. These centres are called *amphidromic* points (meaning: points away from which the tidal wave runs). Some amphidromic points are fairly easy to find, such as is the case with smaller sea basins: there are only three in the North Sea, for example. In the Atlantic, there seems to be one around the area of the Azores, to the east of which the tidal wave turns anticlockwise (which is explained by the fact that it is coming from the south).

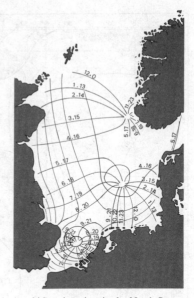

Amphidromic points in the North Sea.

The tidal wave, which can have a wave length of several hundred nautical miles, forms a 'progressive' wave. It is propagated at sea at high speed (400mph in the Atlantic). When it reaches our shores, it slows down and its amplitude increases, since the available volume is suddenly reduced (water cannot be compressed). After this, it spreads out and takes on different forms according to the shape of the sea bed and the coastline. Its propagation can be observed by linking up all the points along the same coast where high water occurs at the same time: this gives you the *co-tidal* lines. It can be observed that, in the Bay of Biscay, high water occurs at about the same time all along the coast, from Penmarch down to the Spanish border. However, the co-tidal lines are especially interesting to follow on a chart of the Channel: the tidal wave takes about 8 hours to go up it from one end to another, slowing considerably in the narrow passage between Cherbourg and the Isle of Wight. Even then, the chart cannot show up all the strange effects that are produced by peculiarities of the sea bed or the coastline, especially in the estuaries. At le Havre, for example, the high water slack lasts an abnormally long time (this is the 'providential' *tenue du plein*, or high water stand, that we referred to earlier), while at Southampton, there is a double high tide, although when the Seine had not been dredged, the tidal wave coming into the estuary caused a tidal bore that was known as the *mascaret*, which went up the Seine as far as Rouen.

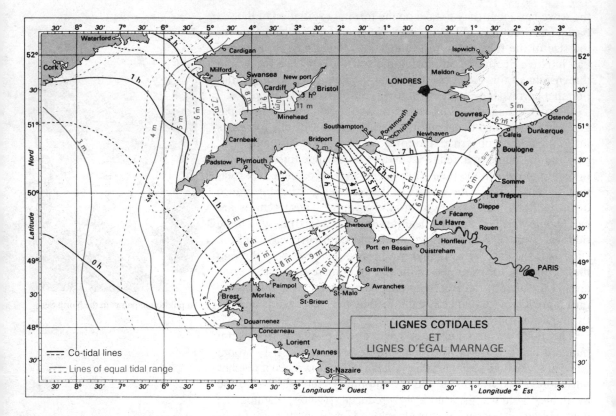

Co-tidal lines and lines of equal tidal range in the Channel (*Guide du navigateur*). Note the growth in amplitude in the bays and the 'theoretical' amphidromic point over the hills of Dorset. See also Admiralty Chart 5058.

Once again, the inertia of water is an important factor. It can quite easily be imagined that the sea does not respond instantly to the impulses of the generative tidal forces, and thus that its movement continues even when the tide has long since ceased to have an effect. A side question is that of the immense amount of energy that is dissipated by the tide against the continental shelf, and which could usefully be tamed as an energy source, according to some. We will leave these questions and turn to things that concern us more directly, namely the prediction of tides.

Tide predictions

The tide tables published by the various countries give a tidal curve each day for all the principal ports, the times of high and low water and the heights to a tenth of a metre. The precision of these can occasionally be somewhat marred by the weather conditions, but it is easy enough to see the general laws that underlie this mass of figures.

Well, yes and no. As surprising as it may seem, at the present time we still cannot predict the tides for the entire planet. As the tide table given out by the august Bureau des longitudes in France notes: 'The use of methods of prediction can be justified by their success, although there is no actual mechanical basis for them … The diversity of these methods furthermore shows that none of them is better than any of the others.' Certainly, the astronomical facts are well known: the movements of the sun, the earth and the moon all obey universal laws which also shape the flow of the tides. However, the different local situations make the whole thing much more complicated.

The general and complicated formulae that allow for the calculation of the tides are applicable for the high seas, although the figures

The English relate all the tides in the world to those at Dover, while the French relate them to those at Brest.

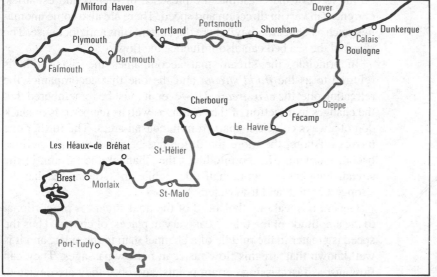

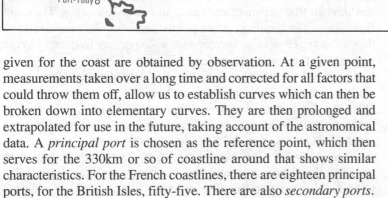

given for the coast are obtained by observation. At a given point, measurements taken over a long time and corrected for all factors that could throw them off, allow us to establish curves which can then be broken down into elementary curves. They are then prolonged and extrapolated for use in the future, taking account of the astronomical data. A *principal port* is chosen as the reference point, which then serves for the 330km or so of coastline that shows similar characteristics. For the French coastlines, there are eighteen principal ports, for the British Isles, fifty-five. There are also *secondary ports*.

This is the paradox of the tides: they obey general laws, and yet can only be calculated by observation.

The principal ports and their attached zones for the Channel.

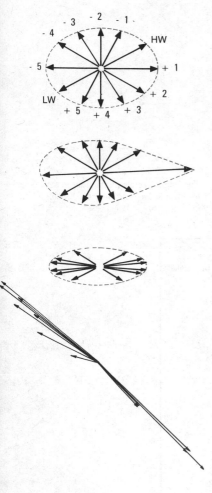

Circular and almost alternating streams (point F on the chart on page 897).

Tidal streams

The periodic streams linked to the phenomenon of the tides are particularly in evidence near the coasts. Further out at sea, they can spread out more easily. They rotate and do a complete rotation during a single tide cycle. In the northern hemisphere, they move in a clockwise direction, in the opposite direction to the southern hemisphere (once again, the Coriolis effect rears its ugly head). The speed varies over the course of the cycle, passing through two opposing maxima and two minima. The rotating current can be progressively transformed into an alternating one, depending on how near the coast is, which is to say that it propagates itself in a particular direction for half the period of the current, and then, after the slack (a short period when there is no current at all), runs in the other direction. Depending on the form of the coastline, the presence of islands and estuaries, currents can vary in direction and speed. There are also some anomalies, such as Quiberon bay, where the current runs anticlockwise. The shape of the sea bed can also influence the flow.

In principle, the stream that accompanies the rising tide is referred to as the *flood stream* and the one that accompanies the retreating one, the *ebb stream*. However, it must be remembered that the changes in direction of the current as well as the periods of slack do not always coincide, apart from in coastal areas. The further one moves offshore, the more the difference between the two periods becomes obvious. In the middle of the Channel, the turning of the stream happens at about half-tide, while the stream reaches its strongest at high and low water.

Generally speaking, the speed of the tidal stream is proportional to the amplitude of the tide. It can vary in places, of course. Thus the speed is greater in the middle of a channel than to the sides, and it is well known that streams flow faster in narrow passages. They can flow just as fast passing certain points, and once they are deviated, they are compressed and accelerated, which occurs frequently in the Channel, in the Portland races and off Lizard Head.

The speed of a stream can also vary according to depth, especially in estuaries. The speeds attained can be considerable in certain channels: 7kn in the Great Russell between Sark and Guernsey, 9kn in the Alderney races, 8kn in le Fromveur near Ushant. The streams are generally weaker on the Atlantic coast than in the Channel, from Audierne onwards (0.5–1kn on average). They are reinforced in river mouths (between 1 and 2.5kn) and between certain islands (les Glénans, Noirmoutier, Ré). The strongest current along this coast is a flood and ebb current in the entrance to Gulf of Morbihan, which can reach 6–8kn.

Tidal streams can seriously upset both navigation and calculations. They can create very difficult seas in certain circumstances. If the stream is fast and the water shallow, then the unevennesses of the sea bed can cause overfalls, pots or kettles, which are always unpleasant, whatever name you give them.

Wind against tide

When the stream runs against the wind, the waves formed by the latter are slowed and stifled between the two. They become shorter and taller, they can curl over excessively to the point of breaking. A stream running against the wind therefore leads to a choppy sea which can be very dangerous: a contrary current of 5kn can cause all the waves to break. In the Alderney race, where the tidal streams are very fast (between 6 and 10 kn), you should never sail when the wind is against the current. A fresh wind can then raise very steep, irregular waves, several metres in height, which are very dangerous for any sailing craft which tries to take advantage of a good following wind and finds itself in the middle of an unnavigable sea. It is also a good idea to give a wide berth to headlands when the wind is against the tide.

When wind and stream run in the same direction, then the waves stretch out and become more gentle, and you do not have to worry about them breaking.

The waves break when the stream is running against the wind.

Making the best use of the tide

The current is not always an adversary, and can even help you. The same points and races that would have been impassable two hours before can easily be passed at slack or when the tide turns.

Rather than getting worn out struggling against them, it is a good idea to make them work for you, and to use these veritable moving pavements whenever they are going in the right direction. Do a little preparation and find out where the back eddies are near the points, in the depths of bays and along estuary coasts. Playing with the streams and the back eddies can be both fascinating or frustrating, depending on whether you know the rules of the game or not.

Some information on the speed and the direction of the streams can be found on the sea charts, and other documents give information whose precision would not disgrace a railway timetable (the French *Instructions nautiques C2* gives the following information for Erquy en Manche: 'At 0200 Saint-Malo, a counter-current comes out of the port'.) However, it should be borne in mind that even though the

LITTLEHAMPTON 10-3-9
W. Sussex

CHARTS
Admiralty 1991, 1652; Stanford 9; Imray C9; OS 197
TIDES
+0015 Dover; ML 2·8; Zone 0 (GMT).

Standard Port SHOREHAM (→)

Times				Height (metres)			
HW		LW		MHWS	MHWN	MLWN	MLWS
0500	1000	0000	0600	6·3	4·9	2·0	0·6
1700	2200	1200	1800				

Differences LITTLEHAMPTON (ENT)
+0010　0000 −0005 −0010 −0·4　−0·4　−0·2　−0·2
LITTLEHAMPTON (NORFOLK WHARF)
+0015 +0005　0000 +0045 −0·7　−0·7　−0·3　+0·2
PAGHAM
+0015　0000 −0015 −0025 −0·7　−0·5　−0·1　−0·1
BOGNOR REGIS
+0010 −0005 −0005 −0020 −0·6　−0·5　−0·2　−0·1

NOTE: Tidal heights inside harbour are affected by flow down River Arun. Tide seldom falls lower than 0·7m above datum.

SHELTER
Good. SE winds cause a certain swell up the harbour; SW winds cause roughness on the bar. Entrance dangerous with strong SE winds.
NAVIGATION
Waypoint 50°47'·50N 00°32'·20W, 166°/346° from/to front Ldg Lt, 0·60M. Bar ½ M offshore. Harbour available from HW−4 to HW+3 for boats with about 2m draught. The ebb stream runs so fast at springs that yachts may have difficulty entering. When Pilot boat with P at the bow displays a RW flag by day or W over R lights at night, all boats keep clear of entrance. Speed limit 6½ kn. Depth over the bar is 0·6m less than depth shown on tide gauges. On departure check tide gauge at East Pier to calculate depth on bar.

LIGHTS AND MARKS
Leading marks for entrance are lighthouse at inshore end of E breakwater and the black steel column for the light at the outer end of E breakwater; Ldg Lts 346°.
Swing bridge FI R Lt—Open
　　　　　　FI R Lt—Closed　　from high mast to port.
The central retractable section of the bridge has 2 FR (vert) to port at each end and 2 FG (vert) to stbd at each end. Opening section is 22m wide. Bridge retracted on request provided notice given before 1630 previous day.
RADIO TELEPHONE
Marinas Ch 80 M (office hours).
TELEPHONE (0903)
Hr Mr 721215/6; MRSC Lee-on-Solent 552100;
☎ (0703) 827350; Marinecall 0898 500 456; Police 716161;
Dr 714113.
FACILITIES
EC Wednesday Littlehampton Marina (120+30 visitors) ☎ 713553, Slip, BH (16 ton), CH, P, D, V, R, Bar, FW, AC, Sh, ME; **Ship and Anchor Marina** (182, some visitors) ☎ Yapton 551262, Slip, FW, C (6 ton), ME, Sh, CH, V, R, Bar (Access HW∓4); **Arun YC** (90+10 visitors) ☎ 714533, Slip, AC, FW, L, M, Bar (Access HW∓3); **E side of Harbour** M, C, FW; **Littlehampton Sailing and Motor Club** ☎ 715859, M, FW, Bar; **Wm Osbornes** ☎ 713996, BY; **Delta Yachts** ☎ 717369, BY; **Arrow Marine** ☎ 721686, FW, ME, El, Sh, P, D; **County Wharf** FW, C (5 ton); **Hillyards** ☎ 713327, M, FW, ME, Sh (Wood), C;
Town P, D, V, R, Bar. ✉; ⊚; ≈; ✈ (Shoreham).

Harbour, coastal and tidal information extract from *Macmillan & Silk Cut Nautical Almanac*, based on British Admiralty information.

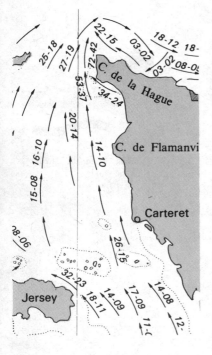

Offshore streams, and back eddies behind headlands (*Atlas des courants de marée*, No 553).

information given by these tables is precise, they cannot take account of the particular conditions created by the weather, and especially the wind. The stream that is observed is rarely identical to the one in the chart. You must therefore learn to observe and deduce the presence and strength of a current. For example, in the North Sea, the *Pilot Book* recommends that you observe the current to know at what stage the tide is. Points of reference are plentiful: lighter streaks on the surface and the movement of weed on the bottom, the water moving past a buoy, the direction in which lobster-pot markers are leaning, differences in the chop, foam and so on. The current is one of the least obvious aspects of the sea, and yet, for the sailor, it is one of the most important elements to be taken into consideration, providing a rhythm to all aspects of sea life and navigation.

Waves and swell

The streams and the tides are constant – they are the secret life of the sea – but there is also a more superficial element, which is shaped by the wind.

When the wind blows on a calm sea, the friction of the air creates small ripples on the surface of the water. These can last only a short time, but if the wind persists, then undulations and wavelets form, followed by waves, which flow across the surface of the water in the direction of the wind.

On a smaller and rather less brutal scale, the wind can have the same effect on the sea as a stone thrown into a puddle: it gives rise to trains of waves. Note that it is the waves that are moving and not the water itself. The particles stay in the same place, and complete a sort of circular movement as each wave passes. This movement can best be illustrated by looking at a bottle floating in the waves. When the wave reaches the bottle, it goes up and a little forwards, then once the crest has passed, it comes back down again and moves a little backwards, returning to its original position. The same sort of motion can be felt on board a boat which is moving in the same direction as the waves, when these are sufficiently large: the boat accelerates as the wave comes up, and then seems to be slowed down as it passes.

Thus the movement of the waves is not purely horizontal as is commonly imagined.

Characteristics of the waves

A wave can be defined by its dimensions: its height, which is the distance between the crest and the bottom of the hollow; its length, which is the distance between two hollows or two crests (waves do actually have wave lengths in the strict sense of the term). The relation between height and length is characterised by the steepness or slope. A wave is always much longer than it is tall, and the slope becomes critical when the ratio of height to length reaches $1:7$. If the height increases, then the wave breaks, at which point there really is horizontal movement of the water.

A wave is also defined by the depth to which its movement reaches. In theory, this movement should be detectable down to a depth equal to half the wave length, but in practice, the movement is very much reduced even a fifth of the wave length down.

The wave also moves (only the form, though, remember!), and is part of a train, with its own rhythm, characterised by a period, which is the time between the two crests passing the same point, and by its speed, which is the distance covered by a wave in a given time.

At sea, there is a direct relation between the length and the characteristics of the waves. This length (L) is equal to the product of the period (T) and the speed (C): $L = TC$, a formula which does not require any information about the depth of the water or the amplitude of the waves, and which can also be written as:

$$C = \frac{L}{T} \text{ or } T = \frac{L}{C}$$

Length L
Short waves: 0–100m.
Medium waves: 100–200m.
Long waves: 200m and greater.

Contrary to appearances, the bottle comes back to its point of departure after having described a circle.

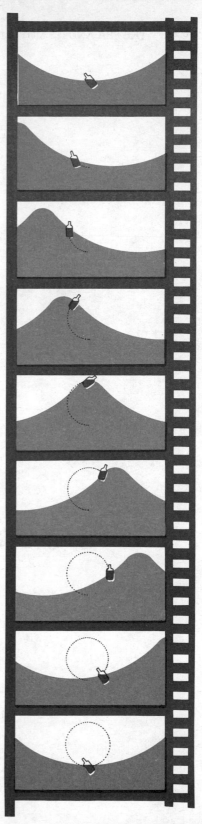

Nearer land on the other hand, the influence of the sea bed becomes much more important. When the depth of the water is less than half the wave length, then the wave slows. The movement of the particles is no longer circular, and describes an ellipse, which gradually becomes a horizontal movement in the shallowest part of the water. The speed only depends on the depth at the point in question: at a given point, all swell is being propagated at the same speed, and the shallower the water, the less the speed. The length also diminishes, and the only remaining constant is the period. We shall see what causes the unfurling of waves closer to the shore.

The sea conditions

The term 'sea conditions' covers any system of waves that forms in a given place under the action of a particular wind.

Suppose that the wind begins to blow on a calm sea at the point where we are. The size of the waves will then depend on three factors:
– the strength of the wind;
– how long it blows for;
– the fetch, which is the distance over which it acts without meeting any obstacle, or without changing direction.

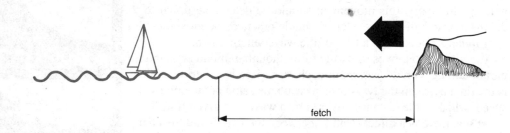

fetch

The waves that are formed begin to get higher. When they are formed, they have a strong camber, because their speed is still not great in relation to the speed of the wind. If the wind persists, then they get longer and longer, and the height, length, period and speed all increase progressively until they reach a maximum which varies according to the strength of the wind. If the wind continues to blow at the same strength for a number of days, then the characteristics of the waves created will not change.

If the fetch is too short, on the other hand, then the waves will not be able to attain their optimal shape. When the first waves

created at the point where the wind starts to blow reach the end of the fetch (the coast for example), then an equilibrium is established. Here again, the time for which the wind continues to blow is no longer an issue, as long as it remains at the same strength. It is easy to see that the shorter the fetch, the less chance the waves have to

A good example of sea conditions off les Glénans, during the storm of 6 July 1969. The fetch is only about 500m, but the wind reaches force 10.

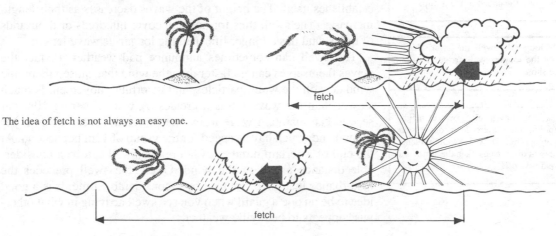

The idea of fetch is not always an easy one.

increase in size. Sailing in a small closed sea is therefore not necessarily more agreeable than sailing out to sea: since the waves cannot stretch out, they are shorter and more abrupt, and the sea is therefore a lot choppier.

Note that the wind is never perfectly regular in either force or direction, so that the sea never appears completely uniform: there are always shorter waves and waves cutting across. When the wind changes direction, then the first wave system only disappears slowly, while another one appears. In the meantime, the two combine, and waves of different generations meet and blend into each other. The sea takes on a rather chaotic appearance and can frequently splash onto the deck of the boat. The situation can become very tricky, as is exemplified by the dreadful sea conditions encountered by the competitors in the 1979 Fastnet race at the entry to the Bristol Channel.

Swell

Sometimes a slower, more langorous pulsation is propagated in a very different direction from that of the present wind, and which seems to have a life of its own: this is the swell.

Waves become swell from the moment that they leave the area where the wind that created them was blowing, or, to put it more technically, when they have left their generating basin. For example, created by a wind far out in the North Atlantic, which has then stopped blowing or changed direction, these waves have stored up a considerable amount of energy (something in the order of millions of horsepower). They therefore only disappear very slowly. The shortest waves disappear first and a regular movement establishes itself. The height of the waves decreases as their length increases. The swell thus formed can cover hundreds or thousands of miles, and has a longer life span the longer its wave length.

The swell can sometimes announce bad weather. In fact the waves themselves can go faster than the wind that caused them: the wind acts on the water particles, and its orbital movement is much slower than the wave trains it creates. A wind covering 10m per second can maintain wave trains that move at speeds of 24m per second and which have a speed for the group of 12m per second. At the end of a certain number of hours, the swell can be a considerable distance ahead of the wind. Often, the swell precedes the disturbance that gave rise to it by a considerable time. It is a good idea to be on one's guard when you see swell arriving in what otherwise appears to be idyllic weather.

Waves are propagated in 'packets' or groups which transport energy and whose speed offshore corresponds to half of that for each individual wave: this gives the speed of the group.

The longer the swell, the faster. This is why the longer swell arrives first on the shore.

If a long, low swell grows in height rapidly, then there is a depression approaching. If the swell remains weak or diminishes, then the storm is a good way off.

Large waves

The description of sea conditions in the Beaufort scale is imprecise about the height of waves, because this depends not only on the wind at that moment, but also on how long it lasts and on its fetch. In order to give some impression, take a wind of about 20–25kn (force 5–6), which stirs up large, crested waves of between 1.5 and 3.5m in height according to how long the wind lasts. A wind of force 8 creates waves of medium height according to the Beaufort scale. These medium heights can be about 4m after 2 hours, 6m after 4 hours and then grow slowly towards 7m. What the weather forecasts refer to as a heavy sea is a height of between 6 and 9m on the open water for the largest waves.

In any event, from the deck of a small boat, it is very difficult to estimate the real height of the waves, because of the angle from which one sees the crest when in a hollow and because of the absence of a horizon. It is all too easy to believe that they are as high as the mast. Generally speaking, it is conventional only to give an indication of the height of the waves, the average being termed the 'significant height'.

Not all the waves that follow on from one another have the same height, because they are part of wave trains of variable speed and period, which can either join together or interfere with one another. Small waves are caught and overtaken by larger ones, which do not always have the same amplitude and period even then. This is why the sea conditions are constantly changing. It is by proceeding from these observations over a period of time that we note that, for each sea of a certain height, there are always waves much taller than average.

Such is the case in the North Atlantic, offshore, where the waves are generally between 3 and 5m in height in summer, and between 5 and 7m in winter. However, certain waves can reach heights over 12m in bad weather with a distance between crests of 200–500m, if not more.

Waves over 18m in height are rare, but it can happen that some waves are really of exceptional height and come roaring out of a gust of wind, or even when the wind is dying down. Although short-lived, some waves can reach heights of 30m – the height of a 10-storey house – and disappear as quickly as they are formed. They are fortunately very rare, and have not been much observed up until present. They are the result of various waves all pursuing their own routes coming together and meeting. Adlard Coles refers to them as monsters, noting that a wave does not actually have to reach such a height to merit the title.

Wave height (international scale)

Code	Sea	Height (in metres)
0	Calm	0
1	Rippled	0–0.2
2	Good	0.2–0.5
3	Slightly formed	0.5–1.25
4	Formed	1.25–2.50
5	Rough	2.5–4
6	Very rough	4–6
7	Heavy	6–9
8	Very heavy	9–14
9	Huge	14 +

Note: this is not the Beaufort scale.

Effect of a 3kn counter-current on a wave:
– its length decreases from 60 to 33m;
– its speed decreases from 18 to 14kn;
– its height increases from 1.2 to 1.8m.
The wave takes on more of a camber.

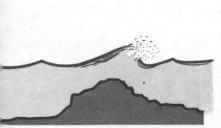

Waves break on a shallow.

The sea and obstacles

Sea conditions, whether there is a swell or not, can vary considerably according to whether there are any obstacles in the way.

First of all, let us remember that the sea can find obstacles within itself: swells that cut across one another, wind against the current, well before there is any question of any land mass in the way, and that these can disturb both waves and swell.

The sea conditions can also change through the influence of the shape of the sea bed. At certain points, where the bottom rises up rapidly, the waves are suddenly slowed, as with a counter-current, they increase in height, and break and unfurl. These are the breakers that are so characteristic of shallows, which are well known for the difficult sea conditions that tend to be found there.

In bad weather, the sea can also be very rough in front of the lines of shallow areas running parallel to the coast. Examples of this can be found in the North Sea and Dover Strait.

Swell waves can also be distorted when they reach an island or a rock. In such situations, refraction or diffraction can occur, something which shows up very clearly on aerial photographs, and which is entirely analogous to the effect of obstacles on light or sound waves. The swell passes on either side of the island and reforms behind it. The interference of the two trains of swell that are thereby created can give quite a difficult sea, even close to the shore.

The end of a quay with vertical walls can create diffraction in the swell, which then pivots sharply, troubling the waters near the pier-head. However, the diffraction is also accompanied by a dispersal of energy. The same is true behind a headland: if the headland is sheer, then the swell pivots against its end as against a pierhead, while if the headland is prolonged by submerged or partly submerged rocks, then the swell breaks and the shelter is good. If the sea bed slopes gently away around the headland, then there will be no shelter.

Along the coast, where the sea bed rises sharply, the waves all break in the same place and constitute what is known as a bar (as on the west coast of Africa, for example). It can also be very much localised, such as in front of an estuary, where the accumulation of sediment forms a barrier over which the waves cannot pass without breaking (examples are the bars at the mouths of the Etel and Adour rivers).

A bar forms where the sea bed rises sharply.

Near the coast, the influence of the sea bed on the movement of the waves is translated into a refraction of the swell: that is to say a change in direction rather like that found when light passes through a denser medium. When the swell strikes at an oblique angle, it gradually pivots, and the crests become more or less parallel to the level lines, and therefore parallel to the shore.

In order to study their direction, lines are traced that run perpendicular to the crests of the waves. These are referred to as swell orthogonals, and are generally constructed in laboratory tanks or from aerial photographs.

Orthogonals are very close together around the points, which indicates a concentration of energy in these areas, while on the other hand they are much further apart in the back of bays where the swell dies down. They also allow us to understand the effect of the contours of the sea bed on the sea. When the swell reaches the deeper part of an undersea valley, then it diverges, and the area is calmer around the edge. On the other hand, there is a concentration above sea ridges nearer the coasts: never anchor there, and don't construct any jetties or barriers (although this has been done for

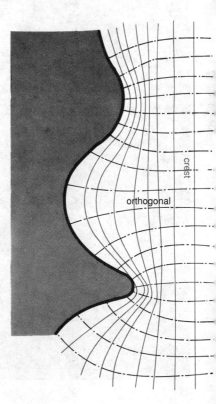

crest

orthogonal

In a bay, even one opening out to sea, the crests of the swell gradually space out (the orthogonals fan out), and the sea becomes calmer. Around a point, the swell tends to be concentrated (the orthogonals are closer together), and so the sea is rougher.

want of prior thought).

On the other hand, the energy of the waves is dissipated over the shallows, which can therefore form a useful protective barrier. To summarise, the careful study of the profile of the sea bed on a chart should give you a good idea what the conditions are likely to be along a given coastline, which is useful if you are looking for places to moor a camping boat which does not draw much water or a coastal cruiser, so as to spend the night quietly.

The last obstacle that the sea can throw up is the shore. Sometimes this can take the form of a vertical wall (sheer coast, or the edge of a quay). When the waves strike it, they reflect and then head back in the opposite direction to crash into the others, creating an area of rather confused wave movements. Things are quite different when they reach shallows after a gentle slope. The movement of the water particles becomes elliptical and then flattens out more and more. Slowed by the sea bed, the waves becomes taller, and then at the last moment it can happen that the leading trough enters shallower water than the crest behind it, slows down and is overtaken by the crest, which then collapses spectacularly.

The longest waves, and therefore the oldest, sense the bottom very quickly, and can grow enormously before reaching the shore. It is the long swell which gives the strongest undertow. On calm days, this swell appears in all its splendour: the sea is smooth and

The swell orthogonals diverge over a sea valley, here at Cap-Breton (on the Landes coast). Although it is open to the sea, this place is a good anchorage.

The swell orthogonals converge on an undersea ridge – here at Long Beach, California. The dike situated at the point of convergence was simply destroyed by the sea, although the swell was much more gentle around that point.

←Aerial photograph of the lagoon at Penfret (Glénan islands) in an east wind.

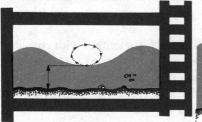

When the wave feels the bottom, then the movement of the water molecules becomes elliptical.

If the slope is steep, then the waves hollow out and break strongly.

If the slope is gentle, then the wave energy is gradually dissipated.

covered by huge, regular undulations, which can be very tall, but which are also very long, and often separated by several hundred metres. When they reach the coast at an angle, then they create a current that runs parallel to the coast, and the more cambered the swell, the more vicious that current can be. Rip currents are created in this way. All these currents carry sediment, depositing it in a saw-tooth pattern, and thereby play an essential role in reshaping the coastline.

So end the waves, sometimes quietly, sometimes with considerable drama. On very gentle slopes, waves can travel for a long time on the point of breaking. It is then that one can share that moment of arrival, by means of a surfboard, balanced on the crest of a wave, coming crashing onto the sand in a shower of spray.

PART VII

Navigation

The term 'navigation', taken in its most limited sense, covers the body of techniques which enable us to find out where we are at sea, to choose the best route, and to be able to be sure at any given moment whether we are following this route or not.

Such a definition should not lead you to believe that navigation is something that only affects those who set sail on the high seas; in fact, we are 'navigating' the minute we turn round to look back at the shore and see how far we've come … Navigational techniques are rarely used aboard a simple sailing dinghy – except perhaps in a few exceptional cases, where it might be useful to know which is the best tack between one buoy and the next. However, if you are out for the day, or going sea-fishing, there is a basic minimum of information that you must know: how to use landmarks along the coast, take account of tides and eddies, how to use a sea chart and a compass. However, even for coastal cruising, this is no longer enough: you must be able to use more complex instruments and methods, in order to plot your position, to see which course to follow, and – if necessary – to take a fix. Such tasks require a substantial grasp of navigation; indeed, when cruising, there is no other way to go, even if one might use other sources and points of reference, such as radio signals and the stars. We will consider such parts of this vast subject that are especially relevant to coastal cruising, trying to put over all the information that might be necessary to a small cruiser.

We have borne two main aims in mind. The first was to emphasise the huge gap between theory and practice in the matter of navigation, especially when one is navigating from the cabin of a small boat. We have therefore always tried to show the easiest way to carry out any particular task, with advice on how to eliminate most errors. If from time to time we have proposed more elaborate methods, then it will become apparent that these are only really of any use in good weather.

Our second main concern has been to cut back to a bare minimum on the use of theoretical material and to illustrate (or even occasionally replace) theory by concrete examples. It seems to us that navigational techniques in themselves are only part of a certain way of thinking about and observing the sea, a sort of sixth sense which is perhaps the most important thing to acquire. As you work through the examples that we give here (some of them are pretty difficult, but no worse than you can expect to meet in real life), it will become apparent that navigation is an art, requiring rigour and intuition, caution and the courage of one's convictions, humility and stubbornness. It will further become apparent why for some it is an abiding obsession, a sort of total discipline, combining the beauties of mathematics with a feel for sea conditions.

CHAPTER 1

Reference points and documents

Nobody is going to embark on a voyage around the world with nothing but a pipe and a penknife for luggage: naturally enough, a certain amount of basic information is necessary. First of all, one must be able to use and recognise the various sorts of reference points available: buoys and beacons, lights, sound signals, radio signals and the stars. Thanks to them, it is quite simple to measure and maintain one's current distance from land. Another distance must also be known: that of the keel from the sea bed. To do this, it is necessary to be able to calculate the tides in order to be able to say how deep the water will be in a given place and at a given time; one should also know about those currents that are associated with, and affected by the ebb and flow of the sea.

Apart from the systems of beacons, whose rules can be learned by heart with little difficulty, none of the different reference points can be used without the various documents which describe both them and their position. The most important references are the *Macmillan & Silk Cut Nautical Almanac*, the *Macmillan & Silk Cut Yachtsman's Handbook*, *Reed's Nautical Almanac*, the *Cruising Association Handbook*, Admiralty Pilots, and the Admiralty *List of Lights and Fog Signals*, and *List of Radio Signals*.

In this chapter we will go through the different land and sea marks, as well as the various reference works, along with the documents and charts that should be used in conjunction with them. This will give an overview of an otherwise rather difficult subject, and will give the reader a starting point. If a more complete guide is required, the reader is directed to Reed's or Macmillan's almanacs (the French equivalent is the SHOM's *Guide du navigateur)* which contains all the information that one could wish to have at one's disposal, and much more than one would ever need or, indeed, know what to do with.

The first and very important thing to bear in mind is the fact that the world described by these documents changes from day to day. *Even the most official documents are unusable, and should therefore not be used under any circumstances, unless they have been rigorously kept up to date* . We shall therefore describe how this is to be done for each of the works the navigator will be required to use. In the first place, it would, however, perhaps be of some use to give the reader an idea of the system set up to provide all this information. Below there follows a summary of the principal types and sources of this information.

Information for navigators

According to the *Guide du navigateur* (the French equivalent of the *Channel Pilot,* the *Macmillan Almanac* or *Reed's*), navigational information can take four forms depending on the degree of urgency involved.

• *Basic information* is to be found in the relevant documents and amendments and the corrections to these published and distributed in fascicule form.

• *'Normal' information* is classed as useful but non-urgent, and not pertaining to matters that would place the safety of the crew in question. It is published every week in small pamphlets entitled *Notices to Mariners*, or, for cruising in France, *Groupes hebdomadaires d'avis aux navigateurs* (*Weekly Update for Navigators*). These pamphlets contain, along with a variety of other information, the latest changes and corrections made to the basic documents, and summary tables of corrections and notices.

• *'Rapid' information* includes important pieces of information, which could affect the safety of the navigator in the short or medium term. In France bulletins known by the acronym DIFRAP can be consulted in any harbourmaster's office, as well as in the local press.

• *Urgent information* covers events that have just occurred and which could put the navigator at considerable and immediate risk: light gone out, buoy disappeared, drifting wreck, etc. This is broadcast by radio in the form of *urgent information for navigators* at fixed times by the coastal stations (le Conquêt, Niton, etc). Details of the bulletins are also posted in all harbourmasters' offices, sometimes in the yacht club and generally in the local newspapers, magazines and local guides.

This system should, in principle, save the navigator from any nasty surprises. However, despite the remarkable work that it does (and with very limited resources, it has to be said), the editors of the

Information for navigators in the UK

Information for navigators in this country is disseminated in much the same way as it is in France. The Admiralty publishes *Notices to Mariners*, which can be consulted in the Mercantile Marine Offices, in customs offices, in the ports and at coastguard stations. Navigational warnings are broadcast by the coastal radio stations, and the list of these stations can be found in Reed's or Macmillan's nautical almanacs.

How to get up to date at the start of the season

It is rare for anyone to keep meticulously up to date with the various changes and notices pertaining to navigation that are published over the winter. However, it is perfectly possible to find out everything that one needs to know without too much difficulty if one takes the following steps:
 • Most publishers of reference works produce regular supplements to update their information. The major almanacs are in any case annual.
 • The Admiralty *Notices to Mariners* are published weekly and give essential updates to Admiralty charts. They are available from Admiralty Chart agents or can be consulted at harbourmasters offices. There is a special *Small Craft Edition of Notices to Mariners* published periodically, which summarises the most relevant information for pleasure sailors.

---

various references would bow to the knowledge and experience of every navigator as to whether they choose to place any confidence in a given piece of information. Furthermore, the organisations do not hesitate to call upon the co-operation of all navigators in order to correct any errors or omissions, and no individual should ever neglect to do so. Addresses will be found in the publications concerned.

The buoyage system

Our ancestors were blessed with good eyes and keen noses. The only reference points available to them were those that lay along the coast itself. It may well have been that the sighting of a particular monument, such as a tumulus, a menhir, an ancient temple, a watchtower, or even a particular rock or clump of trees might have been all that they needed to guide them safely home to their village.

Nowadays, landmarks, that is to say fixed visible points along the coast, are equally precious to us. Simply take into account the fact that the landscape is changing a little faster than before. Steeples, water towers, or factory chimneys, which once were useful guides to navigation, can be hidden from view by trees, or, more frequently, the apparently unstoppable progress of civilisation. Now, only official landmarks provide a reliable guide: whitewashed rocks, lighthouses, all noted in the relevant publications. These are very carefully maintained and kept safe from the unwelcome attention of developers.

On this stretch of coast, there is no lack of landmarks. Next year there will be even more of them.

See fold-out section 5 at the end of the book.

Landmarks are not part of the system of beacons per se. Instead, the term 'beacon' is a blanket term covering all the markers put in place by Trinity House (in France, the Service des phares et balises) for the use of navigators. Those items that come under the general heading of beacons are the buoys, stone towers and genuine beacons, which are perches set into the rock, or fixed to the sea bed.

How to recognise a mark

Every buoy and mark has a precise purpose, indicated by their shape, colour, topmark, and, last but not least, the light on top.

The shape (cone, cylinder, sphere, spar, pillar) is not sufficient to identify the marker alone. There is no strict code, and a good number of the small towers predate such rules as exist.

The colour (red, green, black, yellow) is much more important. A rust-red colour simply means that the marker is badly maintained, but this is rare in Europe.

The topmark (cone, cylinder, sphere, cross) should settle any doubts that still remain, because it gives precise indications which complement those given by the colour.

In 1976, there were about thirty beacon systems in operation throughout the world, but since 1982, a single system has been established as standard. In this, there are two main types of marks: *cardinal* and *lateral,* and then three other types.

Lateral marks

Lateral markers are to be found mainly in channels and at the entry to ports. They are laid out so as to help a navigator *entering* harbour.

When leaving a port, the directions must be read in the oppposite direction. The principle is as follows:

– *any green marker, topped with a conical topmark, point upwards and a green light, must be left to starboard;*
– *any red marker with a cylindrical or can-shaped topmark and a red light must be left to port.*

These markers are usually numbered. The numbering usually starts from out to sea coming in. The red markers have even numbers; and the green markers, uneven numbers.

All of this is fairly easy to remember. However, if your memory is a bit shaky, the following mnemonic may help:

If there is no *red port left*, throw the *green* bottle *starboard right* away.

It is also helpful to bear in mind that the colour of the lights corresponds to the lights on the boat: red to port, green to starboard.

In certain coastal rivers, the markers are covered in a reflective paint, which shows up nicely when hit by a searchlight. Many buoys and turrets are also equipped with a radar reflector.

The world is divided into two zones, each following different conventions for the colouring of lateral marks. France and the UK fall into area A, whose system is discussed here. In area B, which comprises the Americas, Japan, Korea and the Philippines, the colours are reversed. There are also modified lateral markers. These are used in the case of a channel that forks, and indicate the better route to follow. These markers look almost exactly like ordinary ones, but have a horizontal bar in the middle – green on a red marker, red on a green one. Consequently, a green marker with a red band should be to starboard normally, but should be to port if you are following the other channel.

Cardinal marks

Cardinal marks – so named because they refer to the cardinal points – are used to mark dangerous spots along the coast, as well as some dangerous areas at sea. The principle is as follows: *a cardinal marker defines its own position in relation to the blackspot, and therefore indicates where it is safe to navigate. A southern cardinal marker is positioned to the south of the danger area, and you must therefore keep to the south of it.*

All these markers are painted yellow and black, topped by a topmark consisting of two black cones, one on top of the other, along with a white light. The different markers are distinguished by the distribution of colours and topmarks.

The positioning of the north and south markers appears logical, while west and east markers are shaped so that a W or an E can be made out along their left-hand side.

It is easy to see the layout of the colours on the different markers if you remember that black corresponds to the point and yellow to the base of the cones.

It should further be noted that a cardinal marker covers a very specific area. The presence of a west marker, for example, means that the route is clear in the sector NW-SW, but not all the way round between north and south. Furthermore, just because you have identified a cardinal marker correctly does not mean that you can get away without looking at the map.

See fold-out section 5 at the end of the book.

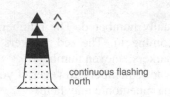

continuous flashing
north

sequences of 9 flashes
9 o'clock west

like a W = west

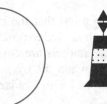

like an E = east

sequences of 3 flashes
3 o'clock east

sequences of 6 short flashes and 1 long
6 o'clock south

yellow

red

How to remember it all.

Isolated danger marks.

Safe water marks.

Other markers

Safe water marks. These markers do not indicate the quality of the water, but rather whether there is any danger in the immediate vicinity. They are generally to be found at the entry to channels (for example, the buoy SN 1, which is the first marker for the channel leading into the port of Saint-Nazaire).

The markers are painted in vertical red and white stripes, sometimes topped with a red sphere (the sphere always indicates that the buoy can be passed on either side).

If the buoys are marked with a light, then this is white and isophase (occulting).

Isolated danger marks. These markers indicate danger in a limited area (they are positioned directly above it). They are painted black with large red horizontal bands, carrying a characteristic topmark: two black spheres one on top of the other. If they have a light, then it is white and gives patterns of two flashes.

Special marks. These mark areas set aside for particular purposes: exercises, cables etc. They are yellow, with a yellow, X-shaped topmark, and sometimes a yellow light.

Lights and signals

Under the heading of lights come lighthouses, light-vessels, beacons and buoys. At night, these lights provide a very simple and clear indication of the coastline, the position of channels and so on. In fact, it is often easier to land by night than by day.

The positions and characteristics of the various lights are defined in the *List of Lights*. On maps, they are shown as magenta-coloured teardrop marks, and are given a brief description.

Lights are distinguished by their colour, type, the rhythm of the flashes and the time between them.

See fold-out section 6 at the end of the book.

Colour. Green, red or white for ordinary beacons. Yellow for special markers, or even bluish-white or violet in some cases.

Type. The principal sorts are: fixed lights (F), flashing lights (Fl), occulting lights (Occ), isophase lights and quick-flashing lights (Qk Fl).
- Fixed lights: continuous light of constant intensity.
- Flashing lights: the flashes are much briefer than the intervals in between.
- Occulting lights: periods of darkness (occultations) are much shorter than the periods of light.
- Isophase lights: the periods of darkness and light are of equal length.
- Quick-flashing lights: isophase lights with a very rapid rhythm (more than forty flashes a minute). Quick-flashing lights can be of the interrupted or fixed kinds.

Rhythm. The division between periods of darkness and periods of light gives the rhythm of the light.

In the case of occulting lights, there are three sorts of rhythm:

1. The periods of brightness between each occultation are always of the same duration. The light is then said to be regular, with 1 occultation: an example is the light on the green tower at Port-Louis (green light, 1 occultation, 4 seconds).
2. The occultations are separated by briefer flashes of light and grouped in twos, threes or fours, with a longer period of light separating each group.
3. The occultations are grouped irregularly, an example being Trévignon (3+1 occultations). The grouped occultations are sepa-

Lens for a group flashing two flashes.

Lens for light visible through 360°. Unlike the light shown above, this lens does not rotate: the rhythm is created by switching the bulb on and off. It can therefore function as an occulting, a flashing, quick-flashing or isophase light.

rated from one another by shorter flashes of light, and these groups are then separated from the single occultation by a longer flash.

The principle is the same for flashing lights.

Period. The period is the time taken for the light to go through one complete sequence of flashes, for example the Trévignon light has a period of 12 seconds from the first occultation of the group of three to the first occultation of the next group of three, or from the first isolated occultation to the next one, and so on.

Special lights

There are a number of lights with special characteristics as follows:
• *Lights with sectors* do not show the same colour in all directions. Each colour covers a particular area. Often, white indicates the clear area (a channel leading into a port, for example), while red and green sector lights indicate danger – this is not always the case, and you should check the relevant charts in each case.
• *Directional lights* are generally placed along the line of a channel (such as is the case with the Beuzec lights at the entry to Concarneau). These lights have a highly focussed beam and are much less bright to the sides than along the line they mark.
• *Leading lights* are laid out to lead the navigator along a line (take, for example, the lights at la Croix, or the Beuzec lights at Concarneau). The light nearer the navigator is known as the *front light*, the light further away is known as the *rear light*.
• *Exit and entry lights* are to be found outside ports to which there is no permanent access (because of locks, large cargo ships, or closure on certain days). These lights are always made up of a combination of red and green lights (flags during daytime). Consult the Pilot Book or Almanac.
• *Auxiliary lights* are based on the same structure as the main light (as at Penfret) and cover an isolated danger or indicate a passageway. These lights are not very powerful, and can only be seen from a short distance away.

Another kind of light that deserves a mention are *alternating lights,* which show colour changes along the same bearing, an example being the Guernsey breakwater. There are also *air obstruction lights* which are switched on as needed and which give out a letter of the Morse code (Portsmouth, Cherbourg, Biarritz). Last but not least, there are certain lights with sectors that do not change colour, but rhythm instead. One of the more notable is the light on the Cape of Corrubedo, not too far from Cape Finisterre; this light shows 3 red flashes in one sector, and 3+2 red flashes in the next. It requires a good deal of attention to see which sector you are in.

The Armen Lighthouse
(provisioning and inspection).

Recognising a light

Theoretically, all harbour lights were standardised in 1990.

In conditions of good visibility, lights give precise information. However, experience has shown that novices can get a bit confused when dealing with them, particularly since they have the tendency to take the first light they see for the one they want to see.

To identify a light, do not start out by assuming that it is the one you are looking for, and then fit the facts to suit. Instead, calmly check the characteristics first, and then identify it.

The colour ought to be obvious. However, in foggy weather, white lights can appear reddish.

It is easy to identify a light's type when dealing with flashing and quick-flashing lights. However, some fixed lights can be drowned out by the lights from a town. Some occulting lights can look as if they are isophase, and vice versa. In order to work out the duration of the periods of light and dark, the best way is to count in your head (any speed will do, but counting quickly usually gives a more regular and accurate estimate).

The rhythm of a light can be calculated in the same way, either during periods of darkness for a flashing light, or during periods of light for an occulting one.

Lens for a directional light. The light is more intense directly in the line of the light than to the sides.

It is rare that anyone should need to know the period of a light (in the waters around France, in any event, no two lights are distinguished by the period alone). If there is still cause for doubt, then the period can be measured by counting in seconds (counting A1, A2, A3, etc will give a fairly accurate indication), or by using a timer.

When the characteristics of the light have been determined, then an attempt can be made to find out its name. In addition, it is a good idea to make other checks (position relative to other lights, bearings) in order to be certain. All this requires a certain amount of practice, and it is important not to miss any opportunity to gain experience in this vital skill.

The *List of Lights*

We are sailing in the vicinity of Concarneau and we see a green light, occultations in groups of 1 and 3, with a period of 12 seconds. We open the *List of Lights*. No possible alternative: it must be the Trévignon light. We also gain a good deal of additional information:
– we can see a green light, but the Trévignon light presents other colours in other directions (white and red): it is a sector light;
– the light is 11m above MHWS;
– its *range of visibility* varies according to colour and sector: white is the most brilliant, and is visible from the greatest distance, then next red and finally green. This is a nominal range, set out by the International Association of Lighthouse Authorities and is given for weather conditions allowing a visibility of 10 miles. Some other countries have different definitions. The *List of Lights* reproduces without any change figures given in foreign documents;
– next, there is the description of the different sectors and their limits. We read that the Trévignon light has six sectors: two red, one obscured, two white, one green. The green sector covers 34°, from 051° to 085°. Be warned: the sector bearings are given *from seawards*; that is, they are the bearings a navigator would take. The green sector of Trévignon therefore covers an area to the WSW of the lighthouse (and not to the ENE, where there are lots of cute herds of cows, and the picturesque chapel of Saint-Philibert, a gem of sixteenth-century architecture);
– the list also gives a description of the structure carrying the light, and its height above ground level. This is useful, because lighthouses are good landmarks by day, and it also saves having to look frantically for a tower when the light is tucked away in a house on a hill;
– a detailed description of the phases of the light is also given. It is often very complicated and will probably confuse you more than it

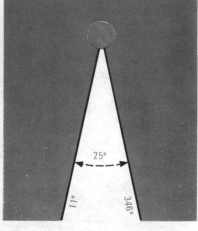

The bearings of light sectors are given from seawards. The sector shown (346° to 11°) sweeps an area to the south of the light.

NUMÉROS	NOM DESCRIPTION — POSITION APPROCHÉE Lat N Long. W	ÉLÉVATION DU FOYER	PORTÉE (milles)	CARACTÈRE — PÉRIODE PHASES — SECTEURS D'ÉCLAIRAGE SIGNAUX DE BRUME — INTENSITÉ LUMINEUSE
	FRANCE — DE LA POINTE DE PENMARCH A LORIENT			115
40374 *D.0944*	Trévignon Tourelle carrée verte et blanche 7 m 47.47,6 3.51,3	11	B. 10 R. 7 V. 6	**B. R. V. (3 + 1) Occ.** 12 s ((1 ; 1) *2 fois* ; (1 ; 3) *2 fois*) 322 - **R.** - 351 - **Obs.** - 004 - **B.** - 051 - **V.** - 085 - **B.** - 092 - **R.** - 127
40378 *D.0945*	— Môle abri - Musoir Colonne blanche sommet vert 3 m 47.47,7 3.51,3	5	5	**F. V. 4 s (1)**
	ILE DE GROIX			
40952 *D.0962*	PEN-MEN - Au NW de l'île Tour carrée blanche, sommet noir 24 m 47.38,9 3.30,5	60	30 *20*	**4 É. B.** 25 s ((0,2 ; 2,8) *3 fois* ; 0,2 ; 15,8) Vis. 309 - 275 (34) SIRÈNE **4 sons** 60 s ((2 ; 3) *3 fois* ; 2 ; 43) 0,2 M Ouest **RADIOPHARE**
40963	*Bouée « Les Chats »* Card. Sud 47.35,7 3.23,6	4	5	**4 É. R.** 12 s ((1 ; 1) *3 fois* ; 1 ; 5) ⌒ **SIFFLET**

helps you – all in all, it's best not to read it;
– for other lights, such as the one at Pen-a-Men, information is also given about fog signals, radio beacons and so on;
– for the bigger lights, where the range of visibility is considerably extended, the *geographical range* of the light is given in italics. This gives the maximum distance at which the light can be seen beyond the visible horizon. The geographical range depends on the height of the tide and the height of the eye of the observer (which in turn depends on the height of the person in question and the size of the boat). The geographical range marked in the book is calculated for an observer who is 4.5m above the surface of the sea at MHWS. It is rare that an observer is so high up, but a table at the front of the *List* gives the relevant compensations.

Most lights are not manned, and in event of failure can therefore be out for several hours at a time. Buoys are not manned either (and the cormorants that generally live on them are not very good at maintenance). Do not therefore forget that the light on a buoy can malfunction, and that some time may pass before it is repaired, especially in bad weather.

Reproduction of a page from the *List of Lights (Livre des feux).*

For the marking of lights on sea charts, see fold-out section 1 at the end of the book.

Keeping the *List of Lights* up to date

The *List of Lights* always comes with either a booklet of corrections, or with replacement pages if it is being sold as a folder with removable pages. In the first instance, cut out the corrections and stick them in place on the page (remember to cross out the old directions and instructions, just in case the glue isn't up to it). If you have bought it in folder format, then simply replace the outdated pages.

In order to keep the work up to date thereafter, you must buy either the replacement pages that are put out every six months, or the pamphlet of corrections that appears every year. To keep up to date on a day-to-day basis, listen to the corrections given as part of the 'Urgent notices to mariners' at the end of weather forecasts from coastal stations, or consult the *Notices to Mariners*.

Fog signals

When buoys and lights disappear in the fog, sound signals take over. Gunshots used to be heard around the Stiff on the NW corner of France on these occasions. Guns are seldom, if ever, used any more, and today the signals are, in decreasing order of power:
– diaphones, with a very deep note (le Creac'h at Ushant, le Guéveur on the island of Sein);
– sirens, usually on lighthouses;
– fog horns, at the end of harbour jetties;
– bells and whistles on buoys.

Lighthouse sirens usually have the same pattern as the light, with a longer period (if it has three flashes every 20 seconds, the siren gives three blasts every minute). Since the bells and whistles on buoys are powered by the sea, they follow its rhythm. The characteristics of fog signals are given in the *List of Lights*.

All these signals do what they can, but in many cases you cannot expect precise information from them, especially concerning their exact position. Fog distorts sounds to the extent that a signal that is quite close can seem a long way off, and a signal that is on the right can appear to be on the left.

Having said that, sound signals can be quite useful, as a group of Mousquetaire yachts from the Glénans centre at Baltimore in Ireland discovered: they were able to go round the Fastnet rock at night in a real peasouper of a fog, without seeing the light once. The important thing in cases like this is to constantly check the information from the signals against frequent soundings, either by lead or by echosounder. Radio bearings are also of help.

Radio signals

There are various systems of radio signals, and different ways of receiving them. The most common technique used by amateur sailors is DF wireless navigation which we will discuss in greater detail in the chapter entitled 'Navigation at sea' in this part. Radio signals are exactly like light signals in the way that they are used for navigation: in both cases, one must establish one's position in relation to the 'active beacons' whose characteristics are already known. Only the methods differ slightly: instead of using light as a signal and the eye to detect it, we use radio waves, put out by radio beacons, and a radio receiver to transform the signals into sound.

Radio beacons are mentioned in the *List of Lights* when they are found in a lighthouse (which is often the case), but their characteristics are not given there. These are to be found in the Admiralty *List of Radio Signals* or in your nautical almanac (in France, vol 91 of the publications of the SHOM, entitled *Radiosignaux à l'usage des navigateurs*). They are also to be found in various unofficial publications which we will discuss in due course.

Information on hyperbolic or satellite navigation is now practically unnecessary, since these now give points directly in terms of geographical co-ordinates, along with the times these satellites will be passing overhead for the next 24 hours. The main reference work for these therefore remains the manufacturer's instructions.

The following works are also of use: *Skippers* for the year in question, which is especially useful for radio beacons and directional VHF receivers, and the *Loisirs nautiques* (special number No 21: Jan 1986), for radio navigation and radar.

The stars

Are the stars lights or signals? This is largely down to one's own personal convictions. They are nonetheless useful points of reference, and allow for very precise navigation. The nautical almanacs publish star charts for navigational purposes, and these are updated annually. (In France, one can also consult the *Éphémérides nautiques*, a large, expensive volume published every year by the Bureau des longitudes (Editions Gauthier-Villars). This work contains tables giving the position of the sun, the moon, four planets and eighty-one stars throughout the year, along with a variety of tables of corrections.)

For navigation by the stars, we will discuss other tables which are essential for the various calculations that can be made from the data given in your almanac. However, it should be noted that there are now calculators available which not only make the work easier, but which also replace certain parts of the almanacs.

The chart

The marine chart is the most basic of documents for the sailor. It gives a very precise graphic representation of the sea and the coasts, and also contains a great deal of information pertaining to markers, buoys, lights, currents and many other things.

The basic principles of map-reading are well known to anyone who paid any attention at all in school. Just in case you didn't, however, we'll go over the basics again.

Basic principles

Seeing that the world is really rather large, and realising that it would be a good idea to know where one is, human beings have invented a simple system of reference points, based on a sort of lattice of lines covering the globe. Some of the lines run parallel to the equator: these are called the *parallels*. In addition, there are the lines running perpendicular to the equator, and which meet at the poles: these are called *meridians*. All one needs to do then is to choose a parallel and a reference meridian – any point on the globe can be found by reference to this system of co-ordinates. Its position with respect to the reference meridian defines its *longitude*. Latitude and longitude are measured in degrees and minutes.[1]

Latitude. The polar axis forms an angle of 90° with the plane of the equator. The equator has a latitude of 0°, and the poles have a latitude of 90° (north or south). All latitudes therefore fall between 0° and 90° north and south, and are measured by reference to the equator. Thus the latitude of the island of Penfret (47°43'N) corresponds to the angle that an imaginary straight line linking Penfret to the centre of the earth makes with the plane of the equator.

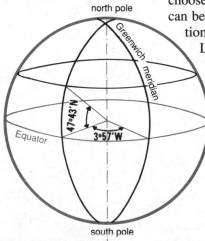

The Penfret Lighthouse is at 47°43'N and 3°57'W.

1. A degree is divided into 60 minutes, a minute into 60 seconds. However, nowadays we generally use degrees, minutes and tenths of a minute.

This angle corresponds to a distance on the earth's surface. A minute of latitude equals 1,852m. This distance is a unit of measurement known as the nautical mile.[2]

1 minute of latitude = 1 sea mile = 1,852m.

The island of Penfret is 2,863 sea miles from the equator.

Longitude. Since there is no meridian that naturally imposes itself as a reference point, the one that passes through Greenwich has been chosen. Since the globe is divided up into 360°, longitude is counted from Greenwich (180° east, 180° west).[3]

The longitude of Penfret is 3°57'W.

Distance cannot be calculated on the basis of longitude since the meridians do not run parallel to one another.

Mercator's projection

On a chart, however, the meridians are parallel. The reason is that a convex surface cannot be reproduced in a plane without some distortion. Either the precise representation of angles, or an exact representation of distance must be sacrificed. As the measurement of angles is indispensable in navigation, charts are normally drawn on Mercator's projection. On the chart, the angles are correct, but the distances are only exact at the equator; the further one moves away from the equator, the more exaggerated the representation is. Around the poles, the distortion is considerable: Greenland seems as big as Africa, whereas it is in fact fourteen times smaller.

On the chart, then, the shortest distance from one point to another is not always a straight line. If you link two points on the same parallel by stretching a string over a globe, then the string follows the *arc of a great circle* (a circle whose centre is in the same position as that of the earth): the shortest course does not follow the parallel. Now, on the chart, the parallels are straight lines running parallel. The navigator who wants to steer a straight line must therefore gradually change course. The straight course is called the *orthodromic*, or *great circle course*. The course by the chart is called the *loxodromic*, or *rhumb line course*. Note that there is no need to take this peculiarity into account on coastal cruises, or even on long passages when the distances are not great enough for the difference between the great circle and the rhumb line courses to make any significant difference to the distance covered.

2. Since the earth is not totally spherical, a minute of latitude can actually vary in length: 1,842.78m at the equator and 1,861.55m at a latitude of 85°.
3. In measures of latitude and longitude, the cardinal points are always referred to as N, S, W, and E by international convention.

The principle of Mercator's projection is that an angle on the globe must be represented by the same angle on a chart.

As a consequence, around that point, the distances on the globe and the distances on the map are reproduced according to the same scale in all directions. There is thus no distortion when dealing with small areas.

The constant distance in millimetres between any two given meridians represents a changing distance in nautical miles between the same meridians on the globe. This distance diminishes as one moves away from the equator. As a result, the actual scale of the map increases with latitude. Large areas, such as oceans, are therefore distorted. To be more exact, the scale of Mercator's projection alters in inverse proportion to the cosine of the latitude.

All the areas A, B, C, D are 15° latitude and 10° longitude. As the latitude increases, their surface area decreases; on the chart, it appears to increase.

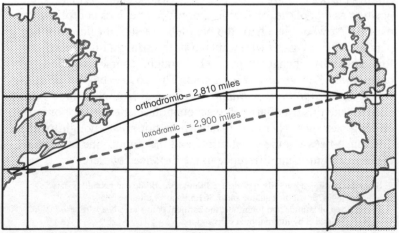

The areas marked A, B, C and D all measure 15° latitude by 10° longitude.

Despite all appearances to the contrary, the orthodromic route is the shortest. This can be easily demonstrated by stretching a string across the surface of a globe.

Reading the chart

Reading charts needs practice. The information contained is often given in the form of conventional signs and abbrevations, which you must be able to decipher without making any mistakes. We will only deal with the subject briefly; the Admiralty publication chart 5011 (INT1) (or, in France, the *Guide du navigateur*) will provide you with all the necessary information.

For an introduction, see the chart of les Glénans, fold-out section 3 at the end of the book.

Scales

The northern and southern edges of a sea chart (north is at the top) give a longitude scale, which allows you to situate yourself in relation to the Greenwich meridian.

The western and eastern edges give the latitude scale. This allows you not only to work out the latitude, but above all to calculate distances.

The latitude scale varies, as we know. One minute of latitude is represented by a greater distance on the chart as we approach the poles. Even if this increase is not apparent just from looking at the map, it must nonetheless be taken into account. In order to measure the distance between the two points, the distance must be measured at the level of the two points in question.

Depths and heights

The three zones on the charts are quite distinct: the sea, that is to say places where there is always water; terra firma, where there is never any water; and the foreshore, which is sometimes under water and sometimes not.

On old charts, the sea is white, the land is an even grey, and the foreshore is shaded grey according to the nature of the sea bed.

On new charts, which are in colour, the sea is blue where it is relatively shallow, with the colour lightening as the water deepens. From a depth of 20m, the sea is represented as white. The land is khaki, and the foreshore is grey-brown (khaki and blue superimposed).

On all maps, the contours of the sea bed are denoted by lines referred to as *depth contours*, and the depth is given by soundings.

The soundings are given in metres, and are based on the lowest astronomical tide (coefficient 120). This level is known as the *chart datum*.

The distances are measured on the latitude scale. The distance from the Bodic light to the light at les Héaux is 6 sea miles as the crow flies (*Admiralty Chart 2668*).

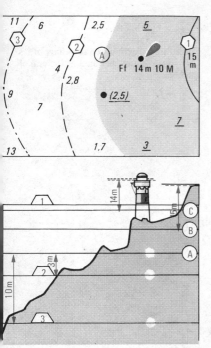

Different datum levels are used for soundings and heights.

A. Datum level for depth, zero on sea charts (lowest tide level).
B. Datum level for heights (level at half-tide).
C. Datum level for height of the lights on lighthouses (mean spring tide, coefficient 95).

Consequently, the height of the light on the lighthouse (14m on the chart) and the height of the top of the slope do not have the same datum level as the one used for depths.
1. High water level.
2. Sounding (3m).
3. Sounding (10m).

There are still a few charts to be had in Britain that give soundings in feet and refer to the average spring tides (coefficient 95). It is therefore just as well to find out which scale is being used on the chart in question.

Drying heights are given in metres, and in relation to the same reference point. However, the height uncovered at low water is underlined on the chart: 3.5 indicates a point emerging 3.5m at low water.

Heights are also given in metres or feet, but relate to mean high water springs, or mean sea level. In order to avoid any possible confusion with the soundings, the figures are followed by an 'm'.

On French charts rocks that are always exposed are represented by a hollow triangle Δ on recent charts, and by a T on the older charts in black and white.

The landscape

Scales and levels give the basic facts, but the chart has many other indications, which, taken together, provide a picture of the landscape that is suited to the needs of navigators. On the chart, the land looks bare, merely an area for landmarks: it consists only of high points, conspicuous buildings and the more stately trees. The world only really begins at the water's edge, with its precise boundaries. It is a curving, uneven region of blank area between particular features. The smallest buoy has the importance normally accorded to a village. The magenta marks showing lights catch the eye in just the same way as the lights do themselves at night. All in all, the landscape is most accurately portrayed by the chart.

There is only one way to learn to read a chart: look at it for a long time, and orientate it to the area it describes. We shall leave it at that. For an example, look at the chart for les Glénans, appended at the end of the book – that is plenty to be going on with for the moment. Don't forget to look at others from time to time: a few good charts are much more entertaining than the TV on winter evenings.

Correction and care of charts

People will be glad to know that the charts produced by the SHOM are divided up into seven categories: from charts for coastal navigation (scale from 1:10,000 up to 1:25,000) right up to charts of shipping lanes and globes (scales from 1:5,000,000 to 1:15,000,000), passing through charts for seagoing, coasting,

LA MANCHE

d'après les travaux français et anglais les plus récents.

SERVICE HYDROGRAPHIQUE DE LA MARINE

Paris _ 1913

Les sondes sont exprimées en mètres.

Les sondes de la côte de France sont réduites au niveau des plus basses mers.
Celles de la côte d'Angleterre au niveau des basses mers moyennes de vive eau.

Echelle de $\frac{1}{797.000}$ (Lat. 49° 55')

5 ___ 0 _____ 10 _____ 20 _____ 3o _____ 4o _____ 5o Kilomètres

· 1947 _ Cette carte n'est pas tenue à jour des épaves

1°   30'   0°

ide à l'Est du méridien international (Greenwich)   2°   30'

48°

landings, sea crossings and maps of the oceans. Every map carries a number, which helps prevent confusion. The Admiralty catalogue of charts (publication number NP 131) lists around six thousand charts, enough to sail safely round the world. A limited edition of the catalogue (NP 109) covers the British Isles and North West Europe, and is published in January each year.

Admiralty charts are kept scrupulously up to date. When buying a map from a registered agent, check the delivery date (marked on the bottom of the chart) and then ask for the *Notices to Mariners* that has appeared since. This will contain a list of the necessary corrections.

Charts that you have had for a while can be corrected from the Admiralty's *Notices to Mariners: Small Craft Edition*, which is published every April. Corrections should be made with indelible ink, preferably magenta; the date and number of corrections made should also be marked in the left-hand margin, so that you can tell how up to date the chart is. You should try to keep all your references up to date with the relevant supplements.

Remember that when buying foreign charts it will not always be possible to keep them precisely up to date, and therefore they must

The title of the chart must be carefully read, particularly for the datum levels and whether it is a metric chart or a fathom chart. Note that this French chart, produced in 1913, gives two different longitude scales. The one on the inside gives the longitude from the Paris meridian, 2°22' east of the one that passes through Greenwich. Note also that the scale indicated is exact at a latitude of 49°55', and for no other latitude.

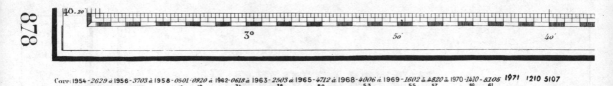

878

Corr: 1954-*2629* à 1956-*3703* à 195 8-*0501-0920* à 1962-*0618* à 1963-*2503* à 1965-*4712* à 1968-*4006* à 1969-*1602* à *4820* à 1970-*1410-5105*   **1971** **1210 5107**
  I   II   18   19   34   36   50   53   55   57   60   61   **62   63**

On this chart, the last correction made in 1971 is denoted by the number group: 5107
                                                                                      63
51: number of the week in which the correction was published in the *Notices to Mariners*.
07: the number that this particular correction had in the list of corrections for that week.
63: the 63rd correction made to the chart since 1954, the year of the last edition. In order to be sure that all the corrections have been made to the chart, the numbers ought to follow in sequence, or groups ought to be linked by the preposition 'to'.

be used with a great deal of care. The plastic-covered charts (coded 'p' by the SHOM) are difficult to keep up to date.

Note that in order to keep a chart reliable, it must remain perfectly legible – taking good care of it is a matter of safety.

The *Notices to Mariners*

The *Notices to Mariners,* in the UK Admiralty Pilots, are the fruit of many centuries of experience. They are the result of observations made at every latitude, by generations of sailors. This body of information is checked and updated every day of the year, and is an irreplaceable source of information.

The *Notices to Mariners* ought to be consulted at the same time as the charts: they are an important aid to understanding them properly. Originally produced for merchant ships, they inevitably see life from a more lofty perspective, which is easy to understand, given that merchant ships are a little taller. Nonetheless, information specifically targeted at the amateur sailor is beginning to appear. In any event, even the information pertaining to large vessels is useful, providing the necessary adjustments are made.

Each volume of the *Notices to Mariners* is divided into two parts. The first is given over to general items of information relating to the region in question: meteorology, oceanography, geography, regulations, sea routes, landings. The second is a description of the coast, with its dangers, markers, buoyage (for daytime), tides, currents, channels, anchorages, ports and what they have available in the way of resources. This information is complemented by sketches and profiles of the coast.

The *Notices to Mariners* in France (*Instructions nautiques*) also contain a volume of plates (charts of ports, panoramic shots of the coast and so on).

Keeping the *Notices to Mariners* up to date

The procedure below describes the situation in France in detail. The British publications are updated regularly in a similar manner. Every volume of the *Notices to Mariners* is designated by a letter and a number. The letter indicates the series to which the volume belongs, and is also keyed into the corresponding *List of Lights*. The number relates to the region described by the volume. Thus, the volume dealing with the northern and western coasts of France carries the reference C2. Those volumes with fixed pages also carry a number giving the year of publication.

Each volume of the *Notices to Mariners* purchased must be accompanied by a pamphlet of corrections or a group of replacement pages (for the volumes published in folder format).

In order to keep the volume up to date, get hold of the pamphlet of corrections or the replacement pages which are updated and published every year.

In addition, in order to be properly up to date, also consult the last summary table that appeared in the *Weekly Notices to Mariners* (groups 10, 20, 30, etc), all the tables that have appeared since the publication of the last summary table, and the last list of notices that is still valid.

Other documents

There are, naturally enough, other documents in addition to the official ones. They are not intended to replace the latter, but often draw together a good deal of information – which would otherwise be spread out through a number of Admiralty publications – in a single volume. These are too numerous to mention here, but a visit to a specialist bookshop or chandlers should enable you to have a look at a selection and see if there is one suited to your needs.

The *Almanach du marin breton*

Published by the discreet Oeuvre du marin breton, this almanac is extremely useful when sailing along the French Atlantic coast. It contains information on buoyage conventions, a table of tides for certain ports, the list of lights and lighthouses from the entry to the North Sea down to Saint-Jean-de-Luz, as well as advice on sailing at night in these waters. There is also a list of radio beacons, with their characteristics and a list of sea charts.

The almanac for the year in progress appears on 1 September for that year, but you can also get supplements on 1 January and 1 June.

Reed's Nautical Almanac, **and** *Macmillan & Silk Cut Nautical Almanac*

Every sailor should have one or other of these standard works. They both give comprehensive information not only for the coasts of the British Isles (as far as Iceland), but also for the Dutch, Belgian and French coasts, down to Saint-Jean-de-Luz.

Much of the work is given over to navigation by the stars (and gives the appropriate tables). They also give detailed information about individual ports and harbours complete with hazards, lights, buoys, marinas and anchorages. There is also a great deal of invaluable information concerning the tides and tidal currents in the Channel.

Cruising Association Handbook

This publication also gives detailed information on harbours, hazards, buoyage systems, leading lights and transits for all major and most minor anchorages likely to be of interest to the cruising sailor.

Documents of interest to amateur sailors

A good deal of additional information directly targeted at amateur sailors can be found in various cruising guides and in the different sailing magazines published throughout Europe. Descriptions of the various areas in which one might be sailing can be found in the appropriate magazines for the country in question. The descriptions will usually be accompanied by photographs and sketches of use to the amateur sailor. These studies are generally put together by responsible people, but it must always be remembered that the information given concerning buoyage and lights can, as with any other yachting publication, go out of date very quickly. So while such magazines can provide a useful supplement to the information given in the more official publications, the more established works on the subject are still of central importance.

Calculating the tides

The tides are an important factor in the life of the sea, and are therefore discussed at some length in Part VI. For the present, we will limit ourselves to a discussion of the means by which the sailor can take account of the tides for the purposes of navigation: documents and methods that allow one to know the depth of water underneath the keel, and practical information on tidal currents.

The *Tide Tables*

Since we know the movement of the planets, it is quite possible to work out the movement of the tides for any given place and any given time, that is to say, the difference between the water levels at high tide and low tide respectively, along with the times at which these highs and lows will occur. The SHOM produces tables of these figures every year: the *Annuaire des Marées*. This is one of the few documents which does not have to be kept up to date (except that it does need to be corrected from time to time).

These tide tables contain:

• A table showing the coefficients for the different tides that year. The *coefficient* is a measure, used in France, indicating the size of the tide in relation to the heavenly bodies. It is given in hundredths, and the coefficients used as reference points are:

C = 120 for the largest tide known (maximum astronomical tide);
C = 95 for average spring tides;
C = 70 for an average tide;
C = 45 for average neap tides;
C = 20 for the smallest tide known (minimum astronomical tide).

The range of the tides varies considerably from one place to another, depending on the bottom and the shape of the coastline. Consequently, on the same day (and therefore for the same coefficient) the range can be 11.2m at Saint-Malo and 4.6m at Lorient. Note, however, that in any given place, the relation between the ranges is equal to the ratio of the coefficients. Accordingly, the range at maximum spring tide is six times greater than the range at maximum neap tide. (120 = 6 x 20).

• The *Annuaire des marées* also gives the depths at high tide and at low tide for the eighteen main French ports, and then the corrections required to estimate the tides in the 215 secondary ports to be found in France, Britain, Belgium, the Netherlands and Spain.

• Figures are also given for the tidal flow, hour by hour, at le Havre and Saint-Malo, where the normal flow is affected by local conditions. There are also graphs for the tides in various ports, and a table of corrections that allow for the effect of air pressure on water levels.

Comment should also be made on times and on levels at half tide.

Times. Always check what time is being used as a reference. At the moment, the time used is GMT + 1 ; add an hour in summer.

Levels. Levels are given in metres, in relation to the reference level. However, this level is not the same for all countries.

Most countries, including France, have chosen the level of the lowest astronomical tide. This seems to be a fairly safe principle to follow, given that, apart from in a few exceptional cases, the actual depth of the water is never less than the depth given in the tables. Sometimes, indeed, it is rather deeper: at Paimpol, for example, the line chosen as zero on the charts is in fact 50cm above the level of the lowest astronomical tide.

However, in certain other countries, there are still documents that use the *mean low water springs* as a reference level. When you calculate the low water depth of above-average spring tides, you will have heights that will be less than the datum.

Half tide level. Note that, *whatever the range is at a given spot, the level of the sea is always the same at half tide*. This half tide level is given in the tide tables for each of the standard ports as well as for most of the secondary ones (it is also to be found on the label of most charts). It can also be referred to as the *mean level*, and is an invaluable reference, as will be seen.

Tidal calculations

When sailing near the coast, there are a variety of possible reasons for wanting to calculate the flow of the tides. One of the main concerns is to keep a sufficient distance between the keel and the sea bed. However, calculating the tide can also be of use in determining the appearance of the coastline you are approaching: it will tell you which rocks will be above water, and which ones will be submerged. Finally, sometimes the combined use of soundings and tidal calculations can give an idea of position – this is especially useful in very foggy conditions.

In practice, it is a matter of finding out:
– the depth of water in a given place at a given time;
– or the time when there will be a certain depth of water in a given place.

The calculations are made on the basis of the times of high and low water. All that is needed now is the method.

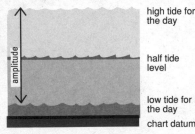

high tide for the day

half tide level

low tide for the day

chart datum

The rule of twelfths

There is no lack of methods for calculating the times and the levels of the tides: there are ones for every occasion and to suit everyone.

We will keep to an explanation of the method that seems simplest, which is known as the *rule of twelfths*. Then we will deal with certain tables which might be useful in areas where the flow of the tides shows some peculiarity.

The rule of twelfths is based on a simple observation: the tidal curve is very like a sine curve. From one slack water to the next, the sea rises or descends by:

1/12 of its range in the 1st hour;
2/12 of its range in the 2nd hour;
3/12 of its range in the 3rd hour;
3/12 of its range in the 4th hour;
2/12 of its range in the 5th hour;
1/12 of its range in the 6th hour.

This is what is known as the rule of twelfths.

Since the range is divided by 12 and the time interval between two slack waters by 6, it is very easy to figure out the depth of water from hour to hour. Note however, that since the interval is, on average, longer than 6 hours, the tide time is different from clock time. Having said that, the difference does not need to be taken into account except when the time interval is very different from this average (which happens in the Channel, for example, where time intervals can be less than 5 hours or more than 7 hours). Practically speaking, one does not need to make corrections unless the time interval is less than $5^{1}/_{2}$ hours or more than $6^{1}/_{2}$ hours.

Given that some navigators hate drawings, and some hate calculations, it is a happy coincidence that the rule of twelfths can be used either by calculation or graphically.

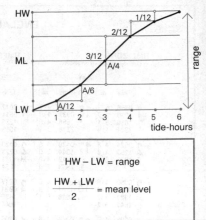

$$HW - LW = range$$

$$\frac{HW + LW}{2} = mean\ level$$

Calculation for a standard port

Supposing we are at Shoreham on 3 July, and we want to know the following things:
– *what will be the depth of water in the port at 1220?*
– *at what time will the water be 4m deep?*

This is an easy example, since Shoreham is one of the standard ports, and the figures for the times and levels of the tides are given in the almanacs. We will come to an example of the calculations required for a secondary port later.

Let us look first of all for the times of high and low tide at Shoreham on 3 July.

High tide	0829	4.8m
Low tide	1446	1.8m

Here we go!

ENGLAND, SOUTH COAST — SHOREHAM

Lat 50°50′ N   Long 0°15′ W

TIME ZONE GMT
For Summer Time add ONE hour in non tinted area

TIMES AND HEIGHTS OF HIGH AND LOW WATERS   YEAR 1986

MAY

Day	Time	m	Time	m	Time	m	Time	m
1 Th ☾	0358	5.1	1030	1.7	1656	5.1	2321	1.9
2 F	0524	4.8	1157	1.8	1825	5.0		
3 Sa	0050	1.9	0656	4.8	1321	1.7	1942	5.2
4 Su	0203	1.7	0810	5.0	1426	1.5	2040	5.4
5 M	0259	1.4	0903	5.3	1515	1.3	2125	5.7
6 Tu	0343	1.1	0944	5.6	1558	1.0	2204	5.9
7 W	0420	0.9	1020	5.7	1635	0.9	2238	5.9
8 Th	0455	0.8	1053	5.8	1708	0.8	2309	6.0
9 F	0526	0.8	1125	5.8	1740	0.9	2339	5.9
10 Sa	0556	0.8	1157	5.8	1810	1.0		
11 Su	0006	5.8	0624	0.9	1229	5.7	1839	1.1
12 M	0034	5.7	0654	1.0	1259	5.6	1911	1.3
13 Tu	0102	5.5	0725	1.2	1333	5.4	1944	1.5
14 W	0136	5.3	0801	1.5	1410	5.2	2025	1.8
15 Th	0219	5.0	0844	1.7	1457	5.0	2116	2.0
16 F	0312	4.7	0937	1.9	1556	4.9	2218	2.1
17 Sa ☽	0420	4.6	1044	2.0	1712	4.9	2333	2.0
18 Su	0540	4.6	1201	1.9	1828	5.1		
19 M	0046	1.8	0653	4.9	1312	1.6	1933	5.4
20 Tu	0147	1.4	0754	5.3	1411	1.2	2026	5.7
21 W	0242	1.0	0844	5.7	1504	0.9	2113	6.0
22 Th	0332	0.7	0932	6.0	1555	0.7	2200	6.3
23 F ○	0421	0.6	1021	6.1	1644	0.6	2247	6.4
24 Sa	0509	0.6	1112	6.2	1731	0.7	2334	6.4
25 Su	0557	0.7	1205	6.3	1819	0.8		
26 M	0021	6.4	0645	0.8	1257	6.2	1908	1.0
27 Tu	0108	6.2	0733	1.0	1347	6.1	1958	1.2
28 W	0157	6.0	0822	1.1	1439	5.9	2052	1.4
29 Th	0249	5.6	0915	1.3	1535	5.6	2152	1.6
30 F ☾	0349	5.3	1016	1.5	1637	5.4	2259	1.7
31 Sa	0458	5.0	1125	1.6	1748	5.2		

JUNE

Day	Time	m	Time	m	Time	m	Time	m
1 Su	0012	1.8	0614	4.8	1236	1.7	1855	5.2
2 M	0120	1.7	0723	4.9	1341	1.6	1954	5.3
3 Tu	0217	1.6	0821	5.0	1435	1.5	2044	5.4
4 W	0305	1.4	0908	5.2	1522	1.3	2128	5.5
5 Th	0348	1.2	0949	5.4	1603	1.2	2208	5.6
6 F	0426	1.1	1028	5.5	1641	1.1	2242	5.6
7 Sa ●	0502	1.0	1106	5.6	1717	1.1	2316	5.7
8 Su	0535	1.0	1141	5.6	1749	1.2	2346	5.7
9 M	0606	1.1	1216	5.6	1823	1.3		
10 Tu	0017	5.6	0638	1.2	1250	5.6	1857	1.4
11 W	0052	5.5	0715	1.3	1325	5.5	1935	1.5
12 Th	0129	5.4	0752	1.4	1403	5.5	2015	1.4
13 F	0210	5.2	0833	1.5	1445	5.4	2101	1.6
14 Sa	0256	5.1	0918	1.5	1534	5.3	2152	1.7
15 Su ☽	0352	5.0	1012	1.6	1632	5.2	2250	1.7
16 M	0453	4.9	1115	1.6	1736	5.2	2357	1.6
17 Tu	0601	5.0	1222	1.5	1841	5.4		
18 W	0104	1.4	0706	5.2	1330	1.3	1943	5.6
19 Th	0207	1.2	0807	5.4	1432	1.1	2040	5.8
20 F	0306	1.0	0906	5.7	1603	0.9	2135	6.0
21 Sa	0402	0.8	1003	5.9	1626	0.9	2228	6.2
22 Su ○	0455	0.7	1100	6.1	1719	0.9	2319	6.3
23 M	0547	0.9	1156	6.1	1811	1.0		
24 Tu	0010	6.2	0637	0.9	1250	6.2	1900	1.1
25 W	0100	6.2	0725	1.0	1342	6.1	1951	1.4
26 Th	0148	6.0	0813	1.1	1429	6.0	2040	1.3
27 F	0237	5.8	0901	1.2	1516	5.8	2131	1.4
28 Sa	0329	5.6	0949	1.3	1604	5.6	2224	1.6
29 Su ☾	0420	5.3	1042	1.5	1658	5.4	2321	1.7
30 M	0518	4.9	1142	1.7	1757	5.1		

JULY

Day	Time	m	Time	m	Time	m	Time	m
1 Tu	0024	1.8	0624	4.7	1246	1.8	1858	5.0
2 W	0127	1.9	0729	4.7	1349	1.9	1958	5.0
3 Th	0225	1.8	0829	4.8	1446	1.8	2052	5.1
4 F	0317	1.6	0921	5.1	1536	1.6	2140	5.3
5 Sa	0402	1.4	1007	5.3	1620	1.5	2223	5.4
6 Su	0442	1.3	1050	5.5	1659	1.4	2300	5.5
7 M ●	0519	1.2	1129	5.6	1734	1.4	2333	5.6
8 Tu	0554	1.2	1205	5.7	1810	1.4		
9 W	0008	5.7	0627	1.2	1240	5.7	1845	1.4
10 Th	0042	5.7	0703	1.2	1316	5.8	1923	1.3
11 F	0119	5.6	0742	1.2	1351	5.8	2001	1.3
12 Sa	0158	5.6	0820	1.1	1429	5.8	2042	1.3
13 Su	0238	5.5	0900	1.2	1509	5.7	2125	1.3
14 M	0323	5.3	0944	1.2	1555	5.5	2215	1.4
15 Tu	0412	5.2	1037	1.4	1650	5.4	2314	1.5
16 W	0513	5.0	1141	1.5	1756	5.3		
17 Th	0025	1.5	0626	5.0	1255	1.5	1909	5.3
18 F	0140	1.4	0743	5.2	1410	1.4	2020	5.5
19 Sa	0251	1.2	0854	5.5	1519	1.2	2123	5.8
20 Su	0354	1.1	0959	5.8	1619	1.1	2221	6.0
21 M ○	0450	1.0	1056	6.0	1714	1.1	2313	6.2
22 Tu	0541	0.9	1150	6.1	1804	1.1		
23 W	0002	6.2	0628	0.9	1239	6.2	1851	1.1
24 Th	0048	6.2	0712	0.9	1324	6.2	1935	1.1
25 F	0132	6.1	0755	0.9	1406	6.2	2019	1.1
26 Sa	0213	5.9	0836	1.0	1444	6.0	2059	1.2
27 Su	0254	5.7	0915	1.1	1521	5.8	2141	1.4
28 M	0334	5.3	0956	1.3	1601	5.6	2227	1.6
29 Tu	0420	5.0	1044	1.7	1651	5.0	2323	1.9
30 W	0517	4.6	1136	1.9	1755	4.7		
31 Th	0030	2.1	0632	4.5	1259	2.2	1908	4.6

AUGUST

Day	Time	m	Time	m	Time	m	Time	m
1 F	0142	2.1	0749	4.5	1411	2.2	2019	4.6
2 Sa	0247	2.0	0856	4.8	1511	2.0	2118	5.0
3 Su	0340	1.7	0950	5.1	1600	1.7	2205	5.3
4 M	0423	1.5	1034	5.4	1641	1.5	2245	5.6
5 Tu ●	0502	1.3	1112	5.7	1717	1.4	2318	5.7
6 W	0536	1.2	1147	5.8	1751	1.2	2351	5.8
7 Th	0611	1.1	1221	5.9	1827	1.1		
8 F	0025	5.9	0647	1.0	1255	6.0	1904	1.0
9 Sa	0102	5.9	0724	0.9	1332	6.1	1941	0.9
10 Su	0140	5.9	0800	0.9	1406	6.1	2019	0.9
11 M	0216	5.8	0837	0.9	1440	6.0	2058	1.0
12 Tu	0255	5.6	0916	1.1	1522	5.8	2142	1.2
13 W	0337	5.3	1004	1.3	1612	5.4	2240	1.5
14 Th	0437	5.0	1109	1.6	1722	5.1	2357	1.7
15 F	0601	4.9	1236	1.8	1849	5.0		
16 Sa	0126	1.7	0735	5.0	1404	1.7	2012	5.3
17 Su	0246	1.5	0855	5.3	1518	1.4	2122	5.6
18 M	0351	1.2	0958	5.7	1618	1.2	2217	5.9
19 Tu ○	0444	1.0	1051	6.1	1708	1.0	2305	6.2
20 W	0531	0.9	1137	6.3	1752	1.0	2347	6.3
21 Th	0612	0.8	1219	6.3	1832	0.9		
22 F	0027	6.3	0651	0.8	1257	6.3	1911	0.9
23 Sa	0105	6.2	0727	0.8	1332	6.2	1947	0.9
24 Su	0141	6.0	0801	0.9	1403	6.1	2021	1.0
25 M	0213	5.8	0834	1.0	1433	5.8	2055	1.2
26 Tu	0246	5.5	0909	1.4	1506	5.4	2133	1.6
27 W ☾	0323	5.0	0950	1.8	1549	5.0	2220	2.0
28 Th	0414	4.6	1045	2.2	1651	4.6	2328	2.3
29 F	0533	4.3	1207	2.5	1817	4.4		
30 Sa	0055	2.4	0710	4.4	1336	2.5	1946	4.5
31 Su	0215	2.2	0829	4.7	1445	2.2	2055	4.8

Chart Datum: 3.27 metres below Ordnance Datum (Newlyn)

Question 1: what will be the depth of the water at 1220?

1. Given that it is summer, we will use GMT + 1 instead of GMT .
   High tide   0929
   Low tide   1546
2. Calculation of a twelfth:
   range: 4.8 − 1.8 = 3.0m (high tide minus low tide)
   twelfth: 3.0/12 = 0.25m (range divided by 12)
3. To calculate the time of the tide (interval divided by 6):
   interval: 1546 − 0929 = 6hr 17min or 377min
   tide-hours: 6hr 17/6min = 1hr 3mins, or 63min by the clock
4. At 1220, the tide has been going down for 2hr 51min, thus 171min by the clock. This time must be converted into tide-minutes by using a rule of three:
   (171 x 60)/63 = 163 tide-minutes, thus 2hr 43 tide-hours

   The sea has therefore gone down by approximately 5/12, or about 1.25m. At 1220, the depth of the water at Shoreham will therefore be:
   4.8 − 1.25 = 3.55m.

Question 2: at what time will the water be 4m in depth?

When the water level is at 4m, the sea will have dropped by 4.8 − 4 = 0.8m, ie just over 3/12.

The sea goes down by 3/12 in 2 tide-hours, or 120 tide-minutes. We can convert tide-minutes into clock-minutes:
   (120 x 63)/60 = 126min, or 2hr 6min
   So, the water level will be 4m at:
   0929 + 0206 = 1135.

The semi-circle

On a vertical scale calibrated in metres, a semi-circle is drawn with a diameter equal to the range of the tide, taking care to make low water and high water fall at the required depth. The half circumference is then divided into six, or better still into twelve, equal parts, corresponding to each hour or half hour of tide.

Depth of water at 1220: point A at 1220 on the semi-circle falls on the horizontal 3.55m.

The time at which there is 4m of water: the horizontal for 4m meets the semi-circle at point B, which is about 1135.

The graph should be drawn on squared paper (preferably in millimetres) if it is to be readable.

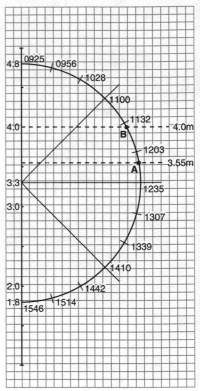

In order to divide the semi-circle into twelve, three radii are marked: one at right angles to the vertical, the others at 45°. With the compasses still adjusted to the radius of the semi-circle, you mark out the required intersections from the five radii (the last two are obtained from the intersections which are on either side of the horizontal radius).

Reproduced from *Macmillan & Silk Cut Nautical Almanac*, based on British Admiralty data.

Calculations and reality

Whatever method is used to calculate the depth of the water, always remember that the results are approximate (different results can be obtained by using different methods). A variety of factors can contribute to this imprecision – atmospheric pressure for example (don't forget to consult the back page of the *Tide Tables*, which has a table that allows you to correct the results according to the atmospheric pressure on that day). Equally, the wind can cause variations that must be allowed for, even though there is no good way of predicting exactly how great the difference will be (it can be between +/–20cm and +/–50cm). Generally speaking, when the atmospheric pressure is high and the wind is from the land, the depth of the water will be less than the figures derived by calculation, and it will be greater when the pressure is lower and the wind is from the sea.

On the other hand, swell causes a variation in level that corresponds to half the height of the wave. If it is remembered that the swell tends to increase in shallower water, then one can always allow a certain safety margin.

All this goes to show that there is no real need to make complicated calculations. If you get seasick, then you'll only make mistakes anyway. Unless one is dealing with a particular case, then it is best to stick to an estimate somewhere around mean level. Caution counsels that this should then be increased by a margin of about 30cm, which is known as the 'pilot's foot'. Remember to include this safety margin in your calculations.

A simple calculation from mean level

Since the mean level of the tide is constant for a given spot, it forms a very useful reference point. This mean level is always indicated in the tide tables for every port, whether standard or secondary.

According to the rule of twelfths, the sea level varies by a quarter of its range during the hour preceding half tide, and by another quarter during the hour following it. All that is needed is to calculate this quarter (in our example 3.0m/4 = 0.75m); this result then gives us two more interesting facts:

– one hour before half tide: 3.3 + 0.75m =3.75m;
– one hour after half tide: 3.3 – 0.75m = 2.55m.

This rule of fourths seems sufficient in most cases, especially if allowance is made for the pilot's foot.

The pilot's foot

A foot on a ruler is about 30cm. In fact, it has been noted that the older a pilot gets, the more his foot grows.

Experience teaches caution, especially as one grows to realise that it is altogether more pleasant to sail without having to worry, rather than to be constantly wondering whether one has allowed a sufficient margin or not. With this in mind, it does seem that the rule of fourths, plus a pilot's foot equal to half the range, ensure complete relaxation (let those who have never gone aground cast the first stones – if they dare). More exact calculations are only necessary when circumstances do not allow for such a safety margin.

In certain cases, indeed, one has to make do with very little. One can reasonably reduce the pilot's foot to less than 30cm if the sea is calm, the bottom sandy, and the tide rising, for example.

Take every possible opportunity to check your calculations by observation. For example, if there is a rock marked on your chart which you can see breaking surface, then this gives a fairly precise indication of the level of the water. In addition, most ports usually have tide gauges.

Specific cases

Calculation for a secondary port

The example we chose to illustrate the rule of twelfths was a standard port: Shoreham. However, nobody spends all their time (thank heavens!) sailing in the immediate vicinity of a standard port – this could get rather dull after a while. Consequently, in order to calculate the tide for other areas, we must look up the *Tide Tables*, which give the range and times for the nearest secondary port.

Note that, here again, the differences are usually negligible. Do not make corrections unless there is a difference of at least 10 minutes or 0.3m between the standard and secondary ports in question.

In some areas, however, corrections do have to be made. Let us take Littlehampton as an example. Littlehampton is a secondary port where the range and hours of the tide are slightly different from those given for the nearest standard port (Shoreham).

Let's run through the same questions as we used for Shoreham: what will be the water level at Littlehampton on 3 July at 1220? From the almanac we can see that different corrections must be applied depending on whether we are in the spring or neap tides. We

> If the coefficient is lower than 70, use the columns marked Np (neap). If the coefficient is greater than 70, use the columns marked Sp (spring).

must begin by checking the coefficient: this is currently .57, and so we must be in a period of neap tides. There is a 10 minute difference between high water at Littlehampton and at Shoreham, and the same (in the other direction) at low water.

This allows us to make the following calculation:

HW Shoreham	0829
Correction	+ 10 min
HW Littlehampton =	0839

LW Shoreham	1446
Correction	− 10 min
LW Littlehampton	= 1456

In order to be able to use this directly, we go from GMT to GMT + 1, which is the time used in summer. Therefore:

HW Littlehampton	0939
LW Littlehampton	1556

The same corrections apply to the depth as well, so:

HW Shoreham	4.8
Correction	− 0.4
HW Littlehampton	= 4.4

LW Shoreham	1.8
Correction	− 0.2
LW Littlehampton	= 1.6

The answers are: at 1220 there will be 3.35m of water; there will be 4m of water at 1105.

All that remains to be done now is to apply the rule of twelfths. It would be good practice if you made the calculations for yourself.

Special tables

Certain places in the Channel have very particular tidal patterns. In France, there is the bay around Saint-Malo, and the estuary of the Seine; in England, there is the Solent, which lies between the Isle of Wight and the mainland. In the *Annuaire des marées*, the water levels are given hour by hour for le Havre and Saint-Malo. Further, the *Table permanente des hauteurs d'eau* (fascicules 530 A and 530 B for the Channel) is a very useful guide. For the Solent, the necessary information can be found in Macmillan's or in Reed's Nautical Almanacs, or in Admiralty *Tide Tables*.

Notes on the British reference books

Some UK publications differ from the French. They give hours and depths of water at high tide for the standard ports, and the relevant corrections for the secondary ports. However, low tide must be calculated from the mean level and the duration of mean rise.

To find the time of low water, subtract the duration of mean rise from the high water time. To find the height at low water, subtract the difference between the high water level and the mean level from the mean level.

Britain has adopted the international system, where the heights are given in metres relative to the lowest astronomical tide (LAT), and most documents have been revised. A few charts still give heights in feet (0.305m) relative to the mean low water springs (MLWS).

Tidal terms in English and French

HW	High water	pleine mer
LW	Low water	basse mer
Sp	Spring	vives-eaux
Np	Neap	mortes-eaux
ML	Mean level	niveau moyen
MHWS	Mean high water springs	pleine mer moyenne de VE
MHWN	Mean high water neaps	pleine mer moyenne de ME
MHW	Mean high water	pleine mer moyenne
MLW	Mean low water springs	basse mer moyenne de VE
MLWN	Mean low water neaps	basse mer moyenne de ME
MLW	Mean low water	basse mer moyenne
LAT	Lowest astronomical tide	plus basse mer connue
CD	Chart datum	zéro des cartes
Ft	Foot, feet	pied, pieds
	Rise	montée
DMR	Duration of mean rise	durée moyenne de la montée
Ht. Diff.	Height difference	correction de hauteur
	Range	amplitude
	Rate	vitesse estimée
	Slack	étale
	Time	heure
Tm. Diff.	Time difference	correction d'heure
GMT	Greenwich mean time	temps universel
BST	British summer time	heure Europe centrale

<table>
<tr><td colspan="3">Example of a tidal calculation for Baltimore</td></tr>
</table>

Example of a tidal calculation for Baltimore		
Reed's gives: high water at Cobh (standard port)		
time:	0441	1706
ht:	4.0	4.1
Tidal differences on Cobh		
Tm. Diff.	−015	
Ht. Diff.	−0.4	
ML	2.0	
DMR	610	
To calculate times:		
HW Cobh time	0441	1706
Tm. Diff.	−015	−015
HW Baltimore		
time	0426	1651
DMR	−610	−610
LW Baltimore		
time	2216	1041
To calculate height:		
HW Cobh ht.	4.0	4.1
Ht. Diff.	−0.4	−0.4
HW Baltimore ht.	3.6	3.7
2 x ML (2 x 2.0)	4.0	−4.0
HW Baltimore ht.	−3.6	−3.7
LW Baltimore ht.	0.4	0.3

British tide tables take this fact into account, and both systems are given where relevant. The old measures will be retained until all charts have been revised. Note that the height of the tide is not given in terms of a coefficient, but rather by the high water level for the port of Dover.

Tidal streams

All kinds of general and specific information on the streams can be found in the nautical almanacs and pilots. Many charts have *insets* in which the speed and direction of the stream are shown, area by area and hour by hour.

However, there are also some more specialised works. For the Channel, there is the *Pocket Tidal Streams Atlas*, published by the Hydrographic Office. This is very useful when crossing the Channel, but is less accurate for coastal areas (except for the Solent and the Channel Islands, which have special sections devoted to them). It nevertheless shows the times at which the tide turns in given areas, and this is usually enough for navigational purposes.

For French waters there are also charts of tidal streams produced by the publisher Éditions maritimes et d'outre-mer. These are very well produced, extremely clear and easy to read, and carry insets for particular streams around le Havre, Cherbourg and the Solent. The main problem is that the Channel is divided up between three maps, which are much more expensive and much more bulky than the *Pocket Tidal Streams Atlas*.

Title No 550 from the SHOM – *Courants de marée dans la Manche et sur les côtes françaises de l'Atlantique* – is also useful. This is complemented by the more extensive *Atlas des courants de marée*, and forms an appendix to the *Notices to Mariners*.

In order to use these works properly, refer back to your almanac from time to time. This gives clear explanations of how to use the information provided. For the present, we will just note the following facts:

– the direction of the tidal stream is the direction in which it is going, not where it is coming from (as is the case with wind direction);

– the times are given by four figures next to each other, preceded by a plus or a minus sign. A plus means 'after high water', and a minus 'before high water'. For example, the almanac may give 'the stream runs WSW at about + 0430 Cherbourg', which means 4 hours 30 minutes after high water at Cherbourg;

– speeds indicated correspond to tides of coefficient 45 or 95 (average neap and spring tides); from this, the speed for a given

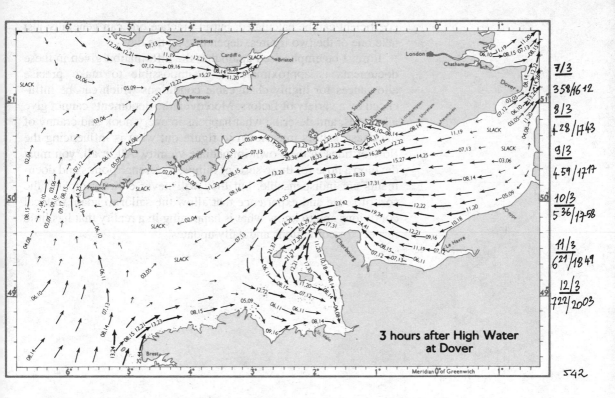

3 hours after High Water at Dover
Swansea
Cardiff
Bristol
Barnstaple
London
Chatham
Dover
Southampton
Portsmouth
Littlehampton
Shoreham
Newhaven
Weymouth
Devonport
Falmouth
Penzance
Cherbourg
Le Havre
Dieppe
St. Malo
Brest
SLACK
Meridian 0° of Greenwich
7/3
358/1612
8/3
428/1743
9/3
459/1717
10/3
536/1758
11/3
621/1849
12/3
722/2003
542

A page from the *Pocket Tidal Streams Atlas, English and Bristol Channels*. In the margin, the navigator has noted the times of day when these tidal conditions will occur for the next 6 days.

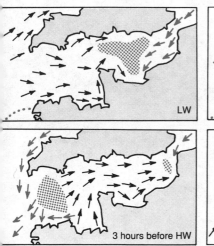

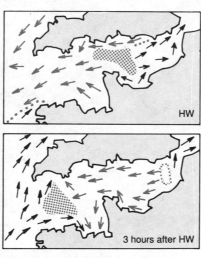

LW
HW
3 hours before HW
3 hours after HW
flood
ebb
slack

Direction of streams at different tide-hours. The hours given are for Dover or Boulogne.

coefficient can be calculated, but in practice one can generally just take one of the two figures, depending on the day.

It must be emphasised again that the information given in these documents is approximate. It is impossible to make precise allowances for highly changeable conditions which can be influenced by a variety of factors. Moreover, the documents cannot give all details, and describe what happens in every nook and cranny of the coast: sailors must learn to figure out what is influencing the flow of tides in their own immediate vicinity. All in all, you must develop a nose for these sorts of things. Reference points and documents are indispensable, but they will never entirely replace the sort of sense and experience that allow the sailor to adapt to local conditions and to know what is happening in a reality that has little respect for corrections and daily updates.

CHAPTER 2

Coastal navigation

Right! Off we go! Now what we learned in the previous chapter can be put to practical use. The landmarks will be used as leading marks for navigating close to the coast. When we are a little further out, we shall take bearings to fix our position accurately on the chart. And in turn, on the chart, we shall see how to take into account factors such as the leeway and tide, and thereby how to set a course to steer by.

Pilotage, fixing and choice of course are the main preoccupations of the navigator in sight of land. Further offshore, navigation is clearly a different problem.

Pilotage

In good visibility, and when there are plenty of landmarks, it is quite easy to navigate and to calculate the distance covered by what one can see. This is known as pilotage.

The essential reference works are, in the first place, the chart, and in addition, the Pilot Book, *Tide Tables* and the *List of Lights*. A piece of whipping twine is the only vital tool, although a bearing compass and a Cras ruler or protractor plotter can come in handy.

Although the pilot's tools are simple, pilotage is an exacting technique, requiring method and discipline. Approximations may well be enough when you are sailing in a completely clear area where there are no immediate dangers. To this end, relative positions can give a reasonably accurate guide that is often enough. However, it is a very different matter when you approach land, enter a narrow channel or sail along a coast strewn with reefs. Trusting to flair and accuracy of vision alone becomes a dangerously hit-or-miss affair, for the simple reason that it is impossible to judge distances of more than twenty metres or so by eye accurately at sea. Something more than guesswork is needed. Essentially, pilotage consists in taking reference points, and making them work for you by a simple system: leading marks or transits.

Leading marks or transits

When two landmarks appear to stand exactly one behind the other, then they are aligned – they form a transit. As a consequence, the observer must be on the extension of the line that links the two marks. All you have to do is to choose good, clear transits on the chart, know where to find them in reality, and the world (well, the coast, anyway) is your oyster. With a decent set of transits to point the way, you can enter the narrowest channels confidently. When you have them to port and starboard, you can steer a course through dangers. With two transits, you can find your position very accurately, because you are at the intersection of two straight lines. By finding a transit, one can also, as we saw at the beginning of the book, observe the leeway of a boat and know what sort of headway is being made against the tide. Further, one can use one transit to find another. In short, for the skilled pilot who can follow a chart well, each rock carries a wealth of possible projected lines which can be joined to lines taken from other rocks. Used this way, they can pilot you through the most treacherous waters and safely into harbour.

However, transit marks must be unmistakable, and for this you need good landmarks.

A buoy is not a good mark, in spite of its exact outline: it moves a little in wind and tide, and should therefore be used with caution. The same applies to a moored boat. Permanently fixed marks are needed.

Landmarks must also be as clear cut as possible: a hill without a clear top is not a good mark. Neither is a house too close to you, but its chimney might be. Lighthouses and beacons are good marks, all the more so because they are easily identifiable.

Rocks are less identifiable, but they are often all you have. Check carefully with the chart, and note their size, height and shape, which all change with the depth of water. A rock lost among a mass of others of the same height is useless – the same goes for a rock obscured by a larger one. A very large rock, an islet or a headland can only be useful if you pick out their profiles, but remember that the tide can deceptively shorten or lengthen their slopes.

The list of possible marks is potentially endless. Generally speaking, transit marks are more precise the further apart they are and the more narrow and/or clearly defined they are.

Note that landmarks on either side of the observer can in no way be considered as transits, unless you are a sea bird, or some other creature with eyes on either side of your head. On the other hand, two marks slightly out of line can serve as perfectly valid transit marks on occasion. One mark is then said to be 'open' in relation to

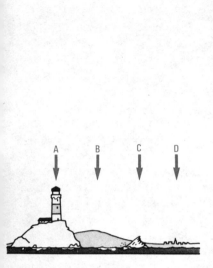

Landmarks A, C and D are good because they present a clear point or a clear vertical line. B is not a good landmark because of the rounded hilltop.

the other. Rock W, for instance, open to the right of beacon X; or lighthouse Y, open two widths to the left of tower Z. This type of transit is used, either because nothing better can be found, or because there is a danger just on the transit of the two marks; all that is needed then is for the leading line to remain open for the danger to be avoided.

When a course has to be plotted in a rock-strewn area, the choice of transit marks must be carefully thought out. Although the surroundings must be used to their best advantage, they were not specifically created for that purpose. The art of pilotage is to turn even potential hazards to good use.

All this requires a certain discipline. Everything must be foreseen in advance on the chart: the course, the leading marks, the means of recognising those marks. Nothing can be left vague or obscure, and a line of reasoning must be pursued to its logical conclusion. Doubt is tantamount to error. Even if everything seems plain sailing, it is still a good idea to have alternative plans. Having said that, do not invent a variation on the spur of the moment, as this always causes problems. Finally, no daydreaming as you watch the world go by: find the marks first and admire the scenery afterwards.

While the rules of the game are simple, playing the game, and thinking through moves is rather less so. Much depends on circumstance, and all the theorising in the world is probably rather less useful than one good example. The one we are going to look at concerns the Glénans islands, a region that is particularly useful for this sort of exercise.

To follow the pilot's working, you must have the same equipment as he has: chart, string, and the desire to get to where you're going. In order to make things easier, we have indicated the transits and marks used on the map of les Glénans in the back of the book.

Open transit: the rock X is open on the right of the tower. To be more exact, we can also say that the rock is open half a width to the right of the tower.

The ramblings of a navigator

To follow the pilot, see fold-out section 3 at the end of the book.

My name is Jézéquel. Let us suppose that I'm coming from Groix, and that I'm heading for the island of Cigogne, which is one of the Glénans islands, to see Sophie, who is on a course at the famous yachting school. The wind is WSW, I don't seem to be moving terribly fast, it's getting late and I'm getting fed up.

The entrance

Now is not the time to get fed up. Consulting the Admiralty Pilot reveals that the area is littered with rocks, and that there isn't much water between them. To help people move about, the book points out some splendid landmarks: on Penfret island, a lighthouse to the north and a signal station to the south; there is another marker on a rock known as le Huic; then there is also the fort and the tower on the island of Cigogne itself – no doubt with Sophie waiting on the ramparts. There is a tower marker on the island of Guéotec, a factory chimney on the island of Loch, a white house on the island of Saint-Nicolas, and last but not least, a marker to the SE of the island of Bananec, on la Baleine point. Not a bad little collection, all in all.

How to use the Admiralty Pilot.

My boat draws 1m. The tide is rising. A quick calculation tells me that there will be about 2.5m of water when I reach the archipelago.

In front of me is the island of Penfret, easily recognisable with its two hills, the lighthouse on one side and the signal station on the left. On which side shall I pass? It is tempting to go in from the south: the wide Brilimec channel, with its leading mark to Cigogne is clearly visible on the chart. However, to get to this channel, I would have to go round some rather less conspicuous dangers lying in wait to the SE, and I don't like the look of that.

Better to go in from the north. I shall pass close to Penfret; its rocky northern point, Pen-a-Men, is sheer. There is no foreshore.

Once past Pen-a-Men, there is a very easy entrance between Penfret and an island called Guiriden, which looks more like a sand bank with a central rock marked at (5.9m) and another marked at (3.4), further over to the east. Here we go: for somebody who isn't that good at maths, it's always very annoying to see two rocks marked in relation to different points of reference: some in relation to the mean water level (figure followed by an 'm'), and others in relation to the lowest astronomical tide (figure underlined). All this because some always emerge and others don't. Of course, it is enough, given the half-tide level for the area, to add about 2.9m to the height given for the first rocks, to have some idea of their height relative to the others (the whole business still gets on my nerves, anyway). In short, the (5.9m) one will be much higher than the (3.4) – enough said.

Between Penfret and Guiriden, there is just water, and one little black mark. The latter is a little rocky plateau, marked (1.8), and called Tête-de-Mort. When I arrive, it will be invisible, and I will have to steer fairly close to Penfret to avoid the little swine.

After that, the route is clear right along to Cigogne. There is a (0.2) marked on the route, but I will have enough water to clear it.

The main problem is finding enough safe leading marks to get round the Tête-de-Mort rock. I shall first need a transit running approximately north–south to avoid going too far west as I sail in; then I will need an east–west line showing me when I have passed the rock and can cross the barrier represented by the first leading line.

First transit: les Méaban by Guéotec

The chart shows an entrance transit. This is splendid, but, as it is right into the wind, I can't easily use it (I shall find out later that this transit is not easily visible from the deck of a small boat anyway). I shall have to find an alternative. The island of Guéotec, which lies to the south of the channel, is surely a good landmark, as the Admiralty Pilot mentions its beacon. All I need to do now is to find another landmark to line up with it.

How to find a transit on a chart.

I take my piece of twine. I put one end on the beacon and I sweep the stretch of water between the Tête-de-Mort rock and Penfret. There is nothing suitable. Likewise, there is nothing to the south of the marker, and, in any event, the height of the island would mean that I could not see anything behind it. I may have a bit better luck with the edges on Guéotec itself. I take my string and pivot left and right, using the western edge as an axis: there is nothing to be seen. I then take the eastern edge and find something straight away: first of all, there is a group of rocks called les Méaban with a nice little 6.5m peak, much higher than any of the surrounding rocks. Lining up its summit with the eastern edge on Guéotec, the string falls bang on Tête-de-Mort. Bingo! All I need to do now is to keep that transit open, that is to say, to make sure that I can always see some open water between the edge on Guéotec and the 6.5m rock, and it will be easy to avoid the rock. Excellent!

However, even if Guéotec is easy to identify, how am I going to identify my 6.5m rock from the ones around it? First of all, I must know in what order the rocks are going to come into view when I arrive. I put one end of my twine on Pen-a-Men and I sweep the channel between Guéotec and Penfret, from west to east. The first thing that I find is Penfret itself: on a level with the lighthouse, there is a foreshore which will be covered when I arrive. Then come the furthest rocks of the Méaban group, which are relatively low-lying (3.9 and 3.2); then there are some taller rocks (4.5m and 4.1m). In fact, it will be only when I have got away from Pen-a-Men a bit that I will be able to make out my (6.5m), which will doubtless be indistinguishable from the mass of the other rocks closer up. However, if I believe my twine, there is a stretch of clear water beyond the 6.5m mark, and then, after that, a (3.3m), after which I will be able to see the rocks at Ruolh. All in all, my (6.5m) rock is much higher than the other ones of the Méaban group, and is also furthest to the left, with water to the left. This seems clear enough.

Turning right: Saint-Nicolas and la Baleine
Now I need an east–west transit so as to know when I should head straight for Cigogne after having passed the Tête-de-Mort.

Are there any notable marks in the west of the group of islands? On the NW of Saint-Nicolas, there is the tower of le Huic. The chart says that it is a former lighthouse. I like lighthouses: they are easy to identify and present a clear outline. There aren't any other marks in the area, and so I will try to use this one. With my string on le Huic, stretching away towards Tête-de-Mort, I find what I want straight away: a (3.5m) rock at the top of the northern foreshore of Bananec. How am I going to identify it, however? I won't be able to see it when I pass Pen-a-Men, because it will be obscured by Guiriden. Will it be any clearer when I get a bit further south, and what will the seascape look like? In order to find out, I put one end of my string on le Huic, and I sweep the other end along the course that I will take, following my first transit. It becomes apparent that le Huic will be obscured first of all by the island of Brunec, then it will appear to its left, and the next rock that appears will be my (3.5m). Easy!

Well, it seems easy enough, but actually, it's a pretty stupid idea. Sophie says that I always like to make things as difficult as possible, and she's not entirely wrong. All of a sudden, I realise that there has to be a much easier transit using the southern coast of the islands of Saint-Nicolas and Bananec, all the more so because there are some much more precise marks: the mark on la Baleine point at the end of the SE foreshore of Bananec, and the white house on Saint-Nicolas, which must be pretty easy to spot because it functions as an official mark for the entry transit by the SE. There are quite a few houses on Saint-Nicolas, but that isn't a problem, since it is clear from their lay-out which one I want. Lining up the southernmost house or group of houses on Saint-Nicolas with the mark on la Baleine is easy enough, but finding the mark is the real trick. It is yellow and black. When I arrive at Pen-a-Men, it will be hard to see because of the island of Drénec. The colour ought to stand out pretty well, but this is not certain because the sun will be fairly low at that point and it will have the Sun behind it. In fact, as I go further south along my first transit, I will see it clearly in the passage between Drénec and Saint-Nicolas; it will appear to cross the passage, and when it touches the coast of Saint-Nicolas, then it will be time to go about anyway.

I have marked the transits on my chart, and, because I don't really have a head for these sorts of things, I have noted in the corner the sorts of things that I have to use as reference points, and in the order that they will appear: Guéotec, the (6.5m) rock from les Méabans, Drénec, Saint-Nicolas and the mark on la Baleine point. I am now ready. Soon, the Tête-de-Mort rock will be behind me. I shall then make some short tacks

How to identify marks in real life.

The view from point A.
Reality is always a little surprising when compared to the chart! However, it is easy to pick out all the elements that allow our sailor to find his first transit. From right to left: the island of Guéotec and its mark, then the (4.5m) and the (4.1m) of les Méabans, then the (6.5m) that we are looking for, which is the largest and the nearest and is followed to the left by a stretch of clear water and the (3.3m).

The transit of the (6.5m) from les Méabans and the eastern edge of Guéotec falls bang on the Tête-de-Mort. All that needs to be done to avoid the danger is to keep the transit open. At the point at which the sighting has been made, all seems well, and there is even enough time to have a quick glance at Penfret, where the signal station indicated on the map is clearly visible.

How to make the landscape move.

The view from point B.
As the navigator heads into the archipelago, he sails south, keeping his first transit open. To his right he notes some characteristic marks mentioned in the Admiralty Pilot. There is the fort on Cigogne, of course, the eastern mark of la Baleine point, and even the top of the tower of le Broc'h (since both are visible, he could even go north around the Tête-de-Mort). The large house on Saint-Nicolas is not visible yet. In the meantime, though, he can see Drénec and Bananec with their respective buildings.

Further to the right, le Huic has just appeared to the left of the island of Brunec. The black rock just to its left should be the (3.5m) on the northern foreshore of Bananec (the smaller, more lightly-coloured rocks between le Huic and the (3.5m) are therefore in the background). He will be much happier when he sees that the darker rock is the first to pass in front of le Huic.

Cures for the lovesick.

The view from point C.
The navigator passes between Cigogne and Drénec. In front of him, between the island of le Loc'h to the left and the island of Quignénec to the right, there is a large group of rocks, called Fourou Loc'h. The largest rock to the right is the (6.6m), which is a useful mark for getting out of the channel.

How to find an emergency exit.

The view from point D.
A rather enigmatic little seascape, this, which will cause the pilot some worries. From the left, it is possible to pick out, to the left of the tower of le Broc'h, Castel Braz and then Castel Bihan, then le Run, and then the first large rock of le Bondiliguet, followed by the (5.3m) we are looking for … To the right, the light-house at le Huic is clearly visible, but where is le Gluet? If things don't get any clearer, then it would be best to leave straight away by the west, on the line to the rear running between the Guéotec beacon and the north edge of la Bombe.

without going too near Vieux-Glénan (an odd name: it can't be much older than the other islands), and finally drop anchor, in triumph, beneath the ramparts of fort Cigogne.

Exit route

Sophie wasn't on the ramparts. She must be much more interested in her bearded companions than in me. I'm off. Sitting round the fire in the evening beneath the vaults of fort Cigogne, I heard tell of a tight little channel between le Huic and le Gluet – I'll use that on the way back. Looking for leading marks will take my mind off the fact that Sophie stood me up.

The wind is ESE this morning. The passage seems possible: I shall have the wind behind me for most of the time: first of all to pass to the west of Drénec, and then to move back up towards le Bondiliguet. At that point, I will have to make a detour to go NE for a while to line myself up to go through the passage in front of le Huic, and the wind may be a little too much on my nose, but it seems there is enough room to make a short tack if necessary. When I am ready, the tide will be low. There will be about 1m of water, so there is no question of going between Drénec and Saint-Nicolas. I will have to go round Drénec to the south – it is quite possible to pass between Cigogne and Drénec. The (3.2) rock on the western point of la Cigogne is perfectly visible, but the (1) in the middle of the passageway is less so. I note that the (1) in the centre of the passage is just in line with the (5.9m) on Guiriden and the (4.5) on la Baleine point, just to the left of the mark that I used yesterday. All I have to do to avoid the (1), therefore, is to keep this transit open.

Consequently, what I will do is get under way while taking a wide sweep to the north, as there isn't much water near Cigogne. I will then follow the open transit that I have just found, and then, when I draw level with the (3.2) on Cigogne, turn slightly south.

A transit to the rear: Guéotec by la Bombe

I now need a line in order to go along the south coast of Drénec. There is a passage with enough water between the shore and a (2.7). I put my string in the passage and straight-away I find a marvellous line to the rear: the Guéotec beacon by la Bombe. Obviously, it is not very easy to follow a line to the rear, but when piloting, it is often the best solution, for the simple reason that one generally knows the leading marks behind better than the ones ahead. I know the Guéotec beacon now, and I saw la Bombe yesterday when I arrived. I can see it quite easily from where I am anchored: it is an isolated rock, and will be easy to find on the other side of Cigogne.

I always use a long enough piece of string to find lines, and today I have reason to be thankful for doing so: stretching my string from the Guéotec beacon to the western edge of my map, I note that my transit from Guéotec by la Bombe has an additional advan-tage: it allows me to pass directly out of the group of islands if I am unable to find leading marks to take me up to le Huic (you never know, and anyway, I slept badly). There is just one rather annoying little (1.2) in the way, lying to the south of the tower on le Broc'h. In order to avoid it, I will have to change my line slightly as I pass to the south of Drénec. This will be relatively simple: I line up the Guéotec beacon with the northern edge of la Bombe instead of with the summit. After that, everything will be hunky-dory.

Rounding the coast of Drénec

Up until now, life has been fairly simple. However, I now need a line so that I can turn north after having rounded Drénec. Among the rocks on the chart, le Gluet appears to offer some possibilities: there is in particular a (9.2m) to the north, right behind a vast (9m). With the two rocks right in front of one another, it ought to be fairly easy to spot them. I find a line very quickly: *le Gluet by the* (5.3m) *of le Bondiliguet*, but spotting it in reality will be another story entirely.

What do I see as soon as I round Drénec? I place one end of my string on the west edge of the island, and sweep round from the west to the north. There appear in turn: the tower on le Broc'h (the only one in the area), and then a more or less unbroken line of large rocks: Castel Braz, Carrec Christophe, Castel Bihan. Castel Bihan ought to be easy to recognise, since it is made up of what appear to be sheer rocks – (7.5m) and (7.2m) – with a wide channel immediately to the right.

From there on in, things seem to get rather more fiddly, however. There are rocks everywhere: in the distance, le Run, le Gluet, le Huic; rather nearer there are the rocks on le Bondiliguet. It will be difficult to figure out what I am looking at. Thinking about it, it seems best to sweep the string back in the other direction from le Huic, whose tower is easy to identify. Keeping one end of the string on the western edge of Drénec, I put the other end on le Huic, and sweep west. I ought to see the following things: the (3.8m) of le Huic, then the (3.7m) on the western foreshore of Saint-Nicolas, then, straight away afterwards, the (6.4m) of le Bondiliguet and the various rocks of le Gluet. The first rock to the left of le Gluet is the (5.3m) on le Bondiliguet that I want. So what I have to remember is this: when I come round Drénec and see the tower on le Huic to the north, the (5.3m) I want will be just to the left of le Gluet.

How to find a more simple solution when things are too complicated.

That is still quite a few things to think about at the same time. I will have to be on my toes when I come round Drénec. It is a good idea to take some precautions: I measure the distance on the chart between the transit using le Huic and the western edge of Drénec to the other (le Gluet and the (5.3m) on le Bondiliguet): it's 200m. With a good following breeze, I will make at least 5–6kn. Roughly speaking, I should cross the 200m in a minute. If at the end of a minute and a half I haven't found anything, I will have to retrace my steps. Besides, I have a final mark – Job rock, which is a single rock ahead of me, and which will be easy to identify, even from a distance. If I can make out limpets coming into transit on Job, then I will have missed my turn by quite a bit.

How to stop in time …

A little breathing space …

All this is not absolutely clear. I think that it would perhaps be a good idea to allow myself a little space to manoeuvre to the SW of Drénec, so that I can circle around until I have found the marks that I am looking for. This turning space can be quite easily marked out by three transit marks, two of which are already known:
– Guéotec by la Bombe, which protects me to the north;
– le Huic by the west edge of Drénec, which protects me to the east;
– finally, le Broc'h by Job, which completes the triangle nicely.

I shall therefore be able to circle as long as I like, and so will have plenty of time to spot the (5.3m) on le Bondiliguet. I will then follow the leading line from le Gluet to the (5.3m), almost right up to the rock itself. At that point, I will have to turn to avoid the (6.4m) of le Bondiliguet, which stands between me and the exit route. Looking at the chart, it seems absurd to want a transit to make a little turn like that, but that's the sort of thinking that lost me my last boat, the *Sophie VII*. In any event, I have to make a tack to make that turn, and I could quite easily be caught out if I try it without having any leading marks.

Another exit channel

I note in passing that I can run clear out to the west if I've really had enough. To do this, I leave the Broc'h beacon to my left, and go out by the les Bluiniers channel. However, just for the hell of it, I think I'll stick to my original plan.

Le Buquet

I place my string between le Bondiliguet and Roc'h ar C'haor (a haunting name, for those who know any Breton) along a SW–NE axis. The north edge of Brunec, or, more exactly, of le Buquet just behind it, appears between two rocks very close to one another – one a (7.4m) and the other an (8.7m) – which should be easily visible, because they are both high and rather narrow.

If I need to tack a little, I can use this gap between the two rocks as a reference point: the north edge of le Buquet, just visible to the right of the (7.4m) will mark my northern limit, and the same edge – this time, hidden by the (8.7m) – will form my southern limit.

The view from point E.
The north edge of le Buquet is framed by the (7.4m) and the (8.7m). The latter cannot really be seen against Brunec, but is easier to make out as the line changes, and the back- and middle-grounds become more separated.

How am I going to recognise all this? Roc'h ar C'haor must be visible immediately on passing the transit line of le Huic by the west edge of Drénec – it's the first rock of any size to the right of le Huic. Then, when I am following the leading line running between le Gluet and the (5.3m) on le Bondiliguet, I will have to watch how the scenery changes to my right. Once I have passed Drénec, I should see Cigogne and then the signalling station on Penfret. At that precise moment, the two rocks that previously framed Buquet will be hidden behind Roc'h ar C'haor. I will see them reappear a moment later, and then, in the distance to their right, the island of Brunec – no problem!

The exit channel

Whether I like it or not, I need a last north–south line to get me through the channel between le Huic and le Gluet, since the foreshore of le Gluet stretches out quite a way to the east.

In order to find something that will be of use, I am forced to look a long way off: to the south of Drénec, there is the large (6.6m) rock of Fourou Loc'h. There are other rocks around it, but it lies furthest to the west and is clearly the largest. Although the (6.6m), visible between the west edge of Drénec and the east edge of the (8m) on Quignénec, is perfect, it is also quite a way away, and I will have to pick it up early as I pass to the south of Drénec. In fact, I notice that I must be heading for Fourou Loc'h as I go south between Cigogne and Drénec. It's the group of rocks just to the right of the island of le Loch, and the (6.6m) is the rock furthest on the right of them. Later, when I am nearer the exit, I will see the other rocks of Fourou Loc'h disappear one by one behind the west edge of Drénec, leaving the (6.6m) alone between Drénec and Quignénec. If I miss it – which won't be too bad, I've some water to play with – then the line between the east edge of Quignénec and the west edge of Drénec will tell me. All I shall need to do is to bear away for it to reappear.

Now, what I need to do is to carefully note down my leading marks in the order in which I will have to look for them.

The view from point F.
The (6.6m) of Fourou Loc'h is unmistakable: it stands out on its own, seen isolated clearly in the background to the left of Quignénec. We are now in the exit channel.

At anchor :	(4.5) rock on Bananec
	(5.9m) Guiriden
	La Bombe
Going south :	(6.6m) of Fournou Loc'h
On the line from Guéotec by la Bombe :	Job rock
	The tower of le Broc'h
	The tower of le Huic
	Le Gluet (4th from le Huic)
	(5.3m) on le Bondiliguet
	Roc'h ar C'haor
On the leading line from le Gluet to le Bondiliguet :	Signal station on Penfret
	(7.4m) and (8.7m) in front of Brunec and le Buquet
On the leading line from Buquet to the (7.4m) and the (8.7m) :	Fournou Loc'h

Epilogue

I have now returned home. The scenery was quite extraordinary, which is not easy to see from my sketches, unfortunately. In all events, what the sketches cannot put over is the joy and pleasure that one gets from identifying a rock in the midst of a group of others, and then being able to put a name to it. It's like being at home all of a sudden.

Whether Sophie is there or not, I will go back to the Glénan islands and do the trip in reverse, by going in through the passage by le Huic. All I have to do is to line up Fournou Loc'h between Drénec and Quignénec, and it's like fitting a key into a lock – you go in and you're at home. It's fun to figure all this out. Anyway, it's time to let you get onto the next section now, dear reader.

Taking a fix

A little way out from the coast, most landmarks become indistinct against the background. Soon all that remain are a few outstanding points, scattered along the horizon. Leading marks become scarce, and there is little likelihood of finding two at the same time to check the course.

If there are no leading marks, then the logical thing is to navigate by bearings. The pilot's twine is replaced by more complicated equipment: the hand-bearing compass and the protractor or a pair of parallel rules. Arithmetic is replaced by geometry, and we move onto the serious business of taking a fix.

Taking a fix by bearings

Fixing a position means:
– taking bearings;
– correcting them as necessary;
– plotting them on the chart;
– checking the result.

Taking a bearing

Taking the bearing of a landmark means measuring the angle at which one sees it in relation to a point of reference (ie north).

Measurements are made with a hand-bearing compass. It has a sight and a prism. A sight is taken on the mark, and the bearing shown on the compass card is read through the prism. Note that this measurement is not very accurate – especially when taken from the deck of a small boat. The further off the mark and the rougher the sea, the greater the potential for error; allow for +/–1° in flat calm, +/–2° in normal weather, and +/–5° at least in heavy weather. In order to reduce this margin of error, it is a good idea to practise using the compass. The main thing is not to tire yourself unnecessarily: if you bring the sight up to your eye first and then sweep the horizon to find a landmark, you will only make your arms ache. It is much easier to work in the following order: find the landmark, raise the compass to the chin and wait for it to settle, bring the sight up to your eye and then read off the bearing from the card.

Take care to stand where the compass will not be thrown off by

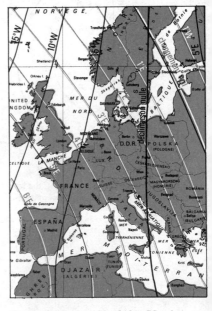

Extract from chart No 0101 GS of the SHOM (in black, lines of equal magnetic variation in 1980; in colour, lines of equal variation in declination in 1980).

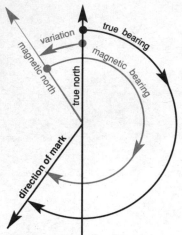

When the variation is to the west, the true bearing is smaller than the magnetic bearing.

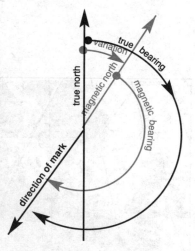

When the variation is to the east, the true bearing is greater than the magnetic bearing.

large amounts of metal. We shall come back to this later when dealing with the ship's compass.

Correcting the bearing

The compass shows *magnetic north*, and we all know that this is not the same as *true north* (direction of the meridians). Before plotting a bearing on the chart, we must first take into account the *variation*, that is to say, the angle between magnetic and true north. This angle varies not only according to where you are, it also varies over time, and changes very slightly from year to year.

According to one's position, the variation can be either east or west. It is marked on the chart along with the annual increase or decrease. In the area of les Glénans, for instance, the variation was 7°30'W in 1975; shifting by 5'E per year, it reached 6°55'W in 1982, and is continuing to decrease.

When the variation is to the east, it must be added to the bearing shown by the compass. When it is to the west, it must be subtracted. In so doing, we convert from magnetic to true bearings.

To remember how to make the correction, the mathematically-minded will recall the formula:

$$T = M + V$$
V positive if it is east
V negative if it is west

Where T = true bearing, M = magnetic bearing and V = variation.

The less mathematically-minded may find the following lines of doggerel helpful:

Variation East, Compass Least
Variation West, Compass Best

The purists can always reproduce the diagram from first principles.

In all events, it is a good idea to find some way of remembering how the correction is to be applied without having to think too long about it. Things that seem obvious in a armchair are less so when the boat is pitching in a rough sea and you are beginning to feel thoroughly seasick.

Plotting the bearing on the chart

In order to plot the bearing on the chart, you will need a protractor to transfer the angle from the meridian or parallel, and a ruler to draw the line. Since using both instruments at once is not exactly convenient, some clever designers have come up with a contraption that combines both pieces. In France, the types of protractor-ruler

Checking the hand-bearing compass: deviation

In an ideal world, the hand-bearing compass ought to indicate magnetic north. Unfortunately, however, it is subject to numerous unwelcome influences: electronics, loudspeakers, watches, the spectacle frames of the person using it, and so on, all of which can produce irregularities in the readings obtained. Even if all these pitfalls are taken into account, there can still be a difference between compass north and magnetic north: this is deviation. In theory, one ought to produce a graph, showing the rate of deviation. Although this is rarely done in practice, the following precautions should nevertheless be taken:

1. Always take your readings at the same place on the boat.
2. When cutting across a leading line, or, better still, at the intersection of two known lines, always take readings. This will allow you to see that the compass is functioning properly, and to see what degree of deviation has to be taken into account, and therefore what sort of error has to be allowed for in the bearings.

used most commonly are the Autocap, the Breton protractor and the *Cras protractor*, named after its inventor, Admiral Jean Cras.

On the Cras ruler, there are two protractors, each with a double scale, which allows you to measure an angle both from a parallel and from a meridian. An arrow indicates the direction in which the rule must be set, and that's it.

The extreme simplicity of the instrument is rather startling first of all, particularly for those not exactly enamoured of figures. However, as you move the ruler over the chart, the principle will quickly become apparent. To plot a bearing, you proceed by stages:

1. Place the chart as straight as possible in front of you, north to the top.
2. Place the ruler on the chart, so that its arrow points roughly in the direction of the mark that you have taken. This assumes that you know in which *quadrant* the mark is: for instance, a mark on a bearing of 312° is in the 4th quadrant.
3. Put one of the edges of the ruler on the mark. The easiest way to do this is to put a pencil point on the mark, and push the ruler up against it.
4. Slide and pivot the ruler so that you have at the same time:
– the most southerly centre of the protractor (this is marked with a small circle) on either a meridian or a parallel;
– on the same meridian or on the same parallel, the graduation corresponding to the bearing taken. There is no need to twist your neck round to read this scale: the upright figures are the ones you want. Note that, of the two scales on each protractor, it is the one on

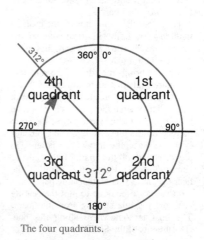

The four quadrants.

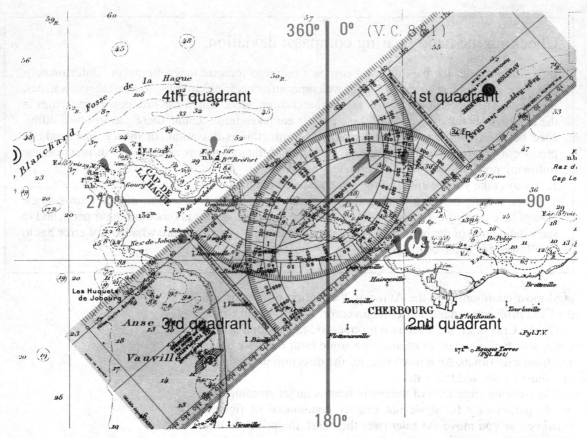

How to use the Cras protractor

A navigator is sailing in the vicinity of the Cap de la Hague. He takes a bearing on the Basse Bréfort buoy at 213° true and wants to plot it on the chart.

1. He places the protractor on the chart so that the arrow points in the direction of the bearing taken. The 213° bearing lies in the 3rd quadrant.

2. He next brings the edge of the rule onto the mark and tries to make the southerly centrepoint of the protractor coincide with a meridian or a parallel. In this instance, he uses a parallel (the bearing must therefore be read on the inner scale). The protractor is now in place: the arrow (1) is pointing in the direction of the mark; the southerly centrepoint (2) is on the parallel; the bearing 213° (3) is on the same parallel.

All that has to be done to plot the bearing is to draw a line starting from the mark. The boat is somewhere along this line. (Documents of the SHOM.)

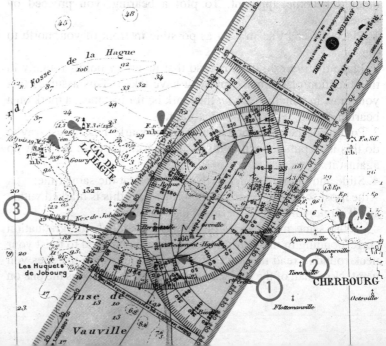

the outside that applies when you are using a meridian, and the inner one when you are using a parallel.

The only problem is to be able to place the ruler exactly in relation to these three reference points: the mark, the meridian (or the parallel), and the figures. When the boat is heaving about, this can be difficult. However, once you have managed it, all that you have to do is to make a mark (or draw a straight line if you prefer) running from the mark to where you are relative to it, ie in the opposite direction to the arrow. You now have a position line and know that the boat is somewhere along that line, or near enough.

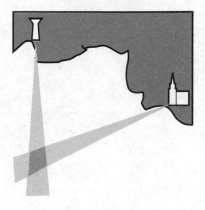

A fix by two bearings.

A two-point fix
Naturally, it takes at least two bearings to make a fix. For the best results, it is important that the two marks should not be too close together. The ideal is to have two bearings at right angles to each other. On the drawing, you can see that inaccuracy in the bearings used gives rise to a quadrilateral of uncertainty, which grows as the marks are further away, and if the boat is pitching.

A three-point fix
A fix with only two bearings is seldom accurate. It is usually necessary to take three bearings to hope for any degree of accuracy. Ideally, these marks should be about 60° apart.

Since the task can take time (and since the boat is still moving), it is a good idea to take the first reading on the mark that appears to be moving the least, which will be the one that is furthest away, or which lies nearest to the axis along which the boat is travelling.

When you plot these bearings on the chart, you get a triangle – a cocked hat. The boat should lie within this triangle. The size of the triangle gives an indication of how good the fix is. If the hat is huge, then there is an error somewhere, either in the identification of the landmarks, or in the bearings themselves. If it is small, then one may assume that no glaring mistakes have been made, but remember that it is still only an approximation. If there is no hat at all, ie the three bearings meet on the same point, then don't get carried away: there's probably some slight error somewhere. Taking a fourth bearing will show how accurate you really were.

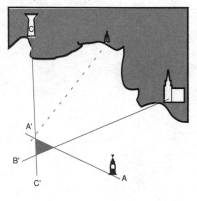

Nothing proves that we are in the cocked hat. The bearing AA' is the most precise, because the tower is closest. A fourth bearing would help.

A fix by two bearings and a transit line
Sometimes one comes across a transit line. The moment that one crosses that line is a good one to take a fix: all you need to do is to take two bearings, and you get not merely a three-cornered hat, but rather a segment bounded by the two bearings on the transit line. This sort of fix is much more precise.

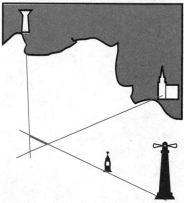

A fix by two bearings and a transit line. The only possible imprecision is in the bearings.

Checking the fix

When you have plotted the bearings on the chart and have not got too ridiculous a cocked hat for your pains, you must next check the fix and, if possible, try and improve on it. This is done by orientating the chart, so that it lines up with the scenery around you. Starting from your fix, the most obvious features should all then lie on the same bearing from you as they do on the chart.

As we are passing Trévignon point, we can use it as an example.

The weather is good, there are marks close at hand, and in exactly the right sort of position: on the left, there is the beacon on les Soldats, in the middle, the Trévignon lighthouse, and on the right, the tower of Men-Du.

We take the following bearings: les Soldats at 342°
the lighthouse at 19°
Men-Du at 69°

The corrections for variation must be included as shown on the chart: 7°30'W in 1975, which gives – with the annual shift of 5'E – 7°05'W in 1980 (about 7°, for the purposes of calculation).

This gives us: les Soldats at 335°
the lighthouse at 12°
Men-Du at 62°

The three bearings give a decent enough sort of hat, and we must now see if the cap fits. Orientating the chart, we see that it corresponds largely to what we see: the château of Trévignon is to the right of the lighthouse; the tower of Men-Du is to the left of Raguénès; the Corn-Vas buoy is to the right of Île Verte.

Since Men-Du is the nearest mark, its bearing is probably the most precise of the three, and therefore it is likely that we are in the northern part of the hat. However, we can improve on this, by tracing the angle of uncertainty of each bearing on the chart. For the current weather conditions, this is probably 2° either side of the bearings we have (see the section entitled 'Taking a Bearing'). Theoretically, we ought to be in the dark-blue diamond in the centre.

In practice, there is no need to be so precise, but if the possibility of inaccuracy is not eliminated, we could equally be to either side. A mistake is easily made: supposing the bearing of Men-Du had read 59° (therefore 52° true) on the compass, instead of 69°. Then the hat would have looked quite different: rather smaller, it is true, but this would not necessarily be a good sign. Nonetheless, the château is definitely to the right of the lighthouse, and Men-Du is to the left of Raguénès. There is only one detail that would allow us to spot the error: on the chart, Corn-Vas almost forms a line with Île Verte, whereas in reality it is definitely to the right.

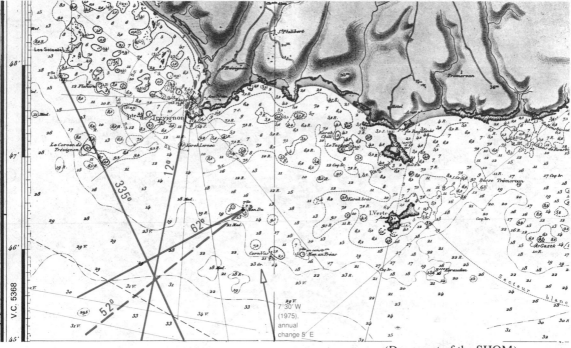

(Document of the SHOM)

Finding new landmarks

However good they may be, all landmarks have one important defect: it doesn't take long before you can't see them any more. The boat moves on, and new landmarks must always be found to form the next links in the chain. When navigating in unfamiliar waters – which is useful practice, and everyone ought to try it – finding them can be quite hard work and takes a bit of thought.

It is a good principle always to check the identity of a new landmark against the chart, even if you think you recognise it.

When you have identified two or three landmarks and you take a bearing on them to make a fix, it is a good idea to take a bearing on one or two marks ahead that you have not yet identified. Then plot these new bearings on the chart and see what they correspond to. The problem can also work the other way round: you notice a useful landmark on the chart, but it is as yet impossible to pick it out. Measure the bearing on the map, and then, on deck, look for the mark with the compass. However, take care that, when taking the bearing from the chart (which is true) and converting it into a compass bearing, that you make the required correction in the other direction. In Brittany, where the variation is west, the degree of

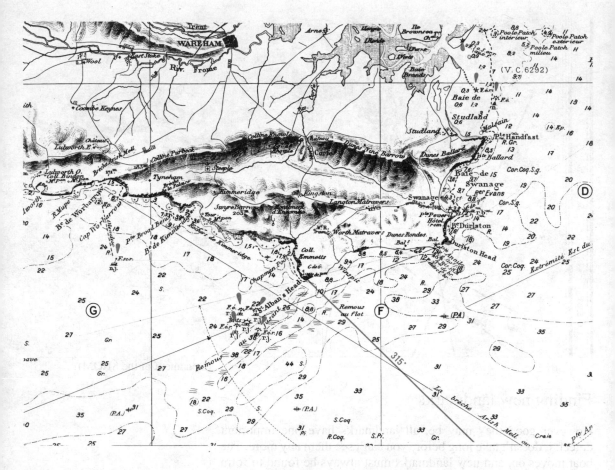

Coming from Cherbourg, you want to make a landfall on Durlston Head to enter Poole harbour. You catch sight of the coastline in the haze, but nothing can be identified except a fairly sheer headland on the left. Its bearing is 315° true, and by moving the ruler over the chart, you see that it must be St Alban's Head. Consequently, you must be further to the west than you thought. (Document of the SHOM.)

variation must be added to the true bearing.

Where the magnetic variation remains west, the important things to remember when making corrections are that:
– when bringing the compass bearing down on the chart, *subtract* the amount of variation;
– when bringing the chart bearing up to the compass, *add* the amount of variation.

So: to go down, subtract; to go up, add.

No matter how careful you are, you can never be sure of not making some sort of glaring mistake. In this, as ever, common sense rules. If the fix shows that you have travelled 32 nautical miles in an hour, then something is not quite right (unless you've bought the wrong sort of boat). The same applies if the fix says that you have 15° of leeway to windward. Anything that seems unlikely is probably wrong.

Using the sextant in coastal navigation

The method of taking a fix by three bearings, described above, is the most common way of fixing position. Now, if there is a sextant on board, and you are just itching to try using it, then you will doubtless be delighted to learn that it is quite possible to use it to make a fix when navigating in sight of the coast. The sextant can even be of considerable use when you only have one mark, or when the marks are too close to one another to allow you to take a precise bearing in any other way. Moreover, there is no need to get a very expensive one – one of the plastic models will do perfectly well.

The great advantage of a sextant over a compass is that it gives a precise and definitive measurement the moment that you can line up the two points that you are trying to use.

Fix by bearing and height

Thanks to the sextant, it is possible to work out your position in relation to one marker, even though you may have no idea of its height. There are many marks whose heights can be found in the various documents, whether it is a mountain or a lighthouse. In general, lighthouses are the most common points of reference, given that their heights can be found in the *List of Lights*.

The principle is as follows: first take a bearing on the mark, which allows you to trace a line on the chart. Then, using the sextant, measure the angle α between the base and the summit of the mark. You can then work out how far away the mark is, and therefore the position of the boat on the line. This can be done by applying the following (simplified) formula (maximum error: 10%):

$$d = (2\,H) \div \alpha$$

where d is the distance in nautical miles, H is the height of the mark in metres, and α is the angle in minutes of arc.

Some special cases can apply:
– the structure is completely visible (for example, a lighthouse) and you know the height. This is easy enough: all you have to do is make sure that the top and the base of the structure are both visible through the lens to know the angle α;
– the base of the mark is not visible, and the height is only given in relation to a reference level – NGF (Nivellement Général de la France) for a hill or a mountain, coefficient 95 (high water) for the top of a lighthouse. In this case, you must first calculate the tide to be able to correct the height of the mark, allowing for the tide. Having done this, you line up both the edge of the water and the top of the mark in the lens; this will give you the angle α;

> **To save time**
> The table for coastal navigation given in *Reed's* gives the distance of the mark derived from its height and the angle measured by the sextant.

– the foot of the mark is over the horizon. This is quite common, since, for an observer at an altitude of 2m, the horizon is only 3 nautical miles away. This time not only does the tide have to be taken into account, but also the curvature of the earth. This can only be done by means of a very complicated formula, so complicated, in fact, that it is usually best to use the relevant tables.

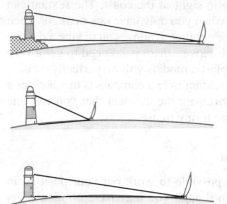

The structure is completely visible, and the height is known: this is the simplest example.

The water is visible at the base of a structure of known height: the state of the tide must be taken into account.

The base of the structure is over the horizon: both the tide and the curvature of the earth must be taken into account.

We are approaching Jersey from the SW, and we can only see the lighthouse at la Corbière. We take a bearing on it of 12°. Glancing at the *List of Lights*, we see that la Corbière is a white tower, 19m in height. The angle measured by the sextant is 7'.3.

We apply the formula: d = (2 x 19) ÷ 7.3 = 5.2 nautical miles.

Fix using horizontal sextant angles (position circles)

Taking a fix by horizontal sextant angles is useful when you have three marks, but which are only separated by a small angle (they are too close to one another).

It is known (or it is about to be) that the geometrical position from which one can see two points, A and B, at an angle α, is along the arc of a circle passing through A and B. In plain English, this means that, having taken the angle subtended by A and B at the observer, it is possible to construct a circle passing through these two marks, and one can then be certain of being on that circle.

Taking in the same way the angle subtended by B and that of another landmark, C, a second circle can be constructed, passing through B and C. This circle cuts the previous one at the position of the observer. Smart, eh?

The angle between A and B is measured by the sextant: 17° (angle α) and then the angle between B and C: 22° (angle β);
– a straight line is drawn joining A and B;
– from A, another straight line is drawn, at an angle of (90° – β) to the line AB;
– the same thing is done at point B;
– the intersection of the lines is the centre, c1, of the circle whose arc passes through both A and B;
– the same procedure is used for B and C, in order to obtain the centre, c2, of the circle whose arc passes through B and C;
– the two circles intersect at M: this is the position of the boat.

　　If you don't have a compass, or if the arcs that have to be drawn are too large for the compasses you have, then you can use the following method:
– draw a line making an angle of (90° – α) with AB through the point B;
– draw a line perpendicular to AB running through A;
– the two lines intersect at a point d1;
– similarly, draw a line through B at an angle of (90° – β) to BC, and then trace a line perpendicular to BC, passing through C. This gives a point d2;
– draw a straight line linking d1 and d2;
– the line perpendicular to the segment d1– d2, passing through B, gives the position of the boat (M).

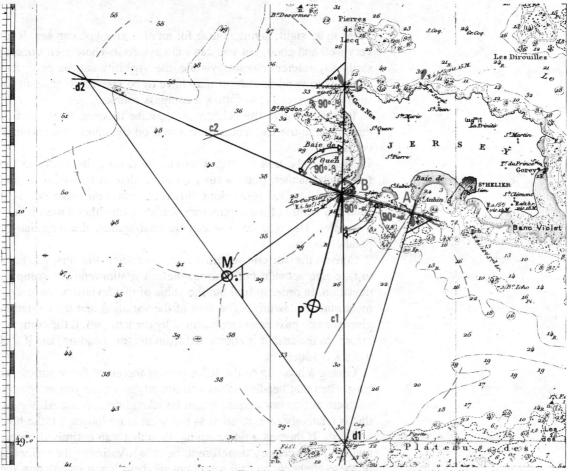

Fix using position circles. The blue lines are marked by compasses, the black lines using a square. At P we have the fix, bearing 12° and distance 5.18 nautical miles. (Document of the SHOM.)

To the SW of Jersey, now that the visibility is a little better, we
can take a fix using this method, using three marks not too far from
one another: A, the lighthouse on Noirmont point; B, the Corbière
lighthouse; C, the lighthouse on Gros-Nez point (on closer examination, it is apparent that we can't see it. Still, there's no holding us
back on account of something like that: we can use the edge of
Gros-Nez point as C).

This time the sextant must be used flat so that the images of the
two marks coincide.

Giving a course to the helmsman

Steering by sight, laying course for an objective you can see, is all
very well and good, but you can't always do it. There aren't necessarily any reference points visible, the visibility can be poor, and
drift due to wind or current may have to be taken into account. In
such cases, you have to follow a compass course.

In order to give the helmsman a course to steer, the navigator
must change the true course measured on the chart to a compass
course:

1. Measure the true course. This can be done quite easily in the
following manner: place a ruler on the course to be followed, and
then slide the Cras ruler along this ruler until you make the most
southerly centre of the protractor coincide with either a meridian or
a parallel. The true bearing can be read against the meridian or
parallel chosen.

2. Convert the true course into a compass course. For this, you have
to take into account both the magnetic variation and the compass
deviation. In order to find out the value of the deviation, the instrument must be 'swung'. The sum of the variation and the deviation
gives the compass error (represented by the letter w). If the compass
error is to the east, it is subtracted from the true heading, and if it is
west, it is added.

Giving a heading to the helmsman is therefore fairly simple, at
least when that heading takes you directly to where you are going,
and neither tide nor current has to be taken into account. However,
this is relatively rare: as soon as the wind is no longer aft, the boat
will drift. If there is a tide running, then that's an entirely different
matter. It is necessary therefore to be able to estimate the influence
of these elements and take account of them when calculating the
heading.

Estimating leeway and current

Estimating leeway comes with experience and familiarity with your boat. You have to watch out for it, and note how it varies according to different speeds, different sail combinations and the strength of the wind. Near to land, there will be no lack of opportunity to calculate leeway precisely. If you are passing very close to a buoy, for instance, keep an eye glued on its bearing in relation to your course away from it. At the end of 10 minutes or so, take a bearing on the buoy: comparing the compass heading and the compass bearing taken will give you an idea of the degree of leeway. Another way is to make a fix, then follow a precise heading, make another fix a little while later and then measure the angle of leeway on the chart.

Estimating the stream is usually more difficult. Here, it is the sea that is moving in one direction or another, taking everything that isn't anchored to the bottom with it. All you can do in this case is to trust the tidal information given in the *Tide Tables* and the insets on charts, which, if local conditions make it necessary, give the strength and direction of the stream hour by hour, along with the tidal coefficient. If it is stated that, for instance, between 6 and 5 hours before high water, the stream is 1.5kn, bearing 306°, then you must take into account the fact that, whatever the heading of the boat, it will be carried 1.5 nautical miles along a bearing of 306° during the hour in question.

This is the distinction that has to be made between *course through the water* and *course made good over the ground*. The course made good over the ground, the only one that counts at the end of the day, equals the course made by the boat (as measured by the log) plus the course made by the sea in the same period. The course made good over the ground can differ wildly from the course through the water in the same period. Laying a course in such circumstances can be a very tricky operation.

The following examples show the kind of difficulties facing the navigator sailing around the coast of northern Brittany, focussing particularly on the stretch between the NW buoy of les Minquiers and the lighthouse at le Grand-Léjon.

The compass error (w) is equal to the sum of the variation (D) and the deviation (d):

$$w = D + d$$

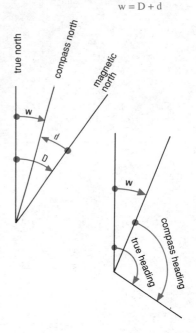

In order not to get mixed up between the true heading and the compass heading, there is a useful little formula:

True heading = compass heading + w

This can also be expressed as: Compass heading = True heading – w

+ if w is east
– if w is west

(assuming for w the same conventions as for D.)

First voyage: no leeway

On this day, the wind is north. The boat will therefore be on a broad reach on starboard tack. Because of the wind, there is no problem with leeway. We are in the period of the neap tides (coefficient 25), and so the current is negligible.

The bearing on the chart is 224°. Our navigator adds the magnetic variation of 7°W. The compass is properly compensated.

The compass course is therefore: 224° + 7° = 231°

Second voyage: with leeway

This time the wind is WNW. The trip will therefore be a close fetch on starboard tack. On this point of sailing, the boat will make considerable leeway. The navigator, who knows the boat, estimates this to be 5°, to port, naturally. To arrive bang on at le Grand-Léjon, he must therefore aim 5° further to starboard – that is, add 5° to the course. The calculation then is:

True course	224°
Correction for variation	+ 7°
Correction for leeway to port	+ 5°
Compass course	= 236°

If the wind were from the SSE, the boat would be close fetching on port tack, and would therefore have 5° leeway to starboard. In this case, you would have to aim 5° extra to the left, that is to say, to subtract 5° from the bearing. Thus:

True course	224°
Correction for variation	+ 7°
Correction for leeway	− 5°
Compass course	= 226°

If the wind were SSW, then you would have to beat. In this case, there would be no point giving a course to the helmsman. It might even be a good idea to cover up the compass: the helmsman should not try to follow a course, but rather simply concentrate on making the best possible course to windward. Apart from that, the navigator should lift the corner of the sail from time to time, to see what is happening.

Third voyage: with constant tidal stream

The wind is weak NE and the tides are neap. We are leaving the NW buoy of les Minquiers 3 hours after high water (HW + 3).

The first thing to work out is the speed of the boat. This can only

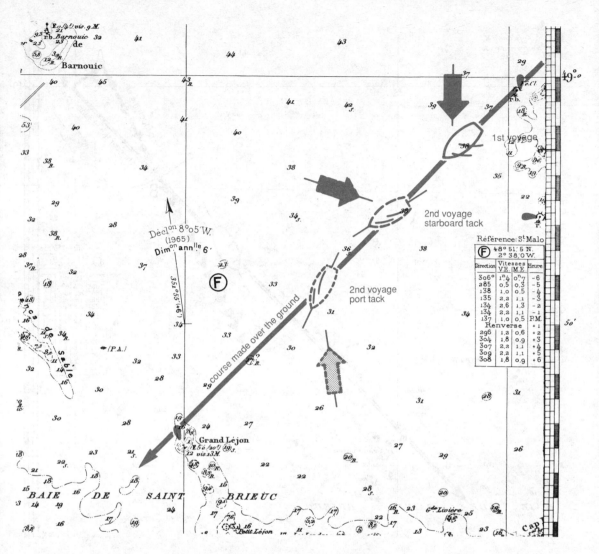

Reference: St Malo

		F	48° 51.5 N.		
			2° 38.0 W.		
Direction	Vitesses			Heure
	VE.	ME.		
306°	1.4	0.7		-6
285	0.5	0.3		-5
138	1.0	0.5		-4
135	2.2	1.1		-3
134	2.6	1.3		-2
134	2.2	1.1		-1
137	1.0	0.5		P.M.
Renverse				
296	1.2	0.6		+1
304	1.8	0.9		+2
307	2.2	1.1		+3
309	2.2	1.1		+4
308	1.8	0.9		+6

really be an estimate and our navigator thinks it will be 5kn. Since we have 19.5 nautical miles to cover, the journey will take about four hours.

In area F, during the 4 hours following HW + 3, the chart inset indicates the direction of the current as varying between 304 and 309°, and its speed between 1.8 and 2.2kn at springs, 0.9 and 1.1kn at neaps. As we are now at medium tides, we can reckon on a constant current of 1.5kn, bearing 307°.

To lay the right course, we shift the departure point on the chart for the distance and direction the tide will take the boat off course during an hour's sailing.

Heading of the boat in relation to the true course, with leeway made due to the wind. (Document of the SHOM.)

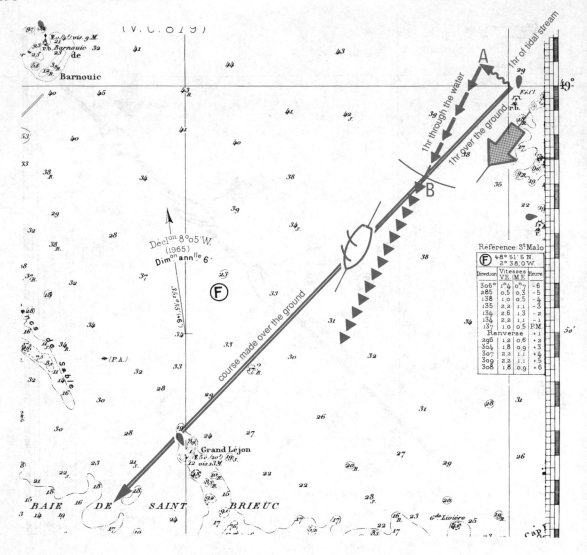

Heading of the boat in relation to the true course in a constant current. (Document of the SHOM.)

1. We plot the direct course from NW Minquiers to Grand-Léjon.

2. From the NW Minquiers buoy, we plot a line representing an hour's current: that gives us point A, 1.5 nautical miles at 307° true from the buoy.

3. Taking point A as a centre, we mark an arc of radius 5 nautical miles (speed of the boat through the water). This arc cuts the direct course at point B.

4. We draw the line ΛB and measure the angle it makes with the north: 206°.

This is the true heading. Now it remains to calculate the compass course. Since the wind is NE, the boat will be running, and there will be no leeway.

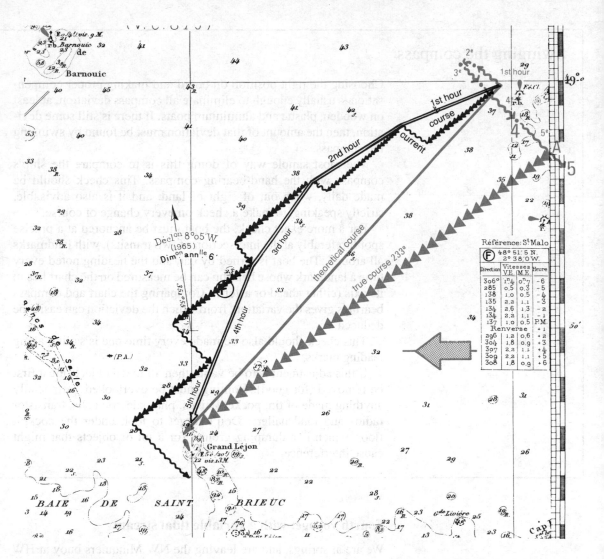

Thus we have:

True course	206°
Correction for variation	+ 7°
Compass course	= 213°

The tide is slightly against us. *The speed over the ground is therefore not as great as the speed through the water.* It is represented by the length of the vector NW Minquiers – point B, ie 4.8kn instead of 5. It will therefore take a little longer to reach Grand-Léjon than if there were no tide.

Heading of the boat in relation to a variable current.

In principle, by calculating the course from point A, it ought to be able to pass le Grand-Léjon without difficulty. However, if the wind drops and the boat slows, then the trip will take longer than estimated. It might well be a good idea to allow for a quarter of an hour of extra tide, and thus calculate the course from point 5. (Document of the SHOM.)

Swinging the compass

Choosing the right position on board and making proper compensation is usually enough to eliminate all compass deviation, at least on wooden, plastic and aluminium boats. If there is still some deviation, then the amount of that deviation must be found by swinging the compass.

The most simple way of doing this is to compare the ship's compass with the hand-bearing compass. This check should be made daily, when out of sight of land, and it is also advisable, strictly speaking, to make a check on every change of course.

For a more exact check, the boat must be anchored at a precise spot (preferably at the intersection of two transits), with landmarks all around. The boat is turned by oar, and the heading noted every time a landmark whose bearing can be measured on the chart lies in its axis (either ahead or astern). Comparing the chart and compass bearings gives the variation, from which the deviation can easily be deduced.

This check should also be made every time one is sailing along leading marks.

If this adjustment is to be valid, then all metal objects must first be removed (for good). Nothing must be overlooked – especially anything made of tin, pocket knives, photoelectric cells, transistor radios and loud hailers. Don't forget to look under the cockpit floor, which is a dumping ground for a lot of objects that might cause interference.

Fourth voyage: with a variable tidal stream

We are at springs, and are leaving the NW Minquiers buoy at HW – 6. This time it is all too obvious that the chart inset shows that there will be considerable tidal variations in the hours to come.

We shall have to calculate the bearing in relation to the whole of the journey: this means shifting the departure point to compensate for all the tidal changes that will take place along the way.

First of all we must calculate the time taken for the voyage.

The wind is east, therefore abaft the beam, but weak. The boat will probably travel at about 4kn. Is it possible to make the trip in about 4 hours?

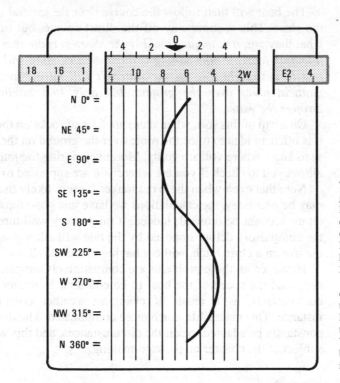

This table is very easy to make and gives compass error without any calculations. First of all, you trace the compass deviation curve, which is obtained by swinging the compass. Here we can see that, when on a heading of NW (315°), the deviation is 3° east.

The small sliding rule is calibrated on the same scale as is used for deviation. The variation for the particular locality is set on the sliding scale, so that it matches up with the arrow (here, 7°W). The compass error for each bearing is then simply read off: at 315°, it is 4° west.

To find out, we shift the departure point, taking into account the tidal variations in the next 4 hours:

1st hour: 1.4kn at 306°
2nd hour: 0.5kn at 285°
3rd hour: 1.0kn at 138°
4th hour: 2.2kn at 135°

From the theoretical point 4, we measure the distance to Grand-Léjon: 18.8 nautical miles – the actual distance to be covered through the water. Four hours is a bit short – add another hour of tide: 2.6kn at 134°.

From point 5, the distance is 19.3 nautical miles. Five hours is then more than we need, so we place our theoretical departure point between points 4 and 5. From there, we plot the line to le Grand-

Léjon and measure the true course: 233°.

Since there is no leeway due to the wind, the compass course is:

$$233° + 7° = 240°$$

The boat will then follow the course over the ground shown on the chart. This is some way off the direct course, but tides being what they are, *it is unquestionably the shortest route that could be found: in fact, the boat sailing in a constant heading will make the trip in a straight line on the water. It will have travelled 20.5 nautical miles over the ground, but only 19.3 nautical miles through the water.*

On a trip of this sort, when there are a lot of rocks on the bottom, it is often an idea to trace the route over the ground on the chart, so as to know where you are going. Moreover, during the journey, this allows you to check if you are where you are supposed to be.

Note that even when the wind makes it seem likely that tacking may be necessary, the calculations we have just gone through must on no account be omitted. Indeed, it might very well turn out that the compulsory detour imposed by the tide will allow you to make the trip on a close fetch, without having to tack at all.

However, all these problems are comparatively simple. We have supposed the speed of the boat to be constant. In reality, it varies continuously, as a result of changing weather conditions for instance. This makes life much more complicated. The theory must constantly be adapted to suit the circumstances, and this will be the subject of the chapter on passage-making.

CHAPTER 3

Navigation at sea

Dick Sand, apprentice on board the brigantine *Pilgrim*, making passage from Auckland to Valparaiso, is promoted captain as a result of dramatic events that resulted in the officers and almost all the crew perishing. Although near to despair, the boy is determined to bring his ship safe into harbour. Not knowing how to make an astronomical fix, Dick has to rely on dead reckoning alone, that is to say, an estimate of the course travelled each day based on the compass and log readings. Unfortunately, there is a treacherous villain on board who has managed to put a piece of iron under the ship's compass. This gives it a deviation of 45° east. The blackguard also arranges for the log line to break. Thereupon, a terrific storm ensues, driving the boat towards the SE, and then to the NE at a speed impossible to estimate. The upshot is that Dick Sand, having passed Cape Horn without realising it, and mistaking Tristan da Cunha for Easter Island, finally runs aground on the shores of Angola, believing he has finally arrived in Bolivia. Such a colossal mistake in dead reckoning is without precedent in the annals of the sea, but that is the tale told by Jules Verne in *A Fifteen-Year-Old Captain*, one of the most gloriously botched-up novels of all time. Nonetheless, the work stands as a parable of navigation: no captain can expect to finish on target if the reckoning is out from the word go.

Nevertheless, provided that there are no blackguards on your boat, dead reckoning is the most accurate way of locating your position when out of sight of land, and it is the method we shall examine in detail in this chapter.

After studying dead reckoning, we shall consider the different techniques for finding your position accurately when approaching land. The only real difficulty about navigation offshore is when it comes to making a landfall. You don't have to have made a particularly long passage for this apparently simple procedure to become problematic: all that has to happen is for the fog to come up when you are a few cables out from land, or for you to be caught at night along a badly lit coast. These methods must be mastered therefore even if you have no intention of sailing offshore: while sailing out of sight of land is the dream of all sailors, it can quickly become a nightmare if you are not prepared, and remains a risk every time you set out.

The other dream of the apprentice sailor is sailing by the stars. Navigating by the stars is only really of any use on long journeys, but knowing the basic principles is a pleasure in itself and contributes to one's knowledge of the sea. It is for this reason that we will attempt to boldly go where no one has gone before …

Dead reckoning

There are now two ways of navigating offshore. There are electronic position-fixing devices, which cost between £1,000 and £20,000, and which allow you, as long as you have enough electrical power, to find out your position to within anything between about 2 nautical miles and 200m simply by pressing a button. There is also the old method of dead reckoning, which is as old as the sea itself. One thing is certain: *while the first of these two methods is not absolutely necessary, the second is indispensable.*

Whatever the quality of equipment, there is always the possibility of a power failure, or, if the boat is struck by lightning for example, of electrical and electronic equipment being disabled or destroyed.

Dead reckoning is a method of calculating the course made good by the boat from its last known position. This is based on the distance run, on the estimated leeway and tidal stream and on the course followed. Transferring the dead reckoning onto the chart – a process known as *plotting the course made good* – is a simple enough operation in itself. It consists of:
– correcting the compass course by the amount of the variation, deviation and leeway, so as to obtain the true course;
– from the true course, plotting the distance made good through the water, and marking on it the distance run;
– finally, adjusting, if necessary, the position arrived at by the amount the boat has drifted because of the tidal stream.

This will then give you the course made good over the ground. In order to lay a course, the navigator had to think ahead and reckon on the conditions you might possibly encounter. When plotting the course made good, the navigator has to take into account what has actually happened, and what the conditions were like. Evidently, these are never quite as foreseen. Correctly assessing the information at hand in order to provide a dead reckoning is clearly the main difficulty, and requires a highly developed feel for sea conditions.

It is obviously not just a question of checking off the thousand-and-one details that allow him to arrive at a dead-reckoning position. At most, all we can do here is to lay out some basic principles to guide the beginning navigator. Of course, the image of the navigator as an artist lost in prophetic contemplation should not be taken too seriously: a dead reckoning is as much the product of the entire crew, especially when they are used to sailing together and all have some experience in navigation.

Appraising the available information

Having an accurate last-known position available is the most important factor in making a dead reckoning or when estimating position. If you make a mistake with the first button, you'll get caught with your pants down, to mix a metaphor.

Even when nobody had any intention of sailing out of sight of land, the navigator must always be on the alert. It is not strictly necessary to be making a fix feverishly every 20 minutes, when visibility is perfect and the forecast is for cool, changeable weather; however, if there is any danger of fog, then it is a good idea to take a fix every hour at least, and at every change of heading.

Is the boat being kept on course?

Is the helmsman following the course accurately? A good question. Keep a discreet eye on the course from the cabin using the handheld compass. Some helmsmen don't like having the wind dead astern, and always tend to come on to a broad reach; others, close-hauled, get too close to the wind, which gives a lot more leeway than you might have expected: note differences of this sort. One helmsman, possibly a novice, always steers 5° too much to starboard, so give them a course 5° to port – and so on. If the boat is yawing too much, then the sails will have to be trimmed to make things easier for the helmsman. When close to the wind, do not give a course – this will make dead reckoning easier: if one is following a course in these conditions, and the wind varies, then it becomes impossible to estimate drift with any degree of accuracy. Steering as the wind dictates means that the leeway remains constant, which is what counts. What really matters on this point of sailing is that the helmsman should be able to say honestly what average heading you have followed. Inexperience is not so enduring a problem as pigheadedness.

Leeway

The strength of the wind, point of sailing, sea conditions, the tuning of the boat, and the skill of the helmsman are all variables that have to be taken into account when estimating leeway. Always check leeway at every opportunity, but don't tell the helmsman what you are doing, as they will concentrate on keeping the course during the check, thus rendering the exercise useless. The thing to check is what the helmsman is doing rather than what they can do when under constant surveillance.

Distance run

Logs are fairly reliable provided that their strengths and weaknesses are taken into account: some are optimistic, and some tend more towards caution. Most of them are inaccurate at lower speeds.

The vane of a patent log has to be carefully watched. It might have suffered a knock since last used, and could then turn faster (or more slowly) than it should. It can also catch up in seaweed and jam as a result. Keep an eye on the dial and take readings regularly – every hour, for instance. Get into the habit of making a mental estimate of the speed of the boat, so that you will be able to assess the distance run if the log breaks down.

Electronic logs are almost always equipped with an alarm which rings whenever the vane or the wheel stops turning. Doppler logs are practically unaffected by seaweed and other floating debris.

The tidal stream

Tidal stream predictions are all very well, but personal observation is better. The information given on tides is only accurate up to a certain point, and, as is well known, the wind can upset all the calculations anyway. Passing a lobster pot or a buoy is a useful chance to check the direction and approximate strength of the tidal stream. When an exact position is required, such as in fog near land, it is well worth a detour to take a closer look at any fixed object.

Offshore, it is sometimes difficult to determine the direction in which the boat is moving. The lead line, or a fishing line with a heavy weight, can then come in handy. Drop the line, giving it plenty of slack; the angle that the line makes with the stern when it touches bottom gives a fair indication of the direction of movement in relation to the bottom.

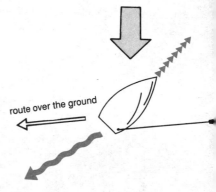

route over the ground

The actual route over the ground does not always correspond to what you thought it was.

Apart from the tidal streams covered in the previous chapter, on coastal navigation, it is a good idea to know the general streams whose strength is given in nautical miles covered per 24 hours in the *pilot charts* and other equivalent documents. One should also take note of the surface currents created when the winds are strong and blow in the same direction for long periods. Tables can be found in the Admiralty Pilots.

The log book

The entries in the ship's log can be followed in reverse back over the course run, rather in the way that Theseus found his way out of the labyrinth. All the details used in laying the course must be entered: courses (the one asked for and the one actually followed), the log readings, strength and direction of the wind, sea conditions, name of the helmsman. All changes should also be noted: going about, changes of sail, changes in the weather, fixes taken (and how they were made), along with any ships met. Nothing must be judged insignificant on an a priori basis.

It is wiser to list only the bare data: that is to say, compass course, rather than true course, the figure read from the log rather than the distance run, and so on. If each individual adds his or her own personal interpretation in the log book, then the risk of error is multiplied by the number of people on board, and the facts can thereby be irrevocably distorted.

The ship's log must also be kept scrupulously up to date, even when dead reckonings are not expected to be made. It is always possible that a reckoning might have to be made. Furthermore, if there is an accident, then the ship's log can be invaluable as evidence of what actually happened. In France, it is compulsory to keep a log for all boats of category 3 and up (ie if sailing over 20 miles from shore), and a good idea for categories 4 and 5 (over 5 miles from shore).

If the boat is equipped with a Loran, Decca, Satnav or other position finder, the log must still be kept up to date, and the position noted at least four times a day. This position can then serve as the starting point for a dead reckoning in case of instrument malfunction or failure.

The uncertainty principle

No matter how great the navigator's flair and precision may be, dead reckoning can seldom give an accurate position. There is a degree of uncertainty in all data, and thus the position is the sum of all those uncertainties. This total can vary according to the conditions encountered. Sailing in an area with little or no tide (or where the tidal streams are precisely known), and running free with a steady, moderate wind on a calm sea, the margin of error is probably as low as 4% for the distance run. On the other hand, if you are tacking in light weather and unfavourable currents, or have had to heave-to in bad weather, then the margin of error can easily be 10% and higher.

When a passage has been made in a straight line, then the area of uncertainty can be marked on the chart with some degree of precision: it is a quadrilateral, longer than it is broad if there is more reason to doubt the distance run than the course followed, or broader than it is long if it is the course rather than the distance that seems open to question. If you have had to tack, however, then the area can only best be represented as a circle, whose diameter corresponds to the maximum amount of possible error. It is assumed for

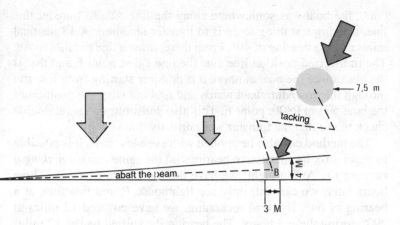

7,5 m

tacking

abaft the beam.

B

4 M

3 M

From A to B, the boat has followed a course with the wind free. In order to calculate the quadrilateral of uncertainty, uncertainty over course (here, about 4 nautical miles) must be distinguished from uncertainty over distance (here, about 3 nautical miles).

From B onwards, because the wind has changed direction, it becomes difficult to maintain the distinction. To make things simpler, the area of uncertainty is taken to be a circle, whose diameter is equal to the maximum degree of uncertainty (here, 7.5 nautical miles).

the purposes of calculation that one is in the middle of this circle, but of course, you could be anywhere within it.

As the distance covered increases, the circle of uncertainty grows, and the reckoning becomes more and more open to error. Obviously, it must be updated at every possible opportunity, particularly when landfall is made. Running fixes and running a line of soundings are rather old-fashioned methods, but are not bad for gathering information, and a radio direction finder can also help. Meeting another boat can also be useful. All these methods allow for greater precision, but the value of this information is minimal unless the actual reckoning is relatively accurate. This is the most important technique to master.

Transferred position line

The position in question is a geometrical one: either a bearing or a position circle, or a measure of height by a sextant.

The principle of the transfer is very simple. We know that at least two of the points must be recognised if a fix is to be made: the point where our bearings cross gives our position. But if there is only one bearing available, it can always be kept in reserve until another is found. The first position line is then transferred according to the course run: it then intersects with the second. However, the fix obtained by this method is only accurate if the dead reckoning has been correctly kept up.

A fix can thereby be made with transferred position lines from two marks. At 8 o'clock a lighthouse A is seen at 120°. At midday, lighthouse A is out of sight, but we can now see lighthouse B on a bearing of 60°. By dead reckoning, we have run 18 miles at 40°. At

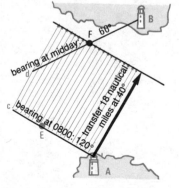

Fix by transferred position line on two marks
While transferring the bearing Ac, the area of uncertainty introduced into the dead reckoning between 0800 and midday must be taken into account.

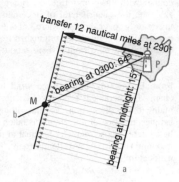

Running fix by different bearings on the same landmark
Here, equally, the transfer of bearing Pa is also subject to uncertainty affecting the dead reckoning between midnight and 0300. Three bearings in succession reduce this area of uncertainty by creating a hat.

0800, the boat was somewhere along the line Ac. To transfer this line, the simplest thing to do is to transfer landmark A 18 nautical miles along a bearing of 40°. From there, draw a line parallel to Ac. The transferred position line cuts the line Bd at point F and that is the position of the boat at noon. It is possible starting from F to run through the procedure backwards and find out what the position of the boat was at 0800: point E. This also constitutes a useful double check to see that the transfer was correctly done.

The method can also be applied with even less data. It is possible to make a fix by successive bearings on the same mark – *making a running fix*. At midnight, we have the lighthouse P at 15°. Three hours later, we can still only see lighthouse P, and this time at a bearing of 64°. By dead reckoning, we have covered 12 miles at 290° during these 3 hours. The bearing Pa, shifted by the 12 miles of the reckoning, cuts the bearing Pb at point M, and this gives the boat's position at 0300.

This system of transferring position lines on the chart has great potential. There is nothing to prevent us from transferring the same position line several times in succession, making it 'tack' with the boat and using it in several different positions. A detailed example will show the kind of working necessary to make a landfall using this kind of method.

On the road to Groix

It is dawn on a June morning. Fog has come down during the night and is still persisting in large patches, although the sun is breaking through in places. We are coming in from Belle-Ile, and want to enter the port of Lorient. The wind is NNE. Because of bad visibility, it is better to go round the west end of Groix and be able to make landfall on an open, easily recognisable coast: the point of Pen-a-Men.

We are making a course of 330° true. At 0500 we catch sight of Groix through the haze, but cannot identify anything precisely. It is time to plot our dead reckoning on the chart. We estimate the margin of error to be 6 or 7%, which gives us, taking the distance run since Belle-Ile into account, a circle of about 2 nautical miles in diameter. This circle is drawn, and in its centre (the estimated position of the boat), we enter the time of the fix (0500) and log reading (53.2).

At 0512, we see the lighthouse at Pen-a-Men for a moment in a clear patch. Its bearing is taken immediately: 50° true. This is bearing I. When this position line is plotted on the chart, it shows that the estimated position (EP) was somewhat optimistic: we have not covered as much ground as we thought. The area of uncertainty is no longer the circle, but only a sector of it, length equal to the diameter

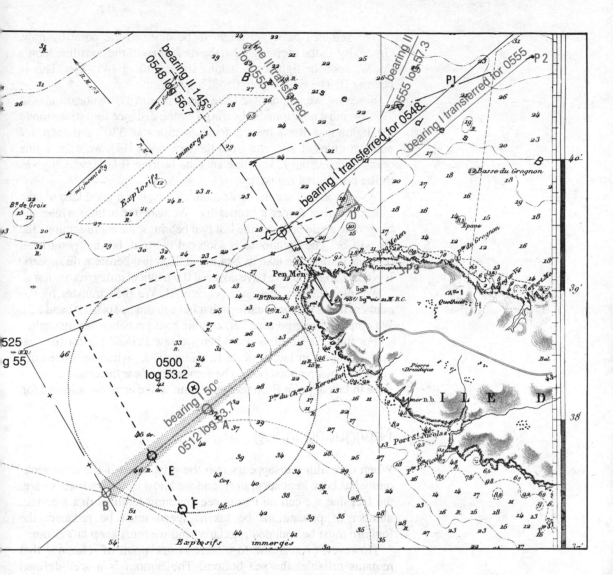

(Document of the SHOM.)

of the circle, and width equal to the possible uncertainty of the bearing. The boat should be at point A.

It is nonetheless wise to reckon on being in the most unfavourable position, that is at point B. To clear Pen-a-Men from point B, we reckon we still have 1.3 nautical miles to go, on a bearing of 330°, before we go about. We shall therefore go about when the log reaches 55. This margin is good enough to avoid any risk of collision, but close enough to have a chance of seeing it.

At 0525, we go about, and proceed on a heading of 70° on port tack.

The minutes pass. We ought to be close to the point by now. Gradually, in the morning mist, the dark mass of the coastline looms up. We spot the lighthouse, taking its bearing at 145° true. This is bearing II. The time is now 0548, log 56.7.

Since we went about we have therefore run 1.7 nautical miles at 70°. We must now transfer bearing I by the distance run, so we move the lighthouse itself by 1.3 nautical miles at 330° and then 1.7 nautical miles at 70°, and from the new point (PI), we draw a line parallel to bearing I. This line cuts the bearing II at C, which gives us the position of the boat.

As we can still see the coast quite clearly, it is a good idea to take a third bearing to get a proper fix. We wait for a little while: the bigger the angle between the last two bearings, the more accurate the fix will be. The lighthouse is soon out of sight, but the point itself remains visible. We take its bearing at 205° just before it disappears. It is 0555, log 57.3. We have covered 0.6 nautical miles from point C.

We plot the new bearing: bearing III. We then transfer by 0.6 nautical miles the two bearings that have given us fix C (P2 and P3). We obtain a three-pointed hat, and the boat probably lies inside it.

For the sake of curiosity: when we saw Pen-a-Men for the first time, we were in fact at point E; and at 0500, when we traced our circle, supposing ourselves to be somewhere near the centre of it, we were in fact at point F, on the outer limit of the error we allowed for.

Navigating in fog

When everything disappears into the mist, even if the dead reckoning has been kept accurately, and we know exactly where we are, the fact that we can no longer see anything requires that a certain number of precautions be taken: speed must be reduced, the foghorn must be sounded regularly, and we must keep an ear out.

However, even in the fog, there is one point of reference that remains reliable: the sea bottom. The bottom is a well-defined stretch of ground, covered with plains and valleys, various sorts of plants and deeper channels, and has the useful characteristic of rising when land is near. It is therefore possible to make landfall in dense fog as long as you are in an area with easily identifiable features on the sea bottom, and you take accurate soundings.

The procedure to follow varies according to the nature of the bottom: sometimes there is a line of soundings that will keep you clear of all the dangers along the coast. Sometimes you need to fix position by running a line of soundings. However, everything depends on the depth sounding equipment you have available.

The echo sounder and the lead line

The echo sounder and the lead line are clearly very different instruments. The echo sounder can take soundings at great depth and gives accurate and continuous readings. The lead line is really only accurate in shallow water (less than 15m) and only gives

How to swing the lead
1. The foredeck hand swings the lead with a pendulum motion …
2. … throws it as far forward as possible …
3. …and lets the line run out through finger and thumb.

information at intervals. For depths greater than 20m, the most that one can know is whether the boat is between different depth markings. It is therefore impossible to use a lead and an echo sounder in the same way. The one allows you to figure out your position with great accuracy, the other registers the approach of dangers.

Another important difference is that the use of the echo sounder needs no special expertise on the part of the operator, while the use of the lead calls for some experience and practice.

When an exact depth has to be taken in shallow water, the procedure is as follows. The line should be ready in a bucket, or laid loose on the deck. To throw the lead you should usually stand on the leeward side of the boat, about amidships. Hold the lead in the leeward hand, with the weight just above the water, then set it swinging with a pendulum motion and throw it as far forward as possible, so that it hits the bottom before the boat overtakes it. The faster the boat is going, the further the lead must be thrown, but take care not to hit anyone with it.

As soon as the lead hits the water, it makes a splash that leaves a ripple. When you come up to this ripple, the line is held straight up and down to mark the depth.

As soon as the water gets fairly deep, then the result becomes

4. The lead must be on the bottom when the boat passes over it.

If the lead brings up sand, the bottom is sandy; if it brings up mud, the bottom is muddy; if it brings up gold, stop and drop anchor at once.

rather hit and miss, since the boat has generally passed before the lead line reaches the bottom. If it is vital to get an exact sounding, then the boat must either slow or stop.

Up to 20m, the lead is particularly useful for finding the depth contours. The technique is then somewhat different. If you want to know, for instance, when you will cross the 20m line, you first make ready the required length of line (20m plus the depth of water above chart datum for that hour of the tide, plus the freeboard and the height of the stern rail to which the line is fastened). One of the crew then throws the lead from the bows of the boat as far forward as possible. The line must be vertical when you pass on a level with the ripple (if it isn't, you're going too fast). Once you have passed the ripple, haul in the line, and you will be able to tell by the tallow smeared on the base whether you have touched bottom or not.

Sounding in deep water

In order to be of real use in deep water cruising, an echo sounder must be capable of registering depths up to at least 100m. If it can do that, then it can supply all kinds of precious information far offshore. When crossing the Channel between Torquay and Paimpol, for example, a dead reckoning which has become pretty shaky owing to periods of calm and a certain amount of beating can be brought up to date again when crossing Hurd Deep, when the sounder will suddenly indicate depths of over 100m for a short distance. Coming in to make landfall at Penmarch in thick weather, in an area littered with rather nasty rocks, you know you have nothing to fear as long as the 100m line has not been reached.

Making a landfall at Groix – described in a previous section by way of illustrating the method of transferring position lines – could have been done in quite a different way, if the sounder had been used. The moment you sight the lighthouse at Pen-a-Men for the first time, the echo sounder will give you an exact fix immediately. Thanks to the bearing, we know that the boat is somewhere along the line drawn from the lighthouse, but as the sounder gives a depth of 45m, we must be somewhere close to point E.

These few examples give a simple idea of what can be done with the echo sounder. Certainly, such a piece of equipment is almost as useful as the DF aerial. Sounders are, furthermore, almost all equipped with an alarm which can be set to a specific depth. This is very useful for tacking safely along the coast, when there is a depth contour running more or less parallel to the coastline.

Following a depth contour

Following a depth contour with an echo sounder is child's play. However, as we have seen, it is equally possible to follow one with a lead line. Obviously, the boat must not be going too fast, nor must it be tacking. In practice, following a depth contour is generally a matter of not moving too far away from it.

Let us take the example of the approach to Groix for the last time, and examine the profile of the depth contours around Pen-a-Men point. Even if the fog had got thicker, it would have been perfectly possible to go round the point in safety by following the 20m contour, which would give us a wide berth around all the possible dangers.

Another example is the entry into the port of Concarneau. Suppose we were caught by the fog 1.5 nautical miles to the south of the Cochon beacon. We take soundings and find less than 10m of water, so we immediately set course NW to find the 10m line again, which we then follow, always leaving it slightly to starboard. It is thereby easy to arrive at the Cochon beacon, and from there enter the channel by dead reckoning, keeping the 5m contours to either side.

Running a line of soundings

Of course, there is not always a depth contour that will lead us directly to where we are going. On many occasions we have to proceed step by step, trying first of all to reach a spot that can be identified with some degree of certainty. This allows us then to fix our position before going any further.

To make a fix by using soundings, the dead reckoning usually has to be made by *running a line of soundings*. To do this, take a piece of squared tracing paper, which can then be moved over the chart parallel to the meridians or the parallels. This effectively forms a blank chart with north at the top.

As we approach landfall, the track made good over the ground is plotted on the tracing paper, along with the soundings taken. Always pay attention to the scale of the chart when marking the track and the soundings. The next step is then to move the tracing paper over the chart, and to try to make the soundings you have marked match up with the ones on the chart. You may find your position very quickly and very accurately, but things may not be so easy and you will then have to backtrack and begin again, always keeping the dead reckoning up to date. The whole thing can tend to become an exercise in perseverance, and so the example we will use will be rather complicated.

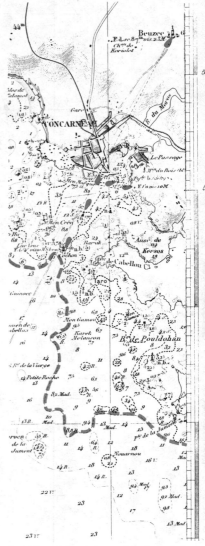

In thick weather, it is possible to reach the Cochon tower by following the 10m depth contour.

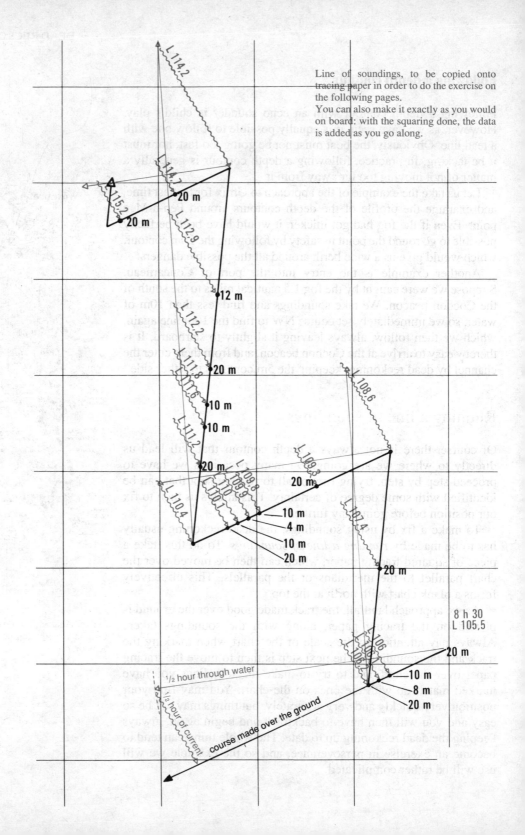

Line of soundings, to be copied onto tracing paper in order to do the exercise on the following pages.
You can also make it exactly as you would on board: with the squaring done, the data is added as you go along.

L 114.2

L 114.7

L 115.2

20 m

20 m

L 112.9

12 m

L 112.2

L 111.8

20 m

L 111.6

10 m

L 111.2

10 m

20 m

L 110.8

L 110.6

L 110.9

L 109.8

L 109.3

20 m

L 110.4

L 101.7

10 m

4 m

10 m

20 m

L 101.4

L 108.6

20 m

8 h 30
L 105,5

106
108
108

20 m

10 m

8 m

20 m

½ hour through water

½ hour of current

course made over the ground

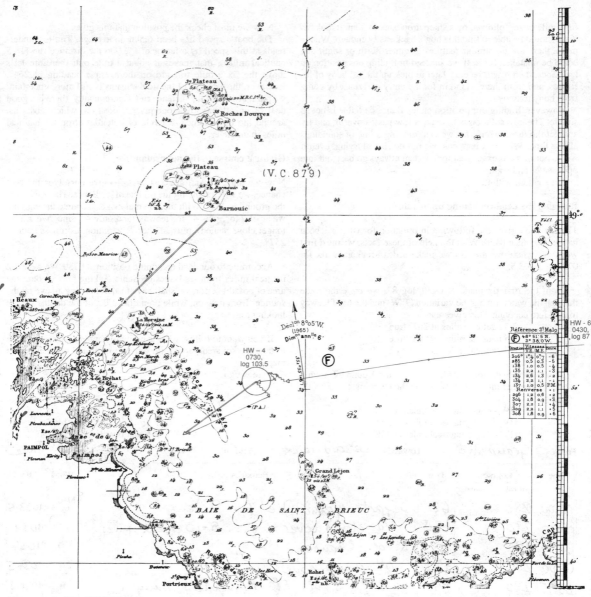

(Document of the SHOM.)

Making a landfall at les Bancs de Sable

We are en route from Granville to Lézardieux. It is neap tides. At 0430 (HW −6) the navigator makes a fix, placing the boat 2.3 nautical miles to the south of the SW Minquiers buoy. The log reads 87. Wind NW force 4. We are close-hauled on the starboard tack and the heading has averaged 280°.

Fine weather, smooth sea and good visibility. The navigator thinks it isn't really necessary to plot the course and goes to bed.

At 0715 the navigator is rudely awoken: fog has come in. A

glance outside is enough to show that, sure enough, visibility has fallen to about half a mile. What should we do? Go on and make a landfall by soundings, or tack around gently, trying not to hit anything until the fog lifts?

First, let's take a look at the chart. Is there a possible point on the coast we are making for, that would serve as a landfall and that is well away from all dangers? Yes! Les Bancs de Sable, off Paimpol. They are very easy to recognise by sounding: the bottom rises slowly up to the 20m line, then continues at less than 20m for a mile or so, followed by a sharp drop back to 30m. It looks as if we should be able to find this hog's back easily enough. What's more, there are no similar features to either north or south that could be mistaken for it. If we succeed in finding our position on les Bancs, then it will be easy later to pick up the SE buoy of les Basses, and from there, stand in for the entry of Trieux by going from buoy to buoy.

However, finding our position on les Bancs de Sable is not so simple. The best solution is to make a few passes over it, and try and get the most precise fix we can, running a line of soundings all the time. Whatever happens, we run no risk in trying: even if we do not find our exact position, we can always go back out into open water and wait.

Let's get on with it.

Bringing the dead reckoning up to date

The log book gives the following information for what has been happening since 0430. With the help of these facts, we must first work out where we are. So we make a dead reckoning fix for 0730, log 103.5.

From the first fix made at 0430, log 87, we trace the route through the water, taking the variation (7°W) and the 6° of leeway to port into account. This gives us:

2.5 nautical miles at 267° true
5.5 nautical miles at 264° true
8.5 nautical miles at 262° true

Then, we trace the route made good over the ground by moving the fix by the tide movement shown on the chart inset:

HW −6: 0.7 nautical miles at 306°
HW −5: 0.3 nautical miles at 285°
HW −4: 0.5 nautical miles at 138°

Now we must check the position that this gives.

The boat's speed has been 6.5kn on average. The log under-reads at this speed by a factor of 6%. On the distance run (16.5 nautical miles), that makes it about a mile out; therefore let's move the fix a mile forward on the average heading of 264°. However, the estimate of the tidal streams is still more uncertain: we put it at 10% of the distance run. Consequently, there is a good deal of uncertainty over our present position, which gives us, around the fix obtained, a circle of potential error 1.7 nautical miles in diameter.

Giving a course to the helmsman

Now we must try and get on target. To give ourselves the best chance, we will try and hit the middle of les Bancs. The track over the ground is 235°. With the tide that makes a course through the water of 246°, plus 4° for leeway (and only 4°, since we are no longer close-hauled), plus another 7° variation. Compass course: 257°.

According to our dead reckoning position at 0730, we were 2.2 nautical miles from les Bancs de Sable. Taking into account the area of possible error, we shall have to start keeping an eye on the sounder from now on, while preparing a list of the depths we are looking for.

If you want to follow what is going to happen, now is the time to take the squared paper with our plot on it and place it on the map.

Here we go!

Extract from a logbook (blank log © 1991, International Log Book A/S).

From	Granville		Towards	Lezardrieux	And at		Date	21 June

Time	Course		Log	Remarks	Wind	Bar
	Ordered	Steered				
00.00	280		62	Depart Grandville for Trieux	NW 4	1033.5
01.00	280		67.5	1/4 cloud cover vis. 5–10 naut. miles	"	1034
02.00	280		73	S of Chausey	"	1034
03.00	280		79.5	0 cloud cover	"	1034.5
03.45	280		84	c. 2m S of SE Minquiers buoy	"	1034.5
04.30	280		87	c. 2.3m S of SW " "	"	1035
05.00	280		89.5	mist on horizon 1/4 cloud cover	"	1035
06.00	277		95	wind heading slightly	"	1035
07.00	275		100.5		"	"
07.15	275		102	fog		1036
07.30	275		103.5	DR 245° true Les Bancs 7.2m uncertainty ±0.85m		

Date	Distance Run	Engine Hours Run	Fuel Remaining

area in which the buoy is visible

**Worst case scenario:
following a depth contour along the coast**

If the dead reckoning becomes completely useless as a result of instrument failure in foggy conditions, then one of the more extreme solutions is to follow a depth contour along the coast, in order to establish position again. As soon as landfall is made on the unidentified coast, then you can follow a line of soundings at either 5 or 10m for a few hours at a low speed, in order to see whether the track obtained corresponds with a section of the relevant depth contour on the chart. This method allowed the boat *Gauloise IV* to identify Miquelon, and then to enter the port of Saint-Pierre when visibility was less than 0.25 of a nautical mile in 1982.

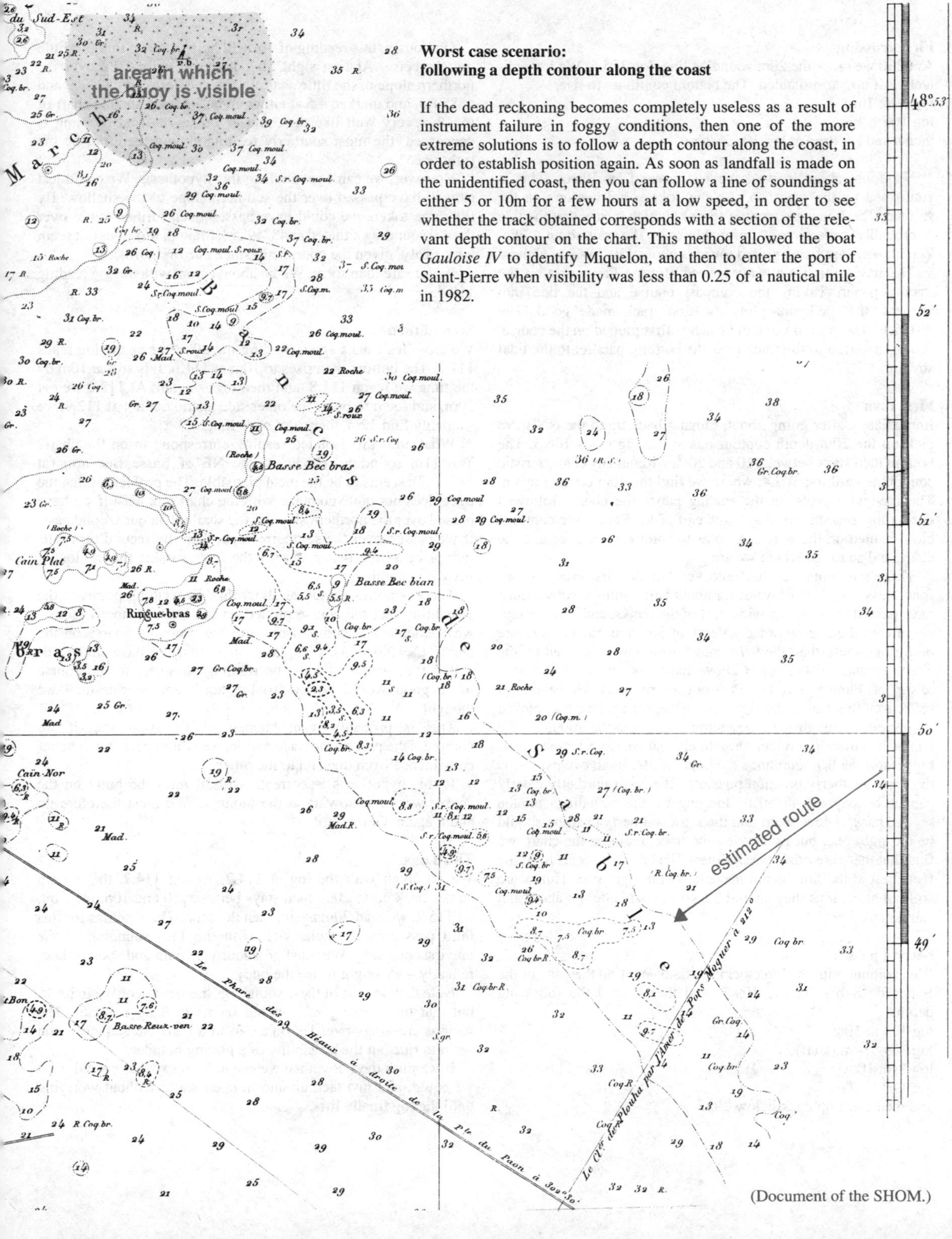

estimated route

(Document of the SHOM.)

First crossing

At 0830 we cross the 20m sounding line, log 105.5. We immediately luff up, close-hauled. The bottom continues to rise:

log 106: 10m
log 106.1: 8m
then a sudden drop at log 106.2: 20m.

No doubt about it, we have just crossed les Bancs. This is confirmed by the presence of a few lobster-pot markers on the surface. The floats are tending to sink, which means that the tide is probably quite strong – probably over 1kn, say about 1.3kn. The markers are being pulled towards about 150°. We go about.

The navigator has already started plotting the course on the tracing paper. Taking the compass course and the tide into account, the navigator plots the first track made good. The distance measured through the water is first plotted on the course, then transferred to the track over the bottom, parallel to the tidal stream.

First turn

Immediately after going about, moving back up to the NNE, we pick up the 20m depth contour again; the log reads 106.3. The bottom then stays between 10 and 20m, without any characteristic soundings until log 107.4, where we find the 20m contour again. The navigator plots on the tracing paper the course followed during this second crossing to the east of les Bancs. We continue close-hauled on the port tack so as to compare the trace and the chart, and so to see where we are.

There's nothing very definite yet. On the first crossing, we found less than 20m of water for about half a mile or so: we must have passed over quite a wide part of the banks, and it is perhaps significant that we recorded a depth of 8m. We cannot therefore be further south than the 9.7m and 8.1m depths recorded on the chart, around 48°48'.8 (just above the transit between the bell-tower of Plouha and the Porsmoguer marker). However, on reflection, this cannot be right, since the 8m reading was picked up just before the drop in the bottom and not in the middle of the banks. It is therefore rather more likely that we have passed a little higher, on the 8.7 soundings at about 48°49'. In all events, this is the most southerly position possible. The most northerly clearly cannot be beyond 48°50'.5. Judging by the soundings on the second pass, it does seem that the most southerly position should be the right one, but by moving the trace about on the chart, we find that there are other possibilities. The one that seems to fit the facts best at the time is not necessarily the right one. Things are still not as clear as they should be, so we had better go about and start again.

Second pass

We go about with the log clocking 108.6. We find the edge of the Bancs de Sables at log 109.3, and then record the following depths:

log 109.8: 10m
log 109.9: 4m (aha!)
log 110: 10m
log 110.1: 20m
and then the drop back below 20m.

Obviously, this reading of 4m will help us make things a little more precise. At first sight, it looks as if we passed over the northern slope of the little shallow situated between 48°49'.9 and 48°50'.3, and marked 4.5 at either end. The trace and the chart fit together very well like that, and as far as the first crossing is concerned, the most southerly reading should therefore be the right one.

However, we can't yet confirm this hypothesis. We could just as well have passed over the southern slope of the shallow. By the same token, we could have passed even further south: over the 4.9 sounding situated at 48°49'.5 (although this does not seem very likely, given the course run since our first turn).

Better safe than sorry. We go about again, with the log reading 110.4.

Second turn

We cross les Bancs again, finding the 20m line as the log reads 111.2. The bottom then rises to 10m at 111.6. It is still at 10m by the time we reach 111.8, and then drops again. At 112.2 we get 20m, and seem to be on the other side again, but no: at 112.9, we suddenly find 12m, then 20m once more.

What does this isolated reading correspond to on the chart? The 11m sounding, shown to the NE of Basse Bec arm (at 48°51'.7), seems to be the most plausible. The problem is that the trace does not quite coincide with the chart, not least if we have passed over the northern slope of the shallow on our second pass. If we passed over the southern slope, then the second turn falls into place a little better, but it's the first crossing that no longer fits with anything.

There is nothing unusual about this. Everything points to the possibility that the course plotted on the tracing paper is somewhat extended in comparison with the probable course on the chart. The most likely explanation is that we have underestimated the current. It must be running stronger, so the course made good would be less to the north and slower than we thought.

This is probably what happened. We guess that if we compress the plot on the trace a little, we would get a much better coincidence from one end to the other.

If this hypothesis is correct, we will miss the buoy on the course we are following at the moment. We must therefore go about again. Geronimo!

Third pass

We go about with the log at 114.2. At log 114.7, the bottom comes back up to 20m, then stays between 20 and 10m for a bit. At 115.2, we read 20m again, then the drop. The readings for this third pass coincide quite well with the 11m sounding of the previous crossing. We must go about yet again and soon – theoretically – we ought to see the buoy.

Note that not one of these soundings has been decisive in itself, but that the working as a whole seems to hang together. The various crossings over les Bancs form a coherent sequence and seem to rule out the possibility of a glaring blunder.

If we miss the buoy, then we can at least say that we did what we could, and just tack around in open water without worrying until the fog finally lifts.

Radio navigation

The log and soundings are not the only means for establishing position in bad conditions. There are also a certain number of radio-electrical navigational aids, which can be of use in keeping a check on the boat's position. The most commonly used in amateur sailing is radio direction finding, whose basic principles are simple enough: with the help of the appropriate type of radio receiver, the bearings of various transmitters are established, and these bearings, when plotted on the chart, allow a fix to be made.

Transmitters

The transmitters used in radio direction finding are known as circular radio beacons, and transmit a specific signal on a predetermined frequency on the long-wave band.

In order to avoid overcrowding the frequencies, radio beacons usually transmit their identification signals three to six times in succession on the same frequency. They transmit in turn and always in the same order. The signal transmitted by each beacon lasts 1 minute in all and consists of:
– a silent period of at least 5 seconds;
– the identification signal of the beacon, a group of two or three Morse letters, repeated several times for 22 seconds;
– a long dash lasting 25 seconds;
– the identification signal repeated once or twice for approximately 8 seconds, after which the next beacon comes in.

The characteristics of the radio beacons are given in the Admiralty *List of Radio Signals*. There are also radio beacon maps

Form of the message for the circular radio beacon for the cape of Antifer (TI). The basic form applies to all other radio signals.

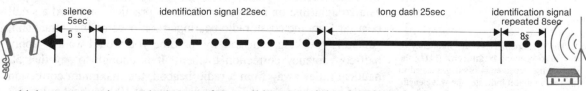

which are convenient and adequate for small boats, and the signals are also given in Macmillan's and Reed's Nautical Almanacs, or, for the French coast of the Channel and the French Atlantic coasts, in the *Almanach du marin breton*.

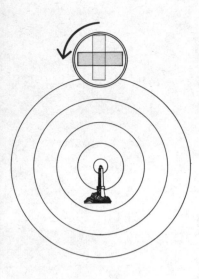

If the ferrite of the DF aerial is in the position marked in blue, then the sound is at its weakest; if it is in the position marked in black, the sound is at its strongest.

The receiver

The receiver is a radio set with a movable aerial plugged into it, referred to as a DF aerial. The aerial used on board small boats is a piece of ferrite rod usually attached to a small HB compass.

When the receiver is tuned to the frequency of a radio beacon,[1] then the radio wave transmitted by the beacon induces a current in the DF aerial, with an intensity that varies according to the position of the aerial. This is exactly what happens in an ordinary transistor radio, which must be orientated in relation to the transmitting aerial if you want to hear the music properly. The strength is at its maximum – and consequently the sound itself is at its maximum – when the ferrite rod is at right angles to the direction of the transmitter. The strength of the signal is at its minimum when the rod is end on to the transmitter. It is this null point that you want to find in order to get the bearing of the beacon: it is a more precise indication of direction than trying to distinguish the point at which the signal is at maximum strength. When the null – the arc of the weakest signal – has some breadth, you rotate the aerial slowly to find the edges of the null, and the bearing of the radio beacon lies in the middle of this arc.

The magnetic bearing is read directly from the compass. Note that some aerials are not fitted with a compass, but rather only a *rotating loop* which gives the heading of the radio beacon in relation to the axis of the boat. In order to obtain the true bearing of the radio beacon, all that then needs to be done is to add this relative bearing to the true heading of the boat (subtracting 360° if necessary).

The bearing obtained is accurate 180° either way, that is to say, you do not know at which end of the ferrite rod the beacon lies. Some receivers are equipped with a device which can tell you the direction of the beacon, but, with the exception of a few unusual situations (such as a radio beacon on a light vessel in dense fog), it should be fairly obvious what the bearing is.

When the boat is a long way away from the beacon, another step can be taken: the navigator must apply half-convergency correction. This enables him to plot the bearing (which is an arc of a great circle) as a straight line on a Mercator chart. In practice, on board a small boat far from the coast, radio bearings soon become inaccurate and, generally speaking, unusable by the time you would want to apply half-convergency correction to them. It is enough to say that 50 nautical miles away from a radio beacon, the maximum correction would be of the order of 1.4 nautical miles; at 100 nautical miles, 3.7 miles; at 200 nautical miles, 5.3 miles. The correction is nil for north and south bearings, because the arcs of a great circle, which make up the meridian, appear as straight lines in Mercator's projection.

1. The documents give the frequency of the radio beacons in kilohertz (kHz); the dial of the receiver is often graduated in metres, so that it indicates the wavelength. To convert from frequency to wavelength, apply the formula:

$$L \text{ (in metres)} = \frac{300,000}{F \text{ (in kHz)}}$$

The value of radio bearings

For various reasons, DF radio bearings are rarely accurate. Some of these reasons pertain to the way in which the radio waves diffuse, others are connected with the process of reception itself.

Wave propagation. Radio waves are not always transmitted in a straight line: they can be deflected by an uneven surface and be refracted when they pass obliquely from the land to the sea. The direct wave can be subject to interference from an indirect wave reflected by the ionosphere (night error).

Error due to refraction can be as much as 5° when the bearing cuts the coast at an angle of less than 30°. Night error is often greater still: it is worst at sunrise and at sunset, so these are bad times to take radio bearings. The best time is in the middle of the day.

Reception. A variety of factors combine to create difficulties at the receiving end. In the first place, radio waves can be deflected around the aerial by any metal objects on board. This is particularly so in steel or concrete boats: it is then necessary to use a fixed aerial, whose margin for error has been calculated in advance by making a deviation curve as for fixed compasses. On other boats, a movable aerial can be used, but it must always be kept away from anything magnetic. Beware of loudspeakers, earphones (especially if they are of the stethoscope variety). If you tend to hold the aerial close to you, then the headphones should be worn behind the head, and not down on the chest.

The quality of the receiver can also create problems – especially its selectivity. If several transmitters are interfering with each other, reception becomes very poor (not to say rather harsh on the ears) if the set has poor selectivity.

Rough seas can also be a source of major error. It is impossible to hear anything in the trough of a wave, and there is consequently a risk of mistaking an incidental null point for a real one.

In short, the skill of the operator is a determining factor in deciding the accuracy of the bearing. If the bearing is to be correct, constant practice is required as well as enormous powers of concentration – not to mention a strong stomach. Eventually, it has to be accepted that even in the best conditions, it is difficult to give a sound estimate of the accuracy of a bearing. If the time of day is right, the reception clear and the null zone only around 5°, one can reckon on a discrepancy of 2° either way in fine weather, and 5° in a rough sea. If the reception is muzzy and the null zone wide (10–20°), one cannot really hope for an accuracy any greater than +/– 4° in fine weather and between +/–7 and 8° in a rough sea. In

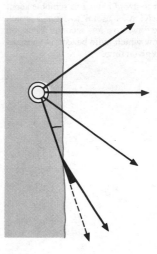

When radio waves reach the coast at an acute angle, there can be considerable refraction.

In order to avoid having to scrabble about needlessly, it is useful to have a watch accurate down to a few seconds. Thus you will know which radio beacon is transmitting at a given time.

really bad conditions, the potential degree of error is generally impossible to assess.

How to make a radio fix

To make a more or less accurate fix, it is a good idea to take several bearings on each radio beacon, and then the most likely one is chosen for each (note: this is not necessarily the average). In good conditions, three bearings on each beacon are probably sufficient, but it may be necessary to get five or six to get an accurate fix. The bearings should not all be taken in quick succession, but rather at an interval of a couple of hours, transferring the fix by the distance run in the meantime.

Since each beacon only transmits every 6 minutes, you have to reckon on taking 30 to 45 minutes to make a fix. This is why good concentration and the ability to cope with seasickness are important factors in the accuracy of the fix. Concentration is easier if you have earphones, which cut you off from what is going on around you to some extent, but the whole job can be much quicker and simpler if you have a set with two different receiving circuits – you can then pass from one band to another at the touch of a button. On a one-circuit receiver, searching for frequencies is frustrating and time-consuming (a useful tip is to mark the frequencies on the dial with a Chinagraph pencil).

For the following example, it just so happens that we are using a double-circuit receiver.

A boat coming from the Fastnet rock is making for Swansea. The sea is heavy and the visibility is poor. As the coast comes up, the navigator decides to get a radio fix to make the dead reckoning position on the chart more accurate. This fix has a potential error reckoned at 7% of the course covered – or a circle of discrepancy 12.5 nautical miles in diameter.

The radio beacons available are: Tuskar Rock (to the SE of Ireland), Mizen Head (SW of Ireland), South Bishop (to the west of Wales), Round Island (on the Scilly Islands), Lundy Island (in the Bristol Channel) and Creac'h (on Ushant).

Radio beacons which transmit at the minutes past the hour given in black also transmit at the times given in blue:

0	6	12	18	24	30	36	42	48	54
1	7	13	19	25	31	37	43	49	55
2	8	14	20	26	32	38	44	50	56
3	9	15	21	27	33	39	45	51	57
4	10	16	22	28	34	40	46	52	58
5	11	17	23	29	35	41	47	53	59

Careless radio-fixing can make you old before your time ...

They are distributed in the following manner:

Minutes	Frequency:	308kHz	296.5kHz
0	....		Tuskar Rock
1	....	Mizen Head	
2	....		South Bishop
3	....	Round Island	
4	....		Lundy Island
5	....	Creac'h	

By tuning the set to these two frequencies, it is possible to pick up the beacons in this order: Mizen Head, South Bishop, Round Island, Lundy Island. You can then take 2 minutes' rest, as there is no point using Tuskar Rock, because it is too far away, as is Creac'h, over the other side of Cornwall (the radio waves can be distorted as they pass over land).

In 24 minutes, we get the following bearings:
Mizen head at: 270°, 275°/277°, 286°/283°/273°
South Bishop at: 346°/349°/356°/345°, 348°
Round Island at: 198°, 197°/210°/208°, 210°/207°, 206°
Lundy Island at: 120°/127°/128°/117°

Radio DF fix for the entry to the Bristol Channel. According to dead reckoning, the boat is to be found within the dotted circle. The bearings on the radio beacons can help to give a more precise fix, but the value of this information is somewhat dependent on the accuracy of the dead reckoning itself.

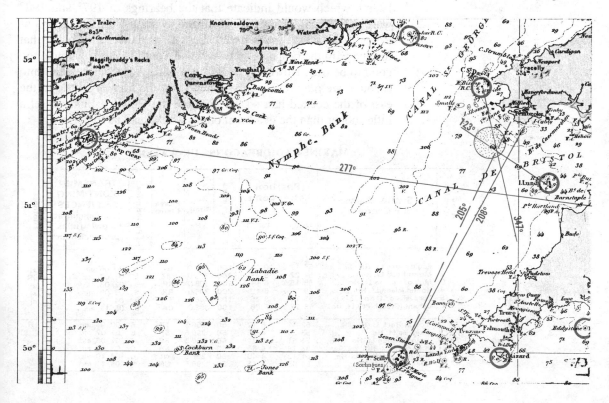

Some of the beacons have been picked up twice in the same transmission, except for Lundy Island, which is not coming through clear.

Now that the bearings have been taken, a little thought is needed to choose the most likely ones:

– Mizen Head: the bearings vary a lot – we choose the average (277°), but without much confidence, since there is a difference of 16° between the highest and lowest readings;

– South Bishop: we will keep 347°, as the 356° bearing seems an accident. The average would be 349°;

– Round Island: 208° is chosen, since it is the average of the five figures, and the 197° and 198° readings are probably wrong;

– Lundy Island: same proceedings as for Mizen Head – we take the average reading (123°).

These bearings are now plotted on the chart, and the result is analysed:

– the bearing of Mizen Head – 277° – is certainly wrong. For the reading to be right, there would have to be an error of at least 40° for Lundy Island, which is quite near. Besides, it also disagrees with the DR;

– it looks as if we must be to the west of the bearing of Round Island, which would indicate that the bearings of 197° and 198° were not all that far out. We therefore average out the bearings of Round Island: that gives us 205°. At first glance, the cocked hat formed with the bearings of Lundy and South Bishop is almost too good to be true. However, taking the bearing of Round Island into account, we may reasonably assume that the boat is a little to the east of the cocked hat, so we may see the Helwick light vessel a little sooner than the dead reckoning would lead us to believe.

Extract from Reed's Nautical Almanac.

MARINE RADIOBEACONS—UK WATERS

Reed's Station No.	Station Name and Grouping	Position Lat. NORTH ° '	Long. WEST ° '	Range miles	Freq. kHz	Morse Ident.	Period mins.	TRANSMIS- SION TIMING SEQUENCES commencing at following mins. past each hour	Footnote
1	Eagle Island Lt. Ho.	54 17	10 05½	100	308.0	GL	6	00, 06, etc.	(a)
2	Mizen Head Lt. Ho.	51 27	9 49	200	308.0	MZ	6	01, 07, etc.	(a)R
3	Mull of Kintyre Lt. Ho.	55 18½	5 48	100	308.0	KR	6	02, 08, etc.	(a)
4	Round Island Lt. Ho.	49 58½	6 19½	200	308.0	RR	6	03, 09, etc.	(a)
5	Tory Island Lt. Ho.	55 16½	8 15	100	308.0	TY	6	04, 10, etc.	(a)
6	Ushant (Creach Pt.) Lt. Ho. ..	48 27½	5 08	100	308.0	CA	6	05, 11, etc.	(a)
77	Tuskar Rock Lt. Ho.	52 12	6 12½	50	296.5	TR	6	00, 06, etc.	R
78	Skerries Lt. Ho.	53 25	4 36½	50	296.5	SR	6	01, 07, etc.	
79	South Bishop Lt. Ho.	51 51	5 24½	50	296.5	SB	6	02, 08, etc.	
80	Kish Bank Lt. Ho.	53 18½	5 55½	50	296.5	KH	6	03, 09, etc.	R
81	Lundy Island North Lt. Ho. ..	51 12	4 40½	50	296.5	NL	6	04, 10, etc.	
82	Cregneish (I.o.M.)	54 05	4 46	50	296.5	CN	6	05, 11, etc.	

Homing on a radio beacon

When there is a radio beacon close to the port you are heading for, or on the course you are following, then it is quite simple to use this beacon as your heading. All you have to do is to keep an eye on the course. Some radio beacons are designed for precisely this sort of thing – they give out a different signal depending on whether you are to either side of the line of the channel or in line with it.

You must be certain that you can home in without running into any dangers along the way – that is to say, if there are no rocks between you and the beacon. It is, for instance, quite possible to home in on the beacon at Round Island if you are coming in from the north, but you should never do so if coming from the south – look at the chart and you'll see why.

Radio fixes are, all in all, a useful aid, but it would be very dangerous to rely on them and nothing else. The *Channel Pilot* puts it very nicely:

'The navigator should not trust blindly indications of position given by one navigational aid alone (radioelectric or otherwise).

It is the navigator's duty, taking account of the degree of precision he can expect from any of these aids when used in combination with dead reckoning, to use [DF radio fixes] along with all the other available methods, to establish a well-considered compromise between the various sorts of information at his disposal.

In particular, the use of radio fixes should not take the place of recognition and observation of marks, when this is possible.'

You can't say better than that.

Morse code made easy

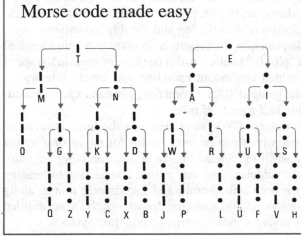

For a dot, look right; for a dash, look left. It might be useful to copy this table out on a larger sheet of paper and stick it up in the chart room.

Electronic navigational aids

Navigating by satellite

Principles: Currently, all devices use the four satellites that make up the Transit system, positioned in a polar orbit of about 1 hour 48 minutes, at 1,000km above the earth's surface. The ground stations program the satellites with the characteristics of the orbits that they will make, and the satellite then transmits the characteristics of the current orbit to the onboard calculator.

The onboard calculator compares the frequency of the satellite's signal with the reference frequency provided by the oscillator on the boat (about 400MHz). The relative motion of the boat and the satellite create a variation in frequency (Doppler effect). If the position of the satellite, the *true course* and the *speed of the boat* are known, then the device can calculate the position of the boat.

Operating instructions: A satellite can be used when its elevation over the horizon falls between 10 and 75°. Outside that bracket, the calculated position is unreliable. Recent units give the times during which the satellite will be passing overhead for the hours and days to come. The unit should be switched on three-quarters of an hour before the satellite passes over, so that the reference frequency provided by the oscillator has stabilised by the time the measurement is taken. Since the unit draws quite a lot of current, then it is best to keep the machine on *standby*, when only the oscillator is drawing power. At full power, which requires quite a good power supply to provide the 10–30W necessary, the dead reckoning can be kept up to date as the satellites pass overhead (every 90 minutes at moderate latitudes), provided that the satellite navigation system is linked in with the log and the ship's compass.

Accuracy: In principle, the system is accurate to within a tenth of a nautical mile, plus 0.2 nautical miles per knot of error in the speed of the boat – which can mount up when you are dealing with a multihulled boat going at 20kn. In practice, you can expect an accuracy of to within half a nautical mile.

Auxiliary functions: The system also tells the time, accurate to within 1 second, which can be very useful for navigating by the stars, but only when the Satnav breaks down. The other auxiliary functions are the calculation of *way points*, comparison of heading and distance for both orthodromic and loxodromic routes, along with a '*man overboard*' function (for details, see the panel entitled 'Auxiliary functions for radioelectrical navigation systems').

Auxiliary functions
for electronic navigation systems

Way points: Anything up to ninety points can be entered into the memory, according to the capacity, which then breaks the route to be followed into stages. One function allows the distance and heading of the next way point to be permanently displayed, and when that one is reached, the next one comes up on the screen. This is the ideal system for lazy navigators.

Orthodromic–loxodromic routes: An additional refinement which allows you to switch between displays giving the orthodromic and loxodromic routes, along with the distance and heading in each case. Pretty useful! Without this clever little gadget, it can take a good quarter of an hour to calculate the orthodromic route.

Man overboard: By pressing a button linked to the cockpit, the point at which the person falls overboard is memorised. As far as the unit is concerned, it's just another way point, and it then displays the distance and heading back to the point in question. Marvellous, but still not a reason to do without your safety harness.

GPS

The global positioning system – operational since 1988 – allows the navigator to use a new network of satellites which have been put into orbit. It is possible to make fixes much more frequently and much more accurately than with the Satnav system. The cost of GPS systems have come down to under £1,000 and will eventually become the dominant electronic navigational aid.

Decca

Principle: The old units were used in conjunction with special charts on which hyperbolas of different colours are printed according to the station in question. The numbers of the hyperbolas and their colour are marked on the unit.

The position of the boat was read from the intersection of the different coloured hyperbolas marked on the unit. Newer equipment gives the position directly in geographical co-ordinates. Coverage is excellent for the Channel and the North Sea, and good for the Eastern Atlantic, with the exception of a couple of gaps in the Bay of Biscay. In the Mediterranean, it is better to use Loran.

Operation: Very simple for the current models. They require relatively little power (less than 10W), and so can be left switched on permanently. The estimated position is entered at departure, to the nearest 15 nautical miles (usually rather better when starting from a port). All you have to do then is to read the position from the display. The machine makes new fixes several times a minute.

Accuracy: To within anything between 0.1 nautical miles and 200m, depending on the distance of the boat from the transmitter. The better units even give the estimated error.

Auxiliary functions: With more advanced units, it is also possible to keep the DR up to date by interfacing them with the log and the compass. Way points and man overboard functions are also available.

Loran C

Principle: "Long Range Navigation C" is a hyperbolic system similar to Decca. As with the latter, the older units require the position to be plotted on special charts, over which the Loran C hyperbolas have been superimposed. Current models give geographical co-ordinates. The area covered extends as far as the coast of the Americas, the Far East and the Mediterranean.

Operation: Switch it on, let it warm up, and then enter the code of the station you want. When on automatic, the unit takes care of all this itself.

Accuracy: A quarter of a nautical mile during the day, half a mile at night. Accuracy varies considerably depending on how far away the transmitter is.

Auxiliary functions: Updating of the DR via interface with log and compass, way points and man overboard.

Meeting merchant ships and ferries

To round off this survey of the ways of establishing your position at sea, we must mention one method that is more unorthodox, but very effective: taking bearings on the courses followed by large merchant ships that you meet. The appearance of a ship on the horizon should not be considered as unusual or a matter of chance. These ships follow lanes whose overall pattern is as precisely laid out as a railway network, with main lines, branch lines and junctions. By taking the bearing of the merchant ship's course, it is usually possible to work out what its heading is, which consequently provides a valuable indication of one's own position.

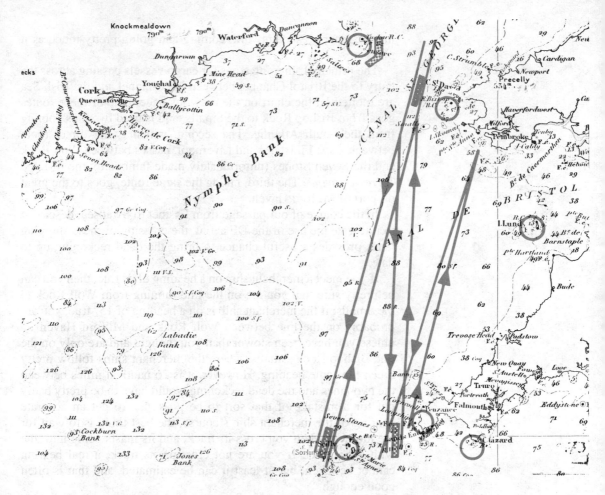

Principal shipping lanes at the entrance to the Bristol Channel.
(Document of the SHOM.)

The main cargo routes are well known, and the most important of these are to be found on the pilot charts. On the East Atlantic, there is Ushant–Cape Finisterre, on the French side of the Channel, there is Ushant–les Casquets–la Bassurelle; on the English side: Bishop Rock (Scilly Islands)–Lizard–Start Point–Royal Sovereign. These routes are the seagoing equivalent of motorways, with traffic going off in different directions at crossroads, marked on the charts by pink lines about 2 miles wide. Other less important routes can easily be deduced from the course of the ship that is met: often all that is needed is to lay the Cras ruler on the chart, along the bearing of the course followed. The *Channel Pilot* also describes the activity of merchant shipping in the various ports, and consequently the sort of ships that will be using them. It is easy to learn the difference between a banana boat (white and heading for Dieppe), a ship carrying ore (black and maybe coming from Cardiff), and a warship in its dapper grey paintwork, coming and going pretty much as it pleases.

The principal shipping lanes for cargo vessels passing across the entry to the Bristol Channel between the Channel and the Irish Sea are plotted on the chart on the previous page. One of these routes goes from Bishop Rock to the Smalls, and is used by ships coming from the South Atlantic. The second, which is the direct route between Cape Finisterre and Liverpool, passes between Wolf Rock and the Seven Stones (unfortunately made famous by the ill-fated *Torrey Canyon*). The third, taking the same route, goes to the great oil port of Milford Haven.

In the course of our passage from Fastnet to Swansea, described to illustrate the use of the DF aerial, the crossing of these shipping lanes provides a useful chance to bring the dead reckoning up to date.

If you meet a merchant ship on a heading of 0° true, then you can be pretty sure that you are on the line running from Wolf Rock to the Smalls; if the merchant ship is on a heading of 15° true, you are probably on the line between Wolf Rock and Milford Haven … unless you have been slower than you thought and are only on the line Bishop Rock–Smalls, where the merchant ships follow pretty much the same heading. However, it is 26 nautical miles between the two lanes and the dead reckoning would have to be pretty badly out for a mistake of that sort to be possible. To get an accurate bearing of the merchant ship's course, the best thing is to wait for the moment when you cross its track, and its masts come into line with each other. If you are not crossing its track, a real bearing cannot be taken, but at least it can be estimated, and that is often good enough.

The lines used by ferries are also followed very precisely. On some of them, the traffic is so intense that the problem is not so much of knowing where you are, but rather knowing where to pass to avoid them all. The Straits of Dover are well marked from that point of view.

Landfall

The first member of the crew to sight land has the right to a double Scotch, and that is a rule never to be forgotten. However, then comes the important job of actually making your landfall. This means that the land you have spotted must be identified, and the boat's position in relation to it fixed before proceeding on to harbour.

If you can, choose an area and an ETA for your landing, then landfall is clearly easier. The ideal is a sheer coastline, with prominent landmarks or profile, approached over a shoaling bottom with characteristic features (like les Bancs de Sable off Paimpol in Brittany). The ideal time is towards dawn: it is easy to establish position by the powerful lighthouses and enter harbour very early. Even if neither of these ideal conditions is fulfilled, other aids are available: positions can be transferred, soundings taken, a radio fix taken, or merchant ships spotted. As a last resort, candles could be lit to your patron saint. However, the important thing is to examine scrupulously all the available information, ensuring that there is nothing contradictory, and that all the facts agree. If something isn't right then don't try to land come what may, but instead, try to find some additional information, keeping a safe distance until you have an idea of what is going on. There are even times when you have to know how to give up the idea of making a landing, when you know – either by experience, or by information gathered – that it is going to be difficult to enter a given port at a given time. After all, is life on shore so wonderful that you are ready to take all sorts of silly risks to get there?

In practice, there is no general advice for making a landfall: they are all quite different, and they can even be quite emotional occasions, depending on the sort of crossing that has just been made. For the navigator, it is the moment of truth, when the validity of the dead reckoning is put to the test. Up until that time, there has always been a margin of uncertainty in the navigation, and it is possible that some slight error may have crept in and upset the calculations. Landfalls always contain a potential for the unexpected, and this is part of their fascination.

IT IS ALWAYS BETTER TO CHECK EVERYTHING
THREE TIMES THAN TO CHECK IT ONLY ONCE
AND WRECK THE BOAT.

CHAPTER 4

Celestial navigation

Observing the stars has allowed us to fix the latitudes and longitudes of many of the most important reference points on the current charts. Equally, the procedure also allows us to find our own position by making a fix using the stars.

The problem about using the stars as marks is that they move. Fortunately, astronomers can predict their position in the heavens for us at any given moment.

> Some people will say that this description is completely wrong, because in reality, it is not the sun but the earth that moves, turning on its own axis once a day, and orbiting the sun every year at an angle (which accounts for the change of the seasons). This is perhaps the case, but there is some value in sticking to older principles, which state that the earth is in the centre of the universe, remaining immobile as the spheres move. It is a reassuring idea, and much easier for the purposes of calculation.

The sun

The Sun rises every day in the east, climbs across the sky, reaches its highest point at midday and finally descends towards the point where it sets in the west. However, its path changes over the course of the year. At the end of December, it remains low over the horizon, and the nights are long. For South Africa, things are the other way round: people there see the sun pass from right to left and reach noon in the north.

> The sun's GP changes by 15° every hour. This means that, at the equinoxes, its speed at the equator is about 900kn. At the same time, the declination changes by about 1' per hour, giving a speed of roughly 1kn for the same GP, either north or south.

The geographical position of the sun

We can compare the sun to the light in a lighthouse, whose *geographical position (GP)* is to be found where the imaginary line joining the sun to the centre of the earth pierces the surface of the planet.

The sun's GP is given in terms of latitude and longitude, like any other reference point. However, unlike the co-ordinates of a lighthouse, the GP for the sun varies with time. To distinguish the co-ordinates for the GP from the co-ordinates for any fixed point, they are referred to as the *Greenwich hour angle (GHA)* and the *declination*. Let us see exactly how they vary:

The sun moves steadily towards the west, and appears to circle the earth in a day. Its GP also moves westwards at an average speed of 360° in 24 hours, or about 15°/hour. As a consequence, the *local*

Opposite: The astrolabe of Ahmad ibn Khalaf (11th century). This is probably the oldest known example of the instrument, although astrolabes must have been in use for many centuries before this.

How to take a noon position: a quick
guide.
1. Estimate time of meridional passage;
2. Correct the height read on the
   sextant;
3. Check the declination of the sun at
   the time the observation is made.

hour angle (LHA) of the sun increases (that is, the angular distance the body is west of the local meridian), on average by 15° every hour, from 0 to 360° starting from the local meridian.

The latitude of the GP of the sun varies in a quite different manner. From the beginning of spring to the end of summer, the sun is north of the equator, its declination is north, as is the latitude of its GP. In autumn and winter, the opposite is true: they all lie to the south.

Since the dawn of time, navigators have known that at a certain time of the year, the nearer the sun is to the horizon at midday, the nearer they are to the pole. We will look at the formula that gives the latitude of the boat in relation to the height of the sun at noon and to the season (or declination of the sun, to be more precise).

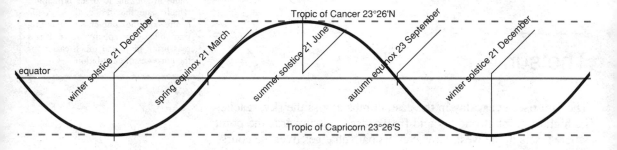

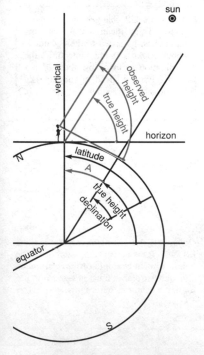

The noon sight

It is local midday when the GP of the sun passes our meridian, reaching its upper culmination. The vertical angular distance from the horizon to the sun is known as its 'height' or 'altitude'. With certain corrections, it is said to be the *true height* of the observed sun.

The ship's angular distance A = 90° – the true height of the GP of the sun.

The ship is to the north of the GP if we have our backs facing north, and in this case, A is given a positive value (+).

If our backs are to the south, the ship is to the south of the GP and A is given a negative value (–).

true height:	60°
back to the north	
A = 90° – true height:	+ 30° (N)
declination D:	+ 20° (N)
latitude L =	+ 50° (N)

Given that the latitude of the GP of the body is equal to its declination, then the latitude L of the boat is :
L (latitude) = D (declination) + A (angular distance: 90° − true height)
D is positive if north, negative if south
A carries the sign indicated above, and we therefore surmise that:
if the result L is positive, then our latitude is north,
if the result L is negative, then our latitude is south.

Example

It is 4 August, and we have left Concarneau very early in the morning, bearing 220° as if we were heading for South America.

Towards about 1130, we are impatient to see our first noon position. Note that if we have kept our watches to the time in use at the moment, then there is no hurry yet: the sun passes the Greenwich meridian between 1145 and 1217 GMT, and not at 1200 exactly, given both the obliquity and the eccentricity of its orbit.

Since we are slightly to the west, it will pass over our meridian a little later (about 2 hours or so).

From here on, we will only use GMT.

At 1130 GMT, it is time to get down to business. We open the *Almanach du marin breton* (or *Reed's*) for the year. We read that the sun will pass over the Greenwich meridian this 4 August at 1206

> In the *Almanach du marin breton*, minutes are abbreviated to *m*, which is sometimes rather confusing.

Août		Déclinaison à 0 h TU		d	AHvo à 0 h TU		V	T. Pass. TU			Lever TU		Coucher TU	
		°	′	′	°	′	°	h	m	s	h	m	h	m
1	M	18	13,4 N		178	25,0		12	06	18	04	21	19	51
2	J	19	58,4		178	25,9		12	06	15	04	23	19	49
				0,6										
3	V	17	43,1		178	26,9		12	06	10	04	24	19	48
4	S	17	27,5		178	28,0		12	06	05	04	26	19	46
5	D	17	11,7		178	29,4		12	06	00	04	27	19	44
							15,001							
6	L	16	55,5		178	30,8		12	05	54	04	28	19	42
7	M	16	39,1		178	32,5		12	05	47	04	30	19	40
				0,7										
8	M	16	22,4		178	34,2		12	05	39	04	34	19	38
9	J	16	05,5		178	36,2		12	05	31	04	33	19	37
10	V	15	48,8		178	38,2		12	05	23	04	35	19	35

Declination and Greenwich hour angle (GHA/AHvo) of the sun at 0000 GMT.
d = hourly variation in declination in minutes and tenths of minutes of arc.
V = hourly change in the hour angle in degrees (fractions expressed in decimals).
T. Pass. = time at which the sun passes over the Greenwich meridian.
Sunrise (lever) and sunset (coucher) for longitude 0° and latitude 50°N.
(Extracted from the *Almanach du marin breton*.)

Table for converting units of arc into units of time (and vice versa) taken from the *Almanach du marin breton*.

0°– 59°			0′– 00		
°	h	m	′	m	s
0	0	00	**35**	2	20
1	0	04	**36**	2	24
2	0	08	**37**	2	28
3	0	12	**38**	2	32
4	0	16	**39**	2	36
5	0	20	**40**	2	40

> Remember to check whether your tables give minutes and seconds or minutes and (decimal) tenths of a minute.

> Other reference works give more detailed corrections, but these are not really worth the extra work.

5sec. It will pass the meridian 4°36'W, on which our dead reckoning position places us, slightly later, but how much later?

The operation is simple given that the GP of the sun is moving west at a rate of 15° per hour. However, this becomes even easier when we consult the table for the conversion of units of arc into units of time:

4° is covered in 0hr 16min, and 36' in 2min 24sec

so 4°36' in 0hr 16min + 2min 24sec = 18min 24sec

Thus the time will be

1206 and 5sec + 18min 24sec = 1224 and 29sec

to observe the sun when it reaches its culmination in the south.

Since we are moving at 4kn on a bearing of 220°, we will have reached 4°40'W and will therefore be 16 seconds early.

Remember that the minutes of arc are divided here not into seconds, but are instead expressed in decimals: the 9 indicates not 9 seconds, but 9/10 of a minute.

True and observed altitude

We get to work about 5 or 10 minutes ahead of the time that the sun should reach the local meridian. We will discuss the use of the sextant further on; let us just say for now that what has to be done is for us to take a series of observations, noting the altitude of the sun each time. *The highest altitude gives us the moment of meridional passage.*

We obtain 59°52'.9 as the highest altitude.

However, this altitude is only the sextant altitude. First of all, we must correct the index error of the sextant. Let us imagine that our sextant has an index error of –2', and we therefore obtain: 59°50'.9, which is the (true) *observed altitude*.

In order to obtain the *true altitude*, we have yet to take account of:

– the height of the observer, which is not at water level at the moment the observation is made. This leads to a degree of 'dip' in the horizon;

– refraction: the sun's rays are refracted by the atmosphere;

HAUTEUR OBSERVÉE	ÉLÉVATION DE L'ŒIL					
	0 m	2 m	4 m	6 m	8 m	10 m
10° 00'	10,8	8,3	7,3	6,5	5,8	5,2
20'	11,0	8,5	7,4	6,6	5,9	5,3
50° 00'	+ 15,3	+ 12,8	+ 11,7	+ 10,9	+ 10,3	+ 9,7
55° 00'	15,4	12,9	11,9	11,1	10,4	9,8
60° 00'	15,5	13,0	12,0	11,2	10,5	9,9
70° 00'	15,7	13,2	12,2	11,4	10,7	10,1

Extract from *Almanach du marin breton*.

– parallax: we are at the surface and not at the centre of the Earth;
– the semi-diameter of the sun: we are measuring the altitude of the lower edge, and not that of the centre.

All this seems rather complicated, but we are sure to find another table in the almanac to help us solve the problem.

• In the first column for observer's height, we find the height corresponding to the height of the eye of the observer, let's say 1.5m. In the next column we see that this corresponds to a dip of 2.2'.

• In the columns for apparent altitude, we look for the figure closest in degrees to the height we have read. Here, it is 60°, but the table stops at 46°. However, in the notes above that, it says that refraction and parallax tend to zero as the height approaches 90°. Let's put it at 0.5'.

• We now add the semi-diameter of the sun, which we will take as 16', as is indicated by the third formula given above the table.

This gives us in the present instance:

Sextant height	59°53'.2
index error	– 2'.0
dip	– 2'.2
refraction & parallax	– 0'.5
semi-diameter	+ 16'.0
the true altitude is therefore	60°04'.2

Declination

Let's take a step backwards in the almanac. We note that on 4 August, the declination of the sun at 0000 is N17°27'.5, and that it is decreasing by 0'.6 per hour. At 1224, it will therefore have decreased by 0'.6 x 12.5, or 7'.5, and will therefore be N17°20'. A quick glance at the figures shows us that this changes very little from one day to the next, that it is north, because we are in the summer, and that it is going down (because we are past the solstice).

At the moment when the sun reaches our local meridian, its declination is certainly no longer the same as it was at 1224, but the difference is negligible.

We now have everything we need to apply the formula L = D + (90° – ta), where D is positive because it is to the north, and 90° – ta is positive also, because the observation has been made with north to our backs.

L = + 17°20' + (90° – 60°4'.2) = + 47°15'.8N

That's all there is to it, but we have accomplished quite a lot. Knowing how to take a noon position, means that there is nothing to stop us heading for Cayenne in French Guiana, for example. All we would have to do is to take noon positions regularly, until we got down onto the latitude of Cayenne, and then head due west ...

If the distance between the latitude of the boat and the GP of the body varies rapidly, then the culmination does not occur at the instant when the body passes the boat's meridian, especially if the body is low over the horizon. As a result, there is an error in the latitude as calculated from the apparent maximum height. The variation in distance is referred to as var./lat.

In order to compensate for the error, add to the height an additional correction as determined by the table below, based on a var./lat.= 20'/hour (= 20kn). If the var./lat. is 10kn, then the correction is reduced by a factor of 4. As you will have gathered, it is proportional to the square of the var./lat.

For var./lat. = 20 knots			
true altitude	declination =		
	lat. –20°	lat. +00°	lat. +10°	lat. +20°
80°	0'2	0'1	0'2	2'2
70°	0'3	0'3	0'3	0'4
60°	0'5	0'5	0'6	0'7
50°	0'6	0'7	0'9	1'2
40°	0'8	1'0	1'3	2'0
30°	1'0	1'5	2'2	4'0
20°	1'3	2'3	4'5	

This table is for northern latitudes. For southern latitudes, reverse the signs.

sa	= sextant altitude
oa	= observed altitude
aa	= apparent altitude
ta	= true altitude

See chart on page 955.

How to use a sextant properly

Getting comfortable

In order to use a sextant properly, you need to be comfortable, without being worried about falling in the water or dropping the instrument. If necessary, modify the heading of the boat, or the set of a sail. Generally speaking, it is best to sit down, or even kneel (take account of this when allowing for the height of the observer). In a rough sea, it is sometimes best to be standing, tied to the mast by your belt, so that you can see the horizon for a sufficient length of time.

Finding the body

First of all, adjust the lens to your eye, aiming at the horizon. If you want to observe the sun, then select the appropriate filters so that the sun is about as bright as the horizon.

If you are having difficulties in finding the sun in the lens, then take out **both** lens and filters: your field of vision will be much wider, and you will be able to see better in which direction to aim. Move the index mirror so that you get the sun reflected into your eye by the two mirrors, then cover up the index mirror, replace the lens, the filters and your eye, and then line up and do any fine tuning necessary. Never look at the sun through the lens without using the filters.

Stars are the hardest to find in the lens. Here, there are two possible things you could do. When you can see the star with your naked eye, but can't find it with the sextant, then turn it the other way up, and move the index mirror to make the horizon line up while sighting on the star. Then turn the sextant the right way up and do any fine tuning. If you can't find the star you're looking for, then work out what altitude it ought to be at, adjust the sextant accordingly, and then sweep the horizon at the relevant time – you should find it more or less immediately, even before night has properly fallen. You can also improve on your night vision by using the method of looking out of the corner of your eye, which is better at spotting movement or flickering, and therefore more useful at night.

Measuring altitude

In order to measure the height of a body, bring its lower (or, in some-cases, upper) edge down to the horizon (or the actual point, if it is a star). The measurement is only valid if the sextant is perfectly vertical at the moment it is taken. How do we know when it is? The answer is to *swing the sextant* with a movement of the wrist (or better still, of the entire upper body) so that the star appears to describe the arc of a circle. The point at which the sextant is vertical is where the body appears touch the horizon at the lowest point of its swing.

Practice

Although measuring altitude is not an easy thing to do, it is nonetheless the hardest part of the whole business. You must therefore try to practise as much as possible, either on land or at sea; take as many measurements as possible and check how good they are. The best solution is to make a graph and plot the measurements on it one after another; the fixes on the graph are good when the points virtually line up. When making a measurement for real, it is important to make at least four measurements in succession, plot them on a graph and take the one that seems best.

Making mistakes

The worst errors are in fact the most common: while completely absorbed in counting minutes and seconds of arc, you arrive at a reading that is one degree out; while taking care to get the measurement right down to the second, you give the time in local time and not GMT. Such things happen! Generally speaking, you usually notice: an error of 1° works out at 60 nautical miles, an error of 1 minute in time is 15 nautical miles. However, there are errors that are less easy to spot straight away, but which can nonetheless be detected with the aid of a graph.

'Landing'

It must be remembered that those famous detectives, the Thompsons, who crossed the Atlantic with Tintin on board the *Sirius* with Captain Haddock in search of the treasure of Rackham the Red, once made a fix that would have placed the boat right in the middle of the choir-stalls of St Peter's basilica in Rome. Even if the stars are fascinating, you have to keep your feet on the ground, and leave out the cosmographical speculations. In astronomical navigation more than anywhere else, an ability to spot the improbable solution is of paramount importance.

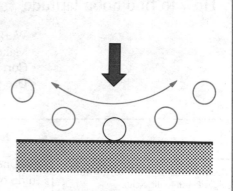

The star should make a tangent with the horizon at the lowest point of the swing.

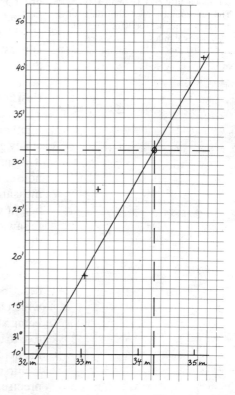

How to find noon latitude

- Work out the time of meridian passage for the body.
- Make the observation.
- Correct to obtain true height.
- Use the rules on p936 to calculate latitude.

Example: 23 Sept. D = 0°, L = 48°.
Speed: 1kn to the south.
The measurements in local time were:

at 1200   ta = 42°
at 1201   ta = 42° − 0.03'
at 1201   ta = 42° − 0.12'
at 1203   ta = 42° − 0.27'

Let's be optimistic, and say that we can spot a difference as small as 0.12'. The uncertainty over the time of zenith is 2 minutes, or 30'of longitude = 20 nautical miles.

One might think that it should be possible to work out the longitude of the noon position, since the time interval between the sun passing over the Greenwich meridian and its passing over the local meridian can be calculated in terms of degrees. Do not forget that the GP of the sun moves quickly, however, and that an error of a minute in time corresponds to 15' of longitude.

Determining the precise moment at which the sun reaches its culmination is very difficult: the degree of uncertainty can be as great as 1 minute (see table left), at which point it is almost better to try and estimate one's longitude.

The sun can also be hidden at noon. We will now see whether it is possible to find one's position relative to the sun at any hour of the day, by tracing what is referred to as a *position line*.

Position circles and position lines

The sun, as we have already said, can be considered as the top of a lighthouse, whose GP is situated somewhere on the earth's surface at any given moment . Now, in coastal navigation we have seen that it is quite possible to work out one's position relative to a lighthouse, on the one hand by taking its bearing (that is to say, by measuring its *azimuth*), and on the other by measuring its apparent height with the aid of a sextant, which allows you to work out how far away you are from its GP. The nearer you get to the lighthouse, the greater its apparent altitude; as you get further away, it decreases. If you go round the lighthouse (supposing that it were at sea), observing constantly the same altitude, then you would describe what is referred to as a *position circle,* all the points along which are at an equal distance from the lighthouse, the GP thereof being at the centre of the circle. In order to find one's position relative to the sun at a given time of day, the same principle applies, but the application is a little more complicated.

First of all, the azimuth of the sun cannot be measured precisely. Secondly, if it is possible to measure its height, and

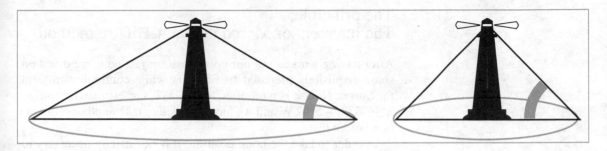

The lighthouse appears smaller to someone standing further away.

The lighthouse appears tall to somebody standing at its GP.

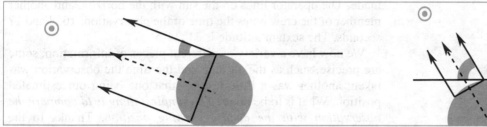

If the star is low over the horizon, then you are a long way away from its GP.

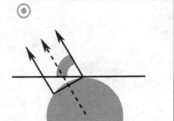

If the star is high above the horizon, then you are near to its GP.

therefore determine the position circle along which one's position lies, then it is apparent that the circle in question is immense. It would just about be possible to trace it on a globe, and even then the globe would have to be enormous, so that the pencil line was not several nautical miles across! As for transferring the part of the circle that interested us to the chart, this would be really rather difficult: you would need a very large compass, and the task would not be made any easier by the Mercator projection used in the making of the charts.

As it happens, it is perfectly possible to get out of the difficulty thanks to a method worked out by the French Admiral, Marcq de Saint-Hilaire.

Position circles around the foot of a lighthouse and the GP of a star.

Around a lighthouse, you are on a surface that may be considered flat when you can see its foot, and the rays of light appear to diverge.
Around the GP of a star, the surface becomes spherical and the light rays appear parallel, because the star is at a point nearer infinity.

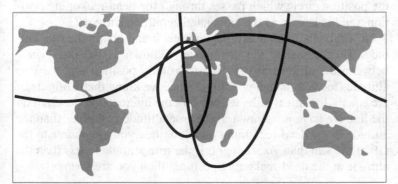

Examples of position circles plotted on a Mercator projection chart.

The principle:
The intercept or Marcq de Saint-Hilaire method

After having worked out our noon position just now, we dined on some exquisitely prepared fish fingers while continuing to head for Suroît. Now it is a bit after 1600 GMT, our estimated position is 46°57'N – 5°02'W and we have decided to take another observation before tea.

In order to take the noon position, it is not strictly necessary to do so on the hour exactly, as we have seen; it is vital, on the other hand, to note the precise instant at which the observation was made. The operator lines up the sun with the horizon, and another member of the crew notes the time of the observation: 1634 and 17 seconds. The sextant altitude is 31°24'.5.

We now have a variety of different pieces of information: some are precise, such as the altitude and the time the observation was taken; another was a little less so, that one being our estimated position. What is to be done? *The simplest thing is to compare the observation with the dead reckoning position.* Thanks to the various reference works, it is perfectly possible for us to work out the altitude at which the sun ought to have been if we had been at the position given by the dead reckoning at 1634 and 17 seconds GMT. *By comparing this altitude at estimated position to the height that we observed, we can then hope to arrive at a more precise idea of where we are.*

The recipe is as follows:

1. Measure the height of the sun by the sextant, noting the time of the observation. Note the sextant altitude at the side.

2. Find out the altitude and azimuth for the sun at the estimated position for the same time.

3. Plot the estimated position on the chart: from that point, draw a straight line in the direction of the sun's GP, according to the azimuth you have just looked up. This straight line is the radius of the position circle which passes through the dead-reckoning position, (and is known as the calculated zenith distance, cZD).

4. Now take the sextant altitude, correct it and obtain the true altitude. Then calculate the difference – known as the *intercept* – between the altitude at the dead-reckoning position and the true altitude (for your actual position). Since we know that 1 minute of arc equals 1 nautical mile, we can plot the intercept on the chart on the line we have just drawn. If the true altitude is *greater* than the altitude at the dead-reckoning position, then you are *nearer* to the GP of the sun than you thought; if the true altitude is *less* than the altitude at the dead-reckoning position, then you are *further away*.

5. All that now has to be done is for you to trace the part of the position circle for the observed altitude that is relevant. Since this circle is of immense size, the arc can be represented as a tangent of the circle, ie at right angles to the radius. This straight line is referred to as the *position line*, and the position of the boat is somewhere along that line.

The means

In order to calculate the noon position, all that was needed, apart from the sextant, was *Reed's* or the *Almanach du marin breton*. In order to work out a position line, you need a good watch, some rather more detailed documents to know what was the position of the sun at the dead-reckoning point at the time of the observation, and something to calculate the altitude of the sun and its azimuth viewed from that position.

Harrison chronometer (18th century). For want of a radio, clocks of this sort were carried on ships so that the time for the point of departure could be known as exactly as possible. The chronometers made by Harrison were the best ones being made in the 1760s: they could survive a 5 month voyage only losing a minute.

Do we actually need an example?
Let us take a watch that is gaining 1min 38sec every 24 hours. If the watch is set to midnight GMT before leaving, then by the end of the seventh day at sea, it will be running 11min 26sec fast. On the eighth day, an observation of the sun is made at 0855 and 7sec, according to the watch in question. What is the GMT time?

We know that 1min 38sec = 98sec, that 24 hours = 1440 minutes and that
8hr 5min 7sec = 535min 7sec
or 535.1min
Since midnight, the watch has gained by
(98 x 535.1) ÷ 1440 = 36sec.

Therefore, by the time the observation is made, it has advanced by:
11min 26sec + 36sec = 12min 2sec

The GMT time is therefore:

8hr 55min 7sec
− 12min 2sec
8hr 43min 5sec

The watch

It is vital to know the exact GMT time at the moment when the observation is made: an error of 4 seconds can lead to an error of a minute of longitude. For a long time, building timepieces sufficiently accurate for the job was the main problem in navigating by the stars: people who had the task of turning the hour glasses over always ended up falling asleep.

Nowadays, this sort of thing is no longer a problem: all you have to do is to listen to the pips on the radio. Of course, the radio can break down, so it is always best to have a good watch. The best thing is a watch that gives the exact time (these are readily available), or at least a watch that always gains or loses by the same amount, and thus which has a regular movement. By checking regularly, it is possible to work out how much the watch is gaining or losing, and thereby to work out the state of the watch, that is to say the difference between the time it shows and the true GMT time.

Set the watch at the beginning of the trip and do not correct it at any point. Check also that the minute hand is on one of the minute marks when the second hand is on the 12: if it is halfway between the two, then eventually you're going to write down the wrong time (of course, if you have a digital watch, then you'll never have these sorts of problems).

Reference works

There are a variety of works that give the GP of the sun at every minute of the day and for the length of the year. We use the *Almanach du marin breton*. The cheaper works are often the most useful, especially when they give a good deal of useful information in addition to that on navigating by the stars.

Reed's Nautical Almanac, which we have already mentioned, is reasonably priced and is useful for a lot of other subjects. This is why we will use it here. In France, there is also an official reference work published by the *Bureau des Longitudes*: the *Éphémérides nautiques* (which used to go under the equally beautiful title of the *Extrait de la connaissance des temps*). A lovely volume, with the sort of large print that is easy on the eye, but which also costs a good deal, it has to be replaced every 3 years and only deals with navigating by the stars.

Since it is a good idea to get experience of using as many documents as possible, we will use the *Éphémérides nautiques* later for the calculation of a position line from the moon.

Tables versus calculators

In order to obtain the altitude and the azimuth of the sun at the dead-reckoning position, we must turn to a few little formulae used in spherical trigonometry.

If you don't mind meeting them head-on, then you can use these tables in combination with a log-table. A variety of others could be used: the ones in *Reed's* for example, or the AP3270 (in the USA, the equivalent is HO 249), all give solutions worked out in advance, are easy to use and don't cost very much. There is always the pocket calculator, and since you can take these into a GCSE exam, then there's no point not using them here. The sort of machine you want shouldn't cost any more than the HO 249 tables, and can be used for all sorts of other things apart from navigating by the stars. We will therefore use a calculator for the first example, and the HO 249 tables and table 1-2-3 later.

The calculation

With both *Reed's* and the calculator in easy reach, let us go back to the example we used previously, remembering the basic facts:
– it is still 4 August;
– it's tea time soon;
– we have made an observation of the sun at 1634 and 17 seconds;
– our dead-reckoning position is 46°57'N by 5°02'W.

In order to be able to draw our position line, we have to know the altitude and the azimuth of the sun at the dead-reckoning position.

This information is easy to get from the calculator, as long as the right information is fed in. It is time to unveil our mysterious trig functions:

One deals with the altitude of the sun at the dead-reckoning position and at the time of the fix, known as the *calculated altitude, ca*:

$$\text{Sin ca} = \sin L \sin D + \cos L \cos D \cos LHA$$

The other deals with its *azimuth, Z*:

$$\cos Z = \frac{\sin D - \sin L \sin ca}{\cos L \cos ca}$$

Of course, for the price of the *Éphémérides nautiques*, you could always buy a calculator programmed with the main facts contained in the navigational tables. However, French regulations specify that craft falling into category 1 have to have tables for astronomical navigation on board.

All times are given in GMT, of course.

According to the log and the helmsman, we have covered 24.4 nautical miles on 220° since 1206.

The hour angle of a body relative to the Greenwich meridian is referred to as GHA in calculations.

We see that the necessary ingredients are:

L: *our estimated latitude* (which we know);
D: *the declination of the sun at the time of the observation;*
LHA: *the local hour angle of the sun, which is its hour angle relative to our estimated longitude. This hour angle is derived from the hour angle at Greenwich.*

All in all, we must start by looking up the hour angle at Greenwich and the declination of the sun's GP at the moment of the observation.

1. The geographical position of the sun

Turn to section II of *Reed's Nautical Almanac* for 4 August. We find that the co-ordinates for the sun's GP, the GHA and the declination, are given for every 2 hours. We must therefore work out the figures for the time of our observation (1634 and 17 seconds) from those given for 1600 and 1800.

The declination is the latitude of the GP of the body, which can be either north and positive or south and negative in the northern hemisphere.

The interpolation of the hour angle can be made from the table entitled 'Sun GHA', the reference for which is given at the bottom of each page. This table is very convenient.

SUN — August — ARIES

Friday, 3rd August

00	178 26.9	N17 **43.1**	310 58.8
02	208 27.0	17 **41.8**	341 03.7
04	238 27.1	17 **40.5**	11 08.6
06	268 27.2	17 **39.2**	41 13.5
08	298 27.2	17 **37.9**	71 18.5
10	328 27.3	17 **36.7**	101 23.4
12	358 27.4	17 **35.4**	131 28.3
14	28 27.5	17 **34.1**	161 33.2
16	58 27.6	17 **32.8**	191 38.2
18	88 27.7	17 **31.4**	221 43.1
20	118 27.8	17 **30.1**	251 48.0
22	148 27.9	N17 **28.8**	281 53.0

Saturday, 4th August

00	178 28.0	N17 **27.5**	311 57.9
02	208 28.1	17 **26.2**	342 02.8
04	238 28.3	17 **24.9**	12 07.7
06	268 28.4	17 **23.6**	42 12.7
08	298 28.5	17 **22.3**	72 17.6
10	328 28.6	17 **20.9**	102 22.5
12	358 28.7	17 **19.6**	132 27.5
14	28 28.8	17 **18.3**	162 32.4
16	58 28.9	17 **17.0**	192 37.3
18	88 29.0	17 **15.7**	222 42.2
20	118 29.1	17 **14.3**	252 47.2
22	148 29.3	N17 **13.0**	282 52.1

Wednesday, 8th August

00	178 34.2	N16 **22.4**	315 54.4
02	208 34.4	16 **21.0**	345 59.4
04	238 34.6	16 **19.6**	16 04.3
06	268 34.7	16 **18.2**	46 09.2
08	298 34.9	16 **16.8**	76 14.2
10	328 35.0	16 **15.4**	106 19.1
12	358 35.2	16 **14.0**	136 24.0
14	28 35.3	16 **12.6**	166 28.9
16	58 35.5	16 **11.1**	196 33.9
18	88 35.7	16 **09.7**	226 38.8
20	118 35.8	16 **08.3**	256 43.7
22	148 36.0	N16 **06.9**	286 48.7

Thursday, 9th August

00	178 36.2	N16 **05.5**	316 53.6
02	208 36.3	16 **04.0**	346 58.5
04	238 36.5	16 **02.6**	17 03.4
06	268 36.7	16 **01.2**	47 08.4
08	298 36.8	15 **59.7**	77 13.3
10	328 37.0	15 **58.3**	107 18.2
12	358 37.2	15 **56.9**	137 23.2
14	28 37.4	15 **55.4**	167 28.1
16	58 37.5	15 **54.0**	197 33.0
18	88 37.7	15 **52.6**	227 37.9
20	118 37.9	15 **51.1**	257 42.9
22	148 38.1	N15 **49.7**	287 47.8

Extracted from *Reed's Nautical Almanac*.

⊙ SUN G.H.A. CORRECTION TABLE ⊙

Min. or Sec.	Add for Minutes	Add for 1 Hour +Minutes	Add for Secs.	Min. or Sec.	Add for Minutes	Add for 1 Hour +Minutes	Add for Secs.
	° ′	° ′	′		° ′	° ′	′
0	0 0.0	15 0.0	0.0	**30**	7 30.0	22 30.0	7.5
1	0 15.0	15 15.0	0.3	**31**	7 45.0	22 45.0	7.8
2	0 30.0	15 30.0	0.5	**32**	8 0.0	23 0.0	8.0
3	0 45.0	15 45.0	0.8	**33**	8 15.0	23 15.0	8.3
4	1 0.0	16 0.0	1.0	**34**	8 30.0	23 30.0	8.5
5	1 15.0	16 15.0	1.3	**35**	8 45.0	23 45.0	8.8
6	1 30.0	16 30.0	1.5	**36**	9 0.0	24 0.0	9.0
7	1 45.0	16 45.0	1.8	**37**	9 15.0	24 15.0	9.3
8	2 0.0	17 0.0	2.0	**38**	9 30.0	24 30.0	9.5
9	2 15.0	17 15.0	2.3	**39**	9 45.0	24 45.0	9.8
10	2 30.0	17 30.0	2.5	**40**	10 0.0	25 0.0	10.0
11	2 45.0	17 45.0	2.8	**41**	10 15.0	25 15.0	10.3
12	3 0.0	18 0.0	3.0	**42**	10 30.0	25 30.0	10.5
13	3 15.0	18 15.0	3.3	**43**	10 45.0	25 45.0	10.8
14	3 30.0	18 30.0	3.5	**44**	11 0.0	26 0.0	11.0
15	3 45.0	18 45.0	3.8	**45**	11 15.0	26 15.0	11.3
16	4 0.0	19 0.0	4.0	**46**	11 30.0	26 30.0	11.5
17	4 15.0	19 15.0	4.3	**47**	11 45.0	26 45.0	11.8
18	4 30.0	19 30.0	4.5	**48**	12 0.0	27 0.0	12.0
19	4 45.0	19 45.0	4.8	**49**	12 15.0	27 15.0	12.3

There is little change in the declination, and it can be estimated by sight, so to speak. Between 1600 and 1800 it changes by 1'.3. At 1630, it will therefore have changed by a quarter of that value, thus 0'.3, which has to be subtracted, since the declination is diminishing.

At 1600, on 4 August, the sun's	*Hour angle*	*Declination*
co-ordinates are:	58°28'.9	17°17'.0 N
Interpolation for 34min 17sec:	8°34'.3	– 0'.3
Thus, at 1634 and 17sec:	67°03'.2	17°16'.7 N

We see that the sun has moved since midday: it looks as if its GP is somewhere over the Antilles, near the coast of Puerto Rico.

In order to convert hours, minutes and seconds into fractions of a day, enter the seconds and divide by 60, add the minutes and divide by 60, and then add the hours. You then have the time in decimal hours. Divide by 24 to obtain this figure as the fraction of a day.

To convert degrees, minutes (and tenths of a minute) into decimal degrees, enter the minutes and their tenths and divide by 60, then add the degrees.

To convert decimal degrees into degrees and minutes, note the part that is in degrees, subtract it and then multiply the remainder by 60, which gives you the minutes.

2. Calculating the local hour angle

In order to calculate the LHA of the sun, that is to say the angle between the meridian of the GP of the sun and that of our estimated position, all that needs to be done is to subtract our estimated longitude from the GHA. We are currently west of Greenwich, and so the

The direction in which the angles are measured is as important as their value!

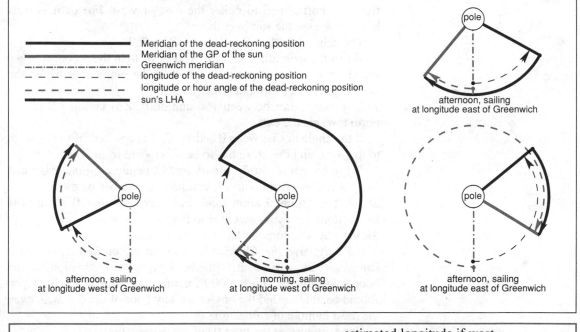

Meridian of the dead-reckoning position
Meridian of the GP of the sun
Greenwich meridian
longitude of the dead-reckoning position
longitude or hour angle of the dead-reckoning position
sun's LHA

afternoon, sailing
at longitude east of Greenwich

afternoon, sailing
at longitude west of Greenwich

morning, sailing
at longitude west of Greenwich

afternoon, sailing
at longitude east of Greenwich

Local hour angle = Greenwich hour angle   – estimated longitude if west
                                           + estimated longitude if east
If necessary, add 360° to the GHA, or subtract 360° from the result.

LHA is smaller than the GHA (if we were east of Greenwich, then it would be greater, and we would have to add our longitude to it).

We therefore have:

$$LHA = 67°03'.2 - 5°02' = 62°01'.2$$

Check to see if we have everything we need:

Estimated latitude: 46°57 N (this is north, therefore positive)
Declination: 17°16'.7 N (this is north, therefore positive)
LHA: 62°01'.2 N

Now all we have to do is to get going on all the sines and cosines.

3. Altitude and azimuth at dead-reckoning position

After having played around on the calculator for a while – the main problem here is making sure you don't enter a figure incorrectly – we obtain the following result:

calculated altitude   =   31°31'.5
                   Z   =   98°.4, rounded down to 98°

First thing to notice: the azimuth is supposed to be 98°, but we can see the sun to the west! Remember that the azimuth is counted from the north, then to either the east or west. For us it is west because we see the sun over there.

The azimuth is therefore $360° - 98° = 262°$.

When the azimuth is close to 180 or 0° then that is because we are close to the noon position, which is the moment at which the hour angle passes through either 0 or 180°.

If the angle lies between 180 and 360°, Z is counted from the north towards the east.

If the angle lies between 0 and 180°, Z is counted from the north to the west, and therefore has to be subtracted from 360°.

If you have a scientific calculator: Depending on the make and the price, these little marvels can have a number of memories, + and –, ( ), decimalisation (and the other way round). Study the instructions with your machine to find the best way of dealing with the various functions we have discussed so far.

If you only have the Almanach du marin breton *and an ordinary calculator:* Since 1986, this little book gives the declination and the hour angle for the sun at 0000 for that day. This means that you should be able to find the angles for any hour of the day with even the most humble of calculators.

For 4 August, at the time (t) of the observation:
t = 1634 and 17sec = 16.571389 hours = 0.6904745 days →
(memory = j)

Declination D:

at 2400	17°11'.7	variation – 15'.8/day
at 0000	17°27 .5	multiplied by (memory) = – 10'.9
	-10'.9	= variation at 1634 and 17sec

D =   17°16'.6   at 1634 and 17sec

Hour angle for the sun:

at 2400	178°29'.4	variation + 1'.4 + 360° = 360°.02333/day
at 0000	178°28'.0	multiplied by (memory) = 248°.58692
	+ 248° 35'.2	= variation at 1634 and17sec

Hour angle for the sun = 427°03'.2
                        = 67°03'.2   at 1634 and 17sec

This gives the same co-ordinates as found in *Reed's* to 0'.1.

4. Tracing the position line

See chart on page 955.

Starting from the dead-reckoning position on the chart, draw a straight line along a heading of 262°, which is the calculated azimuth of the sun.

Take the observed altitude again and convert it into true altitude, as we did for the noon position. (In *Reed's* the table on page 86, entitled 'Sun altitude total correction table', gives a correction to be added.)

SUN ALTITUDE TOTAL CORRECTION TABLE
For correcting the Observed Altitude of the Sun's Lower Limb

ALWAYS ADDITIVE (+)
Height of the eye above the sea. Top line metres, lower line feet

| Obs. Alt. | 0.9 | 1.8 | 2.4 | 3 | 3.7 | 4.3 | 4.9 | 5.5 | 6 | 7.6 | 9 | 12 | 15 | 18 | 21 | 24 |
	3	6	8	10	12	14	16	18	20	25	30	40	50	60	70	80
30	12.7	12.1	11.7	11.4	11.1	10.8	10.6	10.4	10.1	9.6	9.1	8.3	7.6	6.9	6.3	5.7
32	12.9	12.2	11.9	11.5	11.2	11.0	10.7	10.5	10.2	9.7	9.3	8.4	7.7	7.0	6.4	5.8
34	13.0	12.3	12.0	11.6	11.3	11.1	10.8	10.6	10.3	9.8	9.4	8.5	7.8	7.1	6.5	5.9
36	13.1	12.4	12.1	11.7	11.4	11.2	10.9	10.7	10.4	9.9	9.5	8.6	7.9	7.2	6.6	6.0
38	13.2	12.5	12.1	11.8	11.5	11.2	11.0	10.8	10.5	10.0	9.5	8.7	8.0	7.3	6.7	6.1

MONTHLY CORRECTION

Jan.	Feb.	Mar.	Apr.	May	June	July	Aug.	Sept.	Oct.	Nov.	Dec.
+0'.3	+0'.2	+0'.1	0'.0	−0'.1	−0'.2	−0'.2	−0'.2	−0'.1	+0'.1	+0'.2	+0'.3

Extracted from *Reed's Nautical Almanac*.

Sextant altitude	31°24'.5
Index error	− 2'.0
Overall correction	+ 12'.2
Correction for August	− 0'.2
True altitude	31°34'.5

We see that the true altitude is greater than the calculated altitude for the dead-reckoning position (31°31'.5). This means that we are closer to the sun's GP than we thought.

Now calculate the intercept:

   true altitude − calculated altitude = 31°34'.5 − 31°31'.5 = 3'

then plot the intercept on the line corresponding to the azimuth of the sun. This is drawn in the direction of the sun, 3 nautical miles from the dead-reckoning position; then trace a line passing through this point, perpendicular to the radius of the position circle. This is our position line. There you go! We can now go and have our tea.

Position lines made easy

- Observe the body, noting its altitude and the time of the observation.
- Find:
- the boat's latitude by dead reckoning;
- the declination of the body at the time of the observation;
- the LHA of the body.
- Calculate the altitude and azimuth of the body at the dead-reckoning position from these facts.
- Calculate the difference (the intercept) between the true altitude and the calculated altitude.

The fix

It would be a pity not to make the tiny extra effort required to obtain a complete fix, by combining our noon position that we calculated a while back with the position line we have just worked out.

According to the dead reckoning, we have covered 24.4 nautical miles along a bearing of 220° since noon. All that we have to do is to transfer our noon position by 24.4 nautical miles in that direction: it intersects with our position line at a point which gives our position at 1634 and 17 seconds.

Note that we could have taken a fix much earlier, and that it was only the desire to make things clear for the reader that persuaded us to wait until midday to get down to it. In fact, if you can make a position line as early as you like, then obviously it is best to start with the position line, and you will then have a fix as soon as you can obtain a noon position.

In all events, you now have some of the basic procedures for navigating by the stars. Since someone has just pointed out that the moon is rising in the SE, we are of course going to plot a position line using the moon; and since the weather is clear, at dusk we can take a fix on the stars. This time, though, we will go a little faster, since everything is based on the same principle, and only some small details will be new information.

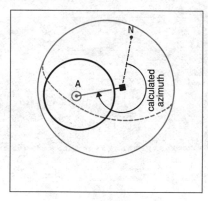

Position circle on a globe.

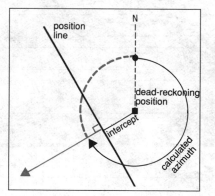

Position line on a chart.

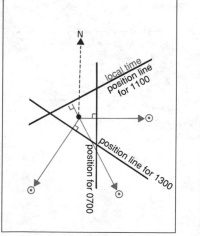

Sun's azimuth at various times. By choosing the times of observation carefully, the position lines can be made to intersect in useful ways.

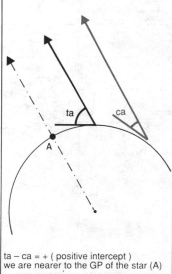

ta − ca = + (positive intercept)
we are nearer to the GP of the star (A)

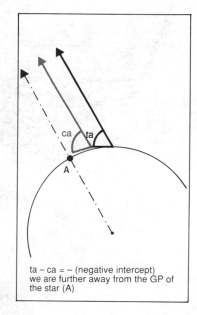

ta − ca = − (negative intercept)
we are further away from the GP of the star (A)

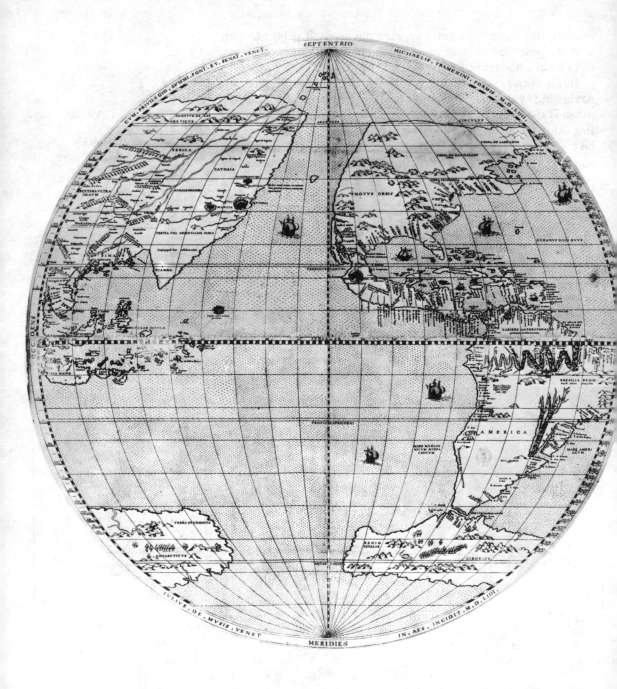

Where are we?
For a better idea see the chart on the next page …

The first fix

1. Noon position at 1224.
2. Dead-reckoning position at 1634.
3. Sun's azimuth at 1634.
4. Sun's position line at 1634.
5. Direction in which noon position is transferred.
6. Noon position transferred for 1634.
(Document of the SHOM.)

Seen from this point, one could wonder whether the log was pessimistic or if we are steering too far to the west. It is best to wait for nightfall to get a better idea.

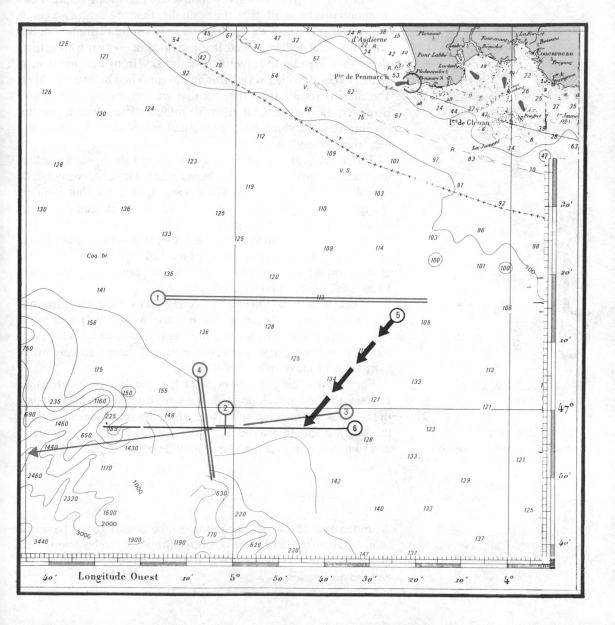

The moon

While we were dealing with the sun, the moon, that dead planet, was rising quietly in the SE.

The moon is deceptive: it appears to be as big as the sun and to pass behind it. All of this gives completely the wrong impression: the moon is very small (fifty times smaller than the earth), and only appears large because we see it close up (Camille Flammarion, the French man of letters, called it a province of the earth). Further, although it appears to travel across the sky from east to west, it actually goes the other way, orbiting the earth in a bit over 29 days. The illusion results from the fact that we are turning even faster. However, each evening it rises 50 minutes later than it did the evening before, which must prove that it has moved east in the meantime, surely?

The moon also always presents the same face (spaceships that have been to look at the far side have come back very disappointed: it looks exactly the same). We nevertheless know that it often changes appearance as the sun's reflected light makes the moon appear to shine. We spoke of all this when we discussed the tides, which are subject to lunar influence. Other influences are attributed to the moon: on how we act (it's just too bad if you've got a lunatic aboard), on the weather (less clear) and on plants (now, gardeners swear this is true, so no sniggering).

Of course, it is the illusion that counts, since the moon , like the sun, is only useful for navigation because we see it appear to do things, even if the truth is quite different. The moon's path across the heavens is a capricious one, however, and there are many irregularities in its movement.

For the time being, the moon has a face for the first quarter, that is to say, the first quarter points in the same direction as the first part of the letter X (this is not surprising, since the sun shines on it from the west). It should also be noted that the lower edge is not clear, and so it is best to take reading of altitude on the upper edge.

Position line by the moon

As in the case of the sun, the moon can be considered as having a foot, or GP on the earth. The position of this GP can be determined at any given instant by the use of the usual co-ordinates: the GHA and the declination.

The moon behaves as if it were crossing the road (in Britain):
   in the first quarter, it looks right;
   in the last quarter, it looks left.

There is no lack of mnemonics like this, but most of them only work in the northern hemisphere.

The moon in the *Éphémérides nautiques*

Let's use the *Éphémérides nautiques* this time, opening them at the page for 4 August. At the bottom of the table dealing with the moon, we read 'PQ', which means that it is in its first quarter, and its age (10.9 days) – the time that has passed since the new moon, and last of all, its apparent semi-diameter (since the orbit it describes is somewhat irregular). (The table is given on page 959.)

Both the GHA and the declination of the moon are subject to variations, v and d, which take account of all its little whims, hour by hour. Last of all, the horizontal parallax has to be taken into account; this is given in the column π.

The moon is effectively too close for us to consider its rays as parallel, as we do with the other stars, and this parallax also varies with time.

The times of the moon's passage over the Greenwich meridian can be found in the very first pages of the *Éphémérides nautiques*; they are given in the sections headed 'Renseignements annuels' ('Information for the year'). In order to calculate the time of passage over the local meridian, the procedure is the same as for the sun, but also adding the duration VP, multiplied by the number of tens of degrees for the longitude west (if east, then the figure is negative).

	Lune	
Date	heure du passage	V.P. 10° G
	h m	m
Août 1	18 16,6	1,4
2	19 06,0	1,5
3	19 58,9	1,5
4	20 55,1	1,6
5	21 54,0	1,7
6	22 54,5	1,7
7	23 54,9	1,6

Times of passage over the Greenwich meridian. Extracted from the *Éphémérides nautiques*. (*Reed's* has a similar table.)

Choosing the time of the observation

The declination of the moon at 1600 is about 18° (south): this means that it won't rise very high over the horizon. At what time is it best to take the observation?

Not too early: it is better that a heavenly body should be well above the horizon, because the refraction is smaller and can be corrected more precisely.

Not too late either: first of all, because (by referring to the column giving the GHA), we note that the moon will pass over the prime meridian a bit before 2100. If we wait too long, we will take a noon position, which will simply double up on the one we took on the sun at 1224. Further, there is no question of taking an observation of the moon at night. This is yet another of its little tricks: the reflection of the moon on the water makes it impossible to see exactly where the horizon is, so the measurement obtained will be inaccurate.

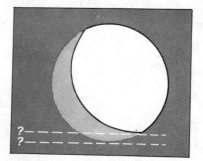

The lower edge of the moon is invisible, and therefore impossible to measure against the horizon.

Since 1634, we have made 13.2 nautical miles on a heading of 220°.

We should be able to take a reasonable sight between 1800 and 1900: at this point the moon will be sufficiently high in the sky, and we will be able to get a position line at a useful angle to our meridian and our recent sightings on the sun.

While waiting for the moon to reach a sufficient height, we can begin to prepare the cabbage for an Auvergne-style broth that we are going to have for dinner. The cabbage was planted under a full moon, of course.

The geographical position of the moon

We bring down on the upper edge of the moon at 1845 and 44sec
The sextant altitude is 16°33'.4.
The dead-reckoning position is 46°44'N by 5°18'W.
We look up the GP of the moon for the time of the observation:

Extracted from the *Éphémérides nautiques* table 4 general interpolations.

CORRECTION	45m	CORRECTION MOYENNE à l'angle horaire			v ou d	CORRECTION
		Soleil Planètes	Point vernal	Lune		
'	s	o '	o '	o '	'	'
1,1	05	11 16,3	11 18,1	10 45,4	1,5	1,1
1,3	06	11 16,5	11 18,4	10 45,7	1,8	1,4
1,6	07	11 16,8	11 18,6	10 45,9	2,1	1,6
1,8	08	11 17,0	11 18,9	10 46,2	2,4	1,8
2,0	09	11 17,3	11 19,1	10 46,4	2,7	2,0
4,5	20	11 20,0	11 21,9	10 49,0	6,0	4,6
4,7	21	11 20,3	11 22,1	10 49,3	6,3	4,8
4,9	22	11 20,5	11 22,4	10 49,5	6,6	5,0
5,1	23	11 20,8	11 22,6	10 49,7	6,9	5,2
5,3	24	11 21,0	11 22,9	10 50,0	7,2	5,5
8,9	40	11 25,0	11 26,9	10 53,8	12,0	9,1
9,1	41	11 25,3	11 27,1	10 54,0	12,3	9,3
9,3	42	11 25,5	11 27,4	10 54,3	12,6	9,6
9,6	43	11 25,8	11 27,6	10 54,5	12,9	9,8
9,8	44	11 26,0	11 27,9	10 54,7	13,2	10,0

GHA:
– at 1800, with v = 6.5, the GHA was .... 317°54'.8
– the interpolation for the 45min 44sec was taken from the table at the end of the *Éphémérides nautiques* (yellow pages). In the column 45min along the line for 44sec we find: .... 10°54'.7
– in the right-hand side of the table, for 45min, we see that the correction for v = 6.5 is: .... 5'.0
this gives us: .... 328°54'.5

Declination:
– at 1800, with d = 2.2: .... 18°19'.3 S
– again, from the table for 45min, for d = 2.2: .... + 1'.6
(the correction is positive because the declination is increasing) this gives us: .... 18°20'.9 S

According to these co-ordinates, the GP of the moon ought to be somewhere in the suburbs of Harare, the capital of Zimbabwe.

If we use a pocket calculator, then the next part of the sum is carried out as for the position line of the sun. However, this time we are going to use the American tables, HO 249.

Azimuth and altitude from the HO 249 tables

We still need the same factors: the *estimated latitude*, the *declination* and the *LHA*. However, the HO 249 tables have one peculiarity in that the tables are expressed in round figures. This means that we must substitute an assumed position for the dead-reckoning position.

1. In order to obtain an LHA in round figures, instead of subtracting our dead-reckoning longitude (5°18'W) from the GHA, we must choose an angle with the same number of minutes as the latter, for example 4°54'.5, which gives us:

$$328°54'.5$$
$$- 4°54'.5$$

LHA   324°

2. Round the declination off to 18°S, for the purpose of this calculation.

3. For the assumed latitude, let us take 47°.

We are at a latitude north, and the moon has a declination of 18°S. We therefore go to the page headed 'Latitude 47°' and enter the table headed 'Declination (15°–29°), Contrary name to latitude'.

In the column 18°, along the line 'LHA = 324', we find three figures:

hc   17° 23'
d   55'
Z   144°

TABLE 5.—Correction to Tabulated Altitude for Minutes of Declination

52 53 54	55 56 57	58 59 60	d /
13 13 14	14 14 14	14 15 15	15
14 14 14	15 15 15	15 16 16	16
15 15 15	16 16 16	16 17 17	17
16 16 16	16 17 17	17 18 18	18
16 17 17	17 18 18	18 19 19	19
17 18 18	18 19 19	19 20 20	20
18 19 19	19 20 20	20 21 21	21
19 19 20	20 21 21	21 22 22	22
20 20 21	21 21 22	22 23 23	23
21 21 22	22 22 23	23 24 24	24
22 22 22	23 23 24	24 25 25	25
23 23 23	24 24 25	25 26 26	26
23 24 24	25 25 26	26 27 27	27
24 25 25	26 26 27	27 28 28	28
25 26 26	27 27 28	28 29 29	29

We could also choose 5°54'.5W, but this value is not so close to 5°18'W.
If we were at a longitude east, then we would have to choose a longitude such that the sum of the two gave us a round figure.

t. {LHA greater than 180°....... Zn=Z													
LHA less than 180°........... Zn=360−Z													

DECLINATION (15°-29°) CONTRARY NAME TO LATITUDE

15°	16°	17°	18°	19°	20°	21°	22°	23°	24°	25°	26°	LHA
Hc d Z	Hc d Z	Hc d Z	Hc d Z	Hc d Z	Hc d Z	Hc d Z	Hc d Z	Hc d Z	Hc d Z	Hc d Z	Hc d Z	
19 53 140	17 56 54 141	17 02 53 141	16 09 54 142	15 15 54 142	14 21 54 142	13 27 53 143	12 34 54 143	11 40 54 144	10 46 54 144	09 52 54 145	08 58 54 145	321
16 54 141	18 22 54 141	17 28 54 142	16 34 54 143	15 40 54 143	14 46 54 143	13 52 54 144	12 58 54 144	12 04 55 145	11 09 54 145	10 15 54 146	09 21 54 146	322
11 54 142	18 47 54 142	17 53 54 143	16 59 54 143	16 05 55 144	15 10 54 144	14 16 54 145	13 22 55 145	12 27 54 145	11 33 55 146	10 38 54 146	09 44 55 147	323
06 54 143	19 12 55 143	18 17 54 144	17 23 55 144	16 28 54 145	15 34 55 145	14 39 54 145	13 45 55 146	12 50 55 146	11 55 54 147	11 01 55 147	10 06 55 148	324
31 −55 144	19 36 −55 144	18 41 −54 145	17 47 −55 145	16 52 −55 146	15 57 −55 146	15 02 −55 146	14 07 −54 147	13 13 −55 147	12 18 −55 148	11 23 −55 148	10 28 −56 148	325

1. Let's deal with d first of all, which is the variation for the calculated altitude when the declination passes from 18 to 19°. We must now take account again of the 20'.9 of our declination which we subtracted in order to make the figure into a round one. Table 5 in the HO 249 ('Correction to tabulated altitude for minutes of declination') indicates that for 21' and d = 55, it is necessary to adjust the calculated altitude by 19'. This correction is to be subtracted, because, as we can see from the columns in the preceding table, the calculated altitude decreases when we go from a declination of 18° to one of 19°.

2. The calculated altitude is therefore: hc = 17°23'−19' = 17°04'.

3. All that remains is the azimuth, Z. Z is counted from north through 0 to 180°, east or west. A note in the top left-hand corner of the page tells us that if the LHA is greater than 180°, then the true azimuth (Zn) equals Z. This is the case here. The azimuth of the moon is therefore 144°, which is reasonable, since we can see it to the SE.

Plotting the position line

First of all, convert the sextant altitude into a true altitude, taking the corrections that must be applied to the moon into account. These are to be found in one of the navigation tables (No IX) in the *Éphémérides nautiques*.

- Sextant altitude   16°33'.4
- Index error   – 2'.   = observed altitude
- First correction (–)
for dip, height of eye at 2m: – 2'.5   = apparent altitude
- Second correction (+) for
refraction (p = 58.8)
and apparent altitude: + 69'.4   = true altitude of top
                                            edge of moon

- Subtract the diameter of the
moon, since observation made
on upper limb: – 32'.1

True altitude (of lower limb) = 17°06'.2

Calculate the intercept:

True altitude – calculated altitude = 17°06'.2 – 17°04' = 2'.2 or 2.2 nautical miles in the direction of the moon, because the true altitude is greater than the calculated altitude, and therefore we are closer to the GP of the moon.

Corrections des hauteurs observées de la Lune.						DEUXIEME CORRECTION. — Bord inférieur (additive)				
PREMIÈRE CORRECTION (négative)						(– Réfraction moyenne + parallaxe + demi-diamètre)				
Dépression apparente de l'horizon.						HAUTEUR apparente	PARALLAXE HORIZONTALE			
							57',5	58'	58',5	59'	59',5

Élévation de l'œil (m)	0	2	4	6	8
Dépression	0',0	−2,5	−3',5	−4',3	−5',0

HAUTEUR apparente	57',5	58'	58',5	59'	59',5
15	67,7	68,4	69,0	69,6	70,2
16	67,7	68,3	68,9	69,6	70,2
17	67,6	68,2	68,8	69,5	70,1
18	67,5	68,1	68,7	69,3	69,9
19	67,3	67,9	68,5	69,2	69,8
DIAMÈTRE de la Lune	31',4	31',7	32',0	32',2	32',5

Pour le bord supérieur, retrancher le diamètre

All that remains to be done is to plot the intercept on the chart, starting from the assumed position chosen (47°N by 4°54'.5 W).

By transferring the noon position and the position line from the sun taken at 1600, the suspicions that arose when we took our first fix are now beginning to be confirmed: the log is at least 5% low.

In any event, we aren't lost. While drawing water to do the washing up after tea, one of the crew remarked that the water had become dark blue: we have left the continental shelf, as the fix plotted on the chart confirms. The moon didn't let us down.

The planets

The planets behave rather like the moon, except that they are less complicated. The variations, v and d, which affect their co-ordinates do not change from hour to hour, but only from day to day. The altitude is corrected from another table in the *Éphémérides nautiques*, and that's all there is to it.

Remember nonetheless that the planets are wanderers, revolving around the sun in their own orbits, and not giving out any light of their own. They do not shine in the way that the stars do (this is very clear in the telescope of the sextant). The earth is a planet, and the eight other planets are Mercury, Venus, Mars, Jupiter, Saturn, Uranus, Neptune and Pluto. Five of them are named after the same gods that give the French the names for days of the week. Only four are of any use in navigating: Venus, the most brilliant, always close to the sun and therefore visible morning and evening, and often called the Morning or Evening Star; Jupiter, the largest; Mars, the red planet and Saturn, with its lead-grey colour and its rings.

Having said that, it's time to prepare the dinner, or we'll never get to bed.

For the line plotted on the chart, see page 975.

The fix is very nice and convenient. However, if we take into account the fact that the log under-reads by 5%, then it is even better (see 13, noon position transferred by 24.4 nautical miles + 13.2 nautical miles + 5%, and 14, position line transferred by 13.2 nautical miles + 5%).

The stars

The ancients considered the sky as a solid vault, which they referred to as the firmament, to which the stars were attached. This image is useful when navigating by the stars, and we shall also consider them fixed to the inside of a large sphere, known as the *celestial sphere*, which centres on the earth. This sphere orbits the earth in about a day or so in the same direction as the sun.

The names of the stars often reflect a rather imagistic line of thought. Our distant ancestors found images of legendary figures and animals from fables in the constellations. The giant Orion can still be found pursuing Taurus, and the seven oxen still draw the chariot of the Great Bear. Particular attention was paid to the regions of the sky that the sun crossed in the course of the year. These were divided into twelve equal parts, each taking the name of the nearest constellation. These names were often those of animals, and the word *zodiac* reflects that, being based on the Ancient Greek for 'animal'. In one year, the sun visits the twelve houses of the zodiac, a course that was said to shape the destinies of men and women. For us this can be nothing more than an interesting excursus, since modern science places a barrier between astrology and astronomy that would not have been acknowledged by the ancient world.

Sailing needs rather more precise forms of reference. This is why the stars are part of the same system of reference as is used for the earth, with two poles and an equator, which are the extensions of the poles and equator on earth. We also needed a prime meridian, a sort of celestial Greenwich. The placing of this meridian is less arbitrary than that of the Greenwich meridian, since it relates to the position of the sun, and its movement across the sphere.

The sun's course is *ecliptic*, because it is that area that produces the eclipses of both sun and moon. If you cast your mind back to what was said of the sun and the tropics, then you will understand that the plane of the ecliptic is at an angle of 23°26' to the plane of the celestial equator (or equinoctial), and that it cuts the latter at two points, corresponding to the two equinoxes. It was naturally convenient for one of these points to be chosen as the prime meridian, and the spring equinox was chosen. This is referred to as the *vernal* or *gamma* point because of the similarity between the Greek letter gamma and the sign for Aries the ram.

With this system, each star can be situated precisely in the sphere, by latitude according to its declination relative to the celestial equator and by longitude according to its *sidereal hour angle* (SHA), that is to say the angle between the meridian of the vernal point and its own meridian. We can then calculate our position relative to the stars.

The position of the stars in the sphere varies very little. This is why there is no heading for each day in the reference works. A page is given over to them for each month, on which between about sixty and eighty stars are described with the basic facts pertaining to each one:

– magnitude, which is how bright the star is (the scale of magnitude is the order in which the stars are listed). Thus the pole star, which is not so bright, at a magnitude of 2.1, appears later than Sirius, the brightest, at magnitude –1.6;
– declination;
– the SHA.

Choosing the time of observation

We now have enough information to make a fix by three stars, for our position on 4 August. We will go back to the tools we used first of all, which is to say *Reed's* and the pocket calculator.

The first thing is to work out the time of twilight. There are only a few minutes when the conditions for making an observation are ideal: *both the horizon and the stars must be visible*.

The times for Civil twilight at 52° of latitude north during the month of August are given in *Reed's*, day by day. For 4 August we find that it is 2026.

AUGUST

G.M.T. (31 days) **G.M.T.**

DATE			Equation of Time		Transit	Semi-diam.	Lat. 52°N.				Lat. Corr. to Sunrise, Sunset, etc.				
Yr.	Day of Mth.	Week	0 h.	12 h.			Twi-light	Sun-rise	Sun-set	Twi-light	Lat.	Twi-light	Sun-rise	Sun-set	Twi-light
			m. s.	m. s.	h. m.		h. m.	h. m.	h. m.	h. m.	°	h. m.	h. m.	h. m.	h. m.
213	1	W	+06 20	+06 18	12 06	15.8	03 39	04 21	19 51	20 32	N70	T.A.N.	–1 50	+1 46	T.A.N.
214	2	Th	+06 17	+06 15	12 06	15.8	03 41	04 23	19 49	20 30	68	–2 28	–1 26	+1 23	+2 26
215	3	F	+06 13	+06 10	12 06	15.8	03 43	04 24	19 48	20 28	66	–1 48	–1 08	+1 06	+1 47
216	4	S	+06 08	+06 05	12 06	15.8	03 45	04 26	19 46	20 26	64	–1 21	–0 53	+0 51	+1 20
217	5	Sun	+06 03	+06 00	12 06	15.8	03 47	04 27	19 44	20 24	62	–1 01	–0 41	+0 39	+1 00
218	6	M	+05 57	+05 54	12 06	15.8	03 48	04 28	19 42	20 22	N60	–0 45	–0 30	+0 29	+0 44
219	7	Tu	+05 50	+05 47	12 06	15.8	03 50	04 30	19 40	20 20	58	–0 32	–0 21	+0 21	+0 30
220	8	W	+05 43	+05 39	12 06	15.8	03 52	04 32	19 38	20 18	56	–0 20	–0 13	+0 13	+0 18
221	9	Th	+05 35	+05 31	12 06	15.8	03 54	04 33	19 37	20 16	54	–0 10	–0 06	+0 06	+0 09
222	10	F	+05 27	+05 23	12 05	15.8	03 56	04 35	19 35	20 14	50	+0 07	+0 06	–0 06	–0 04
223	11	S	+05 18	+05 14	12 05	15.8	03 58	04 37	19 33	20 12	N45	+0 23	+0 18	–0 18	–0 27
224	12	Sun	+05 09	+05 04	12 05	15.8	03 59	04 38	19 31	20 10	40	+0 36	+0 28	–0 28	–0 38
225	13	M	+04 59	+04 54	12 05	15.8	04 01	04 40	19 29	20 07	35	+0 47	+0 37	–0 37	–0 48
226	14	Tu	+04 49	+04 43	12 05	15.8	04 03	04 42	19 27	20 05	30	+0 57	+0 44	–0 45	–0 58
227	15	W	+04 38	+04 32	12 05	15.8	04 04	04 43	19 25	20 03	20	+1 12	+0 57	–0 57	–1 13
228	16	Th	+04 26	+04 20	12 04	15.8	04 06	04 45	19 23	20 01	N10	+1 24	+1 09	–1 08	–1 25

Our dead-reckoning position for that time will be 46°38'N by 5°27'W. The table next to it allows us to make a correction for latitude: 45°N = 0hr 27min. As for the correction for longitude, we

Extracted from *Reed's Nautical Almanac.*

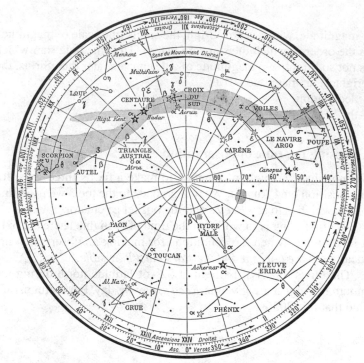

Star charts for the *Éphémérides nautiques*. The principal stars and constellations are easy to find here. On the chart below, it is also possible to find the ecliptic, the course taken by the sun over the year. On the day of the spring equinox, the sun is at the vernal point.

Star chart for the southern celestial hemisphere for declinations from 35°S to 90°S.

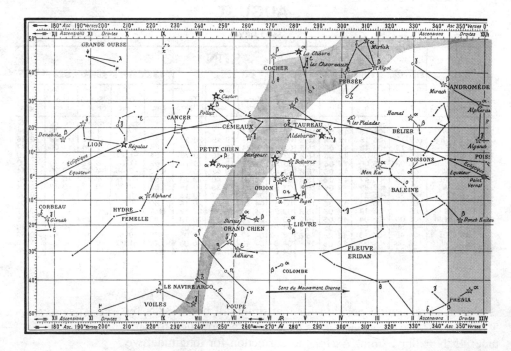

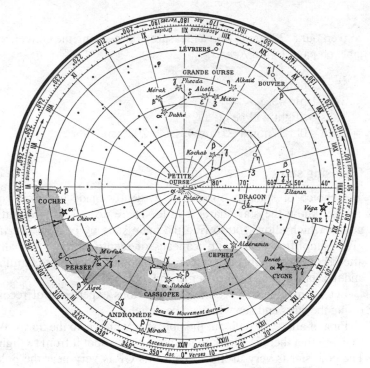

Star chart for the northern celestial hemisphere for declinations from 35°N to 90°N.

The blue band covers the portion of the sky where the stars are not visible on that day. Aquarius will hardly have time to appear: it is very low on the horizon at daybreak. When night falls, Aries lights up for a second, then sets.

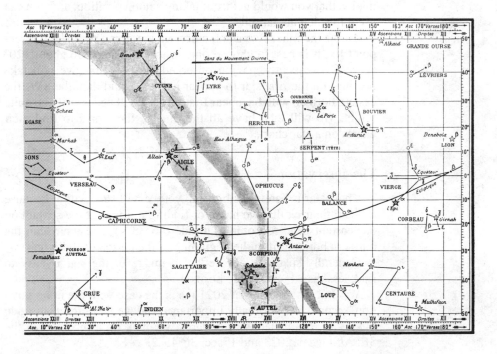

convert our 5°27' of arc into a measure of time using the conversion table on page 154 of *Reed's*:

5° = 20min
27' = 1min 48sec
Thus twilight will be at:
2026 − 0hr 27min + 21min 48sec = 2020 and 48sec

Choosing stars

The choice of stars to observe is evidently made easier if you already know the star charts a little. There are all sorts of little guides which allow you to find the main stars by bearing (*Reed's* gives simplified charts and a means of identification). Actually, after a couple of nights at sea, the sky becomes much more familiar and the stars a good deal easier to pick out.

Let us imagine that we have no previous experience of recognising the stars and see what can be done.

First of all, try to pick out the pole star, which is to the north. We shall see that there is a trick that allows you to spot it from twilight. The pole star is very useful, because its GP is very near the pole. Observing its altitude gives you very much the same sort of information that you would get from taking a noon position, and you can use it to calculate latitude.

As for the other two stars, since we are going to make a three-point fix, it is best to choose ones whose bearings are about 120° apart. Consequently, having observed the pole star, we will take bearings on the first star to appear in the SE and then the SW (the eastern horizon will disappear first). These will necessarily be quite bright. We will then have all the time in the world to find their names on a star chart.

The observation

The pole star is barely visible, and yet we will start with it because of the little trick that we have for finding it. First set the sextant on our current dead-reckoning latitude (46°38'N), and then scan the northern horizon from the beginning of the period of twilight.

Generally speaking, the reflected image of the star is easy to find, less than 1° above the horizon.

We find the pole star at 2021 (as is the case with the noon position, seconds are not really important), and we measure its altitude (46°03'.4). Immediately afterwards, we pick up a nice star in the SE. Altitude at 2023 and 17sec: 36°43'.2.

Finally a third, in the SW at 2025 and 45sec. Altitude: 46°46'.2.

A glance at the star chart suffices for us to identify the stars clearly: they are Altair and Arcturus.

All that remains to be done now is to make the calculations. Since we will need the co-ordinates for our dead-reckoning position in order to make the calculations for Altair and Arcturus, it is best to start with the pole star, since this will allow us to obtain a precise latitude.

Since 1825, we have covered 10 nautical miles on a heading of 220°.

Latitude by the pole star

The GP of the pole star does not fall precisely on the pole, so the altitude from the observation (which we have converted into a true altitude) does not give us a precise figure for our latitude. In order to obtain this, we have to turn to a table in *Reed's*, where we read starting from the LHA of Aries (the vernal point) at the time of the observation (2021). Since the movement of the pole star around the pole is not that large, a LHA in round figures will be perfectly adequate.

On the page for 4 August,
we note that the GHA of Aries is: 252°47'.2
Interpolation for 21min (according
to accompanying tables): 5°15'.9
This gives us: 258°03'.1
Rounded down to: 258°

See table below,
and on page 970.

Since we are west of Greenwich, the LHA is obtained by subtracting our estimated longitude (rounded to 5°) from the GHA.

258°
− 5°
253°

How to calculate latitude from the pole star

1. Look for the star.
2. Look up the LHA of Aries for the time of the observation.
3. Check the necessary correction to be made to the true altitude.

	SUN — August				— ARIES		
	Friday, 3rd August				**Wednesday, 8th August**		
00	178	26.9	N17 43.1	310 58.8	178	34.2	N16 22.4	315 54.4
02	208	27.0	17 41.8	341 03.7	208	34.4	16 21.0	345 59.4
04	238	27.1	17 40.5	11 08.6	238	34.6	16 19.6	16 04.3
06	268	27.2	17 39.2	41 13.5	268	34.7	16 18.2	46 09.2
08	298	27.2	17 37.9	71 18.5	298	34.9	16 16.8	76 14.2
10	328	27.3	17 36.7	101 23.4	328	35.0	16 15.4	106 19.1
12	358	27.4	17 35.4	131 28.3	358	35.2	16 14.0	136 24.0
14	28	27.5	17 34.1	161 33.2	28	35.3	16 12.6	166 28.9
16	58	27.6	17 32.8	191 38.2	58	35.5	16 11.1	196 33.9
18	88	27.7	17 31.4	221 43.1	88	35.7	16 09.7	226 38.8
20	118	27.8	17 30.1	251 48.0	118	35.8	16 08.3	256 43.7
22	148	27.9	N17 28.8	281 53.0	148	36.0	N16 06.9	286 48.7
	Saturday, 4th August				**Thursday, 9th August**		
00	178	28.0	N17 27.5	311 57.9	178	36.2	N16 05.5	316 53.6
02	208	28.1	17 26.2	342 02.8	208	36.3	16 04.0	346 58.5
04	238	28.3	17 24.9	12 07.7	238	36.5	16 02.6	17 03.4
06	268	28.4	17 23.6	42 12.7	268	36.7	16 01.2	47 08.4
08	298	28.5	17 22.3	72 17.6	298	36.8	15 59.7	77 13.3
10	328	28.6	17 20.9	102 22.5	328	37.0	15 58.3	107 18.2
12	358	28.7	17 19.6	132 27.5	358	37.2	15 56.9	137 23.2
14	28	28.8	17 18.3	162 32.4	28	37.4	15 55.4	167 28.1
16	58	28.9	17 17.0	192 37.3	58	37.5	15 54.0	197 33.0
18	88	29.0	17 15.7	222 42.2	88	37.7	15 52.6	227 37.9
20	118	29.1	17 14.3	252 47.2	118	37.9	15 51.1	257 42.9
22	148	29.3	N17 13.0	282 52.1	148	38.1	N15 49.7	287 47.8

Extracted from *Reed's Nautical Almanac*.

On page 91 of *Reed's* we find the table that allows us to determine our latitude from the true altitude of the pole star. We see that for a LHA for Aries of 253°, we have to add 38'.4 to the true altitude. This gives us:

See table below, and
on page 970.

Instrument altitude:	46°03'.9
Index error:	– 2'
Correction for height of observer's eye (1.5m) and an observed altitude of 46°:	– 3'.2
Correction for the pole star:	+ 38'.4
Our latitude is:	46°37'.1N

LATITUDE BY POLE STAR 1979

TABLE FOR DETERMINING APPROXIMATE LATITUDE FROM TRUE ALTITUDE OF POLARIS

L.H.A. Aries Corr.	L.H.A. Aries Corr.	L.H.A. Aries Corr.	L.H.A. Aries Corr.	L.H.A. Aries Corr.	L.H.A. Aries Corr.	L.H.A. Aries Corr.	L.H.A. Aries Corr.
20 –48.7	65 –42.2	110 –11.0	155 +26.5	200 +48.6	245 +42.5	290 +11.5	335 –26.3
21 –48.9	66 –41.7	111 –10.1	156 +27.3	201 +48.8	246 +42.0	291 +10.7	336 –27.0
22 –49.0	67 –41.2	112 –9.3	157 +28.0	202 +48.9	247 +41.5	292 +9.8	337 –27.8
23 –49.2	68 –40.7	113 –8.4	158 +28.7	203 +49.1	248 +41.0	293 +9.0	338 –28.5
24 –49.3	69 –40.2	114 –7.6	159 +29.4	204 +49.2	249 +40.5	294 +8.1	339 –29.2
25 –49.5	70 –39.7	115 –6.7	160 +30.1	205 +49.4	250 +40.0	295 +7.2	340 –29.9
26 –49.6	71 –39.2	116 –5.8	161 +30.8	206 +49.5	251 +39.5	296 +6.4	341 –30.6
27 –49.7	72 –38.6	117 –5.0	162 +31.5	207 +49.6	252 +38.9	297 +5.5	342 –31.3
28 –49.8	73 –38.1	118 –4.1	163 +32.2	208 +49.7	253 +38.4	298 +4.6	343 –31.9
29 –49.8	74 –37.5	119 –3.3	164 +32.8	209 +49.7	254 +37.8	299 +3.8	344 –32.6
30 –49.9	75 –36.9	120 –2.4	165 +33.5	210 +49.8	255 +37.2	300 +2.9	345 –33.2
31 –49.9	76 –36.3	121 –1.5	166 +34.1	211 +49.8	256 +36.7	301 +2.0	346 –33.9
32 –49.9	77 –35.7	122 –0.6	167 +34.7	212 +49.8	257 +36.1	302 +1.2	347 –34.5

Extracted from *Reed's*
Nautical Almanac.

Position line from stars

We have already covered the rest of the procedure required. In order to be able to draw the position lines of the two other stars, we need the same ingredients: *our estimated latitude*, the *declination* and the *LHA* of the star.

In order to find the LHA, we know that we first of all have to find the GHA, and then subtract our estimated latitude from that (we subtract because we are west of Greenwich).

Reed's proposes two methods for arriving at the GHA of the stars:

– one consists of starting with the GHA of the vernal point, and then adding the SHA of the star: this is the classic method;

– the other, which is a speciality of *Reed's*, works by finding the GHA of the star (given in the table of stars for the first day of each month at 0000), and then adding the corrections for the day of the month and the time of the observation.

Either method is good. We will use the first for Altair and the second for Arcturus.

Altair

We will first look up the GHA of the vernal point on 4 August at 2023 and 17sec, which was the time of the observation.

At 2000 it is:	252°47'.2
Correction (p. 89) for 23min:	+ 5°45'.9
and 17sec:	+ 4'.3
	258°37'.4

Add the SHA of
Altair for the month
of August (p. 55):   + 62°32'.9

See tables on pages 967 and 971.

The GHA is therefore:	321°10'.3
minus the estimated longitude:	– 5°27'
The LHA of Altair is:	315°43'.3

August

STARS

★ ★ STARS ★ ★

Oh. G.M.T. AUGUST 1

No.	Name	Mag.	Transit (approx)	DEC.	G.H.A.	R.A.	S.H.A.
			h. m.	° '	° '	h m	° '
39	Menkent	2.3	17 28	S36 16.2	97 38.5	14 05	148 38.0
40	Arcturus	0.2	17 37	N19 17.6	95 19.8	14 14	146 19.3
41	Rigil Kent	0.1	18 03	S60 45.2	89 27.4	14 40	140 26.9
42	Zuben'ubi	2.9	18 12	S15 57.3	86 34.4	14 49	137 33.9
43	Kochab	2.2	18 14	N74 14.8	86 19.8	14 51	137 19.3
44	Alphecca	2.3	18 56	N26 47.3	75 33.2	15 33	126 32.7
45	Antares	1.2	19 51	S26 23.2	61 58.1	16 28	112 57.6
46	Atria	1.9	20 11	S68 59.6	57 22.8	16 48	108 22.3
47	Sabik	2.6	20 32	S15 41.9	51 42.3	17 09	102 41.8
48	Shaula	1.7	20 55	S37 05.3	45 57.0	17 32	96 56.5
49	Rasalhague	2.1	20 57	N12 34.7	45 30.6	17 34	96 30.1
50	Eltanin	2.4	21 19	N51 29.9	39 58.2	17 56	90 57.7
51	Kaus Aust.	2.0	21 45	S34 23.6	33 18.0	18 22	84 17.5
52	Vega	0.1	21 59	N38 46.2	29 56.5	18 36	80 56.0
53	Nunki	2.1	22 16	S26 19.3	25 30.3	18 53	76 29.8
54	Altair	0.9	23 12	N 8 49.1	11 33.4	19 49	62 32.9
55	Peacock	2.1	23 46	S56 48.0	2 59.5	20 23	53 59.0
56	Deneb	1.3	00 07	N45 12.6	358 49.0	20 40	49 48.5

Extracted from Reed's Nautical Almanac.

According to these co-ordinates, at the time of the observation, the GP of Altair was passing over Addis Ababa, a good place for coffee and tobacco among other things.

See table on page 969.

See table below.

STAR OR PLANET ALTITUDE TOTAL CORRECTION TABLE
ALWAYS SUBTRACTIVE (−)
Height of Eye above the Sea. Top line metres—lower line feet

Obs Alt.	1.5	3	4.6	6	7.6
	5	10	15	20	25
9°	8.0	8.9	9.6	10.3	10.7
10°	7.4	8.4	9.1	9.7	10.2
11°	7.0	7.9	8.6	9.2	9.7
12°	6.6	7.5	8.2	8.8	9.3
13°	6.2	7.2	7.9	8.4	9.0
14°	5.9	6.9	7.6	8.1	8.6
15°	5.7	6.6	7.3	7.9	8.4
16°	5.5	6.4	7.1	7.7	8.2
17°	5.3	6.2	6.9	7.5	8.0
18°	5.1	6.0	6.7	7.3	7.8
19°	4.9	5.8	6.5	7.1	7.6
20°	4.8	5.7	6.4	7.0	7.5
25°	4.2	5.1	5.8	6.4	6.9
30°	3.8	4.7	5.4	6.0	6.5
35°	3.5	4.4	5.1	5.7	6.3
40°	3.3	4.2	4.9	5.5	6.0
50°	3.0	3.9	4.6	5.2	5.7
60°	2.7	3.6	4.4	4.9	5.5
70°	2.5	3.4	4.1	4.7	5.3
80°	2.3	3.3	4.0	4.6	5.1
90°	2.2	3.1	3.8	4.4	4.9

Extracted from *Reed's Nautical Almanac*.

This angle fits with the facts because the star is to the east and it has not crossed our meridian.

We now have the information we need to feed into the calculator:
– Our latitude (which we have just found by the pole star): 46°37'.1N
– The declination of Altair (taken from the page for the month of August, and which does not need to be corrected): 8°49'.1N
– The LHA of Altair: 315°43'.3

The calculator replies:
Calculated altitude = 36° 40'.9
Z = 120° 39'.3

The azimuth must mean a bearing of 121°, since we can see Altair in the SE.

Now to calculate the true altitude:
Instrument altitude: 36°43'.2
Index error: − 2'
Overall correction for stars (p. 87): − 3'.5
True altitude: 36°36'.7

The intercept is then plotted: true altitude – calculated altitude = 36°36'.7 – 36°40'.9 = −4'.2

This time, the true altitude is less than the calculated altitude, and the intercept plotted on the chart places us 4.2 nautical miles further from the GP of the star than the dead-reckoning position.

Arcturus

This time we will use the method given in *Reed's* for calculating the GHA of the star.

The GHA can be obtained from the page given over to 1 August, dealing with stars. All that has to be done is to allow for the corrections for the time of the observation (4 August at 2025 and 45sec) using the table on page 89.

1 August at 0000: 95°19'.8
Correction for 4 August: + 2°57'.3
at 2000: + 300°49'.3
at 25min: + 6°16'.0
at 45sec: + 11'.3
405°33'.7

★ STAR AND ARIES G.H.A. CORRECTION TABLE ★ 89

Extracted from *Reed's Nautical Almanac*.

Correction for DATE			Correction for HOURS		Correction for MINS.		Corr. for SECONDS	
Greenwich Date	Correction ° '		Hours	Correction ° '	Mins.	Correction ° '	Secs.	Correction '
1st	+ 0	0·0	19	+ 285 46·8	23	+ 5 45·9	43	+ 10·8
2nd	+ 0	59·1	20	+ 300 49·3	24	+ 6 1·0	44	+ 11·0
3rd	+ 1	58·2	21	+ 315 51·7	25	+ 6 16·0	45	+ 11·3
4th	+ 2	57·3	22	+ 330 54·2	26	+ 6 31·1	46	+ 11·5
5th	+ 3	56·5	23	+ 345 56·7	27	+ 6 46·1	47	+ 11·8

We then subtract 360°, which gives us:

$$405°33'.7$$
$$- \quad 360°$$

GHA: 45°33'.7
Minus the dead-reckoning longitude: − 5°27'.0
LHA of Arcturus: 40°06'.7

At the time of the observation, the GP of Arcturus was actually half way between the Canaries and the Antilles.

This angle makes sense, because the star is in the west and has passed our meridian.

We turn to the calculator again:

− Latitude: 46°37'.1N
− Declination of Arcturus: 19°17'.6N
− LHA: 40°06'.7

The calculator gives us:

    Calculated altitude = 46°39'.1
             Z = 114°50'.9 or 115° rounded

The azimuth Z is in this case 360° − 115° = 245° since we can see Arcturus to the SW.

The calculation of Z and the calculated altitude can also be made by means of the table 1-2-3. The reader will find the method for using this table described on the next page, illustrated by the treatment of the same figures for Arcturus used here, rounded for the purposes of calculation:
− Latitude: 46°37'N
− Declination of the star: 19°18'N
− LHA :   41°07'

The calculations that follow should now be familiar:

Instrument altitude: 46°10'
Index error: − 2'
Overall correction: − 3'.1
True altitude: 46°41'

Calculation for the intercept:

True altitude − calculated altitude = 46°41' − 46°39'.1 = +1'.9

The true altitude is *greater* than the calculated altitude. This means that we are 1.9 nautical miles *nearer* the GP of the star than was originally reckoned.

Altitude and azimuth at the dead-reckoning position by means of the table 1-2-3

This table is used by tutors at les Glénans because it is inexpensive, small and easy to read. We will now show how it is used.

In the extracts on the facing page, for each angle A, three numbers – A1, A2, A3 – are read off from the columns (1), (2) and (3) respectively. If an angle used in the calculations does not lie between 0 and 90°, then it is replaced by an equivalent (its difference from 180° or 360°).

Let's take another look at the calculations for Arcturus, using the data:
Declination D = 19°18'N, LHA = 040°07', Latitude L = 46°37'N

First of all replace LHA = 040°07' by P = 40°07'
D =19°18' we read   D2 =   331.4   D3 = 56012
P = 40°07'   P1 =   2518   P2 =   1537
          add   (+)   (−)   minus
          U1 =   2849   K3 = 54475
K3 is found on the line 24°36' in column (3) of the table.
In column r of the table HZ next to it, on the line 01 which corresponds to the case in hand (L and D north, LHA ≤ 90°), we see that we have to calculate r = L−K, giving 46°37' − 24°36' r = 22°01'. Replace r (following lines RZ of table HZ) by R = 22°01'

We find U1 on the line 37°27' in column (1) of the table.
 U = 37°27' we read   U2 =   1322   U3 = 51528
 R = 22°01'   R2 =   433.8   R1 =   5622
                    (+)   (−)
 H = 47°24'   H1 =   1755.8   Z3 = 45906   Z = 64° (odd!)

To put our azimuth back into the right quadrant, we consult the table HZ which says that Z = 180° + Z, or 244°, which is more sensible.

To calculate	
Convert the LHA into an acute angle P as directed by the column P.	
U1 = D2 + P1	K3 = D3 − P2
r = L ± K (according to column r)	
replace r by R (according to the line RZ)	
H1 = U2 + R2	Z3 = U3 − R1
Convert Z into an azimuth counted as a bearing.	

	19°		
14	6362	329.1	56033
15	6358	329.6	56028
16	6353	330.2	56023
17	6348	330.8	56017
18	6343	331.4	56012
19	6338	332.0	56007
20	6334	332.6	56001
21	6329	333.2	55996
22	6324	333.7	55991
min	(1)	(2)	(3)

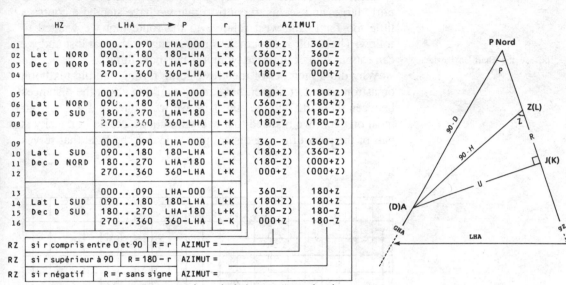

	HZ		LHA ——→ P	r	AZIMUT	
01			000...090	LHA-000	L-K	180+Z	360-Z
02	Lat L	NORD	090...180	180-LHA	L+K	(360-Z)	360-Z
03	Dec D	NORD	180...270	LHA-180	L+K	(000+Z)	000+Z
04			270...360	360-LHA	L-K	180-Z	000+Z
05			000...090	LHA-000	L+K	180+Z	(180+Z)
06	Lat L	NORD	090...180	180-LHA	L-K	(360-Z)	(180+Z)
07	Dec D	SUD	180...270	LHA-180	L-K	(000+Z)	(180-Z)
08			270...360	360-LHA	L+K	180-Z	(180-Z)
09			000...090	LHA-000	L+K	360-Z	(360-Z)
10	Lat L	SUD	090...180	180-LHA	L-K	(180+Z)	(360-Z)
11	Dec D	NORD	180...270	LHA-180	L-K	(180+Z)	(000+Z)
12			270...360	360-LHA	L+K	000+Z	(000+Z)
13			000...090	LHA-000	L-K	360-Z	180+Z
14	Lat L	SUD	090...180	180-LHA	L+K	(180+Z)	180+Z
15	Dec D	SUD	180...270	LHA-180	L+K	(180-Z)	180-Z
16			270...360	360-LHA	L-K	000+Z	180-Z

RZ | si r compris entre 0 et 90 | R = r | AZIMUT =
RZ | si r supérieur à 90 | R = 180 - r | AZIMUT =
RZ | si r négatif | R = r sans signe | AZIMUT =

si la formule pour L'AZIMUT est entre (   ), la hauteur H est négative

	40°				22°				47°	
02	2528	1530	50998	00	5626	433.2	55193	20	1762	2229	49533
03	2526	1531	50995	01	5622	433.8	55188	21	1760	2231	49529
04	2524	1533	50992	02	5618	434.5	55183	22	1759	2232	49526
05	2522	1534	50988	03	5613	435.2	55178	23	1757	2234	49523
06	2520	1535	50985	04	5609	435.9	55173	24	1756	2236	49519
07	2518	1537	50981	05	5605	436.5	55169	25	1754	2238	49516
08	2516	1538	50978	06	5601	437.2	55164	26	1752	2240	49513
09	2514	1540	50975	07	5597	437.9	55159	27	1751	2242	49509
10	2512	1541	50971	08	5593	438.6	55154	28	1749	2243	49506
min	(1)	(2)	(3)	min	(1)	(2)	(3)	min	(1)	(2)	(3)

	24°				37°				63°	
32	5036	542.1	54494	23	2859	1317	51542	52	617.9	4698	45920
33	5032	542.9	54489	24	2857	1319	51538	53	617.1	4701	45916
34	5029	543.6	54485	25	2855	1320	51535	54	616.2	4705	45912
35	5025	544.4	54481	26	2852	1321	51531	55	615.4	4708	45907
36	5021	545.2	54476	27	2850	1322	51528	56	614.6	4711	45903
37	5018	545.9	54472	28	2848	1324	51524	57	613.8	4715	45899
38	5014	546.7	54467	29	2846	1325	51521	58	613.0	4718	45895
39	5010	547.5	54463	30	2844	1326	51517	59	612.2	4722	45890
40	5007	548.2	54459	31	2842	1328	51514	60	611.4	4725	45886
min	(1)	(2)	(3)	min	(1)	(2)	(3)	min	(1)	(2)	(3)

Let us now consider our three position lines. The hat obtained is fairly large, and seems to confirm that we have steered a course a little too far to the west relative to the route that we wanted to follow. The result is nonetheless reassuring: we're not lost and we can eat our dinner in peace, which is the main thing.

Why did a member of the crew, going through an old textbook on astronomy after dinner, have to start talking about the distances between the earth and the stars? As we were quietly digesting our meal on deck, we realised that everything that we see in the sky is part of the past, often the distant past, and that the light that serves

For the fix, see the chart on the facing page.

So as not to spoil the chart and to be able to work on a decent scale, it is better to plot the various lines on a piece of squared paper. The estimated position is placed in the middle of the paper, and a line at the same angle as the latitude is drawn anywhere. It is from this line that the latitudes will be taken, and therefore the distances in nautical miles, while the scale for the longitudes is covered by the squares on the paper.

If you have a calculator, then it is simpler to take 1 square = 1 nautical mile, and then 1' of longitude works out as 1 square cos L. The hat is not too bad for beginners, but we can do better.

The distance plotted on the chart confirms that the log is pessimistic by about 5%, and that we are steering between 1 and 2° too far west.

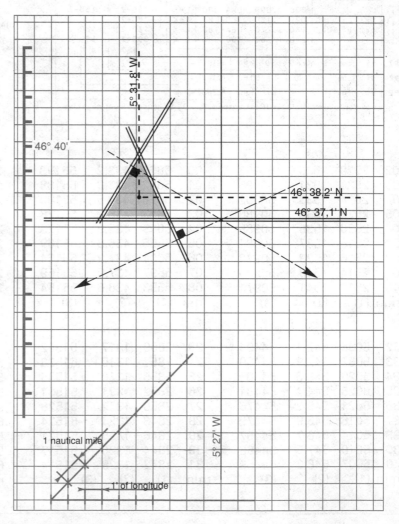

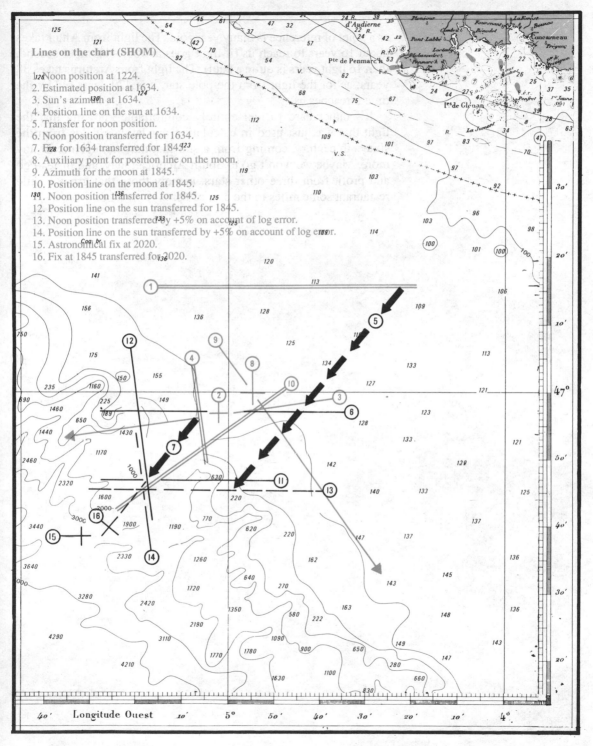

Lines on the chart (SHOM)

1. Noon position at 1224.
2. Estimated position at 1634.
3. Sun's azimuth at 1634.
4. Position line on the sun at 1634.
5. Transfer for noon position.
6. Noon position transferred for 1634.
7. Fix for 1634 transferred for 1845.
8. Auxiliary point for position line on the moon.
9. Azimuth for the moon at 1845.
10. Position line on the moon at 1845.
11. Noon position transferred for 1845.
12. Position line on the sun transferred for 1845.
13. Noon position transferred by +5% on account of log error.
14. Position line on the sun transferred by +5% on account of log error.
15. Astronomical fix at 2020.
16. Fix at 1845 transferred for 2020.

as a point of reference is many years old. The light from Altair takes about 16 years to reach us (if light goes at 300,000km per second, then 16 light years is quite a haul). The light from Arcturus takes 38 years; as for the light from the pole star, it is 470 years old by the time it reaches us.

It's rather hard to feel entirely comfortable knowing that the light that was just used in calculating our latitude dates from the sixteenth century, coming from a star that may not even exist any more. Maybe we won't go to South America today, and instead go and profit from three other stars, namely those that grace a little restaurant some miles to the east of us.

CHAPTER 5

Passage-making

You can choose any route you like at sea. All the reference points
and documents, along with the various techniques that allow you to
find your position, are there to give you the means to exploit that
basic freedom. There is no fixed way of getting from A to B, but
instead the route can be chosen according to circumstances and
taste.

As for taste, well, *chacun à son goût*, as the French say – there's
no saying any route is better than any other from that point of view.
Some people just spend all their time wandering along; others want
to have a comfortable life and therefore choose routes that take
them out of the way of all harsh encounters with the elements, and
others like speed. There are realists and dreamers, old-fashioned
sea dogs and modernists with every sort of technological aid,
people going to the Scilly Islands and people going to Lyonesse.
Mood influences the choice of route greatly, and gives it a certain
colour.

However, there are the particular circumstances of the journey
that must also be taken into account. Even once the leg has been
chosen and the distance that has to be covered calculated, the route
still remains to be finalised. The wind direction can make all the
difference: the trip can either be a short one, or become absolutely
interminable. In fact, the route is rarely defined in terms of distance,
but rather more often in terms of time. A route is a certain number
of days and hours spent at sea in constantly changing conditions:
the water level rises and falls, the current changes direction, the
wind rises, drops or turns, the sea can be choppy here and calm
there, the sun is either to your back or in your eyes, fog can come
and night can fall.

Whatever the state of mind of the sailor, all these circumstances
demand minute preparation: any route can be chosen, but not all are
either possible or reasonable. In other words, the first task is to
make sure that the route chosen is safe. After that we can talk about
the fine details.

Choosing a route

It is very rare to come back from a sea voyage without having learnt anything new. Every route always has something unknown and unexpected about it – there is even an element of risk. Choosing a safe route does not eliminate all possible risks, but it does allow you to foresee as much as possible.

There are various sorts of data to be considered. Some are permanent and given by either the charts or the Pilot Books: these can be the characteristics of the area to be crossed, with the various black-spots that need to be avoided, with sudden shallows, isolated dangers, difficult channels or shipping lanes. Reference points must also be taken into account: beacons, landmarks, lights and radio signals. There are other factors that are variable in nature, but predictable, such as the tides, which can make certain routes impassable at certain times. Others are predictable to a certain extent, such as the wind, visibility, sea conditions in particular places. The rest are unforeseeable: sudden changes in the weather, problems with equipment, human error, and so on.

Choosing a route means facing up to all these factors and seeing how the overall picture shapes up. The order in which they have to be examined cannot be systematised, since one of them will be of predominant importance according to the sort of circumstances you are dealing with. Sometimes there are numerous routes available, sometimes a route suggests itself fairly readily, but you have to make sure that there is an alternative in case of difficulty.

So much for theory, here are some examples.

From la Vilaine to le Palais

We are at Tréhiguier, in the mouth of la Vilaine. The next stop is at le Palais, on Belle-Ile.

The direct route shows a variety of problems. There is a shallow (the shelf at la Recherche), then a large obstacle (the line of rocks jutting out from the headland at Quiberon, with the island of Houat right in the middle). Should we steer a course round la Recherche or not? Everything depends on the weather and the route that we choose in order to cross the reef. There are three possible ways over the reef: la Teignouse, le Béniguet, les Soeurs. There is also a fourth solution, which is to go round the Grands-Cardinaux – this is referred to in the Pilot as the eastern passage.

See fold-out section 2 at the end of the book.

Whatever passage we take, the distance varies very little: 28.5 nautical miles by le Béniguet, 29.5 nautical miles by la Teignouse and by les Soeurs, 30.5 nautical miles by the Grands-Cardinaux.

First choice

The weather is good and seems unlikely to change. There is a steady NE wind, the visibility is good. The boat will probably make 6kn. The trip will probably take about 5 hours.

With these winds, the sea won't be too bad over la Recherche, and we will be able to cross it as long as we keep a pilot's foot of 2m.

Since the route by le Béniguet is the shortest, we will look at this one first of all. With these winds, the passage will be easy. The only problem is that it isn't lit and so we can't do it at night.

The route by les Soeurs seems a little less simple: the landmarks are a good way away, and so there is some danger of confusion. Again, it would be impossible to sail it by night.

La Teignouse can be sailed either day or night, as can the eastern passage.

Should we take account of the tide? The currents are relatively strong in all the channels (except for the eastern passage), and it is best to go through as the tide is falling. The best time to set out is high water, and we will have the current behind us throughout the trip.

All in all, there is a lot to choose from. There don't seem to be any traps or pitfalls and we can always find a port to leeward: either Houat or le Palais. The only precaution that needs to be taken is if we are passing either by le Béniguet or la Teignouse: we should take care not to sail too close to Houat or the reef at Béniguet, where we could be in trouble if there is any kind of mishap.

Second choice

This time the wind is fresh from the west and the visibility is less good. At 5kn (which will give us about 3 nautical miles per hour into the wind), we estimate that the trip will take us 10 hours whatever route we take. If the wind is dead ahead, then by taking the beat into account, the four routes come out about the same.

In this weather, the sea will probably be rather heavy on la Recherche, and it would be better to avoid it. In the passes over the reef, the sea will be dreadful right through the ebb tide, when the tide will be flowing in the opposite direction to the wind. Would it be better to pass over during the flood? It is not yet sure that we would be able to get over beating against the current. The only time it seems possible is either at high or low water.

Advantages and disadvantages of the different routes

• La Teignouse: the passage is wide enough for us to be able to tack on the way through, and we would be sheltered from the reef during most of the trip.

• Le Béniguet: the passage is short, but too narrow for beating; if the wind is west we can go through fast, but if it drops we'd be stuck.

• Les Soeurs: again, we would get little shelter from the reef. The passage itself is long and narrow and the landmarks would be difficult to identify – this is probably not a safe route to take.

• The eastern passage: here the current is not as strong as elsewhere, and if we passed the Grands-Cardinaux at a safe distance, in 30m of water, the sea would probably not be as bad as elsewhere, and we would be able to tack. The problem is that once past the Grands-Cardinaux, we would have no shelter. Furthermore, at night, if visibility was poor, we would have only one light from the Cardinaux.

What time should we then get under way in order to pass over the reef at the right time? Leaving la Vilaine during the flood is out of the question. If we left at high water, then we would miss low water at le Béniguet and la Teignouse. We must therefore get under way at the end of the ebb tide in order to be able to pass over at high water. If we choose the eastern passage, then the choice becomes more simple: we can go round at any time, as long as we give the Cardinaux a wide berth. The best option seems to be to leave Tréhiguier at high water, in order to go through the passage at the end of the ebb.

What options do we have if things don't go to plan? As long as we are in Quiberon bay we can always turn back up into la Vilaine. If anything strange happens around la Teignouse, then we have on our lee either Houat, Port-Navalo, or la Trinité. On the route around the eastern passage, we could drift either towards la Turballe or le Croisic. It is possible to get into any of these ports at any hour of the tide.

If we need an extra option coming out of either la Teignouse or le Béniguet, then we could be in difficulties, since we would have to be well out of any of the channels before we could let ourselves drift towards the SE. In fact, we could always turn right round. All the same it would be better not to go through le Béniguet at the end of the day, because going back through it at night would be sheer lunacy.

Only one last question has to be taken into account, which would be of deciding importance if the visibility were bad: what is there that would allow us to keep an eye on the course we were steering? It would be very difficult to find the entrance to la Teignouse in the murk, and even finding the entry to le Béniguet would not be easy. The only reasonable route is therefore the one that avoids all the dangers, that is the eastern passage. We can make the entire trip navigating by dead reckoning, and then make landfall on Kerdonis point which will be easy to spot.

All in all, given the weather conditions, the eastern passage is the safest. The routes passing by either les Soeurs or le Béniguet are rather perilous. The route passing by la Teignouse is good only if there is sufficient visibility. However, the weather can change. If we were to find ourselves towards the end of a depression and find that the wind picked up from the NW and the visibility improved, then we could look at things in a different light: the route passing through la Teignouse would be the shortest, and as soon as we cleared the passage we could head for le Palais with the wind abaft the beam. On the other hand, if we passed round the Grands-Cardinaux, then we would have to continue to beat for a long time, which would be tiring, the route would not be so safe, and the journey would certainly take longer. Then again, if the wind were to drop from the SW, then the eastern passage would be the best solution. We would still need to be able to see when the wind was going to turn, wonder whether it was going to change in force, and what the sea would be like as a result.

From Concarneau to Royan

It is 185 nautical miles from Concarneau to Royan. The route can be plotted as a straight line, going outside the island group: Groix, Belle-Ile, Noirmoutier, Ré and Oléron. It is the sort of trip that a boat suitable for coastal navigation could do very easily – a Mousquetaire, for example, which does 5.5kn in a good wind, would do it in 34 hours.

However, Mousquetaires are not built for the high seas, and therefore we will need to be able to find shelters that we can get to quickly if the weather starts to deteriorate, or if we simply have to give up the idea of getting to the planned destination.

Using the chart and the Pilot, we draw up a list of ports that would be easy enough to get to if we had to, which would be well marked, open at any hour of the tide, both during the day and at night, and which would give shelter from winds coming in off the sea.

Starting from Concarneau, we find Port-Tudy on Groix, Sauzon and le Palais on Belle-Ile, then le Croisic, Pornic, le Bois-de-la-Chaize on Noirmoutier, Port-Joinville in the isle of Yeu, les Sables d'Olonne, Ars-en-Ré. There is also shelter to be had at le Pertuis d'Antioche (either in la Rochelle or the island of Aix-Château-d'Oléron) and, last of all, there is Royan. Is this enough ports to give us easy access to shelter at any point along the route?

If the weather forecast warns us that conditions are going to get worse, then we have to be able to make port in 3–4 hours, 6 at the outside. We would have to take the possibility of some sort of accident into account, which would mean that the boat would be less manoeuvrable (in the worst possible case it is possible to sail with a jury rig with the wind up to 30° on the quarter).

In these conditions, in the area of each port, there is a safe area which can be plotted on the chart. We see that the direct route from Concarneau to Royan is not entirely covered by these safe areas. There are a few blanks that we will have to look at fairly closely.

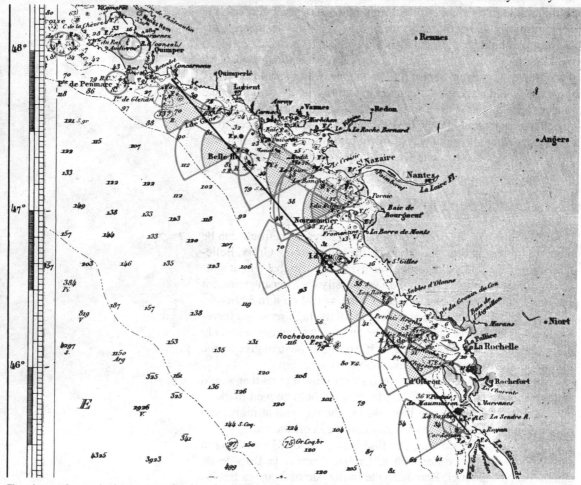

Choosing a safe route is also a matter of seeing where the emergency exits are. If we wanted to make the trip between Concarneau and Royan in a Mousquetaire, for example, then we would have to be sure that there was possible shelter out of the wind all the way along the coast in case of accident or bad weather from the west.

There is a safe area of about 60° in front of each shelter (a Mousquetaire, even when disabled, can still sail with the wind up to about 30° on the weather quarter), and stretching out to 20 nautical miles in front of the port (the shaded areas mark where the boat would be less than 4 hours from port) – up to about 30 nautical miles from port (from the white zone, you can reach port in about 6 hours).

We note that there are three blanks between Concarneau and Royan. These are periods when the boat would not be in easy reach of shelter: between Groix and Belle-Ile, to windward of Belle-Ile and between Chasseron and Royan. (Document of the SHOM.)

The first of these comes straight after Groix: between Lorient and Quiberon there is no shelter along the coast. If the weather is good we can make the trip without worrying too much. However, if the weather is not so good, then it would be a good idea to modify the route considerably to place oneself as fast as possible in the safe area after that stretch, which would be the port of Sauzon.

After les Poulains point, there is another blank: we pass the wild coast of Belle-Ile. This is very pretty, but not much use in a storm. Even in good weather, it's best to give it a decent berth so as to leave a little room to play with on either side in case there is any problem with the boat. If the forecast is not so good, then it would be better to leave the route and pass directly under the wind from the island.

If we pass to windward, then we will be out of safe areas right up to the mouth of the Loire. However, this is a bit of a special case – we're just a little far away from shelter, which is only a problem if the weather is really bad. In all events, we would soon be in the safe area for the island of Yeu, followed immediately by that of les Sables-d'Olonne: it is very clear from this that passing the island of Yeu to leeward would not be a good idea, because we would then be windward of a stretch of coast without any possible shelter.

One blank remains, which is the most serious: between Chasseron point and Royan. Here, it is vital to pay attention to the weather forecasts. If the weather is going to be bad, then it is best to give up and make for le Pertuis d'Antioche, hoping that things will improve. If the weather is reasonable, then it is best to sail out to sea so as to get into the safe area before Royan as fast as possible.

All in all, once the areas have been plotted on the chart, there remain three blanks, where there seem to be no alternative safe options: after Groix, to windward of Belle-Ile, and to windward of Oléron. However, the drawing shows up a solution that would not have been apparent at first glance: in all of the three areas, the solution seems to be to move further out to sea rather than sail nearer into shore. This allows us to reach the next safe area more quickly.

Of course, this solution only works for the sort of boat we have chosen, that is to say a Mousquetaire or a boat of the same category. A smaller boat, a Corsaire for example, could not make the trip in a single go, whatever happened, and for this sort of craft, the problems would be entirely different: in order to make the journey from Groix to Belle-Ile, it would need good weather conditions – if not, the only option would be to wait. For a deep-water cruiser, on the other hand, it is often safest to be out to sea.

These few examples do not show all possible aspects of the problems involved in choosing a route. They simply show the basic principles behind a line of thinking that sometimes has to be pushed a lot farther than we have taken it here. We will therefore have to deal with some of the pitfalls that you might meet, born out of an unhappy mixture of weather and local conditions. A bay that offers no shelter can be a trap when the wind gets up just so as to block the entrance: Porto bay and the mistral have mastered this trick perfectly. There is also the reef with the tide running towards it as the wind dies down – this can happen to the south of the Chaussée de Sein, and can be a very unpleasant experience. The channel with no leading marks (such as the one between Roches de Saint-Quay and the coast) can prove a problem if you have to beat and then night falls before the yacht is through. The Gaine channel (between les Héaux-de-Bréhat and Tréguier) can cause problems, when you suddenly realise that the leading marks cannot be seen against the light on a lovely sunny evening. Other channels can become traps when fog drifts in. What is important to note in all this is that there is nothing baffling or unforeseeable about it all. In most cases, surprises can be avoided by paying attention to the weather forecast and thinking ahead.

To sum up, a safe route is the one that allows you a little room for manoeuvre, so that you can steer away from the dangers of the coast, allow for accidents or tiredness. This is the sort of margin that you should allow with obstacles too: always go about well before you have to (especially after a long tack) and change sail when necessary. The route you should take is the one suggested by the old French sailor's proverb, 'If you want to live long and hale, give wide berths and reduce your sail'. A safe course is where you have both water to manoeuvre in and plenty of escape routes. It should also be, above all, lined with a good number of easily verifiable reference points. However, the most thorough study of the charts and the most perfect grasp of navigational techniques can be reduced to nothing if seasickness sets in, and tiredness can multiply the risks of an accident.

Improving on your course

Both comfort and speed can vary enormously over the same route. As for the former, there is not much to be said: if you want a quiet life, then you soon learn to avoid the open sea and to remember that islands and the coast can offer you some sheltered areas. Also, a course run with the wind free can be much more pleasant than a long, hard beat to windward. If you've tried the latter, then you'll know what is meant by the expression 'battling in the teeth of the wind'.

A comfortable route is also often a safe route, since it allows the crew to save their strength.

Choosing a fast route can be a matter of mood at the time, but it can also be a matter of safety, too. Even if you have settled on the idea of a gentle meander, you should always be in a position to change to a faster course at any moment, so as to be able to get into harbour quickly when bad weather threatens, for example. Going faster can also extend a boat's range: if you gain an hour here and there on a two-week cruise, then you might have time to fit in an extra port of call, which might turn out to be the best part of the trip.

Going fast is also what ocean-racing is all about. Speed is a controversial question in yachting, and opinions seem to fall into two camps. John Illingworth, the famous ocean racer, writes, 'Sailing a boat in an ocean race means driving it at its maximum speed in all weather encountered'. Hilaire Belloc, an old sea salt, whose work is perhaps not as well known as it should be, counters that 'from one's boat (at least from one which is a true companion) one must expect rational behaviour. One must say to oneself that, when she is making seven knots, she is doing well, and when she is making nine, she is upset and will be better for a night's rest'. These two quotations encapsulate remarkably well the two sides of an utterly fruitless, but passionately felt debate. Since it is hardly within the scope of this book to pursue the matter, let us simply refer those interested to John Illingworth's *Offshore* and Hilaire Belloc's *The Cruise of the Nona*.

Suffice it to say that there will come a day when you have had enough of trying to understand why people who have the same type of boat as you can seem to be going rather faster, why you are always badly placed when the wind changes and why you always make that bad tack in a strong tide. The time will come when you want to do better. This does not necessarily require you to have a competitive spirit, but is simply fascinating in itself. It is the challenge of proving yourself equal to that volatile trio of the sea, the wind and the tide – the three forces that make the choice of the fastest course an intriguing puzzle, set to try the ingenuity.

We shall try to lay out the principal rules and give an insight into some of the finer points.

The shortest route

At first sight, the direct course from A to B might seem the fastest. This is indeed often the case, and this is always the eventuality that has to be considered first, even when you know you are capable of devising and steering more complicated courses.

Sometimes, however, it is possible to get from A to B in less time by avoiding the direct route, especially when the wind, the tides and the sea conditions would mean that the boat was going rather more slowly on that route. We already know that it is best to avoid shallows in the interests of safety, but they must also be avoided if you want to sail fast. Shallow waters are likely to be short, steep and choppy, and can even bring the boat to a standstill.

It can also be good policy to move off the direct course in certain wind conditions, enabling you to side-step calm waters and seek a better wind. If you do this, then either the boat will go faster or you will be better able to get into position so that you can benefit from a change in the wind. Similarly, you might want to move off course to take advantage of a current that might help speed you up, or to offset the effects of a current that you are obliged to sail against.

In all events, the question is this: will the detour allow you to reach your destination faster than the course you had originally intended? The answer is not always an obvious one, far from it; indeed, if things are not carefully worked out in advance, you stand a good chance of losing time rather than gaining it.

The time that is lost avoiding shallows is hard to estimate. The real game begins when you change course because of the wind.

Wind tactics

It is easy to talk about avoiding areas of calm or areas where the wind is either too strong or too contrary, but it is much less easy to put it into practice. When the weather is fair and the breezes are fitful, the skill lies in being ready for the slightest breath of wind, and hanging onto it whatever happens. This can lead you off on some very strange detours. Spotting such things depends on acute observation; closer inshore, the art becomes more subtle still, and anyone who does not know the area well can very rapidly become completely bewildered. In these cases, speculating on the wind can be rather a wild goose chase, and the various reference works are not always very helpful. There is nonetheless such a thing as wind psychology, not utterly fanciful, which Jacques Perret, a French specialist in navigation, has studied at some length. The chap maintains that the unity and lapse of time are one and the same thing (or something like that), but this is only really for those of you who believe that a copy of the complete works of Descartes is indispensable for proper navigation (hmm!).

Leaving such weighty matters aside, the use of coastal breezes requires the use of rather more readily accessible facts (but then, what do we mean by a fact anyway?). It is often worthwhile making detours to catch offshore breezes at night and sea breezes that rise in the afternoon when the wind is particularly weak, or when you are in an unfavourable quarter. The problem is to know how far to go out to find them. This depends on the nature of the coastline and what the weather forecast predicts. The distance varies between 5 and 10 nautical miles, sometimes less, rarely more. You also have to think about coming inshore in time.

It is always hard to figure out what there is to be gained by going out of your way when the wind is weak. Covering twice the distance to get near land at night can be worthwhile if you are going to get the benefit of a good breeze throughout the night. On the other hand, it is infuriating to go inshore only to have the wind rise at sea. How do you know which is going to happen?

It is only possible to make predictions when the wind has become fairly settled, and even then the wind can still change direction. Before plunging into complicated calculations and navigational geometry, it is as well to keep up to date with the weather forecasts. Whatever plan you make is based on this information, and this is where the whole thing can become a game of chance.

What it amounts to is that there are considerable gains to be made in gambling with the wind, but that the gambles are only measurable in two basic kinds of situation:
– when moving away from the direct course to get on a faster point of sailing;
– to benefit from an unexpected change of wind.

Looking at things more closely, the second case is simply a variant on the first, and this is the one on which any working must be based.

If you are to decide whether you will gain time by sailing faster along a longer course, you must first estimate the length of the detour, then the anticipated gain in speed as a result, and compare the two.

Estimating the longer course

In the diagram below, it is evident that by moving away from the direct route, AB, by an angle a that the distance to be covered is increased by a distance equalling mC + Cn. The value of this lengthening is naturally directly proportional to the angle a and the distance d, when one is still moving away from the original course.

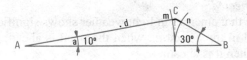

By moving 10° from the direct route for three-quarters of the distance and then rejoining it for the last quarter at an angle of 30°, the first part of the journey is made 1.5% longer and the second part 15%, giving a total increase of 5%.

First impressions are rather encouraging: in the present case, the increase in the distance to be covered seems to be rather small. The calculations for different values of the angles a and b seem to confirm that impression.

for 5°   :   0.4% extra mileage
for 10° :   1.5% extra mileage
for 15° :   3.5% extra mileage
for 20° :   6.4% extra mileage
for 25° :   10.0% extra mileage
for 30° :   15.0% extra mileage

All in all, it can be reckoned that anything up to a departure of 20° from the route does not add an unreasonable extra distance. Beyond that, the increase becomes more considerable, and the possible returns begin to diminish, unless the gain in speed is expected to be significant.

Estimating the speed gained

In order to estimate the gain in speed with any degree of accuracy, you need to know the capabilities of your boat on all points of sailing and at different wind speeds. Clearly it is possible to get by with notional estimates, but you can acquire very precise knowledge for use on an occasion like this by taking the trouble to measure carefully the different speeds of the boat on the different points of sailing and drawing diagrams to illustrate how they compare.

Obviously, a speed diagram only works for the boat on which it is made, and for the conditions in which the measurements were taken (wind speed, sea, etc). The curves given opposite are only examples. They were made on a light displacement boat, 8m on the waterline (whose critical speed is therefore 2.4 x the square root of 8 = 6.8kn). They are nevertheless worth looking at, because they show up certain constants and characteristics shared with the majority of modern boats.

One of the curves was drawn up in rather brisk weather, the other in lighter conditions. The first fact to emerge is that the differences between points of sailing are much more marked in light than in heavier weather. This should go down in the book as rule one:

It is only worth making a detour to go faster in light weather. In heavy weather, it is better to stay on the direct route unless some change is expected.

The curve that emerges in light weather shows significant variation in speed in three sectors: when the wind is ahead, when it is astern and when it is abeam.

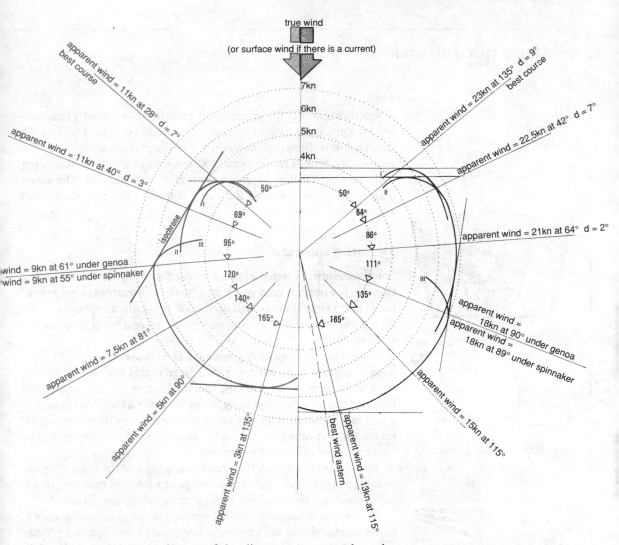

true wind

(or surface wind if there is a current)

apparent wind = 11kn at 28° d = 7°
best course

apparent wind = 11kn at 40° d = 3°

isochrone

wind = 9kn at 61° under genoa
wind = 9kn at 55° under spinnaker

apparent wind = 7.5kn at 81°

apparent wind = 5kn at 90°

apparent wind = 3kn at 135°

best wind astern

apparent wind = 13kn at 115°

apparent wind = 23kn at 135° d = 9°
best course

apparent wind = 22,5kn at 42° d = 7

apparent wind = 21kn at 64° d = 2°

apparent wind = 18kn at 90° under genoa
apparent wind = 18kn at 89° under spinnaker

apparent wind = 15kn at 115°

7kn
6kn
5kn
4kn

50°   50°
69°   64°
95°   86°
120°   111°
140°   135°
165°   165°

Headwind: the gap at the top of the diagram corresponds to the wind in the beating sector.

Wind astern: it appears that the boat goes slightly faster when the wind is on one or the other quarter, which suggests that gybe tacking downwind may be useful.

Wind abeam: the sudden acceleration noticed corresponds to the change from genoa to spinnaker.

Between these sectors, the curve is more or less regular, and the speed varies little. From close fetch to close reach and from reach to broad reach, it is hard to see how a change in direction could lead to an increase in speed. Quite clearly then, on these points of sailing, the direct course is the fastest.

Speed diagrams illustrating the performance of a boat 8m on the waterline (critical speed 6.8kn). In colour, a diagram for a wind of 8 kn. In black, the diagram for a 19kn wind.
Curve I: under jib.
Curve II: under genoa.
Curve III: under spinnaker.

Making a speed diagram

A speed diagram is the graphic representation of a boat's capabilities for a given strength of wind on the different points of sailing. To draw it, start from the centre of the diagram, marking out the vectors of a length proportional to the speed of the boat, according to the headings followed and in relation to the real wind. The speed diagram (or curve) is then the curve that joins the end of all these vectors.

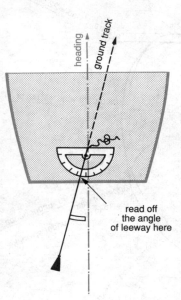

A simple, DIY leeway meter.

Measuring apparatus

Some measuring instruments are needed to draw the diagram, but these do not need to be complicated pieces of electronic equipment: much more simple items will do the job perfectly adequately.

To measure the boat's heading relative to the real wind, you use the steering compass.

To measure the leeway, you can make yourself a leeway meter. Take a schoolboy protractor with a large radius (say about 10cm), fix it to the stern of the boat, the round edge towards the stern of the boat and the straight edge at right angles to the axis of the boat. Fix a thin line about 10m long (fishing line will do) to the centre of the protractor and attach a 100–200g fishing weight to the end. The leeway is read off on the protractor.

To measure the speed, the Dutchman's log and the patent log are usually perfect since they serve the purpose better than electronic logs, which are too sensitive to momentary variations in speed.

In order to measure the wind speed, you need an anemometer: either handheld (not too expensive) or fixed to the mast head (quite pricey). A ventimeter is very cheap and can do the job quite well, the major drawback being that it only detects winds of over 6kn.

To measure the angle between the axis of the boat and the apparent wind, you need a wind vane, which must be at the mast head. This can be a wind sock such as you see in aerodromes or along motorways, or a sheet metal arrow like those you see on the tops of buildings. To get a good measurement of the angle, the support must have two arms on either side, adjusted at appropriate angles (60° and 40° to start with). If you're rich, you can allow yourself the luxury of the sort of electronic apparatus that combines anemometer and wind vane all in one.

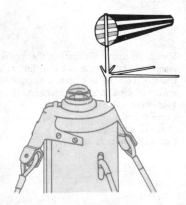

Windsock vane with adjustable arms.

Constructing the diagram

First you need to know the real wind. Its direction can be found either dead astern or by taking the average of the headings followed when close-hauled on both tacks. Its speed is measured with wind astern by taking the sum of the apparent wind speed and that of the boat. If the apparent wind speed is too weak to be measured, then don't worry, as this can be done later.

Next measure the speed and course of the boat for each point of sailing. Follow the heading on the compass, and, if necessary, correct it by the amount of leeway to obtain the true course of the boat. If the diagram is to be realistic, a large number of measurements must be made: every 10 to 15° on a broad reach or on a reach; every 5° when reaching the limit of the spinnaker, and then the same when sailing from anywhere on a close reach to close-hauled.

While this is going on, measure the wind speed at least once. If you have a complete set-up, then note the speed and the apparent wind direction for each heading. If you only have a rudimentary wind vane, then measure the apparent wind speed for angles where its direction is easily identifiable (90°, 60°, 40°). As the apparent wind is much stronger at these points of sailing than with the wind astern, it's only with a dying wind that the ventimeter becomes inadequate.

You can then check the value of these measurements by making a simple diagram. Three curves are drawn: one with the spinnaker, another with the genoa, and a third with the jib. The three curves obtained for the same wind strength are all plotted on the same graph which, without hesitation, allows you to choose the best sail plan for a particular point of sailing and the most advantageous heading to steer.

NB. It is worthwhile (but not essential) to note the strength and direction of the apparent wind for several points of sailing on the diagram, since these are the only knowable factors against which performance can be established.

When several diagrams have been drawn up for different strengths of wind, the arms of the wind vane can be adjusted for two very distinct points of sailing: for instance, the points when the spinnaker can be hoisted and when the genoa must be exchanged for the jib.

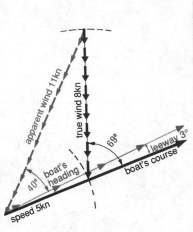

Checking the measurements for an angle between the ship's head and the apparent wind of 40°. The available facts are:

true wind: 10kn
apparent wind: 11kn
speed: 5kn
leeway: 3°

Plot the vector of the apparent wind (2cm per knot, for example), and then the vector for the course. The vector that completes the triangle is the true wind. Measure it and you get 8kn – there is something wrong somewhere.

On the other hand, things are quite different in the three sectors where the speed varies. When the destination you are trying to reach is in the beam wind sector, could you run some of the distance under spinnaker on a broad reach, then finishing on a close reach? When the objective is to leeward, could you get there by two broad reaches rather than going straight for it dead downwind?

As far as the head wind sector is concerned, the problem is clearly quite different. Here, progress can only be made by making a detour, and then it is only a question of working out which detour it is best to take.

The diagram allows for the gain in speed for a given change of course to be reckoned precisely.

Estimating the time gained

Let us take the case of a headwind. The diagram on the left shows that the points can be reached in the same time by beating in a straight line, at right angles to the wind and tangential to the upper edges of the diagram on both sides of the beating sector. The tangential points of the straight line and the diagram indicate precisely the best close-hauled course that can be made on either tack.

According to the same principle, it is possible to know all the targets that can be reached in the same time by tacking on either side of a stern wind. All are situated on a straight line tangential to the curve of the diagram. This straight line – called the *isochrone* – allows for an exact evaluation to be made of the amount of time one gains in relation to the course that would have been run by taking the direct route. Its tangential points with the curve also show which are the best reaches to make.

For all points of sailing where the direct route is the fastest, the isochrone naturally merges with the diagram.

It is time to see what conclusions come out of this in practice, first in a steady wind, and then when a change in the wind is expected.

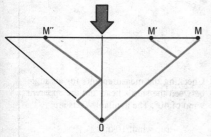

OM = OM′ = OM″. Starting from O, all points that can be reached within the same time by beating are situated on a line at right angles to the wind direction.

Reaching

You are in the vicinity of the buoy SN 1, off the mouth of the Loire, and you are making for Belle-Ile. The wind is light from the SW, your boat is making 5kn, and you are engaged in pondering over the eternal question: to fly or not to fly the kite. You do not know your boat very well. On the other hand, trying out the spinnaker seems like a fun idea, and it seems as if you could carry one on the present point of sailing. Up goes the spinnaker, but alas, it turns out to be a

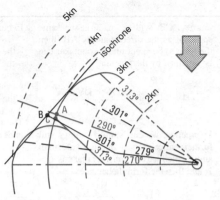

Reaching. The course to be made is 290°. At this speed, it would be impossible to carry the spinnaker; we are making 4kn and will reach our objective in an hour. If we start out at 279°, hoist the spinnaker and do 4.7kn for half an hour, followed by a turn to 301°, putting on the genoa for the next half-hour and make 4kn, then we will reach point B on the isochrone. The average speed is then 4.25kn, thus 6% more than by the direct route. If we wanted to make the best speed with the spinnaker, we would actually be travelling more slowly: half an hour on a bearing of 270° at 5kn followed by another half an hour on 313° at 6kn, which would only take us to point C.

mistake, as it doesn't pull well and the boat does not go any faster. You decide to bear away slightly so that the spinnaker will be of some use after all.

Bearing away by 10°, things go rather better. The spinnaker is pulling correctly, the speed is 6kn and everything is just wonderful.

Nevertheless, you look at the chart to see where this departure from the straight and narrow is taking you. You notice that the difference is not great and you can happily carry on like this for a while. Since the boat is going a bit faster, there will be no real loss.

At this point you notice that the gain in speed is actually quite considerable given the comparatively small extra distance that will have to be covered. If you decide to make half the trip with the spinnaker, and then head directly for Kerdonis, you will have only added 1.5% to the journey while your speed will have increased by 20% over this part of the voyage. In fact, you could quite easily do more than half the trip under spinnaker and you will still gain. You will finish the journey on a close reach, a point of sailing on which your speed will be little different than the one you were making on the direct route, and will be in Kerdonis much earlier than you thought.

If the forecast announces that the wind is going to back southerly you will be able to make the entire trip under spinnaker. If the wind is going to veer north, then it is probably better, given your lack of experience, to do the first part of the journey on a close reach. In order to know when you could then put on the spinnaker and head for Kerdonis you will have to know at what speed your spinnaker will become effective, and then trace on the chart a line from Kerdonis which represents your route at that speed and then join this course on a close reach. In fact, if the wind is due to veer, it is better, given your lack of experience, to give up the idea of the spinnaker and head for Kerdonis by the direct route. Caution counsels you not to move from the direct course unless you are going to profit from it in some immediate way. In any case, you ought to know how to

It is possible to find out very exactly at what moment the gain in speed will be more significant than the amount by which the route is lengthened, but it does require the use of some very complicated formulae which are rather hard to get to grips with at sea! On the other hand, you could get by with just knowing the few following facts. If you know the distance AB, the speed V of the boat over the direct route AB, and therefore the time required for that journey along with the value of the angle α, which is the angle of the detour and the gain in speed delta V which results from the detour, and suppose that the second part of the journey, CB, will be made at the same speed V as the direct journey AB, then the time to be spent under spinnaker can be obtained by the formula:

$$t1 = \frac{AB}{\Delta V} \cdot \frac{\cos \alpha \, (V + DV) - V}{\Delta V + 2V}$$

In practice, we can simplify things still further: since it is a question of small angles, then we can consider that $\cos \alpha = 1$, and then the formula becomes:

$$t1 = \frac{[AB]}{\Delta v + 2V}$$

In our example:

– the distance AB is 24 nautical miles;
– the speed V of the boat over the direct route is 5kn, and the time taken for this journey should be 4hr 48min;
– the angle α is 10° and the gain of speed Δ V is 1 kn.

The time t1 during which we could run under spinnaker is therefore:

$$t1 = \frac{24}{1 + 10} = 2hr \, 11min$$

At 6kn, this gives us 13.1 nautical miles.

assess by how much the wind is going to change and when it will happen. If you think that you will be at Belle-Ile before it happens, then you can chance your luck with the spinnaker, but you risk ending up with the wind dead ahead – it's up to you.

Now, there are less rough-and-ready methods than the ones you are using at the moment. If you are sailing in the region of the buoy SN 1 and you see a racing yacht pass head-down, round the buoy and then break out the spinnaker in double quick time, taking off on the correct course without missing a blink, then you can deduce that there is an expert navigator on board who does not waste his time worrying about the metaphysical dimensions of spinnakers.

Well before arriving at SN 1, this navigator has taken out the speed diagram for today's conditions. This was drawn on tracing paper so that he could lay it on the chart, centring it on the buoy and then orientate it according to the wind. You may be certain that he has immediately discovered the best heading to follow, and what the gain in speed and time would be. He's probably feeling pretty smug about now. Each to his own.

Running

Here the tactic is very simple, as we know: you go faster by gybe tacking than by running right before the wind.

You can be quite satisfied with a rough estimate of the best broad reach (the point of sailing that will give you the maximum speed for the least detour). However, it is also quite possible to make rather more precise estimates without getting too worn out. With the wind astern (and on that point of sailing alone), the true and the apparent winds are in the same direction. We know that if your diagram is to

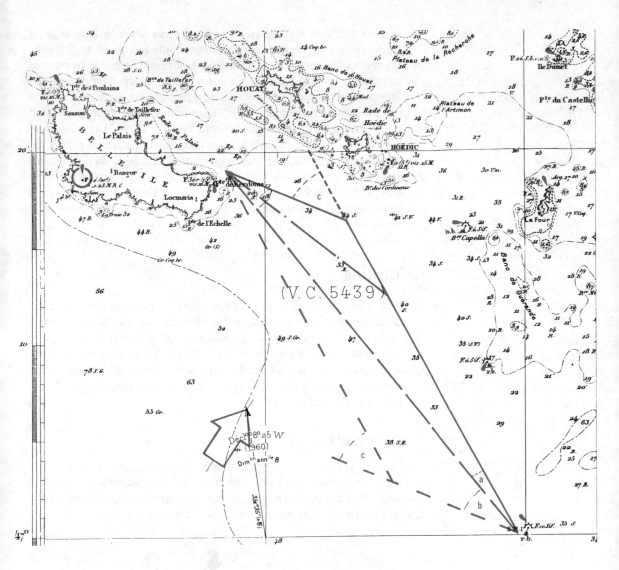

be of any use then it must show the real wind, so all you have to do is to place yourself dead downwind, to log the compass course and speed and then to luff up nice and gently, continuing to record the speed every 5°. In a very short time you will know which is the very best angle of broad reach, for that particular wind strength at least. Even if you don't go so far as to make a diagram, these things can be noted in a corner of the log book for future use.

Should you make short dog legs or long dog legs? Everything depends on what the wind is going to do. If the wind is unlikely to change direction, or if you don't know, then it is probably best to

Between SN 1 and Kerdonis, with a light SW wind, there are three possibilities: take the direct course; bear away and be able to carry the spinnaker, finishing on a close reach; or begin on a close reach and then finish under the spinnaker.

make small dog legs (even though you can actually lose a bit of time gybing). If you move off the direct route too much, then it only takes a small shift in the wind at the last minute for you to have to run the last part with the wind dead astern, which would wipe out all the benefits gained from tacking downwind. However, if you have not moved far from your direct course, then a shift of wind will either have no effect or be beneficial – unless it is more than 80°, in which case you will have to take down the spinnaker. When a change in direction of this magnitude is forecast, then you must give up all idea of gybe tacking, and immediately get on the course that will be imposed on you by the wind backing or veering; in other words, luff up in the direction from which the wind is expected.

Beating

How can you improve on a course when your destination lies in the direction the wind is coming from? Here the question of tactics takes a very peculiar turn: the boat is beating, and it is no longer a matter of asking if a detour will result in a better progress to windward, since, by definition, beating is the point of sailing which provides that. Besides, as long as the wind does not shift, the question is easily answered.

Headwind theorem

Let us take several identical boats, all making 50° to windward. They are spread out on a line m–n and are preparing to beat to windward in order to reach point A. The angle xAy, bisected by the line of the wind, is equal to the beating sector – 100°.

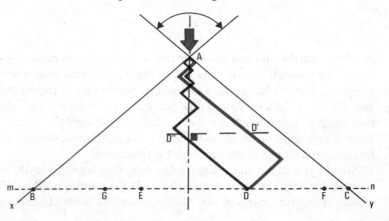

Taking all the tacks to be made into account, all the boats on the line m–n and in the sector xAy are at an equal distance from A.

The important thing is that all the boats on the line m–n are, allowing for the tacks to be made, at an equal distance from A. We can verify from the diagram that two boats setting out from D and tacking differently, would cover the same distance to get to A, and that at any point on the passage (eg D´ and D´´), their progress would be identical. Conversely, any boats to the left of B or the right of C are further away and will take longer to get there.

Close-hauled, the shortest course lies within an angle equal to the beating sector whose bisector is the axis of the wind; all courses within this angle are at an equal distance from A.

Shifting wind theorem

Now the wind backs 15° left, and everything changes. The new beating angle is x´Ay´, and the projection of each boat onto the bisector shows that E is now nearest to A, followed by D, F and C. B is well and truly out of the running. There is some doubt about G, which lies outside the beating angle but slightly to windward of E. If we suppose, to take an example, that the boat G is the one on which the earlier diagrams were based, then it would gain 11% in speed for an extra 9.5% of route.

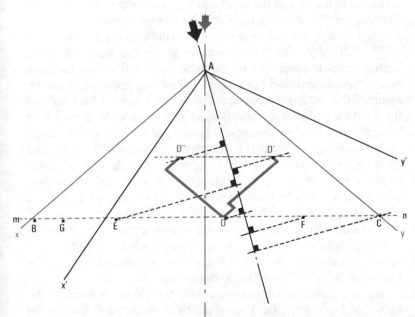

The wind backs 15°, and the picture changes completely. This requires some thought.

The distance of the boats from their objective has also changed, except for D. It is 21% less for E, 24% more for F and 56% more for C. One can imagine that the morale must also have changed quite a bit on the boats D′ and D″: the distance relative to A has been reduced by 12% for D″ and increased by 17% for D′.

These observations add some nuances to the foregoing theorem. If the wind is not going to shift, then tacks can be made in the whole triangle BAC, but in practical terms, it is unwise to pursue that theory, because if the wind changes then there is a better than 50% chance of losing out: either by being too far to windward, as is the case with B, or by being too far to leeward, as is the case with D, F and C.

In practice, experience shows that when it is not known if the wind is going to change, whether backing or veering, the safest option is to tack within a sector of 10°, with the true wind direction as axis.

In this context, when the objective does not lie exactly in the eye of the wind, the question arises of the choice of direction for the first tack. This is simply an extension of the previous rule, for it should be apparent that *the best tack is the one that brings the boat closest to its objective*. In our diagram, it is D″ that has made the best tack.

Now, if a change in wind direction is forecast, and if the direction of the change is known, then the situation changes yet again and we must look back at the diagram: when the change occurs, it is D′ that is nearest to the axis of the wind, but E that wins out. We can therefore deduce the following rule: *When a change in wind direction is forecast, keep to the side from which the wind is going to come*.

The difficulty is to know where to go on that side and which beating sector to adopt. To find the answer, the shift in the wind must be assessed as accurately as possible. Generally speaking, it can be assumed that the angle between the present direction of the wind and the windward edge of the new beating sector cannot be greater than the difference between the present heading of the boat and the angle of the wind shift predicted. If for example, the boat is making 45° into the wind and a wind shift of 30° is predicted, then the difference 45° − 30° = 15° indicates that the direction to windward of the new beating sector must be between 5 and 15° off the axis of the present wind, on the side from which the wind is going to come.

This simple bit of arithmetic throws up another rule: *the greater the shift in the wind is expected to be, the less you should move off the axis of the present wind*. If a wind shift of 40° is forecast, then the calculation 45° − 40° = 5° shows that no change must be made.

Let us return to where we were before, somewhere between the buoy SN 1 and Belle-Ile. Five identical boats are now making for Kerdonis. The wind is to the NW (wind No 1) and the forecast announces that it is going to veer north.

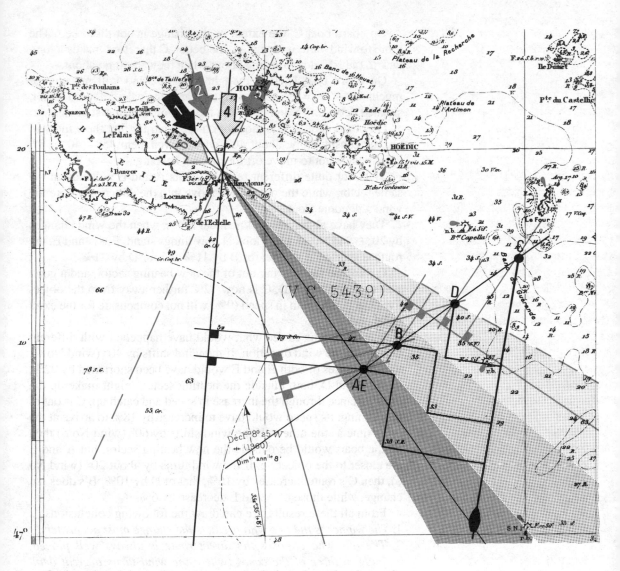

(Document of the SHOM.)

On board each boat, the crews are wondering about the change in the wind, and how they should respond to it.

On board boat A, it is thought that they will have reached Belle-Ile before the wind changes. So they continue to beat within the 10° sector (marked in dark colour) with the present wind as its axis.

On board boat B, it is thought that the wind will veer soon and that it will be about 30°. They therefore make the calculation 45° − 30° = 15°. B then makes a long port tack to then place itself ready for a beat in the grey sector, between 5 and 15° from the axis of the present wind.

On board boat C, the extent of the change is not discussed. The more to windward, it is argued, the better. C therefore makes a long tack to the NE, not worrying about when they are to go about.

On board boat D, it is thought that the wind will not change much: $45° - 20° = 25°$. D sets off to beat in the pale-coloured sector, situated between 15 and $25°$ from the axis of the wind at present.

On board boat E, it is thought on the contrary that the wind will change considerably: about $40°$, which gives them $45° - 40° = 5°$. They decide not to move off the present heading.

Thus, for quite different reasons, boats A and E will stay in the same sector, while the others will move into the direction where the wind will come from.

They have all covered 14 nautical miles, when the wind changes by $20°$ (wind No 2). Let's look at how things stand. For A and E, the route is shortened by 6%, for B by 11% and for D by 21%.

C went too far, moving out of the new beating sector, and a good way to windward of D. C is now 12% further away from the objective than D. The gain in speed (9%) will not compensate for the extra miles added.

It is interesting to see what would have happened with different changes in the wind direction. If the wind shifts by $40°$ (wind No 4), then the routes of both A and E would have been shortened by 22%, while B and D, both outside the beating sector, might make up the extra distance through the increase in speed and catch up. C is out of the running: its speed would have to increase by 18% to arrive at the same time as the others. If the wind shifts by $60°$ (wind No 5) then all the boats would be outside the new beating sector, but A and E are closer to the objective. If the wind turns by about $20°$ (wind No 6), then C's route increases by 16%, that of D by 10%, B's does not change, while those of A and E decrease by 6%.

From all these results, we can draw the following conclusions:
1. *The winner is the one who predicts the change most accurately.*
2. *The one who chooses the direct route is always well placed, winning in three of the cases (where the wind turns a great deal, where it does not turn and where it turns in the other direction).*
3. *In all cases, making a big detour is worse than useless.*

In several cases, it will have been noticed that there were always boats out of the new beating sector, but to windward of the others, and that these stood a chance of making up for lost time, since they were heading for the objective on a close fetch and were therefore sailing faster than those close-hauled. This leads us to consider a particular case: when the objective being made for can be reached in one tack close-hauled. In this case, it can be advisable sometimes to bear away a little to gain speed, if a change in the wind is expected before the end of the passage, either because the wind heads you by more than half the boat's heading or because it frees a little.

According to the distance remaining to be covered, and according to the weather forecast, the line of thinking can change entirely. The further away the objective, the greater the chance that the wind will shift during the trip. If a polar front is active over the area, then you should be thinking in terms of what will happen in the next few hours, whereas in the case of a depression, it's more a question of what will happen in the next few days. If you get caught in a monsoon, then you're looking rather more to the long term.

Crossing the Channel

To sum up what we have covered so far, we will look at how to approach a number of different Channel crossings, in a classic meteorological situation: a depression has just passed and another is on the way. The wind is blowing from the NW and should back soon.

If you are going from the Scilly Islands to Bréhat (course 115°), the direct route obliges you to sail with the wind dead astern – always a bad point of sailing. However, it would be inadvisable to start tacking downwind, since there is a risk of the wind shifting to the point where you would not be able to carry the spinnaker. It is therefore preferable to luff up a little on the starboard tack and keep

(Document of the SHOM.)

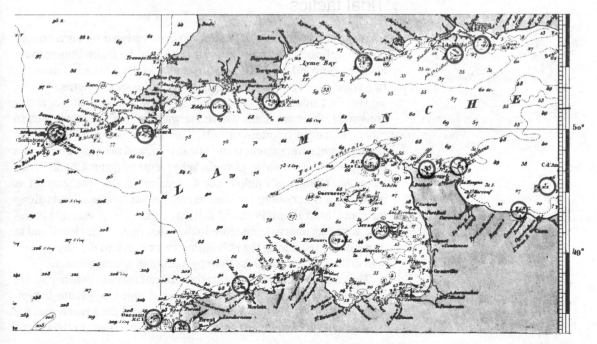

on it – you will then stand a good chance of making the crossing first on a broad reach and then finishing on a reach.

From Torquay to Bréhat (course 169°), the direct route is on a broad reach, but for the same reasons as before, it is better to luff up in the direction from which the wind is going to come. If the forecast is that the wind will change in the first part of the crossing, then it is a good idea to luff up by 15° as soon as you have passed Start Point. If the change in the wind is only going to occur towards the end of the crossing, then you should only luff up by 5°.

From Plymouth to Ushant (course 199°), the direct route is sailed on a reach. Here the choice is difficult and it becomes important to know the latitude over which the forecast depression is going to pass. If it is passing to the north, then the wind will perhaps back no further than west. The most likely plan then seems to luff up as much as possible with the spinnaker from the word go. If the centre of the depression is likely to pass over the Channel, then it is quite probable that the wind will turn south, or even SE. In these conditions, bearing away by 15° in relation to the direct route can be a good tactic. Finally, if you think that the wind is going to settle in the SW, the direct course is the best, trying to make sure that you are as near to Ushant as possible when the wind turns against you.

Tidal tactics

Finding the fastest course in a region criss-crossed by currents can be a complicated business. Everything has to be taken into account at once: the wind, the tidal streams and also the combination of the two which can create a completely new series of problems.

The first thing to bear in mind is that a tidal stream is rarely consistent: there are areas where the water is moving faster than in others, and even counter-currents. The trick is therefore to find the fast area when the current is in your favour, and the slow area or the counter-current when it is foul. When entering the Channel, for example, along the English coast, remember that the current is generally weaker out to sea than nearer the various headlands along the route: Start Point, Portland Bill, St Albans Head, etc. It is therefore advantageous to keep close to the coast during the flood, and to move out to sea during the ebb (either that or go into the bays) – you will make quicker progress than by sailing in a straight line.

The problem begins to get rather more complex when you are caught in a cross-current. If it looks as if you can get no benefit from an alternative cross-current (which would then mean that the boat would be carried first to one side and then back to the other), then it would appear that there would be much to be lost by struggling uselessly against it. The example of the Channel crossing illustrated below shows that instead of struggling, by letting oneself be carried 6 hours in one direction and then 6 hours in another, keeping a constant course all the time, the boat follows a sine curve relative to the bottom, but advances in a straight line through the water, and that this is clearly the shortest possible route.

In order to find the shortest possible route in an alternating cross-current, the principle to follow is always the same: you must total up the currents that you will encounter during the journey, and then displace the point of departure on the chart accordingly. You will then see what heading to keep for the entire trip.

However, the shortest route by this method is not necessarily the fastest, and it might be useful to add a little to the distance in order to get there faster.

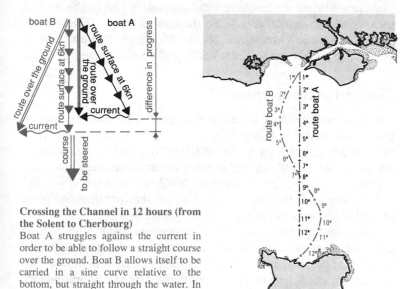

Crossing the Channel in 12 hours (from the Solent to Cherbourg)
Boat A struggles against the current in order to be able to follow a straight course over the ground. Boat B allows itself to be carried in a sine curve relative to the bottom, but straight through the water. In spite of appearances, this is the fastest route.

We must now take account of a new notion, which is the key to all subtle navigation in tidal streams: the notion of resultant wind.

Resultant wind

When a boat enters a tidal stream, the wind changes. As the boat is travelling in a mass of water that is moving as a plane, the wind that is perceived from the boat is no longer the true wind, but rather a combination of the true wind and the wind due to the speed of the tidal stream. This wind is known as the resultant wind. It is not a theoretical force because it is the wind that creates waves in tidal races and that you feel on board a boat that is drifting in the tide.

When the true wind is strong and the tidal stream weak, then the resultant wind is not really significant, but on the other hand, in lighter weather, the difference between the true wind and the resultant wind can become very marked. When a true wind of 5kn, for example, blows against a current of 3kn, then you will feel an 8kn resultant wind on board. If the true wind and the current are running in the same direction, then the resultant wind will only be 2kn. When the true wind and the current are at an angle to one another (and this is the more common case), then the resultant wind differs from the true wind in both strength and direction.

Basic understanding of tidal tactics proceeds from the following observation: since the resultant wind depends in part on the current, then its characteristics vary when the current varies. Therefore, if the variations in current are predictable, then it must also be possible to predict the resultant winds and take advantage of them.

Geometrical constructions

We meet once again the excellent navigator, who in the chapter on coastal navigation in this part, had already made the passage from the NW Minquiers buoy to Grand-Léjon four times. He has kindly agreed to make a fifth trip for us today in conditions very much like the fourth: at spring tides, leaving the NW Minquiers at HW – 6. The only difference is that the wind that was E the first time has come around to the west and has freshened to force 3.

Our man reckons he can do the passage in about 5 hours if he doesn't have to tack. He calculates his course in the same way as he did for the previous trips, displacing the point of departure by the amount of current he will have under him for those 5 hours and then works out his true course, correcting for variation and leeway to get his compass course.

He notes that he can make the trip very easily staring at HW – 6 and that he can make Grand-Léjon on a close fetch. However, the tide is going to turn in the course of the next few hours, and at HW – 3 it will be running at 2.2kn at 135°. So the question arises: when the tide turns, what will be the effect on the resultant wind?

In order to see what the resultant wind might be like at HW – 3, we will have to know its components, that is to say the true wind and the tidal stream at that time. The characteristics of the tidal streams are already known, but as for the true wind, we will have to find that

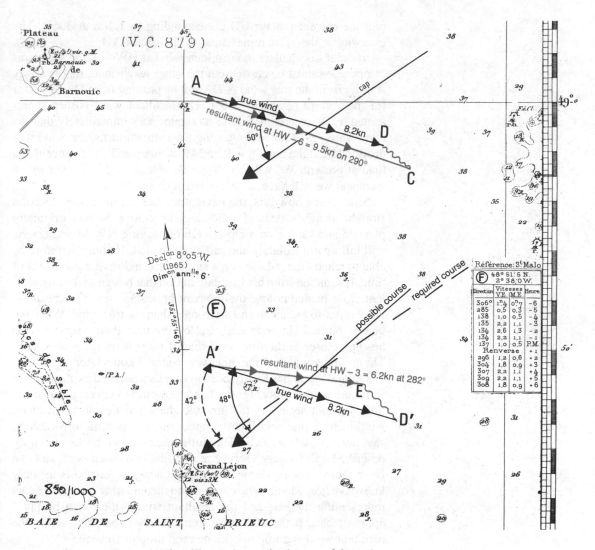

out now (let us suppose that it will not change in the next 3 hours).

Now, when you are sailing in a tidal stream, it is entirely impossible to know what the true wind is (unless you anchor). Rather, it can only be reconstituted from the resultant wind and the current.

You calculate the resultant wind in the same way that you calculate the true wind when drawing up speed diagrams. Since the characteristics of the current are known, all that remains to be done is to draw up a bit of simple geometry on the chart. The resultant wind is plotted as a vector (AC), orientated in the same direction as the wind in question and of a length proportional to the strength of the wind (x knots of windspeed = x nautical miles on the chart). At C, you

Anticipating changes in the resultant wind

Above: from the present resultant wind vector AC and the present current vector CD, we derive the true wind vector AD.

Below: from the true wind A′D′ and the characteristics of the current ED′ at a given hour, we obtain the characteristics of the resultant wind for the time in question. Here we see that the resultant wind will drop and head the boat.

plot the current (vector CD corresponding to 1.4kn at 306°). The true wind is therefore represented by the vector AD.

In order to calculate the resultant wind at HW − 3, the same sort of operation must be carried out the other way round, that is to say starting from the true wind A´D´, and by plotting from D´ the vector for the current (2.2kn at 135°). The resultant wind is then represented by the vector A´E. Our navigator sees immediately that his fears were well-founded: after the tidal stream turns, the wind will drop and head the boat. It will be 34% weaker, and 25° further ahead than at present. We will no longer be able to make the course we want and we will have to tack to reach Grand-Léjon.

Since that's how it is, the navigator takes the necessary decision straight away. Instead of following the course he had originally planned and sailing on a close fetch on leaving NW Minquiers, he will luff up immediately and sail close-hauled. He may therefore be able to reach Grand-Léjon on a single tack and save a good deal of time. He can see from his first calculation that he can make an excellent close-hauled course the moment he leaves, since the resultant wind is not so far ahead and is stronger than the true wind. When the boat is pushed closer to the wind by the tide, then he can steer a heading closer to the true wind than if there were no tidal stream. Things are completely the other way round 3 hours later.

Our navigator has kindly been giving us a detailed explanation to show the sort of working that has to go on. However, most of the time, it is not necessary to know the characteristics of the resultant wind in such fine detail, but is rather more important to be able to say how it will evolve. The little geometrical tricks we have described will be very useful for avoiding confusion later, and can be scribbled down on a piece of paper, taking as your basis the only known vector, which is the current, and then relating it to the vectors representing the true and the resultant winds (these can be fairly approximate). It then becomes immediately apparent whether the resultant wind is going to back or veer, drop or freshen.

Going through la Horaine

Two identical boats are at the NW Minquiers buoy and are travelling together, not to Grand-Léjon, as one might believe, but to la Horaine (distance 24 nautical miles, true course 258°), in order to enter the mouth of the river Trieux. It is springs and the boats are passing the buoy at HW + 4. The wind is WSW, therefore a headwind.

The navigator on the first boat is doing his job quite competently, but not exactly out to break records. Since the forecast does not give any change in the wind for the next few hours, he examines the inset on the chart to see what the tidal movements are (region F). He notes that the tide will turn in 3 hours. He settles on setting off on the starboard tack, which will bring him close to where he is trying to go.

After 2 hours, he realises that the starboard tack has had its day and that it is time to go about. This is an even smarter decision than it first seems since it means that he can take advantage of the end of the ebb in order to be able to position himself so that he doesn't have to struggle against the flood tide. He therefore makes a tack to port, and 1 hour 30 minutes later (3 hours 30 minutes since setting off), estimates that they are in a good position and can go about. They therefore go back over onto the starboard tack, but at the end of 5 hours, the wind begins to head him a bit more, and the course corresponds less and less to what the navigator would have liked. Furthermore, the flood tide is adding to the problems, and he has to tack again. Half an hour later and he is in the right position again, and the boat can go about. However, the course is a disaster, and after another 15 minutes they have to go about yet again. This time they are bang on, and pass la Horaine. The journey has taken 6½ hours.

However, on arriving at Loguivy, they note that the boat that set out from the NW Minquiers buoy with them has already arrived, anchored, is all shipshape and Bristol fashion and that the crew is preparing to go ashore in the dinghy. What did they do to arrive so far ahead?

All the navigator on the second boat did was to ask what influence the variations in current were going to have on the wind. Having drawn up the little diagram that we described in the previous section for the tidal and wind conditions for the next 6 hours, he noticed that the resultant wind was going to back progressively south and lighten: at the end of the trip it would be 25° further south than the true wind and 35% weaker.

In these conditions, it is obvious from the diagram that the best tack to make was the starboard one for the first 3 hours and then the port tack for the fifth and sixth. During the fourth hour, when the current would begin to turn, either tack was as good as the other. However, if they had continued on the starboard tack for that hour, then they would have been too far south in relation to where they wanted to go, and so they went about at the end of the third hour, passing la Horaine three-quarters of an hour ahead of the other boat.

Having chosen their tacks to suit the changes in the resultant wind, note that each time the navigator took the tack that was closest to the true wind. This is because tacking relative to the resultant wind is not so effective, since you do not then progress as fast in relation to the true wind (which is the real measure).

Even in a current, the good tack is always the one that is closest to the true wind. It is therefore the tack on which one makes the best close-hauled course (closer than if there were no current). Here, it is starboard tack before the turn of the tide and port tack after.

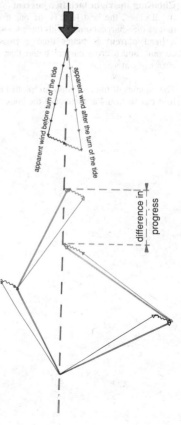

The rule to be drawn from this example is that *when tacking in a current that is variable in both force and direction, the good tack is always the one closest to the true wind*. In our example, the first boat made three bad tacks: port during the fourth hour, and then starboard at the beginning of both the fifth and sixth hours.

This same rule can be expressed in another way by the diagram below, which summarises most of the cases that can occur when tacking in a current.

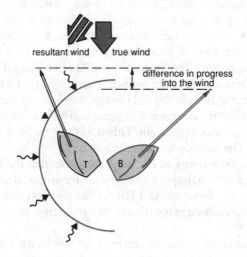

Choosing the right tack in a current
In all cases, the best tack is the one that makes the sharpest angle with the current: a head current is better than a cross-current, and a cross-current better than a current from astern.

The courses of the two boats are plotted in fold-out section 4 at the end of the book.

One can well imagine that in reality, one has to think pretty hard to follow the various rules through to their logical conclusion and determine which is the best tack to take. Nonetheless, it is this little bit of extra thought that makes the difference between otherwise identical boats. As the yachting expert Alain Gliksman put it: 'Some people make good and bad tacks, while others make bad and even worse ones'.

Here we go again …

Our two boats are back at the NW Minquiers buoy again, at HW + 4, in springs, and once more heading for the entry to the river Trieux, but this time the wind is from the NNW and is light.

On board the first boat, the navigator, who has still not learned his lesson from the first trip, is quite happy to calculate the course on the basis of the currents the boat will encounter during the journey. It is 27 nautical miles to the river mouth, the estimated speed is 3.5kn and the trip should therefore take about 8 hours. The true heading is 258°. Here we go.

This time things go well, and even better than had been hoped, since after 4 hours the wind frees and shifts to the north. It is possible to hoist the spinnaker and the speed goes up by a knot. At the end of the sixth hour, it is noted that the tide is carrying the boat west, and we bear away 10°; the speed increases even more and we arrive at the river Trieux going flat out, a good hour earlier than expected.

However, in the quiet waters of Loguivy, we find the other boat, swinging gently on its mooring. It has evidently been there some time as there is no one aboard.

Once again, the navigator of the second boat took into account the evolution of the resultant wind in relation to the current. Using his little sketches, as usual, he calculated that the wind would free and lighten when the tide turned, and that therefore it would be possible to use the spinnaker throughout the entire second half of the journey. Indeed, conditions were such that the question was more: would it not be possible to hoist the spinnaker at the start of the voyage and leave it?

A precise answer to this question requires a little bit of work.

First of all, he needs to work out at what point of sailing it is possible to hoist the spinnaker, and what the speed of the boat is on that point. Next, what will be the route over the bottom if they keep that point throughout the trip?

They can start by hoisting the spinnaker just to see. It becomes apparent that they can carry it at 55° to the apparent wind and that the speed is 4.5kn.

On the basis of these facts and the information about the tidal streams, the navigator makes the little sketch that will allow him to obtain the direction and the strength of the resultant wind for every hour of the journey.

He notes that the resultant wind remains the same for the first 2 hours. Since he knows his present speed and course, he can plot the vector for the route over the ground for the first 2 hours from the vector for the resultant wind and the vector for the speed of the boat.

The navigator then plots on a sheet of tracing paper the angle between the vector for the resultant wind and the vector for the course and speed of the boat. He then displaces the tracing paper over the diagram so that one of the sides of the resultant wind vector coincides with the resultant wind vector for the third hour of the passage; he thereby obtains the vector for the speed and course, and from this, the vector for the route over the ground for the third (shortening the vector for the speed and course as the wind lightens), the navigator only then has to plot them on the chart to figure out where this little wheeze would take them. It becomes apparent that they will pass la Horaine easily and make the trip in 6 hours, arriving an hour ahead of the other boat.

If the other boat is late, it is not that it has made a detour, on the contrary, it followed the direct route through the water; on the other hand, the second boat, which went faster, was subject to the influence of the contrary current for less time, and therefore made a shorter route through the water (1.6 nautical miles less, in fact).

Note that if there are speed diagrams for the boat, then the work is a lot easier. Everything can then be worked out even before arriving at the NW Minquiers buoy, since we already then know at what point of sailing we can hoist the spinnaker and carry it, and what the speed of the boat will be. However, if we want to be entirely strict and methodical, then we ought to take into account the fact that the wind will lighten as it frees, and therefore use different diagrams for the start and finish of the voyage.

However, as you can easily imagine, in the middle of the exercise, the wind could change out of the blue and make the whole bundle of paperwork completely obsolete, leaving the navigator free to go up and take a breath of fresh air.

PART VIII

Cruising

To define 'cruising' properly, we would have to begin by talking about freedom. If we simply said that going on a cruise means spending time at sea on a boat with other people, and in a given place, we would be giving a good description of a passage on a luxury liner. Under sail, on what is bound to be a smaller boat, cruising is characterised, rather, by the fact that you decide to rely entirely on yourself for a certain time, to take certain risks, in full knowledge of the facts – and to get by: to be independent. And independence is demanding, in that it is always forcing you to make decisions.

The first choice, moreover, concerns the measure of independence you want to take on: in space, in time – and in the bad times. How far do you want to go, how long do you want to spend on the water, how prepared are you to face up to problems? Independence really does start straight away: as soon as you set off on an outing beyond the supervised stretches of water, you have to accept this independence, along with the principal demands it makes. This is why we will not hesitate to devote a chapter here to the day trip, an activity which is never discussed, and yet is currently the most widely practised. This is a basic chapter, in so far as the rules of the game are shown quite clearly here. Beyond this, without setting precise limits between the different areas, we will deal with coastal cruising, where sailing time exceeds a single day, then with offshore cruising where, for once, your independence is complete.

In each case, the choices to be made at the outset are the same. Where are you going to sail, with whom, on what? Put differently, every cruise is based on three things: a place, a crew, and a boat. You do not necessarily have to look at them in that order: that depends on the circumstances. What counts is the way they are blended. It is important that the crew and the boat are 'up to' the location, capable of carrying out the programme which has been planned; if not, you have to change the crew, or the boat, or simply devise a more modest programme. This seems perfectly obvious but in fact, at the outset, all this will be strongly coloured by your dreams. And you will have to make a very detailed analysis of all the different factors to come up with the right blend.

The choice of location in which to sail is above all a matter of taste. Certainly, you have every right to dream at first (in fact, dreaming is positively essential!), but a seascape only becomes a cruise location when you have studied its characteristics, the opportunities it offers and the difficulties it conceals. The nature of the coastline and the sea, the meteorological conditions, how to keep the boat still, and to make progress in safety: here you will have to rely on knowledge acquired in the preceding parts of this book and, in addition, study the nautical documents relating to the chosen region. You will then be able to devise a schedule and predict the pace you will take. We will suggest the key points in this kind of analysis.

The crew: this is a factor which we have not yet dealt with, and which will occupy an important place in this part of the book. First, what is a crew? A minimal description of it would state that it is a group of people – relatives, friends, strangers – who are 'in the same boat': the expression has become so much a part of everyday language that there is no need to stress the idea of solidarity it implies. But, beyond this basic observation, we will have to analyse what determines the competence and the coherence of a crew. There are hardly any general rules in this area, where each person's physical capacities, experience, judgement, characteristics and tastes, all interact, along with issues of leadership, and even fanciful ideas. We will deal with the fanciful ideas. Leadership will have its place too – and it will be no small place.

We are left with the boat you are going to sail on. You can imagine that it must be suitable for the kind of cruise you are going to undertake, that it must be seaworthy and reliable, offer acceptable living conditions and, in all, guarantee the independence you desire. Many sailors, even today, think that to have absolute independence, they must in fact have their own boat. This is a very serious choice, as it affects the future in no small way. It is worth pausing here for a while.

Should you own a boat?

When a boat is a kind of all-consuming passion, for which you are prepared to make great sacrifices, the question hardly needs asking: on your own, or with a few friends, scraping the money together, bleeding yourself dry in order to be able to buy an old hull to do up, or to construct some kind of revolutionary craft, this is clearly an essential undertaking. Wanting with all your heart to have a boat, because you derive at least as much pleasure from working on your boat as from sailing it, you can imagine that, too. You have every right to consider that a boat has a soul – and a soul is priceless!

On the other hand, when the passion you feel is more seasonal, it makes sense to reflect for a while before launching into any kind of purchase. On first appearances, you have real freedom when you have a boat of your own: you can do what you want, when you want, where you want. But this assumes in the first place that you have money. Money to buy the boat, but also to buy all the necessary equipment (this can reach 30–50% of the purchase price). Money for insurance, overwintering, security, and above all for maintenance. You have to be ready to pay out almost indefinitely, if only to keep yourself in the position where you started.

Other problems may appear. You may not necessarily manage to find a mooring in a port of your choice (this is, moreover, a point to check on before buying!). It is not necessarily the case, either, that you will always have the proper crew at the desired time: if the most strapping chap on board breaks his leg a couple of days before the departure date for the cruise, are you sure you can replace him? The season can be spoiled; and yet you still have to go on paying … And when, dispirited, you try and resell your dream-boat, you find that the second-hand market is saturated and devilishly depressed. Your dearly bought freedom might prove to be completely illusory in the end.

All in all, these days, buying a boat only seems reasonable if you are absolutely sure you will be spending a lot of time sailing: that is, if you live near the sea. It is reasonable enough, too, if you get hold of a boat which is transportable, which you can take home with you and work on there. Otherwise, why bother? While the coast is getting more and more spoiled by ports full of boats which never sail, do you need to add to them? It seems much wiser to seek alternatives such as a hired boat or a club boat.

You are doubtless deprived of the pleasure of fitting out a boat to your own taste but, on the other hand, you have practically unlimited opportunities to choose the place and the time to go cruising, and the kind of boat most suitable for your cruise. And you commit only a limited amount of money. At sea, it is of course true to the sailor's spirit to act as if the boat belonged to you and to treat it as such; but on returning, everything is over and you can think about something else. In the end you have greater freedom.

Having resolved this important issue, in the following chapters we will take various examples, so as to present as wide a range as possible.

• In 'The day trip', we will deal with getting to know a stretch of water of modest size, with your own boat and a crew of members of the family.

• In 'Coastal cruising', we will set off to look for a cruising area, with a group of friends who have chosen to sail on a hired boat.

• In 'Offshore cruising', we will show what life is like on the open sea, on a club boat, with a crew of people who do not already know each other.

Three different areas, but a single state of mind: in each case, you are sailing 'properly', without having to spend a fortune, and sailing with that sense of safety we defined at the very beginning of the book. It is this sense which is involved whenever there is an important decision to be taken; it is probably the same one which allows you to feel that at sea, in the end, there is no such thing as an unimportant decision.

CHAPTER 1

The day trip

Taking a day trip at sea seems a modest enough aim. It is what the majority of amateur sailors do, on all kinds of boats, large and small. Many do this all their lives, because it suits them perfectly well; others, because circumstances do not allow them to do otherwise; yet others come back to it after having sailed around the world. It is a very simple thing. Unfortunately it is just as simply spoiled, or turns out to be mediocre. What a pity! The freedom you have here is no doubt very limited, but it is all the more prized for that. Knowing how to get the best out of it is a real art, and it is worth taking care over it: compared with so many run-of-the-mill grey days, which are dreary and soon forgotten, a great day at sea, well organised, can sometimes be a kind of masterpiece; such memories last a whole lifetime.

The territory is small, but varied. Several kinds of amateur sailor cross here (and hardly ever mix).

First there are the fishing fanatics, who live the same hours as bakers do. Casting off at night, carving out your path alone at a time when the lamps are lit only for you, the pleasure of finding your markers just before dawn; then a special way of turning and tacking, a solitary wait, particular movements, a scalding cup of coffee, silence; and all of a sudden the wild burst of joy when something suddenly tugs at the end of the line: how glorious, in the first rays of the sun! At midday, often enough, you are already back at home, and the rest of the day is spent in a sort of sleepy limbo, waiting for the next night.

At the other extreme, there are people for whom the sea is above all a sports field, a place for regattas. Here, the essential business is to make your boat perform at its best and, if possible, better than the others. You increase the number of manoeuvres and changes of sail, you try to understand your boat, to fine-tune it, to become one with it; to beat the elements and the people alongside you. Sailing a boat well for a few hours is satisfying enough in itself, it is one more way of feeling good; coming first is even better, of course.

Between these extremes, there are those who quite simply go sailing because they have the urge to get away, to escape the crowds and the petrol fumes and to breathe more freely. You do not have a

very particular goal, and there is no question of tiring yourself out unnecessarily. You don't set off to spend your day clinging to the gunwales: you want to sit down like civilised people. You scoff at performance features, designer sails, and fancy gadgets. You simply go sailing and there are all kinds of people on the boat, young and old, fat and thin; there are things to eat and drink. You want to make the best of the sunshine, enjoy the scenery, or perhaps not even look at it: to be free, in the end, and at ease; you are determined to take your time.

Such definitions are too rigid, in any case, and the day's activities can be infinitely varied according to the place, the time, and the opportunities you have. This is the realm of the imagination, and the mood of the moment. Dad's fishing dinghy, lent to his son and his friends, can quite well be suddenly transformed into a racing boat, covered with flashy borrowed sails, a checked 'big boy', what passes for a 'ghoster', what approximates to a spinnaker and a flying trapeze. The next day, you will have discovered something else: island-hopping; sailing slowly up a river; the simple pleasure of tacking round a distant buoy; or again, the sudden, unexpected chance for a couple to be able to slip away together for a day, alone in the world …

So as not to get side-tracked, let's go on from this last example. The years have passed, they are a married couple now with children of their own. The urge to go sailing has not left them, they are sure enough of this that they decide to buy a small boat. We will try to accompany them on the round of choices they will be faced with: the choice of a boat, of course – a major point; the choice of equipment (and they will need a lot of this even at this stage); then, during the preparation for an outing, the choices to be made regarding the 'crew', the location and the time.

In this chapter, then, we will be dealing with very basic factors – that is to say fundamental ones. Make no mistake: most of the knowledge to be acquired, the precautions to be taken, and the explanations to be given, so you may enjoy yourself and get on well, are already necessary at this stage.

Choosing a boat

In his *Advice to a Humble Sailor*, Hilaire Belloc writes: 'It would not be a bad thing if someone (I am not competent myself) took it on himself to draw up a list of advice for the ignorant man, too poor to sail on a very big boat, or not stupid enough to want one.' Competence notwithstanding, this is advice which has to be given, and has to be given boldly. And our first piece of advice will be this: a boat is not to be chosen like a car, from a catalogue, or by visiting a showroom. A boat is to be chosen at sea.

We give this advice calmly, knowing that you will probably take no notice of it. It is well known that anyone, however level-headed and lucid they may be in ordinary life, is no longer the same person once the urge for a boat overcomes them. You will try in vain to show them point by point that the boat they yearn for is not in the least bit appropriate for what they want to do, the best arguments will serve only to sharpen their desire. The realm of the passions knows no such explanations; a dream is not open to discussion, and that is that.

However, if you still have a little common sense, try at least to ask yourself a few simple questions:
• What will be your exact use of the boat?
• Who will you sail with, not only now, but in 2 or 5 years' time?
• What will you do with it during the winter?

With this, you should already be able to define the basics: the kind of boat, and its size.

And start by making a modest but indispensable investment: get hold of copies of the various statutory texts on the protection of human life at sea (and pollution control): any vessel of 12m in length must carry these statutory texts, as laid down in the *Merchant Shipping Carriage of Nautical Publications Regulations* (1975). The regulations *do* apply to pleasure yachts.

What kind of boat?

What do you prefer, sailing or fishing? Although there are an infinite number of so-called 'sailing/fishing' boats, you cannot be sure that they are all suited to both activities, as soon as you want to do some real fishing or some real sailing. Almost always one will dominate.

A fishing dinghy must have a very deep cockpit, where you can stand upright, spacious enough for everyone to move about easily; it should have narrow gunwales, so you can work over the water, pull up a net, and catch a big specimen in the landing net. It has to be stable, and not get knocked around too much at anchor. It is useful if it has a motor, although, contrary to current popular conceptions, you can fish perfectly well under sail (as has been done for thousands of years!). But on flat calm days it is good, of

---

Authorised fishing equipment

For the coast of the North Sea, the Channel and the Atlantic:

– 1 trammel (net) of a maximum 50m length (except in estuaries and salt water rivers flowing into the sea);
– 2 shellfish pots;
– dipping lines, with a maximum 30 fish hooks;
– 2 trolling lines, each fitted with a maximum 30 hooks;
– 1 pronged harpoon/fish gig;
– 1 landing net.

For the Mediterranean regions, information can be obtained from the local maritime affairs department.
Never forget that you are strictly forbidden from selling what you have caught, be it fish, shellfish or seaweed. (Extracted from the *Almanach du marin breton*.)

course, to be able to move between the fishing grounds with something more powerful than the oars. The motor is useful too when the wind is in the wrong direction or when it is too strong. As it will have to run for a long time while just ticking over, it is better to get a diesel engine rather than an outboard motor.

Clearly, you can go for a quiet sail on such a heavy and well-protected dinghy and you can, in particular, bring people on board who are not very familiar with seafaring matters, and who are easily worried when their faith in their basic stability is disturbed. But if you intend to go sailing often, you should perhaps choose a more adaptable model, one with fold-away seating, for example. You need, above all, a boat which is a real sailing boat, and this requirement should make the choice more clear. Some manufacturers of 'fishing/sailing' boats still think that 90% of their clients will sail exclusively under motor power; consequently, they pay only 10% of their attention to the rigging and sails. You can see that a set of sails of 12sq m on a 500kg boat is completely ineffectual. Choose a boat with sails sufficient to be able to make headway against the wind in fairly blustery weather: this is a basic requirement. You should also be able to shorten sail if need be, so you should have reefing points in the mainsail, and have a storm jib. Even if you intend to be sailing under motor power a good deal, you should be aware that the motor might break down; so it is the sails which provide the real safety backup on the boat. (We should add, at this point, that you should follow this argument through and never go out, under motor power, into places where you would not dare venture under sail …).

Do you want a cabin? Most of the 'fishing/sailing' boats have one; or at least some kind of shelter (this can be little more than a glorified locker). It is a useful place for keeping your equipment, and if someone is ill they can sometimes find a bit of peace there (so long as they keep their eyes tightly closed, and it doesn't smell of petrol or fish). And again, it is pleasant enough to have a little home of your own when you are out at sea. Some people put up curtains or pin prints of naval battles on the partitions, and why shouldn't they? At anchor, bent over double in this cubbyhole so reminiscent of the cabins you made in your childhood, devouring an old adventure story while a heavy shower rattles on the roof, you can sometimes suddenly have, at last, the feeling that you have got your money's worth …

If you prefer a brisker, more sporty style of sailing, you should head for quite a different kind of boat, probably looking for one of the sprightly sailing dinghies. Here, much greater attention is paid to the sails and the way they work. The cleats are not set out so

Capelan-class day cruiser.

Cavale-class day cruiser.

as to leave a comfortable space for the passengers: they are set in the right place, and the passengers sit down where they can. Besides, they are no longer just passengers, but members of the crew. For you cannot expect to sit around on this kind of boat: if you have a serious set of sails, you will not keep the boat balanced without an effort. The hull is naturally more streamlined than that of a fishing boat, and the layout of the deck is quite different: you have to be able to sit out; and the cockpit has to be watertight and self-draining since, as soon as you are sailing at speed against the wind, you will get wet. On this kind of boat, of course, the motor is a mere peripheral (but you should still remember to turn it over from time to time to keep it in condition).

What size of boat?

Less than 4.5m in length, a boat is like a nutshell, which is hardly able to make off safely from the shore. Above 6m, it begins to become unwieldy, especially if you want to be able to tow it on the back of a car. But everyone must still be able to be comfortable on board. There is a delicate compromise to be made. Real wisdom lies, above all, in choosing a boat which you will be able to handle on your own. The crew, even if it is made up of family members, is an eminently unstable thing. Children soon grow up and find other people's boats more attractive …

It must be unsinkable

If you buy a boat of less than 5m in length, it ought to be unsinkable. But the regulation standard of unsinkability really is a minimum. At the time of testing, each member of the crew is replaced on board by a 15kg weight: this means that if the boat is flooded, you will not be able to stay on board, for the boat will be nothing more than a float to hold onto while awaiting rescue. For your own peace of mind, you will have every interest in reinforcing this standard of unsinkability considerably.

If you pick a boat of more than 5m in length, choose for preference one which is certified as being unsinkable: it really is an essential safety measure. If the boat of your dreams is not certified in this way, be ready to make it unsinkable yourself. If you do, you will not be exempted in France from carrying the regulation floats and lifeboats, but you will certainly be more at ease if a problem does crop up!

Some checks to make

Rulebook in hand, you will still have to check that the boat you are interested in conforms to the regulations: this is not always the case, whatever you may think. Make sure, for example, that the sea-cocks in the hull and the fuel taps are easily accessible (you should be able to close them quickly in case of emergency).

We can assume that you do not want a boat which is difficult to maintain (so long as this is not the very thing that turns you on). Check, then, that it is easy to clean, that there are not too many nooks which are impossible to reach, and where fish scales and breadcrumbs will automatically seek refuge …

But, clearly, it is at sea that you will be able to make the decisive observations. First of all, whether the boat moves well, whether its rigging and its gear match up to your expectations; whether you can make your way to the bow without taking foolish risks; whether you can stay up there while you drop anchor without the out-board, which is turning over in neutral at the back, burning out for want of water being fed in … Of course, the ideal boat does not exist. There will always be the badly fixed cleat for the sheet to get jammed in, the useless lockers which, at the first hint of a roll, empty out their contents and, at the second, fill up with water (and stay filled); and all sorts of bits that seem to have been designed for you to bump into. It is up to you to see if you can improve things and if, all things considered, the advantages prevail over the disadvantages. And now, make the decision, the two of you. No one can do it for you.

Piranha-class day cruiser.

Equipment

Sailing zones

1. Voyages made by French-registered pleasure craft are classed in six categories:
1st category: voyages not entering into any of the categories below;
2nd category: voyage during which the boat sails no further than 200 nautical miles from a place of shelter;
3rd category: voyage during which the boat goes no further than 60 nautical miles from a place of shelter;
4th category: voyage during which the boat goes no further than 20 nautical miles from a place of shelter;
5th category: voyage during which the boat goes no further than 5 nautical miles from a place of shelter;
6th category: voyage during which the boat goes no further than 2 nautical miles from a place of shelter.

2. Places of shelter are ports or stretches of water where the craft can easily take refuge and where the people on board will be safe.

Rulebook extract.

For a day trip, you should be equipped for the 5th category; this lets you sail up to 5 nautical miles from a place of shelter. This already offers you considerable scope: you can sail to an island 10 nautical miles out to sea; and if you count on making the outward and the return journeys in one day, your time will already be well filled!

Below, you will find a list of the equipment required for this category – both navigational and safety equipment.

Some commentary is called for.

Navigational equipment

Take navigation seriously from the very start. With only a little expenditure, your trips will be all the more interesting, you will be able to do more, and be safer, too.

• On the documents shelf, be sure to have up-to-date charts, which cover the areas well beyond the zone you intend to explore: you sometimes have to go further than you expected. Rather than the *Tide Tables*, use the *Macmillan & Silk Cut Nautical Almanac* or *Reed's* if you are sailing in the Channel or the Atlantic: you will have all sorts of additional information on the distances between

---

Required equipment for the 5th category

Basic shipboard equipment
– a set of sails, so the boat can make headway;
– a complete set of 'running rigging';
– a storm jib;
– equipment for shortening sail;
– a boat hook;
– an oar and rowlock or two paddles (for boats less than 8m in length);
– a cleat or a bollard, and an anchor rope fairlead at the bow;
– a rope for towing;
– a set of conical wooden plugs;
– a set of tools and spares for the motor.

Navigational equipment
Documents:
– charts of the area where you will be sailing;
– a current set of *Tide Tables*;
– regulations for preventing collisions at sea (text);
– regulations for preventing collisions at sea (plates);
– beacon markers, system A;

– symbols and abbreviations for sea charts.
Instruments: a standard compass.

Safety equipment
– one or two anchor lines (see article 58);
– a signalling mirror;
– flags for letters N and C;
– a waterproof lamp;
– an anchor weight (for boats more than 5.5m in length);
– a conical shape (for boats with a motor);
– a foghorn;
– a bell (for boats more than 12m in length);
– three automatic handheld flares;
– a rescue buoy;
– individual lifejackets;
– a No 1 first aid box (see below);
– a rigid bucket of at least 7 litres capacity, with a rope attached;
– buoyancy bags (except for boats certified as being unsinkable).

ports, proper routes, and the table of lights (see below), because you never know …

• Have a good compass, check that it is correct and, if necessary, calculate its curve of deviation.

• Invest in a plotting compass straightaway; it is worth it. Some standard compasses are dual purpose, but it is always preferable to have two compasses rather than just the one. There are also telescopes containing a plotting compass, which are very useful instruments.

• To take a bearing, all you need now is a protractor or a Cras ruler. It would be a pity not to have one. If you know how to take a bearing you have ten times as many possibilities, you no longer have such a limited scope in respect of the coast, of fog, or other dangers.

• Do not forget your watch, even – and especially – if you want to take your time. It is useful for calculating the depth of the water according to the tide, for checking you have not fallen behind on your schedule, and so as not to miss the meteorological forecast. And you should know that if your compass goes wrong, your watch will tell you where north lies at any time (see diagram).

• A pair of binoculars is very useful (or that telescope with the plotting compass, mentioned above). As soon as you leave the shore behind, it is remarkable how far away everything is that you wanted to identify! The binoculars will let you bring things close while you maintain your distance …

• And have a barometer with you. Even for a simple day trip it is an indispensable piece of equipment. There may be a sudden fall in pressure, which does not occur often, but which is all the worse when it does happen. Even if your barometer only persuades you once, in your sailing career, to call off your plans there and then and make for home in haste, you will not regret having had it with you that day. This is also the instrument which will let you become best familiarised with the conditions in the area where you are sailing, if you calibrate it, and get into the habit of comparing its readings with those given in the weather forecast. The dialogue between the barometer and the weather forecast is essential for anyone who wants to make progress. Do not forget your radio!

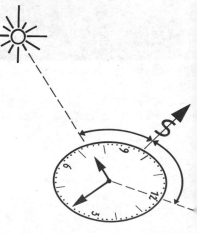

A watch is set to 'solar time' (it is 0720) and laid flat, the hour hand pointing towards the sun. Given that, in this position, south is indicated by bisecting the angle formed by the hour hand and the 12 o'clock position, you can find north.

Safety equipment

The dividing line between basic shipboard equipment and safety equipment is not very clear.

Let's say that with the former, you should be able to avoid getting into a difficult situation; the latter will get you out, if you do unfortunately get into such a situation.

• So, start by having a very good anchor. Or rather two. Yes, even on a small boat. And let the second anchor be heavier than the principal one. If the first anchorline breaks, or if the anchor drags, it will probably not be in flat calm conditions. Again, this will perhaps only ever happen to you once, but you will be so wildly happy to have a second anchor, sturdier than the other, that you will never again find it a burden to have on board.

• The issue of buoyancy aids and lifejackets should be just as clear. According to the regulations, you should wear buoyancy aids on board boats less than 5m in length and 2 tonnes in weight; above this, you should wear lifejackets. But in neither case is it necessary, in the 5th category, to fasten yourself to the boat with a harness. Why should you, then? The water is hardly any warmer when you are less than 5 nautical miles from a place of shelter than it is beyond that, and it is still a long way for you to swim back to shore … So kit yourselves out with lifejackets which have built-in harnesses; and get 'one-size' ones, particularly if the 'crew' you have on board often changes: in a difficult situation, you will have to act quickly, and everyone will have to take the nearest lifejacket to hand, without wasting a second.

Only small children should have their own lifejackets, and they should wear them all the time. If you are worried that this will give them a complex, there is only one solution: do the same yourself.

• You must have on board three automatic red flares: if you do not have to use them during the first 3 years, do not throw them away: although they may be out of date, they can remain in working condition for a long time afterwards. Three regulation flares and three outdated flares makes six chances to be seen, in all.

• We have said you should have a watertight lamp on board. This means that we imagine that darkness may creep up on you. If this eventuality occurs, it is far preferable to have two or three lamps, for a single lamp has very particular characteristics: either it doesn't work, or it falls in the water … But lamps which are really waterproof are rare and expensive. A good idea is to get hold of a number of small, disposable lamps, each kept in a transparent plastic bag which you can have sealed by your butcher or your dry-cleaner.

• Take a boarding ladder with you, too. It is an important accessory which we will come back to soon.

• And everyone should have a knife. It is always useful, and particularly for saving your life if, by misfortune, you fall into the water and are caught up in a sheet.

• Apart from the knife, which you should keep in your pocket, put all of this equipment in an easily transportable box; and protect the fragile equipment with a couple of old sweaters …

The crew

An old Malaysian legend tells how the first human to master the sea was an abandoned child. Floating in the bamboo nest of a wild duck, he had to confront the Seven Torments of the Sea: hunger, thirst, loneliness, self-pity, regret, fear and hope. The story tells how he conquered the first six torments, but never the seventh, for hope clings fast to the heart of man.

For a day trip, problems concerning the crew come down in essence to the various torments which can overwhelm it. In Britain in general, and on a boat in particular, hunger and thirst are rarely to be feared (but all too often you forget to take a small reserve stock of water …). Neither is solitude to be feared. Self-pity and regret generally have one and the same cause: seasickness. In the present case of the day trip, this is treated quite simply, by returning home. Usually the next trip is much better: you begin to get your sea legs. If you do not get any better, you are perhaps in the presence of a deep-sea kind of seasickness; we will come back to this in the relevant chapter.

The Malaysian legend does not say anything about cold or heat, which are nonetheless both formidable torments. At sea, happiness sometimes hangs only by a fragile thread. You should not set off for the day or even for a few hours in only a bathing costume; you have to be able to cover up from head to toe (and you will see how your old sweaters end up tempting the most clothes-conscious of women, or the most designer-dressed of men …).

But a blazing sun on a flat calm day can also be a dreadful torture: you need hats, sunglasses and suncream. Otherwise, by the end of the day, your skin will not be worth living in. It is astonishing how much you have to take with you to be comfortable at sea: you hardly ever have everything you need.

Of the seven torments, there remains fear, which deserves a special mention. Some people are very fearful, others not enough. Without being over-dramatic, however, it is quite right that everyone should have a clear sense of the most likely risk there is when you are on a boat: that of falling overboard.

The risk of falling in the water

If the 'boss' is the only competent sailor on board, the first rule is that he *clip on permanently*. This might appear surprising, or even ridiculous, and yet … !

Otherwise, the issue can be stated in a few simple terms:

For this exercise to be realistic, the fender needs to be rigged to a floating anchor, or it will drift much more quickly than would a man overboard.

– a crew member falling into the water is always a serious matter, which can quickly turn into a crisis;
– it is already less serious if the boss is there to fish them out;
– it is even less serious if that crew member was roped up;
– it is nothing but a slight accident if you have the necessary equipment to get them back on board.

On your first outing, if the people on board are those who will be forming the 'regular' crew, do not hesitate to introduce them to the various aspects of the issue. You can, for example, throw a fender overboard, pass the helm to someone else and quietly count the time it takes to pick it up again … If they go for an early dip in a quiet creek, let them try to get on board on their own: they will probably realise how difficult it can be to do it when they are fully dressed, and tired. And have two crew members, even strong ones, hoist from the water a third, even a light one, deliberately acting as a dead weight: they will see that they need Herculean strength. After this unfunny set of jokes, everyone will probably look on their lifejacket, their harness and the boarding ladder in a new light.

If you take a 'once-off' crew on board, who are little used to the sea, the first rule is to adapt your schedule to suit this crew. And the second is to know how early – well before it is necessary – to take the decision to make everyone put on their lifejackets and harnesses.

For your passengers to see these safety issues in the proper light you will have to cultivate 'the art of being the boss' more generally. Suddenly making them wear a lifejacket, without explaining why, you run the risk of worrying them, and spoiling their good mood. It is essential to 'let them know what's what' and primarily with regard to navigation itself, never miss an opportunity to teach them something, to explain what you are doing, have them join in with handling the boat and look out for seamarks. You have a passion for sailing, why not try to share it? Safety issues will be integrated quite naturally, in such an atmosphere.

A day at sea

A simple day trip in a place you do not already know requires a great deal of preparation. This is not so that you can show off; what you are going to do is in essence fully comparable to a cruise. The preliminary considerations are the same: you will first have to get hold of documents which cover the area where you are going to sail, and discover its characteristic features. And then you will have to plan your itinerary, measure the distances, plan a schedule which takes account of the weather prospects; establish a 'strategy', however modest it may be, imagining variable features and alternative solutions. Make a careful note of the equipment to take with you. And above all, do all your shopping the day before you set off.

The characteristics of the zone

You have decided, for example, to base yourself for a season at la Trinité-sur-Mer, at the far end of the bay of Quiberon.

Don't wait for the fair weather before collecting and studying the documents you will need. Your winter will be transformed!

Documents

Get hold of sea charts of the bay and the surrounding area: the largest scale charts published by the SHOM and the Admiralty. There is a systematic list of them in the *Cruising Association Handbook*.

See fold-out section 2 at the end of the book.

For the kind of sailing you will be doing, many official publications will not be of everyday use; you would do just as well to consult a friend's copy or a club copy. In the French *Instructions Nautiques*, for instance (the equivalent of the Admiralty's *Notices to Mariners*), a mere five pages are devoted to the popular cruising bay of Quiberon. They start with a sentence printed in italic type (evidently an important one) which will no doubt leave you perplexed: 'The bay of Quiberon offers a good sheltered mooring for numerous craft.' So the place for your adventure, the vast stretch of water you will confront when you sail out of la Trinité river is nothing but a good sheltered mooring! This is because such publications are meant essentially for large vessels … All the same, you can deduce from this, for your own interest, that this is a stretch of water where you will not risk meeting any wild seas. You will have to make the same kind of interpretation several times over as you read the following pages.

You will feel much more comfortable consulting other documents meant for amateur sailing, such as the 'Where to sail' articles in nautical magazines. In fact, these articles contain much more information which you will find useful. All the same, you should take account of their date of publication: since then, many things may have changed.

What are the main things you should be looking for in these documents? First of all, general information on the bay: the wind patterns, the tides and currents. And then more detailed information on essential aspects such as hazards, seamarks and places of shelter.

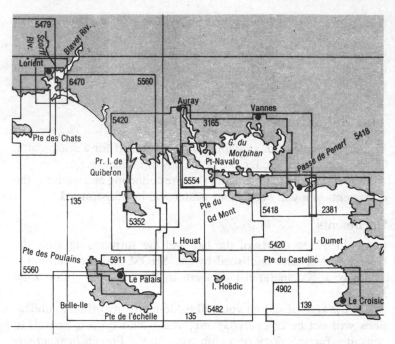

The right map for sailing in the bay of Quiberon is No 5420 (*Instructions Nautiques* C2).

Wind patterns, tides and currents

The chapter on meteorology in the *Instructions Nautiques* shows that the dominant winds in the region are westerlies. The bay is well protected from these winds by the Quiberon peninsula. It is also protected from the less frequent south winds by the islands of Houat and Hoëdic. It is open to the SE, but there is practically no likelihood of south-easterly winds in the summer: this can be seen from the map of wind frequencies for July, and you can check it in more detail against the table of observations made at the closest coastal weather station, the point of Talut on Belle-Ile.

The *Almanach du marin breton* gives Port-Tudy as the reference port for the tide. From the monthly tables, and the maps, you will see that it is a very standard tide, semi-diurnal, with a spring tidal range of less than 5m. The times and heights of tides in the bay of Quiberon are probably not exactly the same as those at Port-Tudy, but with a quick look at the adjacent tables in the almanac you may note that – for Port-Haliguen, for example – the difference really is negligible.

The tidal currents – described in the *Instructions Nautiques* – do not seem to cause great problems, except at the mouth of the Gulf of Morbihan. Nonetheless, you should study the overlay of map 5420: the current can reach 2kn at spring tide in the middle of the zone. Note also, that the winds have a strong influence on the currents.

Frequency of winds in the region in July (*Instructions Nautiques* C2).

French ports (contd.) and English	High tides				Low tides				Reference ports
	Time correction		Height correction		Time correction		Height correction		
	MHWS	MHWN	MHWS	MHWN	MHWS	MHWN	MHWS	MHWN	
	hr min	hr min	m cm	m cm	hr min	hr min	m cm	m cm	
Audierne	−0 07	−0 16	+0 10	0 00	−0 06	+0 03	−0 05	0 00	Port-Tudy
Penmarch	+0 03	−0 12	+0 05	+0 05	+0 02	−0 06	−0 10	−0 05	Port-Tudy
Loctudy	+0 02	−0 06	−0 20	−0 25	+0 02	+0 01	−0 40	−0 35	Port-Tudy
Bénodet	+0 08	−0 07	−0 25	−0 30	−0 07	+0 09	−0 35	−0 35	Port-Tudy
Concarneau	0 00	−0 04	−0 15	−0 10	+0 04	+0 06	−0 15	−0 15	Port-Tudy
Pt.-Haliguen	+0 12	+0 05	+0 10	0 00	+0 08	+0 07	−0 30	−0 15	Port-Tudy
Belle Isle (Le Palais)	+0 05	−0 07	+0 05	−0 05	+0 05	+0 01	−0 15	−0 05	Port-Tudy
Pt.-Navalo	+0 26	+0 27	−0 10	−0 10	+0 23	+0 21	−0 20	−0 20	Port-Tudy

Corrections to be made for Port-Haliguen, to the times and heights of tide at the reference port (Port-Tudy de Groix). (Extracted and translated from the *Almanach du marin breton*.)

What is a hazard at sea?

It might perhaps be interesting to cite here the definition of a hazard, given by Bonnefous and Pâris in their famous *Dictionnaire de la marine à voile*, with the list of local forms: 'Hazard: generic term covering the rocks, sandbanks, shallow waters, sand bars, strands, banks, lookouts, shallows, reefs, shelves and other similar things, which boats run the risk of grounding on and which, under whatever particular kind of name, are found in all waters.'

Pick out the hazards in your chosen zone in the almanac, *Instructions Nautiques* or *Cruising Association Handbook*, and on the chart. At first glance, they seem few and far between. There is, of course, the infamous Teignouse embankment (Chaussée de la Teignouse), in the extension of the Quiberon peninsula, 'the poor man's Cape Horn', as they call it here. But there is no question of venturing off there for the moment. However, you should pay attention to the Méaban embankment (Chaussée de Méaban), which stretches out in the NE of the bay between the end of the channel of la Trinité and the mouth of the Gulf: this is a bad place.

But, in our civilised regions, a hazard is never without its buoy. In the *Cruising Association Handbook* or *Instructions Nautiques*, the name of each hazard is followed immediately by the name of the buoy or buoys which mark it out. These buoys and their characteristic features are also shown on the charts.

How to use seamarks

The documents signal various seamarks. If you have taken a look at the plates volume of the *Instructions Nautiques*, you must have thought these seamarks are not blindingly obvious things ... Well, at the very least, you already have a list of them. And, in any case, one

Kérisper Bridge   Great Crac'h lighthouse (LA TRINITÉ)   005° – Lesser Crac'h lighthouse (47°34'N – 3°00'W) – 0.6
Kernevest farm buildings

M – 1960 (4.1m of water)

Atlantic Hotel   Britannia Hotel   Grand Hotel 309° – CARNAC belltower (47°35'N – 3°05'W) – 3.2
Carnac water tower

M – 1960 (2.2m of water)   Guardroom at Beaumer Point   Saint-Michel chapel   Stuhan Island

Mouth of la Trinité river and Carnac beach
(*Instructions Nautiques* C2).

thing is certain: a seamark only exists when you have identified it.

What is important, in the first instance, is to be able to divide the zone in which you are going to sail into three or four parts, each delimited by clear points of reference: if you have tacked and turned a lot during a fishing trip, if the weather is a bit hazy or you are feeling a bit hazy yourself, this allows you to find out where you are at a single glance. At first sight, the map of the bay offers hardly any possibilities for creating these kinds of sections. However, the alignment of the point of the Petit-Mont and the islet of Méaban must be useful … But you will have to be able to look at this on the spot, to check if you really can see the belltower of Crac'h or Saint-Michel chapel on its tumulus in the hinterland of Carnac. Without any doubt, one of the important points of your first outing will be the moment when you sail out of the channel, at the level of the Petit-Trého buoy. The entire bay will open up before you, but what you really must do is look behind you; for very soon the coast will close up on itself, and hide its inlets and projections. Try to imprint some points of reference in your mind: the lighthouse, of course, and a given house or group of trees. Everyone sees the landscape in their own way, and it is not necessarily the most official of seamarks which you will find striking. You, perhaps, will be more particularly sensitive to certain contours of the coast, which you will be able to recognise without fail later. You may ask yourself why; but do not try to understand, just take advantage of it.

Then, as you head out, the seamarks should gradually begin to stand out against the skyline. It is at this point that you will probably be able to begin to organise your landscape.

What makes a good place of shelter?

A good place of shelter is one which satisfies these four requirements:
– it is easy to spot from a fair distance away;
– it has a clear and well-marked entrance channel;
– it is accessible at any time of the tide;
– it offers protection against all winds.

This of course would be the ideal place of shelter! But there are excellent places which do not satisfy all of these requirements, the last one in particular. Everything might depend on the current conditions: if you are looking for a good place of shelter from the west wind, it does not matter much if it is not well protected from east winds (all the same, it is as well to know this, and to know that you should get out in time if the wind changes).

As far as places of shelter in the bay of Quiberon are concerned, they will only be useful to you if strong northerly winds prevent you from getting back to la Trinité. If this happens, you should look at the shelter offered by Port-Haliguen and Port-d'Orange to the west, and the port of Crouesty to the east. There is also Port-Navalo at the mouth of the Gulf, but can you get in there when the tide is not coming in?

After these preliminary considerations, you probably still do not have a very clear picture of your first outing; but you have an idea of the navigational conditions in the bay, you know the hazards to avoid, you know what are the first things you will have to find out, and you have the escape routes you may need. This is not bad going!

Preparing a programme

There is no special goal on this first outing. The ideal thing would be to take a little cruise around the bay, in order to get to know it: locate the mouth of the Gulf, sail by Carnac, follow the peninsula, have a picnic on a beach somewhere, perhaps.

In which direction should you do this circuit? That depends on the wind. Usually, for this kind of outing, it is better to plan to have the wind behind you on the return leg: it will be a long day, the children will be tired, you should not let it drag on at the end. So you should make straight for the Quiberon peninsula with the west winds, which means that you get a look, on the return journey, at the mouth of the Gulf – but from a little way off, so as to avoid the wind in the la Trinité channel. With east winds, the situation is less obvious. In fact, you have to start to pay more detailed attention to the weather situation.

The weather cover

To begin with, choose a day with top-class, high-pressure weather. The ideal situation, which occurs often in the summer, is when an anticyclone is centred on the British Isles. The pressure is around 1025 millibars, there is no atmospheric disturbance in sight. The good weather is settled, though it is slightly misty in the distance. In fact, it is 'solar breeze' weather, as they say here: the winds change with the movement of the sun. Observe the situation during the days leading up to the outing: in the early morning the wind blows from the NE, sometimes fairly strongly (the weather is not very warm); the wind softens, turning to the east as the morning advances and, about midday (1000 GMT), it disappears more or less completely, in blazing sun. It gets up again slowly in the SW in the afternoon, then settles more firmly in the west. In the evening, it climbs back into the NW, then to the north, freshening quite noticeably.

In these conditions, the choice of a route is fairly simple: you have to follow the wind. You will start by passing beyond the mouth of the Gulf, then you will dip towards Quiberon Point, which you will have to reach with the last breaths of the east wind if you want to be able to take a swim and picnic on the shore. You will roast yourself in the sun until the wind picks up again in the west, then you will follow the coast to Port-d'Orange. Of course, you could go to Port-d'Orange first, then follow the coast to the tip of the peninsula, but that would not be a very good choice: on the return journey, if the wind were to get up a little quickly in the north, you would have to sail very close-hauled to get back. In the end, the best rule is always to put yourself where the wind will be coming from.

Marine 'space-time'…

The sea is the realm of general relativity! Trying to establish a precise relation between a given distance and the time it will take you to cover it is a risky business. A journey can take up to three times as long as it might, depending on whether you have a rear wind or a headwind; the difference can be as big as ten times if the rear wind is strong and the headwind weak!

You may find you have less space than time.

And yet, you should try to plan a schedule, so that you can at least focus your ideas a little. To do this, you will have to work on the basis of what winds are likely, and know what your boat can do. And, in any case, leave yourself a wide margin.

Take a piece of string and measure the distances on the map: six nautical miles between la Trinité and the Méaban Shallows buoy which lies at the mouth of the Gulf; from there, it is 7 nautical miles to Quiberon Point. If you estimate that your boat will do about 4kn, you will need just over 3 hours to reach the picnic spot. Assuming the wind will hold until 1100, you will have to leave at about 0730. But this could be a bit tight if the wind is weaker than expected: you had better plan to leave at 0700. As you make your way, depending on the wind, you might have to change your plans: if you have still not made it to the Méaban Shallows buoy by 0900, too bad, you should go straight on to Quiberon.

For the return journey, it is best to count backwards from the time you have decided to be back at anchor, let's say 1900. It is 3 nautical miles from Quiberon Point to Port-d'Orange, 7 nautical miles from Port-d'Orange to la Trinité: that makes roughly a 3 hour journey. So you need only leave the beach at 1600, if you can see that the wind is picking up again well. You could set off again a bit earlier, so you could press on to the fort at Penthièvre, and explain to the children what a tombolo is, and then round out the route a little to have a look at the amazing swarming crowd on the beach at Carnac. But you should not forget that, if the wind picks up well in the NW, you will have to tack back up la Trinité channel, and that may take quite a time. Of course, things may change again while you are on your way. If the wind is really weak, you can go and see Quiberon Point another day.

Leaving early

'All the pleasure in a day is in the morning,' said Malherbe (better known as a poet than as a sailor). You will certainly have to set off early. And perhaps even earlier than you think. You will have to get to know the pleasure of being at sea at dawn. It is like the beginning of the world. Everyone is happy. And it is usually organisational problems which will deprive you of that happiness. You really do have to do all your shopping the day before. Make sure the bags are ready. If you have decided to set off at 0700, be on board at 0630 at least. And if you are there at 0600, all the better. You will be able to take your time and perhaps even set off early. Yes, be ahead of schedule: you will be amazed at the sharp sense of pleasure it will give you!

Getting back early

'Darkness is already close once midday is past.' This is the next verse of the poem, less well known than the first, but it bears witness to a very refined maritime sensibility. Clearly, Malherbe lived

by GMT: when it is midday by our watches, darkness still seems a long way off, in summer. At 1400, this is no longer the case. As soon as the sun begins to dip towards the west, the atmosphere changes, you are already heading towards the darkness, and your calculations have to head off in the same direction. Do you still have time to do the whole journey? Should you not set off back a little earlier? Is the wind going to hold? Before midday you are exultant, and pensive in the afternoon (such is life). And there is nothing wrong with getting back a little early, so you can hang about on board a while, when everything has been cleared up; the shadows close in gradually on the river, and it is the time when the lions come to the watering hole.

Mist

When the mist begins to lurk in the vicinity, it is essential to keep track of your location. In the first instance, the sectioning we talked of earlier will suffice. But, if the basic reference points begin to look blurred, you will be very fortunate if you know how to take a bearing. And then everything can disappear completely: you know where you are, you know the distance between the coast and the cape you will have to sail around. So you can head inland and, often enough, when you do this, the seamarks reappear and you are saved. Of course, if the mist is thick and you no longer know where you are at all, there is only one solution: drop anchor, pull on a sweater and wait. Don't even think of returning blind. And certainly not by touch.

Darkness

Darkness is less worrying, since there are the lights. Still, you have to know how to use them (if not, there is the same solution: anchor,

---

Crac'h River (la Trinité)
Alignment at 347°. – 2 lights – Isophase light every 4sec. – Synchronous.
– Fore – Mouth – Height 10m, range: Blue 12 miles, Red & Green 9 miles. – Sector light 321°-G.-345°-B.-13.5°-R.-80° – Turret shaft.
– Aft – Directional light B. – Height 21m, range 17 miles. – Turret B., summit G. – Int. from 337° to 357° (20°).
'Petit-Trého' buoy. – 4 E.R. every 12sec. – Red – Rr.
Guidance lights. – Directional light flashing – Height 9m, range B. 14 miles, R. & G. 13 miles. – Sector light 345°-G.-346°-B.-348°-R.-349° – Turret B.
La Trinité-sur-Mer – South Wharf – Pierhead. – 2 eclipse lights every 6sec. – Height 7m, range B. 10 miles, R. 7 miles, – Sector lights 90°-R.-293.5°-B.-300.5°-R.-329° – Turret shaft R. & B.
North Wharf – Pierhead. – Isophase light every 4sec. – Height 8m, range 2 miles – Pyl. B., summit R.

Entrance lights for la Trinité. (Adapted from the *Almanach du marin breton*).

sweater and waiting, without forgetting to put a lantern at the top of the mast).

To become familiarised with the lights, it might be useful to choose to come back a little late one fair evening, at lighting-up time, when it is not yet dark. The mouth of la Trinité is perfect for this, with the series of lights which take you in hand, one after the other, to lead you gently to the south slipway of the port. In one go you will discover alignment lights, isophase lights, synchronous lights, sector lights, directional lights, flashing lights and eclipse lights. Of course, this is not to say that you should go sailing at night on the boat you have, but you will be reassured at the prospect of an evening in which you are becalmed at some distance from the coast: when the wind picks up a little, you will be able to avoid having to spend the night outdoors.

You can also carry out this experiment in the morning, setting out very early. It might even be preferable to do this, for if you get a bit lost, daylight will soon come, at any rate!

Your guardian angel

Remember, even at the time of your secret adventures, when you would make off to sea without your parents' knowledge, you thought of letting an accomplice on shore know that you were going, sensing vaguely that it would be better anyway if someone knew … And your guardian angel would naively accept your secret, without thinking of the unpleasant task which would fall to them if, by chance, you were not to return!

You are grown up now, you are no longer accountable to anyone, but you still need your guardian angel – who will be called the 'shore-based contact' in the following chapters. Don't just choose one at random: they should know something about the sea; in particular, they should know how to evaluate the weather conditions sensibly, so as not to alert the rescue services for the sake of a flat calm sea. They should know your sea-going habits, whether you are capable of coming back in the dark, what you will do if it is misty, or if the weather is bad (you should have considered these possibilities together). It is essential that they know the boat well, its name, its type, the colour of its hull and sails, its sail number. They should also know where to go to raise the alert, if necessary.

This is a role which is not to be taken lightly, by either side. If you return at the appointed time but do not bother to tell your 'angel' until the next day, and if they find this quite normal, you would both do better to spend your holidays playing bowls.

Camping afloat

In the Gulf of Morbihan.

One day you will know the bay of Quiberon like the back of your hand. You will have a prestigious collection of seamarks, and private fishing spots, your own secret passages, almost. You will know how to predict the wind, to weigh the most pessimistic meteorological forecasts against the bay you have come to know. You cannot fail to have made friends who have boats like yours. So perhaps you might want to spend more time in their company; not having to return every evening to la Trinité. Why not spend a night in the Gulf, then, beached on a quiet shore? If your boat is too small for you to be able to sleep on it, you can take a tent and pitch it on the beach. And why not stay there the next day, since you are happy there; looking out for an even quieter shore for the next night? The Gulf is full of practically unknown spots. You can live on the beach, and venture into a world the map does not describe. If it appeals to you, you can spend a whole day on shore, and set off again the next day. And if the weather is favourable, why not go further, why not go straight ahead and spend one night at Houat, and the next at Hoëdic? With two boats, you have more opportunities, and greater safety too: you can even do without a guardian angel, if the two boats really are sailing together.

The only problem is that you are on your way to becoming real nomads: you will have difficulty falling back in line having got used to this unusual and strangely satisfying lifestyle. For the moment, your freedom is limited only by the need to go and stock up on supplies from time to time (and this does not have to be a chore). All the same, do not be surprised if people peer at you in a curious way in the shops: it is a week now since you looked in a mirror. Have you seen the state of your hair?

CHAPTER 2

Coastal cruising

Cruising along the coast means living on board a boat, exploring a chosen area in stages, at a pace which pleases you. The shore is now only the place where you find your ports of call: you will go for a walk around from time to time, then you will go back home, on board, and set off again. You can probably keep the same hours as ordinary people: cast off in the morning and be sensibly at anchor every evening when the landlubbers are sitting down to dinner. You might also slip gradually into a totally different schedule, which will almost certainly be the case if you are sailing intensively. You may end up sleeping during the day because you finished sailing very late the previous evening; or you might cast off after supper because the conditions are favourable for a good night run. You casually settle into a secretive new timescale; and then the shape of your life is changed, no doubt about it.

How long will you sail? That depends. Too many personal factors enter into play here for us to discuss them all. Let's say that a week-long cruise is perhaps a little short: you get your sea legs at last, you find the 'right system', and you stop just when something more is opening up. A fortnight is perhaps enough: beyond this, you have to have a really comfortable boat, and get on well with each other, perhaps even love each other. No doubt it is better for it to be a bit short than for it really to be too long. It is up to each of you to find the right distance and the right pace.

In any case, there are dozens of different ways to carry out a coastal cruise, depending on the precise pace you adopt. It is a question of how you feel. Some crews rarely stop at ports of call, preferring long stretches during which they may lose sight of the shore for a while, where they already feel as if they are on the open sea. Others scarcely break away from the shore, and stop often, but they like to attempt tricky passages, piloting between the rocks. We all know those hearty sail-slappers and fearless salt-water gorillas, who dream only of battling with the elements, of carving out a path in the face of the winds and currents, to reach the goal they set, whatever the cost: fair weather bores them. There are others who devote themselves to perfecting a certain elegance in their life at sea, based on light breezes, refined jokes and general relaxation (if it doesn't work

Off the pointe du Raz.

out well, they will go and have fun on shore). Others again – and we amongst them! – want principally to play it by the elements, to bend to the natural rhythms so as to blend properly into the landscape, to recognise its finest subtleties. And for them, everything is an opportunity and a challenge, flat calm and fresh weather, the flood tide and the ebb tide, whatever the sea has to offer …

It is in this spirit that we will try to highlight the reasons behind the choices to be made when preparing for a cruise. Our starting hypothesis is that we do not have a boat, and we intend to hire one. So in the first place we should choose where we are going to sail, study its potential – and its potential problems – to see if they suit the tastes and the capabilities of the crew; then plan a fairly detailed programme. Then we will have to choose a suitable boat, make preparations and all kinds of other arrangements on land and at sea, before departure.

But first of all, where should you sail ?

Where to sail

Where should you sail? Since you do not have a boat, and you can find hire companies more or less anywhere, for the moment you have total freedom of choice: you can dream away avidly, and it would be a shame not to let yourself do this. A crowd of images jostles in your head, vague desires, other people's say-so's (word-of-mouth information plays an important part at this stage), memories of beautiful photos seen in sailing magazines …

Often, you spontaneously think about the choice of climate, first of all, and the basic factors of temperature, sun or rain. You can gather information on these subjects from all kinds of places; you will quickly find very detailed information if you consult the pages of any cruising guide. For example, one person will enjoy reading, in the volume on Greece and Turkey (*Instructions Nautiques* series D, vol 5): 'On the Greek coasts of the Ionian Sea, whose climate is usually fairly mild in winter, July and August are the warmest months, with the average for maximum daily temperatures reaching 29–32°C … The sky usually remains clear during this period and is often cloudless for several consecutive days … It rarely rains for a whole day … The Mediterranean is a sea of blue and limpid water, and the Ionian Sea is one of its bluest parts … In August, the water temperature can exceed 25°C.' Another person, who has chosen the *Instructions Nautiques* series B, vol 4, for their bedside book, will nod off during the long winter evenings to magical phrases such as: 'The Orkney and Shetland coasts, exposed to bad weather from practically every direction, are beaten by great waves when there are high winds …The sky is very cloudy along all the coasts, and remains three-quarters covered during most of the year …The number of days of rain per month is around 15–17 from April to June, and 20 during the other months.' They are happy to learn that 'after February the frequency of high winds drops and, during the calmest months (June and August), its force rarely exceeds 7 more than one day in three'. And they fall asleep reassured by this final sentence: 'There are few very hot days.'

You can also enjoy less extreme climates! And however much importance you may attach to the idea of getting a suntan or not getting a suntan, the most important thing is the sailing. (We should mention, in passing, that if you are dreaming of the Ionian Islands, you would do well to find out about the characteristics of the wind in this region!)

So you will soon have to set to finding a more detailed form for your desires.

The concept of the cruising area

In your chosen climate, you have to find a suitable navigational zone, which includes at least one large port (if only so you can hire a boat), with interesting and varied journeys to make all around, little ports, anchoring points, or perhaps islands. Even if you are not afraid of difficult sailing, it is desirable that the area should contain sheltered zones, where you can sail under any conditions (after all, it would be stupid to get stranded by bad weather in the same place for a week).

But you might also want to wander about on land, visiting places, meeting other people – and all the better if the coast and the hinterland are interesting …

Briefly, it is a question of finding an area whose parts are both harmonious and diverse, which may be called a cruising area, with a fairly well-defined shape. A more concrete example of this idea may be seen in the cruising areas of southern Brittany, mentioned many times already in this book. One stretches from Penmarc'h to Lorient, a veritable paradise protected by the Glénan and Groix islands, with its main ports (Bénodet, Concarneau, Lorient), a multitude of little fishing ports, anchoring points, and enticing rias. The other – separated from the first by a short and fairly inhospitable zone – stretches from Quiberon to Croisic, including the islands again, and the marvellous stretches of sheltered water of the bay of Quiberon and the Gulf of Morbihan …

But how do you come to 'isolate' such areas, and work out what their shape, their characteristics, and their limits are? And is it possible, at the same time, to plan what kind of cruise you will be able to make there, at what pace, and in what atmosphere?

Shape

You can approach this issue, still in a very general way, essentially by using charts, and with the almanac within arm's reach. Take as your starting point a fairly large port (called a port of reception, and which has the necessary services), and examine the surroundings. This is how basins of different size and shape appear:

• 'Round' basins, very large ones, such as the Aegean Sea or the Danish archipelago; more restricted, such as the Bocce di Bonifacio; or quite small, such as the islands of Charente around la Rochelle.

• 'Long' basins, in a more or less straight line, such as the French Riviera/Côte d'Azur from Marseilles to Genoa and beyond; jagged, such as the Cantabrian coast between San Sebastian and Cabo Ortegal, with Santander as the starting point; or those lined with a string of islands, as in southern or northern Brittany.

• 'Saw-toothed' basins such as the SW coast of Ireland, with its strong capes and deep bays, around Baltimore; or the Galician rias, between la Coruña and Vigo.

There also exist what might be called non-cruising basins, long stretches beaten by the sea and with no places of shelter, such as the coast of the Landes or the Caux region.

At first sight, you might think that a cruise will be more pleasant and more varied in a 'round' basin, which you can cross in any direction, rather than in a 'long' basin where you can only go in one direction or the other, and then turn back the other way. But this is a very rough generalisation which it would be wrong for you to rely on before you have made a more serious study of the characters of these basins!

Character

What factors should you take into account so that you may accurately judge the potential of a cruise in one area or another? Still on a very general level, we can say that there are three principal characteristics:

– meteorological conditions; that is, essentially, the wind patterns:

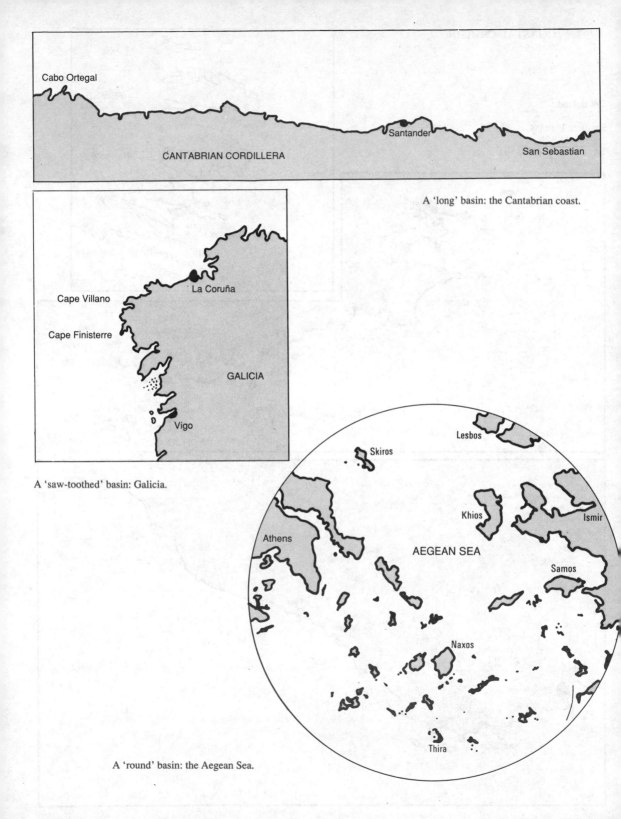

Cabo Ortegal

Santander

San Sebastian

CANTABRIAN CORDILLERA

A 'long' basin: the Cantabrian coast.

La Coruña

Cape Villano

Cape Finisterre

GALICIA

Vigo

A 'saw-toothed' basin: Galicia.

Skiros

Lesbos

Khios

Ismir

Athens

AEGEAN SEA

Samos

Naxos

Thira

A 'round' basin: the Aegean Sea.

SW Ireland

Southern Brittany

The Côte d'Azur/Riviera

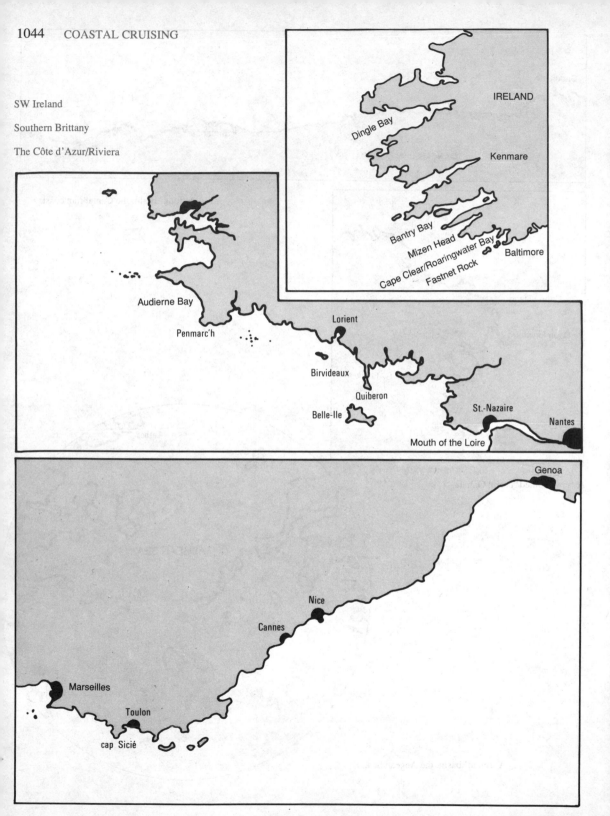

IRELAND

Dingle Bay

Kenmare

Bantry Bay

Mizen Head

Cape Clear/Roaringwater Bay

Fastnet Rock

Baltimore

Audierne Bay

Penmarc'h

Lorient

Birvideaux

Quiberon

Belle-Ile

St.-Nazaire

Nantes

Mouth of the Loire

Genoa

Nice

Cannes

Marseilles

Toulon

cap Sicié

direction, strength, frequency, and the related problem of visibility;
– the nature of the sea: wave- and swell-systems, depending on the fetch and the contours of the sea bottom; the tides and currents;
– the nature of the coast: its 'type', its orientation in relation to the winds and the sea; and the improvements people have made: the marker buoys and ports.

These characteristics can vary in importance and be combined in different ways, depending on the location. For now, we will try to illustrate them by studying the maps relating to basins which are very different from each other: for example southern Brittany, (as already mentioned), SW Ireland and the Côte d'Azur.

Meteorological conditions

Southern Brittany is situated on the edge of the trajectory of the polar front disturbances. Naturally, it suffers the consequences of this but, usually, to a limited and predictable degree: as each disturbance passes, the winds rotate from the SW to the NW in a classic pattern. Otherwise, the disturbances may be pushed back northwards while an anticyclone settles on the British Isles, giving a good north/NE wind, or solar breezes in summer. There is little fog.

Ireland, for its part, is situated right in the path of the disturbances. On the SW coast, you are in a ringside seat to greet the succession of winds turning from the SW to the NW, with fog from the warm sector and violent squalls in its wake ... These disturbances are produced throughout the year, but a glance at the statistical tables relating to the winds shows they are usually less violent in summer. Note that the centre of the cyclonic systems is not far off; thus the winds turn fairly rapidly. If you want to take advantage of a SW wind to complete one stage of your journey, and a NW wind for another, it will be useful for you to follow the changes in the weather conditions very closely.

On the Côte d'Azur, it is completely different. You are on the edge of the mistral region, which is a land wind, occurring mostly in winter and in spring. In summer, you are more likely to enjoy a regime of coastal breezes and, according to the statistics again, the greatest risk is of not having any wind at all for fairly long periods.

The nature of the sea.

In southern Brittany the sea is of a pleasant nature. It is rarely heavy; the swells, from the SW to the west, are not usually very dangerous. The currents are normally negligible. The tidal range is moderate and the tidal currents are only strong at certain particular points: in the estuaries, or as a result of the shape of the coast and the contours of the sea bed. You can familiarise yourself with these without danger, and sail in many places without confronting them.

In Ireland, on the other hand, with the dominant winds from the west, which rush down from Newfoundland without meeting the least obstacle, the seas can be huge! The swell is indeed a constant factor in this landscape, like the breathing of the land. The currents are not inconsiderable and, when they are running against the wind, the swell breaks far out over the continental plate. You simply cannot plough straight through this sea.

On the Côte d'Azur, when a high wind arises (usually without warning), the sea very quickly becomes unpleasant: with a short, deep chop, it makes progress difficult, often forcing you to change course. But as soon as the wind drops, the sea becomes calm. The tide gives you no cause for concern; on the other hand, you have to consider the drift currents, which are difficult to predict.

The nature of the coast

The pace and the atmosphere of a cruise will be very different along a coast with a straight face, where it is difficult to see where you are, and places of shelter are rare, compared with an indented rocky coast, with numerous seamarks and abundant places of shelter. Southern Brittany is the perfect example of this latter type of coast, and sailing there is made even easier by the quality of the markers and the abundance of ports.

A mountainous coast is another thing altogether: the map of SW Ireland is enough to set you dreaming. This succession of high, projecting capes and deep bays suggests a kind of sailing which alternates between violent effort (to pass the capes) and relaxation (in the depth of the bays). The traces of man's passage are discreet: you meet few boats, the markers are sparse, sometimes the lights are lit up late, the ports are rare and sparsely equipped. The only real navigational aid, in this area, is the atmosphere of the pubs.

On the Côte d'Azur, it is more likely the abundance of ports which is surprising, and the services you find there. Here you do not leave civilisation behind: there will be water and electricity available at points spread along the jetty, telephones, and sometimes even a socket for the TV. In many places the coast, viewed from the sea, is nothing but a garland of lights at night, and the problem is recognising among these lights those which are meant for the sailors …

Of course, when you analyse a cruising area for real, its characteristics do not emerge in strict order, they appear at random looking at the map. Sometimes, a dominant characteristic stands out straightaway. In Ireland, it is the swell; on the Côte d'Azur, the effect of man's presence; elsewhere, in northern Brittany for example, it will be the current. In any case, a certain cruising style may determine your choice.

From the outset, southern Brittany seems to be an ideal place for an initiation into coastal cruising. Difficulties can be tackled there progressively, everything is made to measure: the unambiguous weather conditions, the alternation of sheltered zones and open zones where you can get to know the 'real' sea, a perfect distribution of ports. Beyond this initiation, the variety of landscapes allows you to keep planning new programmes, in almost every season.

In Ireland, you can look forward to an austere cruise in a grandiose setting, and great battles with a strong sea. You should have a sea-going boat and a tough, experienced crew with a great deal of skill and fitness to fall back on. Such a cruise is really only a reasonable prospect in the fair season (at the beginning of the summer, the nights are very short – but, from 15 August, it might as well already be September!).

On the Côte d'Azur, you should sail rather in spring or autumn, if you want to have any wind. In the summer, apart from a gust of the mistral, which is always possible, you run the risk of an idle cruise, blissfully sunny, with lots of people around you. And why not, after all?

Limits

To sketch out a steady cruising pattern, you have to think about the limits of the basin you want to navigate. Sometimes, these limits can be seen at first glance, sometimes they are very subtle and are only obvious after detailed study.

Often enough, they are suggested by the shape of the coast. One point may separate two different worlds. This is the case in southern Brittany for example, where the point of Penmarc'h is a real turning point: to the south, it is peaceful, sheltered and welcoming; to the north, wild, open to the high sea and with no place of shelter. In the two areas, the sea is not the same at all.

Sometimes, a point simply presents a difficult obstacle to be overcome, between two basins of similar character. So, on the south coast of England, between Lizard Cape and the Isle of Wight, the monsters of Start Point and Portland Bill separate two basins whose profiles are almost identical. Another possible barrier is the mouth of a river, such as the mouth of the Loire which, with its troubled waters, its sandbanks, and the lack of protection in the face of the open sea, clearly marks the limit of southern Brittany. Another barrier may be formed by a forbidding section of the coast: between Lorient and Quiberon, once you have left the shelter of Groix behind, there is no going back.

Such limits appear clearly on the maps. Others are less clear. In northern Brittany, for example, it seems at first sight that the eastern limit of the basin is marked by the Cotentin coast; but a more attentive examination shows that the limit is really to be found out at sea, on a level with Jersey and the Minquiers. Beyond, towards the east, quite another world of reefs and currents begins, which it is better to leave to the locals (assuming you do not want to specialise in this).

Other limits are quite simply invisible, and they are wind-based. Thus, in the Mediterranean, the cruising basin of south Corsica and north Sardinia is quite precisely delimited, in summer, by a line between Ajaccio and Porto-Vecchio in the north, and a line between Asinara and Olbia in the south: above and below you can scarcely imagine navigating under sail alone. Again, in the Mediterranean, on the French coast, if cap Sicié constitutes an obstacle in its own right, it also marks the limit between a very windy basin, the Gulf of Lyons, and the Côte d'Azur, which is much calmer ...

Often enough the real limits of a basin are those that you fix yourself. The 'natural' limits do not present absolute obstacles, and they are of different degrees of importance: either you do not have a boat or a crew sturdy enough to surmount them, or you simply do not want to. The limit between the two basins in southern Brittany, for example, is far from absolute: in good weather conditions, these two basins beome a single one, from Penmarc'h to the Loire. Similarly, on the southern English coast, if you can get beyond Start Point and Portland Bill, you really have a basin which stretches from the Lizard to the Solent. On the other hand, in Ireland, if you do not feel sufficiently hardened to pass from one bay to another, you may decide that the bay of Kenmare, for example, or the bay of Baltimore are basins which are sufficient in themselves. Or again, in northern Brittany, you may think you are able to go as far as the Channel Islands: the limits are pushed back, and the 'long' basin becomes triangular ... In the end, the best cruising basin is the one you make to measure for yourself.

In any case, at this stage it still does not really exist. So even though you have defined its shape, and worked out its characteristics and its limits, it is an open space, a collection of propositions to which the wind will give a meaning. When the wind changes, in a basin with a varied profile, make sure you are not guided by habit alone. In southern Brittany, how many crews think of Port-Tudy as the only port on Groix Island! Because they are used to reaching it

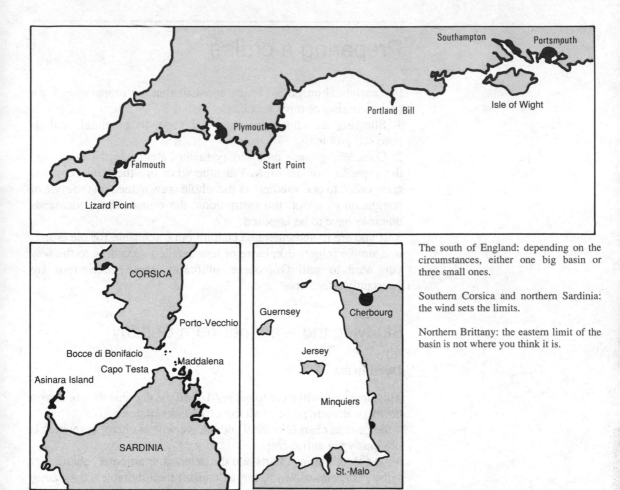

The south of England: depending on the circumstances, either one big basin or three small ones.

Southern Corsica and northern Sardinia: the wind sets the limits.

Northern Brittany: the eastern limit of the basin is not where you think it is.

with the west wind, they insist on trying to get in there (with many misfortunes) even when the wind is in the NE; when at that moment, on the other side of the island, the wild coast has become the peaceful side, and the little port of Locmaria is a perfectly calm port open to the high sea! On a cruise there is no obligatory port of call.

But it is now time to make a decision. Where should you sail? Let's assume that we have already had a lot of experience in southern Brittany, and we want to do something more difficult. Why not simply look to northern Brittany? For years you have heard of the current which dominates up there; at first sight, it seems to constitute a major disadvantage. And yet, there are northern Brittany fanatics, who never stop looking down on us. What is it that fascinates them so much about this place? It is tempting to look a little more closely.

Preparing a cruise

For analytical purposes, let us consider that the preparation for a cruise consists of three sections:
1. Studying the chosen navigational zone, its potential, and its potential problems.
2. Considering these preliminary factors alongside the tastes and the capacities of the crew. Put otherwise: are the landscape and crew suited to one another? Is the whole crew agreed on the style of navigation to adopt, the restrictions, the organisational demands that may have to be imposed?
3. If you are in agreement, sketching out a schedule for the cruise, or a simple framework, more or less detailed according to the way you want to sail. Of course, in reality, these three steps are constantly intertwined.

Studying the area: northern Brittany

Documents

This time, you will have to get hold of all the documents you can on northern Brittany, first of all the official documents:
– the general chart (No 5069) which we will use here, but which is obviously not sufficient;
– the coastal sailing charts and the detailed, 'particular' charts;
– the *Instructions Nautiques*, of course, the tide tables, the *List of Lights*; the *Almanach du marin breton* remains a very useful tool, but is not sufficient with respect to the tide;
– documents concerning the currents: document 550 from the SHOM (this is very detailed; so detailed, in fact, that it is difficult to use); and, above all, the atlas of currents for the region.
    Then look out the documents meant specially for amateur sailing: for example, the *Cruising Association Handbook*, the Adlard Coles guide *North Brittany Pilot*; the 'Where to sail' articles in *Bateaux* (Boats) magazine, the stunning aerial-photographic *Guide de croisière* (Cruising guide) produced by Neptune-Nautisme: not only are the photos beautiful, but they help you understand the structure of the coast better. Such works contain a host of precious information which is much more detailed than that in the *Instructions Nautiques*; but remember that they are not kept up to date, and that reference to the official documents is essential.

And as soon as you become interested in a region, you will find other documents everywhere which are principally concerned with history and geography, gastronomy and folklore. You might be interested to learn, for example, that this north Breton coast saw the arrival, around the fifth century, of strange boats manned by adventurous monks called Malo, Brieuc, Samson, Guirec, and Quémeau. You can amuse yourself by touring the places they are presumed to have landed, but these do not necessarily present good anchoring points: for their boats, it is said, were made of stone and for them it was a one-way trip.

A method

You are not about to draft a new sailing guide to the region with the help of all these documents, since these already exist. In a far more personal way, you will be working step by step to discover the 'profile' of the future cruise, its pace and its atmosphere. Put otherwise: what are we to deduce, for our own purposes, from a study of such aspects as:
– the local meteorological conditions;
– the sea in all its states;
– the characteristics of tide and current in one place and another;
– the shape of the coast;
– the marker buoys, ports and places of shelter?

Meteorological conditions

You should of course reread the chapter on meteorology in the *Instructions Nautiques*. To have a detailed idea of the weather conditions in northern Brittany, it is useful to look at the table of statistics of observations made at the weather station at Bréhat. And since we know southern Brittany, we can compare this table with that of the weather station at Talut – two pages further on – for the month of July, for example. Without being able to call it a different climate, we can see that in northern Brittany:
– the temperature is a bit cooler, about an extra sweater's worth;
– the sky is clouded over more often, and it rains a little more;
– there are 3 misty days on average, instead of 2 in southern Brittany (if you are interested enough to consult the intervening table, relating to the weather station at Créac'h, you will see that Ushant is an infamous mist trap: 9 days in July. This means you run the risk of coming across more mist by going to the west of the area than by going to the east);

WEATHER STATION AT BRÉHAT ISLAND (ILE DE BRÉHAT) (48°51′25″N—03°00′20″W)
Altitude: 29m

Month	Pressure reduced to sea level at 1200 GMT (millibars)	Temperatures					Average relative humidity		Cloud covering				Precipitation	Fog
		Average		Extreme					N < 2/8		N > 6/8		Av. depth mm	Av. no of days (6)	Av. no of days (7)
		°C (1)	min. °C (2)	max. °C (3)	min. °C (4)	max. °C (5)	at 06 %	at 12 %	at 06 %	at 12 %	at 06 %	at 12 %			
January	1,016.1	7.2	5.4	9.0	-9.5	17.5	87	83	16	7	56	65	68	19	1
February	1,015.1	7.0	5.0	9.0	-8.0	19.4	86	80	15	4	61	67	48	14	1
March	1,016.0	8.2	5.9	10.5	-3.0	20.8	88	79	18	16	56	58	43	13	3
April	1,017.9	9.9	7.4	12.4	-0.0	23.5	88	76	21	21	47	39	42	13	2
May	1,015.6	12.2	9.5	14.8	1.0	30.0	91	78	17	15	51	48	45	13	2
June	1,017.5	15.0	12.1	17.9	5.0	28.9	92	79	14	13	60	50	37	10	3
July	1,018.7	16.8	13.9	19.7	5.6	31.8	93	79	17	16	53	45	40	11	3

ÎLE DE BRÉHAT : FRÉQUENCE °/₀₀ DES OBSERVATIONS DE VENT
Année 1949 à 1970

Mois	Calme	1 à 10 nœuds								11 à 21 nœuds								22 à 33 nœuds								34 nœuds et au dessus							
		N	NE	E	SE	S	SW	W	NW	N	NE	E	SE	S	SW	W	NW	N	NE	E	SE	S	SW	W	NW	N	NE	E	SE	S	SW	W	NW
Janvier	28	20	27	30	58	98	130	36	19	29	38	48	44	44	103	62	29	11	25	18	4	3	27	34	20	1	4	0	0	0	1	4	3
Février	43	24	39	59	54	67	96	44	23	27	47	82	33	30	92	58	33	9	19	22	4	6	25	35	21	0	2	0	0	0	1	5	1
Mars	32	35	45	57	78	67	82	60	38	27	58	86	44	23	63	76	33	5	16	18	5	4	15	22	9	0	1	1	0	0.	0	1	0
Avril	41	40	71	63	54	45	73	65	56	34	78	56	20	14	57	96	43	6	20	10	1	1	8	25	20	0	0	0	0	0	0	1	2
Mai	46	48	68	74	59	60	87	85	65	17	55	52	11	18	64	85	55	0	16	8	0	0	4	16	5	0	0	0	0	0	0	1	0
Juin	61	62	89	73	46	34	96	125	82	9	32	39	6	9	46	120	43	0	1	2	0	1	2	17	3	0	0	0	0	0	0	0	0
Juillet	43	70	77	52	36	32	97	125	99	15	31	23	3	6	54	139	62	0	1	1	0	0	6	24	3	0	0	0	0	0	0	1	0

(*Instructions Nautiques* C2.)

– the frequency of winds is about the same: a clear predominance of westerlies (from SW to NW), but also a fair proportion of north-easterly winds at this time of the year. It is not unreasonable to think you could cross the whole basin with a following wind!

The state of the sea

There are two interesting notes in the *Instructions Nautiques*:
1. 'From the mouth of the Channel to the Cotentin, usually, the winds carrying towards the land from the west and SW sectors produce heavy seas along the English coast. The west, NW, north and NE winds cause comparatively high seas on the French coast.'

This means that all the winds against which you were well protected in southern Brittany (and particularly the roughest, the north-westerly) come at you full in the face, here.

In fact, this difference will not necessarily be unpleasant, at least as far as navigation is concerned, if you think of the close relation between seasickness and the chart table: in bad south-westerly weather, with reduced visibility, the sea will be calm and you can work in peace; in north-westerly weather, you might have a hellish sea, but good visibility, and so shorter periods at the chart table!

2. 'The waters from the mouth of the Channel to the Cotentin are characterised by short seas with fairly deep hollows which are caused by strong tidal currents which may be in opposition to the dominant wind direction twice a day.'

And, further on: 'For a wind of a given strength, when the directions of the wind and tide are opposed, the sea is heavier than it would be under the influence of the weather alone; in the opposite case, it would be lighter.'

This means that every day, however little wind there is, you have to expect alternating rough and smooth seas. At first sight, it seems wise to take account of this when choosing mealtimes. Secondly, if there are passages which are a little tricky to pull off, you will do well to be organised so as to face them when the wind and the current are in the same direction. Which is easy enough to say! And no doubt easy enough to do when you are heading eastwards, with the dominant west winds. But in the other direction? Is it possible to make headway against the wind and the current? That is the essential question, and it is time to examine this infamous current more closely.

The tide and the current

What do you find in the *Instructions Nautiques* or Stanfords' or the Admiralty's tidal stream atlas?

The tide-wave comes in from the Atlantic, enters the Channel by a north-easterly route and crosses it in 7 hours. The tide is semi-diurnal, which means that the tidal current pulls for 6 hours in one direction, on average, and 6 hours in the other (but there are strong inequalities in certain spots, as is clearly shown in the table of French coastal tides). The tidal range is considerable and increases as you progress towards the east: on average, 7.7m in spring tides at Morlaix, 8.8m at the Héaux-de-Bréhat, 10.8m at Saint-Malo.

What is the strength of the current? From 1.5 to 4kn in the middle of the Channel. And near land? You only need to look through the paragraph on tides and currents, in each chapter on our

Ports	Marée de vive-eau cœfficient 95					Marée de morte-eau cœfficient 45					Marnage cœfficient 120
	Heures (T. U.)		Montée	Baissée	Marnage	Heures (T. U.)		Montée	Baissée	Marnage	
	P. M.	B. M.				P. M.	B. M.				
Dunkerque....................	12 h 51 mn	7 h 42 mn	5 h 21 mn	6 h 59 mn	5,2 m	6 h 40 mn	13 h 08 mn	5 h 48 mn	6 h 53 mn	3,4 m	5,9 m
Calais.........................	12 h 28 mn	7 h 21 mn	5 h 09 mn	7 h 10 mn	6,3 m	6 h 06 mn	12 h 49 mn	5 h 38 mn	7 h 01 mn	3,9 m	7,0 m
Boulogne.....................	12 h 14 mn	7 h 13 mn	5 h 03 Lın	7 h 17 mn	8,0 m	5 h 40 mn	12 h 32 mn	5 h 35 mn	7 h 05 mn	4,7 m	9,3 m
Dieppe........................	11 h 52 mn	6 h 34 mn	5 h 25 mn	6 h 55 mn	8,5 m	5 h 18 mn	11 h 46 mn	5 h 46 mn	6 h 54 mn	4,7 m	9,8 m
Fécamp.......................	11 h 30 mn	5 h 53 mn	5 h 44 mn	6 h 36 mn	7,2 m	4 h 58 mn	11 h 10 mn	6 h 06 mn	6 h 34 mn	4,0 m	8,1 m
Le Havre.....................	11 h 03 mn	5 h 44 mn	5 h 33 mn	6 h 46 mn	6,6 m	4 h 25 mn	10 h 50 mn	5 h 57 mn	6 h 43 mn	3,7 m	7,9 m
Cherbourg...................	8 h 51 mn	3 h 24 mn	5 h 37 mn	6 h 43 mn	5,2 m	2 h 26 mn	9 h 01 mn	5 h 48 mn	6 h 53 mn	2,5 m	6,5 m
Saint-Malo..................	7 h 05 mn	1 h 56 mn	5 h 21 mn	6 h 58 mn	10,8 m	0 h 20 mn	6 h 49 mn	5 h 48 mn	6 h 53 mn	4,9 m	13,2 m
Les Héaux-de-Bréhat............	6 h 50 mn	0 h 43 mn	6 h 14 mn	6 h 09 mn	8,8 m	0 h 17 mn	6 h 27 mn	6 h 06 mn	6 h 28 mn	4,2 m	11,2 m
Morlaix.......................	6 h 06 mn	0 h 14 mn	6 h 03 mn	6 h 21 mn	7,7 m	23 h 30 mn	5 h 31 mn	6 h 12 mn	6 h 20 mn	3,6 m	9,6 m
Brest..........................	4 h 52 mn	23 h 00 mn	5 h 59 mn	6 h 22 mn	6,1 m	22 h 33 mn	4 h 41 mn	6 h 13 mn	6 h 26 mn	2,9 m	7,7 m
Port-Louis....................	4 h 28 mn	22 h 33 mn	5 h 59 mn	6 h 22 mn	4,4 m	22 h 19 mn	4 h 20 mn	6 h 27 mn	6 h 10 mn	2,1 m	5,6 m
Saint-Nazaire.................	4 h 30 mn	23 h 13 mn	5 h 16 mn	7 h 04 mn	4,9 m	22 h 59 mn	4 h 39 mn	6 h 28 mn	6 h 06 mn	2,5 m	6,0 m
La Rochelle-Pallice.............	4 h 17 mn	22 h 36 mn	5 h 55 mn	6 h 25 mn	5,0 m	23 h 12 mn	4 h 07 mn	7 h 00 mn	5 h 32 mn	2,3 m	6,6 m
Cordouan.....................	4 h 37 mn	22 h 25 mn	6 h 25 mn	5 h 59 mn	4,3 m	22 h 37 mn	4 h 09 mn	6 h 36 mn	5 h 55 mn	2,0 m	5,5 m
Pointe de Grave................	4 h 54 mn	22 h 49 mn	6 h 07 mn	6 h 13 mn	4,4 m	23 h 00 mn	4 h 23 mn	6 h 31 mn	5 h 46 mn	2,2 m	5,5 m
Boucau........................	4 h 24 mn	22 h 18 mn	6 h 19 mn	6 h 04 mn	3,5 m	22 h 25 mn	4 h 06 mn	6 h 31 mn	6 h 02 mn	1,8 m	4,3 m
Socoa.........................	4 h 22 mn	22 h 17 mn	6 h 16 mn	6 h 07 mn	3,8 m	22 h 29 mn	4 h 15 mn	6 h 26 mn	6 h 07 mn	1,9 m	4,9 m

Extracted from the 'Tableau des marées du littoral français' (Table of French coastal tides) (*Instructions Nautiques* C2).

basin, to learn that it is 2, 3, or 4kn, depending where you are. On a small boat you will not be able to fight against currents like these. A boat which would normally make progress against the wind at 3 nautical miles per hour, will be standing still in the face of a current of 3kn. On the other hand, with the current behind, you will progress at 6 nautical miles an hour into the wind. With current and wind behind, you will be flying! This is a very simple thing to note, but it will have its effect on the pace of the cruise: in this region, either you do not advance at all, or you go very quickly. With a Mousquetaire, it is not unrealistic to imagine progressing at 10 nautical miles an hour, with the wind and the current to carry you.

But this remark implies another, less simple one: for example, if the Mousquetaire in question sets off from Primel at low tide and progresses eastwards at an average 9 nautical miles an hour, it might find itself at Erquy at the end of the flood tide, having travelled 63 nautical miles … There is in fact 1 hour's difference between high tide at Primal and high tide at Erquy. Thus the boat will have had the advantage of the tidal current for 7 hours. But for the return leg, if you imagine that it leaves Erquy at high tide in the same excellent conditions of carrying wind and current, and thus at the same speed, our Mousquetaire will scarcely get beyond Ploumanach before the end of the ebb tide: heading into the flood tide, in effect, it will only benefit from the favourable current for a little over 5 hours.

Taking account of the direction of the dominant winds, a clear conclusion is drawn from this: in this area it is much easier to progress eastwards than westwards, easier to dig yourself in than to dig yourself out, as they say. It is one of the principal factors to take into account when organising the cruise!

But there again, these are only general comments about the current. You will have to go over the documents in detail to judge the nuances of its action. Then you will see that it behaves in an infinite variety of ways, depending on the shape of the coast. The current can have completely different characteristics in places which are very close to each other: on the flood tide, for example, it pulls to the SW in the mouth of the Trieux, and ENE at le Ferlas, 2 nautical miles from there (not to mention the counter-currents!). In one place, it may always run in the same direction, in the flood tide and in the ebb tide. In another, the ebb tide may not follow the same channels as the flood tide. It is not that easy at all!

The coast

Now, examining the map, we will look at the kind of coastline beyond the current. You will have to study its general orientation and its nature, the different parts of it and then, in more detail, the zones to be avoided, the tricky passages and the sheltered zones.

To follow this analysis, see fold-out section 4 at the end of the book.

General orientation

From l'Aberwrac'h to the bay of Mont-Saint-Michel, the coast follows a straight line, facing north; more or less parallel, then, to the dominant winds.

All the same, the coast does not face exactly the same way on either side of the projection formed by the Héaux-de-Bréhat, more or less in the middle of the basin. The west side is fully exposed to the NW winds, the 'hard' winds; it will also probably suffer the effects of the Atlantic swell. The east side is undoubtedly more sheltered; in the bay of Saint-Brieuc in particular, the sea will be calmer in a NW wind.

Character

This is a very indented coast, where several rivers meet the sea (it is a coast of rias). So you can imagine that there will be many places of shelter, although, according to the map, a good number of river mouths are dry at low tide.

| Flood tide | Counter-current to the flood tide | Ebb tide | Counter-current to the ebb tide |

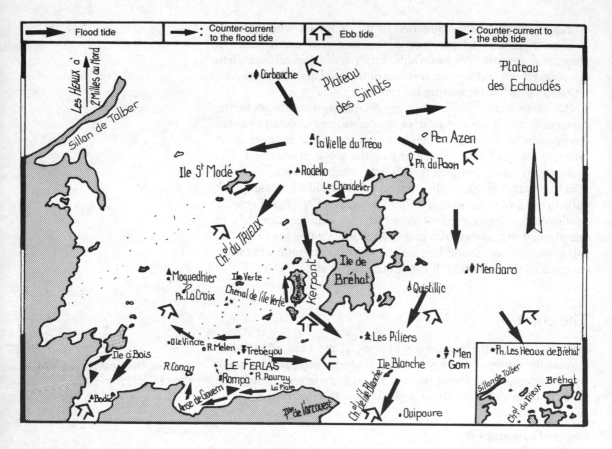

Currents and counter-currents in the Bréhat archipelago. (Extracted from *Glénans*.)

Looking more closely, you can see that this coast is practically bursting with 'hazards' from one end to the other. But think: these hazards certainly present difficulties for navigation, but often they must also offer a certain amount of protection against the open sea. Moreover, given the size of the tidal range, you will be sailing in an ever-changing landscape!

Different sections

Besides the two major areas separated by the Héaux-de-Bréhat, can you pick out any sub-sections, that is, any parts of the coast which have their own character? From east to west you find:
– from l'Aberwrac'h to the Ile de Batz, a coastline which seems to have no ports and few marker buoys;
– two bays separated by a short zone which has no places of shelter: the deep bay of Morlaix which is dotted with islands; and the bay of Lannion which is open to the NW, which looks as if it may be

protected by the Méloine and Triagoz plateaux (but a glance at the documents proves there is no real protection);
– from Trebeurden to Perros-Guirec, a very indented projection (this is the famous 'pink granite coast'), protected by the Triagoz and the Sept-Iles;
– from Port-Blanc to the Héaux, a short, unprotected zone; and the mouth of the Tréguier river;
– then the Bréhat archipelago and the Trieux river, a section which looks very complicated;
– the great bay of Saint-Brieuc, from Paimpol to Cape Fréhel, with a great sandy stretch;
– finally, another very indented zone, with deep bays, and the river Rance, before you reach Saint-Malo.

Zones to avoid

You should certainly avoid the whole section of the coast which

Did you say a 'changing landscape' ? At low tide, the channel is dry. At high spring tide, you disembark at the foot of the pyramid.

stretches from l'Aberwrac'h to the Ile de Batz. Violent currents, hazards from one end to the other, difficulties in identifying the seamarks with any certainty (all the bell-towers of Léon look alike!), no proper places of shelter: the question is settled on a single page in the *Instructions Nautiques*.

The bay of Mont-Saint-Michel, which is not well mapped and increasingly blocked up with sands, is hardly navigable either.

Tricky passages

Without doubt, these are all the places where the current runs fastest:

– points: north of the island of Batz, and the Sept-Iles, Héaux-de-Bréhat, the north coast of Bréhat, Cape Fréhel. You can avoid some of these passages: the islands all have a landward channel. Others are 'inevitable': the Héaux and Cape Fréhel. The *Cruising Association Handbook* says, coyly, 'stream runs fast', or 'fair-weather open anchorage'. But then, for southern Brittany, the *Instructions Nautiques* only make discreet allusions to the difficulties at la Teignouse, where you can remember having learnt a lesson more than once …

– tight passages: this time, the *Instructions Nautiques* are very clear, regarding the passage between the Sept-Iles and the coast: 'The sea is very rough there when the current is running against the wind';

– sudden changes in the depth of water: with a certain combination of the current and the wind, this is often hell. It is likely to happen NE of Bréhat, on the Horaine and Echaudés side.

Very sheltered zones

These are the zones where you can continue to sail if there is bad weather beyond them. These zones have to be easily accessible, and they should be sufficiently large and varied. So they will be the deep bays and rivers. What is there, from west to east?

– the bay of Morlaix: certainly full of potential;

– the Lannion river: surely not. The *Cruising Association Handbook* talks of breaking seas preventing entry, and says that the channel is 'narrow and tortuous';

– on the other hand, the Trieux river and the whole of the Bréhat archipelago seem to be an ideal spot, and abundantly varied;

– the Rance, finally, near Saint-Malo: you should be able to get a long way up it, and even run away to something better by way of the canals to southern Brittany, if it really is no good up here!

All you have to do now is to think of the ports of call.

Ports and shelters

Do you really need to study the marker buoys? A quick look at the documents is enough to tell you that the marking is perfect. Similarly, at the first glance, you can see there are several ports. But the great novelty compared with southern Brittany is that a good number of these ports are not 'open all hours', far from it.

So you will have a bit of a job to find:
– the ports which are accessible at any time of the tide (or which have a good waiting anchorage);
– the ports which are only accessible at certain times;
– the ports which are difficult of access because of the current or the wind. This problem can apply equally to the ports in the preceding categories.

During this exercise, you may make a certain number of observations:
– it is not necessarily the biggest ports which are accessible all the time. Paimpol is not; but nearby Pors-Even and Port-Clos are. Roscoff is dry at low tide whereas, at the other side of the bay of Morlaix, there is always water at Primel;
– certain ports, with flood-tide basins, are not only impossible to enter some of the time: you may not be able to get out of them either. Perros-Guirec and Binic are sometimes closed for three days in a row because of the neap tide. What a trap!
– No doubt it is not easy to sail up the rivers against the wind and the current;
– depending on the direction of the winds, certain ports 'open', others 'close'. In the bay of Saint-Brieuc, in a strong north-westerly wind, it is inadvisable to try Dahouet and Erquy, but Binic and Saint-Quay-Portrieux are welcoming. In a north-easterly wind, the reverse is true. Note that it is a good idea, moreover, to examine the whole coast with the hypothesis of a north-easterly wind: many perspectives change!

An important question: in the event of bad weather, are there ports of refuge for all eventualities? This time, you will have to make a vigorous effort to imagine all the different situations. Here is one example: you leave Saint-Malo at high tide to make for Bréhat, with a fairly fresh south-westerly wind which gradually turns to the west, then gathers strength in the north-west; at the mouth of the bay of Saint-Brieuc, the sea is very rough and it becomes practically impossible to make any headway. What are you going to do? It is low tide, all the ports in the bay of Saint-Brieuc are closed. Will you have to go and look for somewhere to

The crew in question?

shelter over by Saint-Quay, and will you be able to 'hold tight' in front of the port, waiting for it to open? Is it not better to turn round and go back to Saint-Malo on the flood tide, even if it is a long way? It seems that, in this region, the best place of refuge is not necessarily the closest port, and you have to be able to face up to rough weather, in order to reach your place of refuge.

Gradually, when you go into the details, many possibilities appear, besides the official ports and places of shelter. There are doubtless a multitude of 'occasional' anchoring points to be found, where you can spend the night in fair weather, or wait for the current to change, or for a port to open. It is hard to check them all out in advance: there are some things that you can only find out when you have the landscape before your eyes ...

The crew in question

During this study we have made together, the crew – let's say there are five of us – has discovered a whole host of reasons for going to northern Brittany. There are (for example!):
– the woman who wants to see Roscoff at all costs, for the memory of Tristan Corbière and his cutter; and Tréguier, for the sake of Ernest Renan; and who would certainly go as far as the tomb of Chateaubriand on the Grand-Bé at Saint-Malo;
– the passionate ornithologist who dreams of sailing by the island of Rouzic to see gannets, fulmars and puffins up close; and who has spotted in a guide that, 7km from Binic, there is a chapel (ask for the keys at the house next door), where every year a pilgrimage is held, in which the bird-catchers take part;
– the Orkneys fanatic, who has spotted a host of particularly interesting hazards; he really hopes to come upon a 'harsh sea' as promised by the *Instructions Nautiques*, between the Sept-Iles and the coast, a foretaste of the Pentland Firth where, as his bedside reading book tells him, 'when the swell is against the current, a sea rises which is difficult to imagine if you have never seen it';
– the man who dreams of the Ionian Islands but, on balance, prefers to get drenched with his friends rather than sunbathe on his own. He consoles himself with having read somewhere that the climate of Bréhat 'is remarkable for its mildness; aloes, palm trees, mimosas and fig trees grow well there, as well as all the southern flowers';
– and there is the woman who wants 'to go to Dahouet by sea' because she has a friend there who never stops boasting to her of the approach to this little port which is totally invisible from the open sea. And you will have to hurry before Dahouet is transformed into

a marina!

Is all this just fanciful? It is actually like this that plans to go cruising are usually born and start to take shape. But this is only a beginning: beyond the individual wishes, of course, there need to be common goals. For this, the crew will have to ask about its own style of sailing, its capabilities, the organisation which needs doing. Here you are getting into an area where objective factors are not the only things at issue, and where it is difficult to give general rules. Let's try, all the same, to track the thoughts of our crew.

What pace should you adopt ?

Without a doubt, you are about to try something harder than southern Brittany: this is what you wanted. The area seems pretty, and it will be windy: all the better. You risk getting shaken about from time to time: so what? But the great unknown, of course, is the infamous current you cannot fight against. What will be your attitude towards it?

Most of the cruising rhythms we have described, above, would be appropriate. If you like long stretches at sea, it is quite possible, as we have seen, to go a long way in a single stage. You can also make very short stages, without going far offshore, playing with the current among the rocks. If you have assigned yourself a precise goal, you can make for it while the current is favourable, seek shelter when it changes and set off once more when it turns again …

All the same, this last option is not very satisfactory: it amounts to many hours of lost sailing time, even if you take advantage of this time to explore the land. To a certain extent, you are refusing to play the game, trying to have an ordinary cruise in an extraordinary region. Are you not running the risk of missing out on the best part?

As soon as you think about sailing in these waters, it is probably best to decide that the current is not a disadvantage. And what if you were to decide, once and for all, that there is no such thing as a contrary current? All your perspectives would be changed!

Clearly, this means that you are going to be spending your time criss-crossing the bay from one side to the other: the idea of a cruising schedule will take a knocking. However, it is enough to ponder over the map a while: with this attitude, you are not stopped from going wherever you want to go, and no doubt you can do much more besides.

Another objection: with all these comings and goings we will be passing the same spot time and time again. But is this really the case? Let's assume that we have already done enough sailing to

An example of a route in northern Brittany

You have decided to go to Saint-Malo. You leave Tréguier, for example, in the morning at the beginning of the ebb tide. You are out at sea at mid-tide; it is still possible to go to Port-Blanc or to Perros. You set off back for Binic with the flood tide. The next morning you can go sailing round the Bréhat archipelago, and set off again from there at low tide to reach Saint-Malo.

Note that on a fortnight's cruise, it seems wise to go to Saint-Malo during the first week: given the direction of the dominant winds, you may need some time for getting back.

know that at sea, you never pass the same spot twice. Because the wind and sea conditions change; because your mood itself changes (you are a different person after several days at sea); because the second time you pass by, you are sure to discover something you had not noticed until then; and because the hundredth time you pass by you are so happy to recognise 'your' landscape. It is true that you end up getting to love your seamarks, like you did the tower of Fort-Cigogne, or the Saint-Michel tumulus. Here, it will perhaps be the 'slender shaft' of Plougrescant church spire or the 'bell-tower shaped like a peaked cap' at Étables-sur-Mer. There will be a hint of conspiracy in the glance you give them. There we are, in the end: are we discerning, or are we not ? That is the only real question.

Are you 'capable'?

Don't let's get carried away. This landscape is demanding, too:
• The tide waits for no one: you can quickly lose a day's sailing on account of a few minutes' delay in getting up. Are you capable of imposing a modicum of discipline on yourselves as far as time tables are concerned?
• Not all ports are accessible when you would like them to be. Are you capable of staying at sea, if need be, in conditions which may be difficult? If everyone has seasickness, what are you going to do?
• As regards navigation, you can see that you will have to be fairly strict. Some approximate manoeuvres which are acceptable in southern Brittany are not so here, without great risk. Do you have the necessary ability?
    In all, it seems necessary for at least two or three members of the crew to be sturdy and competent. One alone will not be able to deal with everything at once, to steer, to navigate and take a reef.
    However, this is not enough to guarantee that everything will go well. You will have to develop the analysis a little further: what really constitutes the competence of a crew? The fact that everybody is of a high technical standard guarantees nothing at all. (We might even be tempted to say that the opposite is true. Nothing can be more irritating, or more dangerous even, than a crewful of 'little captains', where everyone wants to impose their own point of view. In a crew whose technical level is varied, the ambience is much richer, and knowledge and ignorance can learn things from each other!) In the end, a competent crew is one whose members have diverse and complementary qualities. Nobody knows how to do everything, but one person can make a neat, precise job of the navigation, another can steer marvellously in a close spot; one man

knows no seasickness and at the same time (what luck!) loves cooking; another woman is a DIY freak at heart, and gifted in seamanship; this man derives his pleasure from attending to little practical tasks, he has a wonderful fetish for tidying; and this woman has the strange ability to fall asleep immediately at any time of day, which means she can stay up all night if necessary; this man is a frustrated quartermaster, and this other one is blessed with perfect vision; this woman has the gift of calming the atmosphere with a simple joke when things are not going well ... With such a range, nothing is going to stop you.

Who will be the captain?

'In a storm, the crew should be more afraid of the boss than of the sea,' an old fishing captain once said, when there was still a sane idea of 'group dynamics'. For an amateur crew, the atmosphere on board should, theoretically, be different (though this might not always be the case!). It is all the more likely to be so if the crew is made up of friends who are used to sailing together, as in the present case. However, even here, it is useful to choose a captain: this is an essential commodity. You cannot imagine a pleasant life on board without a certain coherence, co-ordinating all the different issues: manoeuvring, navigation, maintenance of the boat, pace of life; without a certain overall view. How rare it is for five 'overall views' to match perfectly, and how long and tedious it can be to reach agreement, even if it is only one person who is sticking to their guns.

More subtly, it is good for someone to have a clear sense of the level of competence of the crew, throughout the cruise. It is important, since the schedule will have to be adapted to suit this. This level of competence is always changing: it increases if the group works well together, which may allow you to carry out a more ambitious programme than the one you planned; it may also diminish, with tiredness, and even fall by dramatic proportions if disagreement sets in. It is good for someone to be able to stand back and keep an eye out for trouble.

If you always sail together, you can simply change the captain from one cruise to the next. For this cruise, for example, why not choose the woman who has a friend at Dahouet? This friend in Dahouet could then become the sixth member of the crew, who will take part in the cruise in a very special way, without leaving dry land: that is to say, he will be the shore-based contact – your guardian angel.

Who will be the shore-based contact?

The friend in Dahouet will be a perfect shore-based contact:

– if he has already sailed in northern Brittany himself, and knows the problems well;
– if he knows how to judge the nuances in the meteorological situation sensibly;
– and above all, if he knows the captain well.

Experience is the essential thing: he will have to be able to imagine the captain's reactions in a given circumstance, to be able to interpret a silence or a delay correctly, if need be. Let's go further, at the risk of being indiscreet: it is desirable for the relations between the captain and the shore-based contact to be like a kind of complicity, so they can understand each other without having to spell things out. The ideal thing is for them to have sailed together: in this way, the contact knows what kind of 'dream' the captain is pursuing when he goes to sea, they can the see unconscious nuances in the clear intentions stated to them! People's lives can depend on this kind of subtlety and level of understanding.

Of course, we are talking of the ideal contact here. If the friend in Dahouet does not have all these qualities and if you cannot find anyone on the spot who is better suited for the job, you can quite well choose another friend who lives at, let's say, Château-Chinon. Someone who is competent can fulfil this role even from far away. In any case, near or far, a good sailor or not such a good one, you have to have a contact.

The next important thing is to respect strict rules. The captain agrees to telephone at each port of call; they indicate their plans and fix, at least approximately, the time of the next rendezvous. The contact, for their part, really has to watch over the boat, and be on it in their thoughts ... And, of course, know how to alert the rescue services if it becomes necessary.

You will have to let them know the characteristics of the boat you are going to hire: type, name, registration number, the colour of the hull and sails, and the sail number. You will also have to give them the names and addresses of each member of the crew so that they can pass on messages, if necessary.

If the agreements made by the captain and the shore-based contact are carefully respected, this will certainly give you a basic guarantee of safety. The captain should check that the arrangements made are realistic, clearly understood and followed by all concerned.

Cruising canvas

A canvas is a thick cloth sheet of fairly tightly woven threads, which is used as a base for needlework …

Here, the threads of the canvas are of different kinds: they are the attitudes you adopt depending on the competence of the crew and the character of the region, and the pace of life you want to have; they have to do with elementary safety regulations, personal fetishes, and the demands associated with hiring a boat. You have to weave them carefully together.

Directional threads

1. You decide that sailing will take place principally by day. But, given the daily discrepancy in the tides, it is highly probable that you will also be sailing at night, so as not to clock up too many wasted hours in the port: if for any reason, you cannot leave Perros at full tide at 1000, you are not going to wait for 24 hours before setting off! All the same, you should not sail by night in difficult conditions; for example, 'forcing your way through a passage' at night is out of the question.
2. You do not have to set up a watch for the full duration of the cruise, but this may become necessary; you will have to be able to plan ahead for this, and the captain will have to be able to send people to bed early!
3. You will not head into bad weather on purpose: this is ridiculous on a coastal cruise, where you are always close to the shore. If bad weather arrives, you head for shelter, and that's it.
4. Taking account of tidal problems, you will have to plan for a fairly large degree of independence (this consideration will also influence your choice of boat). You should always have things to eat and drink for 2 or 3 days, for you will not always be putting in at places which are well-off for shops – nor at times when the shops are open.
5. We have a principle which we hold dear: at the beginning of the cruise, if you set off with a following wind, you will always have the advantage of the ground gained by this. There are people who imagine that, setting off with a headwind, they will necessarily have a following wind for the return leg. Experience proves, alas, that there is no justice with the wind.
6. There is one last requirement: you must be to windward of your port of destination at least 2 days before the end of the cruise, so as to be sure of returning the boat on time.

There is nothing now other than to define the edges of the canvas, that is, the 'navigational perimeter', and to choose the port of departure. Then we can begin embroidering.

Limits

Studying the zone, you have seen what the limits of the basin are: in the west, there are no places of shelter along the coast from the island of Batz to l'Aberwrac'h; in the east, you should not venture close to the Cotentin coast, which the *Notices to Mariners* describes in quite dramatic terms.

So the perimeter extends, in principle, from Roscoff to Saint-Malo. But these are not absolute limits. Perhaps you will not go as far, perhaps you will go further, depending on the circumstances and the condition of the crew.

If you find yourself at Roscoff with east winds forecast for 24 hours, why not try a quick hop to l'Aberwrac'h, or even to Ushant if the weather is clear and fine? Likewise, if you are at Saint-Malo and the crew is working at full capacity, why not take advantage of a shallow depression to do a tour of the Channel Islands, with a SW wind for the outward leg, and a NW one for the return trip? But in the end, we are not lured by the myth of the Channel Islands, nor that of Ushant: let's say that these are not considered to be normal stages; but if the opportunity presents itself, you need not systematically turn it down.

Choosing the port of departure

Bearing in mind the principles we stated:
– if you want to set off with a following wind, it is better not to choose Saint-Malo …
– if you want to be within wind of the port 2 days before the end of the cruise, it is better not to choose Roscoff.

Clearly, the ideal thing is to choose a port situated approximately in the middle of the basin. You have a choice between Perros-Guirec, Tréguier, Lézardrieux and Paimpol.

Of course, you will have to check that you can hire a boat in one or another of these ports, but check, too, that you will find the things you need to eat and drink there; that it will be easy to transport your equipment on board; and, finally, that you will be able to get back in easily at the end of your first sea trials, to load up additional equipment, if necessary.

Why stop?

First, because life is like that, you set off, you stop, you set off again. You can't always be on the road, can you? And then, for thousands of other, more concrete reasons. The first is that a port opens out its arms to you, it is made for you to stop in.

Of course, there are all the practical and technical reasons: you will have to stock up on food and water, and so on. But this is not a problem, you can do all this at the beginning, if need be. You can also get fed up of being on a smelly, dirty boat, and want to do a big spring clean in the calm of the port. I won't even talk about repairs because there is nothing to say: when something isn't working, it isn't working. And you have to stop.

Good, so I've come to the real reasons. The Human Factor and the Aesthetic Factor, as they say. Dead important, these guys.

You are not there to get shouted at (that old familiar tune). You are there to see the place. The land seen from the sea is not the same at all as the land seen from the land! It's the other side of the coin. And, in this case, the flip side is often much more exciting than the front. As for me, I cannot express it properly, but it is always a thrill. No port is the same as another, but they are all equally attractive. And then, that great fraternity of little boats at anchor. Aah!

That deals with the aesthetics and all that, but as we are not all aesthetes, I'll bring out my second set of arguments.

A port of call means new places, and new changes of place, talking with other people, idling around unknown towns, visiting nice little eating-places, talking in little smoky cafés, clinging for a moment to the illusion of a more sociable, or less solitary, or less artificial life; whatever you like: going somewhere at last.

That goes for the human side, but since we are not all human (good grief, some captains are animals!), I will bring out my third set of arguments.

And I hope I will be able to do this all right, because FORM is sacred.

Well then, let's take it that there is a bit of wind and that, in fact, and as if by chance, you have been setting off into a headwind for a fortnight … I don't need to spell it out, do I?

A listing boat, heavy seas, vinaigrette everywhere, smelly socks, drunks, those who've been throwing up and those who've been thrown up on, the cold, the wind, the rain, the lack of sleep, the lack of living space, the dirt, the mess … I want to go home to my mum!!! and so on … If all this doesn't stop, I'LL FREAK OUT. It's so good to stop from time to time. And I haven't even said anything about the nervous tension.

Because living for a while in a box with six or seven other people is stressful, even if they're good sorts, you have to take a break. Especially when you don't know them from Adam or Eve!

Someone's little fetishes, someone else's little fetishes, everyone's sudden changes of mood, those who aren't getting on with each other, and those who are getting on too well with each other, those who like tea and those who like milk, those who smoke and those who drink, those who like Anne Sylvestre, and those who prefer candyfloss. Those who are always saying the same thing and those who say nothing at all. The girl who is losing the feathers from her sleeping bag, oh, her! and the guy who scratches himself all the time …

AT SEA, GIVE ME SOME SPACE OR I'LL HIT SOMETHING!

Either you blow up or you stop somewhere. Then, how marvellous for a few hours to feel that you are FREE AT LAST, ALONE AT LAST. And then, your mates, they're not at all the same on land as at sea. There are things you don't notice at all on the old tub and which leap out at you on the grass!

So, you have to get some air: it does nobody any harm. It would even do everybody good. And everything is much better afterwards. That said, and since the reply to the first question has been a bit long, let's be more brief for the rest.

• If you stop, you should get off, or it's not worth doing. You are not a barnacle.
• On land, you should go on visits, you should move about. And you can do anything, a tour of the museums and a tour of the cake-shops.
• You can have a chat if you are in the mood for chattering.
• You can go with each other or go alone. As you like, but most of the time, you are so happy to be free that you won't be parted from each other.
• Why do you decide to set off again? Well, that's what you're there for, isn't it? There aren't any arrivals if there's no departure!

(Extracted from a survey on 'L'escale en croisière' (Ports of call on a cruise), which appeared in the review *Glénans*.)

In the lock at Paimpol.

You will easily be able to stock up fully with food and drink at Perros and Paimpol, no doubt, but you cannot get back into these ports at all times. At Lézardrieux, there is no doubt you can get back in, but stocking up on food risks being rather basic. Tréguier is no doubt a pleasant town, but the river mouth is a tricky spot, certainly ill advised for the preliminary tests. You will probably have to choose between Perros and Paimpol.

Hiring a boat

Let's move on to practical problems now. With a touching accord, the crew has seen fit for the captain to deal with the 'formalities' of hiring: to read through the contracts carefully, to study all the clauses, to deal with the issue of the deposit, etc.

When you start on these formalities, you can see that if hiring offers many advantages (maximum freedom, minimum worries) it is not without its problems, all the same. First observation: it would have been far better, if it had been possible, to sail in June rather than in July: the rates are much lower, there is a wider range of choice (and the days are longer!). In any case, to be sure of having a boat in July, you will really have to get on with it early.

The second disadvantage is that unless you live on the spot, or close by, you do not know the exact condition of the boat you are being offered. It is not that you want a brand new boat (on the contrary, on a boat which has sailed a bit, everything which was going to break will have already broken!), but in the end, you want to know what it is like.

In fact, the only real problem is being able to start up a detailed dialogue with the hirer. This is hardly ever done, and it is a pity. If you know exactly what you want, not only in the way of a boat, but also in the way of the boat's on-board equipment, and if you are able to explain why you want it, it is very rare not to manage to come to an agreement.

Choosing a boat

In the first place, you will have to know what kind of boat is suitable for this kind of cruise:

– a 'sea-going' boat, of course, that is to say, a sturdy boat, well-protected, and equipped with robust rigging; a strong boat, capable of making headway into the wind in fairly fresh weather (force 7 at least) without everything on board getting soaked beyond repair. A dry berth is undeniably a safety factor;
– a small-draughted boat, which takes the ground easily, since we have decided to enjoy all the nooks and crannies along the coast! A ballasted sailing dinghy should do the trick;
– what size of boat? It has to be able to guarantee the desired independence, on stages which will not necessarily stop at the end of the day. So it must be sufficiently large and well equipped for you to be able to cook at sea, to sail in good conditions and, above all, be able to rest properly: two or three members of the crew should be able to sleep while the others are on watch.

At the same time, it should not be too big, for various reasons. First, the bigger it is, the more expensive it will be. And if it is too big, you will not be able to get into the anchorages you would like to. If it always needs all the crew to be at work, you will not be able to plan very long stages …

You also have to know if you are willing to make compromises on the question of comfort. Five of you can very comfortably live on a boat less than 8m in length, and headroom is not necessary unless arthritis has already exercised its ravages on you.

Sunrise 34.

Sunlight.

Sunlight 30.

Coco.

And why not an unsinkable boat?

Required equipment

What category of navigation (see page 1021) would we choose for our programme? The 4th category lets you sail up to 20 nautical miles from a place of shelter, the 3rd category, up to 60 nautical miles. Measuring the distances on the map, you can see that the equipment for the 4th category is enough for reaching Jersey from Saint-Malo (with the Chauseys as a possible place of shelter on the way), which it is not possible to do from Paimpol.

There is a choice to be made. In any case, the regulation equipment in France differs little from one category to another. What is most important is to have a detailed knowledge of the quality of the equipment concerned. Sometimes, the hirer merely states that the boat contains the 'regulation equipment for the category'. In the UK there are no legal regulations, but you should be guided by those on page 1022. But you have to know more than this: ask for a detailed list, with descriptions. What kind of compass is it? Does the complete set of sails really contain a genoa, No 1 jib, No 2 jib and storm jib? Besides, as far as safety is concerned, the regulation equipment does not seem sufficient: before committing yourself to the contract, you want to reach an agreement on some basic points.

Anchors

The single anchor which is obligatory for boats less than 9m in length (10kg anchor, 8m of 8mm chain and a 14mm line, of a total length five times the length of the boat) is cutting it a bit fine. First, because there is only the one, and you might lose it. Second, because it runs the risk of being rather short when you have to anchor in places where there are 6–8m of water at low tide, or 15–20m at high tide. The solution lies in having on board what you need to make up a second anchor, or lengthen the first one; that is, another 10kg anchor, and a 100m warp with several metres of chain. A small watch-anchor and a light 100m rope would also be desirable, so you can anchor at sea in a flat calm, if need be.

Lifejackets

We think it is indispensable to have one-size lifejackets with integral harnesses: they are the only ones which provide the security we want.

(In fact, if we are going to continue to sail on hired boats, we will no doubt end up buying our own lifejackets: it will be safer. But if the lifejackets offered by the hirer are as good as or better than your own, there is no point weighing yourselves down!)

How to pull someone out of the sea

To be able to rig the horseshoe lifebelt and its lifebuoy light as indicated in a favourite book of ours (which is not pricey, for that matter) we would want to have a lifebelt equipped with a sea anchor, a fixed (not flashing) lifebuoy light, and a long line.

But does the boat have what you need to be able to pull someone back on board (a boarding ladder, a hoist, or a kicking strap to act as a hoist)?

The lifeboat

Can we get ourselves an unsinkable dinghy? If you do not have one, can you provide us with a class IV dinghy (even if we are sailing in the 4th category)? If we have to settle for a class V liferaft, will it be possible to see one inflated? If not would you tell us what model of raft it is, so we can see one at a dealer's?

The tender

If you cannot get hold of a class IV dinghy, you will have to have a tender. It must be sufficiently seaworthy (with a convenient gusset, and strong paddles) to allow three people to carry an anchor out in rough weather.

Of course, these various demands run the risk of incurring extra costs, and this is normal. But it is no doubt possible to economise on the motor: for what we want to do, it does not seem indispensable.

Preparations

While waiting to get a closer look at the boat, let's think about ourselves for a while. There are two crucial questions: what are we going to wear? What are we going to eat?

Sailing kit

At sea, you may certainly sport fancy gear. Unfortunately, this often leads you to take many unnecessary things and forget what is essential. The essential thing is to have what you need to protect yourself from the cold and wet, and sometimes also from the heat.

Clothing

The simplest thing, perhaps, is to plan to have two complete outfits:
– one resolutely cold-beating outfit: trousers, thick shirt, thick sweater, woollen socks, sensible underwear (it is worth knowing that, though modern textiles have many qualities, they also present serious disadvantages if you have to wear them wet for too long a time, such as in a lifeboat; only pure cotton, pure wool, or pure silk do not cause irritation, even when wet);
– another, lighter outfit: Terylene trousers or shorts, shirt, light pullover, nylon socks.

With these two outfits you can create a third one, if need be, for the really evil icy weather: the sweaters and the socks can be worn on top of each other very effectively, and with a good insulating jacket as well, gloves, if need be, and a hat or balaclava, you are kitted out for Spitzbergen.

All the same, the important thing is for you to be comfortable. Jeans, for example, however fashionable, are not really made for sailing in: they are too tight-fitting, you cannot put anything in the pockets, they take time to dry. A good old pair of cotton trousers is much more suitable.

Waterproofs

Your choice of waterproofs is important. There are waterproofs of all kinds: coats, one-piece combinations, jackets, trousers. On board a small cruising dinghy, it is the jacket and trousers combination which seems to offer the best solution.

The jacket, to be really waterproof, should have a double fastening system (for example buttons or a zipper, and a flap fastened by a Velcro strip); elasticated wrists; pockets (with a Velcro-fitted flap) which do not connect with the inside. All the same, there remains the serious problem of waterproofing at the neck: you need an absorbent collar. A towel will do the job perfectly. You should take several.

The trousers should come up high enough to be properly covered by the jacket; so you need trousers with braces, without flies or side openings.

Footwear

In summer, boots are hardly any use: they are clumsy, dirty, smelly ... Better to take light shoes with non-slip soles, tennis shoes or suchlike, or even those awful plastic sandals which have the

The sea-helmet.

advantage of never slipping, even on an oily slipway. Staying barefoot on the boat is ill-advised, in any case: you do not have so many toes that you can afford to lose them to the thousand obstacles which are lying in wait for them.

Indispensable accessories

– A knife, of course. A folding one (preferably!). And a really ordinary one. Who has never lost their knife?
– a watertight lamp, with new batteries and a spare bulb;
– a small first-aid box of your own to avoid unnecessary raids on the one on board: a few dressings, a bandage, cotton wool, antiseptic, alcohol, aspirins, whatever you use for seasickness …
– a toilet bag (even for the boys);
– a sleeping bag, of course; a swimsuit;
– a rigid case for glasses;
– ID papers;
– and, for the captain, an ALARM CLOCK.

Supplies

Some people, before they set off, plunge into philosophical works which deal with the problem of human relations. For our account, we will say soberly: when you eat well, you get on well.

So this is an issue not to be taken lightly: the question of stocking up on food at the beginning of the cruise should be approached with absolute seriousness, with all the crew present: First of all, you should know what people like, and what they hate. Then you will have to plan the menus: if you go shopping without clear ideas, you are opening the door to the worst kind of mistakes.

How can you get an idea of the number and the size of the meals you are going to want? At sea, it is not quite the same thing as on land: it is rare for people to make lavish meals while they are sailing but, since you are undertaking a fairly large amount of physical activity, you are almost always hungry. Given this, you will have to plan not 3, but more likely 5 or 6 meals: a copious breakfast, which is very important; a slice of sausage and a glass of wine, maybe, at 1000, which keeps up your good humour and keeps you going until midday; lunch, a more or less full one depending on the circumstances; tea-time snack (tea and biscuits, or back to the sausages if you are a country boy at heart); dinner, relaxed and abundant when you are at anchor; and then the night-time snack, if you are still sailing …

How should you organise all this? You know that, at sea, there is a direct relation between gastronomy and meteorology, and therefore there is a fundamental uncertainty, if not in the quality, at least in the quantity of foodstuffs to be taken. Of course, since you are on a coastal cruise, you can go shopping every day if you want to, but then you will hardly have any time for sailing. If you do not want to waste time, a convenient solution for a 2-week cruise, for example, lies in dividing up the time into three 'wedges' of 4 days. At the beginning, you plan the menus for the first two sections and you buy:
– everything you need for the first section: fresh produce and what may be called basic produce: vegetables, preserved foods, condiments, drinks of all kinds;
– the basic produce for the second section.

So, you are set up for all eventualities: if the weather is very good, all the produce for the first section will be eaten up, but the basic produce for the second section will help you to ward off starvation; if the weather is bad, there will be spares, and at the second stocking-up, you can make adjustments, according to the same principles, so as to have everything you need for the second section and the basic goods for the third. After this, in any case, you will be 'run in', and you will know exactly what to buy to keep you going until the final, slap-up meal.

With regard to what you should eat and drink, we think, simply, at the risk of offending the dieticians, that above all, cruising

---

Basic kit

Complete set of waterproofs
3 or 4 towels
Insulating jacket
Hat
2 sweaters (at least)
2 shirts
2 pairs of trousers
1 pair of shorts
Underwear
Handkerchiefs
Swimsuit
3 pairs of socks
Footwear
Pyjamas
Sleeping bag
Toilet bag
Personal first-aid kit
Knife
Waterproof lamp
Alarm clock for the captain

cooking is there to be enjoyed – in moderation. One person must keep a constant eye on how much food remains. And this is not necessarily a girl's job, no more than the cooking is, either. It is truly amazing what the boys show they can do.

(While we are here, let's go further: it is said that some of the old men in charge of the Glénans Sailing Centre, when they take stock of several decades of their career, mutter into their beards that, in the end, the boys are better at cooking and the girls are better at sailing the boats. This is an ideal discussion topic for the interminable night-watches or the late, smoky evenings.)

Storage

Here is the boat. First observation: it is far too small for you to be able to store all your equipment! And yet you will have to be able to manage it; everything must find a well-defined place, and not leave it unless it is to be used, and be put back there straightaway afterwards. This is extremely important for the mood of the cruise: when you store things well, you get on well.

Foodstuffs

It is always said that you should plan the storage of the food, and this is a perfectly respectable suggestion. But, in reality, it is often nothing but a pious wish. It is important for the supplies officer to supervise the food storage, at least, and for everyone to be there when the food is put away: a crew is also a collective memory …

The ideal thing is to find close to the galley, that is, near the stove, various shelves, cupboards and drawers, where you can put away 2 or 3 days' worth of food; a little storage space which you stock up again from other storage points. These are usually found underneath the bunks and in the hold. You should put in the hold (taking care to distribute the weight well) the things which will not be spoiled by water: bottles and tins. It is as well to take the labels off straightaway, before they come off in the water, and mark each tin so as to avoid opening the stew for breakfast.

For the rest, you will have to take account of two essential enemies: water, and the rolling of the boat.

With regard to the wet, you should note first of all that a shelf has the more chance of remaining dry, the further it is away from the hold and the cabin door; then (and this will remain in men's memory as the most useful product of the oil industry) there is the plastic bag. You should take several rolls of these. Note that they

will not really be effective unless they are wrapped over on themselves and secured with an elastic band.

What else do we know? That you shouldn't play with fire. Setting off on a cruise with two or three big boxes of matches is sheer madness. What you need is a large number of little boxes (at least twenty for a fortnight's cruise), divided into several batches, and kept in different places on the boat. Briefly, against the wet there is but one rallying cry: divide and rule!

And then there is rolling. The best of storage systems can prove catastrophic at sea if it has not been carefully thought out with respect to heel and counter-heel: soon the portside products join the starboard ones in the hold, and get mixed up with them there; the supplies officer loses his head, and the dry biscuits lose their adjective. Since you cannot swear that everything will be perfectly housed for the full fortnight, take certain precautions:

– avoid glass packaging (paraphrasing Jacques Prévert, we will say how terrible is the little thud of the jam pot shattering on the deck …);
– choose products with sturdy packaging. And when the packaging is sturdy, don't tinker with it. For example, avoid cutting the point off the top of your detergent bottles: a cruise will be marked for ever by the memory of the sweetish smell of washing-up liquid spilt in the hold.

Personal belongings

Here, there is only one enemy: the wet, and the same solution holds: divide things up as much as you can.

Clothing can be split into three sections:
– everyone's waterproofs and boots, if you have them, should be kept in a box outside the cabin;
– nightclothes: sleeping bag and pyjamas to be rolled in a plastic bag and stored at the end of the bunk;
– dry clothes in a plastic bag, the ideal thing being to have one bag per garment (or one garment per bag).

Note that clothes soaked in sea water will be difficult to dry like that, because the salt encrusted in them attracts damp. It is advisable to rinse them in fresh water as soon as you can. And, of course, those who don't like water will find an excuse here to have a shower fully dressed.

Taking on the boat

In the end, all these domestic issues are quite boring. We're really ready to go! And, although the most important thing still needs doing, that is, checking the boat and all its equipment, we really think that it is high time to go. After all, what is keeping us in the port? All we have to do is:
– do a shipboard inventory, accompanied by the hirer;
– check the rigging: send the best technician of the crew aloft to set about a detailed inspection, check that everything is well secured, that the pins are in good condition, and the halyards are not likely to get stuck between the casing and the sheave, etc;
– store your personal belongings away, since it is dangerous to get under way with an untidy boat.

But now let's go and get some fresh air! We'll set off. It is not even necessary to sort out all the food; you simply take everything you will need for 12 or 24 hours. For this is, of course, a false departure. You will be coming back. But you will really have to set off because, in the port, whether you like it or not, you are not yet 'really with it', you don't know where to start, you hesitate, you waste time, you think like a landlubber. Really taking charge of a boat happens at sea, when you are sailing. Only there will you wake up, will you find your sea legs again, will you be able to check properly how everything works, find out what is not working and what you still need. This is an outing which can last several hours, or a whole day, or even longer: it is certainly not a bad idea to spend the first night at anchor, near the port, if you really want to deal with the issue exhaustively.

Certain checks are particularly concerned with handling the boat, and others are for safety. But, really, everything is a safety issue on this first outing. The order you proceed in matters little, the essential thing is not to forget anything. Let's try.

• Before you set off, position an exercise book open upon the chart table, which you will use for noting down problems as they crop up.

• As you leave, set up sails appropriate for the weather. This is the time to agree on the layout of the halyards in the various cleats.

• Get under way using the sculling oar: it is never too early to check that the old motor is in working condition, that the oar is correct, and its rowlock too.

Under way

• When you are in clear water, get out the lifejackets. Everyone should examine thoroughly the one they have taken, check the end and the clasp, and get out their waterproof lamps (the only way to be sure that no one has forgotten theirs).

• You should clip yourselves on, to get used to the lifelines. Check that they are the proper length, and that they are correctly secured. At the same time, check the guard rails and the stanchions (in the port, everything always seems impeccable).

• Begin to make a systematic test of all the sails.

• Take all the reefs one after another, to be sure you can do this, and that there are enough reefing points.

• Try the various combinations of sails and observe how the boat moves at different speeds.

• Tack about with these different sets of sails. Clock up mistakes on purpose, to see with what degree of error the boat is able to tack.

• During these various trials, carry out exercises of pulling a man back out of the sea (with different sail settings, at different speeds). Check the equipment and how to use it:

– how to use the lifebuoy light / line / horseshoe lifebelt equipment;
– how to use the hoist to heave the person back on board.

• Drop anchor. This lets you check that all the anchors are there, and that they are properly set up.

At anchor

At a calm spot, examine all the rest of the safety equipment:
– hand flares and rocket flares: read the instructions; everyone should pick the things up, and know how they work (by the way, you should ask the hirer if he has a stock of expired hand flares and if he can lend you some);
– the fire extinguisher: where it is, how to get it down, how to use it;
– use the signalling mirror (if it is sunny!);
– use the fog horn;
– set up the 'lightning conductor', that is, see how to rig up the chain around the boat to earth the rigging;
– check the working of the pumps;
– check the navigation lights are working;
– simulate a launch of the liferaft; check how it is secured to the boat; see how to release it; go through the list of equipment to take on it; everyone should know where this equipment is to be found on board;
– try the tender.

One last piece of advice: if you intend hiring with friends, try to have enough people to take two or three boats. Sailing in a flotilla is a basic safety point, and it is often much more fun.

CHAPTER 3

Offshore cruising

On a sea cruise, steering, manoeuvring, maintaining your boat, keeping a check on the weather forecast, and taking a bearing are daily activities just like eating and sleeping: living and sailing are one and the same thing: this is what we dreamed about; and here we are!

At the beginning it is not so very new. The preparation for such a cruise differs very little from that for a coastal cruise: you select your goal and get your documentation, you prepare the boat, you go shopping. Only, at each stage in this preparation, it is important to think much further ahead, as regards one basic point: at sea, you can count only on yourself; this is complete independence. If you have forgotten something at the start, you will not be able to pick it up during the journey. Accidents involving yourselves or your equipment have to be remedied without anyone's help. Bad weather will have to be confronted, if it occurs. You will jolly well have to get over your seasickness on the spot, or die of it! So, first, you will have to plan everything, and be extremely rigorous, so as to create the proper conditions for this independence.

However well prepared you are, what happens next is always a bit of a mystery. Essentially, it is a matter of small details. So above all, we will be discussing these details here, and the rituals which punctuate the passing of the hours on board a boat on the open sea, which is like a kind of floating monastery, with its funny, grinning, hooded monks …

And, this time, we will be preaching what we really believe in: having discussed owning your own boat or hiring a boat in preceding chapters, here we will be presenting life on board a big boat in accordance with our own experience: the club boat. Besides, at the present time, for people with modest incomes, it is just about the only way to get out on the high seas. You have to be a millionaire to buy and maintain a big sailing boat. Hiring one is possible, if need be, but the best agent can only provide what he has, which is: equipment. You would still have to be able to get together a suitable, competent crew, made up of people likely to get on with each other, really committed to going on a stiff cruise – and who are not going to drop out at the last moment! A club offers both the

organisation and the human potential you will need. And something else, which (in our opinion!) is priceless: the possibility of being at sea with people you would not have the chance of meeting in everyday life, and of whom you know only that a single passion animates them. Throwing yourself into an unknown lifestyle in the company of unknown people: without any doubt, it is this kind of escape which interests us!

Before setting off

Let's not get lost in the preliminaries: assume we have a Glénans boat, designed for the high sea and accommodating eight to ten people. Several members of the club really want to go sailing on this boat, and form a crew. From now until departure time, the question of guaranteeing yourselves complete independence will serve as a directional thread, at every stage of preparation.

To be independent, the crew needs, first, to be competent to carry out the programme it is planning. When you do a 1-day stage, repairs can be provisional; they must be pretty well definitive when you have to sail for several days. On a coastal cruise, when the weather is rough, you can wait until the evening to eat; at sea, you need someone to be brave enough still to cook. In drawing up a list of the various qualifications of each member of the crew, do you have a solution to all of the problems which may arise? This is the basic question.

If this competence exists, you will then have to set about complementing it, by getting hold of documents relating to the region you are going to be sailing in. You may note in passing that a club, these days, serves more or less the same purpose once served by the harbour pub: you meet people there, you tell of your adventures, everyone comes out with their sagas and their odyssey ... In this way you can collect a whole set of unpublished information from someone who has already carried out the cruise that you are planning: these oral nautical instructions are all the more precious for coming from the same angle as your own. You would not be able to find their equal in the official documents.

All the same, you will have to get hold of the following documents, and study them.

Documents and any maps necessary for the voyage to be undertaken, to which it is wise to add documents which will let you reach a port of refuge during the voyage, if need be; specific documents

On board the *Sereine*.

on navigation on the open sea: documents on radio signals, nautical calendars, American pilots' charts, if you are undertaking a crossing of some size.

The boat must be equipped for a certain category of sailing: 2nd category if you are not going more than 200 nautical miles from a place of shelter, 1st category if you are going further. It should contain the appropriate navigational equipment: direction finder, sextant … There are all kinds of far more sophisticated equipment, but we can do without them! You might well dream of having the apparatus to produce facsimiles of meteorological charts on demand: after all, it is fascinating to have a clear explanation of what is happening before your eyes at almost exactly the same time as it is happening overhead.

As a safety precaution, you might equally well dream of being watched over by a satellite; as things stand to date, it is cheaper to have a shore-based contact. It will usually be someone in charge at the club, who is used to the high sea.

Now you just have to pack your bags: this is hardly any different from the packing you did for the coastal cruise; you simply change things according to your expected latitude. The adventure really begins when you arrive at the port and, after having walked along the quays looking at the boats, you finally discover yours and you jump on the deck.

Taking charge of the boat

The boat has just come back from a cruise. There will be on board a kind of record book – sometimes called a handing-over book – in which, every day, successive captains have carefully noted the damage sustained, the repairs made; explanations of problems which are difficult to detect, if need be, anomalies which are more obvious (for example: the helm is a bit stiff, but this is to be expected, as the hinges have just been replaced). The ideal thing, of course, is for the previous captain still to be on the spot: this allows for a much more lively handover. For want of anything better, a telephone call can be very useful. You should go over the logbook in detail, in any case. In theory, your predecessors will have left everything in impeccable condition; in practice, certain problems may have been left hanging on and you will have to deal with them yourselves. From now on, it is up to the new crew to write the next part of the story.

There are different ways of going about taking charge of the boat. Some captains want to get everything right before the first

The *Sereine*.

outing. For this the crew is divided into several teams, one team is delegated to get the food, another to inspect the boat in detail, another deals with any repairs which may need doing. Then you organise a collective visit on board so everyone can familiarise themselves with the equipment, then cast off, and go out to check that everything is working.

But you can also adopt the method we suggested for the coastal cruise: cast off as soon as possible and do all the business of taking charge at sea. Since the boat was sailing yesterday, it ought to be able to sail for one more day! You run through the rigging, load enough things to eat for several meals and you set off.

At sea, you should carry out all the possible manoeuvres, try out all the sails, take in all the reefs and study the way the boat behaves, you agree on what methods to use, rehearse the ways of fishing someone back out of the sea, you check the safety equipment, etc. For the crew, this is the chance to get acquainted with the boat. For the captain, this is the chance to get to know the crew, to get an idea of each crew member's qualities; and this will be useful later when they will have to organise the watches.

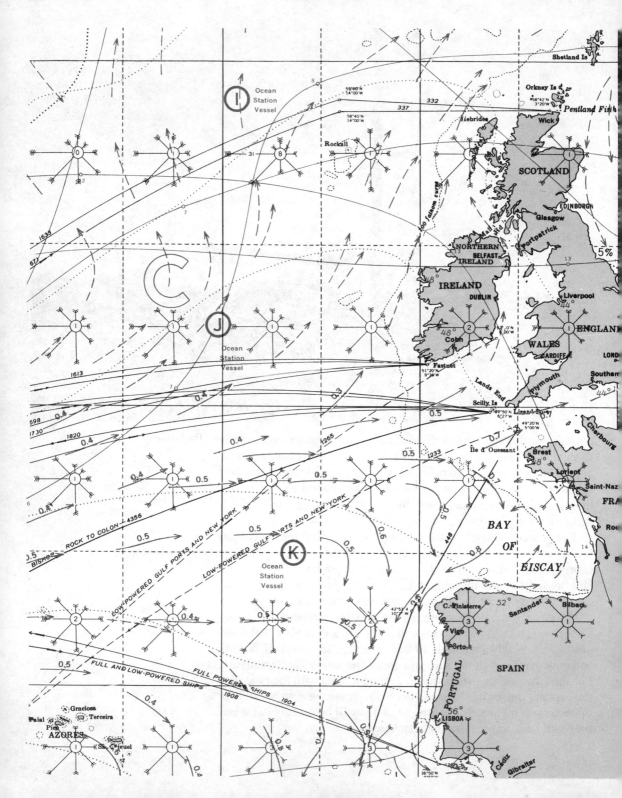

Securing your independence

But more than anything, this is the time to think hard about the equipment, bearing in mind the independence which is to come. In fact, you should be asking yourself the simple question every time you use something: 'If this breaks, what will we do?' And being able to provide an answer every time: either you can repair it, or you will have to replace it, or substitute one thing for another. Let's take some examples from different areas.

The rigging. If the main halyard breaks, what will you do? Will you be able to repair it? Do you know how to make a tail splice, do you have the equipment you need? If you cannot repair it, can you replace it, can you climb to the top of the mast and feed the new halyard down the inside? Could you use the topping lift instead?

The sails. If a jib tears, what will you do? Of course, you can replace it with another one, smaller or bigger. But if it is the storm jib? You have to be able to rely on the storm jib, or be able to repair it. Do you have fabric, thread, and the right implements?

The gear. If a winch gets broken: do you know how it is assembled inside? Can you change one of the parts? If not, can you use another winch? Or rig a purchase to replace it: have you got the pulleys you will need, do you know how to mount it, will you know how to fasten it properly onto the sheet?

The hull. What will you do if you spring a leak? Do you have the wood to repair it? Could the floorboards or parts of the bunks be used? Do you have what you need to make use of them: tools, screws, tacks? And you will perhaps need to work on the outside of the boat: it would not be a bad idea to take a mask and a snorkel.

And if you lose the panel which closes off the cabin? This is very serious, since it is a unique piece of equipment. You cannot afford to lose it, and you will have to look after it very carefully.

The navigational equipment. If the compass goes wrong, can you replace it with the hand-bearing compass, or the compass from the direction finder? Can you set it up correctly?

And if the radio breaks down? You will probably not be able to do anything about that, but this means you will have to have a good watch, or better, two of them, and get to know the way they work pretty quickly, so as to be able to do without the radio time signal.

And the stove? It's a very important thing, the stove: it is a great catastrophe if it breaks down, especially if there is nothing left to eat but noodles and rice. Do you know how to take it apart and replace the parts? Should you not take a spare burner with you?

All the parts of the boat and the equipment should be examined closely in this way. You can make lists so as not to forget anything

Facing page:
The pilots' charts of the American Department of Oceanography cover very large areas (there are four to cover the entire globe). Drawn up on the basis of monthly statistics (thus there are twelve charts per zone, one for each month of the year), they provide a lot of information, principally:

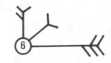

Average winds at the point indicated. The arrow gives the direction; its length indicates frequency; the arrow points indicate its strength on the Beaufort scale; the number in the middle indicates the percentage of calm days or weak winds.

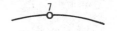

The path of the centre of the depressions which have caused the strongest storms in recent years, with the position at midnight on the day indicated (7).

• • • • • 52°

Average air temperature, in degrees Fahrenheit, for the month in question (here, it is February).

Direction of the usual current and speed in knots; a dotted line means that the information is based only on a small number of measurements.

Sea routes with an indication of the distances from point to point.

These charts are published every year. It is wise to order them fairly well in advance.

Taking charge of the *Glénan*.

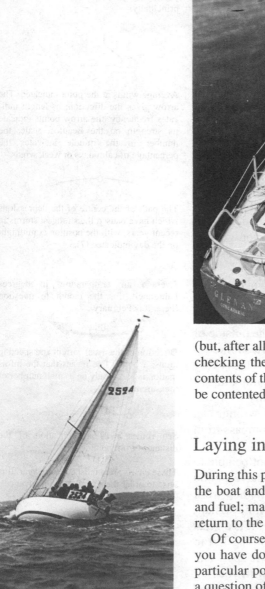

Sainte-Anne.

(but, after all, you are currently holding in your hand a good tool for checking these things: you only have to run through the table of contents of this book!). The important thing is to be rigorous, not to be contented with evasive replies.

Laying in supplies

During this preliminary outing, you will not only be concerned with the boat and its equipment. You will also have to talk food, drink and fuel; make lists of these, too, so as not to waste time when you return to the port.

Of course you will already have some ideas about these issues if you have done some coastal cruising: so here we will only stress particular points regarding the duration of the voyage. In fact, it is a question of thinking as if you were about to undergo a siege: you will have to live on your reserves, you can hardly expect to find things to live off as you go along. Of course, you might think about fishing and take along some serious tackle; perhaps you will also be able to catch fresh water at the bottom of the boom, if a squall comes along to save you. But, in the end, you will have to take these as windfalls and plan as if none of this were to happen.

Water

Let's start with water, since this is the most important question on the open sea; you can go without eating for a certain time, if need be, but you cannot survive without drinking.

The minimum quantity to reckon on is about 1.5 litres per person per day, to be calculated on the basis of the longest possible duration of the crossing. This is an absolute minimum, which is only sufficient if you impose a strict discipline on yourselves.

Washing yourself and washing-up are done in sea water, of course. Cooking too, to a certain extent: a pressure cooker is an indispensable piece of equipment, with which you need only use sea water for everything which can be cooked by steaming. You can also use sea water, in the proportion of 1 part sea water to 3 or 4 parts fresh, for everything cooked in water (which avoids you having to add salt). You will have to take account of this when choosing what to eat: potatoes and rice can be steamed, but not pasta; food which is already salty cannot be cooked in sea water …

Fragola.

Palynodie-Glénans.

Throughout the trip, you will have to make sure you know what position you are in, and compare the amount of water you have with the distance you still have to cover: you should restrict consumption if the boat slows down; on the other hand, you can loosen the reins a little if you have been going more quickly than planned. Shaking the last drops of water into the homecoming Scotch proves you have managed your stock perfectly!

But all these sensible precepts are pointless if you do not first take elementary precautions for loading the drinking water so it will remain fit to drink during the journey.

Before filling the containers, it is important to rinse them carefully with chlorinated water. You should be very careful how you handle it, and taste the water once you have loaded it on the boat. The least negligence can be catastrophic: for example, if you have filled up with a funnel which has been used before for decanting oil … Besides, it is wise to divide up the water stocks as much as possible, to have several reservoirs rather than just one: this avoids polluting it all in case of mishandling. In any case, you should also have several water bottles (three-quarters full so that they will float) to take with you in case of shipwreck.

Food

Everyone has their own idea about what you should eat at sea. Some set about loading a balanced stock of starches, fats and proteins. Others entrust themselves to Saint Émilion and others refuse to set off unless you plan to have soup with every meal (instant soups in individual packets have fortunately solved this serious problem). We have already stated our opinion on this subject: the essential thing is for everyone to be happy. When you know everyone's tastes, the only sure solution, here as on a coastal cruise, consists in planning menus for the full duration of the voyage. And showing a modicum of common sense, in not loading too many perishables which you will not be able to finish before they go off ...

Conservation of the produce on board is a major concern, and we will discuss this again later, when we are at sea. For the moment, you should note that, in the first place, conservation is associated with the quality of the packaging. You will have to take account of this when you go shopping. Plastic bags and plastic boxes will always prove very useful.

Oil, batteries, diesel oil, gas, matches, have you thought of everything? Indeed, has everyone got their own first-aid kit? There is a first-aid box on board, but it is a little bit tight for covering all the crew's needs. Everyone should know their own weak points and take what they might need.

As soon as you get back to the quay, everyone should set off at top speed. There follow several hours of feverish comings and goings, after which you will have to repack everything on board. It might be a good idea to nominate a quartermaster – who would be better called the steward – to organise the system of storage. A telephone call to the shore-based contact and then you cast off for good.

Living at sea

After the great agitation of the preparations, suddenly everything is calm, a kind of great emptiness sets in: there is almost nothing to do, other than guide the boat towards a goal which, for the moment, remains rather unreal. A slight feeling of unease goes with great departures: while the land is getting further away, you are still attached to it by all kinds of invisible links, and habits which you will have to break one by one. You used to live in a stable world. Living on dry land was natural. Night was made for sleeping in. You had living space. Now, everything begins to move, everything which is not held down falls to the bottom of the boat, or to the side; there is an enormous amount of water by your side; it is very wet water which will start getting everywhere if you are not careful. The next night you will still be there, you will have to carry on

The *Glénan*.

WATCH CHARTS

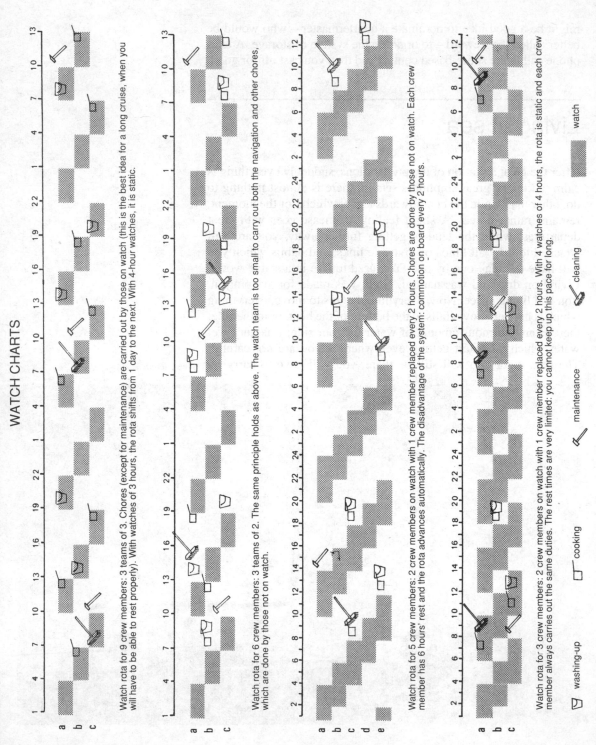

Watch rota for 9 crew members: 3 teams of 3. Chores (except for maintenance) are carried out by those on watch (this is the best idea for a long cruise, when you will have to be able to rest properly). With watches of 3 hours, the rota shifts from 1 day to the next. With 4-hour watches, it is static.

Watch rota for 6 crew members: 3 teams of 2. The same principle holds as above. The watch team is too small to carry out both the navigation and other chores, which are done by those not on watch.

Watch rota for 5 crew members: 2 crew members on watch with 1 crew member replaced every 2 hours. Chores are done by those not on watch. Each crew member has 6 hours' rest and the rota advances automatically. The disadvantage of the system: commotion on board every 2 hours.

Watch rota for 3 crew members: 2 crew members on watch with 1 crew member replaced every 2 hours. With 4 watches of 4 hours, the rota is static and each crew member always carries out the same duties. The rest times are very limited: you cannot keep up this pace for long.

▽ washing-up   ◻ cooking   ⚒ maintenance   🧹 cleaning   ▦ watch sailing. And here is the most surprising thing: while having this immensity around you, you are going to find yourselves heaped up on each other in a narrow and confined space.

All in all, you are going to be hassled from all sides! When you set off, you have a certain stock of physical freshness, patience and good humour, which runs the risk of wearing out quickly. To maintain this stock, you will have to be organised, and positively create a new life for yourselves; one which is regular in the strong sense of the word, that is to say, one founded on a certain sense of order. It is important to establish this sense of order and to get used to it as soon as possible: all sorts of unpredictable things, bad weather in particular, will take it upon themselves to test it soon enough!

The rhythm of the watches

On the high sea, a boat lives a 24 hour day. So you will have to organise a rota, so that part of the crew is resting while another part is busy navigating and carrying out the various everyday tasks: you divide up the crew members into teams, who take the watch in turn.

The composition of the watches/teams can vary according to the type of cruise you are doing, the number of crew members you have available, their energy and their competence. This competence, as you know, is rarely complete. One crew member sets the sails well but is not very strong on navigation, another one keeps a lookout better than he steers: the most important thing is to create even teams, whose crew members have complementary abilities. Beyond this requirement, there are no absolute rules. It is so much the better if there are enough of you to make three watches, but this is rare. And so much the better if there is enough competence for your watches to be of only two crew members, but this is often pushing it a bit. You can create fixed watches, or you may prefer mobile ones where the crew members rotate: during a long crossing, you might not always want the same faces opposite you!

The watches themselves can be of variable length. You can plan a static rota, or a rolling one, so it is not always the same people keeping the most difficult watch, at the end of the night. Briefly, you may plan all sorts of things, and it is for each of you to find the system which suits you. All the same, you may note that the most classic set-up, found in almost every navy in the world, is that of 4-hour watches, with two 'short watches' of 2 hours in the afternoon, so as to ensure a rolling timetable, precisely.

The captain often occupies a special place in this organisation.

When there are enough people on board to make up even watches, it is preferable for the captain to be outside the watch. This lets the captain maintain the overall view which is necessary if the cruise is to go well and, above all, be available at any time in case of need. The fact of being off watch, far from being a privilege, means in the end that the captain is there to do his master's bidding. You have to be able to count on him in times of difficulty, often at night: he may want to be woken at every change of watch, or to replace a weakening crew member, or when a manoeuvre requires the presence of more than two pairs of hands on deck … Given this, it is clear that he should try to sleep whenever he can, which will often be during the day. Besides, he really will not sleep soundly unless he is certain that he will be woken whenever there is the slightest reason. He has the right to expect this! Too bad if he is woken five times in a row for nothing, as long as he is also woken when there really is something up.

The rolling of the watches, the 'dotted' life of the captain: you can imagine the strange atmosphere this will create on board a cruising boat. Three-quarters of the time, there are people sleeping. If you want to try to describe an ordinary day at sea, you would say first that the early morning is usually quiet. Those who have just taken over the watch busy themselves without saying a word, each is still a little withdrawn, unwittingly observing one of the basic recommendations of the monks' order (*De taciturnitate*). A certain amount of movement begins around 1000, with the appearance of a little hole in people's stomachs. The 'sausage and muscadet' comes at the allotted time to sustain the right atmosphere, then there is a period of intense social activity until midday: you attend to various jobs, there is the important business of preparing lunch, then the meal itself, which is a high point in the day. Straight after, those who are not on watch will have a siesta, a certain torpor sets in, there is another period of silence until tea-time approaches, and the activity reasserts itself again until after dinner time. Then there are the long hours of the night, calm below, calm on deck where the people keeping watch are quite still, each one pursuing a solitary train of thought, grunting something from time to time to pass the hours …

You can already see that eating and sleeping are basic preoccupations in this way of life! But you will also have to clean and maintain the boat, keep up the navigation, keep watch, manoeuvre, day and night. How can you manage these activities and carry them all out properly?

We are not going to draw up a doctrine on this subject; we will just give some basic advice.

Keeping dry

Damp will get into everything very quickly, if you do not take care: your belongings, your clothes, your skin, your mind; in the end, it gets to your morale. Combatting this invasion is thus a safety issue: because of this you will have to impose real discipline on yourself, be wildly energetic, and not let yourself be distracted at any time!

• When you get up, seal up your sleeping bag and pyjamas immediately, in a plastic bag.

• On the deck, when the weather is freshening, do not wait until you have got wet to put on your waterproofs (this is often what happens). First, you can just put on the trousers: wetness works up from the bottom. In any case it is wrong to put on just the jacket: you get soaked with sea water at the bottom and sweat on top. When the weather gets worse, you need the whole set of waterproofs: even this will not be effective unless you add an absorbent 'collar', that is a towel, at the neck: without it, the water heads straight for your soul.

• If you have been surprised by the weather, think about drying your clothes as quickly as possible. A wet pair of trousers is not necessarily a crisis; you should keep them on, or put them back on, if it is not cold and you have the advantage of a little dry wind: this is how they will dry out quickest.

In the really foul weather, when you no longer have a hope of drying anything outside, there is a very effective solution which consists in using two sleeping bags (you can choose very light ones if you are worried about being too hot!). You slip into one of them, with your wet clothes on you, or beside you, and you put the second one over the first. This second sleeping bag works like a sponge: it pumps up all the wetness from below (or, in more elegant terms, all the water vapour in the wet clothes condenses there). After 1 or 2 hours, you are dry. Of course, the top sleeping bag is completely soaked, but that does not matter much: you should not hesitate to put it away, even when it is soaked. Let's add that with a careful reading of 'Meteorology' Part V, of this book you will understand that the colder it is, the better this system works!

• You have to fight, too, to keep the inside of the boat as dry as possible. Avoid walking about in there with dripping waterproofs, and do not let your wet clothes drip. Fight against leaks as well. It is rare for the deck to be perfectly waterproof, and it is difficult to eliminate these leaks, but you can at least try to channel the water directly towards the hold, suspending a piece of rope in the appropriate places, or a crepe bandage, or some sort of fabric. If the water is getting in through the coach-roof it is often because the gutters are blocked.

Above all, you must not give up: every point counts, in this tricky combat.

It is better to get a little seasick, by acting in time, than to let the enemy gain the advantage and find yourself later sick as a dog in its hole, soaking in freezing water!

Sleeping

First, it is imperative for everyone to have their quota of 'restorative' sleep (the expression takes on all its weight here). You have to create the conditions to achieve this.

To begin with, the most difficult thing is to change your habits: it seems strange to go to bed at 2000 when on land, at that time, the most interesting part of the day would be beginning. You will have problems getting to sleep. And the next day, you will find it difficult to fight off sleep, especially in the early morning and the beginning of the afternoon. First, then, it is important to create a peaceful atmosphere on board at these times, while you wait for the right rhythm to be established.

Clearly, what spoils this peaceful atmosphere is the noise made by those on watch. Here, there is a whole set of practices to adopt, restrictive ones of course.

For example, it is better to avoid:

– going down into the cabin every five minutes because you have forgotten something: a sweater, something to eat, water, seasickness tablets;

– singing Tyrolean songs and shouting orders when there is no need;

– when you are wearing a lifejacket or harness, letting your clasp drag on the deck: this is just like knocking those who are sleeping on the head;

– using the winches inconsiderately; carrying out manoeuvres or changes of sail which are not absolutely necessary. As far as possible, it is always preferable to let this wait until the change of watch: everyone is up and there are more hands available.

The conditions of silence having been established, you will still have to be properly set up, if you want to sleep well. If all the bunks in the boat are good, all the better; everyone will have their own. But if, as is often the case, some bunks are a bit tight, not really made to be used at sea, it would be stupid to make someone stay in there while the bunks of the people on watch are free. Apart from the captain who, because of his particular lifestyle, needs a bunk of his own, you would be well advised to adopt the principle of the 'warm bunk' – meaning one which doesn't have time to get cold between the one crew member leaving and the other coming down …

A good lee cloth (see page 384), well pulled up, procures you the desired comfort and isolation. Plugs in your ears help you forget the outside world.

In general, after two days, there are hardly any problems: during the interminable night watches, you have so much dreamt of your bunk as a lost paradise that you will not waste any further chance to go back to it again, without waiting for vespers or compline …

Eating

… When matins sounds, the people on watch are usually very attentive towards those who are to replace them. When these latter open their eyes, the wick in the lamp has been turned up a little, the water is singing gently in the kettle, people are busy preparing what everyone wants to eat. They might almost go and cut some flowers.

This attentiveness, even if it is not disinterested, creates the appropriate atmosphere for the first important act of the day: breakfast. At sea, breakfast is a big deal: it will probably be the biggest meal of all, the one where you really do restore your strength.

So it has to be appetising, and for it to be appetising you will have to get what you like to eat. It is notable, moreover, that many

Fresh food

When you set off for a fairly long time, the problem of keeping food on board is such a tricky one that you often choose to stick with the tried and tested: rice, pasta, instant potato, etc. However, it is quite possible not to give up freshness and variety; this can be the very time to question your day-to-day habits, to liberate yourself from the system of 'pre-packaged and ready to serve' food, to prove you have some imagination!

Some suggestions to guide your research:
• Meat. After the first few days, you usually start using the tin-opener. However, smoked ham and raw ham, hung in a well-ventilated spot on board, will not go off. Fresh pork, cut into ribbons and stored in salt in a well-sealed box, stays in an excellent condition for over a year.
• Fish. Gutted, washed and dried or preserved in vinegar, will keep for a long time. And what if you catch a 20kg tuna, for example?

Some people take glass bottles with them, to preserve fish cooked in the pressure cooker. You can even take some home for the winter months.

• Fruit and vegetables. Cabbage, carrots, onions, turnips, apples, grapefruit, bananas and lemons all keep very well, as long as they are not heaped up on each other; they should be properly stacked and the 'fruitshop' visited every day to eliminate the doubtful cases.
• Cheese. The only secret is in the packaging: do not use plastic or aluminium foil, but waxed paper. Split it into several portions to reduce risks.
• Butter. This will not spoil, even in the tropics, if you keep it in a bottle of water covered with a damp cloth, stored in a cool place.

You could go further and rethink your entire eating habits, stocking maize, wheat, barley and oats on board, those grains hardly anyone knows how to use any more! Soya beans sprout very well if you pay them a little attention every day: in this way you can have a fresh salad anywhere, anytime. With a bit of organisation you can grow chives, parsley or tarragon in pots …

Thus, unsuspected gardening skills can sometimes be revealed on the open sea.

people who are not very interested in what makes up the main menus, stick madly by their habits here. Coffee or tea, or hot chocolate, or soup, cereals, eggs, cheese, meat, whatever. Whatever must be, must be. Watching someone wolf down their breakfast, still only just awake, you get the best idea of the child they once were! Afterwards, they become a big boy or a big girl once again, and they are prepared to glance amiably at the people around them.

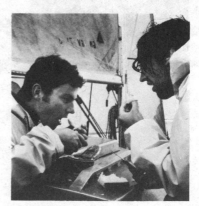

As a general principle, at sea, small meals are more important than the big ones: breakfast, elevenses, tea, and snacks on the night watch are often better accepted and more easily digested than the main meals. So the kitchen should be well stocked with tit-bits which are nourishing and quick to eat.

The main meals are nevertheless important moments in the day. It is good for them to be served at regular times (which is much easier to do than on a coastal cruise) so, set to it on time – not too early, that is – and be organised enough at least for the meat and potatoes to be ready at the same time … The midday meal is a basic feature of communal living: if the weather is good you can all eat together, except perhaps for the person helming. The evening meal can be the most frugal of all (indigestion does not promote good sleep: it is better to stuff yourself at tea time!) and relatively brief, so the washing-up is done before dark: this is essential if you want to avoid mess, and losing cutlery.

In fact, the only problem with meals at sea is that the boat is moving. That is fair enough as long as the weather is good, but as soon as the wind freshens, everything gets complicated. And you begin to make useful observations: for example, at breakfast, it is better to make your toast before filling your coffee mug; afterwards, it is impossible! And it would be very useful to have non-slip paper place mats – at least on civilised boats where you have a table. If not, you are really lucky if you can balance things on your lap.

To cook in blustery weather, on the other hand, you really have to have your heart set on it, and above all you should know that you are exposing yourself to a serious risk: that of scalding yourself. It is indispensable for the cook to be properly equipped, and put on boots and waterproof trousers: the trousers over the boots and not inside, of course!

As soon as the sea stops being very calm, it becomes dangerous to use saucepans: only the kettle and the pressure cooker are still to be trusted. In fact, the time comes fairly quickly, when no one is interested in big meals any more, and you switch to snacks. Then you bless the person who invented powder, be it coffee powder, powdered milk or leek and potato soup: all you have to do is heat up a lot of water, and everyone serves themselves according to taste.

In this perpetual state of bulimia, bad weather comes to constitute a sort of interval, when you are happy to munch away at sweets, toffees, raisins, nougat, barley sugar, fruit pastilles, walnuts, hazelnuts, peanuts and almonds.

Cleaning and maintenance

Eating so much, you will make everything dirty. Cleaning operations, which include washing-up, have to be done three times a day: this is the only way to live on a clean and clean-smelling boat. You don't have to clean everything from top to bottom every day, but you should clean the deck and the cabin bilges, at least. For the rest, you can spread out the work over the seven days of the week, dividing the boat into seven parts, one of which is to be thoroughly cleaned every day .

Cleaning includes tidying up as well. There is nothing like a mess for making life on board perfectly impossible (and it is a question of safety as well). When you wash the deck, you should pick up everything that is lying about, undo any tangles in the sheets, adjust everything which has a tendency to come loose. Inside, you have a permanent fight on your hands to keep the utensils, tools, sails and navigational equipment in their place. You have to be unfailingly attentive: each little negligence or error is punished, not by some superior officer, but by the sea itself; everything which is not put away slips, falls, tips up, gets wet, breaks or disappears. Everything which disappears into the hold goes rusty or goes rotten.

At washing-up time, one question crops up: what to do with the scraps? At sea you can throw overboard everything the fish will eat, everything which is biodegradable. Note that you should try to avoid broken bottles while you are on a continental shelf; fishermen sometimes pick them up in their nets; so it is better to fill them with water and sink them. The rest, especially plastic packaging, must be put in a suitable place and wait for the port (if you scald a plastic bottle, it shrivels and takes up little space).

Besides this, you will have to check and maintain the rigging, the gear and the sails. Here, especially, it is a case of battling against the routine which threatens to set in stealthily day after day. When you keep the same sails up for a long time, it is not a bad idea to pull them down and re-hoist them every so often, to be sure nothing is stuck, and to change the pressure point on the halyard. And inspecting the

---

Making your own bread

Ingredients
– 600–700g of flour;
– 0.5 litres curdled milk (all you have to do is leave a carton of long–life milk open for 2 or 3 days; powdered milk can also be used);
– a teaspoon of salt;
– a teaspoon of sodium bicarbonate.

Method
– Mix together the flour, salt and sodium bicarbonate.
– Add the milk curds and mix everything to a dough which is not sticky.
– Put the dough in a pan (prefloured so it does not stick). Cook for half an hour on one side, 10 minutes on the other.
– Tap the bread with your finger: when it sounds hollow, it is cooked.

Notes
– The bicarbonate is a good substitute for yeast. Ordinary yeast does not keep, and dried yeast makes too heavy a dough.
– You can make this bread in the pressure cooker. An oven is obviously the ideal thing ...
– You can vary the recipe by using buckwheat (1/3 buckwheat, 2/3 wheatflour), sultanas, etc.

rigging in pairs every morning is always a good habit to get into, while on fair days going for a walk aloft is not out of the question: this makes a change! Besides, there is always a sheave to grease, a halyard to turn, a whipping to be redone, a seam to be repaired. On average, to keep the boat in good condition, one in five of the crew should devote an hour to maintenance during a day's sailing. Between elevenses and lunch, between tea and dinner, you can make all the noise you want: this is when to take advantage of it …

Navigation

Getting on so well, we might gradually forget we were heading somewhere, if every day there were not particular rituals to perform, with regard to navigation itself.

In the first instance, this is a case of keeping up the logbook hour by hour, noting the course you are following, the log, the weather, the influential events along the way. It is notable that the logbook is the only standard navigational instrument which completely changes in size between coastal cruising and offshore cruising. Here, you feel the need for it quite keenly: you quickly lose the sense of time on the high sea, soon you no longer know what day it is; it is by means of the logbook that you maintain contact with reality.

Then there are moments of intense concentration when you listen out for the good word on the sky: the time for the meteorological forecasts. And then the three 'offices' which punctuate the day: the bearings taken in the morning, at midday and in the evening. The midday bearing is usually the most important of the three: you take a meridian (not to be confused with the siesta of the same name, which only happens later). Then you collate all the navigational facts you have available: three spoonfuls of astronomy and a pinch of the direction finder, all mixed to the required consistency with a little dead reckoning, and there is our position. On the open sea, extreme precision is not absolutely necessary; the essential thing is to be making progress on the right track …

As far as running the boat is concerned, each watch can devise their own little rituals, and organise a suitable rota to make sure the various tasks are done: steering, lookout, navigation. The important point here is not to slip into a routine! Even at sea, you must not let your attention slip: the 'open' sea is not free of dangers, and collisions occur sometimes in the most unexpected conditions. And what if someone, far away, were calling for help? You should also think about re-trimming the boat and sails, even when the weather is fairly settled and you are still on the same tack. And check it

again before handing over to the next watch. They will perhaps have different ideas, and that is no bad thing! Only, in this little world where subtlety is a cardinal rule, it may be good form to wait for your predecessors to fall asleep before undoing all their work!

The changes of watch are important moments. Because everyone is usually awake, you can take advantage of this to carry out the necessary manoeuvres, and to make a quick inspection of the deck, to check everything is in order and properly secured. You let your successors know how things stand: things which have taken place during the preceding hours, difficulties encountered on account of the weather, the condition of the sea. You explain the route you have been following, and pass on orders. Sometimes, you also have to hand on a particular mood: when you have a real wind, in heavy seas, it might be a good idea for the helmsman coming off the watch and the upcoming helmsman to hold the helm together for a few minutes, so that the newcomer can get the rhythm. You only go to bed when you have passed on to the following team everything which has happened over the last few hours.

Darkness

The watch which is on duty at sunset does the rounds of the deck, checks that everything is in its place and well secured, picks up everything which is lying around. It is the property of darkness to create confusion; it takes over familiar territory, scattering it with traps. This is something you ought to know!

And take the inspection further, into the cockpit and the interior of the boat. Everything breathes innocence in there, all the things remain silent, stored in accordance with the present listing of the boat. In principle there is nothing to worry about. But during the night, the wind changes, you tack to starboard and you pick up the glass from the binoculars on one side of the boat, the mustard minus its bottle on the other, you slip on the pear you were saving for when you were thirsty and you wake everyone up to find the winch handle that you were absolutely sure you put down over there!

Those who take over the first night watch should equip themselves, get out the lifejackets and the lamps, prepare their snack and put it in a safe place, within arm's reach. The others go off to bed. The captain gives his orders and goes to bed too, if the conditions lend themselves to this: it is as well for him to be ready for the hard times in the early morning.

Silence settles in, and you find yourself alone, charging into the unknown, into the dark! We could add some atmospheric comments here: phosphoresences, the screeching of invisible birds, the rasping breath of porpoises. This would make some seasoned sailors smile, for whom there is hardly any difference between night sailing and sailing by day, in the end, and we would run the

Seeing clearly

In the dark, on deck, the lookout must remain in complete darkness; surprised by the flash of an electric lamp, they become useless for many minutes.

It may be as well to remind you here of the way the human eye perceives light. This perception depends on a double system of cells:
– first the 'cones', which are only stimulated by bright light, but let you distinguish colour;
– then the 'rods', which are sensitive to weaker light sources, blinded by bright light and which cannot distinguish colour. The extreme sensitivity of the rods is due to the presence in their cellular body of a vitamin A derivative, visual purple, which is destroyed immediately by bright light and only reconstituted in the dark. Reconstitution is only complete after about 20 minutes. Only red light does not degrade it.

At the centre of the retina, you only find cones, around the outside, cones and rods. Consequently:
– the central section, which allows for the precise perception of things and their colours in day vision, becomes practically useless in night vision if the fixed light source is too weak;
– the peripheral section, which in day vision gives you a hazy perception of your surroundings, becomes the only really useful section at night. It perceives and communicates the weakest source of light, albeit without indicating its colour or its exact shape, as long as the visual purple of the rods is not destroyed by lighting which is too strong.

These facts suggest some practical considerations for night sailing:
• To identify a fine detail, it is better not to look at it directly, but focus your eyes a few degrees away from it; you should systematically doubt your judgement of colours.
• Since red light does not destroy visual purple, it is a good idea to put red bulbs in the compass and the map table lights.
• The lookout should only be replaced by a crew member who has adapted to the dark over at least 10 minutes. To keep the adaptation period as short as possible, it might be a good idea to create 'indirect' lighting inside the boat, by masking the light sources with aluminium foil. The eye adapts easily to this soft light, which also creates a favourable atmosphere for some to rest and others to carry out their muffled activities.

Note that bilberries and carrots are very rich in vitamin A.

risk of giving a false impression to the novice. If they remain objective, they will soon see that in general, the darkness is much less
black than people say – on condition that you do not get dazzled, of
course, as we have discussed.

The risk of confusion becomes more acute at the changes of
watch. Note, first of all, that it would be as well for everyone in the
watch coming off duty, however impatient they may be, to stay on
the bridge until the upcoming watch is ready: it is usually when
everyone is in their pyjamas that something happens. And then you
have to pass on the orders once again and, above all, not forget to
say what action you have taken during the watch: putting a boom
retainer in place, tying up one thing or another to cut down noise ...
If you take advantage of the change in the watch to carry out
manoeuvres, to change sail for example, you will have to carry
them out by the book, without flourishes, and without inventing
variants at the last minute; replace each halyard on its peg, pull
every sheet through where it should normally go. Routine is a good
thing, at night: it allows you to scoff at the monsters which lurk in
the shadows, waiting for someone to gobble up ...

Bad weather

Since we mentioned it, it was bound to happen one day! At least let
it not be at night, which can be more of a nuisance.

You have known fair breezes, good breezes and fresh winds. At
what point might you consider that you are getting into bad
weather? Probably as soon as the strength of the wind and the
condition of the sea no longer let you do exactly what you want to
with the boat; as soon as the pace of life on board starts to be seriously disrupted. So that depends on the boat and, above all, on the
experience of the crew. Often, at the beginning of a cruise, the bad
weather threshold is quickly reached. As you relax, it gradually
draws further back. Bad weather makes everything more difficult:
sleeping, eating, cleaning, taking a bearing; it makes it difficult to
move, to carry out even a simple manoeuvre. The unpredictable
movements of the boat, the spectacle around you and the noises
stupefy your mind: you are not necessarily ill, but not sparkling
either. From this point on, you have to think of simplifying all the
essential activities.

As regards manoeuvring, you have theoretically been ready for
some time. On the trial outing, before setting off, you checked all
the bad weather sails, and tried them all out. If the weather was too
calm that day, you had the bright idea of trying them again en route,

on a breezier day, so as to see how the boat moved in really bad weather. You will have used your lifejacket and harness at the slightest risk of someone falling in the water: it is familiar equipment that you wear almost without thinking about it. As far as this is concerned, there is no risk of you being surprised.

And again, it is rare for bad weather to set in brutally, in a dramatic way. You will have followed the changes in the weather: usually, you have time to get organised, with one primary aim: conserving a normal pace of life for as long as possible.

Getting organised

What have you got to fear, then? After all, in bad weather, you are not so badly off at sea. Probably less well off than in a port, but certainly better off than near the coast. Even when the wind is blowing like the devil, when you are on the open sea, the sea is well formed, regular, and much less dangerous than when you are sailing over sandbanks, for example. And then, if you miss a manoeuvre, or have a minor accident, you do not necessarily put yourself in danger: you have plenty of water around you, you can work it out.

Really, there are two scourges to be feared above all others: two quite ordinary curses, which threaten to take on alarming proportions here – disorder and damp. In bad weather, the inside of the boat should remain a kind of peaceful haven, you should be able to sustain a certain level of comfort there. To prevent disorder you should look at everything again with a fresh eye: tidy everything away, tie everything down. To combat the damp, start by emptying the water from the bilges, and assume that it will try to get back in: check that the panel over the steps holds fast, stop up the air vents, even the hawse-hole. In any case, the water will get back in, because you will have to open the door from time to time to go in and out, and you will come back in soaked. So you should put the things which absolutely must stay dry in a safe place, carefully wrapped up in plastic bags: your change of clothes and the matches.

You should also do the rounds on the deck more carefully than usual, to clear it up, collect everything which is not absolutely necessary for carrying out manoeuvres, check the liferaft is secured, the spinnaker pole, the paddle and the anchor. You should examine everything with a view to leaving the least 'grip' possible to the wind and the sea.

Then you have to think about your day-to-day life. It runs the risk of being disrupted, and primarily on one basic point: the organisation of meals. You will probably not be able to cook properly for a certain time (curiously, you are not so bothered about it, either). But it is better not to wait until you are in the middle of the fray to prepare hot drinks, in Thermos flasks, and put in a place which is easy to reach all those little things which are easy to eat, and which we have already listed.

There is also seasickness: this is a serious matter which may have considerable influence on subsequent events. Those who are subject to it would be well advised to find their pills well before the swell rises, and their stomachs too.

Carrying on

Having taken these precautions, life goes on. Each team carries out its normal watch. You should pay greater attention to keeping the logbook, and it is not a bad idea to try to determine your position while this is still possible: uncertainty on this subject runs the risk of increasing considerably afterwards.

The problems will take a different form depending on where the bad weather is coming from. If it comes from right ahead of you, you can easily judge the stages of its setting in. At first, you can still probably make headway in acceptable conditions: the boat presents its best defended section to the sea, the stem; in the cockpit at the

Seasickness

'At the beginning, you are afraid you will die; at the end, you are afraid you won't.'

If it does not always reach the metaphysical proportions implied by this definition, seasickness is nonetheless a special kind of sickness, very disagreeable, and very common. A privileged few are totally immune to it, but in the end you come across very few of them – at least at sea. More or less serious, more or less frequent, it is in any case a reality you will have to deal with when it sets in on board: some of you, suffering a moderate attack, are still capable of a certain amount of activity between two bouts of throwing up, but others are reduced to limp rags; others still are struck in an insidious way: the sickness only manifests itself in a certain sleepiness, a sort of mental sluggishness which ravages your will. Thus it is that the captain's orders become vague or pass into the conditional: 'Someone ought to take a reef … We should check the route … Watch out!'

Seasickness can have various causes. On the strictly physiological level, it is associated with abnormal stimulations suffered by the system of semi-circular canals which regulates balance, situated in the inner ear. Thus, the movements of the boat will play an essential part: in a flat calm no one on board is ill. But the threshold for the sickness to be triggered off varies a lot between individuals and different circumstances: fear, tiredness, cold, damp or insomnia may be decisive factors. Setting off in good physical condition, dressing warmly, avoiding staying wet, getting a full quota of sleep when you can: these are so many preventive remedies.

There are numerous medicines for seasickness: it is up to each person to find the one that suits them! There are also patent remedies: a small glass of sea water (Slocum); a crust of stale bread, 'to line your stomach' (Breton fishermen); chewing gum … You can add some simple observations: you are not usually as sick on deck as you are inside; you should keep busy: the simple act of taking the helm often stops seasickness in its early stages; if you really are not well, you should lie down, passing as quickly as possible from a standing to a lying position (this is what might be called the 'orthogonal' treatment for seasickness), the seated position being the worst of all. You should also eat something, which is difficult to accept, because, as for your appetite … At least try some fruit, or vegetables, a small amount, and often. And drink salty water or Vichy, because you quickly get dehydrated.

In any case, the adaptive faculties of the human being are astonishing. However frequent at the beginning of the cruise, the severe form of seasickness is almost always a temporary thing. Gradually, you get used to the movements of the boat, you get your sea legs. To such a point that, later, putting your feet back on the ground, you may be struck with a strange distressing feeling, due to the formidable immobility of the ground; this 'land sickness' does not of course constitute any risk, other than that of evoking scornful glances around you, when you are still looking for your first drink.

back, you are relatively sheltered. But gradually the pitching increases, the shock of the waves is rougher and rougher, life inside becomes difficult. The way you should behave is then dictated by two principal concerns: to avoid breaking things, and to handle the crew with care. It is better to shorten sail fairly soon, so as to travel less quickly; try to steer with the waves; go at a less impressive speed, if need be. You can also take various precautions: for example, heighten the tack of the jib to get it out of the way of squalls; double your sheet with the aid of a counter-sheet or any suitable piece of rope.

Pressing head-on into bad weather, you will soon be at battle stations. At least you do not risk being taken by surprise: you have taken account of the strength of the wind and the changes in the weather, and the boat's movements are unambiguous.

This is not the case when the storm catches up on you from behind. At first, life on board is still comfortable enough, since you are heading in the same direction as the wind and the sea. But the danger, here, is precisely that of not realising what is happening quickly enough: the wind seems less violent than it really is; the sea does not really seem that bad. When you start to find that the swell is taking on worrying proportions, when the boat begins to yaw, when it becomes difficult to control it with the helm, when a tonne of water invades the cockpit, this usually means that you should have shortened sail a good while ago ...

In reality, whether you are are heading into it or if the wind is behind you, when the bad weather sets in, you never know exactly what turn it is going to take.

The attitude to take should thus be dictated by that same sense of forward planning which inspired the preparations: the important thing is not the present moment, but what might be likely to happen a little later. From this perspective, it is good to have in mind at least two clear principles:

• Every manoeuvre must be decided on in time, that is to say a little before it becomes absolutely necessary. Taking a reef and changing the jib can be transformed into acrobatic exercises, when they would not have presented any particular problems 5 minutes earlier.

• As long as you have the opportunity to do something, you should not be satisfied with an approximation. The worst thing is, in fact, to suffer the events too passively: letting the boat bob or roll from side to side for hours increases the risk of breaking things, and everyone gets worn out – when a brief effort to modify the sail or to change speed would sometimes be enough to make the situation much more tolerable straightaway.

Hanging on

If the weather continues to get worse, there may come a moment when pushing on ahead becomes unreasonable: it is better not to insist; you had better seek the means of holding out without tiring yourselves too much. You can begin by stalling the jib slightly by trimming its counter-sheet, so as to make headway at a much reduced speed.

And if that is not enough, you should really heave-to: mainsail at the bottom reef trimmed normally, the jib backed, the helm secured to leeward. This is the theory at least, the boat still has to want to apply it. If it is a craft with a lot of weather helm, for example, will it perhaps be calmer under the storm jib alone, or with the helm tied in the centre, or even into the wind a little? You will have to see this

Shipwreck and survival

The big disasters (explosion, fire, collision, irreparable leak), do not happen every day, but they happen all the same. You may be forced to abandon ship, and sometimes very quickly. There is only one thing to ask yourselves: are you really ready, at any moment, for such an eventuality?
• You are not ready if you know nothing about the liferaft you are going to use; if you have never seen one inflated. You are not really ready if you have never had the opportunity to try one out, to see how to launch it, how it inflates, how it moves.
• You are not ready if you have not made a meticulous inspection of the equipment you will have to take on board the liferaft; if you have not thought personally about what else you should take; if you do not know properly how to use the equipment. You are not really ready if all this equipment is not organised so it can be assembled on the bridge in the wink of an eye.

We have discussed liferafts and the requisite equipment in the chapter on gear in Part III, 'The Boat'. It is time to refer to this now. At this point, what you should do is heavily dependent on the circumstances: to be convinced of this, you need only read the stories of shipwrecked people (you should read them anyway; it is rare not to learn something from them). All we can do here is remind you of some basic points, with reference to some well-known facts:
• First, you should only abandon ship if you are really sure that it is going to sink. Some shipwrecked people have died of exhaustion in their inflatable rafts, and their boats have been found later, crippled but still afloat, still containing all that would be necessary to stay alive.

• Loading the raft is a vital time: everything which follows depends on the cool you manage to keep during this manoeuvre. You must not forget anything and not drop anything in the water. Some crew members board the raft; you should pass them the equipment from hand to hand, not throw it. All this equipment must be strapped on board immediately. There are many examples to show that, in bad weather, you run a great risk of capsizing in the very first minutes, because you don't yet know how to distribute yourselves properly to maintain the balance of the raft. Very often, the majority of the equipment is lost at this point.
• Then, you should remember that you still have an enormous range of possibilities. If you have a 'dynamic' raft, you are on a proper boat, capable of crossing an ocean: it has been done. This is the beginning of another cruise, with a programme which usually suits everyone: head for land, or towards a well-frequented seaway. You will have to navigate and fight. Fight against cold: we have already mentioned aluminium blankets and sleeping bags which are remarkably effective. Against hunger: but this is not the principal problem; you know that you can survive for several days without eating. Against thirst: this is much more important. When you run out of water, you should remember what Alain Bombard proved: that you can survive by drinking sea water, in small amounts, and often (two mouthfuls, eight to ten times a day), and that fish flesh contains fresh water …

You should remember above all, and there are many examples of this, that human resistance proves itself to be absolutely incredible, so long as you have the will to live. That, in the end, is what counts!

for yourself, you will have to proceed by trial and error. The essential thing is to achieve the position of equilibrium which clearly improves your living conditions: the boat continues to make a little progress, while it drifts a lot; this is less tiring, as the drift creates turbulence on the windward side of the hull which counteracts the spite of the waves. And then, when the balance has been found, it is no longer necessary to leave someone at the helm: everyone can rest, inside in the warm. The boat will be ready, in any case, for you to put it back on its way in a wink, if need be. All you have to do is wait.

When you are making your way with the wind behind you, everything is very different. First, you should think about striking the mainsail fairly quickly. You will still be going very fast under the jib alone. And if you are still going too quickly, you should strike the jib. From this moment on, the boat is in flight (all the better if this flight takes it in the right direction!). This is not necessarily a comfortable speed, and it is risky in comparison with heaving-to. It requires the constant presence of someone at the helm. If someone falls into the sea, there is practically no chance of fishing them out again; the risk of a wave breaking over the transom is very serious: you will have to put the stair well out of bounds, and reinforce the back hatch of the roof, if need be.

Beyond this stage, it would be indecent to give any more detailed advice. There comes a point where the only things which enter into account are the experience you have been able to accumulate, and the knowledge you have of the behaviour of your boat. You know that there are several ways of trying to improve things: using a floating anchor to keep head-on to the waves, dragging a long warp or line behind as a brake on the boat in flight, to stabilise it. When nothing is any use any more, some people choose to heave-to with the sails down, the boat being left completely to its own devices.[1] Others prefer free flight, considering that after a certain point it becomes dangerous to put brakes on the boat. In fact, after a certain point, you do what you can: you really have to choose one of the two solutions, even if you do still wonder, a long time after, if the other one might not have been better!

One thing is certain: whatever happens, those on board will be suffering. The regular pace of life you imposed on yourselves until now is nothing but a distant memory. You still try to 'take your watch', that is to say, to be ready to take action, if you are not too sick. If not, the people who are capable do things as quickly as they can: there is no longer any question of putting off a manoeuvre until later, and if a repair is necessary at 0300, it doesn't matter how much noise you make!

Above all, you should try to maintain morale, even though the problems posed by communal living become more acute in this sodden little interior where everything is upside down. Here, the role of the captain is obviously a determining one. If they seem to be overcome by events, you should expect the worst: there is no medicine against a bad atmosphere. But if the captain keeps a cool

1. Adlard Coles, in particular, says he has frequently used this method. If you want information on very bad weather, you really should read his book *Heavy Weather Sailing*, which is a veritable Bible on the issue. A series of extraordinary accounts, from the author's experience or which he has collected, this book tries to draw a lesson from the events, point by point, without ever risking to dictate general rules. As exemplary as the accounts themselves seems the author's tone, that inimitable mixture of modesty and composure which is the mark of a true sailor.

head, if he controls the situation well, on the contrary, a new atmosphere may develop, and everyone reveal that they are a match for the circumstances. There is the man who threw up his guts and still manages to come out with a good joke (you have to). The woman who recites, between clenched teeth: 'While you are free, you will always love the sea.' The man who cannot understand how anyone can be ill, but who bravely agrees to put his lifejacket and harness back on to go and eat his sardines in oil on the deck (saying that in the Orkneys, in any case, it was much worse). And the woman who does not say very much, but puts new ribbons in her hair every morning ... Evidently, you still have a certain margin of safety, with these people.

And then, there are no examples, at least that we know of, of the bad weather not coming to an end. One fine day the wind softens, you still do not dare believe it; the sea begins to quieten down, you manage to stand up without holding on ... There will be work to do to put everything back on the right track! You should try to find out where you are, and make a proper meal at last, dry your clothes, take up the rhythm of the watches again, put everything back in order, empty out the water, clean the hold. Cleaning the deck is not worth doing: it has already been done.

Good weather

'He who goes to sea for pleasure would go to hell to pass the time,' said the old long-distance seamen when the first yachtsmen appeared. They may well have been perplexed by seeing people confront tiredness, cold, damp, fights, etc without being forced to. Can this be explained? We would have to suppose that beyond all the constraints of life at sea, something else may surface, something which resembles real freedom for everyone.

Not only do the various activities we have discussed here leave you time to do something else – fish, walk, have a laugh – but the very spirit in which they are carried out usually distracts from their character as chores. Every moment of life at sea, as long as everyone gets on well on board, may take on an incomprehensible new edge. Is it perhaps that, in a world reduced to the bare essentials, every action takes on its full value? Go and find out. There are people who feel transformed as soon as they set foot on a boat, who see everything with a fresh eye, who find themselves curiously relaxed, all the time: in the sun and in rough weather; during the quiet evenings, the long nights, the icy early mornings. They are at ease because the boat is moving on, because they are carrying out a precise piece of navigation, because they are in harmony with the skies.

You may perhaps be at your ease too, because at last you have the leisure to express yourself and to listen to others expressing themselves. We should say more about our own experience. When the people who form a crew do not know each other beforehand, there is, as the days go by, the astonishing experience of getting to know other people, the rich differences and deep similarities between you. There is the birth of a friendship which will not break down. Among all the joys which life at sea has on offer, perhaps this is the truest one, and the most long lasting.

In the end, what makes a successful cruise? We might say that it is a kind of happy conjunction between a group of people, a boat, and the radiance of their meeting. But this is a very abstract way of putting it. It is better to leave to you who are about to put down this book and take to the high seas, the job of discovering it for yourself. We have done what we could to prepare you for it, trying to translate what we know into simple terms, without masking the complexities under the pretext of facilitating the approach.

One day soon, we hope, you will know more about it than we do today. In any case, we will be setting off again ourselves, for when you are at sea and the wind is with you, nothing you may learn is final, truth does not always come on prescription and your own experience will be worth more than any of our assertions.

PART IX

Practical references

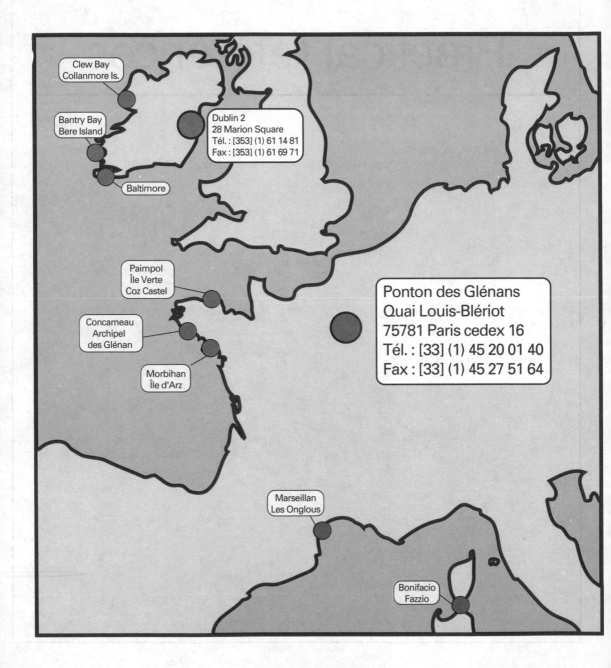

Useful addresses

Les Glénans
Paris: quai Louis-Blériot, 75781 Paris cedex 16
Ireland: Glenan Irish Sailing Centre, 28 Merrion Square, Dublin 2
Paimpol: quai Loti, BP 70, 22500 Paimpol
Glénans archipelago: rue Alfred-Le-Ray, BP 504, 29185
Concarneau cedex
Morbihan: 56840 Ile-d'Arz
Marseillan: BP 36, 34340 Marseillan
Corsica: Maison de la Mer, route de Santa-Manza, 20169
Bonifacio

British Telecom Maritime Radio Services, 43 Bartholomew Close,
London EC1A 7HP (071-583-9416)
Cruising Association, Ivory House, St Catherine's Dock, World
Trade Centre, London E1 9AT (071-481-0881)
HM Coastguard, Sunley House, 80–84 High Holborn, London
WC1V 6LP (071-405-6911)
HM Customs and Excise, Dorset House, Stamford Street, London
SE1 9PS (071-620-1313)
Lloyd's Register of Shipping, Yacht and Small Craft Department,
69 Oxford Street, Southampton SO1 1DL (0703-20353)
Meteorological Office, London Road, Bracknell, Berkshire RG12
2SZ (0344-420242)
Royal National Lifeboat Institution, West Quay Road, Poole,
Dorset BH15 1HZ (0202-671133)
Royal Yachting Association, Romsey Road, Eastleigh, Hampshire
SO5 4YA (0703-629962)

Service hydrographique et océanographique de la Marine
(SHOM), 13 rue du Chatellier, BP 426, 29275 Brest cedex
Secrétariat d'Etat à la mer (direction des ports et de la navigation
maritimes), Bureau de la plaisance, 3 place Fontenoy, 75007 Paris
Fédération française de voile, 55 avenue Kléber, 75008 Paris

Opposite page: Where you can sail with les Glénans.

APPENDIX 2

Select bibliography and further reading

The Practice of Sailing

K. Adlard Coles *Heavy Weather Sailing* Adlard Coles
Alain Gree *Anchoring and Mooring* Adlard Coles
Ian Proctor *Sailing Strategy: Wind and Current* Adlard Coles
Eric Tabarly *Practical Yacht Handling* Stanford Maritime

Maintenance

George Buchanan *The Boat Repair Manual* Pelham
Nigel Calder *Boatowner's Mechanical and Electrical Manual*
Nautical Books
Eric C. Fry *The Shell Combined Book of Knots and Ropework*
David and Charles
H. Janssen *Laying up your Boat* Adlard Coles

The Mechanics of Sailing

Jeremy Howard-Williams *Sails* Adlard Coles
Anne Madden *More Sail Trim* Adlard Coles
C. A. Marchaj *Aero-Hydrodynamics of Sailing* Adlard Coles
Matthew Sheahan *Sailing Rigs and Spars* Haynes

Meteorology

Ray Sanderson *Meteorology at Sea* Stanford Maritime
Alan Watts *Wind Pilots* Nautical Books

The Sea

Paul Tchernia *Descriptive Regional Oceanography* Pergamon

Navigation

Mik Chinery *Simple Electronic Navigation* Fernhurst
Tom Cunliffe *Coastal and Offshore Navigation* Fernhurst
Tom Cunliffe *Inshore Navigation* Fernhurst
Conrad Dixon *Basic Astro Navigation* Adlard Coles
Ephémérides nautiques Gautier-Villars (Dunod)
Mike Harris *Astro Navigation by Pocket Computer* Adlard Coles
Elbert S. Maloney *Dutton's Navigation and Piloting* Naval Institute
Press
Cuthbert Mason *Deep Sea Racing* Phoenix House
RYA *Navigation: an RYA Manual* David and Charles
Kenneth Wilkes *Ocean Yacht Navigator* Nautical Books
Kenneth Wilkes *Practical Yacht Navigator* Nautical Books

Cruising	Jimmy Cornell *World Cruising Handbook* Adlard Coles Cruising Association *Cruising Association Handbook* Eric Hiscock *Cruising Under Sail* Adlard Coles
Pilots (a selection)	*Almanach du marin breton* Oeuvre du marin breton Mark Brackenbury *Normandy and Channel Islands Pilot* Adlard Coles K. Adlard Coles *Channel Harbours and Anchorages* Adlard Coles Brian Goulder *Adlard Coles Pilot Packs* (4 vols) Adlard Coles Eric Guillemot and Michael Le Berre *Guide de croisière, Bretagne-Nord* EMOM-Neptune Gill and Basil Heather *Which? Guide to Harbours and Marinas* Hodder and Stoughton Imray Pilots: *South France* (3 vols); *East Spain*; *Greek Waters; Turkish Waters*; *Italian Waters*; *West Coast of Scotland* (2 vols), etc. Irish Sailing Club *Sailing Directions* Malcolm Robson *Channel Islands Pilot* Nautical Books Malcolm Robson *French Pilot* (4 vols) Nautical Books
Safety and Survival	Michael Cargal *The Captain's Guide to Liferaft Survival* Seafarer Bob Fisher *The Fastnet Disaster and After* Pelham Tom McClean and Alec Beilby *Survival at Sea: A Handbook* Stanley Paul John Rousmaniere *Fastnet Force 10* Nautical Books Charles Wright *Survival at Sea* Brown & Son
General Works (reference)	*Reed's Nautical Almanac* *Macmillan & Silk Cut Nautical Almanac* Macmillan *Macmillan & Silk Cut Yachtsman's Handbook* Macmillan Peter Johnson *The Encyclopedia of Yachting* Dorling Kindersley
General Works (training)	William Barnes *Day Skipper/Competent Crew* Stanford Maritime Mike Bowyer *The Concise Day Skipper Guide* David and Charles
Periodicals	*Sail* *Yachting Monthly* *Yachting World* *Yachts and Yachting*
Other Books	Dermod MacCarthy *Sailing with Mr Belloc* Collins Harvill Joshua Slocum *Sailing Alone Around the World* Century The Bible *The Odyssey* Herman Melville *Moby Dick*

APPENDIX 3

Acknowledgements and translator's note

The Glénans Manual of Sailing is a collectively written work, and has been in print in successively updated editions since 1955. The current edition is the work of:

Text preparation and markup
Cécile Saurin, Catherine Martenot

Text revision
Geneviève Beauvarlet

2nd edition revisions
Jean-Louis Goldschmid

Copy editing
Jacques Morel, Isabelle Prince

Copy editing, English translation
Colin Hutchens

Advice, English translation
John Jameson, Bob Menzies, Richard Ebling, Howard Cheadle, Chris Pilling

Co-ordinating editor
Jean Ginod

Drawings and diagrams
Marine Ginod; Taurus Graphics

Photographs
B.N. Paris 934, 954. – Bateaux 807 b, 1070 c. - Beken of Cowes Ltd. 241 a. - Edouard Berne/ Fotogram 838. - Boudot-Lamotte 784 b, 785 b. - R. Decker 785 a. - Ph. Facque 241 b. - GME 441. - J.-L. Goldschmid 246, 284, 423. - CNG-Bernard Henry 25, 52, 54, 55,

57, 60, 61, 65, 67, 68, 70, 71, 93, 113, 115, 116, 117, 118, 121, 122, 123, 125, 126, 128, 134, 137, 138, 140, 142, 143, 144, 145, 147, 148, 149, 150, 195, 241 b, 279 a, 318 ab, 324, 1070 abcd. - KFS, distr. par Opera Mundi 1014. - Michel Langrognet 805. - Lanoue/Bateaux 358 b, 614. - Gilbert Le Cossec/Bateaux 1021. - Le Guern 165, 279 b, 322. - Charles Lénars 784 a. - Pierre Lieutaghi 802, 803. - D. Maupas/Bateaux 1020 a. - Rosine Mazin/CEDRI 785 c. - Météorologie nationale 162, 683 ab, 686, 687, 706, 707, 708, 709, 712, 720. - Jean Mounicq/Fotogram 800 a. - National Maritime Museum, London 945. - *Neptune Yachting* 360. - Port of Rotterdam 804. - Rhône-Poulenc 242 b. - Rubinstein 241 c, 280, 312, 418 abc, 468, 529, 581. - S. Schneider 276, 277. - Services des phares et balises 848, 849. - © SPADEM 806, 836. - Studio Le Merdy, Concarneau 783. - Éric Twiname 167. - UNESCO/ATL 782. - P. Viannay 242 a.

All other photographs come from the Glénans photographic library and were taken by our members.

We are particularly grateful to Editions Dunod and to the Service hydrographique et océanographique de la Marine (SHOM).

Extracts from *Reed's Nautical Almanac* (Thomas Reed Publications Ltd), *Macmillan & Silk Cut Nautical Almanac* and *Macmillan & Silk Cut Yachtsman's Handbook* (Macmillan) and *International Log Book* (International Log Book A/S) reproduced by kind permission of the publishers.

The New Glénans Sailing Manual (David & Charles, 1978) made the work of the Glénans school accessible to a broad English-speaking public for the first time. The translators of this current volume, in common with thousands of British yachtsmen and yachtswomen, owe a debt of gratitude to the translators of that edition, James MacGibbon and Stanley Caldwell.

Translator's Note

We have tried to make every part of this book accessible to English-speaking yachtsmen and yachtswomen, while maintaining its original flavour and principles intact. The flavour is that of French cooking and Breton cruising; the principles are the international ones of safety, good seamanship and fellowship afloat.

The manual is not the work of one person; and nor has the work of translating it been a solitary endeavour. Jim Simpson's knowledge of French is vast, his work-rate impressive … but most of all I valued his good humour and constant commitment.

Thanks are due also to Ruth Bagnall and Catherine du Peloux Menagé, our co-translators; to my father, John Davison, for giving me (unsolicited) his entire sailing library and for teaching me to sail in the first place; to Neil Hudson at Cambridge University Library; to Jean-Louis Goldschmid who helped with numerous queries; and to our editor, Tim Jaycock, who contributed more to this book than an editor should need to.

Index

Index prepared by
Gerard M-F Hill